11,000 DRINKS

Also by Paul Knorr

10,000 Drinks

Big Bad-Ass Book of Cocktails

Big Bad-Ass Book of Shots

Bomb Squad!

Candy Shots

Momosas

Playboy Book of Shots

Shake, Jiggle & Shoot

The Vodka Bible

11,000 DRINKS

30 YEARS' WORTH OF COCKTAILS

PAUL KNORR

An Imprint of Sterling Publishing Co., Inc.
1166 Avenue of the Americas
New York, NY 10036

STERLING EPICURE is a trademark of Sterling Publishing Co., Inc.
The distinctive Sterling logo is a registered trademark of
Sterling Publishing Co., Inc.

Some recipes in this book contain raw eggs or parts of raw eggs. Consuming raw or undercooked eggs may increase your risk of foodborne illness. The young, elderly, pregnant women, and anyone who may be immunocompromised should not consume them.

ISBN 978-1-4549-0706-0

Distributed in Canada by Sterling Publishing Co., Inc.
c/o Canadian Manda Group, 664 Annette Street
Toronto, Ontario, M6S 2C8, Canada

Distributed in the United Kingdom by GMC Distribution Services
Castle Place, 166 High Street, Lewes, East Sussex, BN7 1XU, United Kingdom

Distributed in Australia by NewSouth Books
45 Beach Street, Coogee, NSW 2034, Australia

For information about custom editions, special sales, and premium and corporate purchases, please contact Sterling Special Sales at 800-805-5489 or specialsales@sterlingpublishing.com.

Manufactured in China

2 4 6 8 10 9 7 5 3 1

www.sterlingpublishing.com

To my three amazing children, Camryn, Colby, and Cooper,
to Jill, and to all of my drinking buddies past and present

CONTENTS

AUTHOR'S NOTE

A lot can happen in a decade. Nearly ten years have passed since *10,000 Drinks* was published, and in that time the cocktail landscape has changed significantly. People have become more aware of and more concerned with what goes into their bodies, including the cocktails they drink. People are taking note of where the ingredients in their favorite beverages come from. The "locavore" trend that started with meats and vegetables has spread to vodka and gin. In response—after updating some post-Prohibition laws—small craft distilleries are becoming as commonplace as craft breweries. The beverage giants have responded with new products and new flavors. Bartenders are combining these in new, creative, and unexpected ways, putting us in the midst of a mixed-drink renaissance!

In the first version of this book, I tried to make sure that it included the most popular drinks of the time. In this updated edition, I have tried once again to identify and include the most popular drinks of the day. Fireball, RumChata, and St. Germain hadn't caught the public's palate ten years ago. A bar today would seem incomplete without them. Those products and more are well represented here, as are many of the vast array of flavored vodkas and rums. The world has far more than 11,000 drinks in it, so decisions had to be made about which to include and which to leave out. I tried to make the right decisions, but I'm sure I'll hear from you if you think I didn't.

New to this revised and expanded edition of the book are a section on garnishing drinks, a section on simple homemade bar mixes, and an index of drinks by name. We eat with our eyes first, so an attractive garnish enhances the overall experience of a drink. Homemade mixes also improve the experience of a drink by making it taste fresher. Simply put, mixes made in-house and juices freshly squeezed make drinks taste better.

An important note: Most drinks in this book list ingredients by proportions rather than exact measurements for two simple reasons: first, to avoid needing to convert between imperial and metric measures; second, to accommodate the wide variety of glassware available. Not all coupe or highball glasses are the same size, so having the ingredients in "parts" instead of ounces, fractions of ounces, or centiliters allows you to adjust a recipe easily for the glassware at hand. That said, fractions of parts can get a bit tricky, so here's a handy conversion chart to help make those small measures a little easier to understand.

Conversion Chart

If 1 part = 1 ounce = 2 tbsp, then

1/2 part = 1 tbsp

1/3 part = 2 tsp

1/6 part = 1 tsp

1/12 part = 1/2 tsp

1/24 part = 1/4 tsp

For metric measures, 1 part = 3 centiliters.

Yes, this book contains 11,000 mixed-drink recipes. Eleven. Thousand. This weighty encyclopedia captures the vast variety of drinks available in the world today. I also hope it sparks your creativity. Browse and explore the different categories, find inspiration, and add a subtle twist that makes a drink your own.

BARTENDING TOOLS

Here are the basic tools that you'll need to make the perfect drink every time.

Bar Mats

Also known as spill stops, these are great for pouring shots. The mat traps the spillage and keeps the bar neat. Don't forget to empty the mats and wash them after each use.

Bar Rags

Always keep a stack of bar rags handy to wipe up inevitable spills and keep the bar clean.

Bar Spoon

This small spoon with a very long handle—sometimes but not always twirled—has many uses behind the bar. Primarily it's for stirring cocktails, but it also helps making layered drinks.

Blender

A stick blender is fine for liquids—as long as you keep the blades below the liquid surface—but use a heavy duty, multi-speed countertop model when blending ice for those fancy frozen drinks, and *always* make sure the lid is completely on before you start the machine.

Garnish Tray

Keep your lemon slices, lime wedges, orange wheels, cherries, and other garnishes on a nice, neat, covered tray.

Ice Scoop

Ice is legally a food, and all the safe-handling procedures apply. Commercial bars must use plastic ice scoops, and they're strongly recommended for home use as well. Using a scoop will keep your hands and glassware from touching the ice. If you don't want to buy a dedicated scoop, *never* use a glass to scoop ice because glass chips. Imagine trying to find a chip of glass in a bin of ice! Use a plastic or paper cup instead.

Jigger

This measuring device consists of two metal cups joined bottom to bottom. One cup measures 1.5 ounces (45 ml), and the other measures 1 ounce (30 ml). Fancier models have a handle attached and may come in varying sizes as well.

Knife

A sturdy, small, sharp knife is essential for cutting fruit for garnish. Some specialty knives have built-in zesters, and some even have a built-in channel knife, used to cut the small strip of citrus peel for a twist garnish.

Liquor Pours or Spouts

These control the flow of liquor from the bottle, providing speed and consistency by producing a steady stream of liquid instead of the uneven gurgling that happens without them. Many different types of pours exist, but they all fit inside the tops of almost any bottle, replacing the cap. Pours do have drawbacks, though: They need to be cleaned frequently; if they don't have built-in screens, they can allow bugs such as fruit flies into the bottle; and thick or syrupy liqueurs can clog them.

Muddler

Muddling is pressing down and twisting ingredients, such as mint leaves or lime slices, in the bottom of a glass to release their flavors. In a pinch, you can use a bar spoon to do this, but if you're making many drinks, a dedicated muddler makes the process faster and easier. A muddler is simply a wooden or metal rod with a flat end. Use the flat end to press and twist the ingredients. Sometimes the end has a hard rubber surface with small grooves. The rubber prevents scratching or accidentally breaking the glass.

Shaker

The most common kind of shaker you'll see is a cocktail shaker, also known as a cobbler or martini shaker. This basic tool for making most cocktails consists of three parts: cup, strainer, and cap. The cap covers the opening of the strainer, which fits onto the cup. Always shake away from your face and away from your guests or customers! When serving, you can leave the strainer on to strain out ice or remove it to pour the drink into a glass as is.

The Boston shaker is a simpler, easier, cheaper, and more reliable alternative to the cocktail shaker. It consists of a metal cup and a pint glass. Ice and liquids go into the cup, and the glass fits tightly over the cup, forming a seal. A Boston shaker doesn't have a built-in strainer, though, so you'll need a separate strainer if the drink needs straining.

Strainer

A Hawthorne strainer has a metal coil around its circular edge and fits over the top of a Boston shaker or any other glass. Pressing forward allows you to adjust the straining level. A julep strainer looks like a big spoon with lots of slots in it and is used primarily for stirred drinks rather than those that are shaken.

Wine Key or Opener

Any bar that serves wine should have a wine opener. Anything will do, from a simple corkscrew to a fancy "estate" wine opener that mounts on the edge of the bar. The most popular is the waiter's corkscrew, sometimes called a wine key, which is small, easy to use, and folds up easily to fit in a pocket.

DRINK STYLES

There are many different categories of alcoholic beverages. These are the most common.

Apéritif

An alcoholic drink taken before a meal or, by association, any of several liqueurs or fortified wines.

Buck

Drink made with an ounce of liquor, with lemon juice and ginger ale, and topped with a lemon twist.

Chaser

Any beverage you drink after doing a shot instead of combining the two. The original chaser was the Boiler-Maker, which was a shot and a beer.

Cobbler

A tall, summer-style drink consisting of ice, wine or liqueur, and a variety of fruit slices, cherries, berries, and so forth.

Collins

Tall, cool, punch-like drinks made with any basic liquor with lime or lemon juice, over ice cubes in a frosted glass, with sugar and club soda added. (A Tom Collins has gin, a John Collins features whiskey, and a Joe Collins contains scotch.)

Cooler

A lower-alcohol drink consisting of a smaller amount of liquor or liqueurs in a tall glass then filled with soda or juice.

Dry

Description of any form of wine or liqueur to denote a lack of sweetness.

Fix

A sour drink, usually made with pineapple juice and crushed ice.

Fizz

Made from liquor, citrus juices, and sugar. Shaken with ice and strained into a highball glass. Then club soda or another carbonated liquid is added. You can use any carbonated beverage, even Champagne, to make the drink fizz.

Flip

An eggnog and fizz combination. Made with liquor, egg, sugar, and shaved ice, shaken well, and sprinkled with nutmeg.

Frappe

A drink made by packing a glass with crushed ice and pouring liqueur over it.

Highball

Any liquor served with ice, soda, ginger ale, or other carbonated beverages. Similar to a Cooler but usually smaller with a higher liquor-to-mixer ratio.

Julep

Made with a liquor (traditionally bourbon) and fresh mint leaves (muddled, crushed, or whole), served in a frosted glass or silver cup with shaved ice and a mint garnish.

Lowball

A short drink consisting of spirits served with ice alone or with water or soda in a short glass. Also known as an on-the-rocks or old-fashioned.

Mist

A glass packed with crushed ice to which spirits are added, usually straight. Similar to a Frappe.

Neat

Served in a small glass without any ice.

Pick-Me-Up

Any concoction designed to allay the effects of overindulgence in alcoholic beverages.

Pousse-Café

A sweet, multi-layered after-dinner drink. Success in making it depends upon keeping each layer separate and distinct from the others. The secret is knowing the relative heaviness of the various liquids that make up the Pousse-café and adding them to the glass from heaviest to lightest.

Rickey

A cross between a Collins and a Sour that consists of lime or lemon juice, club soda, and alcohol. Unlike the Collins and Sour, it contains no added sugar.

Sangaree

Made with whiskey, gin, rum, or brandy, with port, wine, ale, porter, or stout floated on top, with a sprinkle of nutmeg.

Shooter

A straight shot of spirits taken neat or a mixture of spirits and other ingredients chilled and strained into a shot glass.

Sling

Made like Sangarees, with the addition of lemon juice and a twist of lemon peel, and served in a rocks glass.

Smash

Small juleps, served in a rocks glass. Made from muddled sugar; ice cubes; whiskey, gin, rum, or brandy; and club soda.

Sour

Made of lemon juice, ice, sugar, with any basic liquor.

Swizzle

Originally a tall rum cooler filled with cracked ice that was "swizzled" with a long stirring rod or spoon rotated rapidly between the palms to produce frost on the outside of the glass.

Toddy

Originally a hot drink made with spirits, sugar, spices such as cinnamon and cloves, and a lemon peel, mixed with hot water, and served in a tall glass. Toddies can also be cold.

Wine Cooler

A low-alcohol drink consisting of either white or red wine mixed with either lemon-lime soda, ginger ale, club soda, or a citrus juice.

TECHNIQUES

The instructions in this book are all fairly straightforward, but here's a little bit more about how to make the drinks.

Pour ingredients into glass neat (do not chill).

Add all of the ingredients into the glass (typically a shot glass) straight from the bottle. Don't chill them if they're not already cold.

Layer in a shot glass.

Layer each of the ingredients in a shot glass or a pousse-café glass. The layering technique requires practice. The trick is to place a bar spoon upside down against the inner rim of the glass above the first ingredient. Then gently pour the next ingredient over the back of the spoon. This method prevents the next liquor from going into the glass too quickly and therefore helps prevent them from mixing. For layered drinks, order is important. It's much more difficult to layer a heavier ingredient on top of a lighter one.

Layer over ice.

Fill the glass with ice and gently add each ingredient so they mix as little as possible.

Layer over ice. Drink through a straw.

Layer the drink over ice as described, but serve with a straw. These drinks are meant to be consumed quickly with the layers of the drink providing different flavors.

Shake with ice and strain.

Fill the cup of your shaker with ice, add the ingredients, cover it, and shake briskly until the outside begins to frost. Then take the top off (for a cocktail shaker) or remove the pint glass and place a strainer over the cup (for a Boston shaker), and strain the drink into the glass, leaving the ice behind in the shaker. This is the common method for making a martini.

Shake with ice and strain over ice.

Same as shaking with ice above, but you strain the drink into a glass already filled with fresh ice.

Shake with ice and pour.

The same as shake with ice above, but you don't use a strainer and pour the full contents of the shaker into the glass.

Muddle

Mashing in the bottom of the glass. The technique releases flavors and aromas and helps blend ingredients before adding other liquids. To muddle, add the ingredients to bottom of the shaker or glass (depending on the drink), and press down on them while twisting with the back of a bar spoon or a muddler. You want to break up the ingredients and release their flavors—not make a paste in the bottom of the glass! One or two twists should be enough.

Build over ice.

Fill the glass with ice, and add the ingredients allowing them to mix naturally. This method creates the "sunrise" effect in a Tequila Sunrise.

Build over ice and stir.

Fill the glass with ice, add the ingredients, then stir the drink with a bar spoon. Alternatively, you can put a stirrer or straw in the drink, and let the drinker stir it.

Build in the glass with no ice.

Add the ingredients to the glass without ice. This is typically necessary when ingredients are already cold and shouldn't be diluted with ice. Most Champagne-based or beer-based drinks are made this way.

Build in a heatproof cup or mug.

Combine the ingredients in a heatproof container, such as a coffee mug or Irish coffee cup, then add the ingredients in the order listed. This is typically required for hot drinks, such as an Irish coffee.

Stir gently with ice and strain.

In a mixing glass (if you have one) or the cup of a shaker (if you don't), combine the ingredients and ice. Instead of shaking them, stir them gently with a bar spoon before straining the mixture into the appropriate glass.

Stir gently with ice.

In a mixing glass or the cup of a shaker, combine the ingredients and ice. Stir them gently with a bar spoon, and pour everything into the glass.

Combine all ingredients in a blender with ice. Blend until smooth.

Add ice to the blender, then add the ingredients. Blend everything until smooth. This is the method commonly used for most frozen drinks.

Combine all ingredients in a blender. Blend until smooth.

Place all ingredients in the blender without adding any ice. Blend everything until smooth. This is the method commonly used for drinks made with ice cream.

Shake all but X with ice and strain. Top with X.

In this case, X is typically club soda, tonic water, ginger ale, or Champagne. Shake all ingredients with ice, and strain them into a glass. Then fill the glass the rest of the way with X. Whether to add ice to the glass before straining in the drink depends on the type of drink. If ice would dilute the mixer (Champagne for example), then don't add ice.

Fill with

Fill any remaining space in the glass with the specified ingredient. If "Fill with" appears for two ingredients, fill the remaining space with both equally. If "Top with" follows "Fill with," leave a small amount of space at the top.

Top with

Add a splash (less than 1 ounce) of the specified ingredient to the top of the drink before serving.

GARNISHES

A properly made drink pleases all the senses, including sight. Garnishes embellish a cocktail visually and enhance the experience of enjoying it.

Cherries

Some drinks specifically call for cherries as garnish, including the Manhattan and the Shirley Temple. (A Shirley Temple served without a cherry is called a Brooke Shields.) Maraschino cherries are typically red—and the best are dark red rather than neon—but a green variety is available as well. In some drinks, a green maraschino cherry looks nicer than red. Don't add cherries to a drink where the primary flavor of the liquor is the focus, a drink served neat for example. As with olives and onions, spear cherries with a toothpick or similar item before placing them as garnish.

Citrus

Lemons and limes are perhaps the most common garnish. Oranges are also popular. The ingredients of the drink should guide you as to what to use for a garnish. For example, drinks with lemon juice, a lemon liqueur, or lemon-flavored vodka can use a lemon wedge or wheel for garnish. Drinks with triple sec or other orange flavors can use an orange wheel or twist.

Flags

Start with a plastic pick, small plastic sword, or even (in certain tropical cases) a paper umbrella. Take an orange half moon, and spear the edge of one side with the pick. Add a cherry to the pick, then wrap the half moon around the cherry, spearing the opposite edge onto the pick.

Herbs

Sprigs of mint can serve as garnish in any drink with muddled mint leaves in it. Sprigs of thyme or basil also can garnish cocktails, particularly gin-based drinks.

Olives and Onions

Pimento-stuffed olives are the standard garnish for a martini. Use a small cocktail onion in the same exact drink, and it becomes a Gibson instead. Any grocery store has cocktail olives, and the brine from the olives is what makes a Dirty Martini dirty. You usually can find small, pickled cocktail onions in the same place as the olives, but the onions are less common. Spear olives or onions with a toothpick or similar item before placing them, which minimizes contact with the garnish (and is required by some health codes).

Pineapple and other tropical fruit

Tropical drinks deserve tropical garnishes. Pineapple, mangos, kiwi, and other fruits can be used to great effect as a garnish. Pineapple rounds can be cut into wedges. Other tropical fruits should be peeled and cut into wheels, wedges, or spears as desired.

Rimming

This is the process of coating the rim of a glass with a powdered garnish. The most common example of this is the salt on a margarita glass. Glasses can be rimmed with chile powder, cinnamon sugar, coco powder, grated coconut, salt, sugar, and many other options. In a shallow saucer, place your powder so it's about a quarter inch (5 mm) deep. In a second saucer, add water to the same depth. Evenly dip the mouth of the glass in the water. Shake off any excess, then dip the glass in the powdered garnish saucer. The powder will stick to where the glass is wet. Alternately, you can rub the rim of the glass with a piece of fruit garnish first.

Twists

These are thin strips of citrus peel, 1–2 inches long. Using a small paring knife, carefully cut along the circumference of the fruit going deep enough to see a little bit of white but not into the pith, which is bitter. If you can still see the pores of the peel in the white part, you're doing it right. If you no longer see pores and see just white, then you've gone too deep and should trim off the pith. Once the twist is cut, twist it over the drink, releasing the oils from the peel. You can also rub the twist around the rim of the glass before placing it inside the drink.

Wedges

Place wedge-shaped slices of fruit on the edge of any straight-sided glass containing a drinks that matches the fruit flavor. Wedges work best for smaller fruit, such as lemons or limes. First cut the fruit in half, from top (stem) to bottom. Next cut each half in half to make quarters. Then cut each quarter in half across the peel to make eights. Finally, halfway through the fruit, from the center toward the peel, slice the wedge, but make sure you don't cut it in half. This will create a notch used to place the wedge onto the edge of the glass. If the wedge is going into the glass rather than on the rim, squeeze it first, cupping your hand over top it so the juice doesn't spray.

Wheels

Wheels work with fruit up to about the size of a tangerine. Full size oranges should be cut in half first to make half moons instead of wheels. Make a single shallow cut from top to bottom from the peel to just inside the pulp. Next cut the fruit through the diameter making 1/8-inch thick circles (wheels) of fruit and peel. Discard the ends, which have more peel than fruit. The first shallow cut you made provides the notch on which the wheel fits onto the glass.

BASIC BAR MIXES

Syrups and other mixes add sweetness, bitterness, and other flavors to mixtures, helping to ensure a proper flavor balance. Here are the three most common.

Simple Syrup

2 cups water
2 cups granulated sugar

In a medium saucepan, bring the water to a boil over high heat. Reduce heat to low, add the sugar, and stir until the sugar has dissolved completely. Allow to cool to room temperature, and store in an airtight container in the refrigerator for up to a month.

You can make almost any flavored syrup the same way by adding 1–2 teaspoons of flavor extract, such as almond, mint, orange, peppermint, or vanilla, when you add the sugar.

Sweet & Sour Mix (also known as Sour Mix or Bar Mix)

1 cup water
1 cup granulated sugar
1 cup lime juice
1 cup lemon juice

Over high heat, bring the water to a boil in a medium saucepan. Reduce heat to low, add the sugar, and stir until the sugar dissolves completely. Add the juices, and stir to combine. Allow to cool to room temperature, and store in an airtight container in the refrigerator for up to a month.

Note: It's worth the time and effort to squeeze fresh lemons and limes. The flavored water in those plastic bottles won't do the job nearly as well.

Grenadine

4 cups pomegranate juice
2 cups granulated sugar

In a medium saucepan, bring the pomegranate juice to a low simmer over medium to medium low heat. Simmering the juice, stirring occasionally, until the juice reduces by half. Add the sugar, and stir until it has dissolved completely. Allow to cool to room temperature, and store in an air tight container in the refrigerator for up to a month.

Note: Seeding a pomegranate and squeezing the juice from the seed packets isn't worth the time or effort. Buy 100 percent fresh (meaning refrigerated) pomegranate juice from the store for this recipe.

STOCKING YOUR HOME BAR

What you keep in your home bar depends on the tastes of who's drinking, the space available, and of course your budget. But you can keep most people happy with a few basic liquors, liqueurs, wine, and a small assortment of beers.

The Basics

Gin

Buy a recognized brand, such as Tanqueray (sharp), Gordon's (standard), or Bombay Sapphire (soft). For higher-end tastes, try Hendricks (cucumbers and rose petals) or a local craft distilled gin.

Rum

Here you might want at least three different types, a dark (Gosling's, Black Seal, or Myers), light (Bacardi), and spiced (Captain Morgan's). A relative newcomer to the rum category is black spiced rum, such as Captain Morgan Black or Kraken. A black spiced rum will add more intense flavor to drinks that call for either dark or spiced rum.

Flavored Rums

As with vodka, flavor varieties also overrun the rum category. Citrus is also popular here (Bacardi Limon), but go for more tropical flavors, such as pineapple or mango. The best way to avoid having flavors you'll never use is to set a menu and get only what you need.

Tequila

There are two types of Tequila drinkers: the "Lick it, slam it, suck it" crowd—based on the traditional salt-shot-lime sequence—and the 100 percent Blue Agave sipping crowd. To keep both happy, consider a bottle of José Cuervo for the slammers and a more upscale tequila, such as Patrón or Cabo Wabo, for the sipping crowd.

Vodka

You can't go wrong with a premium name brand, such as Absolut or Skyy. If you want to go more upscale, buy a super-premium vodka, such as Grey Goose.

Flavored Vodka

If it exists as a flavor, a vodka probably comes in that flavor. Somewhere around glazed-donut flavor and bacon flavor, it started getting out of hand. The most common flavors are citrus or lemon (Absolut Citron) and vanilla (Stoli Vanil). The best way to tame the confusion is to plan a drink menu and get only the flavors you need to cover your menu.

Whiskey

A good whiskey can be expensive. For some, a basic bottle of Jack Daniel's might suffice, while for others you might want an assortment of American, Canadian, Irish, Scottish, or even Japanese whiskies. As with vodka and rum, flavors have invaded the whiskey category as well. The most popular by far is cinnamon (Fireball) with cherry a close second.

Bourbon

Wild Turkey, Maker's Mark, and Jim Beam are among the biggest names.

Scotch

Choose according to the tastes of your guests and your budget since scotch can be expensive. Cutty Sark, Johnnie Walker, J & B, and Teachers are among the most well known. If your guests appreciate a good whiskey, then you might want to go for a single malt scotch.

Liqueurs

Brandies

Due to the often artificial taste of mass-produced brands, flavored brandies have fallen out of favor in recent years. In most cases, you can substitute a blackberry liqueur for blackberry brandy without any problem. For the unflavored variety, consider a good cognac.

Cream Liqueurs

Irish cream liqueur is used in many different drinks. Rum cream liqueurs, made in the style of traditional horchata (RumChata), are also popular and tasty.

Crèmes

The essentials are Crème de Menthe (green or white), Cacao (Brown or White), and Banana.

Orange Flavored Liqueurs

Many different liqueurs are flavored with orange. They're often lumped together under the name Triple Sec, but they include Cointreau, Curaçao, Grand Mariner, and, yes, basic Triple Sec.

Schnapps

The most commonly used schnapps in America is Peach. It goes into everything from Sex on the Beach to the Woo Woo. After peach, consider melon (Midori), apple, butterscotch, and any other flavors that strike your fancy.

Others

There are literally hundreds of different liqueurs out there in almost every flavor, but Bénédictine, Chambord, Frangelico, Jägermeister, Kahlua, and Rumplemintz, are the common staples.

Wine

When it comes to wine, even mild-mannered people become freakish snobs. You'll never please everyone, so keep it simple. For red, Cabernet Sauvignon and Pinot Noir are safe and easy to find. For white, a nice Chardonnay, Pinot Grigio, or Sauvignon Blanc are also safe and easy-to-find choices. Wine doesn't keep well after being opened, so trying to keep a large selection on hand isn't practical. But if you know that your guests like a particular style—say a fine Mad Dog 20/20 or a good vintage Wild Irish Rose—then base your offerings on your guests' tastes.

Beer

As with wine, what you stock depends on the tastes of your guests. For a large party, I typically offer a lot of Corona and Coors Light along with a small selection of others, such as Sam Adams, Beck's, Bud, and a few cans of Guinness. If you don't know your guests' tastes ahead of time, aim for a selection that includes domestic and imported beer as well as at least one brand of light beer. (You might consider a non-alcoholic beer as well.)

Hard cider, hard lemonade, hard iced tea, and hard root beer have about the same alcohol content as beer but appeal to those who prefer not to drink beer. Again, whether to stock these depends on your guests' tastes.

Mixers

Mixers are almost as important as the liquors themselves. Here are the basics that will satisfy almost any guest. Keep in mind, though, that sodas go flat over time—even if you never open the bottle. This is especially true of club soda and tonic water. As a general rule, if the bottle is more than six months old, consider replacing it.

Bloody Mary Mix

A Bloody Mary is a very personal drink. Every bartender has his or her variation that makes it individual. Spicy vegetable juice, hot sauce, and Worcestershire sauce are most of what it takes to make a good Bloody Mary mix. Keeping these separate behind the bar will allow you to come up with your own signature flavor.

Cola

I get whatever's on sale at the time, Coke or Pepsi. But keep in mind that Coca Cola has more of a vanilla taste profile, while Pepsi tastes more of lemon.

Cranberry Juice

Diet Cola

Some people prefer Diet Coke, some Diet Pepsi. Others like Pepsi Max, Pepsi One, or Coke Zero. I try to keep them all on hand.

Energy Drinks

Some feel that the caffeine in an energy drink masks the effects of the alcohol, making people more intoxicated than they would have been otherwise. Whether to provide these to your guests is your choice, and many popular drinks now make use of them. The most popular brand is Red Bull, but Monster and Rockstar are common as well.

Ginger Ale, Tonic Water, and Club Soda

Unless you use it all the time, get the small bottles for less waste.

Grapefruit Juice

Grenadine (see Basic Bar Mixes)

Lime Juice

Squeeze fresh if possible. Bottled lime juice is OK but not as vibrant. Sweetened lime juice (Rose's for example) isn't the same thing but is good to have as well.

Margarita Mix

As with Sweet & Sour Mix, you can make your own. A margarita needs tequila, triple sec, and lime juice. Margarita mix combines the triple sec and lime so all you need to do is add the tequila. Mix some triple sec and lime juice, and put it in a bottle. You've just made your own top-shelf margarita mix.

Orange Juice

Pineapple Juice

This is available in little cans and keeps for up to a year, so it's easy to keep on hand without going bad.

Sour Mix (See Basic Bar Mixes)

Sprite / 7-Up

GLOSSARY OF INGREDIENTS

99 Schnapps 99 Apples, 99 Bananas, 99 Oranges—a line of 99 proof fruit-flavored schnapps first produced by Barton Brands, now owned by the Sazerac Company.

Absinthe A high-proof (45–75% alcohol by volume) anise-flavored spirit made from several herbs and flowers, including the flowers and leaves of *Artemisia absinthium*, commonly called wormwood. The sale of absinthe was banned in most of the world between 1907 and 1915. By the 1990s, research had shown it wasn't as harmful as originally thought, and production resumed again. More than 200 brands are available today.

Advocaat A creamy Dutch liqueur made from a blend of brandy, herb extracts, sugar, vanilla, and egg yolks. The drink originated in the Dutch colonies in South America, where it was made from avocados. When the drink traveled north, egg yolks replaced the tropical fruit.

Agavero Liqueur A tequila-based liqueur made with damiana flower tea. The liqueur is very sweet with a strong agave flavor.

Alcopop A generic term for clear, malt-based flavored beverages, such as Mike's Hard Lemonade or Smirnoff Ice. The term refers to the often sweet, candy-like flavors that these drinks have.

Alizé® A French brand that offers several varieties of cognac and fruit juice blends. The original flavor ("Alize Gold Passion") blends French cognac and passion fruit juice. Other varieties include Red Passion (with cranberry), Wild Passion (with pink grapefruit), and Alize Bleu with cherry, ginger, and passion fruit.

Amaretto An Italian liqueur made from apricot pits and almond extract steeped in brandy and sweetened with sugar syrup. Amaretto is Italian for "a little bitter."

Amaro Averna® An Italian herbal liqueur based on a secret recipe created in Caltanissetta in 1854. The liqueur has a mild, bitter flavor and is a digestif in Italy.

Amarula® Cream Liqueur A cream liqueur made in South Africa from the fruit of the Marula tree.

Amer Picon® A bittersweet French apéritif made from herbs, with a distinct orange flavor. Produced and sold in France, Amer Picon is rarely exported and is difficult to find.

Ancho Reyes® An 80-proof ancho chile liqueur produced in Puebla, Mexico.

Anisette An Italian anise-flavored liqueur mainly consumed in France and Spain. It's sweeter than most anise-flavored liqueurs (such as pastis or Pernod) and has a lower alcohol content (typically 25% by volume, versus 40%).

Aperol® An Italian apéritif made of neutral spirits infused with bitter orange, gentian, rhubarb, and an array of herbs and roots—according to a secret recipe unchanged since its creation in 1919. It has a bittersweet orange-and-herbs taste and a red-orange color.

Applejack An alcoholic beverage made from apples that originated during the American colonial period. It's made by concentrating hard cider either by the traditional method of freeze distillation or by true evaporative distillation. The name derives from "jacking," a term for freeze distillation.

Aquavit A caraway-flavored liqueur from Scandinavia. Its name comes from *aqua vitae*, the Latin for "water of life."

Armagnac A brandy, similar to Cognac, produced in the Armagnac region of France. It differs from Cognac in that it's distilled once instead of twice. The distillation also occurs at a lower temperature, allowing more of the character of the fruit to remain.

B&B Bénédictine and brandy

Barenjäger® A German neutral spirit–based liqueur sweetened and then flavored with honey. The word means "bear hunter."

Bénédictine® A brandy-based herbal liqueur produced in France, Bénédictine is believed to be the oldest liqueur continuously made, having been developed by Dom Bernardo Vincelli in 1510 at the Bénédictine Abbey of Fécamp in Normandy. Every bottle of Bénédictine bears the initials "D.O.M.," which stand for "Deo Optimo Maximo,"—"To God, the best, the greatest."

Bitters Originally marketed as patent medicines, these bitter herbal flavorings they principally are used now as a flavoring in food recipes and cocktails.

Angostura Bitters® Named for the town of Angostura, Venezuela. It contains no angostura bark, a medicinal bark named after the same town. These are the most widely distributed bar item in the world.

Peychaud's Bitters® Closely associated with New Orleans, Louisiana, but can be difficult to find elsewhere. It has a subtly different and sweeter taste than the Angostura brand.

Orange Bitters Made from the rinds of unripe oranges.

Fee Brothers A line of flavored bitters that include orange, rhubarb, chocolate, and many others. The company was founded in 1864 in Rochester, New York.

Curaçao A liqueur flavored with the dried peels of Larahas, bitter relatives of oranges, grown on the island of Curaçao. The liqueur has an orange flavor and is bottled with various added coloring. The most common color is blue, but it also comes in green, orange, and red.

Bourbon American whiskey made from at least 51% corn, with the remainder being wheat or rye and malted barley. It's distilled to no more than 160 proof and aged in new, charred white oak barrels for at least two years. It must be put into the barrels at no more than 125 proof; in this way, it's similar to scotch, which also ages in charred barrels.

Brandy A strong alcoholic spirit distilled from wine or other fermented fruit juice.

Cachaça A Brazilian spirit made from distilled sugarcane juice. It's the primary ingredient in an authentic Caipirinha.

Calvados Apple brandy from the Lower Normandy region of France.

Campari® Introduced in Italy in 1860 by Gaspare Campari, it is a mild (between 20–24% alcohol by volume) bitters-type apéritif, often drunk with soda, orange juice, or in mixed drinks.

Chambord® A French liqueur made from small black raspberries.

Champagne A sparkling wine produced only in the Champagne region of France. Champagne is made by adding sugar to bottled wine, allowing a secondary fermentation to occur in the bottle, producing carbon dioxide bubbles. Cava, made in the Catalonia region of Spain, is made the same way and has similar regional restrictions on the name. The secondary fermantation of Prosecco, named after a town in Italy, takes place in steel vats.

Chartreuse® A famous French herbal liqueur produced by Carthusian monks in France from a formula dating back to 1605 and containing 130 herbs and spices.

Green Chartreuse 55% alcohol by volume and naturally green in color. Chartreuse the color is named after the liqueur.

Yellow Chartreuse 40% alcohol by volume, it has a milder and sweeter flavor.

Cherry Heering® A Danish cherry liqueur with a brandy base that has been produced since 1818 under several different names, including "Heering" and "Peter Heering."

Clamato® A blend of tomato juice and clam broth sold by Motts.

Cognac A type of brandy produced only in the Cognac region of western France, it's recognized universally as the finest and most elegant liqueur in the world. Not a drop of any other wine or brandy is ever allowed to enter a bottle of Cognac. The Cognac region is divided into six districts, with the Cognac of Grand Champagne considered the best. Cognac labels feature the following letters: V (very), S (superior), O (old), P (pale), E (extra or *especial*), F (fine), X (extra). French law states that Cognac with 3 stars be aged at least 1½ years old to be rated VS and 4 years to be rated VSOP (although 7–10 years is more common). By French law, the words "Extra," "Napoléon," "Réserve," and "Vieille" (old) may not appear on the label unless the cognac has been aged at least 5½ years.

Cointreau® A fine, colorless, orange-flavored liqueur made from the dried skins of oranges grown on Curaçao in the Dutch West Indies. The Generic term is Curaçao, and if redistilled and clarified is called triple sec.

Courvoisier A type of cognac and famous for being the favorite drink of Napoléon Bonaparte.

Crème Liqueurs Crème liqueurs are very sweet with a single flavor that dominates.

- **Crème d'Amand** almond
- **Crème de Banane** banana
- **Crème de Cacao (dark)** chocolate and dark brown in color
- **Crème de Cacao (white)** chocolate and colorless
- **Crème de Cassis** black currant
- **Crème de Coconut** coconut
- **Crème de Menthe (green)** mint and green in color
- **Crème de Menthe (white)** mint but colorless
- **Crème de Noyaux** made from fruit pits with a bitter almond flavor
- **Crème de Violette (or Crème Yvette)** violets

Cream Soda Vanilla-flavored soft drink.

Cream Sherry A style of sweet sherry created by blending dry sherry with sweet wines that results in a dark, rich wine with a soft sweet finish.

Crown Royal® A blended Canadian whisky

Cynar A bitter Italian liqueur made primarily from artichokes.

Drambuie® A famous whiskey liqueur consisting of Highland malt scotch whiskey, heather honey, and herbs.

Dubonnet® A brand of quinquina, a sweetened fortified wine that contains quinine. Produced in France, it comes in two varieties.

- **Blonde** lighter in color and less sweet
- **Rouge** red in color and sweeter

Everclear® A brand of grain alcohol, 95% alcohol by volume (190 proof)

Fernet Branca®An extremely bitter Italian herbal apéritif or digestif made from cinchona bark, gentium, rhubarb, calamus, angelica, myrrh, chamomile, and peppermint, often drunk to settle the stomach and/or as a hangover remedy. It's classified as a bitters.

Fireball® Cinnamon-flavored whiskey-based liqueur produced by the Sazerac Company. It has a Canadian whisky base with sugar and cinnamon flavoring added.

Firewater® Bright red cinnamon-flavored liqueur.

Frangelico® An Italian hazelnut-flavored liqueur packaged in a distinctive monk-shaped bottle.

Galliano® A sweetish, golden, Italian liqueur with an herby, spicy taste.

Gin A neutral spirit redistilled with or filtered through juniper berries and other botanicals, such as coriander seed, cassia bark, orange peels, fennel seeds, anise, caraway, angelica root, licorice, lemon peel, almonds, cinnamon bark, bergamot, and even cocoa. This secondary process imparts to each gin its particular taste.

Dry (or London Dry) Gin Most of the gin produced now is London dry, which is light, dry, and perfect for making martinis and other mixed drinks.

Plymouth Gin A sweeter and milder gin originally produced in Plymouth, England.

Ginger Beer A fermented, carbonated beverage flavored with ginger, lemon, and sugar. Ginger beer reached the height of its popularity in England in the 1900s. It's popular today in Bermuda and is part of the "national drink" of Bermuda: the Dark and Stormy.

Glayva® Scotch liqueur A liqueur made from a blend of Scotch whiskies, spices, tangerines, cinnamon, almonds and honey.

Godiva® Liqueur A neutral spirit-based liqueur flavored with Godiva brand Belgian chocolate and other flavors. It comes in three varieties: dark chocolate, white chocolate, and espresso.

Goldschläger® A cinnamon-flavored liqueur made in Switzerland that includes flakes of real gold in the bottle.

Gosling's Black Seal Rum® An 80 proof dark rum produced in Bermuda. Along with ginger beer, an essential in the Dark and Stormy.

Grain Alcohol An un-aged neutral spirit with a very high alcohol content (greater than 90% alcohol by volume or 180 proof). Grain alcohol cannot be sold legally in many states in America.

Grand Marnier® A French aged orange flavored liqueur (triple sec) with a brandy base.

Grappa An Italian brandy distilled from the pulpy mass of skins, pits, and stalks left in the wine press after the juice of the grapes has been extracted. Young grappa can be harsh, but it mellows with age.

Grenadine A syrup made from pomegranate juice, containing little or no alcohol.

Guinness® Stout A dry stout made from water, barley malt, hops, and brewers yeast. A proportion of the barley is flaked and roasted to give Guinness its dark color and characteristic taste. Draught and canned Guinness both contain nitrogen in addition to the natural CO_2. The nitrogen helps give Guinness its thick head and "waterfall" settling effect.

Hard Apple Cider (or Hard Cider) Fermented apple juice with an alcohol content similar to beer.

Hennessy® A cognac produced in France by James Hennessy and Co. and the Hennessy family.

Horchata The name for several kinds of traditional beverages made from ground almonds, sesame seeds, rice, barley, or tigernuts.

Hot Damn® Cinnamon Schnapps A cinnamon-flavored liqueur with a strong cinnamon flavor and a red color.

Hpnotiq® An American fruit liqueur made from vodka, cognac, and tropical fruit juices, bottled in France by Heaven Hill Distilleries.

Irish Cream Liqueur A mocha-flavored whiskey and double-cream liqueur that combines Irish whiskey, cream, coffee, chocolate, and other flavors.

Irish Mist® A liqueur produced in Ireland, consisting of Irish whiskey flavored with heather honey.

Jack Daniel's® A whiskey made in Tennessee and perhaps the most famous American whiskey. The Jack Daniel's distillery in Lynchburg, Tennessee, dates from 1875 and is the oldest registered distillery in the United States. Jack Daniel's is made using the sour-mash process and the "Lincoln County Process" of filtration through sugar maple charcoal before being aged in charred American Oak casks.

Jägermeister® This complex, aromatic liqueur containing some 56 herbs, roots, and fruits has been popular in Germany since its introduction in 1935. In Germany, it's frequently consumed warm as an apéritif or after dinner as a digestif. In America, due to savvy marketing by the importer, it's widely popular as a chilled shooter.

KeKe Beach® liqueur A key lime–flavored cream liqueur with a hint of graham cracker flavor as well.

Kirschwasser A clear brandy made from double distillation of the fermented juice of the black cherry.

Kümmel® A sweet, colorless liqueur flavored with caraway seed, cumin, and fennel.

Licor 43® (Cuarenta y Tres) A yellow liqueur from Spain made from fruit juices, vanilla, and other aromatic herbs and spices.

Lillet® An apéritif wine from the Bordeaux region of France, Lillet comes in both red and white varieties.

Limoncello An Italian liqueur made from lemons.

Madeira A fortified wine made in the Madeira Islands of Portugal and popular as a dessert wine or for cooking.

Malibu Rum® A Jamaican coconut-flavored rum liqueur.

Mandarine Napoleon Liqueur® A liqueur made from mandarin orange–flavored cognac.

Maraschino A very sweet white cherry liqueur made from the Marasca cherry of Dalmatia, Croatia. This liqueur is sometimes used in sours in place of sugar.

Marsala A fortified wine made in the Italian city of Marsala and traditionally served chilled with a spicy cheese between the first and second course of a meal or warm as a dessert wine. It's also used for cooking.

Melon Liqueur A pale green liqueur that tastes of fresh muskmelon or cantaloupe. The most famous brand, Midori®, is

Japanese and produced by the Suntory Company in Mexico, France, and Japan.

Metaxa A strong, sharp-tasting, aromatic Greek brandy.

Mezcal A Mexican distilled spirit made from the agave plant. Tequila is a mezcal made only from the blue agave plant in the region around Tequila, Jalisco. Spirits labeled "Mezcal" are made from other agave plants and don't belong to the Tequila family.

Mozart® Chocolate Liqueur A line of chocolate liqueurs produced in Salzburg, Austria. Varieties include chocolate cream, white chocolate, dark chocolate and a clear chocolate flavored vodka.

Muscatel A wine, often fortified, produced from the Muscat variety of grape.

Nassau Royale® A rum-based liqueur with a vanilla flavor.

Ouzo An anise-flavored liqueur from Greece, usually served on the rocks. Ouzo can be used as a substitute for absinthe in many cases.

Parfait Amour A cordial made of citrus juices, cinnamon, coriander, and brandy.

Passoa® A passion fruit–flavored liqueur produced by Remy Cointreau.

Pastis A semi-sweet anise-flavored liqueur produced as a substitute for absinthe and lacking the wormwood.

Peach Schnapps A sweet peach-flavored liqueur

Pernod® A brand of pastis produced by the Pernod-Ricard company.

Pimm's® Also known as Pimm's No. 1, it's an English gin-based liqueur made with a secret mixture of herbs. Other varieties, numbered 2 through 6, have various flavor profiles and base spirits, but No. 1 is the most common and best known.

Pisang Ambon® A Dutch liqueur green in color and flavored with banana.

Pisco A brandy made in the wine-producing regions of South America. The most popular spirit in Chile and Peru.

Ponche Kuba® A "ponche" is a homemade cream liqueur similar to eggnog and popular in Caribbean and Latin American countries. Ponche Kuba is a packaged form of this liqueur. It's made from a rum base with cream, eggs, and sugar added and flavored with a proprietary blend of spices.

Port A sweet, fortified wine from the Douro Valley in the northern part of Portugal

Red Bull® A carbonated soft drink with additives and extra caffeine that claim to reduce mental and physical fatigue.

Rock & Rye A blend of rye whiskey with rock candy and fruit juice.

Rose's Lime Juice® A sweetened lime juice syrup used in many cocktails.

Rum A liquor made from fermented and distilled sugar cane juice or molasses. Rum has a very wide range of flavors, from light and dry like a vodka, to dark and complex like a cognac.

Light Rum clear in color and dry in flavor

Dark Rum dark, almost black in color with a rich and complex flavor

Amber Rum gold in color and sweeter than a light rum

Añejo Rum aged in wood

Flavored Rums Like vodka, available in a wide array of flavors. The first flavored rums featured vanilla or lemon. Now almost any flavor can be found.

Rum Cream Cream liqueurs made with a rum base with cream and flavoring added. The flavors are typically tropical such as banana, coconut, and pineapple.

Spiced Rum The original flavored rum. Spiced rum consists of an amber rum with vanilla and cinnamon flavor added.

RumChata® A creamy horchata-based liqueur with added rum.

Rumplemintz® A 100 proof (50% alcohol by volume) peppermint schnapps produced in Germany

Safari® A fruit liqueur flavored with mango, papaya, passion fruit, and lime.

Sake A Japanese alcoholic beverage brewed from rice. It's commonly called "rice wine" in America but its production has more in common with malt liquor.

Sambuca An Italian liqueur flavored with anise and elderberry. It's produced in both clear ("white Sambuca") and dark blue or purple ("black Sambuca") versions.

Schnapps A liqueur distilled from grains, roots, or fruits. Real schnapps has no sugar or flavoring added because the flavor should originate from the base material. Many syrupy sweet fruit liqueurs are called schnapps but aren't true schnapps because of added sugar and flavorings.

Scotch Scotch whiskey is whiskey produced in Scotland. In America, it's commonly called Scotch. In Scotland, however, it's known simply as whisky (note the spelling).

Sherry A type of Spanish wine fortified with brandy.

Simple Syrup (or Sugar Syrup) A combination of equal parts sugar and boiling water, allowed to cool, and bottled as a sweetener for many mixed drinks.

Sloe Gin A liqueur flavored with sloe berries and blackthorn fruit. Traditionally it was made with a gin base and with sugar added. Most modern versions use a neutral spirit base and add flavorings later.

Smirnoff Ice® A clear malt-based beverage that comes in a variety of flavors.

Southern Comfort® A neutral-spirit liqueur with peach and almond flavors.

St. Germain® A French liqueur flavored with elderflowers. It was created in 2007 and is owned by Bacardi, Ltd.

Stout A beer made with roasted barley or malt. Roasting the grain gives the beer a darker color and a stronger flavor.

Strega An Italian herbal liqueur with mint and fennel flavors. Saffron in the recipe gives it a yellow color. The name in Italian means "witch."

Sweet & Sour Mix A syrup made from a blend of sugar and lemon juice. A simple recipe is to mix equal parts simple syrup and lemon juice.

Sweetened Lime Juice Lime juice with added sugar.

T.Q. Hot® A tequila flavored with hot peppers.

Tabasco® Sauce A hot pepper sauce made from a blend of Tabasco peppers, vinegar, and salt that's aged in wood casks.

Tang® An orange-flavored powdered drink mix owned by Kraft Foods. Iintroduced in 1959, it became popular when NASA gave it to astronauts, starting with the Gemini program, in 1965.

Tequila A type of mezcal made only from the blue agave plant in the region surrounding Tequila, a town in the Mexican state of Jalisco. Tequila is made in many different styles, the difference among them mostly depending on how long the distillate ages before being bottled.

- **Silver ("plata" or "blanco")** Clear, unaged tequila that has a very strong flavor.
- **Gold ("oro" or "joven abocado")** Meaning "bottled when young," this is a white tequila with coloring added.
- **Reposado** Meaning "rested," this kind is aged at least 1 year.
- **Añejo** Aged between 1 and 3 years

Tequila Rose® A cream liqueur with a tequila base and a strawberry flavor.

Tia Maria® A coffee-flavored liqueur from Jamaica. The base is Jamaican rum flavored with spices.

Tonic Water Seltzer with quinine added. Originally used to prevent malaria, the amount of quinine in bottled tonic water today is about half of the dose given to malaria patients.

Triple Sec A popular flavoring agent in many drinks, triple sec is the best known form of Curaçao, a liqueur made from the skins of the Curaçao orange.

Vermouth A fortified wine flavored with aromatic herbs and spices. It comes in three common varieties.

- **Dry Vermouth** Clear or pale yellow and very dry
- **Sweet Vermouth** Red and sweeter
- **White Vermouth** Clear or pale yellow but sweeter than dry vermouth

Vodka A neutral spirit that can be distilled from almost anything that will ferment (grain, potatoes, grapes, corn, beets). It's distilled multiple times and filtered to remove as many of the impurities as possible. Then it's diluted with water to bring the alcohol content down before being bottled. Vodka can be found in a wide variety of flavors from birthday cake to watermelon.

Wasabi The root of this member of the cabbage family is ground and used as a potent Japanese spice.

Whiskey (or Whisky) A beverage distilled from fermented grain and aged in oak casks. The location, grain, type of oak, and length of aging all affect the flavor. Spelled with an e in Ireland and America and without the e everywhere else. The four major regions where whiskey is produced: Ireland, Scotland, Canada, and America. Each has a different style that imparts a distinctive flavor.

Wild Turkey® A Kentucky bourbon whiskey available in both 80 proof and 101 proof versions.

Wine An alcoholic beverage produced by the fermentation of fruit juice, typically grapes. The type of grape, where they grew, and the way the wine is stored as it ferments affect the taste and color.

Yukon Jack® A Canadian liqueur made from a whiskey base and flavored with honey.

COCKTAILS

What makes a cocktail different from a martini? What makes it different from a run-of-the-mill mixed drink? Here, a cocktail is a mixed drink shaken or stirred with ice and strained in a cocktail glass. Additionally, none of the drinks below end with "tini."

1 Randini

COCKTAIL GLASS

2 parts Cranberry Juice Cocktail
3 parts Gin
1 part Triple Sec

Shake with ice and strain. Garnish with Lime Wedge.

1001 Nights

COCKTAIL GLASS

1½ parts Crème de Cacao (Dark)
1½ parts Triple Sec

Shake with ice and strain.

1-900-Fuk-Meup

COCKTAIL GLASS

2 parts Currant Vodka
1 part Grand Marnier®
1 part Raspberry Liqueur
1 part Melon Liqueur
1 part Coconut Rum
1 part Amaretto
2 parts Cranberry Juice Cocktail
1 part Pineapple Juice

Shake with ice and strain.

20th Century

COCKTAIL GLASS

2 parts Gin
1 part Crème de Cacao (White)
1 part Lillet®
1 part Lemon Juice

Shake with ice and strain into a chilled glass.

21 Joc

COCKTAIL GLASS

1 part Vodka
½ part Triple Sec
½ part Strawberry Liqueur
splash Lime Juice

Shake with ice and strain.

22 Park Lane

COCKTAIL GLASS

1½ parts Gin
¼ part Sweet Vermouth
¼ part Triple Sec

Shake with ice and strain.

2lips

COCKTAIL GLASS

⅔ part Vodka
½ part Parfait Amour
splash Crème de Cassis
splash Lime Juice
splash Cranberry Juice Cocktail

Shake with ice and strain.

3 Base Hit

COCKTAIL GLASS

1 part Strawberry Liqueur
1 part Orange Liqueur
1 part Crème de Banane

Shake with ice and strain.

3 Commandments

COCKTAIL GLASS

1 part Añejo Rum
1 part Citrus Flavored Rum
1 part Orange Rum

Shake with ice and strain.

3C

COCKTAIL GLASS

1½ parts Cherry Brandy
1 part Cream
3 parts Cranberry Juice Cocktail

Shake with ice and strain.

3 G's

COCKTAIL GLASS

splash Mezcal
1½ parts Gin
1 part St-Germain
½ part Ginger Liqueur
splash Pernod

Rinse a chilled cocktail glass with the Mezcal and dump the excess. Combine remaining ingredients in a shaker with ice, shake, and strain into the cocktail glass. Garnish with Pomegranate Seeds and a Dill Sprig.

420 Kicker

COCKTAIL GLASS

2 parts Absolut® Peppar Vodka
1 part Peppermint Schnapps
1 part Sweet & Sour Mix

Shake with ice and strain.

43 Amigos

COCKTAIL GLASS

1 part Tequila
½ part Licor 43®
½ part Triple Sec
½ part Lime Juice

Shake with ice and strain.

44 Special

COCKTAIL GLASS

1 part Cranberry Vodka
1 part Vodka
1 part Peach Schnapps
2½ parts Grape Juice
2½ parts Pineapple Juice

Shake with ice and strain.

4th Estate Cocktail

COCKTAIL GLASS

1 part Gin
1 part Dry Vermouth
1 part Sweet Vermouth
splash Absinthe

Shake with ice and strain.

4th of July

COCKTAIL GLASS

1½ parts Vodka
½ part Blue Curaçao
½ part Triple Sec
½ part Sweet & Sour Mix

Shake with ice and strain. Top with splash of grenadine.

5 M

COCKTAIL GLASS

1 part Dark Rum
½ part Mandarine Napoléon® Liqueur
½ part Crème de Banane
1 part Cream
splash Grenadine

Shake with ice and strain.

'57 Chevy

COCKTAIL GLASS

1 part Southern Comfort®
1 part Gin
1 part Vodka
splash Orange Juice
splash Pineapple Juice
splash Grenadine

Shake with ice and strain.

73 Bus

COCKTAIL GLASS

3 parts Gin
1 part Triple Sec
1 part Cranberry Juice Cocktail

Shake with ice and strain.

7 Kickers

COCKTAIL GLASS

3 parts Pineapple Juice
1 part Blue Curaçao
1 part Peach Schnapps
½ part Crème de Coconut

Shake with ice and strain.

7th Heaven

COCKTAIL GLASS

1½ parts Gin
½ part Maraschino Liqueur
½ part Grapefruit Juice

Shake with ice and strain.

8th Birthday

COCKTAIL GLASS

¾ part Raspberry Liqueur
¼ part Crème de Cacao (Dark)
1 part Vodka
1 part Milk

Shake with ice and strain.

9½ Weeks

COCKTAIL GLASS

2 parts Citrus Vodka
½ part Triple Sec
1 part Orange Juice
splash Strawberry Liqueur

Shake with ice and strain.

A.J.

COCKTAIL GLASS

1½ parts Grapefruit Juice
3 dashes Grenadine
1½ parts Apple Brandy

Shake with ice and strain.

Abbey in the Hills

COCKTAIL GLASS

⅔ part Vodka
½ part Crème de Cacao (White)
½ part Irish Cream Liqueur
½ part Frangelico®

Shake with ice and strain.

Abe's Tropical Night in Hell

COCKTAIL GLASS

2 parts Vodka
2 parts Banana Liqueur
2 parts Godiva® Liqueur
1 part Grenadine

Shake with ice and strain.

Abigail

COCKTAIL GLASS

1½ parts Bourbon
splash Pernod
2 dashes Angostura Bitters
dash Orange Bitters

Shake with ice and strain. Garnish with Lemon Twist.

Abracadabra

COCKTAIL GLASS

1 part Light Rum
1 part Orange Juice
1 part Grapefruit Juice
splash Amaretto

Shake with ice and strain.

Absinthe Sour

COCKTAIL GLASS

1 part Absinthe
1 Egg White
1 tbsp Sugar
½ part Lemon Juice

Shake with ice and strain.

Absinthe Special Cocktail
COCKTAIL GLASS
1 1/2 parts Anisette
dash Bitters
dash Sugar
1 part Water
Shake with ice and strain.

Absolut® Evergreen
COCKTAIL GLASS
2/3 part Citrus Vodka
1/3 part Pisang Ambon® Liqueur
splash Lemon Juice
Mix with ice and strain.

Absolut® Northern Style
COCKTAIL GLASS
1 part Vodka
splash Apple Brandy
1/2 part Cream
fill with White Wine
Shake with ice and strain.

Absolut® Pissy
COCKTAIL GLASS
2 parts Vodka
1 part Lime Juice
2 parts Pineapple Juice
Shake with ice and strain.

Absolute Dream
COCKTAIL GLASS
3 parts Orange Vodka
1 part Chambord
2 parts Sweet & Sour Mix
Shake with ice and strain.

Absolute Zero
COCKTAIL GLASS
2 parts Vodka
2 parts Coffee Liqueur
1 part Peppermint Schnapps
2 parts Cream
Shake with ice and strain.

Acapulco
COCKTAIL GLASS
1 1/2 parts Tequila
3 parts Pineapple Juice
1 part Grapefruit Juice
Shake with ice and strain.

Accidental Tourist
COCKTAIL GLASS
1 1/2 parts Gin
1 part Vanilla Vodka
1/2 part Apple Brandy
1/2 part Passion Fruit Liqueur
Shake with ice and strain.

Accordion
COCKTAIL GLASS
1 1/2 parts Brandy
1/2 part Sweet Vermouth
1/2 part Dry Vermouth
2 splashes Triple Sec
Shake with ice and strain.

Acme
COCKTAIL GLASS
1/2 part Apricot Brandy
1 1/2 parts Light Rum
1/2 part Lime Juice
dash Powdered Sugar
Shake with ice and strain.

Acrobat
COCKTAIL GLASS
1 part Gin
2/3 part Apricot Brandy
2/3 part Dry Vermouth
splash Lime Juice
Shake with ice and strain.

Across the Stars

COCKTAIL GLASS

1/2 part Light Rum
1/2 part Dark Rum
1/2 part Triple Sec
2/3 part Lemon Juice
2/3 part Pineapple Juice
2/3 part Cranberry Juice Cocktail

Shake with ice and strain.

Adam and Eve

COCKTAIL GLASS

1 part Brandy
1 part Gin
1 part Apple Liqueur
splash Lemon Juice

Shake with ice and strain.

Admiral Cocktail

COCKTAIL GLASS

1 1/2 parts Gin
1 part Cherry Liqueur
2 splashes Lime Juice

Shake with ice and strain over ice.

Admiralens Lile

COCKTAIL GLASS

1/2 part Apricot Brandy
1/2 part Dark Rum
1 part Crème de Banane
1 part Apple Juice
splash Grenadine

Shake with ice and strain.

Admirals Only

COCKTAIL GLASS

1/2 part Citrus Vodka
2/3 part Amaretto
2/3 part Grand Marnier®
1 1/2 parts Cranberry Juice Cocktail

Shake with ice and strain.

The Admiral's Passion

COCKTAIL GLASS

1 part Passoã®
1 part Lemon-Lime Soda
1 part Orange Juice

Shake with ice and strain.

Adriana

COCKTAIL GLASS

1 part Orange Juice
1 part Gin
1/2 part Dry Vermouth
1/2 part Sweet Vermouth

Shake with ice and strain.

Adult's Channel

COCKTAIL GLASS

1 part Gin
1/2 part Strawberry Liqueur
splash Vanilla Liqueur
splash Lemon Juice

Shake with ice and strain.

Aer Rianta

COCKTAIL GLASS

1/2 part Gin
1/2 part Crème de Banane
1/2 part Sweet Vermouth
1/2 part Lemon Juice

Shake with ice and strain.

African Coffee

COCKTAIL GLASS

1 1/2 parts Crème de Cacao (Dark)
1 1/2 parts Hot Coffee
1 1/2 parts Tia Maria®
dash Strawberry Juice

Shake with ice and strain.

After 8

COCKTAIL GLASS

1 part Irish Cream Liqueur
1 part Coffee Brandy
1 part Crème de Menthe (Green)

Shake with ice and strain.

After Dinner Delight
COCKTAIL GLASS
1 part Creme de Menthe (White)
1 part Frangelico®
2 parts Irish Cream Liqueur
Shake with ice and strain.

Afterburner
COCKTAIL GLASS
1 part Vodka
½ part Triple Sec
splash Grapefruit Juice
Shake with ice and strain.

Aftermath
COCKTAIL GLASS
2 parts Vodka
1 part Mandarine Napoléon® Liqueur
4 parts Grapefruit Juice
Shake with ice and strain.

Afternoon Chat
COCKTAIL GLASS
1 part Jim Beam®
1 part Maraschino Liqueur
½ part Peach Schnapps
2 parts Cranberry Juice Cocktail
3 parts Pineapple Juice
Shake with ice and strain.

Afternoon Cocktail
COCKTAIL GLASS
1 part Cognac
1 part Maraschino Liqueur
1 part Fernet-Branca®
Shake with ice and strain.

Agavemon
COCKTAIL GLASS
½ part Tequila Reposado
1 part Melon Liqueur
½ part Triple Sec
1½ parts Lime Juice
Shake with ice and strain.

Agave Suave
COCKTAIL GLASS
1½ parts Gold Tequila
1 part Orange Juice
1 part Pineapple Juice
splash Amaretto
dash Pernod
Shake with ice and strain.

Ahh
COCKTAIL GLASS
1 part Vodka
1 part Parfait Amour
1 part Fruit Juice
Shake with ice and strain.

Ahi, Mi Amor!
COCKTAIL GLASS
1½ parts Dark Rum
½ part Lime Juice
¼ part Parfait Amour
½ part Simple Syrup
Shake with ice and strain.

Air Mail Special
COCKTAIL GLASS
1½ parts Sweet Vermouth
½ part Grappa
Shake with ice and strain.

Airbag
COCKTAIL GLASS
1½ parts Silver Tequila
3 parts Grapefruit Juice
½ part Mango Juice
splash Lemon Juice
splash Triple Sec
Shake with ice and strain.

Airborne Penguin
COCKTAIL GLASS
1½ parts Gin
1½ parts Dry Vermouth
splash Maraschino Liqueur
splash Pernod®
dash Orange Bitters
Shake with ice and strain.

Akuna Matata

COCKTAIL GLASS

2/3 part Crème de Banane
2/3 part Crème de Coconut
2/3 part Frangelico®
2/3 part Spiced Rum
3 parts Cream

Shake with ice and strain.

Alabama

COCKTAIL GLASS

1 part Brandy
1 part Triple Sec
1/2 part Lime Juice
1 tbsp Sugar

Shake with ice and strain.

Alabammy Sammy

COCKTAIL GLASS

1 part Cherry Brandy
1/2 part Sambuca
1 part Sweet & Sour Mix
2/3 part Ginger Ale

Shake with ice and strain.

Aladdin Sane

COCKTAIL GLASS

1 part Citrus Vodka
1/2 part Lime
1/2 part Cointreau®
2 parts Fruit Punch

Shake with ice and strain.

Alaine Cocktail

COCKTAIL GLASS

1 part Lemon Rum
1 part Amaretto
1 part Cranberry Juice

Shake with ice and strain.

Alaskan Cocktail

COCKTAIL GLASS

1 1/2 parts Gin
3/4 part Yellow Chartreuse
2 dashes Orange Bitters

Shake with ice and strain. Garnish with Lemon Twist.

Alberta Warmer

COCKTAIL GLASS

1/2 part Maraschino Liqueur
1/2 part Dry Vermouth
1 part Canadian Whisky
1 part Pineapple Juice

Shake with ice and strain.

Aleluia

COCKTAIL GLASS

1 part Vodka
1/2 part Peach Schnapps
1/2 part Apricot Brandy
1 part Orange Juice

Shake with ice and strain.

Alessandro

COCKTAIL GLASS

1 part Gin
1 part Sambuca
1 part Cream

Shake with ice and strain.

Alexander's Sister

COCKTAIL GLASS

2 parts Gin
1 part Crème de Menthe (Green)
1 part Cream

Shake with ice and strain.

Alexandre le Grand

COCKTAIL GLASS

1 1/2 parts Brandy
1/2 part Triple Sec
1/2 part Mandarine Napoléon® Liqueur
splash Galliano®
1 part Cream

Shake with ice and strain. Top with cream.

Alfa Romeo®

COCKTAIL GLASS

2 parts Sweet Vermouth
1/2 part Gin
1 part Maraschino Liqueur
splash Campari®

Shake with ice and strain.

Alfred's Special Cocktail

COCKTAIL GLASS

2 parts Lemon Vodka
1 part Triple Sec
1 part Pineapple Juice

Shake with ice and strain.

Algebra

COCKTAIL GLASS

1 part Light Rum
½ part Triple Sec
½ part Lemon Juice

Shake with ice and strain.

Alien Autopsy

COCKTAIL GLASS

2 parts Raspberry Vodka
1 part Whipped Cream Vodka
1 part Orange Juice

Shake with ice and strain. Garnish with a green Maraschino Cherry.

Alien Booger

COCKTAIL GLASS

1 part Coconut Rum
1 part Melon Liqueur
1 part Pineapple Vodka
splash Pineapple Juice

Shake with ice and strain.

Alien Sky

COCKTAIL GLASS

1 part Light Rum
1 part Cherry Brandy
½ part Blue Curaçao
2 parts Orange Juice
3 parts Pineapple Juice

Shake with ice and strain.

All Jacked Up

COCKTAIL GLASS

½ part Jack Daniel's®
1 part Sloe Gin
1 part Melon Liqueur
1 part Pineapple Juice

Shake with ice and strain.

All Plucked Up

COCKTAIL GLASS

1½ parts Añejo Rum
1½ parts Coconut Rum
¼ part Grenadine
1 part Lime Juice
2 parts Orange Juice
3 parts Pineapple Juice

Shake with ice and strain.

All Stars

COCKTAIL GLASS

1 part Gin
1 part Triple Sec
1 part Sweet Vermouth

Shake with ice and strain.

All White Frappe

COCKTAIL GLASS

1 part Peppermint Schnapps
1 part Crème de Cacao (White)
1 part Anisette
1 part Lemon Juice

Shake with ice and strain.

All at Once

COCKTAIL GLASS

1 part Licor 43®
1 part Cherry Brandy
½ part Apricot Brandy

Shake with ice and strain.

Allegheny

COCKTAIL GLASS

1 part Dry Vermouth
1 part Blackberry Brandy
½ part Lemon Juice

Shake with ice and strain. Garnish with a Lemon Twist.

Allegro Agitato

COCKTAIL GLASS

1 part Maraschino Liqueur
1 part Grenadine
1 part Grappa
1 part Dry Sherry

Shake with ice and strain.

Alleluia

COCKTAIL GLASS

2 parts Tequila Reposado
1 part Maraschino Liqueur

Shake with ice and strain.

Alley Shooter

COCKTAIL GLASS

1 part Irish Cream Liqueur
1 part Coffee Liqueur
1 part Frangelico®
1 part Amaretto
1 part Vodka

Shake with ice and strain.

Allota Fagina

COCKTAIL GLASS

1 part Butterscotch Schnapps
1 part Irish Cream Liqueur
1 part Coconut Rum

Shake with ice and strain.

Alma Cocktail

COCKTAIL GLASS

2 parts Crème de Cacao (Dark)
1 part Light Rum
1 part Gin
½ part Cream

Shake with ice and strain.

Almodovar

COCKTAIL GLASS

1 part Cherry Brandy
1 part Apricot Brandy
1 part Dry Vermouth
1 part Dry Sherry

Shake with ice and strain.

Almond Colada

COCKTAIL GLASS

3 parts Amaretto
¼ cup Crème de Coconut
1½ parts Vodka
1 part Chocolate Syrup

Shake with ice and strain.

Almond Delight

COCKTAIL GLASS

1½ parts Amaretto
½ part Sambuca

Shake with ice and strain.

Almond Eye

COCKTAIL GLASS

1 part Amaretto
1 part Crème de Cacao (Dark)
1 part Cream

Shake with ice and strain.

Almond Joy®

COCKTAIL GLASS

½ part Amaretto
½ part Crème de Cacao (White)
2 parts Light Cream

Shake with ice and strain.

Almondini

COCKTAIL GLASS

1 part Vodka
1 part Amaretto

Shake with ice and strain.

Alphabet

COCKTAIL GLASS

½ part Drambuie®
⅔ part Apple Brandy
splash Blue Curaçao
splash Chartreuse®

Shake with ice and strain.

Amagansett

COCKTAIL GLASS

1½ parts Gin
½ part Dry Vermouth
½ part Pernod®
splash Crème de Menthe (White)

Shake with ice and strain.

Amaretto Flip

COCKTAIL GLASS

2 parts Amaretto
1 Egg White
1 part Orange Juice
3/4 part Cream

Shake with ice and strain.

Amatitán Monk

COCKTAIL GLASS

2 parts Partida Reposado Tequila
3/4 part St-Germain
1/4 part Bénédictine
1/4 part Lemon Juice
1/4 part Lime Juice

Shake with ice and strain.

Amaretto Stinger

COCKTAIL GLASS

1 1/2 parts Amaretto
3/4 part Crème de Menthe (White)

Shake with ice and strain.

Amba

COCKTAIL GLASS

1 part Scotch
1/2 part Dark Rum
1 part Triple Sec
1 part Sweet Vermouth

Shake with ice and strain.

Ambaraba

COCKTAIL GLASS

1 part Whiskey
1/2 part Light Rum
1/4 part Triple Sec
1/4 part Sweet Vermouth

Shake with ice and strain.

L'Ambassadeur

COCKTAIL GLASS

1 1/2 parts Orange Gin
1/2 part Crème de Banane
1/2 part Dry Vermouth
splash Lemon Juice

Shake with ice and strain.

Ambrosia

COCKTAIL GLASS

2 parts Vodka
1/2 part Melon Liqueur
1/4 part Orange Bitters

Stir gently with ice and strain.

Ambrous

COCKTAIL GLASS

1 part Apricot Brandy
1 part Apple Brandy
1 part Ginger Ale
splash Lime Juice

Shake with ice and strain.

America On Line

COCKTAIL GLASS

1 1/2 parts Jim Beam©
1 1/2 parts Orange Juice
splash Peppermint Liqueur
splash Amaretto

Shake with ice and strain.

American Dragon

COCKTAIL GLASS

1 1/2 parts Gin
1/2 part Peppermint Liqueur
1/2 part Kümmel
1/2 part Lemon Juice
dash Orange Bitters

Shake with ice and strain.

American Pie

COCKTAIL GLASS

1 part Brandy
1/2 part Dry Vermouth
1/2 part Tawny Port
splash Crème de Menthe (White)
1 part Orange Juice

Shake with ice and strain.

American Woman
COCKTAIL GLASS

2 parts Bourbon
1 part Cherry Vodka
1 part Southern Comfort
½ part Cherry Liqueur

Shake with ice and strain.

Amethyst
COCKTAIL GLASS

1 part Parfait Amour
½ part Raspberry Liqueur
½ part Vanilla Vodka

Shake with ice and strain.

Amethyst Mist
COCKTAIL GLASS

2 parts Vodka
1 part Drambuie
1 part Parfait Amour

Shake with ice and strain.

Amigo
COCKTAIL GLASS

1 part Dark Rum
½ part Crème de Banane
½ part Apricot Brandy
1 part Pear Juice
splash Grenadine

Shake with ice and strain.

Amer Picon® Cocktail
COCKTAIL GLASS

1 part Sweet Vermouth
1 part Amer Picon®

Shake with ice and strain.

Amor Brujo
COCKTAIL GLASS

1½ parts Cherry Brandy
1½ parts Chocolate Liqueur
1½ parts Cream

Shake with ice and strain.

Amore Me Amore
COCKTAIL GLASS

1 part Blackberry Liqueur
1 part Currant Vodka
½ part Frangelico®
½ part Lemon Juice
2 parts Raspberry Seltzer

Shake with ice and strain.

Amsterdam
COCKTAIL GLASS

1½ parts Gin
¾ part Triple Sec
½ part Orange Juice

Shake with ice and strain.

Anchor's Seagrit
COCKTAIL GLASS

½ part Dark Rum
1 part Triple Sec
splash Passion Fruit Liqueur
splash Lime Juice
splash Sweet & Sour Mix

Shake with ice and strain.

Andalusia
COCKTAIL GLASS

½ part Light Rum
1½ parts Dry Sherry
½ part Brandy

Shake with ice and strain.

Andicuri Special
COCKTAIL GLASS

1 part Light Rum
1 part Crème de Cacao (White)
1 part Cream
splash Coffee

Shake with ice and strain.

Angel Face
COCKTAIL GLASS

1 part Gin
½ part Apricot Brandy
½ part Apple Brandy

Shake with ice and strain.

Angel with Dirty Face

COCKTAIL GLASS

2/3 part Cherry Brandy
1 1/2 parts Scotch
1 1/2 parts Carpano Punt e Mes Vermouth

Shake with ice and strain.

Angelic Cocktail

COCKTAIL GLASS

1 part Bourbon
1/2 part Crème de Cacao (White)
1/2 part Cream
splash Grenadine

Shake with ice and strain.

Angel's Treat

COCKTAIL GLASS

2 parts Dark Rum
1 part Amaretto
2 parts Whipping Cream

Shake with ice and strain.

Angers Rose

COCKTAIL GLASS

1 part Pineapple Juice
1/2 part Triple Sec
1/2 part Bourbon
splash Campari®
1 Egg White

Shake with ice and strain.

Anisette Cocktail

COCKTAIL GLASS

1 part Anisette
dash Sugar
splash Water

Shake with ice and strain.

Ankle Sprainer

COCKTAIL GLASS

1/2 part Cherry Brandy
splash Crème de Banane
splash Pineapple Juice
splash Orange Juice

Shake with ice and strain.

Ann Sheridan

COCKTAIL GLASS

1 part Light Rum
1/2 part Blue Curaçao
1/2 part Lime Juice

Shake with ice and strain.

Annabelle Special

COCKTAIL GLASS

2 parts Bénédictine
1/4 part Dry Vermouth
1/4 part Lime Juice

Shake with ice and strain.

Año

COCKTAIL GLASS

2/3 part Raspberry Liqueur
2/3 part Vodka
2/3 part Dry Vermouth

Shake with ice and strain.

Antananarivo

COCKTAIL GLASS

1/2 part Amaretto
1/2 part Crème de Cacao (White)
1/2 part Cherry Brandy
1 part Dark Rum
1 part Cream

Shake with ice and strain.

Ante Up

COCKTAIL GLASS

2 parts Apple Brandy
1 part Dubonnet Blanc
1/2 part Triple Sec

Shake with ice and strain.

Antidote

COCKTAIL GLASS

1 part Amaretto
1/2 part Triple Sec
1 1/2 parts Scotch
2 parts Orange Juice
1 part Lemon Juice

Shake with ice and strain.

Aperitivo
COCKTAIL GLASS

1 1/2 parts Gin
1 part Sambuca
2 dashes Orange Bitters

Shake with ice and strain.

Aperol™ '86
COCKTAIL GLASS

1 part Aperol™
1 part Cointreau®
1 part Dry Vermouth

Shake with ice and strain.

Aphrodite
COCKTAIL GLASS

1 1/2 parts Parfait Amour
1/2 part Vanilla Liqueur
1 1/2 parts Cream

Shake with ice and strain.

Appalachia
COCKTAIL GLASS

1 1/2 parts Scotch
1 part Green Ginger Wine
1 part Orange Juice

Shake with ice and strain.

Appian Way
COCKTAIL GLASS

1 1/2 parts Gin
1/2 part Strega®
1/2 part Amaretto

Shake with ice and strain.

Apple Bee
COCKTAIL GLASS

1 1/2 parts Sour Apple Schnapps
1/2 part Applejack
1/2 part Cranberry Juice Cocktail

Shake with ice and strain.

Apple Cream Pie
COCKTAIL GLASS

1 part Apple Vodka
1 part Sour Apple Schnapps
1/2 part Lime Juice
1/2 part Triple Sec
1 part Cream

Shake with ice and strain.

Apple Daiquiri
COCKTAIL GLASS

1/2 part Apple Juice
1/2 part Lime Juice
1 1/2 parts Light Rum
dash Powdered Sugar

Fill a mixing glass with 4 parts of shaved ice and add all ingredients. Shake and strain into a chilled glass.

Apple Jax
COCKTAIL GLASS

1 part Melon Liqueur
1/2 part Whiskey
1/2 part Apple Liqueur

Shake with ice and strain.

Apple Judy
COCKTAIL GLASS

1/2 part Grand Marnier®
1/2 part Vodka
3 parts Apple Juice

Shake with ice and strain.

Apple Juice
COCKTAIL GLASS

1 part Coconut Rum
1 part Peach Schnapps
1 part Pisang Ambon® Liqueur
1 part Lime Juice
1 part Apple Juice

Shake with ice and strain.

Apple Ordeal
COCKTAIL GLASS

1 part Apricot Brandy
1 part Apple Brandy
1/2 part Cream of Coconut
1/2 part Cream

Shake with ice and strain.

Apple Pie
COCKTAIL GLASS

3/4 part Sweet Vermouth
3/4 part Rum
splash Apple Brandy
splash Grenadine
splash Lemon Juice

Shake with ice and strain.

Apple Stone Sour
COCKTAIL GLASS

2 parts Apricot Brandy
1 part Lime Juice
splash Orange Juice
dash Sugar

Shake with ice and strain.

Applecar
COCKTAIL GLASS

1 part Applejack
1 part Triple Sec
1 part Lemon Juice

Shake with ice and strain.

Applejack Manhattan
COCKTAIL GLASS

2 parts Apple Brandy
1/2 part Sweet Vermouth
dash Orange Bitters

Shake with ice and strain.

Apples & Oranges
COCKTAIL GLASS

1 part Apple Liqueur
1 part Orange Vodka
1 part Cranberry Juice

Shake with ice and strain.

Apples to Oranges
COCKTAIL GLASS

1 part Apple Brandy
1 part Dubonnet® Blonde
1/2 part Triple Sec

Shake with ice and strain.

Apricot Blossom
COCKTAIL GLASS

1 part Rum
1/2 part Strawberry Liqueur
1 1/2 parts Apricot Juice
1/2 part Cream

Shake with ice and strain.

Apricot Cocktail
COCKTAIL GLASS

1 part Gin
1 1/2 parts Apricot Brandy
1/4 part Lemon Juice
1/2 part Orange Juice

Shake with ice and strain.

Apricot Moonshine
COCKTAIL GLASS

2 parts Apricot Brandy
1 part Triple Sec

Shake with ice and strain.

Apricot Pie
COCKTAIL GLASS

2 parts Light Rum
1 part Apricot Brandy
1 Egg White
1/2 part Triple Sec
1/2 part Lime Juice

Shake with ice and strain.

April Rain
COCKTAIL GLASS

2 parts Dry Vodka
1/2 part Lime Cordial
1/2 part Vermouth

Shake with ice and strain.

Aprishot
COCKTAIL GLASS

2 parts Vodka
½ part Apricot Brandy
1 part Pineapple Juice

Shake with ice and strain.

Aqua Plunge
COCKTAIL GLASS

½ part Blue Curaçao
1 part Aquavit
½ part Margarita Mix
1 part Cranberry Juice Cocktail

Shake with ice and strain.

Aqueduct
COCKTAIL GLASS

1½ parts Vodka
¾ part Amaretto
¾ part Triple Sec
½ part Lime Juice

Shake with ice and strain.

Arcadia
COCKTAIL GLASS

1½ parts Gin
½ part Galliano®
½ part Crème de Banane
½ part Grapefruit Juice

Shake with ice and strain.

Archimedes
COCKTAIL GLASS

1½ parts Amaretto
1½ parts Orange Juice
1½ parts Cranberry Juice Cocktail

Shake with ice and strain.

Arcimboldo Punch
COCKTAIL GLASS

2 parts Light Rum
1 part Dry Vermouth
2 parts Pineapple Juice
1 part Grape Juice

Shake with ice and strain.

Arena
COCKTAIL GLASS

1 part Dry Vermouth
1 part Sweet Vermouth
1 part Sherry
dash Bitters

Shake with ice and strain.

Ariete
COCKTAIL GLASS

1 part Vodka
1 part Dry Vermouth
½ part Dry Sherry
splash Peach Schnapps
splash Blue Curaçao

Shake with ice and strain.

Aristocracy
COCKTAIL GLASS

1 part Apricot Brandy
1 part Crème de Banane
½ part Crème de Cacao (White)
½ part Cream of Coconut

Shake with ice and strain.

Armagnac Lilie
COCKTAIL GLASS

1½ parts Lillet®
1 part Armagnac

Shake with ice and strain.

Armon
COCKTAIL GLASS

1 part Vodka
½ part Coffee Liqueur
splash Crème de Menthe (White)
splash Blue Curaçao

Shake with ice and strain.

Armour Cocktail
COCKTAIL GLASS

1¾ parts Dry Sherry
1 part Sweet Vermouth

Shake with ice and strain.

Army Cocktail

COCKTAIL GLASS

1 1/2 parts Gin
1 part Sweet Vermouth
2 dashes Grenadine

Shake with ice and strain.

Arnaud

COCKTAIL GLASS

1 part Dry Vermouth
1 part Gin
1 part Crème de Cassis

Shake with ice and strain.

Arrowhead

COCKTAIL GLASS

1/2 part Bourbon
1/2 part Dry Vermouth
1/2 part Sweet Vermouth
1 Egg White

Shake with ice and strain.

Arsenic and Old Lace

COCKTAIL GLASS

1 part Gin
1/2 part Pastis
splash Dry Vermouth
splash Parfait Amour

Shake with ice and strain.

Artificial Satellite

COCKTAIL GLASS

1 part Blue Curaçao
2/3 part Spiced Rum
1/2 part Lime Juice
1 part Pineapple Juice

Shake with ice and strain.

Aruba

COCKTAIL GLASS

1 part Gin
1/2 part Blue Curaçao
1 part Lemon Juice
1 Egg
splash Amaretto

Shake with ice and strain.

Asbach Beauty

COCKTAIL GLASS

3/4 part Brandy
3/4 part Extra Dry Vermouth
splash Crème de Menthe (White)
1 part Port
3/4 part Orange Juice
splash Grenadine

Shake with ice and strain.

Asbury Park

COCKTAIL GLASS

1 1/2 parts Brandy
1/2 part Applejack
1/2 part Sweet Vermouth

Shake with ice and strain.

Ascot

COCKTAIL GLASS

1 part Gin
1/2 part Sweet Vermouth
1/2 part Dry Vermouth
dash Bitters
splash Anisette

Shake with ice and strain. Garnish with Lemon Twist.

Ashcroft

COCKTAIL GLASS

1/2 part Peach Schnapps
1/2 part Goldschläger®
1/2 part Butterscotch Schnapps
1/2 part Irish Cream Liqueur
1 part Milk

Shake with ice and strain.

Asphalt Jungle

COCKTAIL GLASS

1 part Vodka
1/2 part Irish Cream Liqueur
1/2 part Lime Juice

Shake with ice and strain.

Atahualpa

COCKTAIL GLASS

1 part Peach Schnapps
1 part Cachaça
1 part Pineapple Juice
splash Simple Syrup

Shake with ice and strain.

Athenian Night

COCKTAIL GLASS

1½ parts Gin
½ part Cherry Brandy
½ part Madeira
splash Orange Juice

Shake with ice and strain.

Atlantis

COCKTAIL GLASS

1½ parts Citrus Vodka
½ part Blue Curaçao
⅔ part Passion Fruit Juice
⅔ part Grapefruit Juice

Shake with ice and strain.

Atmosphere

COCKTAIL GLASS

1 part Gin
⅔ part Passion Fruit Liqueur
⅔ part Mandarine Napoléon® Liqueur
splash Simple Syrup
½ part Lemon Juice

Shake with ice and strain.

Atomic Powered

COCKTAIL GLASS

1 part Gin
1 part Dry Vermouth
splash Cherry Brandy
splash Pernod®

Shake with ice and strain.

Attention Grabber

COCKTAIL GLASS

1½ parts Gin
½ part Dry Vermouth
splash Passion Fruit Liqueur
splash Chartreuse®
dash Orange Bitters

Shake with ice and strain.

Aussie Boomerang

COCKTAIL GLASS

1 part Melon Liqueur
1 part Kiwi Schnapps
1 part Cream

Shake with ice and strain.

Autumn Buzz

COCKTAIL GLASS

1 part Blue Curaçao
1 part Chambord®
½ part Rémy Martin® VSOP

Shake with ice and strain.

Aviator

COCKTAIL GLASS

1 part Gin
½ part Apricot Brandy
½ part Maraschino Liqueur
1 part Lemon Juice

Shake with ice and strain.

Avion El Humo de Mexico

COCKTAIL GLASS

splash Mezcal
2 parts Avion Añejo Tequila
½ part Dry Vermouth
½ part St-Germain
⅓ part Amaro

Chill a cocktail glass, rinse it with the Mezcal, and dump the excess. In a shaker or mixing glass, add ice, then the Tequila, Dry Vermouth, St-Germain, and Amaro. Stir gently with a bar spoon and strain into the cocktail glass. Flame a Grapefruit Peel and rim the glass with the peel.

Avion G5
COCKTAIL GLASS
2 parts Avion Silver Tequila
1 part St-Germain
2 parts Lime Juice
Shake with ice and strain.

Awesomer
COCKTAIL GLASS
1 part Apple Rum
1 part Orange Rum
1 part Pineapple Rum
1 part Strawberry Rum
dash Pineapple Juice
dash Pomegranate Juice
Shake with ice and strain.

Awesomest
COCKTAIL GLASS
1 part Apple Rum
1 part Orange Rum
1 part Strawberry Rum
dash Pomegranate Juice
Shake with ice and strain.

Aztec Gold
COCKTAIL GLASS
2 parts Gold Tequila
1 part Crème de Banane
1 part Amaretto
1 part Galliano®
Shake with ice and strain.

Azteca
COCKTAIL GLASS
1½ parts Light Rum
1 part Coffee Liqueur
1 part Crème de Cacao (White)
dash Blue Curaçao
Shake with ice and strain.

Azulejo
COCKTAIL GLASS
1 part Vodka
½ part Parfait Amour
½ part Triple Sec
splash Pineapple Juice
dash Bitters
Shake with ice and strain.

B.M. Slider
COCKTAIL GLASS
1 part Coffee Liqueur
1 part Cream
1 part Southern Comfort®
Shake with ice and strain.

B.V.D.
COCKTAIL GLASS
1 part Blackberry Brandy
1 part Gin
1 part Peach Schnapps
1 part Lemon-Lime Soda
1 part Cola
Shake with ice and strain.

B-52
COCKTAIL GLASS
1 part Coffee Liqueur
1 part Irish Cream Liqueur
1 part Amaretto
Layer in a cocktail glass.

Baby
COCKTAIL GLASS
1½ parts Triple Sec
1 part Cream
dash Bitters
Shake with ice and strain.

Baby Aspirin
COCKTAIL GLASS
1½ parts Coconut Rum
½ part Orange Juice
½ part Pineapple Juice
½ part Grenadine
½ part Triple Sec
Shake with ice and strain.

Baby Doll

COCKTAIL GLASS

2 parts Courvoisier®
1½ parts Grand Marnier®
½ part Lemon Juice

Stir gently with ice and strain.

Baby Fingers

COCKTAIL GLASS

2 parts Sloe Gin
1 part Gin
2 dashes Angostura Bitters

Shake with ice and strain.

Baby's Bottom

COCKTAIL GLASS

1½ parts Whiskey
½ part Crème de Cacao (White)
½ part Crème de Menthe (White)

Shake with ice and strain.

Bacardi® Alexander

COCKTAIL GLASS

¾ part Rum
½ part Crème de Cacao (Dark)
½ part Cream
dash Ground Nutmeg

Shake with ice and strain.

Bacardi® Special

COCKTAIL GLASS

2 parts Light Rum
¾ part Gin
splash Lime Juice
splash Grenadine
dash Sugar

Shake with ice and strain.

Bacarra

COCKTAIL GLASS

1½ parts Raspberry Liqueur
⅔ part Grand Marnier®
⅔ part Campari®

Shake with ice and strain.

Baci da Roma

COCKTAIL GLASS

1 part Coffee Liqueur
¼ part Crème de Cacao (White)
¼ part Sambuca
1 part Cream

Shake with ice and strain.

Back in Black

COCKTAIL GLASS

1 part Blackberry Liqueur
1 part Amaretto
1 part Lychee Liqueur
1 part Cream
splash Anisette

Shake with ice and strain.

Back Seater

COCKTAIL GLASS

½ part Apple Brandy
½ part Brandy
½ part Triple Sec
splash Lemon Juice

Shake with ice and strain.

Backstreet

COCKTAIL GLASS

1½ parts Light Rum
½ part Applejack
½ part Sweet Vermouth
½ part Cherry Brandy

Shake with ice and strain.

Bahama-Americana

COCKTAIL GLASS

1 part Light Rum
1 part Southern Comfort®
½ part Crème de Banane

Shake with ice and strain.

Bahia

COCKTAIL GLASS

1 part Dry Sherry
1 part Dry Vermouth
1 part Pastis
dash Orange Bitters

Shake with ice and strain.

Baileys® Comet
COCKTAIL GLASS

1 part Irish Cream Liqueur
1 part Butterscotch Schnapps
1 part Goldschläger®
1/4 part Sambuca
dash Ground Nutmeg

Shake with ice and strain.

Baileys® Cuddler
COCKTAIL GLASS

1 part Irish Cream Liqueur
1/2 part Amaretto

Shake with ice and strain.

Baileys® Tropic
COCKTAIL GLASS

1 part Dark Rum
1 part Blue Curaçao
2 parts Pineapple Juice

Shake with ice and strain.

Baja Bug
COCKTAIL GLASS

1/2 part Crème de Coconut
splash Sloe Gin
splash Raspberry Liqueur
1 part Pineapple Juice
1 part Cranberry Juice Cocktail

Shake with ice and strain.

Bajadera
COCKTAIL GLASS

1 part Blue Curaçao
1 part Silver Tequila
1 part Maraschino Liqueur

Shake with ice and strain.

Bali Dream
COCKTAIL GLASS

1 part Light Rum
1 part Dark Rum
1 part Crème de Banane
1 part Passoã®
1/2 part Crème de Coconut
splash Grenadine
splash Orange Juice

Shake with ice and strain.

Ballack
COCKTAIL GLASS

2 parts Kirschwasser
1 part Cherry Liqueur
1 part Cranberry Juice

Shake with ice and strain.

Ballet Russe Cocktail
COCKTAIL GLASS

2 parts Vodka
1/2 part Crème de Cassis
4 splashes Lime Juice

Shake with ice and strain.

Ballistic Banana
COCKTAIL GLASS

2 parts 99 Bananas Liqueur
1 part Vodka
splash Grenadine

Shake with ice and strain.

Balmoral
COCKTAIL GLASS

1 1/2 parts Scotch
1/2 part Sweet Vermouth
1/2 part Dry Vermouth
2 dashes Bitters

Shake with ice and strain.

Bam Bam
COCKTAIL GLASS

1 1/2 parts Whiskey
1/2 part Crème de Cacao (White)
1/2 part Crème de Menthe (White)

Shake with ice and strain.

Banana Baron

COCKTAIL GLASS

1/2 part Crème de Banane
2/3 part Maraschino Liqueur
1/2 part Anisette

Shake with ice and strain.

Banana Bird

COCKTAIL GLASS

1 part Cream
2 splashes Crème de Banane
2 splashes Triple Sec

Shake with ice and strain.

Banana Boomer

COCKTAIL GLASS

1 part Crème de Banane
1 part Pineapple Juice
1 part Orange Juice
1/2 part Apricot Brandy
1/2 part Cherry Brandy

Shake with ice and strain.

Banana Cow

COCKTAIL GLASS

1 part Light Rum
1 part Crème de Banane
1 1/2 parts Cream
splash Grenadine

Shake with ice and strain.

Banana Girl

COCKTAIL GLASS

1 part Crème de Cacao (White)
1 part Cream
1 part Pisang Ambon® Liqueur
1 part Crème de Coconut

Shake with ice and strain.

Banana Hammock

COCKTAIL GLASS

1 part 99 Bananas Liqueur
1 part Orange Vodka
splash Orange Juice

Shake with ice and strain.

Banana Irlandese

COCKTAIL GLASS

2 parts Banana Juice
1 part Crème de Cacao (White)

Shake with ice and strain.

Banana Mango

COCKTAIL GLASS

1 1/2 parts Light Rum
1 part Crème de Banane
1/2 part Lime Juice
1/2 part Mango Nectar

Shake with ice and strain.

Banana Nut

COCKTAIL GLASS

1 1/2 parts Frangelico®
1/2 part Crème de Banane
1 part Pineapple Juice

Shake with ice and strain.

Banana Rum Cream

COCKTAIL GLASS

1 1/2 parts Dark Rum
1/2 part Crème de Banane
1 part Light Cream

Shake with ice and strain.

Banana Split

COCKTAIL GLASS

1/2 part Vodka
1 1/2 parts Crème de Banane
1 part Crème de Cacao (White)
1 part Light Cream

Shake with ice and strain.

Banana Sunrise

COCKTAIL GLASS

1 part Coconut Rum
1 part Crème de Banane
1 part Piña Colada Mix

Shake with ice and strain.

Bananarama
COCKTAIL GLASS

1/2 part Vodka
1 part Crème de Banane
1/2 part Triple Sec
1 part Light Cream

Shake with ice and strain.

Banff Cocktail
COCKTAIL GLASS

1 1/2 parts Canadian Whisky
1/2 part Grand Marnier®
1/2 part Kirschwasser
dash Bitters

Shake with ice and strain. Garnish with Lemon Twist.

Bank Holiday
COCKTAIL GLASS

1 part Orange Vodka
1 part Crème de Cacao (White)
1 part Blackberry Liqueur

Shake with ice and strain.

Banshee
COCKTAIL GLASS

1 part Crème de Banane
1/2 part Crème de Cacao (White)
1 1/2 parts Light Cream

Shake with ice and strain.

Barbados Cocktail
COCKTAIL GLASS

2 parts Light Rum
1/2 part Triple Sec
1 part Pineapple Juice

Shake with ice and strain.

Barbancourt Winner
COCKTAIL GLASS

2/3 part Amaretto
2/3 part Dark Rum
2/3 part Pineapple Juice
1 part Cranberry Juice Cocktail

Shake with ice and strain.

El Barbarazo
COCKTAIL GLASS

1 part Jim Beam®
1/2 part Triple Sec
1/2 part Sweet Vermouth
1/2 part Dry Vermouth

Shake with ice and strain.

Barbazul
COCKTAIL GLASS

2/3 part Triple Sec
2/3 part Currant Vodka
1 1/2 parts Grapefruit Juice
splash Lime Juice
splash Blue Curaçao

Shake with ice and strain.

Bare Back
COCKTAIL GLASS

3 parts Bourbon
1 part St-Germain
2 dashes Orange Bitters

Shake with ice and strain.

Bare Cheeks
COCKTAIL GLASS

1 part Vodka
1 part Apple Juice
splash Grenadine
splash Lemon Juice

Shake with ice and strain.

Barefoot
COCKTAIL GLASS

1 part Brandy
1/2 part Dry Vermouth
2 splashes Maraschino Liqueur
splash Crème de Menthe (White)

Shake with ice and strain.

Barely Legal
COCKTAIL GLASS

2/3 part Amaretto
1/2 part Peach Schnapps
2/3 part Cranberry Juice Cocktail

Shake with ice and strain.

Baron Cocktail
COCKTAIL GLASS

1/2 part Dry Vermouth
1 1/2 parts Gin
splash Triple Sec
splash Sweet Vermouth

Shake with ice and strain. Garnish with Lemon Wedge.

Barrel of Monkeys
COCKTAIL GLASS

1 part Crème de Banane
1/2 part Crème de Coconut
1 part Light Rum
1 part Cream

Shake with ice and strain.

Bartender's Delight
COCKTAIL GLASS

1 part Dry Vermouth
1 part Gordon's® Orange Vodka
1 part Dry Sherry

Shake with ice and strain.

Basic Bill
COCKTAIL GLASS

1 1/2 parts Añejo Rum
1/2 part Dubonnet® Rouge
1/2 part Grand Marnier®
2 dashes Bitters

Shake with ice and strain.

Basin Street
COCKTAIL GLASS

2 parts Bourbon
1 part Triple Sec

Shake with ice and strain.

Bastardly
COCKTAIL GLASS

1/2 part Vodka
1/2 part Blackberry Liqueur
splash Vanilla Liqueur
splash Amaretto

Shake with ice and strain.

Battery Charger
COCKTAIL GLASS

1 1/2 parts Vermouth
1 part Jamaican Rum
splash Cherry Brandy

Shake with ice and strain.

Bavarian Cherry
COCKTAIL GLASS

1/2 part Kirschwasser
1/2 part Citrus Vodka
1/4 part Crème de Cassis
1 Egg White

Shake with ice and strain.

Bay Dream
COCKTAIL GLASS

1 part Gin
1/2 part Advocaat
1 1/2 parts Dry Vermouth
dash Angostura® Bitters
1/2 part Lemon Juice
splash Simple Syrup

Shake with ice and strain.

BCC
COCKTAIL GLASS

1 1/2 parts Blackberry Liqueur
1 part Triple Sec
1 part Cognac
1 part Grenadine

Shake with ice and strain.

Be Bop a Lula
COCKTAIL GLASS

1 part Vanilla Liqueur
1 part Armagnac
1 part Cream
1 part Pineapple Juice
splash Chocolate Mint Liqueur

Shake with ice and strain.

Beach Blanket Bop

COCKTAIL GLASS

½ part Vodka
½ part Crème de Coconut
½ part Melon Liqueur
½ part Blackberry Liqueur
1 part Pineapple Juice
½ part Cranberry Juice Cocktail

Shake with ice and strain.

Beachbum

COCKTAIL GLASS

2 parts Rum
¾ part Triple Sec
¾ part Lime Juice
splash Grenadine

Shake with ice and strain.

Beachcomber

COCKTAIL GLASS

1½ parts Light Rum
½ part Triple Sec
½ part Lime Juice
splash Maraschino Cherry Liqueur
dash Granulated Sugar

Shake with ice and strain.

Beachcomber's Gold

COCKTAIL GLASS

2 parts Dark Rum
½ part Dry Vermouth
½ part Sweet Vermouth

Shake with ice and strain.

Beadlestone Cocktail

COCKTAIL GLASS

1½ parts Dry Vermouth
1½ parts Scotch

Stir gently with ice and strain.

Beals Cocktail

COCKTAIL GLASS

1½ parts Scotch
½ part Dry Vermouth
½ part Sweet Vermouth

Shake with ice and strain.

Bearded Clam

COCKTAIL GLASS

1 part Amaretto
1 part Canadian Whisky
1 part Cranberry Juice

Shake with ice and strain.

Beau Rivage

COCKTAIL GLASS

1 part Dry Gin
1 part Light Rum
1 part Dry Vermouth
1 part Orange Juice
1 part Sweet Vermouth
1 part Grenadine

Shake with ice and strain.

Beautiful American

COCKTAIL GLASS

1 part Melon Liqueur
1 part Blue Curaçao
1 part Sweet & Sour Mix

Shake with ice and strain.

Beautiful Bateaux

COCKTAIL GLASS

1 part Amaretto
1 part Maraschino Liqueur
3 parts Cranberry Juice Cocktail
2 parts Sweet & Sour Mix

Shake with ice and strain.

Beauty and the Beach

COCKTAIL GLASS

1½ parts Light Rum
1½ parts Southern Comfort®
splash Grand Marnier®
splash Lemon Juice
dash Orange Bitters

Shake with ice and strain.

Beauty Gump
COCKTAIL GLASS

1/2 part Blue Curaçao
1/2 part Peach Schnapps
1/2 part Orange Vodka
splash Sweet & Sour Mix

Shake with ice and strain.

Bee Stinger
COCKTAIL GLASS

1 1/2 parts Blackberry Brandy
1/2 part Crème de Menthe (White)

Shake with ice and strain.

Beeing Frenzy
COCKTAIL GLASS

1 1/2 parts Light Rum
1/2 part Strawberry Liqueur
2/3 part Orange Juice
2/3 part Pineapple Juice
2/3 part Lemon Juice
2/3 part Club Soda

Shake with ice and strain.

Bee's Kiss
COCKTAIL GLASS

1 part Rum
splash Cream
splash Honey

Shake with ice and strain.

Bee's Knees
COCKTAIL GLASS

1 1/2 parts Rum
1/2 part Triple Sec
1/2 part Orange Juice
1 tbsp Powdered Sugar
1/2 part Lime Juice

Shake with ice and strain.

Before Dawn
COCKTAIL GLASS

2 parts Port
1/2 part Amaretto

Shake with ice and strain.

Before Midnight
COCKTAIL GLASS

1/2 part Vodka
1/2 part Orange Juice
1/2 part Gin
splash Apricot Brandy

Shake with ice and strain.

Beige Blindfold
COCKTAIL GLASS

1 1/2 parts Gin
1/2 part Triple Sec
2 splashes Brandy
2 splashes Lemon Juice

Shake with ice and strain.

Bekki's Boobs
COCKTAIL GLASS

1 1/2 parts Melon Liqueur
1 1/2 parts Jamaican Rum
1 part Kiwi Schnapps

Shake with ice and strain.

Belching Dragon
COCKTAIL GLASS

1 part Pepper Vodka
1 part Cinnamon Schnapps
1 part Vanilla Liqueur

Shake with ice and strain.

La Belle Quebec
COCKTAIL GLASS

1 1/2 parts Canadian Whisky
1/2 part Brandy
1/2 part Cherry Brandy
1/2 part Lemon Juice
1/2 tsp Superfine Sugar

Shake with ice and strain.

Belinda
COCKTAIL GLASS

1 part Dark Rum
1/2 part Dry Vermouth
splash Crème de Banane
splash Amaretto

Shake with ice and strain.

Bells of St. Mary's

COCKTAIL GLASS

1 1/2 parts Gin
1 part Triple Sec
1 part Apricot Brandy
splash Lemon Juice

Shake with ice and strain.

Belmont

COCKTAIL GLASS

2 parts Gin
1/2 part Raspberry Syrup

Shake with ice and strain.

Belmont Stakes

COCKTAIL GLASS

1 1/2 parts Vodka
3/4 part Rum
1/2 part Lime Juice
1/2 part Strawberry
1/4 part Grenadine

Shake with ice and strain.

Bénédictine Cocktail

COCKTAIL GLASS

2 parts Bénédictine
dash Angostura Bitters
dash Lemon Juice
1/4 tsp Powdered Sugar

Shake with ice and strain.

Benedictus

COCKTAIL GLASS

1 part Gin
1 part Bénédictine®
1/2 part Maraschino Liqueur

Shake with ice and strain.

Bengal Cocktail

COCKTAIL GLASS

1 1/2 parts Brandy
1/2 part Maraschino Liqueur
1/2 part Triple Sec
1 part Pineapple Juice
2 dashes Bitters

Shake with ice and strain.

Bengal Tiger

COCKTAIL GLASS

1 1/2 parts Brandy
1/2 part Maraschino Liqueur
1/2 part Triple Sec
1 part Pineapple Juice

Shake with ice and strain.

Bent Nail

COCKTAIL GLASS

1 1/2 parts Canadian Whisky
1/2 part Drambuie
1/6 part Kirschwasser

Shake with ice and strain.

Bentley

COCKTAIL GLASS

1 1/2 parts Apple Brandy
1 part Dubonnet® Blonde

Stir gently with ice and strain. Garnish with Lemon Twist.

Bergenline

COCKTAIL GLASS

2 parts Frangelico®
1 part Sweet Vermouth
3/4 part Triple Sec

Shake with ice and strain. Garnish with Lime Wedge.

Berimbau

COCKTAIL GLASS

1 1/2 parts Jägermeister®
1/2 part Cachaça
1/4 part Triple Sec
splash Lemon Juice

Shake with ice and strain.

Bermuda Cocktail

COCKTAIL GLASS

1 3/4 parts Gin
3/4 part Peach Brandy
splash Orange Juice
dash Grenadine

Shake with ice and strain.

Bernardo

COCKTAIL GLASS

2 parts Gin
1/2 part Triple Sec
2 splashes Lemon Juice
2 dashes Bitters

Shake with ice and strain.

Berry Deauville

COCKTAIL GLASS

1 part Vodka
1/2 part Blackberry Liqueur
1/2 part Raspberry Liqueur
1/2 part Peach Schnapps
1 1/2 parts Pineapple Juice

Shake with ice and strain.

Berry Festival

COCKTAIL GLASS

1 part Vodka
1 part Crème de Cacao (White)
1/2 part Blackberry Liqueur
1 part Cream

Shake with ice and strain.

Berry Fusion Cocktail

COCKTAIL GLASS

2 parts Raspberry Vodka
1 part Blackberry Liqueur
1 part Hpnotiq
2 parts Cranberry Juice

Shake with ice and strain.

Berry Harry

COCKTAIL GLASS

1 part Light Rum
1 part Blackberry Liqueur
1 part Crème de Cassis
1 part Raspberry Juice
1 part Blackberry Juice

Shake with ice and strain.

Berry Patch

COCKTAIL GLASS

1 part Currant Vodka
1/4 part Lime Juice
1/4 part Blackberry

Shake with ice and strain.

Beso de Limon

COCKTAIL GLASS

2 parts Crème de Banane
2 parts Dark Rum
1 part Lemon Juice

Shake with ice and strain.

Bethlehem

COCKTAIL GLASS

1 part Dark Rum
1/2 part Bénédictine®
splash Amaretto
splash Drambuie®

Stir gently with ice and strain.

Betsy Ross

COCKTAIL GLASS

1 1/2 parts Brandy
1 1/2 parts Port
splash Triple Sec

Shake with ice and strain.

Better Than Ever

COCKTAIL GLASS

1 part Vodka
1/2 part Triple Sec
1/2 part Lime Juice
1/2 part Pear Liqueur
1/2 part Raspberry Syrup

Shake with ice and strain.

Beware of the Currant

COCKTAIL GLASS

1 1/2 parts Blue Curaçao
1/2 part Raspberry Liqueur
1 part Currant Vodka
1 part Pineapple Juice

Shake with ice and strain.

Bianca Castafiore

COCKTAIL GLASS

1 part Amaretto
1 part Sambuca
1 part Galliano®

Shake with ice and strain.

Bibe '77

COCKTAIL GLASS

1 part Vodka
1 part Sweet Vermouth
1 part Dry Vermouth
½ part Apricot Brandy
splash Amaretto
splash Grenadine

Shake with ice and strain.

Big Band Charlie

COCKTAIL GLASS

1½ parts Dark Rum
½ part Melon Liqueur
½ part Triple Sec
½ part Lime Juice

Shake with ice and strain.

Big Calm

COCKTAIL GLASS

⅔ part Crème de Coconut
⅔ part Melon Liqueur
⅔ part Amaretto
splash Pineapple Juice

Shake with ice and strain.

Big Easy Cocktail

COCKTAIL GLASS

1½ parts Southern Comfort
½ part Raspberry Liqueur
1 part Lemon Juice
½ part Simple Syrup

Shake with ice and strain.

Bijou

COCKTAIL GLASS

1¼ parts Dry Gin
¾ part Chartreuse®
¾ part Vermouth

Shake with ice and strain.

Bikini

COCKTAIL GLASS

1 part Light Rum
2 parts Vodka
½ part Milk
dash Sugar
½ part Lemon Juice

Shake with ice and strain. Garnish with Lemon Twist.

Bikini Top

COCKTAIL GLASS

1½ parts Vanilla Vodka
1 part Blackberry Liqueur
⅔ part Crème de Cacao (White)

Shake with ice and strain.

Billy Hamilton

COCKTAIL GLASS

1 part Crème de Cacao (White)
1 part Cognac
1 part Triple Sec
1 Egg White

Shake with ice and strain.

Biondina

COCKTAIL GLASS

1 part Triple Sec
1 part Anisette

Shake with ice and strain.

Bird of Paradise Cocktail

COCKTAIL GLASS

1 part Silver Tequila
1 part Crème de Cacao (White)
½ part Amaretto
2 parts Cream

Shake with ice and strain.

Biscayne Cocktail

COCKTAIL GLASS

2 parts Gin
1 part Light Rum
1 part Passion Fruit Liqueur
1 part Lime Juice

Shake with ice and strain.

Bishop Brandy

COCKTAIL GLASS

1/2 part Triple Sec
1 part Brandy
1/2 part Maraschino Liqueur
dash Orange Bitters
1 part Pineapple Juice

Shake with ice and strain.

Bitch Fight

COCKTAIL GLASS

1 part Cointreau®
1 part Peach Schnapps
1 part Cranberry Juice Cocktail
splash Lime Juice

Shake with ice and strain.

Bitch on Wheels

COCKTAIL GLASS

2 parts Gin
1/2 part Crème de Menthe (White)
1/2 part Dry Vermouth
splash Pernod

Shake with ice and strain.

Bittersweet

COCKTAIL GLASS

1 part Dry Vermouth
1 part Sweet Vermouth
dash Bitters
dash Orange Bitters

Shake with ice and strain.

Bittersweet Symphony

COCKTAIL GLASS

1 part Light Rum
3/4 part Crème de Cacao (White)
1/2 part Cherry Brandy
1 part Grapefruit Juice
dash Orange Bitters

Shake with ice and strain.

Black and Blue

COCKTAIL GLASS

2 parts Black Death® Vodka
1 part Blue Curaçao
1 part Cranberry Juice Cocktail

Shake with ice and strain.

Black Baltimore

COCKTAIL GLASS

2 parts Brandy
1 part Black Sambuca
1 Egg White

Shake with ice and strain.

Black Bird

COCKTAIL GLASS

3/4 part Gin
1/4 part Sweet Vermouth
1/4 part Crème de Cassis
splash Pernod®

Shake with ice and strain.

Black Bite

COCKTAIL GLASS

1 part Vodka
1 part Blackberry Liqueur
1 part Grapefruit Juice

Shake with ice and strain.

Black Cherry

COCKTAIL GLASS

1 part Vodka
1 part Southern Comfort®
1 part Amaretto
1 part Melon Liqueur
1 part Cranberry Juice Cocktail

Shake with ice and strain.

Black Devil

COCKTAIL GLASS

2 parts Light Rum
1/2 part Dry Vermouth

Stir gently with ice and strain.
Garnish with a Black Olive.

Black Friday

COCKTAIL GLASS

1 part Gin
1 part Black Vodka
1 part Grapefruit Juice
1 part Lime Juice

Shake with ice and strain.

Black Gin

COCKTAIL GLASS

1½ parts Gin
½ part Black Sambuca
splash Sweet Vermouth

Shake with ice and strain.

Black Jack

COCKTAIL GLASS

1½ parts Scotch
1 part Coffee Liqueur
½ part Triple Sec
½ part Lemon Juice

Shake with ice and strain.

Black Jack #2

COCKTAIL GLASS

2 parts Grand Marnier®
½ part Coffee Liqueur
splash Brandy

Shake with ice and strain.

Black Metal

COCKTAIL GLASS

½ part Vodka
½ part Blue Curaçao
½ part Crème de Cassis
½ part Lime Cordial

Shake with ice and strain.

Black Monday

COCKTAIL GLASS

1 part Dark Rum
½ part Black Sambuca
splash Cherry Brandy
½ part Lemon Juice

Shake with ice and strain.

Black Widow

COCKTAIL GLASS

¾ part Dark Rum
½ part Southern Comfort®
1 part Sweet & Sour Mix

Shake with ice and strain.

Black Witch

COCKTAIL GLASS

1½ parts Gold Rum
¼ part Dark Rum
¼ part Apricot Brandy
½ part Pineapple Juice

Shake with ice and strain.

Blackberry Cream

COCKTAIL GLASS

1½ parts Blackberry Liqueur
1 part Dry Gin
1 part Cream
1 Egg Yolk

Shake with ice and strain.

Blackhawk

COCKTAIL GLASS

3 parts Vodka
1 part Chambord
1 part Lime Juice

Shake with ice and strain.

Blackout

COCKTAIL GLASS

1½ parts Gin
1 part Blackberry Brandy
splash Lime Juice

Shake with ice and strain.

Blackthorn

COCKTAIL GLASS

3 parts Sloe Gin
1 part Sweet Vermouth

Shake with ice and strain.

Blade Runner

COCKTAIL GLASS

2 parts Jim Beam®
1½ parts Apricot Brandy
½ part Lemon Juice

Shake with ice and strain.

Blanca Playa

COCKTAIL GLASS

1 part Crème de Banane
1 part Pineapple Juice
1 part Crème de Coconut

Shake with ice and strain.

Blarney Stone Cocktail

COCKTAIL GLASS

2 parts Irish Whiskey
splash Anisette
splash Triple Sec
splash Maraschino Cherry

Shake with ice and strain. Garnish with Orange Peel and Olive.

Blaze of Glory

COCKTAIL GLASS

1½ parts Dark Rum
½ part Grand Marnier®
splash Crème de Cacao (Dark)

Shake with ice and strain.

Bledsko Jezero

COCKTAIL GLASS

1 part Vodka
1 part Sweet Vermouth
1 part Maraschino Liqueur
splash Blue Curaçao

Shake with ice and strain.

Bleeding Ulcer

COCKTAIL GLASS

1 part Dark Rum
1 part Jägermeister
1 part Melon Liqueur
1 part Pineapple Juice

Shake with ice and strain.

Blenheim

COCKTAIL GLASS

1 part Orange Juice
1 part Apricot Brandy
½ part Grenadine
dash Orange Bitters

Shake with ice and strain.

Blimey

COCKTAIL GLASS

2 parts Scotch
½ part Lime Juice
dash Sugar

Shake with ice and strain.

Blind Melon

COCKTAIL GLASS

1 part Melon Liqueur
½ part Vodka
½ part Light Rum
½ part Triple Sec

Shake with ice and strain.

Blitz

COCKTAIL GLASS

1 part Tequila
1 part Triple Sec
1 part Southern Comfort®
1 part Grenadine
1 part Lemon Juice
1 part Orange Juice

Shake with ice and strain.

Blood Shot

COCKTAIL GLASS

1 part Whiskey
1 part Vodka
1 part Apricot Brandy
1 part Sweet Vermouth
2 dashes Bitters

Shake with ice and strain.

Blood Transfusion

COCKTAIL GLASS

1 part Orange Liqueur
2 parts Citrus Vodka
3 parts Orange Juice
splash Lime Cordial

Shake with ice and strain.

Bloody Brain

COCKTAIL GLASS

1½ parts Strawberry Liqueur
½ part Grenadine
½ part Irish Cream Liqueur

Shake all but Irish Cream with ice and strain. Carefully pour the Irish Cream into the center of the drink.

Bloody Lip

COCKTAIL GLASS

1 part Cherry Brandy
½ part Vodka
½ part Maraschino Liqueur

Shake with ice and strain.

Bloody Lip #2

COCKTAIL GLASS

2 parts Cherry Vodka
1 part Sour Cherry Liqueur
½ part Triple Sec
½ part Lime Juice

Shake with ice and strain.

Bloody Matador

COCKTAIL GLASS

1½ parts Tequila
3 splashes Maraschino Liqueur
splash Grenadine
2 splashes Orange Juice

Shake with ice and strain.

Blue Agave

COCKTAIL GLASS

1½ parts Silver Tequila
¾ part Cream
¼ part Blue Curaçao
¼ part Crème de Cacao (White)

Shake with ice and strain.

Blue Alexander

COCKTAIL GLASS

1 part Gin
½ part Blue Curaçao
½ part Cream

Shake with ice and strain.

Blue and Gold

COCKTAIL GLASS

1 part Vodka
½ part Blueberry Schnapps
½ part Pineapple Juice

Shake with ice and strain.

Blue Angel

COCKTAIL GLASS

½ part Blue Curaçao
½ part Brandy
½ part Crème de Cacao (White)
½ part Lemon Juice
½ part Cream

Shake with ice and strain.

Blue Bananas

COCKTAIL GLASS

1½ parts Grapefruit Juice
1 part Whiskey
1 part Crème de Banane
1 part Blue Curaçao
1 Egg White

Shake with ice and strain.

Blue Bayou

COCKTAIL GLASS

⅔ part Blue Curaçao
½ part Coffee Liqueur
1½ parts Dark Rum
1 part Orange Juice
1 part Lemon Juice

Shake with ice and strain.

Blue Belle Babe

COCKTAIL GLASS

1 part Blue Curaçao
1 part Southern Comfort®
½ part Lime Juice

Shake with ice and strain.

Blue Bird
COCKTAIL GLASS

1½ parts Gin
½ part Triple Sec
dash Bitters

Shake with ice and strain. Garnish with Lemon Twist and Cherry.

Blue Buddha
COCKTAIL GLASS

2 parts Vodka
splash Blue Curaçao
splash Sake
splash Grapefruit Juice
½ part Lemon Juice
½ part Lime Juice
splash Simple Syrup

Shake with ice and strain.

Blue Bullet
COCKTAIL GLASS

½ part Maraschino Liqueur
½ part Peach Schnapps
½ part Blue Curaçao

Shake with ice and strain.

Blue Capri
COCKTAIL GLASS

1½ parts Crème de Cacao (White)
½ part Crème de Menthe (Green)
1 part Blue Curaçao

Shake with ice and strain.

Blue Carnation
COCKTAIL GLASS

½ part Crème de Cacao (White)
½ part Blue Curaçao
2 parts Light Cream

Shake with ice and strain.

Blue Chili
COCKTAIL GLASS

2 parts Blue Curaçao
1 part Vodka
½ part Gin
½ part Light Rum

Shake with ice and strain.

Blue Cosmopolitan
COCKTAIL GLASS

2 parts Citrus Vodka
1 part Blue Curaçao
½ part Grapefruit Juice
½ part Simple Syrup

Shake with ice and strain.

Blue Creole
COCKTAIL GLASS

2 parts Light Rum
½ part Goldschläger®
½ part Lime Juice

Shake with ice and strain.

Blue Danube
COCKTAIL GLASS

½ part Vodka
½ part Blue Curaçao
½ part Triple Sec
½ part Crème de Banane
splash Cream

Shake with ice and strain.

Blue Diamond
COCKTAIL GLASS

1 part Blue Curaçao
1 part Dry Gin
1 part Lime Juice
1 part Cream

Shake with ice and strain.

Blue Edisonian
COCKTAIL GLASS

2 parts Campari®
2 parts Brandy
1 part Lemon Juice

Shake with ice and strain.

Blue Fox Trot
COCKTAIL GLASS

1½ parts Light Rum
½ part Lemon Juice
3 dashes Blue Curaçao

Shake with ice and strain.

Blue Grass

COCKTAIL GLASS

2 parts Bourbon
1 part Pineapple Juice
1/2 part Maraschino Liqueur

Shake with ice and strain.

Blue Haze

COCKTAIL GLASS

1 part Dark Rum
1/2 part Dry Vermouth
1/2 part Parfait Amour
1/2 part Triple Sec

Shake with ice and strain.

Blue Is Beautiful

COCKTAIL GLASS

1 1/2 parts Dry Gin
1 part Blue Curaçao
1/2 part Lime Cordial

Shake with ice and strain.

Blue Kontiki

COCKTAIL GLASS

1 part Triple Sec
1 part Grapefruit Juice
splash Blue Curaçao

Shake with ice and strain.

Blue Lagoon

COCKTAIL GLASS

1 part Blueberry Schnapps
1 part Blue Curaçao
splash Pineapple Juice

Shake with ice and strain.

Blue Light Special

COCKTAIL GLASS

3/4 part Sour Apple Schnapps
1/4 part Vodka
1/4 part Blue Curaçao
splash Pineapple Juice

Shake with ice and strain.

Blue Liquid

COCKTAIL GLASS

1 part Coconut Rum
1 part Vanilla Vodka
1/2 part Blue Curaçao
1 part Milk

Shake with ice and strain.

Blue Margarita

COCKTAIL GLASS

1 1/2 parts Tequila
1 part Blue Curaçao
1 part Lime Juice

Shake with ice and pour.

Blue Marine

COCKTAIL GLASS

1 1/2 parts Vodka
1 part Butterscotch Schnapps
1 part Blue Curaçao
splash Lemonade

Shake with ice and strain.

Blue Monday

COCKTAIL GLASS

1 part Vodka
1 part Triple Sec
1 part Blue Curaçao

Shake with ice and strain.

Blue Morning

COCKTAIL GLASS

2 parts Vodka
1 part Blue Curaçao
1 part Peach Schnapps

Shake with ice and strain.

Blue Nuts

COCKTAIL GLASS

1 part Blue Curaçao
1 part Coconut Rum
1 part Grand Marnier
1 part Cream of Coconut

Shake with ice and strain.

Blue Ocean

COCKTAIL GLASS

3/4 part Melon Liqueur
1/2 part Anisette
1/2 part Cognac
3/4 part Grapefruit Juice

Shake with ice and strain.

Blue Panther

COCKTAIL GLASS

2 parts Vodka
1 part Dry Vermouth
1 part Orange Juice
1 Egg White
1/2 part Crème de Cassis

Shake with ice and strain.

Blue Riband

COCKTAIL GLASS

2/3 part Gin
1/2 part Blue Curaçao
2/3 part Triple Sec

Shake with ice and strain.

Blue Rocks

COCKTAIL GLASS

1 1/2 parts Peach Schnapps
3/4 part Blue Curaçao
3/4 part Orange Juice

Shake with ice and strain.

Blue Shark

COCKTAIL GLASS

1 part Silver Tequila
1 part Vodka
splash Blue Curaçao

Shake with ice and strain.

Blue Sky Delight

COCKTAIL GLASS

1 1/2 parts Crème de Coconut
2/3 part Dark Rum
2/3 part Blue Curaçao
1 part Apple Juice

Shake with ice and strain.

Blue Star

COCKTAIL GLASS

1 part Blue Curaçao
1 part Orange Juice
1 part Gin

Shake with ice and strain.

Blue Sunrise

COCKTAIL GLASS

1 1/2 parts Rum
1 part Blue Curaçao
1 part Pineapple Juice
1/2 part Parfait Amour

Shake with ice and strain.

Blue Tartan

COCKTAIL GLASS

1 1/2 parts Scotch
1/2 part Blue Curaçao
1/2 part Crème de Cacao (White)

Shake with ice and strain.

Blue Temptation

COCKTAIL GLASS

1 part Vodka
1 part Blue Curaçao
1 part Pisang Ambon® Liqueur
1/2 part Crème de Banane
2 parts Cream

Shake with ice and strain.

Blue Zone

COCKTAIL GLASS

1 part Citrus Rum
1 part Coconut Rum
1 part Passion Fruit Rum
dash Blue Curaçao

Shake with ice and strain.

Bluebird Tropicale

COCKTAIL GLASS

1 1/2 parts Gin
1/2 part Triple Sec
1/2 part Blue Curaçao
2 dashes Bitters

Shake with ice and strain.

Blueblooded
COCKTAIL GLASS

1½ parts Light Rum
½ part Blue Curaçao
1½ parts Dark Rum
splash Apricot Juice

Shake with ice and strain.

Bluenette
COCKTAIL GLASS

½ part Blue Curaçao
½ part Crème de Coconut
½ part Peach Schnapps
splash Sweet & Sour Mix

Shake with ice and strain.

Blushing Mellow
COCKTAIL GLASS

1 part Vodka
½ part Strawberry Liqueur
½ part Grenadine
1½ parts Cream

Shake with ice and strain.

Blushing Monarch
COCKTAIL GLASS

⅔ part Gin
½ part Blue Curaçao
½ part Campari®
⅔ part Passion Fruit Juice

Shake with ice and strain.

Bobbit
COCKTAIL GLASS

1 part Vodka
1 part Gin
½ part Peach Schnapps
½ part Campari®

Shake with ice and strain.

Boca Chico Banana
COCKTAIL GLASS

½ part Vodka
½ part Pisang Ambon® Liqueur
½ part Crème de Coconut
splash Passion Fruit Nectar
1 part Guava Juice

Shake with ice and strain.

Boccie Bounce
COCKTAIL GLASS

1 part Amaretto
½ part Orange Juice
1½ parts Cream

Shake with ice and strain.

Bodil
COCKTAIL GLASS

1 part Crème de Menthe (White)
1 part Parfait Amour
1 part Crème de Cacao (White)
1 part Cream

Shake with ice and strain.

Body Shiver
COCKTAIL GLASS

1 part Gold Tequila
1 part Passion Fruit Liqueur
1 part Melon Liqueur
splash Lemon Juice

Shake with ice and strain.

Bodyguard
COCKTAIL GLASS

2 parts Jim Beam®
1½ parts Melon Liqueur
⅔ part Pisang Ambon® Liqueur
splash Lemon Juice

Shake with ice and strain.

Bold Gold Monkey
COCKTAIL GLASS

1 part Gold Rum
1 part Vodka
4 parts Orange Juice
splash Grenadine

Shake with ice and strain.

Bolo Blast
COCKTAIL GLASS
½ part Crème de Coconut
½ part Raspberry Liqueur
½ part Crème de Banane
½ part Blackberry Liqueur
½ part Orange Vodka
Shake with ice and strain.

Bolshoi Punch
COCKTAIL GLASS
1 part Vodka
½ part Light Rum
¼ part Crème de Cassis
½ part Lemon Juice
2 splashes Simple Syrup
Shake with ice and strain.

Bombar Cocktail
COCKTAIL GLASS
1½ parts Blue Curaçao
1 part Orange Vodka
1 part Coconut Rum
Shake with ice and strain.

Bon Lis
COCKTAIL GLASS
⅔ part Vodka
⅔ part Passion Fruit Liqueur
2 parts Pear Juice
splash Lemon Juice
Shake with ice and strain.

Bon Voyage
COCKTAIL GLASS
1 part Gin
1 part Tequila
splash Lemon Juice
splash Blue Curaçao
Shake with ice and strain.

Bongo
COCKTAIL GLASS
1 part Citrus Vodka
1 part Lychee Liqueur
1 part Pisang Ambon® Liqueur
1 part Lime Juice
Shake with ice and strain.

Buona Sera
COCKTAIL GLASS
1 part Silver Tequila
½ part Coffee Liqueur
½ part Irish Cream Liqueur
Shake with ice and strain.

Booby Trap
COCKTAIL GLASS
2 parts Bourbon
¾ part Maraschino Liqueur
Shake with ice and strain.

Bosom Caresser
COCKTAIL GLASS
1 part Brandy
½ part Triple Sec
1 part Madeira
Shake with ice and strain.

The Boss's Favorite
COCKTAIL GLASS
⅔ part Gin
1½ parts Apricot Brandy
½ part Crème de Cassis
½ part Lemon Juice
Shake with ice and strain.

Boston Cream Pie
COCKTAIL GLASS
1 part Irish Cream Liqueur
1 part Vanilla Vodka
1 part White Chocolate Liqueur
Shake with ice and strain.

Boston Sidecar
COCKTAIL GLASS
3/4 part Light Rum
3/4 part Brandy
3/4 part Triple Sec
1/2 part Lime Juice
Shake with ice and strain.

Botogo
COCKTAIL GLASS
1 part Gin
1 part Blue Curaçao
splash Vermouth
1 part Pineapple Juice
Shake with ice and strain.

Bounce Heart
COCKTAIL GLASS
1 part Cherry Brandy
1 part Triple Sec
1 part Sweet Vermouth
1 part Lemon Juice
Shake with ice and strain.

Bounty Fresh
COCKTAIL GLASS
1 part Light Rum
1 part Crème de Coconut
1/2 part Amaretto
1 1/2 parts Passion Fruit Juice
Shake with ice and strain.

Bourbon à la Crème
COCKTAIL GLASS
2 parts Bourbon
1 part Crème de Cacao (Dark)
1/2 part Vanilla Liqueur
Shake with ice and strain.

Bourbon del Mar
COCKTAIL GLASS
1 part Jim Beam®
2/3 part Triple Sec
splash Lime Juice
1 part Sweet & Sour Mix
Shake with ice and strain.

Bourbon Sidecar
COCKTAIL GLASS
2 parts Bourbon
1 part Triple Sec
Shake with ice and strain.

Bourbonella
COCKTAIL GLASS
2 parts Bourbon
1 1/2 parts Dry Vermouth
1 1/2 parts Triple Sec
splash Grenadine
Shake with ice and strain.

Bourbonnaise
COCKTAIL GLASS
1 1/2 parts Bourbon
1/2 part Crème de Cassis
splash Dry Vermouth
Shake with ice and strain.

Boyard Boy
COCKTAIL GLASS
1/2 part Southern Comfort®
1/2 part Melon Liqueur
1/2 part Triple Sec
1 part Sweet & Sour Mix
1/2 part Orange Juice
splash Passion Fruit Juice
Shake with ice and strain.

Boys Don't Cry
COCKTAIL GLASS
2 parts Gin
1/2 part Crème de Cacao (White)
splash Grenadine
1 Egg White
Shake with ice and strain.

Brainbow
COCKTAIL GLASS
3/4 part Gin
3/4 part Cherry Brandy
3/4 part Chartreuse®
Shake with ice and strain.

Brainwave

COCKTAIL GLASS

½ part 151-Proof Rum
1 part Amaretto
¼ part Irish Cream Liqueur

Shake with ice and strain.

Brandy Alexander

COCKTAIL GLASS

½ part Brandy
½ part Crème de Cacao (Dark)
2 parts Heavy Cream

Shake with ice and strain.

Brandy Breezer

COCKTAIL GLASS

2 parts Brandy
½ part Triple Sec
½ part Maraschino Liqueur

Shake with ice and strain.

Brandy Classic

COCKTAIL GLASS

1½ parts Brandy
½ part Triple Sec
¼ part Maraschino Liqueur
½ part Lemon Juice
dash Powdered Sugar

Shake with ice and strain.

Brandy Elite

COCKTAIL GLASS

½ part Apricot Brandy
½ part Brandy
½ part Grand Marnier®
½ part Lemon Juice

Shake with ice and strain.

Brandy Rainbow

COCKTAIL GLASS

1 part Apple Brandy
1 part Apricot Brandy
½ part Cherry Brandy

Shake with ice and strain.

Brave Soldier

COCKTAIL GLASS

1 part Cherry Brandy
½ part Passion Fruit Liqueur
½ part Southern Comfort®
½ part Lemon Juice
½ part Sweet & Sour Mix

Shake with ice and strain.

Brazen Hussy

COCKTAIL GLASS

2 parts Vodka
1 part Triple Sec
1 part Lemon Juice

Shake with ice and strain.

Brazilian Daiquiri

COCKTAIL GLASS

2 parts Dark Rum
1 part Light Rum
splash Vanilla Extract
2 dashes Brown Sugar

Shake with ice and strain.

Brazilian Night

COCKTAIL GLASS

1 part Blue Curaçao
1 part Vodka
1 part Crème de Coconut

Shake with ice and strain.

Briar Rabbit

COCKTAIL GLASS

⅔ part Blackberry Liqueur
⅔ part Sweet Vermouth
⅔ part Dry Vermouth
dash Orange Bitters
dash Angostura® Bitters

Shake with ice and strain.

Brisas del Paraíso

COCKTAIL GLASS

1 part Dry Gin
1 part Vodka
1 part Parfait Amour
splash Lemon Juice

Shake with ice and strain.

British Comfort
COCKTAIL GLASS
1½ parts Southern Comfort®
½ part Gin
½ part Lemon Juice
1 part Orange Juice
Shake with ice and strain.

Brittany
COCKTAIL GLASS
1½ parts Gin
1 part Orange Juice
½ part Amer Picon®
Shake with ice and strain.

Broadside
COCKTAIL GLASS
1 part Dark Rum
½ part Vodka
½ part Cherry Brandy
½ part Frangelico®
2 splashes Grenadine
Shake with ice and strain.

Broken Parachute
COCKTAIL GLASS
1 part Raspberry Liqueur
1 part Citrus Rum
dash Powdered Sugar
Shake with ice and strain.

Bronx Ain't So Sweet
COCKTAIL GLASS
1½ parts Gin
splash Dry Vermouth
½ part Orange Juice
Shake with ice and strain.

Bronx Boxer
COCKTAIL GLASS
½ part Apricot Brandy
½ part Cranberry Juice Cocktail
splash Parfait Amour
Shake with ice and strain.

Brood Bloodbath
COCKTAIL GLASS
2 parts Vodka
1 part Cherry Juice
splash Orange Juice
Shake with ice and strain. Garnish with Maraschino Cherry.

Brooklyn
COCKTAIL GLASS
1½ parts Whiskey
1 part Dry Vermouth
1 part Maraschino Liqueur
Shake with ice and strain.

Brown Kitten
COCKTAIL GLASS
1 part Dry Gin
1 part Crème de Cacao (Dark)
1 part Triple Sec
Shake with ice and strain.

Brown Velvet
COCKTAIL GLASS
2 parts Cream
1 part Crème de Cacao (Dark)
1 part Triple Sec
Shake with ice and strain.

Bubble Gum
COCKTAIL GLASS
1 part Southern Comfort®
1 part Crème de Banane
1 part Grenadine
1 part Milk
Shake with ice and strain.

Bubblegum Trouble
COCKTAIL GLASS
1 part Coconut Rum
1 part Melon Liqueur
1 part Passion Fruit Rum
1 part Pomegranate Liqueur
splash Milk
Shake with ice and strain.

Buca Alma

COCKTAIL GLASS

1 1/2 parts Vodka
1 1/2 parts Sambuca
1 part Amaretto

Shake with ice and strain.

Buckle Your Seatbelt

COCKTAIL GLASS

1/2 part Crème de Cassis
1/2 part Grand Marnier®
1/2 part Sweet & Sour Mix
splash Lemon Juice

Shake with ice and strain.

Buddha's Banshee

COCKTAIL GLASS

1/2 part Spiced Rum
1/4 part Crème de Cacao (White)
1/2 part Crème de Banane
3 parts Half and Half

Shake with ice and strain.

Buen Viaje

COCKTAIL GLASS

1 part Dry Gin
1 part Dark Rum
splash Grenadine

Shake with ice and strain.

Buena Vista

COCKTAIL GLASS

1 1/2 parts Grenadine
1 1/2 parts Dark Rum
1 part Sweet Vermouth
1 part Lime Cordial

Shake with ice and strain.

Bull & Bear

COCKTAIL GLASS

1 part Jim Beam®
1 part Peach Schnapps
1 part Pineapple Juice
splash Grenadine
splash Lemon Juice

Shake with ice and strain.

Bull Fighter

COCKTAIL GLASS

1 part Triple Sec
1 part Spanish Brandy
1 part Port
splash Crème de Menthe (White)
splash Strawberry Syrup

Shake with ice and strain.

Bumbo

COCKTAIL GLASS

2 parts Dark Rum
1 part Lemon Juice
splash Grenadine
dash Ground Nutmeg

Shake with ice and strain.

Bunny Bonanza

COCKTAIL GLASS

2 parts Silver Tequila
1 part Apple Brandy
1/2 part Maple Syrup
splash Triple Sec

Shake with ice and strain.

Burning North Pole Breeze

COCKTAIL GLASS

1 part Pepper Vodka
1 part Peppermint Liqueur
1 part Crème de Menthe (White)

Shake with ice and strain.

Burnt Embers

COCKTAIL GLASS

1 1/2 parts Añejo Rum
1/2 part Apricot Brandy
1 part Pineapple Juice

Shake with ice and strain.

Buried Deep

COCKTAIL GLASS

1 part Crème de Cacao (White)
1 part Triple Sec
1 part Milk
1 part Orange Juice

Shake with ice and strain.

Burning Love
COCKTAIL GLASS

1 part Light Rum
1 part Strawberry Vodka
½ part Irish Cream Liqueur
½ part Sambuca
splash Blue Curaçao

Shake with ice and strain.

Bushkill
COCKTAIL GLASS

2 parts Light Rum
½ part Dubonnet Blanc
dash Bitters

Shake with ice and strain. Garnish with Lemon Twist.

Butt Tickler
COCKTAIL GLASS

½ part Goldschläger®
½ part Vanilla Extract
1 part Cranberry Juice Cocktail
1 part Sweet & Sour Mix

Shake with ice and strain.

Butter Nuts
COCKTAIL GLASS

1 part Butterscotch Schnapps
1 part Crème de Cacao (White)
1 part Irish Cream Liqueur

Shake with ice and strain.

Butter Pecan
COCKTAIL GLASS

2 parts Vanilla Vodka
1 part Butterscotch Liqueur
1 part Frangelico

Shake with ice and strain. (Note: A pee-con is a nut. A pee-can is a container.).

Buttered Monkey
COCKTAIL GLASS

2 parts RumChata
1 part Banana Liqueur
1 part Butterscotch Liqueur
1 part Vanilla Vodka

Shake with ice and strain.

Butterfly
COCKTAIL GLASS

1 part Vodka
1 part Crème de Banane
1 part Pineapple Juice
1 part Blackberry

Shake with ice and strain.

Butterfly Kisses
COCKTAIL GLASS

2 parts Peach Schnapps
1 part Sour Cherry Liqueur
1 part Cranberry Juice

Shake with ice and strain.

Butternut
COCKTAIL GLASS

1 part Butterscotch Liqueur
1 part Crème de Cacao (White)
1 part Vanilla Vodka
½ part Chocolate Syrup

Shake with ice and strain.

Buttery Nipple
COCKTAIL GLASS

1 part Irish Cream Liqueur
1 part Butterscotch Schnapps

Shake with ice and strain.

By the Light of the Moon
COCKTAIL GLASS

1½ parts Coffee Liqueur
1 part Cream
1 part Mandarine Napoléon® Liqueur
½ part Simple Syrup

Shake with ice and strain.

Byculla Cocktail
COCKTAIL GLASS
- 1 part Triple Sec
- 1 part Dry Sherry
- 1 part Ginger Liqueur
- 1 part Port

Shake with ice and strain.

Bye Bye Brood
COCKTAIL GLASS
- 1 part Peppermint Liqueur
- 1 part Absinthe

Shake with ice and strain.

Byrrh Bird
COCKTAIL GLASS
- 1 part Advocaat
- 1 part Crème de Banane
- 1 part Sweet & Sour Mix

Shake with ice and strain.

Caballero
COCKTAIL GLASS
- 1 part Pisang Ambon® Liqueur
- 1 part Campari®

Shake with ice and strain.

Cable Car
COCKTAIL GLASS
- 1 part Apricot Brandy
- 1 part Triple Sec

Shake with ice and strain.

Cabo
COCKTAIL GLASS
- 1½ parts Tequila
- fill with Pineapple Juice
- splash Lime Juice

Shake with ice and strain.

Cactus Bite
COCKTAIL GLASS
- 2 parts Tequila
- 2 parts Lemon Juice
- 2 splashes Triple Sec
- 2 splashes Drambuie®
- dash Sugar
- dash Bitters

Shake with ice and strain.

Cactus Flower
COCKTAIL GLASS
- 2 parts Silver Tequila
- ½ part Blue Curaçao
- ½ part Amaretto
- ½ part Vanilla Liqueur
- ½ part Lime Juice

Shake with ice and strain.

Cactus Fruit
COCKTAIL GLASS
- 1 part Grapefruit Vodka
- 1 part Pear Vodka
- 1 part Silver Tequila
- 1 part Grapefruit Juice

Shake with ice and strain.

Cactus Jack
COCKTAIL GLASS
- 1 part Vodka
- ½ part Blue Curaçao
- 1½ parts Pineapple Juice
- 1½ parts Orange Juice

Shake with ice and strain.

Cactus Prick
COCKTAIL GLASS
- 2 parts Silver Tequila
- ½ part Triple Sec
- ⅓ part Drambuie
- 2 parts Lemon Juice

Shake with ice and strain.

Cafe Kirsch Cocktail
COCKTAIL GLASS
1 1/2 parts Dry Gin
1 part Egg White
1/2 part Cream
splash Anisette
Shake with ice and strain.

Café Mocha
COCKTAIL GLASS
1 part Chocolate Vodka
1 part Espresso Vodka
1 part Godiva Chocolate Liqueur
1 part Cream
Shake with ice and strain.

Cafe Trinidad
COCKTAIL GLASS
1 part Dark Rum
1/2 part Amer Picon®
1/2 part Tia Maria®
1 part Cream
Shake with ice and strain.

Caleigh
COCKTAIL GLASS
1 1/2 parts Scotch
1/2 part Blue Curaçao
1/2 part Crème de Cacao (White)
Shake with ice and strain.

California Dream
COCKTAIL GLASS
2 parts Tequila
1 part Sweet Vermouth
1/2 part Dry Vermouth
Shake with ice and strain.

Californian Skateboarder
COCKTAIL GLASS
1 part Light Rum
1/2 part Maraschino Liqueur
1/2 part Grenadine
1 part Pineapple Juice
Shake with ice and strain.

Calin Cocktail
COCKTAIL GLASS
1 part Anisette
1 part Mandarine Napoléon® Liqueur
1 part Orange Juice
Shake with ice and strain.

Calvados Cream
COCKTAIL GLASS
1 1/2 parts Calvados Apple Brandy
1 part Cream
1 Egg White
splash Pineapple Juice
Shake with ice and strain.

Camel Cracker
COCKTAIL GLASS
1 part Black Sambuca
1/2 part Raspberry Liqueur
1/2 part Irish Cream Liqueur
1 part Milk
Shake with ice and strain.

Campay
COCKTAIL GLASS
1 part Campari®
1 part Gin
1/2 part Simple Syrup
2 parts Grapefruit Juice
Shake with ice and strain.

Campeador
COCKTAIL GLASS
1 part Triple Sec
splash Blue Curaçao
splash Amaretto
splash Dry Vermouth
Shake with ice and strain.

Campfire Cocktail
COCKTAIL GLASS
1 1/2 parts Melon Liqueur
1 part Sweet & Sour Mix
splash Lime Juice
dash Powdered Sugar
Shake with ice and strain.

Camptown Races

COCKTAIL GLASS

1 parts Bourbon

1 part Cherry Brandy

½ part Lemon Juice

½ part Orange Juice

Shake with ice and strain.

Canada

COCKTAIL GLASS

1 part Canadian Whisky

½ part Triple Sec

½ part Maple Syrup

Shake with ice and strain.

Canadian Beauty

COCKTAIL GLASS

1½ parts Canadian Whisky

½ part Dry Vermouth

½ part Goldschläger®

splash Crème de Menthe (Green)

splash Port

½ part Orange Juice

Shake all but the Port with ice and strain. Top with the Port.

Canadian Breeze

COCKTAIL GLASS

1½ parts Crème de Coconut

1 part Blue Curaçao

1½ parts Cream of Coconut

1 part Orange Juice

Shake with ice and strain.

Canadian Manhattan

COCKTAIL GLASS

3 parts Canadian Whisky

1 part Sweet Vermouth

Shake with ice and strain. Garnish with Maraschino Cherry.

Cancun Weather

COCKTAIL GLASS

1 part Banana Liqueur

1 part Tropical Tequila

1 part Orange Juice

1 part Pineapple Juice

splash Dark Rum

Shake all but the Rum with ice and strain. Top with a splash Dark Rum.

Candy Apple

COCKTAIL GLASS

1 part Peach Schnapps

1 part Calvados Apple Brandy

½ part Cranberry Juice Cocktail

Shake with ice and strain.

Candy from Strangers

COCKTAIL GLASS

1½ parts Vodka

½ part Triple Sec

½ part Amaretto

½ part Dry Vermouth

Shake with ice and strain.

Canterbury

COCKTAIL GLASS

1 part Gin

1½ parts Kiwi Schnapps

½ part Strawberry Liqueur

½ part Sweet & Sour Mix

Shake with ice and strain.

Cape of Good Will

COCKTAIL GLASS

1½ parts Light Rum

½ part Apricot Brandy

½ part Lime Juice

1 part Orange Juice

2 dashes Orange Bitters

Shake with ice and strain.

Capitán Cienfuegos

COCKTAIL GLASS

1½ parts Light Rum
½ part Lime Juice
½ part Honey
splash Vanilla Liqueur

Shake with ice and strain.

Cappuccino Cocktail

COCKTAIL GLASS

1 part Vodka
1 part Coffee Brandy
1 part Light Cream

Shake with ice and strain.

Caprice

COCKTAIL GLASS

1 part Dry Gin
½ part Apricot Brandy
splash Dry Vermouth
dash Orange Bitters

Shake with ice and strain.

Captain Haddock

COCKTAIL GLASS

1 part Scotch
1 part White Wine
½ part Melon Liqueur
½ part Lime Juice

Shake with ice and strain.

Captain Medellin

COCKTAIL GLASS

1 part Light Rum
1 part Crème de Banane
1 part Orange Juice
splash Sweet & Sour Mix

Shake with ice and strain.

The Captain's Silver Sunrise

COCKTAIL GLASS

1 part Spiced Rum
1½ parts Coconut Rum
splash Orange Juice
splash Cranberry Juice Cocktail

Shake with ice and strain.

Captive

COCKTAIL GLASS

1 part Gin
splash Cherry Brandy
splash Kirschwasser

Shake with ice and strain.

Cara Sposa

COCKTAIL GLASS

1 part Coffee Brandy
1 part Triple Sec
½ part Light Cream

Shake with ice and strain.

Cardicas

COCKTAIL GLASS

2 parts Light Rum
1 part White Port
1 part Cointreau®

Shake with ice and strain.

Cardinal

COCKTAIL GLASS

1½ parts Añejo Rum
½ part Maraschino Liqueur
splash Triple Sec
splash Grenadine

Shake with ice and strain.

Carefree

COCKTAIL GLASS

1 part Cherry Brandy
1 part Apple Juice
1 part Grapefruit Juice
splash Grenadine

Shake with ice and strain.

Caribbean Cruise

COCKTAIL GLASS

¾ part Dark Rum
¾ part Tia Maria®
¾ part Cream of Coconut
1 part Orange Juice
1 part Pineapple Juice

Shake with ice and strain.

Caribbean Kiss

COCKTAIL GLASS

1/2 part Dark Rum
1/2 part Amaretto
1/2 part Coffee Liqueur
1 part Cream
dash Cinnamon
dash Brown Sugar

Shake with ice and strain.

Caribbean Shooter

COCKTAIL GLASS

3/4 part Spiced Rum
1/2 part Brandy
1 part Cranberry Juice Cocktail

Shake with ice and strain.

Caribbean White

COCKTAIL GLASS

1 part Dark Rum
1/2 part Crème de Coconut
1/2 part Crème de Cacao (Dark)
splash Cream

Shake with ice and strain.

Carlton

COCKTAIL GLASS

1 1/2 parts Whiskey
3/4 part Triple Sec
3/4 part Orange Juice

Shake with ice and strain.

Carmencita

COCKTAIL GLASS

1 part Silver Tequila
1/2 part Blue Curaçao
1/2 part Amaretto

Shake with ice and strain.

The Carnal Instinct

COCKTAIL GLASS

1 part Gin
1/2 part Peach Schnapps
splash Limoncello
1/2 part Lemon Juice
1 1/2 parts Apple Juice
splash Simple Syrup

Shake with ice and strain.

Carnegie Melon

COCKTAIL GLASS

1/2 part Crème de Coconut
1/2 part Melon Liqueur
splash Lime Juice

Shake with ice and strain.

Carol

COCKTAIL GLASS

2 parts Gin
1/2 part Apricot Brandy
dash Orange Bitters

Shake with ice and strain.

Carpe Diem

COCKTAIL GLASS

1 1/2 parts 151-Proof Rum
splash Blue Curaçao
splash Mezcal
1/2 part Lemon Juice
1 part Passion Fruit Juice

Shake with ice and strain.

La Carré

COCKTAIL GLASS

1 1/2 parts Vodka
2 splashes Dry Vermouth
2 splashes Kümmel

Shake with ice and strain.

Carta Vieja

COCKTAIL GLASS

1 part Peach Schnapps
1 part Light Rum
1/2 part Lime Juice
splash Simple Syrup

Shake with ice and strain.

Casanova

COCKTAIL GLASS

2 parts Melon Liqueur
2/3 part Crème de Cacao (White)
1 part Cream

Shake with ice and strain.

Castelo dos Mouros

COCKTAIL GLASS

1 1/2 parts Brandy
1/2 part Crème de Cacao (White)
1 part Port

Shake with ice and strain.

Cat and Fiddle

COCKTAIL GLASS

1 1/2 parts Canadian Whisky
1/2 part Cointreau
1/6 part Dry Vermouth
1/6 part Pernod

Shake with ice and strain.

Catcher in the Rye

COCKTAIL GLASS

1 part Irish Whiskey
1 part Apricot Brandy
splash Coffee Liqueur
splash Lemon Juice

Shake with ice and strain.

Catholic Coronation

COCKTAIL GLASS

1 part Vodka
1/2 part Amaretto
1/2 part Butterscotch Schnapps
1/2 part Frangelico®
1/2 part Milk

Shake with ice and strain.

Cavalier

COCKTAIL GLASS

1 1/2 parts Tequila
1/2 part Galliano®
1 1/2 parts Orange Juice
1/2 part Cream

Shake with ice and strain.

Le Cavalier Mysterieux

COCKTAIL GLASS

1 part Calvados Apple Brandy
2/3 part Irish Cream Liqueur
1/2 part Hazelnut Liqueur
splash Amaretto
1 part Cream

Shake with ice and strain.

Celebration

COCKTAIL GLASS

1 1/2 parts Rum
1 part Cognac
1 part Cointreau®
1 part Lemon Juice

Shake with ice and strain.

Celtic Cheer

COCKTAIL GLASS

1 part Butterscotch Schnapps
1 part Peach Schnapps
1 part Irish Cream Liqueur

Shake with ice and strain.

Celtic Twilight

COCKTAIL GLASS

1 part Irish Cream Liqueur
1 part Bushmills® Irish Whiskey
1 part Frangelico®

Shake with ice and strain.

Cessna

COCKTAIL GLASS

1 1/2 parts Gin
1/2 part Dubonnet® Blonde
2 splashes Maraschino Liqueur

Shake with ice and strain.

C'est Parfait

COCKTAIL GLASS

1 part Parfait Amour
2/3 part Amaretto
splash Blue Curaçao
1 part Vanilla Syrup
1 part Cream

Shake with ice and strain.

Chain Lightning
COCKTAIL GLASS

2 parts Gin
1/2 part Triple Sec
2 splashes Lemon Juice

Shake with ice and strain.

Champs Elysées Cocktail
COCKTAIL GLASS

1 part Brandy
1/2 part Yellow Chartreuse®
splash Lemon Juice
dash Powdered Sugar
dash Bitters

Shake with ice and strain.

Chantilly Lace
COCKTAIL GLASS

1 1/2 parts Vanilla Liqueur
1 1/2 parts Maraschino Liqueur
1/2 part Vodka
splash Chocolate Syrup

Shake with ice and strain.

Chaos
COCKTAIL GLASS

2/3 part Blackberry Liqueur
1 1/2 parts Jamaican Rum
2/3 part Lemon Juice
2 parts Raspberry Seltzer

Shake with ice and strain.

Charger
COCKTAIL GLASS

1 1/2 parts Dark Rum
1/2 part Cherry Brandy
1/2 part Lemon Juice
dash Sugar

Shake with ice and strain.

Charging Rhino
COCKTAIL GLASS

1 1/2 parts Vodka
1/2 part Dry Vermouth
1/2 part Campari®

Shake with ice and strain.

Charmer
COCKTAIL GLASS

1 1/2 parts Scotch
1 part Blue Curaçao
splash Dry Vermouth
dash Orange Bitters

Shake with ice and strain.

Cheesecake
COCKTAIL GLASS

1 part Vanilla Vodka
1/2 part Triple Sec
1/2 part Sweet & Sweet & Sour Mix
1 part Cream
splash Crème de Cacao (White)

Shake with ice and strain.

Chellengae
COCKTAIL GLASS

1 part Vodka
1 part Grand Marnier®
1/2 part Lime Juice

Shake with ice and strain.

Cherie
COCKTAIL GLASS

1 part Light Rum
1/2 part Cherry Brandy
1/2 part Triple Sec
1/2 part Lime Juice

Shake with ice and strain.

Cherokee
COCKTAIL GLASS

1 1/2 parts Cognac
1 part Amaretto
1 part Apricot Brandy
splash Grenadine

Shake with ice and strain.

Cherried Cream Rum
COCKTAIL GLASS

1 1/2 parts Light Rum
1/2 part Cherry Brandy
1/2 part Light Cream

Shake with ice and strain.

Cherry Berry

COCKTAIL GLASS

1 part Vodka
1 part Raspberry Liqueur
½ part Cherry Brandy
½ part Blackberry Juice
splash Lime Juice

Shake with ice and strain.

The Cherry Drop

COCKTAIL GLASS

1½ parts Light Rum
½ part Crème de Cacao (White)
1 part Cream
splash Cherry Brandy

Shake with ice and strain.

Cherry Flower

COCKTAIL GLASS

1 part Cognac
1 part Cherry Brandy
1 part Triple Sec
1 part Grenadine

Shake with ice and strain.

Cherry Kid

COCKTAIL GLASS

1 part Cherry Vodka
1 part Amaretto
1 part Cranberry Juice Cocktail

Shake with ice and strain.

Cherry Ripe

COCKTAIL GLASS

1½ parts Vodka
½ part Cherry Brandy
½ part Brandy

Shake with ice and strain.

Cherry Rum Cream

COCKTAIL GLASS

2 parts Cherry Rum
1 part Cherry Liqueur
1 part RumChata

Shake with ice and strain.

Cherry Valley

COCKTAIL GLASS

1 part Cherry Brandy
1 part Cherry Vodka
½ part Triple Sec
1 part Cream
½ part Lime Juice

Shake with ice and strain.

Cherry O

COCKTAIL GLASS

1 part Cream
1 part Coffee Liqueur
1 part Cherry Brandy

Shake with ice and strain.

Cheryl

COCKTAIL GLASS

1 part Triple Sec
1 part Raspberry Liqueur
½ part Grenadine
½ part Sweet & Sour Mix

Shake with ice and strain.

Chicago Style

COCKTAIL GLASS

¾ part Rum
¼ part Triple Sec
¼ part Anisette
½ part Sweetened Lime Juice

Shake with ice and strain.

Chicken Run

COCKTAIL GLASS

1 part Raspberry Liqueur
½ part Triple Sec
½ part Mezcal

Shake with ice and strain.

El Chico

COCKTAIL GLASS

1½ parts Light Rum
½ part Sweet Vermouth
splash Blue Curaçao
splash Grenadine

Shake with ice and strain.

The Child Prodigy

COCKTAIL GLASS

1 1/2 parts Orange Vodka
1/2 part Vanilla Liqueur
1/2 part Crème de Coconut
2/3 part Mango Juice
2/3 part Cream

Shake with ice and strain.

Childhood Memories

COCKTAIL GLASS

1 part Crème de Banane
1 part Blackberry Liqueur
1 part Irish Cream Liqueur

Shake with ice and strain.

Chilly Willy

COCKTAIL GLASS

1 part Melon Liqueur
1 part Coconut Rum
3/4 part Peach Schnapps

Shake with ice and strain.

Chocolate Banana

COCKTAIL GLASS

1 1/4 part Crème de Banane
1 1/4 part Crème de Cacao (White)
splash Milk

Shake with ice and strain.

Chocolate Chip

COCKTAIL GLASS

1 1/2 parts Vodka
1 1/2 parts Frangelico®

Shake with ice and strain.

Chocolate Club

COCKTAIL GLASS

1 part Dark Rum
1 part Chocolate Mint Liqueur
1 part Cream
splash Crème de Cacao (White)

Shake with ice and strain.

Chocolate Cream

COCKTAIL GLASS

1 part Rum
1 part Crème de Cacao (Dark)
1/2 part Crème de Menthe (White)
1 part Cream

Shake with ice and strain.

Chocolate Malt

COCKTAIL GLASS

2 parts RumChata
1 part Chocolate Liqueur
1 part Whipped Cream Vodka

Shake with ice and strain.

Chocolate Mint Rum Cream

COCKTAIL GLASS

1 part Dark Rum
1 part RumChata
1/2 part Chocolate Liqueur
dash Crème de Menthe (Green)

Shake with ice and strain.

Chocolate Princess

COCKTAIL GLASS

1 part Dark Rum
1 part Milk
1/2 part Crème de Menthe (Green)
1/2 part Crème de Cacao (Dark)

Shake with ice and strain.

Chocolate Pudding

COCKTAIL GLASS

1 part Crème de Cacao (White)
1 part Cream
1 part Hazelnut Liqueur

Shake with ice and strain.

Chocolate Rain

COCKTAIL GLASS

1 part Chocolate Liqueur
1 part Chocolate Vodka
1 part Irish Cream Liqueur
1 part Milk

Shake with ice and strain.

Chocolate Rain with Eternal Chaos

COCKTAIL GLASS

1 part Chocolate Vodka
1 part Chocolate Liqueur
1 part Jägermeister
1 part Milk

Shake with ice and strain.

Chocolate Raspberry Delight

COCKTAIL GLASS

1½ parts Irish Cream Liqueur
1½ parts Raspberry Liqueur

Shake with ice and strain.

Chocolate Screwdriver

COCKTAIL GLASS

2 parts Vodka
1 part Crème de Cacao (White)
fill with Orange Juice

Shake with ice and strain.

Choker

COCKTAIL GLASS

2 parts Scotch
2 splashes Pernod®
2 dashes Bitters

Shake with ice and strain.

Cholla Bay

COCKTAIL GLASS

1 part Tequila
dash Sugar
1 part Sweet & Sour Mix
½ part Grenadine

Shake with ice and strain.

Chop-Nut

COCKTAIL GLASS

¾ part Vodka
1 part Crème de Banane
1 part Crème de Coconut
½ part Orange Juice

Shake with ice and strain.

Chorus Lady Cocktail

COCKTAIL GLASS

1 part Dry Gin
1 part Dry Vermouth
1 part Sweet Vermouth
1 part Orange Juice

Shake with ice and strain.

Christ

COCKTAIL GLASS

1½ parts Bourbon
½ part Peach Schnapps

Shake with ice and strain.

Christmas Cookie

COCKTAIL GLASS

3 parts RumChata
1 part Cake Vodka
1 part Cinnamon Schnapps

Shake with ice and strain. Garnish with Rainbow Sprinkles.

Chronic

COCKTAIL GLASS

1 part Canadian Whisky
1 part Hpnotiq
splash Lime Juice

Shake with ice and strain.

Churchill

COCKTAIL GLASS

1½ parts Scotch
½ part Sweet Vermouth

Shake with ice and strain.

Ciao, Baby

COCKTAIL GLASS

2 parts Strawberry Vodka
1 part Dark Rum
1 part Sweetened Lime Juice
dash Grenadine

Shake with ice and strain.

El Cid

COCKTAIL GLASS

1/2 part Gin
1/2 part Melon Liqueur
1/2 part Sweetened Lime Juice
1 part Orange Juice

Shake with ice and strain.

Cielo Nublado

COCKTAIL GLASS

1 part Gin
1/2 part Blue Curaçao
1/2 part Parfait Amour

Shake with ice and strain.

Cinnamon Sugar Toast

COCKTAIL GLASS

3 parts RumChata
1 part Amaretto

Shake with ice and strain.

Cinammon Twist

COCKTAIL GLASS

1 part Vodka
1 part Triple Sec
splash Lemon-Lime Soda

Shake Vodka and Triple Sec with ice and strain. Top with a splash of Lemon-Lime soda and garnish with Cinnamon Candies.

Cinco de Mayo

COCKTAIL GLASS

2 1/2 parts Tequila
1 part Grenadine
1 part Sweetened Lime Juice

Shake with ice and strain.

Circus Flyer

COCKTAIL GLASS

2 parts Vodka
2/3 part Crème de Cassis
splash Blue Curaçao

Shake with ice and strain.

Citizen Kane

COCKTAIL GLASS

1 part Coffee Liqueur
1 part Irish Whiskey
2 parts Cream

Shake with ice and strain.

Citrus Crown

COCKTAIL GLASS

1 1/2 parts Crown Royal® Whiskey
1/2 part Lemon Juice
1 part Orange Juice

Shake with ice and strain.

Citrus Neon

COCKTAIL GLASS

2 parts Citrus Vodka
1 part Blue Curaçao
1 part Melon Liqueur
1 part Sweet & Sweet & Sour Mix
splash Lime Juice

Shake with ice and strain.

City Slicker

COCKTAIL GLASS

2 parts Brandy
1/2 part Triple Sec
splash Lemon Juice

Shake with ice and strain.

The Clan Chieftain

COCKTAIL GLASS

splash Orange Liqueur
1 part Cointreau®
2 parts Scotch

Shake with ice and strain.

Claridge

COCKTAIL GLASS

1 part Dry Vermouth
1 part Gin
3/4 part Triple Sec
3/4 part Apricot Brandy

Shake with ice and strain.

Clash
COCKTAIL GLASS

1 part Light Rum
1 part Maraschino Liqueur
1 part Crème de Menthe (Green)
1 part Dry Vermouth

Shake with ice and strain.

The Classic
COCKTAIL GLASS

1 part Cognac
½ part Lemon Juice
½ part Maraschino Liqueur
1 part Triple Sec

Shake with ice and strain.

Classy Sanctuary
COCKTAIL GLASS

1 part Vodka
1 part Melon Liqueur
1 part Sweet & Sour Mix
splash Passion Fruit Liqueur

Shake with ice and strain.

Cleopatra
COCKTAIL GLASS

1 part Rum
splash Amaretto
½ part Lemon Juice
3 dashes Angostura® Bitters

Shake with ice and strain.

Climax
COCKTAIL GLASS

½ part Vodka
½ part Amaretto
½ part Crème de Cacao (White)
½ part Triple Sec
½ part Crème de Banane
1 part Light Cream

Shake with ice and strain.

Clipper
COCKTAIL GLASS

1 part Whiskey
½ part Simple Syrup
½ part Apricot Brandy
splash Campari®

Shake with ice and strain.

Cloister
COCKTAIL GLASS

1½ parts Gin
1 part Grapefruit Juice
½ tbsp Sugar

Shake with ice and strain.

Closing Time
COCKTAIL GLASS

1 part Peppermint Liqueur
1 part Vanilla Liqueur
1 part Cream

Shake with ice and strain.

Clover Leaf Cocktail
COCKTAIL GLASS

1½ parts Gin
juice of ½ lemon
⅓ part Grenadine
1 Egg White

Shake with ice and strain. Garnish with a Mint Sprig.

Cloud
COCKTAIL GLASS

1 part Crème de Menthe (Green)
1 part Anisette
1 part Milk

Shake with ice and strain.

Clove Cocktail
COCKTAIL GLASS

1 part Sweet Vermouth
½ part Sloe Gin
½ part Muscatel

Shake with ice and strain.

Cocktail DTV
COCKTAIL GLASS
1 part Gin
1 part Cinzano®
1/2 part Grenadine
Shake with ice and strain.

Coco Candy Cane
COCKTAIL GLASS
1 part Vodka
1 part Crème de Cacao (White)
1 part Peppermint Schnapps
Shake with ice and strain.

Coco Poco
COCKTAIL GLASS
1 part Vodka
1 part Crème de Coconut
1 part Tia Maria®
Shake with ice and strain.

Coco Tobacco
COCKTAIL GLASS
1 part Crème de Menthe (Green)
1 part Peach Schnapps
1 part Crème de Banane
Shake with ice and strain.

Cocoa Chanel
COCKTAIL GLASS
1 1/2 parts Cognac
1/2 part Chocolate Liqueur
1/2 part Amaretto
1 1/2 parts Cream of Coconut
Shake with ice and strain.

Coconut Grove
COCKTAIL GLASS
1 part Dark Rum
1/2 part Southern Comfort®
1/2 part Crème de Banane
splash Lime Juice
splash Lemon Juice
Shake with ice and strain.

Coconut's Coffee
COCKTAIL GLASS
1 1/2 parts Crème de Coconut
1/2 part Coffee Liqueur
1/2 part Cream of Coconut
Shake with ice and strain.

Cocoon
COCKTAIL GLASS
2 parts Jamaican Rum
1/2 part Crème de Coconut
2/3 part Vanilla Liqueur
1 part Cream
Shake with ice and strain.

Coffee Alexander
COCKTAIL GLASS
1 part Gin
1 part Coffee Liqueur
1 part Cream
Shake with ice and strain.

Cognac Cocktail
COCKTAIL GLASS
2 parts Cognac
dash Powdered Sugar
splash Triple Sec
Shake with ice and strain.

Cold Kiss
COCKTAIL GLASS
1 1/2 parts Whiskey
1/2 part Peppermint Schnapps
2 splashes Crème de Cacao (White)
Shake with ice and strain.

Cold Plunge
COCKTAIL GLASS
1 part Vodka
1/2 part Triple Sec
1/2 part Apricot Brandy
splash Crème de Banane
Shake with ice and strain.

Collection

COCKTAIL GLASS

1 part Vodka
1 part Citrus Vodka
½ part Blackberry Liqueur
1 part Lime Juice

Shake with ice and strain.

Colonial Retreat

COCKTAIL GLASS

1 part Sloe Gin
½ part Apricot Brandy
½ part Lime Juice

Shake with ice and strain.

Colorado

COCKTAIL GLASS

1 part Cream
1 part Cherry Brandy
1 part Kirschwasser
splash Cherry Juice

Shake with ice and strain.

Columbia

COCKTAIL GLASS

1½ parts Light Rum
½ part Simple Syrup
½ part Kirschwasser

Shake with ice and strain.

Combustible Edison

COCKTAIL GLASS

2 parts Brandy
1 part Campari®
1 part Lemon Juice

Shake with ice and strain.

Comet Dust

COCKTAIL GLASS

½ part Crème de Cacao (Dark)
½ part Crème de Coconut
½ part Hazelnut Liqueur
2 parts Milk

Shake with ice and strain.

Comfort Inn

COCKTAIL GLASS

½ part Gin
1 part Apricot Brandy
1 part Apple Brandy
1 part Sweet & Sour Mix

Shake with ice and strain.

Comfortable

COCKTAIL GLASS

1 part Crème de Cacao (Dark)
1 part Southern Comfort®
1 part Lemon Juice

Shake with ice and strain.

Commando Cocktail

COCKTAIL GLASS

1½ parts Bourbon
¾ part Triple Sec
¾ part Lime Juice
2 dashes Pernod

Shake with ice and strain.

Compadre

COCKTAIL GLASS

1½ parts Tequila
splash Maraschino Liqueur
splash Grenadine
2 dashes Orange Bitters

Shake with ice and strain.

Compel to Work

COCKTAIL GLASS

1 part Citrus Vodka
½ part Orange Liqueur
1 part Grapefruit Juice
½ part Lemon Juice

Shake with ice and strain.

Complicated Lady

COCKTAIL GLASS

1 part Tequila
½ part Apricot Brandy
½ part Grand Marnier®
1 part Lime Juice

Shake with ice and strain.

Conca d'Oro

COCKTAIL GLASS

2 parts Dry Gin
1/2 part Triple Sec
1/2 part Cherry Brandy
1/2 part Maraschino Liqueur

Shake with ice and strain.

Concarde

COCKTAIL GLASS

1 part Gin
1 part Apricot Brandy
1/2 part Campari®
1/2 part Grenadine

Shake with ice and strain.

Concrete Jungle

COCKTAIL GLASS

2 parts Vodka
1/2 part Apricot Brandy
1/2 part Banana Juice

Shake with ice and strain.

Concubine

COCKTAIL GLASS

1 part Cherry Brandy
1 part Amaretto
1 part Cream

Shake with ice and strain.

Connecticut Bulldog

COCKTAIL GLASS

1 part Gin
1/2 part Dark Rum
1/2 part Lemon Juice
1/2 part Maple Syrup

Shake with ice and strain.

Conquistador

COCKTAIL GLASS

1 part Cognac
1/2 part Crème de Cacao (White)
1/2 part Triple Sec
splash Cream
splash Strawberry Syrup

Shake with ice and strain.

Continental

COCKTAIL GLASS

1 3/4 parts Light Rum
splash Crème de Menthe
2 splashes Lime Juice
dash Powdered Sugar

Shake with ice and strain.

Contradiction

COCKTAIL GLASS

1 part Vodka
1/2 part Melon Liqueur
1/2 part Coffee Liqueur
1 part Cream

Shake with ice and strain.

Control Freak

COCKTAIL GLASS

1 1/2 parts Crème de Menthe (White)
3/4 part Amaretto
1/2 part Crème de Cacao (White)
1/4 part Coffee Liqueur

Shake with ice and strain.

Cool Jazz

COCKTAIL GLASS

1 part White Wine
1 part Crème de Banane
1/2 part Lime Juice

Shake with ice and strain.

Cool Summer Breeze

COCKTAIL GLASS

1 part Passion Fruit Liqueur
1 part Vodka
1 part Cranberry Juice Cocktail
1 part Pear Juice

Shake with ice and strain.

Cooper's Rest

COCKTAIL GLASS

1 part Bourbon
1 part Scotch
1 part Whiskey
1 part Cranberry Juice

Shake with ice and strain. For Cooper.

Copper Rivet

COCKTAIL GLASS

1 part Brandy
1/2 part Dry Vermouth
1/2 part Sweet Vermouth
2 splashes Triple Sec

Shake with ice and strain.

Coral Reef

COCKTAIL GLASS

1 1/2 parts Citrus Vodka
1 part Blue Curaçao
3/4 part Tequila
1 part Sweet & Sweet & Sour Mix

Shake with ice and strain.

Corazón

COCKTAIL GLASS

1 part Cherry Brandy
1 part Coffee Brandy
1 part Cherry Juice
1/2 part Brandy

Shake with ice and strain.

Corkscrew

COCKTAIL GLASS

1 1/2 parts Light Rum
1/2 part Peach Brandy
1 1/2 parts Dry Vermouth

Shake with ice and strain.

Cornhole

COCKTAIL GLASS

1 1/2 parts Irish Cream Liqueur
1 1/2 parts Tequila
splash Dubonnet® Blonde

Shake with ice and strain.

Coronado

COCKTAIL GLASS

1 1/2 parts Gin
1/2 part Blue Curaçao
2 parts Pineapple Juice
splash Kirschwasser

Shake with ice and strain.

Cortez Chorus

COCKTAIL GLASS

1/2 part Crème de Coconut
2/3 part Amaretto
1/2 part Spiced Rum
2/3 part Orange Juice
2/3 part Pineapple Juice

Shake with ice and strain.

Cosmo Katie

COCKTAIL GLASS

2 parts Currant Vodka
1 part Grand Marnier®
splash Lime Juice
splash Cranberry Juice Cocktail

Shake with ice and strain.

Cosmopolitan

COCKTAIL GLASS

1 1/4 parts Citrus Vodka
1/4 part Lime Juice
1/4 part Triple Sec
splash Cranberry Juice Cocktail

Shake with ice and strain.

Cosmorita

COCKTAIL GLASS

1 1/2 parts Tequila
1/2 part Triple Sec
1/2 part Lime Juice
1/2 part Cranberry Juice Cocktail

Shake with ice and strain.

Cossack Charge

COCKTAIL GLASS

1 1/2 parts Vodka
1/2 part Cognac
1/2 part Cherry Brandy

Shake with ice and strain.

Costa del Sol

COCKTAIL GLASS

2 parts Gin
1 part Apricot Brandy
1 part Grand Marnier®

Shake with ice and strain.

Cotillion Cocktail

COCKTAIL GLASS

1 part Triple Sec
1 part Orange Juice
1 part Lemon Juice
splash Rum

Shake with ice and strain.

Cotton Candy

COCKTAIL GLASS

2 parts Coconut Rum
1 part Peach Vodka
1 part Pink Lemonade Vodka

Shake with ice and strain.

Cotton Candy Lip Gloss

COCKTAIL GLASS

1 part Blue Raspberry Liqueur
1 part Cotton Candy Vodka
1 part Passion Fruit Liqueur

Shake with ice and strain.

Country Club

COCKTAIL GLASS

1 part Whiskey
½ part Apricot Brandy
½ part Triple Sec
splash Cream
splash Grenadine

Shake with ice and strain.

Countryside Garden

COCKTAIL GLASS

1 part Apricot Brandy
⅔ part Dry Vermouth
⅔ part Grape Juice
splash Lemon Juice

Shake with ice and strain.

County Fair

COCKTAIL GLASS

1 part Melon Liqueur
1 part Sloe Gin
1 part Sweet & Sour Mix

Shake with ice and strain.

Covadonga

COCKTAIL GLASS

1 part Campari®
1 part Sweet Vermouth
1 part Orange Juice
½ part Grenadine

Shake with ice and strain.

Coyote Girl

COCKTAIL GLASS

1½ parts Bourbon
1 part Southern Comfort®
1 part Lemon Juice

Shake with ice and strain.

Cranberry Blast

COCKTAIL GLASS

1½ parts Peach Schnapps
½ part Dark Rum
½ part Vodka
½ part Scotch
½ part Orange Juice
2 parts Cranberry Juice Cocktail
splash Lemon Juice

Shake with ice and strain.

Cranberry Kami

COCKTAIL GLASS

1½ parts Vodka
½ part Triple Sec
½ part Lime Juice
½ part Cranberry Juice Cocktail

Shake with ice and strain.

Cranium Meltdown

COCKTAIL GLASS

1 part Dark Rum
1 part Crème de Coconut
1 part Pineapple Juice

Shake with ice and strain.

Cranmint

COCKTAIL GLASS

¾ part Raspberry Liqueur
½ part Crème de Menthe (White)
½ part Citrus Vodka

Shake with ice and strain.

Crantango Bay
COCKTAIL GLASS
1/2 part Citrus Vodka
1 part Blackberry Liqueur
2 parts Cranberry Juice Cocktail
Shake with ice and strain.

Cranxious
COCKTAIL GLASS
2/3 part Strawberry Liqueur
1 part Sloe Gin
splash Blue Curaçao
1/2 part Lime Juice
2 parts Cranberry Juice Cocktail
Shake with ice and strain.

Crash Landing
COCKTAIL GLASS
1 1/2 parts Vodka
2 splashes Grenadine
splash Lime Juice
splash Lemon Juice
dash Sugar
Shake with ice and strain.

Crawford
COCKTAIL GLASS
2 parts Citrus Rum
1/2 part Melon Liqueur
1/2 part Blue Curaçao
splash Dry Vermouth
Shake with ice and strain.

Crazy Calypso
COCKTAIL GLASS
1 part Peach Schnapps
1 part Orange Vodka
splash Sweet & Sour Mix
Shake with ice and strain.

Crazy Fin
COCKTAIL GLASS
2 parts Vodka
1 part Dry Sherry
1 part Cointreau®
1/2 part Lemon Juice
Shake with ice and strain.

Crazy Idea
COCKTAIL GLASS
1 part Parfait Amour
1 part Ouzo
Shake with ice and strain.

Crazy Janey
COCKTAIL GLASS
1 part Apricot Brandy
1 part Crème de Menthe (White)
1 part Triple Sec
Shake with ice and strain.

Creamberry
COCKTAIL GLASS
1 part Strawberry Liqueur
1/2 part Raspberry Liqueur
splash Cream
Shake with ice and strain.

Creamsicle®
COCKTAIL GLASS
1 1/2 parts Vanilla Liqueur
1/2 part Grand Marnier®
splash Orange Juice
Shake with ice and strain.

Creamy Crispy Crunch
COCKTAIL GLASS
1 part Crème de Cacao (White)
1 part Frangelico®
2 parts Milk
Shake with ice and strain.

Creamy Nut
COCKTAIL GLASS
2 parts Vodka
1 part Frangelico
1 part Cream
Shake with ice and strain.

Creepy Soldier
COCKTAIL GLASS

1 part Coffee Brandy
½ part Butterscotch Schnapps
⅔ part Hazelnut Liqueur
1½ parts Cream
splash Honey

Shake with ice and strain.

Crème de Gin Cocktail
COCKTAIL GLASS

1½ parts Gin
½ part Crème de Menthe (White)
2 splashes Lemon Juice
2 splashes Orange Juice
1 Egg White

Shake with ice and strain.

Creole Lady
COCKTAIL GLASS

1½ parts Madeira
splash Grenadine

Shake with ice and strain.

Creole Scream
COCKTAIL GLASS

1½ parts Light Rum
1 part Dry Vermouth
dash Angostura® Bitters
splash Grenadine

Shake with ice and strain.

Cricket
COCKTAIL GLASS

¾ part Light Rum
¼ part Crème de Cacao (White)
¼ part Crème de Menthe (Green)
1 part Cream

Shake with ice and strain.

Crimson Marsh
COCKTAIL GLASS

1 part Blackberry Liqueur
½ part Vanilla Liqueur
½ part Hazelnut Liqueur
1½ parts Cream
splash Honey

Shake with ice and strain.

Cripple Creek
COCKTAIL GLASS

1½ parts Silver Tequila
1 part Orange Juice
½ part Galliano®

Shake with ice and strain.

Crista Solar
COCKTAIL GLASS

1 part Vodka
1 part Dry Vermouth
1 part Triple Sec
1 part White Port
dash Bitters

Shake with ice and strain.

Cristal Blue
COCKTAIL GLASS

1½ parts Vodka
1 part Parfait Amour
1 part Dry Sherry
dash Bitters

Shake with ice and strain.

Cristalle
COCKTAIL GLASS

1½ parts Silver Tequila
1 part Blue Curaçao
1 part Peach Schnapps
1 part Lemon Juice
1 part Simple Syrup

Shake with ice and strain.

Crossbow

COCKTAIL GLASS

1 1/2 parts Gin
1 part Crème de Cacao (White)
1 part Triple Sec

Shake with ice and strain.

Crouching Tiger

COCKTAIL GLASS

1 1/2 parts Citrus Rum
1/2 part 151-Proof Rum
splash Maraschino Liqueur
1 1/2 parts Cranberry Juice Cocktail

Shake with ice and strain.

Crown Bomb

COCKTAIL GLASS

1/2 part Crème de Coconut
1/2 part White Wine
1/2 part Amaretto
1/2 part Pineapple Juice

Shake with ice and strain.

Crown Jewel

COCKTAIL GLASS

1/2 part Peach Schnapps
1 part Sloe Gin
1 part Orange Juice
1/2 part Sweet & Sour Mix

Shake with ice and strain.

A Crowned Head

COCKTAIL GLASS

2/3 part Blackberry Liqueur
1 part Dry Vermouth
1 1/2 parts Bourbon
splash Lemon Juice

Shake with ice and strain.

Cruel Intentions

COCKTAIL GLASS

2 parts Orange Vodka
1 part Vanilla Liqueur
splash Vermouth

Shake with ice and strain.

Cruzan for a Bruzan

COCKTAIL GLASS

1 part Cruzan Coconut Rum
1 part Cruzan Mango Rum
1 part Cruzan Pineapple Rum

Shake with ice and strain.

Crystal Palace

COCKTAIL GLASS

2 parts Calvados Apple Brandy
1 1/2 parts Grand Marnier®
2/3 part Lemon Juice

Shake with ice and strain.

Cuban Cocktail

COCKTAIL GLASS

2 parts Rum
dash Sugar
1/2 part Lime Juice

Shake with ice and strain.

Cuban Sidecar

COCKTAIL GLASS

1 1/2 parts Rum
3/4 part Lime Juice
1/2 part Triple Sec

Shake with ice and strain.

Cuban Sour

COCKTAIL GLASS

2 parts Rum
dash Powdered Sugar
2 dashes Lime Juice

Shake with ice and strain.

Cuban Special

COCKTAIL GLASS

1 part Light Rum
splash Triple Sec
2 splashes Pineapple Juice
splash Lime Juice

Shake with ice and strain.

Cubano
COCKTAIL GLASS

2 parts Jamaican Dark Rum
1½ parts Cointreau
1 part Lime Juice
1 Egg White

Shake with ice and strain.

The Cubano Cocktail
COCKTAIL GLASS

1½ parts Gin
1½ parts Dry Vermouth
splash Pineapple Syrup

Shake with ice and strain.

Cumdrop
COCKTAIL GLASS

1 part Coffee Liqueur
1 part Irish Cream Liqueur
½ part Crème de Banane

Shake with ice and strain.

Cupcake
COCKTAIL GLASS

2 parts Cake Vodka
2 parts Vanilla Vodka
1 part Citrus Vodka

Shake with ice and strain.

Cupidon
COCKTAIL GLASS

⅔ part Brandy
½ part Raspberry Liqueur
½ part Hazelnut Liqueur
1½ parts Cream

Shake with ice and strain.

Current Event
COCKTAIL GLASS

1 part Orange Liqueur
2 parts Currant Vodka
splash Cranberry Juice Cocktail

Shake with ice and strain.

Cyberlady
COCKTAIL GLASS

1 part Cognac
½ part Triple Sec
½ part Strawberry Liqueur
1 part Orange Juice
splash Lemon Juice

Shake with ice and strain.

Czarina
COCKTAIL GLASS

1 part Vodka
¾ part Apricot Brandy
½ part Dry Vermouth
½ part Sweet Vermouth

Shake with ice and strain.

Daily Mail
COCKTAIL GLASS

2 parts Scotch
dash Sugar
2 splashes Lemon Juice
2 splashes Blue Curaçao
splash Amaretto

Shake with ice and strain.

Dainty Taste
COCKTAIL GLASS

1½ parts Gin
½ part Passion Fruit Liqueur
½ part Limoncello
1 part Guava Juice
½ part Lemon Juice

Shake with ice and strain.

Daiquiri
COCKTAIL GLASS

1½ parts Light Rum
½ part Lime Juice
dash Powdered Sugar

Shake with ice and strain for a basic Daiquri. For a frozen Daiquri, blend with ice intil smooth. For a frozen fruit Daiquri, add fruit (Strawberry, Banana, Apple, etc.) to the blender as well.

Dallas

COCKTAIL GLASS

1½ parts Passion Fruit Juice
1 part Bourbon
1 part Apricot Brandy

Shake with ice and strain.

Danao

COCKTAIL GLASS

1½ parts Light Rum
½ part Triple Sec
2 parts Cream
1 part Pineapple Juice
1 part Orange Juice

Shake with ice and strain.

Dance with the Devil

COCKTAIL GLASS

2 parts Vodka
1 part Blue Curaçao
½ part Sambuca

Shake with ice and strain.

Dancin'

COCKTAIL GLASS

1 part Vodka
1 part Dry Vermouth
1 part Whiskey
splash Triple Sec
splash Cherry Brandy

Shake with ice and strain.

Dandy

COCKTAIL GLASS

1½ parts Dubonnet® Blonde
1½ parts Rye Whiskey
dash Angostura® Bitters
3 splashes Cointreau®

Shake with ice and strain.

Danish Girl

COCKTAIL GLASS

1 part Amaretto
1 part Crème de Cacao (Dark)
1½ parts Milk

Shake with ice and strain.

Dante's Inferno

COCKTAIL GLASS

2 parts Brandy
1 part Raspberry Liqueur
1 part Lemon Juice

Shake with ice and strain.

Darby

COCKTAIL GLASS

½ part Crème de Coconut
⅔ part Amaretto
1 part Dry Sherry
½ part Lime Juice

Shake with ice and strain.

Daring Apricot

COCKTAIL GLASS

2 parts Vodka
½ part Triple Sec
½ part Apricot Brandy
½ part Lime Juice

Shake with ice and strain.

Dark Lord

COCKTAIL GLASS

1 part Chambord
1 part Vodka
1 part Cranberry Juice

Shake with ice and strain.

Dark Qualude

COCKTAIL GLASS

1 part Coffee Liqueur
1 part Frangelico®
1 part Irish Cream Liqueur

Shake with ice and strain.

Dark Star

COCKTAIL GLASS

1 part Scotch
1 part Crème de Cacao (Dark)
splash Cream

Shake with ice and strain.

Dawdle in the Snow

COCKTAIL GLASS

1 1/2 parts Vodka
1/2 part Triple Sec
1 1/2 parts Pear Juice
1 part Cream

Shake with ice and strain.

Daydreaming

COCKTAIL GLASS

1 1/2 parts Light Rum
1/2 part Grenadine
3 parts Grapefruit Juice
2 parts Cream of Coconut

Shake with ice and strain.

Daydream Nation

COCKTAIL GLASS

1/2 part Limoncello
1/2 part Vodka
1/4 part Triple Sec
1/2 part Cream
1/2 part Orange Juice
dash Grenadine

Shake with ice and strain.

Day-O

COCKTAIL GLASS

1/2 part Crème de Banane
1/2 part Strawberry Liqueur
1/2 part Irish Cream Liqueur
1/2 part Chocolate Liqueur

Shake with ice and strain.

De Rigueur Cocktail

COCKTAIL GLASS

1 1/2 parts Whiskey
1 part Honey
1 part Grape Juice

Shake with ice and strain.

Dead Lawyer

COCKTAIL GLASS

1 part Dry Vermouth
1 part Crème de Cacao (White)
1 part Maraschino Liqueur

Shake with ice and strain.

Dead Man's Party

COCKTAIL GLASS

1 1/2 parts Gin
1/2 part Dry Vermouth
1/2 part Sweet Vermouth
splash Peppermint Liqueur
dash Angostura® Bitters

Shake with ice and strain.

Deadly Desires

COCKTAIL GLASS

2/3 part Cherry Brandy
1/2 part Coffee Liqueur
2/3 part Irish Cream Liqueur

Shake with ice and strain.

Deanne

COCKTAIL GLASS

1 part Vodka
1/2 part Sweet Vermouth
1/2 part Triple Sec

Shake with ice and strain. Garnish with Lemon Twist.

Death by Chocolate

COCKTAIL GLASS

1 1/2 parts Crème de Cacao (Dark)
1 1/2 parts Godiva Chocolate Liqueur
1 part Vanilla Vodka
1 part Half and Half

Shake with ice and strain. Rim glass with Chocolate Shavings, Chocolate Sprinkles, or Oreo crumbs.

Debut d'Etre

COCKTAIL GLASS

1 1/2 parts Maraschino Liqueur
2 parts Rémy Martin® VSOP
1 part Cranberry Juice Cocktail
1/2 part Lime Juice
splash Passion Fruit Juice

Shake with ice and strain.

Debutante
COCKTAIL GLASS

1 part Brandy
1 part Pineapple Juice
1/2 part Cherry Brandy

Shake with ice and strain.

Decadence
COCKTAIL GLASS

1 part Vanilla Vodka
1 part Coffee Liqueur
1 part White Chocolate Liqueur
1 part Cherry Cola
1 part Chocolate Milk

Build over ice and stir.

Deep Dark Secret
COCKTAIL GLASS

1 1/2 parts Dark Rum
1/2 part Añejo Rum
1/2 part Coffee Liqueur
1/2 part Heavy Cream

Shake with ice and strain.

Deep Green Dragon
COCKTAIL GLASS

1 1/2 parts Scotch
1 part Dry Gin
1/2 part Blue Curaçao

Shake with ice and strain.

Deep Menace
COCKTAIL GLASS

2/3 part Orange Liqueur
1 part 151-Proof Rum
splash Lime Juice

Shake with ice and strain.

Deep Sea Cocktail
COCKTAIL GLASS

1 part Gin
1 part Dry Vermouth
splash Anisette
dash Orange Bitters

Shake with ice and strain.

Deepest Fears
COCKTAIL GLASS

1 part Coffee Liqueur
1 part Dark Rum
1 part Spiced Rum
1 part Cream

Shake with ice and strain.

Defy Gravity
COCKTAIL GLASS

2/3 part Melon Liqueur
2/3 part Raspberry Liqueur
2/3 part Pineapple Juice
2/3 part Cranberry Juice Cocktail

Shake with ice and strain.

Delicatessen
COCKTAIL GLASS

1 1/2 parts Apricot Brandy
1 1/2 parts Strawberry Juice
1 1/2 parts Cream

Shake with ice and strain.

Delilah
COCKTAIL GLASS

1 1/2 parts Gin
1/2 part Cointreau®
1/2 Lemon

Shake with ice and strain.

Delta Dawn
COCKTAIL GLASS

2 parts Gin
1 part Coffee Liqueur
1/2 part Lemon Juice

Shake with ice and strain.

Demon's Eye
COCKTAIL GLASS

1 1/2 parts Gin
2/3 part Kirschwasser
2/3 part Peppermint Liqueur
splash Lemon Juice

Shake with ice and strain.

Derosier

COCKTAIL GLASS

1 part Añejo Rum
½ part Crème de Cacao (Dark)
½ part Cherry Brandy
1 part Heavy Cream

Shake with ice and strain.

Desert Death

COCKTAIL GLASS

½ part Crème de Coconut
½ part Melon Liqueur
½ part 151-Proof Rum
splash Crème de Banane
1 part Cranberry Juice Cocktail
1 part Pineapple Juice

Shake with ice and strain.

Desert Tumbler

COCKTAIL GLASS

1 part Gin
1 part Blue Curaçao
1 part Lime Juice

Shake with ice and strain.

Desire

COCKTAIL GLASS

1 part Crème de Cacao (Dark)
1 part Coffee Liqueur
½ part Vodka

Shake with ice and strain.

Devil

COCKTAIL GLASS

1½ parts Crème de Menthe (Green)
1½ parts Triple Sec

Shake with ice and strain.

Devil with a Blue Dress On

COCKTAIL GLASS

2 parts Gin
splash Blue Curaçao
splash Grenadine
½ part Lime Juice

Shake with ice and strain.

Devil's Due

COCKTAIL GLASS

1½ parts Light Rum
1 part Vodka
½ part Apricot Brandy
splash Lime Juice
dash Grenadine

Shake with ice and strain.

Dewini

COCKTAIL GLASS

1 part Mountain Dew®
1 part Gin
1 part Sweet Vermouth

Stir gently with ice and strain.

Diablo

COCKTAIL GLASS

1½ parts Dry White Port
1 part Sweet Vermouth
splash Lemon Juice

Shake with ice and strain.

Diabolique

COCKTAIL GLASS

1 part Vodka
splash Crème de Cassis
2 parts Pineapple Juice

Shake with ice and strain.

Diamond Head

COCKTAIL GLASS

1½ parts Gin
½ part Blue Curaçao
2 parts Pineapple Juice
splash Vermouth

Shake with ice and strain.

Dianne-on-the-Tower

COCKTAIL GLASS

2 parts Light Rum
splash Crème de Cacao (Dark)
splash Cherry Brandy

Shake with ice and strain.

Difficult Drake
COCKTAIL GLASS

1/2 part Peppermint Liqueur
1/2 part Coffee Liqueur
2/3 part Crème de Cacao (White)

Shake with ice and strain.

Digging for Gold
COCKTAIL GLASS

1 part Goldschläger®
1/2 part Crème de Cacao (Dark)
1/2 part Cream

Shake with ice and strain.

Dinah Cocktail
COCKTAIL GLASS

1 1/2 parts Whiskey
dash Powdered Sugar
1/4 part Lemon Juice

Shake with ice and strain.

Diplomat
COCKTAIL GLASS

1 1/2 parts Dry Vermouth
1/2 part Sweet Vermouth
splash Maraschino Cherry Liqueur
2 dashes Bitters

Shake with ice and strain.

Dirty Blonde
COCKTAIL GLASS

2 parts Whipped Cream Vodka
1 part Banana Liqueur
1 part Pineapple Vodka
dash Cranberry Juice

Shake with ice and strain.

Dirty Dancer
COCKTAIL GLASS

1 part Crème de Cacao (White)
1 part Cream
1/4 part Crème de Menthe (White)

Shake with ice and strain.

Dirty Maiden
COCKTAIL GLASS

1/2 part Blackberry Liqueur
1/2 part Southern Comfort®
splash Lemon Juice
1/2 part Cranberry Juice Cocktail

Shake with ice and strain.

Dirty Panty
COCKTAIL GLASS

1 part Tequila
1 part Sambuca
1 part Irish Cream Liqueur
1 part Tabasco® Sauce

Shake with ice and strain. Garnish with a sprinkle of Parmesean Cheese.

Dirty Redhead
COCKTAIL GLASS

1 part Crown Royal® Whiskey
1 part Raspberry Liqueur
1 part Southern Comfort®

Shake with ice and strain.

Disaronno®
COCKTAIL GLASS

1 part Amaretto
1 part Cognac
1 1/2 parts Cream

Shake with ice and strain.

Dive Bomb
COCKTAIL GLASS

1 1/2 parts Dark Rum
1/2 part Cherry Brandy
1/2 part Lemon Juice
dash Sugar

Shake with ice and strain.

Divine Comedy
COCKTAIL GLASS

1 part Scotch
1 part Dry Vermouth
1/2 part Triple Sec
1/2 part Lemon Juice

Shake with ice and strain.

Divorzio

COCKTAIL GLASS

1½ parts Brandy
splash Blue Curaçao
1½ parts Grappa

Shake with ice and strain.

Dixie Delight

COCKTAIL GLASS

1 part Gin
1 part Southern Comfort®
1 part Dry Vermouth
splash Simple Syrup
3 dashes Pernod®

Shake with ice and strain.

Dixie Queen

COCKTAIL GLASS

1 part Southern Comfort®
½ part Orange Juice
¼ part Peach Schnapps

Shake with ice and strain.

Do or Die

COCKTAIL GLASS

½ part Brandy
1 part Chocolate Liqueur

Shake with ice and strain.

Doctor-Patient Relationship

COCKTAIL GLASS

1½ parts Whiskey
½ part Triple Sec
dash Powdered Sugar

Shake with ice and strain.

Doctor's Orders

COCKTAIL GLASS

1 part Vodka
1 part Amaretto
splash Kiwi Schnapps
½ part Lime Juice

Shake with ice and strain.

Dodge Special

COCKTAIL GLASS

1½ parts Cointreau®
1½ parts Gin
splash Grape Juice

Shake with ice and strain.

Doggy Style

COCKTAIL GLASS

1 part Vodka
splash Coffee Brandy
splash Cream

Shake with ice and strain.

Dolphin Cove

COCKTAIL GLASS

1 part Blue Curaçao
1 part Coconut Rum
2 parts Piña Colada Mix

Shake with ice and strain. Garnish with Maraschino Cherry.

Dolphin Fin

COCKTAIL GLASS

1 part Vodka
½ part Sweet Vermouth
1 part Orange Juice
¼ part Lemon Juice
2 splashes Grenadine

Shake with ice and strain.

Dolphin's Foam

COCKTAIL GLASS

1 part Blue Curaçao
1 part Piña Colada Mix

Shake with ice and strain.

Don Giovanni

COCKTAIL GLASS

2 parts Mozart Original Chocolate Liqueur
1 part Amaretto
1 part Whipped Cream Vodka

Shake with ice and strain.

Donkey Peppermint
COCKTAIL GLASS
1½ parts Sambuca
1 part Crème de Menthe (White)
1 part Coffee Liqueur
Shake with ice and strain.

Donna
COCKTAIL GLASS
1 part Crème de Coconut
1 part Light Rum
1 part Cream of Coconut
splash Cream
Shake with ice and strain.

Don't Chicken Out
COCKTAIL GLASS
2 parts Light Rum
½ part Peach Schnapps
½ part Apricot Brandy
splash Simple Syrup
1 part Lemon Juice
Shake with ice and strain.

Don't Shoot the Bartender
COCKTAIL GLASS
½ part Amaretto
½ part Sloe Gin
½ part Triple Sec
½ part Vanilla Vodka
Shake with ice and strain.

Doorknob
COCKTAIL GLASS
1½ parts Light Rum
½ part Amaretto
splash Lime Juice
splash Lemon Juice
dash Sugar
Shake with ice and strain.

The Dope Show
COCKTAIL GLASS
⅔ part Passion Fruit Liqueur
½ part Damiana®
splash Lemon Juice
Shake with ice and strain.

Dorothy's Orgasm
COCKTAIL GLASS
⅔ part Vodka
splash Butterscotch Schnapps
splash Coffee Liqueur
½ part Cream
Shake with ice and strain.

Double Apple Barrel
COCKTAIL GLASS
1 part Apple Brandy
1 part Apple Juice
½ part Goldschläger®
½ part Triple Sec
Shake with ice and strain.

Double Trouble
COCKTAIL GLASS
⅔ part Vodka
splash Amaretto
½ part Melon Liqueur
½ part Cranberry Juice Cocktail
½ part Orange Juice
Shake with ice and strain.

Dovjenko
COCKTAIL GLASS
1½ parts Vodka
splash Cherry Brandy
½ part Chartreuse®
½ part Grapefruit Juice
Shake with ice and strain.

Down in the Dumps
COCKTAIL GLASS
3 parts Whiskey
1 part Blackberry Brandy
2 dashes Orange Bitters
Shake with ice and strain.

Down Under
COCKTAIL GLASS
1 part Vodka
2 splashes Brandy
2 splashes Triple Sec
2 splashes Crème de Cassis
Shake with ice and strain.

Downhill Skier

COCKTAIL GLASS

1 part Blackberry Liqueur
1 part Crème de Banane
1/2 part Blue Curaçao
1/2 part Sweet & Sour Mix

Shake with ice and strain.

Downsized

COCKTAIL GLASS

2 parts Jack Daniel's
1 part Peach Schnapps
1/2 part Lime Juice
1/2 part Orange Juice
splash Grenadine

Shake with ice and strain.

Doyen

COCKTAIL GLASS

1 1/2 parts Gin
1 part Maraschino Liqueur
1/2 part Lime

Shake with ice and strain.

Dr. Livingstone

COCKTAIL GLASS

1 1/2 parts Vodka
1 part Kiwi Schnapps
1/2 part Crème de Banane

Shake with ice and strain.

Dracula's Breakfast

COCKTAIL GLASS

1 part Melon Liqueur
1 part Campari®
1/2 part Brandy
1/2 part Pernod®

Shake with ice and strain.

Dragon Fire

COCKTAIL GLASS

1 part Pepper Vodka
1 part Crème de Menthe (Green)

Shake with ice and strain.

Dreaming

COCKTAIL GLASS

1 part Crème de Cacao (White)
1 part Cream
1 part Black Currant Juice

Shake with ice and strain.

Droog's Date Cocktail

COCKTAIL GLASS

1 1/2 parts Light Rum
2 splashes Cherry Brandy
2 splashes Triple Sec
1/2 part Lime Juice

Shake with ice and strain.

Drop Your Halitosis

COCKTAIL GLASS

1/2 part Peppermint Liqueur
splash Sambuca
splash Lemon Juice
splash Simple Syrup
splash Club Soda

Shake with ice and strain.

Drug Test Specimen

COCKTAIL GLASS

3 parts Apple Vodka
1 part Light Rum
1 part Sour Apple Schnapps
splash Sweet & Sweet & Sour Mix
1 drop Cinnamon Schnapps

Shake with ice and strain. The Cinnamon Schnapps can overpower the drink easily, so use as little as possible.

Dry Ice

COCKTAIL GLASS

2/3 part Blackberry Liqueur
2/3 part Citrus Vodka
splash Blue Curaçao
splash Lemon Juice

Shake with ice and strain.

Duchess

COCKTAIL GLASS

1½ parts Anisette
½ part Sweet Vermouth
½ part Dry Vermouth

Shake with ice and strain.

Dune Buggy

COCKTAIL GLASS

1½ parts Vodka
¾ part Cherry Brandy
½ part Lime Juice
dash Powdered Sugar

Shake with ice and strain.

Dunhill 71

COCKTAIL GLASS

¾ part Crème de Banane
¾ part Cognac
½ part Crème de Cacao (Dark)
¼ part Triple Sec

Shake with ice and strain.

Dusty Rose

COCKTAIL GLASS

1 part Cherry Brandy
½ part Crème de Cacao (White)
2 parts Heavy Cream

Shake with ice and strain.

Eagle Cocktail

COCKTAIL GLASS

1½ parts Gin
¾ part Crème de Violette
1 part Lemon Juice
1 Egg White
1 tsp Sugar

Shake with ice and strain.

East India

COCKTAIL GLASS

2 parts Brandy
1 part Triple Sec
1 part Orange Juice

Shake with ice and strain.

East India #2

COCKTAIL GLASS

1½ parts Brandy
¼ part Blue Curaçao
¼ part Pineapple Juice
dash Bitters

Shake with ice and strain.

East of Eden

COCKTAIL GLASS

1 part Amaretto
⅔ part Apricot Brandy
1 part Irish Cream Liqueur
1 part Pineapple Juice

Shake with ice and strain.

East Wing

COCKTAIL GLASS

3 parts Vodka
1 part Cherry Brandy
½ part Campari®

Shake with ice and strain.

Ebony

COCKTAIL GLASS

1½ parts Dark Rum
½ part Crème de Cacao (Dark)

Shake with ice and strain.

Eclipsed Sun

COCKTAIL GLASS

1 part Crème de Cacao (White)
1 part Crème de Banane
1½ parts Orange Juice

Shake with ice and strain.

Eden Eve

COCKTAIL GLASS

1 part Raspberry Liqueur
1 part Vodka
⅔ part Pineapple Juice
⅔ part Cranberry Juice Cocktail

Shake with ice and strain.

Edge of Oblivion
COCKTAIL GLASS

1 part Cherry Brandy
2/3 part Triple Sec
1 part Apple Brandy
1/2 part Sweet & Sour Mix

Shake with ice and strain.

Eight Bells
COCKTAIL GLASS

2 parts Dark Rum
1 part Dry Vermouth
1/2 part Lemon Juice
1/2 part Orange Juice

Shake with ice and strain.

The Eighth Wonder
COCKTAIL GLASS

1 part Kirschwasser
2/3 part Crème de Cacao (White)
2/3 part Hazelnut Liqueur
1 1/2 parts Cream

Shake with ice and strain.

Ekatherina Andreevna
COCKTAIL GLASS

2 parts Vodka
1 part Orange Juice

Shake with ice and strain.

Electric Cafe
COCKTAIL GLASS

1 part Silver Tequila
1 part Lemon Juice
1/2 part Simple Syrup
splash Coffee Liqueur

Shake with ice and strain.

Electric Chair
COCKTAIL GLASS

1/2 part Orange Liqueur
1 part Tequila
1/2 part Lemon Juice
splash Tabasco® Sauce

Shake with ice and strain.

Elephant Gun
COCKTAIL GLASS

1 part Whiskey
1 part Pineapple Juice
splash Lemon Juice
dash Sugar

Shake with ice and strain.

Elevation
COCKTAIL GLASS

1 1/2 parts Crème de Coconut
1 1/2 parts Crème de Banane
3 parts Pineapple Juice

Shake with ice and strain.

Elisa
COCKTAIL GLASS

1 part Dark Rum
1/4 part Apricot Brandy
1/4 part Sparkling White Wine
1/4 part Amaro Averna®
1/4 part Dry Vermouth

Shake with ice and strain.

Elysium
COCKTAIL GLASS

1 part Peach Schnapps
1 part Vodka
1 1/2 parts Orange Juice
1 1/2 parts Pineapple Juice

Shake with ice and strain.

Emanuelle
COCKTAIL GLASS

1 part Crème de Cacao (White)
1 part Bénédictine®
splash Espresso
splash Cream of Coconut

Shake with ice and strain.

Embassy Cocktail
COCKTAIL GLASS

1 part Brandy
1 part Cointreau
1 part Dark Rum
1/2 part Lime Juice
dash Angostura Bitters

Shake with ice and strain.

Embassy Royal
COCKTAIL GLASS

1 part Bourbon
1/2 part Sweet Vermouth
splash Orange Juice

Shake with ice and strain.

Emerald
COCKTAIL GLASS

1 1/2 parts Gin
1/2 part Crème de Menthe (Green)
1/2 part Crème de Menthe (White)

Shake with ice and strain.

Emerald Cut
COCKTAIL GLASS

2 parts Gin
1 part Crème de Menthe (Green)
1 part Vanilla Vodka

Shake with ice and strain.

Emergency Ward
COCKTAIL GLASS

1 part Kiwi Schnapps
1 part Blue Curaçao
1 part Lime Juice

Shake with ice and strain.

Emerson
COCKTAIL GLASS

1 1/2 parts Gin
1 part Sweet Vermouth
1/2 part Lime Juice
splash Maraschino Cherry Juice

Shake with ice and strain.

Empire
COCKTAIL GLASS

1 1/2 parts Gin
3/4 part Apricot Brandy
1/2 part Apple Brandy

Shake with ice and strain.

Empire Strikes Back
COCKTAIL GLASS

2 parts Silver Tequila
1/2 part Vanilla Liqueur
2/3 part Passion Fruit Juice
2/3 part Cream

Shake with ice and strain.

Enchanted
COCKTAIL GLASS

1 1/2 parts Vodka
1 part Banana Liqueur
1/2 part Crème de Cacao (White)
1 part Cream
dash Lemon Juice

Shake with ice and strain.

L'Enclume
COCKTAIL GLASS

1 part Gin
1 part Kirschwasser
1/2 part Rémy Martin® VSOP
1/2 part Grand Marnier®

Shake with ice and strain.

Erotic
COCKTAIL GLASS

1 part Bourbon
splash Crème de Cassis
splash Grenadine
splash Lemon Juice

Shake with ice and strain.

Escape
COCKTAIL GLASS

1 part Whiskey
1 part Orange Juice
1 part Apricot Brandy

Shake with ice and strain.

Escila

COCKTAIL GLASS

1 part Blue Curaçao
1 part Jamaican Rum
½ part Lemon Juice
splash Simple Syrup

Shake with ice and strain.

Esperanza

COCKTAIL GLASS

½ part Triple Sec
½ part Light Rum
1 part Pineapple Juice
1 part Kiwi Liqueur

Shake with ice and strain.

Espresso Cocktail

COCKTAIL GLASS

2 parts Espresso Vodka
1 part Coffee Liqueur
1 part Irish Cream Liqueur

Shake with ice and strain.

Estate Sale

COCKTAIL GLASS

1 part Gin
1 part Blue Curaçao
⅔ part Light Rum
½ part Sweet & Sour Mix

Shake with ice and strain.

Estoril

COCKTAIL GLASS

2 parts Port
1 part Grand Marnier®
½ part Amaretto

Shake with ice and strain.

Estrella Dorado

COCKTAIL GLASS

1 part Dry Gin
1 part Dry Vermouth
1 part Campari®
1 part Cherry Brandy
2 splashes Lemon Juice

Shake with ice and strain.

Eva

COCKTAIL GLASS

1 part Vodka
1 part Crème de Menthe (Green)
1 part Simple Syrup

Shake with ice and strain.

Evans

COCKTAIL GLASS

1 part Rye Whiskey
1 part Triple Sec
1 part Apricot Brandy

Shake with ice and strain.

Evening Delight

COCKTAIL GLASS

2 parts Irish Cream Liqueur
1 part Vodka

Shake with ice and strain.

Everglades Special

COCKTAIL GLASS

1 part Coffee Liqueur
1 part Crème de Cacao (White)
1 part Light Rum
½ part Cream

Shake with ice and strain.

Evergreen

COCKTAIL GLASS

1½ parts Crème de Banane
½ part Blue Curaçao
½ part Gin
2 parts Grapefruit Juice

Shake with ice and strain.

Exorcist Cocktail

COCKTAIL GLASS

2 parts Tequila
1 part Blue Curaçao
1 part Lime Juice

Shake with ice and strain.

Exploration
COCKTAIL GLASS

1 part Scotch
1 part Dry Sherry
½ part Amaretto

Shake with ice and strain.

Eyes Wide Shut
COCKTAIL GLASS

½ part Southern Comfort®
½ part Crown Royal® Whiskey
½ part Amaretto
½ part Orange Juice
½ part Pineapple Juice
½ part Cranberry Juice Cocktail
splash Grenadine

Shake with ice and strain.

Fade to Black
COCKTAIL GLASS

1 part Coffee Liqueur
1 part Vodka
½ part Crème de Menthe (White)

Shake with ice and strain.

Fair Sex
COCKTAIL GLASS

1 part Maraschino Liqueur
1 part Gin
½ part Cherry Brandy
splash Simple Syrup

Shake with ice and strain.

Fairbanks
COCKTAIL GLASS

1 part Apricot Brandy
1 part Gin
splash Grenadine
splash Lemon Juice
1 part Dry Vermouth

Shake with ice and strain.

Fairy Belle Cocktail
COCKTAIL GLASS

¾ part Apricot Brandy
1½ parts Gin
splash Grenadine
1 Egg White

Shake with ice and strain.

Fairy Queen
COCKTAIL GLASS

1 part Vodka
½ part Cream
½ part Coffee Liqueur

Shake with ice and strain.

The Falcon Chaser
COCKTAIL GLASS

1 part Gin
½ part Chambord®
½ part Hazelnut Liqueur
splash Crème de Coconut
splash Galliano®
1½ parts Cream

Shake with ice and strain.

Fantastico
COCKTAIL GLASS

1 part Dark Rum
½ part Triple Sec
½ part Apricot Brandy
splash Pineapple Juice
splash Orange Juice

Shake with ice and strain.

Far West
COCKTAIL GLASS

½ part Brandy
½ part Advocaat
½ part Dry Vermouth
dash Angostura® Bitters

Shake with ice and strain.

Farewell

COCKTAIL GLASS

2/3 part Coffee Liqueur
2/3 part Apricot Brandy
splash Scotch
2/3 part Cream
2/3 part Milk

Shake with ice and strain.

Farinelli

COCKTAIL GLASS

1 1/2 parts Vodka
1/2 part Dry Vermouth
1/2 part Campari®
splash Amaretto

Shake with ice and strain.

Farmer Giles

COCKTAIL GLASS

2 parts Gin
1/2 part Dry Vermouth
1/2 part Sweet Vermouth
2 dashes Bitters

Shake with ice and strain. Garnish with Lemon Twist.

Fast Punch

COCKTAIL GLASS

1 part Blue Curaçao
splash Apricot Brandy
splash Lime Juice
splash Pineapple Juice

Shake with ice and strain.

Fat Friar

COCKTAIL GLASS

3/4 part Apple Brandy
3/4 part Bénédictine®
1/4 part Triple Sec
1/4 part Lemon Juice

Shake with ice and strain.

Favorite

COCKTAIL GLASS

1 part Sweet Vermouth
1/2 part Triple Sec
1/2 part Maraschino Liqueur
dash Orange Bitters

Shake with ice and strain.

Feliz Natal

COCKTAIL GLASS

1 part Port
1 part Amaretto
2 parts Crème de Cacao (White)
1 part Cherry Brandy
1/2 part Brandy

Stir gently with ice and strain.

Femina

COCKTAIL GLASS

1 1/2 parts Brandy
1 1/2 parts Triple Sec
1/2 part Orange Juice

Shake with ice and strain.

Ferndale Fruit

COCKTAIL GLASS

1 part Sloe Gin
1 part Blackberry Liqueur
1 part Sweet & Sour Mix

Shake with ice and strain.

Fernet Jacque

COCKTAIL GLASS

1 1/2 parts Gin
1/2 part Fernet-Branca®
splash Maraschino Liqueur
splash Sweet Vermouth

Shake with ice and strain.

Feroux

COCKTAIL GLASS

1/2 part Apricot Brandy
1 part Crème de Banane
2/3 part Cachaça
1/2 part Lemon Juice

Shake with ice and strain.

Festival Flavor

COCKTAIL GLASS

½ part Crème de Coconut
½ part Melon Liqueur
½ part Blackberry Liqueur
1½ parts Cranberry Juice Cocktail

Shake with ice and strain.

Fiery Manhattan

COCKTAIL GLASS

1 part Buffalo Trace Bourbon
1 part Fireball Cinnamon Whiskey
splash Dry Vermouth
dash Bitters

Shake with ice and strain. Garnish with Maraschino Cherry.

The Fifth Element

COCKTAIL GLASS

1½ parts Jim Beam®
½ part Kirschwasser
½ part Vanilla Liqueur
splash Amaretto
1 part Cream

Shake with ice and strain.

Fifty-Fifty

COCKTAIL GLASS

1½ parts Vanilla Liqueur
1½ parts Orange Juice

Shake with ice and strain.

Fig Newton

COCKTAIL GLASS

½ part Vodka
½ part Grand Marnier®
¼ part Crème de Almond
splash Orange Juice
splash Lemon Juice

Shake with ice and strain.

Final Storm

COCKTAIL GLASS

2 parts Silver Tequila
⅔ part Passion Fruit Liqueur
1½ parts Guava Juice

Shake with ice and strain.

Fire and Ice

COCKTAIL GLASS

1½ parts Pepper Vodka
2 splashes Dry Vermouth

Shake with ice and strain.

Fire Island

COCKTAIL GLASS

1 part Coconut Rum
1 part Fireball Cinnamon Whiskey

Shake with ice and strain.

Fire Island Sunrise

COCKTAIL GLASS

1 part Rum
1 part Vodka
½ part Orange Juice
½ part Lemonade
splash Cranberry Juice Cocktail

Shake with ice and strain.

Fireball Tart

COCKTAIL GLASS

2 parts Fireball Cinnamon Whiskey
1 part Pomegranate Liqueur
splash Lemon Juice

Shake with ice and strain.

Firehammer

COCKTAIL GLASS

1½ parts Vodka
½ part Amaretto
½ part Triple Sec
splash Lemon Juice

Shake with ice and strain.

Firestarter

COCKTAIL GLASS

1 part Coffee Liqueur
1 part Fireball Cinnamon Whiskey
1 part Irish Cream Liqueur

Shake with ice and strain.

Firestick

COCKTAIL GLASS

2 parts Pear Vodka
1 part Fireball Cinnamon Whiskey
1 part Orange Vodka

Shake with ice and strain.

Firing Line

COCKTAIL GLASS

1 part Jim Beam®
½ part Coffee Liqueur
splash Crème de Cacao (White)
splash Galliano®
2 parts Cream

Shake with ice and strain.

Firish Cream

COCKTAIL GLASS

1 part Crème de Menthe (Green)
1 part Fireball Cinnamon Whiskey
1 part Irish Cream Liqueur

Shake with ice and strain.

Fish Lips

COCKTAIL GLASS

1½ parts Vodka
½ part Kirschwasser
½ part Triple Sec
½ part Grapefruit Juice

Shake with ice and strain.

Fjord

COCKTAIL GLASS

1 part Brandy
1 part Orange Juice
½ part Grenadine
½ part Lime Juice
½ part Aquavit

Shake with ice and strain.

Flame of Love

COCKTAIL GLASS

1½ parts Vodka
½ part Dry Sherry

Shake with ice and strain.

Flamingo Shooter

COCKTAIL GLASS

½ part Southern Comfort®
½ part Amaretto
½ part Crème de Banane
1 part Milk
splash Grenadine

Shake with ice and strain.

A Flash of Mellow

COCKTAIL GLASS

½ part Pisang Ambon® Liqueur
½ part Melon Liqueur
2 parts Light Rum
⅔ part Lemon Juice
splash Honey

Shake with ice and strain.

Fleet Street

COCKTAIL GLASS

1½ parts Gin
½ part Sweet Vermouth
splash Dry Vermouth
splash Triple Sec
splash Lemon Juice

Shake with ice and strain.

Les Fleurs du Mal

COCKTAIL GLASS

1½ parts Kirschwasser
1½ parts Dubonnet® Blonde

Shake with ice and strain.

Flipside Beach Bomber

COCKTAIL GLASS

1 part Vodka
½ part Triple Sec
½ part Grapefruit Juice
½ part Orange Juice
½ part Apricot Brandy

Shake with ice and strain.

Florida Beach Breeze

COCKTAIL GLASS

1 part Vodka
½ part Crème de Cacao (White)
½ part Crème de Banane
1 part Orange Juice

Shake with ice and strain.

Florida Keys Cocktail

COCKTAIL GLASS

⅔ part Light Rum
½ part Grand Marnier®
½ part Lime Juice
1 part Passion Fruit Liqueur

Shake with ice and strain.

Florida Man

COCKTAIL GLASS

1 part Sloe Gin
1 part Vodka
1 part Grapefruit Juice
1 part Orange Juice

Shake with ice and strain.

Florida Rain

COCKTAIL GLASS

½ part Gin
2 splashes Kirschwasser
2 splashes Triple Sec
1 part Orange Juice
splash Lemon Juice

Shake with ice and strain.

El Floridita

COCKTAIL GLASS

1½ parts Light Rum
½ part Lime Juice
½ part Sweet Vermouth
splash Crème de Cacao (White)
splash Grenadine

Shake with ice and strain.

Flower of Nippon

COCKTAIL GLASS

1 part Light Rum
1 part Banana Liqueur
splash Cointreau®
splash Lime Juice
splash Grenadine

Shake with ice and strain.

Flower of the Orient

COCKTAIL GLASS

1 part Cream Sherry
1 part Tia Maria®
1 part Cream
½ part Passion Fruit Juice

Shake with ice and strain.

Flowerdance

COCKTAIL GLASS

1 part Gin
1 part Peach Juice
1 part Lychee Liqueur
½ part Lime Juice

Shake with ice and strain.

Fluffy Cocktail

COCKTAIL GLASS

½ part Coconut Rum
¼ part Light Rum
1 part Pineapple Juice
½ part Cranberry Juice

Shake with ice and strain.

Fluffy Ruffles Cocktail

COCKTAIL GLASS

1½ parts Rum
1½ parts Sweet Vermouth

Shake with ice and strain.

Flying Dutchman

COCKTAIL GLASS

3 parts Gin
splash Blue Curaçao
dash Orange Bitters

Shake with ice and strain.

Flying Fancy
COCKTAIL GLASS

1 part Crème de Cacao (White)
1 part Amaretto
1 part Melon Liqueur

Shake with ice and strain.

Flying Grasshopper
COCKTAIL GLASS

1 part Vodka
1 part Crème de Menthe (Green)
1 part Crème de Cacao (White)

Shake with ice and strain.

Flying Horse
COCKTAIL GLASS

1½ parts Vodka
1 part Cream
1 part Cherry Brandy

Shake with ice and strain.

Focal Point
COCKTAIL GLASS

1½ parts Melon Liqueur
1 part Light Rum
½ part Lemon Juice
splash Grenadine

Shake with ice and strain.

Fog at Bowling Green
COCKTAIL GLASS

1 part Peppermint Liqueur
1 part Vodka
1 part Cream

Shake with ice and strain.

Foggy Afternoon
COCKTAIL GLASS

1 part Vodka
½ part Apricot Brandy
½ part Triple Sec
splash Crème de Banane
splash Lemon Juice

Shake with ice and strain. Garnish with Maraschino Cherry.

Foiled Plan
COCKTAIL GLASS

1 part Irish Whiskey
⅔ part Triple Sec
⅔ part Frangelico®
⅔ part Cranberry Juice Cocktail

Shake with ice and strain.

Fondling Fool
COCKTAIL GLASS

1½ parts Brandy
1 part Madeira
½ part Triple Sec

Shake with ice and strain.

La Fontaine des Anges
COCKTAIL GLASS

1 part Jim Beam®
½ part Orange Liqueur
½ part Lemon Juice
1 part Orange Juice

Shake with ice and strain.

Fontainebleau Special
COCKTAIL GLASS

1 part Brandy
1 part Anisette
½ part Dry Vermouth

Shake with ice and strain.

Forbidden Smoke
COCKTAIL GLASS

1 part Gin
splash Grenadine

Shake with ice and strain.

Foreign Dignitary
COCKTAIL GLASS

1½ parts Brandy
½ part Raspberry Liqueur
1 part Lime Juice

Shake with ice and strain.

Formal Wear

COCKTAIL GLASS

1 part Vodka
1 part Blackberry Liqueur
2/3 part Cranberry Juice Cocktail
2/3 part Orange Juice

Shake with ice and strain.

Fort Lauderdale

COCKTAIL GLASS

2 parts Light Rum
1 part Orange Juice
1 part Lime Juice
1/2 part Sweet Vermouth

Shake with ice and strain.

Four Flush

COCKTAIL GLASS

1 part Light Rum
1 part Dry Vermouth
1 part Grenadine
1 part Maraschino Liqueur

Shake with ice and strain.

The Four-Hundred Blows

COCKTAIL GLASS

1 part Vodka
2/3 part Lime Juice
1/2 part Simple Syrup

Shake with ice and strain.

Fox and Hounds

COCKTAIL GLASS

1 part Pernod®
1 part Lemon Juice
splash Sugar
1 Egg White

Shake with ice and strain.

Fox Trot

COCKTAIL GLASS

1 1/4 parts Dark Rum
splash Blue Curaçao
1 part Lemon Juice
dash Sugar

Shake with ice and strain.

Foxy Lady

COCKTAIL GLASS

1/2 part Amaretto
1/2 part Crème de Cacao (Dark)
2 parts Light Cream

Shake with ice and strain.

Francis Anne

COCKTAIL GLASS

1 part Scotch
1 part Dry Vermouth
1 part Cherry Brandy

Shake with ice and strain.

Frankenjack Cocktail

COCKTAIL GLASS

1 part Gin
3/4 part Dry Vermouth
1/2 part Apricot Brandy
splash Triple Sec

Shake with ice and strain. Garnish with Maraschino Cherry.

Free Fly

COCKTAIL GLASS

1 1/2 parts Vodka
1/2 part Parfait Amour
1/4 part Triple Sec
1/4 part Sweet Vermouth
splash Kiwi Juice

Shake with ice and strain.

French Acquisition

COCKTAIL GLASS

1 part Scotch
1 part Sweet Vermouth
1 part Dry Vermouth
splash Orange Liqueur

Shake with ice and strain.

French Advance

COCKTAIL GLASS

2/3 part Gin
2/3 part Blackberry Liqueur
1/2 part Sweet Vermouth
splash Grenadine
splash Pernod®

Shake with ice and strain.

French Cosmopolitan

COCKTAIL GLASS

1 part Citrus Vodka
1/2 part Grand Marnier®
1/2 part Sweet & Sour Mix
1/2 part Cranberry Juice Cocktail
1/4 part Lime Juice
splash Grenadine

Shake all but Grenadine with ice and strain. Place a few drops of Grenadine in the center of the drink.

French Daiquiri

COCKTAIL GLASS

1 part Light Rum
1/2 part Lime Juice
dash Powdered Sugar
splash Crème de Cassis

Shake with ice and strain.

French Sidecar

COCKTAIL GLASS

1 1/2 parts Dry Gin
1/2 part Triple Sec
splash Lemon Juice

Shake with ice and strain.

French Tear

COCKTAIL GLASS

2/3 part Grand Marnier®
2/3 part Spiced Rum
2 parts Pineapple Juice

Shake with ice and strain.

French Tickler

COCKTAIL GLASS

1 part B&B®
1 part Grand Marnier®
1 part Courvoisier®

Shake with ice and strain. Garnish with Maraschino Cherry.

French Vineyard

COCKTAIL GLASS

2/3 part Raspberry Liqueur
splash Vanilla Liqueur
2/3 part Plum Brandy
2/3 part Port
1 part Cream

Shake with ice and strain.

Fresh Mountain Stream

COCKTAIL GLASS

1 part Aquavit
1 part Vodka
1 part Lime Juice
1 part Simple Syrup

Shake with ice and strain.

Friar Tuck

COCKTAIL GLASS

1 part Frangelico®
1 part Crème de Cacao (White)
2 parts Cream

Shake with ice and strain.

Friendly Alien

COCKTAIL GLASS

1 1/2 parts Vodka
1/2 part Crème de Coconut
1/2 part Mango Schnapps
1/2 part Lemon Juice
1 part Pineapple Juice

Shake with ice and strain.

Frightleberry Murzenquest

COCKTAIL GLASS

1 part Vodka
½ part Galliano®
½ part Triple Sec
½ part Lime Juice
splash Maraschino Liqueur
dash Bitters

Shake with ice and strain.

Frisco

COCKTAIL GLASS

2 parts Rye Whiskey
¼ part Bénédictine®
¾ part Lemon Juice

Shake with ice and strain.

Frisky Intern

COCKTAIL GLASS

1 part Raspberry Liqueur
1 part Jim Beam®
1 part Cream
splash Vanilla Extract

Shake with ice and strain.

Frog's Tongue

COCKTAIL GLASS

1½ parts Vodka
½ part Scotch

Shake with ice and strain.

Froot Loops

COCKTAIL GLASS

1½ parts Sour Apple Schnapps
2 parts Orange Juice

Shake with ice and strain.

Frost Bite

COCKTAIL GLASS

2 parts Peppermint Schnapps
1 part Whipped Cream Vodka
dash Blue Curaçao

Shake with ice and strain.

Frosted Blue

COCKTAIL GLASS

2 parts Silver Tequila
½ part Blue Curaçao
½ part Crème de Cacao (White)
1 part Cream

Shake with ice and strain.

Frosty Dawn

COCKTAIL GLASS

½ part Light Rum
½ part Orange Juice
¼ part Maraschino Liqueur
¼ part Ginger Liqueur

Shake with ice and pour.

Froupe

COCKTAIL GLASS

1½ parts Brandy
1½ parts Sweet Vermouth

Shake with ice and strain.

Frozen Blackcurrant

COCKTAIL GLASS

1 part Pineapple Juice
1 part Crème de Cassis
½ part Brandy

Shake with ice and strain.

Frozen Pussy

COCKTAIL GLASS

1 part Irish Cream Liqueur
1 part Strawberry Liqueur
½ part Grenadine

Shake with ice and strain.

Fruhling

COCKTAIL GLASS

1 part Gin
splash Orange Liqueur
splash Grenadine
splash Lemon Juice

Shake with ice and strain.

Fruit Dangereux

COCKTAIL GLASS

1 part Melon Liqueur
splash Lemon Juice
splash Simple Syrup

Shake with ice and strain.

Fuck Me by the Pool

COCKTAIL GLASS

1 part Tropical Punch Schnapps
1 part Peach Schnapps
2 parts Orange Juice

Shake with ice and strain.

Fuck Me to Death

COCKTAIL GLASS

1/2 part Brandy
1/2 part Scotch
1/2 part Vodka
1/2 part Crème de Coconut

Shake with ice and strain.

Funky Doctor

COCKTAIL GLASS

1/2 part Peppermint Liqueur
1 1/2 parts Light Rum
1/2 part Mandarine Napoléon® Liqueur
splash Vanilla Liqueur

Shake with ice and strain.

Fuschia

COCKTAIL GLASS

1 part Peach Schnapps
1 1/2 parts Vodka
splash Passion Fruit Juice

Shake with ice and strain.

Fuzzy Pucker

COCKTAIL GLASS

1 1/2 parts Peach Schnapps
1 part Grapefruit Juice

Shake with ice and strain.

Galactic Trader

COCKTAIL GLASS

1 part Vodka
splash Apricot Brandy
1/2 part Blue Curaçao
1/2 part Lime Juice

Shake with ice and strain.

Galviston

COCKTAIL GLASS

1 part Amaretto
1 part Orange Juice
1 part Milk
1/2 part Cream

Shake with ice and strain.

Gale at Sea

COCKTAIL GLASS

1 1/2 parts Vodka
1/2 part Blue Curaçao
1/2 part Dry Vermouth
1/2 part Galliano

Shake with ice and strain.

Galliano Daiquiri

COCKTAIL GLASS

1 part Gold Rum
3/4 part Galliano
1/2 part Lime Juice
1/2 part Simple Syrup

Shake with ice and strain.

Galway Gray

COCKTAIL GLASS

1 1/2 parts Vodka
1 part Crème de Cacao (White)
1 part Cointreau®
1/2 part Lime Juice
splash Cream

Shake with ice and strain.

Gangplank

COCKTAIL GLASS

1 1/2 parts Vodka
3/4 part Raspberry Liqueur
1/6 part Campari
1/2 part Lemon Juice

Shake with ice and strain.

Garden Party

COCKTAIL GLASS

1 1/2 parts Spiced Rum
1 part Carrot Juice
2/3 part Triple Sec
2/3 part Tomato Juice
splash Tabasco® Sauce

Shake with ice and strain.

Gareth Glowworm

COCKTAIL GLASS

1 1/2 parts Light Rum
1/2 part Crème de Cacao (White)
1 part Heavy Cream
splash Cherry Brandy

Shake with ice and strain.

Gaslight Girl

COCKTAIL GLASS

2 parts Vodka
splash Orange Liqueur
splash Grenadine
1 part Gold Tequila

Shake with ice and strain.

Gatorade

COCKTAIL GLASS

1 1/2 parts Vodka
1 1/2 parts Rum
1 1/2 parts Orange Liqueur
1 part Sweet & Sour Mix
1/2 part Orange Juice

Shake with ice and strain.

Gay Scorpion

COCKTAIL GLASS

1 part Light Rum
splash Peach Schnapps
splash Grenadine
2 parts Pineapple Juice
splash Cream

Shake with ice and strain.

Gazette

COCKTAIL GLASS

1 1/2 parts Brandy
splash Lemon Juice
splash Simple Syrup
1 part Sweet Vermouth

Shake with ice and strain.

Genesis

COCKTAIL GLASS

2/3 part Blue Curaçao
1 1/2 parts Limoncello
2/3 part Mandarine Napoléon® Liqueur
2/3 part Lemon Juice
1/2 part Simple Syrup

Shake with ice and strain.

Geneva Convention

COCKTAIL GLASS

2 parts Vodka
1/2 part Goldschläger®
1/2 part Grain Alcohol

Shake with ice and strain.

Geneva Summit

COCKTAIL GLASS

1 part Southern Comfort®
1 part Vodka
1/2 part Orange Juice
1/2 part Lime Juice
splash Peppermint Schnapps
splash Lemon-Lime Soda

Shake with ice and strain.

Gentle Touch

COCKTAIL GLASS

1½ parts Citrus Rum
½ part Cointreau®
½ part Apricot Brandy
splash Grenadine
1 part Lemon Juice

Shake with ice and strain.

Georgia Cruise

COCKTAIL GLASS

1 part Cherry Brandy
splash Grenadine
1 part Apple Brandy
1 part Sweet & Sour Mix

Shake with ice and strain.

German Chocolate Cake

COCKTAIL GLASS

½ part Coconut Rum
½ part Crème de Cacao (Dark)
2 parts Cream
splash Frangelico®

Shake with ice and strain.

Ghetto Gold

COCKTAIL GLASS

1 part Dark Rum
1 part Goldschläger®
½ part Vanilla Liqueur

Shake with ice and strain.

Ghost of Christmas

COCKTAIL GLASS

2 parts Melon Liqueur
2 parts Vodka
splash Lime Juice

Shake with ice and strain.

Ghostbuster

COCKTAIL GLASS

1 part Vodka
½ part Irish Cream Liqueur
½ part Coffee Liqueur

Shake with ice and strain.

Gimlet

COCKTAIL GLASS

1½ parts Gin
1 part Lime Juice
dash Powdered Sugar

Shake with ice and strain.

Gimme Some

COCKTAIL GLASS

½ part Crème de Coconut
1 part Vanilla Vodka
1 part Chocolate Liqueur
splash Sweet Vermouth

Shake with ice and strain.

Gimp Aid

COCKTAIL GLASS

2 parts Gin
1 part Triple Sec
1 part Pineapple Juice
dash Orange Bitters

Shake with ice and strain.

Gin and Berry It

COCKTAIL GLASS

1½ parts Gin
splash Maraschino Liqueur
2 splashes Raspberry Syrup
splash Lemon Juice

Shake with ice and strain.

Gin Blue Devil

COCKTAIL GLASS

1 part Gin
splash Blue Curaçao
dash Powdered Sugar
splash Maraschino Liqueur

Shake with ice and strain.

Gin Rummy

COCKTAIL GLASS

1 part Gin
¼ part Dry Vermouth
¼ part Sweet Vermouth

Shake with ice and strain.

Ginny
COCKTAIL GLASS

1 part Gin
½ part Dry Vermouth
½ part Apricot Brandy

Shake with ice and strain.

Glacier
COCKTAIL GLASS

1 part Blackberry Liqueur
½ part Crème de Cacao (White)
½ part Light Rum

Shake with ice and strain.

Glacier Mint
COCKTAIL GLASS

1½ parts Vodka
½ part Lemon Vodka
½ part Crème de Menthe (Green)

Shake with ice and strain.

Gladness
COCKTAIL GLASS

1½ parts Vodka
½ part Green Chartreuse®
splash Triple Sec

Shake with ice and strain.

Glasgow
COCKTAIL GLASS

2 parts Scotch
1 part Amaretto
½ part Dry Vermouth

Shake with ice and strain.

Glass Eye
COCKTAIL GLASS

2 parts Peach Vodka
1 part Triple Sec
1 part White Cranberry Juice
splash Lemon Juice
splash Lime Juice

Shake with ice and strain.

Glaucoma
COCKTAIL GLASS

1 part Vodka
1 part Rum
1 part Gin
½ part Coffee Liqueur
splash Lemon Juice
dash Sugar

Shake with ice and strain.

A Glint in Your Life
COCKTAIL GLASS

½ part Vanilla Liqueur
1½ parts Plum Brandy
½ part Sweetened Lime Juice
splash Lemon Juice

Shake with ice and strain.

Gloom Raiser
COCKTAIL GLASS

2 parts Gin
¾ part Dry Vermouth
2 splashes Pernod®
2 splashes Grenadine

Shake with ice and strain.

Gloria
COCKTAIL GLASS

½ part Brandy
½ part Campari®
½ part Scotch
¼ part Amaretto
¼ part Dry Vermouth

Shake with ice and strain.

Glory Box
COCKTAIL GLASS

1 part Gin
1 part Grand Marnier®
1 part Dry Vermouth

Shake with ice and strain.

Gnome Depot
COCKTAIL GLASS

2/3 part Melon Liqueur
2 parts Orange Vodka
splash Dry Vermouth

Shake with ice and strain.

Go Kucha
COCKTAIL GLASS

1/2 part Triple Sec
1/2 part Frangelico®
1/2 part Light Rum
1/2 part Apricot Juice
1 1/2 parts Pineapple Juice

Shake with ice and strain.

Godchild
COCKTAIL GLASS

1 part Amaretto
1 part Vodka
1 part Cream

Shake with ice and strain.

Godfather Dada
COCKTAIL GLASS

2 parts Amaretto
2 parts Grand Marnier®
3 parts Ketel One® Vodka

Shake with ice and strain. Garnish with Orange Twist.

Going Nuts
COCKTAIL GLASS

1/2 part Amaretto
1 1/2 parts Frangelico®
2 parts Cream

Shake with ice and strain.

Gold Card
COCKTAIL GLASS

1 part Brandy
1/2 part Bénédictine®
1/4 part Chartreuse®

Shake with ice and strain.

Gold Zest
COCKTAIL GLASS

1 part Passion Fruit Liqueur
1/2 part Crème de Noyaux
1 part Cachaça
1 1/2 parts Lemon Juice

Shake with ice and strain.

Golden Bird
COCKTAIL GLASS

1 1/2 parts Orange Juice
1 part Light Rum
1 part Pineapple Juice
1 part Mandarine Napoléon® Liqueur
1/2 part Crème de Banane

Shake with ice and strain.

Golden Dream
COCKTAIL GLASS

1 part Galliano®
1/2 part Triple Sec
2 splashes Orange Juice
2 splashes Light Cream

Shake with ice and strain.

Golden Ermine Cocktail
COCKTAIL GLASS

1 1/2 parts Dry Gin
1 part Dry Vermouth
1/2 part Sweet Vermouth

Shake with ice and strain.

Golden Flute
COCKTAIL GLASS

1/2 part Blue Curaçao
splash Peach Schnapps
2 parts Vodka
splash Campari®

Shake with ice and strain.

Golden Glow

COCKTAIL GLASS

2 parts Orange Juice
2 parts Bourbon
1 part Dark Rum
¼ part Simple Syrup
splash Grenadine

Shake with ice and strain.

Golden Purple

COCKTAIL GLASS

1½ parts Gin
1 part Parfait Amour
1 part Goldschläger®

Shake with ice and strain.

Goldfish

COCKTAIL GLASS

1 part Gin
1 part Goldschläger®
½ part Triple Sec
½ part Orange Juice

Shake with ice and strain.

Goldilocks' Cosmo

COCKTAIL GLASS

2 parts Vodka
¼ part Lime Juice
¼ part Triple Sec
splash White Cranberry Juice

Shake with ice and strain.

Goldmine

COCKTAIL GLASS

2 parts Gin
1 part Pineapple Juice
½ part Maraschino Liqueur

Shake with ice and strain.

Golf Cocktail

COCKTAIL GLASS

2 parts Gin
1 part Dry Vermouth
2 dashes Bitters

Shake with ice and strain.

Gonzo Gonzales

COCKTAIL GLASS

1 part Gin
½ part Crème de Banane
½ part Grapefruit Juice

Shake with ice and strain.

Good Morning Jamaica

COCKTAIL GLASS

1 part Dark Rum
2 parts Coffee Liqueur
½ part Lime Juice

Shake with ice and strain.

Good Morning Mexico

COCKTAIL GLASS

1 part Tequila
2 parts Coffee Liqueur
½ part Lime Juice

Shake with ice and strain.

Goody-Goody

COCKTAIL GLASS

½ part Brandy
½ part Crème de Cacao (White)
⅔ part Sloe Gin
1 part Milk

Shake with ice and strain.

Gotham

COCKTAIL GLASS

1 part Crème de Cassis
2 parts Rémy Martin® VSOP
1 part Lime Juice

Shake with ice and strain.

Governing Body

COCKTAIL GLASS

⅔ part Gin
½ part Sweet Vermouth
⅔ part Dry Vermouth
splash Triple Sec
splash Pernod®

Shake with ice and strain.

Graceland

COCKTAIL GLASS

1 part Dry Vermouth
1 part Sweet Vermouth
1/2 part Scotch
dash Bitters

Shake with ice and strain.

Grand Apple

COCKTAIL GLASS

1/2 part Cognac
1/2 part Grand Marnier®
1 part Apple Brandy

Shake with ice and strain.

Grand Casino

COCKTAIL GLASS

2/3 part Peach Schnapps
2/3 part Dry Vermouth
splash Blue Curaçao
splash Crème de Cacao (White)

Shake with ice and strain.

Grand Gate

COCKTAIL GLASS

1 part Coffee Liqueur
1 part Amaretto
splash Goldschläger®
1 part Milk

Shake with ice and strain.

Grand Occasion

COCKTAIL GLASS

1/2 part Crème de Cacao (White)
1/2 part Grand Marnier®
2 splashes Lemon Juice
1 1/2 parts Light Rum

Shake with ice and strain.

Grape Ape

COCKTAIL GLASS

1 part Vodka
1/2 part Crème de Cacao (White)
1 part Grape Juice (red)

Shake with ice and strain.

Grape Essence

COCKTAIL GLASS

2 parts Grape Vodka
1 part White Cranberry Juice
1 part White Grape Juice
dash Lime Juice

Shake with ice and strain.

Grape Popsicle®

COCKTAIL GLASS

1/2 part Raspberry Liqueur
1/2 part Southern Comfort®
2/3 part Cranberry Juice Cocktail
splash Sweet & Sour Mix

Shake with ice and strain.

Grapeshot

COCKTAIL GLASS

1/2 part Blue Curaçao
1 1/2 parts Tequila
1 part Grape Juice

Shake with ice and strain.

Grappa Strega

COCKTAIL GLASS

1 part Grappa
1 part Strega®
splash Lemon Juice
splash Orange Juice

Shake with ice and strain.

Grasshopper

COCKTAIL GLASS

1 part Crème de Menthe (Green)
1 part Crème de Cacao (White)
1 part Light Cream

Shake with ice and strain.

Great Dane

COCKTAIL GLASS

2 parts Gin
1 part Cherry Brandy
1/2 part Dry Vermouth
1/2 part Kirschwasser

Shake with ice and strain.

Greek Cherry Tree

COCKTAIL GLASS

1 part Light Rum
1 part Cherry Brandy
½ part Grenadine
splash Grapefruit Juice

Shake with ice and strain.

Green and Gold

COCKTAIL GLASS

1 part Gin
⅔ part Peppermint Liqueur
splash Goldschläger®
½ part Vermouth
⅔ part Pineapple Juice

Shake with ice and strain.

Green Apple Tequini

COCKTAIL GLASS

1 part Apple Liqueur
2 parts Silver Tequila
splash Lime Juice
splash Melon Liqueur

Shake with ice and strain.

Green Bay

COCKTAIL GLASS

1½ parts Gin
½ part Green Chartreuse®
½ part Yellow Chartreuse®

Shake with ice and strain.

Green Bracer

COCKTAIL GLASS

1 part Peppermint Liqueur
1 part Irish Cream Liqueur
½ part Crème de Cacao (White)
½ part Peach Schnapps

Shake with ice and strain.

Green Cat

COCKTAIL GLASS

1½ parts Kiwi Schnapps
1 part Rum

Shake with ice and strain.

Green Coconut

COCKTAIL GLASS

2 parts Melon Liqueur
1 part Coconut Rum
splash Cream of Coconut
splash Sweet & Sweet & Sour Mix

Shake with ice and strain.

Green Cubed

COCKTAIL GLASS

⅔ part Melon Liqueur
splash Peppermint Liqueur
splash Green Chartreuse®
splash Lime Juice

Shake with ice and strain.

Green Hope

COCKTAIL GLASS

1½ parts Vodka
½ part Blue Curaçao
½ part Crème de Banane

Shake with ice and strain.

Green Iguana

COCKTAIL GLASS

2 parts Silver Tequila
1 part Melon Liqueur
1 part Lime Cordial

Shake with ice and strain.

Green Ireland

COCKTAIL GLASS

1½ parts Crème de Menthe (Green)
1½ parts Whiskey

Shake with ice and strain.

Green Kryptonite

COCKTAIL GLASS

2 parts Vodka
splash Lime Juice
1 part Melon Liqueur

Shake with ice and strain.

The Green Mile

COCKTAIL GLASS

1 part Melon Liqueur
½ part Coconut Rum
½ part Cointreau®
1 part Pineapple Juice

Shake with ice and strain.

Green Mist

COCKTAIL GLASS

1 part Scotch
1 part Crème de Menthe (White)
½ part Lemon Juice

Shake with ice and strain.

Green Scarab

COCKTAIL GLASS

1½ parts Gin
splash Peppermint Liqueur
1½ parts Absinthe

Shake with ice and strain.

Green Whip

COCKTAIL GLASS

1½ parts Maraschino Liqueur
1½ parts Melon Liqueur
splash Lime Juice

Shake with ice and strain.

Green Wood

COCKTAIL GLASS

1½ parts Apple Liqueur
1½ parts Parfait Amour

Shake with ice and strain.

Greenbriar Cocktail

COCKTAIL GLASS

2 parts Sherry
1 part Dry Vermouth

Shake with ice and strain.

Greensleeves

COCKTAIL GLASS

1 part Cream
1 part Crème de Cacao (White)
1 part Crème de Menthe (White)

Shake with ice and strain.

Greta Garbo

COCKTAIL GLASS

2 parts Light Rum
1 part Lime Juice
½ part Simple Syrup
¼ part Maraschino Liqueur

Shake with ice and strain.

Grouse to Death

COCKTAIL.GLASS

1½ parts Scotch
½ part Blackberry Liqueur
dash Angostura® Bitters
½ part Lemon Juice
splash Vanilla Syrup

Shake with ice and strain.

Grumpy Dwarf

COCKTAIL GLASS

1½ parts Gin
½ part Orange Liqueur
splash Dry Vermouth
splash Plum Brandy

Shake with ice and strain.

Guacamayo

COCKTAIL GLASS

½ part Coffee Liqueur
splash Calvados Apple Brandy
splash Cream
splash Cream of Coconut

Shake with ice and strain.

Guadalupe

COCKTAIL GLASS

1½ parts Silver Tequila
½ part Vanilla Liqueur
1 part Cream

Shake with ice and strain.

Guantanamera
COCKTAIL GLASS

1 part Light Rum
1/2 part Cream
1/2 part Coffee
1/2 part Cream of Coconut

Shake with ice and strain.

Guapasipati
COCKTAIL GLASS

1 1/2 parts Vodka
1/2 part Dry Vermouth
1/4 part Crème de Banane
splash Orange Juice
splash Grenadine

Shake with ice and strain.

Guerilla
COCKTAIL GLASS

1/2 part Triple Sec
1 part Tequila
splash Tabasco® Sauce

Shake with ice and strain.

Gulf of Mexico
COCKTAIL GLASS

1 part Blue Curaçao
1 part Melon Liqueur
1 part Vodka
1 part Pineapple Juice

Shake with ice and strain.

Gumdrop Cocktail
COCKTAIL GLASS

2 parts RumChata
1 part Butterscotch Liqueur
2 parts Cream
dash Blue Curaçao

Shake with ice and strain.

Gummy Bear
COCKTAIL GLASS

1 part Raspberry Liqueur
1 part Vodka
1 part Cranberry Juice

Shake with ice and strain.

Gun Barrel
COCKTAIL GLASS

1/2 part Currant Vodka
1/2 part Triple Sec
splash Cranberry Juice Cocktail

Shake with ice and strain.

Gun Shot
COCKTAIL GLASS

1/2 part Blue Curaçao
splash Crème de Coconut
splash Peach Schnapps
splash Sweet & Sour Mix

Shake with ice and strain.

Gypsy Dream Cream
COCKTAIL GLASS

1/2 part Blackberry Liqueur
1/2 part Raspberry Liqueur
1/2 part Irish Cream Liqueur
2 parts Milk

Shake with ice and strain.

H&H Cocktail
COCKTAIL GLASS

2 parts Dry Gin
1 part Lillet®
splash Triple Sec

Shake with ice and strain.

La Habana Affair
COCKTAIL GLASS

1 part Light Rum
1 part Sweet Vermouth
1 part Maraschino Liqueur

Shake with ice and strain.

Haidin-Haidin
COCKTAIL GLASS

2 parts Light Rum
1/2 part Dry Vermouth
dash Bitters

Shake with ice and strain. Garnish with Lemon Twist.

Hair of the Dog

COCKTAIL GLASS

1 part Scotch
½ part Cream
½ part Honey

Shake with ice and strain.

Hairy Armpit

COCKTAIL GLASS

1 part Ouzo
2 parts Grapefruit Juice

Build over ice and stir.

Half Note

COCKTAIL GLASS

1½ parts Gin
⅔ part Melon Liqueur
⅔ part Lime Juice

Shake with ice and strain.

Half on Orange

COCKTAIL GLASS

½ part Blue Curaçao
2 parts Chocolate Liqueur
½ part Light Rum

Shake with ice and strain.

Halloween in Tijuana

COCKTAIL GLASS

2 parts Absinthe
1 part Grand Marnier®
1 part Lime Juice

Shake with ice and strain.

Hammer and Tongs

COCKTAIL GLASS

2 parts Light Rum
2 splashes Lime Juice
splash Grenadine
½ part Cream

Shake with ice and strain.

Hammerhead

COCKTAIL GLASS

1 part Amaretto
1 part Blue Curaçao
1 part Gold Rum
splash Southern Comfort®

Shake with ice and strain.

Happy Daddy

COCKTAIL GLASS

½ part Gin
½ part Crème de Cassis
½ part Crème de Banane
splash Cream
splash Mango Juice

Shake with ice and strain.

Hard Core

COCKTAIL GLASS

1 part Apple Rum
1 part Apple Vodka
1 part Sour Apple Schnapps
½ part Salted Caramel Vodka

Shake with ice and strain.

Harper's Ferry

COCKTAIL GLASS

½ part Blue Curaçao
½ part Light Rum
½ part Southern Comfort®
1½ parts Dry Vermouth

Shake with ice and strain.

Harry's Pick Me Up Cocktail

COCKTAIL GLASS

2 parts Brandy
½ part Grenadine

Shake with ice and strain.

Harvey Wallpaper Hanger

COCKTAIL GLASS

2 parts Vodka
1 part Galliano®

Shake with ice and strain.

Hasty
COCKTAIL GLASS

1½ parts Gin
½ part Dry Vermouth
½ part Grenadine
splash Pastis

Shake with ice and strain.

Hat Trick
COCKTAIL GLASS

1 part Dark Rum
1 part Light Rum
1 part Sweet Vermouth

Shake with ice and strain.

Haute Couture
COCKTAIL GLASS

1½ parts Brandy
1½ parts Crème de Cacao (Dark)

Shake with ice and strain.

Havana Special
COCKTAIL GLASS

1 part Triple Sec
1 part Light Rum
1 part Pineapple Juice
1 part Lime Juice

Shake with ice and strain.

Hawaiian Comfort
COCKTAIL GLASS

1 part Southern Comfort®
1 part Amaretto
2 parts Sweet & Sour Mix
1 part Pineapple Juice
1 part Grenadine

Shake with ice and strain.

Head over Heels
COCKTAIL GLASS

2 parts Aquavit
splash Raspberry Liqueur
splash Lemon Juice
splash Simple Syrup

Shake with ice and strain.

Headlights
COCKTAIL GLASS

1 part Vodka
½ part Chartreuse®
2 splashes Galliano®
2 splashes Blue Curaçao
splash Lemon Juice

Shake with ice and strain.

Healthy Hiatus
COCKTAIL GLASS

1½ parts Amaretto
½ part Apricot Brandy
½ part Dry Vermouth
1 part Sweet & Sour Mix

Shake with ice and strain.

Heaven and Hell
COCKTAIL GLASS

1½ parts Scotch
1 part Coffee Liqueur
½ part Maraschino Liqueur

Shake with ice and strain.

Heavenly Opera
COCKTAIL GLASS

1 part Apricot Brandy
½ part Dry Vermouth
1 part Irish Whiskey
splash Lemon Juice
½ part Sweet & Sour Mix

Shake with ice and strain.

Heaven Spent
COCKTAIL GLASS

1 part Coconut Rum
1 part Light Rum
½ part Blue Curaçao
½ part Peach Schnapps
splash Piña Colada Mix
splash Pineapple Juice

Shake with ice and strain.

Heavy Fuel

COCKTAIL GLASS

1 part Bourbon
1 part Maraschino Liqueur
splash Peppermint Liqueur

Shake with ice and strain.

Heberts Alexander

COCKTAIL GLASS

2 parts Brandy
½ part Crème de Cacao (Dark)
½ part Frangelico®
1 part Cream

Shake with ice and strain.

Hell Frozen Over

COCKTAIL GLASS

1 part Dry Vermouth
1 part Sloe Gin
½ part Apricot Brandy
½ part Mandarine Napoleon Orange Liqueur

Shake with ice and strain.

Hello, Nurse

COCKTAIL GLASS

1½ parts Vodka
½ part Amaretto
½ part Cream of Coconut
½ part Light Cream

Shake with ice and strain.

Hemingway Special

COCKTAIL GLASS

2 parts Light Rum
1 part Grapefruit Juice
½ part Lime Juice
¼ part Maraschino Liqueur

Shake with ice and strain.

Hep Cat

COCKTAIL GLASS

3 parts Currant Vodka
½ part Dry Vermouth
splash Sweet Vermouth

Shake with ice and strain.

Her Name in Lights

COCKTAIL GLASS

1 part Vodka
½ part Chartreuse®
2 splashes Galliano®
2 splashes Blue Curaçao
½ part Lemon Juice

Shake with ice and strain. Garnish with Maraschino Cherry.

Herbie

COCKTAIL GLASS

1 part Dark Rum
⅔ part Strawberry Liqueur
splash Grenadine
splash Cream

Shake with ice and strain.

Heretic

COCKTAIL GLASS

1 part Calvados Apple Brandy
½ part Pear Brandy
splash Blackberry Liqueur

Shake with ice and strain.

Hibernian Special

COCKTAIL GLASS

1 part Blue Curaçao
1 part Triple Sec
1 part Gin

Shake with ice and strain.

Hidden Allies

COCKTAIL GLASS

⅔ part Amaretto
1 part Triple Sec
1 part Rémy Martin® VSOP
½ part Grapefruit Juice

Shake with ice and strain.

High Fashion

COCKTAIL GLASS

2 parts Vodka
1 part Scotch
1 part Triple Sec

Shake with ice and strain.

Highland Fling

COCKTAIL GLASS

1 1/2 parts Scotch
3/4 part Sweet Vermouth
2 dashes Orange Bitters

Shake with ice and strain. Garnish with an Olive.

Highland Victory

COCKTAIL GLASS

1 part Scotch
2/3 part Orange Liqueur
1/2 part Dry Vermouth
1/2 part Grapefruit Juice

Shake with ice and strain.

Hippo in a Tutu

COCKTAIL GLASS

2 parts Currant Vodka
1/2 part Raspberry Liqueur
1/2 part Blue Curaçao

Shake with ice and strain.

Hokkaido Cocktail

COCKTAIL GLASS

1 1/2 parts Gin
1/2 part Triple Sec
1 part Sake

Shake with ice and strain.

Hole in One

COCKTAIL GLASS

1 3/4 parts Scotch
3/4 part Dry Vermouth
splash Lemon Juice
dash Orange Bitters

Shake with ice and strain.

Holland Dyke

COCKTAIL GLASS

1 part Amaretto
1 part Lime Gin
1 part Orange Vodka
1 part Orange Juice

Shake with ice and strain.

Hollywood Shooter

COCKTAIL GLASS

3 parts Vodka
1 part Pineapple Juice

Shake with ice and strain.

Holy Grail

COCKTAIL GLASS

1 part Vodka
1 part Campari®
1/2 part Apricot Brandy
1 1/2 parts Orange Juice
1 Egg White

Shake with ice and strain.

Homecoming

COCKTAIL GLASS

3/4 part Gin
3/4 part Apricot Brandy
3/4 part Dry Vermouth
splash Lemon Juice

Shake with ice and strain.

Honey Blossom

COCKTAIL GLASS

1 1/2 parts Raspberry Liqueur
1 part Citrus Rum
1/2 part Honey
1/2 part Sweet & Sour Mix

Shake with ice and strain.

Honey Dear

COCKTAIL GLASS

2 parts Dark Rum
1 part Barenjäger Honey Liqueur
1/2 part Honey
1/2 part Lemon Juice

Shake with ice and strain.

Honeymoon

COCKTAIL GLASS

3/4 part Bénédictine®
3/4 part Apple Brandy
1 part Lemon Juice
2 splashes Triple Sec

Shake with ice and strain.

Honolulu Hammer

COCKTAIL GLASS

1½ parts Vodka
½ part Amaretto
splash Pineapple Juice
splash Grenadine

Shake with ice and strain.

Honolulu with Fruit

COCKTAIL GLASS

2 parts Gin
¾ part Lime Juice
½ part Orange Juice
½ part Pineapple
dash Sugar

Shake with ice and strain.

Hoochie Mama

COCKTAIL GLASS

1½ parts Vodka
1 part Crème de Menthe (White)
½ part Chocolate Syrup

Shake with ice and strain.

Hootenanny

COCKTAIL GLASS

1 part Bourbon
1 part Jägermeister
1 part Mango Rum
1 part Cherry Juice
splash Cola

Shake all but Cola with ice and strain. Top splash Cola.

Hope and Peace

COCKTAIL GLASS

1½ parts Dark Rum
½ part Pisang Ambon® Liqueur
½ part Kiwi Schnapps
2 parts Cream

Shake with ice and strain.

Hop-Scotch

COCKTAIL GLASS

1 part Scotch
½ part Dry Vermouth
½ part Triple Sec
splash Blue Curaçao

Shake with ice and strain.

Horizon

COCKTAIL GLASS

1½ parts Dark Rum
1 part Anisette
1 part Grenadine

Shake with ice and strain.

Hornet Stinger

COCKTAIL GLASS

1 part Vodka
½ part Melon Liqueur
dash Powdered Sugar
splash Lime Juice

Shake with ice and strain.

Horse and Jockey

COCKTAIL GLASS

1 part Añejo Rum
1 part Southern Comfort®
½ part Sweet Vermouth
2 dashes Bitters

Shake with ice and strain.

Horse Power

COCKTAIL GLASS

1½ parts Whiskey
1 part Mandarine Napoléon® Liqueur
splash Campari®

Shake with ice and strain.

Hot Buttered Snow

COCKTAIL GLASS

2 parts Vanilla Vodka
½ part Amaretto
½ part Butterscotch Liqueur
½ part Crème de Cacao (White)
1 part Heavy Cream

Shake with ice and strain.

Hot Cherry
COCKTAIL GLASS
1½ parts Cherry Brandy
1 part Silver Tequila
Shake with ice and strain.

Hot Deck
COCKTAIL GLASS
2 parts Fireball Cinnamon Whiskey
1 part Ginger Liqueur
½ part Sweet Vermouth
Shake with ice and strain.

Hot Lava
COCKTAIL GLASS
1¼ parts Pepper Vodka
¼ part Amaretto
Shake with ice and strain.

Hot Property
COCKTAIL GLASS
1½ parts Brandy
½ part Grenadine
splash Anisette
splash Sambuca
½ part Lemon Juice
Shake with ice and strain.

Hot Roasted Nuts
COCKTAIL GLASS
1 part Coffee Liqueur
1 part Cinnamon Schnapps
1 part Frangelico®
Shake with ice and strain.

Hot Winter Night
COCKTAIL GLASS
1½ parts Spiced Rum
splash Vanilla Liqueur
splash Goldschläger®
splash Lemon Juice
Shake with ice and strain.

Hotel Plaza Cocktail
COCKTAIL GLASS
1 part Dry Vermouth
1 part Sweet Vermouth
1 part Gin
Shake with ice and strain.

Houla Houla
COCKTAIL GLASS
2 parts Gin
1 part Orange Juice
¼ part Triple Sec
Shake with ice and strain.

House of Usher
COCKTAIL GLASS
1½ parts Brandy
splash Triple Sec
splash Pineapple Juice
splash Maraschino Liqueur
Shake with ice and strain.

Hudson Bay
COCKTAIL GLASS
½ part Cherry Brandy
1 part Gin
splash 151-Proof Rum
2 splashes Orange Juice
splash Lime Juice
Shake with ice and strain.

Humjob
COCKTAIL GLASS
1½ parts Light Rum
¼ part Crème de Cacao (Dark)
¼ part Cherry Brandy
Shake with ice and strain.

The Hunt Master
COCKTAIL GLASS
1 part Jägermeister®
½ part Peppermint Liqueur
½ part Goldschläger®
splash Crème de Coconut
Shake with ice and strain.

Hunter
COCKTAIL GLASS

1 1/2 parts Bourbon
1 part Cherry Brandy

Shake with ice and strain.

Hunting Man
COCKTAIL GLASS

1 1/2 parts Sloe Gin
1/2 part Raspberry Liqueur
1/2 part Frangelico®
2/3 part Lemon Juice
1 1/2 parts Blackberry Juice

Shake with ice and strain.

Hurlyburly
COCKTAIL GLASS

1 1/4 parts Citrus Vodka
1/2 part Cointreau®
1/2 part Orange Juice
1/2 part Cranberry Juice Cocktail
1 part Sweet & Sour Mix

Shake with ice and strain.

Hurricane
COCKTAIL GLASS

1 part Light Rum
1 part Dark Rum
1 part Passion Fruit Nectar
2 splashes Lime Juice

Shake with ice and strain.

Hyde and Seek
COCKTAIL GLASS

2 parts Passion Fruit Liqueur
1/2 part Coffee Liqueur

Shake with ice and strain.

I Love Lucy
COCKTAIL GLASS

1 part Vodka
1/2 part Lime Juice
1/4 part Parfait Amour
1/4 part Triple Sec

Shake with ice and strain.

I Love You
COCKTAIL GLASS

1 part Dark Rum
1 part Apricot Brandy
1/2 part Peach Schnapps
splash Amaretto
splash Orange Juice

Shake with ice and strain.

I Love You, Honeybunny
COCKTAIL GLASS

1 part Barenjäger Honey Liqueur
1 part Gin
1 part Lemon Vodka
splash Grenadine

Shake with ice and strain.

I See Nothing
COCKTAIL GLASS

1 part Brandy
1 part Dry Vermouth
splash Triple Sec
dash Orange Bitters
splash Maraschino Liqueur
splash Pernod®

Shake with ice and strain.

Ice Crystals
COCKTAIL GLASS

1 1/2 parts Vodka
1/2 part Lemon Vodka
1/2 part Crème de Menthe (Green)

Shake with ice and strain.

Iffy Stiffy
COCKTAIL GLASS

1 part Jim Beam®
1 part Cherry Brandy
1/2 part Dry Vermouth
1/2 part Orange Juice
splash Lime Juice

Shake with ice and strain.

Ignition Key

COCKTAIL GLASS

½ part Grenadine
1½ parts Light Rum
½ part Lime Juice

Shake with ice and strain.

Iguana

COCKTAIL GLASS

½ part Vodka
½ part Tequila
¼ part Coffee Vodka
1½ parts Sweet & Sour Mix
½ Lime Slice

Shake with ice and strain.

Immaculata

COCKTAIL GLASS

1½ parts Light Rum
½ part Amaretto
½ part Lime Juice
splash Lemon Juice
dash Sugar

Shake with ice and strain.

In a Nutshell

COCKTAIL GLASS

1 part Amaretto
½ part Vanilla Vodka
½ part Frangelico®
2 parts Cream

Shake with ice and strain.

In Mint Condition

COCKTAIL GLASS

1 part Crème de Menthe (White)
1 part Triple Sec
1 part Apricot Brandy

Shake with ice and strain.

In the Attic

COCKTAIL GLASS

1 part Gin
½ part Cherry Brandy
½ part Bénédictine®
splash Lemon Juice

Shake with ice and strain.

In Trance as Mission

COCKTAIL GLASS

1 part Triple Sec
1 part Brandy
1 part Lemon Juice

Shake with ice and strain.

Inca

COCKTAIL GLASS

1 part Dry Gin
½ part Dry Vermouth
½ part Sweet Vermouth
½ part Dry Sherry
dash Orange Bitters

Shake with ice and strain.

Indecent Proposal

COCKTAIL GLASS

1 part Gold Tequila
½ part Grand Marnier®
½ part Cointreau®
1 part Lemon Juice
1 part Lime Juice

Shake with ice and strain.

Independence

COCKTAIL GLASS

⅔ part Melon Liqueur
½ part Amaretto
⅔ part Peach Schnapps
½ part Lime Juice
fill with Cranberry Juice Cocktail

Shake with ice and strain.

Indy Blanket

COCKTAIL GLASS

1½ parts Cognac
1 part Rum
¾ part Triple Sec
¾ part Simple Syrup
½ part Lemon Juice

Shake with ice and strain.

Ink Street Cocktail
COCKTAIL GLASS
1½ parts Whiskey
1½ parts Orange Juice
Shake with ice and strain.

Inside Out
COCKTAIL GLASS
1 part Peppermint Liqueur
1 part Plum Brandy
2 parts Pear Juice
Shake with ice and strain.

Intermezzo
COCKTAIL GLASS
1 part Crème de Cacao (White)
1 part Advocaat
½ part Milk
½ part Vanilla Liqueur
Shake with ice and strain.

International Cocktail
COCKTAIL GLASS
1½ parts Cognac
1 part Triple Sec
1 part Anisette
½ part Vodka
Shake with ice and strain.

Intimacy
COCKTAIL GLASS
½ part Strawberry Liqueur
splash Crème de Cassis
⅔ part Dark Rum
splash Simple Syrup
splash Lime Juice
Shake with ice and strain.

Intimate Confession
COCKTAIL GLASS
½ part Crème de Coconut
½ part Frangelico®
2 parts White Port
splash Honey
1 part Cream
Shake with ice and strain.

Intrigue Cocktail
COCKTAIL GLASS
1 part Crème de Banane
½ part Coffee
½ part Dry Vermouth
Shake with ice and strain.

Irish
COCKTAIL GLASS
2 dashes Blue Curaçao
dash Cherry Liqueur
1½ parts Rye Whiskey
2 splashes Pernod®
Shake with ice and strain.

Irish Blessing
COCKTAIL GLASS
1 part Irish Cream Liqueur
1 part Irish Whiskey
Shake with ice and strain.

Irish Eyes
COCKTAIL GLASS
2 parts Crème de Menthe (Green)
2 parts Heavy Cream
1 part Irish Whiskey
Shake with ice and strain.

Irish Kilt
COCKTAIL GLASS
2 parts Whiskey
1 part Scotch
1 tbsp Sugar
dash Orange Bitters
Shake with ice and strain.

Irish Rose
COCKTAIL GLASS
2 parts Whiskey
½ part Grenadine
Shake with ice and strain.

Irish Shillelagh

COCKTAIL GLASS

3 parts Irish Whiskey
1 part Sloe Gin
1 part Light Rum
1 part Lemon Juice
dash Powdered Sugar

Shake with ice and strain.

Irish Whiskey

COCKTAIL GLASS

2 parts Irish Whiskey
splash Triple Sec
splash Anisette
splash Maraschino Liqueur
dash Bitters

Shake with ice and strain. Garnish with Olive.

Isla Tropical

COCKTAIL GLASS

1 part Dark Rum
½ part Dry Gin
½ part Crème de Banane
½ part Pineapple Juice
splash Grenadine

Shake with ice and strain.

Island Nation

COCKTAIL GLASS

½ part Triple Sec
½ part Vodka
½ part Peppermint Liqueur
1½ parts Pineapple Juice

Shake with ice and strain.

Island Trader

COCKTAIL GLASS

2 parts Coconut Rum
2 parts Irish Cream Liqueur
½ part Coffee Liqueur

Shake with ice and strain.

Italian Delight

COCKTAIL GLASS

1 part Amaretto
½ part Orange Juice
1½ parts Cream

Shake with ice and strain. Garnish with Maraschino Cherry.

Italian Sombrero

COCKTAIL GLASS

2 parts Amaretto
3 parts Cream

Shake with ice and strain.

It's Now or Never

COCKTAIL GLASS

1 part Vodka
splash Apricot Brandy
splash Campari®
splash Limoncello

Shake with ice and strain.

Jack Pine Cocktail

COCKTAIL GLASS

1 part Dry Gin
1 part Dry Vermouth
1 part Orange Juice
½ part Pineapple Juice

Shake with ice and strain.

Jack Sour

COCKTAIL GLASS

2 parts Jack Daniel's®
splash Cherry Juice
2 parts Sweet & Sour Mix

Shake with ice and strain. Garnish with a Orange Wedge and Maraschino Cherries.

Jack Withers

COCKTAIL GLASS

¾ part Gin
½ part Orange Juice
¾ part Dry Vermouth
¾ part Sweet Vermouth

Shake with ice and strain.

Jackie O's Rose

COCKTAIL GLASS

2 parts Light Rum
½ part Lime Juice
dash Cointreau®
dash Powdered Sugar

Shake with ice and strain.

Jack-O-Fire

COCKTAIL GLASS

1 part Fireball Cinnamon Whiskey
1 part Irish Cream Liqueur Liqueur
1 part Pumpkin Spice Liqueur
1 part Vanilla Vodka

Shake with ice and strain.

Jack-of-All-Trades

COCKTAIL GLASS

⅔ part Peach Schnapps
1½ parts Whiskey
splash Limoncello
splash Almond Syrup

Shake with ice and strain.

Jacqueline

COCKTAIL GLASS

2 parts Dark Rum
1 part Triple Sec
1 part Lime Juice

Shake with ice and strain.

Jade

COCKTAIL GLASS

1½ parts Light Rum
1/12 part Crème de Menthe (Green)
1/12 part Triple Sec
½ part Lime Juice
1 tsp Powdered Sugar

Shake with ice and strain.

Jaded Dreams

COCKTAIL GLASS

1½ parts Light Rum
2 splashes Crème de Menthe (Green)
splash Triple Sec
splash Lime Juice
dash Sugar

Shake with ice and strain.

Jamaica Hoop

COCKTAIL GLASS

1 part Crème de Cacao (White)
1 part Cream
1 part Crème de Coconut

Shake with ice and strain.

Jamaica Hop

COCKTAIL GLASS

1 part Coffee Brandy
1 part Crème de Cacao (White)
1 part Cream

Shake with ice and strain.

Jamaican Breakfast

COCKTAIL GLASS

½ part Coffee Brandy
½ part Vanilla Liqueur
1 part Jamaican Rum
2 parts Cream
splash Caramel syrup

Shake with ice and strain.

Jamaican Cocktail

COCKTAIL GLASS

1 part Dark Rum
½ part Coffee Liqueur
1 part Lime Juice
dash Bitters

Shake with ice and strain.

Jamaican Creamsicle®

COCKTAIL GLASS

1 part Rum Crème Liqueur
1 part Half and Half
1 part Orange Juice
splash Vanilla Extract

Shake with ice and strain.

Jamaican Fever

COCKTAIL GLASS

2/3 part Passion Fruit Liqueur
1 1/2 parts Jamaican Rum
1 1/2 parts Guava Juice
1/2 part Cranberry Juice Cocktail
1/2 part Lemon Juice

Shake with ice and strain.

Jamaican Ginger

COCKTAIL GLASS

2 parts Dark Rum
1/2 part Maraschino Liqueur
1/2 part Triple Sec
splash Grenadine
dash Angostura Bitters

Shake with ice and strain.

Jamaican Green Sunrise

COCKTAIL GLASS

1 1/2 parts Light Rum
1 part Orange Juice
1/2 part Blue Curaçao
1/2 part Pineapple Vodka

Shake with ice and strain.

Jamaican Renegade

COCKTAIL GLASS

1/2 part Sloe Gin
1/2 part Crème de Banane
splash Lime Juice
splash Cream of Coconut

Shake with ice and strain.

Jamaican-Russian Handshake

COCKTAIL GLASS

2 parts Vodka
1/2 part Grenadine
2/3 part Spiced Rum
2/3 part Lemon Juice

Shake with ice and strain.

Jamaican Tennis Beads

COCKTAIL GLASS

1 part Vodka
1 part Coconut Rum
1 part Raspberry Liqueur
1 part Crème de Banane
1 part Pineapple Juice
1 part Half and Half

Shake with ice and strain.

James II Comes First

COCKTAIL GLASS

2 parts Scotch
1/2 part Tawny Port
1/2 part Dry Vermouth
dash Bitters

Shake with ice and strain.

Japanese Cocktail

COCKTAIL GLASS

2 parts Brandy
splash Amaretto
1/2 part Lime Juice
dash Bitters

Shake with ice and strain.

Japanese Slipper

COCKTAIL GLASS

1 part Melon Liqueur
1 part Cointreau®
1 part Lemon Juice

Shake with ice and strain.

Jasmine

COCKTAIL GLASS

1 1/2 parts Gin
1/4 part Cointreau®
1/4 part Campari®
3/4 part Lemon Juice

Shake with ice and strain.

Jazz

COCKTAIL GLASS

2 parts Gin
1 part Crème de Cassis
1/2 part Lime Juice

Shake with ice and strain.

Je T'adore
COCKTAIL GLASS

½ part Crème de Cacao (White)
1 part Rémy Martin® VSOP
½ part Bénédictine®
2 parts Cream

Shake with ice and strain.

Jelly Belly
COCKTAIL GLASS

1 part Blackberry Liqueur
1 part Peppermint Liqueur
½ part Bourbon

Shake with ice and strain.

Jersey Gentleman
COCKTAIL GLASS

2 parts Whiskey
½ part Pernod
1 part Pineapple Juice

Shake with ice and strain.

Jersey Lightening
COCKTAIL GLASS

2 parts Apple Brandy
1 part Sweet Vermouth
1 part Lime Juice

Shake with ice and strain.

Jerusalem Love Cream
COCKTAIL GLASS

1½ parts Guava Juice
1½ parts Vanilla Vodka
½ part Lychee Syrup

Shake with ice and strain.

Jet Black
COCKTAIL GLASS

1½ parts Gin
2 splashes Sweet Vermouth
splash Black Sambuca

Shake with ice and strain.

Jewel of the Nile
COCKTAIL GLASS

1½ parts Gin
½ part Green Chartreuse®
½ part Chartreuse®

Shake with ice and strain.

Joan Miró
COCKTAIL GLASS

1 part Dubonnet® Blonde
1 part Grand Marnier®
1 part Scotch

Shake with ice and strain.

Jockey's Choice Manhattan
COCKTAIL GLASS

2½ parts Bourbon
¾ part Sweet Vermouth
2 dashes Angostura® Bitters

Shake with ice and strain.

Johan
COCKTAIL GLASS

1 part Peppermint Liqueur
1 part Crème de Cacao (White)
splash Bénédictine®
splash Cream

Shake with ice and strain.

John Doe
COCKTAIL GLASS

1 part Gin
splash Apricot Brandy
splash Calvados Apple Brandy
1 part Lemon Juice

Shake with ice and strain.

John Wood Cocktail
COCKTAIL GLASS

1½ parts Dry Vermouth
1 part Whiskey

Shake with ice and strain.

Johnnie Mack Cocktail

COCKTAIL GLASS

2 parts Sloe Gin
1 part Triple Sec

Shake with ice and strain.

Johnny Appleseed

COCKTAIL GLASS

1 part Cherry Brandy
2 parts Apple Juice
1 part Grapefruit Juice

Shake with ice and strain.

La Jolla

COCKTAIL GLASS

1½ parts Brandy
½ part Crème de Banane
2 splashes Lemon Juice
splash Orange Juice

Shake with ice and strain.

Jolly Roger

COCKTAIL GLASS

1 part Dark Rum
1 part Banana Liqueur
2 parts Lemon Juice

Shake with ice and strain.

Joshua Tree

COCKTAIL GLASS

1 part Peach Schnapps
1 part Brandy
1 part Orange Juice
½ part Cranberry Juice Cocktail

Shake with ice and strain.

Josie & the Pussycats

COCKTAIL GLASS

1 part Cranberry Vodka
1 part Triple Sec
½ part Currant Vodka
½ part Citrus Vodka
dash Angostura® Bitters

Shake with ice and strain.

Joulouville

COCKTAIL GLASS

1 part Gin
½ part Apple Brandy
splash Sweet Vermouth
½ part Lemon Juice
2 splashes Grenadine

Shake with ice and strain.

Joy Division

COCKTAIL GLASS

1½ parts Crème de Coconut
½ part Chocolate Liqueur
1½ parts Frangelico®
½ part Cream

Shake with ice and strain.

Joy Jumper

COCKTAIL GLASS

1½ parts Vodka
2 splashes Kümmel
splash Lime Juice
splash Lemon Juice
dash Sugar

Shake with ice and strain. Garnish with Lemon Twist.

Joy to the World

COCKTAIL GLASS

2 parts Dark Rum
1 part Bourbon
1 part Chocolate Liqueur

Shake with ice and strain.

Judgette

COCKTAIL GLASS

1 part Dry Gin
1 part Dry Vermouth
1 part Peach Schnapps
splash Lime Juice

Shake with ice and strain.

Julia
COCKTAIL GLASS

1 part Pineapple Juice
1 part Dark Rum
1/2 part Blue Curaçao
1/2 part Parfait Amour
splash Simple Syrup

Shake with ice and strain.

Juliet
COCKTAIL GLASS

1 part Silver Tequila
1 part Pisang Ambon® Liqueur
1 part Pineapple Juice
splash Grenadine

Shake with ice and strain.

Jump for Joy
COCKTAIL GLASS

1 part Peach Schnapps
1 part Melon Liqueur
1/2 part Sweet & Sour Mix

Shake with ice and strain.

Jumping Bean
COCKTAIL GLASS

1 1/2 parts Tequila
1/2 part Sambuca
3 Coffee Beans

Shake with ice and strain. Top with Coffee Beans.

Juniper Blend
COCKTAIL GLASS

1 part Cherry Liqueur
1 part Gin
splash Dry Vermouth

Shake with ice and strain.

Jupiter Cocktail
COCKTAIL GLASS

2 parts Dry Gin
1 part Dry Vermouth
1/2 part Parfait Amour
1/2 part Orange Juice

Shake with ice and strain.

Just So Presto
COCKTAIL GLASS

1 1/2 parts Apricot Brandy
1/2 part Lemon Juice
1 part Orange Juice

Shake with ice and strain.

Kabut
COCKTAIL GLASS

1 1/2 parts Vanilla Liqueur
1 part Blue Curaçao
1/2 part Vodka

Shake with ice and strain.

Kahlodster
COCKTAIL GLASS

1 part Coffee Liqueur
1 part Vodka
1 part Jägermeister®

Shake with ice and strain.

Kalashnikov
COCKTAIL GLASS

2 parts Lemon Vodka
1/2 part Absinthe
splash Lemon Juice
dash Cinnamon Schnapps
1/2 tsp Powdered Sugar

Shake with ice and strain.

Kama Sutra
COCKTAIL GLASS

3 parts Raspberry Vodka
1 part Triple Sec
splash Chambord
splash Lime Juice

Shake with ice and strain.

Kama-Kura
COCKTAIL GLASS

1 1/2 parts Crème de Banane
1 1/2 parts Pineapple Juice

Shake with ice and strain.

Kangaroo

COCKTAIL GLASS

1 1/2 parts Vodka
3/4 part Dry Vermouth

Shake with ice and strain.

Kashmir

COCKTAIL GLASS

1 part Vodka
1 part Crème de Cacao (White)
2 splashes Grenadine
2 splashes Lemon Juice

Shake with ice and strain.

KC Rum

COCKTAIL GLASS

1 part Light Rum
1 part Coffee Liqueur
1 part Cream

Shake with ice and strain.

Kempinsky Fizz

COCKTAIL GLASS

2 parts Vodka
1 part Crème de Cassis

Shake with ice and strain.

Kentucky Blizzard

COCKTAIL GLASS

1 1/2 parts Bourbon
1 1/2 parts Cranberry Juice
1/2 part Lime Juice
1/2 part Grenadine
1 tsp Sugar

Shake with ice and strain.

Kentucky Blue

COCKTAIL GLASS

2 parts Bourbon
1/2 part Blue Curaçao
splash Lemon Juice
splash Orange Juice
dash Grenadine

Shake with ice and strain.

Kentucky Mint

COCKTAIL GLASS

1 1/2 parts Bourbon
1/2 part Crème de Cacao (White)
1/2 part Crème de Menthe (White)

Shake with ice and strain.

Key Club Cocktail

COCKTAIL GLASS

2 parts Gin
1/2 part Light Rum
1/2 part Lime Juice
1/2 part Fernet-Branca®

Shake with ice and strain.

Kharamazov

COCKTAIL GLASS

1 part Coffee Liqueur
1 part Vodka
1 part Blue Curaçao
splash Orange Juice

Shake with ice and strain.

A Kick in the Bollocks

COCKTAIL GLASS

1 part Rum
1 part Peach Schnapps
1/2 part Cream of Coconut
1 part Cream
1 part Orange Juice

Shake with ice and strain.

Kick in the Pants

COCKTAIL GLASS

1 part Triple Sec
1 part Cognac
1 part Bourbon

Shake with ice and strain.

Kicking Cow

COCKTAIL GLASS

1 part Rye Whiskey
1 part Maple Syrup
1 part Cream

Shake with ice and strain.

Kidney Machine

COCKTAIL GLASS

2/3 part Triple Sec
1 1/2 parts Dubonnet® Blonde
2/3 part Rémy Martin® VSOP

Shake with ice and strain.

Killer Whale

COCKTAIL GLASS

1 1/2 parts Blue Curaçao
splash Orange Vodka
1 part Orange Juice
splash Pineapple Juice
dash Sugar

Shake with ice and strain.

Kilt Club

COCKTAIL GLASS

2/3 part Citrus Vodka
1 part Kiwi Schnapps
1 part Drambuie®
1/2 part Pineapple Juice

Shake with ice and strain.

King Kooba

COCKTAIL GLASS

2 parts Dark Rum
1/2 part Brandy
1/2 part Triple Sec
1/2 part Lemon Juice

Shake with ice and strain.

King of Kingston

COCKTAIL GLASS

1 part Gin
1/2 part Crème de Banane
splash Grenadine
1 part Cream
1 part Pineapple Juice
splash Grapefruit Juice

Shake with ice and strain.

Kings Club

COCKTAIL GLASS

2 parts Bourbon
1/2 part Grenadine
1/2 part Fernet-Branca®

Shake with ice and strain.

Kinky Cherry

COCKTAIL GLASS

1/2 part Vodka
2 parts Cherry Brandy
1/2 part Jim Beam®
1/2 part Sweet Vermouth
1/2 part Lemon Juice

Shake with ice and strain.

Kiss and Tell

COCKTAIL GLASS

1 part Calvados Apple Brandy
1 part Sloe Gin
splash Lemon Juice
1 Egg White

Shake with ice and strain.

Kiss My Monkey

COCKTAIL GLASS

1 1/2 parts Passion Fruit Liqueur
1/2 part Crème de Banane
1/2 part Dry Vermouth

Shake with ice and strain.

Kiss the Boys Goodbye

COCKTAIL GLASS

3/4 part Brandy
3/4 part Sloe Gin
1 Egg White

Shake with ice and strain. Garnish with a Lemon Wedge.

Kissing Game

COCKTAIL GLASS

1 part Kiwi Schnapps
1 part Triple Sec
splash Lime Juice

Shake with ice and strain.

Kiwillingly

COCKTAIL GLASS

1 part Kiwi Schnapps
1/2 part Safari®
1 part Cachaça
1 part Lemon-Lime Soda

Shake with ice and strain.

Klondike

COCKTAIL GLASS

1 1/2 parts Irish Cream Liqueur
1 1/2 parts Yukon Jack®

Shake with ice and strain.

Knight-Errant

COCKTAIL GLASS

1 1/2 parts Gin
1/2 part Crème de Cassis
1 part Dry Sherry

Shake with ice and strain.

Koh-i-Noor

COCKTAIL GLASS

1 part Gin
1 part Maraschino Liqueur
1/2 part Crème de Menthe (White)

Shake with ice and strain.

Koko Smile

COCKTAIL GLASS

1 part Light Rum
1 part Peach Schnapps
1/2 part Kiwi Schnapps
1 part Cranberry Juice Cocktail

Shake with ice and strain.

Kriki

COCKTAIL GLASS

1 part Crème de Cacao (White)
1 part Crème de Menthe (Green)
1 part Cream

Shake with ice and strain.

Kuala Lumpur

COCKTAIL GLASS

1 1/2 parts Vodka
2/3 part Pisang Ambon® Liqueur
1 part Crème de Coconut
fill with Orange Juice
splash Cream

Shake with ice and strain.

Kulio Drink

COCKTAIL GLASS

1/2 part Whiskey
1/2 part Gin
1 part Triple Sec
1 part Lemon Juice

Shake with ice and strain.

Kyoto

COCKTAIL GLASS

1 1/2 parts Gin
1/2 part Apricot Brandy
1/2 part Triple Sec
1/2 part Dry Vermouth

Shake with ice and strain.

LA Cocktail

COCKTAIL GLASS

1 1/2 parts Whiskey
splash Sweet Vermouth
1 Egg White
dash Sugar

Shake with ice and strain.

Labanga

COCKTAIL GLASS

1 part Triple Sec
1 part Melon Liqueur
1/2 part Green Chartreuse®
1/2 part Sweet & Sour Mix
splash Maraschino Liqueur

Shake with ice and strain.

Ladbroke Treaty

COCKTAIL GLASS

$2/3$ part Gin
$2/3$ part Blackberry Liqueur
$1/2$ part Chartreuse®
splash Lemon Juice
1 part Pineapple Juice

Shake with ice and strain.

Ladies' Night

COCKTAIL GLASS

1 part Vodka
$1/2$ part Peach Schnapps
$1/2$ part Triple Sec
$1/2$ part Lemon Juice

Shake with ice and strain.

Lady 52

COCKTAIL GLASS

1 part Coffee Liqueur
1 part Irish Cream Liqueur
$1\frac{1}{2}$ parts Cream
$1/2$ part Cointreau®

Shake with ice and strain.

Lady Bird

COCKTAIL GLASS

splash Coffee Brandy
splash Crème de Cacao (White)
splash Vanilla Liqueur
2 parts Strawberry Juice
$1\frac{1}{2}$ parts Cream

Shake with ice and strain.

Lady Diana

COCKTAIL GLASS

2 parts Gin
$1\frac{1}{2}$ parts Campari®
1 part Lime Juice
$1/2$ part Simple Syrup

Shake with ice and strain.

Lady Finger

COCKTAIL GLASS

1 part Cherry Brandy
1 part Gin
$1/2$ part Kirschwasser

Shake with ice and strain.

Lady Liberty in a Thong

COCKTAIL GLASS

$1\frac{1}{2}$ parts Dark Rum
1 part Coffee Brandy
2 splashes Lemon Juice

Shake with ice and strain.

Lady Man

COCKTAIL GLASS

$1/2$ part Peach Schnapps
1 part Vodka
splash Grenadine
splash Lemon Juice
splash Papaya Juice

Shake with ice and strain.

Lady Scarlett

COCKTAIL GLASS

1 part Gin
1 part Cointreau®
$1/2$ part Dry Vermouth
$1/2$ part Lime Juice
dash Bitters

Shake with ice and strain.

Laguna Cocktail

COCKTAIL GLASS

2 parts Brandy
$1/4$ part Vodka
$1/4$ part Vermouth
splash Campari®
dash Bitters

Shake with ice and strain.

Lake House
COCKTAIL GLASS

1 part Passion Fruit Rum
1 part Coconut Rum
1 part Blue Curaçao
1 part Pineapple Juice

Shake with ice and strain.

Lambino
COCKTAIL GLASS

2/3 part Raspberry Liqueur
splash Blackberry Liqueur
1 part Crème de Cacao (White)
1 part Milk

Shake with ice and strain.

La Manga
COCKTAIL GLASS

1 part Vodka
1 part Apricot Brandy
1 part Licor 43®
splash Grenadine

Shake with ice and strain.

L'amour le Night
COCKTAIL GLASS

3/4 part Blue Curaçao
3/4 part Cream
3/4 part Amaretto
3/4 part Kirschwasser

Shake with ice and strain.

Landed Gentry
COCKTAIL GLASS

1 1/2 parts Dark Rum
1/2 part Tia Maria®
1 part Heavy Cream

Shake with ice and strain.

Lascivious Cream
COCKTAIL GLASS

1 1/2 parts Crème de Cacao (White)
1 1/2 parts Melon Liquer

Shake with ice and strain.

The Last Judgment
COCKTAIL GLASS

2 parts Brandy
1/2 part Amaretto
1/2 part Blue Curaçao
1 part Cream

Shake with ice and strain.

Last Tango
COCKTAIL GLASS

1 1/2 parts Gin
1/2 part Triple Sec
1 part Orange Juice

Shake with ice and strain.

The Last Warrior
COCKTAIL GLASS

2 parts Dark Rum
1/2 part Vanilla Liqueur
1/2 part Blackberry Liqueur
1 part Cream

Shake with ice and strain.

Latin Manhattan
COCKTAIL GLASS

1 part Dark Rum
1 part Sweet Vermouth
1 part Dry Vermouth
dash Bitters

Shake with ice and strain.

Lavender Mist
COCKTAIL GLASS

2 parts Lemon Vodka
1 part Blue Raspberry Liqueur
splash Grenadine
splash Sweetened Lime Juice

Shake with ice and strain.

Lawhill Cocktail
COCKTAIL GLASS

1 1/2 parts Whiskey
3/4 part Dry Vermouth
1/4 splash Anisette
1/4 splash Maraschino Cherry
dash Bitters

Shake with ice and strain.

La-Z-Boy® Comfortable

COCKTAIL GLASS

1 part Amaretto
1 part Apricot Brandy
1 part Southern Comfort®
splash Sweet & Sour Mix

Shake with ice and strain.

Lele Free

COCKTAIL GLASS

2/3 part Amaretto
2/3 part Crème de Cacao (Dark)
1/2 part Amaretto
1 part Milk

Shake with ice and strain.

Lemon Lance

COCKTAIL GLASS

1 part Vanilla Liqueur
1 part Limoncello
splash Citrus Vodka
splash Bacardi® Limón Rum

Shake with ice and strain.

Lemonade Claret

COCKTAIL GLASS

1 1/2 parts Bourbon
1/2 part Sweet Vermouth
1/2 part Dry Vermouth
1/2 part Campari®

Shake with ice and strain.

Let's Party

COCKTAIL GLASS

1 part Melon Liqueur
1/2 part Pineapple Juice
splash Cream of Coconut
splash Sweet & Sour Mix

Shake with ice and strain.

Lexus

COCKTAIL GLASS

2 parts Brandy
1/2 part Triple Sec
1/2 part Vanilla Liqueur

Shake with ice and strain.

Licorice Stick

COCKTAIL GLASS

1 part Black Sambuca
1 part Vodka
1/2 part Crème de Cacao (White)

Shake with ice and strain.

Life Saver

COCKTAIL GLASS

1 part Light Rum
1 part Pineapple Juice
1/4 part Lime Juice
splash Blue Curaçao
splash Triple Sec
splash Simple Syrup

Shake with ice and strain.

Lifeline

COCKTAIL GLASS

1 part Light Rum
1/2 part Apricot Brandy
1/2 part Brandy
1/2 part Sweet Vermouth
1/2 part Triple Sec

Shake with ice and strain.

Light Blue Something

COCKTAIL GLASS

1 1/2 parts Rum
1 part Blue Curaçao
1 part Light Cream

Shake with ice and strain.

Light Saber

COCKTAIL GLASS

1/2 part Vodka
1/2 part 151-Proof Rum
1 part Crème de Banane
1/2 part Triple Sec
1/2 part Vanilla Liqueur

Shake with ice and strain.

Light Years
COCKTAIL GLASS
1½ parts Drambuie®
½ part Blue Curaçao
1 part Cream
Shake with ice and strain.

Lightning
COCKTAIL GLASS
1 part Blue Curaçao
1 part Citrus Vodka
splash Crème de Cassis
splash Lime Juice
Shake with ice and strain.

Lightning Bolt
COCKTAIL GLASS
1 part Galliano
1 part Vodka
Shake with ice and strain.

Lilith
COCKTAIL GLASS
1 part Kirschwasser
1 part Grand Marnier®
1 part Campari®
Stir gently with ice and strain.

Lillet® Pad
COCKTAIL GLASS
1 part Gin
splash Advocaat
1½ parts Lillet®
Shake with ice and strain.

Lime Light
COCKTAIL GLASS
2 parts Vodka
½ part Melon Liqueur
½ part Grapefruit Juice
Shake with ice and strain.

The Limey
COCKTAIL GLASS
2½ parts Vodka
½ part Blue Curaçao
½ part Lime Juice
Shake with ice and strain.

Lino Ventura
COCKTAIL GLASS
1 part Irish Whiskey
½ part Frangelico®
½ part Bénédictine®
splash Vanilla Liqueur
Shake with ice and strain.

Linstead Cocktail
COCKTAIL GLASS
1 part Whiskey
1 part Pineapple Juice
splash Anisette
splash Lemon Juice
½ tsp Sugar
Shake with ice and strain.

Lip Sync
COCKTAIL GLASS
2 parts Vodka
1 part Limoncello
1 part Lime Juice
½ part Simple Syrup
dash Grenadine
Shake with ice and strain.

Liquid Art
COCKTAIL GLASS
2 parts Crème de Cassis
1 part Apricot Brandy
½ part Lemon Juice
Shake with ice and strain.

Liquid Coma
COCKTAIL GLASS
1½ parts Dark Rum
½ part Southern Comfort®
½ part Crème de Cacao (Dark)
Shake with ice and strain.

Liquid Gold
COCKTAIL GLASS
1 part Vodka
½ part Galliano®
½ part Crème de Cacao (White)
1 part Cream
Shake with ice and strain.

Liquid Nail
COCKTAIL GLASS
1 part Amaretto
1 part Coconut Rum
1 part Vodka
Shake with ice and strain.

Liquid Pants Remover
COCKTAIL GLASS
1 part Dark Rum
1 part Vodka
1 part Tequila
1 part Southern Comfort®
1 part Amaretto
Shake with ice and strain.

Liquid Prozac
COCKTAIL GLASS
1 part Apricot Brandy
½ part Orange Juice
½ part Pineapple Juice
splash Amaretto
splash Lemon Juice
Shake with ice and strain.

Little Black Devil
COCKTAIL GLASS
1 part Blue Curaçao
1 part Blueberry Schnapps
1 part Cherry Vodka
1 part Strawberry Liqueur
1 part Vodka
Shake with ice and strain.

Little Green Frog
COCKTAIL GLASS
2 parts Citrus Rum
1 part Banana Liqueur
1 part Coconut Rum
1 part Melon Liqueur
Shake with ice and strain.

Little Princess
COCKTAIL GLASS
1½ parts Light Rum
1½ parts Sweet Vermouth
Shake with ice and strain.

Little Rascal
COCKTAIL GLASS
1 part Gin
½ part Crème de Cassis
splash Peppermint Liqueur
½ part Lemon Juice
½ part Water
Shake with ice and strain.

Little Red Riding Hood
COCKTAIL GLASS
2 parts Gin
1 part Strawberry Liqueur
1 part Orange Juice
Shake with ice and strain.

Little White Lie
COCKTAIL GLASS
2 parts White Rum
1 part Lychee Liqueur
½ part Lime Juice
½ part Passion Fruit Juice
Shake with ice and strain.

Liveliness
COCKTAIL GLASS
½ part Blue Curaçao
1½ parts Irish Whiskey
½ part Orange Juice
½ part Pineapple Juice
Shake with ice and strain.

Living Monument
COCKTAIL GLASS

½ part Amaretto
½ part Drambuie®
½ part Chocolate Liqueur
1½ parts Milk

Shake with ice and strain.

Lola
COCKTAIL GLASS

1 part Rum
½ part Crème de Cacao (White)
½ part Orange Juice
½ part Mandarine Napoléon® Liqueur
½ part Crème

Shake with ice and strain.

Lola Flores
COCKTAIL GLASS

1 part Gin
1 part Raspberry Liqueur
1 part Dry Sherry

Shake with ice and strain.

London Bridges
COCKTAIL GLASS

2 parts Gin
½ part Blue Curaçao
½ part Lime Cordial
1 part Lemon Juice

Shake with ice and strain.

London Buck
COCKTAIL GLASS

2 parts Gin
1/12 part Simple Syrup
splash Maraschino Liqueur
2 dashes Bitters

Shake with ice and strain.

London Kamikaze
COCKTAIL GLASS

1 part Gin
1 part Triple Sec
½ part Sweetened Lime Juice

Shake with ice and strain.

Loop
COCKTAIL GLASS

1 part Apricot Brandy
1 part Sweet Vermouth
1 part Gin
splash Whiskey

Shake with ice and strain.

Lopez
COCKTAIL GLASS

⅔ part Gin
⅔ part Crème de Cassis
½ part Peach Schnapps
½ part Sweet & Sour Mix

Shake with ice and strain.

Lord Suffolk Cocktail
COCKTAIL GLASS

2 parts Dry Gin
½ part Sweet Vermouth
½ part Maraschino Liqueur

Shake with ice and strain.

Lorraine Cocktail
COCKTAIL GLASS

1¾ parts Kirschwasser
½ part Bénédictine®
2 splashes Lime Juice

Shake with ice and strain.

Lost Cherry
COCKTAIL GLASS

1 part Cherry Vodka
1 part Vanilla Vodka
½ part Crème de Cacao (White)
1 part Orange Juice
½ part Cream

Shake with ice and strain.

Louisiana Sour
COCKTAIL GLASS

1½ parts Bourbon
½ part Triple Sec
½ part Passion Fruit Nectar
1 part Pineapple Juice

Shake with ice and strain.

Louisville Cocktail
COCKTAIL GLASS
1 1/2 parts Whiskey
1/2 part Triple Sec
1/2 part Dry Sherry
2 dashes Orange Bitters
Shake with ice and strain.

Louisville Slugger
COCKTAIL GLASS
1 part Blackberry Brandy
1 part Dry Vermouth
1/2 part Lemon Juice
Shake with ice and strain.

Love Boat
COCKTAIL GLASS
1 part Vodka
1 part Cream of Coconut
1 part Pineapple Juice
splash Blue Curaçao
Shake with ice and strain.

Love Bull
COCKTAIL GLASS
1/2 part Tequila Reposado
1/2 part Parfait Amour
1 part Lychee Liqueur
1 part Lime Juice
Shake with ice and strain.

Love Cocktail
COCKTAIL GLASS
2 parts Sloe Gin
splash Raspberry Juice
splash Lemon Juice
1 Egg White
Shake with ice and strain.

The Love Doctor
COCKTAIL GLASS
2 parts Vodka
1 part Crème de Cacao (White)
1/2 part Raspberry Liqueur
Shake with ice and strain.

Love Heart
COCKTAIL GLASS
1 part Vodka
1/2 part Orange Juice
1/2 part Passion Fruit
splash Peach Schnapps
Shake with ice and strain.

Love Story
COCKTAIL GLASS
1 part Whiskey
1/2 part Triple Sec
1/2 part Melon Liqueur
1/2 part Lime Juice
Shake with ice and strain.

Love Supreme
COCKTAIL GLASS
2/3 part Crème de Banane
splash Crème de Cacao (White)
splash Coffee Liqueur
splash Butterscotch Schnapps
splash Galliano®
1 part Cream
Shake with ice and strain.

Lovers Cocktail
COCKTAIL GLASS
2 parts Sloe Gin
1 Egg White
splash Lemon Juice
splash Raspberry Juice
Shake with ice and strain.

Lover's Kiss
COCKTAIL GLASS
1/2 part Amaretto
1/2 part Cherry Brandy
1/2 part Crème de Cacao (Dark)
1 part Cream
Shake with ice and strain.

Lucid
COCKTAIL GLASS
1½ parts Cachaça
1 part Peppermint Liqueur
splash Dry Sherry
splash Simple Syrup
Shake with ice and strain.

Lucky Lady
COCKTAIL GLASS
1 part Dark Rum
½ part Crème de Cacao (White)
½ part Sambuca
1 part Cream
Shake with ice and strain.

Lugger
COCKTAIL GLASS
1 part Apple Brandy
1 part Brandy
1 part Apricot Brandy
Shake with ice and strain.

Luke Skywalker
COCKTAIL GLASS
2 parts Blue Curaçao
1 part Gin
2 parts Dry Vermouth
splash Lemon Juice
Shake with ice and strain.

Luna City
COCKTAIL GLASS
1 part Sloe Gin
1 part Passion Fruit Liqueur
1 part Cranberry Juice Cocktail
splash Sweet & Sour Mix
Shake with ice and strain.

Lunar Landing
COCKTAIL GLASS
1½ parts Light Rum
¾ part Brandy
2 splashes Grenadine
splash Lemon Juice
Shake with ice and strain.

Lust for Life
COCKTAIL GLASS
2 parts Orange Vodka
½ part Galliano
½ part Peach Schnapps
1 part Orange Juice
½ part Cream
Shake with ice and strain.

Luxury
COCKTAIL GLASS
1 part Dry Gin
1 part Crème de Banane
1 part Sweet Vermouth
1 part Lime Juice
1 part Pimm's® No. 1 Cup
dash Bitters
Shake with ice and strain.

Lylyblue
COCKTAIL GLASS
1 part Vodka
1 part Lime Juice
1 part Lychee Liqueur
splash Blue Curaçao
Shake with ice and strain.

Lysogenenis
COCKTAIL GLASS
1 part Light Rum
½ part Crème de Cacao (Dark)
⅔ part Milk
splash Blue Curaçao
Shake with ice and strain.

Ma Bonnie Wee Hen
COCKTAIL GLASS
1½ parts Scotch
½ part Cream Sherry
½ part Orange Juice
½ part Lemon Juice
splash Grenadine
Shake with ice and strain.

Mac Daddy

COCKTAIL GLASS

2 parts Gin
1/2 part Maraschino Liqueur
1 part Pineapple Juice

Shake with ice and strain.

Macaroni Cocktail

COCKTAIL GLASS

1 1/2 parts Absinthe
1 1/2 parts Sweet Vermouth

Shake with ice and strain.

Macaroon

COCKTAIL GLASS

2 parts Vodka
1/2 part Amaretto
1/2 part Crème de Cacao (Dark)

Shake with ice and strain.

Macbeth

COCKTAIL GLASS

2 parts Scotch
2 splashes Blue Curaçao
2 splashes Amaretto
1/2 part Lemon Juice
1 tsp Sugar

Shake with ice and strain.

Machiavelli

COCKTAIL GLASS

1 part Crème de Banane
splash Galliano®
splash Anisette
1 part Lemon Juice

Shake with ice and strain.

Machintoch

COCKTAIL GLASS

1 part Vodka
1/2 part Blackberry Liqueur
1/2 part Apple Brandy
2 parts Cream

Shake with ice and strain.

Macubo

COCKTAIL GLASS

2 parts Whiskey
3/4 part Blue Curaçao
1/2 part Simple Syrup
1/4 part Maraschino Liqueur

Shake with ice and strain.

Madam Delight

COCKTAIL GLASS

1 part Blackberry Liqueur
1 part Amaretto
1/2 part Orange Juice
1/2 part Milk

Shake with ice and strain.

Madame Butterfly

COCKTAIL GLASS

1 part Apple Brandy
1 part Gin
1/2 part Blue Curaçao
1/2 part Dry Vermouth

Shake with ice and strain.

Madeira Cocktail

COCKTAIL GLASS

1 1/2 parts Rye Whiskey
1 1/2 parts Triple Sec
splash Grenadine
splash Lemon Juice

Shake with ice and strain.

Magic Flute

COCKTAIL GLASS

2 parts Mozart White Chocolate Liqueur
1 part Amaretto

Shake with ice and strain.

Magic Star

COCKTAIL GLASS

3/4 part Crème de Cacao (White)
3/4 part Pisang Ambon® Liqueur
1/2 part Cream
1/2 part Kiwi Schnapps
splash Grenadine

Shake with ice and strain.

Magician

COCKTAIL GLASS

1/4 part Cointreau®
1 1/2 parts Gin
1/4 part Grand Marnier®
splash Dry Vermouth
1/2 part Lillet®

Shake with ice and strain.

Mah-Jonng

COCKTAIL GLASS

1/2 part Cointreau®
1 part Gin
1/2 part Dark Rum

Shake with ice and strain.

Mahukona

COCKTAIL GLASS

2 parts Light Rum
1/2 part Triple Sec
1/4 part Amaretto
dash Orange Bitters

Shake with ice and strain.

Maiden's Dream

COCKTAIL GLASS

1 part Gin
1 part Pernod®
1 part Grenadine

Shake with ice and strain.

Majestic

COCKTAIL GLASS

1 part Gin
1 part Grapefruit Juice
1/2 part Crème de Banane

Shake with ice and strain.

Majoba

COCKTAIL GLASS

1 part Dark Rum
1/2 part Triple Sec
1/4 part Crème de Cacao (Dark)
1/4 part Crème de Banane
splash Pineapple Juice

Shake with ice and strain.

Major Tom

COCKTAIL GLASS

1 1/2 parts Vodka
1/2 part Triple Sec
1/2 part Kirschwasser
1/2 part Grapefruit Juice

Shake with ice and strain.

Malibu Wave

COCKTAIL GLASS

1 part Tequila
1/2 part Triple Sec
1 1/2 parts Sweet & Sour Mix
splash Blue Curaçao

Shake with ice and strain.

Malmaison

COCKTAIL GLASS

2 parts Light Rum
1/2 part Cream Sherry
2 splashes Lemon Juice

Shake with ice and strain.

Maltese Skies

COCKTAIL GLASS

1 part Orange Juice
1 part Dark Rum
1/2 part Parfait Amour
1/2 part Passion Fruit

Shake with ice and strain.

Mama Mia

COCKTAIL GLASS

1 1/2 parts Vodka
1 part Amaretto
1/2 part Cream

Shake with ice and strain.

Man Eater

COCKTAIL GLASS

1 1/2 parts Brandy
1/2 part Southern Comfort®
dash Orange Bitters

Shake with ice and strain.

Mañana
COCKTAIL GLASS

1½ parts Light Rum
½ part Apricot Brandy
½ part Grenadine

Shake with ice and strain.

Mandarin Dream
COCKTAIL GLASS

2 parts Orange Vodka
splash Orange Juice
splash Cranberry Juice Cocktail

Shake with ice and strain.

Mandarin Metropolitan
COCKTAIL GLASS

1½ parts Orange Vodka
1 part Cranberry Juice Cocktail
½ part Sweetened Lime Juice

Shake with ice and strain.

Manhasset
COCKTAIL GLASS

1½ parts Whiskey
splash Sweet Vermouth
splash Dry Vermouth
2 splashes Lemon Juice

Shake with ice and strain.

Manhattan South
COCKTAIL GLASS

1 part Gin
½ part Southern Comfort®
½ part Dry Vermouth
dash Angostura® Bitters

Shake with ice and strain.

Manhattan (Perfect)
COCKTAIL GLASS

1½ parts Whiskey
½ part Dry Vermouth
½ part Sweet Vermouth

Shake with ice and strain.

Maple Leaf
COCKTAIL GLASS

1 part Canadian Club® Rye
¼ part Lemon Juice
splash Maple Syrup

Shake with ice and strain.

Maraca
COCKTAIL GLASS

1½ parts Tequila
½ part Lemon Juice
2 splashes Grenadine
1 part Pineapple Juice

Shake with ice and strain.

Mardi Gras
COCKTAIL GLASS

1½ parts Light Rum
½ part Lime Juice
¼ part Crème de Banane
¼ part Southern Comfort®

Shake with ice and strain.

Mariachi-Loco
COCKTAIL GLASS

1½ parts Sweet & Sour Mix
1 part Passion Fruit
½ part Tequila Reposado

Shake with ice and strain.

Marina
COCKTAIL GLASS

1½ parts Dry Gin
1 part Dry Vermouth
2 dashes Parfait Amour
splash Lemon Juice

Shake with ice and strain.

Mariposa
COCKTAIL GLASS

1 part Light Rum
½ part Brandy
splash Grenadine
2 splashes Orange Juice
2 splashes Lemon Juice

Shake with ice and strain.

Marital Bliss
COCKTAIL GLASS

1 part Light Rum
1 part Apricot Brandy
1 part Melon Liqueur

Shake with ice and strain.

Marmalade Cocktail
COCKTAIL GLASS

2 parts Gin
1 part Lemon Juice
2 splashes Orange Marmalade

Shake with ice and strain.

Le Marseillaise
COCKTAIL GLASS

1 part Gin
1 part Blue Curaçao
½ part Pastis
splash Lime Juice

Shake with ice and strain.

Martinez Cocktail
COCKTAIL GLASS

1 part Gin
1 part Dry Vermouth
¼ splash Triple Sec
dash Orange Bitters

Stir gently with ice and strain.

Mary Pickford Cocktail
COCKTAIL GLASS

1 part Light Rum
1 part Pineapple Juice
splash Maraschino Liqueur
splash Grenadine

Shake with ice and strain.

Mary Rose
COCKTAIL GLASS

1½ parts Gin
½ part Lemon Juice
½ part Orange Juice
¼ part Grenadine
dash Bitters

Shake with ice and strain.

Massive Attack
COCKTAIL GLASS

2 parts Silver Tequila
½ part Cherry Brandy
½ part Galliano®
½ part Lemon Juice

Shake with ice and strain.

Matrix
COCKTAIL GLASS

1 part Light Rum
½ part Triple Sec
½ part Passion Fruit
½ part Lime Cordial
splash Grenadine

Shake with ice and strain.

Maurice Cocktail
COCKTAIL GLASS

1 part Gin
½ part Sweet Vermouth
½ part Dry Vermouth
½ part Orange Juice
dash Bitters

Shake with ice and strain.

Max the Silent
COCKTAIL GLASS

1 part Añejo Rum
½ part Brandy
½ part Applejack
splash Anisette

Shake with ice and strain.

Maxim
COCKTAIL GLASS

1½ parts Gin
1 part Dry Vermouth
splash Crème de Cacao (White)

Shake with ice and strain.

Mazatlan Morning

COCKTAIL GLASS

1 part Blackberry Liqueur
1 part Silver Tequila
splash Lime Juice
1 part Lemon-Lime Soda
1/2 part Honey

Shake with ice and strain over ice.

McDuff

COCKTAIL GLASS

1 1/2 parts Scotch
1/2 part Triple Sec
2 dashes Bitters

Shake with ice and strain.

Me Amigo de la Canaria

COCKTAIL GLASS

1/2 part Lychee Liqueur
2/3 part Lemon Juice
2/3 part Mango Juice
1 part Passion Fruit Juice

Shake with ice and strain.

Medical Solution

COCKTAIL GLASS

1 1/2 parts Vodka
1/2 part Parfait Amour
1 part Cream

Shake with ice and strain.

Mediterranean Delight

COCKTAIL GLASS

2 parts Gin
1/2 part Crème de Banane
1/2 part Grapefruit Juice

Shake with ice and strain.

Mellon Collie and the Infinite Gladness

COCKTAIL GLASS

1 part Light Rum
1/2 part Melon Liqueur
1/2 part Coconut Rum
1/2 part Chocolate Syrup
1 part Cream

Shake with ice and strain.

Melon Heaven

COCKTAIL GLASS

1 part Vodka
1 part Melon Liqueur
1/2 part Triple Sec
1/2 part Lime Juice

Shake with ice and strain.

Melon Lychee

COCKTAIL GLASS

1 1/2 parts Melon Liqueur
1/2 part Lychee Liqueur
1 part Grapefruit Juice

Shake with ice and strain.

Melrose Beauty

COCKTAIL GLASS

1 part Vodka
1/2 part Raspberry Liqueur
1/2 part Cranberry Juice Cocktail
splash Pineapple Juice
splash Lemon Juice
splash Lime Juice

Shake with ice and strain.

Memphis Belle Cocktail

COCKTAIL GLASS

1 1/2 parts Brandy
3/4 part Southern Comfort®
1/2 part Lemon Juice
4 dashes Bitters

Shake with ice and strain.

Ménage à Trois

COCKTAIL GLASS

1 part Dark Rum
1 part Triple Sec
1 part Light Cream

Shake with ice and strain.

Mentholated Cognac

COCKTAIL GLASS

1 part Peppermint Liqueur
1 part Rémy Martin® VSOP
1 part Dry Vermouth

Shake with ice and strain.

Merchant Prince

COCKTAIL GLASS

2/3 part Vodka
1 part Cherry Brandy
2/3 part Drambuie®
2/3 part Vanilla Liqueur

Shake with ice and strain.

Merletto

COCKTAIL GLASS

1 part Crème de Cacao (White)
1 part Advocaat
1 part Coffee

Shake with ice and strain.

Mermaid

COCKTAIL GLASS

1 part Aquavit
1/2 part Dry Vermouth
1/2 part Cherry Brandy
1 Egg White
splash Lime Cordial

Shake with ice and strain.

Merry Go Round

COCKTAIL GLASS

1 part Cherry Liqueur
1 part Cherry Vodka
1 part Maraschino Liqueur

Shake with ice and strain.

Merry Widow Cocktail

COCKTAIL GLASS

1 1/2 parts Dry Vermouth
1 1/2 parts Gin
splash Bénédictine®
splash Anisette
dash Bitters

Shake with ice and strain. Garnish with Lemon Twist.

Meteorite

COCKTAIL GLASS

1 1/2 parts Vodka
1/2 part Triple Sec
1/2 part Cherry Brandy
2/3 part Dry Vermouth

Shake with ice and strain.

El Metraya

COCKTAIL GLASS

1 part Tia Maria®
1/2 part Rum
2 parts Simple Syrup

Shake with ice and strain.

Metropolitan

COCKTAIL GLASS

2 parts Brandy
1/2 part Sweet Vermouth
dash Bitters
dash Sugar

Shake with ice and strain.

Mets Manhattan

COCKTAIL GLASS

1 1/2 parts Whiskey
1/4 part Sweet Vermouth
1/4 part Strawberry Liqueur

Shake with ice and strain.

Mexican Bee Sting

COCKTAIL GLASS

1 1/2 parts Tequila
splash Pernod®
splash Crème de Menthe (White)

Shake with ice and strain.

Mexican Clover Club

COCKTAIL GLASS

1 1/2 parts Silver Tequila
1/2 part Grenadine
1/2 part Simple Syrup
1 Egg White

Shake with ice and strain.

Mexican Sheets

COCKTAIL GLASS

2/3 part Silver Tequila
2/3 part Triple Sec
1 part Peach Schnapps
1/2 part Sweet & Sour Mix
splash Lime Juice

Shake with ice and strain.

Mexican Snowball

COCKTAIL GLASS

2/3 part Crème de Cacao (Dark)
2/3 part Silver Tequila
2/3 part Cream
2/3 part Cream of Coconut

Shake with ice and strain.

Mexican Surfer

COCKTAIL GLASS

2 parts Coconut Rum
2 parts Tequila

Shake with ice and strain.

Mexico City Ambulance

COCKTAIL GLASS

1 part Silver Tequila
1 part Melon Liqueur
1/2 part Sweet & Sour Mix
1/2 part Grapefruit Juice

Shake with ice and strain.

Mezzanine

COCKTAIL GLASS

2 parts Brandy
splash Blue Curaçao
splash Kirschwasser
splash Maraschino Liqueur
splash Dark Rum

Shake with ice and strain.

Mi Casa, Su Casa

COCKTAIL GLASS

splash Raspberry Liqueur
1/2 part Grand Marnier®
1/2 part Gold Tequila
splash Lime Juice

Shake with ice and strain.

Mia Vida

COCKTAIL GLASS

1 part Tequila Reposado
1/2 part Cream
1/2 part Crème de Cacao (Dark)

Shake with ice and strain.

Miami Beach Cocktail

COCKTAIL GLASS

1 part Dry Vermouth
1 part Scotch
1 part Grapefruit Juice

Shake with ice and strain.

Miami Special

COCKTAIL GLASS

1 part Light Rum
1/4 part Crème de Menthe (White)
3/4 part Lemon Juice

Shake with ice and strain.

Mickie Walker Cocktail

COCKTAIL GLASS

2 parts Scotch
1 part Sweet Vermouth
splash Grenadine

Shake with ice and strain.

Midnight Cap

COCKTAIL GLASS

2 parts Apricot Brandy
1/2 part Blue Curaçao
1/2 part Lemon Juice

Shake with ice and strain.

Midnight Delight

COCKTAIL GLASS

1 1/2 parts Vodka
1 part Crème de Cacao (White)
1 part Chocolate Mint Liqueur

Shake with ice and strain.

Midnight in Paris
COCKTAIL GLASS

1 part Lemon Vodka
1 part Raspberry Rum
1/2 part Chambord
1/2 part St-Germain
1/2 part Lime Juice
dash Absinthe

Shake with ice and strain.

Midnight Joy
COCKTAIL GLASS

1 1/2 parts Crème de Cacao (White)
1 1/2 parts Black Sambuca

Shake with ice and strain.

Midnight Rhapsody
COCKTAIL GLASS

1/2 part Crème de Cacao (Dark)
1/2 part Whiskey
1/4 part Crème de Menthe (White)
1/4 part Vanilla Vodka
1 part Cream

Shake with ice and strain.

Midnight Sun
COCKTAIL GLASS

2 parts Vodka
1 part Cointreau®
1 part Apricot Brandy
1 part Grenadine
1/2 part Lemon Juice

Shake with ice and strain.

Midsummer Night's Dreamer
COCKTAIL GLASS

2/3 part Blackberry Liqueur
1 part Sloe Gin
1/2 part Lemon Juice
1/2 part Cherry Syrup

Shake with ice and strain.

MILF
COCKTAIL GLASS

1/2 part Irish Cream Liqueur
1/2 part Frangelico®
1/2 part Light Rum
1 part Cream

Shake with ice and strain.

Miller's Special
COCKTAIL GLASS

2 parts Gin
1/2 part Lychee Liqueur
splash Crème de Cassis
splash Lime Juice

Shake with ice and strain.

Millionaire Cocktail
COCKTAIL GLASS

1 1/2 parts Whiskey
1/2 part Triple Sec
splash Grenadine
1 Egg White

Shake with ice and strain.

Mint ChocoChata
COCKTAIL GLASS

3 parts RumChata
1 part Chocolate Vodka
splash Crème de Menthe (Green)

Shake with ice and strain.

Mintzerac
COCKTAIL GLASS

2/3 part Vodka
1 part Peppermint Liqueur
1/2 part Melon Liqueur
1/2 part Lime Juice

Shake with ice and strain.

Mirage
COCKTAIL GLASS

1 part Melon Liqueur
1 part Pineapple Juice
1/2 part Lemon Juice
1/2 part Strawberry Juice

Shake with ice and strain.

Mirror Conspiracy
COCKTAIL GLASS
2 parts Light Rum
1/2 part Amer Picon®
splash Cherry Brandy
splash Pear Liqueur
Shake with ice and strain.

Miss Belle
COCKTAIL GLASS
1 1/2 parts Dark Rum
1/2 part Grand Marnier®
2 splashes Crème de Cacao (Dark)
Shake with ice and strain.

Mississippi Steamboat
COCKTAIL GLASS
1 part Amaretto
1 part Brandy
1 part Pineapple Juice
splash Lime Juice
Shake with ice and strain.

Missouri Mule
COCKTAIL GLASS
1 1/2 parts Bourbon
1 part Crème de Cassis
Shake with ice and strain.

Missouri Rattlesnake
COCKTAIL GLASS
1 part Southern Comfort®
1 part Triple Sec
1/2 part Grenadine
1 part Orange Juice
Shake with ice and strain.

The MochaChata
COCKTAIL GLASS
2 parts Dark Chocolate Liqueur
2 parts RumChata
1 part Espresso Vodka
Shake with ice and strain.

Mocha Mint
COCKTAIL GLASS
1 part Coffee Brandy
1 part Crème de Menthe (White)
1 part Crème de Cacao (White)
Shake with ice and strain.

Mockingbird
COCKTAIL GLASS
1 1/2 parts Tequila
1 part Lime Juice
2 splashes Crème de Menthe (White)
Shake with ice and strain.

Modern Castle
COCKTAIL GLASS
1 part Melon Liqueur
1/2 part Peppermint Liqueur
1 part Irish Cream Liqueur
1 part Milk
Shake with ice and strain.

Moll Flanders Cocktail
COCKTAIL GLASS
1 1/2 parts Gin
1 part Sloe Gin
1 part Dry Vermouth
Shake with ice and strain.

Molly Mounds
COCKTAIL GLASS
1 part Coconut Rum
1 part Cream of Coconut
1 part Dark Chocolate Liqueur
Shake with ice and strain.

Molokini
COCKTAIL GLASS
1 part Kiwi Schnapps
1 part Blue Curaçao
splash Lime Juice
Shake with ice and strain.

Mon Amour

COCKTAIL GLASS

1 1/2 parts Gin
1/2 part Orange Juice
1/4 part Sake

Shake with ice and strain.

Mon Cherie

COCKTAIL GLASS

1 part Crème de Cacao (White)
1 part Cream
1 part Cherry Brandy

Shake with ice and strain.

Monkey Gland Cocktail

COCKTAIL GLASS

2 parts Gin
splash Bénédictine®
1/2 part Orange Juice
splash Grenadine

Shake with ice and strain.

Montmarte

COCKTAIL GLASS

2 parts Gin
1/2 part Triple Sec
1/2 part Sweet Vermouth

Shake with ice and strain.

Montreal after Dark

COCKTAIL GLASS

1 1/2 parts Crème de Cacao (White)
1 1/2 parts Whiskey
splash Cream

Shake with ice and strain.

Moo Moo Land

COCKTAIL GLASS

1 part Light Rum
1 part Crème de Banane
1/4 part Grenadine
1 1/2 parts Cream

Shake with ice and strain.

Moon Quake Shake

COCKTAIL GLASS

1 part Coffee Brandy
1 1/2 parts Dark Rum
2 splashes Lemon Juice

Shake with ice and strain.

Moonglow

COCKTAIL GLASS

1 1/2 parts Crème de Menthe (White)
1 1/2 parts Brandy

Shake with ice and strain.

Moonlight

COCKTAIL GLASS

1 part Cream
1 part Cognac
1 part Chocolate Mint Liqueur
splash Mandarine Napoléon® Liqueur

Shake with ice and strain.

Moonshine Bells

COCKTAIL GLASS

1 1/2 parts Triple Sec
1 part Lime Juice
1 part Triple Sec
splash Blackcurrant Juice

Shake with ice and strain.

Moose River Hummer

COCKTAIL GLASS

1 part Galliano®
1 part 151-Proof Rum
1 part Rye Whiskey
1 part Rumple Minze®

Shake with ice and strain.

Morgan's Mountain

COCKTAIL GLASS

1 1/2 parts Spiced Rum
1/2 part Crème de Cacao (White)
1 part Heavy Cream
splash Coffee Liqueur

Shake with ice and strain.

Morituri Te Salutant

COCKTAIL GLASS

½ part Cherry Brandy
½ part Dry Vermouth
½ part Campari®
1½ parts Light Rum

Shake with ice and strain.

Mortal Kombat®

COCKTAIL GLASS

⅔ part Lychee Liqueur
2 parts Sake
½ part Lemon Juice
splash Tabasco® Sauce

Shake with ice and strain.

Mother Russia

COCKTAIL GLASS

1½ parts Vodka
½ part Maraschino Liqueur
½ part Coconut Rum
1 part Cream
½ part Egg White

Shake with ice and strain.

Mother Tongue

COCKTAIL GLASS

1 part Crème de Banane
1 part Red Curaçao
¼ part Light Rum
splash Simple Syrup

Shake with ice and strain.

Mounds Bar Cocktail

COCKTAIL GLASS

1½ parts Chocolate Vodka
1½ parts Coconut Rum

Shake with ice and strain.

Mousse Cherry

COCKTAIL GLASS

1 part Vodka
1 part Grapefruit Juice
½ part Cherry Brandy

Shake with ice and strain.

Mozart

COCKTAIL GLASS

1½ parts Añejo Rum
½ part Sweet Vermouth
splash Triple Sec
2 dashes Orange Bitters

Shake with ice and strain. Garnish with Lemon Twist.

Mr. Manhattan Cocktail

COCKTAIL GLASS

2 parts Gin
dash Powdered Sugar
½ part Mineral Water
splash Orange Juice
4 Mint Leaves

Muddle the Mint with the Water and Sugar in the bottom of a shaker. Add Gin and Orange Juice. Shake with ice and strain.

Muddy River

COCKTAIL GLASS

1 part Coffee Liqueur
1 part Coconut Rum
1 part Light Cream

Shake with ice and strain.

Mud Wrestle

COCKTAIL GLASS

1 part Brandy
1 part Coffee Liqueur
1 part Crème de Cacao (Dark)
1 part Irish Cream Liqueur
1 part Cream

Shake with ice and strain.

Mulata

COCKTAIL GLASS

2 parts Light Rum
½ part Crème de Cacao (Dark)
½ tbsp Sugar

Shake with ice and strain.

Mulch Muncher

COCKTAIL GLASS

1 part Banana Liqueur
1 part Vodka
½ part Strega
1 part Orange Juice

Shake with ice and strain.

Mule's Hind Leg

COCKTAIL GLASS

¾ part Gin
¾ part Brandy
¾ part Bénédictine®
¾ part Simple Syrup

Shake with ice and strain.

Multi-Colored Smurf®

COCKTAIL GLASS

½ part Blueberry Schnapps
½ part Apricot Brandy
½ part Vodka
½ part Mango Nectar
1 part Orange Juice

Shake with ice and strain.

Muse

COCKTAIL GLASS

1 part Blackberry Liqueur
1 part Advocaat
1 part Apple Brandy

Shake with ice and strain.

Mutiny

COCKTAIL GLASS

1½ parts Dark Rum
½ part Dubonnet® Rouge
2 dashes Bitters

Shake with ice and strain.

Mystic

COCKTAIL GLASS

1½ parts Sloe Gin
½ part Triple Sec
⅔ part Lemon Juice
splash Honey
1 part Apple Juice

Shake with ice and strain.

Mysticism

COCKTAIL GLASS

1 part Scotch
½ part Triple Sec
½ part Sweetened Lime Juice
splash Lemon Juice

Shake with ice and strain.

Nachtmar

COCKTAIL GLASS

1 part Peach Schnapps
1 part Jägermeister®
1 part Cranberry Juice Cocktail

Shake with ice and strain.

Naked Lady

COCKTAIL GLASS

1 part Light Rum
1 part Sweet Vermouth
splash Apricot Brandy
splash Lemon Juice
splash Grenadine

Shake with ice and strain.

Naked Pear

COCKTAIL GLASS

½ part Apple Vodka
½ part Melon Liqueur
½ part Triple Sec
1 part Pineapple Juice
splash Sweet & Sour Mix

Shake with ice and strain.

Napoleon

COCKTAIL GLASS

2 parts Gin
splash Blue Curaçao
splash Dubonnet® Blonde

Shake with ice and strain.

Nasty
COCKTAIL GLASS

1¼ parts Vodka
¾ part Coffee Liqueur
¾ part Wild Turkey® Bourbon
¾ part Crème de Cacao (Dark)
½ part Cream

Shake with ice and strain.

National Cocktail
COCKTAIL GLASS

2 parts Rum
3 splashes Apricot Brandy
½ part Pineapple Juice
3 splashes Lime Juice

Shake with ice and strain.

Nature
COCKTAIL GLASS

1 part Tequila Reposado
1 part Peach Schnapps
1 part Cream

Shake with ice and strain.

Naughty Farmer
COCKTAIL GLASS

1 part Sloe Gin
1 part Kirschwasser
1 part Cream
splash Amaretto

Shake with ice and strain.

Navy Cocktail
COCKTAIL GLASS

1½ parts Light Rum
1 part Orange Juice
1 part Dry Vermouth

Shake with ice and strain.

Negroni
COCKTAIL GLASS

2 parts Gin
¾ part Campari®
½ part Dry Vermouth

Shake with ice and strain. Garnish with an Orange Twist.

NeO
COCKTAIL GLASS

1 part Jim Beam®
1 part Crème de Cassis
½ part Cinzano®
splash Apple Juice

Shake with ice and strain.

Neon Lights
COCKTAIL GLASS

1½ parts Silver Tequila
½ part Melon Liqueur
½ part Blue Curaçao
½ part Lime Juice

Shake with ice and strain.

Neopolitan Cocktail
COCKTAIL GLASS

1½ parts Cranberry Vodka
½ part Cointreau®
splash Raspberry Liqueur
splash Lime Juice

Shake with ice and strain.

Neptune's Pond
COCKTAIL GLASS

1½ parts Vodka
1½ parts Dubonnet® Blonde

Shake with ice and strain.

Network Special
COCKTAIL GLASS

1½ parts Light Rum
½ part Coffee Brandy
splash 151-Proof Rum
¼ part Crème

Shake with ice and strain.

Nevins
COCKTAIL GLASS

1½ parts Bourbon
¾ part Apricot Brandy
¾ part Lemon Juice
½ part Grapefruit Juice
dash Bitters

Shake with ice and strain.

New Gold Dream

COCKTAIL GLASS

1½ parts Goldschläger®
1 part Galliano®
½ part Cream

Shake with ice and strain.

New Mexico

COCKTAIL GLASS

1 part Mezcal
½ part Blue Curaçao
½ part Triple Sec
½ part Grand Marnier®
½ part Lemon Juice

Shake with ice and strain.

New Orleans Cocktail

ROCKS GLASS

2 parts Bourbon
½ part Pernod®
splash Simple Syrup
splash Anisette
dash Orange Bitters

Shake with ice and strain over ice.

New Orleans Hooker

COCKTAIL GLASS

1 part Southern Comfort®
1 part Blackberry Liqueur
splash Vanilla Liqueur

Shake with ice and strain.

New Wave

COCKTAIL GLASS

1 part Peach
1 part Pineapple Juice
1 part Cream

Shake with ice and strain.

New York Lemonade

COCKTAIL GLASS

1 part Citrus Vodka
½ part Grand Marnier®
½ part Lemon Juice
1 part Club Soda

Stir gently with ice and strain.

Newport Chocolate

COCKTAIL GLASS

⅔ part Crème de Cacao (White)
⅔ part Chocolate Mint Liqueur
⅔ part Irish Cream Liqueur
1 part Milk

Shake with ice and strain.

Nicky Finn

COCKTAIL GLASS

1 part Apricot Brandy
1 part Cointreau®
1 part Lemon Juice
splash Pernod®

Shake with ice and strain.

A Night in Corfu

COCKTAIL GLASS

1 part Banana Liqueur
1 part Light Rum
splash Grenadine
1 part Lemon Juice
splash Milk

Shake with ice and strain over ice.

Night Light

COCKTAIL GLASS

1½ parts Rum
1 part Triple Sec
1 Egg Yolk

Shake with ice and strain.

Night of the Demons

COCKTAIL GLASS

2 parts Vodka
1 part Peach Schnapps
½ part Blue Curaçao
½ part Pineapple Juice

Shake with ice and strain.

Night Stars
COCKTAIL GLASS

1 part Brandy
½ part Whiskey
½ part Triple Sec
splash Crème de Banane
splash Apple Juice

Shake with ice and strain.

Nightmare
COCKTAIL GLASS

1½ parts Gin
½ part Cherry Brandy
½ part Madeira
splash Orange Juice

Shake with ice and strain.

Nineteen and Single
COCKTAIL GLASS

⅔ part Raspberry Liqueur
⅔ part Blackberry Liqueur
1 part Irish Cream Liqueur
1 part Milk

Shake with ice and strain.

Nineteen Twenty
COCKTAIL GLASS

1 part Dry Vermouth
1 part Gin
1 part Kirschwasser
splash Pastis

Shake with ice and strain.

Nineteenth Hole
COCKTAIL GLASS

1½ parts Gin
1 part Dry Vermouth
splash Sweet Vermouth
dash Bitters

Shake with ice and strain.

Ninotchka Cocktail
COCKTAIL GLASS

1½ parts Vodka
½ part Crème de Cacao (White)
½ part Lemon Juice

Shake with ice and strain.

Nitro Cocktail
COLLINS GLASS

1½ parts Vodka
¾ part Scotch
1 part Cranberry Juice Cocktail
1 part Orange Juice

Build over ice and stir.

Nocturnal
COCKTAIL GLASS

1½ parts Crème de Cacao (Dark)
1½ parts Cream

Shake with ice and strain.

Nomad
COCKTAIL GLASS

1 part Cointreau®
1 part Melon Liqueur
1 part Lemon Juice

Shake with ice and strain.

Nordic Sea
COCKTAIL GLASS

1 part Dry Gin
1 part Kiwi Schnapps
½ part Blue Curaçao
splash Pineapple Juice

Shake with ice and strain.

North Pole Cocktail
COCKTAIL GLASS

1 part Gin
½ part Maraschino Liqueur
½ part Lemon Juice
1 Egg White

Shake with ice and strain.

Northern Exposure
COCKTAIL GLASS

1½ parts Gin
1 part Apricot Brandy
1 part Triple Sec
2 splashes Lemon Juice

Shake with ice and strain.

Nostromo
COCKTAIL GLASS

1 part Limoncello
1/2 part Apricot Brandy
1/2 part Mandarine Napoléon® Liqueur
1/2 part Lemon Juice
1/2 part Simple Syrup

Shake with ice and strain.

Nostromo's Chaser
COCKTAIL GLASS

1 part Armagnac
1/2 part Vanilla Liqueur
1/2 part Gin
splash Crème de Noyaux
dash Orange Bitters

Stir gently with ice and strain.

Notre Dame
COCKTAIL GLASS

1 part Calvados Apple Brandy
1/2 part Blue Curaçao
splash Lemon Juice

Shake with ice and strain.

Nougat Ice Cream
COCKTAIL GLASS

1 part Cream
1 part Hazelnut Liqueur
1 part Vanilla Liqueur

Shake with ice and strain.

Nuts and Berries
COCKTAIL GLASS

1 part Frangelico®
1 part Raspberry Liqueur
1 part Light Cream

Shake with ice and strain.

Nutty Angel
COCKTAIL GLASS

1 part Hazelnut Liqueur
1 part Irish Cream Liqueur
1 part Vodka
1/2 part Crème de Cacao (Dark)

Shake with ice and strain.

Nutty Stinger
COCKTAIL GLASS

1 1/2 parts Amaretto
1 1/2 parts Crème de Menthe (White)

Shake with ice and strain.

Oakland Cocktail
COCKTAIL GLASS

1 part Vodka
1 part Dry Vermouth
1 part Orange Juice

Shake with ice and strain.

Obsession
COCKTAIL GLASS

1 part Vodka
1/2 part Passion Fruit Liqueur
1/2 part Pisang Ambon® Liqueur
1 part Orange Juice

Shake with ice and strain.

Obsidian
COCKTAIL GLASS

1 part Dark Rum
1/2 part Blackberry Liqueur
1/2 part Black Sambuca
1/2 part Lemon Juice
splash Cherry Brandy

Shake with ice and strain.

Ocean Drive
COCKTAIL GLASS

1 1/2 parts Coconut Rum
3/4 part Blue Curaçao
splash Orange Juice
splash Pineapple Juice
splash Cranberry Juice Cocktail

Shake with ice and strain.

Ocean Spray
COCKTAIL GLASS

2 parts Mango Rum
2 parts Cranberry Juice
1/2 part Lime Juice

Shake with ice and strain.

Oceanographer
COCKTAIL GLASS

½ part Light Rum
½ part Peach Schnapps
½ part Apple Brandy
½ part Cranberry Juice Cocktail
½ part Orange Juice
½ part Pineapple Juice

Shake with ice and strain.

Odin's Juice
COCKTAIL GLASS

1½ parts Coconut Rum
½ part Spiced Rum
splash Grenadine
splash Orange Juice
splash Pineapple Juice

Shake with ice and strain.

Off-White
COCKTAIL GLASS

1 part Vodka
1 part Amaretto
1 part Crème de Coconut
1 part Vanilla Liqueur

Shake with ice and strain.

Old Car
COCKTAIL GLASS

1 part Vodka
½ part Apricot Brandy
½ part Triple Sec
¼ part Grapefruit Juice

Shake with ice and strain.

Old Etonion
COCKTAIL GLASS

1 part Gin
1 part Lillet®
2 splashes Crème de Noyaux
2 dashes Orange Bitters

Shake with ice and strain.

Old Flame
COCKTAIL GLASS

1 part Gin
½ part Cointreau
½ part Sweet Vermouth
2 parts Orange Juice
splash Campari

Shake with ice and strain.

Old San Juan Cocktail
COCKTAIL GLASS

1½ parts Dark Rum
¼ part Grenadine
¼ part Pineapple Juice

Shake with ice and strain.

Old Switzerland
COCKTAIL GLASS

1 part Amaretto
splash Crème de Cacao (White)
splash Chocolate Syrup

Shake with ice and strain.

Olden Times
COCKTAIL GLASS

1½ parts Scotch
1½ parts Carpano Punt e Mes®
½ part Cherry Brandy

Shake with ice and strain.

Ole
COCKTAIL GLASS

2 parts Silver Tequila
1 part Coffee
½ part Simple Syrup

Shake with ice and strain.

Olive in an Olive
COCKTAIL GLASS

1½ parts Gold Tequila
1½ parts Sweet Vermouth
splash Blue Curaçao

Shake with ice and strain. Garnish with Olive.

Omen of Fire

COCKTAIL GLASS

1 part Orange Liqueur
1 part Kirschwasser
1 part Apricot Brandy

Shake with ice and strain.

On the Loose

COCKTAIL GLASS

1 part Light Rum
1 part Triple Sec
1 part Cherry Brandy
splash Banana Juice

Shake with ice and strain.

On Top of the Sheets

COCKTAIL GLASS

½ part Triple Sec
1 part Rémy Martin® VSOP
splash Limoncello
splash Lime Juice
½ part Simple Syrup

Shake with ice and strain.

One Night in Bangkok

COCKTAIL GLASS

1 part Absinthe
1 part Lillet Blanc
1 part Spiced Rum
1 part Lime Juice

Shake with ice and strain.

Oompa Loompa

COCKTAIL GLASS

½ part Vodka
½ part Chocolate Mint Liqueur
½ part Banana Liqueur
1½ parts Light Cream

Shake with ice and strain.

Opa Cocktail

COCKTAIL GLASS

1½ parts Gin
1 part Orange Juice
1 tbsp powdered Sugar
splash Orange Flower Water

Shake with ice and strain.

Opal

COCKTAIL GLASS

1½ parts Vodka
1 part Crème de Banane
splash Campari®
splash Grenadine

Shake with ice and strain.

Openheim

COCKTAIL GLASS

2 parts Bourbon
½ part Dry Vermouth
½ part Grenadine

Shake with ice and strain.

Opening Night

COCKTAIL GLASS

1½ parts Whiskey
½ part Dry Vermouth
½ part Strawberry Liqueur

Shake with ice and strain.

Ophelia

COCKTAIL GLASS

1½ parts Aquavit
1½ parts Orange Juice
½ part Lime Cordial

Shake with ice and strain.

Opium

COCKTAIL GLASS

1 part Vodka
1 part Amaretto
1 part Peach Schnapps

Shake with ice and strain.

Orange Bloom

COCKTAIL GLASS

1 part Gin
½ part Cointreau®
½ part Sweet Vermouth

Shake with ice and strain.

Orange Bomb

COCKTAIL GLASS

1 part Mandarine Napoléon® Liqueur
½ part Chocolate Liqueur
½ part Irish Cream Liqueur
½ part Half and Half

Shake with ice and strain.

Orange Cadillac

COCKTAIL GLASS

½ part Galliano®
½ part Crème de Cacao (White)
1 part Cream
1 part Orange Juice

Shake with ice and strain.

Orange Cream Chata

COCKTAIL GLASS

2 parts RumChata
1 part Orange Vodka

Shake with ice and strain.

Orange Kamikaze

COCKTAIL GLASS

1½ parts Vodka
½ part Triple Sec
½ part Orange Juice

Shake with ice and strain.

Orange Lion

COCKTAIL GLASS

1 part Orange Vodka
1 part Peach Schnapps
1 part Orange Juice

Shake with ice and strain.

Orcabessa

COCKTAIL GLASS

1 part Peach Schnapps
splash Vodka
splash Orange Juice
splash Sweet & Sour Mix

Shake with ice and strain.

Orchidea Nera

COCKTAIL GLASS

1 part Coffee
1 part Cognac
1 part Whiskey

Shake with ice and strain.

Orgasm

COCKTAIL GLASS

½ part Crème de Cacao (White)
½ part Amaretto
½ part Triple Sec
½ part Vodka
1 part Light Cream

Shake with ice and strain.

Orlof

COCKTAIL GLASS

½ part Triple Sec
½ part Melon Liqueur
1 part Brandy
1 part Sweet & Sour Mix

Shake with ice and strain.

Osaka Dry

COCKTAIL GLASS

3 parts Vodka
½ part Sake

Shake with ice and strain.

Ostwind Cocktail

COCKTAIL GLASS

1 part Vodka
1 part Dry Vermouth
1 part Sweet Vermouth
½ part Rum

Shake with ice and strain.

Outlandish Coffee

COCKTAIL GLASS

1 part Vanilla Liqueur
½ part Chocolate Liqueur
1 part Cream
1 part Coffee Liqueur

Shake with ice and strain.

El Pacifico Vasso

COCKTAIL GLASS

1 part Silver Tequila
½ part Crème de Coconut
½ part Hazelnut Liqueur
½ part Lemon Juice

Shake with ice and strain.

Pacific Fleet

COCKTAIL GLASS

½ part Peach Schnapps
½ part Kiwi Schnapps
½ part Vodka
½ part Light Rum
1 part Cranberry Juice Cocktail

Shake with ice and strain.

Pacifist

COCKTAIL GLASS

¾ part Light Rum
¾ part Brandy
¼ part Lemon Juice
2 splashes Raspberry Syrup

Shake with ice and strain.

Paddy Cocktail

COCKTAIL GLASS

1½ parts Irish Whiskey
1½ parts Sweet Vermouth
dash Bitters

Shake with ice and strain.

Paddy's Special

COCKTAIL GLASS

1 part Cognac
½ part Lime Juice
¼ part Crème de Banane
splash Triple Sec

Shake with ice and strain.

Pagoda

COCKTAIL GLASS

1 part Vodka
1 part Mandarine Napoléon® Liqueur
1 part Pineapple Juice

Shake with ice and strain.

Pale Face

COCKTAIL GLASS

2 parts Gin
⅔ part Crème de Banane
½ part Cream

Shake with ice and strain.

Palmera

COCKTAIL GLASS

2 parts White Rum
1 part Pineapple Juice
splash Lime Juice
dash Grenadine

Shake with ice and strain.

Palmetto Cocktail

COCKTAIL GLASS

1½ parts Light Rum
1½ parts Dry Vermouth
2 dashes Bitters

Shake with ice and strain over ice.

Palooka

COCKTAIL GLASS

1 part Apricot Brandy
1 part Apple Brandy
½ part Sweet & Sour Mix
⅔ part Cranberry Juice Cocktail

Shake with ice and strain.

Panama Cocktail

COCKTAIL GLASS

1 part Brandy
1 part Light Cream
1 part Crème de Cacao (White)

Shake with ice and strain.

Pancho Villa

COCKTAIL GLASS

1 part Gin
1 part Light Rum
½ part Apricot Brandy
splash Cherry Liqueur
splash Pineapple Juice

Shake with ice and strain.

Pandora's Box

COCKTAIL GLASS

1 part Gin
1 part Calvados Apple Brandy
1 part White Wine
splash Blue Curaçao
splash Frangelico®

Shake with ice and strain over ice.

Pantomime

COCKTAIL GLASS

1½ parts Dry Vermouth
splash Grenadine
splash Amaretto
1 Egg White

Shake with ice and strain.

Panty Delight

COCKTAIL GLASS

1½ parts Gin
½ part Dry Vermouth
dash Orange Bitters

Shake with ice and strain.

Paradise Cocktail

COCKTAIL GLASS

1 part Apricot Brandy
¾ part Gin
½ part Orange Juice

Shake with ice and strain.

Parallel Universe

COCKTAIL GLASS

1 part Cointreau®
1 part Light Rum
1 part Grapefruit Juice

Shake with ice and strain.

Parfait Cheer

COCKTAIL GLASS

1½ parts Crème de Cassis
1½ parts Parfait Amour
splash Lemon Juice

Shake with ice and strain.

Paris Opera

COCKTAIL GLASS

1 part Blue Curaçao
1 part Grapefruit Juice
1 part Light Rum

Shake with ice and strain.

Parisian

COCKTAIL GLASS

1 part Dry Vermouth
1 part Gin
¼ part Crème de Cassis

Shake with ice and strain.

Parisian Peggy

COCKTAIL GLASS

1½ parts Cherry Brandy
⅔ part Crème de Cacao (White)
1 part Cream

Shake with ice and strain.

Park Lane

COCKTAIL GLASS

1½ parts Dry Gin
1 part Apricot Brandy
1½ parts Orange Juice
½ part Grenadine

Shake with ice and strain.

Parrotti

COCKTAIL GLASS

1 part Vodka
½ part Apricot Brandy
splash Lychee Liqueur
splash Grenadine
splash Lime Juice

Shake with ice and strain.

Passion Girl

COCKTAIL GLASS

½ part Apricot Brandy
½ part Bourbon
½ part Passion Fruit Liqueur
½ part Dark Rum
splash Amaretto

Shake with ice and strain.

Passionate Affair

COCKTAIL GLASS

1 part Orange Liqueur
1 part Aquavit
1 part Passion Fruit Juice

Shake with ice and strain.

Passionate Sunset

COCKTAIL GLASS

1 part Passion Fruit
½ part Orange Juice
½ part Grenadine
½ part Tequila Reposado

Shake with ice and strain.

Passport to Joy

COCKTAIL GLASS

½ part Frangelico®
½ part Strawberry Liqueur
½ part Melon Liqueur
1½ parts Cream

Shake with ice and strain.

Patchanka

COCKTAIL GLASS

1 part Light Rum
splash Crème de Coconut
splash Passonã®
1 part Pineapple Juice

Shake with ice and strain.

Pauline Cocktail

COCKTAIL GLASS

1 part Rum
1 part Lemon Juice

Shake with ice and strain.

Pavarotti

COCKTAIL GLASS

1½ parts Amaretto
½ part Brandy
½ part Crème de Cacao (White)

Shake with ice and strain.

Peace

COCKTAIL GLASS

2 parts Dark Rum
splash Triple Sec
½ part Orange Juice
½ part Lime Juice
dash Sugar

Shake with ice and strain.

Peach Bunny

COCKTAIL GLASS

1 part Peach Brandy
1 part Crème de Cacao (White)
1 part Light Cream

Shake with ice and strain.

Peach Me Tender

COCKTAIL GLASS

1 part Jack Daniel's®
1 part Peach Schnapps
½ part Limoncello
½ part Amaretto
splash Grenadine

Shake with ice and strain.

Peach Slider

COCKTAIL GLASS

1 part Peach Schnapps
½ part Amaretto
½ part Vanilla Liqueur
1 part Cream

Shake with ice and strain.

Peach Valley

COCKTAIL GLASS

2 parts Peach Schnapps
⅔ part Raspberry Juice
1 part Lime Juice

Shake with ice and strain.

Peachtree Square

COCKTAIL GLASS

1 part Vodka
1 part Peach Schnapps
½ part Crème de Cacao (White)
½ part Cream

Shake with ice and strain.

Peagreen

COCKTAIL GLASS

1 part Vodka
1 part Peppermint Liqueur
1 part Cream

Shake with ice and strain.

Peanut Butter Cup

COCKTAIL GLASS

½ part Vodka
½ part Frangelico®
½ part Crème de Cacao (White)
2 parts Light Cream

Shake with ice and strain.

Pear Drop

COCKTAIL GLASS

1½ parts Citrus Vodka
1½ parts Lychee Liqueur

Shake with ice and strain.

Pearls from Jamaica

COCKTAIL GLASS

½ part Amaretto
½ part Crème de Banane
½ part Maraschino Liqueur
½ part Melon Liqueur
splash Grenadine
splash Cranberry Juice Cocktail

Shake with ice and strain.

Peccati Mei

COCKTAIL GLASS

1 part Triple Sec
1 part Campari®
1 part Grappa

Shake with ice and strain.

Pedi Cocktail

COCKTAIL GLASS

2 parts Vodka
splash Triple Sec
⅔ part Campari®

Shake with ice and strain.

Peking Express

COCKTAIL GLASS

1 part Gin
1 part Triple Sec
1 Egg White
½ part Crème de Menthe (White)

Shake with ice and strain.

Pendennis Club Cocktail

COCKTAIL GLASS

1½ parts Gin
¾ part Brandy
½ part Lime Juice
splash Simple Syrup
dash Bitters

Shake with ice and strain.

Pendragon

COCKTAIL GLASS

⅔ part Blackberry Liqueur
½ part Kirschwasser
1½ parts Armagnac
1 part Cream

Shake with ice and strain.

Pepper Perfect

COCKTAIL GLASS

½ part Vanilla Liqueur
½ part Pepper Vodka
½ part Lemon-Lime Soda
1 part Cranberry Juice Cocktail

Shake with ice and strain.

Peppermint Twist

COCKTAIL GLASS

1 part Peppermint Schnapps
1 part Coffee Liqueur
1 part Crème de Cacao (Dark)

Shake with ice and strain.

Peregrine's Peril
COCKTAIL GLASS
1 part Dark Rum
1/2 part Crème de Banane
1/2 part Southern Comfort®
splash Lemon Juice
splash Lime Juice
Shake with ice and strain.

Perfect Cocktail
COCKTAIL GLASS
1 1/2 parts Gin
splash Sweet Vermouth
splash Dry Vermouth
dash Bitters
Shake with ice and strain.

Perfect Lady
COCKTAIL GLASS
1 part Gin
1 1/2 parts Peach Schnapps
1 Egg White
Shake with ice and strain.

Perfect Manhattan
COCKTAIL GLASS
1/2 part Sweet Vermouth
1/2 part Dry Vermouth
dash Bitters
Shake with ice and strain. Garnish with Lemon Twist.

Pernod® Cocktail
COCKTAIL GLASS
2 parts Pernod®
3 dashes Angostura® Bitters
3 splashes Simple Syrup
1/2 part Water
Shake with ice and strain.

Perpetual Motion
COCKTAIL GLASS
1 part Amaretto
2/3 part Triple Sec
1/2 part Passion Fruit Liqueur
splash Southern Comfort®
1/2 part Sweet & Sour Mix
Shake with ice and strain.

Persian Delight
COCKTAIL GLASS
1 part Vodka
1/2 part Crème de Cacao (White)
1/2 part Lychee Liqueur
1/4 part Maraschino Liqueur
1/4 part Sweetened Lime Juice
Shake with ice and strain.

Peruvian White
COCKTAIL GLASS
1 1/2 parts Cointreau®
2/3 part Pisco
splash Peppermint Liqueur
splash Lime Juice
Shake with ice and strain.

Peto Cocktail
COCKTAIL GLASS
1 1/2 parts Dry Gin
1 part Dry Vermouth
1 part Orange Juice
1 part Sweet Vermouth
splash Maraschino Liqueur
Shake with ice and strain.

Petticoat
COCKTAIL GLASS
1 part Vanilla Vodka
1/2 part Crème de Cacao (White)
1/2 part Chocolate Liqueur
1 part Cream
splash Galliano®
Shake with ice and strain.

Pheromone

COCKTAIL GLASS

1 part Dark Rum
1/2 part Crème de Menthe (White)
1/2 part Cream
1/2 part Crème de Cacao (Dark)
1/2 part 151-Proof Rum

Shake with ice and strain.

Phoebe Snow

COCKTAIL GLASS

1 1/2 parts Dubonnet® Blonde
1 1/2 parts Brandy
splash Anisette

Shake with ice and strain.

Picasso

COCKTAIL GLASS

2 1/2 parts Cognac
1/2 part Simple Syrup

Shake with ice and strain.

Piccadilly Cocktail

COCKTAIL GLASS

1 1/2 parts Gin
3/4 part Dry Vermouth
1/4 splash Anisette
1/4 splash Grenadine

Shake with ice and strain.

Pickens' Punch

COCKTAIL GLASS

1 part Crème de Menthe (White)
1 part Peach Schnapps
1 part Cherry Brandy

Shake with ice and strain.

Pie in the Sky

COCKTAIL GLASS

2 parts Light Rum
1 part Pineapple Juice
dash Powdered Sugar

Shake with ice and strain.

Piedra Putamadre

COCKTAIL GLASS

1 part Tequila
1 part Fernet-Branca®
1 part Anisette

Shake with ice and strain.

Pierced Hooter

COCKTAIL GLASS

1/2 part Peach Schnapps
1 1/2 parts Bacardi® Limón Rum
1/2 part Cranberry Juice Cocktail
1/2 part Orange Juice

Shake with ice and strain.

Pilot Boat

COCKTAIL GLASS

1 1/2 parts Dark Rum
1 part Banana Liqueur
2 parts Lime Juice

Shake with ice and strain.

Pimm's® Flower

COCKTAIL GLASS

1 1/2 parts Orange Juice
1 part Pimm's® No. 1 Cup
1 part Gin
1/2 part Grenadine

Shake with ice and strain.

Pimp Cocktail

COCKTAIL GLASS

2 parts Vodka
1 part Blue Curaçao
1 part Peach Schnapps
fill with Orange Juice

Build over ice and stir.

Pineapple Reef

COCKTAIL GLASS

1 part Crème de Coconut
1 part Spiced Rum
1 1/2 parts Pineapple Juice

Shake with ice and strain.

Pineapple Rum Cassis

COCKTAIL GLASS

1 part Light Rum
½ part Crème de Cassis
1 part Pineapple Juice

Shake with ice and strain.

Pink Baby Cocktail

COCKTAIL GLASS

1½ parts Gin
⅔ part Grenadine
1 Egg White
⅔ part Lemon Syrup

Shake with ice and strain.

Pink Creole

COCKTAIL GLASS

1½ parts Light Rum
2 splashes Lime Juice
splash Grenadine
splash Light Cream

Shake with ice and strain.

Pink Fluid

COCKTAIL GLASS

1½ parts Vodka
½ part Crème de Cacao (White)
½ part Strawberry Syrup

Shake with ice and strain.

Pink Mink

COCKTAIL GLASS

1 part Vodka
1 part Rum
1 part Strawberry Liqueur

Shake with ice and strain.

Pink 'n' Tart

COCKTAIL GLASS

1½ parts Rum
½ part Lemon Juice
½ part Lime Juice
splash Grenadine

Shake with ice and strain.

Pink Panther

COCKTAIL GLASS

1 part Amaretto
½ part Vodka
splash Grenadine
2 parts Light Cream

Shake with ice and strain.

Pink Pleasures

COCKTAIL GLASS

1 part Peach Schnapps
1 part Vodka
½ part Triple Sec
½ part Grenadine
½ part Lime Juice
¼ part Sweet & Sweet & Sour Mix

Shake with ice and strain.

Pink Pussycat Cocktail

COCKTAIL GLASS

1½ parts Gin
¾ part Grenadine
1 Egg White

Shake with ice and strain.

Pink Slip

COCKTAIL GLASS

1 part Crème de Cacao (White)
1 part Crème de Noyaux
1 part Cream

Shake with ice and strain.

Pink Squirrel

COCKTAIL GLASS

2 parts Crème de Cacao (White)
1 part Milk
½ part Grenadine

Shake with ice and strain.

Pink Teddy

COCKTAIL GLASS

1 part Vodka
1 part Passion Fruit Liqueur
½ part Lychee Liqueur
½ part Cream
splash Grenadine

Shake with ice and strain.

Pipe and Smoke

COCKTAIL GLASS

1 1/2 parts Drambuie®
1/2 part Crème de Coconut
1/2 part Cherry Brandy
1 part Lemon Juice

Shake with ice and strain.

Piranha

COCKTAIL GLASS

1 1/2 parts Vodka
1 1/2 parts Crème de Cacao (Dark)

Shake with ice and strain.

Pirate Cocktail

COCKTAIL GLASS

1 1/2 parts Rum
1/2 part Sweet Vermouth
2 dashes Angostura® Bitters

Shake with ice and strain.

Pirate's Gold

COCKTAIL GLASS

1 1/2 parts Dark Rum
1 part Dry Vermouth
2 dashes Orange Bitters

Shake with ice and strain.

Pirates Pleasure

COCKTAIL GLASS

1 part Coconut Rum
1 part Dark Rum
1 part Dark Spiced Rum
1 part Lime Juice
1 part Orange Juice
1 part Pineapple Juice

Shake with ice and strain.

Pisa

COCKTAIL GLASS

1 part Amaretto
1 part Cream
splash Apricot Brandy
splash Orange Juice

Shake with ice and strain.

Pixy Stix® Cocktail

COCKTAIL GLASS

1 1/2 parts Light Rum
1/2 part Apricot Brandy
2 splashes Lime Juice
2 splashes Lemon Juice
dash Sugar

Shake with ice and strain.

Plankton

COCKTAIL GLASS

1 1/2 parts Light Rum
1/2 part Galliano®
splash Crème de Cacao (White)

Shake with ice and strain.

Play It Again, Sam

COCKTAIL GLASS

2 parts Light Rum
splash Triple Sec
splash Maraschino Liqueur
splash Lime Juice

Shake with ice and strain.

Playa del Mar

COCKTAIL GLASS

1 part Silver Tequila
1 part Pineapple Juice
1/2 part Lime Juice
1/2 part Strawberry
splash Simple Syrup

Shake with ice and strain.

Playmate

COCKTAIL GLASS

1 part Brandy
1/2 part Apricot Brandy
1/2 part Mandarine Napoléon® Liqueur
1 part Orange Juice
1 Egg White

Shake with ice and strain.

Plaza Cocktail
COCKTAIL GLASS

3/4 part Gin
3/4 part Dry Vermouth
3/4 part Sweet Vermouth

Shake with ice and strain.

Police Brutality
COCKTAIL GLASS

2/3 part Light Rum
2/3 part Crème de Banane
1/2 part Galliano®
1 1/2 parts Pineapple Juice

Shake with ice and strain.

Polish Sidecar
COCKTAIL GLASS

2 parts Gin
1 part Blackberry Liqueur

Shake with ice and strain.

Polly's Cocktail
COCKTAIL GLASS

2 parts Scotch
1/2 part Pineapple Juice
1/2 part Triple Sec

Shake with ice and strain.

Polyanthus
COCKTAIL GLASS

1 part Blackberry Liqueur
1 part Chocolate Liqueur
1 part Cream

Shake with ice and strain.

Polynesian Cocktail
COCKTAIL GLASS

1 1/2 parts Vodka
3/4 part Cherry Brandy
1/2 part Lime Juice
dash Powdered Sugar

Shake with ice and strain.

Polynesian Sour
COCKTAIL GLASS

2 parts Light Rum
1/2 part Orange Juice
1/2 part Guava Juice

Shake with ice and strain.

Ponce de Leon
COCKTAIL GLASS

1 1/2 parts Light Rum
1/2 part Grapefruit Juice
1/2 part Mango Juice

Shake with ice and strain.

Ponche Orinoco
COCKTAIL GLASS

1 part Light Rum
1/2 part Apricot Brandy
1/4 part Vodka
1/4 part Orange Juice
splash Grenadine
dash Bitters

Shake with ice and strain.

Pool Table Sex
COCKTAIL GLASS

1 part Peach Schnapps
1 part Triple Sec
1 part Raspberry Liqueur
1 part Melon Liqueur
1 part Grapefruit Juice

Shake with ice and strain.

Poop Deck
COCKTAIL GLASS

2 parts Gold Rum
1 part Amaretto
splash Grenadine
dash Lime Juice
dash Simple Syrup

Shake with ice and strain.

Popstar

COCKTAIL GLASS

1 part Dark Rum
1 part Strawberry Liqueur
splash Vanilla Liqueur
splash Cream

Shake with ice and strain.

Pornography

COCKTAIL GLASS

1 1/2 parts Passion Fruit Liqueur
1 part Campari®
1 part Lime Juice

Shake with ice and strain.

Port Royal

COCKTAIL GLASS

1 part Spiced Rum
1/2 part Crème de Banane
splash Crème de Cacao (White)
2 parts Cream

Shake with ice and strain.

Potemkin

COCKTAIL GLASS

3 parts Vodka
splash Bénédictine®

Shake with ice and strain.

Potpourri

COCKTAIL GLASS

1 1/2 parts Vodka
1/2 part Cherry Brandy
1/2 part Brandy

Shake with ice and strain.

Potted President

COCKTAIL GLASS

2/3 part Blackberry Liqueur
2/3 part Raspberry Liqueur
2/3 part Sambuca
1 part Sweet & Sour Mix

Shake with ice and strain.

Power-Line

COCKTAIL GLASS

1 part Brandy
1 part Crème de Banane
1 part Orange Juice
splash Cream

Shake with ice and strain.

Prankster

COCKTAIL GLASS

1 part Crème de Banane
1 part Lime Juice
1 part Sweet & Sour Mix

Shake with ice and strain.

Prelude

COCKTAIL GLASS

1 part Dry Vermouth
1/2 part Peach Schnapps
1/4 part Gin
3/4 part Peach Juice
1/4 part Honey
splash Strawberry Juice

Shake with ice and strain.

El Presidente

COCKTAIL GLASS

1 1/4 part Dark Rum
1/2 part Lime Juice
1/2 part Pineapple Juice
1/2 part Grenadine

Shake with ice and strain.

Presto Cocktail

COCKTAIL GLASS

1 1/2 parts Brandy
1/2 part Sweet Vermouth
2 splashes Orange Juice
1/4 splash Anisette

Shake with ice and strain.

Prestwick
COCKTAIL GLASS

2 parts Light Rum
1 part Crème de Cassis
1 part Crème de Noyaux
1 part Orange Juice
1 part Cranberry Juice Cocktail
1 part Pineapple Juice

Shake with ice and strain.

Pretty Angel
COCKTAIL GLASS

1 part Crème de Banane
1/2 part Crème de Menthe (White)
1/2 part Cream
1/2 part Dark Rum
splash Grenadine

Shake with ice and strain.

Pretty Thing
COCKTAIL GLASS

1 1/2 parts Vodka
1/2 part Amaretto
1/2 part Cream of Coconut
1/2 part Heavy Cream

Shake with ice and strain.

Primo Amore
COCKTAIL GLASS

1 part Apricot Brandy
1 part Cognac
1/2 part Orange Juice
splash Grenadine

Shake with ice and strain.

Prince Regent
COCKTAIL GLASS

1 part Apricot Brandy
1 part Crème de Cacao (White)
1 part Chocolate Milk

Shake with ice and strain.

Prince's Smile
COCKTAIL GLASS

1 part Gin
1/2 part Apple Brandy
1/2 part Apricot Brandy
1/4 splash Lemon Juice

Shake with ice and strain.

Princeton Cocktail
COCKTAIL GLASS

1 part Gin
1 part Dry Vermouth
1/2 part Lime Juice

Shake with ice and strain.

Private Meeting
COCKTAIL GLASS

1 1/2 parts Gin
1/2 part Peach Schnapps
1/2 part Mandarine Napoléon® Liqueur
dash Orange Bitters

Stir gently with ice and strain.

Prohibition
COCKTAIL GLASS

1 part Gin
1 part Lillet®
splash Apricot Brandy
2 splashes Orange Juice

Shake with ice and strain.

Proserpine's Revenge
COCKTAIL GLASS

1 1/2 parts Crème de Menthe (White)
1 1/2 parts Cognac

Shake with ice and strain.

Psycho Therapy
COCKTAIL GLASS

1 part Vodka
1 part Rémy Martin® VSOP
1 part Scotch

Shake with ice and strain.

Pulmonia
COCKTAIL GLASS

1 part Gold Tequila
2/3 part Blue Curaçao
2/3 part Maraschino Liqueur
1 part Sweet & Sour Mix

Shake with ice and strain.

Pulsar
COCKTAIL GLASS

1 part Blue Curaçao
1/2 part Crème de Cassis
splash Vodka
splash Lime Juice

Shake with ice and strain.

Punisher
COCKTAIL GLASS

1 1/2 parts Scotch
1 part Crème de Cacao (Dark)
1/2 part Coffee Liqueur

Shake with ice and strain.

Pure Delight
COCKTAIL GLASS

1 part Raspberry Liqueur
1 part Grand Marnier®
1 part Irish Cream Liqueur

Shake with ice and strain.

Puropi
COCKTAIL GLASS

2 parts Silver Tequila
3/4 part Crème de Cassis
1/2 part Crème de Menthe (Green)

Shake with ice and strain.

Purple Bunny
COCKTAIL GLASS

1 1/2 parts Cherry Brandy
1/2 part Crème de Cacao (White)
1/2 part Cream

Shake with ice and strain.

Purple Kiss
COCKTAIL GLASS

1 1/4 parts Gin
3/4 part Lemon Juice
3/4 part Crème de Noyaux
splash Cherry Brandy

Shake with ice and strain.

Purple Mask
COCKTAIL GLASS

1 part Vodka
1/2 part Crème de Cacao (White)
1 part Grape Juice (red)

Shake with ice and strain.

Purple Turtle
COCKTAIL GLASS

1/2 part Blue Curaçao
1 part Coconut Rum
1 part Triple Sec
1 part Cranberry Juice Cocktail

Shake with ice and strain.

Pursuit Plane
COCKTAIL GLASS

1 1/2 parts Vodka
2/3 part Vanilla Liqueur
2/3 part Butterscotch Schnapps

Shake with ice and strain.

Pussy Supreme
COCKTAIL GLASS

3/4 part Irish Cream Liqueur
3/4 part Blue Curaçao
2 parts Half and Half

Shake with ice and strain.

Quattro
COCKTAIL GLASS

1 part Amaretto
1 part Whiskey
1/2 part Dry Vermouth
1/2 part Crème de Cassis

Shake with ice and strain.

Quebec Cocktail
COCKTAIL GLASS
1½ parts Canadian Whisky
½ part Cherry Liqueur
½ part Dry Vermouth
½ part Amer Picon®
Shake with ice and strain.

Queen Bee
COCKTAIL GLASS
1½ parts Citrus Vodka
1 part Coffee Brandy
½ part Cream Sherry
Shake with ice and strain.

Queen of Scots
COCKTAIL GLASS
2 parts Scotch
splash Chartreuse®
splash Blue Curaçao
dash Sugar
2 splashes Water
splash Lemon Juice
Shake with ice and strain.

Quentin
COCKTAIL GLASS
1½ parts Dark Rum
½ part Coffee Liqueur
1 part Light Cream
pinch Ground Nutmeg
Shake with ice and strain.

Quick-Fire
COCKTAIL GLASS
1 part Chocolate Mint Liqueur
1 part Light Rum
½ part Cream
splash 151-Proof Rum
Shake with ice and strain.

Quicksand
COCKTAIL GLASS
1 part Vodka
⅔ part Coffee Liqueur
splash Vanilla Liqueur
Shake with ice and strain.

Quiet Sunday
COCKTAIL GLASS
1 part Vodka
1 part Orange Juice
½ part Amaretto
½ part Grenadine
Shake with ice and strain.

R&B Cocktail
COCKTAIL GLASS
1 part Jack Daniel's®
½ part Triple Sec
½ part Brandy
fill with Cola
splash Grenadine
Build over ice and stir.

Rad Fuck
COCKTAIL GLASS
¾ part Raspberry Liqueur
¾ part Amaretto
½ part Pineapple Juice
½ part Sweet & Sour Mix
splash Lemon-Lime Soda
Stir gently with ice and strain.

Radioactivity
COCKTAIL GLASS
1 part Vodka
½ part Lychee Liqueur
½ part Pisang Ambon® Liqueur
1 part Lemon Juice
Shake with ice and strain.

Ragtime
COCKTAIL GLASS
1 part Coffee Liqueur
1 part Brandy
1 part Half and Half
Shake with ice and strain.

Rainmaker

COCKTAIL GLASS

2 parts Vodka
1 part Coconut Rum
1 part Crème de Banane
1 part Melon Liqueur
1 part Pineapple Juice

Shake with ice and strain.

Rainy Night in Georgia

COCKTAIL GLASS

1 part Cinnamon Schnapps
1 part Pineapple Rum

Shake with ice and strain.

Ramasi

COCKTAIL GLASS

½ part Vodka
½ part Triple Sec
½ part Amaretto
1 part Sweet & Sour Mix
½ part Pineapple Juice

Shake with ice and strain.

Ramos Fizz

COCKTAIL GLASS

2 parts Gin
1½ parts Cream
½ part Lemon Juice
½ part Lime Juice
2 drops Orange Flower Water
dash Powdered Sugar
fill with Club Soda

Shake all but Club Soda with ice and strain. Top with Club Soda.

Rampage

COCKTAIL GLASS

1 part Peach Schnapps
1 part Spiced Rum
½ part Cranberry Juice
½ part Pineapple Juice
splash Cherry Juice

Shake with ice and strain.

Randini

COCKTAIL GLASS

2 parts Cranberry Juice Cocktail
3 parts Gin
1 part Triple Sec
1 part Vodka

Shake with ice and strain. Garnish with Lime Slice.

Ranger Cocktail

COCKTAIL GLASS

1 part Light Rum
1 part Gin
1 part Lemon Juice
dash Sugar

Shake with ice and strain.

Rapture of Rum

COCKTAIL GLASS

1½ parts Coconut Rum
½ part Orange Liqueur
½ part Lime Juice
dash Powdered Sugar

Shake with ice and strain.

Raquel

COCKTAIL GLASS

1 part Vodka
½ part Blue Curaçao
½ part Parfait Amour
½ part Cherry Brandy
splash Cream

Shake with ice and strain.

Rasp Royale

COCKTAIL GLASS

1 part Vodka
½ part Raspberry Liqueur
½ part Coffee Liqueur
½ part Irish Cream Liqueur

Shake with ice and strain.

Raspberry Blush
COCKTAIL GLASS

1 part Dark Rum
½ part Dry Vermouth
1 part Lime Juice
2 splashes Raspberry Syrup

Shake with ice and strain.

Rattlesnake Cocktail
COCKTAIL GLASS

1½ parts Whiskey
splash Lemon Juice
splash Anisette
dash Powdered Sugar
1 Egg White

Shake with ice and strain.

Razzberi Kazi
COCKTAIL GLASS

1 part Raspberry Vodka
1 part Triple Sec
1 part Sweet & Sour Mix
½ part Grenadine

Shake with ice and strain.

Razzmopolitan
COCKTAIL GLASS

1½ parts Vodka
¾ part Raspberry Liqueur
½ part Lime Juice
splash Cranberry Juice Cocktail

Shake with ice and strain.

Rebel Roar
COCKTAIL GLASS

1 part Crème de Banane
1 part Triple Sec
1 part Grape Juice (white)

Shake with ice and strain.

Recession Depression
COCKTAIL GLASS

1½ parts Citrus Vodka
½ part Triple Sec
½ part Lemon Juice
2 splashes Sweetened Lime Juice

Shake with ice and strain.

Red Apple
COCKTAIL GLASS

1 part Vodka
1 part Apple Juice
2 splashes Lemon Juice
splash Grenadine

Shake with ice and strain.

Red Cloud
COCKTAIL GLASS

1½ parts Gin
½ part Apricot Brandy
2 splashes Lemon Juice
splash Grenadine

Shake with ice and strain.

Red Delight
COCKTAIL GLASS

1 part Peach Schnapps
1 part Coconut Rum
1 part Cream
1 part Strawberry Syrup
2 parts Mango Juice

Shake with ice and strain.

Red Finnish
COCKTAIL GLASS

2 parts Orange Juice
1 part Vermouth
¾ part Red Curaçao

Shake with ice and strain.

Red Gaze
COCKTAIL GLASS

½ part Sloe Gin
½ part Crème de Cassis
splash Lemon Juice
splash Lemon-Lime Soda

Shake with ice and strain.

Red Jobber

COCKTAIL GLASS

2 parts Coconut Rum
1 part Crème de Banane
1 part Strawberry Liqueur
1 part Jägermeister®
splash Grenadine

Shake with ice and strain.

Red Knocker

COCKTAIL GLASS

1 part Sloe Gin
1 part Passion Fruit Liqueur
1 part Apple Juice
splash Sweet & Sour Mix

Shake with ice and strain.

Red Light

COCKTAIL GLASS

1 part Gin
½ part Sloe Gin
½ part Dry Vermouth

Shake with ice and strain.

Red Lion Cocktail

COCKTAIL GLASS

1 part Gin
1 part Grand Marnier®
½ part Lemon Juice
½ part Orange Juice

Shake with ice and strain.

Red Panties

COCKTAIL GLASS

1½ parts Vodka
1 part Peach Schnapps
splash Grenadine
1 part Orange Juice

Shake with ice and strain.

Red Raider

COCKTAIL GLASS

2 parts Bourbon
½ part Triple Sec
1 part Lemon Juice
dash Grenadine

Shake with ice and strain.

Red Russian

COCKTAIL GLASS

1 part Vodka
½ part Crème de Cacao (White)
1 part Cranberry Juice Cocktail

Shake with ice and strain.

Red Sonja

COCKTAIL GLASS

1 part Vodka
1 part Raspberry Liqueur
1 part Cranberry Juice Cocktail

Shake with ice and strain.

Red Tulip

COCKTAIL GLASS

⅔ part Gin
splash Triple Sec
splash Apricot Brandy
½ part Dry Vermouth
½ part Sweet Vermouth

Shake with ice and strain.

Red Viking

COCKTAIL GLASS

1 part Maraschino Liqueur
1 part Aquavit
½ part Grenadine

Shake with ice and strain.

Red Whiskey

COCKTAIL GLASS

1 part Whiskey
1 part Sloe Gin
½ part Lemon Juice

Shake with ice and strain.

Redcoat

COCKTAIL GLASS

1½ parts Light Rum
½ part Vodka
½ part Apricot Brandy
½ part Lime Juice
splash Grenadine

Shake with ice and strain.

Redheaded Slut

COCKTAIL GLASS

1 part Jack Daniel's®
1 part Peach Schnapps
1 part Cranberry Juice Cocktail

Shake with ice and strain.

Reformation

COCKTAIL GLASS

1½ parts Parfait Amour
1 part Cherry Brandy
½ part Scotch

Shake with ice and strain.

Remote Control

COCKTAIL GLASS

1 part Galliano®
½ part Cointreau®
1 part Orange Juice
½ part Cream

Shake with ice and strain.

Renaissance Cocktail

COCKTAIL GLASS

1½ parts Gin
½ part Dry Sherry
½ part Light Cream
dash Ground Nutmeg

Shake with ice and strain.

Rendezvous

COCKTAIL GLASS

3 parts Gin
1 part Cherry Brandy
½ part Campari

Shake with ice and strain.

Renton

COCKTAIL GLASS

1 part Sloe Gin
1 part Crème de Cassis
1 part Milk

Shake with ice and strain.

Reunion

COCKTAIL GLASS

1 part Light Rum
½ part Cherry Brandy
½ part Triple Sec
¼ part Lime Juice

Shake with ice and strain.

Reve Satin

COCKTAIL GLASS

1 part Blackberry Liqueur
1 part Strawberry Liqueur
1 part Cream

Shake with ice and strain.

Rhapsody in Blue

COCKTAIL GLASS

1 part Blue Curaçao
1 part Grappa
1 part Amaretto

Shake with ice and strain.

Rheingold

COCKTAIL GLASS

1 part Dry Gin
½ part Dry Vermouth
½ part Campari®

Shake with ice and strain.

Rhett Butler

COCKTAIL GLASS

1½ parts Southern Comfort®
½ part Triple Sec
½ part Lime Juice

Shake with ice and strain.

Riley

COCKTAIL GLASS

1 part Dark Rum
½ part Cointreau®
½ part Lemon Juice
½ part Orange Juice
½ part Lime Juice
splash Crème de Cassis
splash Raspberry Syrup

Shake with ice and strain.

Rin Tin Tin

COCKTAIL GLASS

1 part Cherry Brandy
1 part Sweet & Sour Mix
1 part Cranberry Juice Cocktail

Shake with ice and strain.

Rio Grande

COCKTAIL GLASS

1½ parts Silver Tequila
¾ part Peach Schnapps
½ part Lime Juice

Shake with ice and strain.

Ripe Reagents

COCKTAIL GLASS

½ part Peppermint Liqueur
1 part Triple Sec
1 part Light Rum
½ part Lime Juice
dash Powdered Sugar

Shake with ice and strain.

Risky Business

COCKTAIL GLASS

1½ parts Vodka
splash Raspberry Liqueur
splash Lime Juice
splash Blackberry Juice

Shake with ice and strain.

Roadster

COCKTAIL GLASS

½ part Crème de Cacao (White)
½ part Crème de Banane
½ part Raspberry Liqueur
1 part Orange Juice
1 part Cream

Shake with ice and strain.

Roberta

COCKTAIL GLASS

1 part Vodka
1 part Dry Vermouth
1 part Cherry Brandy
splash Crème de Banane
splash Campari®

Shake with ice and strain.

Robson Cocktail

COCKTAIL GLASS

1 part Dark Rum
splash Grenadine
2 splashes Lemon Juice
1 part Orange Juice

Shake with ice and strain.

Rocket Radium

COCKTAIL GLASS

1½ parts Peppermint Liqueur
1½ parts Ouzo

Shake with ice and strain.

Rococo

COCKTAIL GLASS

1 part Cherry Vodka
½ part Triple Sec
1 part Orange Juice

Shake with ice and strain.

Roller Coaster

COCKTAIL GLASS

1 part Gin
1 part Brandy
½ part Crème de Menthe (Green)
½ part Lemonade
splash Lime Juice

Shake with ice and strain.

Rolling Thunder

COCKTAIL GLASS

1½ parts Light Rum
½ part Vodka
½ part Apricot Brandy
¼ part Lime Juice
¼ part Grenadine

Shake with ice and strain.

Rolls Royce

COCKTAIL GLASS

1 1/2 parts Gin
1/2 part Dry Vermouth
1/2 part Sweet Vermouth
dash Bénédictine

Shake with ice and strain.

Roma Citta Aperta

COCKTAIL GLASS

1 part Grappa
1 part Triple Sec
1/2 part Apricot Brandy
1/2 part Campari®

Shake with ice and strain.

Romance Cocktail

COCKTAIL GLASS

1/4 part Brandy
1/4 part Blue Curaçao
1/2 part Amer Picon®
1/2 part Dry Vermouth
1/2 part Sweet Vermouth

Shake with ice and strain.

Rome under the Snow

COCKTAIL GLASS

1/2 part Crème de Cassis
1/2 part Plum Brandy
2/3 part Grappa
2 parts Cream

Shake with ice and strain.

Ronrico

COCKTAIL GLASS

1 part Passion Fruit Liqueur
2/3 part Dark Rum
2/3 part Coffee Liqueur
splash Cream of Coconut
splash Milk
splash Pineapple Juice

Shake with ice and strain.

Rook Yah

COCKTAIL GLASS

1/2 part Peppermint Liqueur
1 part Triple Sec
1/2 part Jägermeister®
1 1/2 parts Cranberry Juice Cocktail

Shake with ice and strain.

Rose

COCKTAIL GLASS

2 parts Dry Gin
1/2 part Cherry Brandy
splash Sweet Vermouth

Shake with ice and strain.

Rose Bird

COCKTAIL GLASS

1 part Cognac
1/2 part Crème de Banane
1/2 part Apricot Brandy
splash Orange Juice

Shake with ice and strain.

Rose Hall

COCKTAIL GLASS

1 part Orange Juice
1/2 part Banana Liqueur
splash Lime Juice

Shake with ice and strain.

Rose of Warsaw

COCKTAIL GLASS

1 1/2 parts Polish Vodka
1 part Cherry Liqueur
1/2 part Cointreau®
dash Bitters

Shake with ice and strain.

Rose Walk

COCKTAIL GLASS

1 part Maraschino Liqueur
1 part Brandy
1 part Dry Vermouth
1/2 part Sweet & Sour Mix

Shake with ice and strain.

Roseanne

COCKTAIL GLASS

1 part Coffee Brandy
splash Brandy
splash Irish Cream Liqueur
splash Frangelico®

Shake with ice and strain.

Roselin

COCKTAIL GLASS

1 1/2 parts Dark Rum
1/4 part Triple Sec
1/4 part Mandarine Napoléon® Liqueur
splash Pineapple Juice
splash Grenadine
dash Bitters

Shake with ice and strain.

Rosie McGann

COCKTAIL GLASS

1 part Peppermint Liqueur
1 part Irish Whiskey
1 part Sweet & Sour Mix

Shake with ice and strain.

Roy Howard Cocktail

COCKTAIL GLASS

1 part Lillet®
1 part Brandy
1 part Orange Juice
splash Grenadine

Shake with ice and strain.

Royal Clover Club Cocktail

COCKTAIL GLASS

1 1/2 parts Gin
1/2 part Lemon Juice
2 splashes Grenadine
1 Egg Yolk

Shake with ice and strain over ice.

Royal Cocktail

COCKTAIL GLASS

1 1/2 parts Gin
1/2 part Lemon Juice
dash Powdered Sugar
1 Whole Egg

Shake with ice and strain.

Royal Mounted Police

COCKTAIL GLASS

2 parts Canadian Whisky
1/2 part Blue Curaçao
1/2 part Dry Sherry

Shake with ice and strain.

Royal Passion

COCKTAIL GLASS

1 1/2 parts Vodka
3/4 part Raspberry Liqueur
1/2 part Passion Fruit Juice

Shake with ice and strain.

Royal Wedding

COCKTAIL GLASS

1 part Apricot Brandy
1 part Grand Marnier®
1/2 part Lime Juice

Shake with ice and strain.

Rubaiyat

COCKTAIL GLASS

2 parts Gin
1 part Cointreau®
splash Orange Juice

Shake with ice and strain.

Ruben's

COCKTAIL GLASS

1 1/2 parts Whiskey
1 part Apricot Brandy
splash Lemon Juice
splash Simple Syrup

Shake with ice and strain.

Ruby Cocktail

COCKTAIL GLASS

2 parts Gin
3/4 part Applejack Brandy
3 dashes Grenadine

Shake with ice and strain.

Ruby in the Rough

COCKTAIL GLASS

1 1/2 parts Gin
1/2 part Cherry Brandy
splash Sweet Vermouth

Shake with ice and strain.

Ruby Red Lips

COCKTAIL GLASS

1 1/2 parts Gin
1/2 part Sloe Gin
1/2 part Dry Vermouth
splash Grenadine

Shake with ice and strain.

Ruby Relaxer

COCKTAIL GLASS

1 part Coconut Rum
1 part Peach Schnapps
1 part Vodka
splash Cranberry Juice
splash Pineapple Juice

Shake with ice and strain.

Rude Cosmopolitan

COCKTAIL GLASS

1 1/2 parts Silver Tequila
3/4 part Triple Sec
1/2 part Lime Juice

Shake with ice and strain.

Rum Blossom

COCKTAIL GLASS

1 1/2 parts Dark Rum
1 part Orange Juice
1 tbsp Sugar

Shake with ice and strain.

Rum Flare

COCKTAIL GLASS

1 part Rum
1/2 part Brandy
1/2 part Triple Sec
1/2 part Lemon Juice

Shake with ice and strain.

Rum Rummy

COCKTAIL GLASS

1 1/2 parts Light Rum
1 part Orange Juice
1 part Lime Juice
dash Orange Bitters
splash Simple Syrup

Shake with ice and strain.

Rumba

COCKTAIL GLASS

2 parts Dark Rum
1/2 part Crème de Cacao (Dark)
splash Grenadine

Shake with ice and strain.

Rummer

COCKTAIL GLASS

1 1/2 parts Dark Rum
1/2 part Amaretto
1/2 part Triple Sec
1/2 part Lemon Juice

Shake with ice and strain.

Runaway Bay

COCKTAIL GLASS

1 1/2 parts Spiced Rum
2/3 part Blue Curaçao
splash Pernod®
2/3 part Lime Juice

Shake with ice and strain.

Rushkin
COCKTAIL GLASS

1 part Vodka
1 part Raspberry Liqueur
½ part Blackberry Liqueur
½ part Lime Juice
½ part Sweet & Sour Mix

Shake with ice and strain.

Russian Armpit
COCKTAIL GLASS

½ part Orange Vodka
½ part Citrus Vodka
1 part Crème de Banane
1 part Mango Juice

Shake with ice and strain.

Russian Bear
COCKTAIL GLASS

2 parts Vodka
2 parts Cream
splash Crème de Cacao (Dark)
½ tsp Powdered Sugar

Shake with ice and strain.

Russian Cadillac
COCKTAIL GLASS

1 part Vodka
¾ part Galliano
¼ part Crème de Cacao (White)
1 part Cream

Shake with ice and strain.

Russian Cocktail
COCKTAIL GLASS

1 part Vodka
1 part Gin
1 part Crème de Cacao (White)

Shake with ice and strain.

Russian Haze
COCKTAIL GLASS

1 part Vodka
½ part Frangelico®
½ part Irish Cream Liqueur

Shake with ice and strain.

Russian Peach
COCKTAIL GLASS

1 part Vodka
½ part Peach Schnapps
½ part Crème de Cassis
1 part Orange Juice

Shake with ice and strain.

Russian Smooth Side
COCKTAIL GLASS

1 part Vodka
½ part Orange Liqueur
½ part Mandarine Napoléon® Liqueur
½ part Lemon Juice
1 part Orange Juice

Shake with ice and strain.

Russian Satellite
COCKTAIL GLASS

1 part Crème de Cacao (White)
1 part White Rum
½ part Crème de Menthe (White)
1 part Milk
½ part Dark Rum

Shake all but the Dark Rum with ice and strain. Float the Dark Rum on top and garnish with ground Nutmeg.

Russian Twilight
COCKTAIL GLASS

1 part Vodka
1 part Crème de Cacao (White)
1 part Cream

Shake with ice and strain.

Russin' About
COCKTAIL GLASS

1½ parts Vodka
½ part Irish Cream Liqueur
½ part Tia Maria®
¼ part Frangelico®

Shake with ice and strain.

Rye Lane

COCKTAIL GLASS

1 part Triple Sec
1 part Orange Juice
1 part Rye Whiskey

Shake with ice and strain.

Rye Whiskey Cocktail

COCKTAIL GLASS

2 parts Rye Whiskey
dash Powdered Sugar
dash Bitters

Shake with ice and strain.

Sacrifice

COCKTAIL GLASS

1 part Gin
1 part Calvados Apple Brandy
1 part Dry Vermouth
splash Cherry Brandy

Shake with ice and strain.

Safe and Sound

COCKTAIL GLASS

1 part Crème de Cacao (White)
1 part Calvados Apple Brandy
1 part Cream

Shake with ice and strain.

Saigon Sling

COCKTAIL GLASS

1 part Gin
½ part Sloe Gin
1 part Cherry Brandy
½ part Crème de Cassis
½ part Lime Juice

Shake with ice and strain.

Sail Away

COCKTAIL GLASS

1 part Vodka
½ part Peach Liqueur
½ part Melon Liqueur
1 part Lime Juice

Shake with ice and strain.

Sake Cocktail

COCKTAIL GLASS

1 part Melon Liqueur
1 part Sake
1 part Citrus Vodka

Shake with ice and strain.

Sake to Me

COCKTAIL GLASS

2 parts Orange Vodka
½ part Blue Curaçao
splash Sake

Shake with ice and strain.

Salamander

COCKTAIL GLASS

1½ parts Melon Liqueur
1½ parts Pisang Ambon® Liqueur
1 part Lemon Juice

Shake with ice and strain.

Salem

COCKTAIL GLASS

1 part Vodka
1 part Crème de Menthe (Green)
½ part Dry Vermouth
½ part Triple Sec

Shake with ice and strain.

Samarkanda

COCKTAIL GLASS

2 parts Passoã®
⅔ part Lemon Juice
1 part Orange Juice

Shake with ice and strain.

Sammy

COCKTAIL GLASS

½ part Black Sambuca
½ part Blackberry Brandy
½ part Amaretto
1½ parts Light Cream

Shake with ice and strain.

Samson Cocktail

COCKTAIL GLASS

1 part Amaretto
1 part Black Sambuca
1 part Blackberry Brandy
3 parts Light Cream

Shake with ice and strain.

Samurai

COCKTAIL GLASS

2 parts Sake
3/4 part Lime Juice
1/2 part Triple Sec
1/4 part Sweet & Sour Mix

Shake with ice and strain.

San Francisco Cocktail

COCKTAIL GLASS

1 part Sweet Vermouth
1 part Dry Vermouth
1 part Sloe Gin
dash Orange Bitters

Shake with ice and strain.

San Juan Cocktail

COCKTAIL GLASS

1 part Light Rum
1/4 part 151-Proof Rum
1 part Grapefruit Juice
1/2 part Lemon Juice
1/4 part Cream of Coconut

Shake with ice and strain.

San Sebastian

COCKTAIL GLASS

1 part Gin
splash Rum
splash Triple Sec
2 splashes Grapefruit Juice
2 splashes Lemon Juice

Shake with ice and strain.

Sangria

COCKTAIL GLASS

2 parts Orange Vodka
1/2 part Red Wine
splash Cherry Brandy
1/2 part Orange Juice
splash Lemon Juice
splash Lime Juice

Shake with ice and strain.

Sands of Nevada

COCKTAIL GLASS

1 1/2 parts Gin
2/3 part Blue Curaçao
2/3 part Grapefruit Juice
splash Lemon Juice

Shake with ice and strain.

Santa Maria

COCKTAIL GLASS

1 part Gold Tequila
1 part Spiced Rum
dash Sweet Vermouth

Shake with ice and strain.

Sante Fe

COCKTAIL GLASS

1 1/2 parts Brandy
1/2 part Grapefruit Juice
1/2 part Cinzano®

Shake with ice and strain.

Santo Domingo

COCKTAIL GLASS

1 part Cream
1 part Dark Rum
1/2 part Amaretto
1/2 part Coffee Liqueur

Shake with ice and strain.

Saratoga Cocktail
COCKTAIL GLASS

2 parts Brandy
splash Pineapple Juice
splash Lemon Juice
splash Maraschino Liqueur
2 dashes Bitters

Shake with ice and strain.

Saratoga Party
COCKTAIL GLASS

1½ parts Vodka
splash Grenadine
dash Angostura® Bitters
splash Club Soda

Shake with ice and strain.

Sarteano
COCKTAIL GLASS

1 part Galliano®
1 part Orange Liqueur
1 part Triple Sec
1 part Crème de Cassis
splash Lime Cordial
splash Lemon Juice

Shake with ice and strain.

Satan's Whiskers
COCKTAIL GLASS

½ part Gin
½ part Sweet Vermouth
½ part Dry Vermouth
¼ part Grand Marnier®
1 part Orange Juice
dash Orange Bitters

Shake with ice and strain.

Satin Doll
COCKTAIL GLASS

1 part Brandy
½ part Triple Sec
½ part Pineapple Juice

Shake with ice and strain.

Satin Glow
COCKTAIL GLASS

1½ parts Gin
splash Crème de Banane
⅔ part Orange Juice
splash Pineapple Juice

Shake with ice and strain.

Savannah
COCKTAIL GLASS

1 part Gin
splash Crème de Cacao (White)
splash Orange Juice
1 Egg White

Shake with ice and strain.

Save Ferris
COCKTAIL GLASS

1 part Kiwi Schnapps
1 part Scotch
1 part Cream

Shake with ice and strain.

Save the Planet
COCKTAIL GLASS

1 part Vodka
1 part Melon Liqueur
½ part Blue Curaçao
2 splashes Green Chartreuse®

Shake with ice and strain.

Savoy Hotel Cocktail
COCKTAIL GLASS

1 part Crème de Cacao (White)
1 part Brandy
1 part Bénédictine®

Shake with ice and strain.

Saxon Cocktail
COCKTAIL GLASS

1¾ part Light Rum
splash Grenadine
½ part Lime Juice

Shake with ice and strain.

Sayonara

COCKTAIL GLASS

1 part Vodka
½ part Dry Vermouth
¼ part Triple Sec
¼ part Apricot Brandy
splash Papaya Juice

Shake with ice and strain.

Scallywag

COCKTAIL GLASS

3 parts Light Rum
1 part Blue Curaçao
1 part Galliano®
1 part Lime Juice

Shake with ice and strain.

Scanex

COCKTAIL GLASS

2 parts Vodka
1 part Cranberry Liqueur
1 part Lemon Juice
1 part Grenadine
1 part Sugar

Shake with ice and strain.

Scarabeus

COCKTAIL GLASS

1 part Gin
1 part Blue Curaçao
½ part Crème de Banane
½ part Crème de Coconut

Shake with ice and strain.

Scarlet Lady

COCKTAIL GLASS

1½ parts Vodka
¼ part Coffee Liqueur
¼ part Cherry Brandy

Shake with ice and strain.

Scarlett Fever

COCKTAIL GLASS

1½ parts Citrus Vodka
½ part Amaretto
1 part Cranberry Juice Cocktail

Shake with ice and strain.

Schnapple

COCKTAIL GLASS

1 part Gin
½ part Grenadine
1 part Sweet Vermouth
½ part Apple Brandy

Shake with ice and strain.

Scooter

COCKTAIL GLASS

1 part Brandy
1 part Amaretto
1 part Light Cream

Shake with ice and strain.

Scotch Bishop Cocktail

COCKTAIL GLASS

1 part Scotch
½ part Dry Vermouth
splash Triple Sec
2 splashes Orange Juice
dash Powdered Sugar

Shake with ice and strain.

Scotch Citrus

COCKTAIL GLASS

1½ parts Scotch
1 part Grand Marnier®
1 part Lemon Juice
2 splashes Grenadine

Shake with ice and strain.

Scratch and Win

COCKTAIL GLASS

1 part Peach Schnapps
1 part Sambuca
1 part Cranberry Juice Cocktail

Shake with ice and strain.

Screaming Banana Banshee

COCKTAIL GLASS

½ part Banana Liqueur
½ part Vodka
½ part Crème de Cacao (White)
1½ parts Cream

Shake with ice and strain.

Screaming Banshee

COCKTAIL GLASS

1 part Banana Liqueur
1 part Vodka
½ part Crème de Cacao (White)
½ part Cream

Shake with ice and strain.

Screaming Orgasm

COCKTAIL GLASS

1 part Vodka
1 part Amaretto
1 part Crème de Cacao (White)
1 part Triple Sec
2 parts Cream

Shake with ice and strain.

Screaming Viking

COCKTAIL GLASS

2 parts Vodka
1 part Dry Vermouth
1 part Lime Juice

Shake with ice and strain.

Screech Owl

COCKTAIL GLASS

1½ parts Brandy
splash Orange Liqueur
1 part Blue Curaçao
½ part Strawberry Juice
1 part Lemon Juice

Shake with ice and strain.

Screwed and Tattooed

COCKTAIL GLASS

2 parts Silver Tequila
1 part Melon Liqueur
1 part Absinthe
1 part Lemon Juice

Shake with ice and strain.

Scurvy

COCKTAIL GLASS

2 parts Banana Liqueur
2 parts Vodka
splash Orange Juice

Shake with ice and strain.

Scuttle for Liberty

COCKTAIL GLASS

1½ parts Vodka
½ part Lychee Liqueur
⅔ part Pineapple Juice
⅔ part Mango Juice
⅔ part Lemon Juice

Shake with ice and strain.

Sea Foam

COCKTAIL GLASS

1 part Light Rum
½ part Triple Sec
splash Peppermint Liqueur
dash Powdered Sugar
½ part Lime Juice

Shake with ice and strain.

Sea Spray

COCKTAIL GLASS

1½ parts Gin
½ part Melon Liqueur
½ part Pineapple Juice

Shake with ice and strain.

Seaweed

COCKTAIL GLASS

1½ parts Pineapple Vodka
1½ parts Melon Liqueur
¼ part Strawberry Liqueur
¼ part Pineapple Juice

Shake with ice and strain.

Seether

COCKTAIL GLASS

1½ parts Vodka
½ part Cherry Brandy
1 part Orange Juice
dash Orange Bitters

Shake with ice and strain.

Self Starter

COCKTAIL GLASS

2 parts Gin
1 part Dry Vermouth
½ part Apricot Brandy
¼ part Pernod®

Shake with ice and strain.

Semen de Burro

COCKTAIL GLASS

1½ parts Coconut Rum
½ part Lemon Juice
1 part Crème de Coconut

Shake with ice and strain.

Sensation Cocktail

COCKTAIL GLASS

1½ parts Gin
¼ part Lemon Juice
splash Maraschino Cherry Juice

Shake with ice and strain.

Sensitivity

COCKTAIL GLASS

1 part Amaretto
1½ parts Calvados Apple Brandy
splash Green Chartreuse®
splash Cream

Shake with ice and strain.

Sensual Healing

COCKTAIL GLASS

1 part Vanilla Liqueur
1 part Mandarine Napoléon® Liqueur
1 part Cream

Shake with ice and strain.

Seppuku

COCKTAIL GLASS

1½ parts Gin
splash Melon Liqueur
splash Lychee Liqueur
splash Lemon Juice
1 part Grapefruit Juice

Shake with ice and strain.

Serpentine

COCKTAIL GLASS

1 part Light Rum
½ part Brandy
½ part Sweet Vermouth
½ part Lemon Juice
dash Sugar

Shake with ice and strain.

Seventh Heaven Cocktail

COCKTAIL GLASS

1½ parts Vodka
2 splashes Grapefruit Juice
2 splashes Maraschino Cherry Juice

Shake with ice and strain.

Sex Apple

COCKTAIL GLASS

2 parts Vodka
splash Goldschläger®
½ part Apple Liqueur
1 part Apple Juice

Shake with ice and strain.

Sex on the Beach (West Coast)

COCKTAIL GLASS

1 part Melon Liqueur
2 parts Pineapple Juice

Shake with ice and strain.

Sex on the Space Station

COCKTAIL GLASS

1 part Melon Liqueur
1 part Blue Curaçao
1 part Sweet & Sour Mix
splash Lime Juice

Shake with ice and strain.

Sex on the Table

COCKTAIL GLASS

1 part Cognac
½ part Kirschwasser
½ part Banana Juice
1 part Pineapple Juice
dash Orange Bitters

Shake with ice and strain.

Sexual

COCKTAIL GLASS

1 part Crème de Menthe (Green)
1 part Maraschino Liqueur
1/2 part Brandy
1/2 part Gin

Shake with ice and strain.

Sexy

COCKTAIL GLASS

1 part Dry Gin
1 part Triple Sec
1 part Apricot Brandy
splash Grapefruit Juice

Shake with ice and strain.

Sexy Mountain

COCKTAIL GLASS

1 part Strawberry Liqueur
1 part Gin
1/2 part Cream
1/2 part Strawberry Puree

Shake with ice and strain.

Shagger

COCKTAIL GLASS

2 parts Jägermeister
2 parts Orange Juice
1 part Milk

Shake with ice and strain.

Shaker

COCKTAIL GLASS

1 1/2 parts Tequila
1/2 part Lemon Juice
splash Grenadine
1 part Pineapple Juice

Shake with ice and strain.

Shaker Cocktail

COCKTAIL GLASS

1 1/2 parts Tequila
3 parts Pineapple Juice
1/2 part Lemon Juice
1/12 part Grenadine

Shake with ice and strain.

Shakkah Venue

COCKTAIL GLASS

2/3 part Jamaican Rum
2/3 part Lemon Juice
1/2 part Melon Liqueur
1/2 part Pisang Ambon® Liqueur
splash Crème de Coconut
1 1/2 parts Pineapple Juice

Shake with ice and strain.

Shamrock Cocktail

COCKTAIL GLASS

1 1/2 parts Irish Whiskey
1 part Sweet Vermouth
1/2 part Crème de Menthe (Green)
1/2 part Green Chartreuse®

Shake with ice and strain.

Shamrocker

COCKTAIL GLASS

1 part Maraschino Liqueur
1 part Irish Whiskey
2/3 part Sweet Vermouth
2/3 part Club Soda

Shake with ice and strain.

Shark's Breath

COCKTAIL GLASS

1/2 part Vodka
1/2 part Gin
1/2 part Light Rum
1/2 part Blue Curaçao
1/4 part Lime Juice

Shake with ice and strain.

Sharp Soul

COCKTAIL GLASS

1 part Melon Liqueur
1 part Apple Brandy
1 part Sweet & Sour Mix
splash Lime Juice

Shake with ice and strain.

Sheer Elegance

COCKTAIL GLASS

1½ parts Amaretto
1½ parts Blackberry Liqueur
½ part Vodka

Shake with ice and strain.

Sheriff's Shield

COCKTAIL GLASS

1 part Dark Rum
½ part Mandarine Napoléon® Liqueur
½ part Peach Schnapps
1 part Cream
splash Galliano®

Shake with ice and strain.

Shining Star

COCKTAIL GLASS

1 part Gin
1 part Dry Vermouth
½ part Passion Fruit Liqueur
1 part Grapefruit Juice

Shake with ice and strain.

Ship Cocktail

COCKTAIL GLASS

1½ parts Sherry
splash Jim Beam®
splash Dark Rum
splash Plum Wine
dash Powdered Sugar

Shake with ice and strain.

Shiver

COCKTAIL GLASS

1 part Vodka
1 part Crème de Banane
½ part Parfait Amour

Shake with ice and strain.

Shompy

COCKTAIL GLASS

½ part Silver Tequila
½ part Orange Bitters
1 part Apricot Brandy
splash Campari®
dash Bitters

Shake with ice and strain.

Shooting Star

COCKTAIL GLASS

1 part Apricot Brandy
1 part Sweet Vermouth
dash Angostura® Bitters

Shake with ice and strain.

Short Girl

COCKTAIL GLASS

½ part Vodka
¼ part Coconut Rum
¼ part Peach Schnapps
1 part Orange Juice
1 part Pineapple Juice
splash Cranberry Juice Cocktail

Shake with ice and strain.

Shot in the Dark

COCKTAIL GLASS

2 parts Bacardi® Limón Rum
½ part Dry Vermouth
½ part Cherry Brandy
dash Orange Bitters

Shake with ice and strain.

Shotgun Wedding

COCKTAIL GLASS

1 part Gin
1 part Dubonnet® Blonde
2 splashes Cherry Brandy
2 splashes Orange Juice

Shake with ice and strain.

Showbiz
COCKTAIL GLASS

1 part Vodka
1 part Grapefruit Juice
1 part Crème de Cassis

Shake with ice and strain.

Shrek
COCKTAIL GLASS

1/2 part Kiwi Schnapps
1/2 part Melon Liqueur
1/2 part Vanilla Liqueur
1/2 part Absinthe
1 1/2 parts Cream

Shake with ice and strain.

Shut Out
COCKTAIL GLASS

1/2 part Blackberry Liqueur
1/2 part Southern Comfort®
1/2 part Sweet & Sour Mix
1 part Cranberry Juice Cocktail

Shake with ice and strain.

Siberian Express
COCKTAIL GLASS

1 part Dry Vermouth
1/2 part Coffee
1/4 part Simple Syrup
1 part Cold Espresso

Shake with ice and strain.

Siberian Surprise
COCKTAIL GLASS

1 part Vodka
1 part Peach Schnapps
1/2 part Crème de Coconut
1/2 part Sweet & Sour Mix

Shake with ice and strain.

Side Kick
COCKTAIL GLASS

2 parts Gin
1/2 part Cointreau®
1/2 part Crème de Cacao (White)
splash Lemon Juice

Shake with ice and strain.

Siesta
COCKTAIL GLASS

1 1/2 parts Tequila
3/4 part Lime Juice
1/2 part Sloe Gin

Shake with ice and strain.

Silent Broadsider
COCKTAIL GLASS

1 1/2 parts Light Rum
1/2 part Anisette
1/2 part Lemon Juice
splash Grenadine

Shake with ice and strain.

Silk Stocking
COCKTAIL GLASS

1 1/2 parts Tequila
1/2 part Crème de Cacao (Dark)
1/2 part Raspberry Liqueur
1 part Cream

Shake with ice and strain.

Silver Bullet
COCKTAIL GLASS

1 part Kümmel
1 part Gin
2 splashes Lemon Juice

Shake with ice and strain.

Silver Cherries Jubilee
COCKTAIL GLASS

1 1/2 parts Gin
1 1/2 parts Crème de Banane
1/2 part Cherry Brandy
1 1/2 parts Cream

Shake with ice and strain.

Silver Cocktail
COCKTAIL GLASS

1 part Gin
1 part Dry Vermouth
splash Simple Syrup
splash Maraschino Liqueur
2 dashes Orange Bitters

Shake with ice and strain.

Silver Dollar
COCKTAIL GLASS

1 part Crème de Banane
1 part Crème de Menthe (White)
1 part Light Cream

Shake with ice and strain.

Silver Star
COCKTAIL GLASS

1 part Bourbon
½ part Dry Vermouth
splash Cherry Brandy

Shake with ice and strain.

Silver Streak Cocktail
COCKTAIL GLASS

1½ parts Gin
1½ parts Kümmel

Shake with ice and strain.

Simple Charm
COCKTAIL GLASS

1 part Cognac
1 part Coffee Liqueur
1 part Amaretto
½ part Cream

Shake with ice and strain.

Singapore
COCKTAIL GLASS

1 part Goldschläger®
1 part Gin
½ part Sweet & Sour Mix
½ part Blueberry Schnapps

Shake with ice and strain.

Singing in the Rain
COCKTAIL GLASS

1 part Passion Fruit Liqueur
1 part Sloe Gin
1 part Mango Juice

Shake with ice and strain.

Sintra
COCKTAIL GLASS

1 part Melon Liqueur
⅔ part Orange Vodka
1 part Cream

Shake with ice and strain.

Sir Knight
COCKTAIL GLASS

2 parts Cognac
½ part Cointreau®
½ part Chartreuse®
dash Angostura® Bitters

Shake with ice and strain.

Sister Moonshine
COCKTAIL GLASS

1 part Vodka
1 part Dry Vermouth
½ part Apricot Brandy
½ part Grapefruit Juice

Shake with ice and strain.

Sister Soul
COCKTAIL GLASS

1½ parts Sloe Gin
⅔ part Sweet Vermouth
splash Blue Curaçao
dash Angostura® Bitters

Shake with ice and strain.

Sizilia
COCKTAIL GLASS

1 part Bourbon
1 part Crème de Banane
1 part Cherry Brandy
½ part Passion Fruit Juice

Shake with ice and strain.

Skippy Cosmo
COCKTAIL GLASS

1 part Vodka
½ part Cointreau®
¼ part Grenadine

Shake with ice and strain.

Slaughtering the Slothman

COCKTAIL GLASS

1 part Grand Marnier®
1 part Triple Sec
1 part Lemon Juice
splash Grenadine

Shake with ice and strain.

Sledge Hammer

COCKTAIL GLASS

½ part Lemon Juice
½ part Fruit Liqueur
½ part Blue Curaçao
½ part Grand Marnier®
½ part Simple Syrup

Shake with ice and strain.

Sleepwalker

COCKTAIL GLASS

1½ parts Orange Vodka
½ part Blue Curaçao
½ part Chocolate Liqueur
1 part Cream

Shake with ice and strain.

Slick Willy

COCKTAIL GLASS

1 part Light Rum
1 part Brandy
1 part Triple Sec
splash Lemon Juice

Shake with ice and strain.

Slocommotion

COCKTAIL GLASS

2 parts Gin
½ part Sloe Gin
1 part Cranberry Juice Cocktail
½ part Lime Cordial

Shake with ice and strain.

Sloe Advance

COCKTAIL GLASS

1 part Sloe Gin
2 parts Gin
½ part Lychee Liqueur
dash Peychaud's® Bitters

Shake with ice and strain.

Smile Cocktail

COCKTAIL GLASS

1 part Gin
1 part Grenadine
splash Lemon Juice

Shake with ice and strain.

Smiling Ivy

COCKTAIL GLASS

1 part Peach Schnapps
1 part Light Rum
1 part Pineapple Juice
1 Egg White

Shake with ice and strain.

Smokescreen

COCKTAIL GLASS

1 part Dark Rum
1 part Cherry Brandy
¼ part Lime Juice

Shake with ice and strain.

Smooth Canadian

COCKTAIL GLASS

1 part Whiskey
½ part Triple Sec
½ part Lime Syrup
1 part Cherry Juice

Shake with ice and strain.

Smooth Grand

COCKTAIL GLASS

⅔ part Vodka
⅔ part Amaretto
⅔ part Root Beer Schnapps
1 part Cream

Shake with ice and strain.

Smurf® Cum

COCKTAIL GLASS

1 1/2 parts Light Rum
1/2 part Crème de Cacao (White)
1/2 part Blue Curaçao
1 part Cream

Shake with ice and strain.

Snake in the Grass

COCKTAIL GLASS

1 part Gin
1 part Cointreau®
1/2 part Dry Vermouth
1/2 part Lemon Juice

Shake with ice and strain.

Snake in the Pants

COCKTAIL GLASS

1 part Light Rum
1/2 part Brandy
1/2 part Sweet Vermouth
1/2 part Lemon Juice
dash Sugar

Shake with ice and strain.

Snow Fox

COCKTAIL GLASS

3/4 part Vanilla Liqueur
3/4 part Crème de Cacao (White)
1/2 part Cream of Coconut
1/2 part Cream
1/2 part Milk

Shake with ice and strain.

Snow Job

COCKTAIL GLASS

2 parts Pear Liqueur
1 part Cream
dash Cinnamon

Shake with ice and strain.

Snow Ski

COCKTAIL GLASS

1 1/2 parts Blackberry Liqueur
1 part Peppermint Liqueur

Shake with ice and strain.

Snow Slip

COCKTAIL GLASS

1 part Vanilla Liqueur
1 part Melon Liqueur
1 part Orange Juice

Shake with ice and strain.

Snyder

COCKTAIL GLASS

1/2 part Dry Vermouth
1 1/2 parts Gin
1/2 part Triple Sec

Shake with ice and strain.

So-So Cocktail

COCKTAIL GLASS

1 part Gin
1 part Dry Vermouth
1/2 part Apple Brandy
1/2 part Grenadine

Shake with ice and strain.

Society Cocktail

COCKTAIL GLASS

3/4 part Dry Vermouth
1 1/2 parts Gin
splash Grenadine

Shake with ice and strain.

Socrates

COCKTAIL GLASS

2 parts Canadian Whisky
1/2 part Apricot Brandy
1/6 part Cointreau
dash Bitters

Shake with ice and strain.

Sogno d'Autunno

COCKTAIL GLASS

1 1/2 parts Vodka
1/2 part Crème de Banane
1/2 part Dark Rum
splash Blue Curaçao
splash Lime Juice

Shake with ice and strain.

Son of Adam

COCKTAIL GLASS

1 ½ parts Light Rum
½ part Apricot Brandy
½ part Lemon Juice
splash Grenadine
1 tsp Sugar

Shake with ice and strain.

Son of Sam

COCKTAIL GLASS

1 ½ parts Light Rum
½ part Apricot Brandy
¼ part Lemon Juice
2 splashes Grenadine
dash Sugar

Shake with ice and strain.

Sonora Cocktail

COCKTAIL GLASS

1 ½ parts Light Rum
1 ½ parts Calvados Apple Brandy
splash Apricot Brandy

Shake with ice and strain.

Soother Cocktail

COCKTAIL GLASS

1 part Apple Brandy
1 part Brandy
1 part Triple Sec
1 part Lemon Juice
dash Powdered Sugar

Shake with ice and strain.

Sophisticated Lady

COCKTAIL GLASS

1 ½ parts Gin
⅔ part Maraschino Liqueur
⅔ part Raspberry Liqueur
splash Lemon Juice

Shake with ice and strain.

Soul Bossa Nova

COCKTAIL GLASS

1 part Vodka
½ part Crème de Cacao (White)
splash Grenadine

Shake with ice and strain.

Sound of Silence

COCKTAIL GLASS

1 ½ parts Vodka
½ part Lychee Liqueur
½ part Lemon Juice
½ part Simple Syrup
splash Orange Juice

Shake with ice and strain.

Sound the Retreat

COCKTAIL GLASS

½ part Crème de Banane
1 part Brandy
⅔ part Grand Marnier®
1 part Sweet & Sour Mix

Shake with ice and strain.

Sour Apple Cosmopolitan

COCKTAIL GLASS

½ part Sour Apple Schnapps
1 ½ parts Vodka
1 part Cranberry Juice Cocktail
splash Lime Juice

Shake with ice and strain.

Sour French Kiss

COCKTAIL GLASS

1 part Crème de Banane
1 part Kiwi Schnapps
1 part Sweet & Sour Mix

Shake with ice and strain.

Sour Strawberry

COCKTAIL GLASS

1 part Scotch
1 part Sweet & Sour Mix
1 part Strawberry Liqueur

Shake with ice and strain.

South Beach Cosmopolitan

COCKTAIL GLASS

2 parts Citrus Vodka
½ part Raspberry Liqueur
½ part Cranberry Juice Cocktail

Shake with ice and strain.

South Freshness

COCKTAIL GLASS

1½ parts Southern Comfort®
splash Brandy
splash Peppermint Liqueur
splash Grenadine
½ part Lemon Juice
1 part Passion Fruit Juice

Shake with ice and strain.

South Park

COCKTAIL GLASS

1½ parts Southern Comfort®
½ part Apricot Brandy
splash Simple Syrup
1 part Pear Juice
½ part Lemon Juice

Shake with ice and strain.

South Seas Aperitif

COCKTAIL GLASS

1 part Melon Liqueur
½ part Crème de Banane
½ part Crème de Coconut
½ part Lime Juice

Shake with ice and strain.

Southern Bride

COCKTAIL GLASS

1½ parts Gin
1 part Grapefruit Juice
splash Maraschino Cherry Juice

Shake with ice and strain.

Southern Comfort® Cocktail

COCKTAIL GLASS

1¾ parts Southern Comfort®
¾ part Orange Liqueur
½ part Lime Juice

Shake with ice and strain.

Southern Comfort® Manhattan

COCKTAIL GLASS

2 parts Southern Comfort®
1 part Sweet Vermouth
2 dashes Bitters
splash Grenadine

Shake with ice and strain.

Southern Fortune Teller

COCKTAIL GLASS

1 part Southern Comfort®
⅔ part Crème de Cassis
½ part Amaretto
½ part Cream

Shake with ice and strain.

Southern Life

COCKTAIL GLASS

½ part Vodka
½ part Kiwi Schnapps
½ part Southern Comfort®
½ part Cranberry Juice Cocktail
1 part Orange Juice

Shake with ice and strain.

Southern Sparkler

COCKTAIL GLASS

1 part Southern Comfort®
1 part Grapefruit Juice
1 part Pineapple Juice
splash Seltzer

Stir gently with ice and strain.

Southern Sunrise

COCKTAIL GLASS

1 part Southern Comfort®
½ part Grenadine
½ part Lemon Juice
1 part Orange Juice

Shake with ice and strain.

Southern Twist

COCKTAIL GLASS

1 part Passion Fruit Liqueur
1 part Southern Comfort®
1 part Cranberry Juice Cocktail

Shake with ice and strain.

Southwest One
COCKTAIL GLASS

1 part Vodka
1 part Orange Juice
1 part Campari®

Shake with ice and strain.

SpA
COCKTAIL GLASS

1½ parts Apricot Brandy
1½ parts Dry Vermouth

Shake with ice and strain.

Space
COCKTAIL GLASS

1½ parts Gin
1 part Frangelico®

Shake with ice and strain.

Space Age
COCKTAIL GLASS

1 part Light Rum
½ part Triple Sec
½ part Kiwi Schnapps
1½ parts Orange Juice

Shake with ice and strain.

Space Truckin'
COCKTAIL GLASS

1½ parts Kiwi Schnapps
1 part Blue Curaçao
½ part Lemon Juice

Shake with ice and strain.

Spanish Bombs
COCKTAIL GLASS

1½ parts Brandy
1½ parts Dry Sherry
½ part Galliano®

Shake with ice and strain.

Spanish Eyes
COCKTAIL GLASS

⅔ part Blue Curaçao
1 part Licor 43®
splash Orange Juice
splash Cream

Shake with ice and strain.

Spanish Kiss
COCKTAIL GLASS

1 part Brandy
½ part Crème de Banane
½ part Coffee Liqueur
⅔ part Cream

Shake with ice and strain.

Spanish Moss
COCKTAIL GLASS

½ part Silver Tequila
¾ part Coffee Liqueur
½ part Crème de Menthe (Green)

Shake with ice and strain.

Spark in the Night
COCKTAIL GLASS

1½ parts Dark Rum
½ part Coffee Liqueur
2 splashes Lime Juice

Shake with ice and strain.

Special
COCKTAIL GLASS

1 part Rye Whiskey
splash Apricot Brandy
1 part Lemon Juice
dash Sugar

Shake with ice and strain.

Spellbinder
COCKTAIL GLASS

2 parts Citrus Vodka
⅔ part Melon Liqueur
splash Blue Curaçao

Shake with ice and strain.

Spencer Cocktail
COCKTAIL GLASS

1½ parts Gin
¾ part Apricot Brandy
splash Orange Juice
dash Bitters

Shake with ice and strain.

Sphinx
COCKTAIL GLASS

1 part Gin
splash Dry Vermouth
splash Sweet Vermouth

Shake with ice and strain.

Spin Cycle
COCKTAIL GLASS

1 part Gin
1 part Orange Vodka
½ part Blue Curaçao
½ part Mandarine Napoléon® Liqueur

Stir gently with ice and strain.

Spinal Tap
COCKTAIL GLASS

½ part Apricot Brandy
1 part Apple Brandy
splash Orange Juice

Shake with ice and strain.

Spinward Cocktail
COCKTAIL GLASS

1 part Jim Beam®
1 part Irish Cream Liqueur
1 part Peppermint Liqueur
splash Crème de Cacao (White)

Shake with ice and strain.

Spirit Wind
COCKTAIL GLASS

1 part Spiced Rum
1 part Passion Fruit Liqueur
1 part Cranberry Juice Cocktail

Shake with ice and strain.

Spitball
COCKTAIL GLASS

2 parts Gin
½ part Dry Vermouth
2 splashes Maraschino Liqueur

Shake with ice and strain.

Spring Feeling Cocktail
COCKTAIL GLASS

1 part Gin
½ part Green Chartreuse®
2 splashes Lemon Juice

Shake with ice and strain.

Sprint
COCKTAIL GLASS

1½ parts Grappa
1½ parts Amaro Averna®
½ part Grand Marnier®

Shake with ice and strain.

Spruce
COCKTAIL GLASS

⅔ part Peppermint Liqueur
1 part Brandy
½ part Dry Vermouth
½ part Sweet & Sour Mix

Shake with ice and strain.

Spy's Dream
COCKTAIL GLASS

splash Melon Liqueur
1 part Currant Vodka
1 part Bacardi® Limón Rum
splash Lime Cordial

Shake with ice and strain.

Srap Shrinker
COCKTAIL GLASS

1 part Cranberry Vodka
½ part Raspberry Liqueur
splash Orange Liqueur
½ part Lemon Juice
⅔ part Grapefruit Juice

Shake with ice and strain.

Ssimo Suprize

COCKTAIL GLASS

1 part Citrus Vodka
1 part Melon Liqueur
½ part Kiwi Schnapps
½ part Lemon Syrup

Shake with ice and strain.

St-Germain Pineapple Cosmo

COCKTAIL GLASS

1½ parts Vodka
1 part St-Germain
½ part Pineapple Juice
¼ part Lime Juice

Shake with ice and strain. Garnish with a wedge of Pineapple or Lime.

St. Mark Cocktail

COCKTAIL GLASS

1 part Gin
1 part Dry Vermouth
splash Cherry Brandy
splash Vermouth

Shake with ice and strain.

St. Ignes

COCKTAIL GLASS

2 parts Dark Rum
1 part Passion Fruit Liqueur
splash Amaretto
1 part Pineapple Juice
1 part Lime Juice

Shake with ice and strain.

St. Vincent

COCKTAIL GLASS

1 part Vodka
1 part Apricot Brandy
1 part Licor 43®
splash Grenadine

Shake with ice and strain.

Stanley Cocktail

COCKTAIL GLASS

1 part Light Rum
3 parts Gin
1 part Lemon Juice
splash Grenadine

Shake with ice and strain.

Stanley Senior

COCKTAIL GLASS

2 parts Light Rum
½ part Cranberry Liqueur
1 part Grapefruit Juice

Shake with ice and strain.

Star Cocktail

COCKTAIL GLASS

1 part Sweet Vermouth
1 part Apple Brandy
dash Bitters

Shake with ice and strain.

Star Legend

COCKTAIL GLASS

1 part Vodka
¼ part Apricot Brandy
¼ part Campari®
¼ part Raspberry Liqueur
½ part Orange Juice
splash Blue Curaçao

Shake with ice and strain.

Star of Love

COCKTAIL GLASS

1 part Vodka
1 part Crème de Cacao (Dark)
splash Frangelico®
1 part Cream

Shake with ice and strain.

Star System

COCKTAIL GLASS

1½ parts Peach Schnapps
½ part Vanilla Vodka
1 part Orange Juice
1 part Cream

Shake with ice and strain.

Starry Havana

COCKTAIL GLASS

1 part Amarula
1 part RumChata
1 part Spiced Rum

Shake with ice and strain. Garnish with a dusting of Cinnamon.

Starry Night

COCKTAIL GLASS

1 part Blue Curaçao
1 part Cinnamon Schnapps
1 part Rumple Minze®

Shake with ice and strain.

Stratosphere

COCKTAIL GLASS

2 parts Light Rum
1 part Brandy
1 part Cherry Brandy
1 part Simple Syrup

Shake with ice and strain.

Statue of Liberty

COCKTAIL GLASS

1½ parts Apricot Brandy
½ part Light Rum
splash Simple Syrup

Shake with ice and strain.

Steamboat Gin

COCKTAIL GLASS

1½ parts Gin
¾ part Southern Comfort®
½ part Grapefruit Juice
½ part Lemon Juice

Shake with ice and strain.

Steamboat Queen

COCKTAIL GLASS

1 part Whiskey
1 part Gin
½ part Apricot Brandy
dash Bitters
splash Lemon Juice

Shake with ice and strain.

Stella's Stinger

COCKTAIL GLASS

1½ parts Tequila
splash Pernod®
splash Crème de Menthe (White)

Shake with ice and strain.

Step by Step

COCKTAIL GLASS

1 part Light Rum
1 part Blue Curaçao
1 part Lemon Juice
1 part Mango Juice
1 part Passion Fruit Juice
1 part Kiwi Syrup

Shake with ice and strain.

Sterlitamak

COCKTAIL GLASS

1½ parts Cherry Brandy
1½ parts Vodka
splash Dubonnet® Blonde
splash Lemon Juice

Shake with ice and strain.

Stolen Sorrow

COCKTAIL GLASS

1 part Cherry Brandy
⅔ part Gin
splash Passoã®
⅔ part Grapefruit Juice
splash Lemon Juice

Shake with ice and strain.

Stone Cocktail

COCKTAIL GLASS

1 part Dry Sherry
½ part Sweet Vermouth
½ part Light Rum

Shake with ice and strain.

Stonehenge Collins

COCKTAIL GLASS

2½ parts Gin
½ part Simple Syrup
splash Crème de Menthe (White)

Shake with ice and strain.

Stoner on Acid

COCKTAIL GLASS

1 part Coconut Rum
1 part Alizé®
1 part Jägermeister®

Shake with ice and strain.

Stork Club Cocktail

COCKTAIL GLASS

1½ parts Gin
splash Triple Sec
splash Lime Juice
dash Angostura® Bitters

Shake with ice and strain.

Stovocor

COCKTAIL GLASS

1 part Jim Beam®
1 part Triple Sec
2/3 part Sloe Gin
½ part Lemon Juice

Shake with ice and strain.

Strange Brew

COCKTAIL GLASS

1½ parts Gin
splash Crème de Cacao (White)
dash Angostura® Bitters
splash Lemon Juice

Shake with ice and strain.

Stranger in Town

COCKTAIL GLASS

1½ parts Light Rum
½ part Sweet Vermouth
½ part Calvados Apple Brandy
½ part Cherry Brandy

Shake with ice and strain.

Strapple

COCKTAIL GLASS

1½ parts Sloe Gin
splash Strawberry Liqueur
splash Cider
splash Lemon Juice

Shake with ice and strain.

Strawberry Girl

COCKTAIL GLASS

1 part Vodka
1 part Strawberry Liqueur
1 part Crème de Cacao (White)

Shake with ice and strain.

Strawsmopolitan

COCKTAIL GLASS

2 parts Strawberry Vodka
1 part Cointreau®
splash Lime Juice
splash Cranberry Juice Cocktail

Shake with ice and strain.

Stress Buster

COCKTAIL GLASS

½ part Dry Gin
½ part Dry Vermouth
¼ part Triple Sec
¼ part Apricot Brandy
splash Peach Schnapps

Shake with ice and strain.

Strike!

COCKTAIL GLASS

½ part Triple Sec
2/3 part Vodka
2/3 part Passoã®

Shake with ice and strain.

Stupid Cupid

COCKTAIL GLASS

2 parts Citrus Vodka
½ part Sloe Gin
splash Sweet & Sour Mix

Shake with ice and strain.

Stupid Cupid #2

COCKTAIL GLASS

1 part Crème de Cacao (White)
1 part Fireball Cinnamon Whiskey
1 part Irish Cream Liqueur

Shake with ice and strain.

Suavitas

COCKTAIL GLASS

½ part Strawberry Liqueur
½ part Frangelico®
½ part Galliano®
splash Melon Liqueur
1½ parts Cream

Shake with ice and strain.

Sucubus

COCKTAIL GLASS

1½ parts Gin
splash Calvados Apple Brandy
⅔ part White Wine

Shake with ice and strain.

Suffragette City

COCKTAIL GLASS

1½ parts Light Rum
½ part Grand Marnier®
½ part Lime Juice
splash Grenadine

Shake with ice and strain.

Sugar Daddy

COCKTAIL GLASS

2 parts Gin
2 splashes Maraschino Liqueur
1 part Pineapple Juice
dash Bitters

Shake with ice and strain.

Sugar Kiss

COCKTAIL GLASS

1 part Dark Rum
splash Strawberry Liqueur
splash Grenadine
1 part Pineapple Juice

Shake with ice and strain.

Summer Dreams

COCKTAIL GLASS

1 part Midori®
1 part Orange Juice
1 part Lemon Juice

Shake with ice and strain.

Summer Night Dream

COCKTAIL GLASS

2 parts Vodka
1 part Kirschwasser

Shake with ice and strain.

Sun Chaser

COCKTAIL GLASS

1 part Blue Curaçao
1 part Grand Marnier®
1 part Lemon Juice
splash Root Beer Schnapps

Shake with ice and strain.

Sun Ray

COCKTAIL GLASS

1 part Maraschino Liqueur
1 part Amaretto
splash Citrus Vodka

Shake with ice and strain.

Sunburnt Senorita

COCKTAIL GLASS

2 parts Southern Comfort®
¾ part Lime Juice
¼ part Simple Syrup

Shake with ice and strain.

Sunny Coco

COCKTAIL GLASS

1 part Crème de Coconut
1 part Pineapple
1 part Orange Juice
splash Cream of Coconut

Shake with ice and strain.

Sunny River

COCKTAIL GLASS

1 part Apricot Brandy
1 part Banana Puree
1 part Orange Juice
splash Lemon Juice

Shake with ice and strain.

Sunny Sour
COCKTAIL GLASS

2 parts Dark Rum
1/4 part Lemon Juice
dash Powdered Sugar

Shake with ice and strain.

Sunset Beach
COCKTAIL GLASS

1 part Vodka
1 part Melon Liqueur
1 part Crème de Coconut
1 part Apricot Juice

Shake with ice and strain.

Sunshine Cocktail
COCKTAIL GLASS

1 1/2 parts Gin
3/4 part Sweet Vermouth
dash Bitters

Shake with ice and strain.

Super Hero Respite
COCKTAIL GLASS

2/3 part Vodka
1/2 part Crème de Cacao (White)
1/2 part Raspberry Liqueur
1 part Milk

Shake with ice and strain.

Super Whites
COCKTAIL GLASS

1 part Triple Sec
1 part Crème de Coconut
1 part Goldschläger®

Shake with ice and strain.

Supernova
COCKTAIL GLASS

1 1/2 parts Light Rum
3/4 part Apple Brandy
2 splashes Sweet Vermouth

Shake with ice and strain.

Surf Rider
COCKTAIL GLASS

1 part Vodka
1 part Sweet Vermouth
1/2 part Lemon Juice
splash Grenadine
splash Orange Juice

Shake with ice and strain.

Surfing into the Waves
COCKTAIL GLASS

1 part Raspberry Liqueur
1 part Melon liqueur
1 part Crème de Coconut
1 part Lemon Juice
2 parts Cranberry Juice Cocktail

Shake with ice and strain.

Surreal Deal
COCKTAIL GLASS

1 part Apple Brandy
1/2 part Brandy
1/2 part Triple Sec
1/4 part Lemon Juice
dash Powdered Sugar

Shake with ice and strain.

Suspended Animation
COCKTAIL GLASS

1 part Melon Liqueur
1 part Grand Marnier®
splash Lime Juice

Shake with ice and strain.

Swallow
COCKTAIL GLASS

1 part Crème de Cacao (Dark)
1 part Crème de Banane
1 part Banana Purée
splash Scotch

Shake with ice and strain.

Swamp Water
COCKTAIL GLASS

1 part Vodka
1 part Blue Curaçao
1 part Galliano®

Shake with ice and strain.

Swat with a Finger
COCKTAIL GLASS

½ part Mezcal
splash Melon Liqueur
splash Lemon Juice
splash Orange Juice
½ part Club Soda

Shake with ice and strain.

Sweaty Balls
COCKTAIL GLASS

1 part Gin
1 part Apricot Brandy
1 part Dry Vermouth
splash Lemon Juice

Shake with ice and strain.

Swedish Chef
COCKTAIL GLASS

1 part Gin
1 part Grape Juice (red)
1 part Swedish Punch

Shake with ice and strain.

Swedish Lady
COCKTAIL GLASS

1 part Vodka
½ part Strawberry Liqueur
1 part Simple Syrup
½ part Cream

Shake with ice and strain.

Sweet Anne
COCKTAIL GLASS

1 part Apricot Brandy
splash Peach Schnapps
⅔ part Orange Juice
splash Lemon Juice

Shake with ice and strain.

Sweet Box
COCKTAIL GLASS

1 part Goldschläger®
1 part Coffee Liqueur
1 part Irish Cream Liqueur
1 part 151-Proof Rum
1 part Jägermeister®

Shake with ice and strain.

Sweet Charge
COCKTAIL GLASS

1½ parts Dry Vermouth
½ part Southern Comfort®
2 splashes Light Rum
2 splashes Triple Sec

Shake with ice and strain.

Sweet Cherry Cocktail
COCKTAIL GLASS

1 part Scotch
1 part Cherry Brandy
½ part Sweet Vermouth
½ part Orange Juice

Shake with ice and strain.

Sweet Dream Cocktail
COCKTAIL GLASS

1½ parts Vodka
½ part Cream of Coconut
1 part Orange Juice
1 tbsp powdered Sugar
splash Crème de Coconut

Shake with ice and strain.

Sweet Dumbo
COCKTAIL GLASS

1½ parts Blue Curaçao
½ part Light Rum
½ part Crème de Menthe (White)
1 part Cream

Shake with ice and strain.

Sweet Harmony

COCKTAIL GLASS

1 part Melon Liqueur
1 part Kiwi Juice
1 part Maraschino Liqueur

Shake with ice and strain.

Sweet Heart

COCKTAIL GLASS

1 part Parfait Amour
½ part Amaretto
½ part Vanilla Syrup
½ part Cream
1 part Blue Curaçao

Shake with ice and strain.

Sweet Jamaica

COCKTAIL GLASS

1½ parts Dark Rum
½ part Pineapple Juice
¼ part Lime Juice
splash Maraschino Liqueur

Shake with ice and strain.

Sweet Maria

COCKTAIL GLASS

1 part Vodka
1 part Amaretto
1 part Light Cream

Shake with ice and strain.

Sweet Melody

COCKTAIL GLASS

½ part Vanilla Liqueur
½ part Raspberry Liqueur
½ part Irish Cream Liqueur
⅔ part Plum Brandy
1 part Cream

Shake with ice and strain.

A Sweet Peach

COCKTAIL GLASS

2 parts Vanilla Vodka
1 part Peach Schnapps
½ part Sweet & Sour Mix
½ part Orange Juice

Shake with ice and strain.

Sweet Talk

COCKTAIL GLASS

1 part Raspberry Liqueur
1 part Brandy
1 part Cream

Shake with ice and strain.

Sweet William

COCKTAIL GLASS

1 part Apricot Brandy
1 part Pear Brandy
1 part Cream

Shake with ice and strain.

Swinging Spartan

COCKTAIL GLASS

⅔ part Gin
⅔ part Cherry Brandy
½ part Crème de Cassis
½ part Dry Vermouth
splash Lemon Juice

Shake with ice and strain.

Swiss Miss

COCKTAIL GLASS

1 part Vodka
1 part Crème de Cacao (White)
½ part Butterscotch Schnapps
½ part Frangelico®

Shake with ice and strain.

Sword Fish

COCKTAIL GLASS

1 part Melon Liqueur
½ part Dark Rum
½ part Light Rum
½ part Lemon Juice
fill with Club Soda

Shake all but Club Soda with ice and strain. Top with Club Soda.

TNT Cocktail

COCKTAIL GLASS

1 part Cognac
1 part Absinthe
½ part Cointreau®
dash Bitters

Stir gently with ice and strain.

Tadpole

COCKTAIL GLASS

1 part Kiwi Schnapps
1 part Silver Tequila
1 part Sweet & Sour Mix

Shake with ice and strain.

Tahiti Beach Hut

COCKTAIL GLASS

1½ parts Crème de Coconut
½ part Melon Liqueur
splash Cranberry Juice Cocktail
splash Pineapple Juice
⅔ part Sweet & Sour Mix

Shake with ice and strain.

Tailhook

COCKTAIL GLASS

2 parts Gin
⅔ part Maraschino Liqueur
splash Vanilla Liqueur
1 part Lemon Juice

Shake with ice and strain.

Tailspin Cocktail

COCKTAIL GLASS

1 part Gin
1 part Sweet Vermouth
1 part Green Chartreuse®
dash Orange Bitters

Shake with ice and strain.

Tales of the Future

COCKTAIL GLASS

3 parts Jägermeister®
1 part Melon Liqueur
1 part Raspberry Liqueur
1 part Pineapple Juice
splash Cranberry Juice Cocktail

Shake with ice and strain.

Tangarita

COCKTAIL GLASS

1½ parts Gin
3 parts Margarita Mix
splash Triple Sec

Shake with ice and strain.

Tantric

COCKTAIL GLASS

2 parts Vodka
1 part Passion Fruit Liqueur
splash Cranberry Juice Cocktail
splash Pineapple Juice

Shake with ice and strain.

Tap Dance

COCKTAIL GLASS

1 part Vodka
½ part Amaretto
½ part Peach Schnapps
1 part Orange Juice

Shake with ice and strain.

Tara Reed

COCKTAIL GLASS

½ part Peppermint Liqueur
1 part Light Rum
dash Powdered Sugar
½ part Lime Juice
splash Lemon Juice

Shake with ice and strain.

Tartantula

COCKTAIL GLASS

1½ parts Scotch
1 part Sweet Vermouth
½ part Bénédictine®

Shake with ice and strain.

Taste of Paradise
COCKTAIL GLASS
1 part Crème de Cacao (Dark)
1 part Crème de Coconut
1 part Coffee Liqueur
Shake with ice and strain.

Tasty Trinidad
COCKTAIL GLASS
1 part Citrus Flavored Vodka
1 part Blue Curaçao
½ part Sweet & Sour Mix
½ part Orange Juice
Shake with ice and strain.

Tattoo You
COCKTAIL GLASS
1 part Peach Schnapps
1 part Cranberry Vodka
1 part Orange Juice
Shake with ice and strain.

Tattooed Love Goddess
COCKTAIL GLASS
1 part Vodka
1 part Vanilla Liqueur
1 part Chocolate Liqueur
splash Cream
Shake with ice and strain.

Taxi Driver
COCKTAIL GLASS
1½ parts Gin
½ part Crème de Banane
1 part Lemon Juice
splash Simple Syrup
Shake with ice and strain.

Tea Break
COCKTAIL GLASS
2 parts Dark Rum
1 part Cold Tea
splash Lemon Juice
splash Grenadine
Stir gently with ice and strain.

Teenage Lobotomy
COCKTAIL GLASS
1½ parts Jim Beam®
1½ parts Vodka
splash Blue Curaçao
Shake with ice and strain.

Temperature Rise
COCKTAIL GLASS
½ part Peach Schnapps
½ part Amaretto
½ part Dark Rum
1½ parts Cranberry Juice Cocktail
Shake with ice and strain.

Temptations
COCKTAIL GLASS
1 part Light Rum
½ part Lime Juice
½ part Raspberry Liqueur
splash Grenadine
Shake with ice and strain.

Tenderness
COCKTAIL GLASS
⅔ part Vodka
½ part Passoã®
splash Grand Marnier®
splash Crème de Cassis
splash Lemon Juice
Shake with ice and strain.

Tennessee Rye
COCKTAIL GLASS
2 parts Rye Whiskey
1 part Maraschino Liqueur
Shake with ice and strain.

Tequila Mockingbird
COCKTAIL GLASS
1½ parts Tequila
¾ part Crème de Menthe (Green)
splash Lime Juice
Shake with ice and strain.

Tequila Pink

COCKTAIL GLASS

1½ parts Tequila
1 part Dry Vermouth
splash Grenadine

Shake with ice and strain.

Tequila Stinger

COCKTAIL GLASS

2 parts Tequila
½ part Crème de Menthe (White)

Shake with ice and strain.

Tequilini

COCKTAIL GLASS

2½ parts Casa Noble Crystal
splash Dry Vermouth
splash Lime Juice

Shake with ice and strain.

Tequini

COCKTAIL GLASS

3 parts Tequila
1 part Dry Vermouth
dash Bitters

Shake with ice and strain.

Terre Brûlée

COCKTAIL GLASS

1 part Brandy
½ part Blackberry Liqueur
½ part Vanilla Liqueur
1 part Cream

Shake with ice and strain.

Tesary

COCKTAIL GLASS

1 part Silver Tequila
½ part Coffee Liqueur
½ part Licor 43®
1 part Tomato Juice

Shake with ice and strain.

Thanksgiving Special

COCKTAIL GLASS

1 part Apricot Brandy
1 part Dry Vermouth
1 part Gin
splash Lemon Juice

Shake with ice and strain.

Thirst Quencher

COCKTAIL GLASS

splash Gin
splash Triple Sec
1 part Passoã®
1 part Strawberry Liqueur
fill with Club Soda

Shake all but Club Soda with ice and strain. Top with Club Soda.

Thirsty Vampire

COCKTAIL GLASS

½ part Grenadine
2 parts Cranberry Juice Cocktail
½ part Lemon Juice

Shake with ice and strain.

Thorns and More

COCKTAIL GLASS

1 part Gin
½ part Parfait Amour
1 part Orange Juice
splash Lime Juice
splash Cranberry Juice Cocktail

Shake with ice and strain.

Three Count

COCKTAIL GLASS

1 part Vodka
½ part Cherry Brandy
¼ part Crème de Banane
2 splashes Campari®

Shake with ice and strain.

Three Mile Island

COCKTAIL GLASS

3/4 part Vodka
3/4 part Midori®
1/4 part Lime Juice
2 parts Apple Juice

Shake with ice and strain.

Three Miller Cocktail

COCKTAIL GLASS

1 1/2 parts Light Rum
3/4 part Brandy
splash Lemon Juice
splash Grenadine

Shake with ice and strain.

Three Stripes

COCKTAIL GLASS

1 part Gin
1/2 part Orange Juice
1/2 part Dry Vermouth

Shake with ice and strain.

Thriller

COCKTAIL GLASS

1 1/2 parts Scotch
1 part Green Ginger Wine
1 part Orange Juice

Shake with ice and strain.

Thug Heaven

COCKTAIL GLASS

2 parts Alizé®
2 parts Vodka

Shake with ice and strain.

Thunderbolt

COCKTAIL GLASS

3/4 part Gin
3/4 part Apricot Brandy
2 splashes Grenadine
1/4 part Lemon Juice

Shake with ice and strain.

Tierra del Fuego

COCKTAIL GLASS

1 part Dark Rum
1 part Tia Maria®

Shake with ice and strain.

Tiger Juice

COCKTAIL GLASS

2 parts Vodka
1/2 part Triple Sec
1 part Orange Juice
1/2 part Lemon Juice

Shake with ice and strain.

Tiki Torch

COCKTAIL GLASS

1 1/2 parts White Wine
1/4 part Pineapple Juice
3 splashes Maraschino Liqueur

Shake with ice and strain.

Tikini

COCKTAIL GLASS

1 part Vodka
1/2 part Raspberry Liqueur
1/2 part Blue Curaçao
splash Cranberry Juice Cocktail
splash Pear Juice
splash Lime Juice

Shake with ice and strain.

Tilt-a-Whirl®

COCKTAIL GLASS

1 1/2 parts Dark Rum
1/2 part Cherry Brandy
1/2 part Sweet Vermouth
1/4 part Lemon Juice
dash Sugar

Shake with ice and strain.

Time Killer

COCKTAIL GLASS

2 parts Tequila
1 part Crème de Cacao (Dark)
1 part Heavy Cream
dash Cocoa Powder

Shake with ice and strain.

Time Warp
COCKTAIL GLASS

1½ parts Light Rum
½ part Grand Marnier®
¼ part Lime Juice
2 splashes Grenadine

Shake with ice and strain.

Timeless
COCKTAIL GLASS

2 parts Scotch
½ part Triple Sec
½ part Grapefruit Juice

Shake with ice and strain.

Tireless
COCKTAIL GLASS

½ part Vanilla Liqueur
½ part Crème de Coconut
½ part Butterscotch Schnapps
½ part Crème de Banane
1 part Cream

Shake with ice and strain.

Titanic
COCKTAIL GLASS

1½ parts Vodka
½ part Dry Vermouth
½ part Galliano®
½ part Blue Curaçao

Shake with ice and strain.

Titi Pink
COCKTAIL GLASS

⅔ part Passion Fruit Liqueur
2 parts Vanilla Vodka
splash Cranberry Juice Cocktail
splash Orange Juice

Shake with ice and strain.

Toad Cocktail
COCKTAIL GLASS

⅔ part Ginger Brandy
½ part Triple Sec
⅔ part Lemon Juice

Shake with ice and strain.

Tobago Buca
COCKTAIL GLASS

1 part Melon Liqueur
½ part Peach Schnapps
1 part Sambuca
⅔ part Milk

Shake with ice and strain.

Todos Diaz
COCKTAIL GLASS

1 part Cherry Brandy
1 part Gold Tequila
1 part Ginger Ale
splash Lemon Juice

Shake with ice and strain.

Tojo
COCKTAIL GLASS

1 part Triple Sec
1 part Apricot Brandy
1 part Gin
splash Lemon Juice

Shake with ice and strain.

Tokyo Cosmo
COCKTAIL GLASS

1½ parts Vodka
1½ parts Sake
¼ part Pineapple Juice

Shake with ice and strain.

Tomb Raider
COCKTAIL GLASS

1½ parts Peach Schnapps
½ part Dark Rum
1½ parts Kiwi Juice
splash Lemon Juice

Shake with ice and strain.

Top Hat
COCKTAIL GLASS

1½ parts Gin
1 part Apricot Brandy
splash Grenadine

Shake with ice and strain.

Top of the Hill

COCKTAIL GLASS

1½ parts Orange Juice
1½ parts Sweet Vermouth
splash Pineapple Juice
dash Orange Bitters

Shake with ice and strain.

Topaz

COCKTAIL GLASS

2 parts Scotch
1 part Butterscotch Schnapps
2 splashes Galliano®

Shake with ice and strain.

Topps

COCKTAIL GLASS

1 part Crème de Banane
1 part Maraschino Liqueur
1 part Melon Liqueur
1 part Vodka
1 part Sweet & Sour Mix
1 part Orange Juice

Shake with ice and strain.

Tornado

COCKTAIL GLASS

1½ parts Gin
½ part Maraschino Liqueur
1 part Orange Juice

Shake with ice and strain.

Toronto Orgy

COCKTAIL GLASS

1 part Vodka
½ part Coffee Liqueur
½ part Irish Cream Liqueur
½ part Grand Marnier®

Shake with ice and strain.

Torridora Cocktail

COCKTAIL GLASS

1½ parts Light Rum
splash 151-Proof Rum
½ part Coffee Brandy
splash Cream

Shake with ice and strain.

El Torro

COCKTAIL GLASS

2 parts Tequila
1 part Coffee Liqueur

Shake with ice and strain.

Total Eclipse

COCKTAIL GLASS

1 part Dark Rum
1 part Cranberry Juice Cocktail
½ part Lime Juice
½ part Passion Fruit Juice

Shake with ice and strain.

Tovarich

COCKTAIL GLASS

1½ parts Vodka
¾ part Kümmel
2 splashes Lime Juice

Shake with ice and strain.

Tower Topper

COCKTAIL GLASS

2 parts Canadian Whisky
½ part Grand Marnier
1 part Cream

Shake with ice and strain.

Train Stopper

COCKTAIL GLASS

1 part Vodka
1 part Blackberry Liqueur
splash Crème de Cassis
splash Simple Syrup
½ part Lemon Juice

Shake with ice and strain.

Train Wreck

COCKTAIL GLASS

1 part Citrus Vodka
1 part Raspberry Vodka
1 part Vodka
3 parts Cranberry Juice

Shake with ice and strain.

Tranquility Cove

COCKTAIL GLASS

1 part Vodka
1 part Peach Schnapps
2/3 part Cranberry Juice Cocktail
2/3 part Orange Juice

Shake with ice and strain.

Traveling Trocadero

COCKTAIL GLASS

2/3 part Citrus Vodka
1 part Peppermint Liqueur
1/2 part Pineapple Juice
splash Lime Juice

Shake with ice and strain.

Treachery

COCKTAIL GLASS

2/3 part Goldschläger®
1 1/2 parts Apple Liqueur
2/3 part Cream

Shake with ice and strain.

Tresserhorn

COCKTAIL GLASS

1 part Blue Curaçao
1 part Orange Vodka
1 part Absinthe
1 part Sweet & Sour Mix

Shake with ice and strain.

Tribute to Erwin

COCKTAIL GLASS

1 part Lychee Liqueur
1 part Passoã®
1 part Pineapple Juice

Shake with ice and strain.

Trick Pony

COCKTAIL GLASS

1 1/2 parts Vodka
splash Crème de Cassis
splash Amaretto

Shake with ice and strain.

Trifecta

COCKTAIL GLASS

1 1/2 parts Light Rum
1/4 part Dubonnet® Blonde
2 splashes Lemon Juice

Shake with ice and strain.

Trinidad Cocktail

COCKTAIL GLASS

2 parts Light Rum
2 splashes Lime Juice
dash Sugar
dash Bitters

Shake with ice and strain.

Trinity Cocktail

COCKTAIL GLASS

1 part Gin
1 part Dry Vermouth
1 part Sweet Vermouth

Stir gently with ice and strain.

Triple Back Flip

COCKTAIL GLASS

1 part Gin
splash Orange Liqueur
splash Grenadine
1/2 part Lemon Juice
1 Egg Yolk

Shake with ice and strain.

Triplet

COCKTAIL GLASS

1 part Dry Vermouth
1 part Gin
1 part Peach Brandy
2 splashes Lemon Juice

Shake with ice and strain.

Trocadero

COCKTAIL GLASS

1 part Dry Vermouth
1 part Sweet Vermouth
1 part Grenadine
dash Orange Bitters

Shake with ice and strain.

Trojan Horse
COCKTAIL GLASS
3/4 part Brandy
3/4 part Dubonnet® Blonde
2 splashes Maraschino Liqueur
1/2 part Lime Juice
Shake with ice and strain.

Tropical Cachaça
COCKTAIL GLASS
1 part Cachaça
1 part Coffee Liqueur
1/2 part Pineapple Juice
1/2 part Mango Juice
Shake with ice and strain.

Tropical Cream
COCKTAIL GLASS
1 part Melon Liqueur
1 part Peach Liqueur
1 part Light Rum
1 part Crème de Coconut
1 part Frangelico®
1 part Cream
1 part Orange Juice
Shake with ice and strain.

Tropical Dream
COCKTAIL GLASS
1 part Coconut Rum
1 part Blue Curaçao
1 part Pineapple Juice
Shake with ice and strain.

Tropical Gaze
COCKTAIL GLASS
1 part Vodka
1 part Melon Liqueur
2/3 part Cranberry Juice Cocktail
2/3 part Pineapple Juice
Shake with ice and strain.

Tropical Lullaby
COCKTAIL GLASS
1/2 part Irish Cream Liqueur
3/4 part Butterscotch Schnapps
3/4 part Malibu® Rum
3/4 part Pineapple Juice
Shake with ice and strain.

Troubled Water
COCKTAIL GLASS
1 part Gin
1/2 part Blue Curaçao
1/2 part Simple Syrup
1/2 part Grapefruit Juice
Shake with ice and strain.

Tulip Cocktail
COCKTAIL GLASS
1 part Apple Brandy
1/2 part Sweet Vermouth
1/2 part Lemon Juice
1/2 part Apricot Brandy
Shake with ice and strain.

Turf Cocktail
COCKTAIL GLASS
1 part Dry Vermouth
1 part Gin
splash Anisette
2 dashes Bitters
Shake with ice and strain.

Turtle
COCKTAIL GLASS
3 parts Canadian Whisky
1 part Bénédictine
Shake with ice and strain.

Tuscaloosa
COCKTAIL GLASS
1 1/2 parts Whiskey
3/4 part Sweet Vermouth
2 splashes Bénédictine®
Shake with ice and strain.

Tuttosi
COCKTAIL GLASS

1 part Whiskey
1/2 part Brandy
1/2 part Sweet Vermouth
1/4 part Mandarine Napoléon® Liqueur

Shake with ice and strain.

Tuxedo
COCKTAIL GLASS

3 parts Sherry
1/2 part Anisette
splash Maraschino Liqueur
2 dashes Angostura® Bitters

Shake with ice and strain.

Tweety®
COCKTAIL GLASS

2/3 part Kiwi Schnapps
2/3 part Pear Brandy
2/3 part Orange Juice
splash Lemon Juice

Shake with ice and strain.

Tweety® Bird
COCKTAIL GLASS

1 1/2 parts Light Rum
1 part Lime Juice
1/2 part Galliano®
1/2 part Grand Marnier®

Shake with ice and strain.

Twenny
COCKTAIL GLASS

1 part Vodka
1 part Coffee Liqueur
1 part Triple Sec
splash Apricot Brandy

Shake with ice and strain.

Twenty Thousand Leagues
COCKTAIL GLASS

1 1/2 parts Gin
1 part Dry Vermouth
splash Pernod®
2 dashes Orange Bitters

Shake with ice and strain.

Twizzler®
COCKTAIL GLASS

2 parts Vodka
1 part Strawberry Liqueur
splash Grenadine

Shake with ice and strain.

Twizzler® Twist
COCKTAIL GLASS

1 part Cherry Brandy
1/2 part Strawberry Liqueur
splash Grenadine
1 part Anisette
1/2 part Milk

Shake with ice and strain.

Two Drink Minimum
COCKTAIL GLASS

1 part Coffee Brandy
1 part Crème de Cacao (White)
1 part Light Cream

Shake with ice and strain.

Two Sheets to the Wind
COCKTAIL GLASS

1 part Dark Rum
1 part Brandy
1 part Orange Liqueur
1 part Lime Juice

Shake with ice and strain.

Two Turtles
COCKTAIL GLASS

1 1/2 parts Canadian Whisky
1 part Bénédictine
1/2 part Brandy
1/2 part Triple Sec

Shake with ice and strain.

Ugly Virgin

COCKTAIL GLASS

1 part Grapefruit Vodka
1 part Lemonade Vodka
1 part Orange Vodka
dash Cranberry Juice

Shake with ice and strain.

Ulanda

COCKTAIL GLASS

2 parts Gin
1 part Triple Sec
splash Pernod

Shake with ice and strain.

Ultimate Challenger

COCKTAIL GLASS

2/3 part Peach Schnapps
1 part Cream

Shake with ice and strain.

Ultra Violet

COCKTAIL GLASS

2 parts Vodka
1/2 part Parfait Amour

Shake with ice and strain.

Ultrasonic

COCKTAIL GLASS

1 1/2 parts Triple Sec
1 1/2 parts Mandarine Napoléon® Liqueur
1 part Lemon Juice
1/2 part Simple Syrup

Shake with ice and strain.

Unfaithful

COCKTAIL GLASS

1/2 part Blackberry Liqueur
1/2 part Chambord®
2 parts Red Wine
splash Carpano Punt e Mes®
splash Lemon Juice

Stir gently with ice and strain.

Unicorn

COCKTAIL GLASS

1 part Irish Cream Liqueur
1/2 part Coffee Liqueur
1/2 part Whipped Cream Vodka
1 part Milk
dash Cointreau
dash Melon Liqueur

Shake with ice and strain.

Unicorn Horn

COCKTAIL GLASS

1 part Raspberry Liqueur
1/2 part Southern Comfort®
2/3 part Grand Marnier®
1/2 part Lemon Juice

Shake with ice and strain.

Unisphere

COCKTAIL GLASS

1 1/2 parts Coconut Rum
1/2 part Grenadine
splash Pernod®

Shake with ice and strain.

United

COCKTAIL GLASS

2/3 part Apricot Brandy
2/3 part Dry Vermouth
2/3 part Apple Brandy
1/2 part Sweet & Sour Mix

Shake with ice and strain.

Unlimited

COCKTAIL GLASS

1 1/2 parts Apricot Brandy
1 1/2 parts Passion Fruit
1 part Parfait Amour

Shake with ice and strain.

Uranus

COCKTAIL GLASS

1 1/2 parts Vodka
1/2 part Pisang Ambon® Liqueur
1/2 part Passion Fruit Liqueur

Shake with ice and strain.

Uvula
COCKTAIL GLASS

2 parts Brandy
2 splashes Maraschino Liqueur
1/4 part Pineapple Juice
splash Lemon Juice

Shake with ice and strain.

Valize
COCKTAIL GLASS

1 part Alizé®
1 part Vodka

Shake with ice and strain.

Valkyrie
COCKTAIL GLASS

1 1/2 parts Vodka
splash Peppermint Liqueur
1/2 part Jägermeister®
1 part Cream

Shake with ice and strain.

Valle Rojo
COCKTAIL GLASS

1 part Whiskey
1 part Dry Gin
1 part Triple Sec
splash Orange Juice
splash Grenadine

Shake with ice and strain.

Vampire
COCKTAIL GLASS

1 part Vodka
1 part Raspberry Liqueur
1/2 part Sweetened Lime Juice
1/2 part Cranberry Juice Cocktail

Shake with ice and strain.

Van Dusen Cocktail
COCKTAIL GLASS

2 parts Gin
1 part Dry Vermouth
splash Grand Marnier®

Shake with ice and strain.

Vancouver
COCKTAIL GLASS

1 1/2 parts Canadian Whisky
1/2 part Cherry Brandy
1/2 part Orange Juice
1/2 part Lemon Juice

Shake with ice and strain.

Vanilla 43
COCKTAIL GLASS

3/4 part Licor 43®
1 1/4 part Vanilla Vodka
1 part Pineapple Juice

Shake with ice and strain.

Vanilla Cream
COCKTAIL GLASS

1 part Vanilla Liqueur
1 1/2 parts Pineapple Juice
1 part Cream

Shake with ice and strain.

Vanishing Cream
COCKTAIL GLASS

1 part Crème de Cacao (White)
1 part Chocolate Liqueur
1 part Cream
splash Vodka

Shake with ice and strain.

Vanity Fair
COCKTAIL GLASS

1 part Kirschwasser
1 part Amaretto
1 part Maraschino Liqueur

Shake with ice and strain.

Velocity Cocktail
COCKTAIL GLASS

1 part Gin
2 parts Sweet Vermouth
splash Orange Juice

Shake with ice and strain.

Velvet Elvis
COCKTAIL GLASS
2 parts Vodka
splash Amaretto
splash Chocolate Liqueur
½ part Pear Liqueur
Shake with ice and strain.

Velvet Kilt
COCKTAIL GLASS
1 part Butterscotch Liqueur
1 part Scotch
Shake with ice and strain.

Velvet Kiss
COCKTAIL GLASS
1 part Gordon's® Gin
½ part Crème de Banane
½ part Pineapple Juice
1 part Heavy Cream
splash Grenadine
Shake with ice and strain.

Velvet Orchid
COCKTAIL GLASS
1 part Crème de Cacao (White)
1 part Dry Vermouth
splash Blackberry Syrup
Shake with ice and strain.

Velvet Orgasm
COCKTAIL GLASS
1 part Strawberry Liqueur
1 part Crème de Cassis
1½ parts Cream
Shake with ice and strain.

Veneto
COCKTAIL GLASS
1½ parts Brandy
1 part Sugar
1 Egg White
¼ part Sambuca
Shake with ice and strain.

Venice
COCKTAIL GLASS
1 part Scotch
1 part Cherry Brandy
1 part Sherry
Shake with ice and strain.

Venom
COCKTAIL GLASS
2 parts Gin
½ part Mozart Dark Chocolate Liqueur
½ part Simple Syrup
Shake with ice and strain.

Veracruz
COCKTAIL GLASS
2 parts Silver Tequila
splash Crème de Menthe (White)
Shake with ice and strain.

Verboten
COCKTAIL GLASS
3 parts Gin
1 part Passion Fruit Liqueur
1 part Lemon Juice
1 part Orange Juice
Shake with ice and strain.

Vermouth Triple Sec
COCKTAIL GLASS
1 part Dry Vermouth
1 part Gin
½ part Triple Sec
Shake with ice and strain.

Vero Beach
COCKTAIL GLASS
1 part Apricot Brandy
1 part Orange Juice
Shake with ice and strain.

Veruska

COCKTAIL GLASS

1 part Vodka
1/2 part Campari®
1/4 part Crème de Banane
splash Sweetened Lime Juice

Shake with ice and strain.

Vespa

COCKTAIL GLASS

2 parts Sweet Vermouth
3/4 part Gin
1/4 part Dry Vermouth

Shake with ice and strain.

Vesper

COCKTAIL GLASS

3 parts Gin
1 part Vodka
1/2 part Lillet Blanc

Shake with ice and strain. This is James Bond's drink of choice in *Casino Royale*.

VHS

COCKTAIL GLASS

1 1/2 parts Vanilla Liqueur
1 part Scotch
1 part Frangelico®

Stir gently with ice and strain.

Via Veneto

COCKTAIL GLASS

1 3/4 parts Brandy
2 splashes Sambuca
2 splashes Lemon Juice
1 1/2 parts Simple Syrup
1 Egg White

Shake with ice and strain.

Vicious Kiss

COCKTAIL GLASS

3 parts Citrus Vodka
2 splashes Maraschino Cherry Juice
2 splashes Lime Juice

Stir gently with ice and strain.

Victor

COCKTAIL GLASS

2 parts Gin
1/2 part Brandy
1/2 part Sweet Vermouth

Shake with ice and strain.

Victor, Victoria

COCKTAIL GLASS

1 1/2 parts Dry Vermouth
1/2 part Gin
1/2 part Cherry Brandy

Shake with ice and strain.

La Vida Loca

COCKTAIL GLASS

1 part Crème de Banane
1 part Cherry Brandy
1 part Melon Liqueur
1 part Crème de Coconut

Shake with ice and strain.

Villa Beata

COCKTAIL GLASS

1/2 part Coffee Liqueur
1/2 part Crème de Coconut
1 part Dark Rum
splash Cream

Shake with ice and strain.

Vintage 84

COCKTAIL GLASS

1 part Light Rum
1/2 part Pineapple Juice
1/2 part Orange Juice
1 part Apricot Brandy
splash Grenadine

Shake with ice and strain.

Violetta Cocktail

COCKTAIL GLASS

1 part Advocaat
1 part Cream
1 part Crème de Cassis

Shake with ice and strain.

Violetta Comfort
COCKTAIL GLASS

1 part Vodka
1 part Parfait Amour
1 part Southern Comfort®
splash Lime Juice

Shake with ice and strain.

VIP
COCKTAIL GLASS

1 part Gin
1 part Pimm's® No. 1 Cup
1 part Pineapple Juice
splash Dry Vermouth

Shake with ice and strain.

Virgin
COCKTAIL GLASS

1 part Gin
½ part Crème de Menthe (White)
1 part Passion Fruit Juice

Shake with ice and strain.

Virgin's Blood
COCKTAIL GLASS

2 parts Vodka
1 part Red Curaçao
1 part Strawberry

Stir gently with ice and strain.

Visigothic
COCKTAIL GLASS

1 part Goldschläger®
1 part Jägermeister®
2 parts Cream

Shake with ice and strain.

Vixen
COCKTAIL GLASS

2 parts Frangelico®
½ part Grenadine
½ part Coffee Liqueur

Shake with ice and strain.

Vodka Gibson
COCKTAIL GLASS

2 parts Vodka
½ part Dry Vermouth

Shake with ice and strain. Garnish with a pearl onion.

Vodka Grasshopper
COCKTAIL GLASS

1 part Vodka
1 part Crème de Menthe (Green)
1 part Crème de Cacao (White)

Shake with ice and strain.

Vodka Stinger
COCKTAIL GLASS

1½ parts Vodka
1½ parts Crème de Menthe (White)

Shake with ice and strain.

Volatile
COCKTAIL GLASS

2 parts Irish Cream Liqueur
½ part Amaretto
½ part Chocolate Liqueur

Shake with ice and strain.

Volga
COCKTAIL GLASS

1 part Vodka
1 part Pineapple Juice
1 part Orange Juice
splash Grenadine

Shake with ice and strain.

Voodoo Cocktail
COCKTAIL GLASS

1 part Peach Schnapps
1 part Vodka
1 part Cream

Shake with ice and strain.

Voodoo Lady

COCKTAIL GLASS

1 part Triple Sec
1 part Cognac
½ part Lemon Juice

Shake with ice and strain.

Voodoo Pigalle

COCKTAIL GLASS

1 part Absinthe
⅔ part Melon Liqueur
⅔ part Green Chartreuse®
splash Lemon Juice

Shake with ice and strain.

Vorhees Special

COCKTAIL GLASS

1 part Vodka
1 part Coconut Rum
1 part Sambuca
1 part Orange Juice
splash Banana Liqueur
splash Tabasco® Sauce

Shake with ice and strain.

Vulgar Vulcan

COCKTAIL GLASS

1 part Crème de Coconut
½ part Amaretto
1 part Orange Juice
1 part Cream

Shake with ice and strain.

Waikiki Beachcomber

COCKTAIL GLASS

1 part Triple Sec
1 part Gin
2 splashes Pineapple Juice

Shake with ice and strain.

Wakeumup

COCKTAIL GLASS

1½ parts Gin
⅔ part Triple Sec
⅔ part Lillet®
splash Pastis
⅔ part Lemon Juice

Shake with ice and strain.

Waldorf Cocktail

COCKTAIL GLASS

2 parts Bourbon
1 part Pernod®
½ part Sweet Vermouth

Shake with ice and strain.

Walk the Dinosaur

COCKTAIL GLASS

1½ parts Apricot Brandy
1 part Lemon Juice
dash Powdered Sugar
dash Angostura® Bitters

Shake with ice and strain.

Wall Street

COCKTAIL GLASS

1 part Crème de Cacao (White)
1 part Whiskey
1 part Sweet Vermouth
splash Dry Vermouth
2 dashes Bitters

Shake with ice and strain.

Walters

COCKTAIL GLASS

1½ parts Scotch
2 splashes Lemon Juice
2 splashes Orange Juice

Shake with ice and strain.

Warrior Cocktail
COCKTAIL GLASS
1 part Dry Vermouth
1 part Sweet Vermouth
1/2 part Brandy
1/12 part Cointreau
1/12 part Pernod
Shake with ice and strain.

Warsaw Cocktail
COCKTAIL GLASS
1 1/2 parts Vodka
1/2 part Dry Vermouth
1/2 part Blackberry Brandy
splash Lemon Juice
Shake with ice and strain.

Wasting Day
COCKTAIL GLASS
1 1/2 parts Spiced Rum
1/2 part Vanilla Liqueur
1/2 part Grand Marnier®
splash Butterscotch Schnapps
1 part Cream
Shake with ice and strain.

Watchdog
COCKTAIL GLASS
1 1/2 parts Citrus Vodka
splash Maraschino Liqueur
1 part Lemon Juice
Shake with ice and strain.

Waterbury Cocktail
COCKTAIL GLASS
1 1/2 parts Brandy
splash Grenadine
1/4 part Lemon Juice
dash Powdered Sugar
1 Egg White
Shake with ice and strain.

Webster Cocktail
COCKTAIL GLASS
1 part Gin
1/2 part Dry Vermouth
splash Apricot Brandy
1/2 part Lime Juice
Shake with ice and strain.

Wedding Bells Cocktail
COCKTAIL GLASS
1 part Orange Juice
1 part Gin
1/2 part Cherry Brandy
Shake with ice and strain.

Wedding Wish
COCKTAIL GLASS
1 part Gin
1 part Crème de Cassis
1/2 part Sweet & Sour Mix
splash Lemon Juice
Shake with ice and strain.

Weekender
COCKTAIL GLASS
1 part Gin
1 part Triple Sec
1 part Dry Vermouth
1 part Sweet Vermouth
splash Pernod®
Shake with ice and strain.

Weep No More Cocktail
COCKTAIL GLASS
1 part Dubonnet® Blonde
1 part Brandy
splash Maraschino Liqueur
1/2 part Lime Juice
Shake with ice and strain.

Wellington Rose
COCKTAIL GLASS

1 1/2 parts Maraschino Liqueur
1/2 part Ginger Liqueur
1/2 part Grenadine
2/3 part Lime Juice
fill with Club Soda

Shake all but Club Soda with ice and strain. Top with Club Soda.

Wembeldorf
COCKTAIL GLASS

1 part Vodka
1 part Apricot Brandy
1/2 part Lime Juice
1/2 part Sweet & Sour Mix
1/2 part Pineapple Juice

Shake with ice and strain.

West of Eden
COCKTAIL GLASS

1 1/2 parts Peach Schnapps
1 part Scotch
1 part Crème de Coconut
splash Cream

Shake with ice and strain.

Westbrook Cocktail
COCKTAIL GLASS

2 parts Gin
1/2 part Sweet Vermouth
splash Scotch
dash Powdered Sugar

Shake with ice and strain.

Western
COCKTAIL GLASS

1 part Cognac
1 part Lime Cordial
1/2 part Triple Sec
1/2 part Maraschino Liqueur

Shake with ice and strain.

Western Regiment
COCKTAIL GLASS

1 part Amaretto
1/2 part Coffee Brandy
2 parts Milk

Shake with ice and strain.

Western World
COCKTAIL GLASS

1 1/2 parts Drambuie®
1 part Crème de Banane
1/2 part Lemon Juice

Shake with ice and strain.

Westminster
COCKTAIL GLASS

1 part Dry Vermouth
1 part Rye Whiskey
splash Triple Sec

Shake with ice and strain.

Wet Dream Cocktail
COCKTAIL GLASS

1 part Gin
1 part Apricot Brandy
1/2 part Grenadine
splash Lemon Juice

Shake with ice and strain.

When a Man Loves Woman
COCKTAIL GLASS

1 part Passion Fruit Liqueur
1 part Irish Whiskey
splash Passion Fruit Juice
splash Strawberry Syrup

Shake with ice and strain.

Whimsy
COCKTAIL GLASS

1 part Mandarine Napoléon® Liqueur
1/2 part Amaretto
1/2 part Pisang Ambon® Liqueur
1 part Cream

Shake with ice and strain.

Whip Crack

COCKTAIL GLASS

1 part Triple Sec
1 part Advocaat
1 part Sweet & Sour Mix

Shake with ice and strain.

Whiplash

COCKTAIL GLASS

1½ parts Brandy
½ part Sweet Vermouth
½ part Dry Vermouth
2 splashes Triple Sec

Shake with ice and strain.

Whirl Hound

COCKTAIL GLASS

1 part Sloe Gin
1 part Triple Sec
½ part Sweet Vermouth
½ part Dry Vermouth
½ part Lemon Juice

Shake with ice and strain.

Whiskey Tango Foxtrot

COCKTAIL GLASS

1 part Jim Beam®
½ part Amaretto
½ part Pernod®
1 part Pineapple Juice

Shake with ice and strain.

Whisper Cocktail

COCKTAIL GLASS

1 part Scotch
1 part Dry Vermouth
1 part Sweet Vermouth

Shake with ice and strain.

Whispers in the Night

COCKTAIL GLASS

2 parts Cream sherry
2 parts Port
1 part Whiskey
1 tsp Sugar

Shake with ice and strain.

Whispers of the Frost

COCKTAIL GLASS

1 part Blended Scotch Whisky
1 part Cream Sherry
1 part Port
dash Powdered Sugar

Shake with ice and strain.

Whistling Dixie

COCKTAIL GLASS

1 part Crème de Menthe (White)
1 part Triple Sec
dash Powdered Sugar

Shake with ice and strain.

White Castle

COCKTAIL GLASS

1 part Dry Gin
1 part Dry Vermouth
1 part Triple Sec
splash Lime Juice

Shake with ice and strain.

White Chocolate Stinger

COCKTAIL GLASS

1 part Crème de Cacao (White)
1 part Crème de Menthe (White)
1 part Vodka

Shake with ice and strain.

White Cocktail

COCKTAIL GLASS

2 parts Gin
½ part Anisette
dash Orange Bitters

Shake with ice and strain.

White Commie

COCKTAIL GLASS

1 part Brandy
1 part Coffee Liqueur
1 part Cream

Shake with ice and strain.

White Cosmopolitan
COCKTAIL GLASS

2½ parts Vodka
1 part Triple Sec
splash White Cranberry Juice
dash Sweetened Lime Juice

Shake with ice and strain.

White Elephant
COCKTAIL GLASS

1½ parts Gin
1 part Sweet Vermouth
1 Egg White

Shake with ice and strain.

White Flush Cocktail
COCKTAIL GLASS

1½ parts Gin
1 part Maraschino Liqueur
1 part Milk

Shake with ice and strain.

White Goose
COCKTAIL GLASS

1 part Dry Vermouth
1 part Grenadine
1 part Raspberry Liqueur

Shake with ice and strain.

White Heart
COCKTAIL GLASS

1 part Crème de Cacao (White)
1 part Sambuca
2 parts Cream

Shake with ice and strain.

White House
COCKTAIL GLASS

1 part Crème de Coconut
1 part Chocolate Liqueur
1 part Cream
splash Vodka

Shake with ice and strain.

White Knight
COCKTAIL GLASS

1 part Scotch
1 part Coffee Liqueur
1 part Cream

Shake with ice and strain.

White Lightning Cocktail
COCKTAIL GLASS

1 part Crème de Cacao (White)
1 part Light Rum
1 part Cream

Shake with ice and strain.

White Lily Cocktail
COCKTAIL GLASS

1 part Light Rum
1 part Gin
1 part Triple Sec
splash Anisette

Shake with ice and strain.

White Lion Cocktail
COCKTAIL GLASS

1½ parts Light Rum
½ part Lemon Juice
splash Grenadine
dash Powdered Sugar
2 dashes Bitters

Shake with ice and strain.

White Mexican
COCKTAIL GLASS

2 parts Horchata
1 part Irish Cream Liqueur
1 part Vodka

Shake with ice and strain.

White Oak
COCKTAIL GLASS

1 part Light Rum
½ part Crème de Cacao (White)
½ part Jim Beam®
½ part Cream

Shake with ice and strain.

White Rose Cocktail

COCKTAIL GLASS

¾ part Gin
½ part Maraschino Liqueur
2 splashes Orange Juice
1 Egg White

Shake with ice and strain. Garnish with Lime Slice.

White Sands

COCKTAIL GLASS

2 parts Dark Rum
1 part Crème de Banane
1 part Pineapple Juice
splash Coffee Liqueur
splash Lime Juice

Shake with ice and strain.

White Satin

COCKTAIL GLASS

1 part Galliano®
1 part Tia Maria®
1 part Cream

Shake with ice and strain.

White Snow

COCKTAIL GLASS

1 part Cream
1 part Passion Fruit Juice
½ part Crème de Cacao (White)

Shake with ice and strain.

White Spider

COCKTAIL GLASS

1½ parts Vodka
½ part Crème de Menthe (White)

Shake with ice and strain.

White Way Cocktail

COCKTAIL GLASS

2 parts Gin
1 part Crème de Menthe (White)

Shake with ice and strain.

White Wing

COCKTAIL GLASS

2 parts Gin
1 part Crème de Menthe (White)

Shake with ice and strain.

Whitney

COCKTAIL GLASS

2 parts Light Rum
1 part Red Wine
splash Lemon Juice

Shake with ice and strain.

Whizz Bang

COCKTAIL GLASS

1 part Scotch
½ part Dry Vermouth
splash Grenadine
splash Pernod®
dash Orange Bitters

Shake with ice and strain.

Whizz Doodle Cocktail

COCKTAIL GLASS

1 part Gin
1 part Scotch
1 part Crème de Cacao (White)
1 part Cream

Shake with ice and strain.

Who Knows

COCKTAIL GLASS

2 parts Tequila
1 part Triple Sec
½ part Amaretto

Shake with ice and strain.

Whore

COCKTAIL GLASS

1 part Vodka
1 part Triple Sec
½ part Lemon Juice

Shake with ice and strain.

Who's That Girl?

COCKTAIL GLASS

2 parts Gin
2/3 part Apricot Brandy
2/3 part Apple Brandy
splash Lemon Juice

Shake with ice and strain.

Who's Ya Daddy

COCKTAIL GLASS

2 parts Cognac
1 part Coffee Liqueur

Shake with ice and strain.

Why Not?

COCKTAIL GLASS

2 parts Gin
1 part Apricot Brandy
1/2 part Dry Vermouth
dash Lemon Juice

Shake with ice and strain.

Wicked Tasty Treat

COCKTAIL GLASS

2 parts Cinnamon Vodka
1 part Amaretto
1 part Coffee Liqueur
1 part Irish Cream Liqueur
1 part Cream

Shake with ice and strain.

Wide-Awake

COCKTAIL GLASS

1 1/2 parts Fernet-Branca®
1 1/2 parts Chartreuse®
1/2 part Peppermint Liqueur

Shake with ice and strain.

Wiggle Worm

COCKTAIL GLASS

2 parts Vodka
1/2 part Cherry Heering
2 parts Orange Juice

Shake with ice and strain.

Wild Cherry

COCKTAIL GLASS

1 part Vodka
1 part Crème de Cacao (White)
1/2 part Coffee
1/2 part Frangelico®

Shake with ice and strain.

Wild Flower

COCKTAIL GLASS

1 part Apple Brandy
1 part Bacardi® Limón Rum
splash Apricot Brandy
splash Cranberry Juice Cocktail

Shake with ice and strain.

Wild Island

COCKTAIL GLASS

2 parts Bourbon
1 part Tropical Punch Schnapps
1/2 part Orange Vodka
1/2 part Orange Juice

Shake with ice and strain.

Wild Rose

COCKTAIL GLASS

1 1/2 parts Light Rum
1 part Crème de Coconut
splash Grenadine
splash Lemon Juice

Shake with ice and strain.

Wild West

COCKTAIL GLASS

1 1/2 parts Brandy
dash Sugar
1 Egg Yolk

Shake with ice and strain.

Will Rogers

COCKTAIL GLASS

1 1/2 parts Gin
1/2 part Dry Vermouth
splash Triple Sec
2 splashes Orange Juice

Shake with ice and strain.

Willem van Oranje
COCKTAIL GLASS
1 part Brandy
½ part Triple Sec
3 dashes Orange Bitters
Shake with ice and strain.

Wilson Cocktail
COCKTAIL GLASS
1 part Gin
2 splashes Orange Juice
2 splashes Dry Vermouth
Shake with ice and strain.

Wimbledon Cup
COCKTAIL GLASS
1 part Gin
1 part Pimm's
½ part Strawberry Liqueur
1 part Cream
1 part Orange Juice
Shake with ice and strain.

Windy Road
COCKTAIL GLASS
1 part Coffee Liqueur
½ part Apricot Brandy
1½ parts Cream
Shake with ice and strain.

Winston
COCKTAIL GLASS
2 parts Gin
2 parts Spiced Rum
dash Frangelico
dash Rose's Lime Juice
Shake with ice and strain.

A Winter in Armagnac
COCKTAIL GLASS
½ part Blackberry Liqueur
½ part Strawberry Liqueur
1 part Armagnac
2 parts Cream
Shake with ice and strain.

A Winter in Green Park
COCKTAIL GLASS
1 part Melon Liqueur
½ part Maraschino Liqueur
splash Crème de Coconut
½ part Limoncello
2 parts Cream
Shake with ice and strain.

Winter Garden
COCKTAIL GLASS
2 parts Canadian Whisky
1 part Peach Schnapps
1 part Sweet Sherry
Shake with ice and strain.

Wintergreen Breathmint
COCKTAIL GLASS
1 part Peppermint Liqueur
½ part Melon Liqueur
½ part Anisette
splash Chocolate Mint Liqueur
½ part Lime Juice
Shake with ice and strain.

Wiper Fluid
COCKTAIL GLASS
1 part Hpnotiq
½ part Raspberry Vodka
½ part Vanilla Vodka
1 part Pineapple Juice
Shake with ice and strain.

Witch of Venice
COCKTAIL GLASS
1½ parts Vodka
½ part Strega®
2 splashes Crème de Banane
1 part Orange Juice
Shake with ice and strain.

Witchery
COCKTAIL GLASS
2 parts Brandy
½ part Vanilla Liqueur
½ part Chocolate Liqueur
Shake with ice and strain.

Wizardry
COCKTAIL GLASS

1½ parts Kirschwasser
1 part Dry Vermouth
1 part Mandarine Napoléon® Liqueur

Shake with ice and strain.

Wolf Hound
COCKTAIL GLASS

1½ parts Canadian Whisky
½ part Cherry Brandy
½ part Apricot Brandy
½ part Lemon Juice

Shake with ice and strain.

Wolf's Milk
COCKTAIL GLASS

1 part Peach Schnapps
1 part Crème de Noyaux
1 part Milk

Shake with ice and strain.

Womanizer
COCKTAIL GLASS

1½ parts Gin
½ part Parfait Amour
½ part Cherry Brandy
½ part Lime Cordial

Shake with ice and strain.

Wong Tong Cocktail
COCKTAIL GLASS

1 part Vodka
½ part Gin
½ part Dry Vermouth
1 part Lemonade

Shake with ice and strain.

Woodcrest Club
COCKTAIL GLASS

1½ parts Gin
¾ part Sweet Vermouth
2 splashes Pineapple Juice
2 splashes Grenadine
1 Egg White

Shake with ice and strain.

Woodstock
COCKTAIL GLASS

1½ parts Gin
splash Maple Syrup
1 part Lemon Juice
dash Orange Bitters

Shake with ice and strain.

Woodward
COCKTAIL GLASS

2 parts Rye Whiskey
½ part Dry Vermouth
½ part Grapefruit Juice

Shake with ice and strain.

Works of God
COCKTAIL GLASS

1 part Vodka
1 part Strawberry Liqueur
1 part Cream

Shake with ice and strain.

World Trade Center
COCKTAIL GLASS

½ part Apricot Brandy
1½ parts Canadian Whisky
1 part Sweet Vermouth

Shake with ice and strain.

Wormwood
COCKTAIL GLASS

1½ parts Scotch
½ part Apricot Brandy
½ part Campari®
½ part Grand Marnier®

Shake with ice and strain.

Wyoming Swing
COCKTAIL GLASS

1 part Dry Vermouth
1 part SweetVermouth
1 part Orange Juice
½ part Simple Syrup

Shake with ice and strain.

X Files

COCKTAIL GLASS

1 part Licor 43®
½ part Peach Schnapps
splash Limoncello
dash Bitters
splash Lemon Juice

Stir gently with ice and strain.

Xango

COCKTAIL GLASS

1½ parts Light Rum
½ part Triple Sec
1 part Grapefruit Juice

Shake with ice and strain.

Xanthia Cocktail

COCKTAIL GLASS

1 part Gin
1 part Cherry Brandy
1 part Chartreuse®

Shake with ice and strain.

X-Rays

COCKTAIL GLASS

2 parts Light Rum
½ part Blue Curaçao
½ part Grapefruit Juice

Shake with ice and strain.

XYZ Cocktail

COCKTAIL GLASS

2 parts Light Rum
½ part Triple Sec
½ part Lemon Juice

Shake with ice and strain.

Y B Normal?

COCKTAIL GLASS

1 part Brandy
½ part Chartreuse®
¼ part Lemon Juice
dash Powdered Sugar

Shake with ice and strain.

Yankee Yodeler

COCKTAIL GLASS

1 part Blue Curaçao
½ part Maraschino Liqueur
½ part Grapefruit Juice

Shake with ice and strain.

Yellow Boxer

COCKTAIL GLASS

2 parts Tequila
½ part Galliano
1 part Orange Juice
½ part Lemon Juice
½ part Rose's Lime Juice

Shake with ice and strain.

Yellow Jade

COCKTAIL GLASS

3 parts Gin
1 part Blackberry Liqueur
1 part Crème de Banane
1 part Cream

Shake with ice and strain.

Yellow Sea

COCKTAIL GLASS

½ part Dark Rum
½ part Maraschino Liqueur
splash Simple Syrup

Shake with ice and strain.

Yokohama Cocktail

COCKTAIL GLASS

1 part Gin
1 part Vodka
1 part Grenadine
1 part Orange Juice

Shake with ice and strain.

Yolanda

COCKTAIL GLASS

2 parts Sweet Vermouth
1 part Gin
1 part Brandy
1 part Anisette
splash Grenadine

Shake with ice and strain.

Yoshi
COCKTAIL GLASS

1 part Chocolate Mint Liqueur
splash Goldschläger®
splash Vanilla Liqueur
splash Bénédictine®

Shake with ice and strain.

You and Me
COCKTAIL GLASS

2 parts Dry Gin
1 part Dry Vermouth
dash Orange Bitters

Shake with ice and strain.

Yukon Cocktail
COCKTAIL GLASS

1½ parts Canadian Whisky
1 tbsp Sugar
¼ part Triple Sec

Shake with ice and strain.

Yuma
COCKTAIL GLASS

1 part Vodka
1 part Triple Sec
½ part Apricot Brandy
½ part Cognac

Shake with ice and strain.

Zabao
COCKTAIL GLASS

1 part Light Rum
½ part Dry Vermouth
½ part Pineapple Juice
½ part Grenadine

Shake with ice and strain.

Zabriski Point
COCKTAIL GLASS

1 part Vodka
splash Vanilla Liqueur
splash Apple Brandy
1½ parts Apple Juice

Shake with ice and strain.

Zagoo Bears
COCKTAIL GLASS

1 part Peach Schnapps
½ part Sloe Gin
½ part Guava Juice
1 part Pineapple Juice
splash Lychee Syrup

Shake with ice and strain.

Zamba
COCKTAIL GLASS

1½ parts Rum
1 part Sweet Vermouth

Shake with ice and strain.

Zanzibar Cocktail
COCKTAIL GLASS

½ part Gin
1½ parts Dry Vermouth
dash Orange Bitters
½ part Lemon Juice
splash Simple Syrup

Shake with ice and strain.

Zara
COCKTAIL GLASS

⅔ part Gin
⅔ part Maraschino Liqueur
splash Sweet Vermouth
splash Lemon Juice

Shake with ice and strain.

Zazie
COCKTAIL GLASS

1 part Triple Sec
1 part Gin
1 part Dry Vermouth
splash Orange Juice

Shake with ice and strain.

Zephyr
COCKTAIL GLASS

1 part Vodka
1 part Blue Curaçao
½ part Parfait Amour
splash Lemon Juice

Shake with ice and strain.

Zero
COCKTAIL GLASS

1½ parts Blue Curaçao
1 part Crème de Cacao (White)
1 part Vodka

Shake with ice and strain.

Zero Hour
COCKTAIL GLASS

1 part Brandy
½ part Triple Sec
½ part Strawberry Liqueur
1 part Orange Juice

Shake with ice and strain.

Ziga
COCKTAIL GLASS

1 part Gin
1 part Amaretto
½ part Dry Vermouth
½ part Lemon Juice

Shake with ice and strain.

Zip Fastener
COCKTAIL GLASS

1 part Dark Rum
1 part Triple Sec
½ part Coffee

Shake with ice and strain.

Zoot
COCKTAIL GLASS

1 part Gin
1 part Jack Daniel's®
fill with Lemon-Lime Soda

Build over ice.

Zorba
COCKTAIL GLASS

1 part Whiskey
1 Sweet Vermouth
splash Triple Sec

Shake with ice and strain.

Zorro's Revenge
COCKTAIL GLASS

1 part Amaretto
1 part Crème de Cacao (Dark)
1 part Irish Cream Liqueur

Shake with ice and strain.

CLASSIC DRINKS

Invented long ago but still known today, classic drinks have withstood the test of time. Many of these recipes have changed over the years as components became scarce (Peychaud's® Bitters) or were discontinued (Crème Yvette®) or outlawed (Absinthe). Each of the recipes below appear in modern-day bartender's guides, but what makes them unique is that they also appear in bartender guides from before 1940.

Abbey Cocktail

COCKTAIL GLASS

1½ parts Gin
dash Orange Bitters
½ part Orange Juice

Shake all ingredients (except for the cherry) with ice and strain into a cocktail glass. Top with Maraschino Cherry.

Absinthe Cocktail

COCKTAIL GLASS

1½ parts Absinthe
1 Egg White
dash Sugar

Shake with ice and strain.

Absinthe Drip

HIGHBALL GLASS

1½ parts Absinthe
1 Sugar Cube
2 parts Water

Fill a highball glass with crushed ice. Using a french drip spoon, (or other slotted spoon), drizzle Absinthe over the sugar cube so it disolves into the glass. Add water and stir.

Absinthe Flip

COCKTAIL GLASS

1 part Absinthe
1 part Cointreau®
2 splashes Lemon Juice
1 Egg
dash Sugar

Shake with ice and strain.

Adonis

COLLINS GLASS

2 parts Dry Sherry
1 part Sweet Vermouth
dash Orange Bitters

Stir with ice and strain over ice.

Affinity

COCKTAIL GLASS

1½ parts Scotch
1 part Sweet Vermouth
1 part Dry Vermouth
2 dashes Orange Bitters

Shake with ice and strain.

Affinity #2

SHOT GLASS

1 part Dry Vermouth
1 part Sweet Vermouth
1/2 part Crème de Violette

Shake with ice and strain.

Affinity Perfect

COCKTAIL GLASS

1 part Scotch
1/4 part Dry Vermouth
1/4 part Sweet Vermouth

Shake with ice and strain.

After Dinner Cocktail

ROCKS GLASS

1 1/2 parts Apricot Brandy
1 1/2 parts Blue Curaçao
2 parts Lime Juice

Shake with ice and strain over ice.

After Dinner Cocktail #2

COCKTAIL GLASS

1 part Apricot Brandy
1 part Triple Sec

Shake with ice and strain. Garnish with Lime Wedge.

After Dinner Cocktail #3

COCKTAIL GLASS

1 part Prunella Brandy
1 part Cherry Brandy
splash Lemon Juice

Shake with ice and strain.

After Supper Cocktail

COCKTAIL GLASS

1 part Triple Sec
1 part Apricot Brandy
splash Lemon Juice

Shake with ice and strain.

Agincourt

COCKTAIL GLASS

1 part Dry Vermouth
1 part Sweet Vermoutha
1/2 part Amaretto
1/6 part Lemon Juice

Shake with ice and strain.

Alaska

HIGHBALL GLASS

3 parts Gin
1 part Chartreuse®

Build over ice and stir.

Alaska #2

HIGHBALL GLASS

2 dashes Orange Bitters
2 parts Gin
1 part Yellow Chartreuse®

Build over ice and stir.

Alaska #3

COCKTAIL GLASS

2 parts London Dry Gin
1/2 part Green Chartreuse®
1/2 part Dry Sherry

Shake with ice and strain.

Alexander

COCKTAIL GLASS

1/2 part Gin
1/2 part Crème de Cacao (White)
2 parts Light Cream
dash Ground Nutmeg

Shake all ingredients (except Nutmeg) with ice and strain. Top with Ground Nutmeg.

Alexander Special

COCKTAIL GLASS

1 part Brandy
1 part Cream
1 part Coffee

Shake with ice and strain.

Alexander's Brother

COCKTAIL GLASS

1 part Gin
1 part Crème de Cacao (White)
1 part Cream

Shake with ice and strain.

Alfonso #2

COCKTAIL GLASS

1 part Dry Vermouth
1 part Sweet Vermouth
1 part Gin
1 part Mandarine Napoléon® Liqueur

Shake with ice and strain.

Alfonso Special

COCKTAIL GLASS

2 parts Grand Marnier®
1 part Dry Gin
1 part Dry Vermouth
2 splashes Sweet Vermouth
dash Angostura® Bitters

Shake with ice and strain.

Alliance

ROCKS GLASS

1 part Dry Vermouth
1 part Gin
splash Aquavit

Shake with ice and strain over ice.

Allie's Cocktail

COCKTAIL GLASS

1 part Dry Vermouth
1 part Gin
splash Kümmel

Shake with ice and strain.

Amer Picon® Cocktail

COCKTAIL GLASS

1½ part Amer Picon®
splash Grenadine

Shake with ice and strain. Garnish with Lime Wedge.

Amer Picon® Cocktail #2

COCKTAIL GLASS

1 part Amer Picon®
1 part Sweet Vermouth

Shake with ice and strain.

Amer Picon® Cooler

HIGHBALL GLASS

1½ parts Amer Picon®
1 part Gin
½ part Cherry Heering®
splash Lemon Juice
fill with Club Soda

Build over ice and stir.

Amer Picon® Punch

ROCKS GLASS

2½ parts Amer Picon®
splash Grenadine
fill with Club Soda
1 part Brandy

Build over ice and stir. Float Brandy on top.

American Beauty

COCKTAIL GLASS

1 part Brandy
½ part Dry Vermouth
splash Crème de Menthe (White)
1 part Orange Juice
splash Grenadine
½ part Tawny Port

Shake with ice and strain.

American Beauty Special

COCKTAIL GLASS

1 part Triple Sec
1 part Cognac
1 part Rum

Shake with ice and strain.

Angel's Kiss

POUSSE-CAFÉ GLASS

1 part Crème de Cacao (White)
1 part Sloe Gin
1 part Brandy
1 part Light Cream

Layer in a pousse-café glass.

Apparent Cocktail

COCKTAIL GLASS

2 parts Dry Gin
splash Pernod®

Shake with ice and strain.

Appetizer

COCKTAIL GLASS

2 parts Gin
1 part Orange Juice

Shake with ice and strain.

Apple Pie

COCKTAIL GLASS

1 part Light Rum
½ part Sweet Vermouth
splash Applejack
splash Lemon Juice
splash Grenadine

Shake with ice and strain.

Applejack

ROCKS GLASS

1 part Jack Daniel's®
2 parts Apple Liqueur
1 part Sweet & Sour Mix
1 part Club Soda

Build over ice and stir.

Astoria

COCKTAIL GLASS

2 parts Gin
1 part Campari®
1 part Vermouth
2 Olives
dash Orange Bitters

Shake with ice and strain.

Aviation

COCKTAIL GLASS

1½ parts Gin
½ part Lemon Juice
splash Maraschino Cherry Juice
splash Brandy

Shake with ice and strain.

Aviation #2

COCKTAIL GLASS

2 parts Gin
splash Lemon Juice
4 splashes Maraschino Cherry Juice

Shake with ice and strain.

Bacardi® Cocktail

COCKTAIL GLASS

1½ parts Bacardi® Light Rum
splash Grenadine
½ part Lime Juice

Shake with ice and strain.

Bacardi® Cocktail #2

COCKTAIL GLASS

1 part Rum
1 part Sweet & Sour Mix
splash Grenadine

Shake with ice and strain.

Bachelor's Bait Cocktail

COCKTAIL GLASS

1½ parts Gin
splash Grenadine
1 Egg White
dash Orange Bitters

Shake with ice and strain.

Baltimore Bracer

COCKTAIL GLASS

1 part Brandy
1 part Anisette
1 Egg White

Shake with ice and strain.

Bamboo

COCKTAIL GLASS

1 part Dry Vermouth
2 parts Dry Sherry
dash Orange Bitters

Shake with ice and strain.

Barbary Coast

COCKTAIL GLASS

1 part Scotch
1 part Gin
1 part Rum
1 part Crème de Cacao (White)
1 part Light Cream

Shake with ice and strain.

Barbary Coast #2

HIGHBALL GLASS

1 part Scotch
1 part Gin
1 part Light Rum
3/4 part Crème de Cacao (White)

Shake with ice and strain.

Beauty Spot (Dry)

COCKTAIL GLASS

1 part Dry Gin
1 part Dry Vermouth
1 part Sweet Vermouth
1 part Grapefruit Juice
1 part Grenadine

Shake with ice and strain.

Beauty Spot (Sweet)

COCKTAIL GLASS

splash Grenadine
1 part Old Tom's Gin
1/2 part Sweet Vermouth
1/2 part Dry Vermouth
splash Orange Juice

Pour a splash of Grenadine in a cocktail glass. Shake remaining ingredients with ice and strain.

Belle of the Island

COCKTAIL GLASS

2 parts Dry Vermouth
1/2 part Brandy
1/6 part Cointreau
2 dashes Orange Bitters
1/2 tsp Powdered Sugar

Shake with ice and strain.

Belmont Cocktail

COCKTAIL GLASS

2 parts Gin
splash Raspberry Syrup
3/4 part Light Cream

Shake with ice and strain.

Belmont Cocktail #2

COCKTAIL GLASS

2 parts Gin
3/4 part Cream
1/2 part Grenadine

Shake with ice and strain.

Bennett Cocktail

COCKTAIL GLASS

1 1/2 parts Gin
1/2 Lime
dash Powdered Sugar
2 dashes Orange Bitters

Shake with ice and strain.

Bermuda Rose

COCKTAIL GLASS

1 1/4 parts Gin
splash Apricot Brandy
splash Grenadine

Shake with ice and strain.

Between the Sheets

COCKTAIL GLASS

1 part Brandy
1 part Light Rum
1 part Triple Sec
1 part Lemon Juice

Shake with ice and strain.

Between the Sheets #2

COCKTAIL GLASS

1 part Cognac
1 part Crème de Cacao (Dark)
1 part Cream
dash Angostura® Bitters
dash Sugar

Shake with ice and strain.

Between the Sheets #3

COCKTAIL GLASS

1 part Brandy
1 part Triple Sec
1 part Rum

Shake with ice and strain.

Bitter Memories

ROCKS GLASS

2 parts Campari
1 part Dry Vermouth
1 part Triple Sec

Shake with ice and strain over ice.

Black Eye

COCKTAIL GLASS

1½ parts Vodka
½ part Blackberry Brandy

Shake with ice and strain.

Black Hawk

COCKTAIL GLASS

1 part Whiskey
1 part Sloe Gin

Shake with ice and strain.

Black Hawk Collins

COLLINS GLASS

1 part Whiskey
½ part Crème de Cassis
2 parts Sweet & Sour Mix

Shake with ice and strain over ice.

Block and Fall

COCKTAIL GLASS

1 part Cognac
1 part Cointreau®
1 part Apple Brandy
½ part Pernod®

Shake with ice and strain.

Blood and Sand

COCKTAIL GLASS

1 part Scotch
1 part Orange Juice
1 part Cherry Brandy
1 part Sweet Vermouth

Shake with ice and strain.

Bloodhound

COCKTAIL GLASS

2 parts Gin
1 part Dry Vermouth
1 part Sweet Vermouth

Shake with ice and strain.

Blue Devil

HIGHBALL GLASS

1 part Vodka
1 part Blue Curaçao
fill with Sweet & Sour Mix
splash Cherry Juice

Build over ice and stir.

Blue Devil #2

COCKTAIL GLASS

1¼ parts Gin
½ part Blue Curaçao
½ part Sweet & Sour Mix

Combine all ingredients in a blender with ice. Blend until smooth.

Blue Moon

HIGHBALL GLASS

1 part Rum
1 part Blue Curaçao
fill with Pineapple Juice

Shake with ice and pour.

Blue Moon Cocktail

COCKTAIL GLASS

1½ parts Citrus Vodka
1 part Vanilla Vodka
1 part Blue Curaçao

Shake with ice and strain.

Bobby Burns

COCKTAIL GLASS

1 part Scotch
1 part Dry Vermouth
1 part Sweet Vermouth
splash Bénédictine®

Shake with ice and strain.

Bohemian Martini

COCKTAIL GLASS

1 part Anisette
1 part Vodka

Shake with ice and strain.

Bolero

COCKTAIL GLASS

2 parts Light Rum
1 part Apple Brandy
splash Sweet Vermouth

Shake with ice and strain.

Bolero #2

COCKTAIL GLASS

1 part Dark Rum
½ part Apple Brandy
2 splashes Sweet Vermouth

Shake with ice and strain.

Bombay

ROCKS GLASS

1 part Brandy
½ part Dry Vermouth
½ part Sweet Vermouth
½ part Triple Sec
splash Pernod®

Build over ice and stir.

Booster

COCKTAIL GLASS

2 parts Brandy
½ part Blue Curaçao
1 Egg White

Shake with ice and strain.

Boston Cocktail

COCKTAIL GLASS

1 part Gin
1 part Apricot Brandy
splash Grenadine
splash Lemon Juice

Shake with ice and strain.

Boston Cooler

COLLINS GLASS

2 parts Rum
½ part Lemon Juice
dash Sugar
fill with Club Soda

Shake all but club soda with ice and strain. Top with club soda.

Boxcar

ROCKS GLASS

1½ parts Gin
1 part Triple Sec
splash Lemon Juice
splash Grenadine
1 Egg White

Shake with ice and strain.

Brainstorm

COCKTAIL GLASS

2 parts Scotch
½ part Bénédictine®
splash Sweet Vermouth

Shake with ice and strain.

Brainstorm Cocktail

COCKTAIL GLASS

2 parts Whiskey
splash Dry Vermouth

Shake with ice and strain.

Brandy Fizz

HIGHBALL GLASS

2 parts Brandy
dash Powdered Sugar
½ part Lemon Juice
fill with Club Soda

Shake all but Club Soda with ice and strain. Top with Club Soda.

Brandy Flip

ROCKS GLASS

1½ parts Brandy
dash Powdered Sugar
1 Whole Egg
2 splashes Light Cream
dash Ground Nutmeg

Shake all but Nutmeg with ice and strain. Top with Ground Nutmeg.

Brandy Gump

COCKTAIL GLASS

1 part Brandy
1 part Lemon Juice
splash Grenadine

Shake with ice and strain.

Brandy Rickey

HIGHBALL GLASS

1½ parts Brandy
splash Lime Juice
fill with Club Soda

Shake all but Club Soda with ice and strain. Top with Club Soda.

Brandy Stinger

COCKTAIL GLASS

1½ parts Brandy
½ part Crème de Menthe (White)

Shake with ice and strain.

Brazil

COCKTAIL GLASS

1 part Dry Vermouth
1 part Dry Sherry
splash Absinthe

Shake with ice and strain.

Brazil #2

COCKTAIL GLASS

1 part Dry Sherry
1 part Dry Vermouth
splash Anisette
dash Bitters

Shake with ice and strain.

Broken Spur

ROCKS GLASS

1 part Gin
1½ parts Port
1 part Sweet Vermouth
fill with Club Soda

Shake all but Club Soda with ice and strain. Top with Club Soda.

Broken Spur #2

COCKTAIL GLASS

1 part Sweet Vermouth
2 parts Port
splash Triple Sec

Shake with ice and strain.

Bronx

COCKTAIL GLASS

1 part Gin
½ part Dry Vermouth
½ part Sweet Vermouth
1 part Orange Juice

Shake with ice and strain.

Bronx #2

COCKTAIL GLASS

1 part Gin
1 part Sweet Vermouth
1 part Orange Juice
½ Lime

Shake with ice and strain.

Brown Cocktail

COCKTAIL GLASS

1 part Light Rum
1 part Gin
1 part Dry Vermouth

Shake with ice and strain.

Bulldog Cocktail

COCKTAIL GLASS

1½ parts Cherry Brandy
1 part Gin
½ part Lime Juice

Shake with ice and strain.

Bulldog Highball

HIGHBALL GLASS

2 parts Gin
½ part Orange Juice
fill with Ginger Ale

Build over ice and stir.

Button Hook

COCKTAIL GLASS

1 part Crème de Menthe (White)
1 part Brandy
1 part Apricot Brandy

Shake with ice and strain.

Button Hook Cocktail

COCKTAIL GLASS

1 part Brandy
1 part Apricot Brandy
1 part Anisette
1 part Crème de Menthe (White)

Shake with ice and strain.

Cabaret

COCKTAIL GLASS

1½ parts Gin
splash Dry Vermouth
splash Bénédictine®
2 dashes Bitters

Stir gently with ice and strain. Garnish with a Cherry.

Café de Paris

ROCKS GLASS

2 parts Gin
½ part Anisette
1 Egg White
1 part Heavy Cream

Shake with ice and strain over ice.

Cameron's Kick Cocktail

COCKTAIL GLASS

1 part Scotch
1 part Irish Whiskey
splash Lemon Juice
2 dashes Orange Bitters

Shake with ice and strain.

Canadian Cocktail

COCKTAIL GLASS

1½ parts Canadian Whisky
½ part Triple Sec
dash Bitters
dash Powdered Sugar

Shake with ice and strain.

Caruso

COCKTAIL GLASS

1½ parts Gin
1 part Dry Vermouth
½ part Crème de Menthe (Green)

Build over ice and stir.

Caruso Blanco

COCKTAIL GLASS

1½ parts Gin
1 part Dry Vermouth
1 part Crème de Menthe (White)

Build over ice and stir.

Casino

COCKTAIL GLASS

1½ parts Dry Gin
1 part Maraschino Liqueur
dash Orange Bitters

Shake with ice and strain.

Casino #2

COCKTAIL GLASS

2 parts Gin
splash Maraschino Cherry Juice
splash Lemon Juice
2 dashes Orange Bitters

Shake with ice and strain.

Castle Dip Cocktail

COCKTAIL GLASS

1 part Crème de Menthe (White)
1 part Apple Brandy

Shake with ice and strain.

Catastrophe

HIGHBALL GLASS

1 part Goldschläger®
splash Strawberry Liqueur
splash Cranberry Vodka

Build over ice and stir.

Champagne Cocktail

CHAMPAGNE FLUTE

1 Sugar Cube
2 dashes Bitters
fill with Champagne

Soak the sugar cube with bitters. Place the cube in the bottom of a Champagne Flute. Fill with Champagne.

Chelsea Cocktail

COCKTAIL GLASS

1 part Dry Vermouth
3/4 part Bourbon
1/6 part Blackberry Brandy
1/12 part Cointreau
1/3 part Lemon Juice

Shake with ice and strain.

Chelsea Sidecar

COCKTAIL GLASS

1 1/2 parts Gin
1/2 part Triple Sec
2 splashes Lemon Juice

Shake with ice and strain.

Cherry Blossom

COCKTAIL GLASS

1 1/2 parts Brandy
1/2 part Cherry Brandy
2 splashes Lemon Juice
splash Grenadine
splash Triple Sec

Shake with ice and strain. Garnish with Maraschino Cherry.

Cherry Blossom #2

CHAMPAGNE FLUTE

1 part Cognac
1/2 part Kirschwasser
splash Triple Sec
splash Grenadine

Shake with ice and strain.

Classic Cocktail

COCKTAIL GLASS

2 parts Brandy
1/2 part Triple Sec
1/2 part Maraschino Liqueur

Shake with ice and pour.

Clover Club

HIGHBALL GLASS

1 part Gin
4 splashes Grenadine
2 parts Lemon Juice
1 Egg White

Shake with ice and strain.

Club Cocktail

COCKTAIL GLASS

2 parts Gin
1 part Sweet Vermouth

Shake with ice and strain.

Cold Duck

COCKTAIL GLASS

2 parts Brandy
1 part Peppermint Schnapps
1 part Sweet Vermouth

Shake with ice and strain.

Colonial Cocktail

COCKTAIL GLASS

1½ parts Gin
½ part Grapefruit Juice
splash Maraschino Liqueur

Shake with ice and strain.

Commodore

COCKTAIL GLASS

1½ parts Whiskey
¼ part Lemon Juice
dash Powdered Sugar
2 dashes Orange Bitters

Shake with ice and strain.

Cornell Cocktail

COCKTAIL GLASS

1½ parts Gin
splash Lemon Juice
splash Cherry Juice
1 Egg White

Shake with ice and strain.

Coronation Cocktail

COCKTAIL GLASS

1 part Gin
1 part Dry Vermouth
1 part Dubonnet® Blonde

Shake with ice and strain.

Coronation Cocktail #2

COCKTAIL GLASS

1 part Dry Vermouth
1 part Sherry
splash Maraschino Liqueur

Shake with ice and strain.

Coronation Cocktail #3

COCKTAIL GLASS

2 parts Brandy
splash Triple Sec
splash Crème de Menthe (White)

Shake with ice and strain.

Corpse Reviver

COCKTAIL GLASS

2 parts Cognac
1 part Calvados Apple Brandy
1 part Sweet Vermouth

Shake with ice and strain.

Cowboy Cocktail

COCKTAIL GLASS

1½ parts Whiskey
splash Light Cream

Shake with ice and strain.

Creole Cocktail

COCKTAIL GLASS

1 part Coconut Rum
¾ part Vodka
1 part Orange Juice
splash Grenadine

Shake with ice and strain.

Crystal Slipper Cocktail

COCKTAIL GLASS

1½ parts Gin
½ part Blue Curaçao
2 dashes Orange Bitters

Shake with ice and strain.

Cuban

COCKTAIL GLASS

1 part Cognac
1 part Apricot Brandy

Shake with ice and strain.

Cupid

COCKTAIL GLASS

2 parts Gin
1 part Dry Vermouth
1 part Sweet Vermouth

Shake with ice and strain.

Damn the Weather

HIGHBALL GLASS

1 part Gin
½ part Orange Juice
¼ part Triple Sec
½ part Sweet Vermouth

Shake with ice and pour.

Deauville Cocktail

COCKTAIL GLASS

1 part Apple Brandy
1 part Brandy
1 part Triple Sec
½ part Lemon Juice

Shake with ice and strain.

Delmonico

COCKTAIL GLASS

1 part Dry Vermouth
1 part Sweet Vermouth
1 part Brandy
½ part Gin

Shake with ice and strain.

Dempsey Cocktail

COCKTAIL GLASS

1 part Apple Brandy
1 part Gin
splash Anisette
splash Grenadine

Shake with ice and strain.

Depth Bomb

ROCKS GLASS

1 part Apple Brandy
1 part Brandy
splash Lemon Juice
splash Grenadine

Shake with ice and pour.

Devil's Cocktail

COCKTAIL GLASS

1 part Brandy
1 part Dry Vermouth
3 splashes Blue Curaçao
2 dashes Bitters

Shake with ice and strain.

Devil's Cocktail #2

COCKTAIL GLASS

2 parts Port
1 part Dry Vermouth

Shake with ice and strain.

Diana

HIGHBALL GLASS

1 part Brandy
3 parts Crème de Menthe (White)

Build over ice and stir.

Diana #2

WHITE WINE GLASS

2 parts Peppermint Schnapps
3 splashes Cognac

Build over ice and stir.

Diana #3

COCKTAIL GLASS

2 parts Crème de Cacao (White)
1 part Brandy

Build over ice and stir.

Dixie Cocktail

COCKTAIL GLASS

½ part Dry Vermouth
1 part Gin
½ part Orange Juice
2 splashes Anisette

Shake with ice and strain.

Dixie Whiskey

COCKTAIL GLASS

2 parts Bourbon
½ part Crème de Menthe (White)
splash Triple Sec
dash Powdered Sugar

Shake with ice and strain.

Dolores

COCKTAIL GLASS

1 part Brandy
1 part Cherry Brandy
1 part Crème de Cacao (White)

Shake with ice and strain.

Dream Cocktail

COCKTAIL GLASS

2 parts Brandy
1 part Triple Sec
splash Anisette

Shake with ice and strain.

Dubarry Cocktail

COCKTAIL GLASS

2 parts Gin
1 part Dry Vermouth
splash Anisette
dash Bitters

Shake with ice and strain.

Dubonnet® Cocktail

COCKTAIL GLASS

2 parts Dubonnet® Blonde
1 part Gin
dash Bitters
1 Lemon Twist

Shake with ice and strain.

Duke of Marlboro

COCKTAIL GLASS

1½ parts Dry Sherry
1½ parts Sweet Vermouth
dash Orange Bitters

Shake with ice and strain. Garnish with an Orange Twist.

Earthquake

COCKTAIL GLASS

1 part Vodka
1 part Amaretto
1 part Southern Comfort®
½ part Sweetened Lime Juice

Shake with ice and strain.

Earthquake #2

COCKTAIL GLASS

1 part Gin
1 part Whiskey
1 part Pernod®

Shake with ice and strain.

Eclipse

ROCKS GLASS

1 part Gin
1½ parts Sloe Gin
½ part Grenadine

Shake with ice and strain over ice.

Eclipse #2

HIGHBALL GLASS

1 part Vodka
splash Crème de Cacao (White)
splash Strawberry Liqueur
1 part Cream

Shake with ice and strain over ice.

Elk Cocktail

WHITE WINE GLASS

1 part Port
1 part Whiskey
1 Egg White
dash Powdered Sugar

Shake with ice and strain.

Emerald Isle

HIGHBALL GLASS

1 part Vodka
2 parts Melon Liqueur
fill with Mountain Dew®

Build over ice and stir.

English Rose

COCKTAIL GLASS

2 parts Dry Gin
1 part Dry Vermouth
1 part Apricot Brandy
splash Grenadine

Shake with ice and strain.

Ethel Cocktail

COCKTAIL GLASS

1 part Crème de Menthe (White)
1 part Triple Sec
1 part Apricot Brandy

Shake with ice and strain.

Ethel Duffy Cocktail

COCKTAIL GLASS

1 part Crème de Menthe (White)
1 part Apricot Brandy
1 part Triple Sec

Shake with ice and strain.

Eye Opener

COCKTAIL GLASS

1 Egg Yolk
1 part Light Rum
½ part Crème de Cacao (White)
½ part Triple Sec
½ part Sambuca

Shake with ice and strain.

Fair and Warmer Cocktail

COCKTAIL GLASS

2 parts Light Rum
1 part Sweet Vermouth
splash Triple Sec

Shake with ice and strain.

Fallen Angel

COCKTAIL GLASS

1½ parts Gin
½ part Lemon Juice
splash Crème de Menthe (White)
dash Bitters

Shake with ice and strain.

Fallen Angel Cocktail

HIGHBALL GLASS

1½ parts Gin
1 part Lemon Juice
½ part Lime Juice
dash Angostura® Bitters
2 splashes Crème de Menthe (White)

Shake with ice and strain over ice.

Fancy Bourbon

COCKTAIL GLASS

1 part Triple Sec
dash Sugar
2 dashes Bitters
1 Lemon Twist

Shake with ice and strain.

Fancy Brandy

COCKTAIL GLASS

2 parts Brandy
splash Triple Sec
dash Powdered Sugar
dash Bitters

Shake with ice and strain. Garnish with Lemon Twist.

Fancy Brandy #2

COCKTAIL GLASS

2 parts Brandy
½ part Triple Sec
1 tbsp Powdered Sugar

Shake with ice and strain.

Fancy Gin

COCKTAIL GLASS

2 parts Gin
splash Triple Sec
splash Powdered Sugar
dash Bitters

Shake with ice and strain. Garnish with Lemon Twist.

Fancy Scotch

COCKTAIL GLASS

2 parts Scotch
splash Triple Sec
dash Sugar
2 dashes Bitters

Shake with ice and strain. Garnish with Lemon Twist.

Fancy Whiskey

COCKTAIL GLASS

2 parts Whiskey
splash Triple Sec
dash Powdered Sugar
dash Bitters

Shake with ice and strain. Garnish with Lemon Twist.

Farmer's Martini

COCKTAIL GLASS

3 parts Gin
½ part Dry Vermouth
½ part Sweet Vermouth
dash Bitters

Shake with ice and strain.

Fine and Dandy

COUPETTE GLASS

2 parts Gin
1 part Triple Sec
1 part Lemon Juice
dash Angostura® Bitters

Combine all ingredients in a blender with ice. Blend until smooth.

Five Fifteeen Cocktail

COCKTAIL GLASS

1 part Dry Vermouth
1 part Triple Sec
1 part Cream

Shake with ice and strain.

Flamingo Cocktail

COCKTAIL GLASS

½ part Apricot Brandy
1½ parts Gin
½ part Lime Juice
splash Grenadine

Shake with ice and strain.

Flying Scotsman

HIGHBALL GLASS

1 part Scotch
1 part Sweet Vermouth
splash Simple Syrup
dash Angostura® Bitters

Shake with ice and strain over ice.

Fox River Cocktail

HIGHBALL GLASS

1½ parts Rye Whiskey
½ part Crème de Cacao (Dark)
2 dashes Orange Bitters

Shake with ice and strain over ice.

Frackenjack Cocktail

COCKTAIL GLASS

1 part Gin
½ part Triple Sec
½ part Apricot Brandy
½ part Sweet Vermouth

Shake with ice and strain.

French Rose

COCKTAIL GLASS

2 parts Gin
½ part Cherry Liqueur

Shake with ice and strain.

Froth Blower

HIGHBALL GLASS

1 Egg White
1½ parts Gin
splash Grenadine

Shake with ice and strain.

Gibson

COCKTAIL GLASS

3½ parts Gin or Vodka
½ part Dry Vermouth

Shake with ice and strain. Garnish with a Cocktail Onion; otherwise it's a Martini.

Gilroy Cocktail

COCKTAIL GLASS

3/4 part Cherry Brandy
3/4 part Gin
1/2 part Dry Vermouth
1/4 part Lemon Juice
dash Orange Bitters

Shake with ice and strain.

Gin & Tonic

HIGHBALL GLASS

1 1/2 parts Gin
fill with Tonic Water

Build over ice and stir.

Gin Alexander

HIGHBALL GLASS

1 part Gin
1 part Crème de Cacao (White)
1 part Cream

Build over ice and stir.

Gin Buck

ROCKS GLASS

1 1/2 parts Gin
1/2 part Lemon Juice
fill with Ginger Ale

Build over ice and stir.

Gin Fix

HIGHBALL GLASS

2 1/2 parts Gin
dash Powdered Sugar
1/2 part Lemon Juice
1 Lemon Slice
splash Water

Shake with ice and strain over ice.

Gin Fizz

HIGHBALL GLASS

2 parts Gin
1/2 part Lemon Juice
dash Powdered Sugar
fill with Seltzer

Build over ice and stir.

Gin Rickey

HIGHBALL GLASS

1 1/2 parts Gin
1/2 part Lime Juice
fill with Seltzer

Build over ice and stir. Garnish with Lime Wedge.

Gin Sidecar

COCKTAIL GLASS

1 1/2 parts Dry Gin
1 part Triple Sec

Shake with ice and strain.

Gin Sling

ROCKS GLASS

2 parts Gin
1/2 part Lemon Juice
dash Powdered Sugar
splash Water

Shake with ice and strain over ice. Garnish with Orange Twist.

Gin Stinger

COCKTAIL GLASS

2 parts Vodka
1 part Crème de Cacao (White)
1 part Crème de Menthe (Green)

Shake with ice and strain.

Gin Swizzle

COLLINS GLASS

2 parts Gin
1/2 part Lime Juice
dash Powdered Sugar
2 dashes Bitters
fill with Seltzer

Build over ice and stir.

Gin Toddy

ROCKS GLASS

2 parts Gin
2 splashes Water
dash Powdered Sugar

Build over ice and stir. Garnish with Lemon Twist.

Golden Dawn

ROCKS GLASS

1 part Apple Brandy
½ part Apricot Brandy
½ part Gin
1 part Orange Juice
splash Grenadine

Build over ice and stir.

Golden Gate

COCKTAIL GLASS

1 part Brandy
1 part Triple Sec
1 part Light Rum

Shake with ice and strain.

Good Times

COCKTAIL GLASS

1 part Canadian Whiseky
1 part Dry Vermouth
splash Lemon Juice

Shake with ice and strain.

Grapefruit Cocktail

COCKTAIL GLASS

1 part Gin
1 part Grapefruit Juice
splash Maraschino Cherry Juice

Shake with ice and strain.

Green Dragon

WHITE WINE GLASS

1 parts Pernod®
1 parts Milk
1 parts Heavy Cream
½ part Simple Syrup

Shake with ice and strain.

Green Dragon #2

COCKTAIL GLASS

1½ parts Gin
1 part Crème de Menthe (Green)

Shake with ice and strain.

Green Dragon #3

COCKTAIL GLASS

2 parts Gin
½ part Crème de Menthe (White)
1 part Jägermeister®

Shake with ice and strain.

Green Room

COCKTAIL GLASS

1½ parts Dry Vermouth
½ part Brandy
splash Triple Sec

Shake with ice and strain.

Grenadine Cocktail

HIGHBALL GLASS

1 part Grenadine
1 part Orange Juice
1 part Pineapple Juice

Shake with ice and pour.

Guard's Room

COCKTAIL GLASS

2 parts Dry Gin
1 part Dry Vermouth
splash Triple Sec

Shake with ice and strain.

Gypsy Martini

COCKTAIL GLASS

3 parts Gin
¾ part Sweet Vermouth

Shake with ice and strain.

Harlem

COCKTAIL GLASS

2 parts Dry Gin
1 part Pineapple Juice
splash Maraschino Liqueur

Shake with ice and strain.

Harry Lauder
COCKTAIL GLASS

3/4 part Sweet Vermouth
3/4 part Scotch
1/2 part Simple Syrup

Shake with ice and strain.

Harvard Cocktail
COCKTAIL GLASS

2 parts Brandy
1 part Sweet Vermouth
splash Grenadine
2 splashes Lemon Juice
dash Bitters

Shake with ice and strain.

Havana
HIGHBALL GLASS

1 part Vodka
1 part Banana Juice
1 part Wild Berry Schnapps
2 parts Lemonade
1 part Orange Juice

Build over ice and stir.

Havana Club
COCKTAIL GLASS

1 1/2 parts Light Rum
1/2 part Dry Vermouth

Shake with ice and strain.

Havana Cocktail
COCKTAIL GLASS

1 part Light Rum
2 parts Pineapple Juice
splash Lemon Juice

Shake with ice and strain.

Havana Martini
COCKTAIL GLASS

1 1/2 parts Light Rum
1/2 part Lime Cordial
1/2 tbsp Sugar

Shake with ice and strain.

Hawaiian Cocktail
COCKTAIL GLASS

2 parts Gin
1/2 part Triple Sec
2 splashes Pineapple Juice

Shake with ice and strain.

Haymaker
ROCKS GLASS

1 part Dry Vermouth
1 part Maker's Mark Bourbon
1 part Triple Sec
1 part Lime Juice

Shake with ice and strain over ice.

Hoffman House
COCKTAIL GLASS

1 1/2 parts Gin
1/2 part Dry Vermouth
2 dashes Orange Bitters

Shake with ice and strain.

Holland House Cocktail
COCKTAIL GLASS

2 parts Dry Gin
1 part Dry Vermouth
splash Maraschino Liqueur
splash Pineapple Juice

Shake with ice and strain.

Honeymoon Cocktail
COCKTAIL GLASS

3/4 part Apple Brandy
3/4 part Bénédictine®
splash Triple Sec
1/2 part Lemon Juice

Shake with ice and strain.

Honolulu Cocktail
COCKTAIL GLASS

1 1/2 parts Gin
splash Orange Juice
splash Pineapple Juice
splash Lemon Juice
dash Sugar

Shake with ice and strain.

Honolulu Cocktail #2
COCKTAIL GLASS
1 part Gin
1 part Maraschino Liqueur
1 part Bénédictine®
Shake with ice and strain.

Hurricane Cocktail
COCKTAIL GLASS
1 1/4 parts Brandy
3/4 part Pernod®
3/4 part Vodka
Shake with ice and strain.

Imperial
COCKTAIL GLASS
1 part Dry Gin
1 part Dry Vermouth
1/2 part Maraschino Liqueur
dash Bitters
Shake with ice and strain.

Income Tax Cocktail
COCKTAIL GLASS
1 part Gin
2 splashes Sweet Vermouth
2 splashes Dry Vermouth
1/2 part Orange Juice
dash Bitters
Shake with ice and strain.

Jack Rose
HIGHBALL GLASS
1 1/2 part Apple Brandy
1/2 part Grenadine
3/4 part Sweet & Sour Mix
Shake with ice and strain over ice.

Jack Rose Cocktail
COCKTAIL GLASS
1 1/2 parts Apple Brandy
splash Grenadine
1/2 part Lime Juice
Shake with ice and strain.

Jewel Cocktail
COCKTAIL GLASS
1 part Gin
1 part Sweet Vermouth
1 part Green Chartreuse®
dash Orange Bitters
Shake with ice and strain.

Jockey Club
COCKTAIL GLASS
1 1/2 parts Gin
1/2 part Lemon Juice
splash Crème de Cacao (White)
dash Angostura® Bitters
Shake with ice and strain.

Journalist
COCKTAIL GLASS
2 parts Gin
1 part Dry Vermouth
1 part Sweet Vermouth
1 part Triple Sec
splash Lemon Juice
dash Bitters
Shake with ice and strain.

Kentucky Colonel
COCKTAIL GLASS
1 1/2 parts Bourbon
1/2 part Bénédictine®
Shake with ice and strain. Garnish with Lemon Twist.

Kiss in the Dark
COCKTAIL GLASS
1 part Gin
1 part Cherry Brandy
1 part Vermouth
Shake with ice and strain.

Knickerbocker Cocktail
COCKTAIL GLASS
2 parts Dry Gin
1 part Dry Vermouth
splash Sweet Vermouth
Shake with ice and strain.

Knickerbocker Special

COCKTAIL GLASS

2 parts Light Rum
splash Triple Sec
splash Orange Juice
splash Lemon Juice
splash Raspberry Syrup

Shake with ice and strain. Garnish with a Pineapple Slice.

Knockout Cocktail

COCKTAIL GLASS

1 part Gin
1 part Dry Vermouth
½ part Crème de Menthe (White)
½ part Pastis

Shake with ice and strain.

Kretchma Cocktail

COCKTAIL GLASS

1 part Vodka
1 part Crème de Cacao (White)
splash Grenadine
½ part Lemon Juice

Shake with ice and strain.

Ladies Cocktail

COCKTAIL GLASS

1½ parts Whiskey
splash Anisette
dash Bitters

Shake with ice and strain.

Leap Year

COCKTAIL GLASS

1½ parts Gin
½ part Grand Marnier®
splash Lemon Juice
½ part Sweet Vermouth

Shake with ice and strain.

Leave It to Me

COCKTAIL GLASS

1 part Gin
½ part Dry Vermouth
½ part Apricot Brandy
splash Grenadine
splash Lemon Juice

Shake with ice and strain.

Liberal

ROCKS GLASS

1 part Whiskey
1 part Sweet Vermouth
3 splashes Amer Picon®
2 dashes Bitters

Shake with ice and strain over ice.

Liberty Cocktail

COCKTAIL GLASS

1½ parts Apple Brandy
¼ part Light Rum
splash Simple Syrup

Shake with ice and strain.

Little Devil Cocktail

COCKTAIL GLASS

1 part Light Rum
2 splashes Triple Sec
1 part Gin
¼ part Lemon Juice

Shake with ice and strain.

London Martini

COCKTAIL GLASS

3 parts Gin
dash Powdered Sugar
¼ part Maraschino Liqueur

Shake with ice and strain.

Lone Tree Cocktail

COCKTAIL GLASS

1 part Dry Gin
1 part Dry Vermouth
1 part Sweet Vermouth

Shake with ice and strain.

Los Angeles Cocktail

ROCKS GLASS

1 1/2 part Whiskey
1/4 part Sweet Vermouth
1/2 part Lemon Juice
dash Powdered Sugar
1 Egg

Shake with ice and strain.

Mabel Moon

COCKTAIL GLASS

1 part Melon Liqueur
1/2 part Maraschino Liqueur
1/2 part Orange Juice
1 part Sweet & Sour Mix.

Shake with ice and strain.

Magnolia Blossom

HIGHBALL GLASS

1 part Gin
1/2 part Lemon Juice
1 1/2 parts Cream
2 splashes Grenadine

Shake with ice and strain over ice.

Maiden's Blush

COCKTAIL GLASS

1 1/2 parts Gin
1/2 part Triple Sec
splash Cherry Brandy
1 part Lemon Juice
splash Maraschino Cherry Juice

Shake with ice and strain.

Maiden's Prayer

COCKTAIL GLASS

1 1/2 parts Gin
1 part Lemon Juice
1/2 part Triple Sec

Shake with ice and strain.

Manhattan

COCKTAIL GLASS

2 parts Whiskey
1 part Sweet Vermouth
dash Bitters

Shake with ice and strain. Garnish with Maraschino Cherry.

Marconi

COCKTAIL GLASS

1 1/2 parts Gin
1 part Dry Vermouth
dash Bitters

Shake with ice and strain.

Marconi Wireless

COCKTAIL GLASS

1 1/2 parts Apple Brandy
1/2 part Sweet Vermouth
2 dashes Orange Bitters

Shake with ice and strain.

Merry Widow

COCKTAIL GLASS

1 part Gin
1 part Dubonnet® Blonde

Shake with ice and strain.

Miami Beach

COCKTAIL GLASS

2 parts Rum
3/4 part Cointreau®
4 splashes Lemon Juice

Shake with ice and strain.

Miami Cocktail

COCKTAIL GLASS

1 1/2 parts Light Rum
1/2 part Crème de Menthe (White)
splash Lime Juice

Shake with ice and strain.

Miami Cocktail #2

COCKTAIL GLASS

1½ parts Rum
½ part Crème de Menthe (White)
splash Lemon Juice

Shake with ice and strain.

Millionaire

COCKTAIL GLASS

3 splashes Blue Curaçao
1 Egg White
splash Grenadine
½ part Pernod®

Shake with ice and strain.

Minnehaha Cocktail

COCKTAIL GLASS

1 part Dry Gin
1 part Orange Juice
1 part Sweet Vermouth

Shake with ice and strain.

Modern Cocktail

COCKTAIL GLASS

1½ parts Scotch
splash Dark Rum
splash Anisette
splash Lemon Juice
dash Orange Bitters

Shake with ice and strain.

Monte Cristo Cocktail

ROCKS GLASS

1 part Cointreau®
1 part Lemon Vodka

Shake with ice and strain over ice.

Morning

HIGHBALL GLASS

1 part Brandy
1 part Dry Vermouth
2 dashes Orange Bitters
splash Blue Curaçao
splash Cherry Liqueur
splash Pernod®

Shake with ice and strain over ice.

Morning After

COUPETTE GLASS

1 part Crème de Cacao (White)
1 part Dark Rum
½ part Coffee Liqueur
½ part Cream

Shake with ice and strain.

Moulin Rouge

COCKTAIL GLASS

2 parts Sloe Gin
1 part Sweet Vermouth
dash Bitters

Shake with ice and strain.

Mountain Cocktail

COCKTAIL GLASS

1½ parts Whiskey
splash Dry Vermouth
splash Sweet Vermouth
splash Lemon Juice
1 Egg White

Shake with ice and strain.

Nevada Cocktail

COCKTAIL GLASS

1½ parts Light Rum
1 part Grapefruit Juice
½ part Lime Juice
3 dashes Powdered Sugar
dash Bitters

Shake with ice and strain.

New York Cocktail

COCKTAIL GLASS

1½ parts Whiskey
splash Grenadine
½ part Lemon Juice
dash Powdered Sugar

Shake with ice and strain.

Nightcap Cocktail

COCKTAIL GLASS

1 part Brandy
1 part Triple Sec
1 part Amer Picon®
1 Egg Yolk

Shake with ice and strain.

Oasis

HIGHBALL GLASS

1 part Melon liqueur
1 part Coconut Flavored Rum
1/2 part Pisang Ambon® Liqueur
2 parts Lemon Juice
splash Cream

Shake with ice and strain over ice.

Old Fashioned

ROCKS GLASS

2 parts Rye Whiskey
2 dashes Angostura® Bitters
dash Sugar
splash Water

Build over ice and stir. Garnish with Maraschino Cherry, Lemon Twist, and Orange Slice.

Old Pal Cocktail

COCKTAIL GLASS

1 1/4 parts Whiskey
1/2 part Sweet Vermouth
1/2 part Grenadine

Shake with ice and strain.

Opera

COCKTAIL GLASS

1 1/2 parts Gin
1/2 part Cherry Liqueur
1/2 part Dubonnet® Blonde

Shake with ice and strain.

Orange Blossom

COCKTAIL GLASS

2 parts Gin
1 part Orange Juice
dash Sugar

Shake with ice and strain.

Orange Blossom #2

ROCKS GLASS

1 1/2 parts Gin
1/2 part Orange Juice
2 splashes Blue Curaçao
2 splashes Lemon Juice
splash Orange Flower Water
splash Simple Syrup

Shake with ice and strain over ice.

Oriental

COCKTAIL GLASS

1 part Rye Whiskey
1/4 part Cointreau®
1/4 part Sweet Vermouth
1/2 part Lime Juice

Shake with ice and strain.

Pall Mall

ROCKS GLASS

1 1/2 parts Gin
1/2 part Dry Vermouth
1/2 part Sweet Vermouth
1/2 part Crème de Menthe (White)

Shake with ice and strain over ice.

Pall Mall Martini

COCKTAIL GLASS

2 parts Vodka
1/2 part Crème de Menthe (White)
1/2 part Dry Vermouth
1/2 part Sweet Vermouth

Shake with ice and strain.

Palm Beach Cocktail
COCKTAIL GLASS
2 parts Gin
splash Sweet Vermouth
2 splashes Grapefruit Juice
Shake with ice and strain.

Pan American
ROCKS GLASS
1 part Rye Whiskey
½ part Simple Syrup
Shake with ice and strain over ice.

Panama
COCKTAIL GLASS
1 part Crème de Cacao (White)
1 part Heavy Cream
Shake with ice and strain.

Paradise
HIGHBALL GLASS
1 part Apricot Brandy
¾ part Gin
¾ part Orange Juice
Shake with ice and pour.

Parisian Blonde
COCKTAIL GLASS
1 part Jamaican Rum
1 part Triple Sec
½ part Light Cream
Shake with ice and strain.

Peter Pan Cocktail
COCKTAIL GLASS
1 part Dry Vermouth
1 part Gin
1 part Orange Juice
2 dashes Bitters
Shake with ice and strain.

Pick Me Up
HIGHBALL GLASS
1 part Sweet Vermouth
1 part Cherry Brandy
¼ part Gin
Shake with ice and strain over ice.

Pierre Special
ROCKS GLASS
1 part Vodka
1 part Coconut Rum
½ part Passion Fruit Liqueur
½ part Lime Cordial
Shake with ice and strain.

Ping Pong
HIGHBALL GLASS
1 part Melon Liqueur
1½ parts White Wine
fill with Lemon-Lime Soda
Build over ice and stir.

Pink Elephant
CHAMPAGNE FLUTE
1 part Vodka
1 part Galliano®
1 part Crème de Noyaux
1 part Orange Juice
1 part Cream
splash Grenadine
Shake with ice and strain.

Pink Lady
COCKTAIL GLASS
1½ parts Gin
splash Grenadine
splash Light Cream
1 Egg White
Shake with ice and strain.

Pink Whiskers

HIGHBALL GLASS

1 part Apricot Brandy
1 part Port
½ part Dry Vermouth
splash Crème de Menthe (White)
splash Grenadine
fill with Orange Juice

Shake with ice and strain over ice.

Planter's Cocktail

COCKTAIL GLASS

1½ parts Rum
dash Powdered Sugar
¼ part Lemon Juice

Shake with ice and strain.

Plaza

COCKTAIL GLASS

1 part Gin
2 splashes Pineapple Juice
1 part Dry Vermouth
1 part Sweet Vermouth

Shake with ice and strain.

Poker Cocktail

COCKTAIL GLASS

1 part Light Rum
1 part Sweet Vermouth

Shake with ice and strain.

Pollyanna

HIGHBALL GLASS

1½ parts Gin
2 splashes Sweet Vermouth
2 splashes Grenadine

Shake with ice and strain over ice.

Polo

HIGHBALL GLASS

1½ parts Gin
2 splashes Grapefruit Juice
2 splashes Orange Juice

Shake with ice and strain over ice.

Polo #2

COCKTAIL GLASS

1 part Gin
½ part Lemon Juice
½ part Orange Juice

Shake with ice and strain.

Poppy

COCKTAIL GLASS

1½ parts Dry Gin
1 part Crème de Cacao (White)

Shake with ice and strain.

Preakness Cocktail

COCKTAIL GLASS

2 parts Whiskey
1 part Sweet Vermouth
splash Bénédictine®
dash Bitters

Shake with ice and strain.

Presidente Cocktail

COCKTAIL GLASS

1½ parts Light Rum
½ part Dry Vermouth
½ part Blue Curaçao
splash Grenadine

Shake with ice and strain.

Princeton

COCKTAIL GLASS

2 parts Gin
1 part Port
4 dashes Orange Bitters

Shake with ice and strain.

Quaker Cocktail

COCKTAIL GLASS

1 part Brandy
½ part Rum
½ part Lemon Juice
splash Raspberry Syrup

Shake with ice and strain.

Queen Elizabeth
COCKTAIL GLASS

1½ parts Gin
½ part Dry Vermouth
splash Bénédictine®

Shake with ice and strain.

Queens Cocktail
COCKTAIL GLASS

1 part Dry Vermouth
1 part Gin
1 part Sweet Vermouth
1 part Pineapple Juice

Shake with ice and strain.

Racquet Club Cocktail
COCKTAIL GLASS

2 parts Gin
1 part Dry Vermouth
dash Orange Bitters

Shake with ice and strain.

Ritz Bar Fizz
HIGHBALL GLASS

splash Grenadine
1 part Pineapple Juice
1 part Grapefruit Juice
fill with Champagne

Build over ice.

Rob Roy
COLLINS GLASS

2 parts Scotch
½ part Sweet Vermouth
dash Orange Bitters

Shake with ice and strain.

Rock and Rye Cocktail
COCKTAIL GLASS

1 part Rock & Rye
1 part White Port
2 splashes Dry Vermouth

Shake with ice and strain.

Royal Smile
COCKTAIL GLASS

1½ parts Gin
1 part Grenadine
splash Lemon Juice

Shake with ice and strain.

Rum Daisy
ROCKS GLASS

2 parts Dark Rum
1 part Lemon Juice
dash Sugar
splash Grenadine

Shake with ice and strain over ice.

Rum Fix
HIGHBALL GLASS

2½ parts Light Rum
½ part Lemon Juice
dash Powdered Sugar
splash Water

Shake with ice and strain.

Rum Fizz
COLLINS GLASS

1 part Dark Rum
½ part Apricot Brandy
½ part Sweet & Sour Mix
fill with Club Soda

Shake all but Club Soda with ice and strain. Top with Club Soda.

Rum Rickey
HIGHBALL GLASS

1½ parts Light Rum
½ part Lime Juice
fill with Seltzer

Build over ice and stir.

Rum Stinger
COCKTAIL GLASS

1½ parts Dark Rum
1 part Crème de Menthe (White)

Shake with ice and strain.

Rum Swizzle

COLLINS GLASS

2 parts Dark Rum
1/2 part Lemon Juice
dash Powdered Sugar
2 dashes Bitters
fill with Seltzer

Shake all but Seltzer with ice and strain. Top with Seltzer.

Rum Toddy

IRISH COFFEE CUP

2 parts Rum
1 Sugar Cube
1 Lemon Slice
dash Ground Nutmeg
fill with Boiling Water

Build in a heat-proof cup or mug.

Russian

COCKTAIL GLASS

1 part Crème de Cacao (White)
1 part Gin
1 part Vodka

Shake with ice and strain.

Salome Cocktail

COCKTAIL GLASS

1 part Gin
1 part Dry Vermouth
1 part Dubonnet® Blonde

Shake with ice and strain.

Santiago

COCKTAIL GLASS

1 1/2 parts Light Rum
splash Grenadine
dash Powdered Sugar
splash Lime Juice

Shake with ice and strain.

Saratoga

COCKTAIL GLASS

2 parts Brandy
2 splashes Cherry Liqueur
2 dashes Angostura® Bitters
1 part Pineapple Juice

Shake with ice and strain.

Saucy Sue

COCKTAIL GLASS

2 parts Apple Brandy
splash Apricot Brandy
splash Pernod®

Shake with ice and strain.

Savoy Tango

COCKTAIL GLASS

1 1/2 parts Apple Brandy
1 part Sloe Gin

Shake with ice and strain.

Saxon

COCKTAIL GLASS

1 3/4 parts Rum
splash Lime Juice
splash Grenadine

Shake with ice and strain.

Sazerac Cocktail

ROCKS GLASS

1 1/2 parts Rye Whiskey
splash Absinthe
dash Sugar
2 dashes Peychauds® Bitters
2 dashes Angostura® Bitters

Rinse a chilled rocks glass with the Absinthe and dump the excess. In a shaker or mixing glass, mix the Sugar with the Bitters until the Sugar dissolves. Add ice and stir to chill. Add the Rye and the Bitters/Sugar mixture to the rocks glass. Garnish with a Lemon Twist.

September Morn

COCKTAIL GLASS

2 parts Light Rum
½ part Lime Juice
splash Grenadine
1 Egg White

Shake with ice and strain.

Seventh Heaven

COLLINS GLASS

2 parts Canadian Whisky
2 parts Amaretto
1 part Pineapple Juice
1 part Lemon-Lime Soda

Build over ice and stir.

Sevilla

ROCKS GLASS

1 part Dark Rum
1 part Sweet Vermouth

Shake with ice and strain over ice.

Sevilla Cocktail

ROCKS GLASS

1 part Light Rum
1 part Port
dash Powdered Sugar
1 Whole Egg

Shake with ice and strain over ice.

Shamrock

COCKTAIL GLASS

1½ parts Irish Whiskey
½ part Dry Vermouth
splash Crème de Menthe (Green)

Shake with ice and strain.

Shamrock #2

COCKTAIL GLASS

1½ parts Irish Whiskey
½ part Coffee Liqueur
½ part Irish Cream Liqueur

Shake with ice and strain.

Shanghai Cocktail

COCKTAIL GLASS

1½ parts Dark Rum
1 part Lemon Juice
splash Anisette
splash Grenadine

Shake with ice and strain.

Sherry Cocktail

COCKTAIL GLASS

1 part Gin
1 part Cream Sherry

Shake with ice and strain.

Shriner Cocktail

COCKTAIL GLASS

1 part Sloe Gin
1 part Brandy
splash Simple Syrup
2 dashes Bitters

Shake with ice and strain.

Sidecar

ROCKS GLASS

1 part Brandy
1½ part Lemon Juice
½ part Triple Sec

Shake with ice and strain over ice.

Silver King

HIGHBALL GLASS

1 part Gin
1 part Lemon Juice
splash Simple Syrup
2 dashes Orange Bitters
1 Egg White

Shake with ice and strain.

Sir Walter Cocktail

ROCKS GLASS

1½ parts Brandy
½ part Rum
splash Grenadine
splash Lime Juice
splash Blue Curaçao

Shake with ice and strain over ice.

Sky Rocket

COCKTAIL GLASS

1 part Apricot Brandy
1 part Campari®
1 part Dark Rum
1 part Spiced Rum
2 parts Guava Juice

Shake with ice and strain.

Sloe Gin Cocktail

COCKTAIL GLASS

2 parts Sloe Gin
splash Dry Vermouth
dash Orange Bitters

Shake with ice and strain.

Sloppy Joe

COCKTAIL GLASS

1 part Brandy
1 part Port
2 splashes Triple Sec
splash Grenadine
1 part Pineapple Juice

Shake with ice and strain.

Smile

SHOT GLASS

1 part Melon Liqueur
1 part Apple Brandy

Shake with ice and strain.

Smiler Cocktail

COCKTAIL GLASS

1 part Gin
1/2 part Dry Vermouth
1/2 part Sweet Vermouth
splash Orange Juice
dash Bitters

Shake with ice and strain.

Snowball

COCKTAIL GLASS

1 1/2 parts Gin
1/2 part Anisette
1/2 part Light Cream

Shake with ice and strain.

Soul Kiss

COCKTAIL GLASS

1 part Dubonnet® Blonde
1/2 part Sweet Vermouth
1/2 part Dry Vermouth
1 part Orange Juice

Shake with ice and strain.

Southside

COCKTAIL GLASS

1 1/2 parts Gin
1/2 part Lemon Juice
dash Powdered Sugar

Shake with ice and strain.

St. Patrick's Day

COCKTAIL GLASS

1 part Crème de Menthe (Green)
1 part Green Chartreuse®
1 part Irish Whiskey
dash Bitters

Shake with ice and strain.

Stinger

COCKTAIL GLASS

1 1/2 parts Brandy
1/2 part Crème de Menthe (White)

Shake with ice and strain.

Sunshine

ROCKS GLASS

1 1/2 parts Vodka
1/2 part Triple Sec
fill with Grapefruit Juice

Build over ice and stir.

Swiss Family Cocktail

COCKTAIL GLASS

2 parts Whiskey
1 part Dry Vermouth
splash Anisette
2 dashes Bitters

Shake with ice and strain.

Tailspin

COCKTAIL GLASS

2 parts Gin
1½ parts Sweet Vermouth
dash Orange Bitters

Shake with ice and strain.

Tango

ROCKS GLASS

1½ parts Gin
½ part Dry Vermouth
½ part Sweet Vermouth
1 part Orange Juice
splash Blue Curaçao

Shake with ice and strain over ice.

Temptation Cocktail

COCKTAIL GLASS

1½ parts Whiskey
splash Dubonnet® Blonde
splash Triple Sec
splash Anisette

Shake with ice and strain.

Third Rail

ROCKS GLASS

2 parts Dry Vermouth
splash Blue Curaçao
splash Crème de Menthe (White)

Shake with ice and strain over ice.

Thunder Cocktail

COCKTAIL GLASS

2 parts Brandy
1 part Egg Yolk
1 tbsp Powdered Sugar
splash Tabasco® Sauce

Shake with ice and strain.

Thunderclap

COCKTAIL GLASS

1 part Whiskey
1 part Brandy
1 part Gin

Shake with ice and strain.

Tipperary Cocktail

COCKTAIL GLASS

1 part Rye Whiskey
1 part Sweet Vermouth
1 part Green Chartreuse®

Shake with ice and strain.

TnT

COCKTAIL GLASS

2 parts Brandy
1 part Triple Sec
splash Pastis

Stir gently with ice and strain.

Tropical Cocktail

COCKTAIL GLASS

1 part Dry Vermouth
1 part Crème de Cacao (White)
1 part Maraschino Liqueur
dash Bitters

Shake with ice and strain.

Turf

COCKTAIL GLASS

1 part Dry Vermouth
1 part Gin
½ part Pernod®

Shake with ice and strain.

Twin Six

COCKTAIL GLASS

1 part Gin
½ part Sweet Vermouth
2 splashes Grenadine
½ part Orange Juice
1 Egg White

Shake with ice and strain.

Ulysses

COCKTAIL GLASS

1 part Brandy
1 part Dry Vermouth
1 part Cherry Brandy

Shake with ice and strain.

Union Jack Cocktail

COCKTAIL GLASS

2 parts Gin
1 part Sloe Gin
splash Grenadine

Shake with ice and strain.

Up to Date Cocktail

COCKTAIL GLASS

1 part Sherry
1 part Canadian Whisky
dash Angostura® Bitters
splash Grand Marnier®

Shake with ice and strain.

Valencia Cocktail

ROCKS GLASS

2 parts Apricot Brandy
1 part Orange Juice
2 dashes Orange Bitters

Shake with ice and strain over ice.

Vanderbilt

COCKTAIL GLASS

2 parts Brandy
1 part Cherry Liqueur
splash Simple Syrup
2 dashes Angostura® Bitters

Shake with ice and strain.

Vermouth Cocktail

COCKTAIL GLASS

1 part Sweet Vermouth
1 part Dry Vermouth
dash Orange Bitters

Shake with ice and strain.

Virgin Cocktail

COCKTAIL GLASS

1 part Crème de Menthe (White)
1 part Dry Gin
1 part Triple Sec

Stir gently with ice and strain.

Waldorf

COCKTAIL GLASS

3/4 part Pernod®
1/2 part Sweet Vermouth
dash Bitters

Shake with ice and strain.

Wallick Cocktail

COCKTAIL GLASS

1 part Gin
1 part Dry Vermouth
splash Triple Sec

Shake with ice and strain.

Ward Eight

RED WINE GLASS

2 parts Whiskey
1/2 part Lemon Juice
splash Grenadine
dash Powdered Sugar

Shake with ice and strain over ice.

Warday's Cocktail

COCKTAIL GLASS

1 part Gin
1 part Sweet Vermouth
splash Chartreuse®
1 part Apple Brandy

Shake with ice and strain over ice.

Washington

COCKTAIL GLASS

1 part Dry Vermouth
1 part Brandy
splash Simple Syrup
2 dashes Angostura® Bitters

Shake with ice and strain.

Waterbury

ROCKS GLASS

2½ parts Brandy
½ part Lemon Juice
splash Simple Syrup
1 Egg White
splash Grenadine

Shake with ice and strain over ice.

Wedding Belle

COCKTAIL GLASS

1 part Gin
1 part Dubonnet® Blonde
½ part Cherry Brandy
1 part Orange Juice

Shake with ice and strain.

Wedding Bells

ROCKS GLASS

1½ parts Gin
½ part Orange Juice
½ part Kirschwasser

Shake with ice and strain over ice.

Weep No More

ROCKS GLASS

1 part Dubonnet® Blonde
1 part Brandy
1 part Lime Juice
splash Maraschino Liqueur

Shake with ice and strain over ice.

Wembly Cocktail

COCKTAIL GLASS

2 parts Gin
1 part Dry Vermouth
splash Apple Brandy
splash Apricot Brandy

Shake with ice and strain.

Western Rose

COCKTAIL GLASS

1 part Gin
½ part Apricot Brandy
½ part Dry Vermouth
splash Lemon Juice

Shake with ice and strain.

Western Rose Cocktail

COLLINS GLASS

1 part Gin
1 part Apricot Brandy
½ part Dry Vermouth
splash Lemon Juice
fill with Club Soda

Build over ice.

Whip

COCKTAIL GLASS

1½ parts Brandy
½ part Dry Vermouth
½ part Sweet Vermouth
splash Triple Sec
splash Anisette

Shake with ice and strain.

Whiskey Cocktail

COCKTAIL GLASS

2 parts Whiskey
splash Simple Syrup
dash Bitters

Shake with ice and strain.

Whiskey Sour

ROCKS GLASS

1½ parts Whiskey
fill with Sweet & Sour Mix

Shake with ice and strain over ice.

White Cargo

WHITE WINE GLASS

2 parts Gin
1/2 part Maraschino Liqueur
splash White Wine
1 scoop Ice Cream

Combine all ingredients in a blender. Blend until smooth.

White Lady

COCKTAIL GLASS

1 1/2 parts Gin
splash Light Cream
dash Powdered Sugar
1 Egg White

Shake with ice and strain.

White Rose

ROCKS GLASS

1 1/2 parts Gin
1/2 part Lime Juice
1/2 part Maraschino Liqueur
splash Simple Syrup
1 Egg White
fill with Orange Juice

Shake with ice and pour.

White Way

ROCKS GLASS

1 part Brandy
1 part Pernod®
1 part Anisette

Shake with ice and strain over ice.

Widow's Dream

HIGHBALL GLASS

2 parts Bénédictine®
fill with Heavy Cream

Shake with ice and pour.

Widow's Kiss Cocktail

COCKTAIL GLASS

2 parts Calvados Apple Brandy
1/2 part Chartreuse®
1/2 part Bénédictine®

Shake with ice and strain.

Witch Hunt

ROCKS GLASS

2 parts Scotch
1/2 part Dry Vermouth
splash Strega
1 part Lemonade

Build over ice.

---

x.y.z. Cocktail

COCKTAIL GLASS

1 part Light Rum
1/2 part Triple Sec
2 splashes Lemon Juice

Shake with ice and strain.

Xanthia

ROCKS GLASS

1 part Gin
1 part Cherry Brandy
1/2 part Chartreuse®

Shake with ice and strain over ice.

Yale Cocktail

COCKTAIL GLASS

1/2 part Dry Vermouth
1 1/2 part Gin
splash Blue Curaçao
dash Bitters

Shake with ice and strain.

Yellow Parrot

ROCKS GLASS

1 part Apricot Brandy
1 part Pernod®
1/2 part Chartreuse®

Shake with ice and strain over ice.

Yellow Rattler

COCKTAIL GLASS

1 part Gin
1/2 part Sweet Vermouth
1/2 part Dry Vermouth
1/2 part Orange Juice

Shake with ice and strain.

Zanzibar

HIGHBALL GLASS

1 part Gin
2 parts Dry Vermouth
1/2 part Lemon Juice
splash Simple Syrup
dash Orange Bitters

Shake with ice and strain over ice.

Zaza Cocktail

COCKTAIL GLASS

2 parts Gin
1 part Dubonnet® Blonde

Shake with ice and strain.

Zazarac Cocktail

COCKTAIL GLASS

1 part Canadian Whisky
1/2 part Anisette
1/2 part Light Rum
splash Absinthe
1/2 part Simple Syrup

Shake with ice and strain.

MARTINIS

Some people claim that anything other than a combination of gin (or, less strictly, vodka) and vermouth is not and never can be called a "martini." But we live in a world where more people think otherwise, so, for the purposes of this book, a martini is any drink that has "tini" in the name. This category features a broad range of flavors and styles and covers everything from the classic Ian Fleming / James Bond Martini to the questionable Chocolate Banana Martini.

50-50 Martini

COCKTAIL GLASS

1 part Gin
1 part Dry Vermouth

Mix with ice and strain.

Absinthe Martini

COCKTAIL GLASS

2 parts Gin
1/2 part Dry Vermouth
splash Absinthe

Mix with ice and strain.

Absinthe-Minded Martini

COCKTAIL GLASS

3 parts Gin
1/2 part Absinthe
1/2 part Grand Marnier®

Mix with ice and strain.

Absolute Martini

COCKTAIL GLASS

2 1/2 parts Vodka
1/2 part Triple Sec

Shake with ice and strain.

After Eight® Martini

COCKTAIL GLASS

1 1/2 parts Chocolate Mint Liqueur
1 1/2 parts Scotch
1 1/2 parts Cream

Shake with ice and strain.

Alizé Martini

COCKTAIL GLASS

2 1/2 parts Alizé®
1 part Vodka

Shake with ice and strain.

Almond Joy® Martini

COCKTAIL GLASS

2 parts Coconut Rum
splash Frangelico®
1 part Dark Chocolate Liqueur

Shake with ice and strain.

Alterna-tini

COCKTAIL GLASS

2 parts Vodka
1/2 part Crème de Cacao (White)
1/4 part Dry Vermouth
1/4 part Sweet Vermouth

Shake with ice and strain.

Alterna-tini #2

COCKTAIL GLASS

1/2 part Vodka
1/2 part Red Curaçao
1/2 part Blue Curaçao
1 part Apple Juice

Shake with ice and strain.

Ambrosia Martini

HIGHBALL GLASS

1 part Blue Curaçao
1 part Raspberry Liqueur
1 part Raspberry Vodka
fill with Pineapple Juice

Build over ice and stir.

Apollo XI Martini

COCKTAIL GLASS

2 parts Vodka
splash Vermouth
splash Tang®
fill with Gatorade®

Shake with ice and strain. Serve in a cocktail glass rimmed with Tang® granules.

Apple Cintini

COCKTAIL GLASS

1½ parts Apple Vodka
½ part Amaretto
1 part Sweet & Sour Mix

Shake with ice and strain.

Apple Martini

COCKTAIL GLASS

1 part Vodka
1 part Sour Apple Schnapps
splash Lime Juice

Shake with ice and strain.

Apple Martini #2

COCKTAIL GLASS

3 parts Vodka
1 part Sour Apple Schnapps
splash Pineapple Juice
splash Sweet & Sour Mix
splash Melon Liqueur

Shake with ice and strain.

Apple Pie Martini

COCKTAIL GLASS

1⅓ parts Vanilla Vodka
⅔ part RumChata
⅔ part Sour Apple Schnapps

Shake with ice and strain.

Applepuckertini

COLLINS GLASS

2 parts Sour Apple Schnapps
2 parts Vodka
fill with Mountain Dew®

Build over ice and stir.

Apple-tini

COCKTAIL GLASS

1 part Light Rum
1 part Apple Liqueur
1 part Triple Sec

Shake with ice and strain.

Apple-tini #2

COCKTAIL GLASS

2 parts Vodka
1 part Apple Liqueur
splash Lime Juice

Shake with ice and strain.

Aquatini

COCKTAIL GLASS

2 parts Lemon Vodka
1 part Blue Curaçao
splash Sweet & Sour Mix

Shake with ice and strain.

Armada Martini

COCKTAIL GLASS

3 parts Vodka
1 part Cream Sherry

Shake with ice and strain.

Austin Fashion Martini

COCKTAIL GLASS

1½ part Vodka
½ part Dry Vermouth
splash Blue Curaçao

Shake with ice and strain.

B&T's Purple Martini
COCKTAIL GLASS
1 part Vodka
1/2 part Blue Curaçao
splash Cranberry Juice Cocktail
dash Vermouth
Shake with ice and strain.

Baby Face Martini
COCKTAIL GLASS
3 parts Raspberry Vodka
1/2 part Dry Vermouth
1/4 part Maraschino Liqueur
Shake with ice and strain.

Bacon Martini
COCKTAIL GLASS
2 parts Bacon Vodka
1 part Salted Caramel Vodka
splash Olive Juice
splash Tabasco Sauce
Shake with ice and strain.

Banana Coffee Cake Martini
COCKTAIL GLASS
2 1/2 parts RumChata
1/2 part 99 Bananas Liqueur
1/2 part Chocolate Cake Vodka
splash Espresso Vodka
Shake with ice and strain.

Banana Martini
HIGHBALL GLASS
1 part Vodka
1 part Banana Liqueur
Shake with ice and strain.

Banana Nut Bread Martini
COCKTAIL GLASS
2 parts RumChata
1 part Frangelico
1/2 part Banana Liqueur
Shake with ice and strain. Garnish with a few Walnuts floated on top.

Bellini-tini
COCKTAIL GLASS
2 parts Vodka
1/2 part Peach Schnapps
1/2 part Peach Puree
dash Bitters
Shake with ice and strain.

Berlin Martini
COCKTAIL GLASS
2 parts Vodka
1 part Peach Schnapps
splash Black Sambuca
Shake with ice and strain.

Berrytini
COCKTAIL GLASS
3 parts Currant Vodka
1/2 part Raspberry Liqueur
Shake with ice and strain.

Black and White Martini
COCKTAIL GLASS
3 parts Vanilla Vodka
1 part Crème de Cacao (Dark)
Shake with ice and strain.

Black Forest Cake Martini
COCKTAIL GLASS
1 1/2 parts Vodka
1 part Crème de Cacao (White)
splash Raspberry Liqueur
Shake with ice and strain.

Black Martini
COCKTAIL GLASS
1 part Gin
1/2 part Black Sambuca
Shake with ice and strain.

Black Martini #2
COCKTAIL GLASS

1½ parts Vodka
1 part Raspberry Liqueur
1 part Blue Curaçao

Shake with ice and strain.

Black Martini #3
COCKTAIL GLASS

2 parts Blackberry Liqueur
1 part Dry Vermouth

Shake with ice and strain.

Bleu Bling Martini
COCKTAIL GLASS

2 parts Alize Bleu Liqueur
1 part super premium Vodka

Shake with ice and strain.

Blood Orange Martini
COCKTAIL GLASS

1 part Campari®
2 parts Orange Vodka
1 part Orange Juice

Shake with ice and strain.

Bloody Martini
COCKTAIL GLASS

1½ parts Gin
splash Grenadine
splash Lemon Juice
splash Vermouth

Shake with ice and strain. Garnish with Maraschino Cherry.

Blue Jaffa Martini
COCKTAIL GLASS

1 part Vodka
1 part Blue Curaçao
1 part Crème de Cacao (White)

Shake with ice and strain.

Blue on Blue Martini
COCKTAIL GLASS

3 parts Vodka
½ part Blue Curaçao

Shake with ice and strain.

Bond's Martini
COCKTAIL GLASS

3 parts Gin
1 part Vodka
½ part Vermouth

Shake (don't stir) with ice and strain.

Boomerang Martini
COCKTAIL GLASS

3 parts Gin
1 part Dry Vermouth
¼ part Maraschino Liqueur

Shake with ice and strain.

Bootlegger Martini
COCKTAIL GLASS

1½ parts Gin
¼ part Southern Comfort®

Shake with ice and strain.

Brantini
ROCKS GLASS

1½ parts Brandy
splash Dry Vermouth
1 part Gin

Shake with ice and strain. Garnish with Lemon Peel.

Brazen Martini
COCKTAIL GLASS

2 parts Vodka
½ part Parfait Amour®

Shake with ice and strain.

Broadway Martini

COCKTAIL GLASS

3 parts Gin
1 part Crème de Menthe (White)

Shake with ice and strain.

Buckeye Martini

COCKTAIL GLASS

3 parts Gin
1 part Dry Vermouth

Shake with ice and strain.

Burnt Martini

COCKTAIL GLASS

2 parts Gin
1 part Whiskey

Shake with ice and strain.

Cabaret Martini

COCKTAIL GLASS

2 parts Gin
splash Pernod®

Shake with ice and strain.

Café Martini

COCKTAIL GLASS

1 part Amaretto
1 part Butterscotch Liqueur
1 part Coffee Liqueur
1 part Frangelico
1 part Irish Cream Liqueur

Shake with ice and strain over ice.

California Martini

COCKTAIL GLASS

2 parts Vodka
1 part Red Wine
1/4 part Dark Rum

Shake with ice and strain.

Campari® Martini

COCKTAIL GLASS

3 parts Vodka
1 part Campari®

Shake with ice and strain.

The Can-Can Martini

COCKTAIL GLASS

2 parts Vodka
1 1/2 parts St-Germain
1/4 part Dry Vermouth

Shake with ice and strain. Garnish with a Lemon or Orange Twist.

Candy Corn Martini

COCKTAIL GLASS

2 parts Vanilla Vodka
1 part Crème de Cacao (White)
1 part Butterscotch Liqueur
3 parts Orange Juice

Shake with ice and strain into a glass rimmed with Dark Cocoa Powder.

Caramel Apple Martini

COCKTAIL GLASS

2 parts RumChata
1 part Caramel Apple Liqueur

Shake with ice and strain.

Caramel Apple Martini #2

COCKTAIL GLASS

2 parts Butterscotch Schnapps
2 parts Sour Apple Schnapps
1 part Vodka

Shake with ice and strain.

Caribbean Martini

COCKTAIL GLASS

1 1/2 parts Vanilla Vodka
3/4 part Malibu® Rum
splash Pineapple Juice

Shake with ice and strain.

Cheesecake Martini

COCKTAIL GLASS

2 parts Vanilla Rum
1 part Cranberry Juice
1 part Milk
1 part Pineapple Juice

Shake with ice and strain.

Chocolate Banana Martini

COCKTAIL GLASS

2 parts Vodka
1 part Crème de Cacao (White)
1 part 99-Proof Banana Liqueur

Shake with ice and strain.

Chocolate Cream Pie Martini

COCKTAIL GLASS

1 part Godiva Chocolate Liqueur
1 part RumChata
1 part Vanilla Vodka

Shake with ice and strain.

Chocolate Lovers' Martini

COCKTAIL GLASS

1½ parts Irish Cream Liqueur
1½ parts Vodka
1½ parts Crème de Cacao (White)
½ part Chocolate Syrup

Shake with ice and strain.

Chocolate Martini

COCKTAIL GLASS

2 parts Vodka
½ part Crème de Cacao (White)

Shake with ice and strain.

Chocolate Martini #2

COCKTAIL GLASS

1½ parts Vanilla Vodka
1 part Godiva® Liqueur

Shake with ice and strain.

Chocolate Raspberry Martini

1½ parts Raspberry Vodka
1 part Crème de Cacao (White)

Shake with ice and strain.

Christmas Martini

COCKTAIL GLASS

2 parts Vodka
½ part Crème de Menthe (White)
½ part Dry Vermouth

Shake with ice and strain.

Church Lady Martini

COCKTAIL GLASS

2 parts Gin
1 part Orange Juice
1 part Sweet Vermouth

Shake with ice and strain.

Cinnamon Cream Martini

COCKTAIL GLASS

1 part Cinnamon Schnapps
1 part Irish Cream Liqueur
1 part Vanilla Vodka

Shake with ice and strain.

Citritini

COCKTAIL GLASS

1½ parts Citrus Rum
splash Lime Juice
1½ parts Sweet & Sour Mix

Shake with ice and strain.

Cool Yule Martini

COCKTAIL GLASS

3 parts Vodka
½ part Crème de Menthe (White)
½ part Dry Vermouth

Shake with ice and strain.

Copper Illusion Martini

COCKTAIL GLASS

1 part Gin
½ part Triple Sec
½ part Campari®

Shake with ice and strain.

Crantini

COCKTAIL GLASS

1½ parts Vodka
½ part Triple Sec
½ part Vermouth
2 parts Cranberry Juice Cocktail

Shake with ice and strain.

Crantini #2

COCKTAIL GLASS

1 part Sweet Vodka
1 part Cointreau®
1 part Cranberry Juice Cocktail
splash Lime Juice

Shake with ice and strain.

Cream of Coconut Pie Martini

COCKTAIL GLASS

2 parts RumChata
1 part Whipped Cream Vodka
1 part Coconut Rum
splash Ginger Ale

Shake with ice and strain.

Crimson Martini

COCKTAIL GLASS

3 parts Gin
½ part Port
½ part Grenadine

Shake with ice and strain.

Cuban Martini

COCKTAIL GLASS

3 parts Light Rum
½ part Dry Vermouth
1 tbsp Powdered Sugar

Shake with ice and strain.

Dark Chocolate Martini

COCKTAIL GLASS

1 part Vodka
1 part Crème de Cacao (Dark)

Shake with ice and strain.

Daydream Martini

COCKTAIL GLASS

2 parts Citrus Vodka
1 part Orange Juice
½ part Triple Sec
dash Powdered Sugar

Shake with ice and strain.

Deadly Pumpkin Martini

COCKTAIL GLASS

2 parts Fireball Cinnamon Whiskey
1 part Hazelnut Liqueur
1 part Pumpkin Liqueur
pinch nutmeg

Shake with ice and strain.

Dirty Martini

COCKTAIL GLASS

2 parts Gin
1 tbsp Dry Vermouth
2 tbsp Olive Brine

Shake with ice and strain. Garnish with 2 Olives.

Dirty Martini #2

COCKTAIL GLASS

2 parts Gin
splash Olive Brine

Shake with ice and strain.

Double Fudge Martini

COCKTAIL GLASS

3 parts Vodka
½ part Crème de Cacao (Dark)
½ part Coffee Liqueur

Shake with ice and strain.

Dusty Martini

COCKTAIL GLASS

2 parts Gin
⅙ part Scotch
dash Dry Vermouth

Shake with ice and strain.

Elderflower Martini

COCKTAIL GLASS

1 part Dry Vermouth
1 part Gin
1 part St-Germain
½ part Lime Juice

Shake with ice and strain.

Emerald Martini

COCKTAIL GLASS

1½ parts Gin
½ part Dry Vermouth
splash Chartreuse®

Shake with ice and strain.

Espresso Raspberry Chocolate Martini

COCKTAIL GLASS

1 part Espresso Vodka
1 part Godiva Chocolate Liqueur
1 part Raspberry Vodka

Shake with ice and strain.

Euro-tini

COCKTAIL GLASS

1 part Vodka
½ part Triple Sec
1 part Orange Juice
¼ dash Sugar

Shake with ice and strain.

Extra Dry Martini

COCKTAIL GLASS

1½ parts Gin
1 drop Vermouth

Shake with ice and strain.

Fare Thee Well Martini

COCKTAIL GLASS

2 parts Gin
¼ part Dry Vermouth
¼ part Sweet Vermouth

Shake with ice and strain.

Fire-tini Hunter

COCKTAIL GLASS

2 parts Pepper Vodka
1 part Dry Vermouth

Shake with ice and strain.

French Apple Martini

COCKTAIL GLASS

2 parts St-Germain
1½ parts Green Apple Vodka
¼ part Lemon Juice

Shake with ice and strain.

French Martini

COCKTAIL GLASS

1 part Vodka
1 part Raspberry Liqueur
1 part Grand Marnier®
1 part Pineapple Juice
1 part Sweet & Sour Mix

Shake with ice and strain.

French Pear Martini

COCKTAIL GLASS

2 parts Pear Vodka
1 part St-Germain
dash Lemon Juice

Shake with ice and strain.

Fretful Martini

COCKTAIL GLASS

3 parts Blue Curaçao
½ part Amaretto

Shake with ice and strain.

Fruit Blast Martini

COCKTAIL GLASS

1 part Mango Rum
1 part Orange Rum
1½ parts Pineapple Juice
1 part Cranberry Juice

Shake with ice and strain.

Fuzzy Martini

COCKTAIL GLASS

2½ parts Vodka
1 part Peach Schnapps
splash Orange Juice

Shake with ice and strain.

Ginger Apple Martini

COCKTAIL GLASS

1 1/2 parts Apple Vodka
1 part Ginger Liqueur
1 part Apple Juice
1/2 part Lime Juice

Shake with ice and strain.

Gingerbread Martini

COCKTAIL GLASS

3 parts RumChata
2 parts Vanilla Rum
1 part Ginger Liqueur

Shake with ice and strain. Garnish with Gingerbread Cookie crumbles.

Granny Smith Martini

COCKTAIL GLASS

1 1/2 parts Vanilla Vodka
1/2 part Sour Apple Schnapps
1/4 part Melon Liqueur

Shake with ice and strain.

Grape Martini

COCKTAIL GLASS

2 parts Grape Vodka
1 part Whipped Cream Vodka
splash Lime Juice

Shake with ice and strain.

Grappatini

COCKTAIL GLASS

1 1/2 parts Grappa
1/2 part Dry Vermouth

Shake with ice and strain.

Green Apple Martini

COCKTAIL GLASS

1 1/2 parts Sour Apple Schnapps
1 1/2 parts Vodka
splash Vermouth

Shake with ice and strain.

Gumball Martini

COCKTAIL GLASS

2 parts Gin
1 part Vodka
1/2 part Southern Comfort®
1/4 part Dry Vermouth

Shake with ice and strain.

Gumdrop Martini

COCKTAIL GLASS

1 part Citrus Rum
1/2 part Vodka
1/4 part Dry Vermouth
1/4 part Southern Comfort®

Shake with ice and strain.

Harry Denton Martini

COCKTAIL GLASS

1 1/4 parts Gin
1/2 part Green Chartreuse®

Shake with ice and strain.

Hawaiian Martini

COCKTAIL GLASS

2 parts Dirty Gin
1/2 part Triple Sec
splash Pineapple Juice

Shake with ice and strain.

Honeydew Martini

COCKTAIL GLASS

2 parts Vodka
1/2 part Triple Sec
1/2 part Melon Liqueur

Shake with ice and strain.

Horchata Martini

COCKTAIL GLASS

2 parts RumChata
1 part Vanilla Vodka

Shake with ice and strain.

Hot and Dirty Martini

COCKTAIL GLASS

2 parts Absolut® Peppar Vodka
1/2 part Dry Vermouth
1/2 part Olive Brine

Shake with ice and strain.

Hpnotiq® Martini

COCKTAIL GLASS

1 part Cherry Vodka
2 parts Hpnotiq® Liqueur

Shake with ice and strain.

Imperial Martini

COCKTAIL GLASS

3 parts Gin
1 part Dry Vermouth
1/4 part Maraschino Liqueur

Shake with ice and strain.

In and Out Martini

COCKTAIL GLASS

splash Dry Vermouth
3 parts Gin

Rinse a chilled cocktail glass with Dry Vermouth and dump the excess. Shake Gin with ice and strain.

Irish Martini

COCKTAIL GLASS

2 parts Vodka
1/2 part Dry Vermouth
1/4 part Whiskey

Shake with ice and strain.

Island Martini

COCKTAIL GLASS

2 parts Dark Rum
1/2 part Dry Vermouth
1/2 part Sweet Vermouth

Shake with ice and strain.

Jack London Martini

COCKTAIL GLASS

3 parts Currant Vodka
1/2 part Maraschino Liqueur

Shake with ice and strain.

Jacktini

COCKTAIL GLASS

1 part Whiskey
1 part Mandarine Napoleon® Liqueur
1/4 part Lime Juice

Shake with ice and strain.

James Bond Martini

COCKTAIL GLASS

1 1/2 parts Gin
1/2 part Vodka
1/4 part Lillet®

Shake with ice and strain. The original order that Mr. Bond placed was "Three measures Gordon's®, one of Vodka, half a measure of Kina Lillet®. Shake it very well until it's ice-cold, then add a large thin slice of Lemon Peel." (From *Casino Royale* by Ian Fleming, 1953.)

Jamie's Martini

COCKTAIL GLASS

2 parts Vodka
1 part Orange Juice
1/2 part Triple Sec
dash Powdered Sugar

Shake with ice and strain.

Kamitini

COCKTAIL GLASS

1 part Vodka
1/2 part Raspberry Liqueur
1/2 part Vanilla Liqueur
1 part Raspberry Juice
splash Lime Juice

Shake with ice and strain.

Kentucky Martini

COCKTAIL GLASS

3 parts Bourbon
1 part Crème de Cacao (White)

Shake with ice and strain.

Kir Martini

COCKTAIL GLASS

1 part Gin
1 part Extra Dry Vermouth
1 part Crème de Cassis

Shake with ice and strain.

Leap Year Martini

COCKTAIL GLASS

3 parts Citrus Vodka
½ part Sweet Vermouth

Shake with ice and strain.

Lemon Drop Martini

COCKTAIL GLASS

3 parts Citrus Vodka
1 part Triple Sec
½ part Lemon Juice
1 tsp Sugar
Rim the glass with Sugar.

Shake with ice and strain.

Lemon Splash Martini

COCKTAIL GLASS

1½ parts Vodka
½ part Triple Sec
½ part Amaretto

Shake with ice and strain.

Long Kiss Goodnight

COCKTAIL GLASS

1 part Vodka
1 part Vanilla Vodka
1 part Crème de Cacao (White)

Shake with ice and strain.

Lilly Martini

COCKTAIL GLASS

1 part Currant Vodka
1 part Raspberry Vodka
½ part Blueberry Schnapps
½ part Vanilla Vodka
½ part Lemon Juice

Shake with ice and strain. For Lilly.

Low Tide Martini

COCKTAIL GLASS

3 parts Vodka
½ part Dry Vermouth
½ part Oyster Juice

Shake with ice and strain.

Main Beach Martini

HIGHBALL GLASS

1½ parts Orange Vodka
½ part Crème de Cacao (White)

Shake with ice and strain over ice.

Mama's Martini

COCKTAIL GLASS

2 parts Vanilla Vodka
½ part Apricot Brandy

Shake with ice and strain.

Mango Martini

COCKTAIL GLASS

1 part Light Rum
1 part Mango Rum
½ part Triple Sec
½ part Cranberry Juice
½ part Sweetened Lime Juice
splash Mango Puree

Shake with ice and strain.

Mangotini

COCKTAIL GLASS

1½ parts Vodka
½ part Sour Apple Schnapps
1 part Mango Nectar
splash Vermouth

Shake with ice and strain.

Margatini
COCKTAIL GLASS
1 1/2 parts Silver Tequila
1/2 part Triple Sec
splash Lime Juice
Shake with ice and strain.

Martian Martini
COCKTAIL GLASS
2 parts Gin
1 part Melon Liqueur
Shake with ice and strain.

Martini
COCKTAIL GLASS
2 1/2 parts Gin
1/2 part Dry Vermouth
Shake with ice and strain. Garnish with an olive or Lemon Twist. A drier martini uses less (or no) Vermouth. A Vodka martini substitutes Vodka for the Gin. A martini garnished with a cocktail onion instead of an olive is called a Gibson.

Martini Esoterica
COCKTAIL GLASS
2 1/2 parts Gin
1/2 part Dry Vermouth
splash Pernod®
Shake with ice and strain.

Martini Oriental
COCKTAIL GLASS
1 1/2 parts Gin
1/2 part Sake
Shake with ice and strain Garnish with a Lemon Twist.

Martini Patton
COCKTAIL GLASS
2 1/2 parts Gin
1/2 part Sake
Shake with ice and strain Garnish with a Lemon Twist.

Martini Colorado
COCKTAIL GLASS
1/2 part Gin
1/2 part Vodka
1 1/2 parts Vermouth
2 dashes Angostura® Bitters
dash salt
Shake with ice and strain Garnish with two Olives.

Martini Meme
COCKTAIL GLASS
2 parts RumChata
1 part Coconut Rum
2 parts Pineapple Juice
Shake with ice and strain.

Martini Milano
COCKTAIL GLASS
2 parts Gin
1/2 part Dry Vermouth
1/2 part Campari®
1/2 part White Wine
Shake with ice and strain.

Martinique
COLLINS GLASS
1 part Light Rum
1 part Triple Sec
1 part Lime Juice
1 part Orange Juice
fill with Pineapple Juice
Shake with ice and strain over ice.

Ma-tini
COCKTAIL GLASS
1 part Vodka
1/2 part Blackberry Liqueur
1/2 part Cointreau®
1 part Lemonade
Shake with ice and strain.

Mellow Martini

COCKTAIL GLASS

1 1/2 parts Vodka
3/4 part Crème de Banane
splash Lychee Liqueur
2 parts Pineapple Juice

Shake with ice and strain.

Melon Martini

COCKTAIL GLASS

2 1/2 parts Vodka
1/2 part Melon Liqueur

Shake with ice and strain.

Mexicali Martini

COCKTAIL GLASS

1 part Gold Tequila
1/2 part Grand Marnier®
1/2 part Triple Sec
1/2 part Lime Juice
1/2 part Orange Juice

Shake with ice and strain.

Mexico Martini

COCKTAIL GLASS

1 1/2 parts Tequila
1/2 part Dry Vermouth
3 splashes Vanilla Extract

Shake with ice and strain.

Milky Way® Martini

COCKTAIL GLASS

1 part Vanilla Vodka
1 part Chocolate Liqueur
1 part Irish Ceam Liqueur

Shake with ice and strain.

Mint-tini

COCKTAIL GLASS

2 parts Vodka
1 part Crème de Menthe (White)
1/2 part Dry Vermouth

Shake with ice and strain.

Mistletoe Martini

COCKTAIL GLASS

1 part Coconut Rum
1 part Melon Liqueur
1 part Pineapple Juice
1 part Sweet & Sour Mix

Shake with ice and strain.

Mocha Blanca Martini

COCKTAIL GLASS

1 part Vodka
1 part Chocolate Liqueur
1 part Coffee Liqueur

Shake with ice and strain.

Mocha Martini

COCKTAIL GLASS

2 1/2 parts Vodka
1/2 part Coffee Liqueur
1 part Crème de Cacao (White)

Shake with ice and strain.

Monkey Martini

COCKTAIL GLASS

3 parts Dark Rum
1 part Banana Liqueur
1 part Irish Cream Liqueur
1 part Cream

Shake with ice and strain. Garnish with Shredded Coconut.

Monkey Rum Martini

COCKTAIL GLASS

2 parts Dark Spiced Rum
1/2 part Banana Liqueur
1/2 part Irish Cream Liqueur
1/2 part Cream

Shake with ice and strain.

Monk's Martini

COCKTAIL GLASS

1 part Vodka
1 part Crème de Menthe (White)
1 part Crème de Banane
1 part Irish Cream Liqueur

Shake with ice and strain.

Mortini

COCKTAIL GLASS

2 parts Vodka
splash Amaretto
splash Grenadine

Shake with ice and strain.

Motherpucker Martini

COCKTAIL GLASS

1 part Cherry Vodka
1 part Grape Vodka
1 part Sour Apple Vodka

Shake with ice and strain.

Mozart Martini

COCKTAIL GLASS

1 part Crème de Cacao (Dark)
1 part Chocolate Liqueur
2 parts Cream
splash Vodka

Shake with ice and strain.

Neopolitan Martini

COCKTAIL GLASS

1 part Vanilla Vodka
1 part Orange Vodka
½ part Grand Marnier®
½ part Parfait Amour
splash Lime Juice

Shake with ice and strain.

New Orleans Martini

COCKTAIL GLASS

2 parts Vanilla Vodka
½ part Dry Vermouth
½ part Pernod®

Shake with ice and strain.

Nicotini

COCKTAIL GLASS

1 part Crème de Cacao (Dark)
½ part Crème de Banane
½ part Apricot Brandy
½ part Milk
½ part Cream

Shake with ice and strain.

Ninja Martini

COCKTAIL GLASS

2 parts Gin
1 part Sweet Vermouth
1 part Sake

Shake with ice and strain.

Nutty Martini

COCKTAIL GLASS

3 parts Vodka
½ part Frangelico®

Shake with ice and strain.

Nutty Pumpkin Martini

COCKTAIL GLASS

1 part Pumpkin Spice Liqueur
½ part Hazelnut Liqueur
½ part Vanilla Vodka
1 part Cream

Shake with ice and strain.

Old Country Martini

COCKTAIL GLASS

1 part Vodka
1 part Kirschwasser
1 part Madeira

Shake with ice and strain.

Olorosa Martini

COCKTAIL GLASS

2 parts Sherry
½ part Vodka

Shake with ice and strain.

Opera Martini

COCKTAIL GLASS

3 parts Gin
½ part Maraschino Liqueur

Shake with ice and strain.

Orange Martini

COCKTAIL GLASS

3 parts Vodka
1 part Triple Sec
dash Orange Bitters

Shake with ice and strain.

Orangetini

COCKTAIL GLASS

1½ parts Orange Vodka
1½ parts Triple Sec

Shake with ice and strain.

Oyster Martini

COCKTAIL GLASS

3 parts Vodka
1 part Dry Vermouth

Shake with ice and strain Garnish with an Oyster.

Paisley Martini

ROCKS GLASS

2 parts Gin
splash Scotch
½ part Dry Vermouth

Shake with ice and pour. Garnish with Lemon Peel.

Parisian Martini

COCKTAIL GLASS

2 parts Gin
1 part Dry Vermouth
½ part Crème de Cassis

Shake with ice and strain.

Park Avenue Martini

COCKTAIL GLASS

2 parts Gin
½ part Sweet Vermouth
½ part Pineapple Juice

Shake with ice and strain.

Parrothead Martini

COCKTAIL GLASS

3 parts Silver Tequila
1 part Triple Sec

Shake with ice and strain.

Peach Blossom Martini

COCKTAIL GLASS

2 part's Peach Vodka
½ part Maraschino Liqueur

Shake with ice and strain.

Peach Martini

COCKTAIL GLASS

2 parts Vodka
1 part Peach Schnapps

Shake with ice and strain.

Peachtini

COCKTAIL GLASS

2 parts Gin
1 part Peach Schnapps

Shake with ice and strain.

Pear Martini

COCKTAIL GLASS

2 parts Pear Vodka
1 part Ginger Liqueur

Shake with ice and strain.

Peppar Bayou Martini

COCKTAIL GLASS

1½ parts Absolut® Peppar Vodka
¼ part Dry Vermouth

Shake with ice and strain.

Peppermint Martini

COCKTAIL GLASS

2 parts Gin
1 part Peppermint Schnapps

Shake with ice and strain.

Picadilly Martini
COCKTAIL GLASS
2 parts Gin
3/4 part Dry Vermouth
1/2 part Pernod®
splash Grenadine
Shake with ice and strain.

Pineapple Martini
COCKTAIL GLASS
1 part Orange Vodka
1 part Pineapple Rum
1 part Pineapple Juice
Shake with ice and strain.

Platinium Blonde
COCKTAIL GLASS
2 parts Rum
1 part Cream
Shake with ice and strain.

Poached Pear Martini
COCKTAIL GLASS
2 parts Pear Vodka
1 part Caramel Vodka
1 part Ginger Liqueur
Shake with ice and strain.

Pompano Martini
COCKTAIL GLASS
1 part Gin
1/2 part Dry Vermouth
1 part Grapefruit Juice
Shake with ice and strain.

Pontberry Martini
COCKTAIL GLASS
2 parts Vodka
1/2 part Blackberry Liqueur
Shake with ice and strain.

Pretty Martini
COCKTAIL GLASS
2 parts Vodka
1/2 part Dry Vermouth
1/2 part Amaretto
Shake with ice and strain.

Princess Elizabeth Martini
COCKTAIL GLASS
2 parts Sweet Vermouth
1/2 part Dry Vermouth
Shake with ice and strain.

Princess Martini
HIGHBALL GLASS
1 1/2 parts Gin
1 1/2 parts Orange Juice
1 1/2 parts Pineapple Juice
splash Lemon-Lime Soda
Build over ice and stir.

Prospector Martini
COCKTAIL GLASS
1 1/2 parts Vanilla Vodka
3/4 part Goldschläger®
1/2 part Butterscotch Schnapps
splash Vanilla Extract
Shake with ice and strain.

Pumpkin Pie Martini
COCKTAIL GLASS
2 parts RumChata
1 part Vanilla Vodka
1 part Pumpkin Syrup
Shake with ice and strain. Garnish with a sprinkle of Cinnamon.

Raspberry Lady Finger Martini
COCKTAIL GLASS
1 part RumChata
1/2 part Raspberry Vodka
splash Caramel Vodka
splash Chocolate Liqueur
splash Espresso Vodka
Shake with ice and strain.

Really Dry Martini

COCKTAIL GLASS

3 parts Gin
Dry Vermouth

Place Olives in a chilled cocktail glass. Pour Gin in a shaker with ice, hold an open bottle of Vermouth, lean over the shaker, and whisper "Vermouth." Shake and strain the Gin into the glass.

Red Dog Martini

COCKTAIL GLASS

2 parts Vodka
½ part Port
½ part Grenadine

Shake with ice and strain.

Red Passion Martini

COCKTAIL GLASS

1½ parts Passion Fruit Liqueur
½ part Campari®

Stir with ice and strain.

Red Vodkatini

COCKTAIL GLASS

2 parts Vodka
1 part Sweet Vermouth
splash Crème de Cassis

Shake with ice and strain.

Redhead Martini

COLLINS GLASS

2½ parts Vodka
½ part Strawberry Syrup

Shake with ice and strain.

Renaissance Martini

COCKTAIL GLASS

2½ parts Gin
½ part Dry Sherry

Shake with ice and strain.

Resolution Martini

COCKTAIL GLASS

2 parts Gin
1 part Apricot Brandy

Shake with ice and strain.

Reverse Martini

COCKTAIL GLASS

2 parts Gin
1 part Apple Brandy

Shake with ice and strain.

Rice Pudding Martini

COCKTAIL GLASS

2 parts RumChata
1 part Coconut Rum

Shake with ice and strain.

Rontini

HIGHBALL GLASS

1 part Vodka
fill with Mountain Dew®

Build over ice and stir.

Rouge Martini

COCKTAIL GLASS

2 parts Gin
splash Raspberry Liqueur

Shake with ice and strain.

Rum Martini

COCKTAIL GLASS

2½ parts Light Rum
splash Dry Vermouth

Shake with ice and strain. Garnish with Lemon Twist.

RumChata Ultimartini

COCKTAIL GLASS

2 parts RumChata
1 part Vanilla Vodka
½ part Frangelico

Shake with ice and strain.

Rumtini
COCKTAIL GLASS

2 parts Light Rum
½ part Dry Vermouth

Shake with ice and strain.

Russian Peachtini
COCKTAIL GLASS

1½ parts Vodka
splash Peach Schnapps

Shake with ice and strain.

Saketini
COCKTAIL GLASS

2½ parts Gin
splash Sake

Shake with ice and strain.

Salt and Pepper Martini
COCKTAIL GLASS

2 parts Absolut® Peppar Vodka
splash Dry Vermouth

Shake with ice and strain. Serve in a cocktail glass with a salted rim.

Scarlett Martini
COCKTAIL GLASS

1½ parts Southern Comfort®
1½ parts Cranberry Juice Cocktail

Shake with ice and strain.

Scotini
COCKTAIL GLASS

2 parts Gin
½ part Scotch

Shake with ice and strain.

Sea Blue Martini
COCKTAIL GLASS

2 parts Dry Gin
½ part Blue Curaçao
½ part Triple Sec

Shake with ice and strain.

Secret Martini
COCKTAIL GLASS

3 parts Gin
1 part Lillet®

Shake with ice and strain.

Shrimptini
COCKTAIL GLASS

3 parts Gin
1 part Dry Vermouth
splash Tabasco® Sauce

Shake with ice and strain. Garnish with a Cocktail Shrimp hanging over the side.

Smoked Martini
COCKTAIL GLASS

1 part Scotch
1 part Vodka

Stir gently with ice and strain.

Smoky Martini
COCKTAIL GLASS

2½ parts Gin
½ part Scotch

Stir gently with ice and strain.

Smoky Martini #2
COCKTAIL GLASS

2½ parts Gin
splash Scotch

Shake with ice and strain.

Sour Apple Martini
COCKTAIL GLASS

2 parts Sour Apple Schnapps
1 part Vodka
1 part Triple Sec

Shake with ice and strain.

Sour Patch Martini
COCKTAIL GLASS

1 part Raspberry Vodka
1 part Sour Apple Schnapps
1 part Watermelon Schnapps
1 part Sweet & Sour Mix

Shake with ice and strain.

South Beach Martini
COCKTAIL GLASS

1 part Orange Vodka
1 part Citrus Vodka
1/2 part Cointreau®
1/2 part Lime Juice

Shake with ice and strain.

Soviet Martini
COCKTAIL GLASS

2 parts Currant Vodka
1/2 part Dry Vermouth
1/2 part Dry Sherry

Shake with ice and strain.

Spartinique
COCKTAIL GLASS

1 part Cherry Brandy
1 part Jim Beam®
2/3 part Sweet & Sour Mix
splash Lemon Juice

Shake with ice and strain.

Springtime Martini
COCKTAIL GLASS

2 parts Vodka
1 part Lillet®

Shake with ice and strain.

Strawberry Blonde Martini
COCKTAIL GLASS

2 parts Strawberry Vodka
1 part Lillet®

Shake with ice and strain.

Surfer Martini
COCKTAIL GLASS

1 part Rum
1/2 part Coconut Rum
1/2 part Banana Liqueur
1 part Pineapple Juice

Shake with ice and strain.

Sweet and Spicy Martini
COCKTAIL GLASS

2 parts Vodka
1/2 part Sweet Vermouth
1/2 part Triple Sec

Shake with ice and strain.

Sweet Martini
COCKTAIL GLASS

1 1/2 part Gin
1/2 part Sweet Vermouth

Shake with ice and strain.

Tequila Martini
COCKTAIL GLASS

2 1/2 parts Tequila
1/2 part Dry Vermouth

Shake with ice and strain.

Third Degree Martini
COCKTAIL GLASS

1 1/2 parts Gin
1/2 part Dry Vermouth
splash Pernod®

Shake with ice and strain.

Tiajuanatini
COCKTAIL GLASS

2 parts Silver Tequila
splash Triple Sec

Shake with ice and strain.

Tini Rita

COCKTAIL GLASS

1 1/4 parts Vodka
1/4 part Cointreau®
1/4 part Grand Marnier®
splash Lime Juice
splash Sweet & Sour Mix

Shake with ice and strain.

Tiramisu Martini

COCKTAIL GLASS

2 parts RumChata
1 part Espresso Vodka

Shake with ice and strain. Garnish with shaved Chocolate.

Toffee Martini

COCKTAIL GLASS

1 part Frangelico®
1 part Vanilla Liqueur
1 part Vodka

Shake with ice and strain.

Tootsie Roll® Martini

COCKTAIL GLASS

3 parts Dry Vermouth
1/2 part Crème de Cacao (Dark)

Shake with ice and strain.

Transylvanian Martini

COCKTAIL GLASS

1 1/2 parts Vodka
1 1/2 parts Passion Fruit Liqueur

Shake with ice and strain.

Tropical Martini

COCKTAIL GLASS

2 parts Amaretto
2 parts Coconut Rum

Shake with ice and strain.

Tropical Peach Martini

COCKTAIL GLASS

1 part Coconut Rum
1 part Peach Schnapps
1 part Ginger Ale

Shake with ice and strain.

Truffle Martini

COCKTAIL GLASS

3 parts Strawberry Vodka
1/2 part Crème de Cacao (Dark)

Shake with ice and strain.

Ultimate Arctic Martini

COCKTAIL GLASS

2 parts Vodka
1/2 part Dry Vermouth
1/2 part Lemon Juice

Shake with ice and strain.

Valencia Martini

COCKTAIL GLASS

3 parts Gin
1 part Dry Sherry

Shake with ice and strain.

Violet Martini

COCKTAIL GLASS

2 parts Citrus Vodka
1/2 part Parfait Amour
1/4 part Raspberry Syrup

Stir gently with ice and strain.

Vodka Martini

COCKTAIL GLASS

2 1/2 parts Vodka
2 splashes Dry Vermouth

Shake with ice and strain.

Waikiki Martini

COCKTAIL GLASS

2 parts Pineapple Vodka
1/2 part Dry Vermouth
1/2 part Lillet®

Shake with ice and strain.

Yang Martini

COCKTAIL GLASS

3 parts Gin
½ part Sake Rice Wine

Shake with ice and strain.

Yin Martini

COCKTAIL GLASS

3 parts Sake Rice Wine
½ part Gin

Shake with ice and strain.

Zippy Martini

COCKTAIL GLASS

2 parts Vodka
½ part Dry Vermouth
splash Tabasco® Sauce

Shake with ice and strain.

Zorbatini

COCKTAIL GLASS

1½ parts Vodka
1 part Ouzo

Shake with ice and strain.

Z-Tini

COCKTAIL GLASS

½ part Vodka
½ part Irish Cream Liqueur
½ part Strawberry Liqueur
1 part Raspberry Liqueur
1 part Cream

Shake with ice and strain.

SHOTS & SHOOTERS

Served in small glasses and consumed in a single gulp, shots are much easier to define than martinis or cocktails. In this book, the broad category of "shots" has been refined ever so slightly to "shots," "layered shots," "flaming shots," and "Tabasco® shots."

10 Lb. Sledgehammer

SHOT GLASS

1 part Tequila
1 part Jack Daniel's®

Pour ingredients into glass neat (do not chill).

24 Seven

SHOT GLASS

2 parts Melon Liqueur
1 part Green Chartreuse®
4 parts Pineapple Juice
½ part Sweetened Lime Juice

Shake with ice and strain.

252

SHOT GLASS

1 part 151-Proof Rum
1 part Wild Turkey® 101

Pour ingredients into glass neat (do not chill).

3 Wise Men

SHOT GLASS

1 part Jack Daniel's®
1 part Johnnie Walker® Black Label
1 part Jim Beam®

Pour ingredients into glass neat (do not chill).

40 Skit and a Bent Jant

SHOT GLASS

1 part Blue Curaçao
1 part Jägermeister®
1 part Citrus Vodka
1 part Peach Schnapps
1 part Cranberry Juice Cocktail
1 part Pineapple Juice
splash Lime Juice

Shake with ice and strain.

49er Gold Rush

SHOT GLASS

1 part Goldschläger®
1 part Tequila

Shake with ice and strain.

649

SHOT GLASS

Various Ingredients (see below)

Stand facing the bar and count off the bottles: 6th from right, 4th from left, and 9th from right. Pour equal parts of each into a shot glass neat (do not chill).

8 Ball

SHOT GLASS

4 parts Coconut Rum
4 parts Peach Schnapps
4 parts Raspberry Liqueur
4 parts Vodka
splash Lemon-Lime Soda
1½ parts Cranberry Juice Cocktail
1½ parts Sweet & Sour Mix
splash Grenadine

Shake with ice and strain.

---

8 Seconds

SHOT GLASS

1 part Jägermeister®
1 part Goldschläger®
1 part Hot Damn!® Cinnamon Schnapps
1 part Rumple Minze®

Shake with ice and strain.

911

SHOT GLASS

1 part 100-Proof Peppermint Schnapps
1 part 100-Proof Cinnamon Schnapps

Pour ingredients into glass neat (do not chill).

Absohot

SHOT GLASS

½ part Absolut® Peppar Vodka
splash Hot Sauce
1 Beer

Mix Vodka and Hot Sauce in a shot glass. Serve with beer chaser.

Absolut® Antifreeze

SHOT GLASS

1 part Melon Liqueur
2 parts Absolut® Citron Vodka
2 parts Lemon-Lime Soda

Shake with ice and strain.

Absolut® Asshole

SHOT GLASS

2 parts Vodka
1 part Sour Apple Schnapps

Shake with ice and strain.

Absolut® Hunter

SHOT GLASS

2 parts Vodka
1 part Jägermeister®

Shake with ice and strain.

Absolut® Passion

SHOT GLASS

2 parts Vodka
1 part Passion Fruit Juice

Shake with ice and strain.

Absolut® Peppermint

SHOT GLASS

1 part Absolut® Peppar Vodka
splash Peppermint Schnapps

Shake with ice and strain.

Absolut® Testa Rossa

SHOT GLASS

1 part Vodka
½ part Campari®

Shake with ice and strain.

Absolutely Fruity

SHOT GLASS

1 part Vodka
1 part 99-proof Banana Liqueur
1 part Watermelon Schnapps

Shake with ice and strain.

Absolutely Screwed

SHOT GLASS

1 part Orange Vodka
1 part Orange Juice

Shake with ice and strain.

Acid Cookie
SHOT GLASS

1 part Irish Cream Liqueur
1 part Butterscotch Schnapps
1 part Hot Damn!® Cinnamon Schnapps
splash 151-Proof Rum

Shake with ice and strain.

The Action Contraction
SHOT GLASS

1 part Banana Liqueur
1 part Peppermint Schnapps
1 part Sambuca
splash Lemon Juice

Shake with ice and strain.

Adam Bomb
SHOT GLASS

1 part Sour Apple Schnapps
1 part Goldschläger®

Shake with ice and strain.

Adios, Motherfucker
SHOT GLASS

1 part Vodka
1 part Gin
1 part Rum
1 part Tequila
1 part Triple Sec
2 parts Sweet & Sour Mix
splash Cola
splash Blue Curaçao

Shake with ice and strain. Because this recipe includes many ingredients, it's easier to make in volume, about 6 shots.

Adult Lit
SHOT GLASS

1 part Dry Gin
1 part Vodka
1 part Triple Sec
1 part Light Rum

Shake with ice and strain.

Affair Shot
SHOT GLASS

1 part Strawberry Liqueur
1 part Orange Juice

Shake with ice and strain.

After Eight® Shooter
SHOT GLASS

1 part Crème de Cacao (White)
1 part Crème de Menthe (White)
1 part Vodka

Shake with ice and strain.

Afterbirth
SHOT GLASS

1 part Raspberry Liqueur
1 part Grenadine
1 part Irish Cream Liqueur

Build in order. The Irish Cream will curdle when added.

Afterburner
SHOT GLASS

1 part After Shock® Cinnamon Schnapps
1 part 151-Proof Rum

Pour ingredients into glass neat (do not chill).

Afterburner #2
SHOT GLASS

1 part Pepper Vodka
1 part Coffee
1 part Goldschläger®

Pour ingredients into glass neat (do not chill).

Airhead
SHOT GLASS

1½ parts Peach Schnapps
fill with Cranberry Juice Cocktail

Shake with ice and strain.

Alabama Slammer
SHOT GLASS

1 part Coffee Liqueur
1 part Tequila
1 part Lemon-Lime Soda

Shake with ice and strain.

Alabama Slammer #2
SHOT GLASS

1 part Southern Comfort®
1 part Jack Daniel's®
1 part Amaretto
splash Orange Juice
splash Grenadine

Shake with ice and strain.

Alaskan Oil Slick
SHOT GLASS

1 part Blue Curaçao
1 part Peppermint Schnapps
splash Jägermeister®

Chill Blue Curaçao and strain into shot glass. Float Jägermeister® on top.

Alaskan Pipeline
SHOT GLASS

1 part Yukon Jack®
1 part Amaretto

Shake with ice and strain.

Alcoholic Peppermint Pattie
SHOT GLASS

1 part Rumple Minze®
½ part Chocolate Syrup

Pour Chocolate Syrup into your mouth, followed by a shot of Rumple Minze®. Shake it around and swallow.

Alice from Dallas Shooter
SHOT GLASS

1 part Coffee Liqueur
1 part Mandarine Napoléon® Liqueur
1 part Tequila Reposado

Shake with ice and strain.

Alice in Nightmareland
SHOT GLASS

1 part Blue Curaçao
1 part Coffee Liqueur
1 part Jägermeister

Shake with ice and strain.

Alien
SHOT GLASS

1 part Blue Curaçao
splash Irish Cream Liqueur

Pour the Blue Curaçao into a chilled shot glass, then pour the Irish Cream into the center.

Alien Orgasm
SHOT GLASS

1 part Blue Curaçao
1 part Coconut Rum
1 part Coffee Liqueur
1 part Irish Cream Liqueur

Shake with ice and strain.

Alien Secretion
SHOT GLASS

1 part Vodka
1 part Melon Liqueur
1 part Coconut Rum
1 part Pineapple Juice

Shake with ice and strain.

Alligator Sperm
SHOT GLASS

1 part Melon Liqueur
1 part Cream
1 part Pineapple Juice

Shake with ice and strain.

Almond Cookie
SHOT GLASS

1 part Amaretto
1 part Butterscotch Schnapps

Shake with ice and strain.

Almond Kiss

SHOT GLASS

1 part Amaretto
1 part Godiva Chocolate Liqueur

Shake with ice and strain.

Alpine Breeze

SHOT GLASS

1 part Pineapple Juice
1 part Grenadine
½ part Crème de Menthe (White)
½ part Dark Rum

Shake with ice and strain.

Altoid

SHOT GLASS

1 part Peppermint Schnapps
1 part Vodka
splash Triple Sec
splash Sweet & Sour Mix

Shake with ice and strain.

Amaretto Balls

SHOT GLASS

2 parts Fireball Cinnamon Whiskey
1 part Amaretto

Shake with ice and strain.

Amaretto Chill

SHOT GLASS

1 part Vodka
1 part Amaretto
1 part Lemonade
1 part Pineapple Juice

Shake with ice and strain.

Amaretto Kamikaze

SHOT GLASS

1 part Vodka
1 part Amaretto
fill with Sweet & Sour Mix

Shake with ice and strain.

Amaretto Lemondrop

SHOT GLASS

1 part Vodka
1 part Amaretto
fill with Lemonade

Shake with ice and strain.

Amaretto Pie

SHOT GLASS

1 part Amaretto
1 part Orange Juice
1 part Pineapple Juice

Shake with ice and strain.

Amaretto Slammer

SHOT GLASS

1 part Amaretto
1 part Lemon-Lime Soda

Combine in a shot glass. Cover with your hand, slam on the bar, and drink.

Amaretto Slammer #2

SHOT GLASS

1 part Amaretto
1 part Cherry Schnapps

Shake with ice and strain over ice.

Amaretto Sourball

SHOT GLASS

1 part Vodka
1 part Amaretto
1 part Lemonade
1 part Orange Juice

Shake with ice and strain.

Amaretto Sweet Tart

SHOT GLASS

1 part Vodka
1 part Amaretto
1 part Cherry Juice
1 part Wild Berry Schnapps
fill with Lemonade

Shake with ice and strain.

Amenie Mama

SHOT GLASS

3 parts Irish Whiskey
1 part Amaretto

Shake with ice and strain.

American Apple Pie

SHOT GLASS

1 part Cinnamon Schnapps
1 part Apple Juice

Shake with ice and strain.

American Dream

SHOT GLASS

1 part Coffee Liqueur
1 part Amaretto
1 part Frangelico®
1 part Crème de Cacao (Dark)

Shake with ice and strain.

Anabolic Steriods

SHOT GLASS

2 parts Triple Sec
2 parts Melon Liqueur
1 part Blue Curaçao

Shake with ice and strain.

Anaconda

SHOT GLASS

1 part Sambuca
1 part Whiskey

Shake with ice and strain.

Andies

SHOT GLASS

1 part Crème de Cacao (Dark)
1 part Crème de Menthe (White)

Shake with ice and strain.

Angel Dust

SHOT GLASS

2 parts Frangelico
2 parts Vanilla Schnapps
1 part Milk

Shake with ice and strain.

Angel Piss

SHOT GLASS

1 part Canadian Whisky
1 part Southern Comfort

Shake with ice and strain.

Angel Wing

SHOT GLASS

1 part Crème de Cacao (White)
1 part Brandy

Shake with ice and strain.

Angelic Existence

SHOT GLASS

1 part Raspberry Liqueur
1 part Raspberry Vodka
1 part Lemon Juice
1 tsp Powdered Sugar

Shake with ice and strain.

Angel's Lips

SHOT GLASS

1 part Irish Cream Liqueur
2 parts Bénédictine®

Shake with ice and strain.

Angel's Rush Shooter

SHOT GLASS

1 part Cream
1 part Frangelico®

Shake with ice and strain.

Angry Badger

SHOT GLASS

1½ parts Fireball Cinnamon Whiskey
1 part Honey Whiskey

Shake with ice and strain.

The Angry German

SHOT GLASS

1 part Amaretto
1 part Black Haus® Blackberry Schnapps
1 part Jägermeister®
2 parts Lime Juice
dash Salt

Shake with ice and strain.

Angry Orange

SHOT GLASS

1 part Chambord
1 part Orange Vodka
1 part Orange Juice

Shake with ice and strain.

Anita

SHOT GLASS

1 part Apricot Brandy
1 part Maraschino Liqueur
1 part Grenadine
1 part Campari®
1 part Cream

Shake with ice and strain. Because this recipe includes many ingredients, it's easier to make in volume, about 6 shots.

Anonymous

SHOT GLASS

1 part Southern Comfort®
1 part Raspberry Liqueur
1 part Sweet & Sour Mix

Shake with ice and strain.

Antifreeze

SHOT GLASS

1 part Crème de Menthe (Green)
1 part Vodka

Shake with ice and strain.

Apple and Cinnamon Joy

SHOT GLASS

1 part Sour Apple Schnapps
splash Goldschläger®

Pour ingredients into glass neat (do not chill).

Apple and Spice Shooter

SHOT GLASS

1 part Sour Apple Schnapps
1 part Spiced Rum

Shake with ice and strain.

Apple Cobbler

SHOT GLASS

1 part Sour Apple Schnapps
1 part Goldschläger®
1 part Irish Cream Liqueur

Shake with ice and strain.

Apple Fucker

SHOT GLASS

1 part Sour Apple Schnapps
1 part Vodka

Shake with ice and strain.

Apple Jolly Rancher®

SHOT GLASS

1 part Melon Liqueur
1 part Sweet & Sour Mix
1 part Crown Royal® Whiskey

Shake with ice and strain.

Apple Kamihuzi

SHOT GLASS

1 part Tequila
1 part Sour Apple Schnapps
splash Sweet & Sour Mix

Shake with ice and strain.

Apple Kamikaze

SHOT GLASS

1 part Vodka
1 part Sour Apple Schnapps
splash Sweet & Sour Mix

Shake with ice and strain.

Apple Lemondrop

SHOT GLASS

1 part Vodka
1 part Sour Apple Schnapps
splash Lemonade

Shake with ice and strain.

Apple Mule

SHOT GLASS

1 part Amaretto
1 part Jack Daniel's®
1½ parts Lime Juice
2 parts Orange Juice
1 part Southern Comfort®
1 part Triple Sec

Shake with ice and strain. Because this recipe includes many ingredients, it's easier to make in volume, about 6 shots.

Apple Pie

SHOT GLASS

1 part Fireball Cinnamon Whiskey
splash Green Apple Schnapps
splash Pineapple Juice
splash Sweet & Sour mix

Shake with ice and strain.

Apple Pie Shot

SHOT GLASS

1 part Irish Mist
1 part Cinnamon Schnapps
1 part Frangelico®
1 part Amaretto

Shake with ice and strain.

Applecake

SHOT GLASS

1 part Licor 43®
1 part Apple Brandy
1 part Milk

Shake with ice and strain.

Apples and Jacks

SHOT GLASS

1 part RumChata
1 part Sour Apple Schnapps

Shake with ice and strain.

Arctic Brain Freeze

SHOT GLASS

1 part Amaretto
1 part Melon Liqueur

Shake with ice and strain.

Areola

SHOT GLASS

2 parts Peach Schnapps
1 part Canadian Whisky
1 part Sloe Gin

Shake with ice and strain.

Arizona Antifreeze

SHOT GLASS

1 part Vodka
1 part Melon Liqueur
1 part Sweet & Sour Mix

Shake with ice and strain.

Arizona Twister

SHOT GLASS

1 part Vodka
1 part Coconut Rum
1 part Tequila
splash Orange Juice
splash Pineapple Juice
splash Crème de Coconut
splash Grenadine

Shake with ice and strain. Because this recipe includes many ingredients, it's easier to make in volume, about 6 shots.

Arkansas Rattler

SHOT GLASS

1 part Cinnamon Schnapps
1 part Tequila

Pour ingredients into glass neat (do not chill).

Army Green

SHOT GLASS

1 part Goldschläger®
1 part Jägermeister®
1 part Tequila

Shake with ice and strain.

Arturo's Burning Mindtwister

SHOT GLASS

1 part Scotch
1 part Tequila

Shake with ice and strain.

Astro Pop

SHOT GLASS

1 part Blue Curaçao
1 part Raspberry Vodka
1 part Grenadine
1 part Sweet & Sour Mix

Shake with ice and strain.

Astronaut

SHOT GLASS

1 part Dark Rum
1 part Light Rum
1 part Vodka
1 part Lemon-Lime Soda
1 part Pineapple Juice

Shake with ice and strain.

Astronaut Shooter

SHOT GLASS

1 part Vodka (chilled)
1 Lemon Wedge
dash Sugar
dash Instant Coffee Granules

Coat the lemon with sugar on one side and instant coffee on the other, suck lemon and drink the chilled vodka.

Atomic Apple

SHOT GLASS

1 part Apple Schnapps
1 part Fireball Cinnamon Whiskey

Shake with ice and strain.

Atomic Fireball

SHOT GLASS

1 part 151-Proof Rum
1 part Fireball Cinnamon Whiskey
1 part Grenadine

Shake with ice and strain.

The Atomic Shot

SHOT GLASS

1 part Silver Tequila
1 part Goldschläger®
1 part Absolut® Peppar Vodka
splash Club Soda

Shake with ice and strain.

Auburn Headbanger

SHOT GLASS

1 part Jägermeister®
1 part Goldschläger®

Shake with ice and strain.

Avalanche Shot

SHOT GLASS

1 part Crème de Cacao (Dark)
1 part Coffee Liqueur
1 part Southern Comfort®

Shake with ice and strain.

Awwwwwww

SHOT GLASS

1 part Gold Rum
1 part Triple Sec
dash Bitters

Pour ingredients into glass neat (do not chill).

Azurra

SHOT GLASS

1 part Light Rum
splash Blue Curaçao
splash Crème de Cacao (White)

Shake with ice and strain.

B-1B Stealth

SHOT GLASS

1 part Amaretto
1 part Coffee Liqueur
1 part Espresso Vodka
1 part Irish Cream Liqueur

Shake with ice and strain.

B-2 Bomber

SHOT GLASS

1 part Rum
1 part Southern Comfort®
1 part Lemon-Lime Soda
1 part Green or Lemon-Lime Gatorade®

Shake with ice and strain.

B-52

SHOT GLASS

1 part Amaretto
2 parts Irish Cream Liqueur
1 part Rum

Pour the Amaretto, then the Irish Cream Liqueur, and then, carefully, the Rum. Light the shot on fire and drink it with a straw, or slap it to extinguish the flame and then drink.

B-54

SHOT GLASS

1 part Irish Cream Liqueur
1 part Crème de Menthe (Green)
1 part Grand Marnier®
1 part Coffee Liqueur

Shake with ice and strain.

Babymama

SHOT GLASS

1 part 99 Bananas Liqueur
1 part Strawberry Vodka
2 parts Pineapple Juice

Shake with ice and strain.

Babymama Drama

SHOT GLASS

1 part 99 Bananas Liqueur
1 part 151-Proof Rum
1 part Strawberry Vodka
1 part Pineapple Juice

Shake with ice and strain.

Back Shot

SHOT GLASS

1 part Vodka
1 part Raspberry Liqueur
2 parts Sweet & Sour Mix

Shake with ice and strain.

Back Street Romeo

SHOT GLASS

2 parts Whiskey
1 part Irish Cream Liqueur

Shake with ice and strain.

Backdraft Shooter

SHOT GLASS

1 part Rum
1 part Cinnamon Schnapps

Pour ingredients into glass neat (do not chill).

Bad Head

SHOT GLASS

1 part Coffee Liqueur
1 part Jägermeister
2 parts Half and Half

Shake with ice and strain.

Balboa
SHOT GLASS
1 part Absinthe
1 part Mezcal
1 part Vodka
Shake with ice and strain.

Bald Eagle Shooter
SHOT GLASS
1 part Crème de Menthe (White)
1 part Tequila Reposado
Shake with ice and strain.

Bald Taco
SHOT GLASS
1 part Coconut Rum
1 part Silver Tequila
1 part Lemonade
Shake with ice and strain.

Baldheaded Slut
SHOT GLASS
1 part Jägermeister
1 part Peach Schnapps
Shake with ice and strain.

Ball and Chain
SHOT GLASS
1 part Rumple Minze®
1 part Goldschläger®
splash Jägermeister®
Shake with ice and strain.

Ball Breaker
SHOT GLASS
2 parts Cognac
1 part Peach Schnapps
1 part Cranberry Juice
Shake with ice and strain.

Ball Hooter
SHOT GLASS
1 part Tequila
1 part Peppermint Schnapps
Shake with ice and strain.

Ball Sweat
SHOT GLASS
2 parts Tequila
1 part Irish Cream Liqueur
pinch salt
Build in order. Do not chill.

Banamon
SHOT GLASS
1 part Pisang Ambon® Liqueur
½ part Amaretto
½ part Ginger Ale
Stir gently with ice and strain.

Banana Bite
SHOT GLASS
1 part Banana Liqueur
1 part Fireball Cinnamon Whiskey
1 part Cream
Shake with ice and strain.

Banana Boat Shooter
SHOT GLASS
1 part Crème de Menthe (White)
1 part Coffee
1 part Ponche Kuba®
Shake with ice and strain.

Banana Boomer Shooter
SHOT GLASS
1 part Vodka
1 part Crème de Banane
Shake with ice and strain.

Banana Cream Pie
SHOT GLASS
1 part Banana Liqueur
1 part Crème de Cacao (White)
1 part Vodka
1 part Half and Half
Shake with ice and strain.

Banana Cream Pie #2

SHOT GLASS

4 parts RumChata
1 part Banana Liqueur

Shake with ice and strain.

Banana Hammock Shooter

SHOT GLASS

1 part Banana Liqueur
1 part Blue Curaçao
1 part Coconut Rum
1 part Jägermeister
1 part Sambuca

Shake with ice and strain.

Banana Lemon Surprise

SHOT GLASS

1 part Banana Liqueur
3 parts Lemon Juice

Shake with ice and strain.

Banana Licorice

SHOT GLASS

1 part Banana Liqueur
½ part Cherry Brandy
½ part Sambuca

Shake with ice and strain.

Banana Popsicle® Shooter

SHOT GLASS

1 part Vodka
1 part Crème de Banane
1 part Orange Juice

Shake with ice and strain.

Banana Slug

SHOT GLASS

3 parts 99-Proof Banana Liqueur
1 part Pineapple Juice

Shake with ice and strain.

Banana Split Shooter

SHOT GLASS

1 part Banana Liqueur
1 part Vodka

Shake with ice and strain.

Banana Sweet Tart

SHOT GLASS

1 part Vodka
1 part Banana Liqueur
1 part Cherry Juice
fill with Lemonade

Shake with ice and strain.

Bananas and Cream

SHOT GLASS

1 part Coffee Liqueur
1 part Irish Cream Liqueur
1 part 99-Proof Banana Liqueur

Shake with ice and strain.

Banderas

SHOT GLASS

1 part Tomato Juice
1 part Silver Tequila
1 part Lime Juice

Line up the shots to represent the Mexican flag: Tomato (red), Tequila (white), and Lime (green). Consume quickly in order.

Banshee Shooter

SHOT GLASS

1 part Crème de Cacao (White)
1 part Cream
1 part Crème de Banane

Shake with ice and strain.

Barbados Blast

SHOT GLASS

1 part Dark Rum
1 part Triple Sec
1 part Ginger Liqueur

Shake with ice and strain.

Barbed Wire

SHOT GLASS

1 part Goldschläger®
1 part Sambuca

Shake with ice and strain.

Barbie® Naked

SHOT GLASS

1 part Coconut Rum
1 part Strawberry Schnapps
1 part Pineapple Juice

Shake with ice and strain.

Barbie® Shot

SHOT GLASS

1 part Coconut Rum
1 part Vodka
1 part Cranberry Juice Cocktail
1 part Orange Juice

Shake with ice and strain.

Bare Ass

SHOT GLASS

1 part Amaretto
splash Peach Schnapps
½ part Pineapple Juice

Shake with ice and strain.

Barfing Sensations

SHOT GLASS

1 part Blackberry Liqueur
1 part Peach Schnapps
1 part Vodka
1 part Apple Brandy
1 part Raspberry Liqueur

Shake with ice and strain. Because this recipe includes many ingredients, it's easier to make in volume, about 6 shots.

Barney® on Acid

SHOT GLASS

1 part Blue Curaçao
1 part Jägermeister®
splash Cranberry Juice Cocktail

Shake with ice and strain.

Bart Simpson

SHOT GLASS

1 part Coconut Rum
1 part Melon Liqueur
1 part Vodka

Shake with ice and strain.

Bartender's Wet Dream

SHOT GLASS

1 part Grenadine
1 part Coffee Liqueur
1 part Irish Cream Liqueur

Shake with ice and strain. Top with whipped cream.

Bayou Juice

SHOT GLASS

1 part Coconut Rum
1 part Spiced Rum
1 part Amaretto
1 part Cranberry Juice Cocktail
1 part Pineapple Juice

Shake with ice and strain.

Bazooka® Bubble Gum

SHOT GLASS

1 part Southern Comfort®
1 part Banana Liqueur
1 part Cream
1 part Grenadine

Shake with ice and strain.

Bazooka Joe®

SHOT GLASS

1 part Banana Liqueur
1 part Blue Curaçao
1 part Grand Marnier®

Shake with ice and strain.

Bazooka Moe

SHOT GLASS

1 part Blue Curaçao
1 part Crème de Banane

Shake with ice and strain.

Bear Dozer

SHOT GLASS

1 part Tequila
1 part Whiskey
1 part Cherry Brandy

Shake with ice and strain.

Bearded Boy

SHOT GLASS

1 part Southern Comfort®
1 part Vodka
1 part Water
splash Grain Alcohol

Shake with ice and strain.

Beaver Dam

SHOT GLASS

1 part Vodka
1 part Peach Schnapps
1 part Gatorade®

Shake with ice and strain.

Beaver Shot

SHOT GLASS

1 part Spiced Rum
1 part Pineapple Juice
splash Grenadine

Shake with ice and strain.

Beaver Tail

SHOT GLASS

4 parts Canadian Whisky
1 part Maple Syrup

Shake with ice and strain.

Beavis and Butt-head®

SHOT GLASS

1 part Sour Apple Schnapps
1 part Cinnamon Schnapps

Shake with ice and strain.

A Bedrock

SHOT GLASS

1 part Sambuca
1 part Coffee Liqueur
splash Milk

Shake with ice and strain.

Belfast Sniper

SHOT GLASS

1 part Irish Cream Liqueur
1 part Irish Whiskey
1 part Coffee Liqueur

Shake with ice and strain.

Bend Me Over Shooter

SHOT GLASS

1 part Crown Royal® Whiskey
1 part Amaretto
1 part Sweet & Sour Mix

Shake with ice and strain.

Beowulf

SHOT GLASS

1 part Blue Curaçao
1 part Vodka

Shake with ice and strain.

The Berry Kix®

SHOT GLASS

2 parts Currant Vodka
1 part Sweet & Sour Mix

Shake with ice and strain.

Berube's Death

SHOT GLASS

1 part Cinnamon Schnapps
1 part Black Sambuca
1 part Jägermeister®
1 part Rumple Minze®

Shake with ice and strain.

Betty Come Back
SHOT GLASS
2 parts Silver Tequila
1 part Triple Sec
1 part Parfait Amour
Shake with ice and strain.

The Bianca Pop
SHOT GLASS
1 part Coconut Rum
1 part Amaretto
Shake with ice and strain.

Big Baller
SHOT GLASS
2 parts Vodka
1 part Gin
1 part Triple Sec
splash Lemon Juice
Shake with ice and strain.

Big Pine Puss
SHOT GLASS
1 part Spiced Rum
½ part Banana Liqueur
splash Lime Juice
splash Grenadine
splash Cranberry Juice Cocktail
Shake with ice and strain.

Big Red
SHOT GLASS
1 part Irish Cream Liqueur
1 part Goldschläger®
Shake with ice and strain.

Big Roller
SHOT GLASS
1 part Amaretto
1 part Coffee
1 part Crème de Banane
Shake with ice and strain.

Big Shot
SHOT GLASS
1 part Coconut Rum
1 part Jägermeister
1 part Lemon Juice
Shake with ice and strain.

Big Time
SHOT GLASS
1 part Cognac
1 part Pernod®
Shake with ice and strain.

Big Unit
SHOT GLASS
2 parts Tequila
1 part Blue Curaçao
Shake with ice and strain.

The Big V
SHOT GLASS
1 part Vodka
1 part Crème de Cacao (White)
1 part Blue Curaçao
1 part Sweet & Sour Mix
Shake with ice and strain.

Biglower
SHOT GLASS
2 parts Dark Rum
1 part Crème de Cacao (Dark)
1 part Amaretto
Shake with ice and strain.

Bikini Line
SHOT GLASS
1 part Coffee Liqueur
1 part Raspberry Liqueur
1 part Vodka
Shake with ice and strain.

Bilge Water

SHOT GLASS

2 parts Apple Vodka
2 parts Cherry Vodka
1 part Jägermeister
1 part Cranberry Juice

Shake with ice and strain.

Billy Bad Ass

SHOT GLASS

1 part 151-Proof Rum
1 part Tequila
1 part Jägermeister®

Shake with ice and strain.

Bird Shit

SHOT GLASS

1 part Blackberry Brandy
splash Tequila
splash Milk

Fill shot glass about 3/4 full with Blackberry Brandy. Float the Tequila on top of Brandy. Pour in a little bit of Milk for effect.

Bitch Slap

SHOT GLASS

1 part Irish Cream Liqueur
1 part Raspberry Vodka

Shake with ice and strain.

Bite of the Iguana

SHOT GLASS

1 part Tequila
1 part Triple Sec
1/2 part Vodka
2 parts Orange Juice
2 parts Sweet & Sour Mix

Shake with ice and strain.

Bitter Sorrow

SHOT GLASS

1 part Fireball Cinnamon Whiskey
1 part Gin
1 part Jägermeister
1 part Sour Apple Schnapps

Shake with ice and strain.

Black and Blue Shark

SHOT GLASS

2 parts Jack Daniel's®
1 part Gold Tequila
1 part Vodka
1 part Blue Curaçao

Shake with ice and strain.

Black and Gold

SHOT GLASS

1 part Goldschläger®
1 part Jägermeister

Shake with ice and strain.

Black Apple

SHOT GLASS

1 part Blackberry Liqueur
1 part Sour Apple Schnapps
splash Lemon-Lime Soda
splash Sweet & Sour Mix

Shake with ice and strain.

Black Blood

SHOT GLASS

2 parts Blue Curaçao
1 part Jägermeister®
1 part Ruby Red Grapefruit Juice

Shake with ice and strain.

Black Cat

SHOT GLASS

1 part Amaretto
1 part Tequila

Shake with ice and strain.

Black Death

SHOT GLASS

1 part Jack Daniel's®
1 part Tequila

Shake with ice and strain.

Black Death #2

SHOT GLASS

3 parts Vodka
1 part Soy Sauce

Shake with ice and strain.

Black Forest Cake

SHOT GLASS

1 part Cherry Brandy
1 part Coffee Liqueur
1 part Irish Cream Liqueur

Shake with ice and strain.

Black Gold Shooter

SHOT GLASS

1 part Black Sambuca
1 part Cinnamon Schnapps

Shake with ice and strain.

Black Hole

SHOT GLASS

1 part Jägermeister®
1 part Rumple Minze®

Shake with ice and strain.

Black Orgasm

SHOT GLASS

1 part Vodka
1 part Sloe Gin
1 part Blue Curaçao
1 part Peach Schnapps

Shake with ice and strain.

Black Pepper

SHOT GLASS

1 part Pepper Vodka
splash Blackberry Brandy

Shake with ice and strain.

Blackberry Sourball

SHOT GLASS

1 part Vodka
1 part Blackberry Liqueur
splash Lemonade
splash Orange Juice

Shake with ice and strain.

Blazin' Peach

SHOT GLASS

1 part Fireball Cinnamon Whiskey
1 part Peach Schnapps
splash Grenadine
splash Lemon-Lime Soda

Shake all but soda with ice and strain. Top with Lemon-Lime Soda.

Blazing Saddle

SHOT GLASS

3 parts Blackberry Brandy
1 part 151-Proof Rum

Shake with ice and strain.

Bleacher Creature

SHOT GLASS

1 part Butterscotch Schnapps
1 part 151-Proof Rum

Pour ingredients into glass neat (do not chill).

Bleedin' Hell

SHOT GLASS

1 part Vodka
1 part Strawberry Liqueur
1 part Lemonade

Shake with ice and strain.

Blended Frog

SHOT GLASS

Grenadine
Sugar
1 part Jägermeister
2 parts Irish Cream Liqueur
dash Crème de Menthe (Green)

Dip rim of shot glass in Grenadine, then coat with Sugar. Add the Jägermeister and Irish Cream. Carefully add the Crème de Menthe a little at a time.

Blinded by the Light

SHOT GLASS

1 part Absinthe
1 part Pernod
1 part Sambuca
1 part Water

Shake with ice and strain.

Bliss

SHOT GLASS

1 part Vanilla Liqueur
1 part Vanilla Vodka
1 part Vanilla Cola
splash Honey

Shake with ice and strain.

Blister

SHOT GLASS

1 part 151-Proof Rum
1 part Wild Turkey® Bourbon
1 part Blue Curaçao
splash Pineapple Juice
splash Orange Juice

Shake with ice and strain.

Blister in the Sun

SHOT GLASS

2 parts Canadian Whisky
1 part Raspberry Liqueur
1 part Orange Juice
1 part Lemon Juice
1 part Lemon-Lime Soda

Shake with ice and strain. Because this recipe includes many ingredients, it's easier to make in volume, about 6 shots.

Blonde Bimbo

SHOT GLASS

1 part Coconut Rum
1 part Peach Schnapps
1 part Tuaca
1 part Pineapple Juice

Shake with ice and strain.

Blonde-Headed Slut

SHOT GLASS

1 part Jägermeister
1 part Peach Schnapps
1 part Pineapple Juice

Shake with ice and strain.

Blood Bath

SHOT GLASS

1 part Silver Tequila
1 part Strawberry Liqueur

Shake with ice and strain.

Blood Test

SHOT GLASS

1 part Tequila Reposado
1 part Grenadine

Shake with ice and strain.

Blue Altoid

SHOT GLASS

1 part Peppermint Schnapps
1 part Vodka
splash Blue Curaçao
splash Sweet & Sour Mix

Shake with ice and strain.

Blue Balls

SHOT GLASS

2 parts Blue Curaçao
2 parts Coconut Rum
1 part Peach Schnapps
splash Sweet & Sour Mix
splash Lemon-Lime Soda

Shake with ice and strain. Because this recipe includes many ingredients, it's easier to make in volume, about 6 shots.

Blue Balls #2

SHOT GLASS

1 part Blue Curaçao
1 part Dr. McGillicuddy's® Mentholmint Schnapps

Shake with ice and strain.

Blue Banana

SHOT GLASS

1 part Crème de Banane
1 part Blue Curaçao

Shake with ice and strain.

Blue Bastard

SHOT GLASS

2 parts Triple Sec
1 part Blueberry Schnapps
splash Lime Juice
splash Simple Syrup

Shake with ice and strain.

Blue Caboose

SHOT GLASS

1 part Irish Cream Liqueur
1 part Whiskey
1 part Amaretto

Shake with ice and strain.

Blue Ghost

SHOT GLASS

1 part Banana Liqueur
1 part Blue Curaçao
1 part Coconut Rum
1 part Vodka
1 part Crème de Cacao (White)
1 part Light Rum
1 part Triple Sec
4 parts Cream

Shake with ice and strain. Because this recipe includes many ingredients, it's easier to make in volume, about 6 shots.

Blue Kamikaze

SHOT GLASS

1 part Blue Curaçao
1 part Vodka
1 part Sweetened Lime Juice

Shake with ice and strain.

Blue Marlin

SHOT GLASS

1 part Light Rum
½ part Blue Curaçao
1 part Lime Juice

Shake with ice and strain.

Blue Meanie

SHOT GLASS

1 part Blue Curaçao
1 part Vodka
1 part Sweet & Sour Mix

Shake with ice and strain.

Blue Motherfucker

SHOT GLASS

1 part Blue Curaçao
1 part 151-Proof Rum

Pour ingredients into glass neat (do not chill).

Blue Peach

SHOT GLASS

1 part Peach Schnapps
1 part Blue Curaçao

Shake with ice and strain.

Blue Polar Bear

SHOT GLASS

1 part Vodka
1 part Avalanche® Peppermint Schnapps

Shake with ice and strain.

Blue Razzberry Kamikaze

SHOT GLASS

2 parts Raspberry Vodka
1 part Blue Curaçao
splash Lime Cordial

Shake with ice and strain.

Blue Slammer

SHOT GLASS

1 part Blue Curaçao
1 part Sambuca
1 part Vodka
splash Lemon Juice

Pour ingredients into glass neat (do not chill).

Blue Smurf® Piss

SHOT GLASS

1 part Jägermeister®
1 part 151-Proof Rum
1 part Rumple Minze®
1 part Goldschläger®
1 part Blue Curaçao

Shake with ice and strain. Because this recipe includes many ingredients, it's easier to make in volume, about 6 shots.

Blue Spruce

SHOT GLASS

1 part Maple Syrup
1 part Vodka

Pour ingredients into glass neat (do not chill).

Blueberry Breath Mint

SHOT GLASS

1 part Blueberry Schnapps
1 part Blueberry Vodka
1 part Peppermint Schnapps
1 part Milk

Shake with ice and strain.

Blueberry Muffin

SHOT GLASS

2 parts Blueberry Schnapps
2 parts RumChata
1 part Frangelico
1 part Milk

Shake with ice and strain.

Blurricane

SHOT GLASS

1 part Blue Curaçao
1 part Rumple Minze®
1 part Goldschläger®
1 part Jägermeister®
1 part Wild Turkey® Bourbon
1 part Ouzo

Shake with ice and strain. Because this recipe includes many ingredients, it's easier to make in volume, about 6 shots.

Body Bag

SHOT GLASS

1 part 151-Proof Rum
1 part Goldschläger®
1 part Jägermeister®
1 part Rumple Minze®

Pour ingredients into glass neat (do not chill).

Body Shot

SHOT GLASS

1 part Vodka
dash Sugar
1 Lemon Wedge

Using a partner, lick his or her neck, then pour the Sugar onto the moistened spot. Place the wedge of Lemon in his or her mouth with the skin pointed inward. Lick the Sugar from his or her neck, shoot the Vodka, then suck the Lemon from his or her mouth (while gently holding back of the neck).

Bomb

SHOT GLASS

1 part Coffee Liqueur
1 part Goldschläger®
1 part Irish Cream Liqueur

Shake with ice and strain.

Bomb Atomic

SHOT GLASS

1 part Vodka
1 part Coffee
½ part Cold Coffee

Shake with ice and strain.

Bomb #2

SHOT GLASS

1 part Sour Apple Schnapps
1 part Peach Schnapps
1 part Banana Liqueur
1 part Pineapple Juice
1 part Lemon-Lime Soda

Shake with ice and strain. Because this recipe includes many ingredients, it's easier to make in volume, about 6 shots.

Bombshell

SHOT GLASS

2 parts Irish Cream Liqueur
1 part Cointreau®
splash Aquavit

Shake with ice and strain.

Bong Water

SHOT GLASS

1 part Melon Liqueur
1 part Orange Juice
1 part Jägermeister®

Shake with ice and strain.

Bonnie's Berries

SHOT GLASS

1 part Vodka
1 part Amaretto
1 part Raspberry Liqueur

Shake with ice and strain.

Boogers in the Grass

SHOT GLASS

1 part Melon Liqueur
1 part Peach Schnapps
splash Irish Cream Liqueur

Shake all but Irish Cream with ice and strain. Place a few drops of Irish Cream in the center of the drink.

Boom Box

SHOT GLASS

1 part Vodka
1 part White Wine
1 part Hot Coffee

Pour ingredients into glass neat (do not chill).

Boomer

SHOT GLASS

1 part Tequila
1 part Triple Sec
1 part Crème de Banane
1 part Orange Juice
1 part Sweet & Sour Mix

Shake with ice and strain.

Boomerang Shot

SHOT GLASS

1 part Jägermeister®
1 part Yukon Jack®

Shake with ice and strain.

Booster Shot

SHOT GLASS

1 part Cherry Brandy
1 part Chocolate Liqueur
1 part Lemon-Lime Soda

Shake with ice and strain into a chilled shot glass.

Boot to the Head

SHOT GLASS

1 part Drambuie®
1 part Jack Daniel's®
1 part Silver Tequila

Shake with ice and strain.

The Bootlegger

SHOT GLASS

1 part Jack Daniel's®
1 part Southern Comfort®
1 part Sambuca

Shake with ice and strain.

Border Conflict Shooter

SHOT GLASS

2 parts Vodka
2 parts Crème de Menthe (White)
1 part Grenadine

Shake with ice and strain.

Bottle Cap

SHOT GLASS

1 part Butterscotch Schnapps
1 part Raspberry Liqueur
1 part Lime Juice

Shake with ice and strain.

Brain Damage

SHOT GLASS

1 part 151-Proof Rum
1 part Amaretto
splash Irish Cream Liqueur

Shake all but Irish Cream with ice and strain. Place a few drops of Irish Cream in the center of the drink.

Brain Eraser

SHOT GLASS

1 part Jägermeister®
1 part Peppermint Schnapps

Shake with ice and strain.

Brain Hemorrhage

SHOT GLASS

1 part Peach Schnapps
1 part Irish Cream Liqueur
splash Grenadine

Shake all but Grenadine with ice and strain. Place a few drops of Grenadine in the center of the drink.

Braindead

SHOT GLASS

1 part Vodka
1 part Sweet & Sour Mix
1 part Triple Sec

Shake with ice and strain.

Brainmaster

SHOT GLASS

2 parts Light Rum
1 part Crème de Coconut
1 part Crème de Cacao (White)
splash Apricot Syrup

Shake with ice and strain.

Brass Balls

SHOT GLASS

1 part Grand Marnier®
1 part Peach Schnapps
1 part Pineapple Juice

Shake with ice and strain.

Brave Bull Shooter

SHOT GLASS

1 part Tequila
1 part Coffee Liqueur

Pour ingredients into glass neat (do not chill).

Braveheart

SHOT GLASS

1 part Vodka
splash Blue Curaçao

Shake with ice and strain.

Breakfast in Bed

SHOT GLASS

1 part Butterscotch Liqueur
1 part Fireball Cinnamon Whiskey
1 part Orange Juice

Shake with ice and strain.

Breakfast in Hell

SHOT GLASS

1 part Butterscotch Liqueur
1 part Fireball Cinnamon Whiskey
1 part Irish Whiskey

Shake with ice and strain.

Breast Milk

SHOT GLASS

1 part Chocolate Liqueur
1 part Irish Cream Liqueur
1 part Butterscotch Schnapps
splash Half and Half

Shake with ice and strain.

Breath Freshener

SHOT GLASS

1 part Vodka
2 parts Peppermint Schnapps

Shake with ice and strain.

Breathalizer

SHOT GLASS

1 part Peppermint Schnapps
1 part Light Rum

Shake with ice and strain.

Brody's Icy Alien

SHOT GLASS

1 part Rum
1 part Melon Liqueur
1 part Rumple Minze®
splash Cream

Shake with ice and strain.

Broken Down Golf Cart

SHOT GLASS

1 part Amaretto
1 part Melon Liqueur
2 parts Cranberry Juice

Shake with ice and strain.

Brown Lion

SHOT GLASS

1 part Crème de Cacao (Dark)
1 part Coffee Liqueur

Shake with ice and strain.

Bruised Heart

SHOT GLASS

1 part Vodka
1 part Raspberry Liqueur
1 part Peach Schnapps
1 part Cranberry Juice Cocktail

Shake with ice and strain.

Bubba Hubba Boom Boom

SHOT GLASS

1 part Crème de Cacao (White)
1 part Crème de Menthe (White)

Shake with ice and strain.

Bubble Butt

SHOT GLASS

1 part Southern Comfort
1 part Grenadine
1 part Milk

Shake with ice and strain.

Bubble Gum

SHOT GLASS

1 part Melon Liqueur
1 part Vodka
1 part Crème de Banane
1 part Orange Juice

Shake with ice and strain.

Bubbling Pool

SHOT GLASS

1 part 99 Bananas Liqueur
1 part Blue Raspberry Liqueur
1 part Triple Sec
1 part Grenadine

Shake with ice and strain.

Buca Bear

SHOT GLASS

1 part Butterscotch Schnapps
1 part Sambuca

Shake with ice and strain.

Bucaballs

SHOT GLASS

2 parts Fireball Cinnamon Whiskey
1 part Sambuca

Shake with ice and strain.

Buffalo Balls

SHOT GLASS

1 part Buffalo Trace Bourbon
1 part Fireball Cinnamon Whiskey

Shake with ice and strain.

Bull Shot Shooter

SHOT GLASS

1 part Silver Tequila
1 part Coffee
1 part Dark Rum

Shake with ice and strain.

Bull's Milk

SHOT GLASS

1 part Brandy
1 part Dark Rum
1 part Cream

Shake with ice and strain.

Buona Sera Shooter

SHOT GLASS

1 part Amaretto
1 part Coffee
1 part Vanilla Rum

Shake with ice and strain.

Buried under an Avalanche

SHOT GLASS

1 part Ouzo
1 part Rumple Minze®

Shake with ice and strain.

Burning Cherry

SHOT GLASS

1 part George Dickel Whiskey
1 part Irish Cream Liqueur
1 part Jim Beam®
splash Grenadine

Pour ingredients into glass neat (do not chill).

Burning Worm

SHOT GLASS

1 part Mezcal
1 part Goldschläger®

Pour ingredients into glass neat (do not chill).

Burnt Pineapple

SHOT GLASS

1 part Fireball Cinnamon Whiskey
1 part Sour Apple Schnapps
1 part Pineapple Juice

Shake with ice and strain.

Busted Cherry

SHOT GLASS

1 part Coffee Liqueur
1 part Cherry Brandy

Shake with ice and strain.

Busted Nut

SHOT GLASS

1 part Amaretto
1 part Vodka
1 part Lime Juice

Shake with ice and strain.

Butt Pirate

SHOT GLASS

1 part Butterscotch Liqueur
1 part Spiced Rum

Shake with ice and strain.

Butterball

SHOT GLASS

1 part Coffee Liqueur
1 part Irish Cream Liqueur
splash Butterscotch Schnapps

Pour ingredients into glass neat (do not chill).

Butterfucker

SHOT GLASS

1 part Jägermeister®
1 part Butterscotch Schnapps
1 part Irish Cream Liqueur

Shake with ice and strain.

Butternut Rum Lifesaver

SHOT GLASS

1 part Irish Cream Liqueur
1 part Butterscotch Schnapps
1 part Coconut Rum
1 part Pineapple Juice

Shake with ice and strain.

Buttery Nipple

SHOT GLASS

1 part Sambuca
1 part Butterscotch Schnapps

Shake with ice and strain.

Buzzard's Breath

SHOT GLASS

1 part Crème de Menthe (White)
1 part Amaretto
1 part Coffee Liqueur

Shake with ice and strain.

Buzzard's Breath #2

SHOT GLASS

1 part Amaretto
1 part Peppermint Schnapps
1 part Coffee Liqueur

Shake with ice and strain.

C-4 Shot

SHOT GLASS

1 part Coffee Liqueur
1 part Fireball Cinnamon Whiskey

Shake with ice and strain.

Cactus Jack Shooter

SHOT GLASS

1 part Coffee
1 part Light Rum

Shake with ice and strain.

Cactus Thorn

SHOT GLASS

2 parts Tequila
1 part Crème de Menthe (Green)
1 part Lime Juice

Shake with ice and strain.

California Surfer

SHOT GLASS

1 part Jägermeister®
1 part Coconut Rum
2 parts Pineapple Juice

Shake with ice and strain.

Camel Driver
SHOT GLASS
1 part Sambuca
1 part Irish Cream Liqueur
Shake with ice and strain.

Camryn's Cruciatus
SHOT GLASS
1 part Cinnamon Schnapps
1 part Dark Rum
1 part Jägermeister
1 part Peppermint Schnapps
Shake with ice and strain. For Camryn.

Canadian Goose
SHOT GLASS
1 part Canadian Whisky
1 part Peach Schnapps
Shake with ice and strain.

Canadian Hunter
SHOT GLASS
1 part Yukon Jack®
1 part Wild Turkey® 101
Shake with ice and strain.

Canadian Moose
SHOT GLASS
1 part Coffee Liqueur
1 part Irish Cream Liqueur
1 part Crown Royal® Whiskey
Shake with ice and strain.

Canadian Snakebite
SHOT GLASS
1 part Crème de Menthe (White)
1 part Canadian Whisky
Shake with ice and strain.

Candy Apple
SHOT GLASS
1 part Crown Royal® Whiskey
1 part Sour Apple Schnapps
splash Cranberry Juice Cocktail
Shake with ice and strain.

Candy Killer with a Kiss
SHOT GLASS
1 part Ouzo
1 part Jägermeister®
1 part Goldschläger®
Shake with ice and strain.

Captain Jack Sparrow
SHOT GLASS
1 part Spiced Rum
1 part Vodka
1 part Whiskey
Shake with ice and strain.

Captain Louie
SHOT GLASS
1 part Spiced Rum
1 part Coffee Liqueur
splash Vanilla Extract
Pour ingredients into glass neat (do not chill).

Captain Superman
SHOT GLASS
2 parts Peach Schnapps
2 parts Spiced Rum
1 part Orange Juice
1 part Pineapple Juice
dash Grenadine
Shake with ice and strain.

Captain's Treasure
SHOT GLASS
1 part Goldschläger®
1 part Spiced Rum
Shake with ice and strain.

Captain's Treasure Map
SHOT GLASS
1 part Goldschläger®
1 part Spiced Rum
1 part Grenadine
1 part Lime Juice
Shake with ice and strain.

Caramel Candy Shot
SHOT GLASS
1 part Butterscotch Liqueur
1 part Caramel Vodka
1 part RumChata
Shake with ice and strain.

Caramilk
SHOT GLASS
2 parts Crème de Cacao (White)
1 part Crème de Banane
1 part Coffee Liqueur
Shake with ice and strain.

Carolina Vagina
SHOT GLASS
2 parts Coconut Rum
1 part Irish Cream Liqueur
1 part Coffee Liqueur
splash Grenadine
Shake with ice and strain.

Catfish
SHOT GLASS
3 parts Bourbon
1 part Peach Schnapps
Shake with ice and strain.

Cattle Prod
SHOT GLASS
1 part Butterscotch Schnapps
1 part Crown Royal® Whiskey
Pour ingredients into glass neat (do not chill).

Cayman Shooter
SHOT GLASS
1 part Crème de Banane
1 part Melon Liqueur
1 part Irish Cream Liqueur
Shake with ice and strain.

Champerelle
SHOT GLASS
1 part Triple Sec
1 part Anisette
1 part Cognac
Shake with ice and strain.

Chariot of Fire
SHOT GLASS
1 part Vodka
1 part Sambuca
Shake with ice and strain.

Ché Guevara
SHOT GLASS
1 part Goldschläger®
1 part Tequila
1 part Jägermeister®
Shake with ice and strain.

Cheesecake
SHOT GLASS
1 part Cranberry Juice Cocktail
1 part Vanilla Liqueur
Shake with ice and strain.

Cherry Blow Pop®
SHOT GLASS
1 part Southern Comfort®
1 part Amaretto
1 part Grenadine
Shake with ice and strain.

Cherry Bomb
SHOT GLASS

1 part Vodka
1 part Crème de Cacao (White)
1 part Grenadine

Shake with ice and strain.

Cherry Bomb #2
SHOT GLASS

2 parts Vodka
1 part Goldschläger®
1 part Light Rum

Shake with ice and strain. Garnish with Maraschino Cherry.

Cherry Demon
SHOT GLASS

1 part Jägermeister
1 part Silver Tequila
1 part Sour Cherry Liqueur
1 part Lemonade
1 part Orange Juice

Shake with ice and strain.

Cherry LifeSaver®
SHOT GLASS

1 part Southern Comfort®
1 part Amaretto
2 parts Sweet & Sour Mix
splash Grenadine

Shake with ice and strain.

Cherry Pie
SHOT GLASS

1 part Cherry Bourbon or Whiskey
2 parts RumChata

Shake with ice and strain.

Cherry Ripe Shooter
SHOT GLASS

1 part Kirschwasser
1 part Coconut Rum
1 part Irish Cream Liqueur

Shake with ice and strain.

Chi Phi
SHOT GLASS

1 part Peach Schnapps
1 part Southern Comfort®

Shake with ice and strain.

Chicken Drop
SHOT GLASS

1 part Jägermeister®
1 part Peach Schnapps
1 part Orange Juice

Shake with ice and strain.

Chick Lit
SHOT GLASS

1 part Dr. McGillicuddy's® Mentholmint Schnapps
1 part Southern Comfort®

Shake with ice and strain.

Chilly Girl
SHOT GLASS

1 part Melon Liqueur
1 part Gin
1 part Cream

Shake with ice and strain.

Chinese Mandarin
SHOT GLASS

1 part Mandarine Napoléon® Liqueur
1 part Lychee Liqueur

Shake with ice and strain.

Chip Shot
SHOT GLASS

1 part Spiced Rum
1 part Cranberry Juice Cocktail
1 part Pineapple Juice

Shake with ice and strain.

Chiquita

SHOT GLASS

1 part Vodka
2 parts Crème de Banane
1 part Milk

Shake with ice and strain.

Chocolate Banana Shot

SHOT GLASS

1 part Crème de Cacao (White)
1 part Crème de Banane

Shake with ice and strain.

Chocolate Cake

SHOT GLASS

1 part Frangelico®
1 part Vodka
1 Lemon Wedge
dash Sugar

Shake Frangelico® and Vodka with ice and strain. Moisten hand and sprinkle Sugar onto it, drink the shot, lick the Sugar and suck the Lemon.

Chocolate Cake

SHOT GLASS

3 parts RumChata
2 parts Whipped Cream Vodka
1 part Chocolate Liqueur

Shake with ice and strain.

Chocolate Chip

SHOT GLASS

2 parts RumChata
1 part Banana Liquor
1 part Chocolate Liqueur

Shake with ice and strain.

Chocolate Chip Shooter

SHOT GLASS

1 part Swiss Chocolate Almond Liqueur
1 part Crème de Cacao (White)
1 part Irish Cream Liqueur

Shake with ice and strain.

Chocolate-Covered Cherry

SHOT GLASS

1 part Coffee Liqueur
1 part Amaretto
1 part Crème de Cacao (White)
splash Grenadine

Shake with ice and strain.

Chocolate Heaven

SHOT GLASS

1 part Irish Cream Liqueur
1 part Coffee Liqueur
1 part Chocolate Liqueur
splash Caramel Syrup

Shake with ice and strain.

Chocolate Valentine

SHOT GLASS

1 part Vanilla Vodka
1 part Crème de Cacao (Dark)
1 part Cherry Juice
splash Cream
splash Club Soda

Shake with ice and strain. Because this recipe includes many ingredients, it's easier to make in volume, about 6 shots.

Christmas Cheer

SHOT GLASS

1 part Peppermint Schnapps
1 part Eggnog

Shake with ice and strain.

Christmas in Your Mouth

SHOT GLASS

1 part Fireball Cinnamon Whiskey
1 part Vanilla Vodka

Shake with ice and strain.

Chunky Snakebite

SHOT GLASS

1 part Tequila
1 part Salsa

Pour ingredients into glass neat (do not chill).

CinnaBomb
SHOT GLASS
1 part Fireball Cinnamon Whiskey
1 part RumChata
Shake with ice and strain.

Cinnamon Apple Pie
SHOT GLASS
3 parts Sour Apple Schnapps
1 part Cinnamon Schnapps
Shake with ice and strain.

Cinnamon Roll
SHOT GLASS
1 part Irish Cream Liqueur
1 part Cinnamon Schnapps
Shake with ice and strain.

Cinnamon Roll Shooter
SHOT GLASS
4 parts RumChata
1 part Spiced Rum
Shake with ice and strain.

Cinnamon Toast
SHOT GLASS
1 part Fireball Cinnamon Whiskey
1 part RumChata
Shake with ice and strain.

Cinnamon Toast Crunch
SHOT GLASS
2 parts Vanilla Vodka
1 part Goldschläger®
Shake with ice and strain.

Citron My Face
SHOT GLASS
2 parts Citrus Vodka
1 part Grand Marnier®
1 part Sweet & Sour Mix
Shake with ice and strain.

Citron Sour
SHOT GLASS
1 part Citrus Vodka
1 part Lime Juice
Shake with ice and strain.

Closed Casket
SHOT GLASS
2 parts Jägermeister®
2 parts 151-Proof Rum
1 part Fire Water®
1 part Rumple Minze®
Shake with ice and strain.

Cobra Bite
SHOT GLASS
3 parts Yukon Jack®
1 part Lime Cordial
1 part Peppermint Schnapps
Shake with ice and strain.

Cocaine
SHOT GLASS
1 part Vodka
1 part Raspberry Liqueur
1 part Grapefruit Juice
Shake with ice and strain.

Cockroach
SHOT GLASS
1 part Coffee Liqueur
1 part Drambuie®
Shake with ice and strain.

Cockteaser
SHOT GLASS
1 part Triple Sec
1 part Peach Schnapps
1 part Melon Liqueur
Shake with ice and strain.

Coco Bongo

SHOT GLASS

1 part Crème de Cacao (White)
1 part Crème de Coconut
1 part Cream

Shake with ice and strain.

Coconut Cream Pie

SHOT GLASS

1 part Coconut Rum
top with Whipped Cream

Fill a shot glass with chilled Coconut Rum and top it with Whipped Cream. Drink without using your hands.

Coma

SHOT GLASS

1 part Grand Marnier®
1 part Coffee Liqueur
1 part Sambuca

Shake with ice and strain.

Cookies 'n' Cream

SHOT GLASS

1 part Chocolate Vodka
1 part Vanilla Vodka
1 part Milk

Shake with ice and strain.

Cool Cougar

SHOT GLASS

1 part Jack Daniel's®
1 part Peppermint Schnapps

Shake with ice and strain.

Copper Camel

SHOT GLASS

1 part Irish Cream Liqueur
1 part Butterscotch Schnapps

Shake with ice and strain.

Copper Cowboy

SHOT GLASS

1 part Butterscotch Schnapps
1 part Coffee Liqueur

Shake with ice and strain.

Cordless Screwdriver

SHOT GLASS

1 part Vodka
1 Orange Wedge
dash Sugar

Shake the Vodka with ice and strain. Dip the Orange Wedge in the Sugar, drink the shot, and suck on the Orange.

Cornholio's Revenge

SHOT GLASS

1 part Coconut Rum
1 part Banana Liqueur
1 part Cherry Brandy

Shake with ice and strain.

Cortisone

SHOT GLASS

1 part Coffee Liqueur
1 part Rum
splash Vanilla Liqueur

Shake with ice and strain.

Cough Drop

SHOT GLASS

1 part Crème de Menthe (White)
1 part Blackberry Liqueur

Shake with ice and strain.

Cough Syrup

SHOT GLASS

1 part Vodka
1 part Blue Curaçao
1 part Crème de Menthe (White)

Shake with ice and strain.

Cowboy Cocksucker

SHOT GLASS

1 part Butterscotch Schnapps
1 part Irish Cream Liqueur

Shake with ice and strain.

Cowgirl

SHOT GLASS

2 parts Butterscotch Schnapps
1 part Irish Cream Liqueur

Shake with ice and strain.

Crackhouse

SHOT GLASS

1 part Blackberry Liqueur
1 part Cranberry Juice Cocktail

Shake with ice and strain.

Cranapple® Blast

SHOT GLASS

1 part Sour Apple Schnapps
1 part Cranberry Juice Cocktail
1 part Vodka

Shake with ice and strain.

Cranberry Zamboni®

SHOT GLASS

1 part Cranberry Liqueur
1 part Wild Spirit Liqueur

Shake with ice and strain.

Crash Test Dummy

SHOT GLASS

1 part Tequila
1 part Triple Sec
3 parts Margarita Mix

Shake with ice and strain.

Crazy Coco

SHOT GLASS

1 part Crème de Coconut
1 part Irish Cream Liqueur

Shake with ice and strain.

Crazy Noggie

SHOT GLASS

1 part Light Rum
1 part Vodka
1 part Southern Comfort®
1 part Amaretto

Shake with ice and strain.

Cream Hash

SHOT GLASS

1 part Dark Rum
1 part Chocolate Liqueur

Shake with ice and strain.

Cream of Coconut Pie Shooter

SHOT GLASS

3 parts RumChata
1 part Coconut Rum
1 part Whipped Cream Vodka

Shake with ice and strain.

Cream Soda Slammer

SHOT GLASS

1 part Spiced Rum
1 part Lemon-Lime Soda

Pour ingredients into glass neat (do not chill).

Creamy Johnny

SHOT GLASS

1 part Irish Cream Liqueur
1 part Raspberry Liqueur
1 part Milk
splash Grenadine

Shake with ice and strain.

Creamy Nuts

SHOT GLASS

1 part Crème de Banane
1 part Frangelico®

Shake with ice and strain.

Creamy Snatch

SHOT GLASS

1 part Butterscotch Schnapps
1 part Coffee Liqueur
2 parts Half and Half

Shake with ice and strain.

Crimson Tide

SHOT GLASS

1 part Vodka
1 part Coconut Rum
1 part Raspberry Liqueur
1 part Southern Comfort®
1 part 151-Proof Rum
1 part Cranberry Juice Cocktail
1 part Lemon-Lime Soda

Shake with ice and strain. Because this recipe includes many ingredients, it's easier to make in volume, about 6 shots.

Crispy Crunch

SHOT GLASS

1 part Frangelico®
1 part Crème de Cacao (White)

Shake with ice and strain.

Crispy Treat

SHOT GLASS

1 part RumChata
2 parts Marshmallow Vodka

Shake with ice and strain.

Crocket

SHOT GLASS

2 parts Cherry Liqueur
1 part Grenadine
1 part Sweet & Sour Mix

Shake with ice and strain.

Crossbones

SHOT GLASS

2 parts Jägermeister
2 parts Peppermint Schnapps
1 part Vanilla Vodka

Shake with ice and strain.

Crotch Shot

SHOT GLASS

1 part Butterscotch Liqueur
1 part Canadian Whisky

Shake with ice and strain.

Crowbar

SHOT GLASS

1 part Crown Royal® Whiskey
1 part 151-Proof Rum
1 part Tequila

Shake with ice and strain.

Cruz Azul

SHOT GLASS

1 part 151-Proof Rum
1 part Citrus Rum
1 part Citrus Vodka
1 part Rumple Minze®
1 part Blue Curaçao

Shake with ice and strain. Because this recipe includes many ingredients, it's easier to make in volume, about 6 shots.

Crystal Virgin

SHOT GLASS

1 part Yukon Jack®
1 part Amaretto
2 parts Cranberry Juice Cocktail

Shake with ice and strain.

Cuban Cigar

SHOT GLASS

1 part Crème de Cacao (Dark)
1 part Irish Cream Liqueur

Shake with ice and strain.

Cuban Missile Crisis

SHOT GLASS

1 part Coffee Liqueur
1 part RumChata
1 part Vanilla Vodka

Shake with ice and strain.

Cucaracha

SHOT GLASS

1 part Vodka
1 part Coffee Liqueur
1 part Tequila

Shake with ice and strain.

Cum in a Pond

SHOT GLASS

1 part Blue Curaçao
1 part Vodka
splash Irish Cream Liqueur

Shake all but Irish Cream with ice and strain. Place a few drops of Irish Cream in the center of the drink.

Cum Shot

SHOT GLASS

1 part Butterscotch Schnapps
1 part Irish Cream Liqueur

Shake with ice and strain.

Cupid's Bow

SHOT GLASS

1 part Coconut Rum
1 part Strawberry Liqueur
1 part Pineapple Juice

Shake with ice and strain.

Curly Tail Twist

SHOT GLASS

splash 151-Proof Rum
1 part Jägermeister®
1 part Root Beer Schnapps

Shake with ice and strain.

Curtain Call

SHOT GLASS

1 part Jägermeister®
1 part Melon Liqueur
1 part Jack Daniel's®

Shake with ice and strain.

D. O. A.

SHOT GLASS

1 part Crème de Cacao (White)
1 part Peach Schnapps
1 part Frangelico®

Shake with ice and strain.

Daddy's Milk

SHOT GLASS

1 part Crème de Cacao (Dark)
1 part Crème de Cacao (White)
1 part Frangelico®
splash Cream

Shake with ice and strain.

Dakota

SHOT GLASS

1 part Jim Beam®
1 part Tequila

Pour ingredients into glass neat (do not chill).

Dallas Stars

SHOT GLASS

1 part Crème de Menthe (White)
1 part Goldschläger®

Shake with ice and strain.

Damn These Dreams

SHOT GLASS

1 part Amaretto
1 part Canadian Whisky
1 part Southern Comfort
1 part Whiskey

Shake with ice and strain.

Damned If You Do

SHOT GLASS

1 part Whiskey
1 part Cinnamon Schnapps

Pour ingredients into glass neat (do not chill).

Dangerous Grandma

SHOT GLASS

1 part Coffee Liqueur
½ part Whiskey
splash Amaretto

Pour ingredients into glass neat (do not chill).

Dark Angel

SHOT GLASS

1 part Maraschino Liqueur
1 part Blackberry Liqueur
1 part Advocaat

Shake with ice and strain.

Dark Nightmare

SHOT GLASS

2 parts Coffee Liqueur
1 part Goldschläger®
1 part Milk

Shake with ice and strain.

Dawn's Early Light

SHOT GLASS

1 part Amaretto
1 part Cherry Liqueur
1 part Vanilla Schnapps
1 part Sweetened Lime Juice

Shake with ice and strain.

D-Day

SHOT GLASS

1 part 151-Proof Rum
1 part Citrus Vodka
1 part Crème de Banane
1 part Raspberry Liqueur
1 part Orange Juice

Shake with ice and strain. Because this recipe includes many ingredients, it's easier to make in volume, about 6 shots.

Dead Bird

SHOT GLASS

1 part Jägermeister®
1 part Wild Turkey® Bourbon

Shake with ice and strain.

Dead End

SHOT GLASS

1 part Amaretto
1 part Coffee Liqueur
1 part Grain Alcohol
1 part Irish Cream Liqueur

Shake with ice and strain.

Dead Frog

SHOT GLASS

1 part Coffee Liqueur
1 part Irish Cream Liqueur
1 part Crème de Menthe (White)

Shake with ice and strain.

Dead Green Frog

SHOT GLASS

1 part Rumple Minze®
1 part Coffee Liqueur
1 part Crème de Menthe (Green)
1 part Irish Cream Liqueur
1 part Vodka

Shake with ice and strain.

Dear Sperm

SHOT GLASS

1 part Jägermeister®
1 part Irish Cream Liqueur

Shake with ice and strain.

Death from Within

SHOT GLASS

1 part Spiced Rum
1 part Dark Rum
1 part Vodka

Shake with ice and strain.

Death Note

SHOT GLASS

1 part Cinnamon Schnapps
1 part Sambuca
1 part Silver Tequila

Shake with ice and strain.

Death Row

SHOT GLASS

1 part Jack Daniel's®
1 part 151-Proof Rum

Shake with ice and strain.

Death Wish

SHOT GLASS

1 part Wild Turkey® 101
1 part Rumple Minze®
1 part Jägermeister®

Shake with ice and strain.

Deep Blue Something

SHOT GLASS

1 part Blue Curaçao
1 part Peach Schnapps
1 part Sweet & Sour Mix
1 part Lemonade
1 part Pineapple Juice

Shake with ice and strain. Because this recipe includes many ingredients, it's easier to make in volume, about 6 shots.

The Demon Knight

SHOT GLASS

1 part Peppermint Schnapps
1 part Vodka
1 part Fruit Punch

Shake with ice and strain.

Demons Breeding

SHOT GLASS

1 part Black Sambuca
1 part Jägermeister
1 part Peppermint Schnapps

Shake with ice and strain.

Desert Skies

SHOT GLASS

1 part Apricot Brandy
1 part Rum Crème Liqueur
1 part Coffee Liqueur

Shake with ice and strain.

Detox

SHOT GLASS

1 part Peach Schnapps
1 part Vodka
1 part Cranberry Juice Cocktail

Shake with ice and strain.

Devastating Body Rocker

SHOT GLASS

1 part Blackberry Brandy
1 part Gin

Shake with ice and strain.

Devil's Kiss

SHOT GLASS

1 part Dark Rum
1 part Coffee Liqueur
1 part Grand Marnier®

Shake with ice and strain.

Devil's Mouthwash

SHOT GLASS

1 part Black Sambuca
1 part Southern Comfort®

Shake with ice and strain.

Diamond Cutter

SHOT GLASS

1 part 151-Proof Rum
1 part Spiced Rum
1 part Grenadine

Shake with ice and strain.

Diesel Fuel

SHOT GLASS

1 part Rum
1 part Jägermeister®

Shake with ice and strain.

Dirtiest Ernie

SHOT GLASS

1 part 151-Proof Rum
1 part Grain Alcohol
1 part Rumple Minze®

Shake with ice and strain.

Dirty Bong Water
SHOT GLASS

1 part Chambord
1 part Coconut Rum
1 part Sweet & Sour Mix
1 part Pineapple Juice
splash Blue Curaçao

Shake with ice and strain.

Dirty Diaper
SHOT GLASS

1 part Vodka
1 part Amaretto
1 part Southern Comfort®
1 part Melon Liqueur
1 part Raspberry Liqueur
1 part Orange Juice

Shake with ice and strain. Because this recipe includes many ingredients, it's easier to make in volume, about 6 shots.

Dirty Girl Scout Cookie
SHOT GLASS

1 part Coffee Liqueur
1 part Irish Cream Liqueur
1 part Crème de Menthe (White)

Shake with ice and strain.

Dirty Irish Whiskey
SHOT GLASS

1 part Irish Cream Liqueur
1 part Irish Whiskey

Shake with ice and strain.

The Dirty Leprechaun
SHOT GLASS

1 part Jägermeister®
1 part Irish Cream Liqueur
1 part Midori®

Shake with ice and strain.

Dirty Monkey
SHOT GLASS

2 parts RumChata
1 part Banana Liqueur

Shake with ice and strain.

Dirty Navel
SHOT GLASS

1 part Crème de Cacao (White)
1 part Triple Sec

Shake with ice and strain.

Dirty Rotten Scoundrel
SHOT GLASS

1 part Vodka
1 part Melon Liqueur

Shake with ice and strain.

Dirty Toilet
SHOT GLASS

1 part Butterscotch Liqueur
1 part Coffee Liqueur
1 part Irish Cream Liqueur

Shake with ice and strain.

Dirty Whore
SHOT GLASS

1 part Apple Vodka
1 part Jägermeister
1 part Raspberry Vodka

Shake with ice and strain.

Disney® on Ice
SHOT GLASS

1 part Peppermint Schnapps
1 part Grenadine
1 part 151-Proof Rum
splash Lemon Juice

Shake with ice and strain.

Dizzy Damage
SHOT GLASS

1 part Jägermeister®
1 part Rumple Minze®
1 part Goldschläger®

Shake with ice and strain.

The Doc's Medicine
SHOT GLASS
1 part Scotch
1 part Tequila
Shake with ice and strain.

Dolt Bolt
SHOT GLASS
1 part Grain Alcohol
1 part Rumple Minze®
1 part Goldschläger®
Shake with ice and strain.

Dominator
SHOT GLASS
2 parts Crème de Menthe (White)
1 part Coffee
1 part Triple Sec
Shake with ice and strain.

Don't Thrust Me
SHOT GLASS
1 part Goldschläger®
1 part Butterscotch Schnapps
1 part 151-Proof Rum
Shake with ice and strain.

Double Berry Blast
SHOT GLASS
1 part Blueberry Schnapps
1 part Strawberry Liqueur
Shake with ice and strain.

Double Chocolate
SHOT GLASS
1 part Chocolate Liqueur
1 part Crème de Cacao (Dark)
Shake with ice and strain.

Double Gold
SHOT GLASS
1 part Goldschläger®
1 part Gold Tequila
Shake with ice and strain.

Double Homicide
SHOT GLASS
1 part Jägermeister®
1 part Goldschläger®
1 part Orange Juice
Shake with ice and strain.

The Double Team
SHOT GLASS
1 part Amaretto
1 part Rum
Shake with ice and strain.

Doublemint® Blowjob
SHOT GLASS
1 part Coffee Liqueur
1 part Peppermint Schnapps
2 parts Cream
Shake with ice and strain.

Doucet Devil
SHOT GLASS
1 part Amaretto
1 part Southern Comfort®
1 part Crème de Banane
Shake with ice and strain.

Down the Street
SHOT GLASS
1 part Vodka
1 part Grand Marnier®
1 part Raspberry Liqueur
1 part Orange Juice
Shake with ice and strain.

Downinone
SHOT GLASS
2 parts Blavod® Black Vodka
1 part Triple Sec
1 part Gold Rum
Shake with ice and strain.

Dr. Banana

SHOT GLASS

1 part Tequila
1 part Crème de Banane

Shake with ice and strain.

Dragon's Breath

SHOT GLASS

1 part Fire Water®
1 part 151-Proof Rum

Pour ingredients into glass neat (do not chill).

Dragon's Kiss

SHOT GLASS

1 part Fireball Cinnamon Whiskey
1 part Cranberry Juice

Shake with ice and strain.

Drunk Irish Monk

SHOT GLASS

1 part Irish Cream Liqueur
1 part Frangelico®
1 part Brandy

Shake with ice and strain.

Dublin Doubler

SHOT GLASS

1 part Irish Whiskey
1 part Irish Cream Liqueur

Shake with ice and strain.

Duck Call Shooter

SHOT GLASS

1 part 151-Proof Rum
1 part Coconut Rum
splash Cranberry Juice Cocktail
splash Pineapple Juice

Shake with ice and strain.

Duck Fuck

SHOT GLASS

2 parts Gin
1 part Vodka
1 part Beer

Shake with ice and strain.

Dumbfuck

SHOT GLASS

1 part Cinnamon Schnapps
1 part Canadian Whisky

Shake with ice and strain.

Earth Tremor

SHOT GLASS

1 part Gin
1 part Scotch
1 part Pernod®

Shake with ice and strain.

Earthquake Shooter

SHOT GLASS

1 part Sambuca
1 part Amaretto
1 part Southern Comfort®

Shake with ice and strain.

El Diablillo

SHOT GLASS

3 parts Silver Tequila
1 part Crème de Cassis

Shake with ice and strain.

Electric Banana

SHOT GLASS

1 part Silver Tequila
1 part Crème de Banane
1 part Lime Cordial

Shake with ice and strain.

Electric Kamikaze

SHOT GLASS

1 part Triple Sec
1 part Vodka
1 part Blue Curaçao
1 part Lime Juice

Shake with ice and strain.

Electric Smurf®

SHOT GLASS

1 part Coconut Rum
1 part Blue Curaçao

Shake with ice and strain.

Electric Storm

SHOT GLASS

1 part Cinnamon Schnapps
1 part Irish Cream Liqueur
1 part Jägermeister
1 part Peppermint Schnapps

Shake with ice and strain.

Elvis

SHOT GLASS

1 part Banana Liqueur
1 part Hazelnut Liqueur

Shake with ice and strain.

Elvis in Vegas

SHOT GLASS

1 part Banana Liqueur
1 part Hazelnut Liqueur
dash Goldschläger®

Shake with ice and strain.

Elvis Presley

SHOT GLASS

1 part Vodka
1 part Frangelico®
1 part Crème de Banane
splash Irish Cream Liqueur

Shake with ice and strain.

Embryo

SHOT GLASS

1 part Peppermint Schnapps
splash Cream
splash Grenadine

Place a few drops of Cream and a few drops of Grenadine in the center of a shot of Peppermint Schnapps.

Emerald Rocket

SHOT GLASS

1 part Vodka
1 part Coffee Liqueur
1 part Melon Liqueur
1 part Irish Cream Liqueur

Shake with ice and strain.

The End of the World

SHOT GLASS

1 part 151-Proof Rum
1 part Wild Turkey® 101
1 part Vodka

Pour ingredients into glass neat (do not chill).

Epidural

SHOT GLASS

1 part Grain Alcohol
1 part Vodka
1 part Coconut Rum
1 part Crème de Coconut

Shake with ice and strain.

The Equalizer

SHOT GLASS

1 part Peach Schnapps
1 part Pineapple Juice
1 part Orange Juice

Shake with ice and strain.

Erect Nipple

SHOT GLASS

1 part Silver Tequila
1 part Sambuca

Shake with ice and strain.

Eskimo Joe

SHOT GLASS

1 part Cinnamon Schnapps
1 part Crème de Menthe (Green)
1 part Irish Cream Liqueur
1 part Milk

Shake with ice and strain.

Evil Dead

SHOT GLASS

1 part Dark Rum
1 part Jägermeister
1 part Vodka

Build in order. Do not chill.

Explosive

SHOT GLASS

2 parts Tequila Reposado
1 part Triple Sec

Shake with ice and strain.

Extended Jail Sentence

SHOT GLASS

1 part Jack Daniel's®
1 part Southern Comfort®
1 part Tequila
splash Pineapple Juice

Shake with ice and strain.

Eyeball

SHOT GLASS

1 part Irish Cream Liqueur
splash Blue Curaçao
splash Grenadine

Put a splash of Grenadine in the bottom of a shot glass, then top with Irish Cream Liqueur. Place a small splash of Blue Curaçao in the center for the iris.

F-69

SHOT GLASS

1 part Dark Rum
1 part Coffee Liqueur
1 part Amaretto
2 parts Irish Cream Liqueur

Shake with ice and strain.

Fat Box

SHOT GLASS

1 part Crème de Banane
1 part Blue Curaçao
1 part Coconut Rum
1 part Pineapple Juice

Shake with ice and strain.

Fat Cat

SHOT GLASS

2 parts Irish Cream Liqueur
1 part Amaretto
1 part Banana Liqueur

Shake with ice and strain.

Favorite Shooter

SHOT GLASS

1 part Triple Sec
1 part Vanilla Liqueur

Shake with ice and strain.

Fiery Kiss

SHOT GLASS

1 part Cinnamon Schnapps
splash Honey

Shake with ice and strain.

Fifth Avenue

SHOT GLASS

1 part Crème de Cacao (Dark)
1 part Apricot Brandy

Shake with ice and strain.

Fig

SHOT GLASS

1 part Coconut Rum
1 part Pineapple Juice
1 part Cranberry Juice Cocktail

Shake with ice and strain.

Finger Me Good

SHOT GLASS

1 part Butterscotch Schnapps
3 parts Crown Royal® Whiskey

Pour ingredients into glass neat (do not chill).

Fire and Ice

SHOT GLASS

1 part Cinnamon Schnapps
1 part Irish Cream Liqueur

Shake with ice and strain.

Fire & Ice

SHOT GLASS

1 part Fireball Cinnamon Whiskey
1 part Mint Liqueur

Shake with ice and strain.

Fireball

SHOT GLASS

1 part Coffee Liqueur
1 part Ouzo

Shake with ice and strain.

Fireball Oatmeal Cookie

SHOT GLASS

1 part Butterscotch Liqueur
1 part Coffee Liqueur
1 part Fireball Cinnamon Whiskey
1 part Irish Cream Liqueur

Shake with ice and strain.

Fireball Sin-Sation

SHOT GLASS

2 parts Fireball Cinnamon Whiskey
1 part Chocolate Liqueur
1 part Vanilla Liqueur

Shake with ice and strain.

Firetruck

SHOT GLASS

1 part Jägermeister®
1 part Ginger Ale

Pour ingredients into glass neat (do not chill).

Five Aces

SHOT GLASS

1 part Amaretto
1 part Apricot Brandy
1 part Sour Apple Schnapps
1 part Vodka
1 part Lime Juice

Shake with ice and strain.

Five Star General

SHOT GLASS

1 part Jägermeister®
1 part 151-Proof Rum
1 part Rumple Minze®
1 part Goldschläger®
1 part Tequila

Shake with ice and strain. Because this recipe includes many ingredients, it's easier to make in volume, about 6 shots.

Flamethrower

SHOT GLASS

1 part Vodka
2 parts Cinnamon Schnapps

Shake with ice and strain.

Flamethrower #2

SHOT GLASS

1 part Fireball Cinnamon Whiskey
1 part Sweet & Sour Mix

Shake with ice and strain.

Flaming Cocaine

SHOT GLASS

1 part Cinnamon Schnapps
1 part Vodka
splash Cranberry Juice Cocktail

Shake with ice and strain.

Flaming Squeegee

SHOT GLASS

1 part Rum
1 part Vodka
1 part Lemon Juice
1 part Orange Juice

Shake with ice and strain.

Flashfire

SHOT GLASS

1 part Cinnamon Schnapps
1 part Southern Comfort®
1 part Wild Turkey® 101

Pour ingredients into glass neat (do not chill).

Flat Tire

SHOT GLASS

2 parts Tequila
1 part Black Sambuca

Shake with ice and strain.

Flooze Booze

SHOT GLASS

1 part Jägermeister®
1 part Root Beer Schnapps

Shake with ice and strain.

Flügel

SHOT GLASS

1 part Cranberry Vodka
1 part Red Bull® Energy Drink

Pour ingredients into glass neat (do not chill).

Flukeman

SHOT GLASS

1 part Irish Cream Liqueur
1 part Melon Liqueur

Pour ingredients into glass neat (do not chill).

Fog

SHOT GLASS

3 parts Vodka
1 part Lime Juice

Shake with ice and strain.

The Four Horsemen

SHOT GLASS

1 part Jägermeister®
1 part Tequila
1 part Sambuca
1 part Rum

Pour ingredients into glass neat (do not chill).

The Four Horsemen #2

SHOT GLASS

1 part Jack Daniel's®
1 part Sambuca
1 part Jägermeister®
1 part Rumple Minze®

Shake with ice and strain.

Foxy Lady #2

SHOT GLASS

1 part Amaretto
1 part Crème de Banane
1 part Cream

Shake with ice and strain.

Freaking Shot

SHOT GLASS

1 part Raspberry Liqueur
1 part Vodka
1 part Cranberry Juice Cocktail

Shake with ice and strain.

Freddy Krueger®

SHOT GLASS

1 part Sambuca
1 part Jägermeister®
1 part Vodka

Shake with ice and strain.

Freebase
SHOT GLASS
1 part Coffee Liqueur
1 part Light Rum
1 part 151-Proof Rum
Shake with ice and strain.

Freight Train
SHOT GLASS
1 part Tequila
1 part Irish Cream Liqueur
Shake with ice and strain.

French Toast
SHOT GLASS
1 part Irish Cream Liqueur
1 part Cinnamon Schnapps
1 part Butterscotch Schnapps
Shake with ice and strain.

Frigid Alaskan Nipple
SHOT GLASS
1 part Butterscotch Schnapps
1 part Rumple Minze®
2 parts Vodka
Shake with ice and strain.

Frisky Witch
SHOT GLASS
1 part Sambuca
1 part Vodka
Shake with ice and strain.

Froggermeister
SHOT GLASS
1 part Jägermeister
1 part Melon Liqueur
Shake with ice and strain.

Frog in a Blender
SHOT GLASS
2 parts Tequila
1 part Sloe Gin
splash Sweet Vermouth
Shake with ice and strain.

Fruit Loop®
SHOT GLASS
1 part Amaretto
1 part Blue Curaçao
1 part Grenadine
1 part Milk
Shake with ice and strain.

Fruit of the Loom®
SHOT GLASS
1 part Banana Liqueur
1 part Melon Liqueur
1 part Cherry Brandy
1 part Coconut Rum
Shake with ice and strain.

Fruit Salad
SHOT GLASS
1 part Sour Apple Schnapps
1 part Cherry Schnapps
1 part Grape Schnapps
splash Orange Juice
Shake with ice and strain.

Fruit Tongue Fuck
SHOT GLASS
1 part Citrus Rum
1 part Light Rum
1 part Dark Rum
1 part Peach Schnapps
Shake with ice and strain.

Fruity Fairy
SHOT GLASS
1 part Peach Schnapps
1 part Grenadine
1 part Melon Liqueur
Shake with ice and strain.

Fruity Pebbles®
SHOT GLASS
1 part Vodka
1 part Blue Curaçao
1 part Milk
splash Grenadine
Shake with ice and strain.

Fuck Me Running
SHOT GLASS

1 part Jack Daniel's®
1 part Peach Schnapps
1 part Blackberry Brandy

Shake with ice and strain.

Fuck Me Up
SHOT GLASS

1 part Coffee Liqueur
1 part Irish Cream Liqueur
1 part Banana Liqueur

Shake with ice and strain.

Fucking Hot
SHOT GLASS

1 part Pepper Vodka
1 part Cinnamon Schnapps

Pour ingredients into glass neat (do not chill).

Funky Chicken
SHOT GLASS

1 part Tequila
1 part Wild Turkey® Bourbon

Shake with ice and strain.

Furious George
SHOT GLASS

2 parts 99 Bananas Liqueur
2 parts Fireball Cinnamon Whiskey
1 part Chocolate Liqueur

Shake with ice and strain.

Fuzzy Blue Gobbler
SHOT GLASS

1 part Blue Curaçao
1 part Peach Schnapps
1 part Wild Turkey Bourbon

Shake with ice and strain.

Fuzzy Cherry
SHOT GLASS

1 part Peach Schnapps
1 part Sour Cherry Liqueur
1 part Cranberry Juice
dash Lime Juice

Shake with ice and strain.

Fuzzy Irishman
SHOT GLASS

1 part Raspberry Liqueur
1 part Butterscotch Schnapps
1 part Irish Cream Liqueur

Pour ingredients into glass neat (do not chill).

Fuzzy Logic
SHOT GLASS

1 part Coffee Liqueur
1 part Peach Schnapps
2 parts Cream

Shake with ice and strain.

Fuzzy Melon Shooter
SHOT GLASS

1 part Peach Schnapps
1 part Pineapple Juice
1 part Orange Juice
1 part Melon Liqueur
splash Blue Curaçao

Shake with ice and strain. Because this recipe includes many ingredients, it's easier to make in volume, about 6 shots.

Fuzzy Monkey
SHOT GLASS

1 part Vodka
1 part Peach Schnapps
1 part Crème de Banane
1 part Orange Juice

Shake with ice and strain.

Fuzzy Monkey #2

SHOT GLASS

3 parts Crème de Banane
2 parts Orange Juice
1 part Peach Schnapps

Shake with ice and strain.

Fuzzy Nutted Banana

SHOT GLASS

1 part Peach Schnapps
1 part Amaretto
1 part Banana Liqueur
1 part Orange Juice
splash Grenadine

Shake with ice and strain. Because this recipe includes many ingredients, it's easier to make in volume, about 6 shots.

Fuzzy Pirate

SHOT GLASS

1 part Dark Rum
1 part Peach Schnapps
splash Triple Sec

Shake with ice and strain.

Fuzzy Russian

SHOT GLASS

1 part Vodka
1 part Peach Schnapps

Shake with ice and strain.

Fuzzy Smurf®

SHOT GLASS

1 part Blue Curaçao
1 part Peach Schnapps

Shake with ice and strain.

G Spot

SHOT GLASS

1 part Southern Comfort®
1 part Raspberry Liqueur
1 part Orange Juice

Shake with ice and strain.

G. T. O.

SHOT GLASS

1 part Vodka
1 part Rum
1 part Gin
1 part Southern Comfort®
1 part Amaretto
1 part Grenadine
4 parts Orange Juice

Shake with ice and strain. Because this recipe includes many ingredients, it's easier to make in volume, about 6 shots.

Galactic Ale

SHOT GLASS

2 parts Vodka
2 parts Blue Curaçao
1 part Lime Juice
splash Blackberry Liqueur

Shake with ice and strain.

Gasoline

SHOT GLASS

1 part Southern Comfort®
1 part Tequila

Shake with ice and strain.

Gator Cum

SHOT GLASS

1 part Vodka
1 part Crème de Cacao (Dark)
1 part Frangelico®

Shake with ice and strain.

Gator Tail

SHOT GLASS

1 part Melon Liqueur
1 part Rum
1 part Pineapple Juice
1 part Coconut Rum

Shake with ice and strain.

Geiger Counter

SHOT GLASS

1 part 151-Proof Rum
1 part Jägermeister®

Pour ingredients into glass neat (do not chill).

Gentle Bull Shot

SHOT GLASS

1 part Coffee
1 part Tequila Reposado
splash Cream

Shake with ice and strain.

German Burrito

SHOT GLASS

1 part Tequila
1 part Jägermeister®

Shake with ice and strain.

German Death

SHOT GLASS

1 part Jägermeister®
1 parts Rumple Minze®

Shake with ice and strain.

German Fruit Cup

SHOT GLASS

1 part Rum
1 part Blackberry Liqueur
1 part Blue Curaçao
1 part Grenadine
1 part Honey

Shake with ice and strain. Because this recipe includes many ingredients, it's easier to make in volume, about 6 shots.

Gestapo

SHOT GLASS

1 part Rumple Minze®
1 part Jägermeister®

Shake with ice and strain.

Getaway Car

SHOT GLASS

3 parts Peach Schnapps
1 part Citrus Vodka

Shake with ice and strain.

Ghetto Blaster

SHOT GLASS

1 part Coffee Liqueur
1 part Sambuca
1 part Tequila
1 part Rye Whiskey

Shake with ice and strain.

Ghostbuster

SHOT GLASS

1 part Vodka
1 part Melon Liqueur
1 part Pineapple Juice
1 part Orange Juice

Shake with ice and strain.

Gila Monster

SHOT GLASS

1 part Jägermeister®
1 part Tequila
1 part Orange Juice

Shake with ice and strain.

Gilligan

SHOT GLASS

1 part Coconut Rum
1 part Watermelon Schnapps

Shake with ice and strain.

Gin and Beer It

SHOT GLASS

2 parts Gin
1 part Beer

Pour ingredients into glass neat (do not chill).

Gingerbread Man

SHOT GLASS

1 part Goldschläger®
1 part Irish Cream Liqueur
1 part Butterscotch Schnapps
1 part Vodka

Shake with ice and strain.

Gingerbread Man #2

SHOT GLASS

1 part Fireball Cinnamon Whiskey
1 part Ginger Liqueur
1 part RumChata

Shake with ice and strain.

The Girl Mom Warned You About

SHOT GLASS

1 part Grenadine
1 part Triple Sec
1 part Rum
1 part Melon Liqueur
1 part Blue Curaçao

Shake with ice and strain. Because this recipe includes many ingredients, it's easier to make in volume, about 6 shots.

Girl Scout Cookie

SHOT GLASS

1 part Coffee Liqueur
1 part Milk
1 part Rumple Minze®

Shake with ice and strain.

Gladiator's Stinger

SHOT GLASS

3 parts Brandy
2 parts Crème de Menthe (White)
1 part Sambuca

Shake with ice and strain.

Glitterbox

SHOT GLASS

1 part Black Sambuca
1 part Coffee Liqueur

Shake with ice and strain.

Godhead

SHOT GLASS

1 part Rum
1 part Vodka
1 part Raspberry Liqueur
splash Lime Juice
splash 151-Proof Rum

Shake with ice and strain.

Godzilla®

SHOT GLASS

2 parts Silver Tequila
1 part Orange Bitters

Shake with ice and strain.

Gold Baron

SHOT GLASS

3 parts Rumple Minze®
1 part Goldschläger®

Shake with ice and strain.

Gold Fever

SHOT GLASS

1 part Goldschläger®
1 part Gold Tequila

Shake with ice and strain.

Gold Digger

SHOT GLASS

1 part Jack Daniel's®
1 part Goldschläger®

Pour ingredients into glass neat (do not chill).

Gold Digger in Dublin

SHOT GLASS

1 part Fireball Cinnamon Whiskey
1 part Goldschläger®
1 part Irish Cream Liqueur

Shake with ice and strain.

Golden Cinnamon Grahams

SHOT GLASS

3 parts RumChata
1 part Goldschläger®

Shake with ice and strain.

Golden Comfort

SHOT GLASS

1 part Goldschläger®
1 part Southern Comfort®
1 part Jägermeister®

Shake with ice and strain.

Golden Haze

SHOT GLASS

1 part Blue Curaçao
1 part Campari
1 part Goldschläger®

Shake with ice and strain.

Golden Russian

SHOT GLASS

1 part Vodka
1 part Galliano®

Shake with ice and strain.

Golden Sensation

SHOT GLASS

2 parts Amaretto
2 parts Coffee Liqueur
1 part Crème de Banane
1 part Crème de Cacao (Dark)
1 part Goldschläger®

Shake with ice and strain. Because this recipe includes many ingredients, it's easier to make in volume, about 6 shots.

Good and Plenty

SHOT GLASS

1 part Sambuca
1 part Tequila

Shake with ice and strain.

Goody Two Shoes

SHOT GLASS

2 parts Passion Fruit Liqueur
1 part Pineapple Juice
1 part Blue Curaçao

Shake with ice and strain.

Goosebumps

SHOT GLASS

1 part Blueberry Schnapps
1 part Peach Schnapps
1 part Vodka

Shake with ice and strain.

Gorilla Fart

SHOT GLASS

1 part Rum
1 part Wild Turkey® Bourbon

Shake with ice and strain.

Grab My Coconuts

SHOT GLASS

1 part Dark Rum
1 part Crème de Coconut
2 parts Pineapple Juice

Shake with ice and strain.

The Graduate

SHOT GLASS

3 parts Southern Comfort®
2 parts Pineapple Juice
1 part Amaretto

Shake with ice and strain.

Grandma's Candy

SHOT GLASS

1 part Blue Curaçao
1 part Sambuca

Shake with ice and strain.

Grandpa Is Alive

SHOT GLASS

2 parts Amaretto
1 part Vodka

Shake with ice and strain.

Grape Crush

SHOT GLASS

1 part Chambord
1 part Vodka
1 part Sweetened Lime Juice

Shake with ice and strain.

Grape Juice

SHOT GLASS

2 parts Chambord
1 part Blue Curaçao
1 part Cranberry Juice

Shake with ice and strain.

Grape KoolAid®

SHOT GLASS

1 part Blue Curaçao
1 part Southern Comfort®
1 part Raspberry Liqueur
1 part Pineapple Juice
1 part Sweet & Sour Mix
2 parts Cranberry Juice Cocktail

Shake with ice and strain. Because this recipe includes many ingredients, it's easier to make in volume, about 6 shots.

Grapevine Special

SHOT GLASS

1 part Brandy
1 part Apricot Brandy
1 part Banana Liqueur
1 part Cherry Liqueur
1 part Grand Marnier®

Shake with ice and strain. Because this recipe includes many ingredients, it's easier to make in volume, about 6 shots.

Grasshopper Shot

SHOT GLASS

1 part Brandy
1 part Blue Curaçao

Shake with ice and strain.

Grave Digger

SHOT GLASS

1 part 151-Proof Rum
1 part Jim Beam®

Shake with ice and strain.

Grazysurfer

SHOT GLASS

1 part Dark Rum
1 part Goldschläger®
1 part Sambuca

Pour ingredients into glass neat (do not chill).

Greek Fire

SHOT GLASS

3 parts Brandy
1 part Ouzo

Shake with ice and strain.

Greek Lightning

SHOT GLASS

1 part Ouzo
1 part Vodka
1 part Raspberry Liqueur

Shake with ice and strain.

Greek Revolution

SHOT GLASS

1 part Grenadine
1 part Ouzo

Shake with ice and strain.

The Greek Way

SHOT GLASS

2 parts Ouzo
1 part Metaxa®

Shake with ice and strai.

Green Aftermath

SHOT GLASS

1 part Peppermint Schnapps
1 part Mountain Dew®

Pour ingredients into glass neat (do not chill).

Green Apple Kamikazi

SHOT GLASS

1 part Melon Liqueur
1 part Vodka
1 part Sweet & Sour Mix
splash Lime Juice

Shake with ice and strain.

Green Apple Toffee

SHOT GLASS

1 part Vodka
1 part Butterscotch Schnapps
1 part Sour Apple Schnapps

Shake with ice and strain.

Green Booger

SHOT GLASS

1 part Irish Cream Liqueur
1 part Crème de Menthe (White)
splash Lime Juice

Shake with ice and strain.

Green Card

SHOT GLASS

1 part Blue Raspberry Liqueur
1 part Bourbon
1 part Cointreau
1 part Vodka

Shake with ice and strain.

Green Cookie Monster®

SHOT GLASS

2 parts Gin
1 part Melon Liqueur
1 part Rum

Shake with ice and strain.

Green Fairy

SHOT GLASS

1 part Absinthe
1 part Melon Liqueur
1 part Peach Schnapps

Shake with ice and strain.

Green Fly Shooter

SHOT GLASS

1 part Crème de Menthe (Green)
1 part Melon Liqueur

Shake with ice and strain.

Green Gecko

SHOT GLASS

1 part Crème de Menthe (White)
1 part Triple Sec
splash Limoncello

Shake with ice and strain.

Green Gummy Bear

SHOT GLASS

1 part Orange Vodka
1 part Melon Liqueur
splash Lemon-Lime Soda

Shake with ice and strain.

Green Hornet

SHOT GLASS

1 part Melon Liqueur
1 part Butterscotch Liqueur
splash Ginger Ale

Build in order. Do not chill.

Green Jolly Rancher®

SHOT GLASS

1 part Melon Liqueur
1 part Southern Comfort®
splash Sweet & Sour Mix

Shake with ice and strain.

Green Lizard on the Beach

SHOT GLASS

2 parts Crème de Banane
1 part Blue Curaçao
splash Orange Juice

Shake with ice and strain.

Green Machine
SHOT GLASS

1 part Blue Raspberry Liqueur
1 part Vodka
1 part Energy Drink

Shake with ice and strain.

Green Motherfucker
SHOT GLASS

1 part 151-Proof Rum
1 part Crème de Menthe (Green)

Shake with ice and strain.

Green Sneaker
SHOT GLASS

2 parts Vodka
1 part Melon Liqueur
1 part Cointreau®
splash Cream

Shake with ice and strain.

Green Thing
SHOT GLASS

1 part Coconut Rum
1 part Melon Liqueur
2 parts Pineapple Juice

Shake with ice and strain.

Green Voodoo
SHOT GLASS

1 part Melon Liqueur
1 part Malibu® Rum
1 part Lemon-Lime Soda
splash Triple Sec
splash Sweet & Sour Mix

Shake with ice and strain.

Grenade
SHOT GLASS

1 part Vodka
1 part Triple Sec
1 part Grenadine

Shake with ice and strain.

Greyhound
SHOT GLASS

1 part Cointreau®
1 part Drambuie®

Shake with ice and strain.

Gross One
SHOT GLASS

1 part Vodka
1 part Gin
1 part Jack Daniel's®
1 part Amaretto
1 part Sambuca

Shake with ice and strain.
Because this recipe includes many ingredients, it's easier to make in volume, about 6 shots.

Ground Zero
SHOT GLASS

1 part Peppermint Schnapps
1 part Vodka
1 part Coffee Liqueur

Shake with ice and strain.

Gumball Hummer
SHOT GLASS

1 part Raspberry Liqueur
1 part Banana Liqueur
1 part Grapefruit Juice

Shake with ice and strain.

Gumball Shot
SHOT GLASS

1 part Blue Curaçao
1 part Jägermeister
1 part Red Bull Energy Drink

Shake with ice and strain.

Gummy Worm
SHOT GLASS

1 part Blue Curaçao
1 part Mango Vodka
1 part Raspberry Vodka
1 part Lemon-Lime Soda

Shake with ice and strain.

Haggis

SHOT GLASS

1 part Bourbon
1 part Cognac
1 part Southern Comfort®

Shake with ice and strain.

Hail, Caesar

SHOT GLASS

1 part Melon Liqueur
1 part Crème de Banane
1 part Sweet & Sour Mix

Shake with ice and strain.

Hairy Blue Balls

SHOT GLASS

1 part Amaretto
1 part Blueberry Schnapps
1 part Southern Comfort

Shake with ice and strain.

Halloween Shooter

SHOT GLASS

1 part Licor 43®
1 part Sambuca

Shake with ice and strain.

Hangin' Around

SHOT GLASS

1 part Silver Tequila
1 part Triple Sec
1 part Grenadine

Shake with ice and strain.

Happy Camper

SHOT GLASS

1 part Amaretto
1 part Frangelico®
1 part Coffee Liqueur

Shake with ice and strain.

Happy Irish

SHOT GLASS

1 part Crème de Menthe (White)
1 part Sambuca

Shake with ice and strain.

Happy Juice

SHOT GLASS

1 part Lemon Juice
1 part Vodka

Shake with ice and strain.

Happy Tooth

SHOT GLASS

1 part Coffee Liqueur
1 part Sambuca

Shake with ice and strain.

Harley Davidson®

SHOT GLASS

1 part Yukon Jack®
1 part Jack Daniel's®

Shake with ice and strain.

Harley Oil

SHOT GLASS

2 parts Jägermeister®
1 part Coffee Liqueur

Shake with ice and strain.

Harsh

SHOT GLASS

1 part Tequila
1 part Jägermeister®

Shake with ice and strain.

Hawaiian Around

SHOT GLASS

1 part Amaretto
1 part Southern Comfort
1 part Vodka
1 part Orange Juice
1 part Pineapple Juice
splash Grenadine

Shake with ice and strain.

Hawaiian Punch® from Hell

SHOT GLASS

1 part Vodka
1 part Southern Comfort®
1 part Amaretto
splash Orange Juice
splash Lemon-Lime Soda
splash Grenadine

Shake with ice and strain. Because this recipe includes many ingredients, it's easier to make in volume, about 6 shots.

Hawoo-Woo

SHOT GLASS

1 part Vodka
1 part Peach Schnapps
1 part Cranberry Juice Cocktail
1 part Pineapple Juice

Shake with ice and strain.

Head in the Sand

SHOT GLASS

1 part Crème de Menthe (White)
1 part Brandy
1 part Silver Tequila
1 part Grenadine

Shake with ice and strain.

Head Rush

SHOT GLASS

1 part Peach Schnapps
1 part Pear Liqueur
1 part Sambuca

Shake with ice and strain.

Heavenly Orgasm

SHOT GLASS

2 parts Frangelico®
1 part Amaretto
1 part Irish Cream Liqueur

Shake with ice and strain.

Heavy Metal

SHOT GLASS

1 part Jägermeister
1 part Goldschläger®

Build in order. Do not chill.

Heavy Navel

SHOT GLASS

1 part Jägermeister
1 part Goldschläger®
1 part Peach Schnapps

Build in order. Do not chill.

Heilig

SHOT GLASS

1 part Vodka
1 part Blueberry Schnapps
1 part Cranberry Juice Cocktail

Shake with ice and strain.

Helicopter

SHOT GLASS

1 part Green Chartreuse®
1 part 151-Proof Rum

Pour ingredients into glass neat (do not chill).

Hellfire

SHOT GLASS

1 part Fireball Cinnamon Whiskey
1 part Irish Cream Liqueur
1 part Peach Schnapps
3–5 drops Grenadine

Shake all but Grenadine with ice and strain. Slowly add the drops of Grenadine to the center of the shot.

Hellraiser

SHOT GLASS

1 part Melon Liqueur
1 part Black Sambuca
1 part Strawberry Liqueur

Shake with ice and strain.

Hell's Eye

SHOT GLASS

1 part Canadian Whisky
2 parts Coffee Liqueur
1 part Milk

Shake with ice and strain.

Hemorrhaging Brain

SHOT GLASS

2 parts Strawberry Liqueur
1 part Irish Cream Liqueur
splash Grenadine

Shake all but Grenadine with ice and strain. Place a few drops of Grenadine in the center of the drink.

Herman's Special

SHOT GLASS

1 part Vodka
1 part Brandy
3 parts Peach Schnapps
splash Raspberry Liqueur

Shake with ice and strain.

Heroin

SHOT GLASS

1 part Black Sambuca
1 part Grand Marnier®

Shake with ice and strain.

Hide the Banana

SHOT GLASS

1 part Amaretto
1 part Melon Liqueur
1 part Citrus Vodka

Shake with ice and strain.

Hit and Run

SHOT GLASS

1 part Anisette
1 part Gin

Shake with ice and strain.

Hobbled Gobbler

SHOT GLASS

1 part Dark Rum
1 part Wild Turkey Bourbon

Shake with ice and strain.

Hole-in-One Shooter

SHOT GLASS

3 parts Melon Liqueur
1 part Apple Brandy
splash Half and Half

Shake with ice and strain.

The Honey Badger

SHOT GLASS

2 parts Honey Whiskey
1 part RumChata

Shake with ice and strain.

Honey Bear

SHOT GLASS

1 part Cream
1 part Coffee Liqueur
1 part Frangelico®
1 part Honey

Shake with ice and strain.

Honey-Dew-Me

SHOT GLASS

1 part Bärenjäger®
1 part Melon Liqueur
2 parts Orange Juice

Shake with ice and strain.

Honeysuckle Shooter

SHOT GLASS

2 parts Light Rum
1 part Simple Syrup
1 part Sweet & Sour Mix

Shake with ice and strain.

Honolulu Action

SHOT GLASS

1 part Grenadine
1 part Melon Liqueur
1 part Blue Curaçao
1 part Irish Cream Liqueur
1 part Tequila
1 part Vodka
1 part 151-Proof Rum
top with Whipped Cream

Shake with ice and strain. Because this recipe includes many ingredients, it's easier to make in volume, about 6 shots.

Honolulu Hammer Shooter

SHOT GLASS

2 parts Vodka
1 part Amaretto
1 part Pineapple Juice

Shake with ice and strain.

Hooter

SHOT GLASS

1 part Citrus Vodka
1 part Amaretto
1 part Orange Juice
1 part Grenadine

Shake with ice and strain.

Hornet

SHOT GLASS

2 parts Sloe Gin
1 part Peppermint Schnapps

Shake with ice and strain.

Horny Bastard

SHOT GLASS

1 part Vodka
1 part Caramel Liqueur
splash Grenadine

Shake with ice and strain.

Horny Bull

SHOT GLASS

1 part Tequila
1 part Rum

Shake with ice and strain.

Horny Girl Scout

SHOT GLASS

1 part Coffee Liqueur
1 part Peppermint Schnapps

Shake with ice and strain.

Horny Monkey

SHOT GLASS

1 part Banana Liqueur
1 part Black Sambuca

Shake with ice and strain.

Horny Southerner

SHOT GLASS

2 parts Southern Comfort®
2 parts Melon Liqueur
1 part Sweet & Sour Mix
1 part Lemon-Lime Soda

Shake with ice and strain.

Horsemen of the Apocalypse

SHOT GLASS

1 part Jack Daniel's®
1 part Jim Beam®
1 part Tequila
1 part Spiced Rum

Pour ingredients into glass neat (do not chill).

Hot Afternoon

SHOT GLASS

1 part Peach Schnapps
1 part Coffee Liqueur

Shake with ice and strain.

Hot and Spicy Dirty Angel

SHOT GLASS

1 part Butterscotch Liqueur
1 part Cinnamon Schnapps
1 part Frangelico
1 part Irish Cream Liqueur
1 part Jägermeister

Shake with ice and strain.

Hot Apple Crisp

SHOT GLASS

1 part Cinnamon Schnapps
1 part Sour Apple Vodka
1 part Vanilla Vodka
1 part Cranberry Juice

Shake with ice and strain.

Hot Apple Pie

SHOT GLASS

1 part Irish Cream Liqueur
1 part Goldschläger®

Shake with ice and strain.

Hot Apple Sauce

SHOT GLASS

1 part Fireball Cinnamon Whiskey
2 parts Pineapple Juice

Shake with ice and strain.

Hot Beach Shooter

SHOT GLASS

1 part Hot Coffee
1 part Peach
1 part Coconut Rum

Pour ingredients into glass neat (do not chill).

Hot Bomb

SHOT GLASS

3 parts Tequila
1 part Cinnamon Schnapps

Shake with ice and strain.

Hot Brown Lizard

SHOT GLASS

1 part Cinnamon Schnapps
1 part Melon Liqueur

Pour ingredients into glass neat (do not chill).

Hot Damn

SHOT GLASS

1 part Whiskey
1 part Orange Juice
1 part Rum
1 part Vodka

Shake with ice and strain.

Hot Doctor

SHOT GLASS

1 part Hot Damn® Cinnamon Schnapps
1 part Dr. McGillicuddy's® Mentholmint Schnapps

Shake with ice and strain.

Hot Flash

SHOT GLASS

1 part Amaretto
1 part Fireball Cinnamon Whiskey
2 parts Orange Juice

Shake with ice and strain.

Hot Fuck

SHOT GLASS

1 part Hot Damn!® Cinnamon Schnapps
1 part Jägermeister®

Shake with ice and strain.

Hot Fusion

SHOT GLASS

1 part Melon Liqueur
1 part Absolut® Peppar Vodka

Shake with ice and strain.

Hot Georgia Peach
SHOT GLASS

1 part Hot Damn!® Cinnamon Schnapps
1 part Peach Schnapps

Shake with ice and strain.

Hot José
SHOT GLASS

1 part Hot Damn!® Cinnamon Schnapps
1 part Tequila

Shake with ice and strain.

Hot Nuts
SHOT GLASS

1 part Fireball Cinnamon Whiskey
1 part Hazelnut Liqueur

Shake with ice and strain.

Hot Peach Pie
SHOT GLASS

1 part 151-Proof Rum
1 part Peach Schnapps

Shake with ice and strain.

Hot Stuff
SHOT GLASS

1 part Amaretto
1 part Hot Coffee

Pour ingredients into glass neat (do not chill).

Hot Tamale
SHOT GLASS

3 parts Goldschläger®
1 part Silver Tequila

Shake with ice and strain.

Hot to Trot
SHOT GLASS

1 part Cinnamon Schnapps
1 part Tequila
splash Lime Juice

Shake with ice and strain.

Hot Wet Pussy
SHOT GLASS

1 part 151-Proof Rum
1 part Melon Liqueur
1 part Peach Schnapps
1 part Lemon-Lime Soda
2 parts Pineapple Juice

Shake with ice and strain.

Hotcakes
SHOT GLASS

2 parts Fireball Cinnamon Whiskey
1 part Butterscotch Liqueur

Shake with ice and strain.

Howling Coyote
SHOT GLASS

1 part Chambord®
3 parts Tequila

Shake with ice and strain.

The Human Centipede
SHOT GLASS

1 part Amaretto
1 part Cinnamon Schnapps
1 part Jägermeister
1 part Vodka

Shake with ice and strain.

Hunting Party
SHOT GLASS

1 part Tequila Reposado
1 part Jack Daniel's®
1 part Jim Beam®
1 part Whiskey
1 part Wild Turkey® Bourbon

Shake with ice and strain. Because this recipe includes many ingredients, it's easier to make in volume, about 6 shots.

Hyper Monkey
SHOT GLASS

1 part Banana Liqueur
1 part Coffee Liqueur

Shake with ice and strain.

I Love Rosa

SHOT GLASS

1 part Jack Daniel's®
1 part Amaretto
1 part Cola

Pour ingredients into glass neat (do not chill).

Ice Blue Kamikaze

SHOT GLASS

1 part Rumple Minze®
1 part Vodka
1 part Lemon-Lime Soda

Pour ingredients into glass neat (do not chill).

Ice Bolts

SHOT GLASS

1 part Coffee Liqueur
1 part Tonic Water

Pour ingredients into glass neat (do not chill).

Ice Cream Shot

SHOT GLASS

1 part Vanilla Liqueur
1 part Irish Cream Liqueur

Shake with ice and strain.

Iceberg Shooter

SHOT GLASS

1 part Crème de Menthe (White)
1 part Citrus Vodka

Shake with ice and strain.

Iced Blues

SHOT GLASS

1 part Blackberry Liqueur
1 part Blue Curaçao

Shake with ice and strain.

Icy after Eight

SHOT GLASS

2 parts Vodka
1 part Chocolate Syrup
1 part Crème de Menthe (Green)

Shake with ice and strain.

Iguana #2

SHOT GLASS

1 part Vodka
1 part Tequila
1 part Coffee Liqueur

Shake with ice and strain.

The Igniter

SHOT GLASS

1 part Fireball Cinnamon Whiskey
1 part Firefly Sweet Tea Bourbon

Shake with ice and strain.

Illusion

SHOT GLASS

1 part Coconut Rum
1 part Melon Liqueur
1 part Vodka
1 part Cointreau®
splash Pineapple Juice

Shake with ice and strain.

Immaculate Ingestion

SHOT GLASS

1 part Coffee Liqueur
1 part Peppermint Schnapps
1 part Vodka

Shake with ice and strain.

In the Navy

SHOT GLASS

1 part Crème de Cacao (White)
1 part Crème de Menthe (White)

Shake with ice and strain.

In the Ocean

SHOT GLASS

1 part Blue Curaçao
1 part Lemon Vodka
1 part Orange Vodka

Shake with ice and strain.

Ink Spot

SHOT GLASS

3 parts Blackberry Liqueur
1 part Crème de Menthe (White)

Shake with ice and strain.

International Incident

SHOT GLASS

1 part Vodka
1 part Coffee Liqueur
1 part Amaretto
1 part Frangelico®
2 parts Irish Cream Liqueur

Shake with ice and strain.

Into the Blue

SHOT GLASS

1 part Blue Curaçao
1 part Pineapple Juice
1 part Coffee Liqueur

Shake with ice and strain.

Irish Brogue

SHOT GLASS

3 parts Whiskey
1 part Irish Mist®

Shake with ice and strain.

Irish Bulldog #2

SHOT GLASS

1 part Irish Cream Liqueur
1 part Vodka

Shake with ice and strain.

Irish Eyes Are Crying

SHOT GLASS

1 part Irish Cream Liqueur
1 part Jägermeister
1 part Melon Liqueur

Shake with ice and strain.

Irish Hammer

SHOT GLASS

1 part Jack Daniel's®
1 part Irish Mist®
1 part Irish Cream Liqueur

Shake with ice and strain.

Irish Lass

SHOT GLASS

1 part Irish Cream Liqueur
1 part Rumple Minze®

Shake with ice and strain.

Irish Kiss Shot

SHOT GLASS

1 part Whiskey
1 part Irish Mist®

Shake with ice and strain.

Irish Melon Ball

SHOT GLASS

1 part Irish Whiskey
1 part Melon Liqueur

Shake with ice and strain.

Irish Pirate

SHOT GLASS

1 part Spiced Rum
1 part Irish Mist®

Shake with ice and strain.

Irish Potato Famine

SHOT GLASS

1 part Vodka
1 part Irish Whiskey
1 part Irish Cream Liqueur

Shake with ice and strain.

Irish Quaalude

SHOT GLASS

1 part Crème de Cacao (White)
1 part Frangelico®
1 part Citrus Vodka

Shake with ice and strain.

Irish Setter

SHOT GLASS

2 parts Irish Mist®
2 parts Frangelico®
1 part Crème de Menthe (White)
1 part Brandy

Shake with ice and strain.

Irish Slammer

SHOT GLASS

3 parts Crème de Banane
1 part Whiskey

Shake with ice and strain.

Iron Cross

SHOT GLASS

1 part Crème de Menthe (White)
1 part Apricot Brandy

Shake with ice and strain.

Italian Ecstasy

SHOT GLASS

1 part Grappa
1 part Frangelico®
1 part Cream
1 part Espresso

Shake with ice and strain.

Italian Orgasm

SHOT GLASS

1 part Vodka
1 part Amaretto
1 part Irish Cream Liqueur
1 part Frangelico®

Shake with ice and strain.

Italian Russian

SHOT GLASS

1 part Vodka
1 part Sambuca

Shake with ice and strain.

Italian Spear

SHOT GLASS

1 part Crème de Menthe (White)
1 part Amaretto

Shake with ice and strain.

Italian Stallion

SHOT GLASS

2 parts Sambuca
1 part Amaretto
1 part Frangelico®

Shake with ice and strain.

Italian Stallion Shooter

SHOT GLASS

1 part Galliano®
1 part Cream
1 part Crème de Banane

Shake with ice and strain.

Jack and Jill

SHOT GLASS

1 part Jack Daniel's®
1 part Root Beer Schnapps

Shake with ice and strain.

Jack Ass

SHOT GLASS

2 parts Cinnamon Schnapps
1 part Yukon Jack®

Shake with ice and strain.

Jack in the Box

SHOT GLASS

1 part Coffee Liqueur
1 part Jack Daniel's®
1 part Cream de Banane

Shake with ice and strain.

Jackhammer

SHOT GLASS

1 part Jack Daniel's®
1 part Tequila

Pour ingredients into glass neat (do not chill).

Jackhammer #2

SHOT GLASS

1 part Dark Rum
1 part Lemon Juice

Shake with ice and strain.

Jackson 5

SHOT GLASS

1 part Jim Beam®
1 part Jack Daniel's®
1 part Rye Whiskey
1 part Tequila
1 part Jägermeister®

Shake with ice and strain. Because this recipe includes many ingredients, it's easier to make in volume, about 6 shots.

Jäger® Baby

SHOT GLASS

1 part Irish Cream Liqueur
1 part Jägermeister®

Pour ingredients into glass neat (do not chill).

Jäger® Barrel

SHOT GLASS

1 part Jägermeister®
1 part Root Beer Schnapps
1 part Cola

Shake with ice and strain.

Jäger® Buca

SHOT GLASS

1 part Black Sambuca
1 part Jägermeister
1 part Red Bull Energy Drink

Shake with ice and strain.

Jäger® Mint

SHOT GLASS

1 part Jägermeister®
1 part Peppermint Schnapps

Shake with ice and strain.

Jäger® Monster

SHOT GLASS

3 parts Jägermeister
1 part Orange Juice
splash Grenadine

Shake with ice and strain.

Jäger® Oatmeal Cookie

SHOT GLASS

1 part Jägermeister®
1 part Coffee Liqueur
1 part Irish Cream Liqueur
1 part Butterscotch Schnapps

Shake with ice and strain.

Jäger® Shake

SHOT GLASS

1 part Jägermeister®
1 part Crème de Cacao (White)
splash Half and Half

Shake with ice and strain.

Jäger® Shaker

SHOT GLASS

1 part Irish Cream Liqueur
1 part Jägermeister
splash Cola

Shake with ice and strain.

JägerChata

SHOT GLASS

2 parts RumChata
1 part Jägermeister

Shake with ice and strain.

Jägerita

SHOT GLASS

1 part Jägermeister®
1 part Tequila
1 part Lime Juice

Shake with ice and strain.

Jägershock

SHOT GLASS

1 part After Shock® Cinnamon Schnapps
1 part Jägermeister®

Shake with ice and strain.

Jamaica Dust

SHOT GLASS

1 part Southern Comfort®
1 part Tia Maria®
1 part Pineapple Juice

Shake with ice and strain.

Jamaican Bobsled

SHOT GLASS

1 part Vodka
1 part Banana Liqueur

Shake with ice and strain.

Jamaican Dust Buster®

SHOT GLASS

1 part Rum
1 part Coffee Liqueur
2 parts Pineapple Juice

Shake with ice and strain.

Jamaican Lemondrop

SHOT GLASS

1 part Dark Rum
1 part Triple Sec
1 part Lemonade

Shake with ice and strain.

Jamaican Quaalude

SHOT GLASS

1 part Coconut Rum
1 part Frangelico®
1 part Irish Cream Liqueur
1 part Milk

Shake with ice and strain.

Jamaican Wind

SHOT GLASS

1 part Coffee Liqueur
3 parts Dark Rum

Shake with ice and strain.

Jambalaya

SHOT GLASS

1 part Peach Schnapps
1 part Southern Comfort®
1 part Sweet & Sour Mix
splash Grenadine

Shake with ice and strain.

Jamboree

SHOT GLASS

1 part Vodka
1 part Wild Berry Schnapps
1 part Cranberry Juice Cocktail

Shake with ice and strain.

JavaChata

SHOT GLASS

2 parts RumChata
1 part Espresso Vodka

Shake with ice and strain.

Jealous Queen

SHOT GLASS

1 part Triple Sec
2 parts Vodka
dash Bitters
dash Salt

Shake with ice and strain.

Jedi® Mind Treat

SHOT GLASS

1 part Irish Cream Liqueur
1 part Butterscotch Schnapps
1 part Jägermeister®

Pour ingredients into glass neat (do not chill).

Jell-O® Shots

SHOT GLASS

1 package instant Jell-O® (see flavor combinations)
1 part Hot Water
1 part Liqueur (see flavor combinations)

Basic Recipe: Dissolve Jell-O® in hot water. Add liqueur. Pour into small paper cups and chill. Serve after the Jell-O® has set.

Flavor Combinations:
Cape Cod: Cranberry Jell-O® + Vodka
Gimlet: Lime Jell-O® + Gin
Lemonhead: Lemon Jell-O® + Vodka
Coco Blue: Blue Raspberry Jell-O® + Coconut Rum
Coco Island: Island Pineapple Jell-O® + Coconut Rum
Margarita: Lime Jell-O® + Tequila
Melon Sour: Lime Jell-O® + Melon Liqueur.

Jelly Bean

SHOT GLASS

1 part Blackberry Brandy
1 part Peppermint Schnapps

Shake with ice and strain.

Jelly Bean #2

SHOT GLASS

1 part Coffee Liqueur
1 part Anisette
1 part 151-Proof Rum

Shake with ice and strain.

Jelly Fish

SHOT GLASS

1 part Crème de Cacao (White)
1 part Amaretto
1 part Irish Cream Liqueur
2 splashes Grenadine

Shake all but Grenadine with ice and strain. Place a few drops of Grenadine in the center of the drink.

Jesus Juice

SHOT GLASS

1 part Canadian Whisky
1 part Peach Schnapps
1 part Sour Apple Schnapps
1 part Watermelon Schnapps
1 part Cranberry Juice
1 part Lime Juice

Shake with ice and strain.

Jet Fuel

SHOT GLASS

1 part Grand Marnier®
1 part Southern Comfort®

Shake with ice and strain.

Jeweller's Hammer

SHOT GLASS

1 part Vodka
1 part White Grape Juice

Shake with ice and strain.

Jim Morrison

SHOT GLASS

1 part Jack Daniel's
1 part Jim Beam Bourbon
1 part Seagram's 7 Whisky
1 part Wild Turkey Bourbon

Shake with ice and strain.

Jive-Aid

SHOT GLASS

1 part Vodka
1 part Sloe Gin
1 part Cherry Liqueur
1 part Watermelon Schnapps
splash Lemon-Lime Soda
splash Sweet & Sour Mix

Shake with ice and strain.

Jogger

SHOT GLASS

1 part Citrus Vodka
1 part Vodka
1 part Orange Juice
1 part Galliano®

Shake with ice and strain.

Johnny on the Beach

SHOT GLASS

3 parts Vodka
2 parts Melon Liqueur
2 parts Blackberry Liqueur
1 part Pineapple Juice
1 part Orange Juice
1 part Grapefruit Juice
1 part Cranberry Juice Cocktail

Shake with ice and strain. Because this recipe includes many ingredients, it's easier to make in volume, about 6 shots.

Johnny Appleseed

SHOT GLASS

1 part Vodka
1 part Raspberry Liqueur
1 part Melon Liqueur
1 part Peach Schnapps
1 part Pineapple Juice

Shake with ice and strain. Because this recipe includes many ingredients, it's easier to make in volume, about 6 shots.

Johnny G Spot

SHOT GLASS

1 part Vodka
1 part Blue Curaçao
1 part Orange Juice

Shake with ice and strain.

José Flame-O

SHOT GLASS

1 part Tequila
1 part Fire Water®

Pour ingredients into glass neat (do not chill).

José Pache Sombrero

SHOT GLASS

1 part Jack Daniel's®
1 part Brandy
1 part Tequila

Pour ingredients into glass neat (do not chill).

Judgment Day

SHOT GLASS

1 part Coffee Liqueur
1 part Jägermeister®
1 part Rumple Minze®
splash 151-Proof Rum
splash Grain Alcohol

Shake with ice and strain. Because this recipe includes many ingredients, it's easier to make in volume, about 6 shots.

Juicy Fruit®

SHOT GLASS

2 parts Raspberry Liqueur
1 part Triple Sec
1 part Melon Liqueur

Shake with ice and strain.

Juicy Lips

SHOT GLASS

1 part Vodka
1 part Crème de Banane
1 part Pineapple Juice

Shake with ice and strain.

Juicy Pussy

SHOT GLASS

1 part Irish Cream Liqueur
1 part Peach Schnapps
1 part Pineapple Juice

Shake with ice and strain.

Juicy Volkheimer

SHOT GLASS

1 part Vodka
1 part Coconut Rum

Shake with ice and strain.

Jump Shot

SHOT GLASS

2 parts White Rum
1 part Orange Curaçao
1 part Pineapple Juice
2 dashes Angostura Bitters

Shake with ice and strain.

Junior Mint®

SHOT GLASS

1 part Peppermint Schnapps
1 part Crème de Cacao (Dark)

Shake with ice and strain.

Just Shoot Me

SHOT GLASS

1 part Jim Beam®
1 part Jack Daniel's®
1 part Johnnie Walker® Red Label
1 part Tequila
1 part Jägermeister®
1 part 151-Proof Rum

Shake with ice and strain. Because this recipe includes many ingredients, it's easier to make in volume, about 6 shots.

K-Hole

SHOT GLASS

1 part Cinnamon Schnapps
1 part Gold Tequila
1 part Jägermeister
1 part Vodka

Shake with ice and strain.

Kaisermeister

SHOT GLASS

1 part Jägermeister®
1 part Root Beer Schnapps

Shake with ice and strain.

Kalabreeze

SHOT GLASS

1 part Cherry Brandy
1 part Apricot Brandy
1 part Triple Sec

Shake with ice and strain.

Kamihuzi

SHOT GLASS

1 part Tequila
1 part Triple Sec
1 part Sweet & Sour Mix

Shake with ice and strain.

Kamikaze

SHOT GLASS

1 part Vodka
1 part Triple Sec
1 part Lime Juice

Shake with ice and strain.

Kare Bear

SHOT GLASS

1 part Amaretto
1 part Blue Curaçao
1 part Banana Liqueur

Shake with ice and strain.

Ke Largo

SHOT GLASS

1 part KeKe Beach® Key Lime Cream Liqueur
1 part Melon Liqueur

Shake with ice and strain.

Keith Jackson

SHOT GLASS

1 part Amaretto
1 part Southern Comfort®
1 part Peach Schnapps
1 part Sweet & Sour Mix
1 part Lemon-Lime Soda

Shake with ice and strain.

Kentucky Peach

SHOT GLASS

2 parts Bourbon
1 part Peach Schnapps
1 part Orange Juice

Shake with ice and strain.

Keremiki

SHOT GLASS

1 part 151-Proof Rum
1 part Goldschläger®
1 part Rumple Minze®

Shake with ice and strain.

Kermit's Belly Button

SHOT GLASS

1 part Peach Schnapps
1 part Blue Curaçao
1 part Orange Juice

Shake with ice and strain.

Key Lime Pie

SHOT GLASS

2 parts Licor 43®
2 parts Half and Half
1 part Lime Juice

Shake with ice and strain.

Key Lime Shooter

SHOT GLASS

2 parts Licor 43®
1 part Light Rum
1 part Sweet & Sour Mix
splash Sweetened Lime Juice
splash Half and Half

Shake with ice and strain.

Key West Shooter

SHOT GLASS

1 part Vodka
1 part Melon Liqueur
1 part Orange Juice
1 part Pineapple Juice

Shake with ice and strain.

Kick Me in the Jimmy

SHOT GLASS

1 part Jägermeister®
1 part Jack Daniel's®
1 part Tequila
1 part Fire Water®

Shake with ice and strain.

Kickstand

SHOT GLASS

1 part Amaretto
1 part Southern Comfort®
1 part Coffee Liqueur
1 part Irish Cream Liqueur

Shake with ice and strain.

Killer Bee

SHOT GLASS

1 part Jägermeister®
1 part Bärenjäger®

Shake with ice and strain.

Killer Crawdad

SHOT GLASS

1 part Goldschläger®
1 part Cherry Brandy

Shake with ice and strain.

Killer Kool-Aid®

SHOT GLASS

2 parts Vodka
1 part Amaretto
1 part Melon Liqueur
1 part Cranberry Juice Cocktail

Shake with ice and strain.

Killer Oreos®

SHOT GLASS

1 part Jägermeister®
1 part Coffee Liqueur
1 part Irish Cream Liqueur

Shake with ice and strain.

Killer Sniff

SHOT GLASS

1 part Sambuca
1 part Blue Curaçao

Shake with ice and strain.

Killing Spree

SHOT GLASS

1 part Passion Fruit Liqueur
1 part Advocaat

Shake with ice and strain.

Kimber Krush

SHOT GLASS

1 part Vanilla Vodka
1 part Rumple Minze®
1 part Irish Cream Liqueur
1 part Raspberry Liqueur

Shake with ice and strain.

King's Ransom

SHOT GLASS

1 part Goldschläger®
1 part Crown Royal® Whiskey

Shake with ice and strain.

Kish Wacker

SHOT GLASS

1 part Irish Cream Liqueur
1 part Crème de Cacao (Dark)
1 part Vodka
1 part Coffee Liqueur

Shake with ice and strain.

Kitty

SHOT GLASS

1 part Crème de Banane
1 part Triple Sec
1 part Jim Beam®
1 part Lemon Juice

Shake with ice and strain.

Kiwiki

SHOT GLASS

1 part Vodka
1 part Kiwi Schnapps
1 part Triple Sec

Shake with ice and strain.

Klingon® Disrupter

SHOT GLASS

1 part Jim Beam®
1 part Mezcal
1 part Cinnamon Schnapps

Shake with ice and strain.

Klondyke

SHOT GLASS

1 part Irish Cream Liqueur
1 part Jägermeister®

Shake with ice and strain.

Kool-Aid®

SHOT GLASS

1 part Vodka
1 part Amaretto
1 part Melon Liqueur
1 part Raspberry Liqueur

Shake with ice and strain.

Krazy Kat

SHOT GLASS

1 part Coffee Liqueur
1 part Crème de Banane
1 part Crème de Coconut

Shake with ice and strain.

Kreeper

SHOT GLASS

1 part Amaretto
1 part Chambord
1 part Coconut Rum
1 part Southern Comfort
1 part Grenadine
1 part Lime Juice
1 part Orange Juice

Shake with ice and strain.

Kremlin Shooter

SHOT GLASS

1 part Vodka
splash Grenadine

Shake with ice and strain.

Kriaura

SHOT GLASS

1 part Wild Berry Schnapps
1 part Lemon-Lime Soda
1 part Cranberry Juice Cocktail

Shake with ice and strain.

Kris Kringle

SHOT GLASS

1 part Crème de Noyaux
1 part Root Beer Schnapps
1 part Half and Half

Shake with ice and strain.

Kurant Shooter

SHOT GLASS

1 part Melon Liqueur
1 part Currant Vodka
2 parts Pineapple Juice

Shake with ice and strain.

Kurant Stinger

SHOT GLASS

1 part Bärenjäger®
1 part Currant Vodka

Shake with ice and strain.

La Pussy

SHOT GLASS

1 part Light Rum
1 part Cointreau®
1 part Brandy
1 part Sour Apple Schnapps

Shake with ice and strain.

L.A. Water

SHOT GLASS

1 part Gin
1 part Triple Sec
1 part Vodka
dash Chambord
dash Melon Liqueur

Shake with ice and strain.

The Lady in Red

SHOT GLASS

1 part Peppermint Schnapps
1 part Peach Schnapps
1 part Vodka
1 part Grenadine

Shake with ice and strain.

Lady Killer Shooter

SHOT GLASS

1 part Coffee
1 part Melon Liqueur
1 part Frangelico®

Shake with ice and strain.

Land Rover®

SHOT GLASS

1 part Spiced Rum
1 part Coffee Liqueur
1 part Irish Cream Liqueur

Shake with ice and strain.

Landmine

SHOT GLASS

1 part 151-Proof Rum
1 part Jägermeister®

Shake with ice and strain.

Laserbeam

SHOT GLASS

1 part Amaretto
1 part Grand Marnier®
1 part Melon Liqueur
1 part Pineapple Juice
1 part Southern Comfort®

Shake with ice and strain. Because this recipe includes many ingredients, it's easier to make in volume, about 6 shots.

Last Night on Earth

SHOT GLASS

1 part Jägermeister
1 part Mango Rum
1 part Melon Liqueur
1 part Orange Juice

Shake with ice and strain.

The Last Stop

SHOT GLASS

1 part Maraschino Liqueur
1 part Blackberry Liqueur
splash Absinthe

Shake with ice and strain.

Lazer Beam

SHOT GLASS

1 part Amaretto
1 part Peach Schnapps
1 part Orange Juice

Shake with ice and strain.

Leather Whip

SHOT GLASS

1 part Tequila
1 part Triple Sec
1 part Jack Daniel's®
1 part Peach Schnapps

Shake with ice and strain.

Lemon Drop Shooter

SHOT GLASS

1 part Vodka
1 Lemon Wedge
dash Sugar

Shake the Vodka with ice and strain. Pour the Sugar onto the Lemon Wedge. Drink the shot and bite down on the Lemon Wedge.

Lemon Meringue

SHOT GLASS

1 part Vodka
1 part Lemon Juice

Shake with ice and strain. Top with Whipped Cream.

Lemon Meringue Pie

SHOT GLASS

3 parts RumChata
1 part Limoncello
1 part Whipped Cream Vodka

Shake with ice and strain. Garnish with Graham Cracker crumbs.

Leprechaun Shooter

SHOT GLASS

1 part Blue Curaçao
1 part Peach Schnapps
1 part Orange Juice

Shake with ice and strain.

Leprechaun's Gold

SHOT GLASS

1 part Goldschläger®
1 part Irish Cream Liqueur

Shake with ice and strain.

Lethal Injection

SHOT GLASS

1 part Rum
1 part Coconut Rum
1 part Dark Rum
1 part Amaretto
1 part Orange Juice
1 part Pineapple Juice

Shake with ice and strain.

Levite Pepper Slammer
SHOT GLASS
1 part Southern Comfort®
2 parts Dr. Pepper®
Build in the glass with no ice.

Lewinsky Blowjob
SHOT GLASS
1 part Amaretto
2 parts Cola
splash 151-Proof Rum
Shake with ice and strain. Top with whipped cream and drink without using your hands.

Lie Down and Shut Up!
SHOT GLASS
1 part Jägermeister®
1 part Cinnamon Schnapps
1 part Coffee Liqueur
splash Cream
Shake with ice and strain.

Life Line
SHOT GLASS
1 part Canadian Whisky
1 part Gold Tequila
1 part Jägermeister
1 part Cranberry Juice
1 part Sweetened Lime Juice
Shake with ice and strain.

Life Preserver
SHOT GLASS
1 part Blue Curaçao
1 part Vodka
Shake the Vodka and Blue Curaçao with ice and strain. Garnish with a Cheerio.

Light Green Panties
SHOT GLASS
1 part Crème de Menthe (Green)
1 part Vodka
1 part Irish Cream Liqueur
splash Grenadine
Shake all but Grenadine with ice and strain. Place a few drops of Grenadine in the center of the drink.

Light Headed
SHOT GLASS
1 part Blue Curaçao
1 part Crème de Coconut
1 part Strawberry Liqueur
Shake with ice and strain.

Lime Lizard
SHOT GLASS
1 part Vodka
1 part Rum
1 part Lime Juice
1 part Grenadine
Shake with ice and strain.

Liplock
SHOT GLASS
1 part Dark Rum
1 part Coconut Rum
1 part Grenadine
1 part Pineapple Juice
1 part Orange Juice
Shake with ice and strain. Because this recipe includes many ingredients, it's easier to make in volume, about 6 shots.

Lipstick Lesbian
SHOT GLASS
1 part Raspberry Vodka
1 part Watermelon Schnapps
1 part Cranberry Juice Cocktail
1 part Sweet & Sour Mix
Shake with ice and strain.

Liquid Asphalt

SHOT GLASS

1 part Sambuca
1 part Jägermeister®

Shake with ice and strain.

Liquid Candy Cane

SHOT GLASS

1 part Vodka
2 parts Cherry Liqueur
2 parts Peppermint Schnapps

Shake with ice and strain.

Liquid Cocaine

SHOT GLASS

1 part Grand Marnier®
1 part Southern Comfort®
1 part Vodka
1 part Amaretto
1 part Pineapple Juice

Shake with ice and strain. Because this recipe includes many ingredients, it's easier to make in volume, about 6 shots.

Liquid Crack

SHOT GLASS

1 part Jägermeister®
1 part Rumple Minze®
1 part 151-Proof Rum
1 part Goldschläger®

Shake with ice and strain.

Liquid Diet

SHOT GLASS

1 part Blue Curaçao
1 part Chambord
1 part Lemon-Lime Soda

Shake with ice and strain.

Liquid Heroin

SHOT GLASS

1 part Vodka
1 part Rumple Minze®
1 part Jägermeister®

Shake with ice and strain.

Liquid Kryptonite

SHOT GLASS

1 part Cinnamon Schnapps
1 part Green Apple Schnapps
1 part Melon Liqueur

Shake with ice and strain.

Liquid Mentos®

SHOT GLASS

1 part Blue Curaçao
1 part Peach Schnapps
1 part Banana Liqueur

Shake with ice and strain.

Liquid Nitrogen

SHOT GLASS

1 part Sambuca
1 part Ouzo

Shake with ice and strain.

Liquid Quaalude

SHOT GLASS

1 part Jägermeister®
3 parts Irish Cream Liqueur

Shake with ice and strain.

Liquid Rocher®

SHOT GLASS

2 parts Crème de Cacao (White)
1 part Frangelico®
1 part Vanilla Liqueur

Shake with ice and strain.

Liquid Screw

SHOT GLASS

1 part Coconut Rum
1 part Peach Schnapps
1 part Vodka
1 part Lemon-Lime Soda

Shake with ice and strain.

Liquid Valium

SHOT GLASS

1 part Jack Daniel's®
1 part Amaretto
1 part Tequila
1 part Triple Sec

Shake with ice and strain.

Liquid Viagra

SHOT GLASS

1 part Blue Curaçao
1 part Blue Raspberry Liqueur
1 part Vodka
1 part Milk

Shake with ice and strain.

Liquid Watermelon

SHOT GLASS

1 part Melon Liqueur
1 part Vodka
1 part Watermelon Schnapps
1 part Sweet & Sour Mix
splash Grenadine

Shake with ice and strain.

Liquid Xanax

SHOT GLASS

1 part 151-Proof Rum
1 part Canadian Whisky
1 part Cinnamon Schnapps
1 part Jägermeister

Shake with ice and strain.

Listerine Shot

SHOT GLASS

2 parts Melon Liqueur
1 part Blue Curaçao
1 part Lime Juice

Shake with ice and strain.

Lit City

SHOT GLASS

1 part Jägermeister®
1 part Butterscotch Schnapps
1 part Irish Cream Liqueur
1 part Goldschläger®

Shake with ice and strain.

Little Bitch

SHOT GLASS

1 part Southern Comfort®
1 part Amaretto
1 part Cranberry Juice Cocktail
1 part Orange Juice

Shake with ice and strain.

Little Green Man from Mars

SHOT GLASS

1 Green Maraschino Cherry
1 part Jägermeister®
1 part Rumple Minze®

Remove stem from the Green Maraschino Cherry and drop the cherry in the glass. Pour equal parts Jägermeister and Rumple Minze.

Little Green Martian

SHOT GLASS

1 Green Maraschino Cherry
3 parts Vanilla Vodka
1 part Cranberry Juice

Build in order.

Little Leprechaun

SHOT GLASS

1 part Cinnamon Schnapps
1 part Crème de Menthe (Green)
1 part Irish Whiskey

Shake with ice and strain.

A Little Nervous

SHOT GLASS

1 part Vodka
1 part Peach Schnapps
1 part Blackberry Liqueur

Shake with ice and strain.

A Little Piece of Hell

SHOT GLASS

1 part Cinnamon Schnapps
1 part Simple Syrup

Shake with ice and strain.

Lobotomy

SHOT GLASS

1 part Amaretto
1 part Raspberry Liqueur
1 part Pineapple Juice

Shake with ice and strain.

London Pummel

SHOT GLASS

1 part Gin
1 part Tonic Water
splash Lime Juice

Build in a shot glass.

Long Island Shooter

SHOT GLASS

1 part Silver Tequila
1 part Vodka
1 part Light Rum
1 part Gin
1 part Triple Sec
1 part Cola
1 part Sweet & Sour Mix

Shake with ice and strain.

Loopy Fruits Shooter

SHOT GLASS

3 parts RumChata
1 part Blue Curaçao
1 part Raspberry Vodka

Shake with ice and strain.

Love in the Snow

SHOT GLASS

1 part Crème de Cacao (White)
1 part Amaretto
1 part Pisang Ambon® Liqueur

Shake with ice and strain.

Love Is in the Air

SHOT GLASS

1 part Amaretto
1 part Crème de Banane
1 part Crème de Coconut

Shake with ice and strain.

Love Shack Shooter

SHOT GLASS

2 parts Dark Rum
1 part Lemon-Lime Soda
1 part Orange Juice
splash Grenadine

Shake with ice and strain.

Lucky Dragon

SHOT GLASS

1 part Butterscotch Liqueur
1 part Fireball Cinnamon Whiskey
1 part Irish Cream Liqueur

Shake with ice and strain.

Luna Rossa

SHOT GLASS

1 part Peach Schnapps
1 part Campari®
1 part Limoncello

Shake with ice and strain.

M&M®

SHOT GLASS

1 part Amaretto
1 part Coffee Liqueur

Shake with ice and strain.

M. O. Shooter

SHOT GLASS

1 part Cream
1 part Amaretto

Shake with ice and strain.

Mad Cow

SHOT GLASS

1 part Coffee Liqueur
1 part Cream
1 part 151-Proof Rum

Shake with ice and strain.

Mad Hatter

SHOT GLASS

1 part Vodka
1 part Peach Schnapps
1 part Lemonade
1 part Cola

Shake with ice and strain.

Mad Melon Shooter

SHOT GLASS

1 part Watermelon Schnapps
1 part Vodka

Shake with ice and strain.

Mad Russian

SHOT GLASS

1 part Butterscotch Liqueur
1 part Coffee Liqueur
1 part Irish Cream Liqueur
1 part Vodka
1 part Milk

Shake with ice and strain.

Mad Scientist

SHOT GLASS

1 part Blueberry Schnapps
1 part Raspberry Liqueur
splash Irish Cream Liqueur

Shake with ice and strain.

Madman's Return

SHOT GLASS

1 part Triple Sec
1 part Goldschläger®
1 part Cachaça
1 part Gin

Shake with ice and strain.

Mage's Fire

SHOT GLASS

2 parts Vodka
1 part Cinnamon Schnapps
1 part Blue Curaçao

Shake with ice and strain.

Magic Potion

SHOT GLASS

1 part Coffee Liqueur
1 part Amaretto
1 part Crème de Cacao (Dark)

Shake with ice and strain.

Maiden's Prayer Shooter

SHOT GLASS

1 part Gin
1 part Lillet
1 part Calvados Apple Brandy

Shake with ice and strain.

Malibu Thong

SHOT GLASS

2 parts Coconut Rum
1 part Lemon Vodka
splash Pineapple Juice

Shake with ice and strain. Garnish with Whipped Cream and a Cherry.

Marijuana Milkshake

SHOT GLASS

1 part Melon Liqueur
1 part Lime Juice
1 part Milk

Shake with ice and strain.

Masconivich Shooter

SHOT GLASS

1 part Brandy
1 part Triple Sec
1 part Cognac

Shake with ice and strain.

Mass Confusion

SHOT GLASS

1 part Blue Curaçao
1 part Orange Vodka
1 part Raspberry Vodka
1 part Triple Sec
splash Lemon-Lime Soda
splash Sweet & Sour Mix

Shake with ice and strain.

Mattikaze

SHOT GLASS

1 part Vodka
1 part Lime Juice
1 part Triple Sec
1 part Peach Schnapps

Shake with ice and strain.

Max Factor®

SHOT GLASS

1 part Raspberry Liqueur
1 part Cranberry Juice Cocktail
1 part Triple Sec

Shake with ice and strain.

Mean Machine

SHOT GLASS

1 part Crème de Menthe (White)
1 part Triple Sec

Shake with ice and strain.

Meat and Potatoes

SHOT GLASS

1 part Potato Vodka

Shake the Vodka with ice and strain. Garnish with a slice of Pepperoni.

Melaretto

SHOT GLASS

1 part Melon Liqueur
1 part Amaretto

Shake with ice and strain.

Melon Ball Shooter

SHOT GLASS

2 parts Melon Liqueur
1 part Vodka
1 part Orange Juice

Shake with ice and strain.

Melon Cheer

SHOT GLASS

1 part Melon Liqueur
1 part Strawberry Liqueur
1 part Sweet & Sour Mix

Shake with ice and strain.

Melon Kamikaze

SHOT GLASS

1 part Vodka
1 part Melon Liqueur
1 part Sweet & Sour Mix

Shake with ice and strain.

Melonoma

SHOT GLASS

2 parts Vodka
1 part Melon Liqueur

Shake with ice and strain.

Memory Loss

SHOT GLASS

1 part Vodka
1 part Raspberry Liqueur
1 part Banana Liqueur
1 part Cranberry Juice Cocktail
1 part Orange Juice

Shake with ice and strain. Because this recipe includes many ingredients, it's easier to make in volume, about 6 shots.

Menstrual Mint

SHOT GLASS

1 part Gin
1 part Grenadine
1 part Tequila

Shake with ice and strain.

Merry Kay

SHOT GLASS

2 parts Jim Beam®
1 part Blue Curaçao

Shake with ice and strain.

Mexican Apple

SHOT GLASS

1 part Apple Liqueur
1 part Silver Tequila

Shake with ice and strain.

Mexican Cherry Bomb

SHOT GLASS

1 part Coffee Liqueur
1 part Cream
1 part Grenadine

Shake with ice and strain.

Mexican Empire

SHOT GLASS

1 part Silver Tequila
1 part Coffee
1 part Grenadine

Shake with ice and strain.

Mexican Glow Worm

SHOT GLASS

1 part Melon Liqueur
1 part Gold Tequila

Shake with ice and strain.

Mexican Kamikaze

SHOT GLASS

2 parts Tequila
1 part Vodka
1 part Lemon Juice
1 part Lime Juice

Shake with ice and strain.

Mexican Killer

SHOT GLASS

1 part Gold Tequila
1 part Peach Schnapps
1 part Sweetened Lime Juice

Shake with ice and strain.

Mexican Melon

SHOT GLASS

1 part Silver Tequila
1 part Melon Liqueur

Shake with ice and strain.

Mexican Mountie

SHOT GLASS

1 part Tequila
1 part Yukon Jack®

Shake with ice and strain.

Mexican Mouthwash

SHOT GLASS

1 part Tequila
1 part Rumple Minze®

Shake with ice and strain.

Mexican Pebble

SHOT GLASS

1 part Blue Curaçao
1 part Gold Tequila
1 part Raspberry Liqueur
1 part Lemon-Lime Soda

Shake with ice and strain.

Mexican Shake

SHOT GLASS

1 part Tequila
1 part Coffee Liqueur
1 part Cola
1 part Cream

Shake with ice and strain.

Mexican Snowshoe

SHOT GLASS

1 part Peppermint Schnapps
1 part Tequila

Shake with ice and strain.

Mexican Stand-Off

SHOT GLASS

1 part Vodka
1 part Tequila
1 part Passoã®

Shake with ice and strain.

Mexican Thanksgiving

SHOT GLASS

1 part Tequila
1 part Wild Turkey® Bourbon

Shake with ice and strain.

Mexican Thunder

SHOT GLASS

2 parts Black Sambuca
1 part Cinnamon Schnapps
1 part Gold Tequila

Shake with ice and strain.

Mexican Water

SHOT GLASS

1 part Crown Royal® Whiskey
1 part Tequila Reposado
1 part Vodka

Shake with ice and strain.

Mid Island

SHOT GLASS

1 part Amaretto
1 part Coconut Rum
1 part Coffee Liqueur
1 part Dark Spiced Rum

Shake with ice and strain.

Midnight Matinee

SHOT GLASS

1 part Peach Schnapps
1 part Passion Fruit Liqueur
1 part Lemon Juice

Shake with ice and strain.

Midnight Oil

SHOT GLASS

2 parts Amaretto
1 part Jägermeister

Build in a shot glass. Do not chill.

Milano Shooter

SHOT GLASS

1 part Crème de Menthe (White)
1 part Fernet-Branca®
1 part Sambuca

Shake with ice and strain.

Mild Jizz

SHOT GLASS

1 part Vodka
1 part Melon Liqueur
1 part Coconut Rum
1 part Lemon-Lime Soda

Shake with ice and strain.

Milky Nooky

SHOT GLASS

1 part Peppermint Schnapps
1 part Irish Cream Liqueur
1 part Jägermeister®

Shake with ice and strain.

Milky Way®

SHOT GLASS

1 part Amaretto
1 part Crème de Cacao (Dark)
1 part Cream

Shake with ice and strain.

Milky Way® #2

SHOT GLASS

3 parts Irish Cream Liqueur
2 parts Root Beer Schnapps
1 part Goldschläger®

Shake with ice and strain.

Mind Collapse

SHOT GLASS

1 part Crème de Menthe (White)
1 part Whiskey

Shake with ice and strain.

Mind Game

SHOT GLASS

1 part Pernod®
1 part Blue Curaçao
2 parts Milk

Shake with ice and strain.

Mind Probe

SHOT GLASS

1 part 151-Proof Rum
1 part Sambuca
1 part Jägermeister®

Shake with ice and strain.

Mindtrip

SHOT GLASS

1 part Barenjäger Honey Liqueur
1 part Jägermeister
1 part Vanilla Liqueur

Shake with ice and strain.

Mini Margarita

SHOT GLASS

1 part Silver Tequila
1 part Triple Sec
1 part Sweet & Sour Mix

Shake with ice and strain.

Mint Chocolate

SHOT GLASS

2 parts Crème de Menthe (Green)
1 part Coffee Liqueur
1 part Irish Cream Liqueur

Shake with ice and strain.

Mint Desire

SHOT GLASS

1 part Rumple Minze®
1 part Cream of Coconut
2 parts Cream

Shake with ice and strain.

Mint Julep Shot

SHOT GLASS

2 parts Bourbon
1 part Crème de Menthe (Green)

Shake with ice and strain.

Mintarita

SHOT GLASS

1 part Crème de Menthe (White)
1 part Silver Tequila

Shake with ice and strain.

Minty Asshole

SHOT GLASS

1 part Jägermeister
1 part Mint Schnapps
1 part Vanilla Schnapps

Shake with ice and strain.

Minty Nipples

SHOT GLASS

2 parts Irish Cream Liqueur
1 part Butterscotch Liqueur
1 part Peppermint Schnapps

Shake with ice and strain.

Misconavitch

SHOT GLASS

1 part Cointreau®
3 parts Grand Marnier®

Shake with ice and strain.

Misdemeanor

SHOT GLASS

1 part Butterscotch Schnapps
1 part Crown Royal® Whiskey

Shake with ice and strain.

Miss Mounds
SHOT GLASS

1 part Coconut Rum
1 part Dark Chocolate Liqueur

Shake with ice and strain.

Misty Blue Cumming
SHOT GLASS

1 part Vodka
1 part Sloe Gin
1 part Blue Curaçao
1 part Peach Schnapps

Shake with ice and strain.

Mongolian Clusterfuck
SHOT GLASS

1 part Jägermeister®
1 part Goldschläger®
1 part Rumple Minze®

Shake with ice and strain.

Monkey Brain
SHOT GLASS

3 parts Coffee Liqueur
1 part Advocaat
splash Grenadine

Shake all but Grenadine with ice and strain. Place a few drops of Grenadine in the center of the drink.

Monkey Cum
SHOT GLASS

1 part 99 Bananas Liqueur
1 part Vodka
1 part Milk

Shake with ice and strain.

Monkey Poop Shooter
SHOT GLASS

1 part Vodka
1 part Crème de Banane
1 part Pineapple Juice
1 part Orange Juice
1 part Lime Cordial

Shake with ice and strain. Because this recipe includes many ingredients, it's easier to make in volume, about 6 shots.

Monkey Pussy
SHOT GLASS

1 part Irish Cream Liqueur
1 part Banana Liqueur
1 part Crown Royal® Whiskey
1 part Raspberry Liqueur

Shake with ice and strain.

Monkey Shines
SHOT GLASS

1 part Banana Liqueur
1 part Bourbon
1 part Irish Cream Liqueur

Shake with ice and strain.

Monsoon
SHOT GLASS

1 part Currant Vodka
1 part Amaretto
1 part Coffee Liqueur
1 part Frangelico®

Shake with ice and strain.

Montana Stump Puller
SHOT GLASS

2 parts Canadian Whisky
1 part Crème de Cacao (White)

Shake with ice and strain.

Moose Fart

SHOT GLASS

1 part Vodka
1 part Bourbon
1 part Coffee Liqueur
1 part Irish Cream Liqueur

Shake with ice and strain.

Moranguito

SHOT GLASS

1 part Absinthe
1 part Tequila
1 part Grenadine

Shake with ice and strain.

Morgan's Wench

SHOT GLASS

1 part Spiced Rum
1 part Amaretto
1 part Crème de Cacao (Dark)

Shake with ice and strain.

Morning Wood

SHOT GLASS

1 part Vodka
1 part Peach Schnapps
1 part Orange Juice
1 part Sweet & Sour Mix
1 part Raspberry Liqueur

Shake with ice and strain. Because this recipe includes many ingredients, it's easier to make in volume, about 6 shots.

Mother of Dragons

SHOT GLASS

1 part Chambord
1 part Coconut Rum
1 part Jägermeister
1 part Pineapple Juice

Shake with ice and strain.

Mother Load

SHOT GLASS

1 part Vodka
1 part Blackberry Liqueur
1 part Coconut Rum

Shake with ice and strain.

Mother Pucker Shooter

SHOT GLASS

1 part Vodka
1 part Sour Apple Schnapps
splash Lemon-Lime Soda
splash Club Soda

Shake with ice and strain.

Mouth Wash

SHOT GLASS

1 part Crème de Menthe (White)
1 part Vodka
1 part Blue Curaçao

Shake with ice and strain.

Mouthwatering

SHOT GLASS

1 part Amaretto
1 part Melon Liqueur

Shake with ice and strain.

Mr. Bean

SHOT GLASS

1 part Anisette
1 part Blackberry Liqueur

Shake with ice and strain.

Mr. G

SHOT GLASS

1 part Licor 43®
1 part Vodka
2 parts Grenadine

Shake with ice and strain.

Mudslide Shooter

SHOT GLASS

1 part Vodka
1 part Coffee Liqueur
1 part Irish Cream Liqueur

Shake with ice and strain.

Muddy Water

SHOT GLASS

1 part Vodka
1 part Coffee Liqueur
1 part Irish Cream Liqueur

Shake with ice and strain.

Mudguppy

SHOT GLASS

1 part Amaretto
1 part Irish Cream Liqueur
2 parts Bourbon

Shake with ice and strain.

Muff Dive

SHOT GLASS

1 part Vodka
1 part Peach Schnapps
1 part Cranberry Juice Cocktail

Shake with ice and strain.

Mule Kick

SHOT GLASS

1 part Amaretto
1 part Gold Tequila
1 part Peach Schnapps

Shake with ice and strain.

Murky Water

SHOT GLASS

1 part Blue Curaçao
1 part Coconut Rum
1 part Peach Schnapps
1 part Pineapple Rum
1 part Grenadine
1 part Pineapple Juice

Shake with ice and strain.

Mussolini

SHOT GLASS

1 part Goldschläger®
1 part Jägermeister®
1 part Sambuca

Shake with ice and strain.

Mutated Mother's Milk

SHOT GLASS

1 part Jägermeister®
1 part Irish Cream Liqueur
1 part Peppermint Schnapps

Shake with ice and strain.

MVP's Strawberry Bomb

SHOT GLASS

1 part Tequila Rose®
1 part Vodka
1 part Strawberry Liqueur

Shake with ice and strain.

My Johnson Is Ten Inches Long

SHOT GLASS

2 parts Malibu® Rum
2 parts Raspberry Liqueur
2 parts Melon Liqueur
1 part Sweet & Sour Mix
1 part Cranberry Juice Cocktail

Shake with ice and strain.

My Precious

SHOT GLASS

1 part Blue Maui
1 part Goldschläger®
1 part Hpnotiq

Shake with ice and strain.

Nalgas de Oro

SHOT GLASS

1 part Raspberry Liqueur
1 part Vanilla Liqueur
1 part 151-Proof Rum
1 part Grand Marnier®

Shake with ice and strain.

Nasty Stewardess
SHOT GLASS
1 part Licor 43®
2 parts Tonic Water
2 parts Orange Bitters
Build in the glass with no ice.

Natural Disaster
SHOT GLASS
1 part Cinnamon Schnapps
1 part Peppermint Schnapps
Shake with ice and strain.

Naughty Angel
SHOT GLASS
3 parts Chocolate Liqueur
1 part 151-Proof Rum
Shake with ice and strain.

Navy Seal
SHOT GLASS
1 part Crown Royal® Whiskey
1 part Rum
Shake with ice and strain.

El Negro
SHOT GLASS
1 part Dark Rum
1 part Southern Comfort
1 part Spiced Rum
Build in order. Do not chill.

Neon Bull Frog
SHOT GLASS
1 part Vodka
1 part Blue Curaçao
1 part Melon Liqueur
1 part Sweet & Sour Mix
Shake with ice and strain.

Neon Cactus
SHOT GLASS
1 part Cactus Juice Schnapps
1 part Margarita Mix
Shake with ice and strain.

Neon Lizard
SHOT GLASS
1 part Blue Curaçao
1 part Melon Liqueur
Shake with ice and strain.

Nerd
SHOT GLASS
1 part Cream
1 part Black Sambuca
1 part Strawberry Liqueur
Shake with ice and strain.

Nero's Delight
SHOT GLASS
1 part Vodka
1 part Sambuca
Shake with ice and strain.

Neuronium
SHOT GLASS
1 part Crème de Menthe (White)
1 part Vodka
splash Grenadine
Shake all but Grenadine with ice and strain. Place a few drops of Grenadine in the center of the drink.

Never a Seven
SHOT GLASS
2 parts Jack Daniel's®
1 part Tequila
1 part Rum
1 part Goldschläger®
1 part Hot Sauce
Shake with ice and strain.

New England Kamikaze
SHOT GLASS
2 parts Grand Marnier®
1 part Sweet & Sour Mix
Shake with ice and strain.

New York Slammer

SHOT GLASS

1 part Amaretto
1 part Orange Juice
1 part Southern Comfort®
1 part Triple Sec
1 part Sloe Gin

Shake with ice and strain.

A Night at Naughty Nikki's

SHOT GLASS

1 part Vodka
2 parts Lemon-Lime Soda

Place Skittles or other fruity chewy candy in the bottom of a shot glass, then pour Lemon-Lime Soda and Vodka.

Night Flight Shooter

SHOT GLASS

1 part Amaretto
1 part Peach Schnapps
1 part Blackberry Liqueur

Shake with ice and strain.

Night Hunter

SHOT GLASS

1 part Red Bull Energy Drink
1 part Jägermeister

Build in order. Do not chill.

Ninja

SHOT GLASS

3 parts Frangelico®
1 part Melon Liqueur

Shake with ice and strain.

Nitro

SHOT GLASS

1 part Sambuca
1 part Goldschläger®
1 part Brandy

Shake with ice and strain.

No Name

SHOT GLASS

1 part Amaretto
1 part Whiskey
1 part Sweet & Sour Mix

Shake with ice and strain.

Norwegian Pastry

SHOT GLASS

1 part Crème de Cacao (Dark)
1 part Coffee
1 part Aquavit
1 part Vanilla Liqueur

Shake with ice and strain.

Nuclear Accelerator

SHOT GLASS

1 part Citrus Vodka
1 part Crème de Menthe (White)

Shake with ice and strain.

Nuclear Holocaust

SHOT GLASS

1 part Blue Curaçao
1 part Peach Schnapps
1 part Crème de Banane
1 part Dark Rum

Shake with ice and strain.

Nuclear Kamikaze

SHOT GLASS

3 parts Vodka
1 part Lime Juice
1 part Triple Sec
2 parts Melon Liqueur

Shake with ice and strain.

Nuclear Waste

SHOT GLASS

2 parts Vodka
1 part Melon Liqueur
1 part Triple Sec
splash Lime Juice

Shake with ice and strain.

Nuts 'n' Holly

SHOT GLASS

1 part Drambuie®
1 part Irish Cream Liqueur
1 part Frangelico®
1 part Amaretto

Shake with ice and strain.

Nutty Aruban

SHOT GLASS

1 part Frangelico®
1 part Ponche Kuba®

Shake with ice and strain.

Nutty Jamaican

SHOT GLASS

1 part Dark Rum
1 part Frangelico®

Shake with ice and strain.

Nutty Mexican

SHOT GLASS

1 part Silver Tequila
1 part Frangelico®

Shake with ice and strain.

Nutty Orange

SHOT GLASS

1 part Amaretto
1 part Triple Sec

Shake with ice and strain.

Nutty Professor

SHOT GLASS

1 part Grand Marnier®
1 part Frangelico®
1 part Irish Cream Liqueur

Shake with ice and strain.

Nymphomaniac

SHOT GLASS

3 parts Spiced Rum
1 part Peach Schnapps
1 part Coconut Rum

Shake with ice and strain.

Oatmeal Cookie

SHOT GLASS

2 parts Cinnamon Schnapps
1 part Irish Cream Liqueur
1 part Coffee Liqueur
1 part Frangelico®
1 part Cream

Shake with ice and strain.

Obly Gooh

SHOT GLASS

2 parts Crème de Menthe (White)
1 part Brandy

Shake with ice and strain.

An Offer You Can't Refuse

SHOT GLASS

1 part Amaretto
1 part Sambuca

Shake with ice and strain.

Oil Slick

SHOT GLASS

1 part Jägermeister®
1 part Rumple Minze®

Pour ingredients into glass neat (do not chill).

Old Crusty

SHOT GLASS

1 part 151-Proof Rum
1 part Wild Turkey® Bourbon

Shake with ice and strain.

Open Grave

SHOT GLASS

1 part Jägermeister®
1 part Rumple Minze®
1 part Irish Cream Liqueur

Shake with ice and strain.

Opera House Special

SHOT GLASS

1 part Tequila
1 part Gin
1 part Light Rum
1 part Vodka
1 part Pineapple Juice
1 part Orange Juice
1 part Sweet & Sour Mix

Shake with ice and strain. Because this recipe includes many ingredients, it's easier to make in volume, about 6 shots.

Oral Sex

SHOT GLASS

1 part Amaretto
1 part Irish Cream Liqueur

Shake with ice and strain.

Orange Crisis

SHOT GLASS

2 parts Light Rum
2 parts Peach Schnapps
1 part Triple Sec
1 part Apricot Brandy
1 part Cream
splash Grenadine

Shake with ice and strain. Because this recipe includes many ingredients, it's easier to make in volume, about 6 shots.

Orange Crush Shooter

SHOT GLASS

1 part Vodka
1 part Triple Sec
1 part Club Soda

Stir gently with ice and strain.

Orange Monk

SHOT GLASS

3 parts Frangelico®
1 part Grand Marnier®

Pour ingredients into glass neat (do not chill).

Orange Whip

SHOT GLASS

3 parts RumChata
1 part Orange Vodka
1 part Whipped Cream Vodka

Shake with ice and strain.

Orgasm

SHOT GLASS

1 part Amaretto
1 part Coffee Liqueur
1 part Light Cream

Shake with ice and strain.

Orgasm #2

SHOT GLASS

1 part Vodka
1 part Amaretto
1 part Coffee Liqueur
1 part Irish Cream Liqueur

Shake with ice and strain.

Orgasm #3

SHOT GLASS

3 parts Southern Comfort®
2 parts Pineapple Juice
1 part Amaretto

Shake with ice and strain.

Otter Pop

SHOT GLASS

2 parts Light Rum
2 parts Blue Curaçao
1 part Sweet & Sour Mix
1 part Lemon-Lime Soda

Shake with ice and strain.

Paddington Bear Surprise

SHOT GLASS

1 part Bacardi® Limón Rum
1 part Coffee Liqueur
2 splashes Orange Marmalade
dash Brown Sugar

Combine all ingredients in a blender with no ice. Blend until smooth.

Paddy's Day Special

SHOT GLASS

1 part Crème de Menthe (Green)
1 part Triple Sec
1 part Melon Liqueur

Build in the glass with no ice.

Paint Ball

SHOT GLASS

1 part Banana Liqueur
1 part Blue Curaçao
1 part Irish Cream Liqueur
1 part Southern Comfort®
1 part Triple Sec

Shake with ice and strain. Because this recipe includes many ingredients, it's easier to make in volume, about 6 shots.

Paintbox

SHOT GLASS

1 part Banana Liqueur
1 part Blue Curaçao
1 part Cherry Liqueur

Shake with ice and strain.

Pamoyo

SHOT GLASS

1 part Gin
1 part Lemon-Lime Soda
1 part Grape Juice (Red)

Shake with ice and strain.

Pancake

SHOT GLASS

1 part Cinnamon Schnapps
1 part Irish Cream Liqueur
1 part Cream

Shake with ice and strain.

Pancho Villa Shooter

SHOT GLASS

1 part Silver Tequila
1 part Amaretto
1 part 151-Proof Rum

Shake with ice and strain.

Pants on Fire

SHOT GLASS

1 part Vodka
1 part Strawberry Liqueur
1 part Banana Liqueur
1 part Grapefruit Juice
1 part Orange Juice

Shake with ice and strain. Because this recipe includes many ingredients, it's easier to make in volume, about 6 shots.

Panty Burner Shooter

SHOT GLASS

1 part Advocaat
1 part Coffee
1 part Frangelico®

Shake with ice and strain.

Panty Quiver

SHOT GLASS

1 part Jägermeister®
1 part Blackberry Brandy

Shake with ice and strain.

Panty Raid

SHOT GLASS

2 parts Citrus Vodka
1 part Chambord®
splash Lemon-Lime Soda
splash Pineapple Juice

Shake with ice and strain.

Par 4

SHOT GLASS

1 part Amaretto
1 part Southern Comfort
1 part Lime Juice
1 part Sweet & Sour Mix

Shake with ice and strain.

Paralyzer Shooter
SHOT GLASS
1 part Vodka
1 part Coffee Liqueur
1 part Cola
1 part Milk
Shake with ice and strain.

Paranoia
SHOT GLASS
2 parts Amaretto
1 part Orange Juice
Shake with ice and strain.

Party Animal
SHOT GLASS
1 part Parfait Amour
1 part Crème de Coconut
1 part Orange Juice
Shake with ice and strain.

Passion Killer Shooter
SHOT GLASS
1 part Silver Tequila
1 part Melon Liqueur
1 part Passion Fruit Liqueur
Shake with ice and strain.

Passion Slam
SHOT GLASS
1 part Passion Fruit Liqueur
1 part Kiwi Schnapps
1 part Lime Juice
Shake with ice and strain.

Passout
SHOT GLASS
1 part Amaretto
1 part Licor 43®
1 part Southern Comfort®
1 part Triple Sec
1 part Jack Daniel's®
Shake with ice and strain.
Because this recipe includes many ingredients, it's easier to make in volume, about 6 shots.

PB&J
SHOT GLASS
1 part Vodka
1 part Raspberry Liqueur
1 part Frangelico®
Shake with ice and strain.

Peach Cobbler
SHOT GLASS
1 part Peach Schnapps
1 part RumChata
Shake with ice and strain.

Peach Death
SHOT GLASS
1 part Vodka
1 part Peach Schnapps
1 part Amaretto
Shake with ice and strain.

Peach Nehi
SHOT GLASS
1 part Vodka
1 part Peach Schnapps
1 part Cherry Liqueur
1 part Sweet & Sour Mix
1 part Pineapple Juice
1 part Lemon-Lime Soda
Shake with ice and strain.
Because this recipe includes many ingredients, it's easier to make in volume, about 6 shots.

Peaches and Cream Shot
SHOT GLASS
3 parts Peach Schnapps
2 parts Cream
1 part 151-Proof Rum
Shake with ice and strain.

Peachfuzz
SHOT GLASS
1 part Peach Schnapps
1 part Cranberry Juice Cocktail
Shake with ice and strain.

Pearl Diver

SHOT GLASS

1 part Melon Liqueur
1 part Pineapple Juice
1 part Coconut Rum

Shake with ice and strain.

Pearl Harbor

SHOT GLASS

1 part Vodka
1 part Melon Liqueur
1 part Orange Juice

Shake with ice and strain.

Pearl Necklace

SHOT GLASS

1 part Tequila Rose®
1 part Irish Cream Liqueur

Shake with ice and strain.

Pecker Head

SHOT GLASS

1 part Southern Comfort®
1 part Amaretto
1 part Pineapple

Shake with ice and strain.

Pecker Wrecker

SHOT GLASS

1 part Blackberry Brandy
1 part Crème de Noyaux
1 part 151-Proof Rum
1 part Pineapple Juice
1 part Cranberry Juice Cocktail

Shake with ice and strain. Because this recipe includes many ingredients, it's easier to make in volume, about 6 shots.

Pedra

SHOT GLASS

1 part Tequila
1 part Vodka
1 part Dark Rum
1 part Irish Cream Liqueur
1 part Grenadine
1 part Absinthe

Shake with ice and strain. Because this recipe includes many ingredients, it's easier to make in volume, about 6 shots.

Pee Gee

SHOT GLASS

1 part Cinnamon Schnapps
1 part Orange Juice
1 part Vodka

Shake with ice and strain.

Penthouse

SHOT GLASS

1 part Tequila
1 part Bacardi® Limón Rum
1 part Lime Juice

Shake with ice and strain.

Peppermint

SHOT GLASS

3 parts Pepper Vodka
1 part Crème de Menthe (White)

Shake with ice and strain.

Peppermint Bonbon

SHOT GLASS

4 parts Peppermint Schnapps
1 part Chocolate Syrup

Shake with ice and strain.

Peppermint Pattie®

SHOT GLASS

1 part Coffee Liqueur
1 part Peppermint Schnapps
1 part Half and Half

Shake with ice and strain.

Peppermint Rose
SHOT GLASS
1 part Peppermint Schnapps
1 part Tequila Rose®
Shake with ice and strain.

PeptoChata
SHOT GLASS
1 part Cherry Vodka
1 part RumChata
Shake with ice and strain.

Peschino
SHOT GLASS
1 part Peach Schnapps
1 part Strawberry Liqueur
Shake with ice and strain.

Petronius
SHOT GLASS
2 parts Jim Beam®
1 part Vanilla Liqueur
1 part Peppermint Liqueur
Shake with ice and strain.

Pez®
SHOT GLASS
1 part Spiced Rum
1 part Raspberry Liqueur
1 part Sweet & Sour Mix
Shake with ice and strain.

Photon Torpedo
SHOT GLASS
1 part After Shock® Cinnamon Schnapps
1 part Vodka
Shake with ice and strain.

A Piece of Ass
SHOT GLASS
1 part Amaretto
1 part Southern Comfort®
Shake with ice and strain.

Pierced Fuzzy Navel
SHOT GLASS
2 parts Peach Schnapps
1 part Vodka
1 part Orange Juice
Shake with ice and strain.

Pierced Nipple
SHOT GLASS
1 part Sambuca
1 part Irish Cream Liqueur
Shake with ice and strain.

Pigskin Shot
SHOT GLASS
1 part Vodka
1 part Melon Liqueur
1 part Sweet & Sour Mix
Shake with ice and strain.

Piña Crana Kazi
SHOT GLASS
2 parts Vodka
1 part Triple Sec
1 part Pineapple Juice
Shake with ice and strain.

Pineapple Bomb
SHOT GLASS
1 part Southern Comfort®
1 part Triple Sec
1 part Pineapple Juice
Shake with ice and strain.

Pineapple Upside-Down Cake
SHOT GLASS
1 part Irish Cream Liqueur
1 part Vodka
1 part Butterscotch Schnapps
1 part Pineapple Juice
Shake with ice and strain.

Pineapple Upside-Down Cake #2

SHOT GLASS

2 parts RumChata
1 part Whipped Cream Vodka
splash Grenadine
splash Pineapple Juice

Shake with ice and strain.

Pineberry

SHOT GLASS

1 part Cranberry Vodka
1 part Pineapple Vodka

Shake with ice and strain.

Pink Belly

SHOT GLASS

1 part Jim Beam®
1 part Amaretto
1 part Sloe Gin
1 part Irish Cream Liqueur
1 part Lemon-Lime Soda

Shake with ice and strain. Because this recipe includes many ingredients, it's easier to make in volume, about 6 shots.

Pink Cadillac

SHOT GLASS

2 parts Vodka
1 part Cherry Juice
1 part Lemonade
1 part Orange Juice

Shake with ice and strain.

Pink Cod Shooter

SHOT GLASS

1 part Tequila Reposado
1 part Sweet & Sour Mix

Shake with ice and strain.

Pink Cotton Candy

SHOT GLASS

1 part Vodka
1 part Amaretto
splash Grenadine

Shake with ice and strain.

Pink Danger

SHOT GLASS

1 part Butterscotch Schnapps
2 parts Vodka
3 parts Fruit Punch

Shake with ice and strain.

Pink Floyd

SHOT GLASS

1 part Vodka
1 part Peach Schnapps
1 part Cranberry Juice Cocktail
1 part Grapefruit Juice

Shake with ice and strain.

Pink Lemonade Shooter

SHOT GLASS

1 part Vodka
1 part Sweet & Sour Mix
1 part Cranberry Juice Cocktail

Shake with ice and strain.

Pink Nipple Shooter

SHOT GLASS

3 parts Currant Vodka
1 part Sambuca

Shake with ice and strain.

Pink Ranger

SHOT GLASS

2 parts Vodka
1 part Coconut Rum
1 part Peach Schnapps
1 part Cranberry Juice Cocktail
1 part Pineapple Juice

Shake with ice and strain.

Pinkeye

SHOT GLASS

1 part Vodka
1 part Cranberry Juice Cocktail
1 part Sweet & Sour Mix

Shake with ice and strain.

Pinky

SHOT GLASS

3 parts Rumple Minze®
1 part Fire Water®

Shake with ice and strain.

Pissed Off Mexican

SHOT GLASS

1 part Cinnamon Schnapps
1 part Silver Tequila

Shake with ice and strain.

Pistol Shot

SHOT GLASS

1 part Triple Sec
1 part Apricot Brandy
1 part Cherry Brandy

Shake with ice and strain.

Pit Bull and Crank Shooter

SHOT GLASS

1 part Rum
1 part Tequila
1 part Jägermeister®
1 part Seagram's® Crown 7 Whiskey
1 part Peppermint Schnapps

Shake with ice and strain. Because this recipe includes many ingredients, it's easier to make in volume, about 6 shots.

Pit Bull on Crack

SHOT GLASS

1 part Bourbon
1 part Dark Rum
1 part Gold Tequila
1 part Jägermeister

Shake with ice and strain.

Pixy Stix®

SHOT GLASS

2 parts Southern Comfort®
1 part Amaretto

Shake with ice and strain.

Pleading Insanity

SHOT GLASS

1 part Silver Tequila
1 part Vodka
1 part Dark Rum

Shake with ice and strain.

Poco Loco Boom

SHOT GLASS

1 part Vodka
1 part Tia Maria®
1 part Cream of Coconut

Shake with ice and strain.

Point-Blank

SHOT GLASS

1 part Brandy
1 part Crème de Banane
1 part Apricot Brandy
1 part Cherry Brandy

Shake with ice and strain.

Poison Apple

SHOT GLASS

1 part Apple Brandy
1 part Vodka

Shake with ice and strain.

Poison Ivy

SHOT GLASS

1 part Cinnamon Schnapps
1 part Coffee Liqueur

Shake with ice and strain.

Poison Milk

SHOT GLASS

1 part Jägermeister®
1 part Irish Cream Liqueur

Shake with ice and strain.

Polar Bear Shot

SHOT GLASS

1 part Crème de Cacao (White)
1 part Peppermint Schnapps

Shake with ice and strain.

Poop Shoot

SHOT GLASS

2 parts Sambuca
1 part Fruit Punch

Shake with ice and strain.

Popper

SHOT GLASS

1 part Vodka
3 parts Lemon-Lime Soda

Build in the glass with no ice.

Porto Covo

SHOT GLASS

1 part Vodka
1 part Absinthe
1 part Crème de Coconut
1 part Banana Liqueur

Shake with ice and strain.

Pouce Coupe Puddle

SHOT GLASS

2 parts Irish Cream Liqueur
1 part Peach Schnapps
1 part Crème de Menthe (White)

Shake with ice and strain.

Power Drill

SHOT GLASS

1 part Vodka
1 part Orange Juice
1 part Beer

Build in the glass with no ice.

Power Shot

SHOT GLASS

2 parts Vodka
1 part Absolut® Peppar Vodka
dash Wasabi

Build in the glass with no ice.

Prestone

SHOT GLASS

1 part Melon Liqueur
2 parts Citrus Vodka
2 parts Lemon-Lime Soda

Shake with ice and strain.

Prickly Pear

SHOT GLASS

1 part Ginger Liqueur
1 part Gold Tequila
1 part Pear Vodka

Shake with ice and strain.

Protein Smoothie

SHOT GLASS

1 part Scotch
1 part Cream
1 part Clamato® Juice

Shake with ice and strain.

Prozac®

SHOT GLASS

1 part Crown Royal® Whiskey
1 part Melon Liqueur
1 part Lemon-Lime Soda

Shake with ice and strain.

Pucker Sucker

SHOT GLASS

1 part Sour Apple Schnapps
1 part Coffee Liqueur
1 part Orange Juice

Shake with ice and strain.

Puerto Rican Monkey Fuck

SHOT GLASS

2 parts Coffee Liqueur
2 parts Crème de Banane
1 part 151-Proof Rum

Shake with ice and strain.

Puke

SHOT GLASS

1 part Jack Daniel's®
1 part Jim Beam®
1 part Yukon Jack®
1 part Vodka
1 part Tequila

Shake with ice and strain.

Pumpkin Pie

SHOT GLASS

2 parts Coffee Liqueur
1 part Irish Cream Liqueur
1 part Goldschläger®

Shake with ice and strain.

Puppy's Nose

SHOT GLASS

1 part Peppermint Schnapps
1 part Tia Maria®
1 part Irish Cream Liqueur

Build in the glass with no ice.

Purple Alaskan

SHOT GLASS

1 part Amaretto
1 part Jack Daniel's®
1 part Orange Juice
1 part Southern Comfort®
1 part Raspberry Liqueur

Shake with ice and strain. Because this recipe includes many ingredients, it's easier to make in volume, about 6 shots.

Purple Elastic Thunder Fuck

SHOT GLASS

1 part Vodka
1 part Crown Royal® Whiskey
1 part Southern Comfort®
1 part Amaretto
1 part Raspberry Liqueur
1 part Pineapple Juice
1 part Cranberry Juice Cocktail

Shake with ice and strain. Because this recipe includes many ingredients, it's easier to make in volume, about 6 shots.

Purple Haze

SHOT GLASS

1 part Citrus Vodka
1 part Raspberry Liqueur
1 part Lemon-Lime Soda

Shake with ice and strain.

Purple Haze #2

SHOT GLASS

1 part Amaretto
1 part Root Beer Schnapps
1 part Milk
1 part Grape Soda

Shake with ice and strain.

Purple Helmeted Warrior

SHOT GLASS

1 part Gin
1 part Southern Comfort®
1 part Peach Schnapps
1 part Blue Curaçao
1 part Lime Juice
1 part Grenadine
1 part Lemon-Lime Soda

Shake with ice and strain. Because this recipe includes many ingredients, it's easier to make in volume, about 6 shots.

Purple Hooter

SHOT GLASS

1 part Raspberry Liqueur
1 part Vodka
1 part Sweet & Sour Mix

Shake with ice and strain.

Purple Mother Comfort

SHOT GLASS

1 part Amaretto
1 part Blue Curaçao
1 part Southern Comfort
1 part Cranberry Juice

Shake with ice and strain.

Purple Nipple
SHOT GLASS
3 parts Melon Liqueur
1 part Jägermeister®
2 parts Cranberry Juice Cocktail
1 part Orange Juice
Shake with ice and strain.

Purple Panther
SHOT GLASS
3 parts Sour Apple Vodka
1 part Blue Curaçao
Shake with ice and strain.

Purple Penis
SHOT GLASS
2 parts Vodka
1 part Blue Curaçao
1 part Raspberry Liqueur
Shake with ice and strain.

Purple Rain Shooter
SHOT GLASS
3 parts Cranberry Vodka
1 part Blue Curaçao
Shake with ice and strain.

Purple Viper
SHOT GLASS
1 part Sloe Gin
1 part Vodka
2 parts Raspberry Liqueur
Shake with ice and strain.

Purple Wind
SHOT GLASS
1 part Raspberry Liqueur
2 parts Sake
Shake with ice and strain.

Pussy in a Fight
SHOT GLASS
1 part Gin
1 part Frangelico®
Shake with ice and strain.

Pussy Juice
SHOT GLASS
1 part Goldschläger®
1 part Vodka
1 part Vegetable Juice Blend
Shake with ice and strain.

Quaalude
SHOT GLASS
1 part Vodka
1 part Coffee Liqueur
1 part Irish Cream Liqueur
1 part Amaretto
1 part Frangelico®
Shake with ice and strain.
Because this recipe includes many ingredients, it's easier to make in volume, about 6 shots.

Quick Fuck
SHOT GLASS
1 part Coffee Liqueur
1 part Melon Liqueur
1 part Irish Cream Liqueur
Shake with ice and strain.

Quick Silver
SHOT GLASS
1 part Anisette
1 part Triple Sec
1 part Tequila
Shake with ice and strain.

Quicksand Shooter
SHOT GLASS
1 part Black Sambuca
3 parts Orange Juice
Shake with ice and strain.

Rabbit Punch
SHOT GLASS
1 part Campari®
1 part Crème de Cacao (Dark)
1 part Coconut Rum
2 parts Irish Cream Liqueur
Shake with ice and strain.

Raging Indian
SHOT GLASS
1 part Vodka
1 part Coffee Liqueur
1 part Orange Juice
1 part Mango Nectar
Shake with ice and strain.

Raija
SHOT GLASS
1 part Vanilla Liqueur
1 part Coffee Liqueur
1 part Orange Juice
1 part Mango Juice
Shake with ice and strain.

Rambo Shot
SHOT GLASS
1 part Jägermeister®
1 part Rumple Minze®
Shake with ice and strain.

Raspberry Beret
SHOT GLASS
1 part Vodka
1 part Raspberry Liqueur
1 part Cream
Shake with ice and strain.

Raspberry Chocolate Truffle
SHOT GLASS
2 parts Chambord
1 part Coffee Liqueur
1 part Crème de Cacao (Dark)
1 part Irish Cream Liqueur
Shake with ice and strain.

Rat Shooter
SHOT GLASS
3 parts Green Chartreuse®
1 part Rumple Minze®
Build in the glass with no ice.

Ray of Light
SHOT GLASS
1 part Crème de Cacao (White)
1 part Galliano®
1 part Grand Marnier®
Shake with ice and strain.

Razor Blade
SHOT GLASS
1 part Jägermeister®
1 part 151-Proof Rum
Shake with ice and strain.

Ready Set Go
SHOT GLASS
1 part Crème de Banane
1 part Melon Liqueur
1 part Strawberry Liqueur
Shake with ice and strain.

Real Strong Dirty Rotten Scoundrel
SHOT GLASS
1 part Cranberry Vodka
½ part Melon Liqueur
Shake with ice and strain.

Rebel Jester
SHOT GLASS
2 parts Kiwi Schnapps
1 part Goldschläger®
Shake with ice and strain.

Reboot
SHOT GLASS
1 part Crème de Menthe (Green)
1 part Cachaça
2 parts Absolut® Peppar Vodka
Shake with ice and strain.

Red Baron Shooter
SHOT GLASS
2 parts Crown Royal® Whiskey
1 part Amaretto
1 part Cranberry Juice Cocktail
Shake with ice and strain.

Red Beard

SHOT GLASS

2 parts Spiced Rum
2 parts Coconut Rum
1 part Grenadine
1 part Lemon-Lime Soda

Shake with ice and strain.

Red Death

SHOT GLASS

1 part Vodka
1 part Fire Water®
1 part Yukon Jack®
1 part 151-Proof Rum

Shake with ice and strain.

Red Devil Shooter

SHOT GLASS

1 part Vodka
1 part Southern Comfort®
1 part Amaretto
1 part Triple Sec
1 part Grenadine
1 part Orange Juice
1 part Sweet & Sour Mix

Shake with ice and strain. Because this recipe includes many ingredients, it's easier to make in volume, about 6 shots.

Red Dragon's Breath

SHOT GLASS

1 part Cinnamon Schnapps
1 part Whiskey

Shake with ice and strain.

Red-Eyed Heaven

SHOT GLASS

1 part Vanilla Vodka
1 part Peach Schnapps
1 part Grenadine

Shake with ice and strain.

Red-Eyed Hell

SHOT GLASS

1 part Vodka
1 part 151-Proof Rum
1 part Triple Sec
2 parts spicy vegetable Juice

Shake with ice and strain.

Red Frog Roadkill

SHOT GLASS

1 part Raspberry Liqueur
1 part Amaretto
1 part Jim Beam®
2 parts Cranberry Juice Cocktail

Shake with ice and strain.

Red-Headed Leg Spreader

SHOT GLASS

1 part Jägermeister
1 part Tequila
1 part Vodka
1 part Cranberry Juice

Shake with ice and strain.

Red-Headed Princess

SHOT GLASS

1 part Jägermeister®
1 part Peach Schnapps
2 parts Cranberry Juice Cocktail

Shake with ice and strain.

Red-Headed Vamp

SHOT GLASS

1 part Raspberry Liqueur
1 part Jägermeister®
1 part Cranberry Juice Cocktail

Shake with ice and strain.

Red-Line

SHOT GLASS

1 part Silver Tequila
1 part Sambuca
splash Crème de Cassis

Shake with ice and strain.

Red Lobster
SHOT GLASS

1 part Amaretto
1 part Southern Comfort®
1 part Cranberry Juice Cocktail

Shake with ice and strain.

Red Monster
SHOT GLASS

1 part Tequila
1 part Orange Juice

Shake with ice and strain.

Red Mosquito
SHOT GLASS

1 part Vodka
1 part Hot Damn!® Cinnamon Schnapps

Shake with ice and strain.

Red Royal Shot
SHOT GLASS

1 part Crown Royal® Whiskey
1 part Amaretto

Shake with ice and strain.

Red Snapper Shooter
SHOT GLASS

2 parts Canadian Whisky
1 part Amaretto

Shake with ice and strain.

Redneck Killer
SHOT GLASS

1 part Jack Daniel's®
1 part Jim Beam®
1 part Wild Turkey® 101

Build in the glass with no ice.

Regulator
SHOT GLASS

1 part Crown Royal® Whiskey
1 part Melon Liqueur
3 parts Cranberry Juice Cocktail

Shake with ice and strain.

Republica das Bananas
SHOT GLASS

1 part Silver Tequila
1 part Rum
1 part Crème de Banane

Shake with ice and strain.

Retribution
SHOT GLASS

1 part Rumple Minze®
1 part Tequila
1 part Jägermeister®
1 part Fire Water®

Shake with ice and strain.

Roadkill Shot
SHOT GLASS

1 part Tequila
1 part Hot Damn!® Cinnamon Schnapps
1 part Whiskey

Shake with ice and strain.

Roadrunner Punch
SHOT GLASS

1 part Coconut Rum
1 part Blue Curaçao
1 part Peach Schnapps
1 part Fruit Punch

Shake with ice and strain.

Roasted Toasted Almond Shooter
SHOT GLASS

1 part Amaretto
1 part Coffee Liqueur
1 part Cream
1 part Vodka

Shake with ice and strain.

Robot
SHOT GLASS

2 parts Jack Daniel's®
1 part Vodka
1 part Grenadine

Shake with ice and strain.

Rocket Fuel

SHOT GLASS

2 parts 151-Proof Rum
1 part Vodka
1 part Blue Curaçao

Shake with ice and strain.

Rocket Pop

SHOT GLASS

2 parts Bacardi® Limón Rum
1 part Lemon-Lime Soda
1 part Cranberry Juice Cocktail
1 part Sweet & Sour Mix

Shake with ice and strain.

Rocky Mountain

SHOT GLASS

2 parts Southern Comfort®
2 parts Amaretto
1 part Lime Juice

Shake with ice and strain.

Rocky Mountain Bear Fucker

SHOT GLASS

1 part Tequila
1 part Jack Daniel's®
1 part Southern Comfort®

Shake with ice and strain.

Rocky Mountain Mother

SHOT GLASS

1 part Amaretto
1 part Yukon Jack
2 parts Sweetened Lime Juice

Shake with ice and strain.

Romulan Ale Shooter

SHOT GLASS

1 part Vodka
1 part Tropical Punch Schnapps
1 part Cactus Juice Schnapps

Shake with ice and strain.

Roommate Killer

SHOT GLASS

1 part Jägermeister®
1 part Rumple Minze®

Shake with ice and strain.

Rooster Piss

SHOT GLASS

1 part Jack Daniel's®
1 part Cinnamon Schnapps

Shake with ice and strain.

Rooster Tail

SHOT GLASS

1 part Tequila
1 part Orange Juice
dash Salt

Shake with ice and strain.

Root Beer Float Shooter

SHOT GLASS

3 parts RumChata
2 parts Root Beer Vodka
1 part Whipped Cream Vodka

Shake with ice and strain.

Rosso di Sera

SHOT GLASS

1 part Vodka
1 part Strawberry Liqueur
1 part Triple Sec

Shake with ice and strain.

Rosy Cheeks

SHOT GLASS

1 part Strawberry Liqueur
1 part Melon Liqueur
1 part Sweet & Sour Mix

Shake with ice and strain.

Rot Gut

SHOT GLASS

1 part Cinnamon Schnapps
1 part Vodka

Shake with ice and strain.

Rotten Apple
SHOT GLASS

1 part Jägermeister®
1 part Sour Apple Schnapps

Shake with ice and strain.

Rotten Pussy
SHOT GLASS

2 parts Midori®
1 part Amaretto
1 part Southern Comfort®
1 part Coconut Rum
1 part Sweet & Sour Mix
1 part Pineapple Juice

Shake with ice and strain.

Royal
SHOT GLASS

1 part Vodka
1 part Crème de Banane
1 part Blue Curaçao
1 part Lemon Juice

Shake with ice and strain.

Royal Apple
SHOT GLASS

1 part Crown Royal® Whiskey
1 part Sour Apple Schnapps
2 parts Cranberry Juice Cocktail

Shake with ice and strain.

Royal Bitch
SHOT GLASS

1 part Frangelico®
1 part Crown Royal® Whiskey

Shake with ice and strain.

Royal Flush
SHOT GLASS

1 part Crown Royal® Whiskey
1 part Peach Schnapps
2 parts Cranberry Juice Cocktail
2 parts Orange Juice
splash Club Soda

Shake all but Club Soda with ice and strain. Top with Club Soda.

Royal Fuck
SHOT GLASS

1 part Crown Royal® Whiskey
1 part Chambord®
1 part Peach Schnapps
1 part Pineapple Vodka
1 part Cranberry Juice Cocktail

Shake with ice and strain.

Royal Scandal
SHOT GLASS

1 part Crown Royal® Whiskey
1 part Southern Comfort®
1 part Amaretto
1 part Sweet & Sour Mix
1 part Pineapple Juice

Shake with ice and strain. Because this recipe includes many ingredients, it's easier to make in volume, about 6 shots.

Royal Shock
SHOT GLASS

1 part After Shock® Cinnamon Schnapps
2 parts Crown Royal® Whiskey

Build in the glass with no ice.

Royal Sicilian Kiss
SHOT GLASS

2 parts Amaretto
1 part Crown Royal® Whiskey
1 part Southern Comfort®

Shake with ice and strain.

Rubber Biscuit
SHOT GLASS

1 part Crown Royal® Whiskey
1 part Butterscotch Schnapps

Shake with ice and strain.

Ruby Red
SHOT GLASS

2 parts Vodka
2 parts Cranberry Juice Cocktail
1 part Sweet & Sour Mix

Shake with ice and strain.

Rug Burn

SHOT GLASS

1 part Irish Cream Liqueur
1 part Coffee Liqueur
1 part Irish Whiskey

Shake with ice and strain.

Rum Bubblegum

SHOT GLASS

1 part Crème de Banane
1 part Irish Cream Liqueur
1 part Light Rum

Shake with ice and strain.

Rum Runner Shooter

SHOT GLASS

1 part Dark Rum
1 part Spiced Rum
1 part Coconut Rum
1 part Crème de Banane
1 part Blackberry Liqueur
1 part Grenadine
1 part Sweet & Sour Mix
1 part Orange Juice

Shake with ice and strain. Because this recipe includes many ingredients, it's easier to make in volume, about 6 shots.

RumChata Butterworth

SHOT GLASS

1 part Butterscotch Liqueur
1 part RumChata

Shake with ice and strain.

Rumka

SHOT GLASS

1 part Vodka
1 part Spiced Rum

Shake with ice and strain.

RumpleChata

SHOT GLASS

1 part RumChata
1 part Rumple Minze

Shake with ice and strain.

Russian Apple

SHOT GLASS

1 part Cranberry Vodka
1 part Pineapple Vodka
1 part Vodka

Shake with ice and strain.

Russian Ballet

SHOT GLASS

3 parts Vodka
1 part Crème de Cassis

Shake with ice and strain.

Russian Kamikaze

SHOT GLASS

2 parts Vodka
1 part Raspberry Liqueur

Shake with ice and strain.

Russian Quaalude Shooter

SHOT GLASS

1 part Vodka
1 part Frangelico®
1 part Irish Cream Liqueur
1 part Coffee Liqueur
1 part Cream

Shake with ice and strain. Because this recipe includes many ingredients, it's easier to make in volume, about 6 shots.

Russian Roulette

SHOT GLASS

1 part Vodka
1 part Galliano®
1 part 151-Proof Rum

Shake with ice and strain.

Russian Tongue

SHOT GLASS

1 part Goldschläger®
1 part Rumple Minze®
1 part Vodka

Shake with ice and strain.

Rusted Throat
SHOT GLASS

1 part Light Rum
1 part Orange Juice
1 part Passion Fruit Nectar
1 part 151-Proof Rum

Shake with ice and strain.

Rusty Halo
SHOT GLASS

1 part Vodka
1 part Amaretto
1 part Banana Liqueur
1 part Melon Liqueur

Shake with ice and strain.

Rusty Lambada
SHOT GLASS

1 part Butterscotch Liqueur
1 part Spiced Rum
1 part Cranberry Juice
1 part Maple Syrup

Shake with ice and strain.

Rusty Navel
SHOT GLASS

1 part Tequila
1 part Amaretto

Shake with ice and strain.

Rythym & Blues
SHOT GLASS

1 part Jack Daniel's®
1 part Blueberry Schnapps

Shake with ice and strain.

S.H.I.T.
SHOT GLASS

1 part Sambuca
2 parts Crème Liqueur
2 parts Irish Mist®
1 part Tequila

Shake with ice and strain.

Sabra
SHOT GLASS

1 part Godiva Chocolate Liqueur
1 part Orange Vodka

Shake with ice and strain. Named after the Israeli liqueur made from chocolate and Jaffa oranges.

Saikkosen Special
SHOT GLASS

1 part Cointreau®
2 parts Crème de Cassis
2 parts Tia Maria®

Shake with ice and strain.

Sambuca Slide
SHOT GLASS

2 parts Sambuca
1 part Vodka
1 part Light Cream

Shake with ice and strain.

Sambuca Surprise
SHOT GLASS

1 part Crème de Cacao (White)
1 part Crème de Menthe (White)
1 part Sambuca

Shake with ice and strain.

Sammy Slammer
SHOT GLASS

2 parts Southern Comfort®
1 part Vanilla Liqueur
1 part Peach Schnapps

Shake with ice and strain.

A Sample
SHOT GLASS

1 part Grain Alcohol
1 part Gatorade®

Shake with ice and strain.

Sand Bag

SHOT GLASS

1 part Tequila
1 part Jägermeister®
dash Salt

Shake with ice and strain.

Sandblaster

SHOT GLASS

1 part Light Rum
1 part Lime Juice
2 parts Cola

Stir gently with ice and strain.

Sandy Beach

SHOT GLASS

1 part Irish Cream Liqueur
1 part Butterscotch Schnapps
1 part Amaretto
1 part Cream

Shake with ice and strain.

Saratoga Trunk

SHOT GLASS

1 part Silver Tequila
1 part Tia Maria®
1 part Goldschläger®

Shake with ice and strain.

Satan's Mouthwash

SHOT GLASS

1 part Jack Daniel's®
1 part Sambuca

Shake with ice and strain.

Saturnus

SHOT GLASS

1 part Crème de Banane
1 part Gin
1 part Dry Vermouth
2 parts Orange Juice

Shake with ice and strain.

Scarlet O'Hara Shooter

SHOT GLASS

2 parts Southern Comfort®
1 part Sweet & Sour Mix
1 part Grenadine

Shake with ice and strain.

Schwimmer

SHOT GLASS

2 parts Sambuca
1 part Coffee Liqueur
1 part Irish Cream Liqueur
1 part Butterscotch Schnapps
1 part Jägermeister®

Shake with ice and strain.
Because this recipe includes many ingredients, it's easier to make in volume, about 6 shots.

Scooby Shooter

SHOT GLASS

2 parts Coconut Rum
2 parts Peach Schnapps
2 parts Melon Liqueur
1 part Vodka
1 part Orange Juice
1 part Pineapple Juice

Shake with ice and strain.
Because this recipe includes many ingredients, it's easier to make in volume, about 6 shots.

Scorpion Shooter

SHOT GLASS

2 parts Vodka
1 part Blackberry Liqueur

Shake with ice and strain.

Scorpion Suicide

SHOT GLASS

2 parts Cherry Brandy
1 part Whiskey
1 part Pernod®

Shake with ice and strain.

Screamer
SHOT GLASS

1 part Gin
1 part Rum
1 part Tequila
1 part Triple Sec
1 part Vodka

Shake with ice and strain. Because this recipe includes many ingredients, it's easier to make in volume, about 6 shots.

Screaming Blue Messiah
SHOT GLASS

1 part Goldschläger®
1 part Blue Curaçao

Shake with ice and strain.

Screaming Blue Viking
SHOT GLASS

1 part Yukon Jack®
1 part Rumple Minze®
1 part Blue Curaçao

Shake with ice and strain.

Screaming Green Monster
SHOT GLASS

1 part Coconut Rum
1 part Midori®
1 part 151-Proof Rum
1 part Pineapple Juice
1 part Lemon-Lime Soda

Shake with ice and strain. Because this recipe includes many ingredients, it's easier to make in volume, about 6 shots.

Screaming Moose
SHOT GLASS

1 part Jägermeister®
1 part Coffee Liqueur
1 part Irish Cream Liqueur

Shake with ice and strain.

Screaming Nazi
SHOT GLASS

1 part Jägermeister
1 part Peppermint Schnapps

Shake with ice and strain.

Screaming Orgasm
SHOT GLASS

1 part Cream
1 part Vodka
1 part Amaretto
1 part Crème de Banane

Shake with ice and strain.

Screaming Peach
SHOT GLASS

1 part Peach Schnapps
1 part Melon Liqueur
1 part Grenadine
2 parts Pineapple Juice

Shake with ice and strain.

Screaming Purple Jesus
SHOT GLASS

1 part Vodka
1 part Grape Juice (Red)

Shake with ice and strain.

Screaming Yoda®
SHOT GLASS

1 part Melon Liqueur
1 part Jägermeister®
1 part Orange Juice

Shake with ice and strain.

Screw 'n' Mail
SHOT GLASS

1 part Crème de Banane
1 part Cherry Brandy
1 part Chocolate Mint Liqueur

Shake with ice and strain.

Second Childhood

SHOT GLASS

1 part Crème de Menthe (White)
1 part Vodka

Shake with ice and strain.

Secret Heart

SHOT GLASS

1 part Crème de Cacao (White)
1 part Amaretto
1 part Strawberry Liqueur

Shake with ice and strain.

Seeing Stars

SHOT GLASS

1 part Crème de Menthe (White)
1 part Coffee
1 part Crème de Banane

Shake with ice and strain.

Señor Freak

SHOT GLASS

1 part Tequila Reposado
1 part Light Rum
1 part Vodka
1 part Lemon-Lime Soda

Shake with ice and strain.

Sensei on the Rocks

SHOT GLASS

1 part Coffee Liqueur
1 part Coconut Rum
1 part Jack Daniel's®

Shake with ice and strain.

Seven Twenty-Seven

SHOT GLASS

1 part Vodka
1 part Crème de Coconut

Shake with ice and strain.

Sex in the Parking Lot

SHOT GLASS

1 part Raspberry Liqueur
1 part Vodka
1 part Sour Apple Schnapps

Shake with ice and strain.

Sex Machine

SHOT GLASS

1 part Coffee Liqueur
1 part Irish Cream Liqueur
1 part Milk

Shake with ice and strain.

Sex on Acid

SHOT GLASS

2 parts Jägermeister®
1 part Melon Liqueur
1 part Blackberry Liqueur
1 part Pineapple Juice
1 part Cranberry Juice Cocktail

Shake with ice and strain.
Because this recipe includes many ingredients, it's easier to make in volume, about 6 shots.

Sex on a Pool Table

SHOT GLASS

1 part Peach Schnapps
1 part Vodka
1 part Pineapple Juice
1 part Sweet & Sour Mix
1 part Melon Liqueur

Shake with ice and strain.
Because this recipe includes many ingredients, it's easier to make in volume, about 6 shots.

Sex on the Beach Shooter

SHOT GLASS

1 part Vodka
1 part Peach Schnapps
1 part Orange Juice

Shake with ice and strain.

Sex on the Lake

SHOT GLASS

2 parts Crème de Banane
2 parts Crème de Cacao (Dark)
1 part Light Rum
1 part Cream

Shake with ice and strain.

Sex under the Moonlight

SHOT GLASS

2 parts Vodka
1 part Coffee
1 part Port
1 part Cream

Shake with ice and strain.

Sex up against the Wall

SHOT GLASS

2 parts Currant Vodka
1 part Pineapple Juice
1 part Sweet & Sour Mix

Shake with ice and strain.

Sex with an Alligator

SHOT GLASS

1 part Jägermeister®
1 part Melon Liqueur
1 part Raspberry Liqueur
1 part Pineapple Juice

Shake with ice and strain.

Sexual Stimulation

SHOT GLASS

2 parts Rum
1 part Crème de Menthe (Green)
1 part Crème de Banane
1 part Passion Fruit Nectar

Shake with ice and strain.

Sexy Alligator

SHOT GLASS

2 parts Coconut Rum
2 parts Melon Liqueur
1 part Jägermeister®
1 part Raspberry Liqueur
1 part Pineapple Juice

Shake with ice and strain.

Shag Later

SHOT GLASS

2 parts After Shock® Cinnamon Schnapps
1 part Canadian Whisky
1 part Root Beer
splash Chocolate Syrup

Shake with ice and strain.

Shake That Ass

SHOT GLASS

1 part Blue Curaçao
1 part Banana Liqueur
1 part Sweet & Sour Mix
1 part Orange Juice

Shake with ice and strain.

Shampoo

SHOT GLASS

1 part Irish Cream Liqueur
1 part Butterscotch Schnapps

Shake with ice and strain.

Shape Shifter

SHOT GLASS

1 part Crème de Menthe (Green)
1 part Orange Juice
dash Wasabi

Build in the glass with no ice.

Shark Bite Shooter

SHOT GLASS

1 part Dark Rum
1 part Grenadine
2 parts Orange Juice

Shake with ice and strain.

Shazam Shooter

SHOT GLASS

1 part Sour Apple Schnapps
1 part Raspberry Liqueur
1 part Cranberry Juice Cocktail

Shake with ice and strain.

Shipwreck Shooter

SHOT GLASS

1 part Rum
1 part Crème de Banane
1 part Strawberry Liqueur
1 part Sweet & Sour Mix

Shake with ice and strain.

Shit Kicker

SHOT GLASS

1 part Rye Whiskey
1 part Crème de Menthe (Green)
1 part Grenadine

Shake with ice and strain.

Shit Stain

SHOT GLASS

1 part Crème de Cacao (Dark)
1 part Jägermeister®
1 part Vodka

Shake with ice and strain.

Shittin' Blue

SHOT GLASS

1 part Blueberry Schnapps
½ part Blue Curaçao
½ part Blue Raspberry Liqueur
½ part Vodka

Shake with ice and strain.

Shogun Shooter

SHOT GLASS

3 parts Citrus Vodka
1 part Melon Liqueur

Shake with ice and strain.

Short Southern Screw

SHOT GLASS

1 part Orange Vodka
1 part Southern Comfort
splash Orange Juice

Shake with ice and strain.

Short Vodka Breakfast

SHOT GLASS

1 part Triple Sec
1 part Orange Vodka

Shake with ice and strain.

Shot from Hell

SHOT GLASS

1 part Jägermeister®
2 parts Peppermint Schnapps

Shake with ice and strain.

Shot in the Back

SHOT GLASS

3 parts Vodka
1 part Goldschläger®
dash Wasabi

Pour ingredients into glass neat (do not chill).

Shot-Gun

SHOT GLASS

1 part Jim Beam®
1 part Jack Daniel's®
1 part Wild Turkey® Bourbon

Shake with ice and strain.

Shot-o-Happiness

SHOT GLASS

2 parts Goldschläger®
2 parts Raspberry Liqueur
1 part Pineapple Juice
1 part Sweet & Sour Mix
1 part Lemon-Lime Soda

Shake with ice and strain.

Shrewsbury Slammer

SHOT GLASS

1 part Southern Comfort®
1 part Peach Schnapps
2 parts Apple Cider

Shake with ice and strain.

Siberian Gold

SHOT GLASS

2 part Vodka
2 part Goldschläger®
1 part Blue Curaçao

Shake with ice and strain.

Siberian Toolkit

SHOT GLASS

4 parts Vodka
1 part Whiskey

Shake with ice and strain.

Siberian Walrus

SHOT GLASS

2 parts Blue Curaçao
1 part Light Rum
1 part Vodka
1 part Jack Daniel's®
1 part Kirschwasser
1 part Orange Juice

Shake with ice and strain. Because this recipe includes many ingredients, it's easier to make in volume, about 6 shots.

Sicilian Sunset

SHOT GLASS

1 part Southern Comfort®
1 part Amaretto
1 part Grenadine
2 parts Orange Juice

Shake with ice and strain.

Silk Panties

SHOT GLASS

1 part Peach Schnapps
3 parts Vodka

Shake with ice and strain.

Silver Bullet Shooter

SHOT GLASS

2 parts Peppermint Schnapps
1 part Vodka

Shake with ice and strain.

Silver Devil

SHOT GLASS

1 part Tequila
1 part Peppermint Schnapps

Shake with ice and strain.

Silver Nipple

SHOT GLASS

4 parts Sambuca
1 part Vodka

Shake with ice and strain.

Silver Spider

SHOT GLASS

1 part Vodka
1 part Rum
1 part Triple Sec
1 part Crème de Cacao (White)

Shake with ice and strain.

Silver Wilson

SHOT GLASS

1 part Kiwi Schnapps
1 part Passion Fruit Liqueur
1 part Sweet & Sour Mix

Shake with ice and strain.

Simple Green

SHOT GLASS

1 part Blue Curaçao
1 part Galliano®
1 part Jägermeister®

Shake with ice and strain.

Simpson Bronco

SHOT GLASS

4 parts Sambuca
1 part Grenadine
1 part Orange Juice

Shake with ice and strain.

Sin-cicle
SHOT GLASS
1 part Amaretto
1 part RumChata
Shake with ice and strain.

Singles Night
SHOT GLASS
1 part Coffee Liqueur
1 part Crème de Banane
1 part Cointreau®
1 part Irish Cream Liqueur
Shake with ice and strain.

Sing-Sing
SHOT GLASS
1 part Blue Curaçao
1 part Cream
1 part Crème de Banane
1 part Frangelico®
Shake with ice and strain.

Sit Down and Shut Up
SHOT GLASS
1 part Blackberry Liqueur
1 part Peppermint Liqueur
1 part Southern Comfort®
Shake with ice and strain.

Sit in Judgment
SHOT GLASS
1 part Coffee Liqueur
1 part Dark Spiced Rum
1 part Jägermeister
1 part Peppermint Schnapps
1 part Vodka
Shake with ice and strain.

Sit on My Face, Sammy
SHOT GLASS
1 part Crown Royal® Whiskey
1 part Frangelico®
1 part Irish Cream Liqueur
Shake with ice and strain.

Sivitri
SHOT GLASS
1 part Lychee Liqueur
1 part Absinthe
Shake with ice and strain.

Skandia Iceberg
SHOT GLASS
1 part Crème de Menthe (White)
1 part Vodka
Shake with ice and strain.

Ski Jump
SHOT GLASS
2 parts Vodka
1 part Melon Liqueur
1 part Peppermint Schnapps
Shake with ice and strain.

Skid Mark
SHOT GLASS
1 part Coffee Liqueur
1 part Jägermeister®
1 part Rumple Minze®
Shake with ice and strain.

Skittles®
SHOT GLASS
1 part Vodka
1 part Southern Comfort®
1 part Melon Liqueur
1 part Pineapple Juice
1 part Sweet & Sour Mix
Shake with ice and strain.

Skull
SHOT GLASS
1 part Coffee Liqueur
1 part Irish Cream Liqueur
1 part Whiskey
Shake with ice and strain.

Sky Pilot
SHOT GLASS

1 part Vodka
1 part Irish Cream Liqueur
1 part Peppermint Schnapps

Shake with ice and strain.

Slam Dunk Shooter
SHOT GLASS

2 parts Tequila Reposado
1 part Lime Cordial
1 part Club Soda

Shake all but Club Soda with ice and strain. Top with Club Soda.

Slammer
SHOT GLASS

1 part Vodka
1 part Lemon-Lime Soda

Build in the glass with no ice.

Slap Shot
SHOT GLASS

2 parts Southern Comfort®
1 part Peppermint Schnapps

Shake with ice and strain.

Slice of Apple Pie
SHOT GLASS

3 parts Vodka
1 part Apple Juice

Shake with ice and strain.

Slick and Sleezy
SHOT GLASS

1 part Salsa
5 parts Vodka

Build in the glass with no ice.

Slickster
SHOT GLASS

2 parts Southern Comfort®
1 part Peach Schnapps
1 part Lemon-Lime Soda

Stir gently with ice and strain.

Slippery Cricket
SHOT GLASS

1 part Vodka
1 part Blue Hawaiian Schnapps
1 part Tropical Punch Schnapps

Shake with ice and strain.

Slippery Nipple
SHOT GLASS

1 part Coffee Liqueur
1 part Irish Cream Liqueur
1 part Peppermint Schnapps

Shake with ice and strain.

Slippery Nuts Shooter
SHOT GLASS

1 part Amaretto
1 part Butterscotch Liqueur
1 part Frangelico

Shake with ice and strain.

Slippery Saddle
SHOT GLASS

1 part Vodka
1 part Licor 43®
1 part Orange Juice

Shake with ice and strain.

Sloe Southern Fuck
SHOT GLASS

1 part Sloe Gin
1 part Southern Comfort®
1 part Sweet & Sour Mix
1 part Lemon-Lime Soda

Build in the glass with no ice.

Sloppy Vagina
SHOT GLASS

1 part Vodka
1 part Irish Cream Liqueur
2 parts 151-Proof Rum
splash Lime Juice

Shake with ice and strain.

Small Bomb

SHOT GLASS

1 part Vodka
1 part Triple Sec
1 part Grenadine

Shake with ice and strain.

Smartie®

SHOT GLASS

1 part Grape Schnapps
1 part Melon Liqueur

Shake with ice and strain.

Smashing Pumpkin

SHOT GLASS

1 part Coffee Liqueur
1 part Irish Cream Liqueur
1 part Goldschläger®

Shake with ice and strain.

Smeraldo

SHOT GLASS

3 parts Gin
3 parts Fruit Punch
2 parts Blue Curaçao
1 part Cointreau®
1 part Peach Nectar

Shake with ice and strain.

Smiles

SHOT GLASS

1 part Crème de Menthe (White)
1 part Amaretto
1 part Whiskey
1 part Lemon-Lime Soda

Build in the glass with no ice.

Smooth and Sweet

SHOT GLASS

2 parts Amaretto
2 parts Blackberry Liqueur
1 part Pineapple Juice

Shake with ice and strain.

Smooth Dog

SHOT GLASS

3 parts Amaretto
1 part Lemon-Lime Soda

Build in the glass with no ice.

Smoothie

SHOT GLASS

1 part Crown Royal® Whiskey
1 part Amaretto
1 part Triple Sec
1 part Sweet & Sour Mix
1 part Lemon-Lime Soda

Shake with ice and strain.

Smurf® Fart

SHOT GLASS

1 part Blue Curaçao
2 parts Blueberry Schnapps
1 part Cream

Shake with ice and strain.

Smurf® Pee

SHOT GLASS

1 part 151-Proof Rum
1 part Blue Curaçao
1 part Jägermeister®
1 part Rumple Minze®

Shake with ice and strain.

Snakebite

SHOT GLASS

1 part Tequila
1 part Southern Comfort®

Shake with ice and strain.

Sneeker
SHOT GLASS

1 part Raspberry Liqueur
1 part Coconut Rum
1 part 151-Proof Rum
1 part Midori®
1 part Cranberry Juice Cocktail
1 part Lemon-Lime Soda

Shake with ice and strain. Because this recipe includes many ingredients, it's easier to make in volume, about 6 shots.

Snickers®
SHOT GLASS

1 part Crème de Cacao (Dark)
1 part Frangelico®

Shake with ice and strain.

Snoopy® Dog
SHOT GLASS

2 parts Vodka
1 part Grenadine
1 part Amaretto
1 part Crème de Banane

Shake with ice and strain.

Snot Rocket
SHOT GLASS

1 part Apple Brandy
1 part Sour Apple Schnapps
1 part Vodka

Shake with ice and strain.

Snotty Toddy
SHOT GLASS

1 part Midori®
1 part 151-Proof Rum
1 part Orange Juice

Shake with ice and strain.

Snow Drop Shooter
SHOT GLASS

1 part Crème de Cacao (White)
1 part Vodka
1 part Triple Sec

Shake with ice and strain.

Snow in Kentucky
SHOT GLASS

1 part Peppermint Schnapps
1 part Wild Turkey Bourbon

Shake with ice and strain.

Snow Melter
SHOT GLASS

1 part Sambuca
1 part Crème de Cacao (White)
1 part Rum

Shake with ice and strain.

Snow Shoe
SHOT GLASS

1 part Vodka
1 part Peppermint Schnapps

Shake with ice and strain.

Snowball
SHOT GLASS

1 part Jack Daniel's®
1 part Rumple Minze®

Shake with ice and strain.

Snowsnake Juice
SHOT GLASS

1 part Bourbon
1 part Peppermint Schnapps

Pour ingredients into glass neat (do not chill).

SoCo Slammer
SHOT GLASS

1 part Southern Comfort®
2 parts Cola

Build in the glass with no ice.

SoCo & Lime
SHOT GLASS

1 part Southern Comfort®
splash Lime Juice

Shake with ice and strain.

SoCo Peach and Lime

SHOT GLASS

2 parts Peach Schnapps
2 parts Southern Comfort®
1 part Lime Juice

Shake with ice and strain.

Solar Flare

SHOT GLASS

1 part Vodka
1 part Triple Sec

Shake with ice and strain.

Solaris

SHOT GLASS

1 part Spiced Rum
1 part Grenadine
dash Sugar

Shake with ice and strain.

Solo Shot

SHOT GLASS

1 part Peach Schnapps
1 part Raspberry Liqueur
3 parts Cranberry Juice Cocktail

Shake with ice and strain.

Son of a Peach

SHOT GLASS

1 part Vodka
1 part Peach Schnapps
1 part Honey

Shake with ice and strain.

Songbird

SHOT GLASS

1 part Silver Tequila
1 part Vodka
1 part Crème de Banane

Shake with ice and strain.

Soother

SHOT GLASS

2 parts Amaretto
2 parts Melon Liqueur
1 part Vodka
1 part Sweet & Sour Mix

Shake with ice and strain.

Soul Taker

SHOT GLASS

1 part Vodka
1 part Tequila
1 part Amaretto

Shake with ice and strain.

Sour Grapes

SHOT GLASS

1 part Vodka
1 part Raspberry Liqueur
1 part Sweet & Sour Mix

Shake with ice and strain.

Sour Jack

SHOT GLASS

1 part Jack Daniel's®
1 part Raspberry Liqueur

Shake with ice and strain.

Sourball

SHOT GLASS

1 part Vodka
1 part Lemonade
1 part Orange Juice

Shake with ice and strain.

Southern Beamy Brain Damage

SHOT GLASS

1 part Southern Comfort®
1 part Jim Beam®
1 part Tia Maria®
splash Grenadine

Shake all but Grenadine with ice and strain. Place a few drops of Grenadine in the center of the drink.

Southern Bitch

SHOT GLASS

1 part Southern Comfort®
1 part Amaretto
1 part Peach Schnapps
1 part Pineapple Juice
1 part Orange Juice

Shake with ice and strain. Because this recipe includes many ingredients, it's easier to make in volume, about 6 shots.

Southern Bondage

SHOT GLASS

1 part Southern Comfort®
1 part Amaretto
1 part Peach Schnapps
1 part Triple Sec
1 part Cranberry Juice Cocktail
1 part Sweet & Sour Mix

Shake with ice and strain. Because this recipe includes many ingredients, it's easier to make in volume, about 6 shots.

Southern Chase

SHOT GLASS

1 part Galliano®
1 part Southern Comfort®
1 part Jim Beam®

Shake with ice and strain.

Southern Comfort® Kamikaze

SHOT GLASS

3 parts Southern Comfort®
2 parts Triple Sec
1 part Lime Juice

Shake with ice and strain.

Southern Comfort® Pink

SHOT GLASS

1 part Light Rum
1 part Southern Comfort®
1 part Grapefruit Juice
1 part Grenadine

Shake with ice and strain.

Southern Fruity Passion

SHOT GLASS

1 part Southern Comfort®
1 part Triple Sec
1 part Grenadine

Shake with ice and strain.

Southern Ireland

SHOT GLASS

1 part Irish Cream Liqueur
1 part Southern Comfort®

Shake with ice and strain.

Southern Peach

SHOT GLASS

2 parts Peach Schnapps
1 part Southern Comfort®

Shake with ice and strain.

Southern Pink Flamingo

SHOT GLASS

1 part Southern Comfort®
1 part Coconut Rum
1 part Pineapple Juice
splash Grenadine
splash Lemon Juice

Shake with ice and strain.

Southern Pride

SHOT GLASS

2 parts Southern Comfort®
1 part Peach Schnapps

Shake with ice and strain.

Southern Slammer

SHOT GLASS

1 part Peach Schnapps
1 part Vanilla Liqueur
1 part Southern Comfort®

Shake with ice and strain.

Southern Smile

SHOT GLASS

1 part Southern Comfort®
1 part Amaretto
1 part Cranberry Juice Cocktail

Shake with ice and strain.

Southpaw

SHOT GLASS

1 part Brandy
1 part Orange Juice
1 part Lemon-Lime Soda

Build in the glass with no ice.

Space Odyssey

SHOT GLASS

1 part 151-Proof Rum
1 part Coconut Rum
1 part Pineapple Juice

Shake with ice and strain.

Spanish Moss Shooter

SHOT GLASS

2 parts Coffee Liqueur
1 part Crème de Menthe (Green)
1 part Silver Tequila

Shake with ice and strain.

Sparato Milano

SHOT GLASS

2 parts Sambuca
1 part Amaretto
1 part Cherry Brandy

Shake with ice and strain.

Sparkplug

SHOT GLASS

1 part 151-Proof Rum
1 part Rumple Minze®

Pour ingredients into glass neat (do not chill).

Speedy Gonzales® Shooter

SHOT GLASS

1 part Amaretto
1 part Irish Cream Liqueur

Shake with ice and strain.

Sperm

SHOT GLASS

1 part Tequila
1 part Vodka
splash Cream

Shake all but Cream with ice and strain. Place a few drops of Cream in the center of the drink.

Sperm Bank Shooter

SHOT GLASS

1 part Tequila Reposado
splash Irish Cream Liqueur

Pour the Tequila into the shot glass. Place a few drops of Irish Cream Liqueur in the center of the drink.

Sperm Whale

SHOT GLASS

3 parts Rye Whiskey
3 parts Southern Comfort®
1 part Cream

Shake with ice and strain.

Spice Cake

SHOT GLASS

1 part Irish Cream Liqueur
1 part Amaretto
1 part Cinnamon Schnapps

Shake with ice and strain.

Spiced Apple

SHOT GLASS

1 part Apple Brandy
1 part Goldschläger®
2 parts Spiced Rum

Shake with ice and strain.

Spiced Jolly Roger
SHOT GLASS

1 part Goldschläger®
1 part Spiced Rum

Shake with ice and strain.

Spindle
SHOT GLASS

1 part Amaretto
1 part Crown Royal® Whiskey
1 part Peach Schnapps

Shake with ice and strain.

Spiritwalker
SHOT GLASS

1 part Jägermeister®
1 part Rumple Minze®
1 part 151-Proof Rum
1 part Fire Water®

Shake with ice and strain.

Spitfire
SHOT GLASS

1 part Jack Daniel's®
1 part Rum
1 part Vodka

Shake with ice and strain.

Sprawling Dubinsky
SHOT GLASS

1 part Johnnie Walker® Red Label
1 part Johnnie Walker® Black Label
1 part Citrus Vodka
splash Amaretto

Shake with ice and strain.

Spy Catcher
SHOT GLASS

2 parts Whiskey
1 part Sambuca

Shake with ice and strain.

Squirrel's Fantasy
SHOT GLASS

2 parts Amaretto
1 part Frangelico®
1 part Club Soda

Build in the glass with no ice.

Squished Smurf®
SHOT GLASS

2 parts Peach Schnapps
1 part Irish Cream Liqueur
1 part Blue Curaçao
splash Grenadine

Build in the glass with no ice.

Squishy
SHOT GLASS

1 part Raspberry Liqueur
1 part Amaretto
1 part Vodka

Shake with ice and strain.

SR-71
SHOT GLASS

1 part Amaretto
1 part Irish Cream Liqueur

Shake with ice and strain.

St. Clement's Shooter
SHOT GLASS

1 part Triple Sec
1 part Mandarine Napoléon® Liqueur

Shake with ice and strain.

St. Deliah
SHOT GLASS

1 part Crème de Banane
1 part Raspberry Liqueur

Shake with ice and strain.

Stabilizer

SHOT GLASS

1 part 151-Proof Rum
1 part Rumple Minze®

Shake with ice and strain.

Stained Blue Dress

SHOT GLASS

1 part Vodka
1 part Blue Curaçao
splash Irish Cream Liqueur

Shake all but Irish Cream with ice and strain. Place a few drops of Irish Cream in the center of the drink.

Star Wars® II

SHOT GLASS

2 parts Southern Comfort®
1 part Orange Juice

Shake with ice and strain.

Starburst Shooter

SHOT GLASS

2 parts Dark Rum
1 part Pineapple Juice
1 part Vermouth

Shake with ice and strain.

Stardust

SHOT GLASS

1 part Citrus Vodka
1 part Peach Schnapps
1 part Blue Curaçao
1 part Sweet & Sour Mix
1 part Pineapple Juice
1 part Grenadine

Shake with ice and strain. Because this recipe includes many ingredients, it's easier to make in volume, about 6 shots.

Start Me Up

SHOT GLASS

2 parts Vodka
1 part Tequila
1 part Currant Vodka
1 part Dark Rum

Shake with ice and strain.

Steel Shooter

SHOT GLASS

2 parts Cinnamon Schnapps
2 parts Vanilla Liqueur
1 part Whiskey

Shake with ice and strain.

Stevie Ray Vaughan

SHOT GLASS

1 part Jack Daniel's®
1 part Southern Comfort®
1 part Triple Sec
1 part Sweet & Sour Mix
4 parts Orange Juice

Shake with ice and strain.

Stevie Wonder

SHOT GLASS

1 part Coffee Liqueur
1 part Crème de Cacao (Dark)
1 part Amaretto
1 part Galliano®

Shake with ice and strain.

Stiff Dick

SHOT GLASS

1 part Butterscotch Schnapps
1 part Irish Cream Liqueur

Shake with ice and strain.

Stiletto Shooter

SHOT GLASS

1 part Coffee Liqueur
1 part Peppermint Schnapps
1 part Tequila

Shake with ice and strain.

Stinky Weasel

SHOT GLASS

1 part Tequila
1 part 151-Proof Rum
1 part Lemon Juice
2 dashes Sugar

Shake with ice and strain.

Stop Lights

SHOT GLASS

3 parts Vodka
splash Midori®
splash Orange Juice
splash Cranberry Juice Cocktail

Shake Vodka with ice and strain equal parts into three shot glasses. Top the first glass with Melon Liqueur, the second with Orange Juice, and the third one with Cranberry Juice. Drink all three shots rapidly and in order.

Stormtrooper®

SHOT GLASS

1 part Peppermint Schnapps
1 part Jägermeister®

Shake with ice and strain.

Straight Jacket

SHOT GLASS

2 parts Cinnamon Schnapps
1 part Passoã®
1 part Orange Juice

Shake with ice and strain.

Stranded in Tijuana

SHOT GLASS

1 part Sloe Gin
1 part Tequila Reposado
1 part 151-Proof Rum

Shake with ice and strain.

Strawberry Bliss Bomb

SHOT GLASS

1 part Crème de Cacao (White)
1 part Strawberry Liqueur
1 part Crème de Coconut

Shake with ice and strain.

Strawberry Lemondrop

SHOT GLASS

1 part Vodka
1 part Strawberry Liqueur
fill with Lemonade

Build over ice and stir.

Strawberry Lips

SHOT GLASS

1 part Strawberry Liqueur
1 part Crème de Coconut
1 part Cream

Shake with ice and strain.

Stroke

SHOT GLASS

3 parts Banana Liqueur
1 part Irish Cream Liqueur
splash Grenadine

Shake all but Grenadine with ice and strain. Place a few drops of Grenadine in the center of the drink.

Strong Bad

SHOT GLASS

1 part Southern Comfort®
1 part Vanilla Vodka
1 part Tonic Water

Build in the glass with no ice.

Stumble Fuck

SHOT GLASS

1 part Jägermeister®
1 part Rumple Minze®
1 part Cinnamon Schnapps

Shake with ice and strain.

Stumpfucker

SHOT GLASS

1 part Jägermeister®
1 part Rumple Minze®
1 part 151-Proof Rum

Shake with ice and strain.

Sublime

SHOT GLASS

1 part Amaretto
1 part Banana Liqueur
1 part Crème de Cacao (White)

Shake with ice and strain.

Suicide Stop Light

SHOT GLASS

1 part Midori®
1 part Vodka
1 part After Shock® Cinnamon Schnapps
splash Orange Juice

Fill the first of three shot glasses with Midori®, the second one with 1 part Vodka and 1 part Orange Juice, and the last one with After Shock. Drink all three rapidly and in order.

Sun Scorcher

SHOT GLASS

3 parts Butterscotch Schnapps
1 part Vodka

Shake with ice and strain.

Sunny Mexico

SHOT GLASS

1 part Galliano®
1 part Tequila

Shake with ice and strain.

Sunset at the Beach

SHOT GLASS

2 parts Cranberry Vodka
1 part Melon Liqueur
1 part Raspberry Liqueur
2 parts Pineapple Juice

Shake with ice and strain.

Super Dave

SHOT GLASS

1 part Spiced Rum
1 part Coconut Rum
1 part Pineapple Juice
1 part Cola

Shake with ice and strain.

Supermodel

SHOT GLASS

3 parts Bacardi® Limón Rum
1 part Melon Liqueur
1 part Blue Curaçao

Shake with ice and strain.

Surfer on Acid

SHOT GLASS

1 part Jägermeister®
1 part Coconut Rum
1 part Pineapple Juice

Shake with ice and strain.

Surfer on Ecstasy

SHOT GLASS

1 part Jägermeister
1 part Light Rum
1 part Raspberry Liqueur
1 part Pineapple Juice

Shake with ice and strain.

Susu

SHOT GLASS

2 parts Vodka
1 part Irish Cream Liqueur
1 part Crème de Cacao (Dark)
1 part Coffee Liqueur
1 part Grenadine
2 parts Milk

Shake with ice and strain. Because this recipe includes many ingredients, it's easier to make in volume, about 6 shots.

Swamp Thing

SHOT GLASS

1 part Coffee Liqueur
1 part Irish Cream Liqueur
1 part Crème de Menthe (White)

Shake with ice and strain.

Swan Song

SHOT GLASS

1 part Southern Comfort®
1 part Whiskey
1 part Amaretto
1 part Dark Rum
1 part Orange Juice
1 part Cranberry Juice Cocktail
1 part Lime Juice

Shake with ice and strain. Because this recipe includes many ingredients, it's easier to make in volume, about 6 shots.

Swedish Color

SHOT GLASS

1 part Banana Liqueur
1 part Blue Curaçao
1 part Vodka

Shake with ice and strain.

Swedish Fish

SHOT GLASS

1 part Blackberry Liqueur
1 part Triple Sec
1 part Cranberry Juice

Shake with ice and strain.

Sweet and Sour Pussy

SHOT GLASS

1 part Raspberry Liqueur
1 part Cherry Whiskey

Shake with ice and strain.

Sweet Indulgence

SHOT GLASS

1 part Crème de Cacao (Dark)
1 part Cherry Brandy
1 part Cream

Shake with ice and strain.

Sweet Jesus

SHOT GLASS

1 part 151-Proof Rum
1 part Southern Comfort®

Shake with ice and strain.

Sweet Lips

SHOT GLASS

1 part 151-Proof Rum
1 part Whiskey
1 part Tequila Reposado

Shake with ice and strain.

Sweet Pickle

SHOT GLASS

1 part Vodka
1 part Rumple Minze®
1 part Melon Liqueur

Shake with ice and strain.

Sweet Pigeon

SHOT GLASS

1 part Citrus Vodka
2 parts Crème de Cacao (White)
1 part Blue Curaçao
2 parts Cream

Shake with ice and strain.

Sweet Shit

SHOT GLASS

1 part Vodka
1 part Amaretto
1 part Irish Cream Liqueur
1 part Coffee Liqueur
2 parts Chocolate Syrup

Shake with ice and strain. Because this recipe includes many ingredients, it's easier to make in volume, about 6 shots.

Sweet Sting

SHOT GLASS

1 part Goldschläger®
1 part Cream

Shake with ice and strain.

Sweet Tart

SHOT GLASS

1 part Raspberry Liqueur
1 part Sweet & Sour Mix
1 part Southern Comfort®

Shake with ice and strain.

Sweet Tits

SHOT GLASS

1 part Strawberry Liqueur
1 part Apricot Brandy
1 part Pineapple Juice

Shake with ice and strain.

Swell Sex

SHOT GLASS

1 part Vodka
1 part Coconut Rum
1 part Melon Liqueur
1 part Cream
1 part Pineapple Juice

Shake with ice and strain.

Swift Kick in the Balls

SHOT GLASS

1 part Rum
1 part Vodka
1 part Lemon Juice

Shake with ice and strain.

Swiss Peach

SHOT GLASS

1 part Peach Schnapps
1 part Crème de Cacao (White)

Shake with ice and strain.

Tablazo

SHOT GLASS

1 part Vodka
1 part Ginger Ale

Build in the glass with no ice.

Tainted Heart

SHOT GLASS

1 part Cinnamon Schnapps
1 part Chocolate Liqueur

Shake with ice and strain.

Take It and Vomit

SHOT GLASS

1 part Vodka
1 part Peach Schnapps
1 part Blue Curaçao
1 part Grenadine
1 part Orange Juice

Shake with ice and strain.

Tangaroa

SHOT GLASS

3 parts Vodka
1 part Vanilla Liqueur

Shake with ice and strain.

Tank Force

SHOT GLASS

1 part Blue Curaçao
1 part Orange Juice
1 part Goldschläger®

Shake with ice and strain.

Tartan Special

SHOT GLASS

1 part Glayva®
1 part Drambuie®
1 part Irish Cream Liqueur

Shake with ice and strain.

Tarzan® Scream

SHOT GLASS

2 parts Vodka
2 parts 151-Proof Rum
1 part Caramel Syrup
splash Cream

Shake with ice and strain. Top with Cream.

T-Bone

SHOT GLASS

1 part 151-Proof Rum
splash Steak Sauce

Build in the glass with no ice.

Tear Drop

SHOT GLASS

3 parts Pepper Vodka
1 part Triple Sec

Shake with ice and strain.

Teen Wolf

SHOT GLASS

1 part Advocaat
1 part Kirschwasser

Shake with ice and strain.

Temptation Island

SHOT GLASS

1 part Crème de Coconut
1 part Frangelico®
1 part Peach Schnapps

Shake with ice and strain.

Tennessee Apple

SHOT GLASS

2 parts Fireball Cinnamon Whiskey
1 part Sour Apple Schnapps
2 parts Cranberry Juice

Shake with ice and strain.

Ten Snakes in a Lawnmower

SHOT GLASS

1 part 151-Proof Rum
1 part Raspberry Liqueur
1 part Southern Comfort®
1 part Melon Liqueur

Shake with ice and strain.

Tequila Headfuck

SHOT GLASS

1 part Irish Cream Liqueur
2 parts Tequila

Shake with ice and strain.

Tequila Lemondrop

SHOT GLASS

1 part Tequila
1 part Triple Sec
1 part Lemonade

Shake with ice and strain.

Tequila Pickle Shooter

SHOT GLASS

1 part Tequila
1 part Pickle Juice

Build in the glass with no ice.

Tequila Popper

SHOT GLASS

1 part Silver Tequila
1 part Lemon-Lime Soda

Build in the glass with no ice. Place your hand or a napkin over the glass and slam it down on the bar. Drink while it's still fizzing.

Tequila Rose

SHOT GLASS

1 part Tequila
1 part Triple Sec
1 part Cherry Juice
2 parts Sweet & Sour Mix

Shake with ice and strain.

Tequila Shot

SHOT GLASS

1 part Tequila
1 Lemon Wedge
dash Salt

Rub the lemon on the flesh between the thumb and forefinger of your left hand, cover the spot with salt, then hold the Lemon between your thumb and forefinger. Lick the Salt, shoot the Tequila, and suck the Lemon.

Tequila Slammer

SHOT GLASS

1 part Tequila
1 part Lemon-Lime Soda

Build in the glass with no ice.

Terminator

SHOT GLASS

1 part Jägermeister®
1 part Southern Comfort®

Shake with ice and strain.

Tetanus Shot

SHOT GLASS

1 part Irish Cream Liqueur
1 part Cherry Brandy
1 part Peach Schnapps

Shake with ice and strain.

Texas Antifreeze

SHOT GLASS

1 part Coconut Rum
1 part Citrus Vodka
1 part Melon Liqueur

Shake with ice and strain.

Texas Apple

SHOT GLASS

1 part Apple Whiskey
1 part Fireball Cinnamon Whiskey

Shake with ice and strain.

Texas Rattlesnake

SHOT GLASS

1 part Yukon Jack®
1 part Cherry Brandy
1 part Southern Comfort®
1 part Sweet & Sour Mix

Shake with ice and strain.

TGV

SHOT GLASS

1 part Tequila
1 part Gin
1 part Vodka

Build in the glass with no ice.

Third and Goal

SHOT GLASS

1 part Peach Schnapps
1 part Grand Marnier®
1 part Sweet & Sour Mix

Shake with ice and strain.

Third Reich

SHOT GLASS

1 part Jägermeister®
1 part Rumple Minze®
1 part Goldschläger®

Shake with ice and strain.

Thong

SHOT GLASS

2 parts Vodka
1 part Triple Sec
1 part Cream
1 part Orange Juice
1 part Crème de Noyaux
1 part Grenadine

Shake with ice and strain.
Because this recipe includes many ingredients, it's easier to make in volume, about 6 shots.

Thorazine®

SHOT GLASS

1 part Jägermeister®
1 part Rumple Minze®
1 part 151-Proof Rum

Shake with ice and strain.

Thorny Situation

SHOT GLASS

1 part Crème de Coconut
1 part Frangelico®
1 part Sweet & Sour Mix

Shake with ice and strain.

Three Day Weekend

SHOT GLASS

1 part Jägermeister®
1 part Malibu® Rum
1 part Pineapple Juice
1 part Grenadine

Shake with ice and strain.

Three-Dollar Hooker

SHOT GLASS

2 parts Irish Cream Liqueur
1 part Peppermint Schnapps
1 part Spiced Rum

Shake with ice and strain.

Three Leaf Clover

SHOT GLASS

1 part Whiskey
1 part Irish Mist®

Shake with ice and strain.

Three-Legged Monkey

SHOT GLASS

2 parts Bourbon
1 part Cola
1 part Lemon Juice

Shake with ice and strain.

Three Sheets to the Wind

SHOT GLASS

1 part Jägermeister®
1 part Rumple Minze®
1 part Tequila

Shake with ice and strain.

Three Stages of Friendship

SHOT GLASS

1 part Jack Daniel's®
1 part Tequila
1 part 151-Proof Rum

Shake with ice and strain.

Three Wise Men

SHOT GLASS

1 part Jack Daniel's®
1 part Johnnie Walker® Black Label
1 part Jim Beam®

Shake with ice and strain.

Three Wise Brits

SHOT GLASS

1 part Gin
1 part Scotch
1 part Sloe Gin

Shake with ice and strain.

Three Wise Men on a Farm

SHOT GLASS

1 part Jack Daniel's®
1 part Jim Beam®
1 part Yukon Jack®
1 part Wild Turkey® Bourbon

Pour ingredients into glass neat (do not chill).

Three Wise Men and Their Mexican Porter

SHOT GLASS

1 part Jack Daniel's®
1 part Rye Whiskey
1 part Scotch
1 part Tequila

Build in the glass with no ice.

Thumb Press

SHOT GLASS

2 parts Vodka
2 parts Midori®
1 part 151-Proof Rum
splash Grenadine

Shake with ice and strain.

Thumbs Up

SHOT GLASS

1 part Crème de Banane
1 part Cherry Brandy
1 part Mango Schnapps

Shake with ice and strain.

Thumper
SHOT GLASS

1 part Cognac
1 part Amer Picon®

Shake with ice and strain.

Thunder and Lightning
SHOT GLASS

1 part Rumple Minze®
1 part 151-Proof Rum

Shake with ice and strain.

Thundercloud Shooter
SHOT GLASS

1 part Amaretto
1 part Irish Mist®
1 part 151-Proof Rum

Shake with ice and strain.

Thundercloud
SHOT GLASS

2 parts Coffee Liqueur
1 part Southern Comfort®
1 part Peppermint Schnapps
1 part Rum
splash Cream

Shake all but Cream with ice and strain. Place a few drops of Cream in the center of the drink.

Thursday Shooter
SHOT GLASS

1 part Blue Curaçao
1 part Peach Schnapps
1 part Pineapple Juice

Shake with ice and strain.

Tic Tac® Shooter
SHOT GLASS

1 part Crème de Menthe (White)
1 part Ouzo

Shake with ice and strain.

Tidy Bowl
SHOT GLASS

4 parts Blue Curaçao
1 part Dr. McGillicuddy's® Mentholmint Schnapps
1 part Irish Cream Liqueur

Shake with ice and strain.

Tie Me to the Bedpost
SHOT GLASS

1 part Midori®
1 part Citrus Vodka
1 part Coconut Rum
1 part Sweet & Sour Mix

Shake with ice and strain.

Time Bomb
SHOT GLASS

1 part Blue Curaçao
1 part Melon Liqueur

Shake with ice and strain.

Tip Energizer
SHOT GLASS

1 part Passion Fruit Liqueur
1 part Blue Curaçao
1 part Lime Juice

Shake with ice and strain.

Tiramisu
SHOT GLASS

1 part Coffee Liqueur
1 part Chocolate Mint Liqueur

Shake with ice and strain.

Tired Pussy
SHOT GLASS

3 parts Coconut Rum
1 part Pineapple Juice
1 part Cranberry Juice Cocktail

Shake with ice and strain.

TKO
SHOT GLASS

1 part Tequila
1 part Coffee Liqueur
1 part Ouzo

Shake with ice and strain.

Toffee Apple
SHOT GLASS

1 part Vodka
1 part Butterscotch Schnapps
1 part Apple Brandy

Shake with ice and strain.

Tokyo Rose
SHOT GLASS

1 part Vodka
1 part Sake
1 part Melon Liqueur

Shake with ice and strain.

Tongue Twister
SHOT GLASS

2 parts Dark Rum
1 part Triple Sec
1 part Crème de Coconut

Shake with ice and strain.

Toolkit
SHOT GLASS

1 part Crème de Cacao (White)
1 part Irish Cream Liqueur
1 part Amaretto
1 part Coffee Liqueur

Shake with ice and strain.

Tootsie Roll®
SHOT GLASS

1 part Coffee Liqueur
1 part Orange Juice

Shake with ice and strain.

Top Banana Shooter
SHOT GLASS

1 part Crème de Cacao (White)
1 part Vodka
1 part Coffee
1 part Crème de Banane

Shake with ice and strain.

Toro
SHOT GLASS

1 part Spiced Rum
1 part Vodka
1 part Sweet & Sour Mix

Shake with ice and strain.

Tossed Salad
SHOT GLASS

chocolate syrup
1 part Coffee Liqueur
1 part Jägermeister

Dip rim of shot glass in Chocolate Syrup. Add the Coffee Liqueur and Jägermeister. Drink the shot without using your hands (as with the Blowjob shot).

To the Moon
SHOT GLASS

1 part Coffee Liqueur
1 part Amaretto
1 part Irish Cream Liqueur
1 part 151-Proof Rum

Shake with ice and strain.

Toxic Jelly Bean
SHOT GLASS

2 parts Jägermeister®
1 part Ouzo
1 part Blackberry Brandy

Shake with ice and strain.

Toxic Refuse

SHOT GLASS

1 part Vodka
1 part Triple Sec
1 part Midori®
splash Lime Juice

Shake with ice and strain.

Traffic Light

SHOT GLASS

1 part Orange Juice
1 part Peach Schnapps
1 part Grenadine
1 part Blue Curaçao
1 part Vodka

Shake with ice and strain. Because this recipe includes many ingredients, it's easier to make in volume, about 6 shots.

Transmission Overhaul

SHOT GLASS

1 part Vodka
1 part Amaretto
1 part Southern Comfort®
1 part Mountain Dew®
1 part Orange Juice
1 part Grenadine

Stir gently with ice and strain. Because this recipe includes many ingredients, it's easier to make in volume, about 6 shots.

Tree Frog

SHOT GLASS

1 part Citrus Vodka
1 part Blue Hawaiian Schnapps
2 parts Grapefruit Juice

Shake with ice and strain.

Trick or Treat

SHOT GLASS

1 part Coconut Rum
1 part Pumpkin Spice Liqueur
1 part Vanilla Vodka

Shake with ice and strain.

Triplesex

SHOT GLASS

1 part Vodka
1 part Triple Sec
1 part Sweet & Sour Mix
1 part Pineapple Juice

Shake with ice and strain.

Tropical Hooter

SHOT GLASS

1 part Citrus Vodka
1 part Raspberry Liqueur
1 part Watermelon Schnapps
1 part Lemon-Lime Soda

Shake with ice and strain.

Tropical Life Saver

SHOT GLASS

1 part Coconut Rum
1 part Melon Liqueur
1 part Pineapple Juice

Shake with ice and strain.

Tropical Passion

SHOT GLASS

1 part Rum
1 part Peach Schnapps
1 part Sloe Gin
1 part Triple Sec
splash Orange Juice

Shake with ice and strain.

Tropical Waterfall

SHOT GLASS

1 part Wild Berry Schnapps
1 part Orange Juice

Shake with ice and strain.

True Canadian

SHOT GLASS

1 part Vodka
1 part Maple Syrup

Shake with ice and strain.

Tub Thumper
SHOT GLASS
1 part Apricot Brandy
1 part Irish Cream Liqueur
1 part Whiskey

Shake with ice and strain.

Tubboocki
SHOT GLASS
2 parts Galliano®
1 part Sambuca
1 part Wild Turkey® Bourbon

Build in the glass with no ice.

Turkey Shoot
SHOT GLASS
3 parts Wild Turkey® Bourbon
1 part Anisette

Shake with ice and strain.

Turkeyball
SHOT GLASS
1 part Wild Turkey® Bourbon
1 part Amaretto
1 part Pineapple Juice

Shake with ice and strain.

Turn Up the Volume
SHOT GLASS
1 part Citrus Vodka
1 part Blue Curaçao
1 part Peach Schnapps

Shake with ice and strain.

Twin Sisters
SHOT GLASS
1 part Light Rum
1 part Spiced Rum
splash Cola
splash Sweetened Lime Juice

Shake with ice and strain.

Twisted Jack
SHOT GLASS
1 part Amaretto
1 part Jack Daniel's®
1 part Sweet & Sour Mix
1 part Southern Comfort®
1 part Raspberry Liqueur

Shake with ice and strain.

Twister Shooter
SHOT GLASS
1 part Vodka
1 part Cherry Brandy
1 part Ouzo

Shake with ice and strain.

T-Zone
SHOT GLASS
1 part Sloe Gin
1 part 151-Proof Rum

Shake with ice and strain.

U-2
SHOT GLASS
1 part Crème de Menthe (White)
1 part Melon Liqueur

Shake with ice and strain.

Uarapito
SHOT GLASS
2 parts Dark Rum
1 part Grenadine
1 part Apple Juice

Shake with ice and strain.

Unabomber
SHOT GLASS
1 part Gin
1 part Vodka
1 part Triple Sec
1 part Lime Juice

Shake with ice and strain.

The Undertaker

SHOT GLASS

1 part Triple Sec
1 part 151-Proof Rum

Shake with ice and strain.

Under Water

SHOT GLASS

1 part Blue Curaçao
1 part Irish Cream Liqueur
1 part Peach Schnapps

Shake with ice and strain.

Undertow

SHOT GLASS

1 part Blue Curaçao
1 part Raspberry Liqueur

Shake with ice and strain.

Unholy Water

SHOT GLASS

1 part Gin
1 part Spiced Rum
1 part Silver Tequila
1 part Vodka

Shake with ice and strain.

Universal Shooter

SHOT GLASS

1 part Grapefruit Juice
1 part Sweet Vermouth
1 part Maraschino Liqueur

Shake with ice and strain.

Up Chuck

SHOT GLASS

1 part 151-Proof Rum
1 part Tequila
1 part Jägermeister®

Pour ingredients into glass neat (do not chill).

Upside Down Apple Pie Shot

SHOT GLASS

1 part Apple Juice
1 part Cinnamon Schnapps
1 part Vodka
Whipped Cream

Shake all but the Whipped Cream with ice and strain. Sit facing away from the bar and lean your head back onto the bar. Pour the shot into your mouth followed by a squirt of Whipped Cream and then sit up quickly. A towel might be handy.

Upside Down Kamikaze

SHOT GLASS

2 parts Triple Sec
2 parts Vodka
1 part Lime Juice
Whipped Cream

Shake with ice and strain. Sit facing away from the bar and lean your head back onto the bar. Pour the shot into your mouth followed by a squirt of Whipped Cream and then sit up quickly. A towel might be handy.

Upside Down Margarita

SHOT GLASS

2 parts Tequila
2 parts Lime Juice
1 part Triple Sec
Whipped Cream

Shake with ice and strain. Sit facing away from the bar and lean your head back onto the bar. Pour the shot into your mouth followed by a squirt of Whipped Cream and then sit up quickly. A towel might be handy.

Upside Down Oatmeal Cookie

SHOT GLASS

1 part Irish Cream Liqueur
1 part Goldschläger®
Whipped Cream

Shake with ice and strain. Sit facing away from the bar and lean your head back onto the bar. Pour the shot into your mouth followed by a squirt of Whipped Cream and then sit up quickly. A towel might be handy.

Urban Cowboy

SHOT GLASS

1 part Grand Marnier®
1 part Jack Daniel's®
1 part Southern Comfort®

Shake with ice and strain.

Urine Sample Shooter

SHOT GLASS

1 part Galliano®
1 part Midori®
1 part Vodka

Shake with ice and strain.

Valium®

SHOT GLASS

1 part Rye Whiskey
1 part Peach Schnapps
1 part Cranberry Juice Cocktail

Shake with ice and strain.

Vampire Slayer

SHOT GLASS

2 parts Southern Comfort®
1 part Cognac
1 part Rum
1 part Scotch
1 part Jägermeister®

Shake with ice and strain. Because this recipe includes many ingredients, it's easier to make in volume, about 6 shots.

Vanilla Ice

SHOT GLASS

1 part Vanilla Liqueur
2 parts Blueberry Schnapps

Shake with ice and strain.

Vanilla Jack

SHOT GLASS

2 parts Jack Daniel's®
1 part Vanilla Vodka
1 part Root Beer Schnapps

Shake with ice and strain.

Vanilla Milkshake

SHOT GLASS

1 part Crème de Cacao (Dark)
2 parts Milk
2 parts Vanilla Vodka

Shake with ice and strain.

Varadero Especial

SHOT GLASS

1 part Maraschino Liqueur
1 part Grapefruit Juice

Shake with ice and strain.

Varicose Veins

SHOT GLASS

1 part Irish Cream Liqueur
1 part Crème de Menthe (White)

Shake with ice and strain.

Vegas Blowjob

SHOT GLASS

2 parts Rum
2 parts Jägermeister®
1 part Banana Liqueur
1 part Orange Juice
1 part Pineapple Juice

Shake with ice and strain. Because this recipe includes many ingredients, it's easier to make in volume, about 6 shots.

Viagra® Shooter

SHOT GLASS

1 part Vodka
1 part Blue Curaçao
1 part Irish Cream Liqueur

Shake with ice and strain.

Vibrator

SHOT GLASS

1 part After Shock® Cinnamon Schnapps
1 part Avalanche® Peppermint Schnapps
1 part Spiced Rum
splash Ginger Ale

Build in the glass with no ice.

Victoria's Shot

SHOT GLASS

2 parts Vodka
2 parts Passion Fruit Liqueur
1 part Pineapple Juice
splash Lime Juice
pinch Powdered Sugar

Shake with ice and strain.

Vigor

SHOT GLASS

1 part Peach Schnapps
1 part Crème de Cassis
1 part Cranberry Juice Cocktail
1 part Lemon Juice

Shake with ice and strain.

Viking Funeral

SHOT GLASS

1 part Absolut Vodka
1 part Aquavit
1 part Lingonberry Jam

Shake with ice and strain.

Village

SHOT GLASS

1 part Vodka
1 part Passion Fruit Liqueur
1 part Pineapple Juice
1 part Aperol™

Shake with ice and strain.

Vine Climber

SHOT GLASS

2 parts Vodka
2 parts Melon Liqueur
1 part Sweet & Sour Mix

Shake with ice and strain.

Violent Fuck

SHOT GLASS

1 part Grain Alcohol
1 part Cola

Build in the glass with no ice.

Viper

SHOT GLASS

1 part Vodka
1 part Amaretto
1 part Malibu® Rum
1 part Midori®
1 part Pineapple Juice

Shake with ice and strain.

Virgin Breaker

SHOT GLASS

1 part Vodka
1 part Whiskey
1 part Sambuca
1 part Orange Juice
1 part Grenadine

Shake with ice and strain. Because this recipe includes many ingredients, it's easier to make in volume, about 6 shots.

Virgin Pussy

SHOT GLASS

1 part Watermelon Schnapps
1 part Cinnamon Schnapps

Shake with ice and strain.

Virulent Death

SHOT GLASS

1 part Blue Curaçao
1 part Yukon Jack®
1 part Galliano®

Shake with ice and strain.

Vodka Passion

SHOT GLASS

1 part Orange Vodka
1 part Passion Fruit Juice

Shake with ice and strain.

Volvo®

SHOT GLASS

1 part Cointreau®
1 part Grand Marnier®
1 part Vodka
1 part Cognac
1 part Apricot Brandy

Shake with ice and strain. Because this recipe includes many ingredients, it's easier to make in volume, about 6 shots.

Voodoo Doll

SHOT GLASS

1 part Vodka
1 part Raspberry Liqueur

Shake with ice and strain.

Vulcan Death Grip

SHOT GLASS

1 part Goldschläger®
1 part Rum

Shake with ice and strain.

Vulcan Mind Meld

SHOT GLASS

1 part Ouzo
1 part 151-Proof Rum

Shake with ice and strain.

Waffle

SHOT GLASS

1 part Vodka
1 part Butterscotch Schnapps
1 part Orange Juice

Shake with ice and strain.

Wahoo

SHOT GLASS

1 part 151-Proof Rum
1 part Amaretto
1 part Pineapple Juice

Shake with ice and strain.

Wak-Wak

SHOT GLASS

1 part Crème de Cassis
1 part Absinthe

Shake with ice and strain.

Waltzing Matilda Shooter

SHOT GLASS

2 parts Light Rum
1 part Blue Curaçao
1 part Pineapple Juice

Shake with ice and strain.

Wandering Minstrel Shooter

SHOT GLASS

1 part Crème de Menthe (White)
1 part Brandy
1 part Vodka
1 part Coffee

Shake with ice and strain.

Warm and Fuzzy

SHOT GLASS

1 part Triple Sec
1 part Southern Comfort®
1 part Cherry Brandy

Shake with ice and strain.

Warm Carrot Cake

SHOT GLASS

1 part Butterscotch Schnapps
1 part Cinnamon Schnapps
1 part Irish Cream Liqueur

Shake with ice and strain.

A Warm Glass of Shut the Hell Up

SHOT GLASS

1 part Cinnamon Schnapps
1 part Peach Schnapps
1 part Southern Comfort®

Pour ingredients into glass neat (do not chill).

Warm Leatherette

SHOT GLASS

3 parts Black Sambuca
2 parts Amaretto
1 part Grenadine

Shake with ice and strain.

Warp Core Breach

SHOT GLASS

1 part Goldschläger®
1 part Tequila
1 part Jack Daniel's®

Shake with ice and strain.

Washington Red Apple

SHOT GLASS

1 part Canadian Whisky
1 part Sour Apple Schnapps
1 part Vodka
1 part Cranberry Juice Cocktail

Shake with ice and strain.

Water Moccasin

SHOT GLASS

1 part Crown Royal® Whiskey
1 part Peach Schnapps
1 part Sweet & Sour Mix

Shake with ice and strain.

Waterloo

SHOT GLASS

2 parts Mandarine Napoléon® Liqueur
2 parts Spiced Rum
1 part Orange Juice

Shake with ice and strain.

Watermelon Shot

SHOT GLASS

1 part Vodka
1 part Amaretto
1 part Southern Comfort®
1 part Orange Juice

Shake with ice and strain.

Wayne's World

SHOT GLASS

2 parts Jägermeister®
1 part Sambuca

Shake with ice and strain.

Weasel Water

SHOT GLASS

1 part Crème de Banane
1 part Cream

Shake with ice and strain.

Wedgie

SHOT GLASS

2 parts Coffee Liqueur
1 part Crème de Cacao (Dark)
1 part Whiskey

Shake with ice and strain.

Weekend on the Beach

SHOT GLASS

1 part Canadian Whisky
1 part Sour Apple Schnapps
1 part Peach Schnapps
1 part Sweet & Sour Mix

Shake with ice and strain.

Wench
SHOT GLASS
1 part Amaretto
1 part Spiced Rum
Shake with ice and strain.

Werther's®
SHOT GLASS
1 part Irish Cream Liqueur
1 part Butterscotch Schnapps
1 part Bourbon
Shake with ice and strain.

West Side Special
SHOT GLASS
1 part Southern Comfort®
1 part Peppermint Schnapps
Shake with ice and strain.

Wet Back
SHOT GLASS
1 part Coffee Liqueur
1 part Tequila
Shake with ice and strain.

Wet Crotch
SHOT GLASS
1 part Chambord
1 part Irish Cream Liqueur
1 part Triple Sec
Shake with ice and strain.

Wet Dream
SHOT GLASS
1 part Southern Comfort®
1 part Coconut Rum
1 part Cranberry Juice Cocktail
1 part Pineapple Juice
1 part Lemon-Lime Soda
Shake with ice and strain.

Wet Muff
SHOT GLASS
1 part Butterscotch Schnapps
2 parts Cointreau®
2 parts Tia Maria®
1 part Pineapple Juice
Shake with ice and strain.

Wet Spot
SHOT GLASS
1 part Butterscotch Liqueur
1 part Irish Cream Liqueur
1 part Vodka
Shake with ice and strain.

Whip Me Baby
SHOT GLASS
1 part Triple Sec
1 part Dry Vermouth
1 part Rémy Martin® VSOP
Shake with ice and strain.

Whipper Snapper
SHOT GLASS
1 part Melon Liqueur
1 part Apple Brandy
1 part Cranberry Juice Cocktail
Shake with ice and strain.

Whisker Biscuit
SHOT GLASS
1 part 151-Proof Rum
1 part Banana Liqueur
1 part Coconut Rum
1 part Grenadine
2 parts Pineapple Juice
Shake with ice and strain. Because this recipe includes many ingredients, it's easier to make in volume, about 6 shots.

White Cap

SHOT GLASS

1 part Vodka
1 part Cream
1 part Coffee
1 part Port

Shake with ice and strain.

White Cloud

SHOT GLASS

1 part Milk
1 part Peppermint Schnapps

Shake with ice and strain.

White Cotton Panties

SHOT GLASS

1 part Butterscotch Liqueur
1 part Vanilla Vodka
1 part Cream

Shake with ice and strain.

White Death

SHOT GLASS

1 part Crème de Cacao (White)
1 part Vodka
1 part Raspberry Liqueur

Shake with ice and strain.

White Knuckle Ride

SHOT GLASS

2 parts Coffee
1 part Vodka

Shake with ice and strain.

White Mess

SHOT GLASS

1 part Light Rum
1 part Crème de Cassis
1 part Root Beer Schnapps
1 part Coconut Rum
1 part Heavy Cream

Shake with ice and strain.
Because this recipe includes many ingredients, it's easier to make in volume, about 6 shots.

White Orbit

SHOT GLASS

1 part Crème de Cacao (White)
1 part Melon Liqueur
1 part Glayva®
1 part Cream

Shake with ice and strain.

White Satin Shooter

SHOT GLASS

2 parts Tia Maria®
1 part Cream
1 part Frangelico®

Shake with ice and strain.

Wicked Snowshoe

SHOT GLASS

1 part Canadian Whisky
1 part Goldschläger®
1 part Peppermint Schnapps
1 part Wild Turkey® 101

Shake with ice and strain.

Wicked Stepmother

SHOT GLASS

2 parts Pepper Vodka
1 part Amaretto

Shake with ice and strain.

Widget

SHOT GLASS

3 parts Peach Schnapps
1 part Gin

Shake with ice and strain.

Widow Maker

SHOT GLASS

1 part Vodka
1 part Jägermeister®
1 part Coffee Liqueur
splash Grenadine

Shake with ice and strain.

Wild Berry Pop-Tart®

SHOT GLASS

1 part Wild Berry Schnapps
1 part Vodka
1 part Strawberry Liqueur

Shake with ice and strain.

Wild Black Betty

SHOT GLASS

1 part Bourbon
1 part Southern Comfort
1 part Whiskey
1 part Grenadine
1 part Lime Juice

Shake with ice and strain.

Wild Child

SHOT GLASS

1 part Sour Apple Schnapps
1 part Vodka
1 part Lemon-Lime Soda

Build in the glass with no ice.

Wild Peppertini

SHOT GLASS

1 part Wild Turkey® Bourbon
1 part Peppermint Schnapps

Shake with ice and strain.

Wild Thing Shooter

SHOT GLASS

2 parts Vodka
1 part Apricot Brandy
1 part Lemon-Lime Soda

Build in the glass with no ice.

Windex® Shooter

SHOT GLASS

1 part Blue Curaçao
1 part Vodka

Shake with ice and strain.

Windy

SHOT GLASS

1 part Vodka
1 part Blue Curaçao
1 part Pineapple Juice
1 part Sweet & Sour Mix

Shake with ice and strain.

Winter Green Dragon

SHOT GLASS

2 parts Green Chartreuse®
1 part 151-Proof Rum
1 part Rumple Minze®

Shake with ice and strain.

Wolf Pussy

SHOT GLASS

1 part Bourbon
1 part Cinnamon Schnapps

Pour ingredients into glass neat (do not chill).

Wonka

SHOT GLASS

1 part Cherry Brandy
1 part Amaretto
1 part Sweet & Sour Mix

Shake with ice and strain.

Woo Woo Shooter

SHOT GLASS

1 part Vodka
1 part Peach Schnapps
1 part Cranberry Juice Cocktail

Shake with ice and strain.

Wooden Floor

SHOT GLASS

1 part Whiskey
1 part Bourbon
1 part Canadian Whisky
1 part Gold Tequila

Build in order. Do not chill.

Woof
SHOT GLASS

1 part Blue Curaçao
1 part Amaretto
1 part Parfait Amour

Shake with ice and strain.

Woo-Shoo
SHOT GLASS

2 parts Cranberry Vodka
1 part Peach Schnapps

Shake with ice and strain.

World War III
SHOT GLASS

2 parts Blue Raspberry Liqueur
1 part Chambord
1 part Mango Rum
1 part Triple Sec

Shake with ice and strain.

X
SHOT GLASS

2 parts Amaretto
2 parts Wild Berry Schnapps
1 part Sweet & Sour Mix
1 part Cola

Shake with ice and strain.

Xaibalba
SHOT GLASS

1 part Vodka
1 part Butterscotch Schnapps
1 part Vanilla Liqueur
1 part Chocolate Syrup

Shake with ice and strain.

Y2K Shot
SHOT GLASS

1 part Vodka
1 part Melon Liqueur
1 part Raspberry Liqueur

Shake with ice and strain.

Yak Milk
SHOT GLASS

1 part Crème de Cacao (Dark)
1 part Coconut Rum

Shake with ice and strain.

Yaps
SHOT GLASS

1 part Yukon Jack®
1 part Sour Apple Schnapps

Shake with ice and strain.

Yellow Bow Tie
SHOT GLASS

2 parts Vodka
2 parts Amaretto
1 part Triple Sec
1 part Lime Juice

Shake with ice and strain.

Yellow Cake
SHOT GLASS

1 part Vanilla Vodka
1 part Triple Sec
1 part Pineapple Juice

Shake with ice and strain.

Yellow Haze
SHOT GLASS

1 part Gin
1 part Lemon Rum
splash Lime Juice
Mountain Dew

Shake the Gin, Rum, and Lime Juice with ice and strain, filling it about 2/3 full. Top with Mountain Dew.

Yellow Nutter
SHOT GLASS

1 part Lemon-Lime Soda
1 part Bacardi® Limón Rum
1 part Sweet & Sour Mix
dash Sugar

Shake with ice and strain.

Yellow Snow
SHOT GLASS

3 parts Pineapple Vodka
1 part Pineapple Juice

Shake with ice and strain.

Ying Yang
SHOT GLASS

1 part Jägermeister®
1 part Rumple Minze®

Shake with ice and strain.

Yoda®
SHOT GLASS

1 part Vodka
1 part Blue Curaçao
1 part Sweet & Sour Mix
1 part Midori®
2 parts Sour Apple Schnapps

Shake with ice and strain.

Yooha
SHOT GLASS

3 parts Whiskey
1 part Yoo-Hoo® Chocolate Drink

Shake with ice and strain.

Young Grasshopper
SHOT GLASS

1 part Green Apple Schnapps
1 part Triple Sec
1 part Crème de Menthe (Green)

Build in order. Do not chill.

Yukon Cornelius
SHOT GLASS

4 PARTS YUKON JACK
1 part Goldschläger®

Shake with ice and strain.

Yukon Snakebite
SHOT GLASS

3 parts Yukon Jack®
1 part Lime Juice

Shake with ice and strain.

Z Street Slammer
SHOT GLASS

2 parts Crème de Banane
2 parts Pineapple Juice
1 part Grenadine

Shake with ice and strain.

Zeke's Suprise
SHOT GLASS

1 part Grand Marnier®
1 part Scotch
1 part Peppermint Schnapps

Shake with ice and strain.

Zenmeister
SHOT GLASS

1 part Jägermeister®
1 part Root Beer

Stir gently with ice and strain.

Zoo Station
SHOT GLASS

1 part Amaretto
1 part Coffee Liqueur
1 part Irish Cream Liqueur
1 part Banana Liqueur
2 parts Cream

Shake with ice and strain.

Zool
SHOT GLASS

1 part Peach Schnapps
1 part Vodka
1 part Amaretto

Shake with ice and strain.

Zoot Suit Riot
SHOT GLASS

1 part Apricot Brandy
1 part Blackberry Liqueur
1 part Cranberry Juice Cocktail
1 part Southern Comfort®

Shake with ice and strain.

LAYERED SHOTS

Creating a layered shot takes a steady hand and lots of practice. With the back of a bar spoon, a knowledge of which liqueurs are heavier than others, and nerves of steel, you can create art in a very small glass.

4 Horsemen

SHOT GLASS

1 part Goldschläger®
1 part Jägermeister®
1 part Rumple Minze©
1 part 151-Proof Rum

Layer in a shot glass.

10 W 40

SHOT GLASS

1 part Black Sambuca
1 part Goldschläger®

Layer in a shot glass.

50-50 Bar

SHOT GLASS

1 part Irish Cream Liqueur
1 part Coffee Liqueur
splash 151-Proof Rum

Layer in a shot glass.

69er in a Pool

SHOT GLASS

1 part Vodka
1 part 151-Proof Rum
splash Lemon Juice
splash Tabasco® Sauce

Layer in a shot glass.

401

SHOT GLASS

1 part Coffee Liqueur
1 part Crème de Banane
1 part Irish Cream Liqueur
1 part Yukon Jack®

Layer in a shot glass.

A.T.B. (Ask the Barman)

SHOT GLASS

1 part Melon Liqueur
1 part Grenadine
1 part Blue Curaçao
1 part Amaretto
1 part Irish Cream Liqueur

Layer in a shot glass.

ABC

SHOT GLASS

1 part Amaretto
1 part Irish Cream Liqueur
1 part Cognac

Layer in a shot glass.

Absinthe without Leave

SHOT GLASS

1 part Absinthe
1 part Irish Cream Liqueur
1 part Black Sambuca

Layer in a shot glass.

Adios, Motherfucker

SHOT GLASS

1 part Coffee Liqueur
1 part Tequila

Layer in a shot glass.

Advosarry

SHOT GLASS

3 parts Maraschino Liqueur
2 parts Advocaat

Layer in a shot glass.

Aequitas

SHOT GLASS

1 part After Shock® Cinnamon Schnapps
1 part 151-Proof Rum
1 part Jägermeister®
1 part Rumple Minze®

Layer in a shot glass.

After Dark

SHOT GLASS

1 part Coffee Liqueur
1 part Irish Cream Liqueur
1 part Licor 43®

Layer in a shot glass.

After Eight®

SHOT GLASS

1 part Coffee Liqueur
1 part Crème de Menthe (White)
1 part Irish Cream Liqueur

Layer in a shot glass.

After Five

SHOT GLASS

1 part Coffee Liqueur
1 part Peppermint Schnapps
1 part Irish Cream Liqueur

Layer in a shot glass.

After Four

SHOT GLASS

1 part Irish Cream
1 part Peppermint Schnapps
1 part Rumchata

Layer in a shot glass.

Afterburner #3

SHOT GLASS

2 parts Jägermeister
1 part Coconut Rum
1 part Irish Cream Liqueur
1 part 151-Proof Rum

Layer in a shot glass.

Afterlanche

SHOT GLASS

1 part After Shock® Cinnamon Schnapps
1 part Avalanche® Peppermint Schnapps

Layer in a shot glass.

Alaskan Oil Spill

SHOT GLASS

1 part Blue Curaçao
1 part Rumple Minze®
splash Jägermeister®

Shake Blue Curaçao and Rumple Minze® together with ice and strain. Layer the Jägermeister® on top.

Alien Nipple

SHOT GLASS

2 parts Butterscotch Schnapps
1 part Irish Cream Liqueur
1 part Melon Liqueur

Layer in a shot glass.

Alligator Bite

SHOT GLASS

1 part Jägermeister®
1 part Raspberry Liqueur
1 part Vodka
splash Orange Juice
1 part Melon Liqueur

Layer in a shot glass.

Alligator on the Rag

SHOT GLASS

2 parts Melon Liqueur
1 part Raspberry Liqueur
1 part Jägermeister®

Layer in a shot glass.

Almond Joy

SHOT GLASS

1 part Amaretto
1 part Irish Cream Liqueur
1 part Swiss Chocolate Almond Liqueur

Layer in a shot glass.

Altered State

SHOT GLASS

1 part Golden Pear Liqueur
1 part Irish Cream Liqueur
1 part Coffee Liqueur

Layer in a shot glass.

American Flag

SHOT GLASS

1 part Grenadine
1 part Crème de Cacao (White)
1 part Blue Curaçao

Layer in a shot glass.

Amoco Shot

SHOT GLASS

1 part 151-Proof Rum
1 part Grain Alcohol
splash Coffee Liqueur

Layer in a shot glass.

Amy Girl

SHOT GLASS

1 part Banana Liqueur
1 part Butterscotch Schnapps
1 part Frangelico®

Layer in a shot glass.

Andy

SHOT GLASS

1 part Cola
1 part Beer

Layer in a shot glass.

Angel Bliss

SHOT GLASS

3 parts Bourbon
1 part Blue Curaçao
1 part 151-Proof Rum

Layer in a shot glass.

Angel's Delight

POUSSE-CAFÉ GLASS

1 part Grenadine
1 part Triple Sec
1 part Sloe Gin
1 part Light Cream

Layer in a Pousse-Café glass.

Angel's Kiss

SHOT GLASS

1 part Coffee Liqueur
1 part Swiss Chocolate Almond Liqueur
splash Irish Cream Liqueur

Layer in a shot glass.

Angel's Tit

SHOT GLASS

1 part Crème de Cacao (White)
1 part Maraschino Liqueur
1 part Heavy Cream

Layer in a shot glass. Garnish with Maraschino Cherry.

Angel's Wing

POUSSE-CAFÉ GLASS

1 part Crème de Cacao (White)
1 part Brandy
splash Light Cream

Layer in a shot glass.

Apache

SHOT GLASS

1 part Coffee Liqueur
1 part Irish Cream Liqueur
1 part Melon Liqueur

Layer in a shot glass.

Apple Pie

SHOT GLASS

1 part Vodka
1 part Apple Juice

Layer in a shot glass.

Apple Slammer

SHOT GLASS

1 part Sour Apple Schnapps
1 part Lemon-Lime Soda

Layer in a shot glass. Cover with your hand, slam down against the bar, and drink while it fizzes.

Aquafresh

SHOT GLASS

1 part After Shock® Cinnamon Schnapps
1 part Rumple Minze®
1 part Avalanche® Peppermint Schnapps

Layer in a shot glass.

Astropop

SHOT GLASS

1 part Grenadine
1 part Amaretto
1 part Rumple Minze®

Layer in a shot glass.

Aunt Jemima®

POUSSE-CAFÉ GLASS

1 part Brandy
1 part Crème de Cacao (White)
1 part Bénédictine®

Layer in a pousse-café glass.

Autopsy

SHOT GLASS

1 part Melon Liqueur
1 part Irish Whiskey
1 part Tomato Juice

Layer in a shot glass.

B and B

CORDIAL GLASS

1 part Brandy
1 part Bénédictine®

Layer in a cordial glass.

B.B.C.

SHOT GLASS

1 part Bénédictine®
1 part Irish Cream Liqueur
1 part Cointreau®

Layer in a shot glass.

B.B.G.

SHOT GLASS

1 part Bénédictine®
1 part Irish Cream Liqueur
1 part Grand Marnier®

Layer in a shot glass.

B-52

SHOT GLASS

1 part Grand Marnier®
1 part Coffee Liqueur
1 part Irish Cream Liqueur

Layer in a shot glass.

Baby Beer

SHOT GLASS

3 parts Licor 43®
1 part Cream

Layer in a shot glass.

Baby Guinness®

SHOT GLASS

3 parts Coffee Liqueur
1 part Irish Cream Liqueur

Layer in a shot glass.

Backfire

SHOT GLASS

1 part Coffee Liqueur
1 part Irish Cream Liqueur
1 part Vodka

Layer in a shot glass.

Backstabber

SHOT GLASS

1 part Scotch
1 part Melon Liqueur
1 part Irish Mist

Layer in a shot glass.

Bad Sting

SHOT GLASS

1 part Grenadine
1 part Anisette
1 part Grand Marnier®
1 part Tequila

Layer in a shot glass.

Baghdad Café

SHOT GLASS

1 part Coffee Liqueur
1 part Tia Maria®
splash San Marco Cream

Layer in a shot glass.

Baileys® Chocolate-Covered Cherry

SHOT GLASS

1 part Coffee Liqueur
1 part Grenadine
1 part Irish Cream Liqueur

Layer in a shot glass.

Baileys® Comet

SHOT GLASS

1 part Irish Cream Liqueur
1 part Goldschläger®
splash 151-Proof Rum

Layer in a shot glass.

Baker's Delite

SHOT GLASS

3 parts Crème de Cacao (White)
1 part Peach Schnapps

Layer in a shot glass.

Ballistic Missile

SHOT GLASS

1 part Amaretto
1 part Grand Marnier®
1 part Pineapple Juice

Layer in a shot glass.

Banana Cream Pie

SHOT GLASS

1 part Coffee Liqueur
1 part Licor 43®
1 part 99-Proof Banana Liqueur

Layer in a shot glass.

Banana Drop

SHOT GLASS

1 part Crème de Banane
1 part Irish Cream Liqueur
½ part Cream
½ part Chocolate Mint Liqueur

Layer in a shot glass.

Banana Slip

CORDIAL GLASS

1 part Crème de Banane
1 part Irish Cream Liqueur

Layer in a cordial glass.

Bat Blood

SHOT GLASS

splash Grenadine
1 part Jägermeister

Layer in a shot glass.

Battered, Bruised, and Bleeding

SHOT GLASS

1 part Grenadine
1 part Melon Liqueur
1 part Blue Curaçao

Layer in a shot glass.

Bazooka Joe®

SHOT GLASS

1 part Parfait Amour
1 part Crème de Banane
1 part Irish Cream Liqueur

Layer in a shot glass.

B.B. Grand

SHOT GLASS

1 part Irish Cream Liqueur
1 part Banana Liqueur
1 part Grand Marnier®

Layer in a shot glass.

Beam Me Up, Scotty

SHOT GLASS

1 part Coffee Liqueur
1 part Banana Liqueur
1 part Irish Cream Liqueur

Layer in a shot glass.

Beauty and the Beast

SHOT GLASS

3 parts Jägermeister®
1 part Tequila Rose®

Layer in a shot glass.

Bee Bite

SHOT GLASS

1 part Coffee Liqueur
1 part Banana Liqueur
1 part Vodka

Layer in a shot glass.

Belfast Street Map

SHOT GLASS

1 part Coffee Liqueur
1 part Irish Cream Liqueur
1 part Irish Whiskey

Layer in a shot glass.

Bellevue Gangbang

SHOT GLASS

1 part Cinnamon Schnapps
1 part Black Sambuca

Layer in a shot glass.

Bertie Bichberg

SHOT GLASS

1 part Vodka
1 part Crème de Banane

Layer in a shot glass. Garnish with Maraschino Cherry.

Beverly Hills

SHOT GLASS

1 part Swiss Chocolate Almond Liqueur
1 part Irish Cream Liqueur
1 part Grand Marnier®

Layer in a shot glass.

Big 'O'

SHOT GLASS

1 part Peppermint Schnapps
1 part Irish Cream Liqueur

Layer in a shot glass.

Bipple
SHOT GLASS

1 part Butterscotch Schnapps
1 part Irish Cream Liqueur

Layer in a shot glass.

Bitches from Hell
SHOT GLASS

1 part Jägermeister
1 part Banana Liqueur
1 part Half and Half

Layer in a shot glass.

Bit-O-Honey® Shot
SHOT GLASS

1 part Apple Brandy
1 part Frangelico®

Layer in a shot glass.

Black Army
SHOT GLASS

1 part Galliano®
1 part Jägermeister®

Layer in a shot glass.

Blackberry Blossom
SHOT GLASS

1 part Blackberry Liqueur
1 part Irish Cream Liqueur

Layer in a shot glass.

Black Bitch
SHOT GLASS

3 parts Black Sambuca
3 parts Irish Cream Liqueur
2 parts 151-Proof Rum

Layer in a shot glass.

Black Bullet
SHOT GLASS

1 part Peppermint Schnapps
1 part Jägermeister®

Layer in a shot glass.

Black Dragon
SHOT GLASS

1 part Crème de Menthe (White)
1 part Coffee Liqueur
1 part Scotch

Layer in a shot glass.

Black Knight
SHOT GLASS

1 part Coffee Liqueur
1 part Irish Cream Liqueur
1 part Sambuca
splash Advocaat
splash Grenadine

Layer in a shot glass.

Black Magic Cream
SHOT GLASS

1 part Coffee Liqueur
1 part Crème de Cacao (White)
1 part Amarula® Crème Liqueur

Layer in a shot glass.

Black Rain
SHOT GLASS

1 part Black Sambuca
2 parts Champagne

Layer in a shot glass.

Black Sand
SHOT GLASS

1 part Coffee Liqueur
1 part Sambuca
1 part Amaretto

Layer in a shot glass.

Black Tie
SHOT GLASS

1 part Drambuie®
1 part Scotch
1 part Amaretto

Layer in a shot glass.

Black Unicorn
SHOT GLASS

1 part Coffee Liqueur
1 part Butterscotch Schnapps
1 part Irish Cream Liqueur

Layer in a shot glass.

Black Wolf
SHOT GLASS

1 part Black Sambuca
1 part Green Chartreuse
splash Tabasco® Sauce

Layer in a shot glass.

Black Forest
SHOT GLASS

1 part Coffee Liqueur
1 part Grand Marnier®
1 part Cherry Whiskey

Layer in a shot glass.

Blaster
SHOT GLASS

1 part Banana Liqueur
1 part Triple Sec
1 part Coffee Liqueur

Layer in a shot glass.

Bleacher's Twist
SHOT GLASS

1 part Coffee Liqueur
1 part Raspberry Liqueur
1 part Irish Cream Liqueur

Layer in a shot glass.

Blood Clot
SHOT GLASS

2 parts Southern Comfort®
1 part Grenadine

Layer in a shot glass.

Blood of Satan
SHOT GLASS

1 part Jägermeister®
1 part Goldschläger®
1 part Irish Whiskey
1 part Jack Daniel's®

Layer in a shot glass.

Bloodeye
SHOT GLASS

½ part Raspberry Liqueur
1 part Citrus Vodka
½ part Cranberry Liqueur

Layer in a shot glass.

Bloody Frog Cum
SHOT GLASS

1 part Grenadine
splash 151-Proof Rum
1 part Melon Liqueur
splash Irish Cream Liqueur

Layer in a shot glass.

Bloody Psycho
SHOT GLASS

splash Orange Liqueur
splash 151-Proof Rum
1 part Irish Cream Liqueur

Layer in a shot glass.

Bloody Rectum
SHOT GLASS

2 parts Coffee Liqueur
1 part Vodka
splash Grenadine

Layer in a shot glass.

Blow in the Jaw
SHOT GLASS

splash Goldschläger®
splash Calvados Apple Brandy
1 part Spiced Rum

Layer in a shot glass.

Blow Job

SHOT GLASS

1 part Irish Cream Liqueur
1 part Coffee Liqueur

Layer in a shot glass. Top with Whipped Cream. Drink without using your hands.

Blue Ice Breathe

SHOT GLASS

1 part Citrus Vodka
1 part Blue Curaçao
1 part Bitter Lemon

Layer in a shot glass.

Blue Kisok

SHOT GLASS

2 parts Blue Curaçao
1 part Vodka
splash Lime Juice
fill with Lemon-Lime Soda

Layer in a shot glass.

Blue-Eyed Blonde

SHOT GLASS

1 part Banana Liqueur
1 part Blue Curaçao
1 part Irish Cream Liqueur

Layer in a shot glass.

Blue-Eyed Blonde #2

SHOT GLASS

1 part Chocolate Vodka
1 part Banana Liqueur
1 part Blue Curaçao

Layer in a shot glass.

Blue Moon Shooter

SHOT GLASS

1 part Amaretto
1 part Irish Cream Liqueur
1 part Blue Curaçao

Layer in a shot glass.

Blue Neon

SHOT GLASS

3 parts Goldschläger®
1 part Rum
splash Blue Curaçao

Layer in a shot glass.

Bob Marley

SHOT GLASS

1 part Melon Liqueur
1 part Jägermeister®
1 part Goldschläger®

Layer in a shot glass.

Bonfire

SHOT GLASS

1 part Irish Cream Liqueur
splash Goldschläger®
dash Cinnamon

Layer in a shot glass.

Bonobo

SHOT GLASS

1 part Banana Liqueur
1 part Triple Sec
1 part Grand Marnier®

Layer in a shot glass.

Bonsai Pipeline

SHOT GLASS

1 part Wild Turkey® 101
1 part Melon Liqueur
splash 151-Proof Rum

Layer in a shot glass.

Bottom Bouncer

SHOT GLASS

1 part Irish Cream Liqueur
1 part Butterscotch Schnapps

Layer in a shot glass.

Brain Teaser
SHOT GLASS
2 parts Sambuca
2 parts Irish Cream Liqueur
1 part Advocaat
Layer in a shot glass.

Branded Nipple
SHOT GLASS
1 part Butterscotch Schnapps
1 part Irish Cream Liqueur
1 part Goldschläger®
splash 151-Proof Rum
Layer in a shot glass.

Break
SHOT GLASS
1 part Coffee Liqueur
1 part Crème de Banane
1 part Anisette
Layer in a shot glass.

Brimful Rainbow
SHOT GLASS
1 part Blue Curaçao
1 part Amaretto
1 part Grenadine
1 part Melon Liqueur
Layer in a shot glass.

Brush Fire
SHOT GLASS
1 part Fireball Cinnamon Whiskey
1 part Goldschläger
splash Tabasco® Sauce
Layer in a shot glass.

Buckshot
SHOT GLASS
1 part Tequila
1 part Jack Daniel's®
1 part Irish Cream Liqueur
dash Ground Pepper
Layer in a shot glass.

Bulgaria United
SHOT GLASS
1 part Grenadine
1 part Crème de Menthe (Green)
1 part Vodka
Layer in a shot glass.

Bumble Bee
SHOT GLASS
1 part Irish Cream Liqueur
1 part Coffee Liqueur
1 part Sambuca
Layer in a shot glass.

Busted Rubber
SHOT GLASS
1 part Raspberry Liqueur
1 part Irish Cream Liqueur
1 part Grand Marnier
Layer in a shot glass.

Butter Baby
SHOT GLASS
1 part Butterscotch Schnapps
1 part Irish Cream Liqueur
Layer in a shot glass.

Buttery Jäger Ripple
SHOT GLASS
1 part Jägermeister®
1 part Irish Cream Liqueur
1 part Butterscotch Schnapps
Layer in a shot glass.

Buttery Nipple with a Cherry Kiss
SHOT GLASS
1 part Butterscotch Schnapps
1 part Irish Cream Liqueur
splash Cherry Liqueur
Layer in a shot glass.

Camel Hump

SHOT GLASS

2 parts Butterscotch Schnapps
1 part Irish Cream Liqueur

Layer in a shot glass.

Camel's Snot

SHOT GLASS

1 part Red Wine
1 part Irish Cream Liqueur

Layer in a shot glass.

Candy Cane

SHOT GLASS

1 part Grenadine
1 part Crème de Menthe (White)
1 part Peppermint Schnapps

Layer in a shot glass.

Candy Corn

SHOT GLASS

1 part Licor 43®
1 part Blue Curaçao
1 part Cream

Layer in a shot glass.

Candy Raccoon

SHOT GLASS

1 part Cinnamon Schnapps
1 part Black Sambuca

Layer in a shot glass.

Care Bear®

SHOT GLASS

1 part Raspberry Liqueur
1 part Chocolate Liqueur

Layer in a shot glass.

Cement Mixer

SHOT GLASS

2 parts Irish Cream Liqueur
1 part Sweetened Lime Juice

Layer in a shot glass. Shake liquid in your mouth before you swallow.

Cerebellum

SHOT GLASS

4 parts Vodka
1 part Grenadine
1 part Irish Cream Liqueur

Layer in a shot glass.

Cerebral Hemorrage

SHOT GLASS

1 part Strawberry Liqueur
splash Irish Cream Liqueur
splash Grenadine

Layer in a shot glass.

Channel 64

SHOT GLASS

1 part Crème de Banane
1 part Irish Cream Liqueur
1 part Advocaat

Layer in a shot glass.

Chastity Belt

SHOT GLASS

1 part Tia Maria®
1 part Frangelico®
1 part Irish Cream Liqueur
1 part Cream

Layer in a shot glass.

Chill Out Shock

SHOT GLASS

1 part Butterscotch Schnapps
1 part Espresso

Layer in a shot glass.

China White

SHOT GLASS

3 parts Crème de Cacao (White)
1 part Irish Cream Liqueur
dash Cinnamon

Layer in a shot glass.

Chocolate Almond

SHOT GLASS

1 part Amaretto
1 part Crème de Cacao (Dark)
1 part Irish Cream Liqueur

Layer in a shot glass.

Chocolate Cherry Bomb

SHOT GLASS

1 part Crème de Cacao (White)
1 part Cream
1 part Grenadine

Layer in a shot glass.

Chocolate Chimp

SHOT GLASS

1 part Crème de Cacao (White)
1 part Coffee Liqueur
1 part Crème de Banane

Layer in a shot glass.

Chocolate Sundae

SHOT GLASS

1 part Irish Cream Liqueur
1 part Crème de Cacao (White)
1 part Coffee Liqueur

Layer in a shot glass. Top with Whipped Cream.

Chocorange

SHOT GLASS

2 parts Crème de Cacao (Dark)
1 part Raspberry Liqueur
1 part Grand Marnier®

Layer in a shot glass.

Christmas Shot

SHOT GLASS

1 part Melon Liqueur
1 part Raspberry Liqueur

Layer in a shot glass.

Christmas Tree

SHOT GLASS

1 part Crème de Menthe (White)
1 part Grenadine
1 part Irish Cream Liqueur

Layer in a shot glass.

Cinn's Stop Light

SHOT GLASS

1 part Melon Liqueur
1 part Grenadine
1 part Irish Cream Liqueur

Layer in a shot glass.

City Hot Shot

SHOT GLASS

1 part Blue Curaçao
1 part Triple Sec
1 part Grenadine

Layer in a shot glass.

Clear Layered Shot

SHOT GLASS

1 part Lemon-Lime Soda
1 part Grain Alcohol
1 part Grenadine

Layer in a shot glass. The Grenadine will settle in the middle.

Clit Lickin' Cowgirl

SHOT GLASS

1 part Butterscotch Liqueur
1 part Irish Cream Liqueur
3 drops Grenadine

Layer in a shot glass.

Cobra

SHOT GLASS

1 part Irish Cream Liqueur
1 part Jägermeister®
1 part Rumple Minze®

Layer in a shot glass.

Cock-Sucking Cowboy

SHOT GLASS

1 part Butterscotch Schnapps
1 part Irish Cream Liqueur
1 part Whiskey

Layer in a shot glass.

The Colombian

SHOT GLASS

1 part Coffee Liqueur
1 part Amaretto
1 part Hennessy®

Layer in a shot glass.

Concrete

SHOT GLASS

1 part Vodka
1 part Irish Cream Liqueur

Layer in a shot glass.

Cum in a Hot Tub

SHOT GLASS

2 parts Vodka
1 part White Rum
dash Irish Cream Liqueur

Layer in a shot glass.

Cypress

SHOT GLASS

1 part Crème de Cacao (White)
1 part Light Cream

Layer in a shot glass.

Cyrano

SHOT GLASS

1 part Irish Cream Liqueur
1 part Grand Marnier®
splash Raspberry Liqueur

Layer in a shot glass.

Dagger

SHOT GLASS

1 part Tequila
1 part Crème de Cacao (White)
1 part Peach Schnapps

Layer in a shot glass.

Dam Beaver

SHOT GLASS

1 part Irish Cream Liqueur
1 part Crème de Cacao (White)
1 part Crème de Menthe (Green)

Layer in a shot glass.

Dancin' Cowboy

SHOT GLASS

1 part Banana Liqueur
1 part Coffee Liqueur
1 part Irish Cream Liqueur

Layer in a shot glass.

Dancing Mexican

SHOT GLASS

2 parts Tequila
1 part Milk

Layer in a shot glass.

Decadence

SHOT GLASS

1 part Coffee Liqueur
1 part Frangelico®
1 part Irish Cream Liqueur

Layer in a shot glass.

Desert Water

SHOT GLASS

1 part Tabasco® Sauce
fill with Tequila

Layer in a shot glass.

Dirty Bird

SHOT GLASS

1 part Tequila Reposado
1 part Wild Turkey® 101

Layer in a shot glass.

Dirty Nipple

SHOT GLASS

1 part Sambuca
1 part Irish Cream Liqueur

Layer in a shot glass.

Dirty Oatmeal

SHOT GLASS

1 part Jägermeister®
1 part Irish Cream Liqueur

Layer in a shot glass.

Dog Bowl

SHOT GLASS

1 part Amarula® Crème Liqueur
1 part Banana Liqueur
1 part Frangelico®

Layer in a shot glass.

Don Quixote

SHOT GLASS

1 part Guinness® Stout
1 part Tequila

Layer in a shot glass.

Dragon Slayer

SHOT GLASS

1 part Green Chartreuse®
1 part Tequila

Layer in a shot glass.

Dragoon

POUSSE-CAFÉ GLASS

1 part Black Sambuca
1 part Coffee Liqueur
1 part Irish Cream Liqueur

Shake with ice and strain.

Duck Fart

SHOT GLASS

1 part Coffee Liqueur
1 part Irish Cream Liqueur
1 part Canadian Whisky

Layer in a shot glass.

Duck Shit Inn

SHOT GLASS

1 part Coffee Liqueur
1 part Melon Liqueur
1 part Irish Cream Liqueur
1 part Tequila

Layer in a shot glass.

E.T.

SHOT GLASS

1 part Melon Liqueur
1 part Irish Cream Liqueur
1 part Vodka

Layer in a shot glass.

El Revolto

SHOT GLASS

1 part Peppermint Schnapps
1 part Irish Cream Liqueur
1 part Cointreau®

Layer in a shot glass.

Electric Banana

SHOT GLASS

1 part Tequila
1 part Banana Liqueur

Layer in a shot glass.

Eliphino

SHOT GLASS

1 part Sambuca
1 part Grand Marnier®

Layer in a shot glass.

Eskimo Kiss

SHOT GLASS

1 part Chocolate Liqueur
1 part Cherry Liqueur
1 part Amaretto

Layer in a shot glass. Top with Whipped Cream.

Extraterrestrial

SHOT GLASS

1 part Melon Liqueur
1 part Irish Cream Liqueur
1 part Vanilla Vodka
dash 151-Proof Rum

Layer in a shot glass. Light the Rum with a lighter or match. Extinguish by placing an empty glass upside down over the shot glass. Always extinguish the flame before consuming.

Exxon Valdez

SHOT GLASS

1 part Jägermeister
1 part Butterscotch Liqueur
1 part White Sambuca

Layer in a shot glass.

Face Off

SHOT GLASS

1 part Grenadine
1 part Crème de Menthe (White)
1 part Parfait Amour
1 part Sambuca

Layer in a shot glass.

Fahrenheit 5,000

SHOT GLASS

1 part Firewater®
1 part Absolut® Peppar Vodka
3 splashes Tabasco® Sauce

Layer in a shot glass.

Feather Duster

SHOT GLASS

1 part Whiskey
splash Blackberry Liqueur

Layer in a shot glass.

Ferrari® Shooter

SHOT GLASS

1 part Sambuca
1 part Tia Maria®

Layer in a shot glass.

Fifth Avenue

SHOT GLASS

1 part Crème de Cacao (Dark)
1 part Apricot Brandy
splash Light Cream

Layer in a shot glass.

Fightin' Irish Gold Shot

SHOT GLASS

1 part Irish Cream Liqueur
1 part Goldschläger®

Layer in a shot glass.

Fire Extinguisher

SHOT GLASS

1 part Fireball Cinnamon Whiskey
1 part Irish Cream Liqueur

Layer in a shot glass.

Fisherman's Wharf

SHOT GLASS

1 part Grand Marnier®
1 part Courvoisier©
1 part Amaretto

Layer in a shot glass.

The Flag

SHOT GLASS

1 part Grenadine
1 part Maraschino Liqueur
1 part Chartreuse®

Layer in a shot glass.

Flamboyance

SHOT GLASS

½ part Apricot Brandy
1 part Vodka
splash Grand Marnier®

Layer in a shot glass.

Flame Thrower

SHOT GLASS

2 parts Crème de Cacao (White)
1 part Bénédictine®
1 part Brandy

Layer in a shot glass.

Flaming Diamond

SHOT GLASS

1 part Strawberry Liqueur
1 part Peppermint Schnapps
1 part Grand Marnier®

Layer in a shot glass.

Flatliner

SHOT GLASS

1 part Sambuca
splash Tabasco® Sauce
1 part Tequila

Layer in a shot glass.

Flying Monkey

SHOT GLASS

1 part Coffee Liqueur
1 part Banana Liqueur
1 part Irish Cream Liqueur

Layer in a shot glass.

Fool's Gold

SHOT GLASS

1 part Coffee Liqueur
1 part Goldschläger®
1 part Jägermeister®

Layer in a shot glass.

Fourth of July

SHOT GLASS

1 part Grenadine
1 part Cream
1 part Blue Curaçao

Layer in a shot glass.

Francis Drake

SHOT GLASS

1 part Coffee Liqueur
1 part Spiced Rum

Layer in a shot glass.

Freddie's Naughty Neopolitan

POUSSE-CAFÉ GLASS

1 part Coffee Liqueur
1 part Crème de Cacao (White)
1 part Tequila Rose®

Layer in a pousse-café glass.

French Kiss

SHOT GLASS

1 part Amaretto
1 part Crème de Cacao (White)
1 part Irish Cream Liqueur

Layer in a shot glass.

French Pousse-Café

SHOT GLASS

1 part Cognac
1 part Grenadine
1 part Maraschino Liqueur

Layer in a shot glass.

Frozen Bird

SHOT GLASS

1 part Wild Turkey® Bourbon
1 part Rumple Minze®

Layer in a shot glass.

Full Moon

SHOT GLASS

1 part Amaretto
1 part Grand Marnier®

Layer in a shot glass.

German Blowjob

SHOT GLASS

1 part Irish Cream Liqueur
1 part Jägermeister®
1 part Rumple Minze®

Layer in a shot glass. Top with Whipped Cream and drink without using your hands.

German Cherry Bomb

SHOT GLASS

1 part Grenadine
1 part Godiva Chocolate Liqueur
1 part Cream

Layer in a shot glass.

Gingerbread

SHOT GLASS

1 part Irish Cream Liqueur
1 part Goldschläger®
1 part Butterscotch Schnapps

Layer in a shot glass.

Godfather Shooter

SHOT GLASS

1 part Amaretto
1 part Scotch

Layer in a shot glass.

Gold Rush

SHOT GLASS

1 part Swiss Chocolate Almond Liqueur
1 part Vodka
1 part Yukon Jack®

Layer in a shot glass.

Golden Flash

SHOT GLASS

1 part Sambuca
1 part Triple Sec
1 part Amaretto

Layer in a shot glass.

Golden Night

SHOT GLASS

1 part Swiss Chocolate Almond Liqueur
1 part Irish Cream Liqueur
1 part Frangelico®

Layer in a shot glass.

Golden Nipple

SHOT GLASS

1 part Goldschläger®
1 part Butterscotch Schnapps
1 part Irish Cream Liqueur

Layer in a shot glass.

Gone in 60 Seconds

SHOT GLASS

1 part Strawberry Liqueur
1 part Vanilla Liqueur
1 part Cream

Layer in a shot glass.

Gorilla Snot

SHOT GLASS

1 part Port
1 part Irish Cream Liqueur

Layer in a shot glass.

Grand Baileys®

SHOT GLASS

1 part Irish Cream Liqueur
1 part Grand Marnier®

Layer in a shot glass.

Grand Slam

SHOT GLASS

1 part Crème de Banane
1 part Irish Cream Liqueur
1 part Grand Marnier®

Layer in a shot glass.

Great Balls of Fire

SHOT GLASS

1 part Goldschläger®
1 part Cinnamon Schnapps
1 part Cherry Brandy

Layer in shot glass.

Great White North

SHOT GLASS

1 part Coffee Liqueur
1 part Irish Cream Liqueur
1 part Anisette

Layer in a shot glass.

Green Emerald

SHOT GLASS

1 part Crème de Menthe (Green)
1 part Swiss Chocolate Almond Liqueur

Layer in a shot glass.

Green Monkey

SHOT GLASS

1 part Banana Liqueur
1 part Crème de Menthe (Green)

Layer in a shot glass.

Green with Envy

SHOT GLASS

1 part Crème de Menthe (Green)
1 part Sambuca
1 part Irish Cream Liqueur

Layer in a shot glass.

Guillotine

SHOT GLASS

1 part Butterscotch Schnapps
1 part Irish Cream Liqueur
1 part After Shock® Peppermint Schnapps

Layer in a shot glass.

Guilty Conscience

SHOT GLASS

1 part Melon Liqueur
1 part Gold Tequila
splash Grenadine

Layer in a shot glass.

Hard On

SHOT GLASS

1 part Coffee Liqueur
1 part Amaretto
1 part Irish Cream Liqueur

Layer in a shot glass.

Hard Rocker

SHOT GLASS

1 part Vodka
1 part Melon Liqueur
1 part Irish Cream Liqueur

Layer in a shot glass.

Heartbreaker

SHOT GLASS

1 part Amaretto
1 part Irish Cream Liqueur
1 part Peach Schnapps

Layer in a shot glass.

Hot Jizz

SHOT GLASS

1 part Melon Liqueur
1 part Hot Damm!® Cinnamon Schnapps
1 part Grain Alcohol
1 part Lemon-Lime Soda

Layer in a shot glass.

Hot Lips Shooter

SHOT GLASS

3 parts RumChata
1 part Vanilla Vodka
splash Cinnamon Schnapps

Layer in a shot glass.

Icarus

SHOT GLASS

1 part Crème de Cacao (White)
1 part Irish Cream Liqueur
1 part Plum Brandy

Layer in a shot glass.

Ilicit Affair

SHOT GLASS

1 part Irish Cream Liqueur
1 part Peppermint Schnapps

Layer in a shot glass. Top with Whipped Cream.

Inhaler

SHOT GLASS

1 part Courvoisier®
1 part Amaretto

Layer in a shot glass.

Innocent Eyes

SHOT GLASS

1 part Coffee Liqueur
1 part Sambuca
1 part Irish Cream Liqueur

Layer in a shot glass.

Irish Flag

SHOT GLASS

1 part Irish Cream Liqueur
1 part Crème de Menthe (Green)
1 part Brandy

Layer in a shot glass.

Irish Gold

SHOT GLASS

1 part Irish Cream Liqueur
1 part Goldschläger®

Layer in a shot glass.

Irish Headlock

SHOT GLASS

1 part Brandy
1 part Amaretto
1 part Irish Whiskey
1 part Irish Cream Liqueur

Layer in a shot glass.

Irish Monk

SHOT GLASS

1 part Frangelico®
1 part Peppermint Schnapps
1 part Irish Cream Liqueur

Layer in a shot glass.

Jedi® Mind Trick

SHOT GLASS

1 part Goldschläger®
splash Irish Cream Liqueur
splash Melon Liqueur
splash 151-Proof Rum

Layer in a shot glass.

Joe Hazelwood

SHOT GLASS

1 part Rumple Minze®
1 part Jägermeister®

Layer in a shot glass.

KGB

SHOT GLASS

1 part Kahlua Coffee Liqueur
1 part Galliano
1 part Irish Cream Liqueur

Layer in a shot glass.

Kahbula

SHOT GLASS

1 part Coffee Liqueur
1 part Irish Cream Liqueur
1 part Tequila Reposado

Layer in a shot glass.

Kilted Black Leprechaun

SHOT GLASS

1 part Irish Cream Liqueur
1 part Coconut Rum
1 part Drambuie®

Layer in a shot glass.

King Alphonse

SHOT GLASS

1 part Crème de Cacao (Dark)
1 part Coffee Liqueur
1 part Cream

Layer in a shot glass.

Kitty Litter

SHOT GLASS

1 part Advocaat
1 part Irish Cream Liqueur
1 part Coconut Rum

Layer in a shot glass. Garnish with Chocolate Sprinkles.

Kokopa

SHOT GLASS

1 part Coffee Liqueur
1 part Peppermint Schnapps

Layer in a shot glass.

Kuba Lollipop

SHOT GLASS

1 part Peppermint Liqueur
1 part Ponche Kuba®

Layer in a shot glass.

L.A.P.D. Nightshift

SHOT GLASS

1 part Grenadine
1 part Blue Curaçao
1 part Tequila

Layer in a shot glass.

Landslide

SHOT GLASS

1 part Irish Cream Liqueur
1 part Apricot Brandy
1 part Banana Liqueur
1 part Coffee Liqueur

Layer in a shot glass.

Late Bloomer

SHOT GLASS

1 part Triple Sec
1 part Apricot Brandy
1 part Rum

Layer in a shot glass.

Lava Lamp

SHOT GLASS

1 part Coffee Liqueur
1 part Strawberry Liqueur
1 part Frangelico®
1 part Irish Cream Liqueur
splash Advocaat

In a shot glass, pour the Coffee Liqueur, Strawberry Liqueur, and Frangelico®. Layer the Irish Cream Liqueur and place 2 to 3 drops of Advocaat in the center.

Layer Cake

SHOT GLASS

1 part Crème de Cacao (Dark)
1 part Apricot Brandy
1 part Heavy Cream

Layer in a shot glass.

Leather and Lace

SHOT GLASS

1 part Swiss Chocolate Almond Liqueur
1 part Peach Schnapps

Layer in a shot glass.

Lewd Lewinsky

SHOT GLASS

1 part Jägermeister®
1 part Cream

Layer in a shot glass.

Liberace

SHOT GLASS

1 part Coffee Liqueur
1 part Milk
1 part 151-Proof Rum

Layer in a shot glass.

Lickity Clit

SHOT GLASS

1 part Irish Cream Liqueur
1 part Butterscotch Schnapps

Layer in a shot glass.

Licorice Heart

SHOT GLASS

1 part Strawberry Liqueur
1 part Sambuca
1 part Irish Cream Liqueur

Layer in a shot glass.

Little Beer

SHOT GLASS

1 part Licor 43
dash Cream

Layer in a shot glass so the Cream looks like the head on a miniature glass of beer.

Lizard Slime

SHOT GLASS

3 parts Jose Cuervo© Mistico
1 part Melon Liqueur

Layer in a shot glass.

Lonestar

SHOT GLASS

1 part Parfait Amour
1 part Cherry Liqueur
1 part Rum

Layer in a shot glass.

LSD

SHOT GLASS

1 part Cherry Brandy
1 part Vodka
1 part Passoã®

Layer in a shot glass.

Lube Job

SHOT GLASS

1 part Vodka
1 part Irish Cream Liqueur

Layer in a shot glass.

Machine Shot

SHOT GLASS

1 part 151-Proof Rum
splash Mountain Dew®

Layer in a shot glass.

Marijuana Milkshake

SHOT GLASS

1 part Crème de Cacao (White)
1 part Melon Liqueur
1 part Milk

Layer in a shot glass.

Martian Hard On

SHOT GLASS

1 part Crème de Cacao (White)
1 part Melon Liqueur
1 part Irish Cream Liqueur

Layer in a shot glass.

Meet the Parents

SHOT GLASS

1 part Raspberry Liqueur
1 part Crème de Coconut
2 parts Cream

Layer in a shot glass.

Melon Pousse-Café
SHOT GLASS
1 part Crème de Almond
1 part Crème de Cacao (White)
1 part Melon Liqueur
Layer in a shot glass.

Ménage à Trois Shooter
SHOT GLASS
1 part Coffee Liqueur
1 part Frangelico®
1 part Grand Marnier®
Layer in a shot glass.

Meth Lab
SHOT GLASS
1 part Watermelon Schnapps
1 part Peppermint Schnapps
1 part Aquavit
Layer in a shot glass.

Mexican Berry
SHOT GLASS
1 part Coffee Liqueur
1 part Strawberry Liqueur
1 part Tequila
Layer in a shot glass.

Mexican Flag
SHOT GLASS
1 part Grenadine
1 part Crème de Menthe (Green)
1 part Tequila
Layer in a shot glass.

Mexican Motherfucker
SHOT GLASS
1 part Tequila
1 part Irish Cream Liqueur
1 part Frangelico®
1 part Coffee Liqueur
Layer in a shot glass.

Midnight Madness
SHOT GLASS
1 part Triple Sec
1 part Coffee Liqueur
1 part Brandy
Layer in a shot glass.

Miles of Smiles
SHOT GLASS
1 part Amaretto
1 part Peppermint Schnapps
1 part Rye Whiskey
Layer in a shot glass.

Milk of Amnesia
SHOT GLASS
1 part Jägermeister®
1 part Irish Cream Liqueur
Layer in a shot glass.

Mini Guinness®
SHOT GLASS
3 parts Coffee Liqueur
1 part Irish Cream Liqueur
Layer in a shot glass.

Model T
SHOT GLASS
1 part Coffee Liqueur
1 part Crème de Banane
1 part Swiss Chocolate Almond Liqueur
Layer in a shot glass.

Moist and Pink
SHOT GLASS
1 part Sambuca
1 part Tequila Rose®
Layer in a shot glass.

Mom's Apple Pie
SHOT GLASS
3 parts Sour Apple Schnapps
1 part Cinnamon Schnapps
Layer in a shot glass.

Monkey Balls

SHOT GLASS

3 parts Tequila Rose®
1 part 99-Proof Banana Liqueur

Layer in a shot glass.

Mushroom

SHOT GLASS

1 part Grenadine
1 part Irish Cream Liqueur
1 part Melon Liqueur

Layer in a shot glass.

Napalm Death

SHOT GLASS

1 part Cointreau®
1 part Coffee Liqueur
1 part Drambuie®
1 part Irish Cream Liqueur

Layer in a shot glass.

Necrophiliac

SHOT GLASS

1 part Blue Curaçao
1 part Advocaat

Layer in a shot glass.

Nipple on Fire

SHOT GLASS

1 part Firewater®
1 part Butterscotch Schnapps
1 part Irish Cream Liqueur

Layer in a shot glass.

Norwegian Orgasm

SHOT GLASS

1 part Irish Cream Liqueur
1 part Crème de Menthe (White)

Layer in a shot glass.

Nose Opener

SHOT GLASS

3 parts Cinnamon Schnapps
1 part Irish Cream Liqueur

Layer in a shot glass.

Nude Bomb

SHOT GLASS

1 part Coffee Liqueur
1 part Amaretto
1 part Crème de Banane

Layer in a shot glass.

Nutty Buddy

SHOT GLASS

1 part Frangelico®
1 part Swiss Chocolate Almond Liqueur
1 part Peppermint Schnapps

Layer in a shot glass.

Nutty Irishman

SHOT GLASS

1 part Frangelico®
1 part Irish Cream Liqueur

Layer in a shot glass.

Okanagan

SHOT GLASS

1 part Apricot Brandy
1 part Strawberry Liqueur
1 part Blueberry Schnapps

Layer in a shot glass.

Old Glory

SHOT GLASS

1 part Grenadine
1 part Heavy Cream
1 part Blue Curaçao

Layer in a shot glass.

Oreo® Cookie

SHOT GLASS

1 part Coffee Liqueur
1 part Crème de Cacao (White)
1 part Irish Cream Liqueur
splash Vodka

Layer in a shot glass.

P.D.C.

SHOT GLASS

1 part Crème de Menthe (White)
2 parts Black Sambuca
2 parts Green Chartreuse®
1 part Irish Cream Liqueur

Layer in a shot glass.

Pasedena Lady

SHOT GLASS

1 part Swiss Chocolate Almond Liqueur
1 part Amaretto
1 part Brandy

Layer in a shot glass.

Passion Maker

SHOT GLASS

1 part Raspberry Liqueur
1 part Irish Cream Liqueur

Layer in a shot glass.

The Patriot

SHOT GLASS

1 part Blue Curaçao
1 part Crème de Cacao (White)
1 part Grenadine

Layer in a shot glass.

Patriotic Blow

SHOT GLASS

1 part Sloe Gin
1 part Blue Curaçao
1 part Cream

Layer in a shot glass.

Penalty Shot

SHOT GLASS

1 part Crème de Menthe (White)
1 part Tia Maria®
1 part Peppermint Schnapps

Layer in a shot glass.

Peruvian Jungle Fuck

SHOT GLASS

1 part Chocolate Banana Liqueur
1 part Cafe Orange Liqueur
1 part Half and Half

Layer in a shot glass.

Pipeline

SHOT GLASS

1 part Tequila
1 part Vodka

Layer in a shot glass.

Placenta

SHOT GLASS

1 part Amaretto
1 part Irish Cream Liqueur
splash Grenadine

Layer the Amaretto then the Irish Cream in a shot glass. Place a few drops of Grenadine in the center of the drink.

Pleasure Dome

SHOT GLASS

1 part Brandy
1 part Crème de Cacao (White)
1 part Bénédictine®

Layer in a shot glass.

Port and Starboard

SHOT GLASS

1 part Grenadine
1 part Crème de Menthe (Green)

Layer in a shot glass.

Pousse-Café

SHOT GLASS

1 part Crème de Menthe (White)
1 part Crème Yvette®
1 part Grenadine
1 part Chartreuse®

Layer in a shot glass.

Pousse-Café Americain

SHOT GLASS

1 part Red Curaçao
1 part Cognac
1 part Maraschino Liqueur

Layer in a shot glass.

Primordial

SHOT GLASS

1 part Melon Liqueur
1 part Black Sambuca

Layer in a shot glass.

Pumping Station

SHOT GLASS

1 part Coffee Liqueur
1 part Amaretto
1 part 151-Proof Rum

Layer in a shot glass.

Quick Karlo

SHOT GLASS

1 part Amaretto
1 part Whiskey

Layer in a shot glass.

Quick Tango

SHOT GLASS

1 part Coffee Liqueur
1 part Irish Cream Liqueur
1 part Melon Liqueur

Layer in a shot glass.

Race War

SHOT GLASS

1 part Crème de Cacao (White)
1 part Irish Cream Liqueur
1 part Vodka

Layer in a shot glass.

Raging Bull

SHOT GLASS

1 part Coffee Liqueur
1 part Sambuca
1 part Tequila

Layer in a shot glass.

Raider

SHOT GLASS

1 part Irish Cream Liqueur
1 part Grand Marnier®
1 part Cointreau®

Layer in a shot glass.

Rainbow Cocktail

SHOT GLASS

1 part Blue Curaçao
1 part Crème de Menthe (Green)
1 part Cognac
1 part Maraschino Liqueur
1 part Blackberry Liqueur
1 part Crème de Cassis

Layer in a shot glass.

Raspberry's Romance

SHOT GLASS

1 part Raspberry Liqueur
1 part Coffee Liqueur
1 part Irish Cream Liqueur

Layer in a shot glass.

Rattlesnake

SHOT GLASS

1 part Irish Cream Liqueur
1 part Coffee Liqueur
1 part Crème de Cacao (White)

Layer in a shot glass.

Red, White, and Blue

SHOT GLASS

1 part Cinnamon Schnapps
1 part Goldschläger®
1 part Peppermint Schnapps

Layer in a shot glass.

The Red and Black
SHOT GLASS

1 part Coffee Liqueur
1 part Grenadine

Layer in a shot glass.

Redback Shooter
SHOT GLASS

2 parts Sambuca
1 part Advocaat

Layer in a shot glass.

Redhead's Nipple
SHOT GLASS

1 part Vanilla Vodka
1 part Irish Cream Liqueur
2 drops Grenadine

Layer in a shot glass. Place the drops of Grenadine in the center of the Irish Cream layer.

Return of the Yeti
SHOT GLASS

1 part Lychee Liqueur
1 part Parfait Amour
1 part Goldschläger®

Layer in a shot glass.

Rhino
SHOT GLASS

1 part Coffee Liqueur
1 part Amarula® Crème Liqueur
1 part Cointreau®

Layer in a shot glass.

Rhubarb and Custard
SHOT GLASS

1 part Advocaat
1 part Raspberry Liqueur

Layer in a shot glass.

Rock Lobster
SHOT GLASS

1 part Irish Cream Liqueur
1 part Amaretto
1 part Crème de Cacao (White)

Layer in a shot glass.

Rock 'n' Roll
SHOT GLASS

1 part Chocolate Mint Liqueur
1 part Vodka

Layer in a shot glass.

Roly Poly Shooter
SHOT GLASS

1 part Triple Sec
1 part Irish Cream Liqueur
1 part Peach Liqueur

Layer in a shot glass.

Roy Hob Special
SHOT GLASS

1 part Jack Daniel's®
1 part Irish Cream Liqueur
1 part Peppermint Schnapps

Layer in a shot glass.

Rum Roller
SHOT GLASS

1 part Frangelico®
1 part Dark Rum
1 part Espresso

Layer in a shot glass.

Runny Nose
SHOT GLASS

1 part Coffee Liqueur
1 part Irish Cream Liqueur
1 part Cherry Advocaat

Layer in a shot glass.

Russian Candy

SHOT GLASS

1 part Vodka
1 part Peach Schnapps
1 part Grenadine

Layer in a shot glass.

Rusty Spike

SHOT GLASS

1 part Drambuie®
1 part Scotch

Layer in a shot glass.

Saipa

SHOT GLASS

1 part Banana Liqueur
1 part Vodka

Layer in a shot glass.

Santa Shot

SHOT GLASS

1 part Grenadine
1 part Crème de Menthe (Green)
1 part Peppermint Schnapps

Layer in a shot glass.

Savoy Hotel

SHOT GLASS

1 part Bénédictine®
1 part Brandy
1 part Crème de Cacao (White)

Layer in a shot glass.

Screaming Lizard

SHOT GLASS

1 part Tequila
1 part Chartreuse®

Layer in a shot glass.

Sea Monkey

SHOT GLASS

2 parts Goldschläger®
1 part Blue Curaçao

Layer in a shot glass.

Seduction

SHOT GLASS

1 part Frangelico®
1 part Crème de Banane
1 part Irish Cream Liqueur

Layer in a shot glass.

Shamrock Shooter

SHOT GLASS

1 part Crème de Menthe (White)
1 part Crème de Cacao (White)
1 part Irish Cream Liqueur

Layer in a shot glass.

Shit on the Grass

SHOT GLASS

1 part Melon Liqueur
1 part Coffee Liqueur

Layer in a shot glass.

Shorty Sex House

SHOT GLASS

2 parts Ouzo
2 parts Crème de Menthe (Green)
1 part Passion Fruit Nectar

Layer in a shot glass.

Silver Thread

SHOT GLASS

1 part Banana Liqueur
1 part Irish Cream Liqueur
1 part Peppermint Schnapps

Layer in a shot glass.

Sleigh Ride

SHOT GLASS

1 part Grenadine
1 part Green Chartreuse®
1 part Silver Tequila

Layer in a shot glass.

Slippery Sin

SHOT GLASS

1 part Crème de Coconut
1 part Irish Cream Liqueur

Layer in a shot glass.

Snap Shot

SHOT GLASS

1 part Peppermint Schnapps
1 part Irish Cream Liqueur

Layer in a shot glass.

Snow Cap

SHOT GLASS

1 part Irish Cream Liqueur
1 part Tequila

Layer in a shot glass.

Soft Porn

SHOT GLASS

1 part Crème de Cassis
1 part Raspberry Liqueur
1 part Irish Cream Liqueur

Layer in a shot glass.

Solar Plexus

SHOT GLASS

2 parts Vodka
1 part Cherry Brandy
1 part Campari®

Layer in a shot glass.

Southern Belle

SHOT GLASS

1 part Brandy
1 part Crème de Cacao (White)
1 part Bénédictine®

Layer in a shot glass.

Southern Rattler

SHOT GLASS

1 part Crème de Banane
1 part Southern Comfort®
1 part Gold Tequila

Layer in a shot glass.

Spot Shooter

SHOT GLASS

1 part Vodka
1 part Coffee
splash Irish Cream Liqueur

Layer in a shot glass. Place a few drops of Irish Cream in the center of the drink.

Spring Fever

SHOT GLASS

1 part Drambuie®
1 part Swiss Chocolate Almond Liqueur

Layer in a shot glass.

Springbok

SHOT GLASS

3 parts Crème de Menthe (White)
2 parts Amarula® Crème Liqueur
1 part Cream

Layer in a shot glass.

Stars and Stripes

SHOT GLASS

1 part Blue Curaçao
1 part Heavy Cream
1 part Grenadine

Layer in a shot glass.

Stinky Beaver

POUSSE-CAFÉ GLASS

1 part Goldschläger®
1 part Jägermeister®

Layer in a shot glass.

Storm

SHOT GLASS

1 part Light Rum
1 part Blue Curaçao
1 part Irish Cream Liqueur

Layer in a shot glass.

Storm Cloud

SHOT GLASS

2 parts Rum
1 part Tequila
1 part Amaretto

Layer in a shot glass.

Strawberry Freddo

SHOT GLASS

1 part Rumchata
1 part Coffee Liqueur
1 part Strawberry Liqueur

Layer in a shot glass.

Strawberry Kiss

SHOT GLASS

1 part Coffee Liqueur
1 part Strawberry Liqueur
1 part Irish Cream Liqueur

Layer in a shot glass.

Street Car

SHOT GLASS

1 part Crème de Cacao (Dark)
1 part Irish Cream Liqueur
1 part Apricot Brandy

Layer in a shot glass.

Summer Fling

SHOT GLASS

1 part Blue Curaçao
1 part Irish Cream Liqueur

Layer in a shot glass.

Sun and Surf

SHOT GLASS

1 part Coffee Liqueur
1 part Grand Marnier®
1 part Tequila

Layer in a shot glass.

Sunrise Shooter

SHOT GLASS

1 part Parfait Amour
1 part Grenadine
1 part Chartreuse®
1 part Cointreau®

Layer in a shot glass.

Sweet Bull

SHOT GLASS

2 parts Tequila Reposado
2 parts Lychee Liqueur
1 part Grenadine

Layer in a shot glass.

Sweet Burning Eruption

SHOT GLASS

1 part Triple Sec
1 part Butterscotch Schnapps
1 part Irish Cream Liqueur
splash Grenadine

Layer all but Grenadine in a shot glass. Place a few drops of Grenadine in the center of the drink.

Swiss and Whoosh

SHOT GLASS

1 part Tia Maria®
1 part Frangelico®
1 part Irish Cream Liqueur

Layer in a shot glass.

Swiss Hiker

SHOT GLASS

1 part Swiss Chocolate Almond Liqueur
1 part Crème de Banane
1 part Irish Cream Liqueur

Layer in a shot glass.

T-52

SHOT GLASS

1 part Coffee Liqueur
1 part Tequila Rose®
1 part Grand Marnier®

Layer in a shot glass.

Tampa Pond Scum

SHOT GLASS

1 part Peach Schnapps
1 part Melon Liqueur
1 part Rum
1 part Milk

Layer in a shot glass.

Technical Knock Out

SHOT GLASS

1 part Ouzo
1 part Coffee Liqueur
1 part Tequila

Layer in a shot glass.

Tequila Knockout

SHOT GLASS

3 parts Silver Tequila
1 part Grenadine

Layer in a shot glass.

Texas Chainsaw Massacre

SHOT GLASS

1 part Strawberry Liqueur
1 part Vodka

Layer in a shot glass.

Texas Thunderstorm

SHOT GLASS

1 part Amaretto
splash 151-Proof Rum
splash Irish Cream Liqueur

Layer in a shot glass.

Thin Blue Line

SHOT GLASS

1 part Vodka
1 part Triple Sec
splash Blue Curaçao

Layer the Triple Sec on top of the Vodka then gently drip the Blue Curaçao. It will settle between the Vodka and Triple Sec, forming a thin blue line.

Thorny Rose

SHOT GLASS

1 part Tequila Rose®
1 part Peppermint Schnapps
1 part Coffee Liqueur

Layer in a shot glass.

Three's Company

SHOT GLASS

1 part Courvoisier®
1 part Grand Marnier®
1 part Coffee Liqueur

Layer in a shot glass.

Tiger Tail

SHOT GLASS

1 part Tia Maria®
1 part Grand Marnier®
1 part Peppermint Schnapps

Layer in a shot glass.

Toronto Maple Leafs

SHOT GLASS

1 part Blue Curaçao
1 part Irish Cream Liqueur

Layer in a shot glass.

Trap Door

SHOT GLASS

1 part Swiss Chocolate Almond Liqueur
1 part Rum Crème Liqueur

Layer in a shot glass.

Trial of the Century

SHOT GLASS

1 part Jägermeister®
1 part Goldschläger®
1 part Grenadine

Layer in a shot glass.

Tricolore

SHOT GLASS

1 part Crème de Menthe (White)
1 part Apricot Brandy
1 part Maraschino Liqueur

Layer in a shot glass.

Triple Irish Shooter

SHOT GLASS

1 part Irish Whiskey
1 part Irish Cream Liqueur
1 part Irish Mist®

Layer in a shot glass.

Uncle Sam

SHOT GLASS

1 part After Shock® Cinnamon Schnapps
1 part Avalanche® Peppermint Schnapps
1 part Rumple Minze®

Layer in a shot glass.

Undertaker

SHOT GLASS

1 part Jägermeister®
1 part Cointreau®
1 part 151-Proof Rum

Layer in a shot glass.

V-2 Schnieder

SHOT GLASS

1 part Coffee Liqueur
1 part Irish Cream Liqueur
1 part Frangelico®

Layer in a shot glass.

Vibrator

SHOT GLASS

2 parts Southern Comfort®
1 part Irish Cream Liqueur

Layer in a shot glass.

Vice Versa

SHOT GLASS

1 part Pisang Ambon® Liqueur
1 part Passion Fruit Liqueur
1 part Green Chartreuse®

Layer in a shot glass.

Well-Greased Dwarf

SHOT GLASS

1 part Crème de Cacao (White)
1 part Sambuca
1 part Irish Cream Liqueur

Layer in a shot glass.

Wet Kiss

SHOT GLASS

1 part Amaretto
1 part Sweet & Sour Mix
1 part Watermelon Schnapps

Layer in a shot glass.

Whick

SHOT GLASS

1 part Sambuca
1 part Black Sambuca

Layer in a shot glass.

Whipster

SHOT GLASS

1 part Crème de Cacao (White)
1 part Apricot Brandy
1 part Triple Sec

Layer in a shot glass.

Whistle Stop

SHOT GLASS

1 part Grand Marnier®
1 part Jack Daniel's®

Layer in a shot glass.

Whistling Gypsy

SHOT GLASS

1 part Tia Maria®
1 part Irish Cream Liqueur
1 part Vodka

Layer in a shot glass.

White Flag

SHOT GLASS

1 part Frangelico
¼ part Irish Cream Liqueur

Layer in a shot glass.

White Lightning

SHOT GLASS

1 part Tequila
1 part Crème de Cacao (White)

Layer in a shot glass.

White Tornado

SHOT GLASS

3 parts Sambuca
1 part Tequila Rose®

Layer in a shot glass.

Windsurfer

SHOT GLASS

1 part Coffee Liqueur
1 part Triple Sec
1 part Yukon Jack®

Layer in a shot glass.

Winter Break

SHOT GLASS

1 part Peach Schnapps
1 part Banana Liqueur
1 part Southern Comfort®

Layer in a shot glass.

Witch's Tit

SHOT GLASS

3 parts Coffee Liqueur
2 parts Heavy Cream

Layer in a shot glass. Garnish with a Maraschino Cherry.

Wobble Walker

SHOT GLASS

1 part Crème de Banane
2 parts Irish Cream Liqueur
1 part 151-Proof Rum

Layer in a shot glass.

Wookie

SHOT GLASS

1 part Peach Schnapps
1 part Amaretto
½ part Irish Cream Liqueur

Layer in a shot glass.

Yankee's Pousse-Café

SHOT GLASS

1 part Brandy
1 part Red Curaçao
1 part Grenadine
1 part Maraschino Liqueur
1 part Vanilla Liqueur

Layer in a shot glass.

Zipper Shooter

SHOT GLASS

1 part Grand Marnier®
1 part Tequila
1 part Irish Cream Liqueur

Layer in a shot glass.

Zowie

SHOT GLASS

1 part Banana Liqueur
1 part Irish Cream Liqueur
1 part Coconut Flavored Rum

Layer in a shot glass.

FLAMING SHOTS

Flaming shots are dramatic and entertaining, but you're playing with fire. Always follow these simple safety rules:

- Never lift or move the shot while it's lit. A flaming alcohol spill can be *very* dangerous.
- Always extinguish the flame before consuming the shot.
- Use an inverted empty glass or metal cup to extinguish the flame. An empty shot glass or a jigger works well. Never use your hand.

A.S.S. on Flames

SHOT GLASS

1 part Amaretto
1 part Sour Apple Schnapps
1 part Southern Comfort®
splash 151-Proof Rum

Layer in a shot glass. Light the Rum with a lighter or match. Extinguish by placing an empty glass over the shot. Always extinguish the flame before consuming.

Burning Africa

SHOT GLASS

1 part Jägermeister®
1 part 151-Proof Rum

Layer in a shot glass. Light the Rum with a lighter or match. Extinguish by placing an empty glass over the shot. Always extinguish the flame before consuming.

Concord

SHOT GLASS

1 part Coffee Liqueur
1 part Irish Cream Liqueur splash
splash 151-Proof Rum

Layer in a shot glass. Light the Rum with a lighter or match. Extinguish by placing an empty glass over the shot. Always extinguish the flame before consuming.

Everybody's Irish

SHOT GLASS

2 parts Whiskey
½ part Crème de Menthe (Green)

Pour ingredients into a glass neat (do not chill). Light the Whiskey with a lighter or a match. Extinguish by placing an empty glass over the shot. Always extinguish the flame before consuming.

Feel the Burn

SHOT GLASS

1 part Coffee Liqueur
1 part Irish Cream Liqueur
1 part Ouzo
1 part Wild Turkey® Bourbon
1 part 151-Proof Rum

Pour ingredients into glass neat (do not chill). Light the Rum with a lighter or match. Extinguish by placing an empty glass over the shot. Always extinguish the flame before consuming.

Fiery Balls of Death

SHOT GLASS

1 part 151-Proof Rum
1 part Triple Sec

Pour ingredients into glass neat (do not chill). Light the Rum with a lighter or match. Extinguish by placing an empty glass over the shot. Always extinguish the flame before consuming.

Fiery Blue Mustang

SHOT GLASS

1 part Banana Liqueur
1 part Blue Curaçao
1 part 151-Proof Rum

Pour ingredients into glass neat (do not chill). Light the Rum with a lighter or match. Extinguish by placing an empty glass over the shot. Always extinguish the flame before consuming.

Flambé

SHOT GLASS

1 part Grenadine
1 part Crème de Menthe (White)
1 part Vodka
1 part 151-Proof Rum

Layer in a shot glass. Light the Rum with a lighter or match. Extinguish by placing an empty glass over the shot. Always extinguish the flame before consuming.

Flaming Armadillo

SHOT GLASS

1 part Tequila
1 part Amaretto
1 part Rum

Pour ingredients into glass neat (do not chill). Light the Rum with a lighter or match. Extinguish by placing an empty glass over the shot. Always extinguish the flame before consuming.

Flaming Armageddon

SHOT GLASS

1 part Jägermeister
1 part Peppermint Schnapps
1 part Tequila
1 part 151-Proof Rum

Shake all but the 151-Proof Rum with ice and strain. Float the 151-Proof Rum on top. Light the Rum with a lighter or match. Extinguish by placing an empty glass upside down over the shot glass. Always extinguish the flame before consuming.

Flaming Blazer

SHOT GLASS

1 part Crème de Cacao (White)
1 part Southern Comfort®
1 part 151-Proof Rum

Pour ingredients into glass neat (do not chill). Light the Rum with a lighter or match. Extinguish by placing an empty glass over the shot. Always extinguish the flame before consuming.

Flaming Blue

SHOT GLASS

1 part Anisette
1 part Dry Vermouth
1 part 151-Proof Rum

Pour ingredients into glass neat (do not chill). Light the Rum with a lighter or match. Extinguish by placing an empty glass over the shot. Always extinguish the flame before consuming.

Flaming Blue Fuck

SHOT GLASS

3 parts Sambuca
1 part Blue Curaçao

Pour ingredients into glass neat (do not chill). Light the Sambuca with a lighter or match. Extinguish by placing an empty glass over the shot. Always extinguish the flame before consuming.

Flaming Blue Jesus

SHOT GLASS

1 part Peppermint Schnapps
1 part Southern Comfort®
1 part Tequila
2 parts 151-Proof Rum

Pour ingredients into glass neat (do not chill). Light the Rum with a lighter or match. Extinguish by placing an empty glass over the shot. Always extinguish the flame before consuming.

Flaming Courage

SHOT GLASS

1 part Cinnamon Schnapps
1 part Peppermint Schnapps
1 part Melon Liqueur
splash 151-Proof Rum

Pour ingredients into glass neat (do not chill). Light the Rum with a lighter or match. Extinguish by placing an empty glass over the shot. Always extinguish the flame before consuming.

Flaming Dragon

SHOT GLASS

1 part Green Chartreuse®
1 part 151-Proof Rum

Pour ingredients into glass neat (do not chill). Light the Rum with a lighter or match. Extinguish by placing an empty glass over the shot. Always extinguish the flame before consuming.

Flaming Dragon Snot

SHOT GLASS

1 part Crème de Menthe (White)
1 part Irish Cream Liqueur
1 part 151-Proof Rum

Pour ingredients into glass neat (do not chill). Light the Rum with a lighter or match. Extinguish by placing an empty glass over the shot. Always extinguish the flame before consuming.

Flaming Fart

SHOT GLASS

1 part Cinnamon Schnapps
1 part 151-Proof Rum

Pour ingredients into glass neat (do not chill). Light the Rum with a lighter or match. Extinguish by placing an empty glass over the shot. Always extinguish the flame before consuming.

Flaming Fruit Trees

SHOT GLASS

1 part Peach Schnapps
1 part Banana Liqueur
1 part 151-Proof Rum

Pour ingredients into glass neat (do not chill). Light the Rum with a lighter or match. Extinguish by placing an empty glass over the shot. Always extinguish the flame before consuming.

Flaming Giraffe

SHOT GLASS

2 parts Coffee Liqueur
1 part Butterscotch Schnapps
1 part 151-Proof Rum

Pour ingredients into glass neat (do not chill). Light the Rum with a lighter or match. Extinguish by placing an empty glass over the shot. Always extinguish the flame before consuming.

Flaming Glacier

SHOT GLASS

1 part Cinnamon Schnapps
1 part Rumple Minze®

Pour ingredients into glass neat (do not chill). Light the Schnapps with a lighter or match. Extinguish by placing an empty glass over the shot. Always extinguish the flame before consuming.

Flaming Gorilla

SHOT GLASS

1 part Peppermint Schnapps
1 part Coffee Liqueur
1 part 151-Proof Rum

Pour ingredients into glass neat (do not chill). Light the Rum with a lighter or match. Extinguish by placing an empty glass over the shot. Always extinguish the flame before consuming.

Flaming Gorilla Titties

SHOT GLASS

1 part 151-Proof Rum
1 part Coffee Liqueur

Pour ingredients into glass neat (do not chill). Light the Rum with a lighter or match. Extinguish by placing an empty glass over the shot. Always extinguish the flame before consuming.

Flaming Jesus

SHOT GLASS

1 part Vodka
1 part Lime Juice
1 part Grenadine
1 part 151-Proof Rum

Pour ingredients into glass neat (do not chill). Light the Rum with a lighter or match. Extinguish by placing an empty glass over the shot. Always extinguish the flame before consuming.

Flaming Licorice

SHOT GLASS

1 part Jägermeister®
1 part Sambuca
1 part 151-Proof Rum

Pour ingredients into glass neat (do not chill). Light the Rum with a lighter or match. Extinguish by placing an empty glass over the shot. Always extinguish the flame before consuming.

Flaming Nazi

SHOT GLASS

1 part Goldschläger®
1 part Rumple Minze®
1 part 151-Proof Rum

Pour ingredients into glass neat (do not chill). Light the Rum with a lighter or match. Extinguish by placing an empty glass over the shot. Always extinguish the flame before consuming.

Flaming Rasta

SHOT GLASS

1 part Amaretto
1 part Grenadine
1 part 151-Proof Rum

Layer in a shot glass. Light the Rum with a lighter or match. Extinguish by placing an empty glass over the shot. Always extinguish the flame before consuming.

Freakin' Flamin' Fruit

SHOT GLASS

1 part Melon Liqueur
1 part Crème de Banane
1 part Golden Pear Liqueur
1 part 151-Proof Rum

Pour ingredients into glass neat (do not chill). Light the Rum with a lighter or match. Extinguish by placing an empty glass over the shot. Always extinguish the flame before consuming.

Green Lizard

SHOT GLASS

4 parts Green Chartreuse®
1 part 151-Proof Rum

Layer in a shot glass. Light the Rum with a lighter or match. Extinguish by placing an empty glass over the shot. Always extinguish the flame before consuming.

Harbor Light

SHOT GLASS

1 part Coffee Liqueur
1 part Rumchata
1 part 151-Proof Rum

Layer in a shot glass. Light the Rum with a lighter or match. Extinguish by placing an empty glass over the shot. Always extinguish the flame before consuming.

Hot Lesbian Sex

SHOT GLASS

1 part Cherry Vodka
1 part Mango Vodka
1 part Peach Vodka
splash 151-Proof Rum

Shake all but the 151-Proof Rum with ice and strain. Float the 151-Proof Rum on top. Light the Rum with a lighter or match. Extinguish by placing an empty glass upside down over the shot glass. Always extinguish the flame before consuming.

Lighthouse

SHOT GLASS

1 part Coffee Liqueur
1 part Irish Cream Liqueur
1 part 151-Proof Rum

Layer in a shot glass. Light the Rum with a lighter or match. Extinguish by placing an empty glass over the shot. Always extinguish the flame before consuming.

Morphine Drip

SHOT GLASS

1 part Amaretto
1 part Butterscotch Schnapps
splash 151-Proof Rum

Pour ingredients into glass neat (do not chill). Light the Rum with a lighter or match. Extinguish by placing an empty glass over the shot. Always extinguish the flame before consuming.

Napalm

SHOT GLASS

1 part Cinnamon Schnapps
1 part Fire & Ice®
1 part 151-Proof Rum

Pour ingredients into glass neat (do not chill). Light the Rum with a lighter or match. Extinguish by placing an empty glass over the shot. Always extinguish the flame before consuming.

Napalm Crematorium

SHOT GLASS

1 part Cinnamon Schnapps
1 part Rumple Minze®
1 part 151-Proof Rum

Layer in a shot glass. Light the Rum with a lighter or match. Extinguish by placing an empty glass over the shot. Always extinguish the flame before consuming.

Pyro

SHOT GLASS

1 part Vodka
1 part Fire Water®
splash 151-Proof Rum

Build in the glass with no ice. Light the Rum with a lighter or match. Extinguish by placing an empty glass over the shot. Always extinguish the flame before consuming.

Rock Star

SHOT GLASS

1 part Cinnamon Schnapps
1 part Sloe Gin
1 part Triple Sec
1 part Jägermeister®
1 part 151-Proof Rum

Build in the glass with no ice. Light the Rum with a lighter or match. Extinguish by placing an empty glass over the shot. Always extinguish the flame before consuming.

Southern Bound Meteor

SHOT GLASS

Maraschino Cherry
1 part Southern Comfort®
1 part Goldschläger®
splash 151-Proof Rum

Remove the stem from a cherry and drop it in a shot glass. Pour in the Southern Comfort® and Goldschläger®. Top with a splash of 151-Proof Rum. Light the Rum with a lighter or match. Extinguish by placing an empty glass over the shot. Always extinguish the flame before consuming.

Thriller Shooter

SHOT GLASS

1 part Strawberry Liqueur
1 part Dark Rum

Build in the glass with no ice. Light the Rum with a lighter or match. Extinguish by placing an empty glass over the shot. Always extinguish the flame before consuming.

Vesuvius

SHOT GLASS

3 parts Crème de Cacao (Dark)
1 part Green Chartreuse®

Layer in a shot glass. Light the Chartreuse with a lighter or match. Extinguish by placing an empty glass over the shot. Always extinguish the flame before consuming.

TABASCO® SHOTS

These shots induce pain. If you can't stand the heat, offer them to your "friends," or that loud, obnoxious guy at the end of the bar.

911 Ouch

SHOT GLASS

1 part Cinnamon Schnapps
1 part 100-Proof Peppermint Schnapps
splash Tabasco® Sauce

Pour ingredients into glass neat (do not chill).

Absolut Flat Line

SHOT GLASS

1 part Chile Pepper Vodka
1 part Sambuca
5 dashes Tabasco® Sauce

Layer in a shot glass.

Absolution

SHOT GLASS

1 part Vodka
dash Tabasco® Sauce

Pour ingredients into glass neat (do not chill).

Abuse Machine

SHOT GLASS

1 part Tequila
½ part Whiskey
½ part Sambuca
splash Tabasco® Sauce
splash Worcestershire Sauce

Shake with ice and strain.

Afterburner

SHOT GLASS

splash Tabasco® Sauce
1 part Silver Tequila
dash Salt
1 Lime Slice

Pour enough Tabasco® Sauce into the shot glass to cover the bottom completely. Fill the rest of the shot glass with Tequila. Lick your hand and pour some Salt on it. Lick the Salt, slam the shot, then suck the Lime.

Afterburner #2

SHOT GLASS

1 part Vodka
½ part Tabasco® Sauce

Pour ingredients into glass neat (do not chill).

Anaconda #2

SHOT GLASS

1 part Coconut Rum
1 part Crème de Cacao (Dark)
1 part Irish Cream Liqueur
dash Crème de Menthe (Green)
dash Tabasco® Sauce

Shake with ice and strain.

Anus Burner

SHOT GLASS

1 Jalapeño Pepper Slice
1 part Tequila
splash Tabasco® Sauce

Place slice of Jalapeño in shot glass. Add Tequila and enough Tabasco® to make deep red in color.

The Antichrist

SHOT GLASS

1 part Grain Alcohol
1 part 151-Proof Rum
1 part Absolut® Peppar Vodka
3 splashes Tabasco® Sauce

Shake with ice and strain.

Aqua del Fuego

SHOT GLASS

1 part Tequila
1 part Tabasco® Sauce

Pour ingredients into glass neat (do not chill).

Battery Acid

SHOT GLASS

1 part Dark Rum
1 part Gold Tequila
1 part Green Chartreuse
2 drops Tabasco® Sauce

Shake with ice and strain.

Bloody Chicken

SHOT GLASS

1 part Wild Turkey® Bourbon
½ part Tequila
¼ splash Tabasco® Sauce

Pour ingredients into glass neat (do not chill).

Bloody Molly

COLLINS GLASS

2 parts Irish Whiskey
splash Tabasco® Sauce
splash Worcestershire Sauce
dash Lime Juice
1 tsp Fresh Horseradish
fill with Tomato Juice

Shake with ice and pour.

Brave Bull

SHOT GLASS

1 part Tequila
1 part Tabasco® Sauce

Pour ingredients into glass neat (do not chill).

Buffalo Ball Sweat

SHOT GLASS

3 parts Yukon Jack®
3 splashes Tabasco® Sauce

Pour ingredients into glass neat (do not chill).

Buffalo Piss

SHOT GLASS

1 part Tequila
1 part Tabasco® Sauce

Pour ingredients into glass neat (do not chill).

Burn in Hell and Pray for Snow!

SHOT GLASS

for Snow!
2 parts Rum
2 parts Whiskey
1 part Tabasco® Sauce
12 Hot Peppers

Combine all ingredients in a blender with ice. Blend until smooth. Pour into shot glasses and top with a splash of Irish Cream.

Burning Angel

SHOT GLASS

1 part Vodka
1 part Jägermeister®
splash Tabasco® Sauce
dash Salt

Pour ingredients into glass neat (do not chill).

Cajun Bloody Mary

COLLINS GLASS

2 parts Pepper Vodka
1 part Bacon Vodka
8 parts Tomato Juice
1/6 part Lime Juice
dash Tabasco® Sauce
dash Garlic Powder

Shake with ice and strain over ice.

Chuck Wagon

SHOT GLASS

1 part Jägermeister®
1/2 splash Tabasco® Sauce

Pour ingredients into glass neat (do not chill).

Dead Dog

SHOT GLASS

1 part Bourbon
1 part Beer
3 splashes Tabasco® Sauce

Pour ingredients into glass neat (do not chill).

Death by Fire

SHOT GLASS

1 part Peppermint Schnapps
1 part Cinnamon Schnapps
1 part Tabasco® Sauce

Pour ingredients into glass neat (do not chill).

Devil Drink

SHOT GLASS

1 part Irish Cream Liqueur
1 part Sambuca
1 part Vodka
3 splashes Tabasco® Sauce

Pour ingredients into glass neat (do not chill).

Devil's Reject

SHOT GLASS

1 part Peppermint Schnapps
1 part Vodka
3 drops Tabasco® Sauce

Build in a shot glass. Do not chill.

Dia del Amor

HIGHBALL GLASS

1 1/2 parts Tequila Reposado
1 part St-Germain
3/4 part Lime Juice
2 dashes Tabasco® Sauce

Shake with ice and strain. Garnish with a Lime Wheel.

Diablo!

SHOT GLASS

1 part 151-Proof Rum
splash Tabasco® Sauce

Pour ingredients into glass neat (do not chill).

Dragon's Spit

SHOT GLASS

1 part Fireball
1–10 drops of Tabasco® Sauce

Shake with ice and strain.

Estonian Forest Fire

SHOT GLASS

1 part Vodka
6 splashes Tabasco® Sauce
1 Kiwi Slice

Combine the Tabasco® with a shot of Vodka. Chase it with a slice of Kiwi.

Fence Jumper

SHOT GLASS

1 part Tequila
1 part Rum
splash Tabasco® Sauce

Pour ingredients into glass neat (do not chill).

Firecracker Shot

SHOT GLASS

2 parts Tequila
1 part Tabasco® Sauce

Pour ingredients into glass neat (do not chill).

Fire in the Hole

SHOT GLASS

1½ parts Ouzo
3 splashes Tabasco® Sauce

Pour ingredients into glass neat (do not chill).

Fireball

SHOT GLASS

1 part Fire Water®
splash Tabasco® Sauce

Pour ingredients into glass neat (do not chill).

Fireball #2

SHOT GLASS

1 part Sambuca
1 part Tequila
splash Tabasco® Sauce

Pour ingredients into glass neat (do not chill).

Fireball #3

SHOT GLASS

1 part Cinnamon Schnapps
splash Tabasco® Sauce

Pour ingredients into glass neat (do not chill).

Fireball Shooter

SHOT GLASS

1 part Cinnamon Schnapps
1 part 151-Proof Rum
2 splashes Tabasco® Sauce

Pour ingredients into glass neat (do not chill).

Fist Fuck

SHOT GLASS

1 part Tabasco® Sauce
1 part Tequila

Pour ingredients into glass neat (do not chill).

Galaxy

SHOT GLASS

1 part Fireball Whiskey
1 part Tequila
3 splashes Tabasco® Sauce

Pour ingredients into glass neat (do not chill).

Gator Bite

SHOT GLASS

¼ part Cherry Vodka
¼ part Southern Comfort
¼ part Sweet Vermouth
½ part Sweet & Sour Mix
2 dashes Tabasco® Sauce

Shake with ice and strain.

Great White Shark

SHOT GLASS

1 part Jack Daniel's®
1 part Tequila
splash Tabasco® Sauce

Pour ingredients into glass neat (do not chill).

Green Chilli

SHOT GLASS

1 part Cinnamon Schnapps
2 splashes Tabasco® Sauce

Shake with ice and strain.

Gut Bomb

SHOT GLASS

1 part Rum
splash Tabasco® Sauce

Pour ingredients into glass neat (do not chill).

Hellfire

SHOT GLASS

2 parts Rye Whiskey
1 part Tabasco® Sauce

Pour ingredients into glass neat (do not chill).

Hell's Eye

SHOT GLASS

1 part Canadian Whisky
1 part Coffee Liqueur
1 part Milk
2 drops Tabasco® Sauce

Shake with ice and strain.

Hell's Gate

SHOT GLASS

2 parts Brandy
1 part Tabasco® Sauce
dash Wasabi
splash Butterscotch Schnapps

Pour ingredients into glass neat (do not chill).

Hot Bitch

SHOT GLASS

1 part Vodka
1 part Whiskey
1 part Gin
splash Tabasco® Sauce

Pour ingredients into glass neat (do not chill).

Hot Shot

SHOT GLASS

1 part Vodka
1 part Peppermint Schnapps
splash Tabasco® Sauce

Shake with ice and strain.

Hot Shot #2

SHOT GLASS

1 part Crème de Menthe (White)
1 part Vodka
splash Tabasco® Sauce

Shake with ice and strain.

Hot Spot

SHOT GLASS

1 part Vodka
1 part Tequila
1 part Tabasco® Sauce

Pour ingredients into glass neat (do not chill).

Incinerator

SHOT GLASS

2 parts Black Sambuca
1 part 151-Proof Rum
splash Tabasco® Sauce

Pour ingredients into glass neat (do not chill).

Ironman

SHOT GLASS

1 part Green Chartreuse®
1 part Sambuca
1 part Scotch
3 parts Tabasco® Sauce
1 part Tequila

Pour ingredients into glass neat (do not chill).

Jaw Breaker

SHOT GLASS

1 part Goldschläger®
splash Tabasco® Sauce

Pour ingredients into glass neat (do not chill).

Kentucky Hot Tub

SHOT GLASS

1 part Jim Beam®
1 part Cointreau®
1 part Blue Curaçao
splash Tabasco® Sauce

Shake with ice and strain.

Kickstarter

SHOT GLASS

1 part Jack Daniel's®
1 part Fire Water®
splash Tabasco® Sauce

Build in the glass with no ice.

Labia Licker

SHOT GLASS

1 part Rumchata
splash Tabasco® Sauce

Build in the glass with no ice.

Lava

SHOT GLASS

1 part Fire Water®
1 part Grain Alcohol
2 splashes Tabasco® Sauce

Pour ingredients into glass neat (do not chill).

Leggs

SHOT GLASS

1 part Tequila
1 part Jägermeister®
splash Tabasco® Sauce

Pour ingredients into glass neat (do not chill).

Louisiana Shooter

SHOT GLASS

1 part Tequila
1 Raw Oyster
1/4 splash Horseradish
splash Tabasco® Sauce

Pour ingredients into glass neat (do not chill).

Mad Dog

SHOT GLASS

1 part Vodka
1 part Cherry Juice
splash Tabasco® Sauce

Shake with ice and strain.

Mad Pirate

SHOT GLASS

1 part Butterscotch Liqueur
1 part Irish Cream Liqueur
dash Tabasco® Sauce

Shake with ice and strain.

Mexican Jumping Bean

SHOT GLASS

1 part Tequila
splash Tabasco® Sauce
splash Worcestershire Sauce

Pour ingredients into glass neat (do not chill).

Mexican Missile

SHOT GLASS

1 part Silver Tequila
1 part Red Bull Energy Drink
splash Tabasco® Sauce

Shake with ice and strain.

Monkey Fart

SHOT GLASS

1 part Vodka
1 part Coffee Liqueur
splash Tabasco® Sauce

Pour ingredients into glass neat (do not chill).

Napalm Taco

SHOT GLASS

1 part Jägermeister®
1 part Tequila
1 part Tabasco® Sauce

Shake with ice and strain.

Oklahoma Rattler

SHOT GLASS

1 part Silver Tequila
splash Tabasco® Sauce

Pour ingredients into glass neat (do not chill).

Oyster Shot

SHOT GLASS

1 Raw Oyster
1 part Tequila
splash Tabasco® Sauce

Build in the glass with no ice.

Prairie Dog

SHOT GLASS

1 part 151-Proof Rum
3 splashes Tabasco® Sauce

Pour ingredients into glass neat (do not chill).

Prairie Fire

SHOT GLASS

1 part Tequila
5 splashes Tabasco® Sauce

Pour ingredients into glass neat (do not chill).

Psycho Tsunami

SHOT GLASS

1 part Tequila Reposado
1 part Blue Curaçao
1 part Lime Juice
splash Tabasco® Sauce

Build in the glass with no ice.

Red Hot

SHOT GLASS

1 part Cinnamon Schnapps
splash Tabasco® Sauce

Build in the glass with no ice.

Roswell

SHOT GLASS

1 part Tabasco® Sauce
1 part Tequila Reposado
1 part Red Bull® Energy Drink

Build in the glass with no ice.

Russian Bloody Mary

SHOT GLASS

1 part Vodka
splash Tabasco® Sauce

Build in the glass with no ice.

Satan's Piss

SHOT GLASS

1 part 151-Proof Rum
1 part Yellow Chartreuse
3 splashes Tabasco® Sauce

Pour ingredients into glass neat (do not chill).

Satan's Revenge

SHOT GLASS

1 part Tequila
1 part Jack Daniel's®
1 part Goldschläger®
splash Tabasco® Sauce

Pour ingredients into glass neat (do not chill).

Satan's Spawn

SHOT GLASS

1 part Fire Water®
4 splashes Tabasco® Sauce

Pour ingredients into glass neat (do not chill).

Scratchy Asshole

SHOT GLASS

2 parts Jägermeister®
2 parts Peach Schnapps
1 part Tabasco® Sauce
1 part Lemon-Lime Soda

Shake with ice and strain.

Sharpshooter

SHOT GLASS

1 part Ouzo
1 part Vodka
splash Tabasco® Sauce

Pour ingredients into glass neat (do not chill).

Shot of Hell

SHOT GLASS

1 part Vodka
1 part Jägermeister®
splash Tabasco® Sauce

Pour ingredients into glass neat (do not chill).

Shot of Respect

SHOT GLASS

1 part Tequila
1 part 151-Proof Rum
splash Tabasco® Sauce

Pour ingredients into glass neat (do not chill).

Square Furnace

SHOT GLASS

1 part Jim Beam®
1 part Tequila
1 part Irish Cream Liqueur
1 part 151-Proof Rum
1 part Tabasco® Sauce

Shake with ice and strain.

Stomachache

SHOT GLASS

1 part Jägermeister®
2 splashes Tabasco® Sauce

Pour ingredients into glass neat (do not chill).

Sweaty Goat's Ass

SHOT GLASS

3 parts Silver Tequila
splash Tabasco® Sauce
1 part Cream

Build in the glass with no ice.

Sweaty Irishman

SHOT GLASS

1 part Irish Whiskey
1 part Cinnamon Schnapps
splash Tabasco® Sauce

Build in the glass with no ice.

Sweaty Lumberjack

SHOT GLASS

1 part 151-Proof Rum
1 part Tabasco® Sauce
1 part Tequila

Build in the glass with no ice.

Sweaty Melon

SHOT GLASS

1 part Watermelon Schnapps
1 part Vodka
splash Tabasco® Sauce

Build in the glass with no ice.

Sweaty Mexican Lumberjack

SHOT GLASS

3 parts Yukon Jack®
1 part Tequila
splash Tabasco® Sauce

Build in the glass with no ice.

T2

SHOT GLASS

1 part Tequila
1 part Tabasco® Sauce
dash Black Pepper

Pour ingredients into glass neat (do not chill).

Tenement Fire

SHOT GLASS

1 part Vodka
splash Tabasco® Sauce

Build in the glass with no ice.

Tequila Fire

SHOT GLASS

1 part Tequila
½ splash Tabasco® Sauce

Build in the glass with no ice.

Texas Prairie Fire

SHOT GLASS

1 part Tequila
splash Lime Juice
splash Tabasco® Sauce

Build in the glass with no ice.

Texas Roadkill

SHOT GLASS

1 part Wild Turkey® Bourbon
1 part Vodka
1 part Gin
1 part 151-Proof Rum
splash Tabasco® Sauce

Shake with ice and strain.

Toby Wallbanger

SHOT GLASS

1 part Melon Liqueur
1 part Banana Liqueur
1 part Tequila
1 part Gin
1 part Dark Rum
dash Bitters
splash Tabasco® Sauce

Shake with ice and strain. Because this recipe includes many ingredients, it's easier to make in volume, about 6 shots.

Triple Red

SHOT GLASS

1 part Sloe Gin
1 part Amaretto
splash Tabasco® Sauce

Build in the glass with no ice.

Zhivago's Revenge

SHOT GLASS

1 part Cinnamon Schnapps
1 part Pepper Vodka
1 part Tabasco® Sauce

Shake with ice and strain.

MIND ERASER DRINKS

This group of drinks crosses layered shots with mixed drinks by layering the liquor, liqueur, and mixers over ice in a rocks or highball glass. Drink them quickly through a straw.

B-28

ROCKS GLASS

1 part Irish Cream Liqueur
1 part Coffee Liqueur
1 part Amaretto
1 part Butterscotch Schnapps

Layer over ice. Drink through a straw.

Around the World

HIGHBALL GLASS

1 part Gin
1 part Crème de Menthe (Green)
1 part Pineapple Juice

Layer over ice. Drink through a straw.

Atomic Watermelon

HIGHBALL GLASS

1 part Sweet & Sour Mix
1 part Melon Liqueur
1 part Watermelon Vodka

Build over ice. Drink quickly through a straw.

Blue Knickers

ROCKS GLASS

1 part Vodka
1 part Blue Curaçao
1 part Galliano®
splash Cream

Layer over ice. Drink through a straw.

Brain Drain

HIGHBALL GLASS

1 part Coffee Liqueur
1 part Cola
1 part Vodka

Layer over ice. Drink through a straw.

Brain Eraser

HIGHBALL GLASS

½ part Amaretto
½ part Coffee Liqueur
1 part Vodka
fill with Club Soda

Layer over ice. Drink through a straw.

Brain Eraser #2

ROCKS GLASS

1 part Goldschläger®
1 part Coffee Liqueur
1 part Vodka

Layer over ice. Drink through a straw.

Brainteaser

ROCKS GLASS

1 part Sambuca
1 part Cream
splash Advocaat

Layer over ice. Drink through a straw.

Cookie Monster
ROCKS GLASS
1 part Coffee Liqueur
1 part Irish Cream Liqueur
1 part 151-Proof Rum

Layer over ice. Drink through a straw.

Derailer
HIGHBALL GLASS
1 part Vodka
1 part Gold Tequila
1 part Coffee Liqueur

Layer over ice. Drink through a straw.

Disco Ball
ROCKS GLASS
1 part Melon Liqueur
1 part Goldschläger®

Layer over ice. Drink through a straw.

Fat Cat Cooler
HIGHBALL GLASS
1 part Citrus Rum
1 part Cranberry Juice Cocktail
2 parts Lemon-Lime Soda

Layer over ice. Drink through a straw.

Felching Banana
ROCKS GLASS
1 part Vodka
1 part Irish Cream Liqueur
1 part Crème de Cacao (Dark)
splash Banana Liqueur

Layer over ice. Drink through a straw.

Fin 'n' Tonic
HIGHBALL GLASS
1 part Gin
1 part Peppermint Schnapps
1 part Tonic Water

Layer over ice. Drink through a straw.

Flaming Cockroach
HIGHBALL GLASS
1 part Coffee Liqueur
1 part 151-Proof Rum
1 part Tequila

Layer over ice. Drink through a straw.

Flaming Pisser
HIGHBALL GLASS
1 part 151-Proof Rum
1 part Lemon-Lime Soda
1 part Lime Juice

Layer over ice. Drink through a straw.

The Forehead
HIGHBALL GLASS
1 part Coffee Liqueur
1 part Irish Cream Liqueur
1 part Water

Layer over ice. Drink through a straw.

French Kiss Shooter
ROCKS GLASS
1½ parts Vodka
1 part Lime Juice
½ part Grapefruit Juice
¼ part Triple Sec

Layer over ice. Drink through a straw.

Frog
HIGHBALL GLASS
1 part Gin
1 part Triple Sec
1 part Sweet & Sour Mix

Layer over ice. Drink through a straw.

Glenndog
HIGHBALL GLASS
1 part Amaretto
1 part Drambuie®
1 part Tequila
½ part Ouzo

Layer over ice. Drink through a straw.

Green Russian
HIGHBALL GLASS

1 part Vodka
1 part Melon Liqueur

Layer over ice. Drink through a straw.

Heavy Hairy Testicle
HIGHBALL GLASS

1 part Crème de Cacao (White)
1 part Amaretto
1 part Milk

Layer over ice. Drink through a straw.

High Jamaican Wind
HIGHBALL GLASS

1 part Rum
1 part Coffee Liqueur
fill with Cream

Layer over ice. Drink through a straw.

Innocent Girl
HIGHBALL GLASS

1 part Goldschläger®
1 part Vanilla Liqueur
1 part Apple Liqueur

Layer over ice. Drink through a straw.

Irish Egg Cream
COLLINS GLASS

1 part Irish Cream Liqueur
1 part Godiva Chocolate Liqueur
1 part Club Soda

Layer over ice. Drink through a straw.

Jäger Eraser
ROCKS GLASS

1 part Jägermeister®
1 part Vodka
fill with Club Soda

Layer over ice. Drink through a straw.

Jäger Float
ROCKS GLASS

1 part Cola
1 part Irish Cream Liqueur
1 part Jägermeister®

Layer over ice. Drink through a straw.

Kick in the Face
HIGHBALL GLASS

1 part Rum
1 part Lemon Juice
1 part Club Soda

Layer over ice. Drink through a straw.

Knickerbocker
ROCKS GLASS

1 part Amaretto
1 part Citrus Vodka
1 part Crème de Menthe (White)

Layer over ice. Drink through a straw.

Lactating Green Monkey
HIGHBALL GLASS

1 part Crème de Menthe (Green)
1 part Coffee Liqueur
1 part Milk

Layer over ice. Drink through a straw.

Lakokarocha
HIGHBALL GLASS

1 part Coffee Liqueur
1 part Tequila
1 part Club Soda

Layer over ice. Drink through a straw.

London Bus
HIGHBALL GLASS

1 part Vodka
1 part Light Rum
1 part Sweetened Lime Juice

Layer over ice. Drink through a straw.

Macedonian Haircut
HIGHBALL GLASS
1 part Black Sambuca
1 part Ouzo
1 part Jägermeister®
Layer over ice. Drink through a straw.

Milwaukee Stop Light
HIGHBALL GLASS
1 part Cinnamon Schnapps
1 part Jägermeister®
1 part Goldschläger®
Layer over ice. Drink through a straw.

Mind Blanker
ROCKS GLASS
1 part Vodka
1 part Coffee
1 part Lemon-Lime Soda
Layer over ice. Drink through a straw.

Mind Eraser
ROCKS GLASS
1 part Vodka
1 part Coffee Liqueur
1 part Club Soda
Layer over ice. Drink through a straw.

Mind Fuck
HIGHBALL GLASS
1 part Melon Liqueur
1 part Rum
1 part Tequila
Layer over ice. Drink through a straw.

Neuralizer
HIGHBALL GLASS
1 part Sweet & Sour Mix
1 part Whiskey
1 part Ginger Ale
Layer over ice. Drink through a straw.

Nurse
HIGHBALL GLASS
1 part Absolut® Vodka
1 part Licor 43®
1 part Club Soda
Layer over ice. Drink through a straw.

Paralyzer
HIGHBALL GLASS
1 part Vodka
1 part Coffee Liqueur
1 part Cream
1 part Cola
Layer over ice. Drink through a straw.

Peachaholic Popper
HIGHBALL GLASS
1 part Peach Schnapps
1 part Club Soda
1 part Milk
Layer over ice. Drink through a straw.

Purple Haze
COLLINS GLASS
1 part Raspberry Liqueur
1 part Citrus Vodka
1 part Lemon-Lime Soda
Layer over ice. Drink through a straw.

Purple Jumping Jesus
HIGHBALL GLASS
1 part Rum
1 part Peppermint Schnapps
1 part Jägermeister®
Layer over ice. Drink through a straw.

Purple Mexican
HIGHBALL GLASS
1 part Vodka
1 part Tequila
1 part Grand Marnier®
Layer over ice. Drink through a straw.

Raspberry Felch

ROCKS GLASS

1 part Irish Cream Liqueur
1 part Crème de Cacao (Dark)
1 part Raspberry Vodka

Layer over ice. Drink through a straw.

Reptile

HIGHBALL GLASS

1 part Whiskey
1 part Mountain Dew®
1 part Orange Juice

Layer over ice. Drink through a straw.

Scorpion

HIGHBALL GLASS

1 part Grenadine
1 part Blackberry Brandy
1 part Vodka

Layer over ice. Drink quickly through a straw.

Separator

ROCKS GLASS

1 part Brandy
1 part Coffee Liqueur
1 part Cream

Layer over ice. Drink through a straw.

Southampton Slam

HIGHBALL GLASS

1 part Crème de Menthe (Green)
1 part Anisette
1 part Club Soda

Layer over ice. Drink through a straw.

Summer Night

HIGHBALL GLASS

1 part Orange Juice
2 parts Red Wine
1 part Hard Apple Cider

Layer over ice. Drink through a straw.

Traffic Light

ROCKS GLASS

1 part Crème de Menthe (Green)
1 part Cherry Brandy
1 part Triple Sec

Layer over ice. Drink through a straw.

White Irish

ROCKS GLASS

1 part Irish Cream Liqueur
1 part Irish Whiskey
1 part Light Cream

Layer over ice. Drink quickly through a straw.

Yellow Snow Slammer

HIGHBALL GLASS

1 part Cream
1 part Vodka
3 parts Pineapple Juice

Layer over ice. Drink through a straw.

Zebra

HIGHBALL GLASS

1 part Black Sambuca
1 part Silver Tequila

Layer over ice. Drink through a straw.

Zipper

ROCKS GLASS

1 part Cream
1 part Triple Sec
1 part Tequila

Layer over ice. Drink through a straw.

X-RATED DRINKS

What makes a drink X-Rated? According to the Supreme Court, you'll know it when you see it.

69

HIGHBALL GLASS

1 part Licor 43®
5 parts 7-Up®
1 part Seagram's® 7 Crown Whiskey
5 Cubes of Ice

Build over ice. 1 + 43 + 5 + 7 + 1 + 7 + 5 = 69.

69er

HIGHBALL GLASS

1 part Light Rum
1 part Peach Schnapps
1 part Cola

Build over ice.

Absolut® Royal Fuck

ROCKS GLASS

1 part Crown Royal® Whiskey
½ part Currant Vodka
½ part Peach Schnapps
splash Cranberry Juice Cocktail
splash Pineapple Juice

Shake with ice and strain over ice.

Absolut® Sex

HIGHBALL GLASS

1 part Currant Vodka
½ part Cranberry Juice Cocktail
½ part Melon Liqueur
2 parts Lemon-Lime Soda

Build over ice and stir.

Adios Motherfucker

COLLINS GLASS

1 part Gin
1 part Light Rum
1 part Triple Sec
1 part Vodka
fill with Sweet & Sour Mix

Build over ice and stir.

Alien Orgasm

COCKTAIL GLASS

1 part Coconut Rum
1 part Melon Liqueur
1 part Vodka
splash Pineapple Juice

Shake with ice and strain.

American Clusterfuck

COLLINS GLASS

1 part Light Rum
1 part Dark Rum
1 part Tequila
1 part Vodka
1 part Cranberry Juice Cocktail
splash Tropical Punch Schnapps

Build over ice. in Top with a splash of Tropical Punch Schnapps.

Apple Screw

HIGHBALL GLASS

1 part Apple Liqueur
1 part Vodka
fill with Orange Juice

Build over ice and stir.

Ass

HIGHBALL GLASS

2 parts Vodka
1 part Lemon-Lime Soda
1 part Orange Juice
splash Grenadine

Build over ice and stir.

Assmaster 5000+

HIGHBALL GLASS

1½ parts Rum
1 part Grain Alcohol
1½ parts Grenadine
1 part Triple Sec
fill with Orange Juice

Build over ice and stir.

Bag of Filth

ROCKS GLASS

1 part Pernod®
1 part Tia Maria®

Shake with ice and pour.

Bald Pussy

HIGHBALL GLASS

1 part Citrus Vodka
1 part Vodka
1 part Triple Sec
1½ parts Blueberry Schnapps
1½ parts Melon Liqueur
splash Lime Juice
splash Lemon-Lime Soda

Build over ice and stir.

Ballbreaker

ROCKS GLASS

2 parts Vodka
1 part Dry Vermouth
1 part Silver Tequila
1 part Raspberry Syrup
2 parts Vegetable Juice Blend

Shake with ice and pour.

Banana Assmaster

COLLINS GLASS

1 part Vodka
2 parts Milk
1 Banana
4 scoops Ice Cream

Combine all ingredients in a blender. Blend until smooth.

Bare-Naked Lady

COLLINS GLASS

1 part Dark Rum
1 part Apple Brandy
3 parts Sweet & Sour Mix
2 parts Orange Juice

Shake with ice and pour.

Better than Sex

COLLINS GLASS

1 part Frangelico®
1 part Crème Liqueur
½ part Grand Marnier®
1 part Coffee Liqueur
fill with Cream

Shake with ice and pour.

Big Bull Balls

HIGHBALL GLASS

1 part Jägermeister
1 part Goldschläger®
2 parts Red Bull Energy Drink

Build over ice and stir.

Bishop's Nipple

COLLINS GLASS

1 part Orange Vodka
1 part Raspberry Liqueur
1 part Lime Cordial
fill with Lemon-Lime Soda

Build over ice and stir.

Bitch Ass

HURRICANE GLASS

1 1/2 parts Coconut Rum
1 1/2 parts Vanilla Vodka
splash Cranberry Juice Cocktail
1 part Orange Juice
1 part Pineapple Juice

Build over ice and stir.

Blue Motherfucker

COLLINS GLASS

1 part Blue Curaçao
1 part Gin
1 part Light Rum
1 part Silver Tequila
1 part Vodka
splash Lemon-Lime Soda
splash Sweet & Sour Mix

Build over ice and stir.

Blue Screw

HIGHBALL GLASS

1 1/2 parts Orange Vodka
1 part Blue Curaçao
fill with Orange Juice

Build over ice and stir.

Breast Caresser

HIGHBALL GLASS

1 1/2 parts Brandy
1 part Madeira
1/2 part Triple Sec

Shake with ice and pour.

Breast Milk on Acid

ROCKS GLASS

1/2 part Coconut Rum
3/4 part Jägermeister®
1/2 part Melon Liqueur
1 part Sweet & Sour Mix
splash Orange Juice

Shake with ice and strain.

British Clusterfuck

COLLINS GLASS

1 part Gin
1 part Irish Cream Liqueur
1 part Scotch

Shake with ice and pour.

Bunny Fucker

COLLINS GLASS

1 part Tequila
1 part Lemon-Lime Soda
1 part Orange Juice
splash Grenadine

Build over ice and stir.

Butt Munch

COUPETTE GLASS

2 parts Brandy
1/2 dash Cinnamon
1 part Coffee Liqueur
1 part Milk

Combine all ingredients in a blender with ice. Blend until smooth.

Butt Naked

ROCKS GLASS

1 part Amaretto
1 part Southern Comfort®
fill with Cranberry Juice Cocktail

Build over ice and stir.

Buttcrack

COLLINS GLASS

1 part RedRum®
1 part Citrus Vodka

Pour ingredients into glass neat (do not chill).

Buttery Nipple (Frozen)

COUPETTE GLASS

1 part Irish Cream Liqueur
1 part Butterscotch Ice Cream Topping
2 scoops Ice Cream

Combine all ingredients in a blender. Blend until smooth.

Chicken Fucker

HIGHBALL GLASS

2 parts Coconut Rum
1 part Amaretto
1 part Peach Schnapps
fill with Orange Juice

Build over ice and stir.

Clusterfuck

HIGHBALL GLASS

1 part Southern Comfort®
1 part Vodka
splash Grenadine
1 part Orange Juice
1 part Pineapple Juice

Build over ice and stir.

Colorado Motherfucker

HIGHBALL GLASS

1 part Tequila
1 part Coffee Liqueur
fill with Milk
splash Cola

Build over ice and stir.

Comfortable Screw

HIGHBALL GLASS

1 part Vodka
1 part Southern Comfort®
fill with Orange Juice

Shake with ice and pour.

Comfortable Screw Up Against a Fuzzy Wall

HIGHBALL GLASS

½ part Vodka
¾ part Southern Comfort®
½ part Peach Schnapps
¼ part Galliano®
fill with Orange Juice

Shake with ice and pour.

Comfortable Screw Up Against a Wall

HIGHBALL GLASS

¾ part Vodka
¾ part Southern Comfort®
¼ part Galliano®
fill with Orange Juice

Shake with ice and pour.

Cool Summer Sex

COLLINS GLASS

1 part Currant Vodka
1 part Melon Liqueur
1 part Lime Juice
fill with Lemon-Lime Soda

Build over ice and stir.

Cuban Screw

HIGHBALL GLASS

1½ parts Rum
fill with Orange Juice

Build over ice and stir.

Cum Fuck Me Punch

COLLINS GLASS

1 part Amaretto
½ part Southern Comfort®
½ part Vodka
1 part Pineapple Juice
1 part Orange Juice
1 part Sweet & Sour Mix
1 part Grenadine

Build over ice and stir.

Cum in a Bucket

ROCKS GLASS

2 parts Crème de Cacao (White)
2 parts Cream
1 part Milk

Shake with ice and pour.

Cybersex Orgasm

COLLINS GLASS

1 part Peach Schnapps
1 part Amaretto
2 parts Cranberry Juice Cocktail
1 part Grenadine
3 parts Orange Juice

Shake with ice and pour.

Deep Sea Sex

HIGHBALL GLASS

1 part Melon Liqueur
1 part Blue Curaçao
1 part Amaretto
splash Sweet & Sour Mix
splash Lemon-Lime Soda

Shake with ice and pour.

Dick Hard

HIGHBALL GLASS

1 part Vodka
1 part Gin
1 part Light Rum
fill with Lemon-Lime Soda

Build over ice and stir. Garnish with a Lime Wedge.

Dickey Wallbanger

ROCKS GLASS

1 part Silver Tequila
1 part Vodka
fill with Orange Juice

Build over ice and stir.

Dirty Screwdriver

HIGHBALL GLASS

1½ parts Vodka
fill with Orange Juice
2 splashes Cinnamon Schnapps

Build over ice and stir.

Doggy Style on the Beach

ROCKS GLASS

1 part Hpnotiq
1 part Coconut Rum
splash Blue Curaçao
fill with Lemon-Lime Soda

Build over ice and stir.

Edible Panties

HIGHBALL GLASS

1 part Vodka
1 part Cranberry Juice
1 part Pink Grapefruit Juice

Build over ice and stir.

Fancy Panties

COCKTAIL GLASS

1 part Chambord
1 part Orange Vodka
1 part Passion Fruit Vodka
1 part Pear Vodka

Shake with ice and strain.

Fluffy Fucknut

HIGHBALL GLASS

1 part Peach Schnapps
1 part Frangelico®
1 part Amaretto
splash Grenadine
fill with Milk

Shake with ice and pour.

French Nipple

COLLINS GLASS

1 part Coffee Liqueur
1 part Amaretto
1 part Vodka
fill with Milk

Combine all ingredients in a blender with ice. Blend until smooth.

French Screw

HIGHBALL GLASS

1 part Vodka
1 part Raspberry Liqueur
fill with Orange Juice

Build over ice and stir.

Frog Cum

ROCKS GLASS

1 part Vodka
1 part Melon Liqueur
1 part Lemonade
1 part Club Soda

Build over ice and stir.

Frosted Breast

HIGHBALL GLASS

½ part Crème de Banane
⅔ part Blue Curaçao
½ part Hazelnut Liqueur
fill with Milk

Shake with ice and pour.

Frozen Nipples

HURRICANE GLASS

fill with Butterscotch Schnapps
3 scoops Vanilla Ice Cream

Combine all ingredients in a blender. Blend until smooth.

Fruity Fuck

COLLINS GLASS

½ part Vodka
1 part Melon Liqueur
2 parts Orange Juice
2 parts Pineapple Juice
1 part Passion Fruit Liqueur
½ part Lime Juice

Shake with ice and pour.

Fuck in the Graveyard

HIGHBALL GLASS

1 part Vodka
1 part Rum
1 part Blueberry Schnapps
1 part Sour Apple Schnapps
1 part Blue Curaçao
1 part Raspberry Liqueur
fill with Cranberry Juice Cocktail
splash Orange Juice

Shake with ice and pour.

Fuck Me from Behind

COLLINS GLASS

1 part Coconut Rum
1 part Raspberry Liqueur
1 part Pineapple Juice
1 part Cranberry Juice
splash 151-Proof Rum

Build over ice.

Fuck Me Hard

ROCKS GLASS

1 part Vodka
1 part Triple Sec
1 part Amaretto
2 parts Raspberry Liqueur
1 part Southern Comfort®
splash Cranberry Juice Cocktail
splash Orange Juice

Shake with ice and pour.

Fuck Me Rough

COLLINS GLASS

1 part Raspberry Liqueur
1 part Crème de Banane
1 part Irish Cream Liqueur
fill with Cream

Shake with ice and pour.

Fuck Me Sideways

COLLINS GLASS

1 part Lemon Vodka
1 part Peach Vodka
1 part Orange Vodka
1 part Orange Juice
fill with Grapefruit Juice

Build over ice and stir.

Fuck You

HIGHBALL GLASS

1 part Tequila
1 part Jack Daniel's®
1 part Wild Turkey® Bourbon
1 part Goldschläger®
1 part Rum
1 part Blueberry Schnapps

Shake with ice and strain over ice.

Fuck Your Buddy

HIGHBALL GLASS

1 part Amaretto
1 part Coconut Rum
½ part Crown Royal® Whiskey
½ part Jack Daniel's®
splash Grenadine
fill with Pineapple Juice

Shake with ice and strain over ice.

Fucking Monkey

IRISH COFFEE CUP

1 part Irish Cream Liqueur
1 part Banana Liqueur
½ part Coffee Liqueur
fill with Coffee

Build in a heat proof mug or Irish coffee cup.

Fuzzy Ass

COLLINS GLASS

2 parts Citrus Vodka
1½ parts Peach Schnapps
1 part Sweet & Sour Mix
splash Grenadine
1 part Triple Sec
fill with Lemon-Lime Soda

Build over ice and stir.

Fuzzy Cum(fort)

ROCKS GLASS

½ part Peach Schnapps
1½ parts Southern Comfort®
fill with Lemon-Lime Soda

Build over ice and stir.

Fuzzy Fucker

HIGHBALL GLASS

1 part Peach Schnapps
1 part Vodka
1 part Southern Comfort®
2 parts Orange Juice

Build over ice and stir.

Fuzzy Nipple

HIGHBALL GLASS

1½ parts Vodka
1½ parts Peach Schnapps
splash Triple Sec
fill with Orange Juice

Build over ice and stir.

Fuzzy Screw

HIGHBALL GLASS

1 part Vodka
1 part Peach Schnapps
fill with Orange Juice

Build over ice and stir.

Fuzzy Screw Up Against a Wall

HIGHBALL GLASS

1 part Vodka
1 part Peach Schnapps
splash Galliano®
fill with Orange Juice

Build over ice and stir.

Getting Naked

ROCKS GLASS

1 part Blue Curaçao
1 part Peach Schnapps
1 part Rum
fill with Orange Juice

Shake with ice and pour.

Golden Mountain Screw

HIGHBALL GLASS

1 part Banana Liqueur
2 parts Vodka
fill with Mountain Dew®

Build over ice and stir.

Golden Screw
HIGHBALL GLASS

1 1/2 parts Vodka
dash Angostura® Bitters
fill with Orange Juice

Shake with ice and strain over ice.

Good as Sex
COLLINS GLASS

1 part Blue Curaçao
1 part Pisang Ambon® Liqueur
1 part Passoã
3/4 part Orange Vodka
fill with Lemonade

Shake with ice and pour.

Green Pussy
ROCKS GLASS

1 part Light Rum
1 part Melon Liqueur
1 part Sweet & Sour Mix

Build over ice and stir.

Gulf Coast Sex on the Beach
COLLINS GLASS

2 parts Dark Rum
1 part Crème de Banane
1 part Melon Liqueur
fill with Pineapple Juice

Build over ice and stir.

Hard Fuck
HIGHBALL GLASS

1 part Melon Liqueur
1 part Vodka
1 part Blue Curaçao
1 part Blueberries
fill with Orange Juice

Build over ice and stir.

Hawaiian Screw
HIGHBALL GLASS

1 part Vodka
1 part Rum
1 part Orange Juice
1 part Pineapple Juice

Build over ice and stir.

Heavenly Sex
HIGHBALL GLASS

2 parts Spiced Rum
2 parts Amaretto
splash Chocolate Syrup
1/2 part Grenadine

Shake with ice and strain over ice.

Hot Pussy
HIGHBALL GLASS

1/2 part Cinnamon Schnapps
2 dashes Tabasco® Sauce
1 part Alizé®

Shake with ice and strain over ice.

How Many Smurfs® Does It Take to Screw In a Light Bulb?
COLLINS GLASS

1 part Blue Curaçao
1 part Jägermeister®
fill with Smirnoff Ice®

Two, but I don't know how they get in there . . . Build over ice and stir.

Italian Screw
HIGHBALL GLASS

1 1/2 parts Vodka
1 part Galliano®
fill with Orange Juice

Build over ice and stir.

Jamaican Screw
HIGHBALL GLASS

2 parts Coconut Rum
fill with Orange Juice

Build over ice and stir.

Kick in the Balls
COCKTAIL GLASS

1 part Dark Rum
1 part Melon Liqueur
1 part Cream
1 part Cream of Coconut
1 part Orange Juice

Shake with ice and strain.

Kick in the Nuts

COCKTAIL GLASS

1 part Banana Liqueur
1 part Hazelnut Liqueur
1 part Spiced Rum
dash Grenadine

Shake with ice and strain.

Kinky Sex

HIGHBALL GLASS

½ part Whiskey
½ part Southern Comfort
½ part Lime Juice
fill with Ginger Ale

Build over ice and stir.

Kiss My Nipples

ROCKS GLASS

2 parts Butterscotch Liqueur
2 parts Irish Cream Liqueur
1 part Amaretto

Shake with ice and pour. Garnish with 2 Maraschino Cherries.

Let's Get Drunk and Screw

COLLINS GLASS

2 parts Vodka
1 part Raspberry Liqueur
fill with Cranberry Juice Cocktail

Build over ice and stir.

Liquid Panty Remover

HURRICANE GLASS

1 part 151-Proof Rum
½ part Coconut Rum
1 part Raspberry Liqueur
1 part Cranberry Juice Cocktail
1 part Orange Juice
1 part Pineapple Juice
1 part Lemon-Lime Soda

Build over ice and stir.

Mexican Screw

HIGHBALL GLASS

1½ parts Tequila
fill with Orange Juice

Build over ice and stir.

Mindfuck

HIGHBALL GLASS

1 part Jack Daniel's®
1 part Cactus Juice Schnapps
fill with Cola

Build over ice and stir.

Minty Crotch

COLLINS GLASS

1 part White Rum
½ part Banana Liqueur
½ part Green Apple Schnapps
fill with Orange Juice
splash Crème de Menthe (Green)

Build over ice. Top with Crème de Menthe (Green).

Mongolian Motherfucker

HIGHBALL GLASS

1 part Citrus Vodka
1 part Coconut Rum
½ part Blue Curaçao
½ part Peach Schnapps
splash Melon Liqueur
splash Grand Marnier®
splash Banana Liqueur
splash Orange Juice
splash Pineapple Juice
splash Lemonade
splash Piña Colada Mix

Shake with ice and strain over ice.

Mountain Fuck

BEER MUG

2 parts Cinnamon Schnapps
fill with Mountain Dew®

Build over ice and stir.

Mountain Screw

COLLINS GLASS

2 parts Vodka
fill with Mountain Dew®

Build over ice and stir.

Mountain Sex

ROCKS GLASS

1 part Mountain Dew®
1 part Triple Sec

Build over ice and stir.

Mud Fuck

COUPETTE GLASS

2 parts Vodka
½ part Chocolate Syrup
2 parts Dr. Pepper®
1 part Milk

Combine all ingredients in a blender with ice. Blend until smooth.

Naked in Blackberries

BEER MUG

3 parts Blackberry Liqueur
fill with Iced Tea

Build over ice and stir.

Naked Pretzel

ROCKS GLASS

¾ part Vodka
1 part Melon Liqueur
½ part Crème de Cassis
fill with Pineapple Juice

Shake with ice and strain over ice.

Naked Sunburn

HURRICANE GLASS

1 part Melon Liqueur
1 part Coconut Rum
1 part Crème de Noyaux
1 part Cranberry Juice Cocktail
1 part Pineapple Juice
splash Lemon-Lime Soda
splash Sweet & Sour Mix

Build over ice and stir.

Naked Twister

BEER MUG

1 part Melon Liqueur
½ part Vodka
½ part Tuaca®
fill with Pineapple Juice
splash Lemon-Lime Soda

Build over ice and stir.

Oral Sex on the Beach

HIGHBALL GLASS

1 part Melon Liqueur
1 part Raspberry Liqueur
½ part Vodka
fill with Orange Juice

Shake with ice and strain over ice.

Passion Pussy

HIGHBALL GLASS

1½ parts Passion Fruit Liqueur
2 parts Heavy Cream
splash Grenadine

Shake with ice and pour.

Passionate Kiss

COUPETTE GLASS

1 part Southern Comfort®
1 part Peach Schnapps
1 part Raspberry Liqueur
fill with Pineapple Juice

Shake with ice and pour.

Passionate Screw

COLLINS GLASS

2 parts Vodka
1 part Orange Juice
2 dashes Bitters

Shake with ice and strain.

Peppermint Screw

HIGHBALL GLASS

1 part Gin
¾ part Pisang Ambon® Liqueur
splash Peppermint Liqueur
½ part Sweet & Sour Mix

Shake with ice and pour.

Perfect Screw

HIGHBALL GLASS

1 1/4 parts Peach Schnapps
1/4 part Vodka
fill with Orange Juice

Shake with ice and pour.

Piece of Ass

COLLINS GLASS

1 part Amaretto
1 part Southern Comfort®
splash Lime Juice
fill with Lemon-Lime Soda

Build over ice and stir.

Pink Nipple

HURRICANE GLASS

2 parts Raspberry Liqueur
fill with Cream
splash Grenadine

Shake with ice and pour.

Pink Pussy

HIGHBALL GLASS

1 part Campari®
1/2 part Peach Brandy
fill with Lemon-Lime Soda

Build over ice and stir.

Purple Alaskan Thunderfuck

COLLINS GLASS

1 part Jack Daniel's®
1 part Southern Comfort®
1/2 part Raspberry Liqueur
1/2 part Amaretto
1 part Orange Juice
1 part Pineapple Juice

Shake with ice and strain over ice.

Purple Orgasm

ROCKS GLASS

1 part Chocolate Liqueur
1 part Irish Cream Liqueur
1 part Raspberry Liqueur

Shake with ice and strain over ice.

Pussy on Your Face

HURRICANE GLASS

1 part Melon Liqueur
3/4 part Strawberry Vodka
3/4 part Banana Liqueur
1 part Sweet & Sour Mix
1 part Orange Juice
1 part Pineapple Juice

Build over ice and stir.

Raspberry Screw

COLLINS GLASS

1 part Vodka
1 part Raspberry Liqueur
1 part Orange Juice
1 part Lemon-Lime Soda

Build over ice and stir.

Red Hot Lover

HURRICANE GLASS

2 parts Vodka
2 parts Peach Schnapps
splash Grenadine
1 part Strawberry Juice
1 part Orange Juice

Shake with ice and pour.

Red Hot Passion

ROCKS GLASS

1 part Amaretto
1 part Bourbon
1 part Southern Comfort®
1 part Sloe Gin
1 part Triple Sec
1 part Pineapple Juice
1 part Orange Juice

Shake with ice and strain over ice.

Red Raw Ass

HIGHBALL GLASS

3 parts Gin
1 part Triple Sec
1 part Strawberry Daiquiri Mix
splash Lime Juice
fill with Pineapple Juice

Shake with ice and pour.

Russian Pussy

ROCKS GLASS

1 part Vodka
1 part Crème de Cacao (White)

Shake with ice and strain over ice.

Rusty Screw

BRANDY SNIFTER

1½ parts Scotch
½ splash Grand Marnier®

Build in the glass with no ice.

Sand in Your Ass

HIGHBALL GLASS

1 part Rum
1 part Coconut Rum
splash Blue Curaçao
fill with Pineapple Juice

Shake with ice and pour.

Sand in Your Butt

ROCKS GLASS

1 part Southern Comfort®
1 part Melon Liqueur
fill with Pineapple Juice

Shake with ice and pour.

Sand in Your Crack

COUPETTE GLASS

½ part Vodka
½ part Blue Curaçao
½ part Melon Liqueur
4 parts Pineapple Juice

Combine all ingredients in a blender with ice. Blend until smooth.

Screaming Multiple Climax

HURRICANE GLASS

2 parts Vodka
1 part Crème de Cacao (White)
1 part Amaretto
1 part Frangelico®
1 part Crème de Banane
fill with Cream

Shake with ice and pour.

Screaming Nipple Twister

COLLINS GLASS

2 parts Vodka
fill with Dr. Pepper®
1 scoop Ice Cream

Build over ice and stir.

Screw You

HIGHBALL GLASS

1 part Vodka
1 part Coffee Liqueur
1 part Strawberry Liqueur

Combine all ingredients in a blender with ice. Blend until smooth.

Screwed Banana

HIGHBALL GLASS

1 part Banana Liqueur
1 part Peach Schnapps
fill with Orange Juice

Build over ice and stir.

Screwed Driver

ROCKS GLASS

1½ parts Orange Vodka
fill with Lemonade
splash Cranberry Juice Cocktail

Build over ice and stir.

Screwed Strawberry Stripper

COLLINS GLASS

1 part Vodka
2 parts Strawberry Liqueur
fill with Orange Juice

Build over ice and stir.

Sex

ROCKS GLASS

1 part Coffee Liqueur
1 part Grand Marnier®

Shake with ice and pour.

Sex and Candy

COLLINS GLASS

1 part Peach Schnapps
1 part Lemon-Lime Soda

Build over ice and stir.

Sex Appeal

COLLINS GLASS

1 part Light Rum
1 part Coconut Rum
1 part Melon Liqueur
1 part Peach Schnapps
1 part Blue Curaçao
fill with Sweet & Sour Mix
splash Lemonade

Build over ice and stir.

Sex at My House

HIGHBALL GLASS

1 part Amaretto
1 part Raspberry Liqueur
fill with Pineapple Juice

Build over ice and stir.

Sex by the Lake

COLLINS GLASS

1 part Vodka
1 part Peach Schnapps
1 part Pineapple Juice
1 part Orange Juice

Build over ice and stir.

Sex in a Bubblegum Factory

HIGHBALL GLASS

1 part Crème de Banane
1 part Blue Curaçao
1 part Apricot Brandy
1 part Rum
fill with Lemon-Lime Soda

Build over ice and stir.

Sex in a Jacuzzi

HIGHBALL GLASS

2 parts Vodka
1 part Cranberry Juice Cocktail
1 part Orange Juice
1 part Pineapple Juice
fill with Lemon-Lime Soda
splash Raspberry Liqueur
splash Orange Soda

Build over ice and stir.

Sex in a Tent

COLLINS GLASS

1 part Coconut Rum
1 part Spiced Rum
fill with Mountain Dew®

Build over ice and stir.

Sex in a Tree

COLLINS GLASS

1¼ parts Midori®
1 part Banana Liqueur
1 part Coconut Rum
fill with Pineapple Juice

Build over ice and stir.

Sex in the City

COLLINS GLASS

2 parts Blue Curaçao
1½ parts Peach Schnapps
1½ parts Vodka
1 part Pineapple Juice
1 part Raspberry Juice

Shake with ice and pour.

Sex in the Desert

HIGHBALL GLASS

1 part Tequila
1 part Triple Sec
1 part Cherry Juice
1 part Margarita Mix
1 part Cranberry Juice Cocktail

Shake with ice and pour.

Sex in the Forest

HIGHBALL GLASS

1 part Coconut Rum
1 part Peach Schnapps
splash Vodka
splash Crème de Menthe (White)
fill with Lemon-Lime Soda
splash Cream

Build over ice and stir.

Sex in the Jungle

HURRICANE GLASS

1½ parts Vodka
1 part Blue Curaçao
1 part Melon Liqueur
1 part Coconut Rum
1 part Lime Juice
1 part Pineapple Juice
1 part Orange Juice

Shake with ice and pour.

Sex in the Red Zone

HIGHBALL GLASS

1 part Vodka
1 part Sloe Gin
fill with Lemonade

Build over ice and stir.

Sex in the Shower

CHAMPAGNE FLUTE

1 part Blue Curaçao
1 part Triple Sec
1 part Butterscotch Schnapps
fill with Orange Juice

Shake with ice and strain.

Sex in the Sun

COUPETTE GLASS

½ part Coconut Rum
½ part Light Rum
½ part Galliano®
½ part Melon Liqueur
1 part Lemon Juice
1 part Orange Juice

Shake with ice and pour.

Sex, Lies, and Video Poker

HIGHBALL GLASS

1 part Spiced Rum
1 part Amaretto
1 part Whiskey
1 part Orange Juice
1 part Pineapple Juice
1 part Cranberry Juice Cocktail
1 part Grenadine

Shake with ice and strain over ice.

Sex on an Arizona Beach

ROCKS GLASS

1 part Vodka
1 part Peach Schnapps
splash Grapefruit Juice
splash Lime Juice
splash Grenadine

Shake with ice and strain over ice.

Sex on Daytona Beach

HIGHBALL GLASS

1 part Vodka
1 part Peach Schnapps
½ part Grenadine
¼ part Heavy Cream
fill with Pineapple Juice

Shake with ice and pour.

Sex on Malibu Beach

HIGHBALL GLASS

½ part Vodka
½ part Coconut Rum
½ part Peach Schnapps
1 part Cranberry Juice Cocktail
1 part Orange Juice
splash Grenadine

Shake with ice and pour.

Sex on My Face

HIGHBALL GLASS

1 part Yukon Jack®
1 part Coconut Rum
1 part Southern Comfort®
1 part Banana Liqueur
splash Cranberry Juice Cocktail
splash Pineapple Juice
splash Orange Juice

Shake with ice and pour.

Sex on the Beach

HIGHBALL GLASS

1 part Vodka
1 part Peach Schnapps
1 part Cranberry Juice Cocktail
1 part Orange Juice

Shake with ice and pour.

Sex on the Beach (Southern Style)

HIGHBALL GLASS

1 part Peach Schnapps
1 part Sour Apple Schnapps
1 part Cranberry Juice Cocktail
1 part Pineapple Juice

Shake with ice and strain over ice.

Sex on the Beach in Winter

COUPETTE GLASS

1 part Vodka
1 part Peach Schnapps
½ part Crème de Coconut
1 part Cranberry Juice Cocktail
1 part Pineapple Juice

Combine all ingredients in a blender with ice. Blend until smooth.

Sex on the Beach with a California Blonde

COLLINS GLASS

1 part Vodka
½ part Midori®
½ part Raspberry Liqueur
1 part Pineapple Juice
1 part Cranberry Juice Cocktail

Shake with ice and pour.

Sex on the Beach with a Friend

HIGHBALL GLASS

1 part Crème de Cassis
1 part Midori®
1 part Pineapple Juice
1 part Vodka

Shake with ice and pour.

Sex on the Boat

HIGHBALL GLASS

1 part Spiced Rum
½ part Crème de Banane
fill with Orange Juice

Shake with ice and pour.

Sex on the Brain

HURRICANE GLASS

1 part Peach Schnapps
1 part Vodka
1 part Midori®
1 part Pineapple Juice
1 part Orange Juice
splash Sloe Gin

Shake with ice and pour.

Sex on the Dancefloor

HIGHBALL GLASS

1 part Chambord
1 part Melon Liqueur
fill with Pineapple Juice

Shake with ice and strain over ice.

Sex on the Farm

COLLINS GLASS

¼ part Vodka
¼ part Amaretto
¼ part Peach Schnapps
¼ part Coconut Rum
¼ part Midori®
splash Grenadine
1 part Orange Juice
1 part Pineapple Juice

Shake with ice and pour.

Sex on the Grass

HIGHBALL GLASS

1 part Vodka
1 part Peach Schnapps
½ part Southern Comfort®
½ part Blue Curaçao
1 part Melon Liqueur

Shake with ice and pour.

Sex on the Island

COLLINS GLASS

1 part Coconut Rum
1 part Crème de Cassis
1 part Melon Liqueur
1 part Orange Juice
1 part Cranberry Juice

Shake with ice and strain over ice.

Sex on the Pool Table

HIGHBALL GLASS

1 part Chambord
1 part Melon Liqueur
1 part Peach Schnapps
1 part Triple Sec
1 part Grapefruit Juice

Shake with ice and strain over ice.

Sex on the Sidewalk

HIGHBALL GLASS

1 part Melon Liqueur
1 part Raspberry Liqueur
1 part Cranberry Juice Cocktail

Shake with ice and strain.

Sex on the Sofa

ROCKS GLASS

1 part Vodka
1 part Peach Schnapps
fill with Orange Juice

Shake with ice and strain over ice.

Sex under the Boardwalk

ROCKS GLASS

1 part Peach Schnapps
1 part Raspberry Liqueur
1 part Midori®

Shake with ice and strain over ice.

Sex under the Sun

COLLINS GLASS

1 part Light Rum
½ part Dark Rum
1 part Orange Juice
1 part Pineapple Juice
splash Grenadine

Build over ice and stir.

Sex Wax

COLLINS GLASS

1 part Cream of Coconut
1 part Rum
½ part Southern Comfort®
1 part Orange Juice
1 part Pineapple Juice

Shake with ice and pour.

Sex with a Virgin

COUPETTE GLASS

2 parts Butterscotch Schnapps
1 part Crème de Menthe (White)
1½ parts Irish Cream Liqueur
2 scoops Ice Cream

Combine all ingredients in a blender. Blend until smooth.

Sex with the Bartender

COLLINS GLASS

1 part Light Rum
1 part Strawberry Liqueur
splash Cranberry Juice Cocktail
fill with Orange Juice

Shake with ice and pour.

Sex with the Captain

HIGHBALL GLASS

1½ parts Spiced Rum
1 part Amaretto
1 part Peach Schnapps
1 part Cranberry Juice Cocktail
1 part Orange Juice

Shake with ice and pour.

Sexual Chocolate

HIGHBALL GLASS

1 part Coffee Liqueur
1 part Crème de Cacao (Dark)
1 part Irish Cream Liqueur
1/2 part Chambord
splash Club Soda
splash Milk

Shake with ice and strain over ice.

Sexual Deviant

HIGHBALL GLASS

1 part Citrus Vodka
3/4 part Melon Liqueur
1/2 part Raspberry Liqueur
2 parts Orange Juice
2 parts Pineapple Juice
1 part Margarita Mix

Shake with ice and strain over ice.

Sexual Harrassment

HIGHBALL GLASS

1/2 part Crown Royal® Whiskey
1/2 part Amaretto
1/2 part Sloe Gin
1 part Orange Juice
1 part Pineapple Juice

Shake with ice and strain over ice.

Sexual Healing

HURRICANE GLASS

1 part Jägermeister
1/2 part Coconut Rum
1/2 part Peach Schnapps
2 parts Cranberry Juice
2 parts Pineapple Juice
splash Blue Curaçao

Shake with ice and strain over ice.

Sexual Longing

HIGHBALL GLASS

1 part Melon Liqueur
1 part Jägermeister®
fill with Pineapple Juice

Shake with ice and strain over ice.

Sexual Peak

COLLINS GLASS

1/2 part Amaretto
1/2 part Vodka
1/4 part Peach Schnapps
1 part Orange Juice
1 part Pineapple Juice
splash Sweet & Sour Mix

Shake with ice and pour.

Sexual Trance

COLLINS GLASS

1 part Citrus Vodka
1/2 part Midori®
1/2 part Raspberry Liqueur
1 part Orange Juice
1 part Pineapple Juice
splash Sweet & Sour Mix

Shake with ice and pour.

Sexy Blue-Eyed Boy

COUPETTE GLASS

1 part Blue Curaçao
1 part Vodka
1 part Crème de Cacao (Dark)
1 part Rum Cream Liqueur
1 scoop Ice Cream

Combine all ingredients in a blender. Blend until smooth.

Sexy Green Frogs

HIGHBALL GLASS

1 part Vodka
1 part Triple Sec
1 part Melon Liqueur
fill with Lemon-Lime Soda

Build over ice and stir.

Sexy Motherfucker

COLLINS GLASS

1/2 part Melon Liqueur
1/2 part Raspberry Liqueur
1/2 part Light Rum
1 part Pineapple Juice
1 part Orange Juice

Shake with ice and strain over ice.

Shag in the Sand

HURRICANE GLASS

1½ parts Southern Comfort®
1½ parts Sloe Gin
1 part Vodka
1 part Maraschino Liqueur
½ part Red Curacao
fill with Orange Juice

Shake with ice and strain over ice.

Sicilian Sex

HIGHBALL GLASS

1 part Amaretto
1½ parts Southern Comfort®
fill with Cranberry Juice Cocktail

Build over ice and stir.

Silky Screw

COUPETTE GLASS

1 part Gin
1 part Sloe Gin
½ part Crème de Cassis
½ part Cream
2 parts Orange Juice

Combine all ingredients in a blender with ice. Blend until smooth.

Slippery Dick

COLLINS GLASS

1½ parts Butterscotch Schnapps
2 parts Irish Cream Liqueur
fill with Half and Half

Shake with ice and pour.

Slow Comfortable Fuzzy Screw

HIGHBALL GLASS

1 part Vodka
1 part Sloe Gin
1 part Southern Comfort®
1 part Peach Schnapps
fill with Orange Juice

Build over ice and stir.

Slow Comfortable Screw

COLLINS GLASS

1 part Sloe Gin
½ part Southern Comfort®
fill with Orange Juice

Build over ice and stir.

Slow Comfortable Screw 151 Times in the Dark

COLLINS GLASS

1 part Vodka
1 part Sloe Gin
1 part Southern Comfort®
1 part Galliano®
1 part Tequila
1 part Dark Rum
splash 151-Proof Rum
fill with Orange Juice

Build over ice and stir.

Slow Comfortable Screw Up Against the Wall

HIGHBALL GLASS

1 part Sloe Gin
1 part Southern Comfort®
1 part Vodka
splash Galliano®
fill with Orange Juice

Build over ice and stir.

Slow Comfortable Screw Up Against the Wall with a Bang

COLLINS GLASS

¾ part Sloe Gin
¾ part Southern Comfort®
½ part 151-Proof Rum
½ part Galliano®
fill with Orange Juice

Build over ice and stir.

Slow Comfortable Screw Between the Sheets

COLLINS GLASS

1 part Sloe Gin
1 part Southern Comfort®
1 part Vodka
1 part Triple Sec
fill with Orange Juice

Build over ice and stir.

Slow Comfortable Screw Mexican Style

HIGHBALL GLASS

1 part Sloe Gin
1 part Southern Comfort®
1 part Galliano®
1 part Sauza® Tequila
fill with Orange Juice

Build over ice and stir.

Slow Comfortable Screw on a Dogbox

COLLINS GLASS

1 part Southern Comfort®
1 part Jack Daniel's®
1 part Sloe Gin
splash Grenadine
fill with Orange Juice

Build over ice and stir.

Slow Comfortable Screw Up Against a Fuzzy Wall

HIGHBALL GLASS

1 part Vodka
1 part Southern Comfort®
1 part Sloe Gin
1 part Peach Schnapps
½ part Galliano®
fill with Orange Juice

Build over ice and stir.

Slow Fuzzy Screw

HIGHBALL GLASS

1 part Vodka
1 part Sloe Gin
1 part Peach Schnapps
fill with Orange Juice

Build over ice and stir.

Slow Fuzzy Screw Up Against the Wall

HIGHBALL GLASS

1 part Vodka
1 part Sloe Gin
1 part Peach Schnapps
fill with Orange Juice
splash Galliano®

Build over ice and stir.

Slow Passionate Screw

HIGHBALL GLASS

2 parts Sloe Gin
1 part Orange Juice
1 part Passion Fruit Juice

Build over ice and stir.

Slow Screw

HIGHBALL GLASS

1 part Sloe Gin
fill with Orange Juice

Build over ice and stir.

Slow Screw Mildly Comfortable, Slightly Wild

HURRICANE GLASS

1 part Vodka
1 part Sloe Gin
¾ part Bourbon
¾ part Southern Comfort®
1 part Lemonade
1 part Orange Juice

Shake with ice and pour.

Slow Screw Up Against the Wall

HIGHBALL GLASS

1 part Vodka
1 part Sloe Gin
fill with Orange Juice
splash Galliano®

Build over ice and stir.

Smooth and Sexy

COLLINS GLASS

1 part Passion Fruit
1 part Safari®
½ part Amaretto
½ part Blackberry Juice
fill with Orange Juice

Shake with ice and pour.

Soapy Tits

BEER MUG

1 part Rumple Minze®
1 part Goldschläger®
1 part Cinnamon Schnapps
fill with Lemon-Lime Soda

Build over ice and stir.

Southern Sex
HIGHBALL GLASS

2 parts Southern Comfort®
fill with Lemonade

Build over ice and stir.

Stop and Go Naked
ROCKS GLASS

2 parts Triple Sec
1 part Silver Tequila
1 part Vodka
1 part Light Rum
1 part Gin

Shake with ice and pour.

Sweet Sex
HURRICANE GLASS

1 part Raspberry Vodka
1 part 99-Proof Banana Liqueur
1 part Coconut Rum
1 part Tequila Rose®
1 part Watermelon Schnapps
splash Grenadine
fill with Orange Juice

Shake with ice and pour.

A Thumb in the Ass
HIGHBALL GLASS

1 part Butterscotch Schnapps
1 part Cinnamon Schnapps
1 part Peach Schnapps
1 part Peppermint Schnapps
1 part Blueberry Schnapps

Shake with ice and strain over ice.

Thunderfuck
HIGHBALL GLASS

1 part Vodka
1 part Amaretto
1 part Melon Liqueur
1 part Rum
1 part Sweet & Sour Mix
1 part Orange Juice

Shake with ice and strain.

Tropical Screw
HIGHBALL GLASS

1 part Vodka
½ part Triple Sec

Build over ice and stir.

Tropical Sex
HIGHBALL GLASS

1 part Coconut Rum
1 part Midori®
fill with Pineapple Juice

Combine all ingredients in a blender with ice. Blend until smooth.

Twenty-Dollar Blowjob
COLLINS GLASS

¾ part Vodka
¾ part Southern Comfort®
¾ part Peach Schnapps
2 parts Cranberry Juice Cocktail
2 parts Sweet & Sour Mix
½ part Orange Juice

Build over ice and stir.

Twisted Asshole
COLLINS GLASS

1 part Vodka
1 part Melon Liqueur
½ part Peach Schnapps
splash Blue Curaçao
1 part Pineapple Juice
1 part Orange Juice

Shake with ice and pour.

Twisted Screw
HIGHBALL GLASS

2 parts Vodka
fill with Orange Juice
splash Banana Juice

Build over ice and stir.

Virgin Sex on the Beach

HIGHBALL GLASS

1 part Peach Nectar
½ part Grenadine
1 part Orange Juice
1 part Cranberry Juice Cocktail

Build over ice and stir.

Wet Pussy

COLLINS GLASS

1 part Raspberry Liqueur
2 parts Irish Cream Liqueur
fill with Milk

Shake with ice and pour.

Wild Screw

COLLINS GLASS

1 part Vodka
1 part Bourbon
fill with Orange Juice

Build over ice and stir.

Wild Sex

HURRICANE GLASS

1 part Dark Rum
1 part Peach Schnapps
½ part Grenadine
1 part Pineapple Juice
1 part Orange Juice
1 part Crème de Coconut

Shake with ice and pour.

Wild Squirrel Sex

BEER MUG

½ part Lemon Vodka
½ part Strawberry Vodka
½ part Orange Vodka
½ part Raspberry Vodka
1 part Amaretto
1 part Sweet & Sour Mix
1 part Cranberry Juice Cocktail
splash Grenadine

Build over ice and stir.

Wonder Bra

COCKTAIL GLASS

2 parts Gin
1 part Cointreau
1 part Pineapple Juice

Shake with ice and strain.

TIKI DRINKS

The craze for tiki drinks–which hail from the South Pacific and also the Caribbean–comes and goes. Thankfully they're back again. These colorful, fruity, tropical drinks will make you feel like you're on the beach even in the dead of winter.

2-Tonga

HURRICANE GLASS

1 part Cranberry Vodka
1½ parts Red Curacao
1½ parts Mango Schnapps
4 parts Orange Juice
1 part Lime Juice

Shake with ice and strain over ice.

Acapulco Beach

COLLINS GLASS

2 parts Gold Tequila
⅔ part Peach Schnapps
⅔ part Blue Curaçao
1 part Papaya Juice
2 parts Pineapple Juice

Shake with ice and strain over ice.

Acapulco Zombie

COLLINS GLASS

1 part Rum
1 part Tequila
1 part Vodka
splash Crème de Menthe (White)
half fill with Grapefruit Juice
half fill with Orange Juice

Shake with ice and strain over ice.

Admiral's Grog

ROCKS GLASS

2 parts Gosling's Seal® Black Rum

Pour Rum over ice and squeeze the Lime in. Garnish with Lime Slice.

Aloha

COLLINS GLASS

1 part Dark Rum
1½ parts Myers's® Rum Crème Liqueur
½ part Sweetened Lime Juice
2 parts Pineapple Juice
2 parts Orange Juice
1 part Coco López®
1 scoop Vanilla Ice Cream

Combine all ingredients in a blender. Blend until smooth. Garnish with Pineapple Slice.

Amaretto Paradise

HURRICANE GLASS

1 part Amaretto
1 part Coconut Rum
1 part Melon Liqueur
fill with Pineapple Juice

Build over ice and stir.

Amaretto Rum Punch

HIGHBALL GLASS

1 part Rum
1 part Amaretto
1 part Cherry Juice
1 part Orange Juice
1 part Pineapple Juice

Build over ice and stir.

Ambros Lighthouse

HURRICANE GLASS

2 parts Vodka
1 part Parfait Amour
1 part Crème de Coconut
fill with Banana Juice

Build over ice and stir.

Anchors Away

HURRICANE GLASS

1 part Vodka
1 part Amaretto
1 part Blackberry Liqueur
fill with Orange Juice

Combine all ingredients in a blender with ice. Blend until smooth.

Apple Swizzle

ROCKS GLASS

1½ parts Apple Brandy
1 part Rum
¾ part Lime Juice
dash Powdered Sugar

Build over ice and stir.

Aruba Rum Punch

HURRICANE GLASS

1 part Dark Rum
1 part Light Rum
1 part Orange Juice
1 part Pineapple Juice
½ part Sweet & Sour Mix
splash Grenadine
2 dashes Bitters

Shake with ice and pour.

Avery Island

HIGHBALL GLASS

1 part Melon Liqueur
1 part Dark Rum
½ part Guava Juice
½ part Lime Juice

Build over ice and stir.

Bacardi® Spice on the Beach

COLLINS GLASS

1½ parts Spiced Rum
1 part Peach Schnapps
fill with Orange Juice

Build over ice and stir.

Bahama Mama

HURRICANE GLASS

1½ parts Rum
1 part Coconut Rum
½ part Cherry Heering®
½ part Lemon Juice
2 parts Orange Juice
2 parts Pineapple Juice
splash Grenadine

Build over ice and stir.

Bahama Mama Sunrise

COLLINS GLASS

1 part Dark Rum
1 part Spiced Rum
1 part Orange Juice
1 part Pineapple Juice
dash Grenadine

Build over ice.

Bahamas Rum Cocktail

COCKTAIL GLASS

1 part Coconut Rum
1 part Light Rum
1 part Orange Juice
1 part Pineapple Juice
dash Bitters

Shake with ice and strain.

Bahamian Goombay Smash

HURRICANE GLASS

¾ part Coconut Rum
1¼ parts Dark Rum
¼ part Triple Sec
¼ part Lemon Juice
3 parts Pineapple Juice
dash Simple Syrup

Shake with ice and pour.

Balmy Beach

COLLINS GLASS

1½ parts Peach Schnapps
1 part Spiced Rum
½ part Lemon Juice
fill with Orange Juice

Build over ice and stir.

Banana Banshee (Frozen)

COLLINS GLASS

1 part Crème de Cacao (White)
1 part Crème de Banane
2 scoops Vanilla Ice Cream

Combine all ingredients in a blender. Blend until smooth.

Banana Barbados

COUPETTE GLASS

¾ part Mount Gay® Eclipse Rum
½ part Crème de Banane
2 parts Sweet & Sour Mix
2 scoops Vanilla Ice Cream

Combine all ingredients in a blender. Blend until smooth.

Banana Boat

WHITE WINE GLASS

1 part Light Rum
1 part Brandy
1 part Crème de Banane
2 scoops Vanilla Ice Cream

Combine all ingredients in a blender. Blend until smooth.

Banana Bunch

COUPETTE GLASS

2 parts Crème de Banane
1 part Maple Syrup
3 parts Cream
1 part Kiwi Juice
1 part Banana Puree

Combine all ingredients in a blender with ice. Blend until smooth.

Banana Chi Chi

HIGHBALL GLASS

1 part Vodka
1 part Cherry Juice
1 part Banana Juice
fill with Piña Colada Mix
splash Orange Juice

Combine all ingredients in a blender with ice. Blend until smooth.

Banana Colada

COLLINS GLASS

1 part Dark Rum
1 part Light Rum
1 Banana
1 part Crème de Coconut
4 parts Pineapple Juice

Combine all ingredients in a blender with ice. Blend until smooth.

Banana Milk Punch

COLLINS GLASS

1 part Crème de Banane
1 part Dark Rum
1 part Cream
fill with Milk
splash Simple Syrup

Build over ice and stir.

Banana Punch

COLLINS GLASS

2 parts Vodka
1½ splashes Banana Liqueur
½ part Lime Juice
fill with Seltzer

Build over ice and stir.

Banana Rum Punch

HIGHBALL GLASS

1 part Rum
1 part Banana Liqueur
1 part Cherry Juice
1 part Orange Juice
1 part Pineapple Juice

Build over ice and stir.

Banana Surfer

COUPETTE GLASS

2 parts Milk
1 part Frangelico®
1 part Banana Puree
1 part Crème de Cacao (White)

Combine all ingredients in a blender with ice. Blend until smooth.

Bandung Exotic

HURRICANE GLASS

2 parts Crème de Menthe (Green)
1 part Crème de Banane
1 part Cherry Brandy
fill with Ginger Ale

Shake all but Ginger Ale with ice and strain. Top with Ginger Ale.

Barbados Planter's Punch

COLLINS GLASS

3 parts Sparkling Water
3 parts Dark Rum
1 part Lime Juice
dash Powdered Sugar
dash Orange Bitters

Shake with ice and strain over ice.

Barrier Reef

PITCHER

1 part Gin
1 part Cointreau®
1 scoop Vanilla Ice Cream

Combine all ingredients in a blender. Blend until smooth.

Baywatch

HURRICANE GLASS

1 part Vodka
1 part Galliano®
fill with Orange Juice
splash Cream

Build over ice and stir.

Beach Blanket Bingo

HIGHBALL GLASS

1 part Cranberry Juice Cocktail
1 part Grape Juice (Red)

Build over ice and stir.

Beach Bum

COLLINS GLASS

1½ parts Vodka
1 part Apple Juice
1 part Banana Liqueur
2 parts Pineapple Juice
fill with Fruit Punch

Shake with ice and pour.

Beach Cruiser

COLLINS GLASS

1¼ parts Spiced Rum
1 part Pineapple Juice
1 part Cranberry Juice Cocktail

Build over ice and stir.

Beach Dream

HURRICANE GLASS

1 part KeKe Beach® Key Lime Cream Liqueur
1 part Melon Liqueur
1 part Lime Cordial
½ part Crème de Coconut
½ part Grenadine
4 parts Orange Juice
3 parts Pineapple Juice

Combine all ingredients in a blender with ice. Blend until smooth.

Beach Party

COLLINS GLASS

1¼ parts Rum
1 part Pineapple Juice
1 part Orange Juice
1 part Grenadine

Combine all ingredients in a blender with ice. Blend until smooth.

Beach Sunday
HIGHBALL GLASS
2 parts Peach Vodka
1 part Chambord®
3 parts Cranberry Juice Cocktail

Build over ice and stir.

Beach Sweet
ROCKS GLASS
2 parts Vodka
1 part Apricot Brandy
½ part Lime Juice
3 parts Banana Juice

Combine all ingredients in a blender with ice. Blend until smooth.

Beachcomber
HIGHBALL GLASS
1 part Vodka
1½ parts Light Rum
6 Strawberries
1 Banana
½ part Cream of Coconut
splash Lime Juice
½ part Grenadine

Combine all ingredients in a blender with ice. Blend until smooth.

Beachside
HIGHBALL GLASS
1 part Vodka
1 part Melon Liqueur
1 part Strawberry Daiquiri Mix
1 part Orange Juice
1 part Pineapple Juice

Shake with ice and strain over ice.

Beauty on the Beach
COLLINS GLASS
1 part Light Rum
1 part Southern Comfort®
splash Grand Marnier®
splash Lemon Juice
dash Orange Bitters

Shake with ice and strain over ice.

Bender's Sling
COLLINS GLASS
1½ parts Gin
1 part Lemonade
1 part Orange Juice

Build over ice and stir. Garnish with Orange Slice and Maraschino Cherry.

Bermuda Bloom
COCKTAIL GLASS
1 part Gin
½ part Apricot Brandy
½ part Triple Sec
1 part Lemon Juice
1 part Orange Juice
dash Simple Syrup

Shake with ice and strain.

Bermuda Rum Swizzle
PITCHER, GLASSES
2 parts Gosling's Black Seal® Rum
2 parts Light Rum
¼ part Lime Juice
2 parts Pineapple Juice
2 parts Orange Juice
½ part Grenadine
3 dashes Angostura® Bitters

Fill a pitcher⅓ full with crushed ice. Add all ingredients and stir or shake vigorously until a frothing head appears. Strain into glasses.

Berry Buster
COUPETTE GLASS
1½ parts Currant Vodka
½ part Raspberry Liqueur
2 parts Cranberry Juice Cocktail

Shake with ice and strain over ice.

Berry Me in the Sand
HIGHBALL GLASS
1 part Vodka
½ part Blackberry Liqueur
½ part Triple Sec
fill with Orange Juice

Build over ice and stir.

Bird of Paradise

HIGHBALL GLASS

1 part Coconut Rum
1 part Pineapple Rum
1 part Orange Juice

Shake with ice and strain over ice.

Blackbeard's Ghost

HIGHBALL GLASS

1 part Coconut Rum
1 part Dark Rum
1 part Light Rum
1 part Grapefruit Juice
1 part Orange Juice
1 part Mango Syrup
1/4 part Molasses

Shake with ice and strain over ice.

Blackberry Rum Punch

HIGHBALL GLASS

1 part Rum
1 part Blackberry Liqueur
1 part Cherry Juice
1 part Orange Juice
1 part Pineapple Juice

Shake with ice and pour.

Black Magic

ROCKS GLASS

1 1/2 parts Vodka
3/4 part Coffee Liqueur
splash Lemon Juice

Build over ice and stir.

Blowfish

HURRICANE GLASS

1 part Irish Cream Liqueur
1/2 part Banana Liqueur
1/2 part Dark Spiced Rum
1/2 part Triple Sec
1/2 part Grenadine
fill with Orange Juice

Shake with ice and strain over ice.

Blue Hawaiian

HIGHBALL GLASS

1 part Light Rum
2 parts Pineapple Juice
1 part Blue Curaçao
1 part Crème de Coconut

Combine all ingredients in a blender with ice. Blend until smooth.

Blue Jeep® Island

HIGHBALL GLASS

1 part Triple Sec
1 part Raspberry Liqueur
fill with Lemon-Lime Soda

Build over ice and stir.

Bolduc on the Beach

HIGHBALL GLASS

1 part Vodka
1 part Orange Juice
1 part Grapefruit Juice

Shake with ice and pour.

Bora-Bora Island

HURRICANE GLASS

1 part Jamaican Rum
1 part Coffee Liqueur
1 part Coconut-Cream
1/2 part Crème de Banane
1/2 part Crème de Coconut
1 1/2 parts Cream
1 1/2 parts Banana Juice
1/2 part Almond Syrup

Combine all ingredients in a blender with ice. Blend until smooth.

Cannon Beach

COLLINS GLASS

1 part Blackberry Liqueur
1 part Dark Rum
3 parts Pineapple Juice
2 parts Club Soda

Build over ice and stir.

Caribbean Beach Party

HIGHBALL GLASS

1 part Rum
1 part Cherry Juice
1 part Banana Juice
1 part Piña Colada Mix
1 part Pineapple Juice
1 part Cranberry Juice Cocktail

Build over ice and stir.

Caribbean Punch

HIGHBALL GLASS

2 parts Dark Rum
3/4 part Crème de Banane
1 part Pineapple Juice
1 part Orange Juice
1/4 part Sweetened Lime Juice

Shake with ice and pour.

Category 5

HURRICANE GLASS

1 part Light Rum
1 part Dark Rum
1 part Southern Comfort
1 part Spiced Rum
splash Grenadine
splash Lime Juice
half fill with Orange Juice
half fill with Pineapple Juice

Combine all but Orange and Pineapple juices, shake with ice, and strain over ice. Fill with equal parts Orange Juice and Pineapple Juice.

Cherry Sling

ROCKS GLASS

2 parts Cherry Brandy
1/2 part Lemon Juice

Build over ice and stir. Garnish with a Lemon Twist.

Club Tropicana

HURRICANE GLASS

1 part Coconut Rum
1 part Blue Curaçao
1/2 part Triple Sec
1 part Pineapple Juice
1 part Lemon-Lime Soda
splash Grenadine

Build over ice and stir. Garnish with a Maraschino Cherry.

Cocoa Beach

HURRICANE GLASS

1 part Vodka
1 part Blue Curaçao
2 parts Piña Colada Mix
1 part Lemonade
1 part Pineapple Juice

Shake with ice and strain over ice.

Crooked Monkey

BEER MUG

1 part Irish Whiskey
1 part Banana Liqueur
1 part Orange Juice
1 part Lemon-Lime Soda

Build over ice and stir.

Cuban Crime of Passion

HURRICANE GLASS

1 part Spiced Rum
1 part Light Rum
1 part Coconut Rum
1 part Triple Sec
2 parts Pineapple Juice

Shake with ice and pour.

A Day at the Beach

HIGHBALL GLASS

1 part Coconut Rum
1/2 part Amaretto
4 parts Orange Juice
1/2 part Grenadine

Shake with ice and strain over ice.

Daytona Beach

HIGHBALL GLASS

1 part Vodka
1 part Cherry Juice
1 part Wild Berry Schnapps
2 parts Lemonade
1 part Orange Juice

Shake with ice and pour.

Down Home Punch

COLLINS GLASS

1 part Whiskey
1 part Peach Schnapps
2 parts Orange Juice
1 part Lemon-Lime Soda
1 part Sweet & Sour Mix
splash Grenadine

Build over ice and stir.

El Niño

HURRICANE GLASS

1 part Vodka
1 part Peach Schnapps
½ part Blue Curaçao
2 parts Pineapple Juice
2 parts Orange Juice
splash Club Soda
splash of Sour Mix
splash of Cherry Juice
fill with Pineapple Juice

Shake all but Club Soda with ice and strain over ice. Top with Club Soda.

Flirting with the Sandpiper

HIGHBALL GLASS

1½ parts Light Rum
½ part Cherry Brandy
3 parts Orange Juice
2 dashes Orange Bitters

Shake with ice and pour.

Florida Punch

HIGHBALL GLASS

1 part Dark Rum
¼ part Cognac
1 part Grapefruit Juice
1 part Orange Juice

Shake with ice and strain over ice.

Fog Cutter

COLLINS GLASS

1½ parts Light Rum
½ part Gin
½ part Brandy
1 part Orange Juice
3 splashes Lemon Juice
2 splashes Amaretto

Shake with ice and strain over ice.

Fruity Punch

HIGHBALL GLASS

½ part Coconut Rum
½ part Light Rum
½ part Triple Sec
1½ parts Pineapple Juice
splash Grenadine

Shake with ice and pour.

Fun on the Beach

HIGHBALL GLASS

1 part Vodka
1 part Melon Liqueur
splash Raspberry Liqueur
1 part Pineapple Juice
1 part Cranberry Juice Cocktail

Build over ice and stir.

Gay Bartender

PARFAIT GLASS

1½ parts Coconut Rum
½ part Blue Curaçao
½ part Grand Marnier®
½ part Raspberry Liqueur
1 part Apple Juice
1 part Cranberry Juice Cocktail
1 part Orange Juice
½ part Strawberry Liqueur

Shake with ice and strain over ice.

Gilligan's Island®

COLLINS GLASS

1 part Vodka
1 part Peach Schnapps
3 parts Orange Juice
3 parts Cranberry Juice Cocktail

Shake with ice and strain over ice.

Gilligan's Island® Retreat

HIGHBALL GLASS

1 part Melon Liqueur
1 part Coconut Rum
1 part Banana Liqueur
1 part Amaretto
1 part Spiced Rum
splash Sweet & Sour Mix
splash Cherry Juice
fill with Pineapple Juice

Shake with ice and pour.

Gin Beachball

COLLINS GLASS

1½ parts Gin
1 part Grapefruit Juice
1 part Orange Juice

Build over ice and stir.

Golden Pony

COUPETTE GLASS

1 part Scotch
1 part Orange Juice
1 part Apricot Brandy

Shake with ice and pour.

Gringo Swizzle

ROCKS GLASS

2 parts Silver Tequila
2 parts Ginger Ale
1 part Pineapple Juice
1 part Orange Juice
1 part Lime Juice
½ part Crème de Cassis

Shake with ice and strain over ice.

Grog

ROCKS GLASS

2 parts Dark Rum
3 parts Water

Build in the glass with no ice.

Hairy Slut

COUPETTE GLASS

2 parts Rum
1 part Triple Sec
2 parts Pineapple Juice

Shake with ice and pour.

Hawaiian Island Sunset

HIGHBALL GLASS

1 part Amaretto
1 part Coconut Rum
1 part Peach Schnapps
splash Grenadine
2 parts Lemonade
fill with Pineapple Juice
1½ parts Mango Schnapps

Build over ice and stir.

Hawaiian Kisses

HURRICANE GLASS

1½ parts Light Rum
1 part Blue Curaçao
1 part Triple Sec
fill with Orange Juice

Build over ice and stir.

Hawaiian Lust

COLLINS GLASS

1 part Gin
1 part Pineapple Rum
1 part Sour Apple Schnapps
1 part Coconut Rum
½ part Blue Curaçao
splash Lemon Juice
fill with Lemon-Lime Soda

Build over ice and stir.

Hawaiian Punch

HURRICANE GLASS

½ part Vodka
½ part Southern Comfort®
½ part Amaretto
½ part Sloe Gin
1 part Orange Juice
1 part Pineapple Juice

Build over ice and stir.

Hawaiian Shoreline

HURRICANE GLASS

1 part Coconut Rum
½ part Blue Curaçao
fill with Pineapple Juice

Build over ice and stir.

Hawaiian Surf City

HIGHBALL GLASS

1 part Vodka
1 part Wild Berry Schnapps
1 part Peach Nectar
2 parts Lemonade
1 part Pineapple Juice

Build over ice and stir.

Heat Wave

PARFAIT GLASS

1¼ parts Coconut Rum
½ part Peach Schnapps
1 part Pineapple Juice
1 part Orange Juice
½ part Grenadine

Build over ice and stir.

Hoi Punch

COLLINS GLASS

2 parts Vodka
½ part Crème de Cassis
½ part Light Rum
fill with Lemon Juice
1½ parts Simple Syrup

Shake with ice and strain over ice.

Hurricane

HURRICANE GLASS

4 parts Dark Rum
2 splashes Lime Juice
fill with Hawaiian Punch®
1 part 151-Proof Rum

Shake with ice and pour.

Hurricane Leah

HURRICANE GLASS

¼ part Light Rum
¼ part Gin
¼ part Vodka
¼ part Tequila
¼ part Blue Curaçao
splash Cherry Brandy
1 part Sweet & Sour Mix
1 part Orange Juice

Shake with ice and strain over ice.

Hurricane (New Orleans Style)

HURRICANE GLASS

1 part Light Rum
1 part 151-Proof Rum
1 part Orange Juice
1 part Pineapple Juice
½ part Grenadine

Shake with ice and pour.

Iceberg Vacation

HURRICANE GLASS

1½ parts Blue Curaçao
1½ parts Vodka
1 part Cream
1 part Crème de Menthe (White)
1 part Lime Juice
fill with Lemon-Lime Soda

Build over ice and stir.

Island Breeze

COLLINS GLASS

1¼ parts Coconut Rum
fill with Cranberry Juice Cocktail

Build over ice and stir.

Island Hideaway

COLLINS GLASS

1 part Dark Rum
1 part Passion Fruit Liqueur
1 part Pineapple Juice
1 part Orange Juice

Build over ice and stir.

Island Jack

COLLINS GLASS

3/4 part Banana Liqueur
3/4 part Malibu® Rum
1/2 part Jack Daniel's®
1 part Pineapple Juice
1 part Sweet & Sour Mix
2 parts Cola

Build over ice and stir.

Island Oasis

COLLINS GLASS

1/2 part Crème de Coconut
1/2 part Crème de Banane
2/3 part Spiced Rum
2/3 part Dark Rum
3 parts Piña Colada Mix
2 parts Strawberry Puree

Combine all ingredients in a blender with ice. Blend until smooth.

Island Punch

COLLINS GLASS

1 part Light Rum
splash Grenadine
1 part Orange Juice
1 part Pineapple Juice

Build over ice and stir. Garnish with 2 Maraschino Cherries.

Island Toy

HIGHBALL GLASS

1 part Spiced Rum
1/4 part Peach Schnapps
1/4 part Lime Juice
fill with Pineapple Juice

Build over ice and stir.

Islander

COLLINS GLASS

2 parts Gosling's Black Seal® Rum
fill with Pineapple Juice

Build over ice and stir.

Italian Surfer

HIGHBALL GLASS

1 part Coconut Rum
1 part Amaretto
fill with Pineapple Juice
splash Cranberry Juice Cocktail

Build over ice.

Jamaican 10-Speed

HURRICANE GLASS

1 1/2 parts Coconut Rum
1/2 part Banana Liqueur
1 part Melon Liqueur
1 part Cream
fill with Pineapple Juice

Shake with ice and strain over ice.

Jamaican Breakfast

HIGHBALL GLASS

2 parts Dark Rum
1/2 part Cherry Brandy
dash Molasses
splash Falernum
fill with Cola

Build over ice and stir.

Jamaican Crawler

HIGHBALL GLASS

1 part Light Rum
1 part Melon Liqueur
fill with Pineapple Juice
splash Grenadine

Build over ice.

Jamaican Lifesaver

HURRICANE GLASS

1 part Butterscotch Liqueur
1 part Coconut Rum
4 parts Pineapple Juice

Shake with ice and strain over ice.

Jamaican Punch

COLLINS GLASS

3/4 part Spiced Rum
3/4 part Coconut Rum
3/4 part Banana Liqueur
1 part Orange Juice
1 part Pineapple Juice
splash Grenadine

Shake with ice and strain over ice.

Jamaican Sunset

HURRICANE GLASS

1 part Dark Rum
1 part Spiced Rum
1 part Pineapple Juice
1 part Orange Juice
splash Cranberry Juice

Build over ice.

Jamaican Surfer

ROCKS GLASS

1 part Coconut Rum
1/2 part Tia Maria®
1 part Cream

Shake with ice and strain over ice.

Jamaican Zombie

COLLINS GLASS

2 1/2 parts Light Rum
1 part Dark Rum
1 part Apricot Brandy
1 part Lime Juice
1 part Pineapple Juice
1 part Orange Juice

Shake with ice and strain over ice.

Kangeroo Jumper

COUPETTE GLASS

1 part Vodka
1 part Rum
1 part Crème de Coconut
1/2 part Blue Curaçao
fill with Passion Fruit Juice

Shake with ice and strain over ice.

Kon Tiki

HIGHBALL GLASS

2 parts Scotch
1 part Dark Rum
1 part Cointreau®

Shake with ice and strain over ice.

Las Brisas

HURRICANE GLASS

2 parts Rum
1 part Cream of Coconut
1 part Pineapple Juice
1 part Orange Juice

Shake with ice and strain over ice.

Lazy Licker

COUPETTE GLASS

1 part Tequila Reposado
1/2 part Blue Curaçao
1/4 part Peach Schnapps
2 parts Sweet & Sour Mix
fill with Cola

Shake all but Cola with ice and strain. Top with Cola.

Little Bit of Heaven

HURRICANE GLASS

2 parts Hpnotiq
1 part Coconut Rum
splash Orange Juice
splash Pineapple Juice
fill with Cranberry Juice

Build over ice and stir.

Loch Lomond

PARFAIT GLASS

1 part Scotch
1/2 part Peach Schnapps
1 part Blue Curaçao
fill with Grapefruit Juice
1/2 part Lemon Juice

Shake with ice and strain over ice.

London Fog

HIGHBALL GLASS

1 1/2 parts Gin
1/4 part Pernod®

Shake with ice and strain over ice.

Long Island Sunset

HIGHBALL GLASS

1 part Spiced Rum
1 part Peach Schnapps
1 part Sweet & Sour Mix
1 part Cranberry Juice Cocktail

Shake with ice and pour.

Lost in Paradise

HURRICANE GLASS

1 1/2 parts Light Rum
1 part Blue Curaçao
1 part Triple Sec
3 parts Orange Juice
1 part Pineapple Juice

Shake with ice and strain over ice.

Mai Tai

COLLINS GLASS

1 1/2 parts Light Rum
1 part Dark Rum
1/2 part Amaretto
1/2 part Triple Sec
1/2 part Sweet & Sour Mix
fill with Pineapple Juice
splash 151-Proof Rum

Shake with ice and strain over ice. Top with splash of 151-Proof Rum.

Malibu Beach

HIGHBALL GLASS

1 part Vodka
1 part Coconut Rum
1 part Orange Juice
1 part Pineapple Juice

Build over ice and stir.

Marco Island Rum Runner

COLLINS GLASS

3/4 part Crème de Banane
3/4 part Blackberry Brandy
3/4 part Light Rum
2 parts Sweet & Sour Mix
fill with Orange Juice
splash Grenadine

Build over ice and stir.

Maui Sunset

HURRICANE GLASS

1 part Light Rum
1 1/2 parts Apricot Brandy
1 1/2 parts Triple Sec
fill with Pineapple Juice

Build over ice.

Me Hearty Mudslide

HIGHBALL GLASS

1 part Amaretto
1 part Coffee Liqueur
1 part RumChata
1 part Spiced Rum

Shake with ice and strain over ice.

Melon Chiquita® Punch

COLLINS GLASS

1 1/2 parts Crème de Banane
1 1/2 parts Melon Liqueur
1 part Pineapple Juice
1 part Milk

Shake with ice and strain over ice.

Mississippi Planters' Punch
COLLINS GLASS

1 part Brandy
½ part Light Rum
½ part Lemon Juice
dash Powdered Sugar
fill with Seltzer

Shake all but Seltzer with ice and strain. Top with Seltzer.

Monkey Island
COLLINS GLASS

1½ parts Light Rum
1 part Crème de Banane
1 part Pisang Ambon® Liqueur
½ part Simple Syrup
fill with Pineapple Juice

Shake with ice and pour.

Monster on the Beach
HIGHBALL GLASS

1½ parts Tequila
2 parts Cranberry Juice Cocktail
splash Lime Juice
splash Grenadine

Shake with ice and pour.

Myrtle Beach
HIGHBALL GLASS

1 part Vodka
1 part Blue Curaçao
1 part Piña Colada Mix
1 part Lemonade
1 part Orange Juice

Shake with ice and strain over ice.

Naked Surfer
PINT GLASS

2 parts Vodka
1 part Jägermeister
splash Grenadine
fill with Orange Juice

Build over ice and stir.

Navy Grog
COLLINS GLASS

1 part Light Rum
1 part Dark Rum
1 part Spiced Rum
1 part Orange Juice
2 parts Pineapple Juice
1 part Guava Juice
1 part Lime Juice

Shake with ice and pour.

Nutty Surfer
ROCKS GLASS

1 part Coconut Rum
1 part Frangelico®
1 part Cream

Shake with ice and strain over ice.

Orgasm on the Beach
COLLINS GLASS

1 part Light Rum
1 part Coconut Rum
½ part Blue Curaçao
½ part Raspberry Liqueur
fill with Pineapple Juice

Shake with ice and pour.

The Original Hurricane
HURRICANE GLASS

½ part Amaretto
½ part Dark Rum
½ part Gin
½ part Light Rum
2 parts Grapefruit Juice
2 parts Orange Juice
2 parts Pineapple Juice
¼ part Grenadine

Shake with ice and pour.

Oslo Breeze
COUPETTE GLASS

1 part Vodka
1 part Aquavit
dash Orange Bitters
fill with Cider

Build over ice and stir.

Pacific Sunshine

PARFAIT GLASS

1 part Tequila
1 part Blue Curaçao
1 part Sweet & Sour Mix
dash Bitters

Shake with ice and strain over ice.

Palm Island

COUPETTE GLASS

1 part Passion Fruit Liqueur
1 part Melon Liqueur
½ part Dark Rum
½ part Crème de Coconut
2 parts Orange Juice
2 parts Grape Juice (White)
2 parts Pineapple Juice

Combine all ingredients in a blender with ice. Blend until smooth.

Panama Punch

HIGHBALL GLASS

1 part Rum
1 part Piña Colada Mix
1 part Banana Juice
1 part Orange Juice
1 part Pineapple Juice

Build over ice and stir.

Paradise Island

ROCKS GLASS

1 part Gin
½ part Triple Sec
½ part Peach Schnapps
splash Lime Juice
fill with Pineapple Juice

Shake with ice and pour.

Paradise Sunset

HURRICANE GLASS

½ part Grenadine
2 parts Orange Rum
1 part Vanilla Rum
fill with Orange Juice

Build over ice.

Peach May Cocktail

HURRICANE GLASS

1 part Banana Liqueur
2 parts Peach Schnapps
1 part Apple Juice
1 part Pineapple Juice
1 part Lemon-Lime Soda

Build over ice and stir.

Peach on Malibu Beach

HIGHBALL GLASS

1 part Coconut Rum
1 part Peach Schnapps
1 part Orange Juice
1 part Pineapple Juice
1 part Cranberry Juice Cocktail

Build over ice and stir.

Peach on the Beach

HIGHBALL GLASS

1½ parts Vodka
½ part Peach Schnapps
fill with Pineapple Juice

Shake with ice and pour.

Puerto Rican Punch

HURRICANE GLASS

¾ part Vodka
¾ part Gin
¾ part Sloe Gin
¾ part Peach Schnapps
1 part Orange Juice
1 part Pineapple Juice
splash Grenadine

Build over ice and stir.

Red Headed Cheryl

HURRICANE GLASS

2 parts Coconut Rum
1 part Cherry Vodka
½ part Lime Juice
fill with Pineapple Juice
splash Grenadine

Build over ice. For Cheryl.

Red Tide

HIGHBALL GLASS

1 part Silver Tequila
1 part Orange Juice
fill with Pomegranate Juice

Build over ice and stir.

Rio Bamba

HURRICANE GLASS

1 part Vodka
1 part Gin
½ part Passion Fruit Liqueur
½ part Peach Schnapps
½ part Cream
1 part Pineapple Juice
1 part Orange Juice

Shake with ice and pour.

Rockaway Beach

HIGHBALL GLASS

1½ parts Light Rum
½ part Dark Rum
½ part Tequila
splash Crème de Noyaux
½ part Cranberry Juice Cocktail
½ part Pineapple Juice
1 part Orange Juice

Shake with ice and strain over ice.

Rum Dinger

HURRICANE GLASS

1 part Coconut Rum
1 part Melon Liqueur
1 part Orange Juice
1 part Pineapple Juice

Shake with ice and pour.

Rum Punch

HIGHBALL GLASS

1½ parts Rum
1 part Orange Juice
1 part Pineapple Juice
1 part Cranberry Juice Cocktail

Build over ice and stir.

Rum Relaxer

PARFAIT GLASS

1½ parts Light Rum
1 part Pineapple Juice
½ part Grenadine
fill with Lemon-Lime Soda

Shake all but Lemon-Lime Soda with ice and strain. Top with Lemon-Lime Soda.

Sammy Special

HURRICANE GLASS

1 part Coconut Rum
1 part Light Rum
1 part Pineapple Juice
1 part Orange Juice

Shake with ice and pour.

Sandbar Sleeper

HIGHBALL GLASS

1 part Vodka
1 part Irish Crème Liqueur
1 part Coffee Liqueur
1 part Frangelico®
½ part Milk

Shake with ice and strain over ice.

Sandcastle

COLLINS GLASS

2 parts Citrus Vodka
1 part Grenadine
fill with Pineapple Juice

Shake with ice and pour.

Sand in the Cracks

HURRICANE GLASS

2 parts Spiced Rum
2 parts Coconut Rum
fill with Pineapple Juice
splash Cranberry Juice

Shake all but Cranberry Juice with ice and strain over ice. Top with Cranberry Juice.

Sand in Your Shorts

HIGHBALL GLASS

1/2 part Melon Liqueur
1/2 part Peach Schnapps
1/2 part Raspberry Liqueur
1/2 part Triple Sec
1/2 part Vodka
3 parts Cranberry Juice
3 parts Orange Juice
1 part Sweet & Sour Mix

Shake with ice and strain over ice.

Sandpiper

HIGHBALL GLASS

1 part Light Rum
1 part Cherry Brandy
1/2 part Grapefruit Juice
1 part Orange Juice

Shake with ice and strain.

Sanibel Island

HIGHBALL GLASS

1 part Bacardi® Limón Rum
1 part Orange Vodka
1 part Sweet & Sour Mix
1 part Cranberry Juice Cocktail
1 part Lemon-Lime Soda

Shake with ice and pour.

Scotch Bounty

PARFAIT GLASS

1 part Scotch
1 part Coconut Rum
1 part Crème de Cacao (White)
1/2 part Grenadine
fill with Orange Juice

Shake with ice and pour.

Screaming Chocolate Monkey

HIGHBALL GLASS

2 parts Coconut Rum
1 part Banana Liqueur
1/2 part Chocolate Syrup
fill with Milk

Shake with ice and strain over ice.

Sewer Water

PARFAIT GLASS

1 part 151-Proof Rum
1/2 part Gin
3/4 part Melon Liqueur
splash Pineapple Juice
splash Lime Juice
splash Grenadine

Shake with ice and pour.

Shit on the Beach

HIGHBALL GLASS

2 parts Irish Crème Liqueur
1 part Dark Rum
1 part Chocolate Milk
1 part Milk

Shake with ice and pour.

Singapore Sling

COLLINS GLASS

1 1/2 parts Gin
1/2 part Cherry Heering®
1/4 part Cointreau®
1/4 part Bénédictine®
1/2 part Lime Juice
1/3 part Grenadine
dash Bitters
fill with Pineapple Juice

Shake with ice and strain over ice.

Singapore Sting

HURRICANE GLASS

1 part Light Rum
1/2 part Cherry Schnapps
1/4 part Triple Sec
1/2 part Lime Juice
splash Grenadine
fill with Pineapple Juice
dash Angostura Bitters

Shake with ice and pour.

Skull Island

HIGHBALL GLASS

2 parts Coconut Vodka
1 part 99 Bananas Liqueur
fill with Cola

Build over ice and stir.

South Padre Island

HURRICANE GLASS

1 part Vodka
3/4 part Peach Schnapps
1 part Sweet & Sour Mix
fill with Cranberry Juice Cocktail
splash Orange Juice
splash Pineapple Juice

Build over ice.

Spanish Planter's Punch

HIGHBALL GLASS

2 parts Light Rum
2 parts Pineapple Juice
1 part Triple Sec
1/2 part Maraschino Liqueur
splash Dark Rum

Shake with ice and strain over ice.

Spice on the Beach

HIGHBALL GLASS

1 1/2 parts Spiced Rum
1 part Peach Schnapps
1 part Orange Juice
1 part Cranberry Juice Cocktail

Build over ice and stir.

Suede Vixen

COUPETTE GLASS

1 1/2 parts Crème de Cacao (White)
1 1/2 parts Frangelico®
1 part Triple Sec
fill with Cream

Shake with ice and pour.

Sun of a Beach

HIGHBALL GLASS

1 part Gin
1 part Midori®
fill with Orange Juice

Build over ice and stir.

Sunny Beach

ROCKS GLASS

1 part Gin
1 part Apricot Brandy
1/2 part Cherry Brandy
1/2 part Grenadine
fill with Orange Juice

Shake with ice and strain over ice.

Sunrise Sling

COLLINS GLASS

1 part Dry Gin
1 part Blue Curaçao
1 part Apricot Brandy
fill with Lemonade

Shake with ice and strain over ice.

Sunset at the Beach

COLLINS GLASS

1 1/2 parts Cranberry Vodka
1/2 part Melon Liqueur
1/2 part Raspberry Liqueur
3 parts Pineapple Juice
fill with Lemon-Lime Soda

Shake all but Lemon-Lime soda with ice and strain. Top with Lemon-Lime soda.

Sunset on the Beach

HURRICANE GLASS

1/2 part Vodka
1 part Peach Schnapps
1 part Melon Liqueur
1 part Cream of Coconut
1 part Sweet & Sour Mix
fill with Orange Juice

Shake with ice and strain over ice.

Surfin' Safari

HIGHBALL GLASS

1 1/2 parts Light Rum
1/2 part Safari®
splash Grenadine
fill with Mango Juice

Build over ice and stir.

Surfside

WHITE WINE GLASS

1 part Peach Schnapps
1 part Crème de Banane
1 part Orange Juice
1 part Dark Rum
1 part Southern Comfort®
splash Grenadine

Shake with ice and strain over ice.

Survivor Island

HIGHBALL GLASS

1 part Sloe Gin
1 part Melon Liqueur
1 part Currant Vodka
fill with Orange Juice

Shake with ice and strain over ice.

Tahitian Sunset

HIGHBALL GLASS

½ part Vodka
½ part Coconut Rum
½ part Melon Liqueur
½ part Cointreau
1 part Lemonade
1 part Pineapple Juice
dash Chambord

Build over ice.

Tahitian Surfer

HIGHBALL GLASS

½ part Amaretto
½ part Blue Curaçao
1 part Spiced Rum
½ part Lime Juice
fill with Apple Juice

Shake with ice and pour.

Thunder Cloud

HURRICANE GLASS

½ part Crème de Noyaux
½ part Blue Curaçao
½ part Amaretto
¾ part Vodka
2 parts Sweet & Sour Mix
fill with Lemon-Lime Soda

Build over ice and stir.

Tikitini

COLLINS GLASS

1 part Coconut Rum
1 part Gold Tequila
1 part Vodka
1 part Cream of Coconut
fill with Pineapple Juice

Shake with ice and strain over ice. Top with Grenadine.

Trinidad Swizzle

HIGHBALL GLASS

1 part Dark Rum
1 part Grand Marnier®
¼ part Lime Juice
2 splashes Grenadine
½ part Mango Nectar

Shake with ice and strain over ice.

Tropical Blend

HURRICANE GLASS

1 part Crème de Banane
1 part Melon Liqueur
1 part Pineapple Juice
1 part Cream of Coconut

Combine all ingredients in a blender with ice. Blend until smooth.

Tropical Dawn

HIGHBALL GLASS

2 parts Gin
½ part Campari
fill with Orange Juice

Build over ice and stir.

Tropical Delight

WHITE WINE GLASS

1½ parts Rum
¾ part Pineapple Juice
¾ part Cream of Coconut
1 scoop Vanilla Ice Cream
1 scoop Orange Sorbet
½ Banana

Combine all ingredients in a blender. Blend until smooth.

Tropical Flower

HURRICANE GLASS

1½ parts Light Rum
1½ parts Passion Fruit Liqueur
1 part Lychee Liqueur
2 parts Passion Fruit Juice
½ Banana

Combine all ingredients in a blender with ice. Blend until smooth.

Tropical Kick

HURRICANE GLASS

1 part Coconut Rum
1 part Pineapple Vodka
1 part Light Rum
½ part Tropical Punch Schnapps
½ part Raspberry Liqueur
fill with Pineapple Juice

Shake with ice and pour.

Tropical Nat

HURRICANE GLASS

2 parts Spiced Rum
1 part Vodka
1 part Orange Juice
1 part Cranberry Juice Cocktail
splash Pineapple Juice

Build over ice.

Tropical Oasis

WHITE WINE GLASS

2 parts Pineapple Juice
2 parts Papaya Juice
1 part Peach Juice
3 scoops Orange Sorbet

Combine all ingredients in a blender. Blend until smooth.

Tropical Orgasm

HIGHBALL GLASS

½ part Citrus Vodka
½ part Orange Vodka
½ part Peach Schnapps
splash Strawberry Liqueur
splash Cranberry Juice
splash Orange Juice
splash Pineapple Juice

Shake with ice and strain over ice.

Tropical Paradise

HURRICANE GLASS

1¼ parts Spiced Rum
2 parts Orange Juice
2 parts Crème de Coconut
¼ part Grenadine
½ Banana

Combine all ingredients in a blender with ice. Blend until smooth.

Tropical Punch

HIGHBALL GLASS

1 part Rum
1 part Banana Liqueur
2 dashes Brown Sugar
1 part Lemonade
1 part Orange Juice
1 part Pineapple Juice

Shake with ice and pour.

Tropical Toucan

HURRICANE GLASS

1½ parts Light Rum
½ part Crème de Banane
1 part Pineapple Juice
1 part Orange Juice

Shake with ice and pour.

Tung Shing Dragon Scorpion Bowl

SCORPION BOWL

2 parts Vodka
2 parts Gin
2 parts Rum
1 part 151-Proof Rum
3 parts Grenadine
3 parts Pineapple Juice
3 parts Orange Juice

Shake with ice and strain over ice into a Scorpion Bowl. This is a drink for two or more people.

Tuxedo Beach
HIGHBALL GLASS
- 1 part Blue Curaçao
- 1 part Dark Rum
- ½ part Crème de Coconut
- splash Sweet & Sour Mix
- splash Pineapple Juice

Shake with ice and strain over ice.

Vexed
HURRICANE GLASS
- 2 parts Spiced Rum
- 1 part Vanilla Vodka
- 1 part White Cranberry Juice
- 1 part Raspberry Iced Tea
- 1 part Lemonade

Build over ice and stir.

Virgin Islands Rum Punch
HIGHBALL GLASS
- 2 parts Rum
- dash Bitters
- dash Sugar
- ½ part Grenadine
- 1 part Orange Juice
- 1 part Grapefruit Juice

Shake with ice and strain over ice.

Waikiki Hawaiian
HURRICANE GLASS
- 1½ parts Light Rum
- 1½ parts Dark Rum
- 1 part Blue Curaçao
- 1 part Pineapple Juice
- 1 part Orange Juice

Shake with ice and pour.

Waikiki Tiki
HIGHBALL GLASS
- 1½ parts Light Rum
- 1 part Orange Juice
- 1 part Pineapple Juice

Shake with ice and pour.

Walking Zombie
COLLINS GLASS
- ½ part Amaretto
- 2 parts Pineapple Juice
- 2 parts Lime Juice
- 2 parts Guava Juice
- 2 parts Orange Juice
- 1 part Grenadine

Shake with ice and pour.

White Sandy Beach
HURRICANE GLASS
- 1 part Coconut Rum
- 1 part Amaretto
- 1 part Hpnotiq
- 3 parts Pineapple Juice
- fill with Sweet & Sour Mix

Build over ice.

Wiki Waki
HURRICANE GLASS
- 1 part Light Rum
- 1 part Amaretto
- ½ part Silver Tequila
- ½ part Vodka
- ½ part Triple Sec
- 1 part Pineapple Juice
- 1 part Orange Juice

Shake with ice and pour.

Wiki Waki Woo
HURRICANE GLASS
- ½ part Vodka
- ½ part Rum
- ½ part 151-Proof Rum
- ½ part Tequila
- ½ part Triple Sec
- 1 part Amaretto
- 1 part Orange Juice
- 1 part Pineapple Juice
- 1 part Cranberry Juice Cocktail

Shake with ice and pour.

Wild Thang

HURRICANE GLASS

½ part Gin
½ part Light Rum
½ part Dark Rum
½ part Triple Sec
½ part Maraschino Liqueur
½ part Papaya Juice
1 part Pineapple Juice
1 part Orange Juice
splash 151-Proof Rum

Build over ice and stir.

Winter Tropic

HURRICANE GLASS

2 parts Vodka
1 part Cranberry Juice Cocktail
1 part Strawberry Daiquiri Mix

Build over ice and stir.

Yellow Parakeet

HURRICANE GLASS

1 part Midori®
½ part Banana Liqueur
½ part Light Rum
2 parts Orange Juice
1 part Pineapple Juice
splash Sweet & Sour Mix

Build over ice and stir.

Yo Ho

COLLINS GLASS

1 part Vodka
1½ parts Amaretto
1½ parts Grapefruit Juice
splash Amaretto
1 Banana

Combine all ingredients in a blender with ice. Blend until smooth.

You Jelly?

HURRICANE GLASS

1 part Banana Liqueur
1 part Coconut Rum
1 part Dark Spiced Rum
1 part Melon Liqueur
½ part Lime Juice
½ part Simple Syrup
fill with Pineapple Juice

Shake with ice and strain over ice.

Zombie

COLLINS GLASS

1 part Light Rum
½ part Amaretto
½ part Triple Sec
1 part Sweet & Sour Mix
1 part Orange Juice
splash 151-Proof Rum

Shake with ice and pour. Top with 151-Proof rum.

Zombies in the Night

HIGHBALL GLASS

1 part Vodka
1 part Apricot Brandy
1 part Wild Berry Schnapps
1 part Orange Juice
1 part Pineapple Juice

Shake with ice and pour.

A Zubb Hurricane

HURRICANE GLASS

1 part Dark Rum
1 part Light Rum
1 part Triple Sec
1 part Pineapple Juice
1 part Grenadine

Build over ice and stir.

BLENDED & FROZEN DRINKS

Where would we be without the electric blender? From a frozen Margarita to a Cherry Repair Kit, the drinks below pay tribute to the awesome power of those little metal blades. As a general rule, drinks containing ice cream don't need additional ice. However, if a drink seems too watery or thin after blending, add ice or more ice cream to thicken it.

151 Florida Bushwacker

BEER MUG

½ part 151-Proof Rum
½ part Coconut Rum
½ part Light Rum
1 part Crème de Cacao (Dark)
1 part Cointreau®
1 part Crème de Coconut
3 parts Milk
1 scoop Vanilla Ice Cream

Combine all ingredients in a blender. Blend until smooth. Garnish with Chocolate Shavings.

155 Belmont

WHITE WINE GLASS

1 part Dark Rum
2 parts Light Rum
1 part Vodka
1 part Orange Juice

Combine all ingredients in a blender. Blend until smooth.

3rd Street Promenade

HURRICANE GLASS

1½ parts Vanilla Vodka
1 part Gin
1 part Tequila
1 part Triple Sec
½ part Goldschläger®
6 parts Orange Juice

Combine all ingredients in a blender with ice and blend until smooth.

98 Beatle

COLLINS GLASS

1 part Vodka
1 part Peach Schnapps
1 part Grenadine
2 parts Cranberry Juice Cocktail
1 Banana

Combine all ingredients in a blender with ice and blend until smooth.

Abbot's Dream

COUPETTE GLASS

2 parts Irish Cream Liqueur
1 part Frangelico®
½ Banana
½ part Cream

Combine all ingredients in a blender with ice and blend until smooth.

Absinthe Frappé

COUPETTE GLASS

1½ parts Absinthe
1 Egg White
dash Sugar

Combine all ingredients in a blender with ice and blend until smooth.

African Lullaby

COUPETTE GLASS

1½ parts Amarula® Crème Liqueur
½ part Cream of Coconut
3 parts Milk
dash Ground Nutmeg

Combine all ingredients in a blender with ice and blend until smooth.

After Sunset

COLLINS GLASS

1 part Coffee Liqueur
½ part Triple Sec
2 scoops Vanilla Ice Cream
1 scoop Chocolate Syrup
3 parts Cola
2 parts Cream

Combine all ingredients in a blender and blend until smooth.

Afternoon Balloon

COUPETTE GLASS

1½ parts Light Rum
1 part Crème de Banane
1 part Blackberry Liqueur
splash Cream of Coconut
splash Lime Juice
4 parts Pineapple Juice

Combine all ingredients in a blender with ice and blend until smooth.

Agent Orange

HURRICANE GLASS

1 part Vodka
1 part Gin
1 part Yukon Jack®
1 part Sour Apple Schnapps
1 part Melon Liqueur
2 parts Grenadine
6 parts Orange Juice

Combine all ingredients in a blender with ice and blend until smooth.

Alaskan Monk

COUPETTE GLASS

1 part Frangelico®
1 part Irish Cream Liqueur
1 part Coffee Liqueur
1 part Vodka
1 part White Chocolate Liqueur
splash Half and Half

Combine all ingredients in a blender with ice and blend until smooth.

Alaskan Suntan

COUPETTE GLASS

1 part Gin
1 part Rum
1 part Vodka
3 parts Orange Juice
3 parts Pineapple Juice

Combine all ingredients in a blender with ice and blend until smooth.

Albino Baby Snowpiglet

COUPETTE GLASS

1 part Vodka
1 part Butterscotch Schnapps
1 part Crème de Menthe (White)
2 parts Cream

Combine all ingredients in a blender with ice and blend until smooth.

Albuquerque Real

COUPETTE GLASS

1½ parts Tequila
½ part Triple Sec
½ part Sweet & Sour Mix
¼ part Cranberry Juice Cocktail
splash Grand Marnier®

Combine all ingredients in a blender with ice and blend until smooth.

Alien Abduction

COUPETTE GLASS

2 parts Cointreau®
1 part Melon Liqueur
1 part Peach Schnapps

Combine all ingredients in a blender with ice and blend until smooth.

Almond Joey

COUPETTE GLASS

1½ parts Amaretto
1 part Cream of Coconut
1 part Chocolate Syrup
2 scoops Vanilla Ice Cream

Combine all ingredients in a blender. Blend until smooth.

Almond Velvet Hammer

COUPETTE GLASS

2 parts Coffee Liqueur
½ part Chocolate Syrup
2 dashes Chopped Almonds
2 scoops Ice Cream
fill with Cream

Combine all ingredients in a blender. Blend until smooth.

Al's Frozen Amaretto Mudslide

COUPETTE GLASS

2 parts Irish Cream Liqueur
1 part Amaretto
2 parts Coffee Liqueur
2 scoops Ice Cream

Combine all ingredients in a blender and blend until smooth.

Amaretto Big Red Float

COLLINS GLASS

2 parts Amaretto
fill with Strawberry Soda
2 scoops Ice Cream
splash Strawberry Syrup

Combine all but Ice Cream in a pint glass. Top with Ice Cream followed by Strawberry Syrup.

Amaretto Chi Chi

COLLINS GLASS

1 part Vodka
1 part Amaretto
½ part Orange Juice
2 parts Pineapple Juice
2 parts Cream of Coconut

Combine all ingredients in a blender with ice and blend until smooth.

Amaretto Choco-Cream

COUPETTE GLASS

1 part Amaretto
1 part Crème de Cacao (Dark)
1 part Chocolate Syrup
2 scoops Ice Cream

Combine all ingredients in a blender and blend until smooth.

Amaretto Colada

HURRICANE GLASS

1 part Amaretto
½ part Rum
2 parts Pineapple Juice
2 parts Cream of Coconut
1 part Orange Juice

Combine all ingredients in a blender with ice and blend until smooth.

Amaretto Cruise

COUPETTE GLASS

½ part Amaretto
½ part Peach Schnapps
½ part Light Rum
2 parts Orange Juice
2 parts Cranberry Juice Cocktail
1 part Sweet & Sour Mix
1 part Half and Half

Combine all ingredients in a blender with ice and blend until smooth.

Amaretto Cruise #2

COUPETTE GLASS

½ part Amaretto
½ part Banana Schnapps
½ part Light Rum
2 parts Orange Juice
2 parts Cherry Juice
1 part Sweet & Sour Mix
1 part Half and Half

Combine all ingredients in a blender with ice and blend until smooth.

Amaretto Dreamsicle®

HURRICANE GLASS

1 part Cream
1 part Vodka
1 part Amaretto
1 part Orange Juice
1 part Pineapple Juice

Combine all ingredients in a blender with ice and blend until smooth.

Amaretto Freeze

MARGARITA GLASS

2 parts Amaretto
2 scoops Vanilla Ice Cream

Combine in a blender and blend until smooth. Garnish with a Maraschino Cherry.

Amaretto Hurricane

HURRICANE GLASS

1 part Rum
1 part Amaretto
1 part Cherry Juice
2 parts Orange Juice
1 part Pineapple Juice

Combine all ingredients in a blender with ice and blend until smooth.

Amaretto Mud Pie

COUPETTE GLASS

1 part Amaretto
1 part Crème de Cacao (Dark)
fill with Cream
1 Candy Bar
2 scoops Ice Cream

Combine all ingredients in a blender. Blend until smooth. Works with almost any Candy Bar.

Amaretto Mudslide

COUPETTE GLASS

1 part Amaretto
1 part Crème de Cacao (Dark)
fill with Cream
4 Oreo® Cookies
2 scoops Ice Cream

Combine all ingredients in a blender. Blend until smooth.

Ambrosia Pudding

COLLINS GLASS

1 part Vanilla Liqueur
2 parts Crème de Banane
2 parts Milk
fill with Yogurt

Combine all ingredients in a blender. Blend until smooth.

American Leroy

HIGHBALL GLASS

1 part Coffee Liqueur
1 part Vodka
1 part Irish Cream Liqueur
1 part Crème de Cacao (White)

Combine all ingredients in a blender with ice and blend until smooth.

Amore

COUPETTE GLASS

1 part Amaretto
1 part Coffee Liqueur
1 part Cream

Combine all ingredients in a blender with ice and blend until smooth.

Amsterdam Iced Coffee

COLLINS GLASS

2/3 part Crème de Cacao (Dark)
2/3 part Frangelico®
2/3 part Dark Rum
2 parts Coffee
splash Cream

Combine all ingredients in a blender with ice and blend until smooth.

Andrea's Colada Collision

HURRICANE GLASS

1 1/2 parts Light Rum
3 parts Cream of Coconut
6 parts Pineapple Juice
1 Banana

Combine all ingredients in a blender with ice and blend until smooth.

Angel in Harlem

COUPETTE GLASS

1 1/2 parts Vodka
1 part Peach Schnapps
splash Cranberry Juice Cocktail
3 parts Lemonade

Combine all ingredients in a blender with ice and blend until smooth.

Angel's Hug

HURRICANE GLASS

2 parts Pisang Ambon® Liqueur
1 part Crème de Banane
1 part Dark Rum
2 parts Passion Fruit Juice
1 Banana

Combine all ingredients in a blender with ice and blend until smooth.

Anthracite

COUPETTE GLASS

1 part Coffee Liqueur
1 part Vodka
1 scoop Coffee Ice Cream

Combine all ingredients in a blender and blend until smooth.

Any Given Sunday

COLLINS GLASS

1 part Peach Schnapps
1 part Orange Juice
1 part Grape Juice (Red)

Combine all ingredients in a blender with ice and blend until smooth.

Aphrodisiac Dessert

HURRICANE GLASS

2 parts Light Rum
1 part Crème de Cacao (White)
2 scoops Ice Cream
1 Banana

Combine all ingredients in a blender and blend until smooth.

Apple Colada

COLLINS GLASS

1 part Sour Apple Schnapps
1 part Peach Schnapps
1 part Cream of Coconut
1 part Half and Half

Combine all ingredients in a blender with ice and blend until smooth.

Apple Creamsicle®

WHITE WINE GLASS

1 part Cherry Brandy
1 part Cream
1/2 part Pineapple Juice
1/2 part Apple Juice

Combine all ingredients in a blender with ice and blend until smooth.

Apple Daiquiri Sour

COLLINS GLASS

1 1/2 parts Rum
1 1/2 parts Sour Apple Schnapps
1 part Lime Juice
dash Sugar
splash Triple Sec

Combine all ingredients in a blender with ice and blend until smooth.

Apple Granny Crisp

COUPETTE GLASS

1 part Sour Apple Schnapps
1/2 part Brandy
1/2 part Irish Cream Liqueur
2 scoops Vanilla Ice Cream
1 Graham Cracker

Combine all ingredients in a blender. Blend until smooth.

Apple Pie à la Mode

COUPETTE GLASS

3/4 part Spiced Rum
1/2 part Sour Apple Schnapps
2 parts Apple Juice
1 part Cream of Coconut
1 part Heavy Cream
dash Cinnamon Powder

Combine all ingredients in a blender with ice and blend until smooth.

Apple Sauce

HURRICANE GLASS

1 part Spiced Rum
3 parts Apple Sauce
4 parts Sweet & Sour Mix
splash Triple Sec

Combine all ingredients in a blender with ice and blend until smooth.

Apple Slush Puppy

COUPETTE GLASS

2 parts Sour Apple Schnapps
fill with Lemonade

Combine all ingredients in a blender with ice and blend until smooth.

Apricot Freeze

COUPETTE GLASS

2 parts Apricot Brandy
2 scoops Ice Cream

Combine all ingredients in a blender. Blend until smooth.

A-Rang-a-Tang

COUPETTE GLASS

1 part 99-Proof Banana Liqueur
1 part Coconut Rum
1 part Light Rum
3 parts Orange Juice
2 parts Pineapple Juice
3 splashes Tang®
3 dashes Powdered Sugar

Combine all ingredients in a blender with ice and blend until smooth.

Archduchess

COUPETTE GLASS

1 1/2 parts Brandy
1/2 part Raspberry Liqueur
1 scoop Vanilla Ice Cream

Combine all ingredients in a blender. Blend until smooth.

Arctic Mouthwash

COLLINS GLASS

1 part Tropical Punch Schnapps
1 part Mountain Dew®

Combine all ingredients in a blender with ice and blend until smooth.

Arctic Mudslide

COUPETTE GLASS

1 part Coffee Liqueur
1 part Irish Cream Liqueur
1 part Vodka
1 part Crème de Menthe (White)
2 scoops Ice Cream

Combine all ingredients in a blender and blend until smooth. Top with Whipped Cream.

Atlantic Dolphin Shit

COUPETTE GLASS

1 part Rum
1 part Crème de Cacao (White)
1 part Coffee Liqueur
1 part Cream
2 Oreo® Cookies
2 parts Milk

Combine all ingredients in a blender with ice and blend until smooth.

Atomic Smoothie

COUPETTE GLASS

2 parts Vodka
1/2 part Peach Schnapps
2 scoops Ice Cream
1 part Lemon Juice
6 parts Orange Juice

Combine all ingredients in a blender and blend until smooth.

Aurora

COLLINS GLASS

3 parts Vodka
3 scoops Rainbow Sherbert
1 part Orange Juice
2 parts Cranberry Juice Cocktail

Combine all ingredients in a blender and blend until smooth.

Avalanche

COLLINS GLASS

1 1/2 parts Crème de Banane
3/4 part Crème de Cacao (White)
1/2 part Amaretto
2 parts Cream
1/2 Banana

Combine all ingredients in a blender with ice and blend until smooth.

Azure Sky and Sea

HURRICANE GLASS

2 parts Light Rum
1 part Blue Curaçao
4 parts Pineapple Juice
2 parts Cream of Coconut

Combine all ingredients in a blender with ice and blend until smooth.

B3

COLLINS GLASS

1 part Blue Curaçao
1/2 part Crème de Banane
1/2 part Lime Cordial
1 part Passion Fruit Juice
2 parts Pineapple Juice
2 parts Orange Juice

Combine all ingredients in a blender with ice and blend until smooth.

Baby Eskimo

COUPETTE GLASS

2 parts Coffee Liqueur
fill with Milk
2 scoops Vanilla Ice Cream

Combine all ingredients in a blender. Blend until smooth.

Baby Jane

COUPETTE GLASS

1 part Vodka
1 part Butterscotch Schnapps
1 part Irish Cream Liqueur
1 part Grenadine
2 scoops Ice Cream

Combine all ingredients in a blender and blend until smooth.

Bahama Breeze

COLLINS GLASS

1 part Dark Rum
½ part Coconut Rum
½ part Apricot Brandy
½ part Banana Liqueur
¼ part Grenadine
¼ part Honey
½ part Lemon Juice
1 part Orange Juice
1 part Pineapple Juice

Combine all ingredients in a blender with ice and blend until smooth.

Baileys® Banana Colada

COUPETTE GLASS

2 parts Irish Cream Liqueur
1 part Dark Rum
1 part Banana Liqueur
4 parts Piña Colada Mix
1 Banana

Combine all ingredients in a blender with ice and blend until smooth.

Baileys® Blizzard

COUPETTE GLASS

1 part Irish Cream Liqueur
1 part Peppermint Schnapps
½ part Brandy
1 scoop Vanilla Ice Cream

Combine all ingredients in a blender. Blend until smooth.

Baileys® Mud Pie

COUPETTE GLASS

1 part Irish Cream Liqueur
1 part Crème de Cacao (Dark)
fill with Cream
1 Candy Bar
2 scoops Ice Cream

Combine all ingredients in a blender. Blend until smooth. Works with almost any candy bar.

Baileys® Mudslide

COUPETTE GLASS

1 part Irish Cream Liqueur
1 part Crème de Cacao (Dark)
fill with Cream
2 Oreo® Cookies
2 scoops Ice Cream

Combine all ingredients in a blender. Blend until smooth.

Baleares under Snow

COUPETTE GLASS

⅔ part Grenadine
2 parts Light Rum
1½ parts Strawberry Puree
2 parts Cream

Combine all ingredients in a blender with ice and blend until smooth.

Banana Bender

COLLINS GLASS

1 part Coffee Liqueur
1 part Crème de Banane
1 part Irish Cream Liqueur
1 part Banana Puree
2 parts Cream

Combine all ingredients in a blender with ice and blend until smooth.

Banana Blizzard

HURRICANE GLASS

1 part Coconut Rum
1 part Pineapple Rum
3 parts Milk
1 Banana

Combine all ingredients in a blender with ice and blend until smooth. Garnish with a Maraschino Cherry.

Banana Brilliance

HURRICANE GLASS

1 part Crème de Banane
1 part Vanilla Liqueur
1 part Banana Puree
1/4 part Caramel Syrup

Combine all ingredients in a blender with ice and blend until smooth.

Banana Daiquiri

HURRICANE GLASS

2 parts White Rum
1 part Lime Juice
splash Simple Syrup
1/2 Banana

Combine all ingredients in a blender with ice and blend until smooth.

Banana di Amore

RED WINE GLASS

1 part Amaretto
1 part Crème de Banane
2 parts Orange Juice
1 part Sweet & Sour Mix

Combine all ingredients in a blender with ice and blend until smooth.

Banana Dream

COUPETTE GLASS

1 part Vodka
1 part Banana Liqueur
3 parts Orange Juice
1 part Cream

Combine all ingredients in a blender with ice and blend until smooth.

Banana Dreamsicle®

HIGHBALL GLASS

1 part Vodka
1 part Banana Liqueur
1 part Cherry Juice
1 part Orange Juice
1 part Pineapple Juice
1 part Cream

Combine all ingredients in a blender with ice and blend until smooth.

Banana Flip

COUPETTE GLASS

2 parts Banana Liqueur
1 part Cream
2 parts Orange Juice
splash Cherry Liqueur
splash Sour Apple Schnapps
1 scoop Ice Cream

Combine all ingredients in a blender and blend until smooth. Top with Whipped Cream.

Banana Foster

HIGHBALL GLASS

2 scoops Vanilla Ice Cream
1 1/2 parts Spiced Rum
1/2 part Banana Liqueur
1 Banana

Combine all ingredients in a blender and blend until smooth.

Banana Hurricane

HIGHBALL GLASS

1 part Rum
1 part Banana Liqueur
2 parts Orange Juice
1 part Pineapple Juice

Combine all ingredients in a blender with ice and blend until smooth.

Banana Ivanov

HURRICANE GLASS

1½ parts Dry Vermouth
1 part Lime Cordial
½ part Banana Juice
½ Banana

Combine all ingredients in a blender with ice and blend until smooth.

Banana Mama Bumpin

ROCKS GLASS

2 parts Rum
1 scoop Vanilla Ice Cream
1 part Banana Puree
½ part Crème de Coconut
½ part Banana Syrup

Combine all ingredients in a blender and blend until smooth.

Banana Man

HIGHBALL GLASS

2 parts Coconut Rum
2 parts Banana Juice
fill with Lemonade
splash Orange Juice

Combine all ingredients in a blender with ice and blend until smooth.

Banana Margarita

COUPETTE GLASS

1½ parts Silver Tequila
1 part Lime Juice
½ part Crème de Banane

Combine all ingredients in a blender with ice and blend until smooth.

Banana Nutbread

WHITE WINE GLASS

1 scoop Vanilla Ice Cream
1 part Crème de Banane
1 part Frangelico®

Combine all ingredients in a blender. Blend until smooth.

Banana Queen

COLLINS GLASS

2 parts Dark Rum
1½ parts Cream of Coconut
1 part Banana Puree
1 part Cream
2 parts Pineapple Juice

Combine all ingredients in a blender with ice and blend until smooth.

Banana Republic

COUPE

2 parts Spiced Rum
1 part Mango Rum
1 part Ginger Liqueur
2 parts Pineapple Juice
1 Banana

Combine all ingredients in a blender with ice and blend until smooth.

Banana Split

HURRICANE GLASS

2 parts Irish Cream Liqueur
1 part Banana Liqueur
2 parts Coffee Liqueur
fill with Cream

Combine all ingredients in a blender with ice and blend until smooth.

Banana Tree

COLLINS GLASS

1 part Banana Liqueur
1/2 part Crème de Cacao (White)
1/2 part Galliano®
1 scoop Vanilla Ice Cream
1/2 Banana
splash Vanilla Extract

Combine all ingredients in a blender and blend until smooth.

Banana's Milk

COUPETTE GLASS

1 part Vodka
1 1/2 parts Banana Puree
3 parts Milk

Combine all ingredients in a blender with ice and blend until smooth.

Banoffie Dream

COLLINS GLASS

1 part Crème de Banane
1 part Irish Cream Liqueur
1 part Cream
2 parts Milk

Combine all ingredients in a blender with ice and blend until smooth.

Banshee

COUPETTE GLASS

3/4 part Banana Liqueur
3/4 part Crème de Cacao (White)
1/2 part Amaretto
3/4 part Half and Half

Combine all ingredients in a blender with ice and blend until smooth.

Barnaby's Buffalo Blizzard

COUPETTE GLASS

3/4 part Vodka
1 part Crème de Cacao (White)
1 part Galliano®
1 scoop Vanilla Ice Cream
splash Grenadine

Combine all ingredients in a blender. Blend until smooth.

Barnamint Baileys®

COLLINS GLASS

1 part Crème de Menthe (White)
1 part Irish Cream Liqueur
3 scoops Ice Cream
2 Oreo® Cookies
2 parts Milk

Combine all ingredients in a blender. Blend until smooth.

Barney® Fizz

COLLINS GLASS

1 part Raspberry Liqueur
1 part Amaretto
1/2 part Vodka
3 parts Grape Juice (Red)
1 Egg White
1 part Sugar

Combine all ingredients in a blender with ice and blend until smooth.

Barranquillero

HURRICANE GLASS

2 parts Light Rum
1/2 part Crème de Coconut
2 parts Cream
1 part Melon Liqueur

Combine all ingredients in a blender with ice and blend until smooth.

Batida Abaci

WHITE WINE GLASS

1 part Cachaça®
2 parts Pineapple Juice
dash Sugar

Combine all ingredients in a blender with ice and blend until smooth.

Batida de Piña

ROCKS GLASS

3 parts Rum
6 parts Pineapple Juice
1/2 tbsp powdered sugar

Combine all ingredients in a blender with ice and blend until smooth.

Batida Mango

WHITE WINE GLASS

1 part Cachaça®
2 parts Mango Juice
2 dashes Sugar

Combine all ingredients in a blender with ice and blend until smooth.

Bay City Bomber

PARFAIT GLASS

1/2 part Vodka
1/2 part Rum
1/2 part Tequila
1/2 part Gin
1/2 part Triple Sec
1 part Orange Juice
1 part Pineapple Juice
1 part Cranberry Juice Cocktail
1 part Sweet & Sour Mix
splash 151-Proof Rum

Combine all ingredients in a blender with ice and blend until smooth.

Beaconizer

COUPETTE GLASS

1 part Irish Cream Liqueur
1 part Crème de Cacao (Dark)
2 scoops Ice Cream
splash Cream

Combine all ingredients in a blender. Blend until smooth.

Belly-Button Fluff

COUPETTE GLASS

1 part Light Rum
1 1/2 parts Crème de Coconut
3 parts Pineapple Juice
1/2 Banana

Combine all ingredients in a blender with ice and blend until smooth.

Berries 'n' Cream

HURRICANE GLASS

1/2 part Spiced Rum
3/4 part Wild Berry Schnapps
3 parts Strawberry Daiquiri Mix
5 Raspberries
2 parts Heavy Cream

Combine all ingredients in a blender with ice and blend until smooth.

Betty Swallocks

HURRICANE GLASS

1 1/2 parts Butterscotch Schnapps
1 1/2 parts Coffee Liqueur
1 part Brandy
fill with Milk

Combine all ingredients in a blender with ice and blend until smooth.

Big Blue Sky

COUPETTE GLASS

1/2 part Light Rum
1/2 part Blue Curaçao
1/2 part Cream of Coconut
2 parts Pineapple Juice

Combine all ingredients in a blender with ice and blend until smooth.

Big Booty Shake

BEER MUG

1 1/2 parts Southern Comfort®
8 parts Milk
splash Vanilla Extract
2 scoops Chocolate Ice Cream

Combine all ingredients in a blender. Blend until smooth.

Big Chill

PILSNER GLASS

1 1/2 parts Dark Rum
1 part Pineapple Juice
1 part Orange Juice
1 part Cranberry Juice Cocktail
1 part Cream of Coconut

Combine all ingredients in a blender with ice and blend until smooth.

Big John's Special

COUPETTE GLASS

1 part Vodka
1/2 part Gin
3 parts Grapefruit Juice
3 dashes Orange Bitters
3 dashes Maraschino Cherry Juice

Combine all ingredients in a blender with ice and blend until smooth.

Bikini Bottom

HURRICANE GLASS

2 parts Mango Rum
2 parts Pineapple Rum
2 parts Orange Juice
4 parts Papaya Juice

Combine all ingredients in a blender with ice. Blend until smooth.

Bitch Monkey Lost Its Lunch

COUPETTE GLASS

3 parts Crème de Cacao (White)
2 parts Peppermint Schnapps
1 Banana

Combine all ingredients in a blender with ice and blend until smooth.

Black Bear in the Wood

COUPETTE GLASS

1 part Amaretto
1/2 part Crème de Cacao (White)
1/2 part Crème de Cacao (Dark)
splash Vanilla Extract
splash Chocolate Syrup
1 scoop Vanilla Ice Cream

Combine all ingredients in a blender. Blend until smooth.

Black Cherry Margarita

COUPETTE GLASS

1/2 part Tequila Reposado
1/2 part Triple Sec
3/4 part Cherry Liqueur
2 parts Orange Juice
2 parts Sweet & Sour Mix

Combine all ingredients in a blender with ice and blend until smooth.

Black Forest

COUPETTE GLASS

1 part Vodka
1 part Coffee Liqueur
1 part Blackberry Liqueur
1 scoop Chocolate Ice Cream

Combine all ingredients in a blender. Blend until smooth.

Blaster Bates

COLLINS GLASS

1 Banana
5 Blueberries
5 Raspberries
1 part Milk
2 parts Orange Juice
2 parts Mango Rum

Combine all ingredients in a blender with ice and blend until smooth.

Blended Comfort

COLLINS GLASS

1 part Southern Comfort®
½ part Dry Vermouth
1 part Orange Juice
1 part Lemon Juice
splash Peach Schnapps

Combine all ingredients in a blender with ice and blend until smooth.

Blended Georgia Peach

HURRICANE GLASS

¾ part Vodka
¾ part Peach Schnapps
3 parts Orange Juice
2 parts Peach Puree

Combine all ingredients in a blender with ice and blend until smooth.

Blended Puppy Guts

COLLINS GLASS

2 parts Strawberry Puree
2 parts Lemon-Lime Soda
1 part Strawberry Liqueur
1 Strawberry

Combine all ingredients in a blender with ice and blend until smooth.

Blizzard

HIGHBALL GLASS

1 part Gin
1 scoop Vanilla Ice Cream
¼ part Dry Sherry

Combine all ingredients in a blender. Blend until smooth.

Blue Cloud

COUPE

2 parts Amaretto
1 part Blue Curaçao
1 scoop Vanilla Ice Cream

Combine all ingredients in a blender and blend until smooth.

Blue Hurricane

COUPETTE GLASS

½ part Blue Curaçao
½ part Light Rum
4 parts Pineapple Juice
2 parts Blueberries

Combine all ingredients in a blender with ice and blend until smooth.

Blue Max

HURRICANE GLASS

1 part Vodka
1 part Blue Curaçao
½ part Cream of Coconut
3 parts Pineapple Juice
2 parts Cream

Combine all ingredients in a blender with ice and blend until smooth.

Blue Night Shadow

HURRICANE GLASS

1 part Blue Curaçao
1 part Crème de Cacao (White)
1½ parts Cream
1 part Cream of Coconut
fill with Pineapple Juice

Combine all ingredients in a blender with ice and blend until smooth.

Blue Popsicle®

COUPETTE GLASS

1 part Blue Curaçao
1½ parts Sweet & Sour Mix
1 part Triple Sec
1½ parts Blueberry Schnapps

Combine all ingredients in a blender with ice and blend until smooth.

Blue Velvet

PARFAIT GLASS

1 part Blackberry Liqueur
1 part Melon Liqueur
1 scoop Vanilla Ice Cream
splash Blue Curaçao

Combine all ingredients in a blender and blend until smooth.

Blue Whale

COUPETTE GLASS

1 part Vodka
1 part Blue Curaçao
2 parts Sweet & Sour Mix

Combine all ingredients in a blender with ice and blend until smooth.

Blueberry Tango

COLLINS GLASS

1 part Peach Schnapps
1 part Blue Curaçao
fill with Blueberries
2 parts Grapefruit Juice
½ part Lemon Juice

Combine all ingredients in a blender with ice and blend until smooth.

Blushin' Russian

PARFAIT GLASS

1 part Coffee Liqueur
1 part Vodka
1 scoop Vanilla Ice Cream
4 Strawberries

Combine all ingredients in a blender. Blend until smooth.

Bonsai Berries

COUPETTE GLASS

½ part Strawberry Liqueur
½ part Amaretto
½ part Blackberry Liqueur
2 scoops Vanilla Ice Cream
1 part Cream
1 part Blueberries
2 parts Strawberry Puree

Combine all ingredients in a blender and blend until smooth.

Booty Drink

COLLINS GLASS

2 parts Coconut Rum
1 part Grenadine
2 parts Orange Juice
2 parts Pineapple Juice
½ Banana

Combine all ingredients in a blender with ice and blend until smooth.

Border Thrill

COUPETTE GLASS

1 part Southern Comfort®
½ part Tequila
¼ part Triple Sec
1 part Sweet & Sour Mix
fill with Orange Juice
splash Grenadine

Combine all ingredients in a blender with ice and blend until smooth.

Bosco 42DD

HIGHBALL GLASS

2 parts Crème de Cacao (Dark)
2 parts Coffee Liqueur
½ part Brandy
½ part Gin
2 scoops Chocolate Ice Cream

Combine all ingredients in a blender. Blend until smooth.

Boston Freeze

WHITE WINE GLASS

1¼ parts Dark Rum
3 parts Cranberry Juice Cocktail
1 part Cream of Coconut

Combine all ingredients in a blender with ice and blend until smooth.

Bourbon Dessert

COUPETTE GLASS

1½ parts Jim Beam®
⅔ part Strawberry Liqueur
½ part Hazelnut Liqueur
2 parts Cream

Combine all ingredients in a blender with ice and blend until smooth.

Bourbon Rouge

COUPETTE GLASS

1 part Peach Schnapps
1 part Jim Beam®
1 part Espresso
1 scoop Vanilla Ice Cream

Combine all ingredients in a blender. Blend until smooth.

Brain Freeze

COUPE

3 parts Coffee Liqueur
2 parts Vodka
2 scoops Rocky Road Ice Cream

Combine all ingredients in a blender and blend until smooth.

Brass Fiddle

PARFAIT GLASS

2 parts Peach Schnapps
¾ part Jack Daniel's®
2 parts Pineapple Juice
1 part Orange Juice
1 part Grenadine

Combine all ingredients in a blender with ice and blend until smooth.

Brazilian Monk

WHITE WINE GLASS

1 part Crème de Cacao (Dark)
1 part Coffee
1 part Frangelico®
2 scoops Vanilla Ice Cream

Combine all ingredients in a blender. Blend until smooth.

Brown Cow

CHAMPAGNE FLUTE

1 part Light Rum
½ part Crème de Cacao (White)
¼ part Crème de Menthe (White)
1 scoop Chocolate Ice Cream

Combine all ingredients in a blender. Blend until smooth.

Brown Squirrel

WHITE WINE GLASS

1 part Amaretto
1 part Crème de Cacao (Dark)
1 scoop Vanilla Ice Cream

Combine all ingredients in a blender. Blend until smooth.

Bunky Punch

PARFAIT GLASS

1½ parts Vodka
1 part Melon Liqueur
1 part Peach Schnapps
1½ parts Cranberry Juice Cocktail
2 parts Orange Juice
½ part Grape Juice (Red)

Combine all ingredients in a blender with ice and blend until smooth.

Burnt Almond

WHITE WINE GLASS

1 part Amaretto
1 part Coffee Liqueur
2 scoops Vanilla Ice Cream

Combine all ingredients in a blender. Blend until smooth.

Bushwacker

COLLINS GLASS

1 part Chocolate Liqueur
1 part Coconut Rum
1 part Coffee Liqueur
1 part White Rum
1 part Cream
1 part Cream of Coconut

Combine all ingredients in a blender with ice and blend until smooth.

Cabana Club

HURRICANE GLASS

1 part Rum
½ part Cream of Coconut
1 part Pineapple Juice
1 part Cranberry Juice Cocktail
splash Grenadine

Combine all ingredients in a blender with ice and blend until smooth.

Cactus

COUPETTE GLASS

1½ parts Vodka
1 part Melon Liqueur
1 part Cream of Coconut
fill with Pineapple Juice

Combine all ingredients in a blender with ice and blend until smooth.

Cactus Colada

COLLINS GLASS

1½ parts Silver Tequila
⅔ part Melon Liqueur
½ part Grenadine
2 parts Cream of Coconut
1 part Orange Juice
1 part Pineapple Juice

Combine all ingredients in a blender with ice and blend until smooth.

Cactus Love

COUPETTE GLASS

1 part Crème de Banane
1 part Jim Beam®
splash Triple Sec
splash Lemon Juice
2 parts Pineapple Juice

Combine all ingredients in a blender with ice and blend until smooth.

Cactus Salon

COUPE

2 parts Dark Spiced Rum
1 part Amaretto
1 part Light Rum
8 parts Pineapple Juice
4 parts Lime Juice

Combine all ingredients in a blender with ice and blend until smooth.

Cadillac®

HURRICANE GLASS

1½ parts Silver Tequila
½ part Triple Sec
3 parts Sweet & Sour Mix

Combine all ingredients in a blender with ice and blend until smooth.

California Time

HURRICANE GLASS

1 part Coconut Rum
½ part Amaretto
½ part Blue Curaçao
½ part Light Rum
½ part Southern Comfort
8 parts Pineapple Juice

Combine all ingredients in a blender with ice and blend until smooth.

Calm Voyage

CHAMPAGNE FLUTE

½ part Light Rum
½ part Strega®
splash Passion Fruit Nectar
2 splashes Lemon Juice
1 Egg White

Combine all ingredients in a blender with ice and blend until smooth.

Calypso Kick

COUPE

2 parts Dark Rum
2 parts Sweet & Sour Mix
½ part Cream
½ Banana

Combine all ingredients in a blender with ice and blend until smooth.

Camino Real

COUPETTE GLASS

1½ parts Tequila
½ part Banana Liqueur
1 part Orange Juice
splash Lime Juice
splash Cream of Coconut

Combine all ingredients in a blender with ice and blend until smooth.

Cancun All Inclusive

HURRICANE GLASS

½ part Gin
½ part Melon Liqueur
½ part Rum
½ part Tequila
½ part Vodka
4 parts Pineapple Juice
1 Banana

Combine all ingredients in a blender with ice and blend until smooth.

Candy Store

COUPETTE GLASS

2 parts Raspberry Liqueur
2 parts Amaretto
1 part Crème de Noyaux
2 scoops Cookies and Cream Ice Cream

Combine all ingredients in a blender. Blend until smooth.

Canyon Quake

COUPETTE GLASS

1 part Irish Cream Liqueur
1 part Brandy
1 part Amaretto
2 parts Light Cream

Combine all ingredients in a blender with ice and blend until smooth.

Caribbean Threesome

HURRICANE GLASS

½ part Citrus Rum
½ part Coconut Rum
1 part Spiced Rum
fill with Pineapple Juice
1 Banana
3 Strawberries

Combine all ingredients in a blender with ice and blend until smooth.

Carol Ann

HURRICANE GLASS

1 part Vodka
1 part Amaretto
fill with Skim Milk

Combine all ingredients in a blender with ice and blend until smooth.

The Catalina Margarita

MARGARITA GLASS

1 1/4 parts Tequila
1 part Peach Schnapps
1 part Blue Curaçao
4 parts Sweet & Sour Mix

Combine all ingredients in a blender with ice and blend until smooth.

Cavanaugh's Special

HURRICANE GLASS

1 part Coffee Liqueur
1 part Crème de Cacao (White)
1 part Amaretto
2 scoops Vanilla Ice Cream

Combine all ingredients in a blender. Blend until smooth.

Cha Cha Slide

COUPE

2 parts RumChata
1 part Amaretto
1 part Coffee Liqueur
1 part Whipped Cream Vodka
1 scoop Ice Cream

Combine all ingredients in a blender and blend until smooth. Garnish with a dusting of Cinnamon and a drizzle of Chocolate Syrup. Top with Whipped Cream.

Chamborlada

WHITE WINE GLASS

1 part Dark Rum
2 parts Light Rum
2 parts Cream of Coconut
3 parts Pineapple Juice

Combine all ingredients in a blender with ice and blend until smooth.

Cherry Hill

COUPE

2 parts Light Rum
1 part Cherry Liqueur
1 part Lime Juice

Combine all ingredients in a blender with ice and blend until smooth.

Cherry Repair Kit

COUPETTE GLASS

1 part Amaretto
1 part Crème de Cacao (White)
1 part Half and Half
1 part Maraschino Cherry Juice
6 Maraschino Cherries

Combine all ingredients in a blender with ice and blend until smooth.

Chi Chi

COUPETTE GLASS

1 1/2 parts Vodka
1 part Cream of Coconut
3 parts Pineapple Juice

Combine all ingredients in a blender with ice and blend until smooth.

China Doll

COUPETTE GLASS

1 part Tequila
1 part Brandy
fill with Milk

Combine all ingredients in a blender with ice and blend until smooth.

Chiquita® Punch

HURRICANE GLASS

1 part Banana Liqueur
1 part Orange Juice
1 part Heavy Cream
splash Grenadine

Combine all ingredients in a blender with ice and blend until smooth.

Chocolate Almond Cream

PARFAIT GLASS

2 parts Amaretto
2 parts Crème de Cacao (White)
1 scoop Vanilla Ice Cream

Combine all ingredients in a blender. Blend until smooth.

Chocolate Almond Kiss

COUPETTE GLASS

1 part Crème de Cacao (Dark)
1 part Frangelico®
1 part Vodka
2 scoops Vanilla Ice Cream

Combine all ingredients in a blender. Blend until smooth.

Chocolate Orgasm

COUPETTE GLASS

½ part Crème de Cacao (Dark)
1 part Chocolate Mint Liqueur
½ part Irish Cream Liqueur
1 scoop Vanilla Ice Cream

Combine all ingredients in a blender. Blend until smooth.

Chocolate Snow Bear

CHAMPAGNE FLUTE

1 part Amaretto
1 part Crème de Cacao (White)
¼ part Chocolate Syrup
2 splashes Vanilla Extract
1 scoop French Vanilla Ice Cream

Combine all ingredients in a blender. Blend until smooth.

Chocolate Snowman

COUPETTE GLASS

3 parts Crème de Coconut
2 parts Almond Syrup
1 part Maple Syrup
½ part Crème de Cacao (White)
½ part Cream
½ part Crème de Cacao (Dark)
½ part Crème Liqueur
½ part Milk

Combine all ingredients in a blender with ice and blend until smooth.

Cloud 9

PARFAIT GLASS

1 part Irish Cream Liqueur
1 part Amaretto
½ part Raspberry Liqueur
2 scoops Vanilla Ice Cream

Combine all ingredients in a blender. Blend until smooth.

Cocoa Colada

COLLINS GLASS

1½ parts Light Rum
¼ part Coffee Liqueur
½ part Cream of Coconut
½ part Chocolate Syrup
1½ parts Milk

Combine all ingredients in a blender with ice and blend until smooth.

Coco-Mocha Alexander

COUPETTE GLASS

1 part Spiced Rum
½ part Coffee Brandy
1 part Coffee
1 part Cream of Coconut
1 part Cream

Combine all ingredients in a blender with ice and blend until smooth.

Coconut Delight

COUPETTE GLASS

1 part Crème de Coconut
1 scoop Vanilla Ice Cream
1 part Cream of Coconut
fill with Milk

Combine all ingredients in a blender and blend until smooth.

Coconut Kisses

HURRICANE GLASS

1 part Light Rum
1 part Crème de Coconut
1 part Apricot Brandy
1 part Cream of Coconut
1 part Apricot Juice
1 part Pineapple Juice

Combine all ingredients in a blender with ice and blend until smooth.

Colada Trouble

HURRICANE GLASS

1½ parts Light Rum
6 parts Pineapple Juice
3 parts Cream of Coconut
1 Banana

Combine all ingredients in a blender with ice and blend until smooth.

Colorado Avalanche

HURRICANE GLASS

3 parts Blackberry Brandy
1 part Vanilla Liqueur
1 scoop Vanilla Ice Cream

Combine all ingredients in a blender. Blend until smooth.

Columbia Gold

WHITE WINE GLASS

1¼ parts Yukon Jack®
¾ part Strawberry Liqueur
fill with Orange Juice

Combine all ingredients in a blender with ice and blend until smooth.

Comfortably Numb

COUPETTE GLASS

1 part Spiced Rum
1 part Vanilla Vodka
1 part Crème de Coconut
⅔ part Cream of Coconut
2 parts Pineapple Juice
1 part Orange Juice

Combine all ingredients in a blender with ice and blend until smooth.

Coo Coo

COUPETTE GLASS

1½ parts Rum
1½ parts Melon Liqueur
3 parts Piña Colada Mix
3 parts Sweet & Sour Mix

Combine all ingredients in a blender with ice and blend until smooth.

Cookie Dough

COUPETTE GLASS

1 part Gin
1 part Crème de Cacao (White)
2 dashes Angostura® Bitters
1½ parts Cream of Coconut
½ part Cream

Combine all ingredients in a blender with ice and blend until smooth.

Coqui

COUPE

¼ part Coconut Rum
¼ part Melon Liqueur
¼ part Peach Schnapps
¼ part Pineapple Rum
¼ part Triple Sec
4 parts Sweet & Sour Mix
½ part Lime Juice

Combine all ingredients in a blender with ice and blend until smooth.

Country & Western
COUPETTE GLASS

1¼ parts Dark Rum
1 part Cream of Coconut
1 part Pineapple Juice
1 part Orange Juice

Combine all ingredients in a blender with ice and blend until smooth.

Crazy Banana Mama
ROCKS GLASS

1 part Cream
1 part Amaretto
1 part Rum
1 part Banana Puree

Combine all ingredients in a blender with ice and blend until smooth.

Crazy Monkey
HURRICANE GLASS

1 part Banana Liqueur
2 parts Strawberry Daiquiri Mix
2 parts Orange Juice

Combine all ingredients in a blender with ice and blend until smooth.

Creamsicle® Dream
HIGHBALL GLASS

1½ parts Coconut Rum
1 scoop Vanilla Ice Cream
fill with Orange Juice

Combine all ingredients in a blender and blend until smooth.

Creamy Champ
COUPETTE GLASS

1½ parts Melon Liqueur
1 part Light Rum
1 part Cream of Coconut
4 parts Pineapple Juice
2 scoops Vanilla Ice Cream

Combine all ingredients in a blender. Blend until smooth.

Creamy Imperial
COUPETTE GLASS

2 parts Crème de Cacao (White)
1 part Blackberry Liqueur
1 scoop Vanilla Ice Cream
2 parts Milk

Combine all ingredients in a blender and blend until smooth.

Crème de Menthe Parfait
COUPETTE GLASS

½ part Spiced Rum
¼ part Crème de Cacao (White)
½ part Crème de Menthe (Green)
1 part Cream of Coconut
2 parts Heavy Cream

Combine all ingredients in a blender with ice and blend until smooth.

Crickets
COUPETTE GLASS

1½ parts Peach Brandy
2 parts Crème de Cacao (White)
2 scoops Ice Cream

Combine all ingredients in a blender. Blend until smooth.

Cum in a Blender
HURRICANE GLASS

3 parts Coffee Liqueur
3 parts White Chocolate Liqueur
1 part Whiskey
8 parts Milk
4 parts Cola
1 Banana

Combine all ingredients in a blender with ice and blend until smooth.

Dark Indulgence
COUPETTE GLASS

½ part Tia Maria®
3 parts Cola
1 scoop Vanilla Ice Cream

Combine all ingredients in a blender. Blend until smooth.

Dark Shadows

COUPE

2 parts Beer
2 parts Coconut Rum
2 parts Melon Liqueur
1 part Triple Sec
1 part Vodka

Combine all ingredients in a blender with ice and blend until smooth.

The Dark Side

HIGHBALL GLASS

1 part Amaretto
1 part 151-Proof Rum
1 part Crème de Cacao (Dark)
1 part Coffee Liqueur
1 part Triple Sec
3 scoops Vanilla Ice Cream

Combine all ingredients in a blender and blend until smooth.

Dark Web

COUPE

4 parts Jack Daniel's
2 parts Coffee Liqueur
1 part Beer
2 parts Milk
2 parts Tonic Water
2 scoops Chocolate Ice Cream

Combine all ingredients in a blender and blend until smooth.

Delightful Mystery

COUPETTE GLASS

1 part Gin
2/3 part Peach Schnapps
2/3 part Pisang Ambon® Liqueur
4 parts Orange Juice

Combine all ingredients in a blender with ice and blend until smooth.

Derby Special

COUPETTE GLASS

1 1/2 parts Light Rum
1/2 part Cointreau®
1/2 part Lime Juice
1 part Orange Juice

Combine all ingredients in a blender with ice and blend until smooth.

Devil's Gun

COUPETTE GLASS

1 1/2 parts Dark Rum
1 part Light Rum
1 part Pineapple Juice
1/4 part Apricot Brandy
1/4 part Lime Juice
splash Grenadine

Combine all ingredients in a blender with ice and blend until smooth.

Devil's Tail

CHAMPAGNE FLUTE

1 1/2 parts Light Rum
1 part Vodka
2 splashes Grenadine
2 splashes Apricot Brandy
1 part Lime Juice

Combine all ingredients in a blender with ice and blend until smooth. Garnish with a Lemon Twist.

Di Amore Dream

PARFAIT GLASS

1 1/2 parts Amaretto
3/4 part Crème de Cacao (White)
2 parts Orange Juice
2 scoops Vanilla Ice Cream

Combine all ingredients in a blender. Blend until smooth.

Dirty Banana

CHAMPAGNE FLUTE

1 part Light Rum
2 parts Coffee Liqueur
2 parts Half and Half
dash Powdered Sugar
1 Banana

Combine all ingredients in a blender with ice and blend until smooth.

Dirty Dog

COUPETTE GLASS

1 part Hennessy®
1½ parts Vodka
fill with Orange Juice
1 part Cranberry Juice Cocktail

Combine all ingredients in a blender with ice and blend until smooth.

Dominican Coco Loco

COUPETTE GLASS

½ part Amaretto
1 part Cream of Coconut
splash Grenadine
1 part Milk
½ part Pineapple Juice
1½ parts Light Rum

Combine all ingredients in a blender with ice and blend until smooth.

Don Pedro

COUPETTE GLASS

1 part Whiskey
1 part Coffee Liqueur
2 scoops Vanilla Ice Cream

Combine all ingredients in a blender. Blend until smooth.

Donna Reed

COUPETTE GLASS

1 part Absolut® Vodka
2 parts Cranberry Juice Cocktail
2 parts Sweet & Sour Mix

Combine all ingredients in a blender with ice and blend until smooth.

Down Under Snowball

COUPETTE GLASS

1 part Light Rum
1 part Peach Schnapps
½ part Grenadine
3 parts Orange Juice

Combine all ingredients in a blender with ice and blend until smooth.

Dreamy Monkey

PARFAIT GLASS

1 part Vodka
½ part Crème de Banane
½ part Crème de Cacao (Dark)
1 Banana
2 scoops Vanilla Ice Cream
1 part Light Cream

Combine all ingredients in a blender. Blend until smooth.

E Pluribus Unum

COUPETTE GLASS

1 part Frangelico®
1 part Raspberry Liqueur
1 part Coffee Liqueur
2 scoops Chocolate Ice Cream

Combine all ingredients in a blender. Blend until smooth.

The Event Horizon

HIGHBALL GLASS

1 part Peppermint Schnapps
1 part Vodka
1 part Milk
1 scoop Chocolate Ice Cream

Combine all ingredients in a blender. Blend until smooth.

Feeler

CHAMPAGNE FLUTE

1 1/2 parts Light Rum
1/2 part Galliano®
1/4 part Passion Fruit Nectar
1/4 part Pineapple Juice
2 splashes Lemon Juice

Combine all ingredients in a blender with ice and blend until smooth.

Fiery Scream

COUPE

4 parts Fireball Cinnamon Whiskey
2 scoops Vanilla Ice Cream
1/2 tsp Cinnamon Sugar

Combine all ingredients in a blender and blend until smooth. Rim the glass with Cinnamon Sugar or use it as garnish.

Finnish Flash

COUPETTE GLASS

1 part Cranberry Vodka
1/2 part Crème de Menthe (White)
1/2 part Silver Tequila

Combine all ingredients in a blender with ice and blend until smooth.

Fire & Ice Cream

COUPE

1 1/2 parts Fireball Cinnamon Whiskey
4 parts Milk
1/12 part Vanilla extract
3 scoops Vanilla Ice Cream

Combine all ingredients in a blender and blend until smooth.

Flicker

COLLINS GLASS

2 parts Light Rum
1/4 part Passion Fruit Nectar
2 splashes Lemon Juice
2 splashes Lime Juice

Combine all ingredients in a blender with ice and blend until smooth.

Florida Freeze

COUPETTE GLASS

1 1/4 parts Dark Rum
1 1/4 parts Cream of Coconut
1 part Orange Juice
2 parts Pineapple Juice

Combine all ingredients in a blender with ice and blend until smooth.

Florida Rum Runner

COUPETTE GLASS

1 1/2 parts Rum
1 part Blackberry Brandy
1 part Banana Liqueur
1 part Lime Juice
1/2 part Grenadine

Combine all ingredients in a blender with ice and blend until smooth.

Flying Bikini

HURRICANE GLASS

1 part Brandy
1 part Triple Sec
1 part Strawberry Liqueur
1 part Spiced Rum
1 part Amaretto
fill with Orange Juice

Combine all ingredients in a blender with ice and blend until smooth.

Flying Bliss
COUPETTE GLASS

1 part Crème de Banane
1 part Cognac
2 parts Vanilla Liqueur

Combine all ingredients in a blender with ice and blend until smooth.

Flying Carpet
HIGHBALL GLASS

1 part Vodka
1 part Advocaat
1 part Crème de Banane

Combine all ingredients in a blender with ice and blend until smooth.

Flying Gorilla
COUPETTE GLASS

1 part Vodka
1 part Banana Liqueur
1 part Crème de Cacao (White)
2 scoops Vanilla Ice Cream

Combine all ingredients in a blender. Blend until smooth.

Freezy Melons
COUPETTE GLASS

1½ parts Vodka
⅔ part Kiwi Schnapps
⅔ part Melon Liqueur
2 parts Cream

Combine all ingredients in a blender with ice and blend until smooth.

Fresa
COUPETTE GLASS

½ part Parfait Amour
2 parts Cachaça®
1½ parts Strawberry Puree
dash Sugar

Combine all ingredients in a blender with ice and blend until smooth.

Friscket City
COUPETTE GLASS

1½ parts Southern Comfort®
⅔ part Apricot Brandy
½ part Pear Brandy
2 parts Cream

Combine all ingredients in a blender with ice and blend until smooth.

Frozen Arctic Cream
COLLINS GLASS

2 parts Vodka
2 parts Vanilla Liqueur
1 part Blue Curaçao
2 parts Cream
1 scoop Vanilla Ice Cream

Combine all ingredients in a blender. Blend until smooth.

Frozen Banana Smoothie
COLLINS GLASS

1 part Rum
1½ parts Banana Liqueur
½ part Sweet & Sour Mix
½ Banana

Combine all ingredients in a blender with ice and blend until smooth.

Frozen Berkeley
CHAMPAGNE FLUTE

1½ parts Light Rum
½ part Brandy
1 part Passion Fruit Nectar
1 part Lemon Juice

Combine all ingredients in a blender with ice and blend until smooth.

Frozen Black Irish
COUPETTE GLASS

1 part Coffee Liqueur
1 part Irish Cream Liqueur
1 part Vodka
1 scoop Chocolate Ice Cream

Combine all ingredients in a blender. Blend until smooth.

Frozen Blue Daiquiri

ROCKS GLASS

2 parts Light Rum
½ part Blue Curaçao
½ part Lime Juice

Combine all ingredients in a blender with ice and blend until smooth.

Frozen Brandy and Rum

ROCKS GLASS

1½ parts Brandy
1 part Light Rum
splash Lemon Juice
dash Powdered Sugar
1 Egg White

Combine all ingredients in a blender with ice and blend until smooth.

Frozen Cappuccino

PARFAIT GLASS

1 part Irish Cream Liqueur
1 part Coffee Liqueur
1 part Frangelico®
1 scoop Vanilla Ice Cream
splash Light Cream

Combine all ingredients in a blender and blend until smooth.

Frozen Citron Neon

PARFAIT GLASS

1½ parts Citrus Vodka
1 part Melon Liqueur
½ part Blue Curaçao
½ part Lime Juice
1 part Sweet & Sour Mix

Combine all ingredients in a blender with ice. Blend until smooth.

Frozen Citrus Banana

COLLINS GLASS

1½ parts Dark Rum
1½ parts Lime Juice
2 parts Orange Juice
2 parts Milk
2 parts Club Soda
dash Brown Sugar
1 Banana

Combine all ingredients in a blender with ice and blend until smooth.

Frozen Daiquiri

CHAMPAGNE FLUTE

1 part Light Rum
1 part Lime Juice
splash Triple Sec
dash Sugar

Combine all ingredients in a blender with ice and blend until smooth.

Frozen Danube

HURRICANE GLASS

2 parts Vodka
2 parts Melon Liqueur
1 part Blue Curaçao
3 parts Grapefruit Juice
3 parts Melon Puree

Combine all ingredients in a blender with ice and blend until smooth.

Frozen Domingo

COUPETTE GLASS

1½ parts Spiced Rum
2 parts Piña Colada Mix
2 parts Orange Juice
2 parts Cranberry Juice Cocktail

Combine all ingredients in a blender with ice and blend until smooth.

Frozen Fuzzy

CHAMPAGNE FLUTE

1 part Peach Schnapps
½ part Triple Sec
½ part Grenadine
½ part Lime Juice
splash Lemon-Lime Soda

Combine all ingredients in a blender with ice and blend until smooth.

Frozen Girl Scout

COUPETTE GLASS

1½ parts Crème de Menthe (Green)
3 scoops Chocolate Ice Cream
splash Milk

Combine all ingredients in a blender. Blend until smooth.

Frozen Grasshopper

COUPETTE GLASS

1 part Crème de Menthe (Green)
1 part Crème de Cacao (White)
2 scoops Vanilla Ice Cream

Combine all ingredients in a blender. Blend until smooth.

Frozen Irish Mint

WHITE WINE GLASS

1 part Crème de Menthe (Green)
1 part Irish Cream Liqueur
2 scoops Vanilla Ice Cream

Combine all ingredients in a blender. Blend until smooth.

Frozen Mandarin Sour

WHITE WINE GLASS

2 parts Mandarine Napoléon® Liqueur
1 part Cream
1 scoop Vanilla Ice Cream

Combine all ingredients in a blender. Blend until smooth.

Frozen Margarita

COUPETTE GLASS

1½ parts Tequila
½ part Triple Sec
1 part Lemon Juice

Combine all ingredients in a blender with ice and blend until smooth.

Frozen Matador

COUPE

1½ parts Tequila
2 parts Pineapple Juice
splash Lime Juice

Combine all ingredients in a blender with ice and blend until smooth.

Frozen Monk

COUPETTE GLASS

1 part Frangelico®
1 part Coffee Liqueur
1 part Crème de Cacao (White)
2 parts Cream
2 scoops Ice Cream

Combine all ingredients in a blender. Blend until smooth.

Frozen Mudslide

COUPETTE GLASS

1 part Vodka
1 part Coffee Liqueur
1 part Irish Cream Liqueur
2 scoops Vanilla Ice Cream

Combine all ingredients in a blender. Blend until smooth.

Frozen Rum Runner

COUPETTE GLASS

3 parts Dark Rum
3 parts Light Rum
2 parts Crème de Banane
1 part Pineapple Juice
1 part Orange Juice
2 parts Grenadine

Combine all ingredients in a blender with ice and blend until smooth.

Frozen Steppes

COUPE

2½ parts Vodka
1½ parts Crème de Cacao (White)
1 scoop Vanilla Ice Cream

Combine all ingredients in a blender and blend until smooth.

Frozen Strawberry Daiquiri

CHAMPAGNE FLUTE

1 part Rum
1 part Lemon Juice
4 Strawberries
dash Sugar

Combine all ingredients in a blender with ice and blend until smooth.

Frozen Strawberry Margarita

COUPETTE GLASS

3 parts Tequila
1 part Triple Sec
1 part Sweetened Lime Juice
½ part Lemon Juice
1 part Strawberry Liqueur

Combine all ingredients in a blender with ice and blend until smooth.

Frozen Tahiti

WHITE WINE GLASS

2 parts Dark Rum
1 part Pineapple Juice
½ part Passion Fruit Nectar
splash Grenadine

Combine all ingredients in a blender with ice and blend until smooth.

Frozen Vomit

COUPETTE GLASS

2 parts Gin
1 part Grain Alcohol
1 part Banana Liqueur
2 parts Beef Bouillion

Combine all ingredients in a blender with ice and blend until smooth.

Fruit Booty

HIGHBALL GLASS

2 parts 151-Proof Rum
1 part Blue Curaçao
1 part Cranberry Liqueur
1 part Cranberry Vodka
3 parts Apple-Cranberry Juice
3 parts Pineapple Juice
splash Grenadine

Combine all ingredients in a blender with ice and blend until smooth.

Fruit Frosty

COUPETTE GLASS

1 part Sour Apple Schnapps
1 part Peach Schnapps
1 part Orange Liqueur
1 part Cranberry Juice Cocktail
1 part Cream

Combine all ingredients in a blender with ice and blend until smooth.

Fruit Loop®

PARFAIT GLASS

1 part Midori®
1 part Blue Curaçao
½ part Granadine
3 parts Pineapple Juice
1 part Cream
1 Strawberry

Combine all ingredients in a blender with ice and blend until smooth.

Fruit Margarita

COUPETTE GLASS
WITH SALTED RIM

2 parts Tequila
1 part Triple Sec
4 parts Sweet & Sour Mix
Fresh Fruit

Add fruit to the blender until the desired consistency is reached.

Fruity Smash

COUPE

1 part Banana Liqueur
1 part Cherry Vodka
1 scoop Vanilla Ice Cream

Combine all ingredients in a blender and blend until smooth.

Fubuki-So-San

ROCKS GLASS

1 part Crème de Coconut
1 part Sake
1/2 part Blue Curaçao
1/2 part Cream
1/2 part Cream of Coconut
2 parts Pineapple Juice

Combine all ingredients in a blender with ice and blend until smooth.

Funky Freezer

COUPETTE GLASS

1 1/2 parts Tequila Gold
1/2 part Peach Schnapps
splash Apricot Brandy
splash Blue Curaçao
1/2 part Lime Juice

Combine all ingredients in a blender with ice and blend until smooth.

Funky Monkey

COUPETTE GLASS

2 parts Brandy
2 parts Coffee Liqueur
1 part Milk
1 scoop Ice Cream
1 Banana

Combine all ingredients in a blender. Blend until smooth.

Fuzzy Shark

HURRICANE GLASS

1 1/2 parts Peach Schnapps
5 parts Orange Juice
1/2 part Blue Curaçao

Blend all but the Blue Curaçao with ice. Top with Blue Curaçao.

Gauguin

ROCKS GLASS

1 1/4 parts Dark Rum
1/2 part Passion Fruit Nectar
1/2 part Lemon Juice
1/2 part Lime Juice

Combine all ingredients in a blender with ice and blend until smooth.

Geisha Girl

WHITE WINE GLASS

1 part Gin
1 part Melon Liqueur
2 parts Passion Fruit Juice
1/2 Pear

Combine all ingredients in a blender with ice and blend until smooth.

General's Salute

COUPETTE GLASS

1 1/2 parts Silver Tequila
1/2 part Blue Curaçao
dash Sugar

Combine all ingredients in a blender with ice and blend until smooth.

Georgio

COCKTAIL GLASS

1 part Coffee Liqueur
1 part Irish Cream Liqueur
2 parts Cream
1/2 Banana

Combine all ingredients in a blender with ice and blend until smooth.

Glaciermeister

COUPETTE GLASS

1½ part Jägermeister®
3 scoops Vanilla Ice Cream
1 part Milk

Combine all ingredients in a blender. Blend until smooth.

Glass Slipper

WHITE WINE GLASS

1 part Dry Vermouth
1 part Cream
2 scoops Vanilla Ice Cream

Combine all ingredients in a blender. Blend until smooth.

Golden Cadillac

CHAMPAGNE FLUTE

2 parts Crème de Cacao (White)
1 part Galliano
1 part Cream

Combine all ingredients in a blender with ice and blend until smooth.

Golden Cadillac® with White-Walled Tires

CHAMPAGNE FLUTE

1½ parts Vanilla Vodka
1½ parts Chocolate Liqueur
½ part Galliano®
1½ parts Crème de Cacao (White)
1 part Cream
splash Simple Syrup

Combine all ingredients in a blender with ice and blend until smooth.

Golden Star

PARFAIT GLASS

1 part Vanilla Liqueur
¾ part Amaretto
2 scoops Ice Cream

Combine all ingredients in a blender. Blend until smooth.

Great Idea

COUPETTE GLASS

1 part Tequila Gold
1 part Triple Sec
2 parts Strawberry Puree
3 parts Pineapple Juice
1 part Sweet & Sour Mix
1 scoop Vanilla Ice Cream

Combine all ingredients in a blender and blend until smooth.

Green Angel

COUPETTE GLASS

1 part Pisang Ambon® Liqueur
1 part Peach Schnapps
1 part Coconut Rum
splash Lemon Juice

Combine all ingredients in a blender with ice and blend until smooth.

Green Eyes

COUPETTE GLASS

1 part Rum
¾ part Melon Liqueur
½ part Cream of Coconut
½ part Sweetened Lime Juice
1½ parts Pineapple Juice

Combine all ingredients in a blender with ice and blend until smooth.

Greengarita

COUPE

1 part Melon Liqueur
1 part Silver Tequila
1 part Lime Juice

Combine all ingredients in a blender with ice and blend until smooth.

Green Goddess

COUPETTE GLASS

4 parts Melon Liqueur
1 part Milk
1 Banana

Combine all ingredients in a blender with ice and blend until smooth.

Greenhorn

COUPE

2 parts Melon Liqueur
1 part Coconut Rum
1 part Watermelon Schnapps
1 part Pineapple Juice

Combine all ingredients in a blender with ice and blend until smooth.

Green Ocean

HIGHBALL GLASS

1 part Gin
1 part Pisang Ambon® Liqueur
1 part Sweet & Sour Mix
1 part Passion Fruit Juice
1/2 part Orange Juice

Combine all ingredients in a blender with ice and blend until smooth.

Green Weenie

COUPETTE GLASS

1 part Jack Daniel's®
1 part Rum
1 part Tequila
1 part Vodka
fill with Margarita Mix

Combine all ingredients in a blender with ice and blend until smooth.

Grinch

MARGARITA GLASS

2 parts Tequila Reposado
4 parts Margarita Mix
1/2 Apple
1 Banana

Peel the Apple and cut it into chunks. Combine all ingredients in a blender with ice and blend until smooth.

G-Spot

WHITE WINE GLASS

2 parts Advocaat
1 part Cream
1 part Amaretto
1 part Chocolate Mint Liqueur

Combine all ingredients in a blender with ice and blend until smooth.

Guava Colada

COUPETTE GLASS

1 1/4 parts Dark Rum
3 parts Guava Juice
1 part Cream of Coconut

Combine all ingredients in a blender with ice and blend until smooth.

Habit Rogue

COUPETTE GLASS

1 1/2 parts Gin
2 parts Cranberry Juice Cocktail
1 part Grapefruit Juice
splash Honey

Combine all ingredients in a blender with ice and blend until smooth.

Hana Lei Bay

HURRICANE GLASS

2 parts Dark Rum
1 part Raspberry Liqueur
1 part Pineapple Juice
1 part Cream of Coconut

Combine all ingredients in a blender with ice and blend until smooth.

Happy Banana Mama

HURRICANE GLASS

1½ parts Light Rum
1 part Dark Rum
1 part Cream of Coconut
1 part Strawberry Puree
¼ part Crème de Banane
2 parts Pineapple Juice

Combine all ingredients in a blender with ice and blend until smooth.

Havana Banana Fizz

COLLINS GLASS

2 parts Dark Rum
1½ parts Lime Juice
dash Bitters
3 parts Pineapple Juice

Combine all ingredients in a blender with ice and blend until smooth.

Hawaiian Eye

COUPETTE GLASS

½ part Banana Liqueur
1 part Coffee Liqueur
1 part Heavy Cream
1 Egg White
½ part Vodka
splash Pernod®

Combine all ingredients in a blender with ice and blend until smooth.

Hibiscus

COUPETTE GLASS

¾ part Dark Rum
¼ part Raspberry Liqueur
¼ part Crème de Cacao (White)
½ part Grenadine
2 parts Collins Mix

Combine all ingredients in a blender with ice and blend until smooth.

High Flier

HURRICANE GLASS

1 part Blue Curaçao
1 part Triple Sec
1 part Melon Liqueur
1 part Cream of Coconut
1 part Orange Juice
1 part Mango Juice

Combine all ingredients in a blender with ice and blend until smooth.

Highland Winter

COUPETTE GLASS

1½ parts Scotch
splash Cherry Brandy
splash Drambuie®
½ part Cream

Combine all ingredients in a blender with ice and blend until smooth.

Hi-Rise

ROCKS GLASS

1 part Vodka
¼ part Cointreau®
2 parts Orange Juice
1 part Sweet & Sour Mix
¼ part Grenadine

Combine all ingredients in a blender with ice and blend until smooth.

Hocus Pocus

CHAMPAGNE FLUTE

1 part Gin
1 part Cointreau®
1 part Lemon Juice

Combine all ingredients in a blender with ice and blend until smooth.

Holiday Isle

WHITE WINE GLASS

1½ parts Pineapple Juice
1½ parts Piña Colada Mix
1 part Peach Puree
1 scoop Vanilla Ice Cream
1 scoop Orange Sorbet

Combine all ingredients in a blender. Blend until smooth.

Honey Boombastic

HURRICANE GLASS

1½ parts Vodka
1 part Crème de Cacao (Dark)
1 part Frangelico®
1½ parts Honey
1 Egg
½ part Vanilla Extract

Combine all ingredients in a blender with ice and blend until smooth.

Hop in the Space

COUPETTE GLASS

½ part Crème de Cacao (White)
½ part Hazelnut Liqueur
2 parts Cream
⅔ part Honey

Combine all ingredients in a blender with ice and blend until smooth.

Horny Bull

COUPETTE GLASS

1½ parts Tequila
3 parts Orange Juice
1 part Lemonade
½ part Grenadine

Combine all ingredients in a blender with ice and blend until smooth.

Horny Leprechaun

COUPETTE GLASS

1 part Melon Liqueur
1 part Peach Schnapps
1 part Vodka
2 parts Orange Juice

Combine all ingredients in a blender with ice and blend until smooth.

Hot and Creamy

MARGARITA GLASS

1 part Vodka
½ part Cinnamon Schnapps
2 parts Half and Half

Combine all ingredients in a blender with ice and blend until smooth.

Humdinger

COUPETTE GLASS

1½ parts Melon Liqueur
½ part Silver Tequila
3 parts Lime Juice
dash Sugar

Combine all ingredients in a blender with ice and blend until smooth.

Hummer

HIGHBALL GLASS

1 part Coffee Vodka
1 part Light Rum
2 scoops Vanilla Ice Cream

Combine all ingredients in a blender. Blend until smooth.

Hummingbird

COUPETTE GLASS

1 part Rum Crème Liqueur
1 part Amaretto
1 part Milk
½ part Strawberry Syrup
½ Banana

Combine all ingredients in a blender with ice and blend until smooth.

Hydraulic Screwdriver

COUPETTE GLASS

1 can Frozen Orange Juice Concentrate
1 part Vodka
1 part Triple Sec
1 part Water

Make the Orange Juice but instead of refilling container with water 3 times, fill with Vodka once and Triple Sec once. Mix well and serve on the rocks or blend it with ice for a frozen drink.

I Scream the Blues

COLLINS GLASS

splash Blue Curaçao
splash Lychee Liqueur
1 part Dark Rum
3 parts Pear Juice
1 part Cream

Combine all ingredients in a blender with ice and blend until smooth.

Ice Storm

HIGHBALL GLASS

½ part 151-Proof Rum
2 parts Strawberry Liqueur
½ Banana
5 Strawberries
3 scoops Vanilla Ice Cream

Combine all ingredients in a blender. Blend until smooth.

Iceball

COUPETTE GLASS

1½ parts Gin
¾ part Crème de Menthe (White)
¾ part Sambuca
splash Cream

Combine all ingredients in a blender with ice and blend until smooth.

Iceberg in Radioactive Water

COUPETTE GLASS

3 parts Melon Liqueur
1 part Coconut Rum
1 part Banana Liqueur
fill with Pineapple Juice
1 scoop Vanilla Ice Cream

Combine all ingredients in a blender. Blend until smooth.

Icebreaker

COUPETTE GLASS

2 parts Tequila
2 parts Grapefruit Juice
splash Grenadine
2 splashes Cointreau®

Combine all ingredients in a blender with ice and blend until smooth.

Icemeister

COUPETTE GLASS

2 parts Jägermeister®
2 scoops Ice Cream

Combine all ingredients in a blender. Blend until smooth.

Igloo Sue

HURRICANE GLASS

2 parts Vodka
1 part Grenadine
fill with Lemonade

Combine all ingredients in a blender with ice and blend until smooth.

Illegal Cuban

COUPETTE GLASS

2 parts Blue Curaçao
1 part Cream of Coconut
½ part Amaretto
1 part Lemon Juice
1 part Lime Juice

Combine all ingredients in a blender with ice and blend until smooth.

Inertia Creeps

COLLINS GLASS

1½ parts Vodka
2 parts Strega®
⅔ part Pineapple Juice
½ part Cream

Combine all ingredients in a blender with ice and blend until smooth.

Irish Dream

PILSNER GLASS

½ part Frangelico®
½ part Irish Cream Liqueur
¾ part Crème de Cacao (Dark)
1 scoop Vanilla Ice Cream

Combine all ingredients in a blender and blend until smooth.

Italian Dream

COUPE

2 parts Irish Cream Liqueur
1 part Amaretto
dash Limoncello
2 parts Cream

Combine all ingredients in a blender with ice and blend until smooth.

Italian Margarita

COUPETTE GLASS

1 part Amaretto
½ part Tequila Gold
½ part Triple Sec
2 parts Sweet & Sour Mix

Combine all ingredients in a blender with ice and blend until smooth.

Italian Stallion

WHITE WINE GLASS

¾ part Galliano®
¾ part Crème de Banane
1½ parts Heavy Cream

Combine all ingredients in a blender with ice and blend until smooth.

Italian Sunrise

COLLINS GLASS

1 part Galliano®
1 part Banana Liqueur
1 part Triple Sec
fill with Cream

Combine all ingredients in a blender with ice and blend until smooth.

Jackoff

COUPE

2 parts Spiced Rum
4 parts Orange Juice
2 parts Lemon-Lime Soda

Combine all ingredients in a blender with ice and blend until smooth.

Jäger Vacation

COUPETTE GLASS

1 part Jägermeister®
2 parts Piña Colada Mix
2 parts Pineapple Juice

Combine all ingredients in a blender with ice and blend until smooth.

Jamafezzca

COUPETTE GLASS

1 1/2 parts Jamaican Rum
1 1/2 parts Cream
2/3 part Passion Fruit Liqueur
2 parts Guava Juice

Combine all ingredients in a blender with ice and blend until smooth.

Jamaica Safari

COUPETTE GLASS

1/2 part Peach Schnapps
2/3 part Dark Rum
1/2 part Safari®
1 1/2 parts Banana Juice
splash Lime Juice
splash Cream of Coconut
2 parts Passion Fruit Juice

Combine all ingredients in a blender with ice and blend until smooth.

Jamaican Army

COUPE

1 part Crème de Cacao (White)
1/2 part Banana Liqueur
1/2 part Light Rum
1 part Cream
2 scoops Vanilla Ice Cream
1 Banana
2 Strawberries

Combine all ingredients in a blender and blend until smooth.

Jamaican Blues

COUPETTE GLASS

1 part Dark Rum
1/4 part Blue Curaçao
2 parts Cream of Coconut
2 parts Pineapple Juice

Combine all ingredients in a blender with ice and blend until smooth.

Jamaican Toothbrush

COLLINS GLASS

1/2 part Peppermint Liqueur
1/2 part Spiced Rum
splash Crème de Cacao (White)
1 part Cream of Coconut
2 parts Cream

Combine all ingredients in a blender with ice and blend until smooth.

Jen & Berry's

COUPETTE GLASS

1 1/2 parts Blue Curaçao
1 part Crème de Coconut
1/2 part Coffee Liqueur
2 scoops Vanilla Ice Cream

Combine all ingredients in a blender. Blend until smooth.

Jersey Girl

HURRICANE GLASS

1 part Currant Vodka
1 part Strawberry Liqueur
2 parts Pineapple Juice
1 1/2 parts Orange Juice
1 part Strawberry Syrup

Combine all ingredients in a blender with ice and blend until smooth.

Johnny Banana

COUPETTE GLASS

2/3 part Crème de Banane
2/3 part Citrus Rum
1 part Banana Puree
3 parts Mango Juice
1 1/2 scoops Vanilla Ice Cream

Combine all ingredients in a blender and blend until smooth.

Juliet and Romeo

COUPETTE GLASS

1 part Rum
1 part Amaretto
1 part Strawberry Puree
2 parts Cream

Combine all ingredients in a blender with ice and blend until smooth.

Kaunakakai

COUPETTE GLASS

1 part Light Rum
1 part Crème de Coconut
2 parts Strawberry Juice
1 part Banana Puree
2 parts Pineapple Juice
2 parts Cream of Coconut

Combine all ingredients in a blender with ice and blend until smooth.

Key Lime Quencher

HURRICANE GLASS

1¼ parts Dark Rum
1½ parts Lime Juice
3 parts Heavy Cream
1 part Cream of Coconut
dash Powdered Sugar

Combine all ingredients in a blender with ice and blend until smooth.

Key West Margarita

COUPETTE GLASS

1 part Tequila
1 part Cherry Juice
1 part Piña Colada Mix
1 part Margarita Mix
1 part Orange Juice

Combine all ingredients in a blender with ice and blend until smooth.

Killer Colada

HURRICANE GLASS

1½ parts Vanilla Vodka
1 part Coconut Rum
1 part Crème de Banane
fill with Cream

Combine all ingredients in a blender with ice and blend until smooth.

Kiwiquiri

COUPETTE GLASS

½ part Crème de Cacao (White)
1½ parts Kiwi Schnapps
2 parts Spiced Rum

Combine all ingredients in a blender with ice and blend until smooth.

Knuckleduster

WHITE WINE GLASS

1 part Blue Curaçao
1 part Crème de Coconut
fill with Pineapple Juice

Combine all ingredients in a blender with ice and blend until smooth.

Kodiak Sled Dog

HURRICANE GLASS

1 part Irish Cream Liqueur
1 part Crown Royal® Whiskey
1 part Frangelico®
1 part Coffee Liqueur
2 parts Milk

Combine all ingredients in a blender with ice and blend until smooth.

Kokomo Joe

COUPETTE GLASS

1 part Light Rum
1 part Banana Liqueur
1 part Orange Juice
1 part Piña Colada Mix
½ Banana

Combine all ingredients in a blender with ice and blend until smooth.

Latin Beat

COUPETTE GLASS

1½ parts Light Rum
1 part Crème de Coconut
½ part Crème de Banane
3 parts Pineapple Juice
1 part Cream of Coconut
1 part Raspberry Juice

Combine all ingredients in a blender with ice and blend until smooth.

Lavender Lady

MARGARITA GLASS

1 part Chambord
1 part White Rum
2 parts Cream
1 part Cream of Coconut
1 scoop Vanilla Ice Cream

Combine all ingredients in a blender and blend until smooth.

Lazy Luau

ROCKS GLASS

2 parts Coconut Rum
1 part Peach Schnapps
1 part Vodka
1 part Cranberry Juice Cocktail
2 parts Orange Juice
1 part Pineapple Juice
1 can Pineapple Chunks

Combine all ingredients in a blender with ice and blend until smooth.

Lebanese Snow

RED WINE GLASS

1½ parts Strawberry Liqueur
1 part Crème de Banane
1 part Light Cream

Combine all ingredients in a blender with ice and blend until smooth.

Lechery

COUPETTE GLASS

1 part Vodka
½ part Apricot Brandy
½ part Mandarine Napoleon Liqueur
2 parts Lemon Sherbet
2½ parts Orange Juice

Combine all ingredients in a blender and blend until smooth.

Left of Center

COUPETTE GLASS

1½ parts Dark Rum
⅔ part Peach Schnapps
½ part Crème de Coconut
2 parts Orange Juice
1½ parts Pineapple Juice
1½ parts Cream of Coconut

Combine all ingredients in a blender with ice and blend until smooth.

Licorice Mist

PARFAIT GLASS

1¼ parts Sambuca
½ part Crème de Coconut
2 parts Light Cream

Combine all ingredients in a blender with ice and blend until smooth.

Life As We Know It

HURRICANE GLASS

½ part Dark Rum
½ part Gin
½ part Light Rum
½ part Southern Comfort
½ part Vodka
4 parts Orange Juice
2 parts Pineapple Juice
splash Grenadine

Combine all ingredients in a blender with ice and blend until smooth.

Lil Lolita

COUPETTE GLASS

1 part Blue Curaçao
2 parts Triple Sec
2 parts Blackberry Liqueur
2 parts Orange Juice

Combine all ingredients in a blender with ice and blend until smooth.

Limelight

COUPETTE GLASS

½ part Blue Curaçao
¼ part Banana Liqueur
¼ part Vodka
2 parts Orange Juice
2 parts Pineapple Juice

Combine all ingredients in a blender with ice and blend until smooth.

Liquid Temptation

RED WINE GLASS

1½ parts Light Rum
½ part Crème de Banane
1 part Sweet & Sour Mix
5 Strawberries

Combine all ingredients in a blender with ice and blend until smooth.

Little Brother

ROCKS GLASS

2 parts Coffee Liqueur
1 part Vodka
1 scoop Ice Cream
splash Vanilla Extract

Combine all ingredients in a blender. Blend until smooth.

Little Darlin'

COUPETTE GLASS

1 part Crème de Cacao (White)
1 part Crème de Menthe (Green)
1 scoop Vanilla Ice Cream

Combine all ingredients in a blender. Blend until smooth.

Lonely Night

PARFAIT GLASS

1¼ parts Irish Cream Liqueur
1¼ parts Frangelico®
¾ part Coffee Liqueur
1 scoop Vanilla Ice Cream

Combine all ingredients in a blender and blend until smooth.

Loomdog

COLLINS GLASS

1 part Rum
3 parts Orange Juice
2 parts Pineapple Juice

Combine all ingredients in a blender with ice and blend until smooth.

Loose Moose

COUPETTE GLASS

1 part Crème de Cacao (White)
1 part Frangelico®
1 part Strawberry Liqueur
2 parts Cream

Combine all ingredients in a blender with ice and blend until smooth.

Love Birds

ROCKS GLASS

1½ parts Vodka
2 parts Lemon Juice
splash Dark Rum
½ part Grenadine

Combine all ingredients in a blender with ice and blend until smooth.

Luna

COLLINS GLASS

1 part Passion Fruit Liqueur
⅔ part Blue Curaçao
splash Crème de Banane
1 part Orange Juice
1 part Pineapple Juice
splash Lime Juice

Combine all ingredients in a blender with ice and blend until smooth.

Magic Island

COUPE

3 parts Pineapple Vodka
1 part Grapefruit Vodka
1 part Cream of Coconut
½ part Cream
dash Grenadine

Combine all ingredients in a blender with ice and blend until smooth.

Malibu Slide

COCKTAIL GLASS

1 part Coconut Rum
1 part Coffee Liqueur
1 part Irish Cream Liqueur

Combine all ingredients in a blender with ice and blend until smooth.

Malibu Wipeout

PARFAIT GLASS

1 part Coconut Rum
1 part Citrus Vodka
1 part Cranberry Juice Cocktail
1 part Pineapple Juice

Combine all ingredients in a blender with ice and blend until smooth.

Mambo's Dream

COUPETTE GLASS

1 part Dark Rum
½ part Banana Liqueur
1 part Pineapple Juice
½ part Lemon Juice
½ part Triple Sec

Combine all ingredients in a blender with ice and blend until smooth.

Mango Tango

COLLINS GLASS

2 parts Orange Juice
1 part Mango Nectar
1 part Dark Rum
½ part Crème de Coconut
½ part Passion Fruit Juice
½ part Guava Juice

Combine all ingredients in a blender with ice and blend until smooth.

Margarita (Frozen)

COUPETTE GLASS

1½ parts Tequila
½ part Triple Sec
1 part Lime Juice
dash Salt

Rub rim of the glass with Lime Juice and dip rim in Salt. Combine all ingredients in a blender with ice and blend until smooth.

Margarita Imperial

COUPETTE GLASS

2 parts Tequila Reposado
1 part Mandarine Napoléon® Liqueur
1 part Lime Juice

Combine all ingredients in a blender with ice and blend until smooth.

Margarita Madres

COUPETTE GLASS

1 1/4 parts Tequila
1/2 part Cointreau®
1 1/2 parts Sweet & Sour Mix
1 1/2 parts Orange Juice
1 1/2 parts Cranberry Juice Cocktail

Combine all ingredients in a blender with ice and blend until smooth.

Marlin

COLLINS GLASS

1 part Vodka
2 parts Orange Juice
1 part Grapefruit Juice

Combine all ingredients in a blender with ice and blend until smooth.

Marshmallow Blue Hawaiian

COUPETTE GLASS

1 part Rum
1 part Blue Curaçao
1/3 part Pineapple Juice
2/3 part Piña Colada Mix
4 Marshmallows

Combine all ingredients in a blender with ice and blend until smooth.

Marshmallow Piña Colada

COUPETTE GLASS

1 part Rum
1 part Pineapple Juice
2 parts Piña Colada Mix
4 Marshmallows

Combine all ingredients in a blender with ice and blend until smooth.

Mary-Huana

COLLINS GLASS

1 1/2 parts Absinthe
2/3 part Blue Curaçao
2/3 part Lime Juice
2/3 part Passion Fruit Nectar
fill with Orange Juice
splash Simple Syrup

Combine all ingredients in a blender with ice and blend until smooth.

Master Chief

COLLINS GLASS

2 parts Vodka
2 parts Ginger Ale
2 parts Red Bull Energy Drink
1/2 part Lemon Juice
1/2 part Lime Juice

Combine all ingredients in a blender with ice and blend until smooth.

Maui Breeze

PARFAIT GLASS

1/2 part Amaretto
1/2 part Triple Sec
1/2 part Brandy
1 part Sweet & Sour Mix
2 parts Orange Juice
1 part Guava Juice

Combine all ingredients in a blender with ice and blend until smooth.

McMalted

HIGHBALL GLASS

1 part Vanilla Liqueur
2 parts Irish Cream Liqueur
2 scoops Vanilla Ice Cream
dash Ground Nutmeg

Combine all ingredients in a blender. Blend until smooth.

Mello Yello

COUPETTE GLASS

1 part Melon Liqueur
1 part Grapefruit Juice

Combine all ingredients in a blender with ice and blend until smooth.

Melon Colada

COUPETTE GLASS

1½ parts Light Rum
½ part Dark Rum
½ part Melon Liqueur
fill with Pineapple Juice
1 part Cream of Coconut
splash Cream

Combine all ingredients in a blender with ice and blend until smooth.

Melon Cooler

COUPE

1 part Melon Liqueur
½ part Peach Schnapps
½ part Raspberry Liqueur
2 parts Pineapple Juice

Combine all ingredients in a blender with ice and blend until smooth.

Melon Margarita

COUPETTE GLASS

1 part Tequila
1 part Melon Liqueur
1 part Triple Sec

Combine all ingredients in a blender with ice and blend until smooth.

Melon Suprise

HURRICANE GLASS

1½ parts Melon Liqueur
1 part Light Rum
fill with Pineapple Juice

Combine all ingredients in a blender with ice and blend until smooth.

Mexican Dream

COUPETTE GLASS

1 part Coffee Liqueur
1 part Milk
2 scoops Vanilla Ice Cream

Combine all ingredients in a blender. Blend until smooth.

Mexican Mudslide

HIGHBALL GLASS

1 part Coffee Liqueur
1 part Amaretto
2 scoops Ice Cream

Combine all ingredients in a blender. Blend until smooth.

Midnight Lace

WHITE WINE GLASS

1½ parts Light Rum
1 part Cream
¾ part Chocolate Mint Liqueur
2 scoops Vanilla Ice Cream

Combine all ingredients in a blender. Blend until smooth.

Millenium Eclipse

COUPETTE GLASS

1 part Southern Comfort®
1 part Pineapple Syrup
1 part Blue Curaçao

Combine all ingredients in a blender with ice and blend until smooth.

Mississippi Mud

BEER MUG

1 part Southern Comfort®
1 part Coffee Liqueur
2 scoops Ice Cream

Combine all ingredients in a blender. Blend until smooth.

Monkey Bars

HURRICANE GLASS

2 parts Banana Liqueur
2 parts Coffee Liqueur
2 parts Vanilla Vodka
1 part Chocolate Syrup
3 scoops Vanilla Ice Cream
½ Banana

Combine all ingredients in a blender and blend until smooth. Garnish with a Banana Slice and Chocolate Shavings.

Monkey Kingdom

COUPE

2 parts Coffee Liqueur
2 parts Coconut Milk
1 part Chocolate Syrup
½ Banana

Combine all ingredients in a blender with ice and blend until smooth.

Mont Blanc

RED WINE GLASS

1 part Blackberry Liqueur
1 part Vodka
1 part Light Cream
3 scoops Vanilla Ice Cream

Combine all ingredients in a blender. Blend until smooth.

Montezuma

CHAMPAGNE FLUTE

1½ parts Tequila
1 part Madeira®
1 Egg Yolk

Combine all ingredients in a blender with ice and blend until smooth.

Moose Milk

COUPETTE GLASS

1 part Light Rum
1 part Spiced Rum
½ part Coffee Liqueur
2 scoops Ice Cream
2 Strawberries

Combine all ingredients in a blender. Blend until smooth.

Morgan Melon

PARFAIT GLASS

2 parts Spiced Rum
1 part Lemon-Lime Soda
1 part Watermelon Schnapps
splash Lime Juice
splash Sweet & Sour Mix

Combine all ingredients in a blender with ice and blend until smooth.

Morning Milk

COUPETTE GLASS

1 part Milk
3 parts Gin
10 Strawberries
1 Kiwi, peeled and sliced

Combine all ingredients in a blender with ice and blend until smooth.

Mountain Brook

COLLINS GLASS

1 part Citrus Vodka
½ part Blue Curaçao
½ part Lime Syrup
½ part Hard Cider

Combine all ingredients in a blender with ice and blend until smooth.

Mud Pie

COUPETTE GLASS

2 parts Crème de Cacao (Dark)
fill with Cream
1 Candy Bar
2 scoops Ice Cream

Combine all ingredients in a blender. Blend until smooth. Works with almost any candy bar.

Mudslide (Mud Boy Recipe)

COUPETTE GLASS

1 part Coffee Liqueur
1 part Irish Cream Liqueur
1 part Vodka
1/2 part Chocolate Syrup

Combine all ingredients in a blender with ice and blend until smooth.

Multiple Orgasm, Cajun Style

COUPETTE GLASS

2 parts Dark Rum
2 parts Coffee Liqueur
1 part Amaretto
1 part Crème de Cacao (White)
1 part Rum Crème Liqueur

Combine all ingredients in a blender with ice and blend until smooth.

My Blue Heaven

HIGHBALL GLASS

1 part Cinnamon Schnapps
1 part Tropical Punch Schnapps
1 1/2 parts Blueberry Schnapps
fill with Blueberries

Combine all ingredients in a blender with ice. Blend until smooth.

Nappy Rash

HURRICANE GLASS

1 1/2 parts Rye Whiskey
1 1/2 parts Spiced Rum
3/4 part Peach Schnapps
2 dashes Iced Tea Mix
fill with Grapefruit Juice

Combine all ingredients in a blender with ice and blend until smooth.

Negril Bay

ROCKS GLASS

1 1/2 parts Dark Rum
1 part Guava Juice
1/2 part Cream
1/2 part Lime Juice
1/4 part Blackberry Liqueur

Combine all ingredients in a blender with ice and blend until smooth.

Neon Voodoo

COUPETTE GLASS

1 part Vodka
1 part Apple Juice
3 parts Mountain Dew®

Combine all ingredients in a blender with ice and blend until smooth.

Nuclear Slush

COUPETTE GLASS

3/4 part Citrus Vodka
3/4 part Bacardi® Limon Rum
1/2 part Melon Liqueur
1/2 part Blue Curaçao
fill with Sweet & Sour Mix

Combine all ingredients in a blender with ice and blend until smooth.

Nutella®

COUPETTE GLASS

1 part Crème de Cacao (Dark)
1 part Irish Cream Liqueur
1 part Hazelnut Liqueur
1 scoop Vanilla Ice Cream

Combine all ingredients in a blender and blend until smooth.

Nutty Colada

COLLINS GLASS

1 part Amaretto
1 part Cream of Coconut
1 part Fresh Pineapple

Combine all ingredients in a blender with ice and blend until smooth.

Ogre Drink

BEER MUG

3 parts Coconut Rum
2 scoops Vanilla Ice Cream
4 parts Cola

Combine all ingredients in a blender. Blend until smooth.

Old Bailey

COUPETTE GLASS

1 part Light Rum
2 parts Cream
1 part Cream of Coconut

Combine all ingredients in a blender with ice and blend until smooth.

Orange Bonbon

WHITE WINE GLASS

1 part Crème de Cacao (White)
1 part Vodka
1 part Orange Juice
2 scoops Orange Sorbet

Combine all ingredients in a blender. Blend until smooth.

Orange Daiquiri

COLLINS GLASS

2 parts Light Rum
1/2 part Triple Sec
1 part Orange Juice
1/2 part Lime Juice
splash Grenadine

Combine all ingredients in a blender with ice and blend until smooth.

Orange Julius

COUPETTE GLASS

1 part Vodka
1 part Milk
1 part Orange Juice
dash Sugar
splash Vanilla Extract

Combine all ingredients in a blender with ice and blend until smooth.

Orange Margarita

COUPETTE GLASS

1 part Tequila
1/2 part Triple Sec
fill with Orange Juice
splash Lime Juice

Combine all ingredients in a blender with ice and blend until smooth.

Orange Tree

PARFAIT GLASS

1 1/2 parts Amaretto
3/4 part Crème de Noyaux
1 1/2 parts Orange Juice
3/4 scoop Vanilla Ice Cream

Combine all ingredients in a blender and blend until smooth.

Organ Grinder

HIGHBALL GLASS

1 part Dark Rum
1 part Light Rum
1 part Whiskey
splash Crème de Cacao (White)
2 parts Cream of Coconut

Combine all ingredients in a blender with ice and blend until smooth.

Orgasmatron

HURRICANE GLASS

1½ parts Crème de Cacao (White)
1½ parts Crème de Coconut
½ part Advocaat
4 parts Strawberry Puree
2 parts Cream

Combine all ingredients in a blender with ice and blend until smooth.

Orient Express

HURRICANE GLASS

1 part Grand Marnier®
1 part Melon Liqueur
1 part Cream of Coconut
1 part Pineapple Juice

Combine all ingredients in a blender with ice and blend until smooth.

Out of Africa

HURRICANE GLASS

2½ parts Vodka
2½ parts Safari®
1 part Pineapple Juice
1 part Grapefruit
2 splashes Grenadine

Combine all ingredients in a blender with ice and blend until smooth.

Pacific Sunset

HURRICANE GLASS

1½ parts Light Rum
1 part Crème de Coconut
3 parts Pineapple Juice
2 parts Papaya Juice
2 parts Strawberry Puree

Combine all ingredients in a blender with ice and blend until smooth.

Papakea

COLLINS GLASS

1 part Crème de Coconut
1 part Vodka
fill with Pineapple Juice

Combine all ingredients in a blender with ice and blend until smooth.

Parrot Perch

HURRICANE GLASS

1½ parts Coconut Rum
½ part Triple Sec
1 Banana
3 parts Orange Juice
1 part Banana Liqueur

Combine all ingredients in a blender with ice and blend until smooth.

Passion Mama

COUPETTE GLASS

1 part Pineapple Rum
½ part Passion Fruit Liqueur
1½ parts Pineapple Juice
1 part Orange Juice
½ part Cream

Combine all ingredients in a blender with ice and blend until smooth.

Passion on the Nile

COUPETTE GLASS

2 parts Passion Fruit Liqueur
1 part Maraschino Liqueur
2 parts Lime Juice
2 parts Orange Juice
2 parts Pineapple Juice

Combine all ingredients in a blender with ice and blend until smooth.

Patria Colada

COLLINS GLASS

1 part Light Rum
1 part Spiced Rum
1 part Passion Fruit Juice
1 part Cream of Coconut

Combine all ingredients in a blender with ice and blend until smooth.

Peach Tree

COLLINS GLASS

1½ parts Vodka
¾ part Peach Schnapps
1 part Cranberry Juice Cocktail
1 part Orange Juice

Combine all ingredients in a blender with ice and blend until smooth.

Peach Velvet

COUPETTE GLASS

1½ parts Peach Brandy
1 part Crème de Cacao (White)
1 part Heavy Cream

Combine all ingredients in a blender with ice and blend until smooth.

Peaches and Cream

RED WINE GLASS

½ part Vodka
1 part Peach Schnapps
2 parts Cream
3 Peach Slices

Combine all ingredients in a blender with ice and blend until smooth.

Peanut Butter Sundae

COUPETTE GLASS

½ part Amaretto
2 scoops Vanilla Ice Cream
1 part Chocolate Syrup
1 part Peanut Butter
1 part Milk
1 part Rum

Combine all ingredients in a blender. Blend until smooth.

Pebbles

WHITE WINE GLASS

1 part Amaretto
1 part Triple Sec
1 part Milk
1 part Coconut Rum

Combine all ingredients in a blender with ice and blend until smooth.

Pensacola Bushwacker

COUPETTE GLASS

1 part Dark Rum
½ part Cream of Coconut
½ part Coffee Liqueur
½ part Crème de Cacao (White)
fill with Half and Half

Combine all ingredients in a blender with ice and blend until smooth.

Peppermint Penguin

WHITE WINE GLASS

½ part Crème de Menthe (Green)
½ part Crème de Cacao (Dark)
3 parts Cream
3 Oreo® Cookies

Combine all ingredients in a blender with ice. Blend until smooth.

Pest Control Nightmare

COUPETTE GLASS

1 part Light Rum
1 part Orange Juice
1 part Apricot Brandy
½ part Triple Sec
½ part Simple Syrup
½ part Raspberry Syrup

Combine all ingredients in a blender with ice and blend until smooth.

Phish-Phood

HURRICANE GLASS

1 part Bourbon
½ part Crème de Cacao (Dark)
½ part Butterscotch Schnapps
¼ part Vanilla Liqueur
2 scoops Vanilla Ice Cream

Combine all ingredients in a blender and blend until smooth.

Phoenix Paradise

COUPE

1 part Vodka
2 parts Cranberry Juice
2 parts Mango Juice
2 parts Orange Juice
2 scoops Vanilla Ice Cream

Combine all ingredients in a blender and blend until smooth.

Picker's Peach

COLLINS GLASS

1 part Light Rum
1 part Peach Schnapps
1 part Orange Juice
1 part Peach Puree
½ part Dark Rum
splash Simple Syrup
dash Orange Bitters

Combine all ingredients in a blender with ice and blend until smooth.

Pickled Parrot

COLLINS GLASS

1 part Melon Liqueur
1 part Dark Rum
½ part Lime Juice
2 parts Grapefruit Juice
fill with Orange Juice

Combine all ingredients in a blender with ice and blend until smooth.

Piña Colada

COUPETTE GLASS

3 parts Light Rum
2 parts Cream of Coconut
2 parts Crushed Pineapple

Combine all ingredients in a blender with ice and blend until smooth.

Pino Frio

COUPETTE GLASS

1¼ parts Spiced Rum
2 Pineapple Slices
dash Sugar

Combine all ingredients in a blender with ice and blend until smooth.

Piritta
HURRICANE GLASS

1 part Crème de Banane
1 part Pisang Ambon® Liqueur
1 part Citrus Vodka
2 scoops Vanilla Ice Cream

Combine all ingredients in a blender. Blend until smooth.

Plainfield Sleeper
COUPETTE GLASS

1 part Vodka
1 part Coffee Liqueur
3 scoops Vanilla Ice Cream

Combine all ingredients in a blender. Blend until smooth.

Polyester Velvet Hammer
HURRICANE GLASS

1 part Vodka
1 part Bourbon
1 part Raspberry Liqueur
1 scoop Ice Cream
fill with Cream

Combine all ingredients in a blender and blend until smooth.

Poolside Margarita
COUPETTE GLASS

2 parts Tequila
1½ parts Triple Sec
splash Blue Curaçao
½ part Lime Juice
dash Powdered Sugar

Combine all ingredients in a blender with ice and blend until smooth.

Population Killer
HURRICANE GLASS

1 part Crème de Cacao (White)
1 part Crème de Menthe (Green)
1 Egg White
fill with Cream

Combine all ingredients in a blender with ice and blend until smooth.

Port of Call
COLLINS GLASS

2 parts Crème de Coconut
1 part Lime Juice
2 parts Orange Juice
fill with Pineapple Juice

Combine all ingredients in a blender with ice and blend until smooth.

Princess's Pleasure
COLLINS GLASS

1 part Peach Schnapps
2 parts Cream of Coconut
2 parts Pineapple Juice
¼ Banana

Combine all ingredients in a blender with ice and blend until smooth.

Puerto Banana
COUPETTE GLASS

1½ parts Vodka
½ part Cream
¼ part Crème de Banane
¼ part Lime Juice
½ Banana

Combine all ingredients in a blender with ice and blend until smooth.

Pumpkin Eater
PARFAIT GLASS

1½ parts Light Rum
1 part Triple Sec
1 part Orange Juice
½ part Cream

Combine all ingredients in a blender with ice and blend until smooth.

Pure Ecstasy

COUPETTE GLASS

1 part Coffee Liqueur
2 parts Irish Cream Liqueur
1 part Vodka

Combine all ingredients in a blender with ice and blend until smooth.

Ragnampiza

HURRICANE GLASS

1 part Coffee Liqueur
1 part Jamaican Rum
1 part Amaretto
1 part Crème de Cacao (Dark)
2 scoops Vanilla Ice Cream

Combine all ingredients in a blender. Blend until smooth.

Rainbow Dream

WHITE WINE GLASS

2 parts Melon Liqueur
½ part Grenadine
2 scoops Vanilla Ice Cream

Combine all ingredients in a blender. Blend until smooth.

Rainbow Sherbet

WHITE WINE GLASS

½ part Crème de Banane
½ part Melon Liqueur
½ part Strawberry Juice
1 part Grenadine
2 parts Orange Juice
2 scoops Orange Sorbet

Combine all ingredients in a blender. Blend until smooth.

Rama Lama Ding Dong

ROCKS GLASS

1 part Scotch
1 part Triple Sec
fill with Passion Fruit Juice

Combine all ingredients in a blender with ice and blend until smooth.

Raspberry Milkshake

COUPE

1 part Black Raspberry Liqueur
1 part Crème de Cacao (White)
2 scoops Vanilla Ice Cream

Combine all ingredients in a blender and blend until smooth.

Razzbaretto

COUPETTE GLASS

1 part Raspberry Liqueur
1 part Amaretto
2 scoops Ice Cream

Combine all ingredients in a blender. Blend until smooth.

Red Cactus

COUPETTE GLASS

1 part Tequila
4 parts Raspberry Juice
1½ parts Sweet & Sour Mix

Combine all ingredients in a blender with ice and blend until smooth.

Reese's Revenge

COUPETTE GLASS

1 part Crème de Cacao (Dark)
1 part Frangelico®
2 parts Chocolate Syrup
1 part Peanut Butter
2 scoops Vanilla Ice Cream
splash Cream

Combine all ingredients in a blender and blend until smooth.

Release Valve

COUPETTE GLASS

1 part Rum
2 parts Vodka
1 part Grenadine
fill with Pineapple Juice

Combine all ingredients in a blender with ice and blend until smooth.

Roasted Dog
HURRICANE GLASS

2 parts Whiskey
1 part Advocaat
1 part Amaretto
fill with Milk

Combine all ingredients in a blender with ice and blend until smooth.

Robin Hood
COUPETTE GLASS

1 part Tequila Reposado
1 part Vodka
2 splashes Pisang Ambon® Liqueur
3 parts Orange Juice
2 parts Pineapple Juice

Combine all ingredients in a blender with ice and blend until smooth.

Rocky Road
COUPETTE GLASS

1 part Frangelico®
1 part Crème de Cacao (Dark)
fill with Cream

Combine all ingredients in a blender with ice and blend until smooth.

Roll in the Fruit Field
COUPETTE GLASS

1 part Strawberry Liqueur
1 part Triple Sec
1 part Crème de Coconut
3 parts Cream
2 scoops Lemon Sherbet

Combine all ingredients in a blender and blend until smooth.

Rootin' Tootin' Varmint
COLLINS GLASS

1 part Root Beer Schnapps
1/2 part Coffee
splash Amaretto
1 scoop Vanilla Ice Cream

Combine all ingredients in a blender. Blend until smooth.

Rose Runner
COLLINS GLASS

1 part Tequila Rose®
1 part Coconut Rum
splash Lime Juice
splash Lemon-Lime Soda
splash Grenadine
splash 151-Proof Rum

Combine all ingredients execpt the 151-Proof Rum in a blender with ice and blend until smooth. Top with the 151-Proof Rum.

Roses in Blue
COUPETTE GLASS

1 1/2 scoops Vanilla Ice Cream
1 part Crème de Coconut
splash Blue Curaçao
splash Cream of Coconut

Combine all ingredients in a blender and blend until smooth.

Royal Peaches and Cream
COUPETTE GLASS

1/2 parts Peach Schnapps
1/2 part Crown Royal® Whiskey
1/2 part Cointreau®
1 1/2 parts Heavy Cream
2 scoops Vanilla Ice Cream

Combine all ingredients in a blender and blend until smooth.

Royal Temptation

COUPETTE GLASS

4 parts Amaretto
3 parts Coffee Liqueur
2 parts Melon Liqueur
1 part Cream

Combine all ingredients in a blender with ice and blend until smooth.

Rummy Sour

COUPETTE GLASS

1½ parts Spiced Rum
2 parts Lemonade

Combine all ingredients in a blender with ice and blend until smooth.

Russian Coffee

COUPETTE GLASS

1 part Vodka
1 part Coffee Liqueur
1 part Heavy Cream

Combine all ingredients in a blender with ice and blend until smooth.

Russian in Exile

COUPETTE GLASS

1 part Irish Cream Liqueur
1 part Coffee Liqueur
1 part Vodka
2 splashes Chocolate Syrup
2 scoops Vanilla Ice Cream

Combine all ingredients in a blender and blend until smooth.

Sabuzzo

HURRICANE GLASS

1 part Irish Cream Liqueur
1 part Frangelico®
½ part Banana Liqueur
½ part Coffee Liqueur
½ Banana
1 part Espresso
1 part Chocolate Syrup

Combine all ingredients in a blender with ice and blend until smooth.

Sambuca Whirl

CHAMPAGNE FLUTE

1 part Cream
1 part Light Rum
1 part Sambuca
1 part Lime Cordial

Combine all ingredients in a blender with ice and blend until smooth.

San Juan

COUPETTE GLASS

1½ parts Rum
½ part Cream of Coconut
1 part Grapefruit Juice
1 part Lime Juice
splash 151-Proof Rum

Combine all ingredients in a blender with ice and blend until smooth.

Sandman

HURRICANE GLASS

1 part Pineapple Juice
½ part Light Rum
splash Amaretto
splash Strawberry Liqueur
splash Lime Juice

Combine all ingredients in a blender with ice and blend until smooth.

Sandstorm

WHITE WINE GLASS

1 part Cream
1 part Coffee
1 part Triple Sec

Combine all ingredients in a blender with ice and blend until smooth.

Saturday Night Fever

COLLINS GLASS

1½ parts Tequila Reposado
1 part Passion Fruit Liqueur
⅔ part Kiwi Schnapps
2 parts Cream
2 parts Melon Puree

Combine all ingredients in a blender with ice and blend until smooth.

Sauzarily

WHITE WINE GLASS

2 parts Tequila Reposado
splash Lime Juice
fill with Orange Juice
½ Banana

Combine all ingredients in a blender with ice and blend until smooth.

Scarlet Ibis

COUPETTE GLASS

¾ part Rum
1½ parts Sweet Vermouth
fill with Cranberry Juice Cocktail
2 parts Ginger Ale

Combine all ingredients in a blender with ice and blend until smooth.

Scat Man

COUPETTE GLASS

½ part Tequila Gold
2 parts Passion Fruit Liqueur
3 parts Pineapple Juice
2 parts Orange Juice

Combine all ingredients in a blender with ice and blend until smooth.

Seaside Liberty

COUPETTE GLASS

¾ part Coffee Liqueur
2 splashes Half and Half
1 part Cream of Coconut
3 parts Pineapple Juice

Combine all ingredients in a blender with ice and blend until smooth.

Segne

COLLINS GLASS

1 part Light Rum
1 part Coffee Liqueur
2 scoops Vanilla Ice Cream

Combine all ingredients in a blender with ice and blend until smooth.

Sex on Ice

COUPE

1 part Cherry Liqueur
1 part Light Rum
1 part Melon Liqueur
1 part Raspberry Liqueur
1 part Strawberry Liqueur
1 part Vodka
2 strawberries

Combine all ingredients in a blender with ice and blend until smooth.

Sexy Blue-Eyed Boy

COLLINS GLASS

1 part Blue Curaçao
1 part Crème de Cacao (White)
1 part Rum Cream Liqueur
1 part Vodka
1 scoop Vanilla Ice Cream

Combine all ingredients in a blender and blend until smooth.

Sherbet Pervert

COUPETTE GLASS

1 part Vodka
2 parts Lemon-Lime Soda
½ part Grenadine
1 scoop Orange Sorbet

Combine all ingredients in a blender and blend until smooth.

Shipper's Clipper

COUPETTE GLASS

2 parts Blue Curaçao
2 parts Cream of Coconut
2 parts Grapefruit Juice
1 part Lime Juice

Combine all ingredients in a blender with ice and blend until smooth.

Shit on a Hot Tin Roof

COLLINS GLASS

2 parts Vodka
3 parts Irish Cream Liqueur
1 Banana

Combine all ingredients in a blender with ice and blend until smooth.

Sin Industries

COUPETTE GLASS

1½ parts Blue Curaçao
1½ parts Triple Sec
1 part Vodka
1 part Grapefruit Juice

Combine all ingredients in a blender with ice and blend until smooth.

Singing Orchard

HURRICANE GLASS

1¼ parts Dark Rum
1 part Cream of Coconut
½ part Raspberry Liqueur
3 splashes Grenadine
fill with Pineapple Juice

Combine all ingredients in a blender with ice and blend until smooth.

Skinny Tart

COUPETTE GLASS

1¼ parts Dark Rum
2 parts Grapefruit Juice
2 parts Pineapple Juice
1 packet Artificial Sweetener

Combine all ingredients in a blender with ice and blend until smooth.

Slalom

COUPETTE GLASS

1 part Vodka
1 part Crème de Cacao (White)
1 part Sambuca
1 part Heavy Cream

Combine all ingredients in a blender with ice and blend until smooth.

Slapstick

COUPETTE GLASS

3/4 part Spiced Rum
1/2 part Strawberry Liqueur
1 part Cream of Coconut
1 part Strawberry Syrup
2 parts Pineapple Juice

Combine all ingredients in a blender with ice and blend until smooth.

Sleeping Panda

COUPETTE GLASS

1 part Amaretto
1 part Butterscotch Schnapps
1 part Milk
fill with Vanilla Ice Cream

Combine all ingredients in a blender. Blend until smooth.

Sloe Melting Iceberg

COUPETTE GLASS

2/3 part Sloe Gin
2/3 part Crème de Cassis
1 part Light Rum
1 part Club Soda
fill with Pineapple Juice

Combine all ingredients in a blender with ice and blend until smooth.

Sloppy Kiss

COUPETTE GLASS

1 part Raspberry Liqueur
1 part Apple Brandy
1 part Sweet & Sour Mix

Combine all ingredients in a blender with ice and blend until smooth.

Slushy

COUPETTE GLASS

2 parts Light Rum
1 1/2 parts Blue Curaçao
1 part Raspberry Liqueur
4 parts Pineapple Juice

Combine all ingredients in a blender with ice and blend until smooth.

Slushy Hanky

COUPETTE GLASS

1 part Godiva® Liqueur
1 part Irish Cream Liqueur
1 part Coconut Rum

Combine all ingredients in a blender with ice and blend until smooth.

Smooth Banana

HURRICANE GLASS

1 part Rum
1 part Cream of Coconut
1 part Banana Puree
fill with Pineapple Juice

Combine all ingredients in a blender with ice and blend until smooth.

Smooth Operator

COUPETTE GLASS

1 part Frangelico®
1/2 part Coffee Liqueur
1/2 part Irish Cream Liqueur
1/2 Banana
3 parts Cream

Combine all ingredients in a blender with ice and blend until smooth.

Smooth Prospect

COUPETTE GLASS

1 1/2 parts Raspberry Liqueur
1 1/2 parts Cranberry Juice Cocktail
1 part Club Soda
1 scoop Vanilla Ice Cream

Combine all ingredients in a blender. Blend until smooth.

Snow Way

WHITE WINE GLASS

1 1/2 parts Vodka
1 1/2 parts Pineapple Juice
2 scoops Vanilla Ice Cream

Combine all ingredients in a blender. Blend until smooth.

Snowshot

HIGHBALL GLASS

3 parts Citrus Vodka
1 scoop Lemon Sherbet
splash Lemon Juice
dash Sugar

Combine all ingredients in a blender with ice and blend until smooth.

Soft Touch

HURRICANE GLASS

3/4 part Peach Schnapps
1/2 part Banana Syrup
3 parts Piña Colada Mix

Combine all ingredients in a blender with ice and blend until smooth.

Sorbettino

COUPETTE GLASS

1 1/2 parts Vodka
1 part Triple Sec
1/2 part Cream
splash Grenadine
2 scoops Lemon Sherbet

Combine all ingredients in a blender. Blend until smooth.

Spice Me Up Nice

COUPETTE GLASS

1 part Light Rum
1 part Orange Juice
1 part Sweet & Sour Mix
1/2 part Spiced Rum
dash Orange Bitters
fill with Pineapple Juice

Combine all ingredients in a blender with ice and blend until smooth.

Spiced Banana Daiquiri

HURRICANE GLASS

1 part Spiced Rum
1/2 part Crème de Banane
2 parts Sweet & Sour Mix
1/2 Banana

Combine all ingredients in a blender with ice and blend until smooth.

Spider Monkey

HIGHBALL GLASS

1 part Crème de Banane
1 part Coffee Liqueur
1 scoop Ice Cream

Combine all ingredients in a blender. Blend until smooth.

Spookie Juice

HURRICANE GLASS

1 1/2 parts Dark Rum
1 part Crème de Banane
2 parts Cream of Coconut
1 part Banana Juice
1 part Mango Juice

Combine all ingredients in a blender with ice and blend until smooth.

Spotted Chocolate Monkey

COUPETTE GLASS

2 parts Coconut Rum
1 part Banana Liqueur
1/2 part Chocolate Syrup
2 scoops Vanilla Ice Cream
2 Chocolate Chip Cookies

Combine all ingredients in a blender and blend until smooth.

Squinting Daedelus

COLLINS GLASS

1½ parts Silver Tequila
½ part Triple Sec
fill with Sweet & Sour Mix
dash Salt

Combine all ingredients in a blender with ice and blend until smooth.

Straw Hat

COUPETTE GLASS

1 part Vodka
1 part Coconut Rum
¼ cup Strawberries

Combine all ingredients in a blender with ice and blend until smooth.

Strawberries & Cream

COUPETTE GLASS

1 part Strawberry Liqueur
2 dashes Sugar
2 parts Half and Half
2 Strawberries

Combine all ingredients in a blender with ice and blend until smooth.

Strawberry Blush

WHITE WINE GLASS

2 parts Vodka
2 parts Strawberry Liqueur
1 part Strawberries
2 scoops Vanilla Ice Cream

Combine all ingredients in a blender. Blend until smooth.

Strawberry Colada

COLLINS GLASS

1 part Dark Rum
1 part Light Rum
1½ parts Cream of Coconut
4 parts Pineapple Juice
6 Strawberries

Combine all ingredients in a blender with ice and blend until smooth.

Strawberry FrappaChata

COUPE

1 part RumChata
1 part Piña Colada mix
splash Spiced Rum
1 part Frozen Strawberries

Combine all ingredients in a blender with ice and blend until smooth.

Strawberry Patch

COUPETTE GLASS

1½ parts Southern Comfort®
3 parts Frozen Strawberries
2 parts Orange Juice

Combine all ingredients in a blender with ice and blend until smooth.

Strawberry Piña Colada

HIGHBALL GLASS

1 part Rum
1 part Strawberry Liqueur
1 part Piña Colada Mix
1 part Pineapple Juice

Combine all ingredients in a blender with ice and blend until smooth.

Strawberry Shortcake

COUPETTE GLASS

1 part Amaretto
1 part Crème de Cacao (Dark)
3 parts Strawberries
2 scoops Ice Cream

Combine all ingredients in a blender and blend until smooth.

Strawberry Smash

COUPETTE GLASS

1 part Light Rum
1 part Wild Berry Schnapps
½ part 151-Proof Rum
1 part Sweet & Sour Mix
6 Strawberries
1 Banana

Combine all ingredients in a blender with ice and blend until smooth.

Sudberry Blast

HURRICANE GLASS

1 part Amaretto
1 part Coconut Rum
1 part Spiced Rum
1 part Whipping Cream
2 parts Strawberry Daiquiri Mix
splash Pineapple Juice
1½ parts Piña Colada Mix

Combine all ingredients in a blender with ice and blend until smooth. Top with Whipped Cream.

Summer Breeze

WHITE WINE GLASS

1½ parts Rum
1 part Papaya Juice
2 parts Orange Juice
½ Banana

Combine all ingredients in a blender with ice and blend until smooth.

Summer Dream

COLLINS GLASS

1 part Crème de Cacao (White)
1 part Light Rum
1 part Red Curacao
1 scoop Vanilla Ice Cream

Combine all ingredients in a blender and blend until smooth.

A Sundae on Sunday

COUPETTE GLASS

⅔ part Light Rum
⅔ part Amaretto
1 part Cream of Coconut
1 part Cherry Syrup
splash Milk

Combine all ingredients in a blender with ice and blend until smooth.

Sunny Dream

WHITE WINE GLASS

1½ parts Apricot Brandy
¾ part Triple Sec
4 parts Orange Juice
2 scoops Vanilla Ice Cream

Combine all ingredients in a blender. Blend until smooth.

Surf's Up

PARFAIT GLASS

½ part Crème de Banane
½ part Crème de Cacao (White)
1 part Light Cream
fill with Pineapple Juice

Combine all ingredients in a blender with ice and blend until smooth.

Surfside Swinger

WHITE WINE GLASS

1 part Light Rum
1 part Gin
1 part Passion Fruit Juice
¼ part Grenadine

Combine all ingredients in a blender with ice and blend until smooth.

Sweet Love

COLLINS GLASS

- 2/3 part Crème de Cacao (Dark)
- 2/3 part Galliano®
- 2/3 part Vanilla Vodka
- 2 parts Milk
- 1 scoop Vanilla Ice Cream

Combine all ingredients in a blender. Blend until smooth.

Sweet Sunset

HURRICANE GLASS

- 1 1/2 parts Light Rum
- 2 1/2 parts Passion Fruit Nectar
- 2 parts Sweet & Sour Mix
- 1 part Strawberries

Combine all ingredients in a blender with ice and blend until smooth.

Taipan

WHITE WINE GLASS

- 2 parts Brandy
- 1 part Apricot Brandy
- 1 part Mango Juice
- 1/2 part Fresh Papaya

Combine all ingredients in a blender with ice and blend until smooth.

Tan Russian

COUPETTE GLASS

- 8 parts Coffee Liqueur
- 3 scoops Vanilla Ice Cream
- fill with Milk

Combine all ingredients in a blender and blend until smooth.

Teal Squeal

HIGHBALL GLASS

- 1 part Vodka
- 1 part Blue Curaçao
- 2 parts Pineapple Juice

Combine all ingredients in a blender with ice and blend until smooth.

Tennessee Waltz

PARFAIT GLASS

- 1 1/4 parts Peach Schnapps
- 2 parts Pineapple Juice
- 2 scoops Vanilla Ice Cream

Combine all ingredients in a blender. Blend until smooth.

Tequila Bay Breeze

HURRICANE GLASS

- 1 part Tequila Rose®
- 1/2 part Midori®
- 1/2 part Blue Curaçao
- 1/4 part 151-Proof Rum
- 1 part Orange Juice
- 1 part Pineapple Juice

Combine all ingredients in a blender with ice and blend until smooth.

Terrazo

COUPETTE GLASS

- 1 1/2 parts Vodka
- 1/2 part Crème de Banane
- fill with Orange Juice

Combine all ingredients in a blender with ice and blend until smooth.

Terry

HURRICANE GLASS

- 2 parts Tequila
- 2 parts Cream of Coconut
- 3 parts Orange Juice
- 3 parts Pineapple Juice

Combine all ingredients in a blender with ice and blend until smooth.

Thompson

COLLINS GLASS

2 parts Jägermeister®
1 part Coconut Rum
1 part Triple Sec
3 parts Sweet & Sour Mix
3 parts Pineapple Juice

Combine all ingredients in a blender with ice and blend until smooth.

Thurston Howell

HURRICANE GLASS

3/4 part Spiced Rum
1/2 part Crème de Banane
2 parts Orange Juice
1 part Sweet & Sour Mix
1/2 part Simple Syrup
1/2 part Grenadine

Combine all ingredients in a blender with ice and blend until smooth.

Tidbit

HIGHBALL GLASS

1 part Gin
1 scoop Vanilla Ice Cream
splash Dry Sherry

Combine all ingredients in a blender and blend until smooth.

Tire Swing

COUPETTE GLASS

1 part Rum
3 parts Amaretto
fill with Orange Juice

Combine all ingredients in a blender with ice and blend until smooth.

Titanic Monkey

COUPETTE GLASS

1/2 part Light Rum
1/2 part Vodka
1 1/2 parts Banana Liqueur
2 parts Cream of Coconut
2 parts Pineapple Juice

Combine all ingredients in a blender with ice and blend until smooth.

Toblerone®

HIGHBALL GLASS

1 part Frangelico®
1 part Coffee Liqueur
1 part Irish Cream Liqueur
2 parts Cream
1 part Honey

Combine all ingredients in a blender with ice and blend until smooth.

Touchie Feelie

CHAMPAGNE FLUTE

1 1/2 parts Light Rum
1/2 part Brandy
1/4 part Passion Fruit Nectar
2 splashes Lemon Juice

Combine all ingredients in a blender with ice and blend until smooth.

Trolley Car

HIGHBALL GLASS

2 parts Strawberry Vodka
1 part Amaretto
2 scoops Vanilla Ice Cream
2 Strawberries

Combine all ingredients in a blender and blend until smooth.

Tropic Freeze

COUPETTE GLASS

1 1/4 parts Spiced Rum
1 1/2 parts Cream of Coconut
2 parts Orange Juice
2 parts Pineapple Juice
1/2 part Grenadine

Combine all ingredients in a blender with ice and blend until smooth.

Tropical Coffee

COLLINS GLASS

1 part Crème de Coconut
2/3 part Vanilla Liqueur
2 parts Coffee
2/3 part Cream

Combine all ingredients in a blender with ice and blend until smooth.

Tropical Heaven

HURRICANE GLASS

2 parts Coconut Rum
1 part Vodka
6 parts Pineapple Juice
1 scoop Vanilla Ice Cream
1 Banana

Combine all ingredients in a blender and blend until smooth.

Tropical Lust

HURRICANE GLASS

1 1/2 parts Sloe Gin
1 part Vodka
1/2 part Melon Liqueur
1/2 part Southern Comfort
fill with Pineapple Juice

Combine all ingredients in a blender with ice and blend until smooth.

Tumbleweed

COUPETTE GLASS

1 part Amaretto
1 part Crème de Cacao (White)
2 parts Cream

Combine all ingredients in a blender with ice and blend until smooth.

Turtledove

COUPETTE GLASS

1 part Dark Rum
1/4 part Amaretto
fill with Orange Juice

Combine all ingredients in a blender with ice and blend until smooth.

Tutti-Frutti

WHITE WINE GLASS

1 1/2 parts Rum
1 part Papaya Juice
1 part Strawberry Puree
1 part Peach Puree
1/4 Banana
1/2 part Simple Syrup

Combine all ingredients in a blender with ice and blend until smooth.

Up the Duff

HIGHBALL GLASS

1 part Coffee Liqueur
1 part Crème de Cacao (White)
1 part Brandy
1 scoop Vanilla Ice Cream

Combine all ingredients in a blender. Blend until smooth.

Vanilla Jesus

COUPETTE GLASS

2 parts Peach Schnapps
1 part Vodka
1 part Coconut Rum
splash Vanilla Extract

Combine all ingredients in a blender with ice and blend until smooth.

Very Berry Colada
WHITE WINE GLASS

½ part Dark Rum
¾ part Wild Berry Schnapps
2 parts Cream of Coconut
2 parts Pineapple Juice

Combine all ingredients in a blender with ice and blend until smooth.

Very Merry Berry
WHITE WINE GLASS

¾ part Blackberry Liqueur
¾ part Raspberry Liqueur
¾ part Strawberry Liqueur
½ part Amaretto
1 scoop Vanilla Ice Cream

Combine all ingredients in a blender and blend until smooth.

Vulgar Witch
COUPETTE GLASS

1½ parts Passion Fruit Liqueur
1 part Sloe Gin
2 parts Grapefruit Juice
1 part Lime Juice
3 parts Orange Juice

Combine all ingredients in a blender with ice and blend until smooth.

Wedding Cake
HURRICANE GLASS

2 parts Light Rum
1 part Amaretto
1 part Cream
1 part Milk
1 part Cream of Coconut
3 parts Pineapple Juice

Combine all ingredients in a blender with ice and blend until smooth.

A Weekend in Pleasantville
COUPETTE GLASS

2 parts Dark Rum
1 part Crème de Coconut
2 parts Strawberry Puree
½ part Vanilla Syrup
1 part Cream

Combine all ingredients in a blender with ice and blend until smooth.

Wet Blanket
COLLINS GLASS

1 part Crème de Cacao (Dark)
1 part Crème de Banane

Combine all ingredients in a blender with ice and blend until smooth.

Wet Snatch
MARGARITA GLASS

1 part Blue Raspberry Liqueur
1 part Tequila
1 part Vanilla Vodka
2 parts Coconut Milk
2 parts Pineapple Juice

Combine all ingredients in a blender with ice and blend until smooth.

White Dove
COUPETTE GLASS

1 part Amaretto
1 part Crème de Cacao (White)
3 scoops Ice Cream

Combine all ingredients in a blender. Blend until smooth.

White Monkey
HURRICANE GLASS

1½ parts Light Rum
1½ parts Dark Rum
½ part Crème de Banane
1 part Cream of Coconut
4 parts Pineapple Juice

Combine all ingredients in a blender with ice and blend until smooth.

White Mountain

COUPETTE GLASS

1 part Sake
1 part Piña Colada Mix
1 part Half and Half

Combine all ingredients in a blender with ice and blend until smooth.

White Witch

COUPETTE GLASS

1 part Vodka
1 part Crème de Cacao (White)
2 scoops Vanilla Ice Cream

Combine all ingredients in a blender. Blend until smooth.

Whitecap Margarita

COUPETTE GLASS

2 parts Tequila
1½ parts Lime Juice
fill with Cream of Coconut

Combine all ingredients in a blender with ice and blend until smooth.

Wigwam

COUPETTE GLASS

1 part Melon Liqueur
1 part Strawberry Liqueur
1 part Lemon Juice

Combine all ingredients in a blender with ice and blend until smooth.

Wild Banshee

COUPETTE GLASS

1 part Spiced Rum
¼ part Amaretto
1½ parts Half and Half
½ Banana

Combine all ingredients in a blender with ice and blend until smooth.

Wild Tusker

COUPETTE GLASS

1 part Light Rum
1 part Irish Cream Liqueur
½ part Amaretto
splash Crème de Cacao (Dark)
1 scoop Vanilla Ice Cream

Combine all ingredients in a blender. Blend until smooth.

Windy Beach

HURRICANE GLASS

2 parts Crème de Cacao (White)
1 part Spiced Rum
4 parts Milk
4 parts Orange Juice
splash Lime Juice

Combine all ingredients in a blender with ice and blend until smooth.

Winter Sunshine

HURRICANE GLASS

2 parts Rum
2 parts Vodka
fill with Orange Juice
1 Banana

Combine all ingredients in a blender with ice and blend until smooth.

World News

HURRICANE GLASS

2 parts Dark Rum
1 part Crème de Banane
1 part Cream
1½ parts Cream of Coconut
1 part Pineapple Juice
1 part Strawberry Juice
1 part Blue Curaçao

Combine all ingredients except the Blue Curaçao in a blender with ice and blend until smooth. Top with Blue Curaçao.

Wow-Monkey

HIGHBALL GLASS

1 1/2 parts Crème de Banane
2 parts Orange Juice
1 scoop Vanilla Ice Cream
1/2 Banana

Combine all ingredients in a blender and blend until smooth.

Xylophone

COUPETTE GLASS

1 part Tequila
1/2 part Crème de Cacao (White)
1 part Crème
1/2 part Simple Syrup

Combine all ingredients in a blender with ice and blend until smooth.

Yahoo

HURRICANE GLASS

1 part Vodka
1 part Triple Sec
fill with Fruit Punch

Combine all ingredients in a blender with ice and blend until smooth.

Yellow Tiger

HIGHBALL GLASS

1 1/2 part Vodka
2 scoops Ice Cream
2 parts Lemonade

Combine all ingredients in a blender and blend until smooth.

Yo-Yo

COLLINS GLASS

1 part Banana Rum
1 part Cherry Juice
fill with Milk

Combine all ingredients in a blender with ice and blend until smooth.

Yucatán

COLLINS GLASS

1 1/2 parts Tequila Reposado
1 part Crème de Banane
fill with Passion Fruit Juice
splash Galliano®

Combine all ingredients in a blender with ice and blend until smooth.

Yum Yum

COUPETTE GLASS

1 part Melon Liqueur
1 part Banana Liqueur
fill with Cream
2 scoops Ice Cream

Combine all ingredients in a blender. Blend until smooth.

Zodiac

COUPETTE GLASS

1 1/2 parts Light Rum
1 part Triple Sec
1/2 part Banana Liqueur
2 parts Lemon Juice
2 parts Orange Juice

Combine all ingredients in a blender with ice and blend until smooth.

COOLERS

Start with a liquor, add a liqueur or some juice for flavor, and fill the glass with soda.

10 Toes

COLLINS GLASS

3 parts Hpnotiq®
fill with Lemon-Lime Soda

Build over ice.

3001

COLLINS GLASS

1 part Vodka
1 part Blue Curaçao
splash Lime Juice
fill with Lemon-Lime Soda

Mix with ice.

491

HIGHBALL GLASS

1 part Light Rum
1 part Gin
1 part Apricot Brandy
fill with Ginger Ale

Mix with ice.

Absolut® Limousine

COLLINS GLASS

2 parts Citrus Vodka
1 part Lime Juice
fill with Tonic Water

Build over ice and stir.

Absolutely Screwed Up

COLLINS GLASS

1 part Citrus Vodka
1 part Orange Juice
1 part Triple Sec
fill with Ginger Ale

Build over ice and stir.

Affair

HIGHBALL GLASS

2 parts Strawberry Vodka
2 parts Cranberry Juice
2 parts Orange Juice
fill with Club Soda

Build over ice and stir.

Albemarle

COLLINS GLASS

1 part Club Soda
2 parts Gin
1½ parts Lemon Juice
splash Raspberry Syrup
1 tbsp powdered sugar

Shake all but Club Soda with ice and strain over ice. Top with Club Soda.

Algo Especial

COLLINS GLASS

1½ parts Dark Rum
½ part Crème de Cacao (White)
½ part Dry Gin
fill with Tonic Water
splash Grenadine

Shake with ice and strain over ice. Top with a splash of Grenadine.

Alien Secretion
COLLINS GLASS

1 part Melon Liqueur
1 part Vodka
2 parts Pineapple Juice
fill with Club Soda

Build over ice and stir.

Almond Eye
COLLINS GLASS

1 part Brandy
1 part Gin
1 part Amaretto
½ part Grenadine
fill with Club Soda

Build over ice and stir.

Amaretto Cherry Sour
COLLINS GLASS

2 parts Amaretto
1 part Sweet & Sour Mix
splash Grenadine
fill with Cherry Lemon-Lime Soda

Build over ice and stir.

Amaretto Collins
COLLINS GLASS

2 parts Amaretto
½ part Simple Syrup
fill with Club Soda

Build over ice and stir.

Amaretto Cooler
HIGHBALL GLASS

1½ parts Amaretto
1½ parts Vanilla Vodka
fill with Cola

Build over ice and stir.

Amaretto Rose
COLLINS GLASS

1½ parts Amaretto
½ part Lime Juice
fill with Club Soda

Build over ice and stir.

Amaretto Spritzer
COLLINS GLASS

2 parts Amaretto
fill with Club Soda

Build over ice and stir.

Amber Amour
COLLINS GLASS

1½ parts Amaretto
½ part Sweet & Sour Mix
fill with Club Soda

Build over ice and stir.

American Cobbler
COLLINS GLASS

1 part Southern Comfort®
½ part Peach Schnapps
½ part Lemon Juice
½ part Simple Syrup
fill with Ginger Ale

Build over ice and stir.

Americano
HIGHBALL GLASS

1 part Sweet Vermouth
1 part Campari®
fill with Club Soda

Build over ice and stir. Garnish with a Lemon Twist.

An Arif
COLLINS GLASS

1½ parts Rum
½ part Peach Schnapps
2 parts Orange Juice
1 part Cranberry Juice Cocktail
fill with Ginger Ale
splash Lemon Juice

Build over ice and stir.

Angel of Mercy

HIGHBALL GLASS

1½ parts Blue Curaçao
⅔ part Orange Liqueur
⅔ part Lime Juice
fill with Ginger Ale

Build over ice and stir.

Annie

COLLINS GLASS

1 part Vodka
1 part Cranberry Liqueur
½ part Cream
splash Lime Juice
fill with Club Soda

Build over ice and stir.

Apple Blow

COLLINS GLASS

1½ parts Applejack
1 Egg White
dash Powdered Sugar
1 part Apple Juice
fill with Club Soda

Shake all but Club Soda with ice and pour. Top with Club Soda. Garnish with a Lemon Wedge.

Apple Brandy Cooler

HIGHBALL GLASS

2 parts Apple Brandy
fill with Lemon-Lime Soda

Build over ice and stir.

Apple Core

COLLINS GLASS

1½ parts Light Rum
½ part Applejack
½ part Sour Apple Schnapps
½ part Sweetened Lime Juice
fill with Club Soda

Build over ice and stir.

Apple Rum Cooler

ROCKS GLASS

1½ parts Añejo Rum
½ part Applejack
splash Lime Juice
fill with Club Soda

Shake all but Club Soda with ice and strain over ice. Top with Club Soda.

Apple Mojito

COLLINS GLASS

3 fresh Mint Sprigs
2 Lime Wedges
2 tsp Sugar
2 parts Apple Rum
fill with Club Soda

In the glass, muddle the Mint, Lime, and Sugar. Add crushed ice and the Rum and stir. Fill with Club Soda and garnish with a Green Apple Slice.

Apribon

COLLINS GLASS

1½ parts Jim Beam®
splash Apricot Brandy
dash Angostura® Bitters
fill with Club Soda
splash Grapefruit Juice
splash Lemon Juice

Build over ice and stir.

Apricot Breeze

HURRICANE GLASS

1 part Vodka
3 parts Apricot Nectar
fill with Tonic Water

Build over ice and stir.

Apricot Collins

HIGHBALL GLASS

½ part Apricot Brandy
1½ parts Gin
splash Lemon Juice
fill with Club Soda

Build over ice and stir.

Apricot Fizz
HIGHBALL GLASS

2 parts Apricot Brandy
dash Powdered Sugar
½ part Lemon Juice
½ part Lime Juice
fill with Club Soda

Shake all but Club Soda with ice and strain over ice. Top with Club Soda.

April Shower
WHITE WINE GLASS

1½ parts Brandy
2 parts Orange Juice
fill with Club Soda

Build over ice and stir.

Aquafresh
ROCKS GLASS

1½ parts Vodka
½ part Crème de Menthe (Green)
fill with Club Soda

Build over ice and stir.

Aquarium
COLLINS GLASS

1 part Rum
1 part Blue Curaçao
½ part Grapefruit Juice
fill with Tonic Water

Build over ice and stir.

Arawack Slap
HIGHBALL GLASS

½ part Light Rum
½ part Dark Rum
1 part Triple Sec
½ part Sweet & Sour Mix
½ part Pineapple Juice
fill with Ginger Ale

Build over ice and stir.

Arctic Summer
HIGHBALL GLASS

1½ parts Gin
¾ part Apricot Brandy
⅙ part Grenadine
fill with Bitter Lemon Soda

Build over ice and stir.

Arcturian Sunrise
COLLINS GLASS

1 part Blue Curaçao
1 part Blackberry Liqueur
½ part Grenadine
fill with Club Soda

Build over ice.

Arsenic
COLLINS GLASS

1 part Silver Tequila
½ part Passion Fruit Liqueur
splash Peach Schnapps
dash Orange Bitters
⅔ part Lemon Juice
⅔ part Peach Puree
fill with Club Soda

Shake all but Club Soda with ice and strain. Top with Club Soda.

Aunt Flo
HIGHBALL GLASS

1½ parts Sloe Gin
½ part Orange Juice
¼ part Lemon Juice
1 Egg White
dash Powdered Sugar
fill with Club Soda

Shake all but Club Soda with ice and strain. Top with Club Soda.

Auto da Fe
COLLINS GLASS

1½ parts Vodka
splash Lime Juice
fill with Club Soda

Build over ice and stir.

Axelrod's Sweet Concoction

HIGHBALL GLASS

1 part Amaretto
1 part Peach Schnapps
1/2 part Dry Vermouth
fill with Club Soda

Build over ice and stir.

Baby Doc

COLLINS GLASS

1 part Gin
1/2 part Crème de Cacao (White)
1 part Pineapple Juice
1 part Kiwi Juice
fill with Tonic Water

Build over ice and stir.

Back Bay Balm

COLLINS GLASS

1 1/2 parts Gin
3 parts Cranberry Juice Cocktail
1/2 part Lemon Juice
3 dashes Orange Bitters
fill with Club Soda

Shake all but Club Soda with ice and strain. Top with Club Soda.

Back Wash

COLLINS GLASS

1/2 part Kiwi Schnapps
1/2 part Grand Marnier®
1 1/2 parts Mezcal
splash Lemon Syrup
2/3 part Lemon Juice
fill with Club Soda

Shake all but Club Soda with ice and strain. Top with Club Soda.

Backstage Pass

HIGHBALL GLASS

1 part Orange Vodka
1/2 part Triple Sec
1/2 part Cherry Brandy
1 part Citrus Rum
2 parts Orange Juice
fill with Club Soda

Shake all but Club Soda with ice and strain. Top with Club Soda.

Bahama Highball

HIGHBALL GLASS

2 parts Gin
splash Vermouth
fill with Ginger Ale

Build over ice and stir. Garnish with a Lemon Twist.

Banana Balm

COLLINS GLASS

1 1/2 parts Vodka
1/2 part Banana Liqueur
splash Lime Juice
fill with Club Soda

Shake all but Club Soda with ice and strain. Top with Club Soda.

Banana Cooler

HIGHBALL GLASS

2 parts Banana Liqueur
1 part Orange Juice
1 part Lemon-Lime Soda

Build over ice and stir.

Banker's Doom

COLLINS GLASS

1 part Whiskey
1 part Vodka
1 part Melon Liqueur
fill with Club Soda

Shake all but Club Soda with ice and strain. Top with Club Soda.

Barney
COLLINS GLASS

2 parts Grape Vodka
fill with Grape Soda

Build over ice and stir.

Barney Gone Bad
COLLINS GLASS

2 parts Grape Vodka
1 part Jägermeister
fill with Grape Soda

Build over ice and stir.

Barramundy
HIGHBALL GLASS

1 part Vodka
½ part Blackberry Liqueur
½ part Raspberry Liqueur
fill with Club Soda
1 part Cranberry Juice Cocktail

Build over ice and stir.

Bayard Fizz
COLLINS GLASS

2 parts Gin
½ part Maraschino Liqueur
½ part Lime Juice
½ part Raspberry Syrup
fill with Club Soda

Shake all but Club Soda with ice and strain. Top with Club Soda.

Beach Ball Cooler
COLLINS GLASS

1½ parts Vodka
1 part Lime
½ part Crème de Cacao (White)
fill with Ginger Ale

Shake all but Ginger Ale with ice and strain. Top with Ginger Ale.

Beach Beauty
COLLINS GLASS

1½ parts Vodka
1½ parts Orange Juice
1 part Crème de Banane
splash Grenadine
fill with Tonic Water

Build over ice and stir.

Beady Little Eyes
COLLINS GLASS

1½ parts Light Rum
1 part Orange Juice
¼ part Lemon Juice
fill with Ginger Ale

Build over ice and stir.

Beasley
COLLINS GLASS

1 part Brandy
1 part Tequila
1 part Triple Sec
1 part Vodka
2 parts Vanilla Liqueur
½ part Lemon Juice
fill with Tonic Water

Shake all but Club Soda with ice and strain. Top with Club Soda.

Bee
HIGHBALL GLASS

1 part Vodka
1 part Banana Liqueur
fill with Ginger Ale

Build over ice and stir.

Beefeater® Sunrise
COLLINS GLASS

1 part Dry Gin
splash Crème de Banane
fill with Tonic Water
splash Grenadine

Build over ice.

Bermuda Cooler

COLLINS GLASS

1 part Brandy
1 part Dry Gin
fill with Ginger Ale
dash Orange Bitters

Build over ice and stir.

Bermuda Highball

COLLINS GLASS

1 part Brandy
1 part Dry Vermouth
1 part Gin
fill with Ginger Ale

Build over ice and stir.

Big Dipper

ROCKS GLASS

1 part Dark Rum
1 part Brandy
splash Lime Juice
dash Sugar
splash Cointreau®
fill with Club Soda

Shake all but Club Soda with ice and strain. Top with Club Soda.

Big Game

COLLINS GLASS

1½ parts Orange Rum
1½ parts Raspberry Rum
½ part Pineapple Juice
fill with Cranberry Juice
top with Lemon-Lime Soda

Build over ice and stir.

Big Ol' Girl

COLLINS GLASS

1 part Triple Sec
1 part Vodka
splash Lime Juice
fill with Club Soda

Build over ice and stir.

Big Sky

COLLINS GLASS

2 parts Cake Vodka
splash Blue Curaçao
fill with Lemon-Lime Soda

Build over ice and stir.

Billie Holiday

COLLINS GLASS

1 part Vodka
fill with Ginger Ale
splash Grenadine

Build over ice and stir.

Billy Taylor

COLLINS GLASS

2 parts Gin
½ part Lime Juice
fill with Club Soda

Build over ice and stir.

Bingo

COLLINS GLASS

1 part Vodka
1 part Mandarine Napoléon® Liqueur
1 part Apricot Brandy
fill with Club Soda

Build over ice and stir.

Bitter Tears

HIGHBALL GLASS

1½ parts Gin
1 part Maraschino Liqueur
splash Peppermint Liqueur
splash Lemon Juice
fill with Tonic Water

Build over ice and stir.

Black Betty

COLLINS GLASS

1 part Peach Schnapps
1 part Blackberry Liqueur
1 part Lime Juice
fill with Club Soda

Build over ice and stir.

Blue Glory
COLLINS GLASS

2 parts Peppermint Schnapps
½ part Blue Curaçao
fill with Lemon-Lime Soda

Build over ice and stir.

Blue Ice Mountain
HIGHBALL GLASS

2 parts Blue Curaçao
1 part Vodka
fill with Club Soda

Build over ice and stir.

Blue in the Face
ROCKS GLASS

1 part Vodka
1 part Gin
1 part Light Rum
1 part Blue Curaçao
splash Sugar
fill with Tonic Water

Build over ice and stir.

Blue Motorcycle
COLLINS GLASS

½ part Vodka
½ part Gin
½ part Light Rum
½ part Triple Sec
½ part Tequila
½ part Blue Curaçao
½ part Sweet & Sour Mix
fill with Lemon-Lime Soda

Build over ice and stir.

Blue Rose
COLLINS GLASS

1 part Blue Curaçao
1 part Blavod® Black Vodka
1 part Currant Vodka
fill with Tonic Water

Build over ice and stir.

Blue Swan
HIGHBALL GLASS

2 parts Hpnotiq
1 part Watermelon Vodka
fill with Lemon-Lime Soda
dash Lemon Juice

Build over ice and stir. Top with Lemon Juice.

Blue Tears
COLLINS GLASS

2 parts Cake Vodka
fill with Lemon-Lime Soda
splash Blue Curaçao

Build over ice. Top with Blue Curaçao.

Blue Water
HIGHBALL GLASS

1½ parts Vodka
¼ part Blue Curaçao
fill with Club Soda

Build over ice and stir.

Blueberry Kick
COLLINS GLASS

1 part Vodka
2 parts Blueberry Schnapps
splash Cream
fill with Club Soda

Build over ice and stir.

The Blues Brothers
HIGHBALL GLASS

1 part Coconut Rum
½ part Blue Curaçao
4 parts Red Bull Energy Drink
fill with Lemon-Lime soda

Build over ice.

Blues Club
HIGHBALL GLASS

1 part Blueberry Schnapps
1 part Orange Juice
fill with Club Soda

Build over ice and stir.

Bomba

HIGHBALL GLASS

1 part Spiced Rum
1 part Light Rum
fill with Ginger Ale
splash Lime Juice

Build over ice and stir.

Bonanza Fresh

COLLINS GLASS

1½ parts Gin
⅔ part Lychee Liqueur
½ part Sake
½ part Mango Schnapps
splash Orange Bitters
fill with Club Soda
splash Lemon Juice

Build over ice and stir.

Bongofizz

COLLINS GLASS

2 parts Gin
½ part Maraschino Liqueur
½ part Lime Juice
½ part Raspberry Syrup
fill with Club Soda

Shake all but Club Soda with ice and strain. Top with Club Soda.

Bonne Chance

COLLINS GLASS

1 part Cognac
1 part Triple Sec
fill with Club Soda

Build over ice and stir.

The Bottom Line

HIGHBALL GLASS

1½ parts Vodka
½ part Lime Juice
fill with Tonic Water

Build over ice and stir.

Bourbon Rumbo

COLLINS GLASS

1 part Bourbon
1 part Dark Rum
1 part Dry Vermouth
1 part Simple Syrup
fill with Club Soda

Shake all but Club Soda with ice and strain. Top with Club Soda.

Branded Nuts

COLLINS GLASS

1½ parts Apricot Brandy
splash Blue Curaçao
splash Amaretto
splash Orange Liqueur
splash Frangelico®
fill with Club Soda

Shake all but Club Soda with ice and strain. Top with Club Soda.

Brandy Cobbler

ROCKS GLASS

2 parts Brandy
splash Sugar
fill with Club Soda

Shake all but Club Soda with ice and strain. Top with Club Soda. Garnish with a Lemon Slice.

Brighton Punch

COLLINS GLASS

1½ parts Bourbon
1 part Brandy
1 part Orange Juice
fill with Club Soda

Build over ice and stir.

Bronx Cheer

COLLINS GLASS

2 parts Apricot Brandy
1 part Raspberry Syrup
fill with Club Soda

Build over ice and stir.

Buck Jones

HIGHBALL GLASS

1½ parts Light Rum
1 part Sweet Sherry
splash Lime Juice
fill with Ginger Ale

Build over ice and stir.

Buckhead Root Beer

HIGHBALL GLASS

1½ parts Jägermeister®
fill with Club Soda

Build over ice and stir.

Bulldog

HIGHBALL GLASS

1½ parts Gin
fill with Ginger Ale
splash Orange Juice

Build over ice and stir.

Bull's Eye

HIGHBALL GLASS

1 part Brandy
2 parts Hard Apple Cider
fill with Ginger Ale

Build over ice and stir.

Butterfly Bush

COLLINS GLASS

2 parts Lemon Vodka
½ part Strawberry Liqueur
½ part Limoncello
½ part Lime Juice
fill with Lemon-Lime Soda

Build over ice and stir.

Cablegram

HIGHBALL GLASS

2 parts Whiskey
½ part Lemon Juice
dash Powdered Sugar
fill with Ginger Ale

Build over ice and stir.

Caboose Cooler

HURRICANE GLASS

1 part Orange Vodka
1 part Pineapple Juice
1 part Ginger Ale
splash Grenadine

Build over ice.

Café Cabana

COLLINS GLASS

1 part Coffee Liqueur
fill with Club Soda

Build over ice and stir.

Cagnes Sur Mer

COLLINS GLASS

1½ parts Gin
½ part Blue Curaçao
½ part Passion Fruit Nectar
splash Lemon Juice
2 parts Orange Juice
fill with Club Soda

Build over ice and stir.

California Lemonade

COLLINS GLASS

2 parts Whiskey
½ part Lemon Juice
½ part Lime Juice
dash Powdered Sugar
splash Grenadine
fill with Club Soda

Shake all but Club Soda with ice and strain. Top with Club Soda.

California Lemonade #2

COLLINS GLASS

1½ parts Rum
3 parts Lemon Juice
2 dashes Sugar
dash Bitters
fill with Club Soda

Build over ice and stir.

Calypso Cooler
COLLINS GLASS

1/2 part Spiced Rum
1/2 part Peach Schnapps
splash Dark Rum
2 parts Orange Juice
1 part Grenadine
1 part Lime Juice
fill with Lemon-Lime Soda

Build over ice and stir.

Campari® and Soda
HIGHBALL GLASS

2 parts Campari®
fill with Club Soda

Build over ice and stir.

Canal Street Daisy
COLLINS GLASS

1 part Bourbon
1 part Orange Juice
fill with Club Soda

Build over ice and stir.

Candy Crusher
HIGHBALL GLASS

1 part Grape Vodka
1 part Chambord
1/2 part Butterscotch Liqueur
fill with Lemon-Lime Soda

Build over ice and stir.

Candy Isle
HIGHBALL GLASS

1 part Goldschläger®
1 part Amaretto
fill with Club Soda
splash Vanilla Liqueur

Build over ice and stir.

Cannonballer
HIGHBALL GLASS

1/2 part Melon Liqueur
1/2 part Crème de Banane
2 parts Cranberry Juice Cocktail
fill with Club Soda

Build over ice and stir.

Cantaloupe Dizzy
PARFAIT GLASS

1 part Vodka
1 part Melon Liqueur
1 part Peach Schnapps
fill with Club Soda

Build over ice and stir.

Captain Collins
COLLINS GLASS

1 part Bourbon
splash Grenadine
fill with Club Soda

Build over ice and stir.

Captain's Table
COLLINS GLASS

2 parts Gin
1/2 part Campari®
splash Grenadine
1 part Orange Juice
fill with Ginger Ale

Build over ice and stir.

Carat Fizz
COLLINS GLASS

1 part Crème de Cacao (White)
1 part Campari®
fill with Tonic Water

Build over ice and stir.

Caribbean Sling

COLLINS GLASS

2 parts Light Rum
1 part Triple Sec
splash Simple Syrup
fill with Club Soda

Build over ice and stir.

Carthusian Cooler

COLLINS GLASS

1 part Bourbon
fill with Club Soda

Build over ice and stir.

Catalina Cooler

COLLINS GLASS

2 parts Vodka
splash Cranberry Juice
splash Lime Juice
fill with Club Soda

Build over ice.

Cherry Cobbler

ROCKS GLASS

1½ parts Gin
¾ part Cherry Brandy
dash Powdered Sugar
fill with Club Soda

Build over ice and stir.

Cherry Cooler

COLLINS GLASS

2 parts Cherry Vodka
fill with Cola

Build over ice and stir. Garnish with a Lemon Slice.

Cherry Grove

COLLINS GLASS

1 part Cherry Vodka
½ part Gin
½ part Light Rum
½ part Sour Cherry Liqueur
½ part Triple Sec
½ part Lime Juice
fill with Lemon-Lime Soda

Shake all but the Lemon-Lime Soda with ice and strain over ice. Top with Lemon-Lime Soda. For Nicole and Christine.

Chevy® Subbourbon

COLLINS GLASS

2 parts Jim Beam®
splash Blue Curaçao
dash Angostura® Bitters
fill with Club Soda

Build over ice and stir.

Chicago Fizz

HIGHBALL GLASS

1 part Light Rum
1 part Port
½ part Lemon Juice
dash Powdered Sugar
1 Egg White
fill with Club Soda

Build over ice and stir.

Chilton

HIGHBALL GLASS

1 part Vodka
splash Margarita Mix
fill with Club Soda

Build over ice and stir.

Chit Chat

COLLINS GLASS

1 part Gin
½ part Strawberry Liqueur
splash Limoncello
splash Lemon Juice
fill with Tonic Water

Build over ice and stir.

Cielo

COLLINS GLASS

1¼ parts Vodka
¾ part Crème de Cassis
2 dashes Bitters
fill with Ginger Ale

Build over ice and stir.

Cinnamon Road

COLLINS GLASS

1 part Wild Turkey® Bourbon
1 part Apple Liqueur
1 part Goldschläger®
fill with Ginger Ale

Build over ice and stir.

Citron Cooler

COLLINS GLASS

1½ parts Citrus Vodka
½ part Lime Cordial
fill with Tonic Water

Build over ice and stir.

Citrus Rum Cooler

COLLINS GLASS

1½ parts Spiced Rum
1½ parts Coconut Rum
2 parts Orange Juice
1 part Lemon Juice
1 part Lime Juice
½ tsp Sugar
fill with Lemon-Lime Soda

Build over ice and stir.

City Coral

COLLINS GLASS

1 part Dry Gin
½ part Melon Liqueur
splash Blue Curaçao
splash Grapefruit Juice
fill with Tonic Water

Build over ice and stir.

Clear Blue Sea

HIGHBALL GLASS

1 part Vodka
2 parts Blue Raspberry Liqueur
fill with Lemon-Lime Soda

Build over ice.

Clear Distinction

COLLINS GLASS

1 part Dry Gin
1 part Light Rum
1 part Triple Sec
fill with Club Soda

Build over ice and stir.

Cloud Reader

COLLINS GLASS

1½ parts Crème de Cassis
1 part Lime Juice
2 parts Orange Juice
fill with Ginger Ale

Shake with ice and strain over ice.

Clouseau

HIGHBALL GLASS

1 part Vodka
1 part Coffee Liqueur
fill with Ginger Ale

Build over ice and stir.

Clown

HIGHBALL GLASS

1 part Light Rum
1 part Melon Liqueur
1 part Grenadine
fill with Tonic Water

Build over ice and stir.

Coconut Cooler

HIGHBALL GLASS

2 parts Coconut Rum
1 part Orange Juice
1 part Lemon-Lime Soda

Build over ice and stir.

Color Blind

COLLINS GLASS

2 parts Gin
1 part Triple Sec
½ part Blue Curaçao
splash Lime Juice
fill with Tonic Water

Build over ice and stir.

Cool Blue

COLLINS GLASS

1 part Blue Curaçao
1 part Anisette
fill with Club Soda

Build over ice and stir.

Cosmic South

COLLINS GLASS

1 part Southern Comfort®
½ part Lychee Liqueur
½ part Peach Schnapps
½ part Lemon Juice
fill with Club Soda

Build over ice and stir.

Cotton Panties

COLLINS GLASS

1 part Vodka
2 parts Peach Schnapps
1 part Half and Half
fill with Tonic Water

Build over ice and stir.

Cotton Picker's Punch

COLLINS GLASS

1½ parts Dark Rum
1 part Lime Juice
¾ part Whiskey
½ part Apricot Brandy
½ part Simple Syrup
fill with Club Soda

Build over ice and stir.

Country Club Cooler

COLLINS GLASS

2 parts Dry Vermouth
fill with Club Soda
splash Grenadine

Build over ice.

Cream Fizz

HIGHBALL GLASS

2 parts Gin
dash Powdered Sugar
½ part Lemon Juice
splash Light Cream
fill with Club Soda

Shake all but Club Soda with ice and strain. Top with Club Soda.

Cream Puff

HIGHBALL GLASS

2 parts Light Rum
1 part Light Cream
dash Powdered Sugar
fill with Club Soda

Shake all but Club Soda with ice and strain. Top with Club Soda.

Crocodile

COLLINS GLASS

1 part Citrus Rum
2 parts Melon Liqueur
fill with Club Soda

Build over ice and stir.

Crowning Glory
ROCKS GLASS
3/4 part Bourbon
1/2 part Peach Schnapps
1 part Orange Juice
fill with Club Soda

Build over ice and stir.

Crystal Iceberg
COLLINS GLASS
1 1/2 parts Southern Comfort®
1 part Sour Apple Schnapps
2 parts Sweet & Sour Mix
fill with Ginger Ale
splash Grenadine

Build over ice and stir.

Cuban Cooler
COLLINS GLASS
2 parts Light Rum
fill with Ginger Ale

Build over ice and stir.

Cuernavaca Collins
COLLINS GLASS
1 part Silver Tequila
1 part Lime Juice
1 part Gin
fill with Club Soda

Build over ice and stir.

Curaçao Cooler
COLLINS GLASS
1 part Rum
1 part Triple Sec
1 part Lime Juice
fill with Club Soda

Build over ice and stir.

Daisy Cutter
HIGHBALL GLASS
1 1/2 parts Whiskey
1/6 part Lemon Juice
1/6 part Simple Syrup
dash Cointreau
fill with Club Soda

Build over ice and stir.

Dancing Leprechaun
COLLINS GLASS
1 1/2 parts Irish Whiskey
fill with Ginger Ale

Build over ice and stir.

Dark Matter
COLLINS GLASS
1 part Blue Curaçao
1 part Melon Liqueur
fill with Lemon-Lime Soda
top with Grenadine

Build over ice and stir.

Dead Bastard
COLLINS GLASS
1 part Brandy
1 part Gin
1 part Rum
1/2 part Lime Juice
dash Bitters
fill with Ginger Ale

Build over ice and stir.

Derby Fizz
HIGHBALL GLASS
2 parts Scotch
splash Triple Sec
1/2 part Lemon Juice
dash Powdered Sugar
1 Whole Egg
fill with Club Soda

Shake all but Club Soda with ice and strain. Top with Club Soda.

Desert Healer

COLLINS GLASS

1 1/2 parts Dry Gin
1 part Orange Juice
1 part Cherry Brandy
fill with Ginger Ale

Build over ice and stir.

Devil's Advocate

COLLINS GLASS

1 part Fireball Cinnamon Whiskey
1 part Spiced Rum
1 part Apple Schnapps
fill with Lemon-Lime Soda

Build over ice.

Diamond Ale

COLLINS GLASS

1 1/2 parts Gin
1 part Blue Curaçao
1/2 part Cream of Coconut
fill with Ginger Ale

Build over ice and stir.

Dovahkiin

COLLINS GLASS

1 part Fireball Cinnamon Whiskey
1 part Root Beer Schnapps
fill with Cherry Cola

Build over ice.

Dragonfly

HIGHBALL GLASS

1 1/2 parts Gin
fill with Ginger Ale

Build over ice and stir. Garnish with a Lime Wedge.

Dry Hole

COLLINS GLASS

1 part Light Rum
1/2 part Apricot Brandy
1/2 part Cointreau®
1/2 part Lemon Juice
fill with Club Soda

Shake all but Club Soda with ice and strain. Top with Club Soda.

Dusty Dog

HIGHBALL GLASS

2 parts Vodka
1/2 part Crème de Cassis
splash Lemon Juice
fill with Ginger Ale

Build over ice and stir.

Elderflower Collins

COLLINS GLASS

1 1/2 parts St-Germain
1 part Gin
1/2 part Lemon Juice
fill with Club Soda

Shake all but Club Soda with ice and strain over ice. Top with Club Soda and garnish with a Lemon Wedge or Wheel.

Electric Watermelon

COLLINS GLASS

1 part Vodka
1 part Light Rum
1 part Melon Liqueur
1 part Triple Sec
fill with Sweet & Sour Mix
splash Grenadine
splash Lemon-Lime Soda

Build over ice and stir.

Elephant's Eye

COLLINS GLASS

1 part Dark Rum
1 part Dry Vermouth
1 part Triple Sec
1 part Lime Juice
fill with Tonic Water

Build over ice and stir.

Empire Builder

HIGHBALL GLASS

2 parts Apricot Brandy
1 part Lemon Juice
fill with Club Soda

Build over ice and stir.

English Highball

COLLINS GLASS

1 part Brandy
1 part Gin
1 part Dry Vermouth
fill with Ginger Ale

Build over ice and stir.

Eve's Original Sin

COLLINS GLASS

1 part Green Apple Vodka
1 part 99 Apples Liqueur
1 part Sour Apple Schnapps
1 part Lemon Juice
fill with Lemon-Lime Soda

Build over ice and stir.

Eye of the Tiger

COLLINS GLASS

1½ parts Southern Comfort®
⅔ part Raspberry Liqueur
½ part Apple Liqueur
fill with Club Soda

Build over ice and stir.

Fat Man's Cooler

COLLINS GLASS

2 parts Light Rum
½ part Blue Curaçao
½ part Lime Juice
fill with Ginger Ale

Build over ice and stir.

The Feminist

HIGHBALL GLASS

1 part Amaretto
1 part Coffee Liqueur
1 part Peppermint Schnapps
1 part Rum
fill with Ginger Ale

Build over ice and stir.

Fidel Castro

COLLINS GLASS

1½ parts Dark Rum
½ part Lime Juice
fill with Ginger Ale

Build over ice and stir.

Filthy Mind

COLLINS GLASS

1½ parts Gin
½ part Vanilla Liqueur
1 part Cranberry Juice Cocktail
½ part Lemon Juice
fill with Club Soda

Shake all but Club Soda with ice and strain. Top with Club Soda.

Fizzy Navel

HIGHBALL GLASS

2 parts Peach Schnapps
fill with Orange Soda

Build over ice and stir.

Flaming Soda

HIGHBALL GLASS

1 part Vodka
½ part Melon Liqueur
½ part Triple Sec
fill with Club Soda

Build over ice and stir.

Flashing Fizz

COLLINS GLASS

1½ parts Brandy
1 part Crème de Cassis
fill with Club Soda

Build over ice and stir.

Floradora Cooler

COLLINS GLASS

2 parts Dry Gin
splash Grenadine
dash Powdered Sugar
½ part Lime Juice
fill with Club Soda

Build over ice and stir.

Florida Fizz

COLLINS GLASS

1½ parts Southern Comfort®
2 parts Orange Juice
fill with Club Soda

Build over ice and stir.

Flower Power

COLLINS GLASS

1 part Peach Schnapps
1 part Crème de Coconut
fill with Club Soda

Build over ice and stir.

Flying High

COLLINS GLASS

1 part Vodka
1 part Lime Juice
½ part Crème de Banane
fill with Orange Soda

Build over ice and stir.

Flying Purple Squirrel

COLLINS GLASS

1 part Light Rum
½ part Coconut Rum
½ part Blue Curaçao
splash Grenadine
splash Lime Juice
fill with Club Soda

Build over ice and stir.

Fraise Fizz

COLLINS GLASS

2 parts Gin
1 part Strawberry Liqueur
½ tbsp powdered sugar
fill with Club Soda

Build over ice and stir.

Free Bird

HIGHBALL GLASS

1½ parts Canadian Whisky
fill with Ginger Ale
splash Blue Curaçao

Build over ice.

French Colonial

COLLINS GLASS

1½ parts Dark Rum
1 part Triple Sec
1 part Crème de Cassis
fill with Tonic Water

Build over ice and stir.

French Summer

WHITE WINE GLASS

1 part Raspberry Liqueur
fill with Club Soda

Build over ice and stir.

From Russia with Love

COLLINS GLASS

1½ parts Raspberry Vodka
fill with Lemon-Lime Soda
splash Cranberry Juice

Build over ice and stir.

Frontal Lobotomy

COLLINS GLASS

½ part Jack Daniel's®
½ part Tequila
½ part Vodka
1 part Jägermeister®
fill with Club Soda

Shake all but Club Soda with ice and strain. Top with Club Soda.

Furry Purple Squirrel

HIGHBALL GLASS

1 part Light Rum
1 part Coconut Rum
½ part Blue Curaçao
dash Grenadine
dash Lime Juice
fill with Club Soda

Build over ice and stir.

Fuzzy Charlie

COLLINS GLASS

1¼ parts Dark Rum
½ part Crème de Banane
½ part Crème de Coconut
2 parts Pineapple Juice
fill with Ginger Ale

Build over ice and stir.

Fuzzy Feeling

HIGHBALL GLASS

1 part Orange Vodka
⅔ part Blackberry Liqueur
½ part Lemon Juice
fill with Club Soda

Build over ice and stir.

Gables Collins

COLLINS GLASS

1½ parts Vodka
1 part Crème de Noyaux
1 part Pineapple Juice
1 part Lemon Juice
fill with Club Soda

Shake all but Club Soda with ice and strain. Top with Club Soda. Garnish with a Lemon Slice.

Gale Warning

COLLINS GLASS

2 parts Vodka
½ part Lemon Juice
fill with Lemon-Lime Soda

Build over ice and stir.

General Lee

COLLINS GLASS

2 parts Gin
splash Anisette
dash Sugar
1 part Lime Juice
fill with Ginger Ale

Build over ice and stir.

Geting

HIGHBALL GLASS

1 part Vodka
½ part Banana Liqueur
fill with Ginger Ale

Build over ice and stir.

Gilded Lei

HIGHBALL GLASS

⅔ part Crème de Coconut
1 part Parfait Amour
½ part Light Rum
fill with Club Soda

Build over ice and stir.

Gin and Pink

HIGHBALL GLASS

2 parts Gin
fill with Tonic Water
2 dashes Bitters

Build over ice and stir. Garnish with a Lemon Twist.

Gin Chiller

HIGHBALL GLASS

1½ parts Gin
splash Lime Juice
fill with Ginger Ale

Build over ice and stir. Garnish with a Lemon Wedge.

Ginger 'n' Spice

COLLINS GLASS

1½ parts Spiced Rum
fill with Ginger Ale

Build over ice and stir.

Ginger Rum

HIGHBALL GLASS

2 parts Light Rum
fill with Ginger Ale

Build over ice and stir.

Ginger Scotch

HIGHBALL GLASS

2 parts Scotch
fill with Ginger Ale

Build over ice and stir.

Gin-Ger-Ale

HIGHBALL GLASS

2 parts Gin
fill with Ginger Ale

Build over ice and stir.

Gingervitas

COLLINS GLASS

1 part Citrus Vodka
1 part Dry Vermouth
fill with Ginger Ale

Build over ice and stir.

Ginny Cooler

COLLINS GLASS

1 part Dry Gin
1 part Sweet Vermouth
1 part Grenadine
fill with Tonic Water

Build over ice and stir.

The Glen Ridge

COLLINS GLASS

2 parts Irish Whiskey
fill with Ginger Ale

Build over ice and stir.

Golden Fizz

HIGHBALL GLASS

1½ parts Gin
½ part Lemon Juice
1 tbsp sugar
1 Egg Yolk
fill with Club Soda

Shake all but Club Soda with ice and strain. Top with Club Soda.

Golden Friendship

COLLINS GLASS

1 part Amaretto
1 part Sweet Vermouth
1 part Light Rum
fill with Ginger Ale

Build over ice and stir.

Golden Pirate

COLLINS GLASS

3 parts Dark Rum
fill with Ginger Ale

Build over ice and stir.

Gospodin

COLLINS GLASS

1 part Vodka
⅔ part Apricot Brandy
fill with Club Soda

Build over ice and stir.

Grand Master

HIGHBALL GLASS

2 parts Scotch
½ part Peppermint Schnapps
fill with Club Soda

Build over ice and stir. Garnish with a Lemon Twist.

Grandma Happy Bottoms

HIGHBALL GLASS

3 parts Maraschino Liqueur
fill with Club Soda

Build over ice and stir.

Grape Bomb

PINT GLASS

1 part Lemon Vodka
1 part Grape Vodka
½ part Lime Juice
fill with Grape Soda

Build over ice and stir.

The Grass Skirt

HIGHBALL GLASS

1 part Peppermint Liqueur
1 part Light Rum
½ part Lime Cordial
fill with Club Soda

Build over ice and stir.

Grass Snake

COLLINS GLASS

⅔ part Kiwi Schnapps
1½ parts Light Rum
½ part Limoncello
⅔ part Lemon Juice
fill with Club Soda

Build over ice and stir.

Greek Buck

COLLINS GLASS

1½ parts Brandy
splash Ouzo
2 splashes Lemon Juice
fill with Ginger Ale

Build over ice and stir.

Green Dinosaur

HIGHBALL GLASS

1 part Rum
1 part Vodka
1 part Tequila
1 part Gin
1 part Melon Liqueur
splash Lemon Juice
fill with Club Soda

Build over ice and stir.

Green Grass

COLLINS GLASS

1½ parts Gin
1 part Crème de Menthe (White)
fill with Tonic Water

Build over ice and stir.

Green Highlands

COLLINS GLASS

1 part Blue Curaçao
1 part Scotch
2 dashes Orange Bitters
fill with Club Soda

Build over ice and stir.

Green Shark

COLLINS GLASS

1½ parts Dark Rum
1 part Blue Curaçao
½ part Lime Juice
fill with Club Soda

Shake all but Club Soda with ice and strain. Top with Club Soda.

Green Star

COLLINS GLASS

1 part Rum
½ part Blue Curaçao
½ part Mandarine Napoléon® Liqueur
½ part Grapefruit Juice
1 part Pineapple Juice
fill with Tonic Water

Build over ice and stir.

Guava Cooler

COLLINS GLASS

2 parts Light Rum
1½ parts Guava Juice
1 part Pineapple Juice
1 part Maraschino Liqueur
½ part Simple Syrup
fill with Club Soda

Shake all but Club Soda with ice and strain. Top with Club Soda.

Guinness® Cooler

COLLINS GLASS

1 part Coffee Liqueur
1 part Triple Sec
fill with Guinness® Stout

Build in the glass with no ice.

Gumball

COLLINS GLASS

1 part Blue Curaçao
1/2 part Vodka
1/2 part Crème de Banane
fill with Ginger Ale

Build over ice and stir.

Hackensack Lemonade

COLLINS GLASS

2 parts Canadian Whisky
1 part Triple Sec
1 part Lime Juice
1 part Lemon Juice
dash Powdered Sugar
fill with Club Soda

Shake all but Club Soda with ice and strain. Top with Club Soda.

Hard Hat

COLLINS GLASS

1 1/2 parts Light Rum
1 1/2 parts Lime Cordial
1 tbsp sugar
1/4 part Grenadine
fill with Club Soda

Shake all but Club Soda with ice and strain. Top with Club Soda.

Harvard Cooler

COLLINS GLASS

2 parts Apple Brandy
dash Powdered Sugar
fill with Club Soda

Build over ice and stir. Garnish with an Orange Twist and a Lemon Twist.

Hasty Heart

COLLINS GLASS

1 1/2 parts Gin
1 1/2 parts Crème de Cassis
1/2 part Sweet & Sour Mix
fill with Ginger Ale
splash Lemon Juice

Build over ice and stir.

Headhunter

COLLINS GLASS

2 parts Gin
1 part Crème de Menthe (White)
fill with Ginger Ale

Build over ice and stir.

Headless Horseman

COLLINS GLASS

2 parts Vodka
3 dashes Bitters
fill with Ginger Ale

Build over ice and stir. Garnish with an Orange Slice.

Hedgerow Sling

COLLINS GLASS

2 parts Sloe Gin
1/2 part Blackberry Liqueur
1/4 part Simple Syrup
fill with Club Soda

Shake all but Club Soda with ice and strain. Top with Club Soda.

Hell Bender

COLLINS GLASS

1 1/2 parts Scotch
1/2 part Peach Schnapps
1/2 part Dry Vermouth
2 parts Pineapple Juice
fill with Bitter Lemon Soda

Build over ice and stir.

Hidden Dragon
COLLINS GLASS

2/3 part Melon Liqueur
2/3 part Pisang Ambon® Liqueur
1/2 part Sake
fill with Club Soda

Shake all but Club Soda with ice and strain. Top with Club Soda.

High and Dry
HIGHBALL GLASS

1 part Canadian Whisky
fill with Ginger Ale
dash Bitters

Build over ice and stir.

High Moon
COLLINS GLASS

1 1/2 parts Raspberry Liqueur
1 part Apricot Brandy
1/2 part Cognac
1/6 part Grenadine
fill with Bitter Lemon Soda

Build over ice and stir.

High Valley Sneaker
HIGHBALL GLASS

1 part Vodka
1/2 part Banana Liqueur
1/2 part Jägermeister®
fill with Ginger Ale

Build over ice and stir.

Highland Cooler
COLLINS GLASS

2 parts Scotch
dash Powdered Sugar
fill with Seltzer

Build over ice and stir. Garnish with an Orange Twist and a Lemon Twist.

Hillbilly Buttkicker
COLLINS GLASS

1 part Southern Comfort®
1 part Gin
1 part Vodka
1 part Orange Juice
fill with Ginger Ale
1 part Grenadine

Build over ice and stir.

Hillbilly Highball
MASON JAR

2 parts White Whiskey
fill with Mountain Dew

Build over ice and stir.

Hippie
ROCKS GLASS

1 part Gin
1 part Peach Schnapps
1/2 part Sweet Vermouth
splash Grenadine
fill with Ginger Ale

Build over ice and stir.

Holy Water
ROCKS GLASS

2 parts Vodka
1 part Triple Sec
1 part Light Rum
fill with Tonic Water
splash Grenadine

Build over ice and stir.

Honolulu
COLLINS GLASS

1 1/2 parts Peach Schnapps
1 1/2 parts Crème de Banane
1/2 part Peppermint Extract
fill with Club Soda

Build over ice and stir.

Houdini

HIGHBALL GLASS

1 part Raspberry Liqueur
2 parts Southern Comfort®
fill with Ginger Ale

Build over ice and stir.

Howling Wolf

HIGHBALL GLASS

1 part Vodka
1 part Crème de Menthe (White)
½ part Blue Curaçao
fill with Lemon-Lime Soda

Build over ice.

Hudson

HIGHBALL GLASS

1 part Peach Schnapps
½ part Gin
fill with Club Soda

Build over ice and stir.

Imperial Fizz

HIGHBALL GLASS

½ part Light Rum
1½ parts Whiskey
½ part Lemon Juice
dash Powdered Sugar
fill with Club Soda

Shake all but Club Soda with ice and strain. Top with Club Soda.

Incognito

COLLINS GLASS

1½ parts Vodka
1 part Apricot Brandy
fill with Ginger Ale

Build over ice and stir.

Indian Sun

COLLINS GLASS

1½ parts Gin
⅔ part Campari®
⅔ part Lemon Juice
fill with Ginger Ale
splash Grenadine

Build over ice and stir.

Indira

HIGHBALL GLASS

½ part Blue Curaçao
1½ parts Campari®
1½ parts Dry Vermouth
fill with Club Soda

Build over ice and stir.

Intellectual

COLLINS GLASS

2 parts Jim Beam®
fill with Ginger Ale

Build over ice and stir.

Invisible Man

HIGHBALL GLASS

2 parts Gin
½ part Triple Sec
½ part Brandy
2 splashes Orange Juice
fill with Ginger Ale

Build over ice and stir.

Irish Highball

ROCKS GLASS

2 parts Irish Whiskey
fill with Ginger Ale

Build over ice and stir.

Island Soda

COLLINS GLASS

2 parts Vodka
½ part Banana Liqueur
2 parts Pineapple Juice
fill with Ginger Ale

Build over ice and stir.

Italian Cooler

COLLINS GLASS

1½ parts Sweet Vermouth
splash Grenadine
fill with Sparkling Water

Build over ice and stir.

Jack & Ginger

COLLINS GLASS

2 parts Jack Daniel's®
fill with Ginger Ale

Build over ice and stir.

Jackhammer Fizz

HIGHBALL GLASS

1½ parts Whiskey
1 part Powdered Sugar
fill with Club Soda

Shake all but Club Soda with ice and strain. Top with Club Soda.

Jäger Tonic

HIGHBALL GLASS

1½ parts Jägermeister®
fill with Tonic Water

Build over ice and stir.

Jamaica Cooler

COLLINS GLASS

2 parts Dark Rum
½ part Lemon Juice
dash Powdered Sugar
2 dashes Orange Bitters
fill with Lemon-Lime Soda

Build over ice and stir.

Jamaican Collins

COLLINS GLASS

2 parts Dark Rum
1½ parts Pineapple Juice
dash Sugar
fill with Club Soda

Shake all but Club Soda with ice and strain. Top with Club Soda.

Jamaican Fizz

ROCKS GLASS

2 parts Dark Rum
1 part Pineapple Juice
fill with Club Soda

Build over ice and stir.

Japanese Fizz

HIGHBALL GLASS

1½ parts Whiskey
½ part Lemon Juice
dash Powdered Sugar
2 splashes Port
1 Egg White
fill with Club Soda

Shake all but Club Soda with ice and strain. Top with Club Soda.

Jealous Husband

HIGHBALL GLASS

½ part Vodka
⅔ part Peach Schnapps
⅔ part Triple Sec
3 parts Cranberry Juice Cocktail
fill with Ginger Ale

Build over ice and stir.

Jelly Roll

COLLINS GLASS

1 part Coconut Rum
1 part Strawberry Liqueur
1 part Banana Liqueur
1 part Pineapple Juice
fill with Lemon-Lime Soda

Build over ice and stir.

Jersey Shore Cherry Lemonade

HIGHBALL GLASS

1½ parts Vodka
1 part Sweet & Sour Mix
1 tsp Sugar
fill with Lemon-Lime Soda
splash Grenadine

Build over ice and stir.

Johnny Cat

RED WINE GLASS

1 part Gin
1 part Dry Vermouth
½ part Triple Sec
splash Grenadine
fill with Club Soda

Shake all but Club Soda with ice and strain. Top with Club Soda.

Joumbaba

HIGHBALL GLASS

1½ parts Tequila
2 parts Grapefruit Juice
fill with Tonic Water

Build over ice and stir.

Joy Ride

HURRICANE GLASS

1½ parts Citrus Vodka
1 part Campari®
3 parts Sweet & Sour Mix
1 part Sugar
fill with Club Soda

Shake all but Club Soda with ice and strain over ice. Top with Club Soda.

Jubilee

COLLINS GLASS

1 part Tequila
½ part Gin
½ part Vodka
½ part Blue Curaçao
½ part Lemon Juice
1 tsp Sugar
fill with Club Soda

Build over ice and stir.

Kangaroo Kick

HIGHBALL GLASS

2 parts Melon Liqueur
1 part Vodka
fill with Lemon-Lime Soda

Build over ice and stir.

Karla

HIGHBALL GLASS

2 parts Vodka
1 part Cranberry Juice
fill with Club Soda
splash Jägermeister

Build over ice and stir.

Kentucky Tea

COLLINS GLASS

2 parts Bourbon
1 part Triple Sec
1 tbsp sugar
fill with Ginger Ale

Shake all but Ginger Ale with ice and strain. Top with Ginger Ale.

Kirsch and Cassis

WHITE WINE GLASS

2 parts Crème de Cassis
1 part Kirschwasser
fill with Club Soda

Build over ice and stir.

Kiwi Light

HIGHBALL GLASS

1 part Kiwi Schnapps
fill with Tonic Water

Build over ice and stir.

Kurant Collins

COLLINS GLASS

2 parts Currant Vodka
1 part Lemon Juice
dash Powdered Sugar
fill with Club Soda

Shake all but Club Soda with ice and strain. Top with Club Soda.

L.A. Iced Tea

COLLINS GLASS

1 part Vodka
1 part Triple Sec
1 part Melon Liqueur
1 part Gin
1 part Rum
fill with Club Soda

Shake all but Club Soda with ice and strain. Top with Club Soda.

La Coppa de la Passion

COLLINS GLASS

1½ parts Dark Rum
½ part Passion Fruit Liqueur
½ part Mango Schnapps
1½ parts Banana Puree
½ part Lemon Juice
fill with Club Soda

Shake all but Club Soda with ice and strain. Top with Club Soda.

Laffy Taffy

HIGHBALL GLASS

1 part Peach Vodka
1 part Watermelon Vodka
1 part Sour Apple Vodka
½ part Chambord
dash Lemon-Lime Soda
fill with Sweet & Sour Mix

Shake with ice and strain over ice.

Lappland

COLLINS GLASS

1 part Vodka
1 part Apricot Brandy
1 part Sweet & Sour Mix
fill with Ginger Ale

Build over ice and stir.

Leap Frog

HIGHBALL GLASS

1½ parts Gin
splash Lemon Juice
fill with Ginger Ale

Build over ice and stir.

Lei Lani

COLLINS GLASS

1¼ parts Dark Rum
½ part Lemon Juice
½ part Pineapple Juice
½ part Papaya Juice
1 part Orange Juice
splash Grenadine
fill with Club Soda

Shake all but Club Soda with ice and strain. Top with Club Soda.

Leprechaun

ROCKS GLASS

2 parts Irish Whiskey
fill with Tonic Water

Build over ice and stir.

Lilac Cooler

COLLINS GLASS

1 part Triple Sec
1 part Cognac
1 part Sweet Vermouth
fill with Ginger Ale

Build over ice and stir.

Lili

COLLINS GLASS

1 Lime Twist
dash Sugar
Juice from half a Lime
1 part Vodka
1 part Triple Sec
fill with Club Soda

Muddle the Lime, Sugar, and Lime Juice in the bottom of a collins glass. Fill the glass with ice and add the Vodka and Triple Sec. Fill with Club Soda.

Lime Crime

ROCKS GLASS

2 parts Lime Gin
1 part Cherry Liqueur
2 parts Lemon-Lime Soda
fill with Limeade

Build over ice and stir.

Lime Lush

HIGHBALL GLASS

2 parts Grape Vodka
splash Chambord
fill with Lemon-Lime Soda

Build over ice and stir.

Lion Tamer

HIGHBALL GLASS

2 parts Southern Comfort
dash Lemon Juice
fill with Lemon-Lime Soda

Build over ice and stir.

Liquid Pants Remover

HURRICANE GLASS

½ part Spiced Rum
½ part Vanilla Vodka
½ part Sour Apple Schnapps
½ part Cherry Liqueur
½ part Grape Schnapps
½ part Watermelon Schnapps
fill with Lemon-Lime Soda

Build over ice and stir.

Lisbonne

COLLINS GLASS

1 part Silver Tequila
½ part Blue Curaçao
½ part Maraschino Liqueur
fill with Tonic Water

Build over ice and stir.

Loch Ness Monster

HIGHBALL GLASS

1½ parts Scotch
splash Peppermint Schnapps
fill with Club Soda

Build over ice and stir.

Lone Tree Cooler

COLLINS GLASS

2 parts Gin
splash Dry Vermouth
dash Powdered Sugar
fill with Club Soda

Shake all but Club Soda with ice and strain. Top with Club Soda.

Long Joe

COLLINS GLASS

1 part Apricot Brandy
½ part Sweet Vermouth
½ part Gin
fill with Ginger Ale

Build over ice and stir.

Long Vodka

COLLINS GLASS

2 parts Vodka
½ part Lime Juice
4 dashes Angostura® Bitters
fill with Tonic Water

Build over ice and stir.

Lost Heart

HIGHBALL GLASS

1½ parts Crème de Cassis
⅔ part Sweet Vermouth
2 parts Lemon Juice
splash Amaretto
fill with Club Soda

Shake all but Club Soda with ice and strain. Top with Club Soda.

Love 'n' Fizz

COLLINS GLASS

1 part Gin
1 part Lime Cordial
½ part Mango Nectar
splash Grenadine
splash Crème de Menthe (White)
fill with Club Soda

Shake all but Club Soda with ice and strain. Top with Club Soda.

Love Bond
COLLINS GLASS

2/3 part Melon Liqueur
2 parts Dark Rum
1 1/2 parts Melon Purée
2/3 part Lemon Juice
1/2 part Honey
fill with Club Soda

Shake all but Club Soda with ice and strain. Top with Club Soda.

Love in an Elevator
COLLINS GLASS

2 parts Gin
1 part Blue Curaçao
fill with Club Soda

Build over ice and stir.

Lycheeto
COLLINS GLASS

1 part Light Rum
1 part Lychee Liqueur
1 part Simple Syrup
1/2 part Crème de Menthe (Green)
fill with Club Soda

Shake all but Club Soda with ice and strain. Top with Club Soda.

Machete
COLLINS GLASS

1 part Vodka
2 parts Pineapple Juice
fill with Tonic Water

Build over ice and stir.

Maestro
COLLINS GLASS

1 1/2 parts Añejo Rum
1/2 part Cream Sherry
1/2 part Lime Juice
fill with Ginger Ale

Shake all but Ginger Ale with ice and strain. Top with Ginger Ale. Garnish with a Lemon Twist.

Magic Trace
COLLINS GLASS

3/4 part Dry Gin
1/2 part Lemon Syrup
splash Triple Sec
splash Strawberry Juice
fill with Tonic Water

Build over ice and stir.

Magnolia Maiden
ROCKS GLASS

1 part Mandarine Napoléon® Liqueur
1 part Bourbon
splash Simple Syrup
fill with Club Soda

Build over ice and stir.

Maktak Special
COLLINS GLASS

1 1/2 parts Dark Rum
1/2 part Cream Sherry
1/2 part Lime Juice
fill with Ginger Ale

Build over ice and stir.

Malibu Express
HIGHBALL GLASS

1 part Coconut Rum
1 part Light Rum
2 parts Lemon-Lime Soda
fill with Pineapple Juice

Build over ice and stir.

Mamie Gilroy
COLLINS GLASS

2 parts Scotch
1/2 part Lime Juice
fill with Ginger Ale

Build over ice and stir.

Man o' War
HIGHBALL GLASS

1 part Gin
2 parts Rum
1 part Grenadine
1 part Lime Juice
fill with Tonic Water

Build over ice and stir.

Mandarin Delight
COLLINS GLASS

1½ parts Orange Vodka
fill with Tonic Water

Build over ice and stir. Garnish with a Lime Wedge.

Margue Collins
COLLINS GLASS

1½ parts Silver Tequila
½ part Simple Syrup
splash Lime Juice
fill with Club Soda

Shake all but Club Soda with ice and strain. Top with Club Soda.

Mark Pilkinton
HIGHBALL GLASS

1½ parts Vodka
¾ part Triple Sec
1 part Sweet & Sour Mix
fill with Raspberry Ginger Ale

Build over ice and stir.

Matrix (Blue Pill)
COLLINS GLASS

1 part Silver Tequila
1 part Lemon Rum
2 parts Hpnotiq
fill with Lemon-Lime Soda

Build over ice and stir.

Mayan Whore
COLLINS GLASS

1½ parts Tequila
1 part Coffee Liqueur
1 part Pineapple Juice
fill with Club Soda
splash Grenadine

Build over ice.

Melba Tonic
COLLINS GLASS

2 parts Vodka
½ part Peach Schnapps
½ part Grenadine
½ part Simple Syrup
fill with Tonic Water

Build over ice and stir.

Melon Patch
HIGHBALL GLASS

1 part Melon Liqueur
½ part Triple Sec
½ part Vodka
fill with Club Soda

Shake all but Club Soda with ice and strain. Top with Club Soda.

Merry Wives
HIGHBALL GLASS

2 parts Sloe Gin
½ part Lemon Juice
½ part Orange Juice
1 tsp Powdered Sugar
1 Egg White
fill with Club Soda

Shake all but the Club Soda with ice and strain over ice. Fill with Club Soda and stir.

Mexican Bike Race
HIGHBALL GLASS

2 parts Tequila
splash Campari®
fill with Ginger Ale

Build over ice and stir.

Mexican Mule

COLLINS GLASS

1½ parts Tequila Reposado
½ tbsp sugar
splash Lime Juice
fill with Ginger Ale

Build over ice and stir.

Midnight in the Garden

COLLINS GLASS

1 part Amaretto
1 part Peach Schnapps
splash Orange Juice
fill with Club Soda

Shake all but Club Soda with ice and strain. Top with Club Soda.

Mint Fizz

COLLINS GLASS

2 parts Crème de Menthe (White)
fill with Tonic Water

Build over ice and stir.

Mistletoe Warm Up

HIGHBALL GLASS

1 part Peppermint Liqueur
3 parts Grapefruit Juice
splash Lime Juice
½ part Simple Syrup
fill with Club Soda

Shake all but Club Soda with ice and strain. Top with Club Soda.

Monkey Spanker

BEER MUG

3 parts Jack Daniel's®
fill with Ginger Ale

Build over ice and stir.

Montgomery

COLLINS GLASS

1 part Vodka
¼ part Grenadine
2 parts Sweet & Sour Mix
fill with Ginger Ale

Build over ice and stir.

Morgana's Island

HIGHBALL GLASS

2 parts Pineapple Rum
1 part Pineapple Juice
2 parts Fruit Punch
fill with Lemon-Lime Soda

Build over ice and stir.

Morning Fizz

WHITE WINE GLASS

1½ parts Vodka
1 part Simple Syrup
3 parts Grapefruit Juice
fill with Club Soda

Shake all but Club Soda with ice and strain. Top with Club Soda.

Mountain Berry Cooler

COLLINS GLASS

1 part Raspberry Liqueur
1 part Peach Schnapps
1 part Sour Apple Schnapps
1 part Sour Cherry Schnapps
1 part Triple Sec
fill with Lemon-Lime Soda

Build over ice.

Mudskipper

COLLINS GLASS

1 part Dry Gin
fill with Ginger Ale
splash Chocolate Syrup

Build over ice and stir.

Nadir

HIGHBALL GLASS

1 part Gin
½ part Cherry Liqueur
½ part Grenadine
splash Pineapple Juice
splash Lemon Juice
splash Simple Syrup
fill with Club Soda

Shake all but Club Soda with ice and strain. Top with Club Soda.

Naked Truth

COLLINS GLASS

⅔ part Vodka
1 part Melon Liqueur
1 part Lemon Juice
dash Powdered Sugar
fill with Club Soda

Shake all but Club Soda with ice and strain. Top with Club Soda.

Napoli

HIGHBALL GLASS

1 part Vodka
1 part Campari®
½ part Dry Vermouth
splash Sweet Vermouth
fill with Club Soda

Shake all but Club Soda with ice and strain. Top with Club Soda.

Near the Cataclysm

HIGHBALL GLASS

1½ parts Melon Liqueur
½ part Orange Liqueur
½ part Lychee Liqueur
⅔ part Lemon Juice
fill with Club Soda

Shake all but Club Soda with ice and strain. Top with Club Soda.

Neptune's Nectar

COLLINS GLASS

1 part Blue Curaçao
1 part Melon Liqueur
1 part Pineapple Juice
splash Lemon Juice
fill with Lemon-Lime Soda

Build over ice and stir.

New Orleans Buck

COLLINS GLASS

1½ parts Light Rum
1 part Orange Juice
½ part Lemon Juice
fill with Ginger Ale

Build over ice and stir.

Newport Cooler

COLLINS GLASS

2 parts Gin
½ part Brandy
½ part Peach Liqueur
splash Lime Juice
fill with Ginger Ale

Build over ice and stir.

Night Fever

COLLINS GLASS

1 part Blue Curaçao
1 part Vodka
½ part Cachaca
fill with Club Soda

Shake all but Club Soda with ice and strain. Top with Club Soda.

Nirvana

CHAMPAGNE FLUTE

1½ parts Orange Vodka
½ part Melon Liqueur
½ part Passion Fruit Liqueur
splash Lime Cordial
fill with Club Soda

Shake all but Club Soda with ice and strain. Top with Club Soda.

Northside Special

COLLINS GLASS

1 1/4 parts Dark Rum
2 parts Orange Juice
1/2 part Lemon Juice
fill with Club Soda

Build over ice and stir.

Notre Belle Epoque

HIGHBALL GLASS

1/2 part Blue Curaçao
2 1/2 parts White Wine
2/3 part Plum Brandy
2/3 part Lemon Juice
fill with Club Soda

Shake all but Club Soda with ice and strain. Top with Club Soda.

November Sea Breeze

COLLINS GLASS

1 1/2 parts Lime Juice
2 parts Apple Rum
fill with Club Soda

Build over ice and stir.

Nuclear Fizz

COLLINS GLASS

3/4 part Vodka
1/2 part Melon Liqueur
1/2 part Triple Sec
splash Lime Juice
fill with Club Soda

Shake all but Club Soda with ice and strain. Top with Club Soda.

Nuthouse

HIGHBALL GLASS

1 part Vanilla Vodka
1 part Hazelnut Liqueur
1 part Amaretto
fill with Club Soda

Build over ice and stir.

Nutty Ginger

HIGHBALL GLASS

1 part Amaretto
1 part Frangelico®
fill with Ginger Ale

Build over ice and stir.

One over Par

COLLINS GLASS

1 part Rum
1 part Grapefruit Juice
1 part Orange Juice
1 part Pineapple Juice
fill with Club Soda

Build over ice and stir.

Oral Intruder

HIGHBALL GLASS

1 part Coconut Rum
1 part Melon Liqueur
1 part Sweet & Sour Mix
fill with Ginger Ale
splash Lime Juice

Build over ice and stir.

Orange Fizz

COLLINS GLASS

2 parts Gin
2 splashes Triple Sec
2 parts Lemon Juice
1/2 part Orange Juice
2 dashes Orange Bitters
dash Sugar
fill with Club Soda

Shake all but Club Soda with ice and strain. Top with Club Soda.

Oregon Coastline

HIGHBALL GLASS

1 part Amaretto
1 part Passion Fruit Juice
1 part Lime Juice
fill with Club Soda

Build over ice and stir.

Oscar

COLLINS GLASS

1 part Gin
1/2 part Blue Curaçao
1/2 part Orange Juice
fill with Tonic Water

Build over ice and stir.

Pacific Exchange

HIGHBALL GLASS

1 1/2 parts Vodka
1/2 part Raspberry Liqueur
2/3 part Plum Brandy
2/3 part Lemon Juice
fill with Club Soda

Shake all but Club Soda with ice and strain. Top with Club Soda.

Paddlesteamer

COLLINS GLASS

1 part Vodka
1 part Southern Comfort®
2 parts Orange Juice
fill with Ginger Ale

Shake all but Ginger Ale with ice and strain. Top with Ginger Ale.

Painter's Delight

HIGHBALL GLASS

1 part Gin
1 part Blue Curaçao
splash Pernod®
1/2 part Lemon Juice
fill with Club Soda

Shake all but Club Soda with ice and strain. Top with Club Soda.

Palmetto Cooler

COLLINS GLASS

1 part Bourbon
1 part Apricot Brandy
1 part Dry Vermouth
fill with Club Soda

Build over ice and stir.

Passione al Limone

COLLINS GLASS

1 1/2 parts Vodka
1/2 part Passion Fruit Liqueur
1/2 part Simple Syrup
fill with Club Soda

Shake all but Club Soda with ice and strain. Top with Club Soda.

Password to Paradise

COLLINS GLASS

2 parts Gin
dash Powdered Sugar
splash Passion Fruit Nectar
fill with Club Soda

Shake all but Club Soda with ice and strain. Top with Club Soda.

Path of Sorrows

HIGHBALL GLASS

2 parts Apple Rum
1 part Sour Apple Schnapps
fill with Lemon-Lime Soda

Build over ice and stir.

Peabody

COLLINS GLASS

2 parts Gin
1/2 part Campari®
2 splashes Grenadine
1 part Orange Juice
fill with Ginger Ale

Build over ice and stir.

Peach Temptation

COLLINS GLASS

1 1/2 parts Gin
1 part Peach Schnapps
1 part Triple Sec
2 parts Lemon Juice
fill with Club Soda

Shake all but Club Soda with ice and strain. Top with Club Soda.

Peachy Comfort

COLLINS GLASS

1 part Southern Comfort®
1 part Peach Schnapps
fill with Ginger Ale

Build over ice and stir.

Peek in Pandora's Box

ROCKS GLASS

1 part Scotch
1 part Mandarine Napoléon® Liqueur
splash Campari®
splash Strega®
fill with Ginger Ale

Shake with ice and strain over ice.

Penguin

HIGHBALL GLASS

1 part Salted Caramel Vodka
½ part Blue Curaçao
½ part Lemon Juice
fill with Lemon-Lime Soda
splash Banana Liqueur

Build over ice. Top with Banana Liqueur.

Peyton Place

COLLINS GLASS

1½ parts Sloe Gin
1 part Gin
½ part Simple Syrup
2 parts Grapefruit Juice
fill with Club Soda

Shake all but Club Soda with ice and strain. Top with Club Soda.

Phat Louie

COLLINS GLASS

2 parts Vanilla Vodka
½ part Grenadine
fill with Ginger Ale

Build over ice and stir.

Pierre Collins

COLLINS GLASS

2 parts Brandy
1 tbsp sugar
½ part Lime Cordial
fill with Club Soda

Shake all but Club Soda with ice and strain. Top with Club Soda.

Pigs in Space

COLLINS GLASS

1 part Dark Rum
fill with Ginger Ale

Build over ice and stir.

Pimm's Rangoon

HIGHBALL GLASS

1½ parts Pimm's® No. 1 Cup
fill with Ginger Ale

Build over ice and stir. Garnish with a Lemon Twist and a Cucumber Slice.

Pink Cream Fizz

COLLINS GLASS

2 parts Gin
1 part Lemon Juice
dash Sugar
1 part Light Cream
splash Grenadine
fill with Club Soda

Shake all but Club Soda with ice and strain. Top with Club Soda.

Pisco Collins

COLLINS GLASS

2 parts Pisco
1½ parts Lime Cordial
1 tbsp sugar
fill with Club Soda

Shake all but Club Soda with ice and strain. Top with Club Soda.

Planter's Punch

COLLINS GLASS

1½ parts Dark Rum
1½ parts Light Rum
½ part Lemon Juice
½ part Lime Juice
1 part Orange Juice
fill with Club Soda

Shake all but Club Soda with ice and strain. Top with Club Soda.

Playboy Cooler

COLLINS GLASS

1 part Gold Rum
1 part Coffee Liqueur
2 splashes Lemon Juice
fill with Pineapple Juice
splash Cola

Build over ice and stir.

Plugged on Fruit

HIGHBALL GLASS

1 part Orange Vodka
1 part Blue Curaçao
1 part Peach Schnapps
1 part Lime Juice
1 part Lemon Juice
fill with Club Soda

Shake all but Club Soda with ice and strain. Top with Club Soda.

Polar Attraction

COLLINS GLASS

2 parts Brandy
fill with Tonic Water

Build over ice and stir.

Pond Scum

HIGHBALL GLASS

1 part Vodka
fill with Club Soda
½ part Irish Cream Liqueur

Build over ice. Top with Irish Cream Liqueur.

Port Arms

COLLINS GLASS

2 parts Port
1 part Brandy
½ part Triple Sec
1 part Orange Juice
fill with Club Soda

Build over ice and stir.

Prickly Porn Star

HIGHBALL GLASS

1 part Gold Tequila
1 part Pear Vodka
½ part Ginger Liqueur
½ part Raspberry Liqueur
fill with Lemon-Lime Soda

Build over ice and stir.

Princess Morgan

HIGHBALL GLASS

¾ part Spiced Rum
¼ part Crème de Banane
2½ parts Orange Juice
fill with Club Soda

Build over ice and stir.

Province Town

COLLINS GLASS

1 part Vodka
½ part Citrus Vodka
2 parts Grapefruit Juice
2 parts Cranberry Juice Cocktail
fill with Club Soda

Shake all but Club Soda with ice and strain. Top with Club Soda.

Purple Fantasy

HIGHBALL GLASS

2 parts Grape Vodka
½ part Dark Spiced Rum
fill with Grape Soda

Build over ice and stir.

Purple Goddess
HURRICANE GLASS

2 parts Grape Vodka
2 parts Blue Raspberry Liqueur
fill with Grape Soda

Build over ice and stir.

Purple Heather
COLLINS GLASS

2 parts Scotch
splash Crème de Cassis
fill with Club Soda

Build over ice and stir.

Purple Heaven
ROCKS GLASS

1 part Coconut Rum
½ part Blue Curaçao
fill with Lemon-Lime Soda
dash Grenadine

Build over ice and stir.

Purple Honker
HIGHBALL GLASS

2 parts Strawberry Vodka
1 part Blue Raspberry Liqueur
fill with Lemon-Lime Soda

Build over ice and stir.

Rabbit's Revenge
COLLINS GLASS

1 part Bourbon
1 part Pineapple Juice
½ part Grenadine
fill with Tonic Water

Shake all but Tonic Water with ice and strain. Top with Tonic Water.

Ragnar
HIGHBALL GLASS

2 lime wedges
2 parts Currant Vodka
fill with Lemon-Lime Soda

In the glass, muddle the lime wedges with the Vodka. Add ice and fill with the Soda.

Rail Splitter
COLLINS GLASS

1 part Lemon Rum
splash Simple Syrup
fill with Ginger Ale

Build over ice and stir.

Rangoon Ruby
HIGHBALL GLASS

2 parts Vodka
2 parts Cranberry Juice Cocktail
½ part Lime Juice
fill with Club Soda

Build over ice and stir.

Raspberry Watkins
COLLINS GLASS

1½ parts Vodka
½ part Raspberry Liqueur
¼ part Lime Cordial
splash Grenadine
fill with Club Soda

Shake all but Club Soda with ice and strain. Top with Club Soda.

Red Bait
COLLINS GLASS

1 part Sloe Gin
½ part Dark Rum
½ part Lime Juice
1 part Guava Juice
fill with Tonic Water

Build over ice and stir.

Red Devil's Poison
COLLINS GLASS

1½ parts Citrus Vodka
½ part Parfait Amour
1 part Lemon Juice
fill with Tonic Water

Build over ice and stir.

Red Mystery

COLLINS GLASS

1½ parts Pastis
½ part Grenadine
fill with Club Soda

Build over ice and stir.

Red Rattlesnake

HIGHBALL GLASS

1 part Southern Comfort
½ part Amaretto
½ part Triple Sec
splash Grenadine
splash Lemon-Lime Soda
fill with Sweet & Sour Mix

Shake with ice and strain over ice.

Red Rock West

HIGHBALL GLASS

1 part Crème de Cassis
1 part Raspberry Liqueur
1 part Vodka
fill with Club Soda

Build over ice and stir.

Red Tonic

HIGHBALL GLASS

2 parts Vodka
1 part Grenadine
1 part Lemon Juice
fill with Tonic Water

Build over ice and stir.

Redheaded Schoolgirl

ROCKS GLASS

2 parts Canadian Whisky
fill with Cream Soda

Build over ice and stir.

Remsen Cooler

COLLINS GLASS

2 parts Gin
dash Powdered Sugar
fill with Club Soda

Build over ice and stir.

Rhapsody

HIGHBALL GLASS

2 parts Silver Tequila
1 part Passion Fruit Liqueur
1½ parts Kiwi Schnapps
½ part Lemon Juice
fill with Club Soda

Shake all but Club Soda with ice and strain. Top with Club Soda.

Rocky Mountain Cooler

COLLINS GLASS

1½ parts Peach Schnapps
4 parts Pineapple Juice
fill with Lemon-Lime Soda

Build over ice and stir.

Roman Cooler

COLLINS GLASS

2 parts Gin
1 part Sambuca
½ part Simple Syrup
¼ part Sweet Vermouth
fill with Tonic Water

Shake all but Tonic Water with ice and strain. Top with Tonic Water.

Roman Punch

COLLINS GLASS

½ part Dark Rum
½ part Cognac
splash Port
1 part Raspberry Syrup
1 part Lemon Juice
fill with Club Soda

Shake all but Club Soda with ice and strain. Top with Club Soda.

Royal Air Class

HIGHBALL GLASS

1½ parts Gin
½ part Lychee Liqueur
½ part Lemon Juice
½ part Grenadine
fill with Tonic Water

Shake all but Tonic Water with ice and strain. Top with Tonic Water.

Royal Eagle

HIGHBALL GLASS

1½ parts Currant Vodka
½ part Blackberry Liqueur
½ part Kirschwasser
⅔ part Lemon Juice
fill with Ginger Ale

Shake all but Ginger Ale with ice and strain. Top with Ginger Ale.

Royal Sour Kiss

COLLINS GLASS

½ part Crown Royal Canadian Whisky
1 part Sour Apple Schnapps
splash Lime Juice
fill with Lemon-Lime Soda

Build over ice.

Royal Turkey

COLLINS GLASS

1 part Wild Turkey Bourbon
1 part Sloe Gin
1 part Apricot Brandy
2 parts Pineapple Juice
fill with Lemon-Lime Soda

Build over ice.

Royalty Fizz

COLLINS GLASS

2 parts Gin
splash Blue Curaçao
1 part Lemon Juice
dash Sugar
1 Egg
fill with Club Soda

Shake all but Club Soda with ice and strain. Top with Club Soda.

Ruby Slipper

COLLINS GLASS

2 parts Whiskey
splash Grenadine
fill with Lemon-Lime Soda

Build over ice and stir.

Ruddy Scotch

HIGHBALL GLASS

1 part Peach Schnapps
1 part Whiskey
splash Cranberry Juice Cocktail
splash Raspberry Juice
fill with Ginger Ale

Build over ice and stir.

Rum Bubble

COLLINS GLASS

2 parts Rum
1½ parts Triple Sec
splash Cinnamon Schnapps
fill with Club Soda

Build over ice and stir.

Rum Cobbler

ROCKS GLASS

2 parts Dark Rum
dash Sugar
fill with Club Soda

Build over ice and stir.

Salt Lick

HIGHBALL GLASS

2 parts Vodka
2 parts Grapefruit Juice
fill with Bitter Lemon Soda

Build over ice and stir.

Salute

CHAMPAGNE FLUTE

½ part Gin
½ part Crème de Cassis
1½ parts Dry Vermouth
1 part Sweet Vermouth
½ part Campari®
fill with Club Soda

Shake all but Club Soda with ice and strain. Top with Club Soda.

Sambuca Blitz

COLLINS GLASS

1 1/2 parts Sambuca
1 1/2 parts Crème de Cassis
1 part Dry Vermouth
fill with Club Soda

Build over ice and stir.

San Juan Sling

COLLINS GLASS

1 part Light Rum
1 part Cherry Brandy
1 part Lime Juice
fill with Club Soda

Shake all but Club Soda with ice and strain. Top with Club Soda.

Santa Cruz

COLLINS GLASS

2 parts Dark Rum
1/2 part Cherry Brandy
1 part Lime Juice
1/2 part Simple Syrup
fill with Club Soda

Shake all but Club Soda with ice and strain. Top with Club Soda.

Saratoga Cooler

COLLINS GLASS

2 parts Brandy
splash Pineapple Juice
splash Lemon Juice
splash Maraschino Cherry Juice
fill with Ginger Ale

Build over ice and stir.

Satin Slave

HIGHBALL GLASS

2/3 part Light Rum
2/3 part Sloe Gin
1/2 part Apricot Brandy
1 part Sweet & Sour Mix
fill with Ginger Ale

Build over ice and stir.

Schnapp Pop

COLLINS GLASS

1 1/2 parts Wild Berry Schnapps
fill with Club Soda

Build over ice and stir.

Scotch Collins

COLLINS GLASS

2 parts Scotch
1 part Lemon Juice
dash Sugar
splash Grenadine
fill with Club Soda

Shake all but Club Soda with ice and strain. Top with Club Soda.

Scottish Pirate

HIGHBALL GLASS

1 part Scotch
1/2 part Orange Liqueur
1/2 part Crème de Cassis
3 parts Sweet & Sour Mix
fill with Club Soda

Shake all but Club Soda with ice and strain. Top with Club Soda.

Scummy Nut Sack

COLLINS GLASS

1 part Southern Comfort®
1 part Amaretto
1 part Banana Liqueur
1 part Crème de Menthe (White)
1 part Tequila
1 part Peppermint Schnapps
fill with Club Soda

Shake all but Club Soda with ice and strain. Top with Club Soda.

Sea Fizz

HIGHBALL GLASS

1 1/2 parts Absinthe
1/2 part Lemon Juice
dash Sugar
1 Egg White
fill with Tonic Water

Shake all but tonic water with ice and strain. Top with Tonic Water.

Sea Story

COLLINS GLASS

1 part Blue Curaçao
1 part Triple Sec
fill with Tonic Water

Build over ice and stir.

Seadoo

COLLINS GLASS

1 part Vodka
splash Cranberry Juice Cocktail
fill with Club Soda

Build over ice and stir.

Seersucker

HIGHBALL GLASS

2 parts Light Rum
1 part Orange Juice
2 splashes Grenadine
fill with Tonic Water

Build over ice and stir.

Sehangat Senyuman

COLLINS GLASS

1½ parts Crème de Menthe (Green)
1 part Brandy
fill with Club Soda

Build over ice and stir.

Seth Allen

COLLINS GLASS

3 parts Spiced Rum
fill with Ginger Ale

Build over ice and stir.

Seven Seas

COLLINS GLASS

1½ parts Pisang Ambon® Liqueur
1 part Gin
splash Crème de Banane
fill with Tonic Water

Build over ice and stir.

Shady Grove Cooler

COLLINS GLASS

2 parts Gin
1 part Lime Juice
1 tbsp sugar
fill with Ginger Ale

Shake all but Ginger Ale with ice and strain. Top with Ginger Ale.

Shark's Tooth

COLLINS GLASS

2 parts Dark Rum
½ part Lime Juice
½ part Lemon Juice
splash Grenadine
fill with Club Soda

Build over ice and stir.

Sharky Punch

HIGHBALL GLASS

1½ parts Apple Brandy
½ part Rye Whiskey
splash Simple Syrup
fill with Club Soda

Shake all but Club Soda with ice and strain. Top with Club Soda.

Shetland Skye

HIGHBALL GLASS

1 part Sambuca
1 part Amaretto
splash Cherry Brandy
3 parts Orange Juice
fill with Club Soda

Build over ice and stir.

Ship of Fools

HIGHBALL GLASS

1 part Amaretto
1 part Dark Rum
1 part Orange Juice
splash Lemon Juice
fill with Ginger Ale

Build over ice and stir.

Short Dog Cooler
HIGHBALL GLASS

2 parts Peach Schnapps
1 part Lemon-Lime Soda
2 parts Pineapple Juice

Build over ice and stir.

Shotgun Lou
HIGHBALL GLASS

1½ parts Brandy
2½ parts Milk
dash Brown Sugar
fill with Ginger Ale

Shake all but Ginger Ale with ice and strain. Top with Ginger Ale.

Show Tune
COLLINS GLASS

1 part Spiced Rum
¼ part Amaretto
3 parts Grapefruit Juice
splash Grenadine
fill with Club Soda

Shake all but Club Soda with ice and strain. Top with Club Soda.

Sienna
WHITE WINE GLASS

¾ part Spiced Rum
½ part Amaretto
2 parts Orange Juice
fill with Ginger Ale

Build over ice and stir.

Sign of the Times
HIGHBALL GLASS

2 parts Amaretto
1 part Crème de Banane
fill with Tonic Water

Build over ice and stir.

Silly Kentucky
COLLINS GLASS

1½ parts Jim Beam®
½ part Orange Liqueur
splash Apricot Brandy
splash Limoncello
⅔ part Lemon Juice
fill with Club Soda

Shake all but Club Soda with ice and strain. Top with Club Soda.

Silver Fizz
HIGHBALL GLASS

2 parts Gin
½ part Lemon Juice
dash Powdered Sugar
1 Egg White
fill with Club Soda

Shake all but Club Soda with ice and strain. Top with Club Soda.

Sister Starseeker
HIGHBALL GLASS

2 parts Light Rum
1 part Lemon Juice
splash Grenadine
fill with Tonic Water

Build over ice and stir.

Skyscraper
COLLINS GLASS

1½ parts Gin
½ part Crème de Menthe (Green)
½ part Triple Sec
½ part Lime Juice
splash Simple Syrup
fill with Club Soda

Shake all but Club Soda with ice and strain. Top with Club Soda.

Sleepwalker on the Roof

HIGHBALL GLASS

1 1/2 parts Dark Rum
1/2 part Orange Liqueur
1/2 part Passion Fruit Liqueur
2/3 part Lemon Juice
fill with Ginger Ale

Shake with ice and strain over ice.

(S)limey Coconut

COLLINS GLASS

1 part Crème de Coconut
3/4 part Lime Juice
fill with Lemon-Lime Soda

Shake with ice and strain in the glass over ice.

Sloe Gin Sin

HIGHBALL GLASS

1 part Sloe Gin
1 part Orange Liqueur
1 1/2 parts Sweet & Sour Mix
fill with Club Soda

Build over ice and stir.

Slutty Temple

COLLINS GLASS

2 parts Rum
1 part Coconut Rum
splash Grenadine
splash Cherry Juice
fill with Club Soda

Build over ice and stir.

Smith & Kearns

ROCKS GLASS

1 part Cream
1 part Coffee Liqueur
fill with Club Soda

Build over ice and stir.

Smoke on the Water

ROCKS GLASS

1 part Tequila Reposado
1/2 part Pisang Ambon® Liqueur
1/2 part Blue Curaçao
1 part Pineapple Juice
fill with Club Soda

Shake all but Club Soda with ice and strain. Top with Club Soda.

Smurf®-o-Tonic

HIGHBALL GLASS

1 part Gin
1 part Blue Curaçao
fill with Tonic Water

Build over ice and stir.

Southern Ginger

COLLINS GLASS

2 parts Bourbon
1/2 part Ginger Liqueur
fill with Ginger Ale

Build over ice and stir.

South-of-the-Border Iced Tea

COLLINS GLASS

1 part Vodka
1 part Coffee Liqueur
fill with Club Soda

Build over ice and stir.

Soviet Sunset

HIGHBALL GLASS

1 part Lemon Vodka
1 part Triple Sec
1 part Sweetened Lime Juice
fill with Club Soda

Build over ice and stir.

Sparkling Southern Apple

COLLINS GLASS

1 part Southern Comfort®
1 part Sour Apple Schnapps
fill with Club Soda

Build over ice and stir.

Split Beaver

HIGHBALL GLASS

1 part Gin
1 part Peach Schnapps
fill with Tonic Water

Build over ice and stir.

Spring Field

COLLINS GLASS

2/3 part Pear Liqueur
1/2 part Rémy Martin® VSOP
splash Kirschwasser
1/2 part Simple Syrup
fill with Club Soda

Shake all but Club Soda with ice and strain. Top with Club Soda.

Spritzer

HIGHBALL GLASS

1 1/2 parts Vodka
fill with Club Soda

Build over ice and stir.

Squeeze My Lemon

HIGHBALL GLASS

1 1/2 parts Gin
1/2 part Lemon Juice
fill with Ginger Ale

Build over ice and stir.

Star Gazer

COLLINS GLASS

1 1/2 parts Dark Rum
1/2 part Blue Curaçao
1/2 part Triple Sec
1/2 part Simple Syrup
fill with Club Soda

Shake all but Club Soda with ice and strain. Top with Club Soda.

Starseeker

HIGHBALL GLASS

2 parts Light Rum
1 part Orange Juice
splash Grenadine
fill with Tonic Water

Shake all but Tonic Water with ice and strain. Top with Tonic Water.

Steeplejack

COLLINS GLASS

1 1/2 parts Apple Brandy
splash Lime Juice
fill with Club Soda

Build over ice and stir.

Stork Club Cooler

COLLINS GLASS

2 parts Gin
dash Sugar
fill with Club Soda

Build over ice and stir.

Stranded in the Rain

HIGHBALL GLASS

2 parts Tequila Reposado
2/3 part Lychee Liqueur
2/3 part Lemon Juice
1/2 part Lime Juice
fill with Club Soda

Build over ice and stir.

Strawberry Shortcake Cooler

COLLINS GLASS

2 parts Strawberry Liqueur
1/4 part Grenadine
fill with Lemon-Lime Soda
splash Cream

Build over ice and stir.

Submarine Cooler

HIGHBALL GLASS

1½ parts Gin
1 part Ginger Ale
fill with Tonic Water

Build over ice and stir.

Suisesse

ROCKS GLASS

1 part Pernod®
1 part Lemon Juice
1 Egg White
fill with Club Soda

Shake all but Club Soda with ice and strain. Top with Club Soda.

Summer Light

COLLINS GLASS

3 parts White Wine
1½ parts Dry Vermouth
fill with Club Soda

Build over ice and stir.

Summer Scotch

HIGHBALL GLASS

1 part Scotch
3 splashes Crème de Menthe (White)
fill with Club Soda

Build over ice and stir.

Sun 'n' Shade

COLLINS GLASS

2 parts Gosling's Black Seal® Rum
fill with Tonic Water
splash Lime Juice

Build over ice and stir.

Sunken Ship

HIGHBALL GLASS

⅔ part Crème de Banane
⅔ part Blackberry Liqueur
½ part Light Rum
1½ parts Sweet & Sour Mix
fill with Ginger Ale

Build over ice and stir.

Sunnier Sour

HIGHBALL GLASS

1¼ parts Dark Rum
¼ part Lemon Juice
dash Powdered Sugar
1½ parts Grapefruit Juice
fill with Club Soda

Shake all but Club Soda with ice and strain. Top with Club Soda.

Sunny Delight

MASON JAR

1 part Triple Sec
2 parts Lemon Vodka
splash Club Soda
fill with Orange Juice

Build over ice.

Superfly

HIGHBALL GLASS

2 parts Gin
1 part Lime Juice
fill with Ginger Ale

Build over ice and stir.

Surfboard Popper

HIGHBALL GLASS

1 part Kiwi Schnapps
1 part Passion Fruit Liqueur
fill with Ginger Ale

Build over ice and stir.

Swashbuckler

COLLINS GLASS

1½ parts Spiced Rum
1 part Cola
fill with Club Soda
¼ part Lime Juice

Build over ice and stir.

Sweet Concoction

HIGHBALL GLASS

1½ parts Amaretto
1½ parts Peach Schnapps
1 part Dry Vermouth
fill with Club Soda

Build over ice and stir.

Sweet Ginger

HIGHBALL GLASS

1 part Rum
1 part Amaretto
½ part Sweet Vermouth
fill with Ginger Ale

Build over ice and stir.

Sweet Summer

COLLINS GLASS

2 parts Raspberry Vodka
fill with Ginger Ale
splash Cranberry Juice Cocktail

Build over ice and stir.

Sweet Tart Cooler

HIGHBALL GLASS

1 part Vodka
1 part Cherry Juice
1 part Wild Berry Schnapps
1 part Lemonade
1 part Orange Juice
1 part Lemon-Lime Soda

Build over ice and stir.

TNT

HIGHBALL GLASS

1½ parts Tequila
fill with Tonic Water

Build over ice and stir.

Tahitian Treat

HIGHBALL GLASS

1 part Lemon Rum
1 part Amaretto
2 parts Cranberry Juice
fill with Lemon-Lime Soda

Build over ice.

Tall Islander

COLLINS GLASS

2 parts Light Rum
3 parts Pineapple Juice
3 splashes Lime Juice
splash Simple Syrup
fill with Club Soda

Shake all but Club Soda with ice and strain. Top with Club Soda.

Tapico

COLLINS GLASS

1½ parts Silver Tequila
1 part Crème de Cassis
1 part Banana Juice
fill with Tonic Water

Shake all but Tonic Water with ice and strain. Top with Tonic Water.

Tartan Swizzle

COLLINS GLASS

2 parts Scotch
1½ parts Lime Juice
dash Sugar
dash Bitters
fill with Club Soda

Shake all but Club Soda with ice and strain. Top with Club Soda.

Tenderberry

COLLINS GLASS

1 part Strawberry Vodka
1 part Cream
1 part Grenadine
1 part Strawberry Syrup
fill with Ginger Ale

Build over ice and stir.

Tequila Cooler

HIGHBALL GLASS

2 parts Tequila
fill with Lemon-Lime Soda

Build over ice and stir.

Tequila Fizz

COLLINS GLASS

2 parts Tequila
2 splashes Lemon Juice
3/4 part Grenadine
1 Egg White
fill with Ginger Ale

Shake all but Ginger Ale with ice and strain. Top with Ginger Ale.

Tequila Press

COLLINS GLASS

2 parts Tequila
1/2 part Simple Syrup
splash Lime Juice
fill with Club Soda

Build over ice and stir.

Test Drive

HIGHBALL GLASS

1/2 part Amaretto
1 part Banana Liqueur
fill with Tonic Water

Build over ice and stir.

Texas Fizz

COLLINS GLASS

1 1/2 parts Gin
1 part Orange Juice
dash Powdered Sugar
1/4 part Grenadine
fill with Club Soda

Shake all but Club Soda with ice and strain. Top with Club Soda.

Thermometer

HIGHBALL GLASS

2 parts Vodka
1 part Cranberry Juice Cocktail
fill with Club Soda

Build over ice and stir.

Tijuana Iced Tea

COLLINS GLASS

2 parts Tequila
1 part Coffee Liqueur
fill with Club Soda

Build over ice and stir.

Tonic Twist

COLLINS GLASS

1 part Apricot Brandy
1 part Sweet Vermouth
fill with Tonic Water

Build over ice and stir.

Tonica

HIGHBALL GLASS

2 parts Strawberry Liqueur
1 part Lemon Juice
fill with Tonic Water

Build over ice and stir.

Trade Winds

COLLINS GLASS

1 1/2 parts Dark Rum
1/2 part Lime Juice
1/2 part Plum Brandy
1/2 part Simple Syrup
fill with Club Soda

Shake all but Club Soda with ice and strain. Top with Club Soda.

Triad

HIGHBALL GLASS

1/2 part Añejo Rum
1/2 part Sweet Vermouth
1/2 part Amaretto
fill with Ginger Ale

Build over ice and stir.

Trinidad

COLLINS GLASS

1 part Light Rum
1 part Dark Rum
1 part Lime Juice
splash Triple Sec
dash Brown Sugar
fill with Club Soda

Shake all but Club Soda with ice and strain. Top with Club Soda.

Triple Fizz

HIGHBALL GLASS

1½ parts Gin
splash Triple Sec
splash Dry Vermouth
fill with Club Soda

Build over ice and stir.

Triple Iceberg

COLLINS GLASS

1½ parts Triple Sec
fill with Club Soda

Build over ice and stir.

Tropical Rain

COLLINS GLASS

2 parts Dark Rum
⅔ part Grand Marnier®
⅔ part Lemon Juice
splash Blue Curaçao
fill with Club Soda

Shake all but Club Soda with ice and strain. Top with Club Soda.

Tropical Waters

HIGHBALL GLASS

1½ parts Blue Curaçao
1½ parts Melon Liqueur
fill with Lemon-Lime Soda

Build over ice and stir.

TV Special

COLLINS GLASS

2 parts Gin
1 part Triple Sec
1 part Pineapple Juice
fill with Club Soda

Shake all but Club Soda with ice and strain. Top with Club Soda.

Twinkie® Star

COLLINS GLASS

1½ parts Cherry Brandy
fill with Tonic Water

Build over ice and stir.

Undercurrent

HIGHBALL GLASS

1 part Currant Vodka
½ part Blue Curaçao
½ part Sweet & Sour Mix
¼ part Simple Syrup
fill with Lemon-Lime Soda
splash Chambord

Build over ice. Top with Chambord.

Urine

HIGHBALL GLASS

2 parts Gin
1 part Lime Juice
fill with Club Soda

Build over ice and stir.

Valencia Lady

HIGHBALL GLASS

2 parts Vodka
splash Blue Curaçao
splash Cranberry Juice Cocktail
fill with Club Soda

Build over ice and stir.

Vanilla Hell

COLLINS GLASS

2 parts Fireball Cinnamon Whiskey
fill with Cream Soda

Build over ice.

Velvet Tongue

HIGHBALL GLASS

1 part Southern Comfort®
1 part Canadian Club® Classic
fill with Ginger Ale

Build over ice and stir.

Venus on the Rocks

ROCKS GLASS

1 part Amaretto
2 parts Peach Schnapps
fill with Club Soda

Build over ice and stir.

Vermouth Sparkle

COLLINS GLASS

2 parts Dry Vermouth
splash Sweet Vermouth
splash Grenadine
fill with Ginger Ale

Build over ice and stir.

Very Berry Tonic

COLLINS GLASS

1 part Currant Vodka
1/2 part Raspberry Liqueur
fill with Tonic Water

Build over ice and stir.

Victoria's Dream

HIGHBALL GLASS

2/3 part Peach Schnapps
1/2 part Strawberry Liqueur
1/2 part Irish Cream Liqueur
splash Milk
fill with Club Soda

Shake all but Club Soda with ice and strain. Top with Club Soda.

Victory

ROCKS GLASS

2 parts Pernod®
1 part Grenadine
fill with Club Soda

Build over ice and stir.

Viktor

HIGHBALL GLASS

2 parts Currant Vodka
1 part Lime Juice
fill with Ginger Ale

Build over ice and stir.

Violetta

COLLINS GLASS

1/2 part Parfait Amour
1/2 part Anisette
1 part Pineapple Juice
splash Grenadine
fill with Club Soda

Shake all but Club Soda with ice and strain. Top with Club Soda.

Virtual Reality

HIGHBALL GLASS

1 part Gin
1 part Calvados Apple Brandy
1/2 part Grenadine
1/2 part Lemon Juice
fill with Club Soda

Shake all but Club Soda with ice and strain. Top with Club Soda.

Viva Zapata

COLLINS GLASS

2 parts Tequila Reposado
1/2 part Kiwi Liqueur
1/2 part Lime Juice
1/4 part Simple Syrup
fill with Club Soda

Shake all but Club Soda with ice and strain. Top with Club Soda.

Vodka Cooler

COLLINS GLASS

2 parts Vodka
dash Powdered Sugar
fill with Seltzer

Build over ice and stir.

Vodka Highball
ROCKS GLASS
2 parts Vodka
½ part Dry Vermouth
fill with Ginger Ale

Build over ice and stir.

Vodka Rickey
HIGHBALL GLASS
2 parts Vodka
½ part Sweetened Lime Juice
fill with Club Soda

Build over ice and stir.

Walk the Dog
HIGHBALL GLASS
2 parts Rye Whiskey
fill with Club Soda

Build over ice and stir.

Walk the Plank
HURRICANE GLASS
1 part Spiced Rum
1 part Coconut Rum
1 part Passion Fruit Rum
fill with Lemon-Lime Soda

Build over ice and stir.

Wasp
COLLINS GLASS
1 part Vodka
1 part Banana Liqueur
fill with Ginger Ale

Build over ice and stir.

Whirlaway
HIGHBALL GLASS
1 part Blue Curaçao
dash Bitters
fill with Club Soda

Build over ice and stir.

Whirlpool
ROCKS GLASS
1 part Dark Rum
½ part Strawberry Liqueur
fill with Ginger Ale

Build over ice and stir.

Whiskey Cooler
HIGHBALL GLASS
2 parts Whiskey
fill with Lemon-Lime Soda

Build over ice and stir.

White Cactus
ROCKS GLASS
1 part Silver Tequila
½ part Lime Cordial
fill with Club Soda

Build over ice and stir.

White Carnation
HIGHBALL GLASS
2 parts Vodka
½ part Peach Schnapps
2 parts Orange Juice
fill with Club Soda
splash Cream

Build over ice and stir. Top with Cream.

White Gummy Bear
HIGHBALL GLASS
1 part Raspberry Vodka
1 part Pear Vodka
1 part Peach Schnapps
2 parts Sweet & Sour Mix
fill with Lemon-Lime Soda

Build over ice and stir.

Wild at Heart

COLLINS GLASS

1 part Brandy
1 part Vodka
1 part Triple Sec
1 part Gin
fill with Ginger Ale

Build over ice and stir.

Wild Irish Rose

ROCKS GLASS

2 parts Irish Whiskey
3/4 part Lemon Juice
1/2 part Grenadine
fill with Club Soda

Build over ice.

Wild Kiwi

COLLINS GLASS

1 part Light Rum
1 1/2 parts Kiwi Schnapps
fill with Tonic Water

Build over ice and stir.

Wild-Eyed Rose

COLLINS GLASS

2 1/2 parts Whiskey
1 part Grenadine
1/2 part Lime Juice
fill with Club Soda

Build over ice and stir.

Wrench

HIGHBALL GLASS

1 part Canadian Whisky
fill with Ginger Ale
splash Orange Juice

Build over ice and stir.

Yazoo

COLLINS GLASS

2 parts Crème de Coconut
2 parts Safari®
fill with Club Soda

Build over ice and stir.

Yellow Seersucker

HIGHBALL GLASS

2 parts Light Rum
1 part Lemon Juice
2 splashes Grenadine
fill with Tonic Water

Shake all but Tonic Water with ice and strain. Top with Tonic Water.

Yodel

ROCKS GLASS

1 part Fernet-Branca®
1 part Orange Juice
fill with Club Soda

Build over ice and stir.

Yukon Icee

COLLINS GLASS

2 parts Yukon Jack®
fill with Ginger Ale

Build over ice and stir.

Yo Mama Cocktail

HIGHBALL GLASS

2 parts Orange Vodka
fill with Club Soda
splash Orange Juice

Build over ice and stir. Top with Orange Juice.

Zadarade

COLLINS GLASS

2 parts Orange Vodka
1 part Triple Sec
1 part Sweet & Sour Mix
splash Cranberry Juice
splash Pineapple Juice
fill with Lemon-lime soda

Build over ice and stir.

Zanzibar Cooler

COLLINS GLASS

2 parts Vodka
1 part Peach Liqueur
dash Brown Sugar
fill with Ginger Ale

Build over ice and stir.

Zenith

ROCKS GLASS

2½ parts Gin
1 part Pineapple Juice
fill with Club Soda

Build over ice and stir.

ICED TEAS

This collection started with the infamous Long Island Iced Tea in the 1970s and rapidly grew to include a collection of potent drinks containing various ingredients that combined to make a muddy brown color. These drinks don't necessarily contain tea, though some of course do.

3-Mile Long Island Iced Tea

COLLINS GLASS

1 part Gin
1 part Light Rum
1 part Tequila
1 part Vodka
1 part Triple Sec
1 part Melon Liqueur
splash Sweet & Sour Mix
splash Cola

Mix with ice.

Apple Iced Tea

HIGHBALL GLASS

2 parts Sour Apple Schnapps
fill with Iced Tea

Build over ice and stir.

Apricot Iced Tea

HIGHBALL GLASS

2 parts Apricot Brandy
fill with Iced Tea

Build over ice and stir.

Bacardi® South Beach Iced Tea

COLLINS GLASS

3/4 part Spiced Rum
3/4 part Citrus Rum
3/4 part Light Rum
3 parts Sweet & Sour Mix
1 part Cola

Build over ice and stir.

Bambi's Iced Tea

COLLINS GLASS

1 part Vodka
splash Sweet & Sour Mix
1 part Cola
1 part Lemon-Lime Soda

Build over ice and stir.

Binghampton Iced Tea

COLLINS GLASS

1 part Coconut Rum
1 part Vanilla Vodka
1 part Gin
1 part Tequila
1/2 part Rum
fill with Sweet & Sour Mix
splash Cola

Build over ice and stir.

BJ's Long Island Iced Tea

HIGHBALL GLASS

1 part Amaretto
1 part Rum
1 part Triple Sec
1 part Vodka
splash Lime Juice
fill with Cola

Build over ice and stir.

Blue Long Island Iced Tea

COLLINS GLASS

1 part Vodka
1 part Tequila
1 part Rum
1 part Gin
1 part Blue Curaçao

Build over ice and stir.

Boston Iced Tea

COLLINS GLASS

1 part Vodka
1 part Gin
1 part Rum
1 part Tia Maria®
1 part Grand Marnier®
fill with Sweet & Sour Mix
splash Cola

Build over ice and stir.

California Iced Tea

HIGHBALL GLASS

½ part Gin
½ part Light Rum
½ part Tequila
½ part Vodka
½ part Triple Sec
½ part Sweet & Sour Mix
1 part Orange Juice
1 part Pineapple Juice

Build over ice and stir.

Caribbean Iced Tea

HURRICANE GLASS

1 part Gin
1 part Light Rum
1 part Tequila
1 part Vodka
1 part Blue Curaçao
fill with Sweet & Sour Mix

Build over ice and stir.

Caribbean Iced Tea #2

HIGHBALL GLASS

2 parts Coconut Rum
1 part Light Rum
fill with Iced Tea
splash Lemon Juice

Build over ice and stir.

Carolina Iced Tea

HIGHBALL GLASS

1½ parts Southern Comfort®
1 part Spiced Rum
1 part Peach Schnapps
½ part Vodka
fill with Iced Tea

Build over ice and stir.

Channel Island Iced Tea

COLLINS GLASS

1½ parts Vodka
1½ parts Triple Sec
splash Gold Tequila
splash Lime Juice
fill with Cola

Build over ice.

Coney Island Iced Tea

COCKTAIL GLASS

1 part Spiced Rum
2 parts Lemon Iced Tea
splash Lemon Juice

Shake with ice and strain.

Dead Grasshopper

COLLINS GLASS

1 part Crème de Menthe (White)
1 part Crème de Cacao (White)
1 part Milk
fill with Iced Tea
splash Grenadine

Shake all but Grenadine with ice and strain. Place a few drops of Grenadine in the center of the drink.

Dignified Iced Tea

HIGHBALL GLASS

2 parts Citrus Vodka
fill with Iced Tea

Build over ice and stir.

Electric Iced Tea

COLLINS GLASS

1½ parts Rum
1½ parts Vodka
1½ parts Gin
1 part Tequila
1 part Triple Sec
splash Blue Curaçao
fill with Lemon-Lime Soda

Build over ice and stir.

Embassy Iced Tea

COLLINS GLASS

1 part Blue Curaçao
1 part Vodka
1 part Light Rum
1 part Cachaça®
fill with Lemon-Lime Soda

Build over ice and stir.

Ewa Beach Iced Tea

COLLINS GLASS

½ part Gin
½ part Tequila
½ part Spiced Rum
½ part Vodka
½ part Triple Sec
1 part Fruit Punch
1 part Pineapple Juice

Build over ice and stir.

Georgia Peach Iced Tea

COLLINS GLASS

1 part Vodka
1 part Gin
1 part Rum
fill with Sweet & Sour Mix
1 part Peach Schnapps

Shake with ice and pour.

Iced Tea

COLLINS GLASS

1 part Vodka
1 part Gin
½ part Triple Sec
2 parts Sweet & Sour Mix
splash Cola

Build over ice and stir. Garnish with a Lemon Wedge.

Iced Tea Limoni

COLLINS GLASS

1 part Limoncello
fill with Iced Tea

Build over ice and stir.

Iced Teaspoon

COLLINS GLASS

1 part Silver Tequila
1 part Vodka
1 part Triple Sec
1 part Light Rum
1 part Gin
2 parts Sweet & Sour Mix
fill with Iced Tea

Shake with ice and pour.

Jamaican Iced Tea

HURRICANE GLASS

½ part Dark Rum
½ part Gin
½ part Triple Sec
½ part Vodka
1 part Pineapple Juice
1 part Sweet & Sour Mix

Shake with ice and strain over ice.

L.I.E.

COLLINS GLASS

1 part Vanilla Vodka
1 part Raspberry Rum
1 part Gold Tequila
1 part Gin
1 part Triple Sec
splash Orange Juice
splash Cola

Build over ice and stir. A variation of the Long Island Iced Tea, named after the Long Island Expressway, also known as the world's longest parking lot.

Lake George Iced Tea

HIGHBALL GLASS

½ part Tequila
½ part Rum
½ part Vodka
½ part Gin
½ part Triple Sec
1 part Pineapple Juice
fill with Cola

Shake all but Cola with ice and strain. Top with Cola.

Long Austin Iced Tea

HIGHBALL GLASS

½ part Vodka
½ part Gin
½ part Rum
½ part Triple Sec
1 part Ginger Ale
1 part Iced Tea

Build over ice and stir.

Long Beach Ice Tea

HIGHBALL GLASS

1 part Vodka
1 part Rum
1 part Gin
1 part Triple Sec
1 part Melon Liqueur
fill with Cranberry Juice Cocktail

Build over ice and stir.

Long Island Beach

HIGHBALL GLASS

1 part Vodka
1 part Rum
1 part Triple Sec
2 parts Sweet & Sour Mix
1 part Cranberry Juice Cocktail

Build over ice and stir.

Long Island Blue

COLLINS GLASS

½ part Silver Tequila
½ part Vodka
½ part Light Rum
½ part Gin
1 part Blue Curaçao
2 parts Pineapple Juice
fill with Lemonade

Build over ice and stir.

Long Island Fruit Punch

COLLINS GLASS

½ part Cranberry Vodka
½ part Orange Vodka
½ part Raspberry Vodka
¼ part Peach Schnapps
¼ part Sloe Gin
splash Cranberry Juice
splash Pineapple Juice

Shake with ice and strain over ice.

Long Island Iced Berry Tea

HIGHBALL GLASS

1 part Blackberry Brandy
1 part Amaretto
1 part Sloe Gin
½ part 151-Proof Rum
fill with Pineapple Juice

Shake with ice and pour.

Long Island Iced Tea

COLLINS GLASS

1 part Vodka
1 part Tequila
1 part Rum
1 part Gin
1 part Triple Sec
1½ parts Sweet & Sour Mix
splash Cola

Mix ingredients together over ice. Pour into shaker and give one brisk shake. Pour back into glass and make sure there is a touch of fizz at the top. Garnish with Lemon Wedge.

Long Island Iced Tea Boston Style

COLLINS GLASS

1 part Sweet & Sour Mix
1 part Gin
1 part Rum
1 part Grand Marnier®
1 part Tia Maria®
1 part Orange Juice
fill with Cola

Build over ice and stir.

Long Island Spiced Tea

COLLINS GLASS

¾ part Spiced Rum
½ part Vodka
½ part Lime Juice
½ part Gin
¼ part Triple Sec
fill with Cola

Build over ice and stir.

Long Iver Iced Tea

COLLINS GLASS

1 part Coconut Rum
1 part Vodka
1 part Gin
1 part Tequila
1 part Triple Sec
fill with Sweet & Sour Mix
splash Cola

Build over ice and stir.

Mahwah Iced Tea

HIGHBALL GLASS

1 part Jim Beam®
1 part Southern Comfort®
fill with Iced Tea

Build over ice and stir.

Miami Iced Tea

COLLINS GLASS

½ part Vodka
½ part Gin
½ part Rum
½ part Peach Schnapps
1 part Cranberry Juice
fill with Lemon-Lime Soda

Build over ice and stir.

Nuclear Iced Tea

COLLINS GLASS

½ part Vodka
½ part Gin
½ part Rum
½ part Triple Sec
1 part Melon Liqueur
fill with Sweet & Sour Mix
splash Lemon-Lime Soda

Build over ice and stir.

Pop's Hobby Iced Tea

COLLINS GLASS

2 parts Citrus Rum
splash Lemon Juice
fill with Iced Tea

Build over ice and stir. Garnish with a Lemon Wheel.

Radioactive Long Island Iced Tea

COLLINS GLASS

1 part Rum
1 part Vodka
1 part Tequila
1 part Gin
1 part Triple Sec
1 part Raspberry Liqueur
1 part Melon Liqueur
fill with Pineapple Juice
splash Cola

Build over ice and stir.

Raspberry Long Island Iced Tea

HIGHBALL GLASS

1/2 part Gin
1/2 part Vodka
1/2 part Light Rum
1/2 part Tequila
2 parts Sweet & Sour Mix
2 parts Cola
1/2 part Raspberry Liqueur

Build over ice and stir. Float Raspberry Liqueur on top and garnish with Lemon Wedge.

Raspberry Long Island Iced Tea #2

COLLINS GLASS

1 part Vodka
1 part Rum
1 part Tequila
1 part Gin
1 part Triple Sec
1 part Chambord®
fill with Sweet & Sour Mix
splash Cola

Shake with ice and pour.

A Real Iced Tea

HIGHBALL GLASS

3/4 part Vodka
3/4 part Gin
3/4 part Rum
3/4 part Tequila
1/2 part Triple Sec
splash Cranberry Juice Cocktail
splash Sweet & Sour Mix
splash Cola

Build over ice and stir.

Russian Iced Tea

HIGHBALL GLASS

1 part Vodka
fill with Iced Tea

Build over ice and stir.

Short Island Iced Tea

HIGHBALL GLASS

1 part Southern Comfort®
1 part Spiced Rum
splash Sweet & Sour Mix

Shake with ice and strain over ice.

Sidney Iced Tea

COLLINS GLASS

1/2 part Cointreau®
1/2 part Gin
1/2 part Rum
1/2 part Vodka
1 part Peach Schnapps
fill with Cola

Build over ice and stir.

South Beach Iced Tea

COLLINS GLASS

2/3 part Spiced Rum
2/3 part Light Rum
2/3 part Bacardi® Limón Rum
1 part Simple Syrup
2 parts Lemon Juice
fill with Cola

Build over ice and stir.

Southern Long Island Tea

HIGHBALL GLASS

1 part Gin
1 part Silver Tequila
1 part Vodka
1 part Light Rum
1 part Triple Sec
fill with Orange Juice
splash Cola

Shake with ice and pour.

Texas Iced Tea

HIGHBALL GLASS

1 part Tequila
fill with Iced Tea

Build over ice and stir.

Three Mile Island Iced Tea

COLLINS GLASS

1 part Gin
1 part Rye Whiskey
1 part Tequila
1 part Triple Sec
1 part Vodka
fill with Cola

Build over ice and stir.

Tokyo Iced Tea

COLLINS GLASS

½ part Gin
½ part Rum
½ part Vodka
½ part Silver Tequila
½ part Triple Sec
½ part Melon Liqueur
1 part Lime Juice
fill with Lemonade

Shake with ice and pour.

Tropical Iced Tea

COLLINS GLASS

½ part Vodka
½ part Rum
½ part Gin
½ part Triple Sec
1 part Sweet & Sour Mix
1 part Pineapple Juice
1 part Cranberry Juice Cocktail
½ part Grenadine

Shake with ice and pour.

Tropical Spiced Tea

HIGHBALL GLASS

1¼ parts Spiced Rum
fill with Iced Tea
splash Lemon Juice

Build over ice and stir.

Westwood Iced Tea

BEER MUG

1 part Vanilla Vodka
½ part Tequila
½ part Gin
½ part Light Rum
½ part Goldschläger®
½ part 151-Proof Rum
fill with Sweet & Sour Mix
splash Cola

Build over ice and stir.

Zurich Iced Tea

COLLINS GLASS

1½ parts Scotch
1 part Apricot Brandy
1 part Gin
fill with Iced Tea

Build over ice and stir.

SHORT DRINKS

These altitudinally challenged drinks don't fit into any other marketable category.

1-800 Bite the Berry

ROCKS GLASS

1¼ parts Jose Cuervo® 1800 Tequila
½ part Triple Sec
¼ part Raspberry Liqueur
2½ parts Sweet & Sour Mix
2 parts Cranberry Juice Cocktail

Shake with ice and strain over ice.

1-800 Pink Cad

HIGHBALL GLASS

1 part Jose Cuervo® 1800 Tequila
½ part Triple Sec
2½ parts Sweet & Sour Mix
½ part Lime Juice
splash Cranberry Juice Cocktail

Shake with ice and strain over ice.

2 Gs and a Double R

ROCKS GLASS

1½ parts Citrus Rum
1 part Gin
splash 151-Proof Rum
fill with Grapefruit Juice

Build all but 151-Proof Rum over ice. Top with the Rum.

39 Steps

HIGHBALL GLASS

1 part Raspberry Liqueur
1 part Jim Beam®
1 part Lemon Juice

Shake with ice and strain over ice.

3rd Wheel

COUPETTE GLASS

2 parts Alizé®
1 part Grand Marnier®

Shake with ice and strain over ice.

43 Ole

ROCKS GLASS

1 part Brandy
1 part Licor 43®
2 parts Orange Juice

Mix with ice.

'57 T-Bird

ROCKS GLASS

½ part Southern Comfort®
½ part Grand Marnier®
½ part Amaretto
splash Pineapple Juice
splash Orange Juice
splash Grenadine

Build over ice and stir.

77 Sunset Strip

HIGHBALL GLASS

½ part Vodka
½ part Gin
½ part Spiced Rum
½ part Triple Sec
1½ parts Pineapple Juice
½ part Grenadine

Build over ice and stir.

9 to 5

HIGHBALL GLASS

1 part Blackberry Liqueur
1 part Jim Beam®
½ part Lemon Juice
fill with Ginger Ale

Build over ice and stir.

A.B.C.

HIGHBALL GLASS

1 part Amaretto
1 part Irish Cream Liqueur
1 part Cointreau®

Shake with ice and strain over ice.

Abacaxi

ROCKS GLASS

2 parts Cachaca
1 part Simple Syrup
1 part Pineapple Juice
1 part Lime Juice

Build over ice and stir.

Aberfoyle

ROCKS GLASS

2 parts Vodka
1 part Drambuie

Build over ice and stir.

Abilene

HIGHBALL GLASS

1½ parts Dark Rum
2 parts Peach Nectar
3 parts Orange Juice

Build over ice and stir.

Absinthe Friends

HIGHBALL GLASS

2 parts Blackberry Liqueur
1 part Absinthe

Build over ice and stir.

Absinthe-Minded Margarita

MARGARITA GLASS

1 part Absinthe
1 part Triple Sec
1 part Lime Juice

Shake with ice and strain over ice.

Absolero Liqueur

ROCKS GLASS

¾ part Melon Liqueur
¾ part Absolut® Citron Vodka
¾ part Absolut® Kurant Vodka
1 Egg White
¼ part Lime Juice

Shake with ice and strain over ice.

Absolut® Heaven

HIGHBALL GLASS

1½ parts Orange Vodka
fill with Pineapple Juice
splash Cranberry Juice Cocktail

Build over ice and stir.

Absolut® Mixer

HIGHBALL GLASS

1 part Absolut® Citron Vodka
1 part Absolut® Peppar Vodka
1 part Absolut® Kurant Vodka
1 part Absolut® Vodka
fill with Orange Juice

Build over ice and stir.

Absolut® Stress

HIGHBALL GLASS

1 part Vodka
1 part Coconut Rum
1 part Peach Schnapps
splash Cranberry Juice Cocktail
splash Orange Juice

Build over ice and stir.

Absolut® Trouble

ROCKS GLASS

1½ parts Citrus Vodka
1 part Grand Marnier®
1 part Orange Juice
½ part Grenadine

Shake with ice and strain over ice.

Absolut® Vacation

ROCKS GLASS

1 part Vodka
1 part Cranberry Juice Cocktail
1 part Orange Juice
1 part Pineapple Juice

Build over ice and stir.

Absolute Head

HIGHBALL GLASS

1 part Vanilla Vodka
1 part Cherry Vodka
1 part Raspberry Vodka
fill with Orange Juice

Build over ice and stir.

The Abyss

HIGHBALL GLASS

⅔ part Dark Rum
splash Blue Curaçao
splash Cherry Brandy
splash Vermouth
fill with Orange Juice

Shake with ice and strain over ice.

Acapulco

ROCKS GLASS

1½ part Light Rum
2 splashes Triple Sec
2 splashes Lime Juice
dash Sugar
1 Egg White
1 Fresh Mint Leaf

Shake with ice and strain over ice.

Acapulco Clamdigger

ROCKS GLASS

1½ parts Silver Tequila
6 parts Clamato®
splash Lemon Juice
splash Tabasco® Sauce
splash Worcestershire® Sauce
dash Horseradish

Shake with ice and strain over ice.
Garnish with a Lemon Wedge.

Ademar

HIGHBALL GLASS

1 part Dark Rum
1 part Sweet Vermouth
1 part Triple Sec
splash Blue Curaçao
splash Strawberry Liqueur

Shake with ice and strain over ice.

Admiral

ROCKS GLASS

1 part Rye Whiskey
2 parts Dry Vermouth
splash Lemon Juice

Shake with ice and strain over ice.

Adrian Wixcey

WHITE WINE GLASS

1¼ parts Rum
1½ parts Passion-Grapefruit Juice
1½ parts Sweet & Sour Mix
1 part Orange Juice
splash Grenadine

Build over ice and stir.

Aero Bar

HIGHBALL GLASS

1 part Irish Cream Liqueur
1 part Coffee Liqueur
1½ part Crème de Menthe (White)
fill with Milk

Shake with ice and strain over ice.

Affirmative Action
HIGHBALL GLASS

2 parts Vodka
1 part Cognac
1 part Orange Juice

Shake with ice and strain over ice.

African Rumble
HIGHBALL GLASS

1 part Coffee Liqueur
1 part Cream
1 part Irish Cream Liqueur
1 part Tia Maria®

Shake with ice and strain over ice.

After Burner
HIGHBALL GLASS

1 part Rye Whiskey
1 part Tequila
2 parts Scotch
2 parts Tabasco® Sauce
2 parts Lemon Juice

Shake with ice and strain over ice.

After Eighteen
ROCKS GLASS

1 part Coffee Liqueur
1 part Crème de Menthe (White)
fill with Chocolate Milk

Shake with ice and strain over ice.

After Glo
ROCKS GLASS

1 part Everglo Liqueur
1 part Ginger Ale
1 part Pineapple Juice

Build over ice and stir.

Afternoon Pleasure
ROCKS GLASS

1 part Sweet Vermouth
1 part Amaretto
fill with Orange Juice

Build over ice.

Afterwhile Crocodile
HIGHBALL GLASS

1 part Vodka
1 part Melon Liqueur
1 part Blue Curaçao
fill with Margarita Mix

Shake with ice and strain over ice.

Agent Orange
ROCKS GLASS

1 part Southern Comfort®
1 part Irish Cream Liqueur

Build over ice and stir.

Aggie Slammer
HIGHBALL GLASS

1 part Southern Comfort®
1 part Hennessy®
splash Grenadine
splash Sweet & Sour Mix

Build over ice and stir.

Aggravation
HIGHBALL GLASS

1½ parts Scotch
½ part Coffee Liqueur
½ part Cream

Build over ice and stir.

Airborne Lemon Drop
HIGHBALL GLASS

1¼ parts Vodka
¾ part Chambord®
¾ part 151-Proof Rum
dash Sugar

Shake with ice and strain over ice.
Garnish with a Lemon Wedge.

Akis Special
HIGHBALL GLASS

1 part Light Rum
1½ parts Banana Liqueur
1 part Lemon Juice
fill with Lemon-Lime Soda

Build over ice and stir.

Al Capone

RED WINE GLASS

1½ parts Brandy
¾ part Marsala
splash Drambuie®

Shake with ice and strain.

Alabama

ROCKS GLASS

1 part Blue Curaçao
1 part Brandy
½ part Lime Juice
splash Simple Syrup

Shake with ice and strain over ice.

Alabama Fizz

HIGHBALL GLASS

2 parts Gin
dash Powdered Sugar
½ part Lemon Juice
fill with Seltzer
2 Fresh Mint Leaves

Shake with ice and strain over ice.

Alabama Mamma

HIGHBALL GLASS

1 part Crème de Banane
1 part Raspberry Liqueur
½ part Southern Comfort®
fill with Orange Juice

Shake with ice and strain over ice.

The Alamo

ROCKS GLASS

1 part Tequila
¾ part Coffee Brandy
¼ part Lime Juice

Shake with ice and strain over ice.

Albatross

HIGHBALL GLASS

½ part Crème de Banane
⅔ part Silver Tequila
½ part Pineapple Juice
splash Cream
splash Lemon Juice

Shake with ice and strain over ice.

Albino Russian

ROCKS GLASS

1 part Vanilla Vodka
1 part Coffee Liqueur
1 part Light Cream

Shake with ice and pour.

Albysjön

HIGHBALL GLASS

2 parts Vodka
1 part Orange Fanta® Soda
½ part Lemon-Lime Soda
½ part Kiwi Concentrate

Build over ice and stir.

The Alderman

ROCKS GLASS

1 part Citrus Vodka
½ part Strawberry Liqueur
½ part Lemon Juice
1½ parts Apple Juice
⅔ part Sparkling Water

Shake with ice and strain over ice.

Alex Chi-Chi

WHITE WINE GLASS

2 parts Vodka
1 part Cointreau®
1 part Cream of Coconut
2 parts Pineapple Juice

Shake with ice and strain.

Alexander the Great

HIGHBALL GLASS

1½ parts Vodka
½ part Crème de Cacao (White)
½ part Coffee Liqueur
½ part Cream

Shake with ice and strain over ice.

Alexander's Layers

HIGHBALL GLASS

1 part Apricot Brandy
1 part Crème de Cacao (Dark)
1 part Cream

Build over ice and stir.

Algae

HIGHBALL GLASS

½ part Vodka
½ part Melon Liqueur
½ part Raspberry Liqueur
½ part Blue Curaçao
2 parts Sweet & Sour Mix
fill with Lemon-Lime Soda

Shake with ice and strain over ice.

Algonquin

ROCKS GLASS

1½ part Bourbon
1 part Dry Vermouth
1 part Pineapple Juice
dash Bitters

Shake with ice and strain over ice.

Alice in Wonderland

ROCKS GLASS

1 part Amaretto
1 part Grand Marnier®
1 part Southern Comfort®

Shake with ice and strain over ice.

Alien Secretion

HIGHBALL GLASS

1 part Coconut Rum
1 part Melon Liqueur
fill with Pineapple Juice

Build over ice and stir.

Alien Slime

HIGHBALL GLASS

1 part Vodka
2 parts Blue Curaçao
3 parts Orange Juice

Shake with ice and strain over ice.

Alien Sludge

HIGHBALL GLASS

1 part Blue Curaçao
1 part Coconut Rum
1 part Mango Rum
2 parts Pineapple Juice
1 part Orange Juice
1 part Coconut Water

Shake with ice and pour.

All-American

HIGHBALL GLASS

1 part Southern Comfort®
fill with Cola

Build over ice and stir.

All American from Kentucky

ROCKS GLASS

1 part Bourbon
1 part Southern Comfort
fill with Cola

Build over ice and stir.

All Puckered Out

HIGHBALL GLASS

1½ parts Sour Apple Schnapps
fill with Ginger Ale

Build over ice and stir.

Allen Wrench

HIGHBALL GLASS

2 parts Banana Liqueur
1 part Coconut Rum
fill with Pineapple Juice

Build over ice and stir.

Alligator Piss

ROCKS GLASS

1 part Melon Liqueur
1 part Peach Schnapps
1 part Southern Comfort®
1 part Amaretto
splash Sweet & Sour Mix

Shake with ice and strain over ice.

Alligator Tongue

ROCKS GLASS

1 part Vodka
1 1/2 parts Melon Liqueur
2 parts Pineapple Juice
1/2 part Lemon-Lime Soda
1/4 part Lime Juice

Shake with ice and strain over ice.

All-Star Summit

ROCKS GLASS

1 part Light Rum
1/2 part Triple Sec
1/2 part Gin
1/2 part Raspberry Syrup

Shake with ice and strain over ice.

Alma Rosa

WHITE WINE GLASS

1 part Dark Rum
1/2 part Vanilla Ice Cream
1/4 part Triple Sec
1/4 part Crème de Banane

Shake with ice and strain over ice.

Almeria

ROCKS GLASS

1 1/2 parts Rum
1 part Brandy
1 part Coffee
1 Egg

Shake with ice and strain over ice.

Almond Joy®

HIGHBALL GLASS

1/2 part Coconut Rum
1 part Amaretto
1 part Crème de Cacao (White)
2 parts Cream

Shake with ice and strain over ice.

Almond Passion

HIGHBALL GLASS

1 part Dark Rum
1/4 part Crème de Noyaux
splash Apricot Brandy
2 parts Orange Juice

Shake with ice and strain over ice.

Almond Punch

HIGHBALL GLASS

1 part Amaretto
1 part Passion Fruit Liqueur
splash Orange Juice

Shake with ice and strain over ice.

Almond Schwarzenegger

ROCKS GLASS

2 parts Blavod® Black Vodka
1 part Amaretto

Shake with ice and strain over ice.

Almost a Virgin

HIGHBALL GLASS

2/3 part Raspberry Liqueur
2/3 part Amaretto
1 1/2 parts Currant Vodka
splash Pineapple Juice
splash Cranberry Juice Cocktail

Build over ice and stir.

Aloha Screwdriver

HIGHBALL GLASS

1 part Vodka
1 part Orange Juice
2 parts Pineapple Juice

Build over ice and stir.

Alpine Lemon-Lime Soda

HIGHBALL GLASS

2 parts Peppermint Schnapps
fill with Lemon-Lime Soda

Build over ice and stir.

Alternate Root

HIGHBALL GLASS

1 part Root Beer Schnapps
2 parts Orange Juice

Build over ice and stir.

Altoids® in France

HIGHBALL GLASS

1 part Chambord®
1 part Peppermint Liqueur

Build over ice and stir.

Amaretto Alexander

BRANDY SNIFTER

1 part Amaretto
1 part Crème de Cacao (White)
fill with Cream

Shake with ice and strain over ice.

Amaretto Big Red

HIGHBALL GLASS

2 parts Amaretto
fill with Strawberry Soda

Build over ice and stir.

Amaretto Daiquiri

HIGHBALL GLASS

1 part Rum
1 part Amaretto
fill with Sweet & Sour Mix

Shake with ice and strain over ice.

Amaretto '57 Chevy®

HIGHBALL GLASS

1 part Vodka
1 part Amaretto
1 part Cherry Juice
1 part Lemonade
1 part Orange Juice

Build over ice and stir.

Amaretto '57 T-Bird

HIGHBALL GLASS

1 part Vodka
1 part Amaretto
1 part Cherry Juice
1 part Sweet & Sour Mix
1 part Pineapple Juice

Build over ice and stir.

Amaretto Jack

HIGHBALL GLASS

1 part Amaretto
1 part Jack Daniel's
half fill with Orange Juice
half fill with Pineapple Juice
splash Grenadine

Shake Amaretto and Jack Daniel's with ice and strain over ice. Fill with juices and top with Grenadine.

Amaretto Hawaiian Fizz

HIGHBALL GLASS

2 parts Amaretto
1 part Sweet & Sour Mix
1 part Pineapple Juice
fill with Lemon-Lime Soda

Build over ice and stir.

Amaretto Heartwarmer

ROCKS GLASS

2 parts Southern Comfort®
2 Almonds
1 Peach Kernel, Crushed
dash Sugar
1 part Dry Vermouth
1 part Amaretto

Warm the Southern Comfort® and add the Almonds, Peach Kernel, and Sugar. Stir. Allow to cool and add the Vermouth and Amaretto. Stir again and strain over ice.

Amaretto Margarita

HIGHBALL GLASS

1 part Tequila
1 part Amaretto
fill with Margarita Mix

Build over ice and stir.

Amaretto Piña Colada

HIGHBALL GLASS

1 part Rum
1 part Amaretto
½ part Piña Colada Mix
½ part Pineapple Juice

Shake with ice and strain.

Amaretto Pucker

HIGHBALL GLASS

1 part Vodka
1 part Amaretto
1 part Cherry Juice
fill with Grapefruit Juice

Build over ice and stir.

Amaretto Punch

HIGHBALL GLASS

2 parts Amaretto
1 part Cherry Juice
1 part Orange Juice
1 part Pineapple Juice

Build over ice and stir.

Amaretto Pussycat

HIGHBALL GLASS

1 part Vodka
1 part Amaretto
1 part Cherry Juice
fill with Pineapple Juice

Build over ice and stir.

Amaretto Rummy Tea

HIGHBALL GLASS

1 part Rum
1 part Amaretto
1 part Sweet & Sour Mix
fill with Cola

Build over ice and stir.

Amaretto Russian Tea

HIGHBALL GLASS

1 part Vodka
1 part Amaretto
1 part Sweet & Sour Mix
fill with Cola

Build over ice and stir.

Amaretto Slinger

HIGHBALL GLASS

1 part Vodka
1 part Amaretto
1 part Sweet & Sour Mix
fill with Orange Juice

Build over ice and stir.

Amaretto Smooth Sailing

HIGHBALL GLASS

1 part Vodka
1 part Amaretto
1 part Sweet & Sour Mix
1 part Cranberry Juice Cocktail
1 part Orange Juice

Build over ice and stir.

Amaretto Sombrero

ROCKS GLASS

1 part Amaretto
4 parts Cream

Build over ice and stir.

Amaretto Sour

ROCKS GLASS

3 parts Amaretto
1½ parts Lemon-Lime Soda
1½ parts Lime Juice
1½ parts Sweet & Sour Mix

Shake with ice and strain over ice.

Amaretto Stone Sour

HIGHBALL GLASS

1 part Amaretto
1 part Sweet & Sour Mix
1 part Orange Juice

Build over ice and stir.

Amaretto Sunrise

ROCKS GLASS

1 part Amaretto
fill with Orange Juice
splash Grenadine

Build over ice and stir. Top with a splash of Grenadine.

Amaretto Sunset

ROCKS GLASS

3 parts Amaretto
1 part Triple Sec
fill with Apple Cider

Build over ice and stir.

Amaretto Toasted Almond

ROCKS GLASS

1 part Amaretto
1 part Coffee Liqueur
1½ parts Cream

Build over ice and stir.

Amaretto Vodka Hawaiian

HIGHBALL GLASS

1 part Vodka
1 part Amaretto
1 part Sweet & Sour Mix
1 part Lemon-Lime Soda
fill with Pineapple Juice

Build over ice and stir.

Amaretto Vodka Punch

HIGHBALL GLASS

1 part Vodka
1 part Amaretto
1 part Cherry Juice
1 part Orange Juice
1 part Pineapple Juice

Build over ice and stir.

Amaretto White Italian

HIGHBALL GLASS

1 part Vodka
1 part Amaretto
fill with Cream

Build over ice and stir.

Amazontic

ROCKS GLASS

2 parts Ginger Ale
1 part Rum
dash Sugar

Shake with ice and strain over ice.

Ambijaxtrious

ROCKS GLASS

1 part Vodka
1 part Tequila
1 part Coffee Liqueur
fill with Milk
splash Grenadine

Build over ice and stir.

American Cream Soda

HIGHBALL GLASS

1 part Butterscotch Schnapps
1 part Vanilla Liqueur
2 parts Sweet & Sour Mix
1 part Lemonade

Shake with ice and strain over ice.

American Sweetheart

ROCKS GLASS

1 part Southern Comfort®
splash Dry Vermouth
fill with Sweet & Sour Mix

Shake with ice and strain over ice.

American Yakuza

HIGHBALL GLASS

1 part Lychee Liqueur
1 part Jim Beam®
1 part Lemon Juice

Shake with ice and strain over ice.

AmoreAde

RED WINE GLASS

1½ parts Amaretto
¾ part Triple Sec
3 parts Club Soda

Build over ice and stir.

Amsterdam Surprise

HIGHBALL GLASS

½ part Goldschläger®
½ part Amaretto
½ part Vodka
½ part Southern Comfort®
3 parts Pineapple Juice

Build over ice and stir.

Amy's Ambrosia

HIGHBALL GLASS

½ part Currant Vodka
1 part Melon Liqueur
1 part Strawberry Liqueur
fill with Cranberry Juice Cocktail

Build over ice and stir.

Anchors Aweigh

ROCKS GLASS

1 part Bourbon
1 part Triple Sec
1 part Peach Schnapps
1 part Maraschino Liqueur
1 part Cream

Shake with ice and pour.

Andorian Milk

ROCKS GLASS

1 part Blue Curaçao
fill with Milk

Build over ice and stir.

Andy's Blend

HIGHBALL GLASS

2 parts Vodka
1 part Orange Juice
1 part Pineapple Juice

Build over ice and stir.

Añejo Highball

HIGHBALL GLASS

3 parts Añejo Rum
1 part Orange Curaçao Liqueur
splash Lime Juice
2 dashes Angostura Bitters
fill with Ginger Beer

Build over ice and stir. Courtesy of expert bartender Dale DeGroff.

Anesthetic

HIGHBALL GLASS

3 parts Gin
1 part Vermouth
1 part Cognac
dash Orange Bitters

Build over ice and stir.

Angel & Co.

ROCKS GLASS

1½ parts Frangelico®
¼ part Crème de Banane
fill with Pineapple Juice

Shake with ice and strain over ice.

Angel Blue

HIGHBALL GLASS

1 part Hpnotiq
½ part Blue Curaçao
½ part Coconut Rum
fill with Red Bull Energy Drink

Shake with ice and strain over ice.

Angel's Hug

HIGHBALL GLASS

1½ parts Pisang Ambon® Liqueur
1 part Dark Rum
1 part Crème de Banane

Shake with ice and pour.

Angel's Poison

ROCKS GLASS

1 part Raspberry Liqueur
¼ part Triple Sec
splash Lime Juice
fill with Lemon-Lime Soda

Build over ice and stir.

Angie's Dildo
ROCKS GLASS

1 part Vodka
2 parts Triple Sec
dash Sugar

Shake with ice and pour.

Angostura® Sour
ROCKS GLASS

3 parts Lemon-Lime Soda
1½ parts Sweet & Sour Mix
dash Bitters

Build over ice and stir.

Angry Irishman
ROCKS GLASS

1 part Irish Cream Liqueur
1 part Irish Whiskey

Build over ice and stir.

Angry Parakeet
ROCKS GLASS

3 parts Tequila
1½ parts Green Chartreuse®

Shake with ice and pour.

Angry Pirate
HIGHBALL GLASS

1 part Blue Raspberry Liqueur
1 part Coconut Rum
1 part Melon Liqueur
1 part Peach Schnapps
2 parts Pineapple Juice
splash Lemon-Lime Soda

Shake all but Soda with ice and strain over ice. Top with Lemon-Lime Soda.

Animal in Man
HIGHBALL GLASS

½ part Pisang Ambon® Liqueur
½ part Melon Liqueur
1½ parts Aquavit
½ part Lemon Juice

Shake with ice and strain over ice.

Ankle Breaker
ROCKS GLASS

2 parts 151-Proof Rum
1 part Cherry Brandy
1 part Lime Juice
splash Simple Syrup

Shake with ice and pour.

Antifreeze
HIGHBALL GLASS

1 part Vodka
½ part Blue Curaçao
½ part Crème de Banane
fill with Orange Juice

Shake with ice and pour.

Antoine Special
RED WINE GLASS

1 part Dubonnet® Blonde
1 part Dry Vermouth

Shake Dubonnet® with ice and strain. Top with Vermouth.

Anvil
HIGHBALL GLASS

2 parts Vodka
2 parts Cream of Coconut
3 parts Pineapple Juice

Build over ice and stir.

Aperol™ Schuhmann
HIGHBALL GLASS

1½ parts Aperol™
1 part Lemon Juice
1 part Lime Juice
fill with Orange Juice

Shake with ice and strain over ice.

Apfel Orange
HIGHBALL GLASS

1 part Apple Brandy
½ part Vodka
1 part Orange Juice
1 part Lemon-Lime Soda

Build over ice and stir.

Apfelkuchen
HIGHBALL GLASS

1 part Vodka
fill with Apple Juice
splash Grenadine

Build over ice and stir.

Apollo 13
ROCKS GLASS

2 parts Light Rum
2 parts Cream
½ part Grand Marnier®
½ part Galliano®
splash Grenadine

Shake with ice and strain over ice.

Apple Blossom
ROCKS GLASS

1½ parts Sour Apple Schnapps
½ part Cranberry Juice Cocktail

Shake with ice and pour.

Apple Brandy Highball
HIGHBALL GLASS

2 parts Apple Brandy
fill with Seltzer

Build over ice and stir. Garnish with a Lemon Twist.

Apple Brandy Rickey
HIGHBALL GLASS

1½ parts Apple Brandy
½ part Lime Juice
fill with Seltzer

Build over ice and stir.

Apple Brandy Sour
ROCKS GLASS

2 parts Apple Brandy
dash Powdered Sugar
½ part Lemon Juice

Shake with ice and strain over ice. Garnish with a Lemon Slice and a Maraschino Cherry.

Apple Cart
ROCKS GLASS

2 parts Apple Brandy
1 part Cointreau
splash Lemon Juice

Shake with ice and strain over ice.

Apple Chill
HIGHBALL GLASS

2 parts Sour Apple Schnapps
2 parts Lemonade
1 part Pineapple Juice

Shake with ice and pour.

Apple Coconut Sour
ROCKS GLASS

1 part Coconut Rum
1 part Green Apple Vodka
2 parts Sweet & Sour Mix

Shake with ice and strain over ice.

Apple Daiquiri
HIGHBALL GLASS

1 part Rum
1 part Sour Apple Schnapps
fill with Sweet & Sour Mix

Shake with ice and pour.

Apple Delight
ROCKS GLASS

1 part Vodka
1 part Peach Schnapps
1 part Melon Liqueur
½ part Crème de Banane

Shake with ice and pour.

Apple Dew
HIGHBALL GLASS

2 parts Sour Apple Schnapps
fill with Mountain Dew®

Build over ice and stir.

Apple Dreamsicle®

HIGHBALL GLASS

2 parts Sour Apple Schnapps
1 part Cherry Juice
1 part Orange Juice
1 part Pineapple Juice
1 part Cream

Shake with ice and pour.

Apple Eden

HIGHBALL GLASS

1½ parts Vodka
3 parts Apple Juice

Shake with ice and pour.

Apple Fizz

HIGHBALL GLASS

2 parts Sour Apple Schnapps
½ parts Sweet & Sour Mix
splash Orange Juice
fill with Lemon-Lime Soda

Build over ice and stir.

Apple Jack®

ROCKS GLASS

1½ parts Sour Apple Schnapps
1 part Cinnamon Schnapps

Build over ice and stir.

Apple Pie

ROCKS GLASS

3 parts Sour Apple Schnapps
1 part Cinnamon Schnapps

Build over ice and stir.

Apple Pie with a Crust

HIGHBALL GLASS

1 part Coconut Rum
3 parts Apple Juice
3 splashes Cinnamon Schnapps

Shake with ice and pour.

Apple Piña Colada

HIGHBALL GLASS

1 part Rum
1 part Sour Apple Schnapps
1 part Piña Colada Mix
1 part Pineapple Juice

Shake with ice and pour.

Apple Pucker

HIGHBALL GLASS

1 part Vodka
1 part Sour Apple Schnapps
1 part Cherry Juice
fill with Grapefruit Juice

Shake with ice and pour.

Apple Punch

HIGHBALL GLASS

2 parts Sour Apple Schnapps
1 part Cherry Juice
1 part Orange Juice
1 part Pineapple Juice

Shake with ice and pour.

Apple Pussycat

HIGHBALL GLASS

1 part Vodka
1 part Sour Apple Schnapps
1 part Cherry Juice
fill with Pineapple Juice

Shake with ice and pour.

Apple Rum Rickey

HIGHBALL GLASS

1 part Light Rum
1 part Applejack
splash Lime Juice
fill with Seltzer

Build over ice and stir.

Apple Screwdriver

HIGHBALL GLASS

1 part Vodka
1 part Sour Apple Schnapps
fill with Orange Juice

Build over ice and stir.

Apple Sour

HIGHBALL GLASS

2 parts Sour Apple Schnapps
fill with Sweet & Sour Mix

Shake with ice and pour.

Apple Tequila Sunrise

HIGHBALL GLASS

1 part Tequila
1 part Sour Apple Schnapps
fill with Orange Juice
splash Grenadine

Build over ice.

Apres Ski

HIGHBALL GLASS

1 part Coffee Liqueur
1 part Crème de Cacao (White)
1 part Peppermint Schnapps

Shake with ice and pour.

Apricot and Tequila Sour

ROCKS GLASS

1½ parts Tequila
1 part Amaretto
½ part Lime Juice

Shake with ice and pour.

Apricot Hurricane

HIGHBALL GLASS

1 part Rum
1 part Apricot Brandy
1 part Cherry Juice
2 parts Orange Juice
1 part Pineapple Juice

Shake with ice and pour.

Apricot Lady

ROCKS GLASS

1¼ parts Light Rum
1 part Apricot Brandy
splash Triple Sec
splash Lime Juice
1 Egg White

Shake all ingredients except Orange Slice with ice and strain over ice. Top with the Orange Slice.

Apricot Lemondrop

ROCKS GLASS

1 part Vodka
1 part Apricot Brandy
fill with Lemonade

Shake with ice and pour.

Apricot Screwdriver

HIGHBALL GLASS

1 part Vodka
1 part Apricot Brandy
fill with Orange Juice

Build over ice and stir.

Apricot Twist

HIGHBALL GLASS

1½ parts Rum
1 part Apricot Nectar
½ part Lime Cordial
splash Kirschwasser

Shake with ice and pour. Garnish with a Lemon Twist.

Aqua

HIGHBALL GLASS

1 part Vodka
1 part Irish Cream Liqueur
1 part Blue Curaçao
fill with Lemon-Lime Soda

Build over ice and stir.

Aqua Fodie

HIGHBALL GLASS

1 part Gin
1 part Blue Curaçao
fill with Orange Juice

Shake with ice and pour.

Arabian Sunset

CHAMPAGNE FLUTE

½ part Pisang Ambon® Liqueur
½ part Sloe Gin
1 part Cream
splash Blue Curaçao

Shake all but Blue Curaçao with ice and strain. Top with a splash of Blue Curaçao for a sunset effect.

Arawak Cup

ROCKS GLASS

2 parts Dark Rum
½ part Amaretto
½ part Pineapple Juice
½ part Lime Juice

Build over ice and stir.

Arc Welder

HIGHBALL GLASS

2 parts Blue Curaçao
½ part 151-Proof Rum
splash Light Rum

Shake with ice and pour.

Archers Slingback

CHAMPAGNE FLUTE

1½ parts Gin
1½ parts Apple Juice
1 part Peach Puree
½ part Lime Juice
½ tbsp sugar

Shake with ice and strain.

Area 151

PINT GLASS

1 part Southern Comfort
1 part Peach Schnapps
1 part Hpnotiq
fill with Red Bull Energy Drink
top with 151-Proof Rum

Build over ice and stir.

Arizona Evening

HIGHBALL GLASS

1 part Triple Sec
1½ parts Limoncello
2 parts Cranberry Juice Cocktail
2 parts Club Soda

Build over ice and stir.

Arkansas Razorback

ROCKS GLASS

1 part Rum
1 part Vodka
1 part Amaretto
1 part Coffee Liqueur

Shake with ice and strain over ice.

Arlequin

HIGHBALL GLASS

1½ parts Tequila
splash Grenadine
splash Lemon Juice
1 part Orange Juice
1 part Grapefruit Juice

Shake with ice and pour.

Armadillo

HIGHBALL GLASS

1 part Southern Comfort®
1 part Amaretto
½ part Sweet & Sour Mix
fill with Orange Juice

Build over ice and stir.

Arturro's Death

HIGHBALL GLASS

1 part Rum
1 part Tequila
1 part Sweet Vermouth
1 part Vodka
1 part Blue Curaçao
splash Grenadine

Shake with ice and strain.

Aruba Ariba

HIGHBALL GLASS

3/4 part Rum
3/4 part Vodka
1/2 part Grand Marnier®
splash Grenadine
splash Orange Juice
splash Pineapple Juice
splash Grapefruit Juice

Shake with ice and pour.

Asthma Attack

HIGHBALL GLASS

1/2 part Grain Alcohol
1/2 part 151-Proof Rum
1/2 part Raspberry Liqueur
1 part Amaretto

Shake with ice and pour.

Astroturf®

HIGHBALL GLASS

1 part Crème de Menthe (Green)
1 part Crème de Cacao (Dark)
fill with Milk
splash Chocolate Syrup

Build over ice and stir.

A-Team

HIGHBALL GLASS

1 part Vodka
1 part Brandy
1 part Lime Juice
2 parts Sweet & Sour Mix
fill with Fruit Punch

Shake with ice and pour.

Atlanta Belle

ROCKS GLASS

1 part Bourbon
3/4 part Crème de Cacao (White)
3/4 part Crème de Menthe (Green)

Shake with ice and pour.

Atlantean Uprising

HIGHBALL GLASS

1 part Rum
1/2 part Banana Liqueur
1/2 part Raspberry Liqueur
1/2 part Blue Curaçao
splash Grenadine

Build over ice and stir.

Atlantic Sun

HIGHBALL GLASS

1 part Vodka
1 part Southern Comfort®
1 part Grenadine
2 parts Sweet & Sour Mix
splash Club Soda

Shake all but Club Soda with ice and strain. Top with Club Soda.

Atlas

HIGHBALL GLASS

2 parts Vodka
1 part Blue Curaçao
splash Orange Juice
fill with Cranberry Juice Cocktail

Shake with ice and strain over ice.

Atomic Body Slam

HIGHBALL GLASS

1 part Gin
1 part Vodka
1 part Blackberry Brandy
1 part Light Rum
2 parts Strawberry Fruit Drink

Build over ice and stir.

Aunt Jemima®

HIGHBALL GLASS

3 parts Light Rum
1 part Maple Syrup
1 part Lemon Juice

Shake with ice and strain.

Aurelia

HIGHBALL GLASS

½ part Blue Curaçao
½ part Grenadine
⅔ part Cream of Coconut

Build over ice and stir.

Aussie Orgasm

HIGHBALL GLASS

1 part Cointreau®
1 part Irish Cream Liqueur

Shake with ice and pour.

Aussie Tea

HIGHBALL GLASS

1 part Kiwi Schnapps
1 part Strawberry Liqueur
fill with Iced Tea

Build over ice and stir.

Avalanche

HIGHBALL GLASS

1 part Crown Royal® Whiskey
1 part Coffee Liqueur
fill with Cream

Shake with ice and pour.

Aye Are So Dunk

HIGHBALL GLASS

1 part Apricot Brandy
1 part Blackberry Liqueur
1 part Piña Colada Mix
1 part Blueberry Schnapps

Build over ice and stir.

Aztec

ROCKS GLASS

1 part Gin
½ part Cherry Brandy
1 part Piña Colada Mix
1 part Orange Juice

Shake all but Pineapple and Cherries with ice and strain. Top with Pineapple Slice and Maraschino Cherries.

Azur

WHITE WINE GLASS

2 parts Orange Juice
1 part Apricot Brandy
½ part Passion Fruit Nectar
½ part Blue Curaçao

Shake with ice and pour.

B.S. on the Rocks

HIGHBALL GLASS

1 part Light Rum
1 part Peach Schnapps

Build over ice and stir.

B.W. Wrecker

HIGHBALL GLASS

1 part Amaretto
1 part Cranberry Juice Cocktail
1 part Coconut Rum
1 part Southern Comfort®

Shake with ice and strain over ice.

B-53

ROCKS GLASS

1 part Coffee Liqueur
1 part Irish Cream Liqueur
1 part Grand Marnier®
1 part Vodka

Layer in the glass with no ice.

B-69

ROCKS GLASS

1 part Grand Marnier®
1 part Coffee Liqueur
1 part Irish Cream Liqueur
1 part Amaretto
1 part Vodka

Shake with ice and strain.

Baam Scream

SHERRY GLASS

1 part Cinnamon Schnapps
1 part Jim Beam®

Pour ingredients into glass neat (do not chill).

Baby Fioula

CHAMPAGNE FLUTE

½ part Crème de Cacao (White)
½ part Triple Sec
½ part Banana Liqueur
1 part Strawberry Juice

Shake with ice and strain over ice.

Baby's Milk

HIGHBALL GLASS

¼ part Amaretto
1 part Irish Cream Liqueur
¼ part Peppermint Schnapps
½ part Club Soda

Build over ice and stir.

Bacardi® Tu Tu Cherry

ROCKS GLASS

1 part Dark Rum
3 parts Cranberry Juice Cocktail
2 splashes Grenadine
2 parts Orange Juice

Shake with ice and pour.

Backseat Boogie

HIGHBALL GLASS

½ part Gin
½ part Vodka
1 part Cranberry Juice Cocktail
1 part Ginger Ale

Build over ice and stir.

Bacon Margarita

COUPE

2 parts Gold Tequila
1 part Bacon Vodka
½ part Triple Sec
½ part Lemon Juice

Shake with ice and strain over ice.

Bad Monkey

HIGHBALL GLASS

2 parts Hpnotiq
1 part Banana Liqueur
fill with Lemon-Lime Soda

Build over ice.

Baehr Chunky Monkey

HIGHBALL GLASS

½ part Apricot Brandy
½ part Blue Curaçao
1 part Vodka
2 parts Blueberry Schnapps

Build over ice and stir.

Bagpiper's Melody

ROCKS GLASS

1 part Crème de Menthe (Green)
1 part Scotch

Layer over ice.

Bahama Blue

ROCKS GLASS

½ part Light Rum
½ part Dark Rum
1 part Blue Curaçao
1½ parts Pineapple Juice
splash Cream of Coconut

Shake with ice and pour.

Bahama Margarita

HIGHBALL GLASS

1 part Tequila
1 part Triple Sec
1 part Cherry Juice
2 parts Margarita Mix
1 part Pineapple Juice

Shake with ice and pour.

Bahamut Gold

HIGHBALL GLASS

2/3 part Vodka
splash Peppermint Liqueur
1 part Goldschläger®

Build over ice.

Bairn

ROCKS GLASS

2 parts Scotch
1/2 part Triple Sec
2 dashes Bitters

Shake with ice and strain.

Baitreau

ROCKS GLASS

1 part Irish Cream Liqueur
1 part Cointreau®

Layer over ice.

Baja Coktail

HIGHBALL GLASS

2/3 part Melon Liqueur
2/3 part Kiwi Schnapps
2 parts Sparkling Water

Build over ice and stir.

Balalaika

ROCKS GLASS

2 parts Vodka
1 part Triple Sec

Shake with ice and strain.

Balboa Cocktail

HIGHBALL GLASS

2 parts Orange Rum
2 parts Coconut Rum
1 part Melon Liqueur
fill with Red Bull Energy Drink

Build over ice and stir.

Ball Banger

HIGHBALL GLASS

1 1/2 parts Ouzo
fill with Orange Juice

Build over ice and stir.

Banana Apple Pie

HIGHBALL GLASS

1 part Vodka
1 part Banana Liqueur
fill with Apple Juice

Build over ice and stir.

Banana Banshee

HIGHBALL GLASS

1 part Banana Liqueur
1 part Crème de Cacao (White)
1 part Cream

Shake with ice and strain over ice.

Banana Berry Felch

ROCKS GLASS

1 part Irish Cream Liqueur
splash Banana Liqueur
1 part Crème de Cacao (Dark)
1 part Strawberry Vodka

Build over ice and stir.

Banana Breeze

HIGHBALL GLASS

1 part Vodka
1 part Banana Liqueur
1 part Pineapple Juice
1 part Cranberry Juice Cocktail

Build over ice and stir.

Banana Caipirinha

ROCKS GLASS

1 Lime Wedge
1/2 part Lime Juice
1 part Banana Liqueur
2 tsp Sugar
2 parts Cachaça

Muddle the Lime Wedge, Lime Juice, Banana Liqueur, and Sugar in the glass. Fill with ice and add the Cachaça.

Banana Cream Soda

HIGHBALL GLASS

2 parts Banana Liqueur
fill with Cream Soda

Build over ice and stir.

Banana D.A.

HIGHBALL GLASS

1 part Rum
1 part Cherry Juice
1 part Banana Juice
fill with Piña Colada Mix
splash Pineapple Juice

Build over ice and stir.

Banana Irish Cream

ROCKS GLASS

1 part Crème de Cacao (Dark)
½ part Cream
½ part Banana Puree

Shake with ice and pour.

Banana Jabs

HIGHBALL GLASS

1 part Banana Liqueur
1 part Malibu® Rum
fill with Mountain Dew®

Build over ice and stir.

Banana Lemonade

HIGHBALL GLASS

2 parts Banana Liqueur
fill with Lemonade

Build over ice and stir.

Banana LifeSaver®

HIGHBALL GLASS

1 part Coconut Rum
1 part Melon Liqueur
1 part Banana Liqueur
½ part Sweet & Sour Mix
fill with Pineapple Juice

Shake with ice and pour.

Banana Marble Drop

BRANDY SNIFTER

1 part Crème de Cacao (White)
1 part Crème de Cacao (Dark)
1 part Banana Syrup

Shake with ice and strain. Top with Whipped Cream.

Banana Paraiso

HIGHBALL GLASS

1 part Rum
2 parts Banana Juice
fill with Orange Juice
splash Pineapple Juice

Build over ice and stir.

Banana Pop

HIGHBALL GLASS

1 part Vodka
1 part Cherry Juice
1 part Banana Juice
fill with Orange Juice

Build over ice and stir.

Banana Pudding

HIGHBALL GLASS

1 part Banana Liqueur
1 part Crème de Cacao (White)
3 parts Milk
1 part Tia Maria®
1 part Vodka

Shake with ice and strain.

Banana Rainstorm

HIGHBALL GLASS

1 part Vodka
1 part Blue Curaçao
2 parts Lemon-Lime Soda
1 part Pineapple Juice

Build over ice and stir.

Banana Rum Sour

HIGHBALL GLASS

1 part Rum
1 part Banana Liqueur
fill with Sweet & Sour Mix

Build over ice and stir.

BananaChata

ROCKS GLASS

2 parts RumChata
1 part Banana Liqueur
1 part Caramel Vodka

Shake with ice and pour. Garnish with a Banana Slice caramelized with RumChata and Brown Sugar.

Banango

ROCKS GLASS

1½ parts Light Rum
½ part Mango Juice
½ part Lime Juice
¼ part Crème de Banane

Shake with ice and strain.

Banangrove

HIGHBALL GLASS

1 part Vodka
1 part Crème de Banane
1 part Orange Juice

Shake with ice and strain.

Banshee

ROCKS GLASS

1 part Irish Whiskey
1 part Irish Mist®

Build over ice and stir.

Barkeep Special

HIGHBALL GLASS

¾ part Amaretto
1½ parts Jack Daniel's®
3 parts Pineapple Juice

Shake with ice and strain over ice.

Barn Door

ROCKS GLASS

3 parts Scotch
1 part Cointreau
dash Orange Bitters

Shake with ice and strain over ice.

Barnum & Baileys®

HIGHBALL GLASS

1 part Irish Cream Liqueur
1 part Banana Juice
fill with Cream

Build over ice and stir.

Barracuda Bite

HIGHBALL GLASS

1½ parts Dark Rum
½ part Cherry Brandy
1 part Lemon Juice

Build over ice and stir.

Bartender's Delight

HIGHBALL GLASS

1 part Orange Vodka
1 part Dry Vermouth
1 part Dubonnet® Blonde
1 part Dry Sherry

Shake with ice and strain over ice.

Bartender's Revenge

HIGHBALL GLASS

1 part Brandy
1 part Cognac
1 part Rum
1 part Tequila
splash Tabasco® Sauce
dash Horseradish
splash Lemon Juice

Build over ice and stir.

Bartender's Root Beer

HIGHBALL GLASS

½ part Coffee Liqueur
½ part Galliano®
3 parts Club Soda
1 part Cola

Build over ice and stir.

Basic Instinct

ROCKS GLASS

1 part Light Rum
1 part Gin
½ part Blue Curaçao
½ part Southern Comfort®
2 parts Pineapple Juice
2 parts Passion Fruit Juice

Shake with ice and strain over ice.

Bat Bite

HIGHBALL GLASS

1 part Dark Rum
splash Lime Juice
fill with Cranberry Juice

Build over ice and stir.

Batman®

HIGHBALL GLASS

1 part Melon Liqueur
1 part Frangelico®
1 part Coconut Rum
1 part Cream

Shake with ice and pour.

Battering Ram

HIGHBALL GLASS

1 part Vodka
1 part Tequila
fill with Red Bull® Energy Drink

Build over ice and stir.

Bavarian Alps

HIGHBALL GLASS

2 parts Blackberry Liqueur
1 part Chocolate Liqueur
1 part Milk

Shake with ice and strain over ice.

Bawdy Baboon

HIGHBALL GLASS

1 part Melon Liqueur
½ part Blue Curaçao
½ part Crème de Banane
½ part Crème de Coconut
splash Lemon Juice

Shake with ice and strain over ice.

Bay Breeze

ROCKS GLASS

1½ parts Vodka
fill with Grapefruit Juice
splash Cranberry Juice Cocktail

Shake with ice and pour.

Bay Horse

ROCKS GLASS

1½ parts Whiskey
½ part Pernod®
½ part Crème de Cacao (Dark)
1 part Heavy Cream
dash Ground Nutmeg

Shake with ice and strain.

Bay Spritzer

HIGHBALL GLASS

1½ parts Coconut Rum
fill Lemon-Lime Soda
splash Grenadine
splash Lime Juice

Build over ice and stir.

Beam Me Up

HIGHBALL GLASS

1 part Vodka
1 part Peach Schnapps
1 part Cherry Juice
fill with Lemon-Lime Soda

Build over ice and stir.

Beam Me Up Scotty (Smooth 'n' Painless)

ROCKS GLASS

1 part Whiskey
½ part Vodka
½ part Amaretto
½ part Crème de Banane
splash Southern Comfort®

Build over ice and stir.

Beautiful Day

ROCKS GLASS

1 part Apple Liqueur
1 part Irish Mist®
1 part Parfait Amour®

Shake with ice and strain over ice.

Bec

HIGHBALL GLASS

2 parts Tequila
fill with Dr. Pepper®
splash Lime Juice

Build over ice and stir.

Bed Spinner

ROCKS GLASS

1 part Tia Maria®
1 part Amaretto
splash Sweet & Sour Mix

Shake with ice and strain.

Beekman's Beeker

HIGHBALL GLASS

1 part Jim Beam®
1 part Sweet & Sour Mix
1½ parts Passion Fruit Liqueur

Build over ice and stir.

Belfast Bomber

ROCKS GLASS

1 part Irish Cream Liqueur
1 part Cognac

Build over ice and stir.

Belgian Blue

HIGHBALL GLASS

1 part Vodka
½ part Crème de Coconut
½ part Blue Curaçao
fill with Lemon-Lime Soda

Build over ice and stir.

Belgian Brownie

ROCKS GLASS

1 part Gin
½ part Cognac
1 part Chocolate Liqueur
fill with Heavy Cream

Build over ice and stir.

Belinda's Fuzzy Melon

HIGHBALL GLASS

1 part Peach Schnapps
1 part Melon Liqueur
splash Lime Juice
splash Grenadine

Shake with ice and strain.

Bella Italia

HIGHBALL GLASS

⅔ part Blackberry Liqueur
splash Sambuca
splash Galliano®
fill with Mango Juice

Shake with ice and pour.

Bellas Noches De Mai

HIGHBALL GLASS

1 part Vodka
½ part Parfait Amour
½ part Maraschino Liqueur

Shake with ice and strain over ice.

Bend Me Over

HIGHBALL GLASS

1 part Amaretto
1 part Vodka
1 part Sweet & Sour Mix
4 parts Orange Juice

Build over ice and stir.

Bénédictine® Scaffe

HIGHBALL GLASS

1 part Bénédictine®
1 part Jim Beam®

Build over ice and stir.

Bermuda Bouquet

HIGHBALL GLASS

1½ parts Gin
1 part Apricot Brandy
splash Triple Sec
splash Grenadine
dash Powdered Sugar
1 part Orange Juice
1 part Lemon Juice

Shake with ice and strain over ice.

Bermuda Triangle

ROCKS GLASS

1 part Peach Schnapps
½ part Spiced Rum
fill with Orange Juice

Build over ice and stir.

Berry Blitz

HIGHBALL GLASS

1 part Blackberry Vodka
1 part Blueberry Vodka
1 part Raspberry Vodka
1 part Strawberry Vodka
fill with Pineapple Juice

Shake with ice and strain over ice.

Berry Sour

ROCKS GLASS

1 part Raspberry Liqueur
½ part Kirschwasser
½ part Crème de Cassis
½ part Simple Syrup

Shake with ice and strain over ice.

Bessemer

ROCKS GLASS

½ part Jack Daniel's®
½ part Jim Beam®
½ part Southern Comfort®
2 parts Sweet & Sour Mix

Shake with ice and strain.

Beth and Jen's Sleigh Ride

HIGHBALL GLASS

1 part Vodka
1 part Lemon-Lime Soda
1 part Cranberry Juice Cocktail

Build over ice and stir.

Betsy Clear

HIGHBALL GLASS

1 part Vodka
1 part Peach Schnapps
fill with Lemon-Lime Soda

Build over ice and stir.

Better Bachelor

HIGHBALL GLASS

1 part Sloe Gin
1 part Apricot Brandy
⅔ part Lemon Juice
splash Sweet & Sour Mix

Build over ice and stir.

Bible Belt

ROCKS GLASS

2 parts Southern Comfort®
½ part Triple Sec
2 parts Sweet & Sour Mix

Shake with ice and pour.

Big Bad Voodoo Kooler

HIGHBALL GLASS

2 parts Malibu® Rum
1 part RedRum®
1 part Melon Liqueur
1 part Orange Juice
1 part Pineapple Juice
splash Club Soda

Build over ice and stir.

Big Bang Boom

ROCKS GLASS

1 part Vodka
1 part Crème de Banane
1 part Melon Liqueur
1 part Pineapple Juice
1 part Orange Juice
½ part Grenadine

Shake with ice and strain.

Big Bird

HIGHBALL GLASS

1 part Banana Liqueur
1 part Pineapple Juice
1 part Orange Juice

Build over ice and stir.

The Big Booty
HIGHBALL GLASS

1 part Gin
2/3 part Lychee Liqueur
1/2 part Orange Liqueur
1/2 part Lemon Juice
1 part Papaya Juice

Build over ice and stir.

Big Bull
ROCKS GLASS

1 part Tequila
1 part Coffee Liqueur

Build over ice and stir.

Big Dog
HIGHBALL GLASS

1 1/2 parts Vodka
1 part Coffee Liqueur
fill with Milk
splash Cola

Build over ice and stir.

Big Easy
HIGHBALL GLASS

1 part Southern Comfort
1/2 part Raspberry Liqueur
fill with Cola

Build over ice and stir.

Big Fat One
ROCKS GLASS

1 part Vodka
1 part Triple Sec
1 part Melon Liqueur
splash Orange Juice

Shake with ice and pour.

Big Red Chevy
HIGHBALL GLASS

1 part Vodka
1 part Sweet & Sour Mix
1 part Strawberry Soda
splash Orange Juice

Build over ice and stir.

Big Sammie
HIGHBALL GLASS

1 part Sambuca
1/2 part Crème de Coconut
splash Gin

Build over ice and stir.

Bijoux
HIGHBALL GLASS

1 part Vodka
1 part Melon Liqueur
splash Triple Sec
splash Lemon Juice
splash Pineapple Juice

Shake with ice and pour.

Bikini on the Rocks
HIGHBALL GLASS

1 part Cherry Brandy
1/2 part Blackberry Liqueur
2/3 part Frangelico®
1 part Milk

Shake with ice and strain over ice.

Bill Clinton Zipper Dropper
ROCKS GLASS

1 part Coffee Liqueur
1 part Crème de Cacao (White)
1 part Crème de Menthe (White)

Shake with ice and pour.

Bill's Bongobay
HIGHBALL GLASS

1 part Coconut Rum
1 part Melon Liqueur
fill with Pineapple Juice
splash Grenadine

Build over ice and stir.

Binky
HIGHBALL GLASS

1 part Coffee Liqueur
1 part Crème de Cacao (White)
1 part Irish Cream Liqueur

Build over ice and stir.

Bionda
HIGHBALL GLASS

2/3 part Triple Sec
splash Maraschino Liqueur
fill with Orange Juice

Build over ice and stir.

The Bionic Drink
HIGHBALL GLASS

2 parts Vodka
fill with Grapefruit Juice
splash Lemon Juice

Build over ice and stir.

Birth Control
ROCKS GLASS

1 part Whiskey
1 part Gin

Build over ice and stir.

Bishop's Silk
ROCKS GLASS

1 1/2 parts Amaretto
1 1/2 parts Hazelnut Liqueur
1 part Butterscotch Schnapps

Build over ice and stir.

Bison
HIGHBALL GLASS

1 part Vodka
splash Blue Curaçao
splash Campari®
splash Sweet Vermouth

Shake with ice and strain.

Bitch
HIGHBALL GLASS

1 part Cinnamon Schnapps
1 part Orange Juice

Shake with ice and pour.

Bitter Apple
ROCKS GLASS

1 1/2 parts Apple Brandy
1 part Club Soda

Build over ice and stir.

Bitter Canadian
HIGHBALL GLASS

1 1/2 parts Canadian Whisky
4 parts Sweet & Sour Mix
2 dashes Bitters

Shake with ice and strain over ice.
Garnish with a Lemon Wedge.

Bitter End
ROCKS GLASS

2 parts Sweet Vermouth
3 dashes Angostura® Bitters

Build over ice and stir.

Bitter Pill
HIGHBALL GLASS

1 part Vodka
1 part Jack Daniel's®
splash Lemon Juice
fill with Cola

Build over ice and stir.

Bittersweet Italian
ROCKS GLASS

1 1/2 parts Vodka
1 part Amaretto
1 part Grapefruit Juice
1/2 part Lemon Juice
dash Sugar
fill with Pineapple Juice

Shake with ice and strain.

Bitty Orange
HIGHBALL GLASS

1 part Coffee Liqueur
1 part Cointreau®

Build over ice and stir.

Bizmark

HIGHBALL GLASS

1 part Jim Beam®
1 part Triple Sec
1 part Cherry Brandy
2 parts Sweet & Sour Mix
2 parts Club Soda

Build over ice and stir.

Black Blonde

HIGHBALL GLASS

2 parts Amaretto
splash Crème de Menthe (White)
fill with Orange Juice

Shake with ice and pour.

Black Cactus

ROCKS GLASS

1 part Tequila
1 part Blackberry Brandy
1 part Club Soda

Build over ice and stir.

Black Charro

HIGHBALL GLASS

2 parts Tequila
1 part Lemon Juice
fill with Cola

Build over ice and stir.

Black Cherry

HIGHBALL GLASS

1 part Vodka
1 part Raspberry Liqueur
1 part Irish Cream Liqueur
1 part Coffee Liqueur
1 part Half and Half
splash Cola

Shake with ice and pour.

Black Christmas

HIGHBALL GLASS

1½ parts Black Sambuca
fill with Eggnog

Build over ice and stir.

Black Death

HIGHBALL GLASS

2 parts Jack Daniel's®
splash Sambuca
fill with Cola

Build over ice and stir.

Black Dog

ROCKS GLASS

3 parts Bourbon
1 part Sweet Vermouth
½ part Blackberry Liqueur

Build over ice and stir.

Black Fruit Tree

HIGHBALL GLASS

1 part Blue Curaçao
1 part Amaretto
1 part Triple Sec
1 part Blackberry Brandy
1 part Grenadine

Build over ice and stir.

Black Irish

ROCKS GLASS

3 parts Irish Whiskey
1 part Coffee Liqueur

Build over ice and stir.

Black Lagoon

HIGHBALL GLASS

1 part Citrus Vodka
1 part Blackberry Liqueur
fill with Orange Juice
splash Cranberry Juice Cocktail

Build over ice and stir.

Black Mexican

ROCKS GLASS

1 part Tequila
1 part Coffee Liqueur

Shake with ice and strain.

Black of Night

HIGHBALL GLASS

1 part Vodka
1 part Wild Berry Schnapps
2 parts Lemonade
1 part Cola

Build over ice and stir.

Black Opal

HIGHBALL GLASS

1/2 part Gin
1/2 part Rum
1/2 part Vodka
1/2 part Triple Sec
2 parts Sweet & Sour Mix

Build over ice and stir.

Black Orchid

ROCKS GLASS

2 parts Black Sambuca
1/2 part Cream

Layer over ice.

Black River Boogie

HIGHBALL GLASS

1 part Peach Schnapps
1 part Raspberry Liqueur
2 1/2 parts Sweet & Sour Mix

Build over ice and stir.

Black Russian

ROCKS GLASS

1 1/2 parts Vodka
1 part Coffee Liqueur

Build over ice and stir.

Black Tartan

ROCKS GLASS

1 part Johnnie Walker® Black Label
1 part Irish Whiskey
1 part Drambuie®
1 1/2 parts Coffee Liqueur

Shake with ice and strain over ice.

Black Watch

HIGHBALL GLASS

1 part Coffee Liqueur
1 part Scotch
splash Club Soda

Build over ice and stir.

Black Widow

ROCKS GLASS

1 part Dark Rum
1 part Coffee Liqueur

Shake with ice and strain.

Blackbeard

HIGHBALL GLASS

1 part Spiced Rum
1 part Root Beer Schnapps
fill with Cola

Build over ice and stir.

Blackberry Breeze

HIGHBALL GLASS

1 part Vodka
1 part Blackberry Liqueur
1 part Pineapple Juice
1 part Cranberry Juice Cocktail

Shake with ice and pour.

Blackberry Chill

HIGHBALL GLASS

1 part Vodka
2 parts Blackberry Juice
2 parts Lemonade
1 part Pineapple Juice

Shake with ice and pour.

Blackberry Hill

HIGHBALL GLASS

1 1/2 parts Blackberry Liqueur
fill with Cola

Build over ice and stir.

Blackberry Jack
HIGHBALL GLASS

1 part Jack Daniel's®
1 part Blackberry Liqueur
2 parts Lemon-Lime Soda
splash Grenadine

Build over ice and stir.

Blackberry Lifesaver
HIGHBALL GLASS

1½ parts Vodka
1 part Blackberry Liqueur
fill with Orange Juice

Build over ice and stir.

Blackberry Punch
HIGHBALL GLASS

2 parts Black Haus® Blackberry Schnapps
1 part Rum
splash Lemon Juice
dash Powdered Sugar

Shake with ice and pour.

Blackberry Pussycat
HIGHBALL GLASS

1 part Vodka
1 part Blackberry Liqueur
1 part Cherry Juice
fill with Pineapple Juice

Shake with ice and pour.

Blackberry Sour
HIGHBALL GLASS

2 parts Blackberry Liqueur
fill with Sweet & Sour Mix

Build over ice and stir.

Blackberry Tequila
HIGHBALL GLASS

1 part Tequila
1 part Blackberry Liqueur
1 part Cherry Juice
fill with Orange Juice

Build over ice and stir.

Blackjack
HIGHBALL GLASS

½ part Brandy
1 part Kirschwasser
1 part Coffee Liqueur

Shake with ice and strain.

Blackjack #2
ROCKS GLASS

1½ parts Scotch
1 part Coffee Liqueur
½ part Triple Sec
½ part Lemon Juice

Shake with ice and strain.

Blackjack #3
ROCKS GLASS

½ part Brandy
1 part Cherry Vodka
1 part Coffee Liqueur

Shake with ice and strain over ice.

Blackula
HIGHBALL GLASS

1½ parts Blavod® Black Vodka
fill with Bloody Mary Mix

Shake with ice and pour.

Blazing Probe
HIGHBALL GLASS

1 part 151-Proof Rum
1 part Honey
1 part Strawberry Juice

Build over ice and stir.

Bleeding Heart
HIGHBALL GLASS

2 parts Sloe Gin
¼ part Lemon Juice
2 splashes Grenadine
dash Powdered Sugar
1 Egg White

Shake with ice and pour.

Blessed Event

HIGHBALL GLASS

2 parts Applejack
2 parts Bénédictine®
splash Lime Juice
splash Blue Curaçao

Shake with ice and pour.

Blind Russian

HIGHBALL GLASS

3/4 part Irish Cream Liqueur
3/4 part Godiva® Liqueur
3/4 part Coffee Liqueur
1/2 part Butterscotch Schnapps

Shake with ice and pour.

Blinders

ROCKS GLASS

2 parts Scotch
fill with Grapefruit Juice
splash Grenadine

Build over ice.

Blindside

HIGHBALL GLASS

2 parts Vodka
2 parts Orange Juice
2 parts Grapefruit Juice
1 part Strawberry Syrup

Build over ice and stir.

Blonde Bombshell

HIGHBALL GLASS

1 part Vodka
1 part Brandy
1/2 part Sour Apple Schnapps
1/2 part Peach Schnapps

Shake with ice and pour.

Blonde Ron

HIGHBALL GLASS

1 part Light Rum
fill with Lemon-Lime Soda

Build over ice and stir.

Bloody Biker

ROCKS GLASS

2 parts Vodka
5 parts Spicy Vegetable Juice Blend
splash Worchestershire Sauce
splash Hot Sauce
splash Olive Brine

Shake with ice and pour. Garnish with a Lime Wedge.

Bloody Bitch

HIGHBALL GLASS

2 parts Grapefruit Juice
1 part Vodka
1 part Grenadine

Shake with ice and pour.

Bloody Californian

HIGHBALL GLASS

1 part Raspberry Liqueur
1 part Orange Liqueur
2 parts Pineapple Juice
fill with Cranberry Juice Cocktail

Build over ice and stir.

Bloody Knuckle

HIGHBALL GLASS

1 part Irish Cream Liqueur
1 part Cherry Whiskey

Build over ice and stir.

Bloody Maria

HIGHBALL GLASS

1 1/2 parts Tequila
splash Tabasco® Sauce
splash Worchestershire Sauce
dash Horseradish
dash Celery Salt
dash Pepper
splash Lemon Juice

Build over ice and stir. Garnish with a Celery Stalk and a Lime Wedge.

Bloody Mary

HIGHBALL GLASS

1 part Vodka
1 part Sherry
splash Worchestershire Sauce
dash Salt
splash Tabasco® Sauce
dash Pepper

Build over ice and stir. There are many different variations on the Bloody Mary. This is the basic recipe that you can adjust to your taste. Garnish with a Celery Stalk and a Lime Wedge.

Bloody Navel

HIGHBALL GLASS

1½ parts Peach Schnapps
1½ parts Vodka
dash Grenadine
fill with Orange Juice

Shake with ice and strain over ice.

Bloody Passion

HIGHBALL GLASS

1 part Hennessy®
1 part Alizé® Red Passion

Build over ice.

Bloody Smurf®

HIGHBALL GLASS

1½ parts Blueberry Schnapps
fill with Cranberry Juice Cocktail

Build over ice and stir.

Bloody Sunday

HIGHBALL GLASS

1 part Tropical Punch Schnapps
1 part Grenadine
1 part Piña Colada Mix
1½ part Vodka

Shake with ice and pour.

Bloody Temple

HIGHBALL GLASS

2 parts Vodka
1 part Grenadine
1 part Lemon-Lime Soda

Build over ice and stir.

Blue Almond

CHAMPAGNE FLUTE

2 parts Scotch
1 part Amaretto
½ part Kirschwasser

Shake with ice and strain.

Blue Ball

ROCKS GLASS

1 part Blue Curaçao
1 part Coconut Rum
1 part Raspberry Vodka

Build over ice and stir.

Blue Bermuda

HIGHBALL GLASS

1 part Blue Curaçao
1 part Light Rum
3 parts Pineapple Juice

Shake with ice and pour.

Blue Bike

HIGHBALL GLASS

1 part Vodka
½ part Light Rum
1 part Blue Curaçao
½ part Triple Sec
½ part Sweet & Sour Mix

Shake with ice and pour.

Blue Blarney

ROCKS GLASS

1¼ parts Tequila
¾ part Blue Curaçao
1 part Triple Sec
fill with Sweet & Sour Mix

Build over ice and stir. Garnish with a Lime Wedge.

Blue Cadillac Margarita

COUPE

2 parts Gold Tequila
1 part Blue Curaçao
1 part Lime Juice
splash Grand Marnier

Shake all but Grand Marnier with ice and strain over ice. Top with Grand Marnier.

Blue Denim

HIGHBALL GLASS

splash Blue Curaçao
½ part Dry Vermouth
2 dashes Angostura® Bitters

Shake with ice and strain over ice.

Blue Dolphin

HIGHBALL GLASS

2 parts Dry Vermouth
½ part Blue Curaçao
fill with Lemonade
splash Grenadine

Shake with ice and pour. Garnish with a Lemon Slice.

Blue Eye

HIGHBALL GLASS

1½ parts Vodka
1 part Battery® Energy Drink
1 part Sweet & Sour Mix
splash Blue Curaçao

Shake with ice and strain over ice.

Blue Flannel

HIGHBALL GLASS

1 part Blue Curaçao
1 part Peppermint Liqueur
1 part Cream

Shake with ice and pour.

A Blue Gold Banana

HIGHBALL GLASS

1 part Goldschläger®
1 part Blue Curaçao
splash Crème de Banane

Build over ice and stir.

Blue Hawaiian

HIGHBALL GLASS

1 part Rum
1 part Blue Curaçao
1 part Piña Colada Mix
1 part Pineapple Juice

Build over ice and stir.

Blue Hurricane Highball

HIGHBALL GLASS

1 part Rum
1 part Blue Curaçao
2 parts Orange Juice
1 part Pineapple Juice

Build over ice and stir.

Blue Ice

HIGHBALL GLASS

1 part Coconut Rum
1 part Triple Sec
1 part Hpnotiq®

Build over ice and stir.

Blue Lagoon

HIGHBALL GLASS

1 part Vodka
1 part Blue Curaçao
fill with Lemonade

Build over ice and stir. Garnish with a Maraschino Cherry.

Blue Mango

HIGHBALL GLASS

1 part Blue Curaçao
1 part Vodka
1 part Mango Nectar
fill with Orange Juice

Build over ice and stir.

Blue Monkey

HIGHBALL GLASS

1 part Orange Vodka
1 part Banana Liqueur
1 part Cream
splash Blue Curaçao

Shake with ice and strain over ice.

Blue Mountain
ROCKS GLASS

1½ parts Añejo Rum
½ part Tia Maria®
½ part Vodka
1 part Orange Juice
splash Lemon Juice

Shake with ice and strain over ice.

Blue Note
ROCKS GLASS

1½ parts Gin
¼ part Blue Curaçao
splash Triple Sec
fill with Pineapple Juice

Build over ice and stir.

Blue Poison
HIGHBALL GLASS

1 part Silver Tequila
1 part Vodka
1 part Blue Curaçao
fill with Lemonade

Build over ice and stir.

Blue Russian
ROCKS GLASS

1 part Blue Curaçao
1 part Vodka
fill with Cream

Shake with ice and pour.

Blue Steel
ROCKS GLASS

1 part Hpnotiq
½ part Blue Curaçao
½ part Blue Raspberry Liqueur
splash Lemon-Lime Soda
splash Sweet & Sour Mix

Shake with ice and strain over ice.

Blue Sunset
HIGHBALL GLASS

1 part Tequila
1 part Blue Curaçao
1 part Lemon-Lime Soda
1 part Sweet & Sour Mix
2 parts Orange Juice

Build over ice and stir.

Blue Valium
ROCKS GLASS

½ part Canadian Whisky
½ part 151-Proof Rum
½ part Blue Curaçao
1 part Lemonade
1 part Sweet & Sour Mix

Build over ice and stir.

Blueberry Pucker
HIGHBALL GLASS

1 part Vodka
1 part Blueberry Schnapps
1 part Cherry Juice
fill with Grapefruit Juice

Build over ice and stir.

Bluegrass Cooler
HIGHBALL GLASS

1 part Bourbon
¼ part St-Germain
4 parts Apple Juice

Build over ice and stir.

Blue-Woo
HIGHBALL GLASS

1 part Vodka
1 part Blueberry Schnapps
fill with Cranberry Juice Cocktail

Build over ice and stir.

Blushing Bride
HIGHBALL GLASS

1 part Vodka
2 parts Cranberry Juice Cocktail
3 parts Orange Juice
2 parts Lemon-Lime Soda

Build over ice and stir.

BMW
HIGHBALL GLASS

1 part Irish Cream Liqueur
1 part Coconut Rum
1 part Rye Whiskey

Build over ice and stir.

Boardwalk Breezer
HIGHBALL GLASS

1 part Rum
1 part Banana Liqueur
1 part Cherry Juice
1 part Margarita Mix
1 part Pineapple Juice

Shake with ice and pour.

Boat Drink
HIGHBALL GLASS

2 parts Rum
1 part Pineapple Juice
1 part Orange Juice

Shake with ice and pour.

Bocci Ball
CORDIAL GLASS

1 part Amaretto
fill with Orange Juice

Build over ice and stir.

Bocci Ball #2
HIGHBALL GLASS

1 part Amaretto
1 part Vodka
fill with Orange Juice

Build over ice and stir.

Bon Bini
HIGHBALL GLASS

1 part Dark Rum
1 part Blue Curaçao
fill with Pineapple Juice

Shake with ice and pour.

Bonfire
HIGHBALL GLASS

2/3 part Apricot Brandy
splash Sweet Vermouth
splash Bénédictine®
splash Orange Vodka

Shake with ice and pour.

Bongo Congo
ROCKS GLASS

1 part Crème de Cassis
fill with Orange Juice

Build over ice and stir.

Bongobay
ROCKS GLASS

1 part Melon Liqueur
1 part Coconut Rum
fill with Pineapple Juice
splash Grenadine

Build over ice and stir.

Bonny Doon
CORDIAL GLASS

1 1/2 parts Scotch
1/2 part Vermouth
2 splashes Bénédictine®

Shake with ice and strain.

Boogy Woogy
HIGHBALL GLASS

2 parts Blue Curaçao
2/3 part Orange Vodka
fill with Lemon-Lime Soda

Build over ice and stir.

Boomerang
WHITE WINE GLASS

1 part Rye Whiskey
3/4 part French Vermouth
dash Powdered Sugar
splash Lemon Juice
dash Angostura® Bitters

Shake with ice and pour.

Booster Blaster

HIGHBALL GLASS

1 part Jack Daniel's®
1 part Southern Comfort®
1 part Yukon Jack®
fill with Cola

Build over ice and stir.

Bootlegger

ROCKS GLASS

1 part Tequila
1 part Southern Comfort®

Build over ice and stir.

Booty Juice

ROCKS GLASS

1 part Coconut Rum
1 part Spiced Rum
1 part Melon Liqueur
½ part 151-Proof Rum

Shake with ice and pour.

Border Crossing

HIGHBALL GLASS

1½ parts Tequila
splash Lime Juice
splash Lemon Juice
fill with Cola

Build over ice and stir. Garnish with a Lime Wedge.

Borinquen

ROCKS GLASS

1½ parts Light Rum
splash 151-Proof Rum
splash Passion Fruit Nectar
1 part Orange Juice
1 part Lime Juice

Shake with ice and pour.

Bosom's Caress

HIGHBALL GLASS

1 part Brandy
½ part Triple Sec
1 Egg White
splash Grenadine

Shake with ice and strain.

Boston Tea Party

HIGHBALL GLASS

½ part Vodka
½ part Scotch
½ part Dry Vermouth
½ part Triple Sec
½ part Rum
½ part Gin
½ part Tequila
1 part Orange Juice
1 part Cola
splash Sweet & Sour Mix

Build over ice and stir.

Botany Bay

ROCKS GLASS

2 parts Gin
1 part Orange Juice
1 part Grapefruit Juice
splash Simple Syrup

Shake with ice and strain over ice.

Bottom Rose

HIGHBALL GLASS

1 part Vodka
splash Apricot Brandy
splash Sweet Vermouth

Build over ice and stir.

Bouquet de Paris

HIGHBALL GLASS

1 part Brandy
½ part Apricot Brandy
splash Grenadine
splash Lemon Juice

Shake with ice and pour.

Bourbon Delight

ROCKS GLASS

3 parts Bourbon
1 part Sweet Vermouth
½ part Crème de Cassis

Shake with ice and strain.

Bourbon Sour

ROCKS GLASS

1 part Bourbon
1 part Lemon Juice
dash Sugar

Shake with ice and strain over ice. Garnish with an Orange Slice and a Maraschino Cherry.

Brain Booster

HIGHBALL GLASS

1 part Coffee Liqueur
1 part Irish Cream Liqueur
½ part Grappa

Build over ice and stir.

Brain Damager

HIGHBALL GLASS

1 part Jamaican Rum
1 part Triple Sec
splash Banana Juice

Build over ice and stir.

Bramble

ROCKS GLASS

2 parts Gin
½ part Blackberry Liqueur
dash Sugar

Shake with ice and strain over ice.

Brandy Daisy

ROCKS GLASS

2 parts Brandy
1 part Lemon Juice
dash Sugar
splash Grenadine

Build over ice and stir. Garnish with an Orange Slice and a Maraschino Cherry.

Brandy Fino

ROCKS GLASS

1½ parts Brandy
½ part Dry Sherry

Shake with ice and strain.

Brass

HIGHBALL GLASS

1 part Tequila
1 part Passion Fruit Liqueur

Build over ice and stir.

Brass Monkey

HIGHBALL GLASS

1 part Vodka
1 part Light Rum
fill with Orange Juice

Shake with ice and pour.

Brave Bull

ROCKS GLASS

1½ parts Tequila
1 part Coffee Vodka

Layer over ice. Garnish with a Lemon Twist.

Brazilian Beast

ROCKS GLASS

2 parts Rum
splash Lime Juice
2 dashes Sugar

Shake with ice and pour.

Breeze

ROCKS GLASS

1 part Vodka
½ part Blue Curaçao
½ part Crème de Menthe (Green)

Shake with ice and pour.

Brimstone

HIGHBALL GLASS

1 part Dark Rum
1½ parts Cherry Brandy
1 part Light Rum
½ part Triple Sec
½ part Crème de Noyaux
1½ parts Sweet & Sour Mix
1½ parts Orange Juice

Shake with ice and pour.

Broadway

HIGHBALL GLASS

½ part Vodka
½ part Apricot Brandy
1 part Mango Juice

Shake with ice and strain.

Broken Heart

HIGHBALL GLASS

1 part Vodka
1 part Raspberry Liqueur
fill with Orange Juice
splash Grenadine

Shake with ice and pour.

Broken Nose

HIGHBALL GLASS

1 part Tequila
1½ parts Advocaat
2 parts Grenadine
fill with Lemonade

Shake with ice and pour.

Brooke Shields

HIGHBALL GLASS

1 part Lemon Vodka
2 parts Lemon-Lime Soda
1 part Ginger Ale
splash Grenadine

Build over ice and stir for a Shirley Temple without the cherry. Garnish with an Orange Slice.

Brown

HIGHBALL GLASS

1½ parts Dry Vermouth
2 dashes Orange Bitters

Shake with ice and strain.

Brown Russian

ROCKS GLASS

1 part Chocolate Liqueur
2 parts Vodka

Layer over ice.

Bruja Cubana

HIGHBALL GLASS

3 Fresh Mint Leaves
dash Sugar
splash Lime Juice
1 part Whiskey
½ part Coffee Liqueur
fill with Lemon-Lime Soda

Muddle the Mint, Sugar, and Lime Juice in the glass. Add the Whiskey and Coffee Liqueur and fill with Lemon-Lime Soda.

Bubblegum Smash

ROCKS GLASS

1½ parts Light Rum
1 part Sweet & Sour Mix
½ part Triple Sec
¼ part Lemonade
splash Grenadine

Shake with ice and pour.

Bubble Guppies

ROCKS GLASS

1 part 99 Bananas Liqueur
1 part Southern Comfort
fill with Red Bull Energy Drink

Build over ice and stir.

Bubbly Irish Nut

HIGHBALL GLASS

1 part Irish Cream Liqueur
1 part Amaretto
4 parts Club Soda

Build over ice and stir.

Bull Rider

HIGHBALL GLASS

1 part Malibu® Rum
1 part Coffee Liqueur
½ part Crème de Banane
½ part Jägermeister®

Shake with ice and pour.

Bull Shot

ROCKS GLASS

1 1/2 parts Vodka
fill with Chilled Beef Bouillion
splash Worcestershire Sauce
dash Salt
dash Pepper

Shake with ice and pour.

Bull Stuff

HIGHBALL GLASS

1 1/2 parts Brandy
1 part Light Rum
fill with Milk
splash Cinnamon Schnapps

Shake with ice and pour.

Bullfrog

HIGHBALL GLASS

1 part Vodka
1 part Margarita Mix
fill with Lemon-Lime Soda

Build over ice and stir.

Bun Warmer Jack

HIGHBALL GLASS

1 part Yukon Jack®
fill with Cola

Build over ice and stir.

Bunny Hop

HIGHBALL GLASS

1 part Jim Beam®
1/2 part Peach Schnapps
1 part Cranberry Juice Cocktail
1 part Pineapple Juice

Build over ice and stir.

Bunny Killer

HIGHBALL GLASS

1 part Rum
2 parts Coconut Rum
1 part Pineapple Juice
1 part Orange Juice

Build over ice and stir.

Burlesque

HIGHBALL GLASS

1 part Jim Beam®
1/2 part Triple Sec
1/2 part Parfait Amour
splash Lemon Juice

Shake with ice and pour.

Burning Sun

HIGHBALL GLASS

1 1/2 parts Strawberry Liqueur
fill with Pineapple Juice

Build over ice.

Bushmaster

HIGHBALL GLASS

2 parts Vodka
2 parts Blueberry Pomegranate Juice
1/2 part Lime Juice
fill with Lemonade

Shake with ice and strain over ice.

Bushwacker

HIGHBALL GLASS

1 part Light Rum
1 part Amaretto
1 part Coffee Liqueur
1 part Grand Marnier®
1 part Irish Cream Liqueur

Shake with ice and strain over ice.

Buster

ROCKS GLASS

2 parts Goldschläger®
1 part Anisette
1/2 part Amer Picon®

Shake with ice and strain.

Butterfinger®

HIGHBALL GLASS

1 1/2 parts Butterscotch Schnapps
1 1/2 parts Irish Cream Liqueur
fill with Milk

Build over ice and stir.

Butternut Scotch

ROCKS GLASS

1 part Scotch
1 part Butterscotch Schnapps
1 part Amaretto

Build over ice.

Buttered Toffee

ROCKS GLASS

1 part Coffee Liqueur
1 part Irish Cream Liqueur
1 part Amaretto
fill with Half and Half

Build over ice and stir.

By the Pool

HIGHBALL GLASS

1 part Melon Liqueur
1 part Peach Schnapps
1 part Orange Juice
fill with Lemon-Lime Soda

Build over ice and stir.

Cabo Wabo

MARGARITA GLASS

1 1/2 parts Cabo Wabo Reposado Tequila
3/4 part Grand Marnier
3 parts Cranberry Juice
1 part Lime Juice

Shake with ice and strain over ice.

Cacatoes

ROCKS GLASS

1 part Cognac
1/2 part Mandarine Napoléon® Liqueur
1/4 part Crème de Banane
1/2 part Orange Juice
splash Grenadine

Shake with ice and pour.

Cadillac Margarita

HIGHBALL GLASS

1 part Jose Cuervo® 1800 Tequila
1/2 part Grand Marnier®
1/2 part Cointreau®
fill with Margarita Mix

Shake with ice and pour.

Cadiz

ROCKS GLASS

1 part Blackberry Brandy
1 part Dry Sherry
1/2 part Triple Sec
splash Light Cream

Shake with ice and pour.

Caipirissima

ROCKS GLASS

1 Lime
2 dashes Sugar
2 parts Light Rum

Cut the Lime into wedges and put into a mixing glass with the Sugar. Muddle the Lime until the Lime Juice and Sugar develop a rich froth. Add ice and the Rum and shake vigorously.

Caipiroska

ROCKS GLASS

2 parts Vodka
1 Lime
2 dashes Sugar

Cut the lime into wedges and put into a mixing glass with the Sugar. Muddle the Lime until the Lime Juice and Sugar develop a rich froth. Add ice and the Vodka and shake vigorously.

Cajun Comforter

ROCKS GLASS

1 1/2 parts Southern Comfort®
1/2 part Old Grand-Dad®
splash Tabasco® Sauce

Build over ice.

Cake and Ice Cream

HIGHBALL GLASS

1 part RumChata
1 part Cake Vodka

Build over ice and stir.

Cake Mix

HIGHBALL GLASS

2 parts Cake Vodka
fill with Ginger Ale

Build over ice.

Caledonia

ROCKS GLASS

1 part Brandy
1 part Crème de Cacao (Dark)
1 part Milk
1 Egg Yolk
dash Cinnamon

Shake with ice and pour.

Calico Cat

HIGHBALL GLASS

1 part Rum
1 part Orange Juice
1 part Cola

Build over ice.

California Kool-Aid®

HIGHBALL GLASS

1 part Rum
1 part Raspberry Liqueur
1 part Cherry Juice
1 part Lemonade
1 part Orange Juice

Build over ice and stir.

Californian

HIGHBALL GLASS

1 part Vodka
1 part Orange Juice
1 part Grapefruit Juice

Build over ice and stir.

Calimero

WHITE WINE GLASS

1 part Brandy
1 part Orange Juice
1 Egg White
splash Coffee Liqueur

Shake with ice and strain.

Calypso Beat

HIGHBALL GLASS

1 part Spiced Rum
1 part Peach Schnapps
fill with Orange Juice
splash Grenadine

Build over ice.

Calypso Kool-Aid®

HIGHBALL GLASS

1 part Vodka
1 part Raspberry Liqueur
1 part Cherry Juice
2 parts Lemonade
1 part Pineapple Juice

Build over ice and stir.

Campobello

HIGHBALL GLASS

1½ parts Gin
1 part Campari®
1 part Sweet Vermouth

Shake with ice and strain over ice.

Canada Dream

ROCKS GLASS

1 part Apricot Brandy
1 part Amaretto
3 parts Orange Juice

Shake with ice and strain over ice.

Canadian, Eh?

ROCKS GLASS

2 parts Canadian Whisky
½ part Sour Cherry Liqueur
½ part Lemon Juice
fill with Pineapple Juice

Shake with ice and strain over ice.

Canado Saludo

HIGHBALL GLASS

1½ parts Light Rum
1 part Orange Juice
1 part Pineapple Juice
½ part Lemon Juice
½ part Grenadine
dash Bitters

Build over ice and stir.

Candy Apple

HIGHBALL GLASS

1 part Butterscotch Schnapps
fill with Apple Cider

Build over ice and stir.

Candy Bar

HIGHBALL GLASS

1 part Coffee Liqueur
1 part Cream
½ part Crème de Cacao (White)
½ part Frangelico®

Shake with ice and strain over ice.

Canyon de Chelly

HIGHBALL GLASS

1½ parts Tequila
splash Triple Sec
fill with Cranberry Juice Cocktail
splash Pineapple Juice
splash Orange Juice

Build over ice and stir.

Cape Cod

HIGHBALL GLASS

2 parts Vodka
fill with Cranberry Juice

Build over ice and stir.

Cape Grape

HIGHBALL GLASS

1½ parts Vodka
1 part Cranberry Liqueur
fill with Grapefruit Juice

Build over ice and stir.

Capri

ROCKS GLASS

1 part Crème de Cacao (White)
1 part Crème de Banane
1 part Light Cream

Shake with ice and strain over ice.

Captain Caribbean

HIGHBALL GLASS

1 part Spiced Rum
1 part Coconut Rum
1 part Strawberry Liqueur
fill with Orange Juice

Build over ice and stir.

Captain Climer

HIGHBALL GLASS

1½ parts Spiced Rum
¾ part Irish Cream Liqueur
fill with Root Beer

Build over ice and stir.

Captain Crunch

ROCKS GLASS

1 part Tequila Rose®
1 part Vanilla Liqueur
1 part Coffee Liqueur
1 part Cream
splash Grenadine

Shake with ice and strain over ice.

Captain Hamilton

HIGHBALL GLASS

1½ parts Spiced Rum
2 parts Coconut Rum
½ part Lime Juice

Shake with ice and strain over ice.

Captain Jack on the Rocks

ROCKS GLASS

1 part Spiced Rum
1 part Southern Comfort
fill with Pineapple Juice
splash 151-Proof Rum

Build over ice and stir.

Captain Jack Sparrow

HIGHBALL GLASS

2 parts Añejo Tequila
1 part Dark Rum
3 parts Limeade
splash Maraschino Cherry Juice
½ part 99 Oranges Liqueur

Build over ice and stir.

Captain Kangaroo

HIGHBALL GLASS

1 part Coconut Rum
1 part Spiced Rum
1 part Orange Juice
1 part Pineapple Juice
splash Lemon-Lime Soda

Shake all but the Soda with ice and strain over ice. Top with Lemon-Lime Soda.

Caramel

HIGHBALL GLASS

2 parts Coffee Liqueur
fill with Pineapple Juice

Shake with ice and pour.

Carebear Stare

HIGHBALL GLASS

1 part Raspberry Rum
1 part Watermelon Rum
1 part Orange Juice
1 part Pineapple Juice
½ part Passion Fruit Syrup
fill with Cranberry Juice

Build over ice and stir.

Caribbean Bliss

HIGHBALL GLASS

1 part Vodka
1 part Tequila
fill with Orange Juice

Build over ice and stir.

Caribbean Chat

HIGHBALL GLASS

1 part Spiced Rum
¼ part Crème de Cacao (White)
1 part Orange Juice
1 part Club Soda

Build over ice and stir.

Caribbean Romance

HIGHBALL GLASS

1½ parts Light Rum
1 part Amaretto
1 part Orange Juice
1 part Pineapple Juice
splash Grenadine

Build over ice and stir.

Carilia

HIGHBALL GLASS

1 part Dark Rum
1 part Crème de Banane
1 part Cherry Brandy
1 part Lemon Juice

Shake with ice and pour.

Carmalita

ROCKS GLASS

1 part Vodka
1 part Coffee
1 part Frangelico®

Shake with ice and pour.

Carmen

HIGHBALL GLASS

1 part Gin
splash Apricot Brandy
splash Triple Sec
½ part Dry Vermouth

Shake with ice and strain over ice.

Carrot Cake

HIGHBALL GLASS

1 part Butterscotch Schnapps
1 part Cinnamon Schnapps
1 part Irish Cream Liqueur

Build over ice and stir.

Casa Vieja

HIGHBALL GLASS

1 part Gin
splash Apricot Brandy
splash Grenadine
1 part Apricot Juice

Shake with ice and pour.

Casablanca

HIGHBALL GLASS

1 part Vodka
½ part Southern Comfort®
½ part Amaretto
¾ part Orange Juice
splash Grenadine

Shake with ice and pour.

Cascade Special

HIGHBALL GLASS

⅔ part Gin
½ part Triple Sec
splash Dry Vermouth
1 part Pineapple Juice

Shake with ice and pour.

Casino d'Amsterdam

HIGHBALL GLASS

1 part Gin
1 part Triple Sec
splash Kirschwasser
1 part Dry Vermouth
splash Pineapple Juice

Shake with ice and pour.

Casino Royale

ROCKS GLASS

1 part Gin
1 part Apricot Brandy
1 part Pineapple Juice

Shake with ice and pour.

Castaway

HIGHBALL GLASS

1½ parts Light Rum
1 part Dark Rum
½ part Blue Curaçao
splash Apricot Brandy
splash Grenadine
½ part Lemon Juice
2 parts Pineapple Juice

Shake with ice and pour.

Cato

HIGHBALL GLASS

1 part Dark Rum
1 part Sweet Vermouth
splash Blue Curaçao
splash Campari®
1 part Lemon Juice

Shake with ice and strain.

Cat's Eye

HIGHBALL GLASS

2 parts Dry Vermouth
½ part Chartreuse®
2 dashes Orange Bitters

Shake with ice and strain over ice.

Caucasian

ROCKS GLASS

2 parts Vodka
1½ parts Coffee Liqueur
splash Cream

Shake with ice and strain.

Cayman Sunset

HIGHBALL GLASS

1½ parts Light Rum
½ part Piña Colada Mix
fill with Pineapple Juice
½ part Grenadine

Build over ice and stir.

Celtic Comrade

HIGHBALL GLASS

1 part Coffee Liqueur
1 part Drambuie®
1 part Irish Cream Liqueur
1 part Vodka

Shake with ice and strain over ice.

Chapala

ROCKS GLASS

1½ parts Tequila
splash Triple Sec
2 splashes Grenadine
2 splashes Orange Juice
2 splashes Lemon Juice

Shake with ice and strain. Garnish with an Orange Slice.

Charlie Chaplin

ROCKS GLASS

1 part Apricot Brandy
1 part Sloe Gin
1 part Lemon Juice

Shake with ice and strain.

Charlie's Angel

HIGHBALL GLASS

1½ parts Mezcal
1 part Grand Marnier®
dash Orange Bitters
1 part Orange Juice
1 part Grapefruit Juice
1 part Club Soda

Build over ice and stir.

The Cheap Date

HIGHBALL GLASS

1 part Light Rum
1 part Peach Schnapps
1 part Melon Liqueur
½ part Triple Sec
fill with Apple Juice

Build over ice and stir.

Chattanooga

ROCKS GLASS

1½ parts Vodka
½ part Apricot Brandy
½ part Lime Juice
fill with Pineapple Juice

Shake with ice and strain over ice.

Cheap Sunglasses

ROCKS GLASS

1 part Vodka
1 part Cranberry Juice Cocktail
1 part Lemon-Lime Soda

Build over ice and stir.

Cheerio

HIGHBALL GLASS

1 part Jim Beam®
½ part Cherry Brandy
½ part Lemon Juice
splash Grenadine

Shake with ice and strain over ice.

Cherry Breeze

HIGHBALL GLASS

1 part Vodka
1 part Cherry Liqueur
1 part Pineapple Juice
1 part Cranberry Juice Cocktail

Shake with ice and strain over ice.

Cherry Malibu

ROCKS GLASS

1 part Coconut Rum
½ part Cherry Brandy
2 parts Lime Juice

Build over ice and stir.

Cherry Popper

HIGHBALL GLASS

2 parts Cherry Vodka
fill with Red Bull Energy Drink

Build over ice and stir.

Cherry Pucker

HIGHBALL GLASS

1 part Vodka
1 part Cherry Liqueur
1 part Cherry Juice
fill with Grapefruit Juice

Build over ice and stir.

Cheshire Cat

WHITE WINE GLASS

1 part Spiced Rum
1 part Peach Schnapps
1 part Orange Juice

Shake with ice and strain.

Chi Chi

HIGHBALL GLASS

1½ parts Light Rum
½ part Blackberry Liqueur
fill with Pineapple Juice

Build over ice and stir.

ChocoChata

HIGHBALL GLASS

1 part Frangelico
1 part Godiva Chocolate Liqueur
1 part RumChata

Shake with ice and strain over ice.

Chocoholic

HIGHBALL GLASS

1 part Chocolate Syrup
2 parts Coffee Liqueur
1 part Irish Cream Liqueur
1 part Rum

Shake with ice and strain over ice.

Chocolate-Covered Banana

HIGHBALL GLASS

1 part Vodka
1 part Crème de Cacao (Dark)
1 part Crème de Banane
1 part Cream

Shake with ice and pour.

Chocolate-Covered Cherry

HIGHBALL GLASS

½ part Crème de Cacao (Dark)
½ part Amaretto
2 parts Milk
splash Grenadine

Shake with ice and strain over ice.

Chocolate-Covered Strawberries

ROCKS GLASS

1 part Godiva® Liqueur
1 part Tequila Rose®

Shake with ice and strain.

Chocolate Milwaukee

ROCKS GLASS

1 part Coffee Liqueur
1 part Tia Maria®
1 part Crème de Cacao (White)
1 part Half and Half

Shake with ice and pour.

Christmas Rum Punch

HIGHBALL GLASS

1 part Rum
1 part Cherry Juice
1 part Cranberry Juice Cocktail
1 part Pineapple Juice

Build over ice and stir.

Cinnamon Apple Turnover

HIGHBALL GLASS

2 parts Apple Vodka
1 part Fireball Cinnamon Whiskey
1 part Orange Juice

Shake with ice and strain over ice.

Cinnamon Bun

ROCKS GLASS

3 parts RumChata
1 part Coffee Liqueur

Build over ice and stir.

Cinnamon Pussycat

HIGHBALL GLASS

1 part Vodka
1 part Cinnamon Schnapps
1 part Cherry Juice
fill with Pineapple Juice

Build over ice and stir.

Cinnamon Roll

ROCKS GLASS

1 part RumChata
1 part Cake Vodka
splash Half and Half

Build over ice and stir.

Cinniberry Crasher

HIGHBALL GLASS

1 part Goldschläger®
fill with Cranberry Juice Cocktail

Build over ice and stir.

Citrus Twist on Fire

HIGHBALL GLASS

1 part Goldschläger®
1 part Citrus Vodka

Build over ice and stir.

City Lights

HIGHBALL GLASS

1 part Vodka
1 part Raspberry Liqueur
1 part Cherry Juice
fill with Lemonade

Build over ice and stir.

Clamdigger

HIGHBALL GLASS

1 part Vodka
½ part Clamato®
splash Worchestershire Sauce
dash Salt
dash Pepper

Shake with ice and pour. Garnish with a Lime Wedge.

Class

HIGHBALL GLASS

1 part Scotch
¾ part Sambuca
fill with Iced Coffee

Shake with ice and pour.

Class Act

ROCKS GLASS

1 part Advocaat
½ part Coconut Rum
splash Southern Comfort®
fill with Pineapple Juice

Shake with ice and pour.

Classic

HIGHBALL GLASS

1½ parts Brandy
¼ part Cherry Liqueur
¼ part Cointreau®
splash Lemon Juice

Shake with ice and pour.

Clear Blue Sky

HIGHBALL GLASS

2 parts Blue Curaçao
½ part Grain Alcohol
fill with Milk

Shake with ice and pour.

Cleveland Steamer

ROCKS GLASS

1 part Vodka
1 part Dark Rum
fill with Sweet & Sour Mix
splash 151-Proof Rum

Build over ice and stir.

Clockwork Orange

HIGHBALL GLASS

2 parts Vodka
2 parts Orange Juice
1½ parts Peach Schnapps
splash Campari®

Shake with ice and strain over ice.

Cloudy Sunset

HIGHBALL GLASS

1 part Peach Brandy
2 parts Orange Juice
2 parts Cranberry Juice Cocktail

Build over ice and stir.

Clueless

HIGHBALL GLASS

2 parts Vodka
1 part Orange Juice
1 part Strawberry Juice
fill with Lemon-Lime Soda

Build over ice and stir.

Coastline

HIGHBALL GLASS

1 part Blue Curaçao
1 part Vodka
fill with Pineapple Juice
splash Lemon-Lime Soda

Build over ice and stir.

Cobbler

HIGHBALL GLASS

2 parts Gin
splash Blue Curaçao
splash Simple Syrup

Build over ice and stir.

Cobra Venom

ROCKS GLASS

1 part Sambuca
1 part Rumple Minze®

Shake with ice and strain.

Cocaine Lady

HIGHBALL GLASS

1/2 part Vodka
1/2 part Amaretto
1/2 part Coffee Liqueur
1 part Cream
fill with Cola

Build over ice and stir.

Cocaine Shooter

ROCKS GLASS

1 1/2 parts Vodka
3/4 part Raspberry Liqueur
1/2 part Southern Comfort®
1 part Orange Juice
1 part Cranberry Juice Cocktail

Shake with ice and strain.

Coco Butter

HIGHBALL GLASS

1 1/2 parts Butterscotch Schnapps
1 part Coffee Liqueur
fill with Milk

Shake with ice and pour.

Coco Colada

ROCKS GLASS

1 part Dark Rum
1 part Crème de Cacao (Dark)
1 part Cream of Coconut
fill with Pineapple Juice

Build over ice and stir.

Coco Miami

HIGHBALL GLASS

1 part Crème de Coconut
1 part Orange Juice
1 part Grapefruit Juice

Build over ice and stir.

Coconut Apple Pie

HIGHBALL GLASS

1 part Vodka
1 part Coconut Rum
fill with Apple Juice

Shake with ice and pour.

Coconut Dream

ROCKS GLASS

2 parts Crème de Coconut
1 part Vanilla Liqueur
1/2 part Crème de Cacao (Dark)
2 parts Pineapple Juice
1 part Cream of Coconut

Shake with ice and pour.

Coconut Macaroon

HIGHBALL GLASS

1 part RumChata
1 part Malibu Rum
1 part Coffee Liqueur
1 part Cream

Build over ice and stir.

Coffee Alexander

HIGHBALL GLASS

1 part Coffee Brandy
1 part Crème de Cacao (White)
1 part Cream

Shake with ice and strain over ice.

Coffee Fantasy

HIGHBALL GLASS

1 part Irish Cream Liqueur
1 part Coffee Liqueur
1 part Milk

Build over ice and stir.

Coffin Nail

ROCKS GLASS

1½ parts Whiskey
½ part Amaretto
½ part Drambuie®

Build over ice and stir.

Colby's Delight

ROCKS GLASS

1 part Gin
splash Cranberry Juice
fill with Apple Juice

Build over ice and stir. For Colby.

Cold Comfort Coffee

HIGHBALL GLASS

¾ part Dark Rum
¾ part Southern Comfort
¼ part Crème de Cacao (Dark)
4 parts Cold Coffee

Build over ice and stir.

Cold Fusion

HIGHBALL GLASS

1 part Vodka
1 part Triple Sec
½ part Melon Liqueur
1½ parts Sweet & Sour Mix
½ part Lime Juice

Shake with ice and strain over ice.

Cold Lips

HIGHBALL GLASS

1½ parts Gin
⅔ part Lemon Juice
1 part Ginger Ale
1 part Grape Juice (Red)

Build over ice and stir.

Cold Shoulder

HIGHBALL GLASS

1 part Southern Comfort®
1 part Cherry Brandy
splash Orange Juice
1 part Sweet & Sour Mix
2 parts Pineapple Juice
2 parts Ginger Ale

Build over ice and stir.

Colorado Kool-Aid®

HIGHBALL GLASS

1 part Vodka
1 part Southern Comfort®
½ part Sloe Gin
1 part Amaretto
1 part Orange Juice
2 parts Cranberry Juice Cocktail
splash Lemon-Lime Soda

Build over ice and stir.

Combo

ROCKS GLASS

2½ parts Dry Vermouth
splash Brandy
½ splash Triple Sec
½ dash Powdered Sugar
dash Bitters

Shake with ice and strain over ice.

Comfortable Fuzz
ROCKS GLASS

1 part Peach Schnapps
1 part Southern Comfort®
1 part Cranberry Juice Cocktail
1 part Orange Juice

Build over ice and stir.

Communicator
ROCKS GLASS

1½ parts Dark Rum
½ part Galliano®
2 splashes Crème de Cacao (Dark)

Build over ice and stir.

Confidence Booster
HIGHBALL GLASS

1 part Dark Rum
1 part Peach Schnapps
1½ parts Pineapple Juice

Build over ice and stir.

Continental Sour
ROCKS GLASS

1½ parts Rye Whiskey
½ part Simple Syrup
1 Egg White

Shake with ice and strain.

Cool Jerk
HIGHBALL GLASS

1 part Vodka
1 part Amaretto
2 parts Orange Juice
1 part Lemon-Lime Soda

Build over ice and stir.

Cool of the Evening
HIGHBALL GLASS

1 part Rum
1 part Peach Schnapps
1 part Cranberry Juice Cocktail
1 part Pineapple Juice

Build over ice and stir.

Cool Running
HIGHBALL GLASS

1 part Vodka
1 part Blue Curaçao
fill with Lemonade
splash Cola

Build over ice and stir.

Cool Summer
HIGHBALL GLASS

1 part Vodka
1 part Peach Schnapps
1 part Cherry Juice
1 part Lemonade
1 part Orange Juice

Build over ice and stir.

Cordial Daisy
HIGHBALL GLASS

1 part Vodka
1 part Cherry Liqueur
1 part Lemonade
1 part Club Soda

Build over ice and stir.

The Cornell
HIGHBALL GLASS

1 part Vodka
½ part Watermelon Schnapps
½ part Sweet & Sour Mix

Shake with ice and strain over ice.

Cowboy Killer
HIGHBALL GLASS

1¼ parts Tequila
¾ part Irish Cream Liqueur
½ part Butterscotch Schnapps
fill with Half and Half

Build over ice and stir.

Cowpoke
HIGHBALL GLASS

1 part Whiskey
1 part Southern Comfort®
1 part Orange Juice
splash Lemon Juice
dash Sugar

Shake with ice and pour.

Crack Whore
HIGHBALL GLASS

1 part Vodka
1 part Triple Sec
fill with Orange Soda

Build over ice and stir.

Cracklin' Rosie
HIGHBALL GLASS

1 part Light Rum
½ part Passion Fruit Juice
splash Pineapple Juice
splash Lime Juice
splash Crème de Banane

Shake with ice and strain over ice.

Cranberry Lemondrop
HIGHBALL GLASS

1 part Vodka
1 part Triple Sec
1 part Lemonade
1 part Cranberry Juice Cocktail

Shake with ice and pour.

Cran-Collins
ROCKS GLASS

1½ parts Vodka
2 parts Cranberry Juice Cocktail
2 parts Collins Mix

Shake with ice and strain over ice.

Cranial Meltdown
HIGHBALL GLASS

1 part Rum
1 part Raspberry Liqueur
1 part Coconut Rum

Shake with ice and strain over ice.

Cranilla Dew
HIGHBALL GLASS

1 part Vanilla Vodka
1 part Cranberry Juice Cocktail
1 part Mountain Dew®

Build over ice and stir.

Crazy Caribbean Gentleman
HIGHBALL GLASS

1 part 151-Proof Rum
1 part Frangelico®
fill with Sweet & Sour Mix

Build over ice and stir.

Crazy Man
HIGHBALL GLASS

1 part Gin
1 part Orange Liqueur
½ part Lemon Juice
splash Apple Juice

Shake with ice and pour.

Crazy Orgasm
HIGHBALL GLASS

1 part Vodka
1 part Triple Sec
1 part Cranberry Juice Cocktail
1 part Orange Juice

Shake with ice and pour.

Creamsicle®
HIGHBALL GLASS

2 parts Amaretto
1 part Triple Sec
2 parts Sweet & Sour Mix
4 parts Orange Juice
splash Club Soda

Build over ice and stir.

Creamy Kiss
HIGHBALL GLASS

1 part Amaretto
1 part Irish Cream Liqueur
1 part Peach Schnapps
1 part Cream

Shake with ice and pour.

Creamy Mimi

HIGHBALL GLASS

1 part Vodka
1 part Sweet Vermouth
2 splashes Crème de Cacao (White)
2 splashes Triple Sec

Shake with ice and pour.

Creamydreams

HIGHBALL GLASS

1 part Irish Cream Liqueur
splash Advocaat
½ part Cream
2 parts Banana Juice

Shake with ice and pour.

Creeping Death

HIGHBALL GLASS

1 part Vodka
1 part Extra Dry Vermouth
dash Salt
fill with Orange Juice

Shake with ice and pour.

Crème d'Amour

HIGHBALL GLASS

1 part Vodka
1 part Crème de Banane
splash Cherry Brandy
1 part Pineapple Juice
splash Cream

Shake with ice and pour.

Crème de Café

ROCKS GLASS

1 part Coffee Brandy
½ part Rum
½ part Anisette
1 part Light Cream

Shake with ice and pour.

Creole

ROCKS GLASS

1½ parts Light Rum
splash Lemon Juice
splash Tabasco® Sauce
splash Beef Bouillion
dash Salt
dash Pepper

Shake with ice and pour.

Crillon

ROCKS GLASS

1½ parts Dry Vermouth
½ part Campari®
½ part Kirschwasser

Shake with ice and strain over ice.

Crime of Passion

ROCKS GLASS

½ part Sweet Vermouth
½ part Cherry Brandy
1 part Passion Fruit Liqueur

Shake with ice and strain over ice.

Critical Mass

HIGHBALL GLASS

1 part Vodka
1 part Blue Curaçao
1 part Cherry Juice
fill with Lemonade

Build over ice and stir.

Crooked Golf Cart

HIGHBALL GLASS

2 parts Gold Rum
1 part Amaretto
fill with Cranberry Juice

Build over ice.

The Crown Cherry

HIGHBALL GLASS

1½ parts Crown Royal® Whiskey
1 part Cherry Brandy
½ part Cherry Vodka
fill with Cherry Cola

Build over ice and stir.

Crowned Bull

HIGHBALL GLASS

1 part Crown Royal® Whiskey
fill with Red Bull® Energy Drink

Build over ice and stir.

Cruise

HIGHBALL GLASS

1 part Gin
1 part Dry Vermouth
splash Peach Schnapps

Shake with ice and strain.

Cruise Control

HIGHBALL GLASS

½ part Apricot Brandy
½ part Cointreau
1 part Light Rum
1 part Club Soda
¼ part Lemon Juice

Build over ice and stir.

Crunchy Captain

ROCKS GLASS

2 parts RumChata
1 part Spiced Rum

Shake with ice and pour.

Crunk Juice

ROCKS GLASS

1½ parts Hennessy Cognac
fill with Red Bull Energy Drink

Build over ice and stir.

Cry No More

HIGHBALL GLASS

1 part Vodka
1 part Cherry Brandy
1½ parts Orange Juice
fill with Lemon-Lime Soda

Build over ice and stir.

Crypto Nugget

ROCKS GLASS

¾ part Sour Apple Schnapps
½ part Vodka
¼ part Blue Curaçao
¼ part Sweetened Lime Juice

Shake with ice and pour.

Crystal de Amour

HIGHBALL GLASS

1½ parts Vodka
½ part Parfait Amour

Build over ice and stir.

C-Team

HIGHBALL GLASS

1 part Grand Marnier®
1 part Crème de Menthe (White)
1 part Melon Liqueur
1 part Licor 43®
fill with Cranberry Juice Cocktail

Shake with ice and pour.

Cuba Libre

HIGHBALL GLASS

2 parts Light Rum
splash Lime Juice
fill with Cola

Build over ice and stir.

Cuban Breeze

HIGHBALL GLASS

1 part Vodka
1 part Amaretto
fill with Pineapple Juice

Build over ice and stir.

Cuban Kirschwasser

HIGHBALL GLASS

1½ parts Kirschwasser
fill with Cola
splash Lime Juice

Build over ice and stir.

Cuff and Buttons

ROCKS GLASS

2 parts Southern Comfort®
½ part Lime Juice
4 splashes Sweet Vermouth

Shake with ice and strain.

Cumulous

HIGHBALL GLASS

1 part Drambuie®
1 part Tia Maria®
½ part Cream
1 Egg Yolk
2 dashes Sugar

Shake with ice and strain.

Curious Comfort

HIGHBALL GLASS

1 part Southern Comfort®
2 parts Blue Curaçao
3 parts Pineapple Juice

Shake with ice and pour.

Curled Satan's Whiskers

HIGHBALL GLASS

1 part Gin
1 part Sweet Vermouth
1 part Dry Vermouth
1 part Orange Juice
splash Orange Bitters
1 part Blue Curaçao

Shake with ice and strain.

D.A.

HIGHBALL GLASS

1 part Rum
1 part Cherry Juice
1 part Piña Colada Mix
1 part Orange Juice

Build over ice and stir.

Da Rasta Slamma

HIGHBALL GLASS

2 parts Coconut Rum
1 part Blue Curaçao
½ part Pineapple Juice

Build over ice and stir.

Dambuster

HIGHBALL GLASS

1 part Rum
1 part Coffee Liqueur
1 part Ginger Ale
fill with Milk

Shake with ice and pour.

Damn the Torpedoes

HIGHBALL GLASS

1 part Cinnamon Schnapps
1 part Dark Rum
2 parts Orange Juice
2 parts Pineapple Juice

Shake with ice and strain over ice.

Dances with Wenches

HIGHBALL GLASS

2 parts Spiced Rum
⅓ part Margarita Mix
fill with Cranberry Juice Cocktail

Shake with ice and pour.

Dancing Dawn

HIGHBALL GLASS

½ part Strawberry Liqueur
splash Crème de Banane
½ part Kiwi Schnapps

Shake with ice and pour.

Dangerous Liaisons

SHERRY GLASS

1 part Tia Maria®
1 part Cointreau®
½ part Sweet & Sour Mix

Shake with ice and strain.

Danini

HIGHBALL GLASS

2 parts Vodka
1 part Lime Cordial
fill with Cola

Build over ice and stir.

Danish Gin Fizz

HIGHBALL GLASS

2 parts Gin
½ part Cherry Brandy
1 tbsp powdered sugar
½ part Lime Juice
½ part Kirschwasser

Shake with ice and strain over ice.

Danish Kiss

ROCKS GLASS

1½ parts Vanilla Vodka
½ part Amaretto
2 parts Orange Juice
fill with Red Bull® Energy Drink

Build over ice and stir.

Danish Slammer

ROCKS GLASS

1½ parts Vodka
1½ parts Kirschwasser
1 part Aquavit

Shake with ice and strain.

Darien Librarian

HIGHBALL GLASS

1 part Whiskey
1 part Cola
1 part Ginger Ale

Build over ice and stir.

Dark Eyes

BRANDY SNIFTER

1 part Vodka
¼ part Blackberry Brandy
splash Sweetened Lime Juice

Shake with ice and strain.

Dark Morning

HIGHBALL GLASS

1 part Rum
1 part Coffee Liqueur
3 splashes Chocolate Syrup
2 dashes Sugar
fill with Milk

Shake with ice and pour.

Dark Soul

HIGHBALL GLASS

1 part Amaretto
1 part Peach Schnapps
1 part Triple Sec
fill with Cola

Build over ice and stir.

Daytona 501

HIGHBALL GLASS

1½ parts Dark Rum
½ part Vodka
½ part Triple Sec
2 parts Orange Juice

Shake with ice and pour.

Daytona Daydream

HIGHBALL GLASS

1¼ parts Spiced Rum
3 parts Pink Grapefruit Juice
2 parts Crème de Coconut
½ part Grenadine

Shake with ice and pour.

Dead Bitches

HIGHBALL GLASS

1 part Vodka
1 part Canadian Mist®
1 part Jack Daniel's®
1 part Coffee Liqueur

Shake with ice and pour.

Dead Hand

ROCKS GLASS

2 parts Melon Liqueur
1 part Rum
1 part Vodka
1 part Whiskey

Shake with ice and strain over ice.

Death Kiss

CHAMPAGNE FLUTE

1 part Crème de Cacao (White)
1 part Crème de Menthe (Green)
fill with Cream

Shake with ice and strain.

Deceiver

HIGHBALL GLASS

1 part Tequila
½ part Galliano®

Build over ice.

Deep Freeze

HIGHBALL GLASS

1 part Blue Curaçao
1 part Raspberry Liqueur
fill with Lemon-Lime Soda

Build over ice and stir.

Deep in the Forest

ROCKS GLASS

1½ parts Gin
1 part Blue Curaçao
1 part Grapefruit Juice
1 part Pineapple Juice
1 part Orange Juice
1 part Passion Fruit Nectar

Shake with ice and pour.

Deep Pearl Diver

HIGHBALL GLASS

1 part Vodka
1 part Melon Liqueur
1 part Coconut Rum
fill with Cream

Shake with ice and pour.

Deerslayer

HIGHBALL GLASS

1½ parts Whiskey
½ part Jägermeister®

Shake with ice and strain.

Deja Vu

ROCKS GLASS

2 parts Vanilla Vodka
fill with Root Beer

Build over ice and stir.

Delta

ROCKS GLASS

1½ parts Whiskey
1 part Lime Juice
1 tbsp powdered sugar
½ part Southern Comfort®

Shake with ice and strain.

Denver Bulldog

HIGHBALL GLASS

1 part Vodka
1 part Coffee Liqueur
⅔ part Cream
⅓ part Lemon-Lime Soda

Shake with ice and pour.

Desert Shield

HIGHBALL GLASS

1½ parts Vodka
½ part Cranberry Liqueur
fill with Cranberry Juice Cocktail

Shake with ice and pour.

Desperation Cocktail

HIGHBALL GLASS

2 parts Vanilla Vodka
1 part Ginger Liqueur
½ part Dry Vermouth
1 part Lime Juice

Shake with ice and strain over ice.

Devil's Advocate

ROCKS GLASS

1 part Citrus Rum
1 part Triple Sec
¾ part Sweet & Sour Mix
½ part Grenadine
fill with Cranberry Juice Cocktail

Shake with ice and pour.

Devotion

HIGHBALL GLASS

1 part Watermelon Schnapps
1 part Apple Vodka
fill with Lemon-Lime Soda

Build over ice and stir.

Dewpond
CHAMPAGNE FLUTE

1 part Blue Curaçao
1 part Crème de Coconut
1 part Lime Juice
2 parts Orange Juice

Shake with ice and strain.

Diamond Romeo
ROCKS GLASS

1 1/2 parts Coconut Rum
1 1/2 parts Sour Apple Schnapps
fill with Lemon-Lime Soda
splash Cherry Juice

Shake with ice and strain over ice.

Dictator
HIGHBALL GLASS

1 part Vodka
2/3 part Cherry Brandy
splash Apricot Brandy

Build over ice and stir.

Diesel Power
ROCKS GLASS

1 part Jägermeister
1 part Yukon Jack
fill with Energy Drink

Build over ice and stir.

Dingo
HIGHBALL GLASS

1/2 part Light Rum
1/2 part Amaretto
1/2 part Southern Comfort®
2 parts Sweet & Sour Mix
2 parts Orange Juice
splash Grenadine

Shake with ice and pour.

Dirty Ashtray
HIGHBALL GLASS

1/2 part Gin
1/2 part Vodka
1/2 part Light Rum
1/2 part Tequila
1/2 part Blue Curaçao
1/2 part Grenadine
1 1/2 parts Pineapple Juice
2 parts Sweet & Sour Mix

Shake with ice and pour.

Dirty Bastard
HIGHBALL GLASS

1 1/2 parts Vodka
1/2 part Blackberry Brandy
splash Lime Juice

Shake with ice and pour.

Dirty Dimebag
HIGHBALL GLASS

2 parts Rum
splash Tabasco® Sauce
dash Black Pepper

Pour ingredients into glass neat (do not chill).

Dirty Girl Scout
HIGHBALL GLASS

1 part Irish Cream Liqueur
1 part Coffee Liqueur
1 part Vodka
splash Crème de Menthe (Green)

Shake with ice and strain.

Dirty Grandpa
ROCKS GLASS

1 part Bourbon
1 part Coffee Liqueur
1 part Irish Cream Liqueur
1 part Root Beer Schnapps

Shake with ice and strain over ice.

Dirty Grasshopper

HIGHBALL GLASS

1 part Crème de Menthe (White)
1 part Coffee Liqueur
fill with Milk

Build over ice and stir.

Dirty Irishman

HIGHBALL GLASS

1 part Irish Cream Liqueur
1 part Irish Whiskey

Build over ice and stir.

Dirty Margarita

MARGARITA GLASS

1 part Tequila
1 part Triple Sec
1 part Sweet & Sour Mix
splash Coffee Liqueur

Shake with ice and pour.

Dirty Mexican

HIGHBALL GLASS

2 parts Tequila
1 part Lime Juice
fill with Cola

Build over ice and stir.

Dirty Momma

HIGHBALL GLASS

1 part Coffee Liqueur
1 part Brandy
1 part Vodka
fill with Milk

Build over ice and stir.

Dirty Mother

HIGHBALL GLASS

3 parts Brandy
1 part Coffee Liqueur

Shake with ice and strain over ice.

Dirty Sock

ROCKS GLASS

1 part Scotch
1 part Pineapple Juice

Build over ice and stir.

Dirty Virgin

HIGHBALL GLASS

1½ parts Gin
½ part Crème de Cacao (Dark)

Build over ice and stir.

Dirty White Mother

HIGHBALL GLASS

3 parts Brandy
1 part Coffee Liqueur
1 part Cream

Build over ice. Float the Cream on top.

Disappointed Lady

HIGHBALL GLASS

1 part Brandy
1 part Tia Maria®
1 part Orange Juice
1 part Crème de Noyaux
splash Grenadine

Shake with ice and strain over ice.

Dizzy Blonde

ROCKS GLASS

1 part Advocaat
½ part Pernod
2 parts Lemonade
1 part Orange Juice

Shake with ice and strain over ice.

Dizzy Blue

HIGHBALL GLASS

1 part Vodka
1 part Lemon-Lime Soda
½ part Blue Curaçao
½ part Kiwi Schnapps
½ part Lychee Liqueur

Build over ice and stir.

Doctor Dawson

HIGHBALL GLASS

2 parts Tequila
½ part Lemon Juice
dash Sugar
dash Bitters
1 Egg
3 parts Club Soda

Shake all but Club Soda with ice and strain. Top with Club Soda.

Dog House Dew

HIGHBALL GLASS

3 parts Vodka
fill with Mountain Dew®
3 splashes Lemon Juice

Build over ice and stir.

Dog Nuts

HIGHBALL GLASS

1½ parts Bourbon
1½ parts Crown Royal® Whiskey
1½ parts Jamaican Rum
1 part Dr. Pepper®
1 part Red Bull® Energy Drink

Build over ice and stir.

Dolce Vita

HIGHBALL GLASS

1 part Jim Beam®
½ part Apricot Brandy
⅔ part Sweet Vermouth

Shake with ice and pour.

Dollar Bill

ROCKS GLASS

1 part Vodka
1 part Melon Liqueur
½ part Lime Cordial

Shake with ice and pour.

Double Standard Sour

ROCKS GLASS

1 part Whiskey
1 part Gin
splash Grenadine
½ part Lemon Juice
dash Powdered Sugar

Shake with ice and strain over ice.

Downhill Racer

HIGHBALL GLASS

1 part Rum
1 part Orange Juice
1 part Pineapple Juice

Shake with ice and pour.

Dr. Nut

HIGHBALL GLASS

2 parts Amaretto
fill with Dr. Pepper®

Build over ice and stir.

Drag Queen

HIGHBALL GLASS

½ part Triple Sec
1 part Vodka
dash Angostura® Bitters
dash Salt

Shake with ice and pour.

Dragon Breath

HIGHBALL GLASS

2 parts Vodka
1 part Ouzo
½ part Jägermeister®

Shake with ice and pour.

Dragon Slayer

ROCKS GLASS

1/2 part Vodka
1/2 part Coconut Rum
3/4 part Blueberry Schnapps
1/4 part Blue Curaçao
1 part Pineapple Juice
1 part Orange Juice
fill with Lemon-Lime Soda
splash Grenadine

Build over ice and stir.

Drainpipe

HIGHBALL GLASS

1 part Irish Cream Liqueur
1 part Blue Curaçao
fill with Cola

Build over ice and stir.

Dreamsicle®

HIGHBALL GLASS

1 part Vodka
1 part Cherry Juice
1 part Orange Juice
1 part Pineapple Juice
splash Cream

Shake with ice and pour.

Drink

HIGHBALL GLASS

3/4 part Sour Apple Schnapps
1 part Melon Liqueur
1 part Cranberry Juice Cocktail
1 part Orange Juice

Shake with ice and pour.

Drink If You Dairy

HIGHBALL GLASS

1 part Fireball Cinnamon Whiskey
1 part Half and Half
1 part Milk
1/24 part Vanilla Extract
1/4 tsp Powdered Sugar

Shake with ice and strain over ice.

Drink of the Gods

HIGHBALL GLASS

2 parts Vodka
1 part Blueberry Schnapps
1 part Pineapple Juice

Shake with ice and pour.

Drunk Monkey

HIGHBALL GLASS

3/4 part Banana Liqueur
3/4 part Coconut Rum
3/4 part Watermelon Schnapps
2 parts Cranberry Juice Cocktail
3 parts Pineapple Juice

Build over ice and stir.

Drunk on Christmas

ROCKS GLASS

3 parts Melon Liqueur
2 parts Irish Whiskey
1 part Sour Apple Schnapps
4 parts Sweet & Sour Mix

Build over ice and stir.

Drunken Monkey's Lunch

ROCKS GLASS

1 part Banana Liqueur
1 part Coffee Liqueur
1 part Vodka
fill with Milk

Build over ice and stir.

Dry Hump

HIGHBALL GLASS

1 part Vodka
1 part Coffee Liqueur
1 part Amaretto

Shake with ice and pour.

Dublin Driver

HIGHBALL GLASS

1 part Irish Mist®
fill with Orange Juice

Shake with ice and strain over ice.

Dulcet

WHITE WINE GLASS

1 part Blue Curaçao
1 part Crème de Coconut
2 parts Grapefruit Juice
1½ parts Passion Fruit Juice
1 part Amaretto

Shake with ice and pour.

Dundee Cocktail

ROCKS GLASS

1½ parts Gin
1 part Scotch
⅓ part Drambuie
⅙ part Lemon Juice

Shake with ice and strain over ice. Garnish with a Lemon Twist.

Dunlop

HIGHBALL GLASS

2 parts Light Rum
1½ parts Sherry
2 dashes Bitters

Shake with ice and strain over ice.

Durango

ROCKS GLASS

1 part Tequila
1 part Grapefruit Juice
splash Amaretto
fill with Spring Water

Build over ice and stir.

Eagle Eye

HIGHBALL GLASS

2 parts Passoa
2 parts Vodka
1 part Cranberry Juice
1 part Orange Juice

Shake with ice and strain over ice.

Easter Bunny

ROCKS GLASS

1½ parts Crème de Cacao (Dark)
½ part Vodka
splash Chocolate Syrup
splash Cherry Brandy

Shake with ice and strain over ice.

Eastern Night

HIGHBALL GLASS

1 part Gin
1 part Crème de Banane
1 part Parfait Amour

Shake with ice and strain over ice.

Ecstasy

ROCKS GLASS

1 part Peach Schnapps
1 part Cherry Brandy
1 part Pear Liqueur
fill with Cranberry Juice Cocktail

Shake with ice and strain over ice.

Ectoplasm

HIGHBALL GLASS

2 parts Vodka
1 part Blue Curaçao
1 part Grand Marnier
splash Orange Juice

Shake with ice and strain over ice.

Edison

HIGHBALL GLASS

1 part Strawberry Liqueur
1 part Vodka
1 part Grand Marnier®
splash Grapefruit Juice
fill with Lemon-Lime Soda

Build over ice and stir.

The Eel Skin

ROCKS GLASS

1 part Coconut Rum
½ part Citrus Vodka
2 parts Pineapple Juice
½ part Smirnoff® Citrus Twist
1 part Midori®

Shake with ice and strain.

The Egret

HIGHBALL GLASS

2 parts Vodka
2 parts Apple Juice
1 part Cola

Build over ice and stir.

Eight-Inch Tongue

HIGHBALL GLASS

1 part Southern Comfort®
1 part Vodka
1 part Peach Schnapps
1 part Brandy
1 part Amaretto
fill with Cranberry Juice Cocktail

Shake with ice and pour.

El Morocco

ROCKS GLASS

1 part Gin
1 part Crème de Banane
1 part Campari®

Shake with ice and strain over ice.

Elder Margarita

COUPE

1½ parts St-Germain
1 part Tequila
2 parts Sweet & Sour mix

Shake with ice and strain.

Electric Bubblegum

HIGHBALL GLASS

1 part Banana Liqueur
1 part Blue Raspberry Liqueur
fill with Pineapple Juice
splash Lime Juice

Shake all but Lime Juice with ice and strain over ice. Top with Lime Juice.

Electric Dreams

HIGHBALL GLASS

1 part Vodka
1 part Amaretto
1 part Lemonade
1 part Orange Juice

Shake with ice and pour.

Electric Jam

HIGHBALL GLASS

1¼ parts Vodka
½ part Blue Curaçao
2 parts Sweet & Sour Mix
2 parts Lemon-Lime Soda

Shake with ice and pour.

Electric Kool-Aid®

ROCKS GLASS

1 part Amaretto
1 part Triple Sec
1 part Cherry Brandy
1 part Melon Liqueur
1 part Southern Comfort®
1 part Sweet & Sour Mix
splash Grenadine

Shake with ice and strain over ice.

Electric Slide

ROCKS GLASS

1 part Blue Curaçao
1 part Coconut Rum
fill with Blue Sports Drink
splash Pineapple Juice

Shake all but Juice with ice and strain over ice. Top with Pineapple Juice.

Elf Tea

HIGHBALL GLASS

1 part Peppermint Liqueur
fill with Iced Tea
splash Lemon Juice

Build over ice and stir.

Elmer Fud® Pucker

HIGHBALL GLASS

2 parts Apricot Brandy
1 part Orange Juice
1 part Pineapple Juice
1 part Cranberry Juice Cocktail

Shake with ice and strain over ice.

Elmo

HIGHBALL GLASS

1 part Southern Comfort®
1 part Amaretto
1 part Vodka

Shake with ice and pour.

Emerald

HIGHBALL GLASS

4 parts Brandy
2 parts Crème de Menthe (Green)
1 part Lemon Juice

Shake with ice and strain over ice.

Emerald City

ROCKS GLASS

1½ parts Vodka
1 part Banana Liqueur
½ part Blue Curaçao
4 parts Pineapple Juice
top with Orange Juice

Build over ice and stir.

Emerald Eyes

HIGHBALL GLASS

1 part Coconut Rum
1 part Melon Liqueur
splash Lime Juice
dash Simple Syrup
fill with Ginger Ale

Build over ice and stir. Garnish with a Lime Wedge.

Endless Summer

HIGHBALL GLASS

1 part Vodka
1 part Peach Schnapps
1 part Strawberry Daiquiri Mix
2 parts Lemonade
1 part Orange Juice

Shake with ice and pour.

English Water

HIGHBALL GLASS

1 part Extra Dry Gin
fill with Lemonade

Build over ice and stir.

Entrust Your Heart

HIGHBALL GLASS

½ part Blue Curaçao
½ part Apricot Brandy
1½ parts Dark Rum
½ part Lemon Juice
fill with Orange Juice

Shake with ice and strain over ice.

Estrella del Caribe

ROCKS GLASS

1 part Light Rum
½ part Melon Liqueur
¼ part Strawberry Liqueur
1 part Orange Juice
1 part Passion Fruit Juice

Shake with ice and pour.

Estridentista

COUPE

1½ parts Dry Vermouth
¾ part Anchos Reyes Chile Liqueur
¾ part St-Germain
2 dashes Grapefruit Bitters

Build over ice and stir. Strain into a chilled coupe and garnish with a Lemon Twist expressed over the cocktail and rubbed around the rim.

Evil Blue Thing

HIGHBALL GLASS

1½ parts Crème de Cacao (White)
1 part Blue Curaçao
½ part Cream of Coconut
½ part Light Rum

Shake with ice and strain over ice.

Evil Blue Thing #2

ROCKS GLASS

1½ parts Crème de Cacao (White)
1 part Blue Curaçao
½ part Light Rum

Shake with ice and pour.

Evil Canadian

HIGHBALL GLASS

2 parts Canadian Whisky
½ part Maple Syrup
dash Cinnamon Schnapps
fill with Apple Juice

Shake with ice and strain over ice.

Evil Tongue

WHITE WINE GLASS

1½ parts Gin
1 part Melon Liqueur
splash Sweet & Sour Mix
splash Lemon-Lime Soda

Build over ice and stir.

Exit the Brain

HIGHBALL GLASS

1½ parts 151-Proof Rum
1½ parts Coconut Rum
1 part Grenadine
3 parts Passion Fruit Juice
1 part Red Bull® Energy Drink

Build over ice and stir.

Exotic

HIGHBALL GLASS

1 part Gin
½ part Crème de Cacao (Dark)
½ part Crème de Banane

Build over ice and stir.

Eyes of a Stranger

HIGHBALL GLASS

1 part Gin
splash Lime Juice
1 part Apple Juice

Shake with ice and strain over ice.

Fairy Godmother

HIGHBALL GLASS

1 part Amaretto
1 part Vodka

Build over ice and stir.

Falling Star

HIGHBALL GLASS

1¼ parts Spiced Rum
¼ part Lime Juice
2 parts Orange Juice
2 parts Tonic Water

Shake with ice and strain over ice.

Family Jewels

HIGHBALL GLASS

2 parts Goldschläger®
1 part Raspberry Liqueur
1 part Chocolate Mint Liqueur

Build over ice and stir.

Fantasia

HIGHBALL GLASS

1¼ parts Orange Vodka
¾ part Peach Schnapps
fill with Orange Soda

Build over ice and stir. Garnish with a Lemon Twist.

Fat Face

ROCKS GLASS

1½ parts Gin
½ part Apricot Brandy
splash Grenadine
1 Egg White

Shake with ice and strain over ice.

Fat Hooker

HIGHBALL GLASS

1 part Vodka
½ part Peach Schnapps
½ part Coconut Rum
fill with Orange Juice

Build over ice and stir.

Fatkid on the Rocks

HIGHBALL GLASS

1 part Goldschläger®
1 part Tequila
1 part Vodka
1 part Water

Shake with ice and pour.

Federal Law

HIGHBALL GLASS

1½ parts Currant Vodka
1½ parts Chambord
1½ parts Sweet & Sour Mix
splash Tonic Water
fill with Cranberry Juice

Build over ice and stir.

Federation

HIGHBALL GLASS

1 part Vodka
1½ parts Peach Schnapps
2 parts Cranberry Juice Cocktail
fill with Lemon-Lime Soda

Build over ice and stir.

Fern Gully

HIGHBALL GLASS

1 part Dark Rum
1 part Light Rum
½ part Crème de Noyaux
½ part Cream of Coconut
splash Lime Juice
1 part Orange Juice

Shake with ice and strain over ice.

Ferndale Road

HIGHBALL GLASS

½ part Vanilla Liqueur
1 part Brandy
½ part Grenadine
fill with Apple Juice
splash Lemon Juice

Shake with ice and strain over ice.

Ferrari®

ROCKS GLASS

2 parts Dry Vermouth
1 part Amaretto

Shake with ice and strain over ice.
Garnish with a Lemon Twist.

Fickle Pickle

HIGHBALL GLASS

¾ part Vodka
¾ part Melon Liqueur
¼ part Crown Royal® Whiskey
½ part Triple Sec
splash Sweet & Sour Mix

Shake with ice and strain over ice.

Fidel Castro Special

HIGHBALL GLASS

1 part Dark Rum
½ part Melon Liqueur
½ part Blue Curaçao
1 part Pear Juice
½ part Cream of Coconut

Shake with ice and strain over ice.

Fiery Mule

COPPER MUG

1 part Fireball Cinnamon Whiskey
2 parts Ginger Beer
splash Pineapple Juice
splash Lime Juice

Build over ice and stir.

Figaro

HIGHBALL GLASS

1 part Crème de Cacao (White)
1 part Crème de Menthe (White)
1 part Triple Sec

Build over ice and stir.

Fiji Fizz

HIGHBALL GLASS

1½ parts Dark Rum
3 dashes Orange Bitters
splash Cherry Liqueur
fill with Cola

Build over ice and stir.

Fiorenza

HIGHBALL GLASS

1 part Dark Rum
¼ part Amaretto
fill with Cola

Build over ice and stir.

Fire on the Mountain

HIGHBALL GLASS

1 part Fireball Cinnamon Whiskey
fill with Mountain Dew

Build over ice.

Fire-Rita

MARGARITA GLASS

1 part Fireball Cinnamon Whiskey
1 part Orange Liqueur
1 part Tequila
1 part Lime Juice

Shake with ice and strain.

Fireball

ROCKS GLASS

1 part Coffee Liqueur
1 part Ouzo

Shake with ice and pour.

Fireball Glory

HIGHBALL GLASS

1 part Cinnamon Schnapps
1 part Vodka
3 parts Cranberry Juice Cocktail

Shake with ice and pour.

Firebomb

HIGHBALL GLASS

1 part Tequila
1 part Jack Daniel's®
1 part Vodka
splash Tabasco® Sauce

Shake with ice and pour.

Firecracker

ROCKS GLASS

1 part Cinnamon Schnapps
1 part Cherry Brandy
splash Tabasco® Sauce

Shake with ice and strain over ice.

Firefighter

HIGHBALL GLASS

1 part Triple Sec
1 part Raspberry Liqueur
1 part Kirschwasser

Build over ice and stir.

Firefly

HIGHBALL GLASS

1¼ parts Vodka
2 parts Grapefruit Juice
splash Grenadine

Build over ice and stir.

Firestorm

ROCKS GLASS

1 part Cinnamon Schnapps
1 part Peppermint Schnapps
1 part Rum

Build over ice and stir.

First Avenue

ROCKS GLASS

1½ parts Sweet Sherry
½ part Cointreau
¾ part Club Soda
dash Campari

Build over ice and stir.

Fishbone

HIGHBALL GLASS

1 part Coconut Rum
1 part Blue Curaçao
1 part Melon Liqueur
2 parts Orange Juice
2 parts Sweet & Sour Mix
splash Lemon-Lime Soda

Build over ice and stir.

Fizzetti

HIGHBALL GLASS

1 part Triple Sec
½ part Cherry Brandy
2 parts Cream Sherry
1 part Club Soda

Build over ice and stir.

Flaming Iceberg

HIGHBALL GLASS

splash Blue Curaçao
2 parts Sambuca

Build over ice and stir.

Flamingo

HIGHBALL GLASS

4 parts Cranberry Juice Cocktail
2 parts Pineapple Juice
½ part Lemon Juice
2 parts Club Soda

Shake all but Club Soda with ice and strain. Top with Club Soda and garnish with a Lime Wedge.

Flapper

HIGHBALL GLASS

1 part Rum
1 part Sweet Vermouth
dash Angostura® Bitters

Shake with ice and pour.

Flash Gordon®

HIGHBALL GLASS

2 parts Gin
splash Melon Liqueur
fill with Lemon-Lime Soda

Build over ice and stir.

Flim Flam

HIGHBALL GLASS

1½ parts Light Rum
¾ part Triple Sec
½ part Lemon Juice
½ part Orange Juice

Shake with ice and strain over ice.

Flor de Mayo

HIGHBALL GLASS

1 part Crème de Banane
½ part Dark Rum
½ part Dry Vermouth

Build over ice and stir.

Florida Gold

HIGHBALL GLASS

1 part Tequila Gold
fill with Orange Juice

Build over ice and stir.

Florida Tracksuit

ROCKS GLASS

½ part Orange Vodka
½ part Raspberry Liqueur
fill with Red Bull Energy Drink

Build over ice and stir. From OnTap in Ottawa, Canada.

Fly Away
HIGHBALL GLASS

1 part Vanilla Liqueur
1 part Licor 43®
2 parts Banana Juice

Build over ice and stir.

Flyin' Hawaiian
HIGHBALL GLASS

1 part Melon Liqueur
1 part Light Rum
2 parts Lemon-Lime Soda
3 parts Pineapple Juice

Build over ice and stir.

Flying Dutchman
ROCKS GLASS

2 parts Gin
splash Triple Sec

Shake with ice and strain over ice.

Flying Fortress
WHITE WINE GLASS

1 part Brandy
3/4 part Vodka
1/2 part Absinthe
1/2 part Triple Sec

Shake with ice and pour.

Flying Grapefruit
HIGHBALL GLASS

1 part White Rum
1/2 part Dry Vermouth
1/2 part Vodka
1 part Cranberry Juice
1 part Lemon Juice
fill with Grapefruit Juice

Build over ice and stir.

Flying Squirrel
HIGHBALL GLASS

1 1/2 parts Tequila
1 part Triple Sec
splash Sweet & Sour Mix
splash Sweetened Lime Juice
fill with Orange Juice

Build over ice and stir.

Flying Swan
HIGHBALL GLASS

1 part Coconut Rum
1 part Sour Apple Schnapps
fill with Orange Juice

Build over ice and stir.

Fonso
HIGHBALL GLASS

1/2 part Amaretto
1 1/2 parts Whiskey
3 parts Club Soda

Build over ice and stir.

Foolish Pleasure
HIGHBALL GLASS

2 parts Parfait Amour
1/2 part Coffee Liqueur
1/2 part Peppermint Liqueur
1/2 part Irish Cream Liqueur

Build over ice and stir.

Fort Lauderdale
ROCKS GLASS

1 1/2 parts Light Rum
1/2 part Sweet Vermouth
1/2 part Orange Juice
splash Lime Juice

Shake with ice and strain over ice.

Foxhaven Suprise
HIGHBALL GLASS

1 1/2 parts Vodka
1 part Gin
1/4 part Grenadine
2 parts Orange Juice

Shake with ice and strain.

Foxhound
HIGHBALL GLASS

1 1/2 parts Brandy
1/2 part Cranberry Juice Cocktail
splash Lemon Juice
splash Kümmel

Shake with ice and strain over ice.

Foxy Balls

HIGHBALL GLASS

2 parts Fireball Cinnamon Whiskey
fill with Ginger Ale
2 dashes Bitters

Build over ice and stir.

Freak Me

HIGHBALL GLASS

½ part Cherry Brandy
⅔ part Apricot Brandy
⅔ part Campari®

Build over ice and stir.

Freddie Fudpucker

HIGHBALL GLASS

1 part Tequila
fill with Orange Juice
½ part Galliano®
½ part Coffee Liqueur

Build over ice and stir.

French Afternoon

HIGHBALL GLASS

1 part Coffee Liqueur
1 part Pernod®

Shake with ice and strain over ice.

French Alps

WHITE WINE GLASS

1½ parts Passion Fruit Liqueur
¼ part Crème de Cacao (Dark)
2 parts Pineapple Juice
3 parts Cream

Shake all but Cream with ice and strain. Top with Cream.

French Bubbles

HIGHBALL GLASS

1½ parts Amaretto
⅔ part Grand Marnier®
1 part Simple Syrup
1 part Lemon Juice

Shake with ice and strain over ice.

French Connection

ROCKS GLASS

1½ parts Cognac
¾ part Amaretto

Build over ice and stir.

French Cream

ROCKS GLASS

3 parts RumChata
1 part Cognac

Build over ice.

French Fantasy

HIGHBALL GLASS

1 part Blackberry Liqueur
1 part Grand Marnier®
2 parts Cranberry Juice Cocktail
2 parts Orange Juice

Build over ice and stir.

French Orgasm

BRANDY SNIFTER

2½ parts Cognac
1½ parts Irish Cream Liqueur

Pour ingredients into glass neat (do not chill).

French Sailor

HIGHBALL GLASS

1 part Cointreau®
1 part Vodka
1 Sugar Cube

Build over ice and stir.

French Toast

HIGHBALL GLASS

3 parts RumChata
1 part Maple Whiskey

Shake with ice and strain over ice.

Friday Harbor

HIGHBALL GLASS

1 part Vodka
1 part Peach Schnapps
1 part Cranberry Juice Cocktail
1 part Grapefruit Juice

Build over ice and stir.

Friendly Foe

HIGHBALL GLASS

1 part Canadian Whisky
½ part Passion Fruit Liqueur
½ part Silver Tequila
1 part Lime Juice

Build over ice and stir.

Frisco Sour

ROCKS GLASS

2 parts Whiskey
½ part Bénédictine®
¼ part Lemon Juice
½ part Lime Juice

Shake with ice and pour.

Frisky Whiskey

HIGHBALL GLASS

1 part Whiskey
1 part Gin
splash Lemon Juice

Shake with ice and strain over ice.

Frogster

HIGHBALL GLASS

1½ parts Blue Curaçao
1 part Tequila

Shake with ice and strain over ice.

Froot Loop®

ROCKS GLASS

½ part Vodka
½ part Cherry Brandy
1 part Apple Brandy
1 part Orange Juice

Shake with ice and pour.

Frozen Rainforest

HIGHBALL GLASS

1 part Mango Vodka
1 part Orange Vodka
1 part Pineapple Juice
½ part Lime Juice
splash Blue Curaçao

Shake with ice and strain over ice.

Fruit Grenade

HIGHBALL GLASS

1 part Blackberry Liqueur
½ part Light Rum
1 part Orange Vodka
½ part Sweet & Sour Mix
fill with Cranberry Juice Cocktail

Build over ice and stir.

Fruit of the Loons

ROCKS GLASS

1 part Blackberry Liqueur
1 part Orange Juice
1 part Grape Juice (Red)

Shake with ice and strain over ice.

Fudgesicle

HIGHBALL GLASS

1 part Coffee Vodka
1 part Chocolate Liqueur
fill with Milk

Build over ice and stir.

Fuji Apple

ROCKS GLASS

1 part Melon Liqueur
¾ part Spiced Rum
splash Blue Curaçao
fill with Apple Juice

Shake with ice and strain over ice.

The Full Monty

HIGHBALL GLASS

1 part Vodka
½ part Pisang Ambon® Liqueur
½ part Passoa®
fill with Orange Juice
splash Grenadine

Build over ice.

Full Moon Fever

HIGHBALL GLASS

½ part Spiced Rum
1 part Light Rum
2 parts Coconut Rum
1 part Melon Liqueur
splash Sweet & Sour Mix
fill with Pineapple Juice

Build over ice and stir.

Full Nelson

HIGHBALL GLASS

½ part Crème de Menthe (Green)
1 part Lime Juice
dash Sugar
fill with Seltzer

Build over ice and stir.

Fun Squeeze

HIGHBALL GLASS

½ part 151-Proof Rum
1 part Blue Curaçao
fill with Orange Juice

Build over ice and stir.

Fury

ROCKS GLASS

1 part Vodka
1 part Spiced Rum
splash Sweet & Sour Mix
2 parts Orange Juice

Build over ice and stir.

Fuzzy Balls

ROCKS GLASS

½ part Peach Schnapps
½ part Vodka
½ part Melon Liqueur
1½ parts Grapefruit Juice
1½ parts Cranberry Juice Cocktail

Build over ice and stir.

Fuzzy Banana

HIGHBALL GLASS

2 parts Orange Juice
1 part 99-Proof Banana Liqueur
1 part Peach Schnapps

Build over ice and stir.

Fuzzy Bull

ROCKS GLASS

1½ parts Vanilla Vodka
1 part Peach Schnapps
1 part Orange Juice
fill with Red Bull Energy Drink

Build over ice and stir.

Fuzzy Comfort

HIGHBALL GLASS

1½ parts Rum
½ part Sloe Gin
½ part Southern Comfort®
½ part Peach Schnapps
fill with Orange Juice

Shake with ice and pour.

Fuzzy Mexican

HIGHBALL GLASS

1½ parts Silver Tequila
½ part Peach Schnapps
fill with Orange Juice

Build over ice and stir.

Fuzzy Navel

HIGHBALL GLASS

2 parts Peach Schnapps
fill with Orange Juice

Build over ice and stir. Garnish with an Orange Slice.

Fuzzy Navel #2

HIGHBALL GLASS

1 part Vodka
1 part Peach Schnapps
fill with Orange Juice

Build over ice and stir.

Fuzzy Peach

ROCKS GLASS

1 part Vodka
1 part Peach Schnapps
fill with Grapefruit Juice
splash Grenadine

Shake with ice and pour.

Fuzzy Rita

HIGHBALL GLASS

1½ parts Tequila
½ part Peach Schnapps
½ part Cointreau®
1½ parts Lime Juice

Shake with ice and pour.

Gadzooks

HIGHBALL GLASS

1 part Vodka
1 part Raspberry Liqueur
1 part Cherry Juice
2 parts Lemonade
1 part Cola

Build over ice and stir.

Gallant Bull

HIGHBALL GLASS

1 part Galliano
fill with Red Bull Energy Drink

Build over ice and stir.

Gallina

HIGHBALL GLASS

⅔ part Gin
splash Blue Curaçao
splash Apricot Brandy
splash Dry Vermouth

Build over ice and stir.

Gangbuster Punch

HIGHBALL GLASS

1½ parts Vodka
1½ parts Peach Schnapps
1 part Cranberry Juice Cocktail
splash Lemon-Lime Soda

Shake with ice and pour.

Gangrene

HIGHBALL GLASS

1 part Spiced Rum
1 part Johnnie Walker® Red Label
fill with Mountain Dew®

Build over ice and stir.

Gates of Hell

ROCKS GLASS

3 parts Tequila
splash Lime Juice
splash Lemon Juice
splash Cherry Brandy

Build over ice.

Gator Milk

HIGHBALL GLASS

1 part KeKe Beach® Key Lime-Cream Liqueur
1 part Coconut Rum
1 part Piña Colada Mix
fill with Mountain Dew®

Build over ice and stir.

Gattaca

HIGHBALL GLASS

1 part Gin
1 part Blue Curaçao
1 part Peach Schnapps
1 part Lemon Juice

Build over ice and stir.

Gay Pirate
HIGHBALL GLASS

1 part Apricot Brandy
1 part 151-Proof Rum
1 part Coconut Rum
splash Lemon Juice
fill with Pineapple Juice

Shake with ice and strain over ice.

Geezer!
ROCKS GLASS

1 part Citrus Vodka
1 part Triple Sec
½ part Lime Juice

Shake with ice and strain over ice.

Gemini Dream
HIGHBALL GLASS

1½ parts Citrus Vodka
splash Blue Curaçao
2½ parts Passoã®
3 parts Orange Juice
splash Lime Juice

Shake with ice and strain.

Gene Splice
HIGHBALL GLASS

1 part Vodka
½ part Triple Sec
½ part Raspberry Liqueur
2 parts Pineapple Juice
¼ part Lime Juice

Shake with ice and pour.

Gentle Bull
HIGHBALL GLASS

1½ parts Tequila
1 part Heavy Cream
¾ part Coffee Liqueur

Shake with ice and pour.

Gentleman's Club
ROCKS GLASS

1½ parts Gin
1 part Brandy
1 part Sweet Vermouth
1 part Club Soda

Build over ice and stir.

Gentlemen of the Jury
HIGHBALL GLASS

2 parts Gin
½ part Cherry Brandy
½ part Lemon Juice
dash Bitters
fill with Pineapple Juice

Build over ice and stir.

Georgia Peach
HIGHBALL GLASS

¾ part Southern Comfort®
1 part Peach Schnapps
4 parts Orange Juice
splash Grenadine

Shake with ice and pour.

Georgia Pie
HIGHBALL GLASS

½ part Peach Schnapps
½ part Southern Comfort®
½ part Malibu® Rum
1½ parts Orange Juice

Shake with ice and pour.

German Bliss
HIGHBALL GLASS

2 parts Coffee Liqueur
1 part Jägermeister
fill with Root Beer

Build over ice.

Get in my Belly

HIGHBALL GLASS

1 part Vodka
1 part Sour Cherry Liqueur
1 part Peach Schnapps
1 part Orange Juice
1 part Pineapple Juice
1 part Lemon-Lime Soda

Build over ice and stir.

Get Laid

HIGHBALL GLASS

1 part Vodka
¾ part Raspberry Liqueur
fill with Pineapple Juice
splash Cranberry Juice Cocktail

Build over ice and stir.

Ghost

HIGHBALL GLASS

2 parts Vanilla Vodka
1 part Jack Daniel's®
fill with Cream Soda

Build over ice and stir.

Gin and Juice

HIGHBALL GLASS

2 parts Gin
1 part Orange Juice
1 part Grapefruit Juice

Shake with ice and pour.

Gin Blossom

ROCKS GLASS

1½ parts Peach Schnapps
1 part Gin
fill with Lemon-Lime Soda

Build over ice and stir.

The Ginfather

ROCKS GLASS

1 part Amaretto
1 part Gin

Shake with ice and strain over ice.

Gin Mint Fix

ROCKS GLASS

1½ parts Gin
½ part Crème de Menthe (White)
½ part Simple Syrup

Shake with ice and strain over ice.

Gin Smash

ROCKS GLASS

1 Sugar Cube
1 part Seltzer
4 Fresh Mint Leaves
2 parts Gin

Muddle Sugar with Seltzer and Mint leaves in the glass. Add Gin and 1 ice cube. Stir, add the Orange Slice and the Maraschino Cherry.

Ginger Jack Sour

ROCKS GLASS

2 parts Jack Daniel's
½ part Lime Juice
½ part Simple Syrup
fill with Ginger Ale

Build over ice and stir.

Gingerbread Zip

ROCKS GLASS

1 part Butterscotch Liqueur
1 part Goldschläger®
1 part Irish Cream Liqueur
1 part Vodka
fill with Eggnog

Shake with ice and strain over ice.

Gingersnap

HIGHBALL GLASS

1 part Coffee Liqueur
1 part Irish Cream Liqueur
1 part Frangelico®
1 part Jägermeister®
fill with Cola

Build over ice and stir.

Gladiator

HIGHBALL GLASS

½ part Amaretto
½ part Southern Comfort®
2 parts Orange Juice
fill with Lemon-Lime Soda

Build over ice and stir.

Glitch

ROCKS GLASS

2 parts Vodka
fill with Mango Juice
1 part Lemon Juice
2 parts Blue Curaçao

Build over ice and stir.

Gloom Lifter

HIGHBALL GLASS

1 part Whiskey
½ part Brandy
splash Raspberry Syrup
½ part Lemon Juice
dash Sugar
1 Egg White

Shake with ice and strain over ice.

Glowworm

HIGHBALL GLASS

1½ parts Melon Liqueur
1½ parts Southern Comfort®
3 parts Orange Juice
3 parts Pineapple Juice
1½ parts Blue Curaçao

Build over ice and stir.

Goblin Bowl

BRANDY SNIFTER

1 part Dubonnet® Blonde
1 part Applejack
½ part Raspberry Liqueur
fill with Apple Cider
dash Bitters

Shake with ice and strain over ice.

Godfather

ROCKS GLASS

1½ parts Scotch
¾ part Amaretto

Shake with ice and strain over ice.

Godmother

ROCKS GLASS

3 parts Vodka
1 part Amaretto

Shake with ice and pour.

God's Great Creation

HIGHBALL GLASS

2½ parts Whiskey
1 part Peach Schnapps
2 parts Fruit Punch
½ part Lemon Juice
fill with Cola

Build over ice and stir.

Going Blue

BRANDY SNIFTER

1½ parts Grenadine
¾ part Blue Curaçao
¾ part Light Rum
½ part Crème de Banane

Shake with ice and strain.

Gold Carp

HIGHBALL GLASS

1 part Apricot Brandy
1 part Jim Beam®
1 part Dry Vermouth
1 part Silver Tequila

Build over ice and stir.

Golden Beauty

ROCKS GLASS

1 part Apricot Brandy
1 part Peach Schnapps
splash Remy Martin VS®
splash Pineapple Juice

Build over ice and stir.

Golden Bronx

ROCKS GLASS

2 parts Gin
splash Dry Vermouth
splash Sweet Vermouth
1/2 part Orange Juice
1 Egg Yolk

Shake with ice and strain over ice.

Golden Comet

HIGHBALL GLASS

1 part Gin
1/2 part Blue Curaçao
1/2 part Lime Juice

Shake with ice and pour.

Golden Dreamer

HIGHBALL GLASS

1 part Triple Sec
splash Brandy
splash Dry Vermouth
1 part Light Rum

Shake with ice and strain over ice.

Golden Hornet

ROCKS GLASS

2 parts Gin
1/2 part Cream Sherry
1/2 part Scotch

Shake with ice and strain over ice.

Golden Lilly

HIGHBALL GLASS

1 part Brandy
1 part Gin
1 part Triple Sec
splash Pernod®

Shake with ice and strain over ice.

Golden Miller

ROCKS GLASS

1 part Amaretto
1 part Grand Marnier®
1 part Crème de Cacao (White)
1 part Orange Juice

Shake with ice and strain over ice.

Golden Nugget

HIGHBALL GLASS

2 parts Yukon Jack
fill with Grapefruit Juice

Build over ice and stir.

Golden Panther

HIGHBALL GLASS

2/3 part Gin
2/3 part Brandy
2/3 part Whiskey
1/2 part Dry Vermouth
1 part Orange Juice

Shake with ice and strain over ice.

Golden Rooster

ROCKS GLASS

2 parts Gin
1/2 part Dry Vermouth
1/2 part Apricot Brandy

Shake with ice and strain over ice.

Golden Sunrise

HIGHBALL GLASS

1/4 part Amaretto
1/4 part Spiced Rum
1/4 part Wild Berry Schnapps
1/4 part Key Largo® Schnapps
1/4 part Raspberry Liqueur
1 part Orange Juice
1 part Pineapple Juice

Shake with ice and pour.

Golden Volcano

HIGHBALL GLASS

1/2 part Galliano®
1/2 part Silver Tequila
splash Triple Sec
splash Cream
splash Lemon Juice
splash Orange Juice

Shake with ice and pour.

Goldfinger
HIGHBALL GLASS

1 part Goldschläger®
1 part Amaretto
fill with Lemonade

Shake with ice and pour.

Good Morning Sunshine
HIGHBALL GLASS

1 part Vodka
fill with Cranberry Juice Cocktail

Build over ice and stir.

Good Vibrations
HIGHBALL GLASS

2 parts Tequila
fill with Orange Soda

Build over ice and stir.

Goodnight Kiss
HIGHBALL GLASS

2 parts Raspberry Liqueur
2 parts Strawberry Vodka
1 part Dark Rum
half fill with Cranberry Juice
half fill with Lemon-Lime Soda

Shake all but the Juice and Soda with ice and strain over ice. Fill with equal parts Cranberry Juice and Lemon-Lime Soda.

Gooseberry Jam
HIGHBALL GLASS

1 part Vodka
1 part Southern Comfort®
2 parts Blue Curaçao
fill with Orange Juice

Build over ice and stir.

Gorilla Milk
HIGHBALL GLASS

1 part Coffee Liqueur
1 part Amaretto
1 part 99 Bananas Liqueur
fill with Milk

Build over ice and stir.

Grace of Monaco
HIGHBALL GLASS

1 part Apricot Brandy
1 part Mandarine Napoléon Liqueur
1 part Silver Tequila

Shake with ice and strain over ice.

Grainne
HIGHBALL GLASS

1 part Vodka
1 part Maraschino Liqueur
1 part Crème de Banane
splash Lemon Juice
splash Orange Juice

Shake with ice and strain over ice.

Grand Blue
ROCKS GLASS

1 part Coconut Rum
1 part Peach Schnapps
1 part Blue Curaçao
1 part Sweet & Sour Mix

Shake with ice and strain over ice.

Grand Canard
HIGHBALL GLASS

½ part Grand Marnier®
1 part Southern Comfort®
1 part Tia Maria®
fill with Milk

Build over ice and stir.

Grand Midori®
HIGHBALL GLASS

splash Crème de Banane
splash Melon Liqueur
splash Dry Vermouth
1 part Remy Martin® VSOP

Shake with ice and strain over ice.

Grandma in a Wheelchair

ROCKS GLASS

2 parts Grand Marnier®
1 part Tequila
1 part Lemon-Lime Soda
splash Lime Juice

Build over ice and stir.

Grandpa's Ol' Cough Syrup

HIGHBALL GLASS

1 part Old Grand-Dad®
fill with Orange Juice

Build over ice and stir.

Granny Smith

ROCKS GLASS

2 parts Apple Vodka
1 part Sour Apple Schnapps
fill with Tonic Water

Build over ice and stir.

Granny Smith Cocktail

ROCKS GLASS

1½ parts Sour Apple Vodka
1 part Salted Caramel Vodka
fill with Tonic Water

Build over ice and stir.

Grape Expectations

HIGHBALL GLASS

1 part Melon Liqueur
1 part Vodka
1 part Grape Juice (Red)
1 part Lemon-Lime Soda

Build over ice and stir.

Grape Lifesaver

HIGHBALL GLASS

1 part Coconut Rum
1 part Melon Liqueur
1 part Sweet & Sour Mix
1 part Pineapple Juice
1 part Grape Juice (Red)

Build over ice and stir.

Grape Rainstorm

HIGHBALL GLASS

1 part Vodka
1 part Blue Curaçao
1 part Pineapple Juice
1 part Lemon-Lime Soda

Build over ice and stir.

Grappa Gimlet

HIGHBALL GLASS

2 parts Gin
2 parts Sweetened Lime Juice
1 part Grappa

Shake with ice and pour.

Grass Skirt

ROCKS GLASS

1½ parts Gin
1 part Triple Sec
1 part Pineapple Juice
splash Grenadine

Shake with ice and strain over ice.
Garnish with a Pineapple Slice.

Grateful Dead

HIGHBALL GLASS

½ part Gin
½ part Vodka
½ part Triple Sec
½ part Rum
2 parts Sweet & Sour Mix
1 part Raspberry Liqueur

Shake with ice and pour.

Graveyard Shift

ROCKS GLASS

2 parts Passion Fruit Vodka
1 part Cynar
½ part Amaretto
splash Orange Juice

Shake with ice and strain over ice.

Great Head

HIGHBALL GLASS

1½ parts Whiskey
½ part Applejack

Shake with ice and pour.

Greek Passion

HIGHBALL GLASS

2 parts Vodka
2/3 part Vanilla Liqueur
2/3 part Passion Fruit Liqueur
splash Triple Sec
fill with Orange Juice

Build over ice and stir.

Green Alien

HIGHBALL GLASS

2 parts Melon Liqueur
1 part Lemon Juice
1 part Lime Cordial

Shake with ice and strain over ice.

Green and Sour

HIGHBALL GLASS

1 part Pisang Ambon® Liqueur
1 part Melon Liqueur
1 part Kibowi
splash Lemon Juice

Shake with ice and strain over ice.

Green Arrow

ROCKS GLASS

1 part Blue Curaçao
1 part Tequila Gold
1 part Lemon Juice
1/2 part Lime Juice

Shake with ice and pour.

Green Babe

HIGHBALL GLASS

1 1/2 parts Citrus Rum
1 1/2 parts Vodka
1 part Melon Liqueur
fill with Cranberry Juice Cocktail
splash Sweet & Sour Mix

Build over ice and stir.

Green Cow

ROCKS GLASS

1 part Vodka
1 part Pisang Ambon® Liqueur
1/2 part Milk
fill with Lemon-Lime Soda

Build over ice and stir.

Green Delight

HIGHBALL GLASS

1 part Vodka
1 part Pisang Ambon® Liqueur
1 part Lemon-Lime Soda
1 part Orange Juice

Build over ice and stir.

Green Demon

HIGHBALL GLASS

1 part Vodka
1 part Rum
1 part Melon Liqueur
fill with Lemonade

Build over ice and stir. Garnish with a Maraschino Cherry.

Green Devil

ROCKS GLASS

1 1/2 parts Gin
1 1/2 parts Crème de Menthe (Green)
splash Lime Juice
3 Mint Leaves

Shake with ice and strain.

Green Eggs and Ham

HIGHBALL GLASS

2 parts Melon Liqueur
1/2 part Sweet & Sour Mix
fill with Cranberry Juice Cocktail
splash Cola

Build over ice and stir.

Green-Eyed Lady

HIGHBALL GLASS

1 part Vodka
1 part Melon Liqueur
1 part Lemonade
1 part Lemon-Lime Soda

Build over ice and stir.

Green Hornet

HIGHBALL GLASS

1½ parts Vodka
½ part Sweetened Lime Juice
splash Crème de Menthe (Green)

Shake with ice and strain.

Green Killer

RED WINE GLASS

1 part Vodka
1 part Crème de Banane
1 part Blue Curaçao
fill with Orange Juice

Shake with ice and pour.

Green Sea

ROCKS GLASS

1 part Crème de Menthe (Green)
1 part Vodka
1 part Dry Vermouth

Shake with ice and strain over ice.

Green Slime

HIGHBALL GLASS

2 parts Vodka
1 part Limeade
1 part Orange Juice

Build over ice and stir.

Green Stinger

ROCKS GLASS

1 part Crème de Menthe (Green)
1 part Brandy

Shake with ice and pour.

Green Sunset

HIGHBALL GLASS

1½ parts Coconut Rum
splash Lemon-Lime Soda
splash Cranberry Juice Cocktail
fill with Pineapple Juice
1 part Melon Liqueur

Build over ice.

Green Swamps

RED WINE GLASS

2 parts Light Rum
1 part Blue Curaçao
2 splashes Cherry Juice
fill with Pineapple Juice

Build over ice and stir.

Greenback

ROCKS GLASS

1½ parts Gin
1 part Crème de Menthe (Green)
1 part Lemon Juice

Shake with ice and strain over ice.

Greenham's Grotto

ROCKS GLASS

2 parts Gin
1 part Brandy
2 splashes Amaretto
2 splashes Lemon Juice

Shake with ice and strain over ice.

Gremlin Fixer

ROCKS GLASS

1 part Vodka
1 part Dry Vermouth
1 part Apricot Brandy
1 part Pisang Ambon® Liqueur
fill with Pineapple Juice

Build over ice and stir.

Grinch

HIGHBALL GLASS

1 part Melon Liqueur
1 part Banana Liqueur
1 part Malibu® Rum
splash Lemon-Lime Soda

Build over ice and stir.

G-Strings

HIGHBALL GLASS

1 part 151-Proof Rum
1 part Vodka
1 part Grenadine
1 part Pineapple Juice

Shake with ice and strain over ice.

GTV

ROCKS GLASS

1 part Gin
1 part Tequila
1 part Vodka

Shake with ice and strain over ice.

Guatacarazo

ROCKS GLASS

1 part Dark Rum
½ part Vodka
¼ part Crème de Banane
¼ part Pineapple Juice
splash Lemon Juice

Shake with ice and strain over ice.

Gulf Air

ROCKS GLASS

1 part Light Rum
1 part Triple Sec
1 part Melon
1 part Pernod®

Shake with ice and strain over ice.

Gull's Breath

ROCKS GLASS

2 parts Jägermeister®
½ part Crème de Banane
½ part Lemon Juice

Shake with ice and strain over ice.

Gull's Wing

ROCKS GLASS

2 parts Tequila
½ part Crème de Banane
½ part Lemon Juice

Build over ice and stir.

Gumby®

HIGHBALL GLASS

1 part Melon Liqueur
fill with Apple Cider

Build over ice and stir.

Gummiberry Juice

HIGHBALL GLASS

1½ parts Peach Schnapps
1½ parts Strawberry Liqueur
½ part Triple Sec
fill with Fruit Punch
splash Lemon Juice

Build over ice and stir.

Gummy Bears

HIGHBALL GLASS

1 part Gin
1 part RedRum®
fill with Pink Lemonade

Build over ice and stir. Garnish with a Maraschino Cherry.

Hairy Happy Trail

HIGHBALL GLASS

1 part Vodka
1 part RedRum®
½ part Limoncello
½ part Lime Juice
fill with Orange Juice

Build over ice and stir.

Hairy Navel

HIGHBALL GLASS

1 part Vodka
1 part Peach Schnapps
fill with Orange Juice

Build over ice and stir.

Halloween
HIGHBALL GLASS

2 parts Vodka
1 part Scotch
fill with Orange Juice

Shake with ice and strain over ice.

Halloween Spiced Cider
ROCKS GLASS

3/4 part Spiced Rum
1/2 part Tequila Reposado
fill with Apple Cider

Shake with ice and pour.

Hammer
HIGHBALL GLASS

1 part Orange Juice
1 part Sloe Gin

Build over ice and stir.

Hammerhead
HIGHBALL GLASS

2 parts Scotch
1/2 part Gin
fill with Orange Juice

Build over ice and stir.

Hang Ten
HIGHBALL GLASS

1 part Black Sambuca
1 part Light Rum
1/2 part Crème de Banane
1 part Cranberry Juice Cocktail
1 part Pineapple Juice

Build over ice and stir.

Happy Captain's Ball
ROCKS GLASS

1 part Blue Curaçao
1 part Peach Liqueur
1 part Crème de Coconut
fill with Pineapple Juice

Shake with ice and strain over ice.

Happy Hawaiian
ROCKS GLASS

1 1/2 parts Coffee Liqueur
1 1/2 parts Irish Cream Liqueur
fill with Pineapple Juice

Shake with ice and pour.

Happy Mascot
HIGHBALL GLASS

1 part Apricot Brandy
1 part Light Rum
1 1/2 parts Sweet & Sour Mix
fill with Orange Juice

Build over ice and stir.

Harbor Lights
HIGHBALL GLASS

1 part Vodka
2 parts Peach Nectar
2 parts Lemonade
1 part Cranberry Juice Cocktail

Shake with ice and pour.

Hari Kari
HIGHBALL GLASS

1 part Brandy
1 part Cointreau®
1 part Orange Juice

Shake with ice and strain over ice.

Harlequin Frappé
ROCKS GLASS

1 part Vodka
1 part Crème de Cacao (Dark)
1 part Triple Sec

Build over ice and stir.

Harry Boy
ROCKS GLASS

1 part Cointreau®
1 part Coffee Liqueur
1 part Whiskey
fill with Milk

Shake with ice and pour.

Harry Potter
HIGHBALL GLASS
1 part Blackberry Liqueur
1 part Butterscotch Liqueur
1 part Chambord
splash Cranberry Juice
Shake with ice and strain over ice.

Harvey Cowpuncher
HIGHBALL GLASS
1 part Vodka
½ part Galliano®
fill with Milk
Build over ice and stir.

Haus Special
HIGHBALL GLASS
2 parts 100-Proof Blackberry Schnapps
fill with Cranberry Juice Cocktail
Build over ice and stir.

Hawaiian Jesus
HIGHBALL GLASS
1 part Chambord
1 part Light Rum
2 parts Lemon-Lime Soda
2 parts Pineapple Juice
Shake with ice and strain over ice.

Hawaiian Russian
HIGHBALL GLASS
2 parts Vodka
1 part Hawaiian Punch
1 part Pineapple Juice
1 part Lemon-Lime Soda
Build over ice and stir.

Hawaiian Volcano
HIGHBALL GLASS
1 part Amaretto
1 part Southern Comfort®
½ part Vodka
2 parts Orange Juice
1 part Pineapple Juice
Build over ice and stir. Garnish with a Maraschino Cherry.

Headache
ROCKS GLASS
1 part 151-Proof Rum
1 part Vodka
fill with Energy Drink
Build over ice and stir.

Headkick
HIGHBALL GLASS
1 part Cognac
2 parts Rum
fill with Red Bull® Energy Drink
Build over ice and stir.

Heads Up
HIGHBALL GLASS
1 part Gin
1 part Raspberry Vodka
2 parts Cranberry Juice
2 parts Orange Juice
Shake with ice and strain over ice.

Headshot
HIGHBALL GLASS
1 part Grape Vodka
1 part Raspberry Vodka
1 part Vanilla Vodka
3 parts Orange Juice
Shake with ice and pour

Headspin
ROCKS GLASS
1 part Vodka
1 part Crème de Banane
1 part Apricot Brandy
fill with Orange Juice
Shake with ice and pour.

Heartbeat
HIGHBALL GLASS
1 part Triple Sec
1 part Jamaican Rum
splash Mango Juice
Build over ice and stir.

Heatseeker

HIGHBALL GLASS

1 part Crème de Cacao (White)
2/3 part Butterscotch Schnapps
1 part Irish Cream Liqueur
fill with Coffee

Build over ice and stir.

Hell Raiser

HIGHBALL GLASS

1 part Jack Daniel's®
1 part Tequila
1 part Vodka

Shake with ice and strain over ice.

Hell's Kitchen

ROCKS GLASS

1 part Bushmills® Irish Whiskey
1 1/2 parts Irish Cream Liqueur

Build over ice and stir.

Her Name Was Lola

HIGHBALL GLASS

1 1/2 parts Silver Tequila
1 part Lime Juice
splash Honey
splash Orange Liqueur

Shake with ice and pour.

High Rise

HIGHBALL GLASS

1 part Vodka
1/4 part Cointreau
2 parts Orange Juice
1 part Sweet & Sour Mix
1/4 part Grenadine

Build over ice and stir.

High Road

ROCKS GLASS

1 1/2 parts Scotch
1/2 part Drambuie
1/2 part Dry Sherry
1/6 part Lemon Juice

Shake with ice and strain over ice.

High Roller

HIGHBALL GLASS

1 1/2 parts Vodka
3/4 part Grand Marnier®
fill with Orange Juice
splash Grenadine

Build over ice.

Highland Cream

ROCKS GLASS

1 part Scotch
1/2 part Crème de Cacao (White)
1/4 part Peppermint Schnapps
1/4 part Galliano
1/6 part Glayva Scotch Liqueur
1 part Whipping Cream

Shake with ice and strain over ice.

Highland Margarita

HIGHBALL GLASS

1 1/2 parts Tequila
1/2 part Grand Marnier®
1/2 part Drambuie®
fill with Sweet & Sour Mix

Shake with ice and pour.

Highspeed

HIGHBALL GLASS

1/2 part Absinthe
1/2 part Silver Tequila
1/2 part White Rum
1/2 part Vodka
fill with Red Bull Energy Drink

Build over ice and stir.

Hispaniola

HIGHBALL GLASS

1 part Dark Rum
1 part Blue Curaçao
2 splashes Sweet & Sour Mix

Shake with ice and pour.

Hit in the Face

HIGHBALL GLASS

2 parts Coconut Rum
1 part Southern Comfort®
1 part Jägermeister®
fill with Dr. Pepper®

Build over ice and stir.

Hollywood

HIGHBALL GLASS

1½ parts Vodka
1½ parts Raspberry Liqueur
1 part Triple Sec
splash Sweetened Lime Juice

Shake with ice and strain over ice.

Holy Cow

HIGHBALL GLASS

2 parts Irish Cream Liqueur
½ part Irish Whiskey
1 part Coffee Liqueur
fill with Root Beer

Build over ice and stir.

Homewrecker

HIGHBALL GLASS

1 part Melon Liqueur
1 part Tequila
1 part Jägermeister®
fill with Cranberry Juice Cocktail

Shake with ice and pour.

Honey Drop

ROCKS GLASS

½ part Blue Curaçao
½ part Melon Liqueur
1 part Margarita Mix
fill with Lemonade

Build over ice and stir.

Honeymoon Sunrise

WHITE WINE GLASS

1 part Light Rum
1 part Passion Fruit Nectar
½ part Crème de Coconut
fill with Orange Juice

Shake with ice and strain over ice.

Hoo Doo

ROCKS GLASS

1 part Southern Comfort®
1 part Vodka
½ part Orange Juice
½ part Lime Juice
splash Peppermint Schnapps
splash Lemon-Lime Soda

Shake with ice and strain over ice.

Hop Frog

ROCKS GLASS

2 parts Vodka
1 part Crème de Menthe (Green)
1 part Dry Vermouth

Shake with ice and strain over ice.

Horny Toad

HIGHBALL GLASS

2 parts Vodka
½ part Triple Sec
fill with Lemonade

Shake with ice and strain over ice.

Horse Feathers

HIGHBALL GLASS

2 parts Whiskey
2 dashes Bitters
fill with Ginger Ale

Build over ice and stir.

Hose Wallbanger

HIGHBALL GLASS

1½ parts Tequila
fill with Orange Juice
½ part Galliano®

Build over ice and stir.

Hot and Spicy Men

HIGHBALL GLASS

1 part Cinnamon Schnapps
1 part Jack Daniel's®
1 part Jim Beam®
1 part Spiced Rum
fill with Dr. Pepper®

Build over ice and stir.

Hot Bull

ROCKS GLASS

2 parts Fireball Cinnamon Whiskey
fill with Red Bull Energy Drink

Build over ice and stir.

Hot Night

HIGHBALL GLASS

1 part Crème de Cacao (Dark)
splash Sambuca
splash Absinthe

Shake with ice and strain over ice.

Hot Pants

ROCKS GLASS

1½ parts Tequila
½ part Peppermint Schnapps
splash Grapefruit Juice
1 tsp Sugar

Shake with ice and strain over ice.

Hot Summer Breeze

HIGHBALL GLASS

1 part Vodka
1 part Orange Juice
1 part Ginger Ale

Build over ice and stir.

Hot Tub

HIGHBALL GLASS

1 part Vodka
1 part Grand Marnier
1 part Chambord
fill with Cranberry Juice

Build over ice and stir.

Hula Hoop

HIGHBALL GLASS

1 part Vodka
1 part Peach Schnapps
1 part Lemonade
1 part Orange Juice
1 part Cranberry Juice Cocktail

Shake with ice and pour.

Hulkster

HIGHBALL GLASS

1 part Vodka
1 part Melon Liqueur
1 part Kiwi Schnapps
fill with Lemon-Lime Soda

Build over ice and stir.

Las Special

HIGHBALL GLASS

1 part Banana Liqueur
1 part Aquavit
1½ parts Lime Juice
fill with Lemon-Lime Soda

Build over ice and stir.

Iblis

HIGHBALL GLASS

2 parts Campari®
1 part Gin
splash Lemon Juice

Build over ice and stir.

Ice Blue Aqua Velva®

ROCKS GLASS

¾ part Vodka
¾ part Gin
½ part Blue Curaçao
fill with Lemon-Lime Soda

Build over ice and stir.

Ice Breaker

HIGHBALL GLASS

1 part Peppermint Schnapps
1 part Vodka

Shake with ice and pour.

Iceberg

HIGHBALL GLASS

1 part Crème de Menthe (White)
½ part Peppermint Schnapps
½ part Goldschläger®
fill with Milk

Build over ice and stir.

Iced Latte

HIGHBALL GLASS

1 part Crème de Cacao (Dark)
1/2 part Coffee Liqueur
1/2 part Cherry Brandy
fill with Cream

Shake with ice and pour.

Illiad

HIGHBALL GLASS

1 part Amaretto
2 parts Ouzo
splash Strawberry Liqueur

Shake with ice and strain.

Impatient Virgin

ROCKS GLASS

1 part Vanilla Vodka
1 part Frangelico
1 part Crème de Cacao (White)
3 parts Cream

Shake with ice and strain over ice.

Incredible Hulk®

HIGHBALL GLASS

2 parts Melon Liqueur
1 part Vodka
fill with Mountain Dew®

Build over ice and stir.

Indian Summer

HIGHBALL GLASS

1 part Vodka
1 part Coffee Liqueur
fill with Pineapple Juice

Shake with ice and strain over ice.

Indigo

ROCKS GLASS

1 1/2 parts Gin
1 part Triple Sec
2 splashes Blue Curaçao

Build over ice.

Infernal Love

HIGHBALL GLASS

1/2 part Scotch
1 part Apricot Brandy
1/4 part Grenadine
3 parts Orange Juice

Shake with ice and strain over ice.

International Airport

HIGHBALL GLASS

splash Grenadine
1 part Citrus Rum
2 parts Passion Fruit Juice
2 parts Mango Juice

Shake with ice and strain over ice.

Irish Breakfast

HIGHBALL GLASS

1 part RumChata
1 part Jameson Irish Whiskey

Shake with ice and strain over ice.

Irish Canadian Sangee

ROCKS GLASS

2 parts Whiskey
1 part Orange Juice
1 part Irish Mist®

Shake with ice and strain over ice.

Irish Coconut

HIGHBALL GLASS

1 part Irish Cream Liqueur
1 part Coconut Rum
fill with Cream

Shake with ice and pour.

Irish Curdling Cow

HIGHBALL GLASS

1 part Irish Cream Liqueur
1 part Vodka
1 part Irish Whiskey
fill with Orange Juice

Build over ice and stir.

Irish Fix

ROCKS GLASS

2 parts Whiskey
1 part Irish Mist®
½ part Pineapple Juice

Shake with ice and strain over ice.

Irish Hooker

ROCKS GLASS

1 part Irish Whiskey
splash Irish Cream Liqueur
splash Irish Mist®
splash Coffee Liqueur
splash Frangelico®

Shake with ice and strain over ice.

Irish Russian

HIGHBALL GLASS

1 part Vodka
1 part Coffee Liqueur
splash Cola
fill with Guinness® Stout

Build in the glass with no ice.

Irish Shillelagh

ROCKS GLASS

1½ parts Whiskey
½ part Light Rum
1 tbsp powdered sugar
½ part Sloe Gin

Shake with ice and strain over ice.

Irish Whiskey Highball

HIGHBALL GLASS

2 parts Irish Whiskey
fill with Seltzer

Build over ice and stir. Garnish with a Lemon Twist.

Irish Winter Coffee

ROCKS GLASS

2 parts Irish Cream Liqueur
1 part Coffee Liqueur
fill with Coffee

Build in a heat-proof cup or mug. Top with Whipped Cream.

Iron Butterfly

HIGHBALL GLASS

1 part Vodka
1 part Coffee Liqueur
1 part Irish Cream Liqueur

Shake with ice and strain.

Iron Curtain

HIGHBALL GLASS

2 parts Vodka
½ part Apricot Brandy

Shake with ice and strain over ice.

Isle of Blue

HIGHBALL GLASS

1 part Gin
1 part Blue Curaçao
splash Lemon Juice
splash Lime Juice

Build over ice and stir.

Italian Heather

ROCKS GLASS

1½ parts Scotch
1 part Galliano®

Build over ice and stir. Garnish with a Lemon Wedge.

Italian Ice

ROCKS GLASS

1 part Vodka
1 part Blue Curaçao
1 part Raspberry Liqueur
1 part Sweet & Sour Mix
fill with Lemon-Lime Soda

Build over ice.

Italian Nut

HIGHBALL GLASS

1 part Coconut Rum
1 part Amaretto
fill with Orange Juice
splash Grenadine

Shake with ice and pour.

Jack Be Nimble

HIGHBALL GLASS

1 part Jack Daniel's®
½ part Triple Sec
splash 151-Proof Rum
½ part Cranberry Juice Cocktail

Build over ice and stir.

Jack Dempsey

ROCKS GLASS

1 part Dry Gin
1 part Triple Sec
splash Grenadine
splash Pastis

Shake with ice and strain.

Jack Lemmon, M.D.

HIGHBALL GLASS

2 parts Jack Daniel's®
½ part Lemon Juice
fill with Dr. Pepper®

Build over ice and stir.

Jack-O'-Lantern

ROCKS GLASS

1 part Amaretto
1 part Pineapple Juice
1 part Orange Juice
1 part Southern Comfort®
splash Grenadine

Shake with ice and pour.

Jack the Ripper

BRANDY SNIFTER

2½ parts Crown Royal® Whiskey
¾ part Butterscotch Schnapps

Shake with ice and strain.

Jackhammer

HIGHBALL GLASS

1½ parts Vodka
fill with Pineapple Juice

Build over ice and stir.

Jacobs Haze

HIGHBALL GLASS

1 part Jägermeister®
1 part Currant Vodka
fill with Red Bull® Energy Drink

Build over ice and stir.

Jade Lady

CHAMPAGNE FLUTE

1 part Dark Rum
1 part Gin
½ part Crème de Menthe (Green)
½ part Simple Syrup

Shake with ice and strain over ice.

Jaffa Frost

HIGHBALL GLASS

1 part Vodka
1 part Crème de Cacao (Dark)
1 part Triple Sec

Shake with ice and strain over ice.

Jagasm

ROCKS GLASS

1 part Advocaat
1 part Sweet Vermouth
1 part Crème de Coconut
splash Grenadine

Shake with ice and strain over ice.

Jager Monster

HIGHBALL GLASS

1½ parts Jägermeister®
½ part Amaretto
fill with Orange Juice
splash Grenadine

Build over ice and stir.

Jägerenade

ROCKS GLASS

1 part Jägermeister
1 part Blue Raspberry Liqueur
splash Grenadine
fill with Red Bull Energy Drink

Build over ice and stir.

Jaguar

HIGHBALL GLASS

1 part Vodka
1 part Crème de Banane
fill with Lemon-Lime Soda

Build over ice and stir.

Jailbait

HIGHBALL GLASS

1 part Spiced Rum
1 part Orange Juice
1 part Passion Fruit Liqueur

Shake with ice and pour.

Jamaican

HIGHBALL GLASS

1 part Rum
1 part Coffee Liqueur
1 part Lime Juice
dash Angostura® Bitters
fill with Lemon-Lime Soda

Build over ice and stir.

Jamaican Gravel

HIGHBALL GLASS

1 part Coffee Liqueur
1 part Rum
1 part Canadian Mist®
1 part Cream

Shake with ice and strain over ice.

Jamaican Honeymoon

HIGHBALL GLASS

1 part Crème de Banane
2 parts Lemon-Lime Soda
2 parts Pear Juice
2 parts Orange Juice
splash Lemon Juice

Build over ice and stir.

Jamaican Mountain Bike

HIGHBALL GLASS

1 part Vodka
1 part Melon Liqueur
1 part Crème de Banane
1 part Coconut Rum
fill with Cream

Shake with ice and strain over ice.

Jamaican Sourball

HIGHBALL GLASS

1 part Dark Rum
1 part Triple Sec
1 part Lemonade
1 part Orange Juice

Build over ice and stir.

Jamaican Tea

HIGHBALL GLASS

1 part Dark Rum
1 part Triple Sec
2 parts Sweet & Sour Mix
1 part Cola

Build over ice and stir.

Jamaican Vacation

HIGHBALL GLASS

1 1/2 parts Light Rum
1/3 part Sweet & Sour Mix
splash Sweetened Lime Juice
splash Cherry Juice
1 part Pineapple Juice
1 part Lemon-Lime Soda

Build over ice and stir.

Jamaican Yo Yo

HIGHBALL GLASS

1 part Rum
1 part Tia Maria®

Shake with ice and strain over ice.

Javahopper

ROCKS GLASS

1 part Coffee Brandy
1 part Crème de Menthe (White)
1 part Light Cream

Shake with ice and strain over ice.

Jazzy Green

HIGHBALL GLASS

1 part Citrus Vodka
1 part Blue Curaçao
1 part Peach Schnapps
1 part Orange Juice
1 part Pineapple Juice

Shake with ice and pour.

Jeremiah

HIGHBALL GLASS

1 part Crème de Cacao (White)
1 part Crème de Menthe (White)
1 part Coffee Liqueur

Shake with ice and strain over ice.

Jericho's Breeze

HIGHBALL GLASS

1 part Vodka
3/4 part Blue Curaçao
2 1/2 parts Sweet & Sour Mix
splash Lemon-Lime Soda
splash Orange Juice

Build over ice and stir.

Jersey Shore Cherry Lemonade

HIGHBALL GLASS

1 1/2 parts Vodka
1 1/4 parts Sweet & Sour Mix
dash Sugar
fill with Lemon-Lime Soda
splash Grenadine

Build over ice and stir.

Jesus

HIGHBALL GLASS

1 part Southern Comfort®
splash Grenadine
splash Lemon Juice
fill with Orange Juice

Build over ice.

Jewel

HIGHBALL GLASS

1 part Gin
1 tbsp. Green Chartreuse®
1 part Sweet Vermouth
2 dashes Orange Bitters

Shake with ice and strain over ice.

Jitterbug

HIGHBALL GLASS

2 parts Gin
1 1/2 parts Vodka
3 splashes Grenadine
splash Lime Juice
dash Sugar
3 splashes Simple Syrup
fill with Seltzer Water

Build over ice and stir.

Jo Jo Original

ROCKS GLASS

1 part Myers's® Rum
1/2 part Amaretto
fill with Cola
splash 151-Proof Rum

Build over ice.

Jock-in-a-Box

ROCKS GLASS

1 1/2 parts Scotch
1/2 part Sweet Vermouth
1/2 part Lemon Juice
1 Egg White

Shake with ice and strain.

Joker

ROCKS GLASS

1 part Scotch
1 part Triple Sec

Shake with ice and strain over ice.

Jolly Holliday

HIGHBALL GLASS

2 parts Peppermint Schnapps
1 part Vodka
1 part Watermelon Schnapps
fill with Cranberry Juice

Shake with ice and strain over ice.

Jolly Rancher®

ROCKS GLASS

1 1/2 parts Melon Liqueur
1/2 part Peach Schnapps
fill with Sweet & Sour Mix
splash Grenadine

Shake with ice and pour. Garnish with a Maraschino Cherry.

Jolly Walrus

HIGHBALL GLASS

1 part Orange Vodka
splash Grenadine
splash Orange Juice
fill with Energy Drink

Build over ice and stir.

John Lee Hooker

HIGHBALL GLASS

1 part Spiced Rum
1 part Triple Sec
1 part Peach Schnapps
splash Strawberry Syrup
fill with Lemon-Lime Soda

Build over ice and stir.

A Joy of Almond

ROCKS GLASS

1 part Coffee Liqueur
1/2 part Amaretto
1/2 part Crème de Almond

Build over ice.

Juan Blue

HIGHBALL GLASS

1 1/2 parts Tequila
1/2 part Lemon Juice
2 parts Orange Juice
1 part Grapefruit Juice
dash Bitters
splash Blue Curaçao

Shake with ice and strain over ice.

Juice Juice

HIGHBALL GLASS

1 part Vodka
1 part Triple Sec
1 part Grape Juice (Red)
1 part Orange Juice
1 part Cranberry Juice Cocktail

Build over ice and stir.

Juicy Fruit Remix

HIGHBALL GLASS

1/2 part Banana Liqueur
1/2 part Peach Schnapps
1/2 part Vodka
1/2 part Cranberry Juice Cocktail
1 part Lemonade
1 1/2 parts Orange Juice

Shake with ice and pour.

Juicy Melon

HIGHBALL GLASS

1 1/2 parts Peach Schnapps
1 1/2 parts Melon Liqueur
1 part Orange Juice
1 part Grapefruit Juice
1 part Cranberry Juice Cocktail
splash Melon Liqueur
splash Grenadine

Build over ice and stir.

Juicy Red Lips

CHAMPAGNE FLUTE

1 part Rum
1 part Advocaat
½ part Triple Sec
½ part Red Curacao
1 part Cream
1 part Orange Juice

Shake with ice and strain.

Jumpin' Jack Flash

ROCKS GLASS

1 part Brandy
1 part Blackberry Liqueur
1 part Orange Juice
dash Sugar

Shake with ice and strain.

Jungle Lust

HIGHBALL GLASS

½ part Vodka
1 part Melon Liqueur
1 part Peach Schnapps
1 part Orange Juice
1 part Pineapple Juice

Build over ice and stir.

Just Like Romeo

HIGHBALL GLASS

1 part Vodka
1 part Raspberry Liqueur
1 part Strawberry Daiquiri Mix
2 parts Lemonade
1 part Orange Juice

Build over ice and stir.

Just Married

HIGHBALL GLASS

1 part Dark Rum
1 part Melon Liqueur
fill with Orange Juice

Shake with ice and pour.

Ka-Boom

HIGHBALL GLASS

1½ parts Coconut Rum
1 part Banana Liqueur
1 part Grenadine
fill with Pineapple Juice
½ part Lime Juice

Shake with ice and pour.

Kansas City Ice Water

HIGHBALL GLASS

¾ part Gin
¾ part Vodka
½ part Lime Juice
fill with Lemon-Lime Soda

Build over ice and stir.

Kappa Colada

HIGHBALL GLASS

1 part Brandy
1 part Cream of Coconut
fill with Pineapple Juice

Shake with ice and strain over ice.

Karen's Melons

HIGHBALL GLASS

1½ parts Melon Liqueur
1 part Vodka
fill with Lemon-Lime Soda

Build over ice and stir.

Karma Chameleon

HIGHBALL GLASS

1 part Vodka
1 part Peach Schnapps
fill with Lemon-Lime Soda
splash Grenadine

Build over ice and stir.

Kenai Campfire

ROCKS GLASS

1 part Canadian Whisky
1 part Irish Cream Liqueur
1 part Butterscotch Schnapps

Shake with ice and strain over ice.

Kentucky Appleseed

HIGHBALL GLASS

1½ parts Kentucky Bourbon
fill with Apple Juice

Build over ice and stir.

Kentucky B & B

BRANDY SNIFTER

1½ parts Bourbon
½ part Bénédictine®

Build in the glass with no ice.

Kentucky Cousins

ROCKS GLASS

1 part Sour Apple Schnapps
1 part Bourbon
½ part Mango Rum
fill with Pineapple Juice

Shake with ice and strain over ice.

Kentucky Mule

HIGHBALL GLASS

2 parts Bourbon
splash Sweetened Lime Juice
fill with Ginger Beer

Build over ice and stir.

Kentucky Orange Blossom

ROCKS GLASS

2 parts Bourbon
1 part Orange Juice

Shake with ice and strain over ice.

Kermit the Frog® Piss

HIGHBALL GLASS

1 part Melon Liqueur
½ part Coconut Rum
2 parts Sweet & Sour Mix
fill with Lemon-Lime Soda

Build over ice and stir.

Kevorkian

HIGHBALL GLASS

½ part Spiced Rum
½ part Dark Rum
½ part Coconut Rum
½ part Crème de Noyaux
1 part Orange Juice
1 part Cranberry Juice Cocktail

Shake with ice and strain over ice.

Key West Lemonade

ROCKS GLASS

1 part Vodka
1 part Sweet & Sour Mix
splash Lemon-Lime Soda
splash Cranberry Juice Cocktail

Build over ice and stir.

Kialoa

HIGHBALL GLASS

½ part Rum
1 part Coffee Liqueur
1 part Cream

Shake with ice and strain over ice.

Kid Creole

ROCKS GLASS

1½ parts Light Rum
1 part Mango Juice
1 part Papaya Juice
¼ part Passion Fruit Juice
splash Strawberry Syrup

Shake with ice and strain over ice.

Kilt Lifter

ROCKS GLASS

1 part Drambuie®
1 part Butterscotch Schnapps

Shake with ice and strain.

Kingdom Come

HIGHBALL GLASS

1½ parts Dry Vermouth
¾ part Gin
splash Crème de Menthe (White)
splash Grapefruit Juice

Shake with ice and strain over ice.

King Cole Cocktail
ROCKS GLASS

1 Orange Wedge
1 tbsp Crushed Pineapple
½ tsp Sugar
2 parts Whiskey

Muddle the Orange Wedge, Pineapple, and Sugar in the glass. Add ice and Whiskey and stir.

King's Crown
HIGHBALL GLASS

2 parts Crown Royal® Whiskey
splash Lime Juice
fill with Lemon-Lime Soda

Build over ice and stir.

Kinky Orgasm
HIGHBALL GLASS

1 part Irish Cream Liqueur
1 part Amaretto
1 part Coffee Liqueur
fill with Milk

Build over ice and stir.

Kinky Russian
ROCKS GLASS

1 part Coconut Rum
1 part Coffee Liqueur
1 part Half and Half

Shake with ice and strain over ice.

Kirchoff's Law
HIGHBALL GLASS

1 part Coffee Liqueur
½ part Godiva® Liqueur
fill with Chocolate Milk

Build over ice and stir.

Kirios
HIGHBALL GLASS

1 part Dark Rum
1 part Blue Curaçao
splash Maraschino Liqueur

Build over ice and stir.

Kiss 'n' Tell
HIGHBALL GLASS

1 part Calvados Apple Brandy
1 part Sloe Gin
splash Lemon Juice
1 Egg White

Shake with ice and strain over ice.

Kiss Off
HIGHBALL GLASS

1 part Gin
1 part Cherry Liqueur
splash Dry Vermouth

Shake with ice and strain over ice.

Kiwi Pussycat
HIGHBALL GLASS

1 part Vodka
1 part Kiwi Schnapps
1 part Cherry Juice
fill with Pineapple Juice

Build over ice and stir.

Kiwi Screwdriver
HIGHBALL GLASS

1 part Vodka
1 part Kiwi Schnapps
fill with Orange Juice

Build over ice and stir.

Klingon Battlejuice
ROCKS GLASS

2 parts Vodka
1 part Lemon Juice
splash Orange Juice

Build over ice and stir.

Knockout
ROCKS GLASS

1 part Southern Comfort®
1 part Apricot Brandy
1 part Sloe Gin
splash Orange Juice

Shake with ice and strain.

Kokomo
HIGHBALL GLASS

1 part Vodka
1 part Triple Sec
1 part Margarita Mix
1 part Orange Juice
1 part Cranberry Juice Cocktail

Shake with ice and pour.

Kos Kos Ponch
ROCKS GLASS

1 part Dark Rum
½ part Pineapple Juice
¼ part Crème de Banane
¼ part Cream of Coconut
2 dashes Bitters

Shake with ice and strain over ice.

Kosak's Milk
HIGHBALL GLASS

1 part Vodka
1 part Coffee Liqueur
fill with Milk

Shake with ice and pour.

K-Otic
HIGHBALL GLASS

1½ parts Vodka
1½ parts Grand Marnier®
1 part Lemon Juice

Shake with ice and strain over ice.

Krypto Kami
HIGHBALL GLASS

1 part Currant Vodka
1 part Melon Liqueur
1 part Peach Schnapps
1 part Pineapple Juice
1 part Sweet & Sour Mix

Shake with ice and pour.

Kryptonite
HIGHBALL GLASS

1 part Vodka
½ part Melon Liqueur
fill with Pineapple Juice

Shake with ice and pour.

Kurant Affair
ROCKS GLASS

1 part Currant Vodka
1 part Orange Juice
1 part Cranberry Juice Cocktail

Shake with ice and strain over ice.

KY Special
HIGHBALL GLASS

2 parts Peach Vodka
1 part Orange Juice
1 part Lemon-Lime Soda

Build over ice and stir.

La Bamba
HIGHBALL GLASS

1 part Vodka
1 part Frangelico®
fill with Orange Juice

Shake with ice and pour.

La Ligne Maginot
HIGHBALL GLASS

½ part Peach Schnapps
1 part Armagnac
½ part Pear Brandy
½ part Lemon Juice
fill with Apple Juice

Shake with ice and strain over ice.

Lacy Blue
HIGHBALL GLASS

1 part Vodka
1 part Blue Curaçao
1 part Cream
1 part Orange Juice
1 part Pineapple Juice

Shake with ice and pour.

Ladder
HIGHBALL GLASS

1 part Gin
1 part Pisang Ambon® Liqueur
1 part Crème de Banane
1 part Blue Curaçao
fill with Lemon-Lime Soda

Build over ice and stir.

Lady in Green

HIGHBALL GLASS

1 1/2 parts Anisette
1 1/2 parts Vodka
1/2 part Blue Curaçao
fill with Orange Juice

Shake with ice and strain over ice.

Lady-Killer

CHAMPAGNE FLUTE

1 part Gin
1/2 part Cointreau®
1/2 part Apricot Brandy
fill with Pineapple Juice

Shake with ice and strain.

Lafayette

ROCKS GLASS

2 parts Bourbon
1/2 part Dry Vermouth
1 Egg White
dash Powdered Sugar

Shake with ice and strain.

Lake Louise

HIGHBALL GLASS

1 part Crème de Cassis
1 part Southern Comfort®
1 part Orange Juice
1 part Grapefruit Juice

Shake with ice and pour.

Lara Croft®

ROCKS GLASS

1 1/2 parts Jim Beam®
1 part Crème de Menthe (White)
splash Lime Juice
splash Triple Sec

Shake with ice and strain over ice.

Laser Beam

HIGHBALL GLASS

1 part Amaretto
1 part Galliano®
1 part Peppermint Schnapps

Shake with ice and strain over ice.

Latino Americano

HIGHBALL GLASS

1 part Silver Tequila
splash Grenadine
splash Cream
fill with Orange Juice

Shake with ice and pour.

Lawn Bowler

BRANDY SNIFTER

1/2 part Blue Curaçao
1 part Jägermeister®
fill with Orange Juice
fill with Sweet & Sour Mix
1/2 part Melon Liqueur

Build over ice and stir. Garnish with a Lime Wedge.

Lazy Sunday

HIGHBALL GLASS

1 1/2 parts Tequila
1 part Ginger Ale
fill with Cranberry Juice Cocktail

Build over ice and stir.

Le Blue Dream

HIGHBALL GLASS

2/3 part Gin
1/2 part Blue Curaçao
splash Crème de Banane
1/2 part Pineapple Juice

Shake with ice and strain over ice.

Leche de Pantera

HIGHBALL GLASS

1/2 part Gin
splash Crème de Banane
1/2 part Crème de Cassis
splash Cream
splash Mango Juice

Shake with ice and strain over ice.

LeFreak

HIGHBALL GLASS

1½ parts Butterscotch Schnapps
1½ parts Amaretto
fill with Milk

Shake with ice and pour.

Legspreader

HIGHBALL GLASS

1 part Melon Liqueur
1 part Coconut Rum
fill with Pineapple Juice
splash Lemon-Lime Soda

Build over ice and stir.

Lemon Beat

ROCKS GLASS

2 parts Cachaca
1 part Lime Juice
1 part Honey

Shake with ice and strain over ice.

Lemon Cake

HIGHBALL GLASS

3 parts RumChata
1 part Limoncello

Shake with ice and strain over ice.

Lemon Highlander

ROCKS GLASS

½ part Limoncello
1 part Scotch
½ part Drambuie®

Shake with ice and strain over ice.

Lemon Loop

HIGHBALL GLASS

2 parts Citrus Vodka
½ part Melon Liqueur
½ part Kiwi Schnapps
2 parts Sweet & Sour Mix
2 parts Lemon-Lime Soda
splash Lemon Juice
dash Sugar

Build over ice and stir.

Lemon PineSol®

HIGHBALL GLASS

1 part Gin
1 part Lemon Juice
1 part Water

Shake with ice and pour.

Lemon Tree

HIGHBALL GLASS

1 part Wild Berry Schnapps
1 part Melon Liqueur
fill with Lemonade

Shake with ice and pour.

Lemon Zip

HIGHBALL GLASS

1 part Gin
1 part Jack Daniel's®
½ part Brandy
½ part Grenadine

Shake with ice and strain over ice.

Lemonade Lush

HIGHBALL GLASS

1 part Tequila
1 part Triple Sec
1 part Lemon Juice
1 part Sweet & Sour Mix

Shake with ice and pour.

Lemonado Denado

HIGHBALL GLASS

1 part Citrus Vodka
1 part Bacardi® Limón Rum
splash Grenadine
fill with Lemon-Lime Soda
splash Sweet & Sour Mix

Build over ice and stir.

Lethal Weapon

HIGHBALL GLASS

½ part 151-Proof Rum
1 part Vodka
fill with Mountain Dew®
splash Triple Sec

Build over ice and stir.

Lethal Weapon Shooter

ROCKS GLASS

1 part Vodka
½ part Peach Schnapps
splash Lime Cordial

Build over ice and stir.

Lick Me Silly

HIGHBALL GLASS

1 part Blue Curaçao
1 part Cointreau®
1 part Gin
1 part Vodka
1 part Melon Liqueur
fill with Lemonade

Shake with ice and pour.

Licorice Twist

HIGHBALL GLASS

1 part Black Currant Cordial
1 part Pernod®
2 parts Lemonade

Build over ice and stir.

Liebestraum

HIGHBALL GLASS

1 part Peach Schnapps
1 part Blue Curaçao
1 part Crème de Coconut
splash Lemon Juice
fill with Pineapple Juice

Shake with ice and pour.

Lifesaver

ROCKS GLASS

1 part Melon Liqueur
1 part Light Rum
fill with Pineapple Juice

Shake with ice and pour.

Lightning Lemonade

HIGHBALL GLASS

1 part Citrus Vodka
1 part Triple Sec
fill with Lemonade
splash Sweet & Sour Mix

Build over ice and stir.

Limbo Calypso

ROCKS GLASS

1½ parts Light Rum
splash Lime Juice
splash Crème de Banane
fill with Passion Fruit Juice

Shake with ice and strain over ice.

Limo Driver

HIGHBALL GLASS

2 parts Cherry Brandy
splash Lemon Juice
fill with Cola
splash Ginger Ale

Build over ice and stir.

Lindsay Lohan

HIGHBALL GLASS

2 parts Jägermeister
1 part Peach Schnapps
fill with Cranberry Juice
splash Cola

Build over ice.

Liquid Assets

HIGHBALL GLASS

2 parts Vodka
1 part Melon Liqueur
1 part Triple Sec

Shake with ice and strain over ice.

Liquid Big Red

HIGHBALL GLASS

1 part Goldschläger®
1 part Jägermeister®
fill with Dr. Pepper®

Build over ice and stir.

Liquid Candy

HIGHBALL GLASS

1 part Peach Schnapps
1 part Apple Liqueur
fill with Cranberry Juice Cocktail

Build over ice and stir.

Liquid Dessert

ROCKS GLASS

1 part Whipped Cream Vodka
2 parts Melon Liqueur
fill with Mountain Dew

Build over ice and stir.

Liquid Ecstasy

HIGHBALL GLASS

1 part Citrus Rum
½ part Blue Curaçao
½ part Melon Liqueur
½ part Lemon Juice
fill with Pineapple Juice

Shake with ice and strain over ice.

Liquid Grass

HIGHBALL GLASS

1 part Blue Curaçao
1 part Gin
1 part Orange Juice
splash Grapefruit Juice
splash Apple Juice
splash Melon Liqueur

Shake with ice and strain over ice.

Liquid Snickers®

ROCKS GLASS

1 part Crème de Cacao (Dark)
½ part Irish Cream Liqueur
½ part Frangelico®
½ part Light Cream

Build over ice and stir.

Little Bigman

HIGHBALL GLASS

1 part Dark Rum
2 splashes Galliano®
2 parts Orange Juice

Shake with ice and strain over ice.

A Little Dinghy

HIGHBALL GLASS

2 parts Coconut Rum
splash Orange Juice
splash Cranberry Juice Cocktail
splash Pineapple Juice

Build over ice and stir.

Little Dix Mix

ROCKS GLASS

2 parts Dark Rum
½ part Triple Sec
½ part Crème de Banane
½ part Lime Juice

Shake with ice and strain over ice.

Little Venus

HIGHBALL GLASS

2 parts Gin
⅔ part Passion Fruit Liqueur
½ part Cranberry Juice Cocktail
fill with Guava Juice

Shake with ice and strain over ice.

Loco Lemonade

HIGHBALL GLASS

1½ parts Tequila
1 part Grenadine
fill with Lemonade
½ part Lemon Juice

Build over ice and stir.

Log Cabin

HIGHBALL GLASS

1½ parts Canadian Whisky
½ parts Triple Sec
½ part Cream
fill with Orange Juice

Shake with ice and strain over ice.

Lollapalooza

HIGHBALL GLASS

1 part Vodka
1 part Triple Sec
1 part Lemonade
1 part Cola

Build over ice and stir.

Lollipop

HIGHBALL GLASS

1 part Cointreau®
1 part Kirschwasser
splash Green Chartreuse®
splash Cherry Liqueur

Shake with ice and strain over ice.

London Trio

ROCKS GLASS

1 part Pineapple Juice
1 part Gin
½ part Triple Sec

Shake with ice and strain over ice.

Lone Marshall

HIGHBALL GLASS

1 part Jim Beam®
1 part Peach Schnapps
½ part Southern Comfort®
½ part Sweet & Sour Mix
2 parts Orange Juice

Shake with ice and strain over ice.

Long John Silver

HIGHBALL GLASS

2 parts Spiced Rum
½ part Crème de Cacao (White)
fill with Orange Juice

Shake with ice and pour.

Long Summer Night

HIGHBALL GLASS

1 part Southern Comfort®
1 part Triple Sec
1 part Sweet & Sour Mix
fill with Mountain Dew®

Build over ice and stir.

Looking for Love

HIGHBALL GLASS

1½ parts Gin
1 part Parfait Amour
splash Lime Juice

Shake with ice and strain over ice.

Loosie Goosie

ROCKS GLASS

2 parts Rum
1 part Amaretto
1 part Cream of Coconut

Shake with ice and pour.

Lorelee

HIGHBALL GLASS

1 part Peach Schnapps
1 part Cherry Brandy
1 part Sweet & Sour Mix
fill with Cranberry Juice Cocktail

Shake with ice and pour.

Lost Wallet

HIGHBALL GLASS

⅔ part Melon Liqueur
½ part Grenadine
1½ parts Cointreau®
fill with White Port

Build over ice and stir.

Lotus Elixir

HIGHBALL GLASS

⅔ part Passion Fruit Liqueur
1½ parts Sake
1 part Raspberry Seltzer
⅔ part Lemon Juice
fill with Orange Juice

Shake with ice and strain over ice.

Louisiana Bayou

HIGHBALL GLASS

1 part Irish Cream Liqueur
½ part Coffee Liqueur
½ part Crème de Cacao (White)
fill with Cream

Shake with ice and strain over ice.

Love

ROCKS GLASS

2 parts Sloe Gin
splash Raspberry Syrup
splash Lemon Juice
1 Egg

Shake with ice and strain over ice.

Love Junk

ROCKS GLASS

1 part Vodka
3/4 part Peach Schnapps
3/4 part Melon Liqueur
fill with Apple Juice

Build over ice and stir.

Love Potion Number 9

HIGHBALL GLASS

1 part Vodka
1 part Raspberry Liqueur
1 part Lemonade
1 part Orange Juice
1 part Cranberry Juice Cocktail

Shake with ice and pour.

Lovely

HIGHBALL GLASS

1 part Jim Beam®
1/2 part Cherry Brandy
1/2 part Apricot Brandy
1/2 part Cream

Shake with ice and strain over ice.

Lucky Lemon

ROCKS GLASS

1 part Vodka
fill with Lemon-Lime Soda
splash Lemonade

Build over ice and stir.

Lucky Night

HIGHBALL GLASS

2/3 part Peach Schnapps
2/3 part Orange Liqueur
1 part Lemon Juice

Shake with ice and strain over ice.

Ludwig and the Gang

ROCKS GLASS

1 part Añejo Rum
1 part Vodka
1/2 part Amaretto
1/2 part Southern Comfort®
dash Bitters

Shake with ice and strain.

Lulu

HIGHBALL GLASS

1 part Vodka
1 part Light Rum
1 part Peach Schnapps
1 part Triple Sec
1 part Sweet & Sour Mix

Shake with ice and strain over ice. Garnish with a Maraschino Cherry.

Lumberjack

WHITE WINE GLASS

1 1/2 parts Vermouth
2 parts Club Soda
1 tbsp sugar

Blend Vermouth with crushed ice, pour over ice, and top with Club Soda. Garnish with 2 Maraschino Cherries.

Lynchburg Lemonade®

HIGHBALL GLASS

1 part Jack Daniel's®
1 part Sweet & Sour Mix
1 part Triple Sec
1 part Lemon Juice
fill with Lemon-Lime Soda

Build over ice and stir.

Macorix

HIGHBALL GLASS

2/3 part Cherry Brandy
1/2 part Jim Beam®
dash Orange Bitters
2 parts Lemon-Lime Soda

Build over ice and stir.

Mad Hatter

HIGHBALL GLASS

1 part Vodka
1 part Peach Schnapps
2 parts Lemonade
1 part Cola

Shake with ice and pour.

Madras

HIGHBALL GLASS

1½ parts Vodka
4 parts Cranberry Juice Cocktail
1 part Orange Juice

Shake with ice and pour.

Maeek

HIGHBALL GLASS

1 part Whiskey
1 part Campari®
fill with Orange Juice

Shake with ice and pour.

Mafia's Kiss

HIGHBALL GLASS

1 part Amaretto
1 part Sweet & Sour Mix
1 part Southern Comfort®

Shake with ice and strain over ice.

Magic Cider

HIGHBALL GLASS

½ part Goldschläger®
1 part Cherry Brandy
fill with Apple Juice

Build over ice and stir.

Magpie

HIGHBALL GLASS

1 part Cream
½ part Crème de Cacao (White)
1 part Melon Liqueur
1 part Vodka

Shake with ice and strain.

Maipo

ROCKS GLASS

splash Gin
1 part Cherry Brandy
½ part Grand Marnier®
2 parts Black Currant Juice

Shake with ice and strain over ice.

Major Bailey

ROCKS GLASS

2 splashes Lime Juice
2 splashes Lemon Juice
dash Sugar
4 Fresh Mint Leaves
2 parts Gin

Muddle all ingredients except the Gin and pour over ice. Add Gin and stir until glass is frosted. Decorate with a Mint Leaf and serve with a straw.

Malawi

HIGHBALL GLASS

1 part Vodka
½ part Crème de Coconut
½ part Passoã®
fill with Pineapple Juice

Build over ice and stir.

Malibu Bay Breeze

HIGHBALL GLASS

1½ parts Coconut Rum
1 part Cranberry Juice Cocktail
1 part Pineapple Juice

Build over ice and stir.

Malibu Coral Reef

HIGHBALL GLASS

1 part Rum
1 part Coconut Rum
1 part Cherry Juice
fill with Pineapple Juice

Build over ice and stir.

Malibu Cove

HIGHBALL GLASS

2 parts Coconut Rum
1 part Lemonade
1 part Cranberry Juice Cocktail

Build over ice and stir.

Malibu Sea Breeze

HIGHBALL GLASS

2 parts Coconut Rum
1 part Cranberry Juice Cocktail
1 part Grapefruit Juice

Build over ice and stir.

Malizia

HIGHBALL GLASS

1 part Gin
1 part Triple Sec
½ part Blue Curaçao
fill with Grapefruit Juice

Shake with ice and pour.

Mama Latte

ROCKS GLASS

2 parts RumChata
2 parts Coffee Tequila
1 part Skim Milk

Build over ice.

Man

HIGHBALL GLASS

⅔ part Vodka
splash Grenadine
1½ parts Mandarine Napoléon® Liqueur
⅔ part Lemon Juice

Build over ice and stir.

Man Overboard

HIGHBALL GLASS

2 parts Vodka
½ part Melon Liqueur
1 part Raspberry Liqueur
fill with Pineapple Juice

Shake with ice and strain over ice.

Mande-vile

ROCKS GLASS

1½ parts Light Rum
1 part Dark Rum
splash Galliano®
splash Sweetened Lime Juice
splash Cola
splash Grenadine

Shake with ice and strain over ice.

Mandeville

ROCKS GLASS

1½ parts Light Rum
1 part Dark Rum
splash Anisette
splash Cola
splash Grenadine
splash Lemon Juice

Shake with ice and strain over ice.

Maracaibo

ROCKS GLASS

2 parts Pineapple Juice
1½ parts Spiced Rum
½ part Lime Juice
¼ part Apricot Brandy

Shake with ice and strain over ice.

Marble Spice Cake

HIGHBALL GLASS

3 parts RumChata
2 parts Cake Vodka
1 part Whipped Cream Vodka

Shake with ice and strain over ice.

March Hare

HIGHBALL GLASS

1 part Vodka
1 part Wild Berry Schnapps
2 parts Lemonade
1 part Cola

Build over ice and stir.

March Madness

HIGHBALL GLASS

1 part Peach Schnapps
1½ parts Vodka
1 part Triple Sec
fill with Green Apple Gatorade®

Build over ice and stir.

Mario Driver

ROCKS GLASS

1 part Myers's® Rum
1 part Grand Marnier®
fill with Orange Juice

Shake with ice and pour.

Marionette

HIGHBALL GLASS

1 part Light Rum
1 part Cherry Heering®
1 part Apricot Brandy
1 part Dry Sake

Shake with ice and pour.

Marlboro®

HIGHBALL GLASS

1 part Sour Apple Schnapps
1 part Peach Schnapps
splash Orange Juice
splash Grenadine

Shake with ice and pour.

Marlon Brando

ROCKS GLASS

1½ parts Scotch
½ part Amaretto
1 part Cream

Shake with ice and strain.

Maserati®

HIGHBALL GLASS

1 part Citrus Vodka
1 part Cranberry Juice Cocktail
fill with Lemon-Lime Soda

Build over ice and stir.

Masked Mirror

HIGHBALL GLASS

1 part Citrus Vodka
1 part Blackberry Liqueur
2 parts Cranberry Juice Cocktail
2 parts Sweet & Sour Mix
fill with Lemon-Lime Soda

Build over ice and stir.

Massacre

HIGHBALL GLASS

2 parts Tequila
½ part Campari
fill with Ginger Ale

Build over ice and stir.

Master and Commander

ROCKS GLASS

1 part Spiced Rum
1 part Vodka
½ part Gin
½ part Whiskey
fill with Coconut Water

Shake with ice and strain over ice.

Masturbation

ROCKS GLASS

1 part Pernod®
1 part Crème de Banane
fill with Cola

Build over ice and stir.

Matador

HIGHBALL GLASS

1½ parts Tequila
2 parts Pineapple Juice
½ part Lime Juice

Shake with ice and strain over ice.

Matinee

ROCKS GLASS

1 part Gin
1 part Sambuca
¾ part Cream
1 Egg White
1 part Lime Juice

Shake with ice and strain over ice.

Matisse

ROCKS GLASS

2½ parts Orange Vodka
splash Raspberry Liqueur

Shake with ice and strain over ice.

Mattapoo Shooter

HIGHBALL GLASS

2 parts Vodka
1 part Melon Liqueur
1 part Grapefruit Juice
1 part Pineapple Juice

Shake with ice and strain.

Mayan

ROCKS GLASS

1½ parts Silver Tequila
½ part Coffee
fill with Pineapple Juice

Build over ice and stir.

Mean Green Lovemaking Machine

HIGHBALL GLASS

1 part Vodka
1 part Melon Liqueur
1 part Blue Curaçao
fill with Orange Juice

Shake with ice and pour.

Meet Joe Black

HIGHBALL GLASS

1 part Whiskey
⅔ part Amaretto
⅔ part Lemon Juice
fill with Cola

Build over ice and stir.

Mega Mixer

HIGHBALL GLASS

2 parts Vodka
1 part Cranberry Juice Cocktail
2 parts Lemonade

Build over ice and stir.

Megalomaniac

HIGHBALL GLASS

1½ parts Jim Beam®
½ part Vanilla Liqueur
splash Honey
splash Lemon Juice
fill with Apple Juice

Shake with ice and strain over ice.

Mellow Hiker

HIGHBALL GLASS

1 part Melon Liqueur
½ part Watermelon Schnapps
½ part Banana Liqueur
½ part Coconut Rum
fill with Mountain Dew®

Build over ice and stir.

Melon Ball

HIGHBALL GLASS

1 part Vodka
1 part Melon Liqueur
fill with Pineapple Juice

Shake with ice and strain over ice.

Melon Citron

ROCKS GLASS

1 part Citrus Vodka
¾ part Melon Liqueur
splash Raspberry Liqueur
1 part Grapefruit Juice

Shake with ice and strain over ice.

Melon Madness

HIGHBALL GLASS

1½ parts Dark Rum
⅔ part Melon Liqueur
½ part Grenadine
1 part Pineapple Juice
1 part Orange Juice

Shake with ice and pour.

Melon Snowball
ROCKS GLASS

3/4 part Melon Liqueur
3/4 part Citrus Vodka
1/2 part Pineapple Juice
1/4 part Cream

Shake with ice and strain over ice.

The Melville
ROCKS GLASS

1 part Rum
1 part Sambuca

Shake with ice and strain over ice.

Memories
HIGHBALL GLASS

1 part Amaretto
1 part Melon Liqueur
fill with Cream

Shake with ice and pour.

Mental Enema
HIGHBALL GLASS

1 part Melon Liqueur
1 part Peach Schnapps
1 part 151-Proof Rum
1 part Coconut Rum
fill with Pineapple Juice

Shake with ice and strain over ice.

Mental Hopscotch
ROCKS GLASS

2 parts Spiced Rum
1/2 part Crème de Banane
1/2 part Frangelico®

Shake with ice and strain over ice.

Menthe Breeze
ROCKS GLASS

1 1/2 parts Crème de Menthe (Green)
fill with Orange Juice

Shake with ice and strain over ice.

Merry Moron
HIGHBALL GLASS

2 parts Raspberry Liqueur
2 parts Vodka
2 parts Grape Juice
fill with Orange Juice

Shake with ice and pour.

Merry Mule
HIGHBALL GLASS

1 part Maraschino Liqueur
1 1/2 parts Peach Schnapps
1 part Anisette
1 part Club Soda

Build over ice and stir.

Metrosexual
ROCKS GLASS

1 part Orange Rum
1 part Mango Rum
1/2 part Banana Liqueur
fill with Pineapple Juice

Build over ice and stir.

Mexican Iceberg
ROCKS GLASS

1 1/2 parts Canadian Whisky
1 1/2 parts Gold Tequila
1/2 part Triple Sec
splash Lime Juice

Shake with ice and strain over ice.

Mexican Gold
ROCKS GLASS

1 1/2 parts Tequila
3/4 part Galliano®

Shake with ice and strain over ice.

Mexican Grasshopper
HIGHBALL GLASS

1 part Crème de Menthe (White)
1 part Coffee Liqueur
1 part Cream

Shake with ice and strain over ice.

Mexican Madras

ROCKS GLASS

1 part Tequila Gold
3 parts Cranberry Juice Cocktail
1 part Orange Juice
splash Lime Juice

Shake with ice and strain over ice.

Mexican Rose

HIGHBALL GLASS

1 part Tequila
1 part Strawberry Liqueur
1 part Cherry Juice
fill with Milk

Shake with ice and strain over ice.

Mexicano

HIGHBALL GLASS

2 parts Light Rum
2 splashes Kümmel
2 splashes Orange Juice
4 dashes Angostura® Bitters

Shake with ice and strain over ice.

Midwinter

HIGHBALL GLASS

splash Triple Sec
1 part Dark Rum
½ part Lemon Juice
splash Passion Fruit Nectar
½ part Honey

Build over ice and stir.

Midnight

BRANDY SNIFTER

1 part Black Sambuca
1 part Vodka

Build over ice.

Midnight Express

ROCKS GLASS

1½ parts Dark Rum
½ part Cointreau®
¾ part Lime Juice
splash Sweet & Sour Mix

Shake with ice and strain over ice.

Midnight Manx

ROCKS GLASS

1 part Coffee Liqueur
1 part Irish Cream Liqueur
splash Goldschläger®
1 part Heavy Cream
1 part Hazlenut Coffee

Shake with ice and strain over ice.

Midnight Train to Georgia

HIGHBALL GLASS

1½ parts Whiskey
1 part Peach Schnapps
1 part Orange Juice
1 part Cranberry Juice Cocktail

Build over ice and stir.

A Midsummer Night's Dream

HIGHBALL GLASS

2 parts Vodka
1 part Kirschwasser
½ part Strawberry Liqueur
2 parts Strawberry Puree

Shake with ice and strain over ice.

Mikado

ROCKS GLASS

1½ parts Brandy
½ part Triple Sec
splash Crème de Noyaux
splash Grenadine
dash Bitters

Shake with ice and strain over ice.

Mike Tyson

HIGHBALL GLASS

1 part Tia Maria®
1 part Jägermeister®
1 part Pernod®

Shake with ice and strain over ice.

Milky Way®

HIGHBALL GLASS

1 part Irish Cream Liqueur
1 part Butterscotch Schnapps
fill with Milk

Shake with ice and pour.

Millennium

HIGHBALL GLASS

1 part Cinnamon Schnapps
1 part Blue Curaçao
fill with Lemon-Lime Soda

Build over ice and stir.

Mimi

HIGHBALL GLASS

1 part Cherry Brandy
1 part Crème de Banane
1 part Dark Rum

Shake with ice and strain over ice.

The Mind Bender

ROCKS GLASS

1 part Jack Daniel's®
1 part Jim Beam®
1 part Wild Turkey 101®
fill with Orange Juice

Shake with ice and strain over ice.

Mint Chip

ROCKS GLASS

1 part Peppermint Schnapps
1 part Coffee Liqueur

Shake with ice and pour.

Mir

HIGHBALL GLASS

1 part Vodka
1 part Jack Daniel's®
fill with Cola

Build over ice and stir.

Missing Fortune

ROCKS GLASS

1 part Peach Schnapps
1 part Southern Comfort®
1 part Cranberry Juice Cocktail
1 part Orange Juice
3 parts Club Soda

Build over ice and stir.

Mission Accomplished

HIGHBALL GLASS

2 parts Vodka
1 part Triple Sec
splash Lime Juice
splash Grenadine

Shake with ice and strain over ice.

Mississippi Rum Punch

HIGHBALL GLASS

1 part Rum
1 part Cherry Juice
1 part Orange Juice
1 part Pineapple Juice
1 part Cola

Build over ice and stir.

Misty Dew

ROCKS GLASS

1 part Whiskey
1 part Irish Mist®

Shake with ice and strain over ice.

Mix-O

BRANDY SNIFTER

3/4 part Southern Comfort®
3/4 part Strawberry Syrup
1/4 part Grenadine

Shake with ice and strain.

Moat Float

ROCKS GLASS

1 part Vodka
1 part Amaretto
fill with Cola

Build over ice and stir.

Mockingbird

WHITE WINE GLASS

1 part Silver Tequila
1 part Triple Sec
1/2 part Grapefruit Juice
1/2 part Sweet & Sour Mix

Shake with ice and strain over ice.

Mocos
HIGHBALL GLASS

1 part Melon Liqueur
1 part Crème de Banane
splash Irish Cream Liqueur
1 part Coconut Rum

Shake with ice and strain over ice.

Molly Brown
HIGHBALL GLASS

½ part Blue Curaçao
1 part Aquavit
½ part Lime Juice

Shake with ice and strain over ice.

Mombasa
CHAMPAGNE FLUTE

1 part Light Rum
1 part Sweet Vermouth
½ part Crème de Cassis
1½ parts Grapefruit Juice
1½ parts Pineapple Juice

Shake with ice and strain.

Mona Lisa
HIGHBALL GLASS

2 parts Amaretto
fill with Pineapple Juice
1 part Cream

Shake with ice and pour.

Monkey Doo
HIGHBALL GLASS

3 parts Banana Liqueur
fill with Mountain Dew®

Build over ice and stir.

Monkey See, Monkey Doo
ROCKS GLASS

1½ parts Orange Juice
½ part Crème de Banane
½ part Dark Rum

Shake with ice and strain over ice.

Monkey Wrench
ROCKS GLASS

1 part Light Rum
½ part Orange Juice
¼ part Sweet & Sour Mix
splash Grenadine

Shake with ice and strain over ice.

Monkey Wrench #2
ROCKS GLASS

1½ parts Light Rum
3 parts Grapefruit Juice
dash Bitters

Shake with ice and strain over ice.

Monk's Man
ROCKS GLASS

1 part Silver Tequila
1 part Frangelico®

Shake with ice and pour.

Montana Fire
HIGHBALL GLASS

2 parts Cinnamon Schnapps
2 parts Peppermint Schnapps
½ part Tabasco® Sauce
1 part Tequila

Shake with ice and pour.

Montana Smoothie
ROCKS GLASS

1 part Butterscotch Schnapps
1 part Canadian Whisky

Pour ingredients into glass neat (do not chill).

Monte Carlo
HIGHBALL GLASS

1½ parts Rye Whiskey
½ part Bénédictine®
4 dashes Angostura® Bitters

Shake with ice and pour.

Monterey Bay

HIGHBALL GLASS

1 part Vodka
1 part Melon Liqueur
1 part Cherry Juice
1 part Banana Juice
fill with Orange Juice

Shake with ice and pour.

Montreal Gin Sour

ROCKS GLASS

1 part Gin
1 part Lemon Juice
dash Powdered Sugar
1 Egg White

Shake with ice and strain over ice. Garnish with a Lemon Slice.

Moo Moo

HIGHBALL GLASS

1 part Irish Cream Liqueur
1 part Crème de Cacao (White)
fill with Cream

Shake with ice and pour.

Moonlight

ROCKS GLASS

2 parts Apple Brandy
½ part Lemon Juice
dash Powdered Sugar

Shake with ice and strain over ice.

Moonraker

HIGHBALL GLASS

1 part Rum
1 part Blue Curaçao
fill with Pineapple Juice

Build over ice.

Moon River

HIGHBALL GLASS

1 part Vodka
1 part Blue Curaçao
⅔ part Lemon Juice
fill with Grape Juice (White)

Shake with ice and pour.

Moose Gooser

HIGHBALL GLASS

1 part Crème de Banane
1 part Blue Curaçao
splash 151-Proof Rum

Build over ice and stir.

Morango

HIGHBALL GLASS

1 part Vodka
1 part Strawberry Daiquiri Mix
1 part Lemonade
1 part Orange Juice
1 part Cranberry Juice Cocktail
1 part Wild Berry Schnapps

Build over ice.

More Orgasms

HIGHBALL GLASS

1 part Irish Cream Liqueur
1 part Vodka
1 part Coconut Rum

Shake with ice and pour.

Morgan Madras

HIGHBALL GLASS

1¼ parts Spiced Rum
fill with Orange Juice
splash Cranberry Juice Cocktail

Shake with ice and pour.

Morgan's Booty

HIGHBALL GLASS

½ part Goldschläger®
1 part Spiced Rum
⅔ part Lime Juice
fill with Grapefruit Juice

Shake with ice and strain over ice.

Morning Glory Fizz

HIGHBALL GLASS

2 parts Scotch
splash Anisette
dash Powdered Sugar
1 Egg White
fill with Seltzer

Shake all but Seltzer with ice and strain. Top with Seltzer. Garnish with a Lemon Wedge.

Morning Macintyre

HIGHBALL GLASS

½ part Blackberry Liqueur
½ part Raspberry Liqueur
⅔ part Frangelico®
⅔ part Irish Cream Liqueur
fill with Milk

Shake with ice and strain over ice.

Morro

ROCKS GLASS

1 part Gin
½ part Dark Rum
splash Lime Juice
splash Pineapple Juice
½ tsp Sugar

Shake with ice and strain over ice.

Moscow Dawn

WHITE WINE GLASS

2 parts Vodka
1 part Crème de Menthe (White)
¼ part Triple Sec

Shake with ice and strain.

Mother

HIGHBALL GLASS

1 part Vodka
1 part Gin
1 part Sweet & Sour Mix
1 part Grenadine

Shake with ice and strain over ice.

Mother's Love

HIGHBALL GLASS

1 part Sour Apple Schnapps
1 part Sour Watermelon Schnapps
1 part Lemon-Lime Soda

Build over ice and stir.

Motor Oil

ROCKS GLASS

1 part Jägermeister®
½ part Peppermint Schnapps
½ part Goldschläger®
½ part Coconut Rum

Shake with ice and pour.

Motown Smash

HIGHBALL GLASS

1 part Spiced Rum
1 part Raspberry Liqueur
1 part Pineapple Juice
1 part Lemon-Lime Soda

Build over ice and stir.

Mountain Cider High

BEER MUG

1 part Vodka
1 part Apple Cider
1 part Mountain Dew®

Build over ice and stir.

Mountain Sunset

HIGHBALL GLASS

2 parts Wild Berry Schnapps
1 part Grenadine
fill with Mountain Dew®

Build over ice and stir.

Mountaineer on Acid

HIGHBALL GLASS

1 part Jägermeister®
1 part Coconut Rum
1 part Pineapple Juice

Shake with ice and strain over ice.

Mousse
HIGHBALL GLASS
2 parts Apricot Brandy
splash Blue Curaçao
Build over ice and stir.

Mud Puddle
HIGHBALL GLASS
1 part Vanilla Vodka
2/3 part Coffee Liqueur
1/2 part Irish Cream Liqueur
1 part Cream
Shake with ice and strain over ice.

Muddy Jake
HIGHBALL GLASS
1 1/2 parts Amaretto
1 part Jägermeister®
fill with Lemon-Lime Soda
Build over ice and stir.

Mudslide
HIGHBALL GLASS
2 parts Vodka
2 parts Coffee Liqueur
2 parts Irish Cream Liqueur
Shake with ice and pour.

Muff Diver
HIGHBALL GLASS
1 1/4 parts Crème de Cacao (White)
1 1/4 parts Cream
1 part Lime Juice
1 part Lemon Juice
Shake with ice and strain over ice.

Mulligan Stew
HIGHBALL GLASS
1 part Irish Cream Liqueur
1/2 part Crème de Cacao (Dark)
1/2 part Amaretto
splash 151-Proof Rum
Build over ice and stir.

Mumbo Jumbo
ROCKS GLASS
1 1/2 parts Dark Rum
1/2 part Applejack
1/2 part Lemon Juice
dash Sugar
dash Cinnamon
dash Ground Nutmeg
Shake with ice and strain over ice.

Mummy Dust
HIGHBALL GLASS
2 parts Goldschläger®
2 parts Lemonade
1 part Cola
Build over ice and stir.

Muppet®
HIGHBALL GLASS
2 parts Tequila
1 1/2 parts Lemon-Lime Soda
Build over ice and stir.

Muscle Relaxer
ROCKS GLASS
2 parts Canadian Whisky
1 part Amaretto
1/2 part Irish Cream Liqueur
Shake with ice and strain over ice.

Mustang Sally
HIGHBALL GLASS
1 part Vodka
1 part Strawberry Liqueur
1 part Raspberry Liqueur
fill with Lemonade
Shake with ice and pour.

Mutual Orgasm
HIGHBALL GLASS
2 parts Amaretto
1 part Crème de Cacao (White)
1 part Vodka
fill with Half and Half
Shake with ice and pour.

MVP

HIGHBALL GLASS

1 part Melon Liqueur
1 part Coconut Rum
1 part Vodka
1 part Pineapple Juice

Shake with ice and strain.

Mystical Marquee

HIGHBALL GLASS

1 part Jack Daniel's®
1 part Peach Schnapps
1 part Vodka
fill with Lemon Juice

Shake with ice and strain over ice.

Nail Puller

HIGHBALL GLASS

2 parts Coffee Liqueur
1 part Vodka
fill with Dr. Pepper®

Build over ice and stir.

Napoleon on the Back

ROCKS GLASS

1 part Dark Rum
1 part Cognac

Shake with ice and strain over ice.

Napoli Citric Flip

HIGHBALL GLASS

1 part Silver Tequila
1/2 part Triple Sec
2/3 part Galliano®
fill with Orange Juice

Shake with ice and strain over ice.

Narragansett

ROCKS GLASS

2 parts Bourbon
1 part Sweet Vermouth
1/12 part Anisette

Build over ice and stir.

Narcissist

HIGHBALL GLASS

1 1/2 parts Raspberry Liqueur
1/2 part Vanilla Liqueur
fill with Apple Juice

Shake with ice and strain over ice.

National Aquarium

HIGHBALL GLASS

1/2 part Rum
1/2 part Vodka
1/2 part Gin
1/2 part Blue Curaçao
2 parts Sweet & Sour Mix
fill with Lemon-Lime Soda

Build over ice and stir.

Naval Broadside

HIGHBALL GLASS

1 part Fireball Cinnamon Whiskey
1 part Rum

Build over ice and stir.

Navsky at Noon

HIGHBALL GLASS

1 part Vodka
1 part Blackberry Liqueur
1 part Orange Juice
1/2 part Lime Juice
splash Grenadine
fill with Sweet & Sour Mix

Shake with ice and strain over ice.

Nazzy Baby

HIGHBALL GLASS

1 part Coconut Rum
1 part Peach Schnapps
1 part Vodka
splash Lemon Juice
fill with Orange Juice

Shake with ice and pour.

Near Death

HIGHBALL GLASS

1 part Jägermeister
1 part Triple Sec
1 part Vodka
1 part Cranberry Juice
dash Bitters

Shake with ice and strain.

Neck Roll

HIGHBALL GLASS

2 parts Jack Daniel's®
fill with Lemonade

Build over ice and stir.

Neckbrace

HIGHBALL GLASS

2 parts Light Rum
½ part Triple Sec
fill with Orange Juice

Build over ice and stir.

Neiler

HIGHBALL GLASS

1 part Banana Liqueur
1 part Melon Liqueur
fill with Milk

Shake with ice and pour.

Nelson Special

HIGHBALL GLASS

1½ parts Gin
1 part Cranberry Juice Cocktail
1 part Tonic Water

Build over ice and stir.

Neon

HIGHBALL GLASS

1 part Gin
1 part Raspberry Liqueur
1 part Lemon Juice

Shake with ice and strain over ice.

Neon Chrysanthemum

HIGHBALL GLASS

1 part Blue Curaçao
1 part Coconut Rum
1 part Mango Rum
1 part Vodka
1 part Orange Juice
1 part Pineapple Juice

Shake with ice and strain over ice.

Neon Iguana

HIGHBALL GLASS

1 part Spiced Rum
1 part Coconut Rum
1 part Blue Curaçao
1½ parts Lime Juice
fill with Orange Juice

Shake with ice and strain over ice.

Neon Nights

HIGHBALL GLASS

1½ parts Coconut Rum
1 part Melon Liqueur
1 part Orange Juice
1 part Pineapple Juice
1 part Cranberry Juice Cocktail

Shake with ice and pour.

Neon Smurf®

HIGHBALL GLASS

¾ part Blue Curaçao
¾ part Blueberry Schnapps
2 parts Lemon-Lime Soda
1 part Sweet & Sour Mix

Build over ice and stir.

Netherland

ROCKS GLASS

1 part Triple Sec
1 part Brandy
dash Bitters

Shake with ice and strain over ice.

New Moon

ROCKS GLASS

1½ parts Gin
1½ parts Triple Sec
2½ parts Tonic Water
½ part Rose's Lime Juice

Shake with ice and strain over ice.

New Orleans Fizz

HIGHBALL GLASS

1 part Rum
1 part Simple Syrup
1 part Sweet & Sour Mix
1 part Orange Juice
1 part Lemon-Lime Soda

Build over ice and stir.

New World

HIGHBALL GLASS

1½ parts Rye Whiskey
½ part Lime Juice
splash Grenadine

Shake with ice and strain over ice.

New York

ROCKS GLASS

1 part Rye Whiskey
½ part Simple Syrup
splash Grenadine

Shake with ice and strain over ice.

New York Sour

ROCKS GLASS

2 parts Whiskey
½ part Lemon Juice
dash Sugar
splash Claret

Shake with ice and pour. Garnish with a Lemon Slice and a Maraschino Cherry.

Newman

HIGHBALL GLASS

1 part Gin
1 part Ginger Ale
1 part Lemon Juice
splash Orange Juice

Build over ice and stir.

Newport Punch

HIGHBALL GLASS

1 part Amaretto
1 part Peach Schnapps
1 part Southern Comfort®
1 part Ketel One® Vodka
splash Cranberry Juice Cocktail
splash Orange Juice

Build over ice and stir.

Night Bird

HIGHBALL GLASS

1 part Crème de Coconut
½ part Coffee Liqueur
½ part Butterscotch Schnapps
fill with Cream

Shake with ice and strain over ice.

Night Vampire

HIGHBALL GLASS

1½ parts Sweet Vermouth
1½ parts Scotch
1 part Orange Juice
1 part Cherry Brandy

Shake with ice and strain over ice.

Nightingale

HIGHBALL GLASS

1 part Banana Liqueur
½ part Blue Curaçao
1 part Cream
1 Egg White

Shake with ice and strain over ice.

A Night in Old Mandalay

HIGHBALL GLASS

1 part Light Rum
1 part Añejo Rum
1 part Orange Juice
½ part Lemon Juice
3 parts Ginger Ale

Shake with ice and strain over ice. Garnish with a Lemon Twist.

Nightmare Shooter

ROCKS GLASS

1 part Gin
1 part Cherry Brandy
1 part Orange Juice

Shake with ice and strain over ice.

Nikita

ROCKS GLASS

1 part Coconut Rum
1 part Key Lime Liqueur
½ part Blue Curaçao
1 part Piña Colada mix
fill with Sweet & Sour Mix

Shake with ice and strain over ice.

Nilla® Wafer

HIGHBALL GLASS

2 parts Vodka
2 parts Cream
½ part Vanilla Liqueur
½ dash Brown Sugar

Shake with ice and strain over ice.

Ninety-Nine Palms

HIGHBALL GLASS

1 part Vodka
1 part Peach Schnapps
1 part Piña Colada Mix
1 part Lemonade
1 part Pineapple Juice

Shake with ice and pour.

Ninja Turtle

HIGHBALL GLASS

1½ parts Gin
½ part Blue Curaçao
fill with Orange Juice

Shake with ice and pour.

No Way

HIGHBALL GLASS

½ part Gin
½ part Grand Marnier®
½ part Light Rum
½ part Peach Schnapps
½ part Vodka
1 part Cranberry Juice Cocktail
1 part Sweet & Sour Mix

Shake with ice and pour.

Noche de Amor

HIGHBALL GLASS

1 part Brandy
1 part Crème de Banane
1 part Blue Curaçao

Build over ice and stir.

Noche de Phoof

HIGHBALL GLASS

1 part Vodka
½ part Light Rum
½ part Crown Royal® Whiskey
1 part Pineapple Juice
1 part Cranberry Juice Cocktail
splash Melon Liqueur

Shake with ice and strain over ice.

Nokia

CHAMPAGNE FLUTE

1 part Blackberry Liqueur
½ part Vodka
1½ parts Milk
1 Egg Yolk

Shake with ice and strain.

North Dakota Special

HIGHBALL GLASS

1 part Wild Turkey® Bourbon
1 part Black Velvet® Whiskey
1 part Canadian Whisky
1 part Southern Comfort®
1 part Jack Daniel's®
fill with Cola

Build over ice and stir.

North Polar

HIGHBALL GLASS

1 part Gin
1 part Cointreau®
1 part Campari®

Build over ice and stir.

Nothing Is Eternal

HIGHBALL GLASS

1½ parts Orange Vodka
½ part Apricot Brandy
½ part Lemon Juice
fill with Orange Juice
dash Bitters

Build over ice and stir.

Notre Dame Pick-Me-Up

HIGHBALL GLASS

1 part Vodka
1 part Light Rum
1 part Triple Sec
fill with Orange Juice
dash Powdered Sugar

Build over ice and stir.

Notte a Mosca

HIGHBALL GLASS

1½ parts Vodka
½ part Campari®
splash Blue Curaçao

Shake with ice and strain over ice.

Nouvelle Vague

HIGHBALL GLASS

½ part Peach Schnapps
2 parts Calvados Apple Brandy

Shake with ice and strain over ice.

Nuclear Blue

HIGHBALL GLASS

½ part Blue Curaçao
½ part Southern Comfort
½ part Wild Turkey Bourbon
fill with Sweet & Sour Mix

Shake with ice and strain over ice.

Nuclear Kool-Aid®

HIGHBALL GLASS

1½ parts Southern Comfort®
¾ part Amaretto
1 part Lemon-Lime Soda
1 part Cranberry Juice Cocktail

Shake with ice and pour.

Nuclear Screwdriver

HIGHBALL GLASS

1 part Vodka
1 part Grand Marnier®
fill with Orange Juice

Build over ice and stir.

Nude Beach

HIGHBALL GLASS

2 parts Lemon Vodka
1 part Triple Sec
1 part Cranberry Juice
splash Lime Juice

Shake with ice and strain over ice.

Null and Void

HIGHBALL GLASS

1 part Vodka
½ part Wild Berry Schnapps
½ part Peach Schnapps
splash Southern Comfort®
fill with Fruit Punch

Shake with ice and pour.

Numbnut

ROCKS GLASS

1½ parts Dark Rum
½ part Galliano®
2 splashes Crème de Cacao (Dark)

Shake with ice and strain over ice.

Nutcracker

HIGHBALL GLASS

1 part Vodka
1 part Coffee Liqueur
1 part Irish Cream Liqueur
1 part Amaretto

Shake with ice and strain over ice.

Nutty Belgian

ROCKS GLASS

1 part Chocolate Liqueur
1 part Frangelico®
½ part Vodka

Shake with ice and strain over ice.

Nutty Russian

HIGHBALL GLASS

1 part Vodka
1 part Frangelico®
1 part Coffee Liqueur

Shake with ice and strain over ice.

Nyquil®

ROCKS GLASS

2 parts Triple Sec
1 part Sambuca
1 part Grenadine

Shake with ice and strain over ice.

Oaxaca

ROCKS GLASS

2 parts Gin
1 part Grapefruit Juice
1 part Orange Juice
2 dashes Orange Bitters

Shake with ice and strain over ice.

Ocean Water

HIGHBALL GLASS

¾ part Blue Curaçao
1 part Coconut Rum
fill with Lemon-Lime Soda

Shake with ice and strain over ice.

October Sky

HIGHBALL GLASS

1 part Vodka
½ part Wild Berry Schnapps
2 parts Lemonade
1 part Orange Juice

Shake with ice and pour.

Octopus in the Water

HIGHBALL GLASS

1 part Vodka
1 part Blue Curaçao
1 part Lemonade
1 part Margarita Mix
1 part Wild Berry Schnapps

Build over ice and stir.

Odwits

HIGHBALL GLASS

1½ parts Mezcal
1½ parts Vodka
1 part Southern Comfort®
splash Galliano®
fill with Orange Juice

Shake with ice and pour.

Oh Oh

HIGHBALL GLASS

1 part Light Rum
1 part Blue Curaçao
1 part Limeade
1 part Orange Juice
½ part Passion Fruit Nectar

Shake with ice and strain over ice.

Oil Spill

HIGHBALL GLASS

1 part Vodka
1 part Blue Curaçao
1 part Irish Cream Liqueur
fill with Cola

Build over ice and stir.

Okinawa Special

HIGHBALL GLASS

1 part Coconut Rum
1 part Light Rum
1 part Vodka
1 part Orange Juice
1 part Pineapple Juice

Shake with ice and pour.

Oklahoma Bulldog

HIGHBALL GLASS

1 part Tequila
1 part Coffee Liqueur
2 parts Cream
1 part Cola

Build over ice and stir.

Old Bastard

ROCKS GLASS

1½ parts Scotch
½ part Triple Sec
1 part Orange Juice

Shake with ice and strain over ice.

Old Dirty Surprise

HIGHBALL GLASS

1 part Vodka
½ part Bacardi® Limón Rum
½ part Melon Liqueur
fill with Pineapple Juice

Shake with ice and strain over ice.

Old Green and Gold

CHAMPAGNE FLUTE

1 part Galliano®
1 part Tequila
splash Blue Curaçao

Build over ice.

Old Hag's Cackle

HIGHBALL GLASS

1 part Vodka
1 part Raspberry Liqueur
1 part Lemonade
1 part Cola

Build over ice and stir.

Old James

ROCKS GLASS

1½ parts Triple Sec
1 part Light Rum
fill with Banana Juice

Shake with ice and strain over ice.

Old Nick

ROCKS GLASS

1 part Rye Whiskey
¼ part Orange Juice

Shake with ice and strain over ice.

Old Pal

ROCKS GLASS

1 part Dry Vermouth
1 part Whiskey
1 part Campari®

Shake with ice and strain over ice.

Old Pirate

ROCKS GLASS

1½ parts Vodka
1 part Coconut Rum
1 part Irish Cream Liqueur
½ part Orange Juice
½ part Pineapple Juice
½ part Mango Juice

Shake with ice and pour.

Old Spice®

ROCKS GLASS

1 part Gin
1 part Vodka
1 part Applejack

Shake with ice and strain over ice.

Old Yellow Pages

ROCKS GLASS

1½ parts Gin
splash Pernod®
2 parts Pineapple Juice

Shake with ice and strain over ice.

On Deck

HIGHBALL GLASS

1 part Light Rum
1 part Melon Liqueur
½ part Sloe Gin
1 part Orange Juice
1 part Pineapple Juice

Shake with ice and strain over ice.

One Bad Mutha

HIGHBALL GLASS

2 parts Whiskey
1 part Cranberry Juice Cocktail
fill with Cola

Build over ice and stir.

One Exciting Night

WHITE WINE GLASS

1 part Gin
1 part Dry Vermouth
1 part Sweet Vermouth
1 part Orange Juice

Shake with ice and pour.

Ooh-La-La

HIGHBALL GLASS

1 part Vodka
1 part Cherry Juice
1 part Piña Colada Mix
2 parts Lemonade
1 part Cola

Build over ice and stir.

Opaline

HIGHBALL GLASS

1 part Gin
splash Blue Curaçao
splash Pear Liqueur

Shake with ice and strain over ice.

Orange Bliss

ROCKS GLASS

1½ parts Orange Vodka
1 part Grand Marnier®
fill with Orange Juice

Shake with ice and strain over ice.

Orange Bonnie

HIGHBALL GLASS

2 parts RumChata
1 part Orange Juice

Shake with ice and strain over ice.

Orange Clockwork

ROCKS GLASS

1½ parts Orange Vodka
½ part Triple Sec
½ part Orange Juice
¼ part Lime Juice

Shake with ice and strain over ice.

Orange Crush

ROCKS GLASS

3 parts Triple Sec
1 part Cranberry Juice Cocktail

Shake with ice and strain over ice.

Orange Freestyle

HIGHBALL GLASS

1 part Gin
1 part Dry Vermouth
fill with Orange Juice

Shake with ice and pour.

Orange Glow

HIGHBALL GLASS

½ part Blue Curaçao
½ part Triple Sec
1 part Remy Martin® VSOP
fill with Orange Juice

Shake with ice and pour.

Orange Oasis

HIGHBALL GLASS

1½ parts Gin
½ part Cherry Brandy
2 parts Orange Juice
fill with Ginger Ale

Build over ice and stir.

Orange Outrage

HIGHBALL GLASS

1½ parts Dark Rum
½ part Triple Sec
½ part Vanilla Liqueur
fill with Orange Juice

Build over ice and stir.

Orange Rum Daiquiri

HIGHBALL GLASS

1 part Rum
1 part Triple Sec
2 parts Sweet & Sour Mix
1 part Orange Juice

Shake with ice and pour.

Orange Smartie®

HIGHBALL GLASS

1 part Vodka
1 part Coffee Liqueur
1 part Triple Sec
fill with Orange Juice

Shake with ice and pour.

Orange Spew

HIGHBALL GLASS

2 parts Rum
1 part Cranberry Juice Cocktail
1 part Orange Juice

Shake with ice and pour.

Orange Surprise

HIGHBALL GLASS

1 part Vodka
1 part Peach Schnapps
2 parts Sweet & Sour Mix
fill with Lemon-Lime Soda

Build over ice and stir.

Orange Whip

HIGHBALL GLASS

1 part Rum
1 part Vodka
1 part Cream
fill with Orange Juice

Shake with ice and strain over ice.

Orchard

HIGHBALL GLASS

2 parts Raspberry Liqueur
1 part Apple Brandy
1 part Cherry Brandy
1 part Orange Juice

Shake with ice and strain over ice.

Orchard Punch

HIGHBALL GLASS

1 part Rum
1 part Cherry Juice
1 part Peach Nectar
1 part Orange Juice
1 part Pineapple Juice
1 part Cranberry Juice Cocktail

Shake with ice and pour.

Orchid

HIGHBALL GLASS

1 part Vodka
1 part Peach Schnapps
1 part Cherry Juice
1 part Lemonade
1 part Orange Juice
1 part Cranberry Juice Cocktail

Shake with ice and pour.

Orlando Amethyst

ROCKS GLASS

1 part Gin
½ part Chambord®
fill with Pineapple Juice

Shake with ice and pour.

Orlando Sun

HIGHBALL GLASS

1 part Light Rum
½ part Vodka
½ part Grand Marnier®
1 part Orange Juice
¼ part Lemon Juice

Shake with ice and strain over ice.

Oscar's Flame

ROCKS GLASS

1½ parts Amaretto
½ part Crème de Banane
splash Strawberry Liqueur

Shake with ice and strain over ice.

Out of the Blue

ROCKS GLASS

½ part Vodka
½ part Blueberry Schnapps
½ part Blue Curaçao
1 part Club Soda
splash Sweet & Sour Mix

Build over ice and stir.

Outrigger

HIGHBALL GLASS

1 part Peach Brandy
1 part Vodka
1 part Pineapple Juice
splash Lime Juice

Shake with ice and strain over ice.

Overdose

HIGHBALL GLASS

1½ parts Gin
splash Crème de Banane
splash Kiwi Schnapps
splash Raspberry Liqueur
splash Campari®

Build over ice and stir.

Oxygen Mask

HIGHBALL GLASS

2 parts Melon Liqueur
1 part Amaretto
3 parts Orange Juice
2 parts Pineapple Juice

Shake with ice and strain over ice.

Oxymoron

ROCKS GLASS

1 part Vodka
½ part Lemon Juice
splash Honey

Shake with ice and strain over ice.

P.T.O.

HIGHBALL GLASS

1½ parts Dark Rum
½ part Vodka
½ part Triple Sec
fill with Orange Juice

Shake with ice and strain over ice.

Pacific Blue

HIGHBALL GLASS

1 part Crème de Banane
1 part Blue Curaçao
splash Vodka
splash Crème de Coconut

Build over ice and stir.

Pacific Pacifier

ROCKS GLASS

1 part Triple Sec
½ part Crème de Banane
½ part Light Cream

Shake with ice and strain over ice.

Paducah Punch

HIGHBALL GLASS

½ part Light Rum
1 part Amaretto
1 part Maraschino Liqueur
2 parts Pineapple Juice
2 parts Orange Juice
2 parts Grapefruit Juice

Shake with ice and strain over ice.

Paisano

HIGHBALL GLASS

1 part Vodka
1 part Frangelico®
fill with Milk

Shake with ice and pour.

Pajama Jackhammer

HIGHBALL GLASS

1 part Vodka
1 part Blue Curaçao
1 part Peach Schnapps
fill with Pineapple Juice

Shake with ice and strain over ice.

Palisades Park

HIGHBALL GLASS

1 part Vodka
1 part Peach Schnapps
1 part Banana Juice
2 parts Lemonade
1 part Orange Juice

Shake with ice and pour.

Palmetto

HIGHBALL GLASS

1½ parts Light Rum
½ part Sweet Vermouth
2 dashes Orange Bitters

Shake with ice and strain over ice.

Pamplemousse

ROCKS GLASS

1 part Whiskey
1 part Southern Comfort®
1 part Pineapple Juice
2 parts Grapefruit Juice

Shake with ice and strain over ice.

Panama Jack

HIGHBALL GLASS

2 parts Coconut Rum
1 part Banana Juice
1 part Orange Juice
1 part Pineapple Juice

Build over ice and stir.

Panama Red

ROCKS GLASS

1 part Tequila Reposado
¼ part Grenadine
¼ part Sweet & Sour Mix

Shake with ice and strain over ice.

Panda King

HIGHBALL GLASS

½ part Crème de Cacao (White)
1½ parts Amaretto
1½ parts Milk
1½ parts Club Soda

Shake with ice and strain over ice.

Panic on Board

HIGHBALL GLASS

1½ parts Plum Brandy
⅔ part Apricot Brandy
splash Goldschläger®
fill with Raspberry Seltzer

Build over ice and stir.

Panther

ROCKS GLASS

2 parts Tequila
1 part Sweet & Sour Mix

Shake with ice and strain over ice.

Panty Ripper

ROCKS GLASS

1 part Coconut Rum
splash Cherry Juice
2 parts Pineapple Juice

Shake with ice and strain over ice.

Paradise Bliss

HIGHBALL GLASS

1½ parts Vodka
1½ parts Coconut Rum
1 part Cranberry Juice Cocktail
1 part Pineapple Juice

Shake with ice and pour.

Paradise Punch

HIGHBALL GLASS

1 part Coconut Rum
2 parts Cranberry Juice Cocktail
1 part Pineapple Juice

Build over ice and stir.

Parfait Punch

HIGHBALL GLASS

1 part Parfait Amour
2½ parts Light Rum
dash Powdered Sugar
fill with Milk

Shake with ice and strain.

Paris Burning

BRANDY SNIFTER

1 part Raspberry Liqueur
1 part Hennessy®

Build in the glass with no ice.

Parisian Blond

ROCKS GLASS

1 part Light Rum
1 part Dark Rum
1 part Triple Sec

Shake with ice and strain over ice.

Park West

ROCKS GLASS

1½ parts Gin
2 parts Grapefruit Juice
2 parts Pineapple Juice

Shake with ice and strain over ice.

Parrot

ROCKS GLASS

1 part Vodka
1 part Gin
3 splashes Tabasco® Sauce

Shake with ice and strain over ice.

Partly Cloudy

HIGHBALL GLASS

1 part Vodka
1 part Blue Curaçao
1 part Piña Colada Mix
fill with Lemonade

Shake with ice and pour.

Pascal's Passion

WHITE WINE GLASS

1 part Amaretto
1 part Irish Cream Liqueur
½ part Blue Curaçao
fill with Milk

Shake with ice and pour.

Passion Cup

WHITE WINE GLASS

2 parts Vodka
2 parts Orange Juice
1 part Passion Fruit Juice
½ part Pineapple Juice
½ part Cream of Coconut

Shake with ice and strain over ice.

Passionate Slopes

HIGHBALL GLASS

1½ parts Southern Comfort®
1½ parts Dark Rum
2 parts Passion Fruit Liqueur
fill with Iced Tea
splash Lemon Juice

Build over ice and stir.

Pastis Rouge

HIGHBALL GLASS

splash Grenadine
⅔ part Pastis
fill with Water

Build over ice and stir.

Paul and Jill

ROCKS GLASS

1 part Vodka
splash Lime Juice
fill with Tonic Water
splash Cranberry Juice

Build over ice. For Jill.

Pavlova

ROCKS GLASS

1 part Vodka
½ part Crème de Cacao (White)
½ part Cream

Shake with ice and strain over ice.

Peach Blossom

HIGHBALL GLASS

2 parts Gin
splash Lemon Juice
dash Powdered Sugar
½ part Peach Schnapps
fill with Seltzer

Shake all but Seltzer with ice and strain. Top with Seltzer.

Peach Crush

ROCKS GLASS

1 part Vodka
1 part Peach Schnapps
1½ parts Sweet & Sour Mix

Shake with ice and strain over ice.

Peach Fuzz

HIGHBALL GLASS

1 part Peach Schnapps
1 part Cranberry Juice Cocktail

Shake with ice and pour.

Peach Pit

ROCKS GLASS

1 part Peach Schnapps
1 part Apple Brandy

Shake with ice and strain over ice.

Peacher

HIGHBALL GLASS

⅔ part Peach Schnapps
⅔ part Citrus Vodka
1 part Lemon-Lime Soda
1 part Club Soda

Build over ice and stir.

Peacock

CHAMPAGNE FLUTE

1 part Crème de Cacao (White)
1 part Parfait Amour
1 part Triple Sec
½ part Cream

Layer in a champagne flute.

Peanut Butter-Chocolate Chip Cookie

HIGHBALL GLASS

1 part Frangelico®
1 part Tia Maria®
1 part Coffee Liqueur

Shake with ice and strain over ice.

Pee Wee's Beamer

ROCKS GLASS

¾ part Vodka
¾ part Coconut Rum
½ part Orange Juice

Shake with ice and strain over ice.

Peeled Watermelon

HIGHBALL GLASS

1 part Watermelon Schnapps
1 part Jägermeister
2 parts Orange Juice
fill with Red Bull Energy Drink

Build over ice. Garnish with Whipped Cream

Peep Show

ROCKS GLASS

1 part Dubonnet® Blonde
1 part Brandy
1 part Pernod®
splash Lime Juice

Shake with ice and strain over ice.

Pelican

HIGHBALL GLASS

1 part Bourbon
½ part Triple Sec
1 tbsp sugar
fill with Orange Juice

Shake with ice and strain over ice.

Pensacola

HIGHBALL GLASS

1 part Rum
1 part Lemonade
1 part Orange Juice
1 part Guava Nectar

Shake with ice and pour.

Pentecostal

ROCKS GLASS

1 part Vodka
1 part Bourbon
fill with Lemon-Lime Soda

Build over ice and stir.

Peppermint Crisp

HIGHBALL GLASS

1 part Crème de Menthe (White)
1 part Coffee Liqueur
fill with Milk

Shake with ice and pour.

Peppermint Stick

CHAMPAGNE FLUTE

1 part Peach Schnapps
1½ parts Crème de Cacao (White)
1 part Light Cream

Shake with ice and strain.

Perestroika

ROCKS GLASS

1½ parts Vodka
1 part Vanilla Liqueur
1 part Crème de Cacao (White)

Shake with ice and strain over ice.

Pernod® Riviera

ROCKS GLASS

1 part Pernod®
½ part Gin
2 parts Lemonade

Shake with ice and strain over ice.

Perpetual Depth

HIGHBALL GLASS

⅔ part Blackberry Liqueur
⅔ part Raspberry Liqueur
1 part Orange Vodka
1 part Pineapple Juice

Shake with ice and strain over ice.

Perroquet

ROCKS GLASS

1½ parts Pernod®
splash Peppermint Schnapps

Shake with ice and strain over ice.

Persian Prince

HIGHBALL GLASS

1 part Vodka
1 part Citrus Rum
1 part Sweet & Sour Mix
1 part Orange Juice
1 part Lemon-Lime Soda

Shake with ice and strain over ice.

Petit Caprice

HIGHBALL GLASS

1 part Vodka
½ part Melon Liqueur
½ part Limoncello
½ part Lemon Juice
1½ parts Apple Juice

Shake with ice and strain over ice.

Philishake

HIGHBALL GLASS

1 part Sloe Gin
1 part Triple Sec
splash Cherry Brandy
splash Strawberry Juice

Shake with ice and strain over ice.

Phillips Head Screwdriver

HIGHBALL GLASS

2 parts Vodka
1 part Orange Juice
1 part Pineapple Juice

Shake with ice and pour.

Philofan

HIGHBALL GLASS

1 part Root Beer Schnapps
1 part Amaretto
1 part Cola

Build over ice and stir.

Phoenix Rising

ROCKS GLASS

1½ parts Gold Tequila
1 part Melon Liqueur
splash Grenadine
fill with Orange Juice

Build over ice and stir.

Pier 66

HIGHBALL GLASS

1 part Vodka
1 part Wild Berry Schnapps
1 part Piña Colada Mix
2 parts Lemonade
1 part Orange Juice

Shake with ice and pour.

Pierced Navel

HIGHBALL GLASS

1 part Vodka
1 part Peach Schnapps
1 part Orange Juice
1 part Cranberry Juice Cocktail

Shake with ice and strain over ice.

Pillow Mint

ROCKS GLASS

2 parts Irish Whiskey
½ part Coffee Liqueur
splash Crème de Menthe (White)

Shake with ice and strain over ice.

Pimm's® Cup

WHITE WINE GLASS

1½ parts Pimm's Cup No. 1®
splash Lemon Juice
splash Lime Juice
1 part Lemon-Lime Soda
1 part Ginger Ale

Build over ice and stir.

Pimp Juice

ROCKS GLASS

1 part Alizé®
1 part Hpnotiq®

Build over ice and stir.

Piña

HIGHBALL GLASS

1½ parts Tequila
1 part Lime Juice
splash Simple Syrup
fill with Pineapple Juice

Build over ice and stir.

Piñata

HIGHBALL GLASS

1 part Tequila
splash Banana Liqueur
1 part Lime Juice

Shake with ice and strain over ice.

Pineapple Princess

HIGHBALL GLASS

1½ parts Melon Liqueur
1 part Passion Fruit Liqueur
1 part Lime Juice
2 parts Orange Juice
fill with Pineapple Juice

Build over ice and stir.

Pineapple Slapper

HIGHBALL GLASS

1 part Crème de Coconut
½ part Lemon Juice
½ part Lime Juice
2 parts Sweet & Sour Mix
fill with Pineapple Juice

Shake with ice and strain over ice.

Pinetree Martyr

HIGHBALL GLASS

1 part Vodka
½ part Peach Schnapps
fill with Pineapple Juice

Shake with ice and strain over ice.

Pink

HIGHBALL GLASS

1 part Vodka
1 part Grenadine
fill with Milk

Shake with ice and pour.

Pink Almond

HIGHBALL GLASS

1 part Rye Whiskey
1/2 part Amaretto
1/2 part Crème de Noyaux
1/2 part Kirschwasser
1/2 part Lemon Juice

Shake with ice and strain over ice.

Pink Cloud

HIGHBALL GLASS

1 part Vodka
1 part Crème de Almond
2 parts Piña Colada Mix
fill with Lemonade

Shake with ice and pour.

Pink Drink

HIGHBALL GLASS

2 parts Vodka
fill with Lemon-Lime Soda
splash Cranberry Juice Cocktail

Build over ice and stir.

Pink Elephants on Parade

HIGHBALL GLASS

2 parts Vodka
1/2 part Melon Liqueur
dash Sugar
fill with Pink Lemonade

Shake with ice and strain over ice.

Pink Explosion

WHITE WINE GLASS

1 1/2 parts Cream
3/4 part Dry Vermouth
1/2 part Pernod®
splash Grenadine

Shake with ice and strain over ice.

Pink Fix

ROCKS GLASS

2 parts Gin
2 parts Lemon Juice
3/4 part Grenadine

Shake with ice and strain over ice.

Pink Forest

HIGHBALL GLASS

1 part Gin
1/2 part Cream
1/2 part Triple Sec
fill with Strawberry Juice

Shake with ice and pour.

Pink Goody

HIGHBALL GLASS

1 part Gin
1 part Dark Rum
1 part Lime Juice
splash Cherry Juice
splash Club Soda

Build over ice and stir.

Pink Jinx

ROCKS GLASS

1 part Gin
1 part Lemon Juice
splash Grenadine

Shake with ice and pour.

Pink Lemonade

HIGHBALL GLASS

1 1/2 parts Citrus Vodka
1/2 part Raspberry Liqueur
fill with Sweet & Sour Mix

Shake with ice and pour.

Pink Missile

HIGHBALL GLASS

2 parts Vodka
1 part Raspberry Liqueur
1 part Cranberry Juice Cocktail
1 part Ginger Ale
1 part Grapefruit Juice

Build over ice and stir.

Pink Moon

HIGHBALL GLASS

2 parts Light Rum
1 part Triple Sec
splash Grenadine
fill with Pineapple Juice

Build over ice and stir.

Pink Panty Pulldown
HIGHBALL GLASS

1½ parts Vodka
1 part Sweet & Sour Mix
splash Lemon-Lime Soda
splash Grenadine

Build over ice.

Pink Russian
HIGHBALL GLASS

1 part Tequila Rose®
1 part Coffee Liqueur
1 part Vodka

Shake with ice and pour.

Pink Top
HIGHBALL GLASS

1½ parts Gin
¾ part Grand Marnier®
¼ part Lemon Juice
splash Grenadine

Shake with ice and strain over ice.

Pink Veranda
HIGHBALL GLASS

1 part Gold Rum
1½ parts Cranberry Juice Cocktail
1 part Lime Juice
1½ parts Simple Syrup

Shake with ice and strain over ice.

Pinocchio
HIGHBALL GLASS

1½ parts Gin
½ part Blackberry Liqueur
⅔ part Dubonnet® Blonde
fill with Raspberry Seltzer

Build over ice and stir.

Piper at the Gates of Dawn
ROCKS GLASS

1½ parts Scotch
1 part Coffee Liqueur
½ part Maraschino Liqueur
1 part Heavy Cream

Shake with ice and strain over ice.

Pirate Float
HIGHBALL GLASS

1 part Spiced Rum
1 part Root Beer Schnapps
1 part Vanilla Vodka
1 part Cream

Shake with ice and pour.

Pirate Jenny
HIGHBALL GLASS

1½ parts Light Rum
1 part Orange Liqueur
splash Lime Juice
splash Simple Syrup
fill with Pineapple Juice

Shake with ice and pour.

Pisa
ROCKS GLASS

1 part Dry Vermouth
1 part Amaretto
1 part Scotch
1 part Crème de Banane
1 part Lime Cordial

Shake with ice and strain over ice.

Pisco Kid
ROCKS GLASS

1½ parts Pineapple Juice
1½ parts Pisco
¾ part Dark Rum

Shake with ice and strain over ice.

Planet of the Apes
HIGHBALL GLASS

1 part Dark Rum
½ part Crème de Banane
½ part Cream of Coconut
fill with Pineapple Juice

Shake with ice and strain over ice.

Plastic Gangster

WHITE WINE GLASS

1 part Blue Curaçao
1 part Silver Tequila
1 part Lemonade
1 part Sweet & Sour Mix

Shake with ice and strain over ice.

Plum

HIGHBALL GLASS

½ part Amaretto
½ part Peach Schnapps
1 part Cranberry Juice Cocktail
1 part Sweet & Sour Mix

Shake with ice and pour.

Pluto

ROCKS GLASS

1 part Vodka
1 part Peach Schnapps
1 part Lime Cordial
½ part Blue Curaçao

Shake with ice and strain over ice.

Plutonium Q 26 Space Modulator

HIGHBALL GLASS

1 part Vodka
1 part Cherry Juice
1 part Lemonade
1 part Orange Juice
1 part Cola

Build over ice and stir.

Pocket Ball

ROCKS GLASS

1 part Apricot Brandy
1 part Orange Juice
1 part Sweet & Sour Mix

Shake with ice and strain over ice.

Poison Sumac

HIGHBALL GLASS

2 parts Vodka
1 part Blue Curaçao
1 part Orange Juice

Shake with ice and strain over ice.

Poker Face

HIGHBALL GLASS

1½ parts Tequila
½ part Triple Sec
fill with Pineapple Juice

Build over ice and stir.

Polar Bear

HIGHBALL GLASS

1 part Vodka
1 part Triple Sec
1 part Maraschino Liqueur
1 scoop Vanilla Ice Cream
1 Egg White

Shake with ice and pour.

Polish Red Hair

ROCKS GLASS

1 part Vodka
½ part Amaretto
½ part Lime Cordial
splash Grenadine
fill with Cola

Build over ice and stir.

Polly's Special

HIGHBALL GLASS

1½ parts Scotch
½ part Triple Sec
½ part Grapefruit Juice

Shake with ice and strain.

Polonaise

ROCKS GLASS

1½ parts Brandy
½ part Dry Sherry
splash Blackberry Brandy
splash Lemon Juice

Shake with ice and strain over ice.

Polynesian
HIGHBALL GLASS

1 part Rum
1 part Banana Juice
1 part Piña Colada Mix
1 part Lemonade
1 part Pineapple Juice

Shake with ice and pour.

Pompeii
ROCKS GLASS

1 part Brandy
¾ part Crème de Cacao (White)
½ part Amaretto
1 part Cream

Shake with ice and strain over ice.

Pompier Highball
COLLINS GLASS

1 part Triple Sec
1 part Crème de Cassis
fill with Sparkling Water

Build over ice and stir.

Pontiac
HIGHBALL GLASS

1 part Crème de Coconut
1 part Parfait Amour
1 part Cranberry Juice Cocktail
1 part Lemon-Lime Soda

Build over ice and stir.

Poolside Tropical
ROCKS GLASS

1½ parts Tequila Reposado
½ part Blue Curaçao
½ part Crème de Coconut
fill with Orange Juice

Shake with ice and strain over ice.

Popsicle®
HIGHBALL GLASS

1 part Amaretto
1 part Orange Juice
1 part Cream

Shake with ice and pour.

Porcupine
HIGHBALL GLASS

1 part Scotch
1 part Cointreau®
½ part Amaretto
1½ parts Grapefruit Juice
1½ parts Pineapple Juice

Shake with ice and strain over ice.

Porky Bone
HIGHBALL GLASS

1 part Vodka
½ part Maple Syrup
1 part Cinnamon Schnapps
2 parts Coffee Liqueur

Stir gently with ice.

Porn Star
HIGHBALL GLASS

1 part Blue Curaçao
1 part Raspberry Liqueur
fill with Lemon-Lime Soda

Build over ice and stir.

Port Light
ROCKS GLASS

1 part Bourbon
1 part Honey
1 Egg White

Shake with ice and strain over ice.

Portuguese in Love
ROCKS GLASS

1 part Raspberry Liqueur
2 parts White Port
1 part Apple Juice

Shake with ice and strain over ice.

Prado
ROCKS GLASS

1½ parts Tequila
¾ part Lemon Juice
splash Grenadine
splash Maraschino Liqueur
1 Egg White

Shake with ice and strain over ice.

Prairie Pearl

HIGHBALL GLASS

1 part Amaretto
½ part Limoncello
½ part Galliano®
fill with Milk

Shake with ice and strain over ice.

Praline & Cream

HIGHBALL GLASS

2 parts Praline Liqueur
fill with Cream

Shake with ice and strain over ice.

Praying for Liberty

HIGHBALL GLASS

1 part Currant Vodka
½ part Triple Sec
½ part Plum Brandy
½ part Lemon Juice
fill with Pineapple Juice

Shake with ice and strain over ice.

Praying Mantis

HIGHBALL GLASS

1½ parts Tequila
2 splashes Lime Juice
splash Lemon Juice
fill with Cola

Build over ice and stir.

Predator

HIGHBALL GLASS

1 part Brandy
1 part Light Rum
½ part Apricot Brandy
½ part Bénédictine®
1 part Lemon Juice
½ part Simple Syrup

Shake with ice and strain over ice.

Presbyterian

HIGHBALL GLASS

1 part Whiskey
1 part Club Soda
1 part Ginger Ale

Build over ice and stir.

Pretty in Pink

ROCKS GLASS

2 parts Dark Rum
1 part Cream

Shake with ice and strain over ice.

Prima Donna

HIGHBALL GLASS

½ part Galliano®
2 parts Passion Fruit Liqueur
2 parts Orange Juice
splash Lemon Juice

Shake with ice and strain over ice.

Primavera

HIGHBALL GLASS

1 part Dry Gin
1 part Grapefruit Juice
½ part Blue Curaçao
½ part Triple Sec

Shake with ice and strain over ice.

Prince of Darkness

ROCKS GLASS

1½ parts Scotch
1 part Coffee Liqueur
splash Club Soda

Build over ice and stir.

Prince of Norway

HIGHBALL GLASS

¾ part Vodka
¾ part Apricot Brandy
¼ part Lime Juice
fill with Lemon-Lime Soda

Build over ice and stir.

Princess

HIGHBALL GLASS

1 part Crème de Banane
1 part Dark Rum
1 part Lemon Juice

Shake with ice and strain over ice.

Professor and Mary Ann

HIGHBALL GLASS

1½ parts Vodka
½ part Apricot Brandy
¼ part Lime Juice
fill with Seltzer

Build over ice and stir.

Prussian Winter

HIGHBALL GLASS

1 part Vanilla Liqueur
½ part Goldschläger®
splash Lemon Juice
fill with Cranberry Juice Cocktail
splash Honey

Shake with ice and strain.

Psycho

HIGHBALL GLASS

1 part Light Rum
1 part Galliano®
1 part Orange Juice
1 part Pineapple Juice
splash Grenadine

Shake with ice and pour.

Public Library

BRANDY SNIFTER

1 part Sambuca
1 part Black Currant Syrup
fill with Piña Colada Mix

Shake with ice and pour.

Pucker Up

HIGHBALL GLASS

1 part Apple Liqueur
2 parts Sour Apple Schnapps
3 parts Lemon-Lime Soda
splash Lemon Juice

Build over ice and stir.

Puerto Plata

HIGHBALL GLASS

2 parts Light Rum
½ part Blue Curaçao
½ part Dark Rum
2 parts Pineapple Juice
1½ parts Orange Juice

Shake with ice and strain over ice.

Puerto Rican Sky Rocket

HIGHBALL GLASS

1 part Vodka
1 part Tequila Reposado
½ part Galliano®
fill with Orange Juice

Shake with ice and strain over ice.

Punch Drunk

HIGHBALL GLASS

1 part Spiced Rum
1 part Light Rum
splash Blackberry Liqueur
fill with Pineapple Juice
½ part Lemon Juice
dash Powdered Sugar

Shake with ice and strain over ice.

Purple

ROCKS GLASS

1 part Southern Comfort®
1 part Blue Curaçao
1 part Blueberry Schnapps
1 part Sloe Gin
splash Lime Juice
splash Sweet & Sour Mix
splash Lemon-Lime Soda

Shake with ice and strain over ice.

Purple Cactus

ROCKS GLASS

1½ parts Gold Tequila
½ part Blue Raspberry Liqueur
1½ parts Passion Fruit Juice
dash Grenadine

Shake with ice and strain over ice.

Purple Chevy

HIGHBALL GLASS

1 part Vodka
1 part Cherry Juice
1 part Wild Berry Schnapps
1 part Sweet & Sour Mix
2 parts Orange Juice

Shake with ice and pour.

Purple Cow

HIGHBALL GLASS

1 part Vodka
1 part Raspberry Liqueur
fill with Milk

Shake with ice and pour.

Purple Death

HIGHBALL GLASS

1 part Blue Curaçao
2 parts Wild Berry Schnapps
splash Grenadine
fill with Red Bull® Energy Drink

Build over ice and stir.

Purple Devil

HIGHBALL GLASS

1 part Triple Sec
1 part Cointreau®
1 part Amaretto
fill with Cranberry Juice Cocktail
splash Lemon-Lime Soda

Shake with ice and strain over ice.

Purple Dinosaur

HIGHBALL GLASS

1 part Vodka
1 part Blue Curaçao
1 part Wild Berry Schnapps
1 part Orange Juice
1 part Cranberry Juice Cocktail

Shake with ice and strain over ice.

Purple Dream

ROCKS GLASS

1 part Chambord
1 part Crème de Cacao (White)
1 part Cream

Shake with ice and strain over ice.

Purple Hard-on

HIGHBALL GLASS

1 part Cherry Liqueur
1 part Southern Comfort®
fill with Sweet & Sour Mix
splash Lemon-Lime Soda

Build over ice and stir.

Purple Jesus

HIGHBALL GLASS

2 parts Vodka
1 part Ginger Ale
1 part Grape Juice (Red)

Build over ice and stir.

Purple Lobster

HIGHBALL GLASS

1½ parts Crown Royal® Whiskey
1½ parts Raspberry Liqueur
1 part Cranberry Juice Cocktail
1 part Lemon-Lime Soda

Build over ice and stir.

Purple Magic

HIGHBALL GLASS

1 part Blue Raspberry Liqueur
1 part Light Rum
1 part Watermelon Schnapps
1 part Cranberry Juice
1 part Pomegranate Juice

Shake with ice and strain over ice.

Purple Moon

HIGHBALL GLASS

1 part Vodka
1 part Blue Curaçao
1 part Cherry Juice
1 part Lemonade
1 part Cranberry Juice Cocktail

Shake with ice and pour.

Purple Nurple

HIGHBALL GLASS

1 part Vodka
1 part Grape Juice (Red)
2 parts Wild Berry Schnapps

Shake with ice and pour.

Purple Passion Tea

HIGHBALL GLASS

1/4 part Vodka
1/4 part Rum
1/4 part Gin
1/2 part Blackberry Liqueur
1 part Sweet & Sour Mix
1 part Lemon-Lime Soda

Build over ice and stir.

Purple People Eater

HIGHBALL GLASS

2 parts Chambord
1 part Amaretto
1 part Cherry Brandy
1 part Citrus Vodka
splash Orange Juice
splash Pineapple Juice
splash Grapefruit Juice

Shake with ice and strain over ice.

Purple Pussycat

HIGHBALL GLASS

1 part Vodka
1 part Cherry Juice
1 part Wild Berry Schnapps
fill with Pineapple Juice

Shake with ice and strain over ice.

Purple Rose of Cairo

HIGHBALL GLASS

1 part Citrus Vodka
1 part Raspberry Liqueur
fill with Cranberry Juice Cocktail

Shake with ice and strain over ice.

Purple Russian

HIGHBALL GLASS

2 parts Vodka
2 parts Raspberry Liqueur
1 part Cream

Shake with ice and pour.

Push Up

HIGHBALL GLASS

2 parts Vodka
splash Grenadine
1 part Lemon-Lime Soda
1 part Orange Juice

Build over ice and stir.

Pushkin

ROCKS GLASS

1 part Crème de Cacao (White)
1 part Vodka
1 part Gin

Shake with ice and strain over ice.

Putting Green

HIGHBALL GLASS

1 1/2 parts Melon Liqueur
3/4 part Gin
1 1/2 parts Lemon Juice
1 1/2 parts Orange Juice

Shake with ice and pour.

Quarter Deck

HIGHBALL GLASS

1 1/2 parts Light Rum
splash Sherry
splash Lime Juice

Shake with ice and strain over ice.

Quashbuckler

HIGHBALL GLASS

2 parts Vodka
1 part Gin
1 part Orange Juice
1 part Strawberry Juice

Shake with ice and strain over ice.

Queen of Hearts
HIGHBALL GLASS

1 part Amaretto
1 part Melon Liqueur
1 part Blue Curaçao
fill with Cranberry Juice Cocktail

Shake with ice and pour.

Qui Oui
HIGHBALL GLASS

2/3 part Kiwi Schnapps
1 1/2 parts Orange Juice

Shake with ice and strain over ice.

Quick Slammer
ROCKS GLASS

1 part Whiskey
1 part Sloe Gin
1/2 part Sour Apple Schnapps
fill with Cola

Build over ice and stir.

Quickset
HIGHBALL GLASS

1 1/2 parts Gin
1 part Blackberry Liqueur
1 part Cranberry Juice Cocktail
1 part Pineapple Juice

Shake with ice and strain over ice.

Quicksilver
HIGHBALL GLASS

1 part Anisette
1 part Triple Sec
1 part Tequila

Shake with ice and strain over ice.

R&B
HIGHBALL GLASS

1 1/2 parts Spiced Rum
1 part Orange Juice
1 part Pineapple Juice
splash Grenadine

Build over ice and stir.

Race Day Tea
HIGHBALL GLASS

1 part Light Rum
2/3 part Crème de Cacao (Dark)
1/2 part Lemon Juice
dash Powdered Sugar
fill with Iced Tea

Build over ice and stir.

Radical Sabatical
HIGHBALL GLASS

1 part Amaretto
1 part Blackberry Liqueur
2 parts Sweet & Sour Mix
3 parts Pineapple Juice

Shake with ice and strain over ice.

Radioactive Lemonade
HIGHBALL GLASS

1 part Vodka
1 part Amaretto
fill with Lemonade
splash Wild Berry Schnapps

Build over ice.

Raggae Sunsplash
HIGHBALL GLASS

2 parts Gin
2 splashes Strawberry Syrup
2 splashes Melon Liqueur
fill with Pineapple Juice

Shake with ice and strain over ice.

Raggedy Andy®
ROCKS GLASS

1 part Cranberry Vodka
1 part Cream
1 part Crème de Cacao (Dark)
1/2 part Crème de Banane

Shake with ice and strain over ice.

Ragin' Cajun
ROCKS GLASS

1 part Silver Tequila
1 part Vodka
dash Cayenne Pepper
dash Salt

Shake with ice and strain over ice.

Raging Ratoga
HIGHBALL GLASS

1 part Melon Liqueur
1 part Amaretto
1 part Cranberry Vodka
fill with Pineapple Juice

Build over ice and stir.

Rainbow Brite®
ROCKS GLASS

1 part Gin
2 parts Tonic Water
1 scoop Rainbow Sherbert

Build in the glass with no ice.

Rainstorm
HIGHBALL GLASS

1 part Vodka
1 part Blue Curaçao
2 parts Lemonade
1 part Cola

Shake with ice and strain over ice.

Rainy Day Marley
HIGHBALL GLASS

1 part Vodka
1 part Triple Sec
1 part Coconut Rum
fill with Orange Juice

Build over ice and stir.

Rampancy
HIGHBALL GLASS

2 parts Silver Tequila
2/3 part Crème de Coconut
fill with Pineapple Juice

Shake with ice and strain over ice.

Raspberry Breeze
HIGHBALL GLASS

1 part Vodka
2 parts Raspberry Liqueur
1 part Pineapple Juice
1 part Cranberry Juice Cocktail

Shake with ice and pour.

Raspberry Lynchburg
ROCKS GLASS

1 1/2 parts Whiskey
2/3 part Raspberry Liqueur
1 part Lemon Juice
1/2 part Simple Syrup

Shake with ice and pour.

Raspberry Romance
ROCKS GLASS

3/4 part Coffee Liqueur
3/4 part Blackberry Liqueur
1 1/4 parts Irish Cream Liqueur

Build over ice and stir.

Rastafari
ROCKS GLASS

1 part Crème de Banane
1 part Spiced Rum
fill with Cream

Shake with ice and strain over ice.

Rattlesnake Shake
HIGHBALL GLASS

1 part Kiwi Schnapps
1 part Light Rum
1 part Cranberry Juice Cocktail
fill with Orange Juice

Shake with ice and strain over ice.

Rauhreif
HIGHBALL GLASS

1 part Gin
1 part Blue Curaçao
2 splashes Grenadine
3 splashes Lemon Juice

Shake with ice and pour.

Real World

HIGHBALL GLASS

1 part Calvados Apple Brandy
½ part Frangelico®
½ part Hazelnut Liqueur
splash Amaretto
2 parts Cream

Shake with ice and strain over ice.

Rebel Charge

ROCKS GLASS

½ part Triple Sec
splash Lemon Juice
splash Orange Juice
1 Egg White

Shake with ice and strain over ice.

Rebel Russian

HIGHBALL GLASS

1 part Southern Comfort®
1 part Coffee Liqueur
fill with Half and Half

Shake with ice and pour.

Rebel Yell

ROCKS GLASS

2 parts Bourbon
½ part Triple Sec
1 part Lemon Juice
1 Egg White

Shake with ice and strain over ice.

Recrimination

HIGHBALL GLASS

½ part Crème de Cassis
1 part Calvados Apple Brandy
½ part Armagnac
⅔ part Lemon Juice
2 parts Raspberry Seltzer

Build over ice and stir.

Red Alert

HIGHBALL GLASS

½ part Silver Tequila
½ part Banana Liqueur
1 part Sloe Gin
fill with Sweet & Sour Mix

Shake with ice and pour.

Red Baby

HIGHBALL GLASS

1 part Southern Comfort®
1 part Vodka
1 part Amaretto
½ part Grenadine
1 part Orange Juice
1 part Lemon Juice

Shake with ice and pour.

Red Baron

HIGHBALL GLASS

1½ parts Vodka
fill with Orange Juice
splash Grenadine

Build over ice.

Red Devil

HIGHBALL GLASS

1 part Vodka
1 part Southern Comfort®
1 part Triple Sec
1 part Banana Liqueur
1 part Sloe Gin
splash Lime Juice
fill with Orange Juice

Shake with ice and pour.

Red Dwarf

HIGHBALL GLASS

2 parts Light Rum
1 part Peach Schnapps
½ part Crème de Cassis
½ part Lemon Juice
fill with Orange Juice

Shake with ice and pour.

Redhead on the Moon
HIGHBALL GLASS

½ part Vodka
½ part Melon Liqueur
½ part Sour Apple Schnapps
1 part Sweet & Sour Mix
splash Cranberry Juice Cocktail
fill with Lemon-Lime Soda

Build over ice and stir.

Red Hope
ROCKS GLASS

2 parts Gin
1 part Crème de Banane
½ part Apricot Brandy
splash Strawberry Syrup

Shake with ice and strain over ice.

Red Hot Mama
HIGHBALL GLASS

1½ parts Light Rum
2 parts Cranberry Juice Cocktail
1 part Club Soda

Build over ice and stir.

Red Hurricane
HIGHBALL GLASS

1 part Bacardi® Limón Rum
1 part Tequila
fill with Cranberry Juice Cocktail

Build over ice and stir.

Red Jewel
HIGHBALL GLASS

splash Cinnamon Schnapps
1 part Amaretto
1 part Bourbon

Shake with ice and strain over ice.

Red Rage
HIGHBALL GLASS

1 part Jägermeister®
1 part Vodka
fill with Red Bull® Energy Drink

Build over ice and stir.

Red Rasputin
HIGHBALL GLASS

2 parts Vodka
1 part Grenadine
fill with Cola

Build over ice and stir.

Red Rum
HIGHBALL GLASS

2 parts Gold Rum
1 part Grenadine
fill with Orange Juice

Build over ice and stir.

Red Snapper
HIGHBALL GLASS

1 part Crown Royal® Whiskey
1 part Amaretto
fill with Cranberry Juice Cocktail

Shake with ice and pour.

Red Tea Stinger
HIGHBALL GLASS

2 parts Cinnamon Schnapps
fill with Iced Tea

Build over ice and stir.

Red Velvet
HIGHBALL GLASS

1 part Gin
½ part Pisang Ambon® Liqueur
½ part Lime Juice
fill with Lemon-Lime Soda
splash Grenadine

Build over ice.

Redheads and Blondes
HIGHBALL GLASS

1 part Strawberry Liqueur
1 part Peach Schnapps
1 part Coconut Rum
1 part Strawberry Juice
1 part Pineapple Juice

Build over ice and stir.

Redneck Margarita

ROCKS GLASS

1 part Jack Daniel's
1 part Triple Sec
1 part Lime Juice

Shake with ice and strain over ice.

Reggata the Blank

ROCKS GLASS

1 part Dry Gin
1 part Light Rum
1 part Amaretto
1 part Pineapple Juice
1 part Orange Juice
dash Orange Bitters

Shake with ice and pour.

Rest in Peace

HIGHBALL GLASS

1 part Jack Daniel's®
½ part Vodka
½ part Tequila
½ part Jim Beam®

Shake with ice and strain over ice.

Richelieu

ROCKS GLASS

1 part Bourbon
½ part Vanilla Liqueur
¼ part Lillet®

Shake with ice and strain over ice.

Riedinger

HIGHBALL GLASS

1½ parts Light Rum
1 part Midori®
1 part Lime Juice
fill with Cola

Build over ice and stir.

Rigor Mortis

ROCKS GLASS

1½ parts Vodka
¾ part Amaretto
1 part Pineapple Juice
1 part Orange Juice

Shake with ice and strain over ice.

Rio Blanco

ROCKS GLASS

1 part Dark Rum
½ part Crème de Cacao (Dark)
½ part Triple Sec
splash Lime Juice

Shake with ice and strain over ice.

Rio's Carnival

HIGHBALL GLASS

1½ parts Cachaça®
½ part Vanilla Liqueur
splash Lemon Juice
½ part Sweetened Lime Juice
1½ parts Orange Juice

Shake with ice and strain over ice.

Ritz Bellboy

ROCKS GLASS

⅔ part Crème de Banane
½ part Dry Vermouth
1 part Jim Beam®
1 part Orange Juice

Shake with ice and strain over ice.

Rivaldinho

HIGHBALL GLASS

2 parts Cachaça®
splash Crème de Coconut

Build over ice and stir.

Roadkill

ROCKS GLASS

3 parts Amaretto
1 part Grenadine
fill with Dr. Pepper®

Build over ice and stir.

Roadrunner

ROCKS GLASS

1 part Tia Maria®
1 part Grand Marnier®

Shake with ice and strain over ice.

Roadrunner #2

CHAMPAGNE FLUTE

1 part Vodka
½ part Amaretto
½ part Cream of Coconut

Shake with ice and strain over ice.

Robert Paulsen

HIGHBALL GLASS

2 parts Southern Comfort®
2 parts Cola
1 part Cranberry Juice Cocktail

Build over ice and stir.

Robitussin®

HIGHBALL GLASS

1 part Cherry Liqueur
1 part Root Beer Schnapps

Shake with ice and strain over ice.

Robson

ROCKS GLASS

1½ parts Rum
splash Grenadine
splash Lemon Juice
splash Orange Juice

Shake with ice and strain over ice.

Rocking Root Beer

HIGHBALL GLASS

1½ parts Root Beer Schnapps
⅔ part Crème de Cacao (Dark)
3 parts Cream
1 part Cola

Shake with ice and strain over ice.

Rocky Dane

ROCKS GLASS

1 part Gin
1 part Cherry Brandy
1 part Kirschwasser
½ part Dry Vermouth

Shake with ice and strain over ice.

Rocky Mountain High

HIGHBALL GLASS

1 part Southern Comfort®
1 part Amaretto
fill with Cranberry Juice Cocktail

Build over ice and stir.

Roller

HIGHBALL GLASS

1½ parts Vodka
splash Amaretto
splash Melon Liqueur
fill with Cranberry Juice Cocktail

Shake with ice and pour.

Rolling Green Elixer

HIGHBALL GLASS

1½ parts Peach Schnapps
1 part Blue Curaçao
½ part Vodka
fill with Cranberry Juice Cocktail

Build over ice and stir.

Roman Candle

ROCKS GLASS

1 part Brandy
1 part Dark Rum
½ part Port
1 part Raspberry Syrup
¾ part Lemon Juice

Shake with ice and strain over ice.

Roman Riot

ROCKS GLASS

1 part Sambuca
1 part Galliano®
1 part Amaretto

Shake with ice and strain.

Romantica

HIGHBALL GLASS

1 part Bacardi® Limón Rum
1 part Sweet Vermouth

Shake with ice and strain over ice.

Romulan Ale

HIGHBALL GLASS

1½ parts Light Rum
1 part Blue Curaçao
fill with Lemon-Lime Soda
splash Tabasco® Sauce

Build over ice.

Romulan Dream

HIGHBALL GLASS

1 part Grand Marnier®
1 part Blue Curaçao
1 part Lemon Juice

Shake with ice and strain over ice.

Root Beer

HIGHBALL GLASS

1 part Coffee Liqueur
1 part Galliano®
1 part Lemon Juice
dash Powdered Sugar
fill with Cola

Build over ice and stir.

Rooty Tooty

HIGHBALL GLASS

2 parts Root Beer Schnapps
fill with Orange Juice

Shake with ice and pour.

Rosalita

HIGHBALL GLASS

1½ parts Tequila
1 part Campari®
½ part Sweet Vermouth
½ part Dry Vermouth

Shake with ice and pour.

Roscoe

HIGHBALL GLASS

1 part Jack Daniel's®
1 part Melon Liqueur

Shake with ice and pour.

Rose Hall Nightcap

ROCKS GLASS

2 parts Cognac
1 part Pernod®
½ part Crème de Cacao (Dark)

Shake with ice and strain over ice.

Rosemary

HIGHBALL GLASS

1 part Jim Beam®
1 part Apricot Brandy
splash Crème de Banane
splash Lemon Juice

Shake with ice and strain over ice.

Round Robin

WHITE WINE GLASS

1 part Absinthe
1 part Brandy
1 Egg White
dash Sugar

Shake with ice and strain.

Rowdy German

HIGHBALL GLASS

1 part Coffee Liqueur
1 part Bacardi® Limón Rum
1 part Jägermeister®

Shake with ice and strain over ice.

Roxanne

HIGHBALL GLASS

¾ part Vodka
¾ part Peach Schnapps
½ part Amaretto
½ part Orange Juice
½ part Cranberry Juice Cocktail

Shake with ice and strain over ice.

Royal Gin Fizz

ROCKS GLASS

2 parts Gin
½ part Lemon Juice
dash Powdered Sugar
1 Whole Egg
fill with Seltzer

Shake all but Seltzer with ice and strain. Top with Seltzer.

Royal Lemon

HIGHBALL GLASS

1 part Crown Royal® Whiskey
fill with Pink Lemonade

Shake with ice and pour.

Royal Nightcap

HIGHBALL GLASS

2 parts Goldschläger®
dash Powdered Sugar
fill with Milk

Shake with ice and pour.

Rub-a-Dub-Dub

HIGHBALL GLASS

1 part Dark Rum
½ part Apricot Brandy
½ part Galliano®
½ part Lime Juice
fill with Pineapple Juice

Shake with ice and strain over ice.

Rubber Chicken

HIGHBALL GLASS

3 parts Rye Whiskey
1 part Limeade
1 part Ginger Ale

Build over ice and stir.

Rubber Ducky

HIGHBALL GLASS

1½ parts Melon Liqueur
1½ parts Peach Schnapps
3 parts Cranberry Juice

Build over ice and stir.

Rubbermeister

HIGHBALL GLASS

1 part Jägermeister
2 parts Cherry Cola

Build over ice and stir.

Rubenstein's Revenge

HIGHBALL GLASS

1 part Vodka
1 part Cranberry Juice Cocktail
1 part Gin
1 part Orange Juice
1 part Tonic Water

Shake with ice and strain over ice.

Ruby Fizz

HIGHBALL GLASS

2 parts Sloe Gin
splash Grenadine
½ part Lemon Juice
dash Powdered Sugar
1 Egg White
fill with Seltzer

Shake all but Seltzer with ice and strain. Top with Seltzer.

Ruby Tuesday

HIGHBALL GLASS

2 parts Gin
2 splashes Grenadine
fill with Cranberry Juice Cocktail

Build over ice and stir.

Rudolph the Red-Nosed Reindeer®

HIGHBALL GLASS

1¼ parts Light Rum
1½ parts Lemon Juice
½ part Grenadine

Shake with ice and strain over ice.

Rum Boogie

HIGHBALL GLASS

1 part Dark Rum
½ part Amaretto
splash Lime Juice
fill with Cola

Build over ice and stir.

Rum Cure
HIGHBALL GLASS
1 part 151-Proof Rum
1 part Brandy
splash Blue Curaçao
1 part Pineapple Juice
1 part Orange Juice
1 part Lemon Juice
splash Grenadine
Shake with ice and strain over ice.

Rum Runner
ROCKS GLASS
½ part Light Rum
½ part Spiced Rum
½ part Crème de Banane
½ part Blackberry Brandy
1 part Sweet & Sour Mix
1 part Orange Juice
Shake with ice and pour.

Rum Scoundrel
ROCKS GLASS
1 part Light Rum
½ part Lime Juice
dash Sugar
Shake with ice and pour.

Rum Sour
ROCKS GLASS
2 parts Light Rum
½ part Lemon Juice
dash Powdered Sugar
Shake with ice and strain over ice.

Rum Spice Whacker
ROCKS GLASS
1 part Spiced Rum
1 part Coffee Liqueur
2 parts Cream of Coconut
Shake with ice and strain over ice.

Rum Ta Tum
HIGHBALL GLASS
1 part Rum
1 part Cherry Juice
1 part Lemonade
1 part Pineapple Juice
Shake with ice and pour.

RumChata Blind Russian
HIGHBALL GLASS
1 part Coffee Liqueur
1 part RumChata
1 part Vanilla Vodka
Shake with ice and strain over ice.

RumChata Colada
ROCKS GLASS
3 parts RumChata
1 part Light Rum
1 part Pineapple Juice
splash Cream of Coconut
Shake with ice and strain over ice.

RumChata Oatmeal Cookie
HIGHBALL GLASS
1 part RumChata
1 part Goldschläger®
splash Jägermeister
Build over ice and stir.

RumChata White Russian
ROCKS GLASS
1 part Coffee Liqueur
1 part RumChata
1 part Vodka
1 part Milk or Cream
Shake with ice and pour.

Rumple
HIGHBALL GLASS
1 part Light Rum
1 part Coconut Rum
1 part Bacardi® Limón Rum
fill with Orange Juice
Build over ice and stir.

Runaway
HIGHBALL GLASS

1 part Triple Sec
1 part Tequila Gold
fill with Grape Juice (Red)

Build over ice and stir.

Runaway Train
HIGHBALL GLASS

1 part Rum
1 part Triple Sec
1 part Sweet & Sour Mix
1 part Grapefruit Juice
1 part Cola

Build over ice and stir.

Ruptured Duck
HIGHBALL GLASS

1 part Crème de Noyaux
1 part Banana Liqueur
1 part Cream

Shake with ice and strain over ice.

Russian Banana
HIGHBALL GLASS

1 part Vodka
1 part Crème de Cacao (White)
1 part Banana Liqueur
fill with Cream

Shake with ice and strain over ice.

Russian Chameleon
HIGHBALL GLASS

1 part Blue Curaçao
2 parts Vodka
fill with Orange Juice

Build over ice and stir.

Russian Cream
ROCKS GLASS

2 parts Vodka
1 part Coffee Liqueur
1 part Irish Cream Liqueur

Shake with ice and pour.

Russian Fireman
HIGHBALL GLASS

1 part Fireball Cinnamon Whiskey
1 part Coffee Liqueur
3 parts Half and Half or Milk

Build over ice and stir.

Russian Iceberg
ROCKS GLASS

1 part Crème de Menthe (White)
1 part Peppermint Schnapps
1 part Vodka

Shake with ice and strain over ice.

Russian Jack
HIGHBALL GLASS

1 part Vodka
1 part Jack Daniel's®
fill with Sweet & Sour Mix

Shake with ice and pour.

Russian Hypnotist
HIGHBALL GLASS

1 part Vodka
1 part Irish Cream Liqueur
1 part Frangelico®

Shake with ice and strain over ice.

Russian Quaalude
HIGHBALL GLASS

1 part Coffee Liqueur
1 part Frangelico
1 part Irish Cream Liqueur
1 part Vodka
1 part Cream

Shake with ice and strain over ice.

Russian Quartet
ROCKS GLASS

1 part Vodka
1 part Peppermint Schnapps
1 part Coffee Liqueur
1 part Irish Cream Liqueur
1 part Amaretto
1 part Half and Half

Shake with ice and strain over ice.

Russian Turkey

ROCKS GLASS

1 part Vodka
1 part Cranberry Juice Cocktail

Shake with ice and strain over ice.

Rusty Mist

ROCKS GLASS

1 part Drambuie®
1 part Irish Mist®

Build over ice.

Rusty Nail

ROCKS GLASS

1½ parts Scotch
½ part Drambuie®

Build over ice and stir.

Rye and Dry

ROCKS GLASS

1 part Dry Vermouth
½ part Whiskey

Shake with ice and strain over ice.

Safari Juice

HIGHBALL GLASS

1 part Cointreau®
1 part Midori®
fill with Orange Juice
splash Grenadine

Build over ice.

Saint Paul

HIGHBALL GLASS

1 part Gin
1 part Light Rum
dash Angostura® Bitters

Shake with ice and strain over ice.

Salisbury Special

CORDIAL GLASS

1 part Vodka
1 part Raspberry Liqueur
1 part Cola
1 part Orange Juice

Build over ice and stir.

Salty Dog

HIGHBALL GLASS

1½ parts Gin
dash Salt
fill with Grapefruit Juice

Shake with ice and pour.

Samba

HIGHBALL GLASS

1½ parts Light Rum
½ part Triple Sec
¼ part Grenadine
1 part Pineapple Juice
1 part Orange Juice

Shake with ice and pour.

Samba de Janeiro

ROCKS GLASS

1½ parts Gin
½ part Apricot Brandy
½ part Lime Juice

Shake with ice and strain over ice.

Sambario

HIGHBALL GLASS

1 part Vodka
½ part Apricot Brandy
½ part Dry Vermouth

Build over ice and stir.

Sambrazinha

ROCKS GLASS

2 parts Cachaca®
½ part Lime Juice
fill with Cola

Build over ice and stir.

San Diego Silver Bullet

ROCKS GLASS

1 part Vodka
1 part Sambuca

Shake with ice and strain over ice.

San Francisco Driver

HIGHBALL GLASS

1 part Vodka
1 part Sweet & Sour Mix
1 part Orange Juice

Shake with ice and pour.

San Salvador

ROCKS GLASS

1½ parts Dark Rum
1 part Triple Sec
1½ parts Orange Juice
½ part Lime Juice

Shake with ice and strain over ice.

Sancho Panza

SHERRY GLASS

2 parts Cream Sherry
¾ part Campari®
dash Angostura® Bitters

Build in the glass with no ice.

Sanctuary

ROCKS GLASS

1½ parts Dubonnet® Blonde
¾ part Cointreau®
¾ part Amer Picon®

Shake with ice and strain over ice.

Sandra Buys a Dog

HIGHBALL GLASS

1 part Dark Rum
1 part Añejo Rum
3 parts Cranberry Juice Cocktail
1 part Orange Juice
dash Bitters

Shake with ice and strain over ice.

Santa Fe

HIGHBALL GLASS

1¼ parts Tequila
½ part Triple Sec
fill with Lemon-Lime Soda

Build over ice and stir.

Saratoga Swim

HIGHBALL GLASS

1 part Citrus Vodka
1 part Peach Schnapps
½ part Passion Fruit Liqueur
1 part Sweet & Sour Mix
fill with Orange Juice

Build over ice and stir.

Saronnada

WHITE WINE GLASS

1½ parts Vodka
1½ parts Pineapple Juice
¾ part Amaretto
¾ part Cream of Coconut

Shake with ice and strain.

Satin Angel

HIGHBALL GLASS

1 part Frangelico®
fill with Cream
splash Cola

Build over ice and stir.

Saturn's Rings

HIGHBALL GLASS

1 part Vodka
1 part Raspberry Liqueur
1 part Lemon-Lime Soda
1 part Orange Juice
1 part Cranberry Juice Cocktail

Shake with ice and pour.

Scarecrow
HIGHBALL GLASS

1 1/2 parts Light Rum
1 part Peach Schnapps
splash Crème de Cassis
splash Lemon Juice
fill with Orange Juice

Shake with ice and strain over ice.

Scarlet O'Hara
HIGHBALL GLASS

2 parts Southern Comfort®
fill with Cranberry Juice Cocktail

Build over ice and stir.

Schmegma
HIGHBALL GLASS

1 1/2 parts 151-Proof Rum
1 part Pineapple Juice
1 part Cranberry Juice Cocktail
splash Triple Sec
splash Grenadine
splash Orange Juice
splash Lemon-Lime Soda

Shake with ice and strain over ice.

Schnorkel
HIGHBALL GLASS

2 parts Dark Rum
1/2 part Pernod®
1 part Lime Juice
dash Sugar

Shake with ice and strain over ice.

Scooby Snack®
HIGHBALL GLASS

1 part Melon Liqueur
1 part Rum
1 part Milk

Shake with ice and pour.

Scooley Slammer
ROCKS GLASS

1 part Triple Sec
1 part Peach Schnapps
2 parts Sweet & Sour Mix
fill with Lemon-Lime Soda

Stir gently with ice.

Scotch Bird Flyer
CHAMPAGNE FLUTE

1 1/2 parts Scotch
1/2 part Triple Sec
1 part Light Cream
dash Powdered Sugar
1 Egg Yolk

Shake with ice and strain.

Scotch Cobbler
ROCKS GLASS

2 parts Scotch
1 part Brandy
1 part Blue Curaçao

Shake with ice and strain over ice.

Scotch Dream
HIGHBALL GLASS

1 part Scotch
splash Orange Liqueur
splash Crème de Banane

Shake with ice and strain over ice.

Scotch Explorer
ROCKS GLASS

1 1/2 parts Scotch
1/2 part Amaretto
1/2 part Sherry

Shake with ice and strain over ice.

Scotch Rickey
HIGHBALL GLASS

1 1/2 parts Scotch
1/2 part Lime Juice
fill with Seltzer

Build over ice and stir.

Scotch Sour

ROCKS GLASS

1 1/2 parts Scotch
1/2 part Lime Juice
dash Powdered Sugar

Shake with ice and strain over ice. Garnish with a Lemon Slice.

Scottish Surprise

ROCKS GLASS

2 parts Scotch
2 parts Passion Fruit Juice
1/2 part Grenadine
dash Bitters

Shake with ice and strain over ice.

Scratch and Sniff

HIGHBALL GLASS

1 1/2 parts Tequila
1/2 part Raspberry Liqueur
1 part Pineapple Juice
1 part Orange Juice

Shake with ice and pour.

Screamin' Blue

HIGHBALL GLASS

1 part Gin
1 part Vodka
1 part Light Rum
1 part Triple Sec
1 part Banana Liqueur
1 part Blue Curaçao
1 part Pineapple Juice
1 part Sweet & Sour Mix

Shake with ice and strain over ice.

Screamin' Coyote

ROCKS GLASS

1 part Crème de Menthe (White)
1 part Goldschläger®
1 part Absolut® Peppar Vodka
splash Tabasco® Sauce

Shake with ice and strain over ice.

Screaming Banana

ROCKS GLASS

2 parts 99 Bananas Liqueur
3 parts Pineapple Juice
fill with Orange Juice

Build over ice and stir.

Screaming Blue Monkey

HIGHBALL GLASS

3/4 part Vodka
1 part Blue Curaçao
1 part Banana Liqueur
fill with Sweet & Sour Mix

Shake with ice and strain over ice.

Screaming Mimi

HIGHBALL GLASS

3 parts Irish Cream Liqueur
3 parts Crème de Cacao (White)
1 part Grenadine

Shake with ice and strain over ice.

Screaming White Orgasm

HIGHBALL GLASS

1 part Irish Cream Liqueur
1 part Coffee Liqueur
1 part Rum
splash Cointreau®
splash Milk

Shake with ice and strain over ice.

Screwdriver

HIGHBALL GLASS

2 parts Vodka
fill with Orange Juice

Build over ice and stir.

Screwdriver Boricua

HIGHBALL GLASS

2 parts Vodka
1 part Orange Juice
1 part Cranberry Juice Cocktail

Build over ice and stir.

Screwlimer
HIGHBALL GLASS

2 parts Vodka
splash Lime Juice
fill with Orange Juice

Build over ice and stir.

Sea Breeze
HIGHBALL GLASS

1½ parts Vodka
3 parts Cranberry Juice Cocktail
1 part Grapefruit Juice

Build over ice and stir.

Sea Dragon
HIGHBALL GLASS

1 part Triple Sec
1 part Vodka
½ part Blue Raspberry Liqueur
1 part Sweet & Sour Mix

Shake with ice and strain over ice.

Sea Eagle
ROCKS GLASS

1 part Crème de Cacao (White)
splash Blue Curaçao
splash Scotch
⅔ part Cream
splash Strawberry Syrup

Shake with ice and strain over ice.

Sea Horses
HIGHBALL GLASS

⅔ part Blue Curaçao
splash Irish Cream Liqueur
1 part Orange Vodka

Shake with ice and strain over ice.

Sea Siren
ROCKS GLASS

1 part Light Rum
1 part Pineapple Juice
1 part Guava Juice
splash Grenadine

Shake with ice and strain over ice.

Sea Turtle
ROCKS GLASS

1 part Melon Liqueur
1 part Vodka
2 parts Pineapple Juice
splash Grenadine

Shake with ice and strain over ice.

Seaboard
ROCKS GLASS

1 part Whiskey
1 part Gin
splash Lemon Juice
dash Powdered Sugar

Shake with ice and strain over ice.

Seamen Special
ROCKS GLASS

1 part Gin
1 part Sour Apple Schnapps
1 part Lemon Juice
2 parts Apple Cider

Shake with ice and strain over ice.

Secret Blue
HIGHBALL GLASS

1½ parts Vodka
½ part Lime
dash Sugar
splash Blue Curaçao

Shake with ice and strain over ice.

Seduction on the Rocks
ROCKS GLASS

½ part Butterscotch Schnapps
½ part Lemon-Lime Soda
fill with Orange Juice

Build over ice and stir.

Seesaw

HIGHBALL GLASS

1 part Vodka
1 part Light Rum
½ part Dark Rum
2 parts Cranberry Juice Cocktail
2 parts Orange Juice
dash Bitters

Build over ice and stir.

Señor Frog

ROCKS GLASS

1 part Melon Liqueur
½ part Blue Curaçao
fill with Apple Juice

Shake with ice and strain over ice.

Serena

HIGHBALL GLASS

1 part Vodka
½ part Strawberry Vodka
½ part Dry Vermouth
½ part Pineapple Juice
½ part Blue Curaçao
splash Lemon Juice

Shake with ice and pour.

Serendipity

HIGHBALL GLASS

1 part Vodka
½ part Grand Marnier®
½ part Amaretto
½ part Triple Sec
¼ part Grenadine
fill with Orange Juice

Shake with ice and pour.

Serpent's Tooth

ROCKS GLASS

2 parts Whiskey
1 part Sweet Vermouth

Shake with ice and strain over ice.

Seven & Seven

HIGHBALL GLASS

2 parts Canadian Whisky
fill with Lemon-Lime Soda

Build over ice and stir.

Seven Deadly Sins

ROCKS GLASS

1 part Vodka
½ part Sour Apple Schnapps
½ part Raspberry Liqueur
½ part Watermelon Schnapps
1 part Orange Juice
1 part Sweet & Sour Mix
1 part Papaya Juice

Shake with ice and pour.

Seville

ROCKS GLASS

2 parts Gin
½ part Simple Syrup
½ part Lemon Juice
½ part Orange Juice
½ part Sherry

Shake with ice and strain over ice.

Shadowstorm

ROCKS GLASS

1 part Pisco
splash Triple Sec
splash Black Currant Juice

Shake with ice and strain over ice.

Shady Lady

HIGHBALL GLASS

1 part Melon Liqueur
1 part Tequila
fill with Grapefruit Juice

Build over ice and stir.

Shalom

ROCKS GLASS

1½ parts Vodka
1 part Madeira
splash Orange Juice

Shake with ice and strain over ice.

Shark Bite

HIGHBALL GLASS

1 part Rum
fill with Orange Juice
splash Grenadine

Build over ice.

Shark in the Water

HIGHBALL GLASS

1 part Vodka
1 part Blue Curaçao
fill with Lemonade
splash Strawberry Daiquiri Mix

Shake with ice and pour.

Shark's Nipple

HIGHBALL GLASS

1 part Spiced Rum
1 part Mountain Dew
1 part Cranberry Juice

Build over ice and stir.

Shavetail

HIGHBALL GLASS

1½ parts Peppermint Schnapps
1 part Pineapple Juice
1 part Light Cream

Shake with ice and strain over ice.

Shogun

BRANDY SNIFTER

1 part Sake
1 part Grand Marnier®
1 part Sweetened Lime Juice

Build in the glass with no ice.

Shoot

HIGHBALL GLASS

1 part Sherry
1 part Scotch
splash Lemon Juice
splash Orange Juice
dash Powdered Sugar

Shake with ice and strain over ice.

Short-Sighted

HIGHBALL GLASS

1 part Vodka
1½ parts Dry Vermouth
⅔ part Calvados Apple Brandy
½ part Triple Sec

Shake with ice and strain over ice.

Shotgun

BRANDY SNIFTER

1 part Citrus Vodka
1 part Grand Marnier®
1 part Lime Juice

Shake with ice and strain over ice.

Shuddering Orgasm

HIGHBALL GLASS

1 part Amaretto
1 part Coffee Liqueur
1 part Irish Cream Liqueur

Shake with ice and pour.

Siberian Sleighride

HIGHBALL GLASS

1¼ parts Vodka
¾ part Crème de Cacao (White)
½ part Crème de Cacao (Dark)
3 parts Light Cream

Shake with ice and strain over ice.

Siberian Slider

ROCKS GLASS

1 part Crème de Menthe (White)
1 part Vodka
1 part Light Rum

Shake with ice and strain over ice.

Sid Vicious

ROCKS GLASS

1 part Whiskey
1 part Gin
½ part Sweet Vermouth
dash Bitters
splash Worcestershire Sauce

Build over ice and stir.

Silver Bronx
ROCKS GLASS

2 parts Gin
splash Orange Juice
½ part Dry Vermouth
½ part Sweet Vermouth
1 Egg White

Shake with ice and strain over ice.

Silver Fox
HIGHBALL GLASS

1 part Triple Sec
1 part Crème de Cacao (Dark)
1 part Cream

Shake with ice and strain over ice.

Silverado
ROCKS GLASS

1½ parts Vodka
1½ parts Campari®
1 part Orange Juice

Shake with ice and strain over ice.

Sing Sing
CHAMPAGNE FLUTE

2 parts Scotch
1 part Triple Sec
1 part Sweet Vermouth

Shake with ice and strain.

Sink or Swim
ROCKS GLASS

1½ parts Brandy
2 splashes Vermouth
dash Bitters

Shake with ice and strain over ice.

Sino Soviet Split
ROCKS GLASS

2 parts Vodka
1 part Amaretto
fill with Milk

Build over ice and stir.

Sir Francis
HIGHBALL GLASS

1 part Raspberry Vodka
1 part Peach Vodka
1 part Vanilla Vodka
fill with Lemonade
1 part Grenadine

Build over ice and stir.

Skedattle
HIGHBALL GLASS

1½ parts Scotch
1 part Amaretto
1 part Triple Sec
splash Maraschino Liqueur
⅔ part Lemon Juice
1½ parts Orange Juice

Shake with ice and strain over ice.

Skeleton
HIGHBALL GLASS

½ part Silver Tequila
⅔ part Lemon-Lime Soda
⅔ part Blackberry Juice

Build over ice and stir.

Ski Slope
HIGHBALL GLASS

1 part Vodka
1 part Amaretto
½ part Jack Daniel's®
½ part Southern Comfort®
½ part Sloe Gin

Shake with ice and pour.

Skinny Dipper
ROCKS GLASS

2 parts Midori®
fill with Cranberry Juice Cocktail

Build over ice and stir.

Skinny Pirate
HIGHBALL GLASS

3 parts Spiced Rum
splash Lemon Juice
fill with Diet Cola

Build over ice and stir.

Sky Symphony
CHAMPAGNE FLUTE

1 part Blue Curaçao
1½ parts Grapefruit Juice
1½ parts Pineapple Juice

Layer over ice.

Skylab
HIGHBALL GLASS

1 part Vodka
½ part Peach Schnapps
splash Blue Curaçao
1 part Pineapple Juice
1 part Orange Juice
1 part Lemon-Lime Soda

Build over ice and stir.

Slacker's Slammer
HIGHBALL GLASS

1 part Vodka
1 part Root Beer Schnapps
fill with Root Beer
1 scoop Ice Cream

Build over ice.

Slapshot
HIGHBALL GLASS

1 part Vodka
splash Banana Liqueur
splash Pineapple Juice
fill with Orange Juice

Build over ice and stir.

Sled Ride
HIGHBALL GLASS

1½ parts Vodka
1½ parts Sloe Gin
½ part Sour Apple Schnapps
fill with Lemon-Lime Soda

Build over ice and stir.

Sleepy Lemon Glegg
HIGHBALL GLASS

½ part Crème de Banane
1½ parts Dark Rum
½ part Lemon Juice
1 part Orange Juice
1 part Pineapple Juice

Build over ice and stir.

Sleezy Bitch
HIGHBALL GLASS

3 parts Strawberry Liqueur
fill with Orange Juice

Build over ice and stir.

Slime
ROCKS GLASS

2 parts Vodka
1 part Cream
1 part Melon Liqueur

Shake with ice and strain over ice.

Slippery Golden Egg
HIGHBALL GLASS

1 part Goldschläger®
1 part Chartreuse®
1 Egg Yolk

Shake with ice and pour.

Slippery Lips
ROCKS GLASS

1 part Sweet Vermouth
½ part Triple Sec
½ part Orange Juice
½ part Sweet & Sour Mix

Shake with ice and pour.

Slippery Panties
ROCKS GLASS

1 part Butterscotch Liqueur
1 part Frangelico
1 part Vanilla Vodka

Shake with ice and strain over ice.

Sloe Brandy
ROCKS GLASS

2 parts Brandy
2 splashes Sloe Gin
splash Lemon Juice

Shake with ice and strain over ice.

Sloe Gin Fizz
HIGHBALL GLASS

2 parts Sloe Gin
½ part Lemon Juice
dash Powdered Sugar
fill with Seltzer

Build over ice and stir.

Sloehand
HIGHBALL GLASS

1½ parts Sloe Gin
1 part Vodka
1½ parts Orange Juice
½ part Lemon Juice
2 splashes Grenadine

Shake with ice and strain over ice.

Slow Tequila
ROCKS GLASS

1 part Silver Tequila
1 part Sloe Gin
½ part Lime Cordial

Build over ice and stir.

Small Sand
HIGHBALL GLASS

1 part Gin
1 part Midori®
½ part Strawberry Liqueur
fill with Sweet & Sour Mix

Shake with ice and strain over ice.

Smashed Pumpkin
HIGHBALL GLASS

1 part Vodka
1 part Orange Juice
1 part Cranberry Ginger Ale

Shake with ice and pour.

Smiling Irish
HIGHBALL GLASS

2 parts Irish Cream Liqueur
1 part Cognac
1 part Cream

Shake with ice and pour.

Smith & Kerns
HIGHBALL GLASS

1 part Coffee Liqueur
fill with Cola

Build over ice and stir. Top with Cream.

Smith & Wesson®
HIGHBALL GLASS

½ part Coffee Liqueur
½ part Vodka
fill with Cola

Build over ice and stir. Top with Cream.

Smooth Sailing
HIGHBALL GLASS

1½ parts Vodka
1½ parts Triple Sec
½ part Cherry Brandy
1 part Orange Juice
1 part Cranberry Juice Cocktail

Build over ice and stir.

Smoothberry
HIGHBALL GLASS

1 part Vodka
1 part Strawberry Liqueur
fill with Lemonade
1 part Pear Juice

Build over ice and stir.

Smurf®
HIGHBALL GLASS

1 part Vodka
1 parts Orange Juice
2 splashes Grenadine
splash Strawberry Daiquiri Mix
fill with Lemon-Lime Soda

Build over ice and stir.

Smurf® Piss
ROCKS GLASS
1 part Light Rum
1 part Blueberry Schnapps
1 part Blue Curaçao
1 part Sweet & Sour Mix
1 part Lemon-Lime Soda
Shake with ice and strain.

Sneaky Bastard
HIGHBALL GLASS
1 part Coconut Rum
1 part Melon Liqueur
1 part Vodka
½ part Blue Curaçao
fill with Pineapple Juice
Shake with ice and pour.

Sneaky Pete
HIGHBALL GLASS
1 part Coffee Liqueur
1 part Rye Whiskey
fill with Milk
Build over ice and stir.

Sno-Cone
HIGHBALL GLASS
2 parts Raspberry Liqueur
fill with Lemon-Lime Soda
1 part Grenadine
1 part Blue Curaçao
Build over ice.

Snooker
HIGHBALL GLASS
1 part Gin
1 part Sloe Gin
½ part Orange Liqueur
fill with Orange Juice
Shake with ice and strain over ice.

Snoopy®
HIGHBALL GLASS
1 part Vodka
splash Crème de Banane
splash Amaretto
Shake with ice and strain over ice.

Snowflake
HIGHBALL GLASS
1 part Frangelico®
1 part Crème de Cacao (White)
fill with Cream
Shake with ice and pour.

Snow White
HIGHBALL GLASS
2 parts Southern Comfort®
1 part Vodka
1 part Pineapple Juice
½ part Orange Juice
Shake with ice and strain over ice.

Socket Wrench
HIGHBALL GLASS
2½ parts Vodka
fill with Apple Juice
Shake with ice and pour.

Soda Cracker
ROCKS GLASS
2 parts Vodka
1 part Frangelico®
Build over ice and stir.

Soft Love
HIGHBALL GLASS
1 part Crème de Banane
1 part Cherry Brandy
1 part Cream
splash Grenadine
Shake with ice and strain over ice.

Soho
HIGHBALL GLASS
1½ parts Crème de Cassis
⅔ part Triple Sec
1 part Grapefruit Juice
1 part Orange Juice
Build over ice and stir.

Sombrero

ROCKS GLASS

1½ parts Coffee Brandy
1 part Light Cream

Build over ice.

Sonora Sunset

HIGHBALL GLASS

1 part Melon Liqueur
1 part Amaretto
1 part Vodka
4 parts Orange Juice
2 parts Cranberry Juice Cocktail

Build over ice.

Soprano Sour

ROCKS GLASS

2 parts Whiskey
1 part Amaretto
½ part Simple Syrup
splash Campari®

Shake with ice and strain over ice.

Souless Ginger

HIGHBALL GLASS

2 parts Amaretto
½ part Triple Sec
1 part Sweetened Lime Juice
fill with Ginger Beer

Build over ice and stir.

Soup

HIGHBALL GLASS

1 part Vodka
1 part Coconut Rum
1 part Cointreau®
1 part Peach Schnapps
fill with Red Bull® Energy Drink

Build over ice and stir.

Sour Bee

ROCKS GLASS

2 parts Whiskey
½ part Bénédictine®
¼ part Lemon Juice
¼ part Lime Juice

Shake with ice and strain over ice.

Sour Kiss

HIGHBALL GLASS

1 part Vodka
1 part Sour Apple Schnapps
fill with Sweet & Sour Mix

Build over ice and stir.

Sour Melon Skittle

HIGHBALL GLASS

1 part Melon Liqueur
1 part Raspberry Liqueur
½ part Blue Curaçao
fill with Cranberry Juice

Shake with ice and strain over ice.

South of the Border

ROCKS GLASS

1 part Tequila
¾ part Coffee Brandy
½ part Lime Juice

Shake with ice and strain over ice. Garnish with a Lime Slice.

South Pacific

HIGHBALL GLASS

1 part Vodka
2 parts Brandy
3 parts Pineapple Juice
splash Grenadine

Shake with ice and strain over ice.

South Side Fizz

HIGHBALL GLASS

½ part Gin
½ part Lemon Juice
dash Sugar
fill with Seltzer

Shake all but Seltzer with ice and strain. Top with Seltzer.

Southern Cross

HIGHBALL GLASS

1 part Advocaat
1 part Southern Comfort®
1 part Cranberry Juice Cocktail
1 part Pineapple Juice

Shake with ice and strain over ice.

Southern Harmony

ROCKS GLASS

1¼ parts Jack Daniel's®
¾ part Southern Comfort®
fill with Sweet & Sour Mix
splash Lemon-Lime Soda

Build over ice and stir.

Southern Lady

ROCKS GLASS

1 part Southern Comfort®
1 part Amaretto
fill with Lemon-Lime Soda

Build over ice and stir.

Southern Salutation

HIGHBALL GLASS

2 parts Southern Comfort®
1 part Peach Schnapps
fill with Lemonade

Build over ice and stir.

Soviet Holiday

HIGHBALL GLASS

2 parts Vodka
½ part Coconut Rum
¼ part Tequila Rose®
fill with Fruit Punch

Build over ice and stir.

Sparkling Iceberg

HIGHBALL GLASS

1 part Peppermint Liqueur
1 part Coffee Liqueur
2 parts Cream
2 parts Ginger Ale

Build over ice and stir.

Special K®

HIGHBALL GLASS

1 part Vodka
½ part Blue Curaçao
½ part Triple Sec
dash Sugar
fill with Lemonade

Shake with ice and pour.

Special Reserve

HIGHBALL GLASS

1 part Goldschläger®
1½ parts Apple Brandy
fill with Cranberry Juice Cocktail

Shake with ice and pour.

Spice and Ice

HIGHBALL GLASS

1 part Citrus Vodka
1 part Goldschläger®
fill with Dr. Pepper®

Build over ice and stir.

Spice Whip

HIGHBALL GLASS

1 part Peppermint Liqueur
splash Goldschläger®
½ part Crème de Cacao (Dark)
fill with Hot Cocoa

Build in a heat-proof cup or mug.

Spicy Tiger

HIGHBALL GLASS

1½ parts Peach Schnapps
1½ parts Vodka
2 parts Lemon-Lime Soda
1 part Cranberry Juice Cocktail
1 part Orange Juice

Build over ice and stir.

Spiky Cactus

HIGHBALL GLASS

1 part Blue Curaçao
1 part Vodka
1 part Triple Sec
fill with Mountain Dew®

Build over ice and stir.

Spinster's Delight

HIGHBALL GLASS

1 part Vodka
1 part Brandy
1 part Crème de Cacao (White)
1 part Cream

Shake with ice and strain over ice.

A Splash of Nash

HIGHBALL GLASS

½ part Crème de Banane
1 part Melon Liqueur
2 parts Cranberry Juice Cocktail
2 parts Club Soda

Build over ice and stir.

Spoodie Oodie

HIGHBALL GLASS

1 part Scotch
2 parts Port

Stir gently with ice.

Spooky Juice

HIGHBALL GLASS

1 part Vodka
2 splashes Blue Curaçao
splash Grenadine
fill with Orange Juice

Build over ice and stir.

Spymaster

ROCKS GLASS

1½ parts Vodka
½ part Crème de Banane
½ part Lemon Juice
1 Egg White

Shake with ice and strain over ice.

Squashed Frog

ROCKS GLASS

1 part Melon Liqueur
1 part Strawberry Liqueur
splash Crème de Menthe (White)
splash Crème de Cacao (White)
splash Irish Cream Liqueur

Build in the glass with no ice.

St. John

ROCKS GLASS

1 part Coffee Liqueur
1 part Gin

Shake with ice and strain over ice.

St. Louis Blues

HIGHBALL GLASS

1 part Vodka
1 part Blue Curaçao
1 part Lemonade
1 part Lemon-Lime Soda

Build over ice and stir.

St. Lucian Delight

HIGHBALL GLASS

1 part Rum
2 parts Blue Curaçao
1 part Lime Juice
fill with Pineapple Juice

Build over ice and stir.

St. Paul Punch

HIGHBALL GLASS

2 parts Melon Liqueur
1 part Vodka
1 part Lime Juice
fill with Lemonade

Build over ice and stir.

St. Peter

ROCKS GLASS

1 part Vodka
1 part Coffee Liqueur

Shake with ice and strain over ice.

St. Valentine's Day

ROCKS GLASS

⅔ part Peach Schnapps
⅔ part Citrus Vodka
1 part Cream

Shake with ice and strain over ice.

St. Zipang

CHAMPAGNE FLUTE

4 parts Zipang Sparkling Sake
1 part St-Germain

Build in order and garnish with a Raspberry.

A Star Is Shining

HIGHBALL GLASS

1 part Gin
1 part Pernod®
1 part Crème de Banane
3 parts Orange Juice
2 parts Passion Fruit Nectar

Shake with ice and strain over ice.

Star Kiss

HIGHBALL GLASS

2 parts Strawberry Liqueur
splash Grenadine
splash Cream
fill with Lemon-Lime Soda

Build over ice and stir.

Star Wars

HIGHBALL GLASS

1 part Southern Comfort®
1 part Amaretto
1 part Sweet & Sour Mix
1 part Lemon-Lime Soda

Build over ice and stir.

Starry Starry Night

HIGHBALL GLASS

1 part Vodka
1 part Wild Berry Schnapps
fill with Lemon-Lime Soda

Build over ice and stir.

Stay Up Late

HIGHBALL GLASS

2 parts Gin
½ part Brandy
½ part Lemon Juice
½ part Club Soda

Build over ice and stir.

Stiletto

ROCKS GLASS

1½ parts Whiskey
1½ parts Amaretto
½ part Lemon Juice

Shake with ice and strain over ice.

Stirrup Cup

ROCKS GLASS

1 part Brandy
1 part Cherry Brandy
1 part Lemon Juice
1 tsp Sugar

Shake with ice and strain over ice.

Stock Market Crash

HIGHBALL GLASS

1 part Jack Daniel's®
1 part Yukon Jack®
1 part Southern Comfort®
1 part Wild Turkey® Bourbon
1 part Dark Rum
fill with Cola

Build over ice and stir.

Stomach Reviver

ROCKS GLASS

2 parts Brandy
½ part Fernet-Branca®

Shake with ice and strain over ice.

Stop & Go

ROCKS GLASS

1 part Apricot Brandy
1 part Campari®
fill with Orange Juice

Shake with ice and pour.

Storm at Sea

HIGHBALL GLASS

1 part Vodka
1 part Apricot Brandy
½ part Melon Liqueur
1 part Sweet & Sour Mix
1 part Orange Juice

Build over ice and stir.

Stormtrooper

HIGHBALL GLASS

1 part Vodka
1 part Coconut Rum
fill with Milk

Build over ice and stir.

Storybook Ending
HIGHBALL GLASS

1 part Light Rum
1 part Apricot Brandy
splash Grenadine
1 part Sweet & Sour Mix
1 part Orange Juice

Shake with ice and strain over ice.

Strawberry Assassin
HIGHBALL GLASS

1 part Vodka
fill with Cranberry Juice Cocktail
1 scoop Ice Cream

Shake with ice and pour.

Strawberry Fair
ROCKS GLASS

1 part Silver Tequila
½ part Cream
½ part Strawberry Puree

Shake with ice and pour.

Strawberry Fields Forever
HIGHBALL GLASS

2 parts Strawberry Liqueur
½ part Brandy
fill with Seltzer

Build over ice and stir.

Strawberry Pussycat
HIGHBALL GLASS

1 part Vodka
1 part Strawberry Liqueur
1 part Cherry Juice
fill with Pineapple Juice

Shake with ice and pour.

Strawberry Starburst®
HIGHBALL GLASS

1 part Strawberry Liqueur
1 part Watermelon Schnapps
fill with Lemonade

Build over ice and stir.

Strawgasm
ROCKS GLASS

1 part Cointreau®
1 part Strawberry Liqueur
1 part Galliano®
1 part Coconut Rum
fill with Cream

Shake with ice and pour.

Stress Ball
HIGHBALL GLASS

1 part Vodka
½ part Rum
¼ part Galliano®
¼ part Irish Cream Liqueur
fill with Orange Juice

Shake with ice and pour.

Strudel
HIGHBALL GLASS

2 parts Vanilla Rum
dash Fireball Cinnamon Whiskey
fill with Apple Juice

Build over ice and stir.

Stubbly Beaver
HIGHBALL GLASS

1 part Vodka
1 part Irish Cream Liqueur
splash Butterscotch Schnapps
fill with Milk

Build over ice and stir.

Stumplifter
ROCKS GLASS

1 part Blackberry Brandy
1 part Amaretto
1 part Southern Comfort®
1 part Sloe Gin
fill with Orange Juice
splash Lemon-Lime Soda

Build over ice and stir.

Sucker Punch
HIGHBALL GLASS

2 parts Vodka
1 part Sour Apple Schnapps
splash Cranberry Juice Cocktail
fill with Lemon-Lime Soda

Build over ice and stir.

Suffering Bastard
ROCKS GLASS

1½ parts Rum
¾ part Orange Curaçao Liqueur
½ part Amaretto
1 part Lime Juice
fill with Orange Juice

Shake with ice and strain over ice.

Sugar and Spice
HIGHBALL GLASS

1 part Gin
1½ parts Coffee Liqueur
1 part Tequila Rose®
1 part Tropical Punch Schnapps
fill with Lemon-Lime Soda

Build over ice and stir.

Sugar Reef
HIGHBALL GLASS

1½ parts Orange Vodka
½ part Triple Sec
1 part Pineapple Juice
1 part Cranberry Juice Cocktail
1 part Orange Juice
splash Lime Juice

Shake with ice and strain over ice.

Sukiaki
HIGHBALL GLASS

1 part Amaretto
1 part Butterscotch Schnapps
1 part Irish Cream Liqueur
1 part Triple Sec
1 part Lemon-Lime Soda

Shake with ice and pour.

Summer Bahia Baby
ROCKS GLASS

1 part Vodka
1 part Pisang Ambon® Liqueur
½ part Triple Sec
fill with Pineapple Juice

Shake with ice and strain over ice.

Summer in the City
HIGHBALL GLASS

1 part Vodka
1 part Cherry Juice
1 part Lemonade
1 part Iced Tea

Build over ice and stir.

Summer of 69
HIGHBALL GLASS

1 part Vodka
1 part Strawberry Liqueur
1 part Lemonade
1 part Cola

Build over ice and stir.

Summer Sensation
HIGHBALL GLASS

1 part Banana Liqueur
fill with Orange Juice
splash Grenadine

Build over ice and stir.

Summer Share
HIGHBALL GLASS

1 part Light Rum
1 part Vodka
½ part Tequila
splash Apricot Brandy
1 part Cranberry Juice Cocktail
1 part Orange Juice
fill with Lemon-Lime Soda

Build over ice and stir.

Summer Splash
HIGHBALL GLASS
1½ parts Gin
splash Lemon-Lime Soda
fill with Lemonade
Build over ice and stir.

Sun Burn
HIGHBALL GLASS
2 parts Cinnamon Schnapps
1 part Cherry Juice
fill with Pineapple Juice
Shake with ice and pour.

Sun on the Rocks
HIGHBALL GLASS
2 parts Tequila
dash Sugar
fill with Orange Juice
splash Lemon Juice
Shake with ice and pour.

Sunblock 42
HIGHBALL GLASS
1 part Peach Schnapps
1 part Amaretto
fill with Cranberry Juice Cocktail
Build over ice and stir.

Sundance
HIGHBALL GLASS
1 part Apricot Brandy
1 part Vodka
splash Passion Fruit Nectar
splash Lemon Juice
fill with Pineapple Juice
Shake with ice and pour.

Sundown
ROCKS GLASS
1 part Vodka
1 part Apricot Brandy
fill with Pineapple Juice
Build over ice and stir.

Sunniest Sour
HIGHBALL GLASS
1¼ parts Dark Rum
½ part Lemon Juice
dash Powdered Sugar
1 part Orange Juice
1 part Club Soda
Shake all but Club Soda with ice and strain. Top with Club Soda.

Sunny Campari®
HIGHBALL GLASS
½ part Campari®
1½ parts Orange Juice
Shake with ice and strain over ice.

Sunrise
HIGHBALL GLASS
1 part Gin
splash Sweet Vermouth
1 part Orange Juice
splash Grenadine
Shake with ice and strain over ice.

Sunset Sour
ROCKS GLASS
1½ parts Whiskey
3 parts Sweet & Sour Mix
splash Grenadine
Shake with ice and strain over ice.

Sunset Strip
HIGHBALL GLASS
2 parts Dark Rum
¼ part Grenadine
2 parts Orange Juice
2 parts Pineapple Juice
Shake with ice and pour.

Superman
ROCKS GLASS
1 part Scotch
1 part Vodka
1 part Gin
1 part Grenadine
splash Orange Juice
Shake with ice and strain over ice.

Supersonic Sunshine

HIGHBALL GLASS

1 part Coconut Rum
1 part Vodka
fill with Chocolate Milk

Shake with ice and pour. Garnish with an Orange Slice.

Surprise Me

HIGHBALL GLASS

1 part Sour Apple Schnapps
1 part Vodka
½ part Spiced Rum
splash Triple Sec
fill with Cranberry Juice

Shake with ice and strain over ice. Make this when someone says, "Surprise me." They'll probably like it, and you don't have to think about it too much.

Surrey Slider

HIGHBALL GLASS

1½ parts Añejo Rum
½ part Peach Schnapps
fill with Orange Juice

Build over ice and stir.

Sweaty Belly

HIGHBALL GLASS

1½ parts Amaretto
1 part Orange Juice
1 part Cranberry Juice Cocktail

Build over ice and stir.

Swedish Bear

ROCKS GLASS

¾ part Vodka
½ part Crème de Cacao (Dark)
fill with Heavy Cream

Shake with ice and pour.

Swedish Pinkie

CHAMPAGNE FLUTE

1 part Currant Vodka
1 part Cranberry Juice Cocktail
1 part Sweet & Sour Mix

Shake with ice and pour.

Sweet and Sour Rum

HIGHBALL GLASS

1 part Light Rum
1 part Dark Rum
1 part Orange Juice
½ part Lemon Juice
½ part Lime Juice

Shake with ice and strain over ice.

Sweet Candy Apple

HIGHBALL GLASS

¾ part Southern Comfort®
¾ part Amaretto
¾ part Melon Liqueur
½ part Grenadine
2 splashes Sweet & Sour Mix

Shake with ice and strain over ice.

Sweet Caroline

HIGHBALL GLASS

1 part Vodka
1 part Strawberry Liqueur
1 part Peach Schnapps
1 part Lemonade
2 parts Lemon-Lime Soda

Build over ice and stir.

Sweet City

HIGHBALL GLASS

1 part Vodka
1 part Apricot Brandy
1 part Sweet Vermouth

Build over ice and stir.

Sweet Death

HIGHBALL GLASS

1 part Coconut Rum
1 part 151-Proof Rum
1 part Vodka
1 part Sweet & Sour Mix
1 part Cranberry Juice Cocktail

Shake with ice and pour.

Sweet Jane

WHITE WINE GLASS

2 parts Lime Juice
2 parts Orange Juice
1 part Amaretto
1 part Cream of Coconut

Shake with ice and pour.

Sweet Kiss

HIGHBALL GLASS

1 part Amaretto
fill with Pineapple Juice
splash Grenadine

Shake with ice and pour.

Sweet Patootie

ROCKS GLASS

2 parts Gin
1 part Triple Sec
1 part Orange Juice

Shake with ice and strain over ice.

Sweet Revenge

HIGHBALL GLASS

1 part Cointreau®
1 part Melon Liqueur
fill with Orange Juice

Build over ice and stir.

Sweet Satisfaction

HIGHBALL GLASS

1 part Coconut Rum
1 part Irish Cream Liqueur
1 part Amaretto
1 part Butterscotch Schnapps

Shake with ice and strain over ice.

Sweet Scotch

HIGHBALL GLASS

1 1/2 parts Scotch
1/2 part Bénédictine®
splash Honey
fill with Peach Nectar

Shake with ice and pour.

Sweet Sensation

HIGHBALL GLASS

1 1/2 parts Southern Comfort®
fill with Lemon-Lime Soda

Build over ice and stir.

Sweet Surrender

HIGHBALL GLASS

1 part Coconut Rum
1 part Amaretto
1 part Orange Juice
1 part Pineapple Juice
1 part Lemon-Lime Soda

Build over ice and stir.

Sweet Temptation

HIGHBALL GLASS

2 parts Triple Sec
1 part Peach Schnapps
fill with Lemon-Lime Soda
splash Sweet & Sour Mix

Build over ice and stir.

Sweet Water

HIGHBALL GLASS

1 part Extra Dry Gin
1 part Butterscotch Schnapps
2 parts Triple Sec
2 parts Vodka

Shake with ice and strain over ice.

Sweetie Pie

ROCKS GLASS

1 1/2 parts Apricot Brandy
1/2 part Gin
3/4 part Orange Juice

Shake with ice and strain over ice.

Sword of Damocles

ROCKS GLASS

1 part Rum
1 part Melon Liqueur
1 part Lime Juice

Shake with ice and strain.

T-Bird

HIGHBALL GLASS

1 part Canadian Whisky
3/4 part Amaretto
2 parts Pineapple Juice
1 part Orange Juice
2 splashes Grenadine

Shake with ice and strain.

T.K.O.

ROCKS GLASS

1 part Tequila
1 part Coffee Liqueur
1 part Ouzo

Shake with ice and strain over ice.

Tachyon

HIGHBALL GLASS

1 part Pernod®
1 part Tequila
splash Lemon Juice

Shake with ice and strain over ice.

Tahiti Rainstorm

HIGHBALL GLASS

1 part Rum
1 part Blue Curaçao
1 part Margarita Mix
1 part Lemon-Lime Soda

Build over ice and stir.

Tahiti Vacation

HIGHBALL GLASS

1 part Rum
1 part Wild Berry Schnapps
1 part Cherry Juice
1 part Margarita Mix
2 parts Pineapple Juice

Shake with ice and pour.

Tainted Cherry

HIGHBALL GLASS

1 part Vodka
1 part Cherry Brandy
fill with Orange Juice

Shake with ice and strain over ice.

Tanahgoyang

HIGHBALL GLASS

1 part Vodka
1/2 part Pisang Ambon® Liqueur
1/2 part Crème de Coconut
1 part Lemon Juice
fill with Orange Juice

Shake with ice and strain over ice.

Tango & Cash

HIGHBALL GLASS

1/2 part Crème de Cassis
1 part Vanilla Vodka
2/3 part Lemon Juice
2 parts Raspberry Seltzer

Stir gently with ice.

Tart and Tangy

ROCKS GLASS

1 part Sweet & Sour Mix
1 part Bacardi® Limon Rum
splash Grenadine

Shake with ice and strain over ice.

Tattooed Smurf®

HIGHBALL GLASS

2 parts Blueberry Schnapps
fill with Lemon-Lime Soda

Build over ice and stir.

Tawny Russian

HIGHBALL GLASS

1 part Amaretto
1 part Vodka

Build over ice and stir.

Tea Bag

HIGHBALL GLASS

1½ parts Dark Rum
½ part Crème de Cacao (Dark)
¼ part Lemon Juice
2 dashes Sugar
fill with Iced Tea

Shake with ice and strain over ice.

Tea Spike

HIGHBALL GLASS

1½ parts Rum
½ part Crème de Cacao (Dark)
fill with Iced Tea

Shake with ice and strain over ice.

Technicolor®

HIGHBALL GLASS

½ part Melon Liqueur
½ part Blue Curaçao
1 part Cointreau®
2 parts Orange Juice

Shake with ice and strain over ice.

Tee Off

ROCKS GLASS

1 part Brandy
1 part Crème de Menthe (White)
1 part Pineapple Juice
1 part Orange Juice

Shake with ice and pour.

Temptress

HIGHBALL GLASS

1 part Vodka
1 part Grenadine

Shake with ice and strain over ice.

Ten Quidder

ROCKS GLASS

1½ parts Gin
1 part Triple Sec
dash Bitters
splash Blue Curaçao

Shake with ice and strain over ice.

Tennessee

HIGHBALL GLASS

2 parts Rye Whiskey
½ part Cherry Liqueur
½ part Lemon Juice

Shake with ice and strain.

Tennessee Lemonade

HIGHBALL GLASS

1 part Jack Daniel's®
1 part Triple Sec
fill with Lemonade

Build over ice and stir.

Tennessee Tea

HIGHBALL GLASS

1 part Vodka
1 part Rum
1 part Gin
1 part Triple Sec
1 part Jack Daniel's®
fill with Sweet & Sour Mix
splash Orange Juice
splash Cola

Shake with ice and strain over ice.

Tequila Aloha

HIGHBALL GLASS

½ part Blue Curaçao
1 part Tequila Reposado
½ part Triple Sec
fill with Pineapple Juice

Build over ice and stir.

Tequila Ghost

ROCKS GLASS

½ part Lemon Juice
2 parts Tequila
1 part Pernod®

Shake with ice and strain over ice.

Tequila Manhattan

ROCKS GLASS

2 parts Tequila
1 part Sweet Vermouth
splash Lime Juice

Shake with ice and strain over ice.

Tequila Matador
CHAMPAGNE FLUTE

1½ parts Tequila
3 parts Pineapple Juice
½ part Lime Juice

Shake with ice and strain.

Tequila Mirage
HIGHBALL GLASS

1 part Tequila
1 part Raspberry Liqueur
1 part Orange Juice
1 part Lemon-Lime Soda

Build over ice and stir.

Tequila Old-Fashioned
ROCKS GLASS

1½ parts Gold Tequila
splash Simple Syrup
2 dashes Angostura® Bitters
splash Club Soda

Build over ice and stir.

Tequila Paralyzer
HIGHBALL GLASS

1 part Tequila
1 part Coffee Liqueur
splash Milk
fill with Cola

Build over ice and stir.

Tequila Razz
HIGHBALL GLASS

1½ parts Tequila
½ part Raspberry Liqueur
1 part Orange Juice
1 part Pineapple Juice

Build over ice and stir.

Tequila Sour
ROCKS GLASS

2 parts Tequila
½ part Lemon Juice
dash Powdered Sugar

Shake with ice and strain over ice.

Tequila Sunrise
HIGHBALL GLASS

2 parts Tequila
fill with Orange Juice
splash Grenadine

Build over ice.

Tequila Vertigo
HIGHBALL GLASS

1 part Tequila
1 part Triple Sec
½ Sour Mix
fill with Cranberry Juice Cocktail

Shake with ice and pour.

Tequiria
HIGHBALL GLASS

2 parts Silver Tequila
1 part Raspberry Liqueur
1 part Ginger Ale
1 part Lime Juice
1 part Simple Syrup

Build over ice and stir.

Ter
HIGHBALL GLASS

1 part Peach Schnapps
2 parts Sake

Shake with ice and strain over ice.

Texas Cool-Aid
HIGHBALL GLASS

1 part Vodka
1 part Midori®
1 part Crème de Noyaux
splash Cranberry Juice Cocktail

Shake with ice and pour.

Texas Ice Pick
HIGHBALL GLASS

1 part Tequila
1 part Lemonade
2 parts Iced Tea

Shake with ice and pour.

Texas Sundowner

ROCKS GLASS

1 part Light Rum
½ part Grenadine
½ part Sambuca

Build over ice.

Texas Tea

HIGHBALL GLASS

1 part Gin
1 part Tequila
1 part Rum
1 part Sweet & Sour Mix
fill with Cola

Build over ice and stir.

They Killed Kenny!

HIGHBALL GLASS

2 parts Jack Daniel's®
1½ parts Sour Apple Schnapps
2 parts Apple Juice
fill with Lemon-Lime Soda

Build over ice and stir.

Think Tank

HIGHBALL GLASS

½ part Vodka
1 part Coffee Liqueur
1 part Cream
fill with Seltzer

Build over ice and stir.

Three Fifths

ROCKS GLASS

2 parts Vodka
1½ parts Grape Soda
1½ parts Club Soda

Build over ice and stir.

Three Wise Men Go Hunting

HIGHBALL GLASS

1 part Jack Daniel's®
1 part Jim Beam®
1 part Johnnie Walker® Black Label
1 part Wild Turkey® Bourbon

Pour ingredients into glass neat (do not chill).

Threesome

HIGHBALL GLASS

1½ parts Vodka
1 part Amaretto
splash Sweet & Sour Mix
splash Blue Curaçao
splash Grenadine

Shake all but Blue Curaçao and Grenadine with ice. Place the Blue Curaçao in the glass, fill the glass with ice, and strain the shaken mixture into the glass. Top with Grenadine.

Thunder King

ROCKS GLASS

1 part Citrus Vodka
1 part Whiskey
½ part Coffee Liqueur
fill with Milk

Shake with ice and pour.

Thunder Road

HIGHBALL GLASS

1½ parts Applejack
¾ part Light Rum
¼ part Amaretto
¼ part Lime Juice

Shake with ice and pour.

Thursday Night Juice Break

HIGHBALL GLASS

1½ parts Peach Schnapps
1½ parts Grapefruit Juice
3 parts Lemonade
3 parts Orange Juice
splash Maraschino Cherry Juice

Build over ice and stir.

Tickle Me Elmo®

HIGHBALL GLASS

1 part Strawberry Liqueur
fill with Pineapple Juice

Build over ice and stir.

Tidal Wave
HIGHBALL GLASS

1 part Vodka
1 part Blue Curaçao
2 parts Margarita Mix
1 part Lemon-Lime Soda

Shake with ice and pour.

Tie-Dyed
HIGHBALL GLASS

1 part Blueberry Schnapps
1 part Raspberry Vodka
1 part Cranberry Juice Cocktail
1 part Orange Juice
1 part Lemon-Lime Soda

Build over ice and stir.

Tiffany's
HIGHBALL GLASS

1 1/2 parts Vodka
2/3 part Crème de Cassis

Build over ice and stir.

Tiger's Milk
WHITE WINE GLASS

2 parts Dark Rum
1 1/2 parts Cognac
1/2 part Simple Syrup
fill with Milk

Shake with ice and pour.

Tijuana Bulldog
HIGHBALL GLASS

1 part Tequila
1 part Coffee Liqueur
1 part Cola
1 part Cream

Build over ice and stir.

Tijuana Taxi
HIGHBALL GLASS

2 parts Tequila Gold
1 part Blue Curaçao
1 part Tropical Punch Schnapps
fill with Lemon-Lime Soda

Build over ice and stir.

Tijuana Tea
HIGHBALL GLASS

3/4 part Tequila
1/2 part Triple Sec
1 part Sweet & Sour Mix
fill with Cola

Build over ice and stir.

Time of the Month
ROCKS GLASS

1 part Vodka
1 part Gin
1 part Peach Schnapps
1 part Triple Sec
2 parts Orange Juice
fill with Pineapple Juice
dash Grenadine

Build over ice.

Tiny Tim
HIGHBALL GLASS

1 part Brandy
1 part Dry Vermouth
1/2 part Triple Sec
dash Sugar

Shake with ice and strain over ice.

Tiptoe
ROCKS GLASS

2 parts Light Rum
2 parts Pineapple Juice
1 part Triple Sec

Build over ice and stir.

Titan
HIGHBALL GLASS

1 part Crème de Cacao (Dark)
1 part Amaretto
1 part Light Rum
1 part Cream

Shake with ice and strain over ice.

Tivoli Cola

HIGHBALL GLASS

1 part Light Rum
1 part Triple Sec
½ part Raspberry Liqueur
½ part Sweet & Sour Mix
fill with Cola

Build over ice and stir.

Toast the Ghost

HIGHBALL GLASS

1 part Vodka
1 part Crème de Coconut
1 part Amaretto
1 part Irish Cream Liqueur
fill with Milk

Shake with ice and strain over ice.

Toasted Almond

HIGHBALL GLASS

1 part Amaretto
1½ parts Coffee Liqueur
fill with Light Cream

Shake with ice and pour.

Tokyo at Dawn

ROCKS GLASS

1 part Mango Schnapps
1 part Coconut Rum
1 part Orange Juice
½ part Pineapple Juice

Shake with ice and strain over ice.

Tokyo Tea

HIGHBALL GLASS

½ part Vodka
½ part Rum
½ part Triple Sec
½ part Gin
1 part Melon Liqueur
fill with Sweet & Sour Mix

Shake with ice and pour.

Tomahawk

HIGHBALL GLASS

1 part Vodka
½ part Crème de Cacao (White)
½ part Triple Sec
2 splashes Lime Juice
1 part Cream

Shake with ice and strain over ice.

Tomakazi

ROCKS GLASS

¾ part Vodka
¾ part Gin
½ part Lime Cordial
splash Sweet & Sour Mix
splash Cola

Build over ice and stir.

Tom-Tom

HIGHBALL GLASS

1 part Coffee Liqueur
1 part Whiskey
fill with Cold Coffee

Shake with ice and pour.

Top o' the Morning

HIGHBALL GLASS

1 part Vodka
1 part Triple Sec
¼ part Tequila
1 part Orange Juice
1 part Cranberry Juice Cocktail

Shake with ice and strain over ice.

Top Spinner

WHITE WINE GLASS

1 part Cognac
1 part Lime Juice
1 part Pineapple Juice
1 part Orange Juice

Shake with ice and pour.

Topshelf

ROCKS GLASS

1 part Gin
½ part Orange Juice
½ part Sloe Gin

Shake with ice and strain over ice.

Topsy-Turvy

HIGHBALL GLASS

1½ parts Crème de Coconut
½ part Vanilla Liqueur
½ part Jägermeister®
2 parts Pineapple Juice

Shake with ice and strain over ice.

Toreador

ROCKS GLASS

1½ parts Tequila
½ part Crème de Cacao (White)
dash Cocoa Powder

Shake with ice and strain. Top with Whipped Cream and Cocoa Powder.

Torombolo

HIGHBALL GLASS

2 parts Chocolate Milk
1 part Licor 43®

Build over ice and stir.

Touchdown Tea

HIGHBALL GLASS

2 parts Peach Schnapps
1 part Lemon Juice
fill with Iced Tea

Build over ice and stir.

The Train

HIGHBALL GLASS

1 part 151-Proof Rum
1 part Coconut Rum
1 part Jägermeister
1 part Peach Schnapps
1 part Vodka
1 part Cranberry Juice
1 part Pineapple Juice

Shake with ice and strain over ice.

Traffic

HIGHBALL GLASS

1 part Apricot Brandy
1 part Peach Schnapps
splash Angostura® Bitters
1 part Lemon Juice
fill with Passion Fruit Juice

Shake with ice and strain over ice.

Transmission

HIGHBALL GLASS

1 part Apricot Brandy
⅔ part Orange Liqueur
3 parts Passion Fruit Liqueur
2 parts Orange Juice
splash Lemon Juice

Shake with ice and pour.

Treasure Hunt

ROCKS GLASS

1 part Crème de Menthe (Green)
1 part Whiskey
1 tbsp sugar

Shake with ice and strain over ice.

Tremor

HIGHBALL GLASS

1 part Midori®
1 part Spiced Rum
1 part Vodka
1 part Crème de Noyaux
fill with Orange Juice

Shake with ice and pour.

Trinidad Punch

HIGHBALL GLASS

3 parts Rum
1 part Simple Syrup
1 part Lime Juice
4 dashes Bitters

Shake with ice and strain over ice.

Triple Jump
ROCKS GLASS

1½ parts Vodka
½ part Triple Sec
½ part Apricot Brandy
½ part Strawberry Liqueur
fill with Orange Juice

Build over ice and stir.

Triple Pleasure
HIGHBALL GLASS

1 part Vodka
1 part Tequila
1 part Yukon Jack®
1 part Cranberry Juice Cocktail
1 part Orange Juice
1 part Pineapple Juice

Build over ice and stir.

Trois Rivières
ROCKS GLASS

1½ parts Canadian Whisky
½ part Dubonnet® Blonde
splash Triple Sec

Shake with ice and strain over ice.

Trojan Horse
ROCKS GLASS

1 part Triple Sec
1 part Dry Vermouth
1 part Gin
1 part Kirschwasser
1 part Pineapple Syrup

Shake with ice and strain over ice.

Tropical 2x4
HIGHBALL GLASS

1 part Light Rum
1 part Triple Sec
1 part Pineapple Juice
1 part Orange Juice

Build over ice and stir.

Tropical Blue
ROCKS GLASS

½ part Gin
½ part Dark Rum
½ part Blue Curaçao
½ part Apricot Brandy
½ part Crème de Coconut
1 part Grapefruit Juice
1 part Pineapple Juice
1 part Orange Juice

Shake with ice and strain over ice.

Tropical Daydream
HIGHBALL GLASS

1 part Vodka
1 part Peach Schnapps
½ part Amaretto
1 part Cranberry Juice Cocktail
1 part Orange Juice

Build over ice and stir.

Tropical Itch
HIGHBALL GLASS

1 part Light Rum
1 part Dark Rum
1 part Vodka
1 part Grand Marnier®
1 part Lemon Juice
fill with Mango Nectar

Shake with ice and pour.

Tropical LifeSaver®
HIGHBALL GLASS

¾ part Midori®
¾ part Coconut Rum
½ part Citrus Vodka
2 parts Pineapple Juice
1 part Sweet & Sour Mix
splash Lemon-Lime Soda

Build over ice and stir.

Tropical Rainstorm
HIGHBALL GLASS

1 part Vodka
1 part Blue Curaçao
2 parts Lemon-Lime Soda
1 part Pineapple Juice

Build over ice and stir.

Tropical Sunset

HIGHBALL GLASS

1 part Vodka
1 part Cherry Juice
1 part Wild Berry Schnapps
fill with Orange Juice

Build over ice and stir.

Tropical Torpedo

HIGHBALL GLASS

3/4 part Spiced Rum
3/4 part Melon Liqueur
3/4 part Peach Schnapps
1 part Piña Colada Mix
1 part Pineapple Juice

Build over ice and stir.

Tsunami

HIGHBALL GLASS

1 part Spiced Rum
1/2 part Coconut Rum
1/2 part Meyers's® Rum
fill with Pineapple Juice
splash Grenadine

Build over ice and stir.

Tu Tu Can Can

HIGHBALL GLASS

1 part Gin
1 part Blue Curaçao
1/2 part Dry Vermouth
1/2 part Lime Juice
fill with Orange Juice

Shake with ice and strain over ice.

Tuaca® Nutter

HIGHBALL GLASS

1 part Tuaca®
1 part Frangelico®
1 part Coffee Liqueur
2 parts Cream

Shake with ice and strain over ice.

Tumbled Marble

ROCKS GLASS

1 part Apricot Brandy
1 part Port
1 part Remy Martin® VSOP
1 Egg Yolk
splash Simple Syrup

Shake with ice and strain over ice.

Tumbleweed

HIGHBALL GLASS

1 part Vodka
1 part Peach Schnapps
1 part Raspberry Liqueur
2 parts Lemonade
1 part Cola

Build over ice and stir.

Turkey on Fire

HIGHBALL GLASS

1 part Jim Beam®
1 part Blue Curaçao
1 part Coffee Liqueur
splash Triple Sec

Build over ice and stir.

Twat in the Hat

HIGHBALL GLASS

1 1/2 parts Rum
1 part Lemon Juice
3 parts Orange Juice
fill with Lemon-Lime Soda

Build over ice and stir.

Twilight Zone

HIGHBALL GLASS

1 part Vodka
1 part Blue Curaçao
splash Lemon Juice

Shake with ice and strain over ice.

Twin Hills
ROCKS GLASS

1½ parts Whiskey
1½ splashes Lemon Juice
1½ splashes Lime Juice
2 splashes Bénédictine®
dash Sugar

Shake with ice and strain over ice.

Twinkle My Lights
HIGHBALL GLASS

1 part Amaretto
1 part Raspberry Liqueur
1 part Lemon-Lime Soda

Shake with ice and strain over ice.

Twisted Delight
HIGHBALL GLASS

2 parts Gin
1 part Lemon-Lime Soda
1 part Orange Juice

Build over ice and stir.

Twister
HIGHBALL GLASS

1 part Triple Sec
1 part Vodka
fill with Orange Juice
splash Grenadine

Build over ice.

Two by Four
ROCKS GLASS

1 part Southern Comfort
1 part Whiskey
3 drops Angostura Bitters

Build over ice and stir.

Two Wheeler
HIGHBALL GLASS

1¼ parts Dark Rum
fill with Orange Juice

Build over ice and stir.

Ultra Z
ROCKS GLASS

2 parts Brandy
1 part Crème de Banane
2 parts Pear Juice
1 part Lemon Juice

Shake with ice and strain over ice.

Umbrella Man Special
HIGHBALL GLASS

1 part Vodka
1 part Coffee Liqueur
1 part Irish Cream Liqueur
1 part Grand Marnier®
1 part Drambuie®

Shake with ice and strain over ice.

Uncle Wiggley
HIGHBALL GLASS

½ part Crown Royal® Whiskey
½ part Amaretto
1 part Cranberry Juice Cocktail
1 part Sweet & Sour Mix

Shake with ice and strain over ice.

Unconventional Bloody Mary
HIGHBALL GLASS

1½ parts Citrus Vodka
splash Lime Juice
fill with Tomato Juice
splash Tabasco® Sauce
splash Worcestershire Sauce
dash Salt
dash White Pepper

Shake with ice and pour.

Under the Sea
ROCKS GLASS

1 part Light Rum
1 part Crème de Banane
¾ part Blue Curaçao
1 part Simple Syrup
splash Lemon Juice

Shake with ice and strain.

Underdog

HIGHBALL GLASS

2 parts Coffee Liqueur
fill with Apple Juice

Build over ice and stir.

Union League

HIGHBALL GLASS

2 parts Gin
1 part Port
2 dashes Orange Bitters

Stir gently with ice.

Up on the Roof

HIGHBALL GLASS

1 part Vodka
1 part Cherry Juice
1 part Lemonade
1 part Cola

Build over ice and stir.

Upper-Class

ROCKS GLASS

1 part Amaretto
2 parts Southern Comfort®

Shake with ice and strain over ice.

Upper Cut

ROCKS GLASS

1 part Amaretto
1 part Coffee Liqueur
1 part Espresso Vodka
1 part Irish Whiskey

Shake with ice and strain over ice.

Upside Down Pineapple

ROCKS GLASS

1 part Southern Comfort®
1 part Coconut Rum
splash Pineapple Juice
fill with Orange Juice

Build over ice and stir.

Usual Suspect

ROCKS GLASS

1 part Cream
splash Vodka
splash Crème de Banane

Shake with ice and strain over ice.

Utter Butter

HIGHBALL GLASS

2 parts Coffee Liqueur
1 part Butterscotch Schnapps
2 parts Cream

Build over ice and stir.

V8® Caesar's

HIGHBALL GLASS

1 part Vodka
1 part V8® Vegetable Juice Blend
1 part Clamato® Juice
1/4 part Worcestershire® Sauce
dash Salt
dash Pepper
splash Lime Juice

Shake with ice and pour.

V8® Mary

HIGHBALL GLASS

1 part Vodka
fill with V8® Vegetable Juice Blend
1/4 part Worcestershire® Sauce
dash Salt
dash Pepper
splash Lime Juice

Shake with ice and pour.

Valentine

RED WINE GLASS

2 parts Banana Liqueur
1 part Vodka
fill with Cranberry Juice Cocktail

Shake with ice and strain.

Vampire's Kiss
ROCKS GLASS

2 parts Vodka
½ part Dry Gin
½ part Dry Vermouth
½ part Tequila
dash Salt

Shake with ice and strain over ice.

Vaughn Purple Haze
HIGHBALL GLASS

2 parts Vodka
1½ parts Raspberry Liqueur
fill with Cranberry Juice Cocktail

Build over ice and stir.

VCG
ROCKS GLASS

1 part Vodka
fill with Cranberry Juice Cocktail
splash Grenadine

Build over ice and stir.

Velociraptor
HIGHBALL GLASS

1½ parts Vodka
splash Chicken Broth
3 splashes Tabasco® Sauce

Shake with ice and strain over ice.

Velvet Hammer
HIGHBALL GLASS

1 part Coffee Liqueur
1 part Cointreau
1 part Half and Half

Shake with ice and strain over ice.

Velvet Tu-Tu
HIGHBALL GLASS

1½ parts Black Velvet® Whiskey
1 part Amaretto
1 part Orange Juice
1 part Pineapple Juice

Shake with ice and pour.

Venetian Peach
HIGHBALL GLASS

1 part Spiced Rum
1 part Peach Schnapps
fill with Lemonade
splash Strawberry Daiquiri Mix

Shake with ice and pour.

Ventura Highway
HIGHBALL GLASS

1 part Vodka
2 parts Raspberry Liqueur
1 part Lemonade
1 part Orange Juice

Shake with ice and strain over ice.

Vermont Maple Blaster
HIGHBALL GLASS

1 part Rum
1 part Maple Syrup
1 part Water

Shake with ice and strain over ice.

Vermouth Cassis
HIGHBALL GLASS

1½ parts Dry Vermouth
¾ part Crème de Cassis
fill with Seltzer

Build over ice and stir.

Vernal Equinox
ROCKS GLASS

2 parts Port
1 part Grand Marnier®
½ part Triple Sec

Stir gently with ice.

Vesuvio
ROCKS GLASS

1 part Light Rum
½ part Sweet Vermouth
½ part Lemon Juice
dash Powdered Sugar
1 Egg White

Shake with ice and strain over ice.

Veteran

ROCKS GLASS

2 parts Dark Rum
½ part Cherry Brandy

Shake with ice and strain over ice.

Victoria's Secret®

ROCKS GLASS

1 part Currant Vodka
1½ parts Sweet Vermouth
¼ part Sweet & Sour Mix

Shake with ice and strain.

Viking Blood

HIGHBALL GLASS

1 part Aquavit
1 part Tia Maria®
fill with Lemon-Lime Soda

Build over ice and stir.

Viking Warmer

ROCKS GLASS

1½ parts Vodka
½ part Aquavit
½ part Blueberry Syrup
1 part Lemonade
¼ part Lime Juice

Shake with ice and strain over ice.

Viking's Helmet

HIGHBALL GLASS

1½ parts Aquavit
¾ part Vodka
¾ part Lime Juice
⅓ part Pineapple Syrup
fill with Ginger Ale

Shake with ice and strain over ice.

Villa Park

HIGHBALL GLASS

1 part Bourbon
1 part Pineapple Juice
1 part Orange Juice

Build over ice and stir.

Vincow Somba

HIGHBALL GLASS

1 part Vodka
1 part Triple Sec
1 part Pineapple Juice

Build over ice and stir.

Vinyl Sunset

HIGHBALL GLASS

1 part Absinthe
½ part Crème de Cassis
½ part Lime Juice
fill with Lemonade

Build over ice and stir.

Viper Venom

ROCKS GLASS

1½ parts Yukon Jack®
½ part Triple Sec
1 part Sweetened Lime Juice
1 part Lemon Juice

Shake with ice and strain over ice.

Virgin Maiden

HIGHBALL GLASS

1 part Blue Curaçao
1 part Grenadine
1 part Bénédictine®
1 part Chartreuse®
1 part Crème de Noyaux

Build over ice and stir.

Virgo

HIGHBALL GLASS

1 part Vodka
1 part Wild Berry Schnapps
2 parts Lemonade
1 part Cola

Build over ice and stir.

Viva Villa

ROCKS GLASS

1½ parts Tequila
1 part Lime Juice
1 tsp Sugar

Shake with ice and pour.

Vodka Boatman

HIGHBALL GLASS

1 part Vodka
1 part Cherry Brandy
fill with Orange Juice

Build over ice and stir.

Vodka Dog

HIGHBALL GLASS

1 part Vodka
fill with Grapefruit Juice

Build over ice and stir.

Vodka Red Bull®

HIGHBALL GLASS

2½ parts Vodka
fill with Red Bull® Energy Drink

Build over ice and stir.

Vodka Salty Dog

HIGHBALL GLASS

1½ parts Vodka
fill with Grapefruit Juice
dash Salt

Shake with ice and pour.

Vodka Screw-Up

HIGHBALL GLASS

1 part Vodka
1 part Lemon-Lime Soda
1 part Orange Juice

Build over ice and stir.

Vodka Sour

ROCKS GLASS

2 parts Vodka
½ part Lemon Juice
dash Sugar

Shake with ice and strain over ice.

Vodka Sourball

ROCKS GLASS

1½ parts Lemon Vodka
½ part Triple Sec
½ part Pineapple Juice

Shake with ice and strain over ice.

Vodka Sunrise

HIGHBALL GLASS

1 part Vodka
fill with Orange Juice
splash Grenadine

Build over ice.

Vodka Sunset

HIGHBALL GLASS

1½ parts Vodka
fill with Grapefruit Juice
2 splashes Grenadine

Build over ice.

Vodka Volcano

HIGHBALL GLASS

2 parts Vodka
1 part Grapefruit Juice
splash Grenadine

Build over ice.

Waffle Dripper

ROCKS GLASS

1½ parts Vodka
1 part Butterscotch Schnapps
fill with Orange Juice

Shake with ice and strain.

Wake-Up Call

HIGHBALL GLASS

1 part Jack Daniel's®
1 part Vodka
½ part Lemon Juice

Shake with ice and strain.

A Walk on the Moon
HIGHBALL GLASS
2 parts Blackberry Liqueur
1 part Vodka
3 parts Cola
3 parts Milk
Shake with ice and strain over ice.
Serve with a straw.

Walkover
HIGHBALL GLASS
1½ parts Frangelico®
1 part Coffee Brandy
½ part Cream of Coconut
fill with Pineapple Juice
Shake with ice and strain over ice.

Wallis Blue Cocktail
ROCKS GLASS
1 part Gin
1 part Triple Sec
½ part Lime Juice
Shake with ice and strain over ice.

Walterbury
HIGHBALL GLASS
1 part Kiwi Schnapps
1 part Dark Rum
fill with Lemon-Lime Soda
Build over ice and stir.

Waltzing Matilda
ROCKS GLASS
1 part Dry Sherry
1 part Dry Gin
1 part Passion Fruit Liqueur
½ part Triple Sec
Shake with ice and strain over ice.

Warm Summer Rain
HIGHBALL GLASS
1½ parts Vodka
½ part Crème de Coconut
fill with Pineapple Juice
splash Orange Juice
Shake with ice and strain over ice.

Warrior's Cup
ROCKS GLASS
1 part Amaretto
½ part Scotch
1 part Tequila
Build over ice and stir.

Washington Apple
HIGHBALL GLASS
1 part Canadian Whisky
1 part Sour Apple Schnapps
fill with Apple-Cranberry Juice
Shake with ice and pour.

Wasp Sting
HIGHBALL GLASS
1 part Brandy
1 part Crème de Cacao (White)
fill with Cola
Build over ice and stir.

Waterslide
HIGHBALL GLASS
1 part Amaretto
½ part Light Rum
½ part Lime Juice
fill with Pineapple Juice
Build over ice and stir.

Wave Breaker
ROCKS GLASS
1 part Vodka
1 part Cream of Coconut
splash Lime Juice
Shake with ice and strain over ice.

Wedding Day
HIGHBALL GLASS
1 part Gin
½ part Vodka
1 part Jägermeister®
fill with Apple Cider
Build over ice and stir.

Weeping Willow
HIGHBALL GLASS

1½ parts Gin
½ part Pisang Ambon® Liqueur
splash Crème de Coconut
fill with Orange Juice

Shake with ice and strain over ice.

West Indies Russian
HIGHBALL GLASS

1 part Vodka
1 part Rum
1 part Coffee Liqueur
fill with Cola

Build over ice and stir.

Wet & Wild
WHITE WINE GLASS

1½ parts Silver Tequila
½ part Triple Sec
fill with Grapefruit Juice

Shake with ice and strain.

Wet T-Shirt
HIGHBALL GLASS

1 part Light Rum
½ part Orange Liqueur
2 parts Orange Juice
1 part Pineapple Juice
½ part Lemon Juice

Shake with ice and strain over ice.

Whammy
HIGHBALL GLASS

1 part Rum
1 part Peach Schnapps
1 part Cherry Juice
2 parts Orange Juice
1 part Cola

Build over ice and stir.

What the Hell
ROCKS GLASS

1 part Apricot Brandy
1 part Dry Vermouth
1 part Gin
dash Lemon Juice

Shake with ice and strain over ice.

Wheelbarrow
HIGHBALL GLASS

2 parts Rum
1 part Drambuie®

Shake with ice and strain over ice.

Where's My Kilt
HIGHBALL GLASS

1 part Scotch
⅔ part Crème de Cacao (White)
½ part Cream of Coconut
splash Lemon Juice
3 parts Orange Juice

Shake with ice and strain over ice.

Whippet
HIGHBALL GLASS

1 part Vodka
fill with Orange Juice
splash Raspberry Liqueur

Build over ice.

Whirly Bird
ROCKS GLASS

1 part Pineapple Juice
1 part Melon Liqueur
1 part Southern Comfort®
1 part Citrus Vodka

Shake with ice and strain over ice.

Whiskey Cobbler
ROCKS GLASS

2½ parts Whiskey
½ part Lemon Juice
½ part Grapefruit Juice
½ part Amaretto

Shake with ice and strain over ice.

Whiskey Daisy
HIGHBALL GLASS

1 Lemon Wedge
1 Lime Wedge
½ part Yellow Chartreuse
splash Simple Syrup
1½ parts Whiskey

Muddle the Lemon Wedge, Lime Wedge, Simple Syrup, and Yellow Chartreuse in the glass. Add ice and the Whiskey.

Whiskey Lover
ROCKS GLASS

1 part Scotch
1 part Amaretto

Shake with ice and strain over ice.

Whispering Shadow
ROCKS GLASS

1 part Amaretto
½ part Lemon Juice
1½ parts Pineapple Juice
1 Egg White

Shake with ice and strain over ice.

White Bat
HIGHBALL GLASS

1½ parts White Rum
½ part Coffee Liqueur
1½ parts Milk
fill with Cola

Build over ice and stir.

White Bull
HIGHBALL GLASS

1 part Tequila
1 part Coffee Liqueur
fill with Cream

Shake with ice and pour.

White Chocolate
BRANDY SNIFTER

1 part Vanilla Vodka
2 parts Crème de Cacao (White)

Shake with ice and strain over ice.

White Christmas
HIGHBALL GLASS

1 part Gin
1 part Milk

Shake with ice and strain over ice.

White German
HIGHBALL GLASS

1 part Coffee Liqueur
1 part Vodka
splash Jägermeister
fill with Milk

Build over ice and stir.

White Girl
ROCKS GLASS

2 parts Irish Cream Liqueur
1 part Coffee Liqueur
½ part Vodka
fill with Milk

Build over ice and stir.

White Heat
HIGHBALL GLASS

1 part Gin
½ part Triple Sec
½ part Dry Vermouth
1 part Pineapple Juice

Shake with ice and strain over ice.

White Lily
ROCKS GLASS

1 part Gin
1 part Light Rum
1 part Triple Sec
splash Pernod®

Shake with ice and strain over ice.

White Lizard
HIGHBALL GLASS

2 parts Silver Tequila
1 part Lime Juice
fill with Grapefruit Juice

Shake with ice and pour.

White Mint and Brandy Frappé

HIGHBALL GLASS

1 part Brandy
2 parts Crème de Menthe (White)

Build over ice and stir.

White Out

HIGHBALL GLASS

2 parts Crème de Menthe (White)
1 part Cointreau®
1 part Cognac

Build over ice and stir.

White Rabbit

ROCKS GLASS

1 part Light Rum
½ part Irish Cream Liqueur
½ part Amaretto
½ part Coffee Liqueur
fill with Cream

Shake with ice and pour.

White Russian

ROCKS GLASS

1 part Vodka
1 part Coffee Liqueur
fill with Light Cream

Build over ice and stir.

White Stinger

ROCKS GLASS

2 parts Vodka
¾ part Crème de Cacao (White)

Shake with ice and strain over ice.

White Wedding

ROCKS GLASS

1½ parts Gin
⅔ part Peppermint Liqueur

Shake with ice and strain over ice.

Wicked Apple

HIGHBALL GLASS

1 part Jägermeister
1 part Vodka
splash Ginger Ale
fill with Apple Juice

Build over ice and stir.

Wicked Manhattan

ROCKS GLASS

2 parts Jim Beam®
1 part Sweet Vermouth
dash Bitters

Shake with ice and strain.

Wicked Witch

ROCKS GLASS

1½ parts Whiskey
¼ part Maraschino Liqueur
¼ part Pineapple Juice
splash Lemon Juice

Shake with ice and strain over ice.

Wild Beaver

HIGHBALL GLASS

1 part Amaretto
1 part Whiskey
1 part Cranberry Juice
1 part Sweet & Sour Mix

Shake with ice and strain over ice.

Wild Buttery Squirrel

ROCKS GLASS

1 part Amaretto
1 part Butterscotch Liqueur
1 part Vodka

Shake with ice and strain over ice.

Wild Irish Buttery Squirrel

ROCKS GLASS

1 part Butterscotch Liqueur
1 part Vodka
½ part Amaretto
½ part Irish Cream Liqueur

Shake with ice and strain over ice.

Wild Jackalope

ROCKS GLASS

2 parts Canadian Whisky
1 part Peppermint Schnapps
1/2 part Amaretto
1/2 part Pernod

Shake with ice and strain over ice.

Wild Sacramento

HIGHBALL GLASS

1 part Vodka
1/2 part Tequila
1/2 part Triple Sec
splash Gin
splash Sweet & Sour Mix
dash Angostura Bitters
dash Lemon Juice

Shake with ice and strain over ice.

Wild Thing

ROCKS GLASS

1 1/2 parts Tequila
1 part Cranberry Juice Cocktail
1 part Club Soda
1/2 part Lime Juice

Build over ice and stir.

Wild Wild West

HIGHBALL GLASS

1 1/2 parts Jack Daniel's®
1 part Peach Schnapps
fill with Cranberry Juice Cocktail

Build over ice and stir.

Windex®

HIGHBALL GLASS

2 parts Vodka
1 part Light Rum
1/2 part Blue Curaçao
1/2 part Lime Juice

Shake with ice and strain over ice.

Windjammer

ROCKS GLASS

1 part Amaretto
2 parts Pineapple Juice
2 parts Orange Juice

Build over ice and stir.

Winning Horse

HIGHBALL GLASS

1 part Southern Comfort
1/2 part Dark Rum
1/2 part Sweet Vermouth
fill with Cola

Build over ice and stir.

Wisconsin Dells

HIGHBALL GLASS

1 part Southern Comfort®
1/2 part Sloe Gin
1/2 part Crème de Banane
fill with Pineapple Juice
splash Orange Juice

Shake with ice and strain over ice.

Wishing Well

HIGHBALL GLASS

1 part Apricot Brandy
1 part Crème de Cassis
1 part Sweet & Sour Mix
splash Simple Syrup
1 part Club Soda
1 part Cranberry Juice Cocktail

Build over ice and stir.

Witch's Brew

HIGHBALL GLASS

1 part Vodka
1 part Raspberry Liqueur
1 part Cranberry Juice Cocktail
1 part Sweet & Sour Mix

Build over ice and stir.

Wolf
ROCKS GLASS

1 part Blue Curaçao
½ part Crème de Menthe (White)
½ part Vodka
fill with Lemon-Lime Soda

Build over ice and stir.

Wolf's Lair
CHAMPAGNE FLUTE

1 part Brandy
1 part Peach Schnapps
½ part Honey Liqueur
1 part Whipping Cream

Shake with ice and strain.

Wolfsbane
HIGHBALL GLASS

2 parts Vodka
1½ parts Cherry Brandy
½ part Cream
1 Egg White

Shake with ice and strain over ice.

Woman in Blue
HIGHBALL GLASS

1 part Vodka
1 part Crème de Cacao (White)
1 part Frangelico®
splash Blue Curaçao

Shake with ice and strain over ice.

Wombat
ROCKS GLASS

2 parts Dark Rum
½ part Strawberry Liqueur
1 part Pineapple Juice
1 part Orange Juice

Shake with ice and pour.

Woo Woo
HIGHBALL GLASS

1 part Vodka
1 part Peach Schnapps
fill with Cranberry Juice Cocktail

Shake with ice and strain over ice.

Wookiee
HIGHBALL GLASS

1 part Rum
½ part Vodka
½ part Tequila
½ part Vermouth
1 part Orange Juice
1 part Cola

Build over ice and stir.

Woolly Navel
HIGHBALL GLASS

¾ part Peach Schnapps
1½ parts Vodka
fill with Orange Juice

Build over ice and stir.

Working Man's Zinfandel
WHITE WINE GLASS

1 part Tequila
1 part Scotch
½ part Cinnamon Schnapps
½ part Peach Schnapps
fill with Lemon-Lime Soda

Build over ice and stir.

Wrightsville Sunset
WHITE WINE GLASS

1 part Rum
1 part Tequila
½ part Lime Juice
½ part Grenadine
dash Bitters
fill with Orange Juice

Shake with ice and strain over ice.

X Marks the Spot
HIGHBALL GLASS

1 part Rum
1 part Amaretto
1 part Lemonade
1 part Cola

Build over ice and stir.

X-Wing

HIGHBALL GLASS

1 part Scotch
1 part Coffee Liqueur
1 part Crème de Cacao (White)
splash Irish Cream Liqueur

Shake with ice and strain over ice.

Yabba Dabba Doo

HIGHBALL GLASS

1 part Rum
1 part Strawberry Liqueur
1 part Wild Berry Schnapps
1 part Sweet & Sour Mix
1 part Orange Juice

Shake with ice and pour.

Yankee Dutch

HIGHBALL GLASS

1 part Cherry Brandy
1 part Triple Sec
1 part Vodka
1 part Jim Beam®

Shake with ice and strain over ice.

Yellow Bird

HIGHBALL GLASS

1 part Coconut Rum
1 part Crème de Banane
1 part Apricot Brandy
fill with Orange Juice

Shake with ice and pour.

Yellow Dog

HIGHBALL GLASS

1 part Vodka
1 part Coconut Rum
1 part Mountain Dew®
1 part Pineapple Juice

Build over ice and stir.

Yellow Fever

HIGHBALL GLASS

2 parts Vodka
½ part Galliano
½ part Lemon Juice
fill with Pineapple Juice

Shake with ice and strain over ice.

Yellow Pages

ROCKS GLASS

1½ parts Gin
fill with Pineapple Juice
splash Pernod®
splash Lemon Juice
dash Bitters

Shake with ice and strain over ice.

Yellow Peril

HIGHBALL GLASS

1 part Lime Vodka
1 part Galliano
1 part Banana Liqueur
1 part Cointreau

Build over ice and stir.

Yellow Sock

HIGHBALL GLASS

1 part Vodka
1 part Pisang Ambon® Liqueur
fill with Orange Juice

Build over ice and stir.

Yellow Sunset

HIGHBALL GLASS

1 part Vodka
1 part Grand Marnier®
fill with Pineapple Juice
1 part Cherry Juice

Build over ice.

Yeoman's Passion

ROCKS GLASS

½ part Pisang Ambon® Liqueur
½ part Gin
¼ part Dry Vermouth
1 part Passion Fruit Juice

Shake with ice and strain over ice.

Yorktown Yell
HIGHBALL GLASS

1 part Whiskey
1 part Raspberry Liqueur
1 part Cranberry Juice Cocktail
1 part Lemon-Lime Soda

Build over ice and stir.

Young Nobleman
HIGHBALL GLASS

1 part Grand Marnier®
1 part Southern Comfort®
2/3 part Crème de Cacao (White)
splash Galliano®

Build over ice and stir.

Yuppidoo
HIGHBALL GLASS

1 part Irish Cream Liqueur
1 part Coffee Liqueur
1 part Galliano®
1 part Vanilla Liqueur
splash Half and Half

Shake with ice and strain over ice.

Yup-Yupie
HIGHBALL GLASS

1 1/2 parts Vodka
1/2 part Melon Liqueur
1/2 part Maraschino Liqueur
1/2 part Crème de Cassis

Shake with ice and strain over ice.

Za Za
HIGHBALL GLASS

1 part Gin
1 part Dubonnet® Rouge
dash Angostura® Bitters

Shake with ice and strain over ice.

Zebra Fizz
HIGHBALL GLASS

1 part Vodka
1 part Lemonade
1 part Lemon-Lime Soda

Build over ice and stir.

Zocolo
HIGHBALL GLASS

1 part Rum
1 part Cherry Juice
1 part Lemonade
1 part Cola

Build over ice and stir.

Zoned Out
HIGHBALL GLASS

1 part Pineapple Vodka
1 part Chambord
1/2 part Peach Schnapps
2 parts Cranberry Juice
1 part Orange Juice

Build over ice and stir.

Zoom Bang Boom
HIGHBALL GLASS

1 part Vodka
1 part Wild Berry Schnapps
1 part Lemonade
2 parts Lemon-Lime Soda

Build over ice and stir.

Zoom Shooter
HIGHBALL GLASS

1 part Vodka
1 part Grand Marnier®
1 part Cherry Juice
fill with Orange Juice

Build over ice and stir.

TALL DRINKS

Drinks served in a tall glass that don't fit into any other category fall into this "catch-all" collection.

007

COLLINS GLASS

1 part Orange Vodka
1 part Lemon-Lime Soda
1 part Orange Juice

Mix with ice.

187 Urge

COLLINS GLASS

1 part Jack Daniel's®
1 part Vodka
fill with Dr. Pepper®

Mix with ice.

2001

COLLINS GLASS

½ part Apricot Brandy
½ part Crème de Cassis
2 parts Pineapple Juice
1 part Rum

Mix with ice.

319 Special

COLLINS GLASS

1 part Vodka
1 part Orange Juice
1 part Lemon-Lime Soda
splash Lime Juice

Mix with ice.

.357 Magnum

COLLINS GLASS

1 part Vodka
1 part Spiced Rum
fill with Lemon-Lime Soda
1½ parts Amaretto

Mix with ice and float Amaretto on top.

3 A.M. on a School Night

COLLINS GLASS

2 parts Wild Turkey® Bourbon
fill with Fruit Punch

Mix with ice.

435 French

COLLINS GLASS

1 part Citrus Rum
2 parts Lemon-Lime Soda
2 parts Cranberry-Raspberry Juice

Mix with ice.

The 5th Element

BEER MUG

½ part 151-Proof Rum
½ part Southern Comfort®
½ part Vodka
1 part Pineapple Juice
1 part Lemon-Lime Soda

Build over ice and stir.

50/50

COLLINS GLASS

2½ parts Vanilla Vodka
splash Grand Marnier®
fill with Orange Juice

Build over ice and stir.

500 Proof

COLLINS GLASS

½ part Vodka
½ part Southern Comfort®
½ part Bourbon
½ part 151-Proof Rum
1 part Orange Juice
½ part Simple Syrup

Shake with ice and strain over ice.

501 Blues
COLLINS GLASS
1 part Lemon-Lime Soda
1 part Blue Curaçao
1 part Blueberry Schnapps
½ part Club Soda
Shake with ice and strain over ice.

'57 Chevy® (In Ohio)
HURRICANE GLASS
1 part Amaretto
1 part Sloe Gin
1 part Southern Comfort®
splash Grapefruit Juice
fill with Cranberry Juice Cocktail
Shake with ice and strain over ice.

'57 T-Bird with Florida Plates
COLLINS GLASS
1 part Vodka
1 part Amaretto
1 part Grand Marnier®
fill with Orange Juice
Build over ice and stir.

612 Delight
COLLINS GLASS
1 part Vodka
1 part Diet Lemonade
fill with Cola
Build over ice and stir.

7&7
COLLINS GLASS
2 parts Seagram's® 7 Whiskey
fill with 7-Up®
Build over ice.

A&W Ryebeer
BEER MUG
1 part A & W® Root Beer
1 part Crown Royal® Whiskey
Mix with ice.

A Capella
COLLINS GLASS
1 part Blue Curaçao
1 part Grapefruit Juice
½ part Lime Juice
fill with Tonic Water
Shake all but Tonic with ice and strain into a Collins Glass filled with ice. Fill with Tonic.

Aaron Insanity
COLLINS GLASS
1 part Jägermeister®
¼ part Triple Sec
½ part Cachaça
fill with Lemonade
Build over ice and stir.

The Abba
COLLINS GLASS
2 parts Citrus Vodka
fill with Lemon-Lime Soda
Build over ice and stir.

Abbie Dabbie
COLLINS GLASS
2 parts Vodka
2 parts Melon Liqueur
3 parts Apple Juice
Build over ice and stir.

Abe Froman
COLLINS GLASS
3 parts Vodka
½ part Grenadine
fill with Lemonade
Build over ice and stir.

A-Bomb
BEER MUG

2 parts Tequila
1 part Vodka
3 parts Root Beer Schnapps
fill with Root Beer
1 scoop Ice Cream

Combine all but Ice Cream in a large beer mug over ice and stir. Top with a scoop of Ice Cream and drizzle Root Beer Schnapps over the top.

Absinthe Curaçao Frappé
COLLINS GLASS

1 part Blue Curaçao
2 parts Absinthe
1 part Orange Juice
splash Lemon Juice

Shake with ice and strain over ice.

Abso Bloody Lutly
COLLINS GLASS

1½ parts Absolut® Vodka
4 parts Tomato Juice
splash Worchestershire Sauce
dash Horseradish

Shake with ice and strain over ice.

Absolut® Apple
COLLINS GLASS

1 part Absolut® Vodka
1 part Sour Apple Schnapps
3 parts Lemon-Lime Soda
3 parts Apple Juice

Build over ice and stir.

Absolut® Can Dew
COLLINS GLASS

2 parts Vodka
1 part Blue Curaçao
½ parts Mountain Dew®

Build over ice and stir.

Absolut® Hollywood
COLLINS GLASS

1½ parts Vodka
1 part Raspberry Liqueur
fill with Pineapple Juice

Build over ice and stir.

Absolut® Lemonade
COLLINS GLASS

1 part Citrus Vodka
1 part Amaretto
splash Sweet & Sour Mix
splash Lemon-Lime Soda

Build over ice and stir.

Absolut® Nothing
COLLINS GLASS

1 part Vodka
fill with Lemon-Lime Soda

Build over ice and stir.

Absolut® Orgasm
COLLINS GLASS

2 parts Vodka
1 part Triple Sec
fill with Lemon-Lime Soda
1 part Sweet & Sour Mix

Build over ice and stir.

Absolut® Power Juice
COLLINS GLASS

2 parts Vodka
2 parts Peach Schnapps
1 part Raspberry Liqueur
1 part Lemonade

Build over ice and stir.

Absolut® Russian
COLLINS GLASS

1 part Vodka
3 parts Tonic Water
splash Currant Syrup

Build over ice and stir.

Absolut® Slut

COLLINS GLASS

1 part Vodka
2 parts Orange Juice
2 parts Pineapple Juice

Build over ice and stir.

Absolut® Stress

COLLINS GLASS

½ part Vodka
½ part Coconut Rum
½ part Peach Schnapps
1 part Orange Juice
1 part Pineapple Juice
1 part Cranberry Juice Cocktail

Build over ice and stir.

Absolut® Summer

COLLINS GLASS

1½ parts Citrus Vodka
⅔ part Blue Curaçao
3 parts Grapefruit Juice
3 parts Orange Juice

Build over ice and stir.

Absolut® Summertime

COLLINS GLASS

1½ parts Citrus Vodka
¾ part Sweet & Sour Mix
½ part Lemon-Lime Soda
3 parts Club Soda

Shake with ice and strain over ice. Garnish with a Lemon Wedge.

Absolut® Viking

COLLINS GLASS

1 part Currant Vodka
1 part Crème de Cassis
fill with Ginger Ale

Build over ice and stir.

Absolutly Horny

COLLINS GLASS

1 part 99-Proof Banana Liqueur
1 part Crown Royal® Whiskey
1 part Peach Schnapps
1 part Vodka
1½ parts Cranberry Juice Cocktail
1½ parts Pineapple Juice

Build over ice and stir.

Acapulco Blue

COLLINS GLASS

1½ parts Silver Tequila
¾ part Blue Curaçao
½ part Simple Syrup
fill with Lemon-Lime Soda

Build over ice and stir.

Acapulco Blue #2

COLLINS GLASS

1½ parts Silver Tequila
⅔ part Blue Curaçao
½ part Simple Syrup
1½ parts Lemon Juice

Shake with ice and strain over ice.

Acapulco Gold

COLLINS GLASS

½ part Silver Tequila
½ part Rum
½ part Crème de Cacao (Dark)
½ part Grapefruit Juice
1 part Pineapple Juice

Build over ice and stir.

Ace

HURRICANE GLASS

1 part Vodka
1 part Rum
2 parts Pineapple Juice
2 parts Orange Juice
1 part Lime Juice
½ part Grenadine
1 tbsp sugar

Shake with ice and strain over ice.

Acid Banana

COLLINS GLASS

½ part Crème de Banane
½ part Pisang Ambon® Liqueur
½ part Sour Apple Schnapps
3 parts Lemon-Lime Soda
1 part Grape Juice (White)

Shake with ice and strain over ice.

Adam's Apple

COLLINS GLASS

2 parts Galliano
fill with Apple Juice

Build over ice and stir.

Adam's Apple #2

COLLINS GLASS

1 part Blackberry Liqueur
1 part Sour Apple Schnapps
fill with Cranberry Juice

Build over ice and stir.

Adam's Bomb

COLLINS GLASS

2 parts Gin
1 part Jägermeister®
3 parts Orange Gatorade®
4 parts Orange Juice
4 parts Club Soda

Build over ice and stir.

Adam's Hawaiian Monster

COLLINS GLASS

1 part Rum
1 part Banana Liqueur
1 part Peach Schnapps
fill with Pineapple Juice

Build over ice and stir.

Addington

COLLINS GLASS

1 part Dry Vermouth
1 part Sweet Vermouth
fill with Club Soda

Build over ice and stir.

Adelle's Delight

COLLINS GLASS

1 part Apple Juice
1 part Hard Apple Cider
1 part Ginger Ale
fill with Rum

Build over ice and stir.

Adios

COLLINS GLASS

1 part Dry Gin
1 part Vodka
1 part Rum
1 part Blue Curaçao
1 part Sweet & Sour Mix
fill with Lemonade

Build over ice and stir.

Adios Mother

HURRICANE GLASS

1 part Vodka
1 part Gin
1 part Light Rum
1 part Blue Curaçao
2 parts Sweet & Sour Mix
fill with Lemon-Lime Soda

Build over ice and stir.

Adrienne's Dream

COLLINS GLASS

2 parts Brandy
½ part Crème de Cacao (White)
½ part Peppermint Schnapps
1½ parts Club Soda
½ part Lemon Juice
dash Sugar

Shake with ice and strain over ice.

Adult Kool-Aid®

COLLINS GLASS

1 part Amaretto
1 part Grenadine
1 part Melon Liqueur
2 parts Pineapple Juice
1½ parts Sweet & Sour Mix

Build over ice and stir.

African Knight

COLLINS GLASS

1 part Orange Liqueur
1 part Dark Rum
2 parts Banana Puree
splash Lime Juice
2 parts Mango Juice

Shake with ice and strain.

African Queen

COLLINS GLASS

2 parts Crème de Banane
1 part Triple Sec
fill with Orange Juice

Build over ice and stir.

After Party

COLLINS GLASS

1 part Vodka
2 parts Pineapple Juice
2 parts Cranberry Juice Cocktail
2 parts Ginger Ale
dash Sugar

Build over ice and stir.

Afternoon Delight

COLLINS GLASS

1 part Dark Spiced Rum
1 part Southern Comfort
splash Blue Raspberry Liqueur
splash Cranberry Juice
fill with Ginger Ale

Build over ice and stir.

Aftershock

COLLINS GLASS

1 part Drambuie®
1 part Coconut Rum
1 part Cherry Brandy
fill with Lemonade

Shake with ice and strain over ice.

Agavalada

COLLINS GLASS

1½ parts Agavero®
1 part Jamaican Rum
fill with Pineapple Juice
¾ part Crème de Coconut

Shake with ice and strain over ice. Garnish with a Pineapple Slice and a Maraschino Cherry.

Agave's Cup

COLLINS GLASS

1¾ parts Silver Tequila
¾ part Crème de Menthe (Green)
1 part Sweet & Sour Mix
2 parts Club Soda

Build over ice and stir.

Agent Orange

COLLINS GLASS

1 part Vodka
1 part Rum
1 part Gin
1 part Southern Comfort®
1 part Yukon Jack®
1 part Sour Apple Schnapps
1 part Melon Liqueur
fill with Orange Juice
splash Grenadine

Build over ice and stir.

Agent G

COLLINS GLASS

1 part Vodka
1 part Rum
1 part Gin
1 part Southern Comfort®
1 part Yukon Jack®
2 parts Grenadine
fill with Grapefruit Juice

Build over ice and stir.

Aggie Punch

COLLINS GLASS

2 parts Tequila
splash Lime Juice
fill with Apple-Cranberry Juice

Build over ice and stir.

AK-47

COLLINS GLASS

1 part Sour Apple Schnapps
1 part Rum
1 part Sambuca
1 part Tequila
1 part Tia Maria®

Build over ice and stir.

Alabama Riot

COLLINS GLASS

2 parts Southern Comfort®
1 part Peppermint Schnapps
1 part Vodka
fill with Fruit Punch
1 part Lime Juice

Shake with ice and strain over ice.

Alabama Slammer

COLLINS GLASS

1 part Southern Comfort®
1 part Amaretto
1 part Grenadine
6 parts Orange Juice
6 parts Pineapple Juice

Shake with ice and strain over ice.

Alamo Splash

COLLINS GLASS

1½ parts Tequila
1 part Orange Juice
½ part Pineapple Juice
splash Lemon-Lime Soda

Shake with ice and strain over ice.

Alaska White

COLLINS GLASS

2 parts Tequila
2 parts Vodka
1 part Gin
1 part Sambuca
fill with Lemon-Lime Soda

Build over ice and stir.

Albemarle Fizz

COLLINS GLASS

2 parts Gin
splash Raspberry Liqueur
½ part Raspberry Syrup
3 parts Sparkling Water

Shake with ice, strain over ice, and top with Sparkling Water.

Alcudia

HURRICANE GLASS

2 parts Pineapple Juice
1 part Cream
1 part Crème de Banane
½ part Amaretto
½ part Grenadine

Shake with ice and strain over ice.

Alexandra

COLLINS GLASS

1 Tia Maria®
1 Cream
1 Rum
1 Cream of Coconut

Build over ice and stir.

Alex's Super Stinger

COLLINS GLASS

1 part Honey
3 parts Rum
3 parts Vodka
fill with Apple Juice

Build over ice and stir.

Ali Baba

COLLINS GLASS

1 part Crème de Cacao (White)
1 part Peppermint Liqueur
1 part Frangelico®
1 part Cream

Shake with ice and strain.

Alice Milkshake

COLLINS GLASS

1 part Vodka
2 parts Pineapple Juice
2 parts Orange Juice
½ part Cream
½ part Cherry Syrup

Build over ice and stir.

Alien Urine

COLLINS GLASS

1 part Coconut Rum
½ part Melon Liqueur
½ part Peach Schnapps
1 part Sweet & Sour Mix
1 part Orange Juice

Shake with ice and strain over ice.

All Night Long

HURRICANE GLASS

½ part Vodka
½ part Coconut Rum
½ part Coffee Liqueur
½ part Crème de Cacao (White)
4 parts Pineapple Juice
2 parts Sweet & Sour Mix

Shake with ice and strain over ice.

Alleluia

COLLINS GLASS

2 parts Silver Tequila
1 part Blue Curaçao
1 part Maraschino Liqueur

Shake with ice and strain over ice.

Almond Soda

COLLINS GLASS

2 parts Amaretto
fill with Cream Soda

Build over ice and stir.

Almost Alcoholic

HURRICANE GLASS

3 parts Orange Juice
1½ parts Light Rum
1 part Blue Curaçao
1 part Pisang Ambon® Liqueur

Shake with ice and strain over ice.

Almost Heaven

COLLINS GLASS

1 part Currant Vodka
3 parts Amaretto
3 parts Raspberry Liqueur
splash Pineapple Juice
splash Cranberry Juice Cocktail

Shake with ice and strain over ice.

Aloha Joe

COLLINS GLASS

1 part Dark Rum
1 part Peach Schnapps
½ part Almond Syrup
splash Goldschläger®
fill with Passion Fruit Juice

Build over ice and stir.

Amando IV

COLLINS GLASS

1½ parts Citrus Vodka
⅔ part Blue Curaçao
2 parts Orange Juice
1 part Lemon Juice
splash Simple Syrup

Shake with ice and strain over ice.

Amaretto Backflip

COLLINS GLASS

1 part Amaretto
2 parts Lemon-Lime Soda
2 parts Lemonade
splash Sweet & Sour Mix

Build over ice and stir.

Amaretto Cheesecake

COLLINS GLASS

2 parts Amaretto
1 part Chocolate Syrup
fill with Milk

Build in the glass with no ice and stir.

Amaretto Fizz

COLLINS GLASS

3 parts Orange Juice
2 parts Lemonade
1½ parts Amaretto
fill with Lemon-Lime Soda

Build over ice and stir.

Amaretto Stiletto

COLLINS GLASS

2 parts Amaretto
1 part Vodka
1 part Lemon-Lime Soda
1 part Lime Juice
1 part Sweet & Sour Mix

Build over ice and stir.

Amaretto Stone Sweet

COLLINS GLASS

1½ parts Amaretto
1 part Cherry Syrup
2 parts Orange Juice
fill with Lemon-Lime Soda

Build over ice and stir.

Amaretto Vodka Collins

COLLINS GLASS

1 part Vodka
1 part Amaretto
½ part Sweet & Sour Mix
fill with Lemon-Lime Soda

Build over ice and stir.

Amarissimo

COLLINS GLASS

2 parts Dry Gin
1 part Triple Sec
2 parts Orange Juice
dash Bitters

Shake with ice and strain over ice.

Amarita

COLLINS GLASS

2 parts Amaretto
fill with Margarita Mix

Shake with ice and strain over ice.

Amaya

HURRICANE GLASS

1 part Vodka
1 part Apricot Brandy
½ part Grenadine
½ part Passion Fruit Nectar
2 parts Orange Juice

Shake with ice and strain over ice.

Amazing Pepper

COLLINS GLASS

2 parts Amaretto
1 part Vodka
fill with Cola

Build over ice and stir.

Ambulance

COLLINS GLASS

2 parts Vodka
1 part Coffee Liqueur
1½ parts Coffee
fill with Cola

Build over ice and stir.

Amelia Airhart
COLLINS GLASS

2 parts Gin
1 part Apricot Brandy
splash Triple Sec
splash Grenadine
1/2 part Lemon Juice
1/2 part Orange Juice
dash Sugar

Build over ice and stir.

Amigos Para Siempre
COLLINS GLASS

1 part Citrus Rum
1 part Crème de Coconut
splash Grenadine
splash Cream
fill with Pineapple Juice

Shake with ice and strain over ice.

Amor a la Mexicana
COLLINS GLASS

1 1/2 parts Coffee Liqueur
1/2 part Silver Tequila
1/4 part Vanilla Liqueur
1/4 part Simple Syrup
fill with Milk

Build over ice and stir.

Amore Mio
COLLINS GLASS

1 1/2 parts Dark Rum
1/2 part Maraschino Liqueur
fill with Orange Juice
splash Grenadine

Build over ice and stir.

Amorosae
COLLINS GLASS

1 part Parfait Amour
1 part Vodka
splash Crème de Cassis
splash Lime Juice
fill with Lemon-Lime Soda

Shake with ice and strain over ice.

Amy's Tattoo
COLLINS GLASS

1/2 part Dark Rum
1/2 part Light Rum
2 parts Pineapple Juice
2 parts Orange Juice
splash Grenadine

Shake with ice and pour.

Anamer
COLLINS GLASS

1 part Dark Rum
1/2 part Triple Sec
1/2 part Apricot Brandy
fill with Pineapple Juice

Build over ice and stir.

Ananas Exotic
COLLINS GLASS

1 part Light Rum
1/2 part Cherry Brandy
fill with Pineapple Juice

Build over ice and stir.

Anastavia
COLLINS GLASS

1 part Vodka
splash Triple Sec
splash Grenadine
1 part Orange Juice
splash Lemon Juice

Shake with ice and pour.

Andees Candees Magical Mix
COLLINS GLASS

2 parts Prepared Mudslide Mix
1 part Peppermint Schnapps
fill with Milk

Build over ice and stir.

Andersson
COLLINS GLASS

1 part Vodka
1 part Melon Liqueur
fill with Milk

Build over ice and stir.

Andes® Mint

COLLINS GLASS

1½ parts Peppermint Schnapps
fill with Cola

Build over ice and stir.

Andrea

COLLINS GLASS

1½ parts Blue Curaçao
fill with Orange Juice
splash Amaretto

Shake with ice and strain over ice.

Andy Pandy

COLLINS GLASS

1 part Vodka
1 part Peach Schnapps
1 part Blue Curaçao
1 part Lemonade
1 part Orange Juice

Build over ice and stir.

Angel Affinity

COLLINS GLASS

2 parts Raspberry Liqueur
½ part Blackberry Liqueur
2 parts Cream of Coconut
fill with Milk

Blend ingredients with crushed ice.

Angel's Milk

COLLINS GLASS

4 parts Raspberry Liqueur
2 parts Peach Juice
1 Egg
½ part Amaretto

Shake with ice and pour.

Angry Chameleon

BEER MUG

2 parts Light Rum
2 tsp Cherry Kool-Aid® Granules
fill with Mountain Dew®

Dissolve Kool-Aid® in Rum and add Mountain Dew®.

Anna's Wish

COLLINS GLASS

1 part Dark Rum
½ part Triple Sec
fill with Pineapple Juice

Build over ice and stir.

Anne's Black Rose

COLLINS GLASS

1 part 100-Proof Blackberry Schnapps
fill with Sweet & Sour Mix
splash Cherry Juice

Build over ice and stir.

Anon

COLLINS GLASS

2 parts Light Rum
1 part Melon Liqueur
1 part Crème de Coconut
1 part Apple Brandy
1 part Pineapple Juice
1 part Apple Juice

Build over ice and stir.

Anti-Arctic

COLLINS GLASS

1½ parts Citrus Vodka
½ part Triple Sec
fill with Iced Tea

Shake with ice and pour.

Anu

COLLINS GLASS

1 part Apricot Brandy
½ part Dry Vermouth
½ part Triple Sec
fill with Lemonade

Build over ice and stir.

Aphrodite's Love Potion
COLLINS GLASS

1½ parts Metaxa®
dash Angostura® Bitters
fill with Pineapple Juice

Shake with ice and strain over ice. Garnish with a Maraschino Cherry and an Orange Slice.

Apple Cider Surprise
COLLINS GLASS

2 parts Vodka
1 part Apple Juice
1 part Ginger Ale

Build over ice and stir.

Apple Cola
COLLINS GLASS

1 part Triple Sec
1 part Apple Liqueur
fill with Cola

Build over ice and stir.

Apple Knocker
COLLINS GLASS

1½ parts Vodka
splash Lemon Juice
splash Strawberry Liqueur
fill with Apple Cider

Shake with ice and strain over ice.

Apple Rancher
COLLINS GLASS

½ part Blue Curaçao
⅔ part Melon Liqueur
⅔ part Peach Schnapps
fill with Sweet & Sour Mix
splash Orange Juice

Shake with ice and pour.

Apple to the 3rd Power
COLLINS GLASS

1 part Rum
1 part Cranberry Liqueur
2 parts Lemon-Lime Soda
1½ parts Apple Juice

Build over ice and stir.

Apple-Dew
COLLINS GLASS

1 part Apple Liqueur
1 part Vodka
fill with Mountain Dew®

Build over ice and stir.

Applehawk
COLLINS GLASS

2 parts Apple Brandy
fill with Grape Soda
splash Simple Syrup

Build over ice and stir.

Apple-Snake Nuts
COLLINS GLASS

1 part Vodka
1 part Amaretto
1 part Sour Apple Schnapps
1 part Triple Sec
splash Sweetened Lime Juice

Shake with ice and pour.

Apricanza
COLLINS GLASS

1 part Vodka
½ part Apricot Brandy
fill with Lemon-Lime Soda
splash Grenadine

Build over ice and stir.

Apricot Anise Collins
COLLINS GLASS

½ part Apricot Brandy
1½ parts Gin
2 splashes Anisette
1 part Lemon Juice
fill with Seltzer

Build over ice and stir. Garnish with a Lemon Slice.

Apricot Brandy Sour
COLLINS GLASS

1 part Apricot Brandy
1 part Lemon Juice
fill with Orange Juice

Shake with ice and pour.

Apricot Dandy

COLLINS GLASS

2 parts Light Rum
1 part Crème de Banane
1 part Apricot Brandy
splash Grenadine
splash Apricot Juice

Shake with ice and pour.

Apricot Fiesta

COLLINS GLASS

1 part Cherry Brandy
3 parts Grapefruit Juice
2 parts Orange Juice
splash Simple Syrup

Shake with ice and pour.

Apricot Girl

COLLINS GLASS

1½ parts Rum
1 part Triple Sec
fill with Apricot Juice
1 Egg White

Shake with ice and pour.

April's Apple

COLLINS GLASS

1 part Sour Apple Schnapps
1 part Grenadine
fill with Lemonade

Build over ice and stir.

Aquamarine

COLLINS GLASS

1 part Vodka
½ part Peach Schnapps
splash Blue Curaçao
splash Triple Sec
fill with Apple Juice

Build over ice and stir.

Arbogast

COLLINS GLASS

1 part Vodka
½ part Rumple Minze®
½ part Coffee Liqueur
½ part Irish Cream Liqueur
fill with Milk

Shake with ice and pour.

Arcadian Lovemaker

COLLINS GLASS

1 part Citrus Vodka
1 part Sloe Gin
1 part Southern Comfort®
1 part Orange Juice

Shake with ice and pour.

Arctic

COLLINS GLASS

1 part Blue Curaçao
½ part Crème de Menthe (White)
½ part Triple Sec
splash Lime Juice
fill with Lemon-Lime Soda

Build over ice and stir.

Arctic Circle

COLLINS GLASS

2 parts Vodka
1 part Lime Juice
3 parts Ginger Ale

Build over ice and stir.

Arctic Sunset

COLLINS GLASS

1 part Rye Whiskey
1 part Peppermint Schnapps
fill with Cranberry Juice Cocktail
2 parts Orange Juice

Build over ice.

Arriba Arriba

COLLINS GLASS

1½ parts Dark Rum
1 part Crème de Banane
fill with Lemon-Lime Soda

Build over ice and stir.

Ashtray

COLLINS GLASS

1 part Vodka
1 part Blavod® Black Vodka
1½ parts Blackberry Liqueur
2 parts Milk
2 parts Blackberry Juice

Shake with ice and pour.

Assassin

COLLINS GLASS

1 part Lemon Rum
1 part Citrus Vodka
1 part Lemon-Lime Soda
1 part Orange Juice

Build over ice and stir.

ASU Girls

COLLINS GLASS

1½ parts Vodka
½ part Peach Schnapps
fill with Pineapple Juice

Build over ice and stir.

Atlantic Shore

COLLINS GLASS

1 part Light Rum
½ part Galliano
1 part Lemon Juice
fill with Pineapple Juice
dash Grenadine

Build over ice.

Atlantico

COLLINS GLASS

1 part Blue Curaçao
2 parts Grapefruit Juice
2 parts Passion Fruit Juice
1½ parts Banana Juice

Build over ice and stir.

Atomic Dog

COLLINS GLASS

1 part Light Rum
½ part Melon Liqueur
½ part Crème de Coconut
fill with Pineapple Juice

Shake with ice and pour.

Atomic Kool-Aid®

COLLINS GLASS

½ part Melon Liqueur
½ part Vodka
½ part Amaretto
splash Grenadine
1 part Orange Juice
1 part Pineapple Juice

Shake with ice and pour.

Atomic Lokade

COLLINS GLASS

1 part Vodka
½ part Blue Curaçao
½ part Triple Sec
fill with Lemonade

Build over ice and stir.

Atomic Shit

COLLINS GLASS

1 part Vodka
1 part Grapefruit Juice
fill with Lemonade
splash Jack Daniel's®

Build over ice and stir.

Attitude

HURRICANE GLASS

1 part Amaretto
1 part Southern Comfort®
1 part Lemon Vodka
1 part Melon Liqueur
½ part Sloe Gin
fill with Orange Juice
splash Cranberry Juice Cocktail

Shake with ice and pour.

Attitude Adjustment

COLLINS GLASS

1 part Vodka
1 part Gin
1 part Triple Sec
1 part Amaretto
1 part Peach Schnapps
1 part Sweet & Sour Mix
splash Cranberry Juice Cocktail

Shake with ice and strain over ice.

Authentic Shut the Hell Up

COLLINS GLASS

1 part 151-Proof Rum
1 part Southern Comfort®
1 part Tequila
fill with Cranberry Juice Cocktail

Shake with ice and pour.

Autumn Day

COLLINS GLASS

1 part Rum
1 part Orange Juice
1 part Grape Juice (Red)

Build over ice and stir.

Avalon

COLLINS GLASS

3 parts Vodka
1 part Pisang Ambon® Liqueur
1½ parts Lemon Juice
fill with Apple Juice

Build over ice and stir.

Aviator Fuel

COLLINS GLASS

1 part Vodka
1 part Lemonade
1 part Lemon-Lime Soda

Build over ice and stir.

Azteken Punch

COLLINS GLASS

1½ parts Pineapple Juice
1 part Vodka
1 part Crème de Cacao (Dark)
fill with Orange Juice

Build over ice and stir.

Azurro

COLLINS GLASS

1½ parts Pineapple Juice
1½ parts Passion Fruit Juice
1 part Blue Curaçao
1 part Pisang Ambon® Liqueur
1 part Safari®

Shake with ice and strain over ice.

Bacardi® Gold

COLLINS GLASS

1½ parts Dark Rum
fill with Cola

Build over ice and stir. Garnish with a Lemon Slice.

Bac Bug

COLLINS GLASS

½ part Light Rum
½ part Crème de Banane
½ part Coconut Rum
1½ parts Sweet & Sour Mix
fill with Pineapple Juice

Shake with ice and strain over ice.

Bacio & Kiss

COLLINS GLASS

1 part Vodka
splash Lychee Liqueur
splash Peach Schnapps
2 parts Grapefruit Juice
2 parts Cranberry Juice Cocktail

Shake with ice and strain over ice.

Bad Attitude

COLLINS GLASS

½ part Rum
½ part Vodka
½ part Gin
½ part Tequila
½ part Triple Sec
1 part Amaretto
1 part Pineapple Juice
1 part Orange Juice
1 part Cranberry Juice Cocktail
splash Grenadine

Build over ice and stir.

Bad North Disaster

BEER MUG

1 part Tequila
1 part Triple Sec
fill with Lemon-Lime Soda
splash Lime Juice
splash Lemon Juice

Build over ice and stir.

Bahama Mama

COLLINS GLASS

½ part Coffee Vodka
1 part Dark Rum
1 part Coconut Rum
1 part Lemon Juice
fill with Pineapple Juice
splash 151-Proof Rum

Build over ice and stir.

Bahama Todd

COLLINS GLASS

1 part Light Rum
1 part Dark Rum
1 part Spiced Rum
1 part Coconut Rum
1 part 151-Proof Rum
1 part Blue Curaçao
fill with Pineapple Juice

Shake with ice and pour.

Bahia

COLLINS GLASS

1 part Light Rum
1 part Pineapple Juice
1 part Cream of Coconut
¾ part Triple Sec

Shake with ice and pour.

Bahia de Plata

COLLINS GLASS

1 part Dark Rum
1 part Vodka
1 part Triple Sec
fill with Pineapple Juice
splash Grenadine

Build over ice and stir.

Baja Mar

COLLINS GLASS

1½ parts Dark Rum
¼ part Vodka
¼ part Crème de Banane
fill with Orange Juice
splash Grenadine

Build over ice and stir.

Ballet Russe

COLLINS GLASS

1½ parts Vodka
½ part Crème de Cassis
3 parts Sweet & Sour Mix

Shake with ice and pour.

Balmy Days

COLLINS GLASS

¾ part Coffee Liqueur
1 part Spiced Rum
fill with Fruit Juice

Build over ice and stir.

Balou

COLLINS GLASS

1 part Pisang Ambon® Liqueur
1 part Dry Gin
1 part Apricot Brandy
2 parts Orange Juice

Shake with ice and strain over ice.

Baltic

COLLINS GLASS

1 part Vodka
½ part Passion Fruit Juice
splash Blue Curaçao
fill with Orange Juice

Build over ice and stir.

Baltic Murder Mystery

COLLINS GLASS

1 part Vodka
1 part Crème de Cassis
fill with Lemon-Lime Soda

Build over ice and stir.

Baltic Sea Breeze

COLLINS GLASS

1½ parts Grapefruit Juice
1 part Apple Liqueur
1 part Cranberry Vodka
½ part Melon Liqueur

Build over ice and stir.

Baltimore Eggnog

COLLINS GLASS

1 part Jamaican Rum
1 part Brandy
1 part Madeira
1 Whole Egg
dash Powdered Sugar
1 part Milk

Shake with ice and strain.

Baltimore Zoo

COLLINS GLASS

1 part Vodka
1 part Rum
1 part Tequila
1 part Triple Sec
1 part Sweetened Lime Juice
1 part Grenadine
1 part Sweet & Sour Mix
1 part Root Beer
1 part 151-Proof Rum

Build over ice and stir.

Bam-Bam Special

COLLINS GLASS

1 part Rumple Minze®
1 part Cola

Build over ice and stir.

Bambola Hawaiana

COLLINS GLASS

1 part Rum
1 part Grape Juice (White)
½ part Cherry Brandy
1 part Pineapple Juice
½ part Grenadine
½ part Vanilla Syrup

Build over ice and stir.

Bamby

COLLINS GLASS

1 part Dark Rum
1 part Vodka
1 part Crème de Menthe (Green)
1 part Crème de Banane
fill with Pineapple Juice

Build over ice and stir.

Banana Coffee

COLLINS GLASS

2 parts Banana Juice
1½ parts Orange Juice
1 part Coffee
1 part Crème de Banane
1 part Cognac

Shake with ice and strain over ice.

Banana Cool

COLLINS GLASS

1 part Blue Curaçao
1 part Crème de Banane
fill with Orange Juice

Build over ice and stir.

Banana Rama
COLLINS GLASS

1 part Vodka
1 part Banana Liqueur
½ part Coconut Rum
fill with Milk

Build over ice and stir.

Bananarita
MARGARITA GLASS

1 part Crème de Banane
2 parts Gold Tequila
splash Blue Curaçao
splash Lime Juice
splash Banana Juice

Shake with ice and strain over ice.

Bananes Royalle
COLLINS GLASS

1½ parts Crème de Banane
½ part Light Rum
fill with Pineapple Juice

Build over ice and stir.

Banoffee Milkshake
COLLINS GLASS

1 part Banana Liqueur
1 part Butterscotch Schnapps
fill with Milk

Shake with ice and pour.

The Bantam
COLLINS GLASS

2 parts Jack Daniel's®
1 part Coconut Rum
fill with Cola

Build over ice and stir.

Barbarian
COLLINS GLASS

2 splashes Grenadine
splash Lime Juice
1 part Tequila
1 part Pineapple Juice

Build over ice and stir.

Barbie®
COLLINS GLASS

1 part Gin
1 part Vodka
fill with Lime Soda
splash Grenadine

Build over ice and stir.

Barbisonia
COLLINS GLASS

1 part Dark Rum
½ part Cherry Brandy
½ part Ponche Kuba®
fill with Orange Juice
splash Grenadine

Build over ice and stir.

Baretto Juice
COLLINS GLASS

1 part Light Rum
¾ part Amaretto
fill with Pineapple Juice

Build over ice and stir.

Barking Spider
COLLINS GLASS

1½ parts Tarantula Azul Tequila
1½ parts Blue Curaçao
¾ part 151-Proof Rum
splash Orange Juice
dash Triple Sec
dash Sweet & Sour Mix

Build over ice or blend with ice for a frozen version.

Barlin McNabbsmith
COLLINS GLASS

4 parts Jack Daniel's®
3 parts Scotch
2 parts Molasses
1 part Bitters

Shake with ice and strain over ice.

Barney's® Revenge

COLLINS GLASS

1 part Vodka
1 part Blue Curaçao
splash Apricot Brandy
fill with Raspberry Seltzer

Build over ice and stir.

Barnstormer

COLLINS GLASS

1½ parts Whiskey
½ part Peppermint Schnapps
2 splashes Crème de Cacao (Dark)
½ part Lemon Juice

Build over ice and stir.

Baron Samedi

COLLINS GLASS

1½ parts Dry Gin
½ part Cherry Brandy
3 parts Ginger Ale
2 parts Orange Juice

Build over ice and stir.

Barracuda

COLLINS GLASS

2 parts Vodka
2 parts Grapefruit Juice
1 part Tonic Water

Build over ice and stir.

Bartender in a Cup

COLLINS GLASS

2 parts Vodka
1 part Triple Sec
1 part Pineapple Juice
1 part Orange Juice
1 part Sweet & Sour Mix
1 part Grenadine

Shake with ice and pour.

Barton's

COLLINS GLASS

1½ parts Calvados Apple Brandy
splash Gin
splash Orange Liqueur
splash Scotch
2 parts Ginger Ale

Shake with ice and strain over ice.

Baseball Pleasure

COLLINS GLASS

2 parts Vodka
1½ parts Whiskey
1½ parts Amaretto
fill with Orange Juice

Build over ice and stir.

Bay of Passion

COLLINS GLASS

1 part Vodka
2 parts Pineapple Juice
1 part Passion Fruit Liqueur

Build over ice and stir.

Bayou Backwater

COLLINS GLASS

2 parts Southern Comfort®
fill with Lemonade

Build over ice and stir.

Bayou Self

COLLINS GLASS

1 part Spiced Rum
1 part Butterscotch Schnapps
fill with Pineapple Juice
splash Grenadine

Build over ice and stir.

Bazooka Bull

COLLINS GLASS

1 part Blue Curaçao
1 part Crème de Banane
fill with Red Bull® Energy Drink

Build over ice and stir.

B-Bob
HURRICANE GLASS

1½ parts Peach Schnapps
1 part Dark Rum
1 part Grenadine
1 part Lime Juice
fill with Orange Juice

Build over ice and stir.

Beakers Blue
HURRICANE GLASS

1 part Citrus Rum
1 part Blue Curaçao
1 part Triple Sec
splash Lemon-Lime Soda
splash Sweet & Sour Mix

Shake with ice and pour.

Beam & Cream
COLLINS GLASS

1½ parts Jim Beam®
fill with Cream Soda

Build over ice and stir.

Beam Me Up
COLLINS GLASS

1 part Jim Beam®
1 part Amaretto
fill with Cola

Build over ice and stir.

Bean's Blast
COLLINS GLASS

1 part Blackberry Liqueur
2 parts Coffee Liqueur
1½ parts Cognac
fill with Milk

Build over ice and stir.

The Beatle
COLLINS GLASS

1 part Scotch
fill with Cola

Build over ice and stir.

Beatle Juice
HURRICANE GLASS

½ part Gin
½ part Tequila Reposado
½ part Light Rum
½ part Vodka
1 part Melon Liqueur
splash Grenadine
fill with Sweet & Sour Mix
top with Lemon-Lime Soda

Shake all but Soda with ice and strain. Top with Soda.

Beekers Fruit
COLLINS GLASS

1 part Jack Daniel's®
1 part Vodka
1 part Sloe Gin
1 part Pineapple Juice
1 part Passion Fruit Nectar

Shake with ice and pour.

Beekers Poison
COLLINS GLASS

1 part Spiced Rum
1 part Triple Sec
1 part Lemon Juice
fill with Cola

Build over ice and stir.

Beep
COLLINS GLASS

1 part Vodka
3 parts Orange Juice
fill with Lemon-Lime Soda

Build over ice and stir.

Beer Nuts
COLLINS GLASS

1 part Frangelico®
1 part Root Beer Schnapps

Shake with ice and pour.

Beetlejuice

COLLINS GLASS

1 part Vodka
1 part Melon Liqueur
1 part Blue Curaçao
1 part Raspberry Liqueur
1 part Cranberry Juice Cocktail
fill with Sweet & Sour Mix

Build over ice and stir.

Before the Kiss

COLLINS GLASS

½ part Vodka
½ part Triple Sec
1 part Melon Liqueur
1 part Pear Syrup
fill with Apple Juice

Shake all but Apple Juice with ice and strain. Top with Apple Juice.

Bejia Flor

COLLINS GLASS

1½ parts Vodka
¼ part Parfait Amour
¼ part Southern Comfort®
splash Crème de Banane
splash Apricot Brandy
fill with Lemon-Lime Soda

Build over ice.

Bella

HURRICANE GLASS

1 part Coconut Rum
1 part Sour Apple Schnapps
1 part Spiced Rum
splash Grenadine
fill with Pineapple Juice

Shake with ice and pour.

Belladonna

COLLINS GLASS

1 part Light Rum
1 part Dark Rum
1 part Cranberry Juice Cocktail
1 part Pineapple Juice
1 part Orange Juice

Build over ice and stir.

Bent Bum

COLLINS GLASS

1½ parts Gin
1½ parts Vodka
1 part Orange Juice
1 part Grapefruit Juice
splash Cola

Build over ice and stir.

Berlin Wall

COLLINS GLASS

1 part Goldschläger®
1 part Rumple Minze®
1 part Jägermeister®

Shake with ice and strain.

Berry Blast

COLLINS GLASS

2 parts Rye Whiskey
1 part Cola
1 part Cranberry Juice Cocktail

Build over ice and stir.

Berry Lemonade

COLLINS GLASS

1 part Vodka
splash Strawberry Liqueur
fill with Lemonade

Build over ice and stir.

Berrynice

COLLINS GLASS

1 part Strawberry Liqueur
½ part Peach Schnapps
½ part Melon Liqueur
½ part Cream of Coconut
splash Simple Syrup
½ part Cream
2 parts Fruit Juice

Shake with ice and pour.

Berta's Special

COLLINS GLASS

2 parts Silver Tequila
1 Egg White
1 part Lime Juice
1/2 part Honey
3 parts Club Soda

Shake all but Club Soda with ice and strain. Top with Club Soda.

Best Year

COLLINS GLASS

1 part Vodka
1/2 part Blue Curaçao
1/2 part Licor 43
1/2 part Lime Juice
fill with Pineapple Juice

Shake with ice and pour.

Betsy

COLLINS GLASS

1 part Whiskey
1 part Triple Sec
1/2 part Crème de Banane
fill with Passion Fruit Juice

Build over ice and stir.

Bette Davis Eyes

COLLINS GLASS

1 part Vodka
1/2 part Blue Curaçao
1/2 part Crème de Coconut
fill with Lemon-Lime Soda

Build over ice and stir.

The Betty Ford

COLLINS GLASS

1 1/2 parts Citrus Vodka
fill with Lemon-Lime Soda
1/2 part Grenadine

Build over ice.

Big Apple

COLLINS GLASS

2 parts Vodka
fill with Apple Juice
splash Crème de Menthe (White)

Build over ice and stir.

Big Daddy

COLLINS GLASS

1/2 part Vodka
1/2 part Light Rum
1/2 part Tequila
1/2 part Whiskey
fill with Lemon-Lime Soda

Build over ice.

Big Hawaiian

COLLINS GLASS

3/4 part Rum
3/4 part Coconut Rum
1/2 part Melon Liqueur
fill with Pineapple Juice
splash Grenadine

Build over ice and stir.

A Big Pink Dink

HURRICANE GLASS

1 part Coconut Rum
fill with Milk
splash Grenadine

Build over ice and stir.

Big Red Hooter

COLLINS GLASS

1 part Tequila
3/4 part Amaretto
fill with Pineapple Juice
splash Grenadine

Build over ice.

The Big Robowski

BEER MUG

1 part Jack Daniel's®
1 part Southern Comfort®
1 part Goldschläger®
1 part Dark Rum
1 part Amaretto
fill with Cola

Build over ice and stir.

Big Stick

COLLINS GLASS

½ part Southern Comfort
½ part Sloe Gin
½ part Peach Schnapps
fill with Orange Juice
splash Grenadine

Build over ice.

Bikini Bomber

COLLINS GLASS

1½ parts Dry Gin
½ part Blue Curaçao
½ part Triple Sec
fill with Grapefruit Juice

Shake with ice and pour.

Bill's Tropical Depression

COLLINS GLASS

1 part Coconut Rum
1 part Raspberry Liqueur
½ part Crème de Banane
fill with Pineapple Juice
splash Orange Juice
splash Cranberry Juice Cocktail

Build over ice and stir.

Billy Belly Bomber

COLLINS GLASS

1 part Vodka
3 parts Pineapple Juice
splash Lemon Juice

Build over ice and stir.

Bine's Brain Blower

COLLINS GLASS

1 part Amaretto
1 part Brandy
2 parts Cream
1 part Jägermeister®

Shake all but Jägermeister® with ice and strain. Top with Jägermeister®.

Bingo Bongo

COLLINS GLASS

1½ parts Dark Rum
½ part Triple Sec
2 parts Pineapple Juice
1 part Guava Juice
½ part Lime Juice
½ part Passion Fruit Juice

Build over ice and stir.

Birdy Num-Num

COLLINS GLASS

1 part Coconut Rum
1 part Pineapple Juice

Build over ice and stir.

Bitch Slap

COLLINS GLASS

½ part Gin
½ part Light Rum
½ part Vodka
splash Lemon-Lime Soda
fill with Lemonade
splash Grenadine

Build over ice.

Bitch's Brew

BEER MUG

1 part 151-Proof Rum
1 part Whiskey
1 part Brandy
2 parts Dr. Pepper®
1 part Ginger Ale
splash Lime Juice

Build over ice and stir.

Bitter Bourbon Lemonade
COLLINS GLASS

2 parts Bourbon
1 part Lime Juice
½ part Grenadine
½ part Simple Syrup

Build over ice and stir.

Bitter Kraut
COLLINS GLASS

1 part Jägermeister®
1 part Campari®
1 part Club Soda
2 dashes Bitters

Build over ice and stir.

Bitter Sweet Symphon-Tea
COLLINS GLASS

1½ parts Citrus Vodka
splash Orange Liqueur
fill with Iced Tea
splash Lemon Juice

Shake with ice and strain over ice.

Black Bottom
COLLINS GLASS

¼ part Brandy
¼ part Cointreau®
¼ part Blackberry Brandy
splash Gin
1 part Lemon Juice
1 part Orange Juice

Shake with ice and pour.

Black Butterfly
HURRICANE GLASS

1 part Blackberry Brandy
1 part Cranberry Juice Cocktail
2 parts Lemon-Lime Soda

Build over ice and stir.

Black Cow
COLLINS GLASS

1 part Coffee Liqueur
1 part Half and Half
1½ parts Cola

Build over ice and stir.

Black Forest
COLLINS GLASS

1 part Crème de Cacao (White)
1 part Cherry Liqueur
1 part Kirschwasser
1 part Cream

Shake with ice and pour.

Black Jacket
COLLINS GLASS

1 part Coffee Liqueur
splash Vodka
splash Crème de Noyaux
⅔ part Cream

Shake with ice and pour.

Black Temple
HURRICANE GLASS

2 parts Blackberry Liqueur
1 part Lemon-Lime Soda
1 part Ginger Ale
splash Grenadine

Build over ice and stir.

Black-Eyed Susan
COLLINS GLASS

1 part Vodka
1 part Light Rum
1 part Triple Sec
splash Lime Juice
1 part Pineapple Juice
1 part Orange Juice

Shake with ice and strain over ice.

Blanqita
COLLINS GLASS

1½ parts Coffee Liqueur
1 part Anisette
fill with Pineapple Juice

Build over ice and stir.

Blast-Off

COLLINS GLASS

1 part Vodka
½ part Cointreau®
½ part Galliano®
4 parts Orange Juice
2 parts Pineapple Juice

Build over ice and stir.

Bleach

COLLINS GLASS

1 part Light Rum
½ part Apricot Brandy
½ part Peach Schnapps
½ part Blue Curaçao
fill with Red Bull® Energy Drink
splash Lemon Juice

Build over ice and stir.

Bleeker

COLLINS GLASS

1 part Vodka
½ part Lillet®
½ part Triple Sec
1 Egg White

Shake with ice and pour.

Blind White Russian

COLLINS GLASS

¾ part Irish Cream Liqueur
¾ part Godiva® Liqueur
¾ part Coffee Liqueur
½ part Butterscotch Schnapps
fill with Milk

Shake with ice and pour.

Blinkert

COLLINS GLASS

1 part Cherry Brandy
1 part Sloe Gin
½ part Whiskey
fill with Lemonade

Build over ice and stir.

Bloody Caesar

COLLINS GLASS

1½ parts Vodka
fill with Clamato® Juice
dash Tabasco® Sauce
2 dashes Worcestershire Sauce
dash Salt
dash Pepper

Build over ice and stir. Garnish with a Lime Wedge and a Celery Stalk.

Bloody Maru

COLLINS GLASS

2 parts Sake
2 splashes Worcestershire Sauce
splash Tabasco® Sauce
dash Horseradish
splash Lime Juice

Build over ice and stir.

Blue Aegean

COLLINS GLASS

1 part Blue Curaçao
1 part Vodka
1 part Triple Sec
fill with Pineapple Juice

Build over ice and stir.

Blue Breeze

COLLINS GLASS

1 part Light Rum
1 part Orange Juice
1 part Sweet & Sour Mix
½ part Blue Curaçao
¼ part Coconut Rum
fill with Pineapple Juice

Build over ice and stir.

Blue Bunny

COLLINS GLASS

1 part Rum
1 part Vodka
splash Sweet & Sour Mix
splash Blue Curaçao

Shake with ice and strain.

Blue Cobra

COLLINS GLASS

1 part Blue Curaçao
1½ parts Crème de Coconut
1½ parts Pineapple Juice
3 parts Tonic Water

Build over ice and stir.

Blue Cruncher

COLLINS GLASS

1 part Gin
1 part Blue Curaçao
1½ parts Sweet & Sour Mix
fill with Lemon-Lime Soda

Build over ice and stir.

Blue Fairy

COLLINS GLASS

1 part Blue Curaçao
1 part Absinthe
splash Lime Juice
1 part Grapefruit Juice

Shake with ice and pour.

Blue Harbor

COLLINS GLASS

1 part Rum
1 part Lime Syrup
½ part Blue Curaçao
½ part Triple Sec
fill with Lemon-Lime Soda

Build over ice and stir.

Blue Heaven

COLLINS GLASS

1 part Rum
1 part Amaretto
1 part Blue Curaçao
fill with Pineapple Juice

Shake with ice and pour.

Blue Horizon

COLLINS GLASS

1 part Spiced Rum
1 part 151-Proof Rum
1 part Blue Curaçao
splash Grenadine
fill with Orange Juice

Build over ice and stir.

Blue Ice with Wings

HURRICANE GLASS

1 part Vodka
¾ part Blue Curaçao
½ part Crème de Coconut
½ part Sweet & Sour Mix
fill with Red Bull® Energy Drink

Build over ice and stir.

Blue Jeans

COLLINS GLASS

1 part Vodka
1 part Blue Curaçao
1 part Grapefruit Juice
1 part Pineapple Juice

Build over ice and stir.

Blue Malibu®

COLLINS GLASS

½ part Gin
½ part Rum
½ part Vodka
½ part Blue Curaçao
2 parts Sweet & Sour Mix
splash Lemon-Lime Soda

Build over ice and stir.

Blue Mother Pucker

COLLINS GLASS

½ part Blue Raspberry Liqueur
½ part Sour Apple Schnapps
½ part Light Rum
splash Blue Curaçao
fill with Lemon-Lime Soda

Build over ice and stir.

Blue Mouth

COLLINS GLASS

1 part Dry Vermouth
½ part Southern Comfort®
fill with Orange Juice
splash Blue Curaçao

Build over ice.

Blue Nerfherder

COLLINS GLASS

1 part Tequila
1 part Blue Curaçao
fill with Lemonade

Build over ice and stir.

Blue Nuke

COLLINS GLASS

1 part Vodka
1 part 151-Proof Rum
1 part Gin
1 part Blue Curaçao
1 part Blueberry Schnapps
fill with Sweet & Sour Mix

Build over ice and stir.

Blue Owl

COLLINS GLASS

½ part Vodka
1 part Blue Curaçao
1 part Crème de Banane
splash Cherry Brandy
fill with Lemonade

Shake with ice and pour.

Blue Paradiso

HURRICANE GLASS

1½ parts Blue Curaçao
1½ parts Orange Vodka
½ parts Coconut Rum
fill with Pineapple Juice

Shake with ice and pour.

Blue Passion

COLLINS GLASS

¾ part Spiced Rum
½ part Blue Curaçao
fill with Sweet & Sour Mix

Shake with ice and pour.

Blue Pussycat

COLLINS GLASS

2 parts Scotch
1 part Blue Curaçao
fill with Orange Juice

Build over ice and stir.

The Blues

COLLINS GLASS

1 part Vodka
1 part Coconut Rum
¾ part Blue Curaçao
½ part Triple Sec
fill with Pineapple Juice

Shake with ice and strain over ice.

Blue Shadow

COLLINS GLASS

1½ parts Rum
1 part Parfait Amour
fill with Lemon-Lime Soda

Build over ice and stir.

Blue Sky

COLLINS GLASS

1 part Blue Curaçao
fill with Milk

Shake with ice and pour.

Blue Spider

COLLINS GLASS

2 parts Cranberry Vodka
fill with Red Bull® Energy Drink

Build over ice and stir.

Blue Suede Juice

COLLINS GLASS

1 part Citrus Vodka
¼ part Blue Curaçao
¾ part Triple Sec
fill with Sweet & Sour Mix
splash Lemon-Lime Soda

Build over ice and stir.

Blue Sweden

COLLINS GLASS

1 part Blue Curaçao
1 part Vodka
1 part Crème de Banane
fill with Orange Juice

Build over ice and stir.

Blue Wave

HURRICANE GLASS

1 part Gin
1 part Rum
½ parts Blue Curaçao
1 part Lime Juice
fill with Pineapple Juice

Build over ice and stir.

Blue with You

HURRICANE GLASS

1 part Citrus Rum
1 part Blue Curaçao
1 part Lychee Liqueur
1 part Pernod®
fill with Pineapple Juice

Shake with ice and pour.

Blueberry Hill

COLLINS GLASS

½ part Vodka
½ part Raspberry Liqueur
¼ part Blackberry Liqueur
1 part Sweet & Sour Mix
splash Peach Schnapps
fill with Lemonade

Build over ice and stir.

Boardwalk Breeze

HURRICANE GLASS

1½ parts Coconut Rum
1½ parts Amaretto
1 part Orange Juice
1 part Pineapple Juice
splash Grenadine

Shake with ice and pour.

Boca Chica

COLLINS GLASS

½ part Vodka
splash Pisang Ambon® Liqueur
splash Crème de Coconut
1 part Guava Juice
splash Passion Fruit Nectar

Shake with ice and strain over ice.

Bodega Blues

COLLINS GLASS

1 part Melon Liqueur
1 part Vodka
1 part Peach Schnapps
1 part Orange Juice
1 part Passion Fruit Juice

Build over ice and stir.

Bog Ale

COLLINS GLASS

1½ parts Gin
3 parts Cranberry Juice Cocktail
fill with Ginger Ale

Build over ice and stir. Garnish with a Lime Slice.

Bolster

COLLINS GLASS

1 part Sake
½ part Peach Schnapps
fill with Orange Juice
splash Cherry Brandy

Build over ice and stir.

Bonaire Punch

COLLINS GLASS

½ part Crème de Coconut
1 part Dark Rum
1 part Ponche Kuba®
fill with Pineapple Juice

Build over ice and stir.

Bongo Drum

COLLINS GLASS

1 part Rum
¼ part Blackberry Brandy
fill with Pineapple Juice

Build over ice and stir.

Bonneti

COLLINS GLASS

1 part Scotch
1 part Crème de Cacao (White)
1 part Caramel Syrup
splash Cream

Shake with ice and pour.

Booda's Black Brew

HURRICANE GLASS

1 part Coconut Rum
¾ part Blue Curaçao
¾ part Raspberry Liqueur
½ part Grenadine
fill with Cranberry Juice Cocktail

Build over ice and stir.

Boogie Beck

COLLINS GLASS

1 part Vodka
1 part Amaretto
1 part Southern Comfort®
½ part Lime Juice
1 part Pineapple Juice
1 part Orange Juice

Build over ice and stir.

Boot Blaster

COLLINS GLASS

1 part Light Rum
1 part Gin
1 part Vodka
1 part Triple Sec
fill with Lemonade
splash Cola

Build over ice and stir.

Bootlegger Tea

COLLINS GLASS

¾ part Vodka
¾ part Rum
¾ part Triple Sec
1 part Sweet & Sour Mix
1 part Lemon-Lime Soda
splash Grenadine

Build over ice and stir.

Bootyshaker

COLLINS GLASS

1 part Dark Rum
1 part Crème de Banane
1 part Lime Juice
½ part Triple Sec

Shake with ice and pour.

Borisov

COLLINS GLASS

1 part Jack Daniel's®
1 part Vodka
½ part Brandy
½ part Campari®
½ part Cognac
fill with Red Bull® Energy Drink

Build over ice and stir.

Bossa Nova

COLLINS GLASS

¾ part Dark Rum
¼ part Apricot Brandy
¼ part Galliano®
fill with Pineapple Juice
splash Lemon Juice

Build over ice and stir.

Bottleneck

COLLINS GLASS

1 part Vodka
1 part Parfait Amour
1 part Crème de Banane
1 part Melon Liqueur
splash Lime Juice
fill with Lemon-Lime Soda

Build over ice and stir.

Bowl Hugger

COLLINS GLASS

1 part Tequila
1 part Gin
1 part Rum
1 part Triple Sec
splash Sweetened Lime Juice
1 part Orange Juice
1 part Pineapple Juice
1 part Sweet & Sour Mix

Build over ice and stir.

Brain Candy

COLLINS GLASS

1 part Vodka
1 part Crème de Menthe (White)
fill with Mountain Dew®

Build over ice and stir.

Brainwash

COLLINS GLASS

1 part Gin
1 part Vodka
1 part Jägermeister®
1 part Blue Curaçao
fill with Pineapple Juice

Shake with ice and pour.

Brandy Eggnog

COLLINS GLASS

2 parts Brandy
1 Whole Egg
dash Powdered Sugar
dash Ground Nutmeg
fill with Milk

Shake all but Milk with ice and strain. Top with Milk.

Break the Rules

COLLINS GLASS

1 part Gin
½ part Kiwi Schnapps
½ part Melon Liqueur
fill with Orange Juice

Build over ice and stir.

Breezy Spring

COLLINS GLASS

1½ parts Gin
1 part Crème de Coconut
fill with Grapefruit Juice

Build over ice and stir.

Brewer Street Rascal

COLLINS GLASS

1 part Mandarine Napoléon® Liqueur
½ part Vermouth
3 parts Grapefruit Juice
1 Egg White

Shake with ice and pour.

Bridge to the Moon

COLLINS GLASS

1 part Currant Vodka
1 part Apple Liqueur
1 part Passion Fruit Liqueur
fill with Lemon-Lime Soda

Build over ice and stir.

Bridget in the Buff

COLLINS GLASS

2 parts Vodka
1½ parts Raspberry Liqueur
fill with Lemon-Lime Soda
splash Sweet & Sour Mix

Build over ice and stir.

Brief Bikini

COLLINS GLASS

1½ parts Triple Sec
fill with Lemonade

Build over ice and stir.

Brittle Fracture
BEER MUG
2 parts Root Beer Schnapps
fill with Lemon-Lime Soda
Build over ice and stir.

Broken-Down Golf Cart
COLLINS GLASS
1 part Vodka
1 part Melon Liqueur
1 part Amaretto
fill with Cranberry Juice Cocktail
Shake with ice and pour.

Brown Derby
COLLINS GLASS
1¼ parts Vodka
fill with Cola
Build over ice and stir.

Brown Stain
COLLINS GLASS
1 part Dark Rum
1 part Chocolate Liqueur
1 part Coffee Liqueur
fill with Cola
Build over ice and stir.

Bubba Collins
COLLINS GLASS
2 parts Scotch
1 part Sweet & Sour Mix
fill with Cola
Build over ice and stir.

Bubblicious®
COLLINS GLASS
⅔ part Crème de Cacao (White)
½ part Vanilla Vodka
⅔ part Southern Comfort®
½ part Sweet & Sour Mix
1 part Pineapple Juice
1 part Orange Juice
Shake with ice and pour.

Bud's Beverage
COLLINS GLASS
1 part Lime Rum
1 part Lime Vodka
fill with Mountain Dew
Build over ice and stir. For Bud.

Buena Carmencita
COLLINS GLASS
1 part Crème de Banane
1 part Brandy
fill with Milk
Build over ice and stir.

Bueno
COLLINS GLASS
1 part Crème de Coconut
1 part Passoã®
2 parts Orange Juice
2 parts Pineapple Juice
splash Lemon Juice
Shake with ice and pour.

Buenos Noches
COLLINS GLASS
2 parts Tequila
1 part Crème de Banane
½ part Lemon Juice
Shake with ice and pour.

Bugix
HURRICANE GLASS
1½ parts Vodka
½ part Crème de Banane
1 part Pineapple Juice
1 part Strawberry Juice
Shake with ice and pour.

Bull Blaster
COLLINS GLASS
1 part Jägermeister®
fill with Red Bull® Energy Drink
Build over ice and stir.

Bull Frog
COLLINS GLASS

1½ parts Whiskey
fill with Lemonade

Build over ice and stir.

Bullpup
COLLINS GLASS

1 part Rum
1 part Orange Juice
1 part Ginger Ale

Build over ice and stir.

Burning Bitch!
COLLINS GLASS

1 part Vodka
1 part Irish Cream Liqueur
½ part Lemon Juice
splash Maraschino Cherry Juice

Shake with ice and pour.

Burning Embers
COLLINS GLASS

1½ parts Silver Tequila
1 part Spiced Rum
½ part Worcestershire Sauce
dash Wasabi
fill with Tomato Juice

Build over ice and stir.

Buster Cherry
COLLINS GLASS

1½ parts Whiskey
½ part Cherry Brandy
1 part Orange Juice
1 part Lemon Juice

Shake with ice and strain over ice.

But I Know the Owner
COLLINS GLASS

1½ parts Spiced Rum
½ part Amaretto
1 part Orange Juice
1 part Pineapple Juice

Build over ice and stir.

Butcherblock
COLLINS GLASS

1½ parts Tequila
1½ parts Coffee Liqueur
fill with Half and Half

Build over ice and stir.

Butter Cream
COLLINS GLASS

1½ parts Butterscotch Schnapps
fill with Cream Soda

Build over ice and stir.

Buzz Lightyear
COLLINS GLASS

1 part Vodka
1 part Melon Liqueur
fill with Orange Juice

Build over ice and stir.

Bye-Bye Honey
COLLINS GLASS

1 part Citrus Rum
1 part Orange Vodka
2 parts Blue Curaçao
1 part Orange Juice
fill with Lemon-Lime Soda

Build over ice and stir.

Bye-Bye New York
COLLINS GLASS

1 part Vodka
1 part Dark Rum
1 part Hazelnut Syrup
fill with Orange Juice

Build over ice and stir.

Bygone Era

COLLINS GLASS

2 parts Gin
½ part Sloe Gin
splash Triple Sec
splash Lime Juice
fill with Tonic Water

Shake all but Tonic with ice and strain over fresh ice. Fill with Tonic Water and garnish with a Lime Wheel or Cherry.

C.O.P.

COLLINS GLASS

1 part Crème de Coconut
1 part Triple Sec
½ part Lime Juice
fill with Pineapple Juice

Build over ice and stir.

Caballo

COLLINS GLASS

1½ parts Silver Tequila
1 part Amaretto
fill with Grapefruit Juice

Build over ice and stir.

Caballo Viejo

COLLINS GLASS

1 part Dark Rum
1 part Apricot Brandy
½ part Dry Gin
fill with Pineapple Juice

Build over ice and stir.

Cactus Breeze

COLLINS GLASS

1 part Vodka
1 part Cranberry Juice Cocktail
1 part Pineapple Juice
1 part Sweet & Sour Mix

Build over ice and stir.

Cactus Cafe

COLLINS GLASS

1 part Silver Tequila
2 parts Coffee Liqueur
fill with Lemonade

Build over ice and stir.

Cactus Juice

COLLINS GLASS

1½ parts Tequila
1 part Amaretto
fill with Sweet & Sour Mix

Build over ice and stir.

Cactus Pear

COLLINS GLASS

1 part Pear Vodka
½ part Triple Sec
fill with Red Bull Energy Drink

Build over ice and stir.

Caesar

COLLINS GLASS

1 part Vodka
4 parts Clamato® Juice
splash Tabasco® Sauce
splash Worcestershire Sauce

Build over ice and stir.

Calico Jack

COLLINS GLASS

2 parts Dark Rum
½ part Crème de Coconut
1½ parts Pineapple Juice
1 part Orange Juice
½ part Lime Juice

Build over ice and stir.

California Coastline

COLLINS GLASS

1 part Peach Schnapps
1 part Coconut Rum
½ part Blue Curaçao
1 part Pineapple Juice
1 part Sweet & Sour Mix

Build over ice and stir.

California Dreaming
COLLINS GLASS
½ part Vodka
½ part Coffee Liqueur
½ part Vanilla Liqueur
2 parts Sweet & Sour Mix
1½ parts Cola

Build over ice and stir.

California Gold Rush
COLLINS GLASS
2 parts Vodka
1½ parts Goldschläger®
fill with Lemon-Lime Soda

Build over ice and stir.

California Monkey
COLLINS GLASS
1½ parts Coconut Rum
½ part Crème de Banane
fill with Cola

Build over ice and stir.

California Rattlesnake
COLLINS GLASS
½ part Malibu® Rum
½ part Southern Comfort®
½ part Amaretto
splash Sweet & Sour Mix
splash Lemon-Lime Soda
splash Grenadine

Build over ice and stir.

California Root Beer
BEER MUG
1 part Galliano®
1 part Triple Sec
1 part Coffee Liqueur
1 part Cola
1 part Ginger Ale

Build over ice and stir.

California Screwdriver
COLLINS GLASS
1½ parts Grand Marnier®
2 parts Vodka
1 part Club Soda
1 part Orange Juice

Build over ice and stir.

Call Girl
COLLINS GLASS
½ part Light Rum
½ part Dark Rum
½ part Coconut Rum
½ part Melon Liqueur
½ part Crème de Banane
1 part Pineapple Juice
1 part Orange Juice

Shake with ice and pour.

Campari® Punch
COLLINS GLASS
1 part Campari®
1 part Triple Sec
1 part Grapefruit Juice
1 part Orange Juice

Build over ice and stir.

Campechuela
COLLINS GLASS
1 part Dark Rum
2 parts Orange Juice
3 parts Cranberry Juice Cocktail
splash Cherry Brandy

Build over ice and stir.

Camurai
COLLINS GLASS
1 part Vodka
½ part Blue Curaçao
½ part Cream of Coconut
fill with Sparkling Water

Build over ice and stir.

Canadian Apple

COLLINS GLASS

3 parts Apple Schnapps
2 parts Canadian Whisky
1 tsp Powdered Sugar
top with Tonic Water

Shake all but Tonic with ice and strain over ice. Top with Tonic Water.

Canadian Zombie

COLLINS GLASS

1 part Dark Rum
1 part White Rum
½ part 151-Proof Rum
½ part Green Curaçao Liqueur
splash Grenadine
splash Lemon Juice
fill with Orange Juice

Shake with ice and strain over ice.

Candy

COLLINS GLASS

1¼ parts 151-Proof Rum
1 part Amaretto
fill with Dr. Pepper®

Build over ice and stir.

Cantagallo

COLLINS GLASS

1 part Gin
splash Blue Curaçao
splash Amaretto
½ part Sweet Vermouth
splash Papaya Juice

Shake with ice and pour.

Cape Cod Crush

COLLINS GLASS

2½ parts Southern Comfort®
fill with Cranberry Juice Cocktail

Build over ice and stir.

Cape Cod Sour Squishy

COLLINS GLASS

1 part Light Rum
½ part Sour Apple Schnapps
1 part Cranberry Juice Cocktail
1 part Sweet & Sour Mix
fill with Lemon-Lime Soda

Build over ice and stir.

Cape Driver (or Screw Codder)

COLLINS GLASS

1 part Vodka
1 part Cranberry Juice Cocktail
1 part Orange Juice

Build over ice and stir.

Cape May

COLLINS GLASS

1½ parts Gin
½ part Cherry Brandy
1 part Orange Juice
1 part Ginger Ale

Build over ice and stir.

Captain Billy's Kool-Aid®

COLLINS GLASS

1 part Southern Comfort®
1 part Amaretto
1 part Lemon-Lime Soda
fill with Cranberry Juice Cocktail

Build over ice and stir.

Captain Hawk

COLLINS GLASS

1 part Light Rum
½ part Amaretto
½ parts Crème de Banane
splash Passion Fruit Liqueur
1 part Orange Juice
1 part Pineapple Juice

Shake with ice and strain over ice.

Captain Hook
COLLINS GLASS

1 part Gin
½ part Amaretto
½ part Strawberry Liqueur
1 part Orange Juice
1 part Peach Juice

Shake with ice and strain over ice.

Captain Kirsch
COLLINS GLASS

1 part Vodka
1 part Kirschwasser
1 part Black Currant Syrup
fill with Lemonade

Build over ice and stir.

Captain's Cruiser
COLLINS GLASS

1¼ parts Coconut Rum
3 parts Orange Juice
2 parts Pineapple Juice

Shake with ice and strain over ice.

Captain's Crush
COLLINS GLASS

2 parts Spiced Rum
1 part Amaretto
3 parts Pineapple Juice

Shake with ice and strain over ice.

Captain's First Mate
COLLINS GLASS

1 part Spiced Rum
1 part Southern Comfort
splash Crème de Cacao (White)
fill with Vanilla Cola

Build over ice.

Caputo Special
COLLINS GLASS

1 part Gin
1 part Vodka
1 part Tequila
1 part Blue Curaçao
1 part Peach Schnapps
fill with Lemon-Lime Soda
splash Lime Juice

Build over ice and stir.

Carabinieri
COLLINS GLASS

1 part Tequila
¾ part Galliano®
½ part Cointreau®
splash Sweetened Lime Juice
3 parts Orange Juice
1 Egg Yolk

Shake with ice and strain over ice.

Caribbean Breeze
COLLINS GLASS

2 parts Coconut Rum
1 part Vodka
fill with Orange Juice
splash Grenadine

Build over ice and stir.

Caribbean Queen
COLLINS GLASS

1½ parts Watermelon Schnapps
½ part Coconut Rum
1½ parts Triple Sec
1 part Orange Juice
1 part Lemonade
splash Lemon Juice

Build over ice and stir.

Caribbean Screwdriver
COLLINS GLASS

½ part Peach Schnapps
½ part Crème de Banane
½ part Coconut Rum
2 parts Orange Juice
1 part Pineapple Juice
splash Cream

Build over ice and stir.

Caribbean Smuggler

HURRICANE GLASS

3/4 part Dark Rum
1/2 part Triple Sec
1 part Orange Juice
1 part Margarita Mix
1/2 part Simple Syrup
fill with Lemon-Lime Soda

Shake all but Soda with ice and strain. Top with Soda.

Carlin

COLLINS GLASS

1 part Citrus Vodka
1 part Triple Sec
3 parts Lime Juice

Shake with ice and pour.

Carman's Dance

MASON JAR

1 part Vodka
1 part Gin
1 part Cranberry Juice Cocktail
1 1/2 parts Strawberry Daiquiri Mix
fill with Orange Juice

Build over ice and stir.

Casco Bay Lemonade

COLLINS GLASS

1 1/2 parts Citrus Vodka
fill with Sweet & Sour Mix
splash Cranberry Juice Cocktail
splash Lemon-Lime Soda

Build over ice and stir.

Catalina Margarita

MARGARITA GLASS

1 1/2 parts Tequila
1 part Peach Schnapps
1 part Blue Curaçao
fill with Sweet & Sour Mix

Shake with ice and pour.

Catuche

COLLINS GLASS

1 part Dark Rum
1/2 part Dry Gin
1/2 part Triple Sec
fill with Orange Juice

Build over ice and stir.

Cave Blue

COLLINS GLASS

1 1/2 parts Blue Curaçao
1 part Vodka
fill with Pineapple Juice

Build over ice and stir.

Cervino

COLLINS GLASS

1 part Vodka
1/2 part Coffee Liqueur
1/2 part Crème de Coconut
fill with Pineapple Juice

Build over ice and stir.

Change of Heart

COLLINS GLASS

1 part Light Rum
1 part Crème de Banane
1 part Red Curaçao
dash Sugar
fill with Cola

Build over ice and stir.

Chapman

COLLINS GLASS

1 part Gin
1 part Rum
1/2 part Blue Curaçao
fill with Lemon-Lime Soda

Build over ice and stir.

Charlott

COLLINS GLASS

2 parts Triple Sec
1 part Crème de Banane
1 part Pineapple Juice
1 part Orange Juice

Build over ice and stir.

Charm City Classic

COLLINS GLASS

1 1/2 parts Grand Marnier
1 part Iced Tea
1 part Lemonade

Build over ice and stir.

Cherry Cough Syrup

COLLINS GLASS

1 part Vodka
1 part Peach Schnapps
1 part Triple Sec
1 part Grenadine

Build over ice and stir.

Cherry Spice

COLLINS GLASS

1 part Cherry Brandy
1 part Spiced Rum
fill with Cola

Build over ice and stir.

Cherry Tree Fireball

COLLINS GLASS

2 Fresh Pitted Cherries
1 part Fireball Cinnamon Whiskey
2 parts Cherry Lemonade

Muddle the Cherries in the Whiskey, then strain over ice. Fill with Cherry Lemonade and garnish with a Lemon and Cherry Spear.

Cherry-Bucko

COLLINS GLASS

1 part Cherry Brandy
1/2 part Vodka
1/2 part Lemon Juice
1/2 part Lime Juice
fill with Lemonade

Build over ice and stir.

China Blue

COLLINS GLASS

1 1/2 parts Blue Curaçao
3/4 part Lychee Liqueur
fill with Grapefruit Juice

Build over ice and stir.

Chippendale

COLLINS GLASS

1/2 part Light Rum
1 1/2 parts Pineapple Juice
splash Blue Curaçao
splash Crème de Cacao (Dark)
splash Lime Cordial

Shake with ice and pour.

Chocolate Banana Splitter

COLLINS GLASS

2 parts Crème de Banane
1 part Crème de Cacao (Dark)
2 parts Irish Cream Liqueur
1 part Frangelico®
1 part Cherry Syrup
3 parts Cream

Shake with ice and pour.

Chocolate Monk

COLLINS GLASS

1 part Frangelico®
1 part Créme de Cacao (Dark)
1 part Coffee Liqueur
1 part Irish Cream Liqueur

Shake with ice and strain.

Christmas Elf

COLLINS GLASS

2 parts White Sambuca
1 part Cinnamon Schnapps
1 part Apple Schnapps
1 part Ginger Liqueur
fill with Apple Juice

Build over ice and stir. Garnish with a sprinkle of Cinnamon.

Cinco de Rob-O

BEER MUG

2½ parts Tequila
1½ parts Triple Sec
1 part Sweet & Sour Mix
1 part Ginger Ale

Build over ice and stir.

Cinderella

COLLINS GLASS

1 part Cream
1 part Grenadine
1 part Pineapple Juice
1 part Orange Juice

Shake with ice and strain over ice.

Citrus Breeze

COLLINS GLASS

1½ parts Citrus Vodka
1 part Cranberry Juice Cocktail
1 part Grapefruit Juice

Build over ice and stir.

Citrus Smack

COLLINS GLASS

1½ parts Rum
1½ parts Triple Sec
1 part Sweet & Sour Mix
fill with Grapefruit Juice

Build over ice and stir.

Classic Jack

COLLINS GLASS

2 parts Jack Daniel's®
fill with Cola

Build over ice and stir. Garnish with a Lime Wedge.

Club Coke

COLLINS GLASS

1½ parts Vodka
½ part Peach Schnapps
2 parts Orange Juice
fill with Cola

Build over ice and stir.

Coco Cherry

COLLINS GLASS

1 part Cherry Brandy
⅔ part Crème de Coconut
3 parts Milk
3 parts Cherry Juice

Shake with ice and pour.

Coco Flirt

COLLINS GLASS

2 parts Crème de Coconut
½ part Blue Curaçao
fill with Orange Juice

Build over ice and stir.

Coco Kiss

COLLINS GLASS

1½ parts Crème de Coconut
1 part Light Rum
1 part Passion Fruit Nectar
1 part Pineapple Juice
1 part Orange Juice

Build over ice and stir.

Coconut Almond

COLLINS GLASS

1 part RumChata
1 part Coconut Rum
2 parts Root Beer

Build over ice and stir.

Coconut Almond Margarita

MARGARITA GLASS

1¼ parts Tequila
2½ parts Sweet & Sour Mix
½ part Crème de Coconut
¼ part Amaretto
½ part Lime Juice

Shake with ice and pour.

Coconut Bra

COLLINS GLASS

1 part Coconut Rum
1 part Raspberry Liqueur
splash Lemon-Lime Soda
fill with Sweet & Sour Mix

Build over ice and stir.

Coffee Orange

COLLINS GLASS

1½ parts Coffee Liqueur
fill with Orange Juice

Build over ice and stir.

Cokaretto

COLLINS GLASS

1 part Amaretto
fill with Cola

Build over ice and stir.

Cold Kentucky

COLLINS GLASS

1 part Amaretto
1 part Southern Comfort®
splash Orange Juice
fill with Pineapple Juice

Build over ice and stir.

Collins

COLLINS GLASS

1½ parts Vodka
3 parts Sweet & Sour Mix
1 part Club Soda

Build over ice and stir.

Colorado Bulldog

COLLINS GLASS

1½ parts Butterscotch Liqueur
1 part Coffee Liqueur
2 parts Cola
fill with Half and Half

Build over ice and stir.

Colorado Crush

COLLINS GLASS

1 part Rum
1 part Amaretto
1 part Sloe Gin
fill with Iced Tea

Build over ice and stir.

Colt Cruiser

COLLINS GLASS

1 part Dark Rum
1 part Amaretto
1 part Crème de Banane
fill with Lemonade

Build over ice and stir.

Columbian Necktie

COLLINS GLASS

1 part 151-Proof Rum
2 parts Southern Comfort
fill with Ginger Ale
splash Grenadine

Build over ice.

Cool by the Pool

COLLINS GLASS

1 part Light Rum
¾ part Coconut Rum
¼ part Lime Cordial
2 parts Pineapple Juice
2 parts Orange Juice
splash Grenadine

Build over ice and stir.

Cool Carlos

COLLINS GLASS

1½ parts Dark Rum
1 part Blue Curaçao
2 parts Cranberry Juice Cocktail
2 parts Pineapple Juice
splash Sweet & Sour Mix

Build over ice and stir.

Copabanana

COLLINS GLASS

2 parts Rum
½ part Crème de Banane
½ part Apricot Brandy
1 part Pineapple Juice
1 part Orange Juice

Build over ice and stir.

Coral Sea
COLLINS GLASS

1 part Light Rum
1 part Pineapple Juice
1 part Cream of Coconut
splash Blue Curaçao

Shake with ice and strain over ice.

Costa Dorada
COLLINS GLASS

1 part Vodka
1 part Spiced Rum
½ part Strawberry Liqueur
fill with Lemon-Lime Soda

Build over ice and stir.

Costanza
COLLINS GLASS

1½ parts Vodka
½ part Peach Schnapps
½ part Grenadine
fill with Carrot Juice

Build over ice and stir.

Cow Puncher
COLLINS GLASS

1 part Dark Rum
1 part Crème de Cacao (White)
fill with Milk

Build over ice and stir.

Cowgirl's Prayer
COLLINS GLASS

2 parts Silver Tequila
1 part Lime Juice
fill with Lemonade

Build over ice and stir.

Cran Daddy
HURRICANE GLASS

1 part Vanilla Vodka
1 part Lemon-Lime Soda
1 part Cranberry Juice Cocktail

Build over ice and stir.

Cranberry Kiss
COLLINS GLASS

¾ part Spiced Rum
½ part Peppermint Schnapps
1 part Collins Mix
1 part Cranberry Juice Cocktail

Shake with ice and pour.

Cranberry Margarita
MARGARITA GLASS

1½ parts Tequila
1 part Lime Juice
1½ parts Triple Sec
1½ parts Sweet & Sour Mix
2 parts Cranberry Juice Cocktail

Shake with ice and pour.

Cranmeister
COLLINS GLASS

2 parts Jägermeister
½ part Lime Juice
fill with Cranberry Juice

Build over ice and stir.

Crawling up the Wall
COLLINS GLASS

1½ parts Scotch
½ part Raspberry Liqueur
½ part Lemon Juice
1 part Apple Juice
1 part Raspberry Seltzer

Build over ice and stir.

Crazy Coconut
COLLINS GLASS

1½ parts Crème de Coconut
1 part Crème de Banane
½ part Blue Curaçao
1 part Grapefruit Juice
1 part Pineapple Juice

Shake with ice and pour.

Crazy Horse's Neck
COLLINS GLASS

1 part Fireball Cinnamon Whiskey
fill with Ginger Beer
2 dashes Peychaud's Bitters

Build over ice.

Creamsicle®
COLLINS GLASS

1½ parts Vanilla Vodka
1½ parts Milk
fill with Orange Juice

Shake with ice and strain over ice.

Creamy Avalanche
HURRICANE GLASS

¼ part Rum
¼ part Coconut Rum
¼ part Coffee Liqueur
¼ part Irish Cream Liqueur
¼ part Frangelico®
1 part Half and Half
1 part Cola

Shake with ice and pour.

Creamy Dream
COLLINS GLASS

1 part Coffee Liqueur
1 part Crème de Cacao (White)
1 part Crème de Menthe (White)
1 part Irish Cream Liqueur
fill with Milk

Shake with ice and pour.

Crimson Flow
COLLINS GLASS

2 parts Cranberry Liqueur
fill with Cranberry Juice Cocktail
splash Grenadine

Build over ice and stir.

Croc Punch
HURRICANE GLASS

1 part Melon Liqueur
1 part Crème de Banane
1 part Vodka
1 part Parfait Amour
fill with Lemon-Lime Soda
splash Lime Juice

Build over ice and stir.

Crossing the Line
COLLINS GLASS

2 parts Cherry Brandy
1 part Dry Gin
fill with Apple Juice

Build over ice and stir.

Cruiser
COLLINS GLASS

1¼ parts Coconut Rum
1 part Orange Juice
1 part Pineapple Juice

Build over ice and stir.

Crystal Cranberry
COLLINS GLASS

1 part Vodka
¼ part Bourbon
¼ part Gin
¼ part Amaretto
1 part Orange Juice
1 part Cranberry Juice Cocktail

Build over ice and stir.

Cuban Planter's
COLLINS GLASS

2 parts Light Rum
4 parts Orange Juice
1 part Strawberry Puree
½ part Lime Juice

Shake with ice and pour.

Cupid's Disease

COLLINS GLASS

2 parts Sour Grape Schnapps
1 part Strawberry Vodka
1 part Lemonade
1 part Lemon-Lime Soda

Build over ice and stir.

Curbfeeler

COLLINS GLASS

1 part Peach Schnapps
1 part Light Rum
1 part Vodka
fill with Iced Tea

Build over ice and stir.

Cyclone

COLLINS GLASS

1 part Amaretto
1 part Grenadine
fill with Orange Juice

Shake with ice and pour.

D J Special

COLLINS GLASS

1 part Vodka
1 part Triple Sec
1 part Amaretto
1 part Southern Comfort®
1 part Sloe Gin
fill with Pineapple Juice

Build over ice and stir.

D.P.R.

COLLINS GLASS

1 part Vodka
1 part Triple Sec
fill with Cranberry Juice Cocktail
splash Club Soda

Build over ice and stir.

Daddy's Home

COLLINS GLASS

½ part Amaretto
½ part Coconut Rum
½ part Southern Comfort
½ part Spiced Rum
2 parts Orange Juice
2 parts Pineapple Juice
½ part Grenadine

Shake with ice and strain over ice.

Daily Double

COLLINS GLASS

1 part Southern Comfort®
1 part Amaretto
1 part Orange Juice
1 part Cranberry Juice Cocktail

Shake with ice and strain over ice.

Dallas

COLLINS GLASS

1 part Blue Curaçao
1 part Crème de Banane
1 part Cream of Coconut
fill with Pineapple Juice

Shake with ice and pour.

Damn Gumby®

BEER MUG

1 part Melon Liqueur
1 part Vodka
fill with Hard Apple Cider

Build in the glass with no ice.

Daredevil

COLLINS GLASS

1 part 151-Proof Rum
½ part Dark Rum
2 parts Orange Juice
1 part Cranberry Juice
1 part Pineapple Juice
splash Lemon-Lime Soda

Build over ice and stir.

Darth Maul®

COLLINS GLASS

1 part Gin
1 part Light Rum
1 part Silver Tequila
1 part Vodka
1 part Triple Sec
1 part Jägermeister®
2 splashes Grenadine
fill with Sweet & Sour Mix

Shake with ice and pour.

Darth Vader®

COLLINS GLASS

½ part Vodka
½ part Gin
½ part Light Rum
½ part Silver Tequila
½ part Triple Sec
1 part Jägermeister®
fill with Sweet & Sour Mix

Shake with ice and pour.

David and Goliath

COLLINS GLASS

2 parts Orange Rum
1 part Gold Tequila
fill with Pink Lemonade

Build over ice and stir.

Death from Above

COLLINS GLASS

1 part 151-Proof Rum
1 part Gin
fill with Cola

Build over ice and stir.

Debutante

COLLINS GLASS

1 part Silver Tequila
⅔ part Peach Schnapps
splash Peppermint Liqueur
½ part Lemon Juice

Shake with ice and strain.

Deep Blue Sea

COLLINS GLASS

2 parts Vodka
2 parts Blue Curaçao
1 part Passion Fruit Juice
1 part Grapefruit Juice

Shake with ice and strain over ice.

Deep Brain Stimulation

HURRICANE GLASS

1 part Amaretto
1 part Gin
1 part Light Rum
1 part Melon Liqueur
1 part Triple Sec
1 part Vodka
fill with Orange Juice

Shake with ice and strain.

Deer Hunter

COLLINS GLASS

2 parts Jägermeister
splash Lemon Juice
fill with Root Beer

Build over ice and stir.

Delkozak

COLLINS GLASS

2 parts Vodka
1 part Grapefruit Juice
1 part Lemon Juice
1 part Lime Juice
1 part Orange Juice

Build over ice and stir.

Derby Daze

HURRICANE GLASS

1 part Vodka
1 part Kiwi Schnapps
1 part Blackberry Liqueur

Shake with ice and strain over ice.

Desert Rose

COLLINS GLASS

1 1/2 parts Raspberry Liqueur
2 parts Orange Juice
2 parts Mango Juice
2 parts Pineapple Juice

Shake with ice and pour.

Desert Sunrise

COLLINS GLASS

3/4 part Vodka
1 part Orange Juice
1 part Pineapple Juice
splash Grenadine

Build over ice.

Devil in Miss Jones

COLLINS GLASS

1 1/2 parts Brandy
1/2 part Triple Sec
2 splashes Crème de Noyaux
2 splashes Grenadine

Shake with ice and strain over ice.

Dew Me

COLLINS GLASS

1 part Jack Daniel's®
1 part Southern Comfort®
splash Lemon Juice
fill with Mountain Dew®

Build over ice and stir.

Dewin' the Captain

COLLINS GLASS

1 1/2 parts Spiced Rum
fill with Mountain Dew®

Build over ice and stir.

Dewrunrum

COLLINS GLASS

1 1/2 parts 151-Proof Rum
fill with Mountain Dew®

Build over ice and stir.

Diamond-Studded Screwdriver

COLLINS GLASS

1 1/2 parts Vodka
fill with Orange Soda

Build over ice and stir.

Diaz

COLLINS GLASS

1 1/2 parts Vanilla Vodka
2 parts Apple Juice
2 parts Ginger Ale

Build over ice and stir.

Diego Garcia

COLLINS GLASS

1 part Light Rum
1 part Mandarine Napoléon® Liqueur
1 part Dark Rum
1/2 part Triple Sec
fill with Pineapple Juice

Build over ice and stir.

Dirty Mop

COLLINS GLASS

1/2 part Blavod® Black Vodka
1/2 part Blue Curaçao
1/2 part Passoã®
1 1/2 parts Orange Juice
1 1/2 parts Cranberry Juice Cocktail

Build over ice and stir.

Disco Lemonade

COLLINS GLASS

2 parts Vodka
1/2 part Blue Curaçao
fill with Lemonade

Build over ice and stir.

Diva

COLLINS GLASS

1 1/2 parts Vodka
1/2 part Lime Juice
splash Maraschino Cherry Juice
fill with Lemon-Lime Soda

Build over ice and stir.

Dixieland Tea

MASON JAR

2 parts Whiskey
1/2 part Amaretto
fill with Iced Tea

Build over ice and stir.

Dizzy Tart

HURRICANE GLASS

1 part 151-Proof Rum
1 part Crème de Banane
1 part Crème de Coconut
splash Grenadine
1 part Orange Juice
1 part Pineapple Juice
1 part Papaya Juice

Shake with ice and pour.

Dog Biscuit

COLLINS GLASS

1/2 part Cinnamon Schnapps
1/2 part Root Beer Schnapps
fill with Lemon-Lime Soda
splash Irish Cream Liqueur

Build over ice and stir.

Dominican Goddess

COLLINS GLASS

1 1/2 parts Light Rum
1/2 part Pink Grapefruit Juice
fill with Lemon-Lime Soda

Build over ice and stir.

Don Frederico

COLLINS GLASS

1 part Dark Rum
1/2 part Grenadine
fill with Orange Juice
splash Apricot Brandy

Build over ice and stir.

Donkey Ride

HURRICANE GLASS

1 part Tequila Reposado
1/2 part Blue Curaçao
1/2 part Triple Sec
1 part Pineapple Juice
1 part Orange Juice

Shake with ice and pour.

Dorothy

COLLINS GLASS

1 part Dark Rum
1/2 part Amaretto
1/2 part Crème de Banane
fill with Pineapple Juice
splash Cream of Coconut

Build over ice and stir.

Double Vision

COLLINS GLASS

1 part Currant Vodka
1 part Citrus Vodka
fill with Apple Juice

Build over ice and stir.

Downshift

HURRICANE GLASS

2 parts Tequila
2 parts Fruit Punch
1 part Lemon-Lime Soda
splash 151-Proof Rum

Build over ice and stir.

Dragon Piss

COLLINS GLASS

3/4 part Butterscotch Schnapps
1 part Cinnamon Schnapps
fill with Mountain Dew®

Build over ice and stir.

Drink of the Year

COLLINS GLASS

1 part Vodka
1/2 part Triple Sec
1/2 part Raspberry Syrup
splash Blue Curaçao

Shake with ice and pour.

Dumpster™ Juice

COLLINS GLASS

1 part Vodka
1 part Light Rum
1 part Raspberry Liqueur
1 part Melon Liqueur
1 part Cranberry Juice Cocktail
1 part Orange Juice
1 part Pineapple Juice

Shake with ice and pour.

Early Riser

COLLINS GLASS

1 part Melon Liqueur
1 part Silver Tequila
fill with Orange Juice

Shake with ice and strain over ice.

El Cerro

COLLINS GLASS

1 part Light Rum
1 part Dark Rum
1½ parts Pineapple Juice
splash Triple Sec
splash Grenadine

Build over ice and stir.

El Dorado

COLLINS GLASS

2 parts Silver Tequila
1½ parts Pineapple Juice
1½ parts Orange Juice
1½ parts Banana Juice
splash Triple Sec
splash Crème de Banane

Shake with ice and strain over ice.

El Gringo Loco

COLLINS GLASS

1½ parts Tequila
½ part Cherry Brandy
2 splashes Lemon Juice
2 splashes Lime Juice

Shake with ice and strain over ice.

Ecstasy

COLLINS GLASS

1 part Blue Curaçao
1 part Melon Liqueur
1 part Lime Juice
fill with Cranberry Juice Cocktail

Shake with ice and pour.

Eldorado

COLLINS GLASS

2 parts Tequila
1½ parts Lemon Juice
½ part Honey
fill with Tonic Water

Shake all but Tonic with ice and strain over ice. Fill with Tonic Water.

Electric Lemonade

COLLINS GLASS

1¼ parts Vodka
½ part Blue Curaçao
2 parts Sweet & Sour Mix
splash Lemon-Lime Soda

Build over ice and stir.

Electric Lizard

COLLINS GLASS

1 part Melon Liqueur
1 part Vodka
fill with Sweet & Sour Mix

Build over ice and stir.

Electric Margarita

MARGARITA GLASS

1½ parts Tequila
½ part Blue Curaçao
½ part Sweetened Lime Juice

Shake with ice and pour.

Electric Popsicle

COLLINS GLASS

2 parts Melon Liqueur
2 parts Blue Curaçao
fill with Lemon-Lime Soda

Build over ice and stir. Garnish with a Lime Slice.

Electric Screwdriver

COLLINS GLASS

1 part Southern Comfort®
2 parts Amaretto
fill with Orange Juice

Build over ice and stir.

Electric Tea

COLLINS GLASS

1 part Vodka
1 part Gin
1 part Light Rum
1 part Tequila
1 part Blue Curaçao
2 parts Sweet & Sour Mix
1½ parts Lemon-Lime Soda

Shake with ice and pour.

Eliana

COLLINS GLASS

1½ parts Dry Gin
1 part Grapefruit Juice
1 part Pineapple Juice
½ part Lime Juice
½ part Raspberry Liqueur

Build over ice and stir.

Eliminator

COLLINS GLASS

1 part Wild Turkey® 101
1 part Tequila
fill with Orange Soda

Build over ice and stir.

Emerald Caribbean

COLLINS GLASS

¾ part Coconut Rum
½ part Melon Liqueur
¼ part Crème de Banane
¾ part Blue Curaçao
2 parts Pineapple Juice
1 part Orange Juice

Shake with ice and pour.

Emerald Lily

HURRICANE GLASS

1 part Vodka
1 part Rum
½ part Crème de Menthe (Green)
½ part Lime Juice
fill with Pineapple Juice

Build over ice and stir.

Esclava

COLLINS GLASS

1½ parts Dark Rum
1 part Triple Sec
1 part Crème de Coconut
fill with Pineapple Juice
splash Grenadine

Build over ice and stir.

Excitabull

COLLINS GLASS

1 part Vodka
1 part Peach Schnapps
fill with Red Bull® Energy Drink
splash Cranberry Juice Cocktail

Build over ice and stir.

Exciting Night in Georgia

COLLINS GLASS

1 part Peach Schnapps
½ part Apricot Brandy
1 part Southern Comfort®
fill with Cranberry Juice Cocktail

Build over ice and stir.

Executive Gimlet

COLLINS GLASS

1½ parts Jim Beam®
1 part Triple Sec
½ part Lemon Juice
½ part Lime Juice

Shake with ice and strain.

Eye
COLLINS GLASS

1 part Vodka
2/3 part Passion Fruit Liqueur
2/3 part Triple Sec
2 parts Passion Fruit Juice
1 part Orange Juice

Shake with ice and pour.

Eye of the Storm
COLLINS GLASS

2 parts Spiced Rum
1 part Lime Juice
fill with Cola

Build over ice and stir.

Fairy from Hell
COLLINS GLASS

2 parts Absinthe
1/2 part Lemon Juice
1 part Apple Juice
1 part Ginger Ale
2 parts Red Bull Energy Drink

Build over ice and stir.

Fantastico
COLLINS GLASS

1 1/2 parts Dark Rum
1/2 part Crème de Banane
splash Lemon Juice
fill with Pineapple Juice

Build over ice and stir.

Fatality
COLLINS GLASS

1 part Rum
1 part Blue Curaçao
1 part Peach Schnapps
1 part Sweet & Sour Mix

Shake with ice and strain.

Father's Milk
HURRICANE GLASS

3 parts Tia Maria®
2 parts Crème de Banane
1 part Crème de Menthe (Green)
fill with Milk

Shake with ice and pour.

Femme Fatale
COLLINS GLASS

2 parts Light Rum
1 part Amaretto
1/2 part Blue Curaçao
fill with Pineapple Juice

Shake with ice and pour.

Field of Green
COLLINS GLASS

1 part Sloe Gin
1 part Amaretto
fill with Lemon-Lime Soda

Build over ice and stir.

Fino Mint
COLLINS GLASS

1/2 part Vodka
2/3 part Coffee Liqueur
1/2 part Peppermint Liqueur
fill with Milk

Shake with ice and strain over ice.

Fire & Iced Tea
COLLINS GLASS

1 part Fireball Cinnamon Whiskey
splash Lemon Juice
fill with Iced Tea

Build over ice.

Fire Eater
COLLINS GLASS

1 part Triple Sec
1 part Silver Tequila
1 part Orange Juice
1 part Cranberry Juice Cocktail

Build over ice and stir.

Fire in the Hills

COLLINS GLASS

2/3 part Melon Liqueur
1 part Spiced Rum
2 parts Orange Juice
2 parts Pineapple Juice
1 part Cranberry Juice Cocktail

Build over ice and stir.

First Sight

COLLINS GLASS

1 part Blue Curaçao
1 part Vodka
1 part Tequila Reposado
fill with Lemon-Lime Soda

Build over ice and stir.

Flamin' Beaver

PINT GLASS

2 parts Fireball Cinnamon Whiskey
fill with Woodchuck Cider

Build in order.

Flaming Jesse (Tropical Sunshine)

COLLINS GLASS

1 part Coconut Rum
1/2 part Vodka
1/2 part Irish Cream Liqueur
fill with Orange Juice

Build over ice and stir.

Flaming Scotsman

COLLINS GLASS

1 part Melon Liqueur
1 part Coconut Rum
1 part Raspberry Liqueur
fill with Sweet & Sour Mix

Shake with ice and pour.

Florida Daiquiri

COLLINS GLASS

1 1/2 parts Light Rum
1 part Orange Juice
2 splashes Lime Juice
dash Sugar

Shake with ice and pour.

Florida Sunrise

COLLINS GLASS

1 1/4 parts Light Rum
1/2 part Grenadine
fill with Orange Juice

Build over ice.

Florida Sunshine

COLLINS GLASS

1 1/2 parts Lemon Vodka
1/2 part Peach Schnapps
1 part Cranberry Juice
1 part Orange Juice

Build over ice and stir.

Flubber

COLLINS GLASS

1 part Sambuca
2 parts Vodka
fill with Orange Juice

Build over ice and stir.

Flying Bull

COLLINS GLASS

1 part Dark Rum
1 part Light Rum
1 part Red Bull® Energy Drink
1 part Orange Juice

Build over ice and stir.

Flying Kangaroo

COLLINS GLASS

1 1/2 parts Pineapple Juice
1 part Vodka
1 part Light Rum
1 part Orange Juice
1/2 part Cream
1/2 part Crème de Coconut

Shake with ice and strain over ice.

Flying Meister

COLLINS GLASS

1 part Jägermeister®
fill with Red Bull® Energy Drink

Build over ice and stir.

Forest Funk

COLLINS GLASS

1½ parts Citrus Vodka
¾ part Peach Schnapps
fill with Grapefruit Juice

Build over ice and stir.

Forest Nymph

COLLINS GLASS

1½ parts Gin
½ part Blue Curaçao
2 parts Pineapple Juice
2 parts Mango Juice

Build over ice and stir.

Forever Yours

COLLINS GLASS

1½ parts Vodka
1 part Passion Fruit Liqueur
1 part Lime Juice
fill with Orange Juice

Shake with ice and pour.

Formula 1

COLLINS GLASS

2 parts Vodka
½ part Peach Brandy
½ part Raspberry Liqueur
2 parts Grapefruit Juice
fill with Tonic Water

Build over ice and stir.

Free Fall

COLLINS GLASS

1 part Scotch
⅔ part Crème de Coconut
fill with Pineapple Juice
splash Passion Fruit Juice
splash Lemon Juice

Shake with ice and pour.

French Margarita

MARGARITA GLASS

½ part Silver Tequila
¼ part Triple Sec
2 parts Passion Fruit Liqueur
2 parts Lime Cordial

Shake with ice and pour.

Frenchy

COLLINS GLASS

1½ parts Cognac
1 part Crème de Banane
½ part Strawberry Syrup
2 parts Pineapple Juice
2 parts Orange Juice

Shake with ice and strain over ice.

Frequency

COLLINS GLASS

⅔ part Passion Fruit Liqueur
½ part Lemon Juice
⅔ part Papaya Juice
fill with Sparkling Water

Build over ice and stir.

Fresh

COLLINS GLASS

1 part Citrus Vodka
1 part Amaretto
1½ parts Orange Juice
fill with Apple Cider

Build over ice and stir.

Fresh Coconut

COLLINS GLASS

1½ parts Coconut Rum
fill with Grapefruit Juice
3 splashes Grenadine
3 splashes Lemon-Lime Soda

Build over ice and stir.

Freshness
COLLINS GLASS

1 part Light Rum
1/2 part Amaretto
1/2 part Crème de Banane
fill with Lemonade

Build over ice and stir.

Frog in the Well
COLLINS GLASS

1 part Orange Vodka
1 part Pineapple Vodka
1 part Pineapple Juice
fill with Mountain Dew

Build over ice and stir.

Froggy Potion
COLLINS GLASS

1 part Rum
1 part Vodka
1 part Gin
1 part Tequila
fill with Orange Juice
splash Cola

Build over ice and stir.

Frosty Death
COLLINS GLASS

2 parts Peppermint Schnapps
1 part Vodka

Shake with ice and strain.

Frosty Rain
COLLINS GLASS

1 part Vodka
1 part Parfait Amour
1 part Triple Sec
fill with Lemonade
splash Crème de Banane

Build over ice and stir.

Fruit Collins
COLLINS GLASS

1 part Strawberry Liqueur
1 part Gin
splash Simple Syrup
1 part Lemon Juice

Shake with ice and strain over ice.

Fruit Lush
COLLINS GLASS

1 1/2 parts Light Rum
1 1/2 parts Peach Schnapps
1 1/2 parts Wild Berry Schnapps
1/2 part Crème de Banane
2 1/2 parts Pineapple Juice
fill with Lemon-Lime Soda

Build over ice and stir.

Fruit Tickler
COLLINS GLASS

1 part Peach Schnapps
2/3 part Melon Liqueur
2/3 part Vodka
1 part Orange Juice
1 part Cranberry Juice Cocktail
fill with Lemon-Lime Soda

Build over ice and stir.

Fruit Tingle
COLLINS GLASS

1 part Blue Curaçao
1 part Raspberry Liqueur
fill with Lemonade

Build over ice and stir.

Fruity Bitch
COLLINS GLASS

1 1/2 parts Vodka
1 1/2 parts Triple Sec
1 part Peach Schnapps
fill with Fruit Punch
splash Cola

Build over ice and stir.

Fubar

COLLINS GLASS

1 part Gin
2 parts Rum
2 parts Tequila
2 parts Vodka
fill with Apple Cider

Build over ice and stir.

Funkmaster 2000

COLLINS GLASS

1 part Peach Schnapps
2 parts Vodka
fill with Cranberry Juice Cocktail

Build over ice and stir.

Funky Cold Medina

COLLINS GLASS

1/2 part Blue Curaçao
1/2 part Melon Liqueur
1/2 part Peach Schnapps
1 part Cranberry Juice Cocktail
1 part Orange Juice
1 part Pineapple Juice

Shake with ice and pour.

Funky Filly

HURRICANE GLASS

3/4 part Vodka
3/4 part Melon Liqueur
3/4 part Cherry Liqueur
3/4 part Triple Sec
2 parts Cranberry Juice Cocktail
2 parts Lemon-Lime Soda
1 1/2 parts Lime Juice

Build over ice and stir.

Funny Duck

COLLINS GLASS

1 part Crème de Coconut
splash Grenadine
splash Cream
fill with Pineapple Juice

Shake with ice and pour.

Furry Reggae

COLLINS GLASS

1 part Crème de Coconut
1/2 part Vodka
1/2 part Peach Schnapps
fill with Orange Juice

Build over ice and stir.

The Future Is Bright

COLLINS GLASS

3/4 part Red Curaçao
3/4 part Triple Sec
1/2 part Blue Curaçao
fill with Orange Juice

Shake with ice and pour.

Fuzzy Almond

COLLINS GLASS

1 1/2 parts Amaretto
1 1/2 parts Light Rum
1 part Cranberry Juice Cocktail
1 part Club Soda

Build over ice and stir.

Fuzzy Charlie

COLLINS GLASS

3/4 part Spiced Rum
3/4 part Peach Schnapps
2 parts Piña Colada Mix
fill with Orange Juice

Shake with ice and pour.

Fuzzy Hippo

HURRICANE GLASS

1 part Peach Schnapps
1 part Vodka
2 parts Hpnotiq®
splash Lemon-Lime Soda
fill with Pineapple Juice

Build over ice and stir.

Fuzzy Pierced Navel

COLLINS GLASS

1 part Tequila
1 1/2 parts Peach Schnapps
fill with Orange Juice

Shake with ice and pour.

Fuzzy Prick

COLLINS GLASS

2 parts Peach Schnapps
fill with Pineapple Juice

Build over ice and stir.

A Fuzzy Thing

COLLINS GLASS

2 parts Citrus Vodka
1 part Triple Sec
1½ parts Peach Schnapps
splash Orange Juice
splash Pineapple Juice
splash Sweet & Sour Mix

Build over ice and stir.

G String

COLLINS GLASS

2 parts Vodka
1 part Blue Curaçao
1 part Blackberry Liqueur
2 parts Lemonade
2 parts Lime Juice
2 parts Sweet & Sour Mix

Shake with ice and pour.

Gadfly

COLLINS GLASS

1 part Crème de Banane
1 part Melon Liqueur
1 part Crème de Coconut
1 part Vanilla Liqueur
fill with Pineapple Juice

Build over ice and stir.

Gandy Dancer

COLLINS GLASS

1 part Canadian Whisky
1 part Amaretto
1 part Banana Liqueur
fill with Pineapple Juice

Build over ice and stir.

Gatsby

COLLINS GLASS

1 part Southern Comfort®
splash Lime Juice
fill with Lemonade

Build over ice and stir.

Geisha Cup

COLLINS GLASS

1½ parts Gin
1 part Apricot Brandy
2 parts Grapefruit Juice
2 parts Orange Juice

Build over ice and stir. Garnish with a Maraschino Cherry.

Gekko

COLLINS GLASS

1 part Vodka
1 part Crème de Cassis
2 parts Grapefruit Juice
fill with Ginger Ale

Build over ice and stir.

The General

COLLINS GLASS

1½ parts Cherry Brandy
½ part Grenadine
1 part Cranberry Juice Cocktail
1 part Seltzer

Build over ice and stir.

Generation X

HURRICANE GLASS

1 part Tequila
1 part Jim Beam®
1 part Triple Sec
1 part Blue Curaçao
1 part Melon Liqueur
fill with Smirnoff Ice®

Build over ice and stir.

Geng Green Xu

COLLINS GLASS

1 part Gin
1 part Green Chartreuse®
1 part Vodka
1 part Lemon-Lime Soda
splash Lemon Juice

Build over ice and stir.

Gentle Ben

COLLINS GLASS

1 part Gin
1 part Vodka
1 part Tequila
fill with Orange Juice

Build over ice and stir. Garnish with an Orange Slice and a Maraschino Cherry.

Genuine Risk

COLLINS GLASS

½ part Vodka
½ part Coffee Liqueur
½ part Amaretto
½ part Crème de Coconut
½ part Frangelico®
3 parts Cream

Build over ice and stir.

Georgia Swamp Water

MASON JAR

2 parts White Whiskey
fill with Lemonade

Build over ice and stir.

German Tower

COLLINS GLASS

1 part Triple Sec
1 part Gold Tequila
½ part Jägermeister®
fill with Sweet & Sour Mix
½ part Lime Juice

Shake with ice and strain over ice.

Get Fruity

COLLINS GLASS

1 part Limoncello
1 part Melon Liqueur
1 part Tropical Punch Schnapps
fill with Lemon-Lime Soda

Build over ice and stir.

Get'cha Laid

COLLINS GLASS

1 part Vodka
2 parts Peach Schnapps
1 part Cranberry Juice Cocktail
1 part Orange Juice

Build over ice and stir.

Gettin' Loose

COLLINS GLASS

1½ parts Amaretto
2 parts Vodka
fill with Lemon-Lime Soda

Build over ice and stir.

Gibbs

COLLINS GLASS

1 part Vodka
1 part Watermelon Schnapps
fill with Lemon-Lime Soda

Build over ice and stir.

Gideon's Green Dinosaur

COLLINS GLASS

1 part Dark Rum
1 part Vodka
1 part Triple Sec
1 part Tequila
1 part Melon Liqueur
fill with Mountain Dew®

Build over ice and stir.

Gigantic White

COLLINS GLASS

1 part Irish Cream Liqueur
3 parts Piña Colada Mix
fill with Milk
splash Sloe Gin

Shake all but Sloe Gin with ice and strain. Top with Sloe Gin.

Gilligan

COLLINS GLASS

1 part Light Rum
1/2 part Crème de Banane
1/2 part Lemon Juice
1 part Orange Juice
1 part Pineapple Juice

Build over ice and stir.

Gin Breeze

COLLINS GLASS

1 1/2 parts Gin
1 part Grapefruit Juice
fill with Cranberry Juice Cocktail

Build over ice and stir.

Ginger Balls

COLLINS GLASS

2 parts Fireball Cinnamon Whiskey
fill with Ginger Ale

Build over ice and stir.

Ginger Bite

COLLINS GLASS

1 Lemon Slice
1/2 tsp Fresh Ginger
1/2 tsp Powdered Sugar
1 part Ginger Liqueur
1/2 part Gold Tequila
1/2 part Lime Liqueur
top with Ginger Beer

Muddle the Lemon, Ginger, and Sugar. Add the spirits, shake with ice, and strain over ice. Top with Ginger Beer and garnish with a Lemon Wheel.

Ginger Heat

COLLINS GLASS

2 parts Fireball Cinnamon Whiskey
1 part Peach Schnapps
fill with Ginger Beer

Build over ice and stir.

Giraffe

HURRICANE GLASS

1 part Melon Liqueur
1 part Vodka
fill with Pineapple Juice
splash Cranberry Juice Cocktail

Build over ice and stir.

Glass Tower

COLLINS GLASS

1 part Vodka
1 part Peach Schnapps
1 part Rum
1 part Triple Sec
1/2 part Sambuca
fill with Lemon-Lime Soda

Build over ice and stir.

The Gobbler

COLLINS GLASS

2 parts Wild Turkey® 101
fill with Lemon-Lime Soda

Build over ice and stir.

Golden Blizzard

COLLINS GLASS

1 part Goldschläger®
1 part Peppermint Schnapps
fill with Eggnog

Shake with ice and pour.

Golden Girl

COLLINS GLASS

1 part Apricot Brandy
1 part Vodka
fill with Orange Juice

Shake with ice and pour.

Golden Margarita

MARGARITA GLASS

2 parts Tequila
1 part Simple Syrup
2 parts Sweetened Lime Juice
1/4 part Grand Marnier®
1/4 part Cointreau®
1/4 part Blue Curaçao

Shake with ice and strain over ice.

Golden Moment

COLLINS GLASS

1 part Orange Vodka
splash Goldschläger®
splash Apricot Brandy
splash Vanilla Liqueur
fill with Orange Juice

Shake with ice and strain over ice.

Golden Skyway

COLLINS GLASS

1 part Apricot Brandy
1/2 part Triple Sec
1/2 part Gin
dash Bitters
fill with Lemonade

Shake with ice and pour.

Golden Sunset

COLLINS GLASS

4 parts Grapefruit Juice
1 part Grenadine
dash Powdered Sugar

Shake with ice and pour.

Golden Years

COLLINS GLASS

1 part Crème de Banane
1 part Galliano®
1 part Milk
2 parts Orange Juice
2 parts Pineapple Juice

Shake with ice and pour.

The Gold, the Bad, and the Ugly

COLLINS GLASS

1 1/2 parts Coffee Liqueur
1 part Irish Cream Liqueur
fill with Milk
1 1/2 parts Goldschläger®

Build over ice.

Golfer's Passion

COLLINS GLASS

2 parts Gin
2 parts Passion Fruit Liqueur
2 parts Campari®
fill with Orange Juice

Shake with ice and pour.

Gombay Smash

COLLINS GLASS

1 part Light Rum
1 part Dark Rum
1 part Vodka
1/2 part Triple Sec
1 part Pineapple Juice
1 part Apricot Brandy
dash Powdered Sugar

Shake with ice and strain over ice.

Goober

COLLINS GLASS

1 1/2 parts Vodka
1 1/2 parts Blackberry Liqueur
1 1/2 parts Melon Liqueur
1 part Triple Sec
1 part Grenadine
1 part Pineapple Juice
1 part Orange Juice

Shake with ice and strain over ice.

Good Fortune

HURRICANE GLASS

1 1/4 parts Citrus Vodka
3/4 part Alizé® Gold Passion
fill with Lemonade

Shake with ice and strain over ice.

Good Time Charlie

COLLINS GLASS

1 part Light Rum
1 part Dark Rum
1 part Cranberry Juice Cocktail
1 part Pink Grapefruit Juice
1 part Pineapple Juice
1 part Sweet & Sour Mix

Build over ice and stir.

Goodnight Joyce

COLLINS GLASS

2 parts Vodka
1 part Raspberry Liqueur
fill with Orange Juice
splash Cranberry Juice Cocktail

Build over ice and stir.

Google Juice

COLLINS GLASS

1 part Vodka
1 part Amaretto
1 part Cranberry Vodka
fill with Cranberry Juice Cocktail

Build over ice and stir.

Gorilla Punch

COLLINS GLASS

1 part Vodka
½ part Blue Curaçao
2 parts Orange Juice
2 parts Pineapple Juice

Shake with ice and strain over ice. Garnish with a Maraschino Cherry.

Governor

COLLINS GLASS

1 part Rye Whiskey
2 parts Sweet Vermouth
fill with Apple Cider

Build over ice and stir.

Graffiti

COLLINS GLASS

1½ parts Pisang Ambon® Liqueur
1½ parts Passion Fruit Liqueur
splash Chartreuse®
3 parts Orange Juice
1 part Lime Juice

Build over ice and stir.

Grand Marshall

COLLINS GLASS

1 part Brandy
1 part Rum
1 part Root Beer Schnapps
fill with Cola

Build over ice and stir.

Grandma's Peach Fuzz

HURRICANE GLASS

1½ parts Sour Apple Schnapps
1 part Southern Comfort®
½ part Peach Schnapps
splash Lemon-Lime Soda
fill with Cranberry Juice Cocktail

Build over ice and stir.

Granny's Rocker

COLLINS GLASS

1½ parts Melon Liqueur
½ part Citrus Vodka
splash Blue Curaçao
½ part Lime Cordial
2 parts Margarita Mix

Shake with ice and pour.

Grape Gazpacho

COLLINS GLASS

1 part Vodka
1 part Apricot Brandy
1 part Ginger Ale
1 part Grape Juice (White)

Build over ice and stir.

11,000 DRINKS
TALL DRINKS

Grape Margarita

MARGARITA GLASS

1 part Tequila
1 part Grape Schnapps
fill with Margarita Mix

Shake with ice and pour.

Grape Soda

COLLINS GLASS

1 part Blueberry Schnapps
1 part Raspberry Liqueur
1 part Vodka
splash Lemon-Lime Soda
fill with Cranberry Juice Cocktail

Build over ice and stir.

Grapefruit Teaser

COLLINS GLASS

4 parts Coconut Rum
splash Lime Juice
fill with Grapefruit Juice

Build over ice and stir.

Grapes of Wrath

COLLINS GLASS

1½ parts Grain Alcohol
1 part Grape Juice (Red)
1 part Club Soda

Build over ice and stir.

Grass Widower

COLLINS GLASS

1 part Light Rum
1 part Blue Curaçao
fill with Orange Juice

Build over ice and stir.

Green Anita

COLLINS GLASS

1 part Banana Liqueur
1 part Blue Curaçao
1 part Melon Liqueur
splash Lemon Juice
splash Lime Juice
fill with Lemon-Lime Soda

Build over ice and stir.

Green Banana

COLLINS GLASS

1½ parts Pisang Ambon® Liqueur
fill with Orange Juice

Build over ice and stir.

Green Bull

COLLINS GLASS

2 parts Vanilla Vodka
1 part Peach Vodka
1 part Orange Juice
1 part Passion Fruit Vodka
1 part Pineapple Juice
fill with Red Bull Energy Drink

Shake all but Red Bull with ice and strain over ice. Fill with Red Bull.

Green Doodoo

COLLINS GLASS

1 part Coffee Liqueur
1 part Melon Liqueur
½ part Peppermint Schnapps
½ part Vodka
fill with Cream

Build over ice and stir.

Green Dream

COLLINS GLASS

1 part Crème de Banane
1 part Pisang Ambon® Liqueur
1 part Pineapple Juice
1 part Orange Juice

Shake with ice and pour.

Green Eyes

COLLINS GLASS

1 part Vodka
1 part Blue Curaçao
2 parts Orange Juice

Build over ice and stir.

Green Field

COLLINS GLASS

1 part Melon Liqueur
½ part Blue Curaçao
½ part Triple Sec
½ part Crème de Coconut
fill with Orange Juice

Shake with ice and pour.

Green Fire

COLLINS GLASS

1 part Fireball Cinnamon Whiskey
splash Blue Curaçao
fill with Mountain Dew

Build over ice and stir.

Green Fjord

COLLINS GLASS

1 part Gin
1 part Melon Liqueur
½ part Triple Sec
2 parts Sweet & Sour Mix
fill with Lemon-Lime Soda

Build over ice and stir.

Green Force Five

COLLINS GLASS

1½ parts Rum
½ part Crème de Banane
½ part Melon Liqueur
1½ parts Orange Juice
7 parts Lemon-Lime Soda

Build over ice and stir.

Green Gilli

COLLINS GLASS

2 parts Melon Liqueur
1 part Kiwi Liqueur
1 part Gin
1 Egg White
fill with Lemonade

Shake with ice and strain over ice.

Green Haze

COLLINS GLASS

1 part Light Rum
1 part Spiced Rum
1 part Pineapple Juice
1 part Orange Juice
splash Blue Curaçao

Build over ice and stir.

Green Hell

HURRICANE GLASS

1 part Blue Curaçao
1 part Gin
1 part Vodka
1 part Rum
1 part Triple Sec
1 part Silver Tequila
fill with Orange Juice

Shake with ice and pour.

Green Lantern®

COLLINS GLASS

2 parts Melon Liqueur
1 part Orange Juice
1 part Lemon-Lime Soda

Build over ice and stir.

Green Lantern® #2

COLLINS GLASS

3 parts Hpnotiq®
fill with Red Bull® Energy Drink

Build over ice and stir.

Green Meanie

COLLINS GLASS

1 part Rum
1 part Blue Curaçao
fill with Orange Juice

Build over ice and stir.

Green Mexican

COLLINS GLASS

1 part Tequila
1 part Melon Liqueur
fill with Sweet & Sour Mix

Build over ice and stir.

Green Peace

COLLINS GLASS

1 part Vodka
1 part Dry Vermouth
1 part Pisang Ambon® Liqueur
1 part Apricot Brandy
fill with Pineapple Juice

Build over ice and stir.

Green Scorpion

COLLINS GLASS

1 part Jack Daniel's®
1 part Vodka
2 splashes Blue Curaçao
fill with Lemon-Lime Soda

Build over ice and stir.

Green Tuberia

COLLINS GLASS

2 parts Vodka
1 part Melon Liqueur
1 part Lemon Juice
fill with Lemon-Lime Soda

Build over ice and stir.

Green Velvet

HURRICANE GLASS

1 part Gin
1 part Blue Curaçao
1 part Crème de Coconut
fill with Pineapple Juice
½ part Cream

Build over ice and stir.

Green Wave

COLLINS GLASS

¾ part Coconut Rum
¾ part Spiced Rum
¾ part Blue Curaçao
1 part Pineapple Juice
1 part Orange Juice
1 part Sweet & Sour Mix

Shake with ice and pour.

Green Whale

COLLINS GLASS

1½ parts Blue Curaçao
splash Vodka
dash Sugar
1 part Pineapple Juice
1 part Orange Juice

Shake with ice and pour.

Greeny

COLLINS GLASS

1½ parts Blue Curaçao
1 part Southern Comfort®
fill with Pineapple Juice

Build over ice and stir.

Gremlin

COLLINS GLASS

1½ parts Citrus Rum
1½ parts Lemon-Lime Soda
1 part Melon Liqueur
1 part Sweet & Sour Mix
fill with Pineapple Juice

Build over ice and stir.

Grendel

COLLINS GLASS

½ part Vodka
½ part Rum
½ part Cointreau®
½ part Blue Curaçao
½ part Crème de Menthe (White)
½ part Advocaat
1 part Cream
fill with Lemonade

Shake with ice and pour.

Grinch

HURRICANE GLASS

1½ parts Melon Liqueur
1 part Malibu® Rum
1 part Gin
1 part Vodka
1 part Lemon-Lime Soda
1 part Sweet & Sour Mix
1 part Blue Curaçao

Build over ice and stir.

Grizzly Bear

COLLINS GLASS

1 part Amaretto
1 part Jägermeister®
1 part Coffee Liqueur
fill with Milk

Shake with ice and pour.

Gumby's® Ruby Red

COLLINS GLASS

1 part Light Rum
1 1/2 parts Pink Grapefruit Juice
1 part Pineapple Juice
fill with Lemon-Lime Soda

Build over ice and stir.

The Gummy Bear

BEER MUG

2 parts Vodka
1 part Lemon-Lime Soda
2 parts Fruit Punch

Build over ice and stir.

Gump

COLLINS GLASS

1 1/2 parts Whiskey
1/2 part Pernod®
1/2 part Crème de Cacao (Dark)
1 part Cream
dash Ground Nutmeg

Build over ice and stir.

Hail Mary

COLLINS GLASS

2 parts Vodka
splash Grenadine
fill with Orange Juice
splash Tabasco® Sauce
1 Egg

Shake with ice and pour.

Hairy Lime

COLLINS GLASS

3 parts Gin
splash Grenadine
1/2 part Lemon Juice
1/2 part Lime Juice
fill with Cola

Build over ice and stir.

Hairy Sunrise

COLLINS GLASS

3/4 part Tequila
3/4 part Vodka
1/2 part Triple Sec
fill with Orange Juice
splash Grenadine

Build over ice.

Hala-Balloo

COLLINS GLASS

1 part Brandy
1 part Scotch
fill with Lemonade

Build over ice and stir.

Halaballoosa

COLLINS GLASS

2 parts Citrus Vodka
1 part Jamaican Rum
2 parts Blue Curaçao
1 part Orange Juice
1 part Clamato®

Shake with ice and pour.

Hale & Hearty

COLLINS GLASS

1/2 part Vodka
1/2 part Blue Curaçao
1 1/2 parts Maple Syrup
splash Honey
fill with Grapefruit Juice

Shake with ice and strain over ice.

Half Moon

COLLINS GLASS

2 parts Coconut Rum
1½ parts Crème de Banane
1½ parts Cream of Coconut
1 part Lime Juice

Shake with ice and pour.

Halfway Special

HURRICANE GLASS

1 part Citrus Vodka
1 part Coconut Rum
1 part Blackberry Liqueur
fill with Orange Juice
splash Grenadine

Build over ice and stir.

Hamlet

COLLINS GLASS

1 part Vodka
½ part Campari®
fill with Orange Juice

Build over ice and stir.

Hangover Cure

BEER MUG

1 part Amaretto
2 parts Tequila Reposado
1 part Spiced Rum
1 part Cream of Coconut
2 parts Raspberry Juice

Build over ice and stir.

Happy Daze

COLLINS GLASS

1 part Rye Whiskey
1 part Brandy
1 part Apricot Brandy
1 part Lemon-Lime Soda
1 part Orange Juice
splash Grenadine

Build over ice and stir.

Happy Morning

COLLINS GLASS

1 part Apricot Juice
2 parts Orange Juice
splash Grenadine

Build over ice and stir.

Hard Fireball Razzyade

COLLINS GLASS

2 parts Fireball Cinnamon Whiskey
fill with Mike's Hard Raspberry Lemonade

Build over ice and stir.

Harvey Wallbanger

COLLINS GLASS

1 part Vodka
½ part Galliano®
fill with Orange Juice

Build over ice and stir.

Hasta la Vista

COLLINS GLASS

1 part Crème de Coconut
1 part Licor 43®
½ part Crème de Cacao (White)
fill with Cherry Juice

Build over ice and stir.

Hasta Luego

COLLINS GLASS

1½ parts Spiced Rum
1 Egg Yolk
½ part Crème de Cacao (White)
½ part Simple Syrup
fill with Milk

Shake with ice and pour.

Havana 3 A.M.

COLLINS GLASS

1 part Passion Fruit Liqueur
1 part Tequila Reposado
½ part Mango Nectar
fill with Pineapple Juice

Shake with ice and pour.

Hawaiian Barbie
COLLINS GLASS
2 parts Coconut Rum
1 part Pineapple Juice
1 part Tonic Water
Build over ice and stir.

Hawaiian Hurricane Volcano
COLLINS GLASS
1 part Amaretto
1 part Southern Comfort®
1 part Vodka
splash Grenadine
Shake with ice and pour.

Haywire
COLLINS GLASS
2 parts Lemon Rum
½ part Cherry Liqueur
fill with Lemon-Lime Soda
Build over ice and stir.

Headcrack
HURRICANE GLASS
3 parts Hennessy®
2 parts Coffee Liqueur
fill with Milk
Build over ice and stir.

Headway
COLLINS GLASS
1 part Triple Sec
1 part Peach Schnapps
1 part Light Rum
fill with Orange Juice
Shake with ice and pour.

Healing Garden
COLLINS GLASS
1½ parts Vodka
⅔ part Galliano®
⅔ part Bénédictine®
fill with Pineapple Juice
Shake with ice and pour.

Heartbreaker
COLLINS GLASS
1 part Dark Rum
1 part Cherry Brandy
1 part Pineapple Juice
1 part Orange Juice
Shake with ice and pour.

Heatwave
COLLINS GLASS
1 part Dark Rum
½ part Peach Schnapps
fill with Pineapple Juice
splash Grenadine
Build over ice.

Heavenly Days
COLLINS GLASS
2 parts Amaretto
½ part Grenadine
fill with Sparkling Water
Build over ice and stir.

Heavy Flow
COLLINS GLASS
1 part Vodka
1 part Gin
1 part Peach Schnapps
1 part Orange Juice
1 part Lemon-Lime Soda
splash Grenadine
Build over ice.

Hector Special
COLLINS GLASS
1½ parts Vodka
1 part Silver Tequila
1 part Grenadine
fill with Orange Juice
Build over ice and stir.

Hi Rise

COLLINS GLASS

1 part Vodka
splash Cointreau®
1 part Sweet & Sour Mix
fill with Orange Juice
splash Grenadine

Build over ice and stir.

High Stakes

COLLINS GLASS

1 part Cherry Brandy
1 part Mango Rum
1 part Vodka
2 parts Orange Juice
2 parts Pineapple Juice
splash Jägermeister

Shake with ice and strain over ice.

Hillbilly Kool-Aid

MASON JAR

2 parts White Whiskey
1 part Lemon-Lime Soda
1 part Fruit Punch

Build over ice and stir.

Hillinator

COLLINS GLASS

3 parts Spiced Rum
1 part Fire Water®
fill with Mountain Dew®

Build over ice and stir.

Hippity Dippity

COLLINS GLASS

1½ parts Spiced Rum
½ part Triple Sec
½ part Lime Juice
fill with Orange Juice
splash Grenadine

Build over ice and stir.

Hitchhiker

COLLINS GLASS

1 part Vodka
1 part Mandarine Napoléon® Liqueur
½ part Crème de Banane
½ part Campari®
½ part Crème de Coconut
fill with Lemonade

Build over ice and stir.

A Hint of Mint

COLLINS GLASS

3 parts Lemonade
1 part Peppermint Schnapps
1 part Crème de Coconut

Build over ice and stir.

Hoarfrost Palace

COLLINS GLASS

⅔ part Apricot Brandy
1½ parts Light Rum
⅔ part Galliano®
fill with Pineapple Juice
½ part Lemon Juice

Shake with ice and strain over ice.

Hokes Royal Flush

COLLINS GLASS

2 parts Crown Royal® Whiskey
1 part Peach Schnapps
fill with Cranberry Juice Cocktail

Build over ice and stir.

Hollywood & Vine

COLLINS GLASS

1½ parts Citrus Vodka
⅔ part Orange Liqueur
⅔ part Lime Juice
fill with Grapefruit Juice
dash Powdered Sugar

Shake with ice and strain over ice.

Hollywood Tea

COLLINS GLASS

1 part Gin
1 part Light Rum
1 part Tequila
1 part Vodka
fill with Lemon-Lime Soda

Build over ice and stir.

Home Alone

COLLINS GLASS

½ part Blue Curaçao
⅔ part Plum Brandy
⅔ part Lemon Juice
fill with Pear Juice

Shake with ice and strain over ice.

Home by the Sea

COLLINS GLASS

1 part Blue Curaçao
1 part Pernod®
1 part Crème Liqueur
1 part Orange Juice
1 part Mango Juice

Shake with ice and strain over ice.

Homicidal Maniac

BEER MUG

2 parts Peach Schnapps
2 parts Vodka
1 part Cranberry Juice Cocktail
1 part Apple Juice

Shake with ice and pour.

Honey Dew This

COLLINS GLASS

1½ parts Vodka
½ part Melon Liqueur
splash Crème de Banane
fill with Pineapple Juice

Shake with ice and strain over ice.

Honey Driver

COLLINS GLASS

1½ parts Vodka
1 part Melon Liqueur
fill with Orange Juice
splash Honey

Shake with ice and strain over ice.

Honey Getter

COLLINS GLASS

2 parts Gin
1 part Cranberry Juice Cocktail
1 part Orange Juice

Build over ice and stir.

Hong Kong Fuey

COLLINS GLASS

1 part Silver Tequila
1 part Vodka
1 part Light Rum
1 part Melon Liqueur
1 part Gin
½ part Lime Cordial
fill with Lemonade

Shake with ice and pour.

Honky Tonk

COLLINS GLASS

1½ parts Light Rum
1½ parts Pineapple Juice
½ part Triple Sec
fill with Cola

Build over ice and stir.

Honolulu Juicy Juicer

COLLINS GLASS

1½ parts Pineapple Juice
1½ parts Rum
1½ parts Southern Comfort®
1 part Lime Juice

Shake with ice and strain over ice.

Hoochekoo

COLLINS GLASS

1 part Banana Liqueur
1 part Raspberry Liqueur
1 part Watermelon Schnapps
fill with Fruit Punch

Build over ice and stir.

Horny Juice

COLLINS GLASS

4 parts Peach Schnapps
fill with Cola

Build over ice and stir.

Horseshoe

COLLINS GLASS

2 parts Tequila
1 part Southern Comfort®
fill with Orange Juice
splash Grenadine

Build over ice and stir.

Hot Damn! Dew

COLLINS GLASS

1 part Hot Damn!® Cinnamon Schnapps
fill with Mountain Dew®

Build over ice and stir.

Hot Land

COLLINS GLASS

1½ parts Absolut® Peppar Vodka
2 splashes Amaretto
¾ part Peach Schnapps
fill with Orange Juice

Build over ice and stir.

Hot Young Lady

COLLINS GLASS

1 part Coffee Liqueur
1 part Irish Cream Liqueur
1 part Cinnamon Schnapps
1 part Rumple Minze®

Shake with ice and strain over ice.

Hotel Riviera

COLLINS GLASS

1 part Vodka
1 part Blackberry Liqueur
½ part Sweet & Sour Mix
fill with Lemon-Lime Soda

Build over ice and stir.

Howling Dingo

COLLINS GLASS

2 parts Amaretto
1 part 151-Proof Rum
fill with Dr. Pepper®

Build over ice and stir.

Hulk

COLLINS GLASS

1 part Melon Liqueur
1 part Vanilla Vodka
2 parts Pineapple Juice
splash Lime Juice

Shake with ice and strain over ice.

Hulk Smash!

COLLINS GLASS

1 part Vodka
1 part Gin
1 part Melon Liqueur
fill with Mountain Dew®

Build over ice and stir.

Humboldt Sunset

COLLINS GLASS

1½ parts Orange Vodka
½ part Lemon Juice
1 part Pineapple Juice
1 part Cranberry Juice Cocktail

Build over ice and stir.

Hurricane Carole

COLLINS GLASS

1 part Coconut Rum
1 part Spiced Rum
1 part Light Rum
1 part Orange Juice
1 part Cranberry Juice Cocktail
splash 151-Proof Rum

Shake with ice and pour.

Hypnotoad

COLLINS GLASS

1 part Spiced Rum
1 part Southern Comfort
1 part Passion Fruit Liqueur
½ part Bourbon
fill with Red Bull Energy Drink

Build over ice and stir.

I Am Not Sure

COLLINS GLASS

2 parts Tequila
fill with Root Beer

Build over ice and stir.

IBO Cream

COLLINS GLASS

1 part Blackberry Liqueur
1 part Peach Schnapps
fill with Milk

Build over ice and stir.

Ice Palace

COLLINS GLASS

1 part Light Rum
½ part Galliano®
½ part Apricot Brandy
¼ part Lemon Juice
fill with Pineapple Juice

Build over ice and stir. Garnish with an Orange Slice.

Iced Lemon

COLLINS GLASS

1 part Vodka
1 part Sweet & Sour Mix
½ part Vanilla Liqueur
fill with Lemon-Lime Soda

Build over ice and stir.

Illusions

COLLINS GLASS

1 part Melon Liqueur
1 part Coconut Rum
1 part Cointreau®
½ part Vodka
fill with Pineapple Juice

Shake with ice and pour.

The Incredible Hulk®

COLLINS GLASS

2 parts Spiced Rum
dash Sugar
fill with Mountain Dew®

Build over ice and stir.

In the Sack

COLLINS GLASS

3 parts Cream Sherry
2 parts Apricot Nectar
3 parts Orange Juice
½ part Lemon Juice

Build over ice and stir. Garnish with an Orange Slice.

Infidelity

COLLINS GLASS

2 parts Vodka
½ part Triple Sec
½ part Lime Juice
1 part Fruit Punch
1 part White Grape Juice

Build over ice and stir.

Instant Karma

COLLINS GLASS

2 parts Spiced Rum
fill with Mountain Dew®
splash Cola

Build over ice and stir.

Intercourse

COLLINS GLASS

2 parts Vodka
1 part Orange Juice
1 part Hawaiian Punch®
1 part Mountain Dew®

Build over ice and stir.

Inverted Cherry

COLLINS GLASS

1 part Gin
½ part Grenadine
¼ part Light Rum
¼ part Cherry Brandy
fill with Apple Juice

Build over ice and stir.

Irish Bulldog

COLLINS GLASS

1 part Amaretto
¾ part Coffee Liqueur
¾ part Crème de Cacao (White)
1 part Irish Cream Liqueur

Shake with ice and strain over ice.

Irish Mudslide

BEER MUG

1 part Irish Cream Liqueur
fill with Root Beer

Build over ice and stir.

Irish Spring

COLLINS GLASS

1 part Irish Whiskey
½ part Peach Brandy
1 part Orange Juice
1 part Sweet & Sour Mix

Shake with ice and strain over ice. Garnish with an Orange Slice and a Maraschino Cherry.

Irish Whip

BEER MUG

1 part Vodka
1 part Pernod®
1 part 151-Proof Rum
1 part Crème de Menthe (White)
1 part Lemon-Lime Soda
1 part Orange Juice

Build over ice and stir.

Island Jim

COLLINS GLASS

1 part Jim Beam
½ part Coconut Rum
½ part Banana Liqueur
1 part Pineapple Juice
1 part Sweet & Sour Mix
1 part Pink Lemonade
fill with Cola

Build over ice and stir.

Isle of the Blessed Coconut

COLLINS GLASS

2 parts Light Rum
½ part Orange Juice
½ part Lime Juice
½ part Amaretto
½ part Cream of Coconut

Shake with ice and pour.

Isle of Tropics

COLLINS GLASS

2 parts Coconut Rum
1 part Orange Juice
1 part Pineapple Juice

Shake with ice and pour.

Italian Beauty

COLLINS GLASS

1 part Sambuca
½ part Parfait Amour
½ part Grenadine
fill with Pineapple Juice

Build over ice and stir.

The Italian Job

MASON JAR

2 parts Vodka
1 part Cointreau®
1 part Pineapple Juice
1 part Orange Juice
splash Cream

Build over ice and stir.

Italian Canary

COLLINS GLASS

½ part Vodka
½ part Amaretto
½ part Rum
½ part Vanilla Liqueur
2 parts Sweet & Sour Mix
fill with Lemon-Lime Soda

Build over ice and stir.

Izcaragua

COLLINS GLASS

1 part Dark Rum
½ part Crème de Banane
½ part Dry Vermouth
fill with Orange Juice

Build over ice and stir.

J & P

COLLINS GLASS

2 parts Peach Schnapps
1½ parts Dark Rum
1 part Lemon Juice
splash Simple Syrup
fill with Pineapple Juice

Build over ice and stir.

Jack & Coke

COLLINS GLASS

2 parts Jack Daniel's®
fill with Cola

Build over ice and stir.

Jack Frost

COLLINS GLASS

2 parts Jack Daniel's®
1 part Drambuie®
splash Grenadine
1 part Sweet & Sour Mix
1 part Orange Juice

Shake with ice and pour.

Jack Hammer

COLLINS GLASS

2 parts Jack Daniel's®
fill with Orange Juice

Build over ice and stir.

Jack-O'-Lantern Juice

HURRICANE GLASS

1 part Rum
½ part Crème de Banane
2 parts Lemonade
1½ parts Pineapple Juice
1½ parts Orange Juice
fill with Lemon-Lime Soda

Build over ice and stir.

Jack the Legend

COLLINS GLASS

1 part Jack Daniel's®
1 part Amaretto
fill with Pineapple Juice

Shake with ice and pour.

Jack Your Melon

COLLINS GLASS

2 parts Watermelon Schnapps
1 part Jack Daniel's®
fill with Mountain Dew®

Build over ice and stir.

Jade Isle

HURRICANE GLASS

2 parts Melon Liqueur
1 part Blue Curaçao
1 part Currant Vodka
1 part Sweet & Sour Mix
1 part Lemon-Lime Soda

Build over ice and stir. Garnish with a Maraschino Cherry.

Jäger Bomb

COLLINS GLASS

1 part Jägermeister®
fill with Red Bull® Energy Drink

Build over ice and stir.

Jamaharon

COLLINS GLASS

1 part Blue Curaçao
1 part Melon Liqueur
fill with Cola

Build over ice and stir.

Jamaica Sunset

COLLINS GLASS

1 part Dark Rum
1 part Coffee Liqueur
fill with Pineapple Juice
splash Grenadine

Build over ice and stir.

Jamaican Jambaylaya

COLLINS GLASS

2 parts Spiced Rum
fill with Fruit Punch

Build over ice and stir.

Jamaican Me Crazy

COLLINS GLASS

1 part Dark Rum
1 part Tia Maria®
fill with Pineapple Juice

Build over ice and stir.

Jamaican Me Crazy #2

COLLINS GLASS

1 part Light Rum
1 part Coconut Rum
1 part Banana Liqueur
splash Cranberry Juice Cocktail
splash Pineapple Juice

Shake with ice and strain over ice.

Jamaican Sunrise

COLLINS GLASS

2 parts Vodka
2 parts Peach Schnapps
fill with Orange Juice
1 part Cranberry Juice Cocktail

Build over ice.

Java's Punch

COLLINS GLASS

1 part Vodka
1 part Pisang Ambon® Liqueur
1 part Crème de Coconut
fill with Orange Juice

Build over ice and stir.

Jeannie's Dream

HURRICANE GLASS

2 parts Malibu® Rum
1 part Sloe Gin
1 part Orange Juice
1 part Pineapple Juice
1 part Lemon-Lime Soda

Build over ice and stir.

Jet Ski®

COLLINS GLASS

1 part Crème de Coconut
splash Blue Curaçao
splash Cream
fill with Pineapple Juice

Shake with ice and strain over ice.

Jinx

COLLINS GLASS

2 parts Vodka
1 part Blueberry Schnapps
½ part Irish Cream Liqueur
2 parts Lemon-Lime Soda
1 part Grape Juice (Red)

Build over ice and stir.

Joe Collins

COLLINS GLASS

1 part Scotch
2 parts Sweet & Sour Mix
fill with Cola

Build over ice and stir. Garnish with a Maraschino Cherry.

Joe Falchetto

COLLINS GLASS

1 part Vodka
½ part Triple Sec
½ part Vanilla Liqueur
½ part Strawberry Syrup
fill with Pineapple Juice

Shake with ice and strain over ice.

John Cooper Deluxe

COLLINS GLASS

2 parts Vodka
1 part Orange Juice
1 part Root Beer

Build over ice and stir.

John Daly

COLLINS GLASS

1¼ parts Citrus Vodka
¼ part Triple Sec
1 part Lemonade
1 part Iced Tea

Build over ice and stir.

Johnnie Red

COLLINS GLASS

1 part Vodka
½ part Parfait Amour
½ part Crème de Banane
fill with Orange Juice
splash Grenadine

Build over ice and stir.

Jolly Jumper

COLLINS GLASS

1 part Whiskey
1 part Vodka
1 part Gin
1 part Passion Fruit Liqueur
fill with Orange Juice

Build over ice and stir.

Juicy Lucy

BEER MUG

1 part Vodka
1 part Gin
1 part Blue Curaçao
1 part Orange Juice
1 part Lemon-Lime Soda

Build over ice and stir.

Jump Start

COLLINS GLASS

2 parts Cherry Vodka
1 part Mountain Dew
1 part Red Bull Energy Drink

Build over ice and stir.

Jump Up and Kiss Me

BEER MUG

1 part Apricot Brandy
1 part Galliano®
1 part Rum
fill with Pineapple Juice
splash Grenadine

Build over ice.

Jumper Cable
COLLINS GLASS

2 parts Dark Rum
1 part Red Bull Energy Drink
1 part Cola

Build over ice and stir.

June Bug
COLLINS GLASS

1 part Coconut Rum
½ part Melon Liqueur
½ part Crème de Banane
1 part Pineapple Juice
1 part Sweet & Sour Mix

Build over ice and stir.

Jungle Boogie
COLLINS GLASS

1 part Vodka
1 part Southern Comfort
1 part Fruit Punch
fill with Mountain Dew

Build over ice and stir.

Jungle Juice
COLLINS GLASS

1 part Vodka
1 part Rum
½ part Triple Sec
splash Sweet & Sour Mix
1 part Cranberry Juice Cocktail
1 part Orange Juice
1 part Pineapple Juice

Build over ice and stir.

Jungle Rumble
COLLINS GLASS

1 part Crème de Banane
½ part Blue Curaçao
½ part Light Rum
½ part Lime Juice
fill with Pineapple Juice

Shake with ice and strain over ice.

Kamaniwanalaya
COLLINS GLASS

1 part Amaretto
1 part Light Rum
1 part Dark Rum
fill with Pineapple Juice

Shake with ice and pour.

Kamehameha Rum Punch
COLLINS GLASS

1 part Light Rum
½ part Dark Rum
½ part Blackberry Liqueur
½ part Amaretto
1 part Lime Juice
fill with Pineapple Juice

Shake with ice and pour.

Kanarie
COLLINS GLASS

2 parts Crème de Banane
fill with Pineapple Juice

Build over ice and stir.

Kansas Tornado
HURRICANE GLASS

1 part Light Rum
1 part Dark Rum
½ part Gin
½ part Amaretto
1 part Pineapple Juice
1 part Grapefruit Juice
1 part Orange Juice
splash Grenadine

Build over ice and stir.

Karma Killer
COLLINS GLASS

1 part Dark Rum
½ part Triple Sec
½ part Peach Brandy
1 part Fruit Punch
1 part Orange Juice
1 part Pineapple Juice
1 part Grapefruit Juice

Build over ice and stir.

Kenny McCormick

COLLINS GLASS

1 part Rum
1 part Tequila
1 part Tia Maria®
fill with Cola

Build over ice and stir.

Kentucky Swampwater

COLLINS GLASS

2 parts Jim Beam
splash Blue Curaçao
5 parts Orange Juice
dash Sweet & Sour Mix

Build over ice and stir.

Kentucky Top Hat

COLLINS GLASS

2 parts Bourbon
1 part Amaretto
1 part Frangelico
fill with Cola

Build over ice and stir.

Kentucky Wildcat

HURRICANE GLASS

½ part Jack Daniel's®
½ part Southern Comfort®
½ part Yukon Jack®
½ part Jim Beam®
1 part Sweet & Sour Mix
1 part Cola

Build over ice and stir.

Kermit®

COLLINS GLASS

½ part Vodka
½ part Whiskey
½ part Gin
fill with Orange Juice
1 part Blue Curaçao

Build over ice and stir.

Kermit® Green

COLLINS GLASS

1 part Vodka
1 part Melon Liqueur
fill with Lemon-Lime Soda

Build over ice and stir.

Kermit's® Revenge

HURRICANE GLASS

1 part Rum
1 part Tequila
1 part Vodka
1 part Gin
1 part Triple Sec
1 part Crème de Menthe (Green)
fill with Lemonade

Build over ice and stir.

Kick in the Glass

BEER MUG

2 parts Light Rum
splash Cranberry Juice Cocktail
fill with Orange Juice
1 scoop Vanilla Ice Cream

Build over ice.

Kingston Spritzer

COLLINS GLASS

splash Melon Liqueur
1 part Spiced Rum
fill with Pineapple Juice

Shake with ice and strain over ice.

Kinky Monday

COLLINS GLASS

1 part Vodka
½ part Blackberry Liqueur
½ part Crème de Cassis
½ part Raspberry Liqueur
1 part Lime Juice
fill with Lemon-Lime Soda

Build over ice and stir.

Kiss Me Deadly
COLLINS GLASS

2 parts Vodka
1 part Chambord
1 part Orange Juice
1 part Pineapple Juice

Build over ice and stir.

Kiss of Blue
COLLINS GLASS

1 part Citrus Vodka
1 part Blue Curaçao
1 part Lime Cordial
fill with Orange Juice

Shake with ice and pour.

Kitchen Sink
COLLINS GLASS

1 part Blue Curaçao
1 part Gin
1 part Light Rum
1 part Sour Apple Schnapps
1 part Vodka
1 part Triple Sec
splash Lemon-Lime Soda
splash Sweet & Sour Mix
splash Lemon Juice
splash Melon Liqueur

Build over ice and stir.

Kiwi Kicker
COLLINS GLASS

1 part Advocaat
1 part Kiwi Schnapps
1 part Melon Liqueur
fill with Pineapple Juice

Build over ice and stir.

Kiwi River
COLLINS GLASS

1½ parts Kiwi Schnapps
fill with Lemonade

Build over ice and stir.

Kiwi Wee Wee
COLLINS GLASS

1 part Kiwi Schnapps
¾ part Crème de Coconut
½ part Crème de Banane
½ part Lemon Juice
½ part Lime Cordial
fill with Pineapple Juice

Shake with ice and pour.

Klingon® Blood Wine
BEER MUG

1 part Tequila
1 part Spiced Rum
splash Grenadine
splash Tabasco® Sauce
fill with Cranberry Juice Cocktail

Build over ice and stir.

KMart® Screwdriver
COLLINS GLASS

2 parts Vodka
fill with Orange Soda

Build over ice and stir. Use the cheapest Vodka available and a store brand Soda.

Knoxville Lemonade
COLLINS GLASS

1 part Vodka
1 part Peach Schnapps
fill with Lemonade
splash Ginger Ale

Build over ice and stir.

Kodachrome
COLLINS GLASS

1 part Vodka
1 part Blue Curaçao
splash Lemonade
splash Orange Juice
splash Cranberry Juice Cocktail

Shake with ice and pour.

Kona

COLLINS GLASS

1 part Crème de Coconut
1 part Melon Liqueur
1 part Sweet & Sour Mix
1 part Orange Juice
fill with Lemon-Lime Soda

Build in the glass with no ice.

Konloo

COLLINS GLASS

1 part Light Rum
½ part Blackberry Liqueur
½ part Crème de Banane
splash Crème de Coconut
fill with Pineapple Juice

Build over ice and stir.

Konoko

COLLINS GLASS

1 part Gin
1 part Crème de Coconut
½ part Kiwi Schnapps
1 part Pineapple Juice
1 part Orange Juice

Build over ice and stir.

Kosmo

COLLINS GLASS

1½ parts Orange Vodka
½ part Triple Sec
fill with Cranberry Juice Cocktail
splash Lime Juice
splash Lemon Juice

Shake with ice and pour.

Krazy Kool-Aid®

COLLINS GLASS

1 part Currant Vodka
1 part Amaretto
1 part Melon Liqueur
fill with Pineapple Juice

Shake with ice and pour.

Kuaui King

COLLINS GLASS

2 parts Crème de Coconut
splash Grenadine
fill with Pineapple Juice

Shake with ice and strain over ice.

Kung Fu

COLLINS GLASS

1 part Jägermeister®
1 part Pisang Ambon® Liqueur
fill with Cola

Build over ice and stir.

Kurant Mellow

COLLINS GLASS

1 part Southern Comfort®
1 part Currant Vodka
fill with Lemon-Lime Soda

Build over ice and stir.

L.A. Sunrise

COLLINS GLASS

1 part Vodka
½ part Crème de Banane
1 part Pineapple Juice
1 part Orange Juice
splash Dark Rum

Build over ice.

L.A. Sunset

COLLINS GLASS

1 part Jägermeister
½ part Amaretto
½ part Pineapple Rum
1 part Pineapple Juice
1 part Orange Juice

Build over ice.

La Bomba

COLLINS GLASS

1¼ parts Tequila Gold
¾ part Cointreau®
1 part Pineapple Juice
1 part Orange Juice
splash Grenadine

Build over ice and stir.

La Musa

COLLINS GLASS

1 part Dark Rum
1/2 part Crème de Banane
1/2 part Sweet Vermouth
fill with Orange Juice
splash Grenadine

Build over ice.

Labyrinth

COLLINS GLASS

1 part Advocaat
1 part Whiskey
1 part Kiwi Liqueur
fill with Lemonade

Build over ice and stir.

Lady Killer

COLLINS GLASS

1 1/4 parts Gin
3/4 part Sweet Vermouth
3/4 part Dry Vermouth
3 dashes Orange Bitters

Shake with ice and strain.

Lady Love Fizz

COLLINS GLASS

2 parts Gin
2 splashes Light Cream
dash Powdered Sugar
1/2 part Lemon Juice
1 Egg White
fill with Seltzer

Shake all but Seltzer with ice and strain. Top with Seltzer.

A Laid-Back Drink

COLLINS GLASS

1 part Vodka
1 part Lemon-Lime Soda
1 part Orange Juice

Build over ice and stir.

Laid Back Limeade

COLLINS GLASS

1 1/2 parts Jack Daniel's®
1/2 part Triple Sec
1 part Lime Juice
fill with Lemon-Lime Soda

Build over ice and stir.

Lait Grenadine

COLLINS GLASS

1 part Light Rum
1 part Grenadine
fill with Milk

Build in the glass with no ice and stir.

Lake Water

COLLINS GLASS

1/2 part Gin
1/2 part Jack Daniel's®
1/2 part Tequila
1/2 part Vodka
1 part Blueberry Schnapps
1 part Cola
1 part Lemon-Lime Soda

Build over ice and stir.

Lamoone

COLLINS GLASS

1 part Dry Vermouth
1 part Whiskey
1 part Crème de Banane
splash Lime Juice
fill with Sparkling Water

Build over ice and stir.

Land Shark

COLLINS GLASS

1 1/2 parts Rum
3/4 part Coconut Rum
1/4 part Grenadine
fill with Pineapple Juice

Shake with ice and pour.

Latin Dream
COLLINS GLASS

1 part Light Rum
1 part Dry Sherry
splash Grenadine
1 part Pineapple Juice
1 part Ginger Ale

Build over ice and stir.

Leaving Las Vegas
HURRICANE GLASS

1 part Triple Sec
1 part Vodka
1 part Light Rum
1 part Gin
fill with Lemonade
splash Lemon-Lime Soda

Build over ice and stir.

Left Handed Screwdriver
COLLINS GLASS

2 parts Gold Rum
fill with Orange Juice

Build over ice and stir.

Leg Spreader
COLLINS GLASS

1 part Coconut Rum
1 part Apricot Brandy
1 part Melon Liqueur
1 part Cranberry Juice Cocktail
1 part Pineapple Juice

Shake with ice and pour.

Lemon Fizz
HURRICANE GLASS

1½ parts Vodka
1½ parts Triple Sec
2 parts Seltzer
fill with Lemonade

Build over ice and stir. Garnish with a Lemon Wedge.

Lennart
COLLINS GLASS

1½ parts Pear Brandy
1 part Sweetened Lime Juice
fill with Lemon-Lime Soda

Build over ice and stir.

Lesbian Baseball Team
COLLINS GLASS

1 part Dark Rum
1 part Southern Comfort®
1 part Amaretto
1 part Banana Liqueur
1 part Blackberry Liqueur
fill with Pineapple Juice

Shake with ice and pour.

Lethal Injection
COLLINS GLASS

2 parts Light Rum
1 part Orange Juice
1 part Grapefruit Juice
splash Grenadine

Shake with ice and pour.

Light Bulb
COLLINS GLASS

1½ parts Blue Curaçao
splash Lime Juice
fill with Lemon-Lime Soda

Build over ice and stir.

Lightning Bug
COLLINS GLASS

1 part Lychee Liqueur
1 part Blue Curaçao
½ part 151-Proof Rum
2 parts Sweet & Sour Mix
1 part Orange Juice

Shake with ice and strain over ice.

Lights of Havana

COLLINS GLASS

1 part Coconut Rum
½ part Melon Liqueur
1 part Pineapple Juice
1 part Orange Juice
splash Sparkling Water

Build over ice and stir.

Lilly Pad

COLLINS GLASS

2 parts Coconut Rum
1 part Melon Liqueur
fill with Pineapple Juice
dash Blue Curaçao

Build over ice.

Lime and Coke

COLLINS GLASS

1 part Lime Juice
1 part Lemon Rum
fill with Cola

Build over ice and stir. Garnish with a Lime Slice.

Lime Green

COLLINS GLASS

1 part Mango Rum
1 part Melon Liqueur
fill with Limeade

Build over ice and stir.

Limelon

COLLINS GLASS

1 part Melon Liqueur
1 part Vodka
fill with Limeade

Build over ice and stir.

Linux®

COLLINS GLASS

1½ parts Vodka
½ part Lime Juice
fill with Cola

Build over ice and stir.

Lipstick

COLLINS GLASS

1 part Vodka
½ part Apricot Brandy
½ part Grenadine
1 part Lemon Juice
fill with Orange Juice

Shake with ice and pour.

Liquid Bomb

COLLINS GLASS

½ part Vodka
½ part Citrus Rum
1 part Alizé®
1 part Peach Schnapps
1 part Cranberry Juice Cocktail
1 part Orange Juice

Build over ice and stir.

Liquid Marijuana

HURRICANE GLASS

1 part Blue Curaçao
1 part Coconut Rum
1 part Spiced Rum
fill with Pineapple Juice
splash Sweet & Sour Mix
1 part Melon Liqueur

Shake with ice and pour.

Lively Shamrock

COLLINS GLASS

1 part Whiskey
1 part Crème de Menthe (Green)
fill with Milk

Shake with ice and pour.

Loco in Acapulco

COLLINS GLASS

1½ parts Aperol™
½ part Silver Tequila
splash Crème de Banane
fill with Banana Juice

Build over ice and stir.

London Fever

COLLINS GLASS

1 part Dry Gin
1 part Light Rum
1 part Lime Juice
splash Grenadine
fill with Sparkling Water

Build over ice and stir.

Long Hot Night

COLLINS GLASS

2 parts Bourbon
1 part Cranberry Juice Cocktail
1 part Pineapple Juice

Build over ice and stir.

Long Pan

COLLINS GLASS

1 part Light Rum
1 part Gin
1 part Grenadine
fill with Cola

Build over ice and stir.

Long Suit

COLLINS GLASS

2 parts Southern Comfort®
1 part Grapefruit Juice
1 part Tonic Water

Build over ice and stir.

Long Vacation

COLLINS GLASS

1 part Dry Gin
1 part Amaretto
1 part Red Curaçao
½ part Triple Sec
fill with Pineapple Juice

Build over ice and stir.

Longaberger® Lemonade

COLLINS GLASS

1 part Cranberry Vodka
1 part Triple Sec
1 part Sweet & Sour Mix
fill with Lemon-Lime Soda

Build over ice and stir.

Loose Caboose

COLLINS GLASS

2 parts Vodka
1 part Cranberry Juice Cocktail
1 part Lemonade
splash Grenadine

Build over ice and stir. Garnish with a Maraschino Cherry.

Loretto Lemonade

COLLINS GLASS

1½ parts Bourbon
½ part Melon Liqueur
½ part Lime Juice
fill with Apple Juice

Shake with ice and pour.

Losing Your Cherry

COLLINS GLASS

1½ parts Vodka
½ part Cherry Brandy
1 part Sweet & Sour Mix
1 part Lemonade

Build over ice and stir.

Loudmouth

COLLINS GLASS

1 part Tequila
1 part Coffee Liqueur
fill with Cranberry Juice Cocktail

Build over ice and stir.

Lounge Lizard

COLLINS GLASS

1 part Dark Rum
½ part Amaretto
fill with Cola

Build over ice and stir.

Love Dream

COLLINS GLASS

1 part Blue Curaçao
1 part Peach Schnapps
⅔ part Crème de Coconut
fill with Pineapple Juice
splash Lemon Juice

Shake with ice and pour.

Love Juice

COLLINS GLASS

½ part Vodka
½ part Passion Fruit Liqueur
¼ part Pisang Ambon® Liqueur
1 part Pineapple Juice
1 part Orange Juice
½ part Grenadine

Build over ice and stir.

Love on the Lawn

COLLINS GLASS

1 part Blue Curaçao
1 part Cranberry Vodka
fill with Orange Juice
splash Grenadine

Shake with ice and pour.

Love Shack

COLLINS GLASS

1½ parts Dark Rum
1 part Orange Juice
fill with Lemon-Lime Soda
splash Grenadine

Build over ice and stir.

Lucky Driver

COLLINS GLASS

½ part Crème de Coconut
1 part Lemon Juice
1 part Pineapple Juice
1 part Grapefruit Juice
1 part Orange Juice
splash Simple Syrup

Shake with ice and strain over ice.

Lucy

COLLINS GLASS

1 part Crème de Banane
1 part Blue Curaçao
1 part Crème de Coconut
fill with Pineapple Juice

Shake with ice and pour.

Luisita

COLLINS GLASS

1½ parts Blue Curaçao
½ part Cream
fill with Sparkling Water

Build over ice and stir.

Lunapop

COLLINS GLASS

¾ part Vodka
½ part Crème de Menthe (Green)
¼ part Vanilla Liqueur
splash Amaretto
fill with Milk

Build over ice and stir.

M.V.P.

HURRICANE GLASS

1 part Vodka
½ part Melon Liqueur
½ part Coconut Rum
fill with Pineapple Juice

Build over ice and stir.

Macambo

COLLINS GLASS

2 parts Dark Rum
1½ parts Orange Gin
1 part Orange Juice
1 part Papaya Juice
splash Grenadine

Build over ice and stir.

Macarena

COLLINS GLASS

1 part Tequila
½ part Coconut Rum
3 parts Sweet & Sour Mix
1 part Orange Juice
1 part Pineapple Juice
splash Cranberry Juice Cocktail

Build over ice and stir.

Made in Heaven
HURRICANE GLASS

1 part Cream
1 part Vodka
1 part Crème de Coconut
1 part Strawberry Liqueur
fill with Lemon-Lime Soda

Build over ice and stir.

Madeleine
COLLINS GLASS

1 part Passoa
1 part Gin
1 part Crème de Coconut
fill with Pineapple Juice

Build over ice and stir.

Madison Mule
COLLINS GLASS

1 part Amaretto
½ part Chambord
½ part Melon Liqueur
½ part Dark Spiced Rum
fill with Ginger Beer

Build over ice and stir.

Magic Wonder
COLLINS GLASS

1 part Rum
1 part Strawberry Syrup
fill with Lemon-Lime Soda

Build over ice and stir.

Magnolia
COLLINS GLASS

2 parts Coconut Rum
1 part Grenadine
fill with Dr. Pepper®

Build over ice and stir.

Main Attraction
COLLINS GLASS

½ part Orange Juice
1 part Peach Schnapps
4 parts Orange/Pineapple Juice
1 part Cranberry Liqueur
1 part Wild Berry Schnapps

Build over ice and stir.

Maka Hua Hula
COLLINS GLASS

1 part Crème de Coconut
½ part Crème de Banane
1 part Light Rum
fill with Pineapple Juice
½ part Cranberry Juice Cocktail

Build over ice and stir.

Malibu Barbie®
COLLINS GLASS

1 part Peach Schnapps
1 part Coconut Rum
2 parts Mango Juice

Build over ice and stir.

A Malibu Twist
COLLINS GLASS

1 part Rum
1 part Lime Juice
fill with Lemonade

Build over ice and stir.

Mama Jama
COLLINS GLASS

splash Triple Sec
splash Grenadine
½ part Spiced Rum
1 part Orange Juice
2 parts Apple Juice
splash Cream of Coconut

Shake with ice and pour.

Mamacita

HURRICANE GLASS

1½ parts Malibu® Rum
½ part Passoã®
½ part Cointreau®
fill with Guava Juice

Shake with ice and pour.

Mambo

COLLINS GLASS

1½ parts Sweet & Sour Mix
1 part Lemonade
1 part Melon Liqueur
½ part Light Rum

Shake with ice and strain over ice.

Man in the Melon

COLLINS GLASS

2 parts Melon Liqueur
1 part Vodka
½ part Triple Sec
fill with Tonic Water

Build over ice and stir.

Mandarin Sunrise

COLLINS GLASS

1½ parts Orange Vodka
1 part Peach Schnapps
2 parts Pineapple Juice
1 part Orange Juice

Build over ice and stir.

Mandy Sea

COLLINS GLASS

1½ parts Amaretto
½ part Triple Sec
1 part Sweet & Sour Mix
1 part Orange Juice
1 part Pineapple Juice
splash Grenadine
splash Lemon-Lime Soda

Shake with ice and strain over ice.

Mangorita

MARGARITA GLASS

2 parts Tequila
½ part Triple Sec
1½ parts Mango Nectar

Shake with ice and pour.

Maple Queen

COLLINS GLASS

1 part Scotch
1 part Triple Sec
½ part Maple Syrup
dash Bitters
fill with Lemonade

Shake with ice and pour.

Maracas

COLLINS GLASS

1½ parts Vodka
¼ part Blackberry Liqueur
splash Parfait Amour
fill with Pineapple Juice

Build over ice and stir.

Margarita

MARGARITA GLASS

1½ parts Tequila
½ part Triple Sec
1 part Lime Juice

Rub rim of the glass with Lime Wedge and dip rim in Salt. Shake all ingredients with ice and strain into the salt-rimmed glass.

Maria

COLLINS GLASS

1 part Crème de Banane
1 part Strega®
1 part Orange Juice
1 part Pineapple Juice

Shake with ice and strain over ice.

Marienne

COLLINS GLASS

1 part Crème de Menthe (Green)
1 part Crème de Cacao (Dark)
fill with Milk

Shake with ice and pour.

Marion Barry

COLLINS GLASS

½ part Blackberry Liqueur
1½ parts Currant Vodka
fill with Cranberry Juice Cocktail
1 part Cola

Shake with ice and pour.

Marrakech Express

COLLINS GLASS

1½ parts Gin
splash Grenadine
splash Orange Flower Water
fill with Orange Juice

Shake with ice and pour.

Martian Urine Sample

COLLINS GLASS

1 part Banana Liqueur
1 part Blue Curaçao
1 part Melon Liqueur
1 part Pineapple Juice
1 part Club Soda

Build over ice.

Masroska

COLLINS GLASS

2 parts Vodka
1 part Orange Juice
2 parts Apple Juice

Build over ice and stir.

Mattapoo

COLLINS GLASS

1 part Vodka
½ part Melon Liqueur
1 part Grapefruit Juice
1 part Pineapple Juice

Build over ice and stir.

Maverick

COLLINS GLASS

1½ parts Vodka
½ part Amaretto
½ part Triple Sec
2 splashes Galliano®
fill with Pineapple Juice

Shake with ice and strain over ice.

Meema

COLLINS GLASS

1 part Amaretto
1 part Peach Schnapps
1 part Vodka
fill with Cranberry Juice Cocktail

Build over ice and stir.

Melon Highball

COLLINS GLASS

1½ parts Melon Liqueur
1 part Vodka
fill with Orange Juice

Shake with ice and strain over ice.

Melon Illusion

COLLINS GLASS

2 parts Melon Liqueur
½ part Vodka
½ part Triple Sec
1 part Lemon Juice
fill with Pineapple Juice

Shake with ice and strain over ice.

Melon Spritz

COLLINS GLASS

1 part Spiced Rum
¼ part Melon Liqueur
fill with Pineapple Juice
splash Club Soda

Build over ice and stir.

Mentholyzer

COLLINS GLASS

1 part Vodka
1 part Tia Maria®
¼ part Crème de Menthe (White)
2 parts Cream
fill with Cola

Build over ice and stir.

Merlin

COLLINS GLASS

1 part Peach Schnapps
splash Strawberry Syrup
fill with Pineapple Juice

Shake with ice and strain over ice.

Merlin's Monkey

COLLINS GLASS

1 part Irish Cream Liqueur
1 part 99-Proof Banana Liqueur
1 part Butterscotch Schnapps
½ part Crème de Cacao (Dark)
fill with Milk

Shake with ice and strain over ice.

Mexicali Rose

COLLINS GLASS

⅔ part Raspberry Liqueur
2 parts Tequila
1 part Margarita Mix
splash Lime Juice

Shake with ice and pour.

Mexican Mockingbird

COLLINS GLASS

1½ parts Silver Tequila
1 part Crème de Menthe (Green)
fill with Sparkling Water

Build over ice and stir.

Mexicola

COLLINS GLASS

2 parts Tequila
½ part Lime Juice
fill with Cola

Build over ice and stir.

Miami Ice

COLLINS GLASS

½ part Vodka
½ part Peach Schnapps
½ part Gin
½ part Rum
2 parts Sweet & Sour Mix
fill with Orange Juice

Shake with ice and pour.

Midnight Lemonade

COLLINS GLASS

1½ parts Raspberry Liqueur
fill with Lemonade
splash Lemon-Lime Soda

Build over ice and stir.

Milk Punch

COLLINS GLASS

2 parts Whiskey
dash Powdered Sugar
dash Ground Nutmeg
fill with Milk

Shake with ice and strain over ice.

Mind Twist

COLLINS GLASS

⅔ part Blue Curaçao
⅔ part Absinthe
⅔ part Black Currant syrup
1 part Grapefruit Juice
1 part Pineapple Juice

Shake with ice and pour.

Minnesota Slammer

HURRICANE GLASS

1 part Cherry Brandy
1 part Peach Schnapps
1 part Sour Apple Schnapps
2 parts Sweet & Sour Mix
fill with Lemon-Lime Soda

Build over ice and stir.

Mint Chocolate Milk

COLLINS GLASS

2 parts Crème de Cacao (Dark)
1/2 part Light Rum
1 part Crème de Menthe (White)
fill with Milk

Build over ice and stir.

Mint Julep

COLLINS GLASS

3 Fresh Mint Leaves
dash Powdered Sugar
2 splashes Water
2 parts Bourbon

Muddle the Mint Leaves, Powdered Sugar, and Water in the glass. Fill with crushed ice and add Bourbon. Garnish with a Mint Leaf and serve with a straw.

Misty Ice

COLLINS GLASS

1 part Pernod®
1/2 part Crème de Menthe (White)
fill with Lemon-Lime Soda

Build over ice and stir.

Misty You

COLLINS GLASS

1 part Light Rum
1/2 part Peach Schnapps
splash Blue Curaçao
dash Sugar
fill with Sparkling Water

Build over ice and stir.

Mizzy

COLLINS GLASS

splash Melon Liqueur
splash Citrus Vodka
1/4 part Pineapple Juice
splash Simple Syrup
fill with Orange Juice

Shake with ice and pour.

Mojito

COLLINS GLASS

1 Mint Sprig
1/2 part Lime Juice
1 1/4 parts Dark Rum
dash Sugar
2 parts Club Soda

Muddle Mint Sprig with Lime Juice and Sugar in bottom of the glass. Fill with crushed ice. Add Rum, stir, and top with Club Soda. Garnish with a Mint Leaf.

Mojito Parisian

COLLINS GLASS

10 Mint Leaves
2 parts Light Rum
2 parts St-Germain
1 part Lime Juice
Simple Syrup

Lightly muddle the Mint in the glass. Add the spirits and Juice. Half fill the glass with crushed ice and stir. Fill with more crushed ice and stir again. Add Simple Syrup to taste and garnish with a Lime Wedge.

Monkey Dance

COLLINS GLASS

1 part Rum
1 part Crème de Cacao (Dark)
1 part Crème de Banane
splash Cream
fill with Cola

Build over ice and stir.

Monkey Poop

COLLINS GLASS

3/4 part Vodka
3/4 part Crème de Banane
1/2 part Lime Cordial
1 part Pineapple Juice
1 part Orange Juice

Shake with ice and strain over ice.

Monk's Habit

COLLINS GLASS

1 part Light Rum
1 part Raspberry Liqueur
½ part Triple Sec
¼ part Grenadine
fill with Pineapple Juice

Shake with ice and pour.

Monolith

COLLINS GLASS

1½ parts Dark Rum
½ part Crème de Cacao (White)
½ part Lemon Juice
1 part Orange Juice
fill with Pineapple Juice

Shake with ice and strain over ice.

Moon Tea

COLLINS GLASS

1 part Gin
1 part Rum
1 part Triple Sec
1 part Vodka
fill with Orange Juice

Shake with ice and pour.

Mount Red

COLLINS GLASS

1 part Vodka
1 part Light Rum
1 part Gin
1 part Peach Schnapps
fill with Cranberry Juice Cocktail
splash Lime Juice

Build over ice and stir.

Mountaineer

COLLINS GLASS

1½ parts Rum
1 part Orange Juice
½ part Ginger Ale
¼ part Milk
¼ part Lemon Juice
dash Pepper

Build over ice and stir.

Mouse Trap

COLLINS GLASS

2 parts Vodka
1½ parts Triple Sec
2 parts Orange Juice
1½ parts Grenadine
fill with Lemon-Lime Soda

Build over ice and stir.

Mr. Freeze

COLLINS GLASS

1 part Black Haus® Blackberry Schnapps
1 part Vodka
1 part Blue Curaçao
3 parts Sweet & Sour Mix
1 part Lemon-Lime Soda

Build over ice and stir.

Mr. Wilson

COLLINS GLASS

1 part Apple Brandy
1 part Coconut Rum
fill with Orange Juice

Build over ice and stir.

Muff Rider

COLLINS GLASS

2 parts Sake
1 part Light Rum
3 parts Pineapple Juice
fill with Lemon-Lime Soda

Build over ice and stir.

Mundo Fine

COLLINS GLASS

1½ parts Whiskey
1 part Melon Liqueur
1½ parts Cream
splash Lemon Juice
splash Grenadine
fill with Orange Juice

Shake with ice and pour.

My Own Worst Enemy

COLLINS GLASS

1 part Barenjäger Honey Liqueur
1 part Jägermeister
fill with Energy Drink

Build over ice and stir.

A Mystery

COLLINS GLASS

1 part Coconut Rum
fill with Milk

Build over ice and stir.

Nantucket

COLLINS GLASS

2 parts Brandy
1 part Cranberry Juice Cocktail
1 part Grapefruit Juice

Shake with ice and pour.

Nashville Eggnog

COLLINS GLASS

2 parts Advocaat
1 part Brandy
1 part Dark Rum
½ part Bourbon
fill with Milk

Shake with ice and strain over ice.

Nashville Low Rider

COLLINS GLASS

1 part Triple Sec
1 part Southern Comfort®
1 part Simple Syrup
fill with Lemonade

Shake with ice and strain over ice.

Naval Lint

COLLINS GLASS

2 parts Amaretto
1 part Vodka
splash Lime Juice
fill with Cola

Build over ice and stir.

Navel Caribbean Love

COLLINS GLASS

2 parts Coconut Rum
fill with Orange Juice

Build over ice and stir.

Nectar of the Gods

COLLINS GLASS

½ part Apricot Brandy
½ part Peach Schnapps
½ part Coconut Rum
½ part 151-Proof Rum
1 part Pineapple Juice
1 part Cranberry Juice Cocktail
1 part Orange Juice

Shake with ice and strain over ice.

Needle in Your Eye

COLLINS GLASS

1 part Gin
1 part Vodka
splash Lemon Juice
splash Lime Juice
splash Orange Juice
fill Lemon-Lime Soda

Build over ice and stir.

Nell Gwynne

COLLINS GLASS

2 parts Apricot Brandy
fill with Orange Juice

Shake with ice and pour.

Neon Green

COLLINS GLASS

1 part Melon Liqueur
1 part Crème de Coconut
½ part Crème de Menthe (Green)
fill with Lemon-Lime Soda

Build over ice and stir.

Neon Nightmare

HURRICANE GLASS

1 1/4 parts Coconut Rum
1/2 part Melon Liqueur
1/4 part Blue Curaçao
fill with Pineapple Juice

Shake with ice and strain over ice.

Neon Tea

COLLINS GLASS

1/2 part Gin
1/2 part Sour Apple Schnapps
1/2 part Vanilla Vodka
1/2 part Light Rum
1/4 part Triple Sec
1 part Sweet & Sour Mix
1/4 part Melon Liqueur

Shake with ice and pour.

New Madonna

COLLINS GLASS

1 part Sloe Gin
fill with Lemonade
splash Cherry Brandy

Build over ice and stir.

New Orleans Fizz

COLLINS GLASS

2 parts Gin
2 splashes Lime Juice
2 splashes Lemon Juice
dash Sugar
1 part Cream
1 Egg White
splash Seltzer Water

Shake with ice and pour.

Nickel

COLLINS GLASS

1 part Currant Vodka
1 part Melon Liqueur
1 part Orange Juice
1 part Lemon-Lime Soda

Build over ice and stir.

Nickel Fever

COLLINS GLASS

1/2 part Blue Curaçao
2/3 part Southern Comfort®
2/3 part Galliano®
1 part Cream
1 part Orange Juice

Build over ice and stir.

Nikko

COLLINS GLASS

1 1/2 parts Vodka
1/2 part Blue Curaçao
1/2 part Pineapple Juice
fill with Orange Juice

Build over ice and stir.

No Pressure

HURRICANE GLASS

1 part 151-Proof Rum
1 part Blue Curaçao
1 part Strawberry Daiquiri Mix
1 part Piña Colada Mix

Build over ice and stir.

No Reason to Live

COLLINS GLASS

1 part Tequila
1 part Vodka
1 part Gin
1 part Sambuca
2 splashes Tabasco® Sauce
fill with Orange Juice

Build over ice and stir.

No. 7

COLLINS GLASS

1 part Amaretto
1 part Peach Schnapps
1 part Iced Tea
1 part Cola

Build over ice and stir.

North Dakota Summer

COLLINS GLASS

2 parts Cinnamon Schnapps
fill with Lemonade

Build over ice and stir.

Northern Lights

COLLINS GLASS

1½ parts Yukon Jack®
1 part Cranberry Juice Cocktail
1 part Orange Juice

Build over ice and stir.

Norwegian Iceberg

BEER MUG

2 parts Vodka
fill with Lemon-Lime Soda
1 part Blue Hawaiian Schnapps

Build over ice and stir.

Norwich Collins

COLLINS GLASS

2 parts Gin
1 part Lemon Juice
dash Sugar
fill with Cola

Build over ice and stir.

Nothing at All

COLLINS GLASS

1 part Peach Schnapps
½ part Blue Curaçao
½ part Raspberry Liqueur
½ part Orange Juice
fill with Sweet & Sour Mix

Shake with ice and pour.

Nuclear Meltdown

COLLINS GLASS

1 part Gin
1 part Silver Tequila
1 part Vodka
1 part Light Rum
1 part Sweet & Sour Mix
1 part Melon Liqueur
fill with Lemon-Lime Soda

Build over ice and stir.

Nuclear Sensation

COLLINS GLASS

1 part Dry Gin
1 part Vodka
1 part Rum
1 part Blue Curaçao
fill with Sweet & Sour Mix

Build over ice and stir.

Nut Twister

COLLINS GLASS

1 part Banana Liqueur
1 part Coconut Rum
fill with Orange Juice

Build over ice and stir.

Nutty Cola

COLLINS GLASS

2 parts Amaretto
1 part Lime Juice
fill with Cola

Build over ice and stir.

O&O

COLLINS GLASS

2 parts Orange Vodka
fill with Orange Soda

Build over ice and stir.

Oak Tree

COLLINS GLASS

1 part Brandy
1 part Amaretto
1 part Tia Maria®
fill with Milk

Shake with ice and pour.

Ocean Breeze

COLLINS GLASS

2 parts Coconut Rum
1 part Raspberry Vodka
2 parts Pineapple Juice
fill with Cranberry Juice

Build over ice and stir.

Ocean Waves

COLLINS GLASS

1 part Mango Rum
1 part Cranberry Juice
fill with Mountain Dew

Build over ice and stir.

Ocho Rios

COLLINS GLASS

1½ parts Dark Rum
1 part Cream
1 part Lime Juice
1 part Guava Juice
1 tbsp sugar

Shake with ice and strain over ice.

Odie

COLLINS GLASS

1 part Coffee Liqueur
1 part Frangelico®
1 part Irish Cream Liqueur
1 part Rye Whiskey
fill with Milk

Build over ice and stir.

Okennatt

COLLINS GLASS

1 part Blue Curaçao
1 part Parfait Amour
2 parts Bitter Lemon Soda
1 part Sparkling Water

Build over ice and stir.

Omnibus

COLLINS GLASS

1 part Kirschwasser
1 part Raspberry Syrup
fill with Sparkling Water

Build over ice and stir.

On the Deck

BEER MUG

1¼ parts Spiced Rum
¾ part Dark Rum
½ part Cointreau®
fill with Lemonade
splash Cranberry Juice Cocktail

Build over ice and stir.

OOO

HURRICANE GLASS

1 part Orange Vodka
1 part Orange Juice
1 part Orange Soda

Build over ice and stir.

Oral Invasion

HURRICANE GLASS

1 part Spiced Rum
1 part Coconut Rum
½ part Banana Liqueur
½ part Peach Schnapps
1 part Lemonade
1 part Sweet & Sour Mix

Build over ice and stir.

Orange Delight

COLLINS GLASS

3 parts Maraschino Liqueur
fill with Orange Juice

Shake with ice and pour.

Orange Jolie

COLLINS GLASS

1 part Gin
½ part Triple Sec
½ part Crème de Coconut
fill with Orange Juice

Shake with ice and pour.

Orange Passion

COLLINS GLASS

1 part Vodka
2 parts Passion Fruit Liqueur
fill with Orange Juice

Build over ice and stir.

Orlando
HURRICANE GLASS

1 part Vodka
½ part Crème de Banane
1 part Pineapple Juice
1 part Cream
fill with Orange Juice

Shake with ice and pour.

Orlando Quencher
COLLINS GLASS

1½ parts Rum
1 part Orange Juice
½ part Lime Juice
½ part Simple Syrup
fill with Lemon-Lime Soda

Build over ice and stir.

Oslo Nights
COLLINS GLASS

1 part Citrus Vodka
1 part Blue Curaçao
1 part Aquavit
1 part Cider
1 part Lime Juice
fill with Lemonade

Build over ice and stir.

Othello
COLLINS GLASS

1 part Southern Comfort®
1 part Parfait Amour
½ part Crème de Banane
fill with Lemonade
splash Pineapple Juice
splash Triple Sec

Build over ice and stir.

Over the Top
COLLINS GLASS

1 part Cachaça
½ part Blue Curaçao
½ part Crème de Banane
½ part Crème de Coconut
fill with Pineapple Juice

Build over ice and stir.

Oyster Bay
COLLINS GLASS

1 part Dark Rum
1 part Grapefruit Juice
1 part Pineapple Juice
1 part Papaya Juice
1 part Lime Juice
½ part Simple Syrup
splash Anisette
fill with Mango Juice

Shake with ice and strain over ice.

Paddy's Day Mooch
COLLINS GLASS

1½ parts Whiskey
½ part Peach Schnapps
1 part Orange Juice
1 part Ginger Ale

Build over ice and stir.

Painkiller
COLLINS GLASS

¼ part Rum
¼ part Crème de Coconut
1 part Pineapple Juice
1 part Orange Juice
dash Ground Nutmeg

Build over ice and stir.

Painkiller #2
COLLINS GLASS

1½ parts Rum
3 parts Orange Juice
3 parts Pineapple Juice
splash Coco Lopez®
dash Ground Nutmeg

Shake with ice and pour.

Palm Tree
COLLINS GLASS

1 part Passion Fruit Liqueur
splash Cream
1 part Mango Juice
1 part Orange Juice

Shake with ice and pour.

Paloma

COLLINS GLASS

2 parts Tequila Gold
fill with Grapefruit Juice
1/2 part Lime Juice
splash Club Soda

Build over ice and stir.

Pan Galactic Gargle Blaster

HURRICANE GLASS

1 part Vodka
1 part Tia Maria®
1/2 part Cherry Brandy
splash Lime Juice
1 part Lemon-Lime Soda
1 part Apple Cider

Build over ice and stir.

Panama Jack

COLLINS GLASS

1 1/2 parts Spiced Rum
1 part Dark Rum
splash Strawberry Liqueur
fill with Orange Juice

Build over ice and stir.

Pancho Sanchez

COLLINS GLASS

1 part Peach Schnapps
1 part Sloe Gin
fill with Orange Juice

Build over ice and stir.

Panty Dropper

COLLINS GLASS

1 part Vodka
1 part Coconut Rum
1 part Peach Schnapps
1 part Pineapple Juice
1 part Orange Juice

Build over ice and stir.

Papa Yaya

COLLINS GLASS

1 1/2 parts Gin
1/4 part Lime Juice
1/4 part Papaya Syrup
1/2 part Pineapple Juice
fill with Seltzer

Shake all but Seltzer with ice and strain. Top with Seltzer.

Paradise Is Calling

COLLINS GLASS

1 part Rum
1 part Passion Fruit Liqueur
fill with Mango Juice

Build over ice and stir.

Paradise Quencher

COLLINS GLASS

1 part Spiced Rum
1/4 part Apricot Brandy
2 parts Pineapple Juice
1 part Orange Juice
1 part Cranberry Juice Cocktail

Build over ice and stir.

Parrot Head

COLLINS GLASS

1 part Spiced Rum
1 part Light Rum
1 part Blackberry Liqueur
fill with Pineapple Juice

Shake with ice and pour.

Part-Time Lover

COLLINS GLASS

1 1/2 parts Coconut Rum
1/2 part Raspberry Liqueur
1/2 part Cranberry Juice Cocktail
fill with Cream

Shake with ice and pour.

Partymeister

COLLINS GLASS

1 part Gin
1 part Coconut Rum
splash Lime Juice
fill with Lemonade

Build over ice and stir.

Passion

COLLINS GLASS

1½ parts Coconut Rum
1½ parts Rum
dash Sugar
1 part Pineapple Juice
1 part Sweet & Sour Mix
splash Lemon-Lime Soda

Build over ice and stir.

Passionate Cherry

COLLINS GLASS

1½ parts Cherry Brandy
½ part Vodka
fill with Sweet & Sour Mix

Shake with ice and strain over ice.

Passionate Dream

COLLINS GLASS

1½ parts Light Rum
1 part Passion Fruit Liqueur
1 part Strawberry Liqueur
1 part Grapefruit Juice
1 part Pineapple Juice

Shake with ice and pour.

Passover

COLLINS GLASS

1 part Vodka
2 parts Passion Fruit Juice
fill with Grapefruit Juice

Build over ice and stir.

Patriot Missile

PINT GLASS

½ part Blackberry Liqueur
½ part Blue Curaçao
fill with Smirnoff Ice®
splash Grenadine

Build over ice and stir.

Peaceful Treasure

COLLINS GLASS

1 part Dark Rum
¾ part Lemon Juice
splash Simple Syrup
splash Grenadine
fill with Orange Juice

Build over ice and stir.

Peach Beseech

COLLINS GLASS

1 part Vodka
1½ parts Peach Schnapps
½ part Crème de Cacao (White)
fill with Milk

Shake with ice and pour.

Peach Bomber

COLLINS GLASS

1½ parts Peach Schnapps
1 part Vodka
½ part Blue Curaçao
1 part Pineapple Juice
1 part Orange Juice

Shake with ice and pour.

Peach Margarita

MARGARITA GLASS

1 part Tequila
1 part Peach Schnapps
1 part Sweet & Sour Mix
splash Grenadine

Shake with ice and pour.

Peachberry Crush

COLLINS GLASS

1 part Peach Schnapps
1 part Orange Juice
1 part Black Currant Juice
1 part Sweet & Sour Mix
½ part Strawberry Liqueur

Build over ice and stir.

Peachface

COLLINS GLASS

1 part Vodka
1 part Peach Schnapps
fill with Cranberry Juice Cocktail

Build over ice and stir.

Peach's Up

COLLINS GLASS

1 part Peach Schnapps
1 part Light Rum
1 part Apricot Brandy
1 part Lime Juice
1 part Strawberry Syrup
fill with Lemonade

Build over ice and stir.

Peachy

COLLINS GLASS

1 part Vodka
1 part Peach Schnapps
1 part Melon Liqueur
1 part Orange Juice
1 part Pear Juice

Shake with ice and pour.

Peachy Keen

COLLINS GLASS

2 parts Peach Schnapps
1 part Orange Juice
1 part Lemonade

Build over ice and stir.

Peanut Butter and Jelly

COLLINS GLASS

1 part Frangelico®
1 part Raspberry Liqueur

Shake with ice and strain.

Peariphery

COLLINS GLASS

⅔ part Triple Sec
1½ parts Cachaça
½ part Lime Juice
fill with Pear Juice

Shake with ice and strain over ice.

Pedro Collins

COLLINS GLASS

1½ parts Bacardi® Limón Rum
splash Sweet & Sour Mix
1 part Lemon-Lime Soda
1 part Club Soda

Build over ice and stir.

Pegasus

COLLINS GLASS

1 part Vodka
1 part Peach Schnapps
½ part Lime Juice
½ part Lemon Juice
½ part Cherry Juice
fill with Red Bull® Energy Drink

Build over ice and stir.

Pepe Ramon

COLLINS GLASS

1 part Tequila Reposado
1 part Crème de Banane
1 part Melon Liqueur
½ part Grenadine
fill with Orange Juice

Shake with ice and pour.

Pepito Lolito

COLLINS GLASS

1 part Gin
1 part Blue Curaçao
1 part Tonic Water
1 part Club Soda

Build over ice and stir.

Pepper Eater

COLLINS GLASS

1½ parts Silver Tequila
½ part Triple Sec
fill with Orange Juice
splash Cranberry Juice Cocktail

Build over ice and stir.

Peppermint Milk Punch

COLLINS GLASS

1 part Crème de Menthe (White)
1 part Dark Rum
1 part Cream
splash Simple Syrup
fill with Milk

Shake with ice and pour.

Peruvian Elder Sour

COLLINS GLASS

3 parts Pisco Quebranta
2 parts St-Germain
1 part Lime Juice

Shake with ice and strain over ice. Garnish with a Lime Wedge.

Pervert

COLLINS GLASS

1 part Orange Rum
¾ part Apricot Brandy
¾ part Banana Liqueur
fill with Pineapple Juice

Shake with ice and pour.

Phantasm

COLLINS GLASS

1½ parts Vodka
½ part Galliano®
½ part Cream
fill with Cola

Build over ice and stir.

Phillips Screwdriver

COLLINS GLASS

2 parts Vodka
fill with SunnyD® Orange Drink

Shake with ice and pour.

Piece of Cake

COLLINS GLASS

1½ parts Rye Whiskey
splash Lime Juice
fill with Cola

Build over ice and stir.

Pimp Punch

COLLINS GLASS

1 part Raspberry Liqueur
1 part Currant Vodka
fill with Lemon-Lime Soda

Build over ice and stir.

Piña Rita

MARGARITA GLASS

2 parts Tequila
½ part Triple Sec
fill with Pineapple Juice

Shake with ice and pour.

Piña Verde

COLLINS GLASS

1 part Rum
¼ part Melon Liqueur
fill with Pineapple Juice

Build over ice and stir.

Pineapple Plantation

COLLINS GLASS

¾ part Amaretto
¾ part Southern Comfort®
1½ parts Sweet & Sour Mix
fill with Pineapple Juice

Shake with ice and pour.

Pineapple Splash

COLLINS GLASS

1 part Peach Schnapps
1 part Vodka
1 part Orange Juice
1 part Pineapple Juice

Shake with ice and pour.

Pink Banana

COLLINS GLASS

1 part Crème de Banane
fill with Pink Lemonade

Build over ice and stir.

Pink Cadillac Margarita

MARGARITA GLASS

2 parts Tequila
1 part Triple Sec
2 parts Lime Juice
1 part Cranberry Juice Cocktail
1 part Powdered Sugar

Shake with ice and pour.

Pink Cat

HURRICANE GLASS

1 part Light Rum
1 part Crème de Cacao (White)
1 part Crème de Banane
1 part Passion Fruit Liqueur
½ part Grenadine
fill with Milk

Shake with ice and strain over ice.

Pink Cello

COLLINS GLASS

1 part Vodka
½ part Limoncello
fill with Cranberry Juice Cocktail

Build over ice and stir.

Pink Creamsicle®

COLLINS GLASS

1 part Vodka
1 part Orange Juice
fill with Cream Soda

Build over ice and stir.

Pink Flamingo

COLLINS GLASS

1 part Vodka
1 part Cointreau®
fill with Orange Juice

Shake with ice and pour.

Pink Paradise

HURRICANE GLASS

1½ parts Coconut Rum
1 part Amaretto
1 part Pineapple Juice
1 part Cranberry Juice Cocktail

Build over ice and stir.

Pink Pillow

COLLINS GLASS

2 parts Vodka
splash Grenadine
1 part Sweet & Sour Mix
1 part Ginger Ale

Build over ice and stir.

Pink Pussycat

COLLINS GLASS

1½ parts Vodka
splash Grenadine
fill with Pineapple Juice

Build over ice and stir.

Pink Surprise

COLLINS GLASS

1 part Gin
1 part Cherry Brandy
fill with Lemonade
dash Bitters

Shake with ice and pour.

Pink Tutu

COLLINS GLASS

1 part Peach Schnapps
½ part Vodka
½ part Campari®
dash Powdered Sugar
fill with Grapefruit Juice

Shake with ice and pour.

Pirate's Revenge

COLLINS GLASS

1 part Cachaça
½ part Blue Curaçao
½ part Coconut Rum
splash Vanilla Extract
1 part Pineapple Juice
1 part Orange Juice

Shake with ice and pour.

Pirate's Treasure

COLLINS GLASS

2 parts Spiced Rum
1½ parts Crown Royal® Whiskey
fill with Cola

Build over ice and stir.

Piss in the Snow

COLLINS GLASS

1 part Vodka
1 part Peppermint Schnapps
fill with Mountain Dew®

Build over ice and stir.

Pixie-Hood

COLLINS GLASS

1 part Crème de Banane
1 part Cherry Brandy
1 part Crème de Coconut
fill with Lemon-Lime Soda

Build over ice and stir.

Pixy Stix®

COLLINS GLASS

1 part Vodka
1 part Apricot Brandy
1 part Blue Curaçao
1 part Grape Schnapps
fill with Lemonade

Shake with ice and pour.

Platinum Liver

COLLINS GLASS

½ part Gin
½ part Blue Curaçao
½ part Vodka
½ part Dark Rum
½ part Silver Tequila
1 part Sweet & Sour Mix
1 part Lemon-Lime Soda

Build over ice and stir.

Play with Fire

COLLINS GLASS

1½ parts Brandy
1 part Amaretto
½ part Grenadine
1 part Orange Juice

Shake with ice and pour.

Playball

COLLINS GLASS

1 part Spiced Rum
1 part Vodka
1 part Peach Schnapps
fill with Orange Juice

Shake with ice and pour.

Plutonic

COLLINS GLASS

1 part Vodka
1 part Light Rum
1 part Gin
1 part Tequila Reposado
splash Grenadine
fill with Milk

Shake with ice and pour.

Polar Bear Collar

COLLINS GLASS

2 parts Dark Rum
1 part Sweet Vermouth
1 part Orange Juice
fill with Lemon-Lime Soda

Build over ice and stir.

Polkagris
COLLINS GLASS

1 part Vodka
1 part Crème de Menthe (White)
½ part Grenadine
fill with Lemon-Lime Soda

Build over ice and stir.

Pollenade
COLLINS GLASS

1 part Tequila
1 part Drambuie®
1 part Raspberry Liqueur
fill with Lemonade

Shake with ice and pour.

Pomegranate Blush
COLLINS GLASS

2 parts Pomegranate Vodka
1 part Ginger Liqueur
fill with Tonic Water
dash Pomegranate Juice

Build over ice.

Pomme Rouge
COLLINS GLASS

1½ parts Scotch
fill with Apple Cider
splash Grenadine

Build over ice and stir.

Ponche Tropical
COLLINS GLASS

1 part Dark Rum
1 part Apricot Brandy
1 part Cherry Brandy
1 part Triple Sec
fill with Orange Juice
splash Grenadine

Build over ice and stir.

Poop
COLLINS GLASS

1 part Raspberry Liqueur
1 part Citrus Vodka
fill with Lemon-Lime Soda

Build over ice and stir.

Popo-Naval
COLLINS GLASS

3 parts Peach Schnapps
1½ parts Vodka
fill with Orange Juice

Build over ice and stir.

Popped Cherry
COLLINS GLASS

1 part Vodka
1 part Cherry Liqueur
1 part Cranberry Juice Cocktail
1 part Orange Juice

Build over ice and stir.

Poppin's
COLLINS GLASS

1 part Dark Rum
½ part Triple Sec
1 part Pineapple Juice
1 part Orange Juice
dash Bitters

Build over ice and stir.

Port Milk Punch
COLLINS GLASS

2 parts Port
dash Powdered Sugar
fill with Milk
dash Ground Nutmeg

Shake with ice and strain.

Portland Poker
HURRICANE GLASS

1 part Blackberry Liqueur
1 part Citrus Vodka
½ part Vanilla Liqueur
1 part Mango Juice
1 part Peach Puree
1 part Club Soda

Shake all but Club Soda with ice and strain over ice. Top with Club Soda.

The Power of Milk

COLLINS GLASS

3 dashes Sugar
1 part Vodka
fill with Milk

Build over ice and stir.

Power Play

COLLINS GLASS

1½ parts Orange Vodka
1 part Raspberry Liqueur
½ part Lemon Juice
fill with Orange Juice

Shake with ice and pour.

Prav Da

COLLINS GLASS

½ part Blue Curaçao
½ part Goldschläger®
1 part Sweet & Sour Mix
fill with Apple Juice

Shake with ice and strain over ice.

Premium Herbal Blend

COLLINS GLASS

2 parts Citrus Vodka
½ part Grenadine
fill with Sweet & Sour Mix
top with Club Soda

Build over ice and stir.

Prom Night Virgin

COLLINS GLASS

2 parts Southern Comfort®
½ part Lemon Juice
1 part Smirnoff Ice®
2 parts Mountain Dew®

Build over ice and stir.

Psycho Citrus

COLLINS GLASS

1 part Vodka
1 part Tequila
½ part Crème de Menthe (White)
splash Lime Juice
splash Grand Marnier®
fill with Orange Juice

Shake with ice and pour.

Puckered Parrot

COLLINS GLASS

1 part Coconut Rum
1 part Sour Apple Schnapps
fill with Mountain Dew®

Build over ice and stir.

Puerto Escondido

COLLINS GLASS

1½ parts Silver Tequila
½ part Triple Sec
fill with Pineapple Juice

Build over ice and stir.

Pulp Friction

MARGARITA GLASS

1½ parts Gold Tequila
½ part Cointreau®
½ part Lime Juice
½ part Margarita Mix
½ part Orange Juice

Shake with ice and pour.

Punch in the Stomach

COLLINS GLASS

3 parts Tequila Reposado
fill with Lemon-Lime Soda
splash Fruit Punch

Build over ice and stir.

Punta Gorda

COLLINS GLASS

1 1/2 parts Dark Rum
1 part Lime Juice
1 part Sloe Gin
1/2 part Grenadine
fill with Pineapple Juice

Shake with ice and pour.

Purple Fairy Dream

HURRICANE GLASS

1/2 part Currant Vodka
1 part Blue Curaçao
1 part Raspberry Liqueur
2 parts Cream of Coconut
fill with Lemon-Lime Soda
splash Cranberry Juice Cocktail

Build over ice and stir.

Purple Gecko

MARGARITA GLASS

1 1/2 parts Tequila
1/2 part Blue Curaçao
1 part Cranberry Juice Cocktail
1 part Sweet & Sour Mix
1/2 part Lime Juice

Shake with ice and pour.

Purple Margarita

MARGARITA GLASS

2 parts Tequila
2 parts Raspberry Liqueur
2 parts Sweet & Sour Mix
1 part Lime Juice
1 part Cranberry Juice Cocktail

Shake with ice and pour.

Purple Pancho

MARGARITA GLASS

1 part Tequila
1/2 part Blue Curaçao
1/2 part Sloe Gin
2 parts Lime Juice
2 parts Sweet & Sour Mix

Shake with ice and pour.

Purple Passion

COLLINS GLASS

1 1/2 parts Vodka
dash Sugar
1 part Grape Juice (Red)
1 part Grapefruit Juice

Shake with ice and pour.

Purple Problem Solver

HURRICANE GLASS

1 part Vodka
1 part Rum
1 part Melon Liqueur
1 part Blue Curaçao
1 part Sour Apple Schnapps
1 part Peach Schnapps
1 part Sweet & Sour Mix
fill with Pineapple Juice
splash Grenadine

Shake with ice and strain over ice.

Purple Pussycat Juice

HURRICANE GLASS

3/4 part Tequila Reposado
3/4 part Vodka
1/2 part Triple Sec
1/2 part Raspberry Liqueur
1 part Pineapple Juice
1 part Sweet & Sour Mix

Shake with ice and pour.

Purple Rain

COLLINS GLASS

1 part Vodka
1 part Gin
1 part Rum
1 part Blue Curaçao
1 part Cranberry Juice Cocktail
fill with Lemon-Lime Soda

Build over ice and stir.

Pussycat

COLLINS GLASS

1 1/2 parts Bourbon
splash Grenadine
1 part Sweet & Sour Mix
1 part Orange Juice

Build over ice and stir.

Pussyfoot

COLLINS GLASS

1 part Light Rum
1 part Pineapple Juice
1 part Orange Juice
1 part Grapefruit Juice
½ part Grenadine

Build over ice.

Quantum Theory

COLLINS GLASS

¾ part Rum
½ part Strega®
¼ part Grand Marnier®
2 parts Pineapple Juice
fill with Sweet & Sour Mix

Shake with ice and pour.

Queen's Blossom

COLLINS GLASS

1½ parts Dry Gin
1 part Crème de Banane
fill with Lemonade

Build over ice and stir.

Quikster's Delight

COLLINS GLASS

1½ parts Bacardi® Limón Rum
1 part Orange Juice
1 part Pineapple Juice
½ part Grenadine

Build over ice.

Racer's Edge

COLLINS GLASS

1 part Sweetened Lime Juice
fill with Pineapple Juice
splash Crème de Menthe (Green)

Build over ice.

Rainbow

COLLINS GLASS

1¼ parts Citrus Vodka
1 part Grapefruit Juice
1 part Grape Juice (Red)

Build over ice.

Rainforest

COLLINS GLASS

1 part Blue Curaçao
1 part Crème de Coconut
½ part Crème de Menthe (White)
fill with Lemon-Lime Soda

Build over ice.

Raleigh Autumn

COLLINS GLASS

1 part Light Rum
½ part Galliano®
½ part Apricot Brandy
fill with Pineapple Juice
splash Lemon Juice

Shake with ice and strain over ice.

Ramsey

COLLINS GLASS

1 part Tequila
1 part Coffee Liqueur
1 part Irish Cream Liqueur
fill with Milk

Shake with ice and pour.

Raspava Berry

COLLINS GLASS

1 part Raspberry Liqueur
2 parts Lime Juice
fill with Guava Juice

Shake with ice and pour.

Raspberry Bulldozer

COLLINS GLASS

1 part Raspberry Liqueur
fill with Red Bull® Energy Drink

Build over ice and stir.

Raspberry Drop

COLLINS GLASS

1 part Raspberry Liqueur
½ part Amaretto
1 part Lemon-Lime Soda
3 parts Orange Juice

Build over ice and stir.

Rasta's Revenge

COLLINS GLASS

1 part Light Rum
1 part Spiced Rum
½ part Dark Rum
splash 151-Proof Rum
½ part Grenadine
1 part Pineapple Juice
1 part Mango Juice

Build over ice and stir.

Rattler

COLLINS GLASS

1½ parts Tequila
splash Triple Sec
¼ part Lime Juice
fill with Grapefruit Juice

Build over ice and stir.

Razzberry Ice

COLLINS GLASS

2 parts Raspberry Liqueur
fill with Lemonade

Build over ice and stir.

Razzerini

COLLINS GLASS

1 part Coconut Rum
½ part Raspberry Liqueur
1 part Pineapple Juice
1 part Cranberry Juice Cocktail

Build over ice and stir.

Reason to Believe

COLLINS GLASS

1 part Gin
½ part Bénédictine®
fill with Orange Juice

Build over ice and stir.

Recliner

COLLINS GLASS

1 part Vodka
1 part Whiskey
1 part Sweet & Sour Mix
1 part Cranberry Juice Cocktail
2 parts Pineapple Juice
2 parts Orange Juice
½ part Grenadine

Shake with ice and pour.

Red Bessie

COLLINS GLASS

1½ parts Gin
1 part Strawberry Liqueur
1 part Strawberry Puree
1 part Simple Syrup
fill with Passion Fruit Juice

Shake with ice and strain over ice.

Red Colada

HURRICANE GLASS

1 part Light Rum
1 part Triple Sec
½ part Cream
2 parts Pineapple Juice
2 parts Cream of Coconut

Shake with ice and pour.

Red Crusher

HURRICANE GLASS

1 part Silver Tequila
1 part Vodka
1 part Strawberry Syrup
1 part Mango Juice
1 part Strawberry Juice

Shake with ice and pour.

Red Haze

COLLINS GLASS

1 part Rum
1 part Cherry Liqueur
1 part Cranberry Juice Cocktail
1 part Orange Juice

Shake with ice and pour.

Red Kawasaki®

COLLINS GLASS

1 part Gin
1 part Rum
1 part Sloe Gin
1 part Triple Sec
1 part Vodka
fill with Sweet & Sour Mix
splash Club Soda

Shake all but Club Soda with ice and strain. Top with Club Soda.

Red Ox

BEER MUG

1 part Light Rum
1/2 part Coconut Rum
1 part Pineapple Juice
1/2 part Cranberry Juice Cocktail
fill with Sweet & Sour Mix
splash Grenadine

Build over ice and stir.

Red Point

COLLINS GLASS

1 part Vodka
1 part Sloe Gin
splash Kiwi Schnapps
fill with Cranberry Juice Cocktail
splash Lemon Juice

Shake with ice and pour.

Red Racer

COLLINS GLASS

1 part Vodka
1 part Amaretto
1 part Southern Comfort®
1 part Sloe Gin
fill with Orange Juice

Shake with ice and pour.

Red Rooster

COLLINS GLASS

1 1/4 parts Rum
1/2 part Crème de Noyaux
fill with Guava Juice
splash Grenadine

Build over ice and stir.

Red Royal

COLLINS GLASS

1 part Crown Royal® Whiskey
1 part Amaretto
fill with Cranberry Juice Cocktail
splash Lemon-Lime Soda

Build over ice and stir.

Red Sea

COLLINS GLASS

1 1/2 parts Red Curacao
1 part Pineapple Juice
1 part Orange Juice

Shake with ice and pour.

Red Shock

COLLINS GLASS

2 parts Cinnamon Schnapps
fill with Red Bull® Energy Drink

Build over ice and stir.

Red Stinger Bunny

COLLINS GLASS

1 part Bacardi® Limón Rum
1 part Peach Schnapps
1 part Lime Juice
splash Grenadine
fill with Lemon-Lime Soda

Build over ice and stir.

Red Umbrella

COLLINS GLASS

1 part Campari®
1 part Maraschino Liqueur
1/2 part Crème de Banane
fill with Banana Juice

Shake with ice and pour.

Redneck

COLLINS GLASS

2 parts Southern Comfort®
fill with Mountain Dew®

Build over ice and stir.

Redneck Blitzkreig

COLLINS GLASS

2 parts Southern Comfort
1 part Jägermeister
fill with Tonic Water

Build over ice and stir.

Redneck Martini

MASON JAR

2 parts Southern Comfort
1 part Everclear
fill with Mountain Dew

Build over ice and stir.

Redstar

COLLINS GLASS

½ part Vodka
fill with Red Bull® Energy Drink

Build over ice and stir.

Reef Juice

HURRICANE GLASS

1½ parts Dark Rum
1 part Crème de Banane
½ part Vodka
1 part Grenadine
½ part Lime Juice
fill with Pineapple Juice

Shake with ice and pour.

Reggae Summer

COLLINS GLASS

1 part Light Rum
1½ parts Strawberry Liqueur
fill with Sparkling Water

Build over ice and stir.

Reindeer's Tear

COLLINS GLASS

1 part Vodka
1 part Blue Curaçao
1 part Lemon Juice

Build over ice and stir.

Relaxer

COLLINS GLASS

1 part Cognac
fill with Cola

Build over ice and stir.

Rémy Cup

COLLINS GLASS

1½ parts Cognac
½ part Grenadine
fill with Passion Fruit Juice

Shake with ice and strain over ice.

Return to Bekah

COLLINS GLASS

1 part Vodka
½ part Blue Curaçao
½ part Grape Juice (Red)
fill with Sweet & Sour Mix
½ part Cranberry Juice Cocktail

Build over ice and stir.

Rewstar

COLLINS GLASS

1½ parts Spiced Rum
1½ parts Coconut Rum
½ part Frangelico®
1 part Pink Grapefruit Juice
1 part Orange Juice

Shake with ice and pour.

A Ride in a Bumpy Lowrider

COLLINS GLASS

1 part Melon Liqueur
1 part Tequila
1 part Vodka
splash Grenadine

Build over ice and stir.

Ride in the Desert

COLLINS GLASS

1½ parts Silver Tequila
1 part Triple Sec
1 part Grapefruit Juice
fill with Orange Juice

Build over ice and stir.

Right Field Bleachers

COLLINS GLASS

2 parts Bacardi® Limón Rum
fill with Cherry Cola

Build over ice and stir.

Rising Sun

COLLINS GLASS

2 parts Sake
fill with Orange Juice
½ part Grenadine

Build over ice.

Riviera

COLLINS GLASS

1 part Dark Rum
1 part Passion Fruit Liqueur
1 part Crème de Coconut
fill with Lemonade

Build over ice and stir.

Robicheaux

COLLINS GLASS

1½ parts Bourbon
½ part Lime Juice
splash Cherry Juice
fill with Cola

Build over ice and stir.

Rodeo Tea

COLLINS GLASS

1 part Citrus Vodka
2 parts Blackberry Liqueur
1 tbsp powdered sugar
½ part Lemon Juice
fill with Iced Tea

Shake with ice and strain over ice.

Roly Poley

COLLINS GLASS

2 parts Rum
fill with Dr. Pepper®

Build over ice and stir.

Root Beer Fizz

COLLINS GLASS

2 parts Gin
1 part Lemon Juice
dash Sugar
fill with Root Beer

Build over ice and stir.

Root Beer Float

COLLINS GLASS

1 part Vodka
½ part Galliano
½ part Light Cream
fill with Cola

Build over ice. Top with Whipped Cream.

Root Canal

HURRICANE GLASS

2 parts Root Beer Schnapps
¼ part Peppermint Schnapps
fill with Dr. Pepper®

Build over ice and stir.

Rosarita Margarita

MARGARITA GLASS

1½ parts Tequila Reposado
¾ part Grand Marnier®
½ part Cranberry Juice Cocktail
½ part Sweetened Lime Juice
1½ parts Sweet & Sour Mix

Shake with ice and pour.

Rosebud

COLLINS GLASS

2 parts Citrus Vodka
½ part Triple Sec
1 part Lime Juice
fill with Grapefruit Juice

Build over ice and stir.

Rosette Merola

COLLINS GLASS

1 part Dry Gin
1 part Goldschläger®
1 part Kiwi Liqueur
1 part Aperol™
fill with Orange Juice

Build over ice and stir.

Rovert

COLLINS GLASS

1½ parts Coconut Rum
½ part 151-Proof Rum
2 parts Cranberry Juice Cocktail
1 part Orange Juice

Build over ice and stir.

Roy Roger'd

COLLINS GLASS

splash Grenadine
1 part Dark Rum
fill with Cola

Build over ice and stir.

Royal Fizz

COLLINS GLASS

1 part Gin
2 parts Sweet & Sour Mix
1 Whole Egg
fill with Cola

Shake all but Cola with ice and strain. Top with Cola.

A Royal Sour Kiss

COLLINS GLASS

½ part Crown Royal® Whiskey
1 part Sour Apple Schnapps
splash Lime Juice
fill with Lemon-Lime Soda

Build over ice and stir.

Rudolph's Nose

COLLINS GLASS

1¼ parts Light Rum
1½ parts Lemon Juice
½ part Grenadine
fill with Cranberry Juice Cocktail

Build over ice and stir.

Rum Butter Balls

COLLINS GLASS

2 parts Rum
1 part Butterscotch Schnapps
fill with Root Beer

Build over ice and stir.

Rum Collins

COLLINS GLASS

2 parts Light Rum
½ part Lime Juice
dash Powdered Sugar
fill with Club Soda

Shake all but Club Soda with ice and strain. Top with Club Soda.

Rum Cow

COLLINS GLASS

1¼ parts Dark Rum
dash Sugar
2 dashes Bitters
fill with Milk

Shake with ice and pour.

RumChata Mocha Latte

COLLINS GLASS

2 parts Room-Temperature Espresso
2 parts RumChata
2 parts Skim Milk
1 part Chocolate Syrup

Shake with ice and pour. Garnish with optional Whipped Cream. For added visual effect, drizzle lines of Chocolate Syrup on the sides of the glass before adding the drink mixture.

RumChata Root Beer Float

COLLINS GLASS

1 part RumChata
3 parts Root Beer

Build over ice.

Russian Elektric

COLLINS GLASS

1 part Vodka
1 part Strawberry Liqueur
fill with Red Bull® Energy Drink

Build over ice and stir.

Russian Roadrage

COLLINS GLASS

1 part Jägermeister
1 part Vanilla Vodka
fill with Red Bull Energy Drink

Build over ice and stir.

Russian Sunset

COLLINS GLASS

1 part Vodka
1 part Triple Sec
fill with Sweet & Sour Mix
splash Grenadine

Build over ice.

Russian Virgin Fizz

COLLINS GLASS

2 parts Vodka
1 part Lemon-Lime Soda
1 part Lemonade

Build over ice and stir.

Rusted Root

COLLINS GLASS

2 parts Gin
1/4 part Lemon Juice
dash Powdered Sugar
1 Egg White
fill with Root Beer

Shake all but Root Beer with ice and strain. Top with Root Beer.

S and M

COLLINS GLASS

2 parts Southern Comfort®
fill with Mountain Dew®

Build over ice and stir.

Sabor Latino

COLLINS GLASS

1 part Light Rum
1 part Dark Rum
splash Raspberry Liqueur
1/2 part Mango Juice
1/2 part Lime Juice
1/2 part Papaya Juice
fill with Pineapple Juice

Shake with ice and pour.

Sake Sunshine

COLLINS GLASS

1 part Brandy
1 part Sake
fill with Grapefruit Juice
splash Grenadine

Build over ice.

Salem Witch

COLLINS GLASS

1/2 part Vodka
1/2 part Raspberry Liqueur
1/2 part Midori®
splash Lime Juice
splash Grenadine
1 part Sweet & Sour Mix
1 part Club Soda

Build over ice and stir.

Salim

COLLINS GLASS

1 part Dry Gin
1/2 part Crème de Banane
1/2 part Southern Comfort®
1 part Pineapple Juice
fill with Orange Juice

Build over ice and stir.

Salty Balls

COLLINS GLASS

1 1/2 parts Vodka
1 part Midori®
2 parts Orange Juice
fill with Grapefruit Juice
pinch Salt

Build over ice and stir.

Samovar Sass

COLLINS GLASS

1 1/2 parts Raspberry Liqueur
3 parts Banana Puree
2/3 part Lemon Juice
fill with Orange Juice

Shake with ice and strain over ice.

San Diego Seabreeze

COLLINS GLASS

1 part Vodka
1/2 part Raspberry Liqueur
1/2 part Blueberry Schnapps
1 part Orange Juice
1 part Pineapple Juice
top with Blackberry Brandy

Build over ice.

San Francisco

COLLINS GLASS

1 part Vodka
1 part Triple Sec
1 part Crème de Banane
1 part Pineapple Juice
1 part Orange Juice
1/4 part Grenadine

Shake with ice and pour.

San Juan Tea

COLLINS GLASS

1 1/2 parts Bacardi® Limón Rum
1/2 part 151-Proof Rum
fill with Sweet & Sour Mix
splash Cola

Build over ice.

Sanders' Special

COLLINS GLASS

1 part Vodka
1 part Sour Apple Schnapps
1 part Peach Schnapps
fill with Fruit Punch

Shake with ice and pour.

Sans Souci

COLLINS GLASS

1 1/2 parts Triple Sec
splash Vodka
splash Lime Juice
fill with Lemonade

Shake with ice and pour.

Santa Esmeralda

COLLINS GLASS

1 1/2 parts Vodka
1/4 part Kiwi Schnapps
fill with Grapefruit Juice

Build over ice.

Santa Fe Express

COLLINS GLASS

1 1/2 parts Tequila Reposado
1/2 part Triple Sec
fill with Sweet & Sour Mix

Build over ice and stir.

Santa's Little Helper

COLLINS GLASS

1 part Apple Rum
1 part Fireball Cinnamon Whiskey
1 part Butterscotch Liqueur
fill with Apple Juice

Build over ice and stir.

Santa's Pole

COLLINS GLASS

1 part Peppermint Schnapps
1 part Vodka
2 splashes Grenadine
fill with Lemon-Lime Soda

Build over ice.

Sapphire Blues
HURRICANE GLASS
1½ parts Gin
½ part Blue Curaçao
½ part Lime Cordial
½ part Peach Schnapps
fill with Lemon-Lime Soda
Build over ice and stir.

Satin Sheet
COLLINS GLASS
2 parts Brandy
1 part Peach Schnapps
splash Grenadine
fill with Orange Juice
Build over ice and stir.

Schlägerfloat
COLLINS GLASS
2 parts Goldschläger®
2 scoops Vanilla Ice Cream
fill with Root Beer
Build in the glass with no ice.

Schnapp It Up
COLLINS GLASS
1 part Peach Schnapps
1 part Wild Berry Schnapps
1 part Vodka
fill with Cranberry Juice Cocktail
Build over ice and stir.

Schwartzy
COLLINS GLASS
1 part Peach Schnapps
1 part Southern Comfort®
fill with Orange Juice
splash Pineapple Juice
Build over ice and stir.

Scorpion's Tail
COLLINS GLASS
1 part Coconut Rum
1 part Banana Liqueur
splash Pineapple Juice
fill with Cranberry Juice
Build over ice and stir.

Scotch Milk Punch
COLLINS GLASS
2 parts Scotch
dash Powdered Sugar
dash Ground Nutmeg
fill with Milk
Shake with ice and pour.

Scottie's Popsicle®
COLLINS GLASS
1 part Crème de Cacao (Dark)
1 part Crème de Banane
1 part Raspberry Liqueur
splash Vodka
fill with Half and Half
Shake with ice and pour.

Screaming in the Dark
COLLINS GLASS
1½ parts Black Vodka
1 part Coffee Liqueur
½ part Brandy
½ part Bourbon
fill with Cola
Build over ice and stir.

Screaming Toilet
COLLINS GLASS
1½ parts Tequila Reposado
1 part Peach Schnapps
1 part Triple Sec
1 part Melon Liqueur
fill with Pineapple Juice
Build over ice and stir.

Screw Up
COLLINS GLASS
1 part Vodka
1 part Orange Juice
1 part Lemon-Lime Soda
Build over ice and stir.

Screwball
COLLINS GLASS
2 parts Whiskey
fill with Orange Juice
Build over ice and stir.

Screwdriver with a Twist

COLLINS GLASS

2 parts Vodka
1 part Lemon-Lime Soda
1 part Orange Juice

Build over ice and stir.

Seattle Smog

COLLINS GLASS

1 part Midori®
1 part Peach Schnapps
1 part Blue Curaçao
2 parts Cranberry Juice Cocktail
1 part Orange Juice

Build over ice and stir.

Secret

COLLINS GLASS

1½ parts Scotch
splash Crème de Menthe (White)
fill with Sparkling Water

Build over ice and stir.

Serrera

COLLINS GLASS

1 part Vodka
1 part Blue Curaçao
fill with Sparkling Water

Build over ice and stir.

Set the Juice Loose

COLLINS GLASS

1 part Apricot Brandy
1 part Cherry Brandy
1 part Crème de Banane
1 part Pineapple Juice
1 part Orange Juice

Build over ice and stir.

Seven Year Itch

COLLINS GLASS

2 parts Spiced Rum
splash Lemon Juice
fill with Lemon-Lime Soda

Build over ice and stir.

Sewer Rat

COLLINS GLASS

1 part Vodka
½ part Peach Schnapps
½ part Coffee Liqueur
fill with Orange Juice

Build in the glass with no ice.

Sgt. Pepper

COLLINS GLASS

2 parts Southern Comfort®
fill with Dr. Pepper®

Build over ice and stir.

Shag by the Shore

COLLINS GLASS

½ part Melon Liqueur
½ part Peach Schnapps
1 part Cranberry Juice Cocktail
1 part Orange Juice

Build over ice and stir.

Shamrock Juice

HURRICANE GLASS

1 part Gin
1 part Tequila
1 part Rum
1 part Vodka
1 part Blue Curaçao
fill with Orange Juice

Build over ice and stir.

Shark Tank

COLLINS GLASS

2 parts Vodka
1 part Grenadine
fill with Lemonade

Build over ice and stir.

Shattered Dreams

COLLINS GLASS

1 part Vodka
1½ parts Blueberry Schnapps
splash Grenadine
splash Lemon-Lime Soda
fill with Grape Juice (Red)

Build over ice and stir.

Shipwreck

COLLINS GLASS

1 part Rum
1/4 part Triple Sec
1/4 part Crème de Banane
fill with Sweet & Sour Mix

Build over ice and stir.

Shirley Temple Black

COLLINS GLASS

1 part Coffee Liqueur
fill with Lemon-Lime Soda
splash Grenadine

Build over ice and stir.

Shirley Temple of Doom

COLLINS GLASS

2 parts Vodka
splash Grenadine
fill with Lemon-Lime Soda

Build over ice and stir.

Shock-a-Bull

BEER MUG

1 part Peppermint Schnapps
1 part Vodka
fill with Red Bull® Energy Drink

Build over ice and stir.

Shoo In

COLLINS GLASS

1/2 part Light Rum
1/2 part Dark Rum
1/2 part Brandy
1/2 part Maraschino Liqueur
1 part Grapefruit Juice
1 part Pineapple Juice

Build over ice and stir.

Shoot to the Moon

COLLINS GLASS

2 1/2 parts Light Rum
1 part Club Soda
1 part Cranberry Juice Cocktail
splash Grenadine

Build over ice and stir.

Sierra Nevada

COLLINS GLASS

1 part Dark Rum
1/2 part Apricot Brandy
1/2 part Triple Sec
splash Grenadine
fill with Pineapple Juice

Build over ice and stir.

Silk Boxers

COLLINS GLASS

1 part Light Rum
1/2 part Cherry Brandy
1/4 part Crème de Cacao (White)
fill with Cream

Shake with ice and pour.

Silly Orange

COLLINS GLASS

1 part Hazelnut Liqueur
1 part Strawberry Liqueur
fill with Orange Juice

Build over ice and stir.

Silver Cloud

COLLINS GLASS

1 part Amaretto
1 part Coffee Liqueur
fill with Milk

Shake with ice and pour. Top with Whipped Cream.

Silver Whisper

COLLINS GLASS

1 part Gin
1/2 part Sloe Gin
splash Blackberry Liqueur
1/2 part Lime Juice
splash Simple Syrup
fill with Grapefruit Juice

Shake with ice and pour.

Simple Pimm's®

COLLINS GLASS

1 part Pimm's® No. 1 Cup
1 part Ginger Ale
fill with Lemonade

Build over ice and stir.

Sirocco

COLLINS GLASS

1 part Gin
1 part Lychee Liqueur
1 part Cointreau®
splash Kirschwasser
fill with Lemon-Lime Soda

Build over ice.

Sister Havana

COLLINS GLASS

1½ parts Spiced Rum
½ part Passion Fruit Liqueur
½ part Lemon Juice
fill with Pineapple Juice

Shake with ice and pour.

Sit and Spin

COLLINS GLASS

1½ parts Dark Rum
¼ part Lime Juice
2 splashes Lemon Juice
dash Sugar
fill with Grapefruit Juice

Shake with ice and strain over ice.

Ska Club

COLLINS GLASS

1½ parts Whiskey
½ part Light Rum
fill with Orange Juice

Shake with ice and pour.

Skeet Shooter Special

COLLINS GLASS

1½ parts Dark Rum
½ part Light Rum
1 part Lemon-Lime Soda
1 part Pineapple Juice
1 part Grapefruit Juice
1 part Orange Juice
dash Cinnamon

Build over ice and stir.

Skittle®

COLLINS GLASS

1 part Vodka
1 part 99-proof Banana Liqueur
fill with Fruit Punch

Build over ice and stir.

Sky Blue Fallout

HURRICANE GLASS

½ part Blue Curaçao
½ part Gin
½ part Vodka
½ part Triple Sec
½ part Tequila
½ part 151-Proof Rum
1 part Sweet & Sour Mix
1 part Lemon-Lime Soda

Build over ice and stir.

Sky Walker

COLLINS GLASS

1 part Spiced Rum
1 part Sloe Gin
1½ parts Triple Sec
1 part Grenadine
fill with Orange Juice

Build over ice and stir.

Slice O' Heaven

COLLINS GLASS

1 part Kiwi Liqueur
1 part Melon Liqueur
fill with Apple Juice

Shake with ice and pour.

Slimy Worm

COLLINS GLASS

1 part Blueberry Schnapps
1/2 part Brandy
fill with Apple Juice

Build over ice and stir.

Slippery Giraffe

COLLINS GLASS

1 part Light Rum
fill with Cream Soda

Build over ice and stir.

Sloe Ahead

COLLINS GLASS

1 1/2 parts Light Rum
1/2 part Melon Liqueur
1/4 part Sloe Gin
1 part Pineapple Juice
1 part Orange Juice

Build over ice and stir.

Sloe Coach

HURRICANE GLASS

1 part Vodka
1 part Southern Comfort®
1 part Sloe Gin
fill with Orange Juice

Shake with ice and strain over ice.

Sloe Smack in the Face

COLLINS GLASS

1 1/2 parts Southern Comfort®
1 1/2 parts Sloe Gin
1 part Red Curaçao
1 part Orange Juice
1 part Lemon-Lime Soda

Build over ice and stir.

Sludge

COLLINS GLASS

1 part Vodka
1 part Triple Sec
1/2 part Blue Curaçao
1/2 part Peach Schnapps
1 part Cranberry Juice Cocktail
1 part Orange Juice
splash Melon Liqueur

Build over ice and stir.

Smile Maker

COLLINS GLASS

1 part Amaretto
1 part Orange Juice
1 part Passion Fruit Liqueur
fill with Sweet & Sour Mix

Build over ice and stir.

Smooch

COLLINS GLASS

1 part Coconut Rum
1 part Midori®
1 part Sloe Gin
1 part Amaretto
1 part Peach Schnapps
fill Orange Juice
splash Pineapple Juice

Shake with ice and pour.

Smoove

COLLINS GLASS

1 part Vodka
1 part Peach Schnapps
fill with Lemon-Lime Soda

Build over ice and stir.

Snapper

COLLINS GLASS

2 parts Vodka
1 part Peppermint Schnapps
1 part Lime Juice
fill with Cola

Build over ice and stir.

Sniper

COLLINS GLASS

1 part Tia Maria®
1 part Triple Sec
fill with Orange Juice

Build over ice and stir.

Sno Cone

COLLINS GLASS

1½ parts Coconut Rum
½ part Blue Curaçao
½ part Sweet & Sour Mix
fill with Pineapple Juice

Shake with ice and pour.

Snowball

COLLINS GLASS

2 parts Advocaat
fill with Lemon-Lime Soda

Build over ice and stir.

Something Peachie

COLLINS GLASS

¾ part Vodka
¾ part Peach Schnapps
¾ part Triple Sec
1 part Pineapple Juice
1 part Orange Juice

Shake with ice and pour.

Something to Lose

COLLINS GLASS

1 part Dark Rum
1 part Southern Comfort®
½ part Apricot Brandy
1 part Pineapple Juice
1 part Orange Juice

Shake with ice and pour.

Somewhere in Time

COLLINS GLASS

1 part Lychee Liqueur
1 part Passion Fruit Liqueur
1½ parts Spiced Rum
fill with Papaya Juice
⅔ part Lemon Juice

Build over ice and stir.

Sonic Blaster

COLLINS GLASS

½ part Vodka
½ part Light Rum
½ part Banana Liqueur
1 part Pineapple Juice
1 part Orange Juice
1 part Cranberry Juice Cocktail

Shake with ice and pour.

Sonoma

COLLINS GLASS

1 part Vodka
1 part Grape Juice (Red)
fill with Mountain Dew®

Build over ice and stir.

Sophie's Choice

COLLINS GLASS

1 part Vodka
1 part Peach Schnapps
1 part Melon Liqueur
fill with Sweet & Sour Mix

Build over ice and stir.

Sour Appleball

COLLINS GLASS

1½ parts Sour Apple Schnapps
½ part Vodka
½ part Triple Sec
fill with Lemon-Lime Soda

Build over ice and stir.

Sour Squishy

COLLINS GLASS

1 part Light Rum
½ part Sour Apple Schnapps
2 parts Sweet & Sour Mix
½ part Grenadine
fill with Lemon-Lime Soda

Shake all but Lemon-Lime Soda with ice and strain. Top with Lemon-Lime Soda.

Sourkraut's Heaven

COLLINS GLASS

1½ parts Apple Brandy
1 part Apple Juice
1 part Tonic Water

Build over ice and stir.

South End Lemonade

COLLINS GLASS

1 part Rum
1 part Triple Sec
1 part Vodka
1 part Raspberry Liqueur
fill with Lemon-Lime Soda

Build over ice and stir.

Southern Decadence

COLLINS GLASS

1 part Jack Daniel's®
1 part Southern Comfort®
fill with Lemon-Lime Soda

Build over ice and stir.

Southern Dew

COLLINS GLASS

2 parts Southern Comfort®
fill with Mountain Dew®

Build over ice and stir.

Southern Doctor

COLLINS GLASS

2 parts Southern Comfort®
fill with Dr. Pepper®

Build over ice and stir.

Southern Isle

COLLINS GLASS

¾ part Blue Curaçao
½ part Southern Comfort®
½ part Citrus Vodka
fill with Orange Juice

Build over ice and stir.

Southern Raspberry Tart

HURRICANE GLASS

1 part Southern Comfort®
1 part Jack Daniel's®
1 part Raspberry Liqueur
fill with Sweet & Sour Mix
splash Lemon-Lime Soda

Shake all but Lemon-Lime Soda with ice and strain over ice. Top with Lemon-Lime Soda.

Southern Stirrup

COLLINS GLASS

1½ parts Southern Comfort®
½ part Lemon Juice
1½ parts Cranberry Juice Cocktail
1 part Grapefruit Juice
1 part Club Soda

Build over ice and stir.

Space Orbiter

HURRICANE GLASS

1½ parts Crème de Menthe (Green)
1 part Maple Syrup
½ part Amaretto
fill with Grapefruit Juice

Build over ice and stir.

Spanish Love

COLLINS GLASS

½ part Melon Liqueur
½ part Peach Schnapps
½ part Damiana®
fill with Orange Juice
⅔ part Mango Juice

Build over ice and stir.

Sparkling Garden

COLLINS GLASS

1½ parts Citrus Vodka
⅔ part Parfait Amour
splash Lime Juice
splash Lemon Juice
fill with Sparkling Water

Build over ice and stir.

Sparkling Red Driver

COLLINS GLASS

1 part Vodka
1 part Grapefruit Juice
1 part Ginger Ale

Build over ice and stir.

Special Margarita

MARGARITA GLASS

1 part Tequila
1 part Calvados Apple Brandy
1 part Grand Marnier®
1 part Grenadine
1 part Lemon Juice

Shake with ice and pour.

Speedy Gonzales®

COLLINS GLASS

1 part Blue Curaçao
1 part Grapefruit Juice
1 part Passion Fruit Juice
1 part Banana Juice

Shake with ice and strain over ice.

Sperm Count

COLLINS GLASS

1½ parts Scotch
1 part Crème de Cacao (Dark)
fill with Milk

Shake with ice and pour.

Spice Orgasm

COLLINS GLASS

1 part Spiced Rum
1 part Crème de Banane
1 part Banana Puree
fill with Milk

Shake with ice and strain over ice.

Spiced Cherry

COLLINS GLASS

1½ parts Spiced Rum
fill with Cherry Cola

Build over ice and stir.

Splash and Crash

COLLINS GLASS

2 parts Amaretto
3 parts Cranberry Juice Cocktail
1 part Orange Juice
½ part 151-Proof Rum

Build over ice.

Splendid Brandy

COLLINS GLASS

1 part Brandy
splash Vanilla Liqueur
½ part Strawberry Liqueur
½ part Crème de Coconut
½ part Lemon Juice
fill with Raspberry Seltzer

Build over ice and stir.

Spritsor

BEER MUG

2 parts Canadian Whisky
fill with Lemon-Lime Soda

Build over ice and stir.

Spunky Monkey

COLLINS GLASS

½ part Rum
½ part Crème de Banane
½ part Crème de Cacao (Dark)
½ part Triple Sec
1 part Sweet & Sour Mix
1 part Orange Juice
1 part Cranberry Juice Cocktail

Shake with ice and pour.

Sputnik

COLLINS GLASS

1¼ parts Vodka
1¼ parts Peach Schnapps
1 part Orange Juice
1 part Light Cream

Shake with ice and pour.

Squeeze
COLLINS GLASS

1½ parts Citrus Vodka
1 part Pineapple Juice
1 part Orange Juice

Build over ice and stir.

St. Charles Punch
COLLINS GLASS

1 part Brandy
½ part Triple Sec
½ part Lemon Juice
dash Sugar
fill with Port

Shake all but Port with ice and strain. Top with Port.

St. Zipaine
COLLINS GLASS

2 parts Zipang Sparkling Sake
1½ parts St-Germain
2 parts Club Soda

Build over ice and stir. Garnish with a Lemon Twist.

Staggering Squirrel
COLLINS GLASS

1 part Southern Comfort®
½ part Amaretto
fill with Cola

Build over ice and stir.

Stale Perfume
COLLINS GLASS

1 part Raspberry Vodka
1 part Raspberry Liqueur
fill with Lemon-Lime Soda

Build over ice and stir.

Star Light
COLLINS GLASS

1 part Apricot Brandy
1 part Gin
1 part Dry Vermouth
fill with Grapefruit Juice

Build over ice and stir.

Steady Eddie
COLLINS GLASS

1 part Vodka
1 part Coconut Rum
splash Passion Fruit Liqueur
fill with Orange Juice

Shake with ice and pour.

Stiffy
COLLINS GLASS

1 part Vodka
1 part Pink Lemonade
fill with Mountain Dew®

Build over ice and stir.

Stimulator
COLLINS GLASS

1 part Coffee Liqueur
1 part Irish Cream Liqueur
1 part Galliano®
1 part Frangelico®
1 part Tuacã®
fill with Milk

Shake with ice and pour.

Sting
COLLINS GLASS

1 part Vodka
1 part Crème de Banane
fill with Lemonade

Shake with ice and pour.

Stone Cold
COLLINS GLASS

1 part Vodka
1 part Peach Schnapps
2 parts Orange Juice
½ part Strawberry Syrup
fill with Lemon-Lime Soda

Build over ice and stir.

Strawberry Fruitcup

COLLINS GLASS

2/3 part Strawberry Liqueur
2/3 part Apricot Brandy
1/2 part Lemon Juice
2/3 part Cream
1 1/2 parts Apricot Juice
1 part Pineapple Juice
1 part Passion Fruit Juice

Shake with ice and pour.

Strawberry Heart

HURRICANE GLASS

1 part Strawberry Liqueur
1 part Apricot Brandy
1 part Lime Juice
1 1/2 parts Pineapple Juice
1 1/2 parts Orange Juice
fill with Sparkling Water

Build over ice and stir.

Strawberry Margarita

MARGARITA GLASS

1 part Tequila
1/2 part Strawberry Liqueur
1/2 part Triple Sec
1 part Lemon Juice

Shake with ice and pour.

Strawberry Marsh

COLLINS GLASS

1 part Strawberry Liqueur
1 part Dark Rum
fill with Cranberry Juice Cocktail

Shake with ice and pour.

Strawberry Screwdriver

COLLINS GLASS

2 parts Vodka
1 part Strawberry Liqueur
fill with Orange Juice

Shake with ice and pour.

Strawberry Storm

HURRICANE GLASS

1 part Coffee Liqueur
1 1/2 parts Strawberry Liqueur
1 1/2 parts Cream
fill with Pineapple Juice

Shake with ice and pour.

Stress Killer

COLLINS GLASS

splash Blue Curaçao
2 parts Pineapple Juice
2 parts Grapefruit Juice
1 1/2 parts Passion Fruit Juice
1 1/2 parts Orange Juice

Shake with ice and strain over ice.

Stretcher Bearer

COLLINS GLASS

1 part Myers's® Rum
1 part Malibu® Rum
1 part Cointreau®
1 part Crème de Banane
fill with Pineapple Juice
1 part 151-Proof Rum

Build over ice and stir.

String Bikini

COLLINS GLASS

1/2 part Rum
1/2 part Coconut Rum
1/2 part Melon Liqueur
1/2 part Raspberry Liqueur
1 part Orange Juice
1 part Pineapple Juice

Shake with ice and pour.

Stroumf

COLLINS GLASS

1 part Apricot Brandy
1 part Gin
1/2 part Amaretto
splash Lemon Juice
fill with Orange Juice

Build over ice and stir.

Stumblebum

COLLINS GLASS

½ part Tequila Reposado
½ part Light Rum
½ part Triple Sec
fill with Sweet & Sour Mix
splash Lemon-Lime Soda
½ part Melon Liqueur

Build over ice and stir.

Sugar High

COLLINS GLASS

½ part Crème de Cacao (White)
½ part Blue Curaçao
½ part Midori®
½ part Crème de Banane
2 parts Watermelon Schnapps
2 dashes Sugar
fill with Lemon-Lime Soda

Shake all but Lemon-Lime Soda with ice and strain over ice. Top with Lemon-Lime Soda.

Summer Delight

COLLINS GLASS

½ part Orange Vodka
¼ part Peach Schnapps
1 part Cranberry Juice Cocktail
1 part Orange Juice
¾ part Melon Liqueur

Build over ice and stir.

Summer Fun

COLLINS GLASS

1 part Cognac
¾ part Crème de Banane
1 part Pineapple Juice
1 part Orange Juice

Build over ice and stir.

Summer Hummer

COLLINS GLASS

2 parts Citrus Vodka
2 parts Lemonade
1 part Lemon-Lime Soda

Build over ice and stir.

Summer Slider

COLLINS GLASS

2 parts Dark Rum
1 part Peach Schnapps
fill with Orange Juice

Build over ice and stir.

Summer Smile

COLLINS GLASS

1 part Vodka
1 part Crème de Coconut
fill with Orange Juice

Build over ice and stir.

Summer Sunset

COLLINS GLASS

2 parts Light Rum
1 part Fruit Punch
1 part Ginger Ale

Build over ice and stir.

Summertime

COLLINS GLASS

1 part Gin
1 part Mandarine Napoléon® Liqueur
fill with Orange Juice
splash Grenadine

Build over ice and stir.

Sun Fire

COLLINS GLASS

2 parts Gin
½ part Blue Curaçao
splash Grenadine
fill with Pineapple Juice

Build over ice and stir.

Sun-Kissed Virgin

COLLINS GLASS

½ part Amaretto
1 tbsp sugar
1 part Lime Juice
1 part Pineapple Juice
1 part Orange Juice

Build over ice and stir.

Sunblock

COLLINS GLASS

1½ parts Vodka
1 part Triple Sec
fill with Grapefruit Juice

Build over ice and stir.

Sundowner Delight

COLLINS GLASS

2 parts Dark Rum
1 part Mango Juice
1 part Pineapple Juice
1 part Orange Juice

Build over ice and stir.

Sunfire Bird

COLLINS GLASS

1½ parts Coconut Rum
½ part Crème de Noyaux
fill with Pineapple Juice

Shake with ice and pour.

Sunflowers

COLLINS GLASS

2 parts Gin
⅔ part Caramel Syrup
1 part Lemon Juice
1 part Pineapple Juice
1 part Passion Fruit Juice

Shake with ice and pour.

Sunny Day

COLLINS GLASS

1½ parts Peach Schnapps
1 part Maraschino Liqueur
½ part Lime Juice
1 part Orange Juice
1 part Cranberry Juice Cocktail

Shake with ice and strain over ice.

Sunny Sam

COLLINS GLASS

1 part Vodka
½ part Sambuca
fill with Orange Juice

Shake with ice and pour.

Sunrise Surprise

COLLINS GLASS

2 parts Coconut Rum
splash Grenadine
1 part Orange Juice
1 part Pineapple Juice

Build over ice.

Sunset

COLLINS GLASS

1 part Vodka
1 part Apricot Brandy
fill with Orange Juice
splash Grenadine

Build over ice.

Sunset Boulevard

COLLINS GLASS

1½ parts Vodka
¾ part Peach Schnapps
fill with Orange Juice

Build over ice and stir.

Sunset on the Coast

COLLINS GLASS

1 part Light Rum
1 part Melon Liqueur
1 part Sweet & Sour Mix
fill with Lemon-Lime Soda
splash Sloe Gin

Build over ice.

Sunsplash

COLLINS GLASS

2 parts Orange Vodka
½ part Cointreau®
1 part Lime Juice
1 part Cranberry Juice Cocktail
1 part Orange Juice

Build over ice and stir.

Sunstroke

COLLINS GLASS

2 parts Vodka
fill with Grapefruit Juice
splash Cointreau®

Build over ice.

Superjuice
COLLINS GLASS

1 part Vodka
1 part Gin
1/2 part Lime Juice
1 part Orange Juice
1 part Tonic Water

Build over ice and stir.

Survivor
COLLINS GLASS

1 1/2 parts Light Rum
1/4 part Crème de Cacao (White)
fill with Pineapple Juice
1/4 part Lime Juice

Build over ice and stir.

Swamp Juice
COLLINS GLASS

1 part Vodka
1 part Blue Curaçao
1 part Triple Sec
1 part Orange Juice
1 part Pineapple Juice

Shake with ice and pour.

Sweat Heat
COLLINS GLASS

1 part Crème de Banane
1 part Pisang Ambon® Liqueur
1 part Crème de Coconut
fill with Orange Juice

Shake with ice and strain over ice.

Swedish Apple Pie
COLLINS GLASS

1 1/2 parts Cream
1/2 part Goldschläger®
1/2 part Vanilla Liqueur
1/2 part Apple Liqueur
fill with Milk

Shake with ice and pour.

Swedish Blue
COLLINS GLASS

1 1/2 parts Vodka
1/2 part Blue Curaçao
fill with Pineapple Juice
splash Lime Juice

Build over ice and stir.

Sweet Creams
COLLINS GLASS

1 1/2 parts Blackberry Liqueur
1 1/2 parts Crème de Banane
1 part Orange Juice
1 part Milk

Shake with ice and strain over ice.

Sweet Dream
COLLINS GLASS

2 parts Coconut Rum
1 part Strawberry Juice
1 part Banana Juice
1 part Orange Juice

Shake with ice and pour.

Sweet Escape
COLLINS GLASS

1 part Citrus Vodka
1 part Peach Schnapps
1 part Aquavit
1 part Lime Cordial
fill with Pear Juice

Build over ice and stir.

Sweet Flamingo
HURRICANE GLASS

1 part Gin
1 part Cherry Brandy
1 part Cream of Coconut
1 part Pineapple Juice
1 part Orange Juice

Shake with ice and strain over ice.

Sweet Mary

COLLINS GLASS

1½ parts Crème de Banane
½ part Gin
fill with Lemonade
splash Crème de Cassis

Shake with ice and pour.

Sweet Melissa

HURRICANE GLASS

1½ parts Coconut Rum
1½ parts Vanilla Vodka
splash Cranberry Juice Cocktail
1 part Orange Juice
1 part Pineapple Juice

Shake with ice and strain over ice.

Sweet Passion

COLLINS GLASS

1 part Parfait Amour
1 part Strawberry Liqueur
½ part Amaretto
¼ part Maraschino Liqueur
fill with Apple Juice

Build over ice and stir.

Sweet Passoã®

COLLINS GLASS

1 part Vodka
1 part Passoã®
1 part Tonic Water
fill with Pineapple Juice
splash Orange Juice

Build over ice and stir.

Sweet Pea

HURRICANE GLASS

2 parts Citrus Vodka
1 part Melon Liqueur
2 parts Cream
1 part Melon Puree

Build over ice.

Sweet Ranger

HURRICANE GLASS

2 parts Coconut Rum
1 part Orange Juice
1 part Lemon-Lime Soda

Build over ice and stir.

Sweet Smell of Success

COLLINS GLASS

1 part Passion Fruit Liqueur
½ part Campari®
fill with Apple Juice

Build over ice and stir.

Sweet Submission

COLLINS GLASS

2 parts Amaretto
fill with Apple Juice

Build over ice and stir.

Sweet Tooth

COLLINS GLASS

2 parts Godiva® Liqueur
fill with Milk

Shake with ice and pour.

Sweets for My Sweet

COLLINS GLASS

1 part Amaretto
1 part Whiskey
½ part Crème de Cacao (White)
½ part Strawberry Liqueur
fill with Milk

Shake with ice and pour.

Swift Kick in the Crotch

COLLINS GLASS

1 part Dark Rum
1 part Light Rum
1 part Orange Juice
fill with Cranberry Juice Cocktail

Shake with ice and pour.

Swimming Pool

COLLINS GLASS

1 part Vodka
1 part Gin
1 part Rum
1 part Blue Curaçao
fill with Lemon-Lime Soda

Build over ice and stir.

Take the A Train

COLLINS GLASS

1½ parts Citrus Vodka
½ part Vodka
1 part Grapefruit Juice
1 part Cranberry Juice Cocktail

Shake with ice and pour.

Takemoto Twister

COLLINS GLASS

1 part Vodka
1 part Sour Apple Schnapps
1 part Strawberry Liqueur
1 part Grapefruit Juice
2 parts Orange Juice

Shake with ice and pour.

Tall Blonde

COLLINS GLASS

1 part Aquavit
½ part Apricot Brandy
fill with Lemon-Lime Soda

Build over ice and stir.

Tall Sunrise

COLLINS GLASS

1½ parts Silver Tequila
½ part Triple Sec
½ part Lime Juice
½ part Crème de Cassis
fill with Orange Juice

Shake with ice and pour.

Tangeri

COLLINS GLASS

1½ parts Orange Vodka
½ part Passion Fruit Liqueur
fill with Grape Juice (Red)

Build over ice and stir.

Tartan Sword

COLLINS GLASS

1½ parts Scotch
1 part Dry Vermouth
fill with Pineapple Juice

Shake with ice and strain over ice.

Teddy Bear

COLLINS GLASS

2 parts Pisang Ambon® Liqueur
splash Bacardi® Limón Rum
fill with Orange Soda
splash Lemon Juice

Build over ice and stir.

Telenovela

COLLINS GLASS

⅔ part Crème de Coconut
splash Dark Rum
1 part Cachaça
2 parts Passion Fruit Juice
splash Cream of Coconut

Shake with ice and strain over ice.

Tell It to the Navy

COLLINS GLASS

1 part Coffee
1 part Whiskey
1 part Apricot Brandy
splash Light Rum
fill with Lemonade

Build over ice and stir.

Templar
COLLINS GLASS

1 part Vodka
½ part Kiwi Schnapps
½ part Triple Sec
splash Dry Vermouth
fill with Orange Juice

Shake with ice and pour.

Tenedor del Diablo
COLLINS GLASS

1 part Tequila Reposado
½ part Blue Curaçao
½ part Triple Sec
½ part Lime Juice
fill with Pineapple Juice

Shake with ice and strain over ice.

Teq and Tea
COLLINS GLASS

1 part Tequila
fill with Iced Tea

Shake with ice and strain over ice.

Tequila Caliente
COLLINS GLASS

1½ parts Silver Tequila
1 part Grenadine
1 part Crème de Cassis
fill with Sparkling Water

Build over ice and stir.

Tequila Canyon
COLLINS GLASS

1½ parts Tequila
splash Triple Sec
¼ part Pineapple Juice
¼ part Orange Juice
fill with Cranberry Juice Cocktail

Build over ice and stir.

Tequila Colagallo
COLLINS GLASS

1½ parts Tequila Gold
splash Lemon Juice
dash Salt
fill with Cola

Build over ice and stir.

Tequila Collins
COLLINS GLASS

2 parts Tequila
½ part Lemon Juice
dash Powdered Sugar
fill with Seltzer

Shake all but Seltzer with ice and strain. Top with Seltzer.

Tequila Fever
COLLINS GLASS

1½ parts Tequila Reposado
½ part Triple Sec
1 part Mango Nectar
fill with Passion Fruit Juice

Shake with ice and strain over ice.

Tequila Sunset
COLLINS GLASS

1 part Tequila
fill with Orange Juice
splash Blackberry Brandy

Build over ice.

Texas Mud Slammer
COLLINS GLASS

2 parts Jack Daniel's®
1 part Cola
fill with Orange Juice

Build over ice and stir.

Thais
COLLINS GLASS

1 part Dark Rum
1 part Crème de Banane
1 part Pineapple Juice
1 part Frangelico®

Shake with ice and strain over ice.

Thaitian Tea

HURRICANE GLASS

1 part Vodka
1 part Triple Sec
1 part Gin
1 part Rum
fill with Orange Juice

Shake with ice and strain over ice.

Thompson Tonic

COLLINS GLASS

1 part Peach Schnapps
1 part Spiced Rum
1 part Vodka
fill with Mountain Dew®

Build over ice and stir.

Tiajuana Taxi

COLLINS GLASS

2 parts Tequila Reposado
½ part Crème de Cassis
½ part Blackberry Liqueur
fill with Orange Juice

Shake with ice and pour.

Tie Die

COLLINS GLASS

2 parts Sour Apple Schnapps
splash Cranberry Juice Cocktail
fill with Lemonade

Build over ice.

Tiger's Tail

COLLINS GLASS

1½ parts Pernod®
fill with Orange Juice

Build over ice and stir.

Timberwolf

COLLINS GLASS

1 part Light Rum
1 part Tequila
1 part Gin
1 part Vodka
1 part Crème de Noyaux
fill with Orange Juice

Shake with ice and pour.

Timor

COLLINS GLASS

2 parts Light Rum
1 part Crème de Banane
1 part Cream
1 part Pineapple Juice

Shake with ice and pour.

To the Core

COLLINS GLASS

1 part Mandarine Napoléon® Liqueur
1 part Southern Comfort®
½ part Lime Juice
fill with Lemon-Lime Soda

Build over ice and stir.

Tolle

COLLINS GLASS

1 part Vodka
1 part Crème de Banane
fill with Hard Apple Cider

Build over ice and stir.

Tom Collins

COLLINS GLASS

2 parts Gin
½ part Lemon Juice
dash Powdered Sugar
fill with Seltzer

Shake all but Seltzer with ice and strain. Top with Seltzer.

Tombstone Special

COLLINS GLASS

1½ parts Southern Comfort®
splash Lemon Juice
splash Lime Juice
fill with Mountain Dew®

Build over ice and stir.

Tongue Tangler

COLLINS GLASS

1 part Irish Cream Liqueur
½ part Brandy
fill with Heavy Cream

Build over ice and stir.

Top Gun

COLLINS GLASS

1½ parts Spiced Rum
1 part Orange Juice
1 part Pineapple Juice
½ part 151-Proof Rum

Build over ice and stir.

Torch

COLLINS GLASS

1 part Cream
1 part Raspberry Liqueur
fill with Lemon-Lime Soda

Build over ice and stir.

Toucan

COLLINS GLASS

1 part Coconut Rum
1 part Peach Schnapps
1 part Lemon-Lime Soda
1 part Orange Juice

Build over ice and stir.

Toxic Antifreeze

COLLINS GLASS

1 part Vodka
1 part Triple Sec
1 part Midori®
fill with Lemonade

Build over ice and stir.

Toxic Blue-Green Algae

COLLINS GLASS

1 part Blue Curaçao
1 part Cointreau®
1 part Green Chartreuse®
1 part Vodka
1 part Light Rum
1 part Melon Liqueur
fill with Pineapple Juice

Shake with ice and pour.

Toxic Waste

COLLINS GLASS

1 part Vodka
½ part Southern Comfort®
¼ part Blue Curaçao
1 part Orange Juice
1 part Pineapple Juice

Shake with ice and pour.

Trang Tricot

COLLINS GLASS

1 part Vodka
1 part Pineapple Juice
½ part Crème de Banane
fill with Grape Soda

Build over ice and stir.

Transfusion

COLLINS GLASS

1¼ part Vodka
fill with Grape Juice (Red)

Build over ice and stir.

Trevell

COLLINS GLASS

1 part Coconut Rum
1 part Vodka
fill with Lemon-Lime Soda

Build over ice and stir.

Triple B

COLLINS GLASS

1 part Dark Rum
½ part Blue Curaçao
½ part Crème de Coconut
fill with Pineapple Juice

Build over ice and stir.

Triple Sec and Brandy

COLLINS GLASS

1 part Brandy
1 part Triple Sec
1 Sugar Cube

Build over ice and stir.

Triple XXX

COLLINS GLASS

1 part Red Curaçao
1 part Triple Sec
2 parts Passion Fruit Juice
fill with Apricot Juice

Shake with ice and strain over ice.

Triple XYZ

COLLINS GLASS

2 parts Coconut Rum
1 part Raspberry Liqueur
1/4 part Triple Sec
fill with Pineapple Juice

Build over ice and stir.

Troia

COLLINS GLASS

1 part Vodka
1 part Crème de Coconut
1 part Strawberry Syrup
fill with Lemon-Lime Soda

Build over ice and stir.

Tropic Moon

COLLINS GLASS

1 part Dry Gin
1/2 part Crème de Banane
1/2 part Apricot Brandy
fill with Orange Juice
splash Grenadine

Build over ice and stir.

Tropic Purple Haze

COLLINS GLASS

1 1/2 parts Raspberry Liqueur
1/2 part Vodka
1/2 part Triple Sec
2 parts Cranberry Juice Cocktail
1 part Pineapple Juice

Shake with ice and pour.

Tropic Star

COLLINS GLASS

1 part Cognac
1/2 part Crème de Banane
1/2 part Apricot Brandy
splash Pastis
fill with Lemonade

Build over ice and stir.

Tropic Twister

COLLINS GLASS

3/4 part Southern Comfort®
3/4 part Melon Liqueur
3/4 part Passion Fruit Liqueur
1 part Pineapple Juice
1 part Orange Juice

Build over ice and stir.

Tropical Blue Moon

COLLINS GLASS

1 part Dark Rum
1 part Blue Curaçao
splash Lemonade
fill with Pineapple Juice

Shake with ice and pour.

Tropical Fruits

COLLINS GLASS

1 part Rum
1 part Apricot Brandy
1 part Melon Liqueur
1 part Crème de Coconut
fill with Orange Juice

Shake with ice and strain over ice.

Tropical Growlers

COLLINS GLASS

2 parts Blackberry Liqueur
2/3 part Crème de Coconut
fill with Pineapple Juice

Shake with ice and pour.

Tropical Hit

COLLINS GLASS

2 parts Triple Sec
1 part Mango Schnapps
1 part Simple Syrup
splash Blue Curaçao
fill with Pineapple Juice

Build over ice and stir.

Tropical Leprechaun

COLLINS GLASS

1 part Vodka
½ part Coconut Rum
fill with Lemon-Lime Soda
splash Melon Liqueur

Build over ice and stir.

Tropical Melody

COLLINS GLASS

½ part Cognac
½ part Dark Rum
½ part Blackberry Liqueur
1 part Orange Juice
1 part Mango Juice

Shake with ice and pour.

Tropical Pear Fizz

COLLINS GLASS

2 parts Pear Liqueur
1 part RedRum®
½ part Apple Brandy
½ part Banana Liqueur
fill with Lemon-Lime Soda

Build over ice and stir.

Tropical Red

COLLINS GLASS

1½ parts Blue Curaçao
1 part Gin
1 part Orange Juice
1 part Grapefruit Juice

Shake with ice and pour.

Tropical Storm

COLLINS GLASS

1 part Passion Fruit Liqueur
splash Amaretto
1 part Pineapple Juice
1 part Lime Juice

Build over ice and stir.

Tropical Sunrise

COLLINS GLASS

2 parts Spiced Rum
1 part Triple Sec
1 part Orange Juice
1 part Pineapple Juice
½ part Grenadine

Build over ice and stir.

Tropical Trance

COLLINS GLASS

½ part Crème de Cassis
1 part Crème de Banane
1½ parts Dark Rum
½ part Passion Fruit Nectar
2 parts Grapefruit Juice
1 part Orange Juice

Shake with ice and strain over ice.

Tropicetto

COLLINS GLASS

2 parts Amaretto
1 part Coffee Liqueur
1 part Heavy Cream
fill with Orange Juice

Shake with ice and pour.

Truman State Mouthwash

COLLINS GLASS

1 part Peppermint Schnapps
1 part Mountain Dew®
1 part Fruit Punch

Build over ice.

Try Soft and Hard

COLLINS GLASS

1 part Light Rum
1 part Jamaican Rum
1 part Passion Fruit Nectar
1½ parts Pineapple Juice
fill with Cherry Juice

Shake with ice and pour.

Tukky Tukky Wookiee

COLLINS GLASS

3 parts Irish Whiskey
fill with Mountain Dew®

Build over ice and stir.

Turbo

COLLINS GLASS

1 part Coconut Rum
½ part Passoã®
½ part Pisang Ambon® Liqueur
½ part Piña Colada Mix
fill with Pineapple Juice

Shake with ice and strain.

Turbocharger

COLLINS GLASS

2 parts Spiced Rum
2 parts Sweet & Sour Mix
fill with Orange Juice
½ part Grenadine

Build over ice.

Turbocharged

COLLINS GLASS

1 part Sambuca
1 part Vodka
1 part Blue Curaçao
2 parts Cream of Coconut
fill with Pineapple Juice

Build over ice and stir.

Turkish Cola

COLLINS GLASS

2 parts Jack Daniel's®
fill with Cola

Build over ice and stir.

Turlock Bulldog

COLLINS GLASS

1 part Irish Cream Liqueur
1 part Coffee Liqueur
fill with Root Beer

Build over ice and stir.

Turn Off

COLLINS GLASS

1 part Gin
1 part Apricot Brandy
fill with Apple Juice

Build over ice and stir.

Turquoise Blue

COLLINS GLASS

1½ parts Sweet & Sour Mix
1½ parts Rum
½ part Blue Curaçao
½ part Triple Sec
fill with Pineapple Juice

Shake with ice and pour.

Tutti Fruiti LifeSaver®

COLLINS GLASS

1½ parts Crème de Banane
1 part Pineapple Juice
1 part Orange Juice

Shake with ice and pour.

Twist and Shout

COLLINS GLASS

1 part Vodka
1 part Peach Schnapps
1½ parts Orange Juice
fill with Cola

Build over ice and stir.

Twisted Balls

COLLINS GLASS

2 parts Fireball Cinnamon Whiskey
fill with Twisted Tea

Build over ice and stir. Garnish with a Lemon Wheel.

Twisted Breeze

COLLINS GLASS

1 1/2 parts Citrus Vodka
1 1/2 parts Kiwi Schnapps
1 part Grapefruit Juice
1 part Cranberry Juice Cocktail

Shake with ice and pour.

Twisted Pink Lemonade

BEER MUG

1 1/2 parts Smirnoff® Citrus Twist
3/4 part Triple Sec
1 part Cranberry Juice Cocktail
1 part Sweet & Sour Mix

Shake with ice and pour.

Two Seater

COLLINS GLASS

2/3 part Vodka
1/2 part Apricot Brandy
splash Triple Sec
1 part Orange Juice
1 part Grapefruit Juice

Shake with ice and pour.

Umbongo

COLLINS GLASS

1 part Vodka
2 parts Passion Fruit Liqueur
1 part Orange Juice
1 part Passion Fruit Juice

Build over ice and stir.

Uncle Art

COLLINS GLASS

2 parts Lime Juice
1 part Vodka
dash Sugar
1 part Ginger Ale
1 part Lemon-Lime Soda

Build over ice and stir.

Uncle John

COLLINS GLASS

1 part Gin
splash Triple Sec
1 part Lemon Juice
fill with Orange Juice

Shake with ice and pour.

Uncle Vanya

COLLINS GLASS

1 1/2 parts Vodka
1/2 part Blackberry Liqueur
fill with Sweet & Sour Mix

Build over ice and stir.

The Unforgettable Fire

COLLINS GLASS

1 part Vodka
1/2 part Apricot Brandy
1/2 part Orange Liqueur
1 part Orange Juice
1 part Red Bull® Energy Drink

Build over ice and stir.

Urine Sample

COLLINS GLASS

2 parts Vodka
fill with Malt Liquor

Build in the glass with no ice.

Valldemossa

COLLINS GLASS

1 part Triple Sec
1 part Crème de Banane
1 part Apricot Brandy
splash Lime Juice
fill with Sparkling Water

Build over ice and stir.

Valletta

COLLINS GLASS

1 part Scotch
1/2 part Amaretto
1/2 part Coffee Brandy
1 part Pineapple Juice
1 part Apple Juice

Shake with ice and pour.

Vampire Juice
COLLINS GLASS

1 part Coconut Rum
1 part Blue Curaçao
1 part Bacardi® Limón Rum
fill with Orange Juice

Shake with ice and pour.

Van Gogh's Ear
COLLINS GLASS

2 parts Absinthe
1 part Grenadine
fill with Grapefruit Soda

Build over ice and stir.

Vanilla Rose
COLLINS GLASS

1½ parts Vanilla Vodka
fill with Cola
splash Tuaca®

Build over ice and stir.

Vegan Milk
COLLINS GLASS

1½ parts Irish Cream Liqueur
1 part Frangelico®
1 part Coffee Liqueur
fill with Milk

Shake with ice and pour.

Venus Flytrap
MARGARITA GLASS

2 parts Tequila
1 part Melon Liqueur
1 part Triple Sec
1 part Lime Juice

Shake with ice and pour.

Vertical Horizon
COLLINS GLASS

1 part Vodka
1 part Gin
1½ parts Orange Liqueur
½ part Lemon Juice
fill with Cranberry Juice Cocktail

Shake with ice and strain over ice.

Very Screwy Driver
COLLINS GLASS

1 part Vodka
½ part Silver Tequila
½ part Gin
fill with Orange Juice

Build over ice and stir.

Vaya con Dios
PILSNER GLASS

2 parts Vodka
1 part Pineapple-Orange Juice
1 part Strawberry Daiquiri Mix

Shake with ice and pour.

Vietnam Acid Flashback
HURRICANE GLASS

1 part Apple Liqueur
1 part 151-Proof Rum
1 part Jim Beam®
1 part Light Rum
1 part Vodka
1 part Yukon Jack®
1 part Triple Sec
splash Grenadine
fill with Orange Juice

Shake with ice and pour.

Vile Green Stuff
COLLINS GLASS

1 part Melon Liqueur
1 part Peach Schnapps
2 parts Seltzer
2 parts Orange Juice

Build over ice and stir.

Violet Symphony
COLLINS GLASS

1 part Parfait Amour
1 part Grenadine
fill with Sparkling Water

Build over ice and stir.

Virgin Bloody Mary

COLLINS GLASS

splash Tabasco® Sauce
dash Celery Salt
dash Pepper
2 splashes Worcestershire Sauce
fill with Tomato Juice

Shake with ice and pour.

Vitamin C

COLLINS GLASS

1½ parts Orange Vodka
1 part Sweet & Sour Mix
1 part Orange Juice

Shake with ice and pour.

Viva Mexico

COLLINS GLASS

½ part Tequila
½ part Crème de Cacao (White)
½ part Melon Liqueur
1 part Pineapple Juice
1 part Orange Juice

Build over ice and stir.

Vlad the Impaler

COLLINS GLASS

2 parts Vodka
⅔ part Peach Schnapps
fill with Cranberry Juice Cocktail

Shake with ice and pour.

Vodka 7

COLLINS GLASS

2 parts Vodka
½ part Lime Juice
fill with Lemon-Lime Soda

Build over ice and stir.

Vodka Collins

COLLINS GLASS

2 parts Vodka
½ part Lemon Juice
dash Powdered Sugar
fill with Seltzer

Shake all but Seltzer with ice and strain. Top with Seltzer.

Vodka Paralyzer

COLLINS GLASS

¾ part Vodka
¾ part Coffee Liqueur
2 parts Milk
fill with Cola

Build over ice and stir.

Vodka Smooth

COLLINS GLASS

1½ parts Vodka
½ part Triple Sec
fill with Orange Juice
splash Grenadine

Build over ice.

Vodka Storm

COLLINS GLASS

1 part Vodka
1 part Raspberry Liqueur
fill with Cola

Build over ice and stir.

Vodka with Wings

COLLINS GLASS

1½ parts Vodka
fill with Red Bull® Energy Drink

Build over ice and stir.

Vodka Yummy

COLLINS GLASS

2 parts Vodka
1 part Cinnamon Schnapps
fill with Apple Juice

Build over ice and stir.

Volcano

COLLINS GLASS

½ part Vodka
½ part Jim Beam®
½ part Gin
½ part Rum
½ part Tequila
1 part Orange Juice
1 part Pineapple Juice
splash Grenadine
splash Lemon-Lime Soda

Build over ice and stir.

Vomit Juice

BEER MUG

1 part Cinnamon Schnapps
½ part Irish Whiskey
½ part Southern Comfort®
½ part Silver Tequila
½ part Vodka
fill with Red Bull® Energy Drink

Build over ice and stir.

Voodoo Dew

COLLINS GLASS

2 parts 151-Proof Rum
fill with Mountain Dew®

Build over ice and stir.

Voodoo Sunrise

COLLINS GLASS

1 part Vodka
1 part Rum
2 parts Grenadine
fill with Orange Juice

Build over ice.

Vulgar Virgin

COLLINS GLASS

2 parts Bacardi® Limón Rum
fill with Pink Lemonade

Shake with ice and strain over ice.

Wagon Burner

COLLINS GLASS

3 parts Yukon Jack®
½ part Lime Juice
1 part Lemon-Lime Soda
1 part Cranberry Juice Cocktail
splash Sweet & Sour Mix

Build over ice and stir.

Waikiki

COLLINS GLASS

1 part Light Rum
1 part Passion Fruit Liqueur
1 part Campari®
fill with Orange Juice

Build over ice and stir.

Waikiki Tease

COLLINS GLASS

1 part Dark Rum
1 part Orange Juice
1 part Pineapple Juice

Shake with ice and pour.

Walking Home

COLLINS GLASS

½ part Vodka
½ part Rum
½ part Tequila
½ part Sloe Gin
1 part Lime Juice
splash Maraschino Cherry Juice

Shake with ice and pour.

Warrior Angel

COLLINS GLASS

1½ parts Crème de Banane
⅔ part Gin
splash Apricot Brandy
splash Lemon Juice
fill with Orange Juice

Shake with ice and pour.

Water Buffalo
COLLINS GLASS

1½ parts Vodka
½ part Grand Marnier®
fill with Orange Juice

Build over ice and stir.

Watermelon Crawl
COLLINS GLASS

1 part Southern Comfort
1 part Amaretto
1 part Watermelon Schnapps
4 parts Orange Juice
fill with Pineapple Juice

Build over ice and stir.

Watermelon Slice
HURRICANE GLASS

½ part Grenadine
½ part Rum
½ part Gin
½ part Triple Sec
½ part Vodka
1 part Orange Juice
1 part Cranberry Juice Cocktail
1 part Melon Liqueur

Build over ice and stir.

Wave Rider
COLLINS GLASS

1½ parts Coconut Rum
splash Cranberry Juice Cocktail
1 part Grapefruit Juice
1 part Pineapple Juice

Build over ice and stir.

Wave Runner
COLLINS GLASS

1 part Light Rum
1 part Cranberry Juice Cocktail
fill with Lemon-Lime Soda

Build over ice and stir.

Wayang Dream
COLLINS GLASS

1 part Cherry Brandy
1 part Pisang Ambon® Liqueur
fill with Lemonade

Build over ice and stir.

Wedding Anniversary
COLLINS GLASS

1 part Vodka
1 part Galliano®
1 part Campari®
fill with Orange Juice

Shake with ice and strain over ice.

Weekend Passion
COLLINS GLASS

1½ parts Gin
1 part Sweet & Sour Mix
1 part Passion Fruit Nectar
fill with Lemon-Lime Soda

Build over ice and stir.

Weightlessness
COLLINS GLASS

1½ parts Vodka
1 part Peach Schnapps
1 part Sweet & Sour Mix
1 part Cream of Coconut
1 part Cranberry Juice Cocktail

Shake with ice and strain over ice.

A Wellidian
COLLINS GLASS

1 part Apple Liqueur
1 part Jamaican Rum
1 part Kiwi Juice
fill with Orange Fanta® Soda

Build over ice and stir.

West Indies Yellowbird

COLLINS GLASS

2 parts Dark Rum
½ part Crème de Banane
½ part Galliano®
1 part Pineapple Juice
1 part Orange Juice

Shake with ice and strain over ice.

West Salem Cider

COLLINS GLASS

1 part Peach Brandy
1 part Vodka
fill with Apple Cider

Build over ice and stir.

Western Iced Tea

COLLINS GLASS

½ part Vanilla Vodka
½ part Gin
½ part Light Rum
½ part Cinnamon Schnapps
splash Cola
splash 151-Proof Rum

Build over ice.

Wet and Wild Lip Tickler

COLLINS GLASS

½ part 151-Proof Rum
1 part Melon Liqueur
½ part Amaretto
1 part Triple Sec
fill with Orange Juice

Build over ice.

Whale Orgasm

COLLINS GLASS

1 part Vodka
1 part Crème de Menthe (White)
2 parts Piña Colada Mix

Shake with ice and pour.

Whambam

COLLINS GLASS

¼ part Amaretto
¼ part Peach Schnapps
¼ part Coconut Rum
¼ part Butterscotch Schnapps
¼ part Cherry Liqueur
¼ part Irish Cream Liqueur
1 part Milk
1 part Orange Juice

Shake with ice and pour.

Whammy Kiss

COLLINS GLASS

½ part Crème de Banane
½ part Crème de Coconut
½ part Frangelico®
½ part Spiced Rum
fill with Cream

Shake with ice and pour.

Whiskey Collins

COLLINS GLASS

2 parts Whiskey
dash Powdered Sugar
½ part Lemon Juice
fill with Seltzer

Build over ice and stir.

White Jamaican

COLLINS GLASS

1½ parts Coconut Rum
¾ part Dark Rum
¾ part Crème de Cacao (White)
fill with Milk

Shake with ice and pour.

White Plush

COLLINS GLASS

2 parts Blended Scotch Whiskey
fill with Milk
dash Powdered Sugar

Shake with ice and strain over ice.

White Puerto Rican

COLLINS GLASS

1 part Rum
1 part Coffee Liqueur
fill with Milk

Shake with ice and strain over ice.

White Trash

COLLINS GLASS

2 parts Vodka
fill with Ginger Ale

Build over ice.

White Widow

COLLINS GLASS

1 part Coffee Liqueur
½ part Coconut Rum
fill with Cream

Shake with ice and strain over ice.

Whiting Sunset

COLLINS GLASS

2 parts Vodka
1 part Tequila
fill with Orange Juice
splash Grenadine

Build over ice and stir.

Why Santa Has a Naughty List

COLLINS GLASS

1 part Amaretto
1 part Banana Liqueur
1 part Gin
½ part Grenadine
fill with Lemon-Lime Soda

Build over ice and stir.

Wild Dog

COLLINS GLASS

1 part Dark Rum
1 part Southern Comfort®
fill with Pineapple Juice

Build over ice and stir.

Wild Fling

COLLINS GLASS

1½ parts Wild Berry Schnapps
2 parts Pineapple Juice
1 part Cranberry Juice Cocktail

Build over ice and stir.

Wile E. Coyote

COLLINS GLASS

1 part Dark Rum
1 part Banana Liqueur
1 part Blackberry Liqueur
1 part Pineapple Juice
1 part Cranberry Juice

Build over ice and stir.

Windward Isles

COLLINS GLASS

1½ parts Light Rum
½ part Kiwi Schnapps
splash Blue Curaçao
fill with Pineapple Juice

Shake with ice and strain over ice.

Winona Ryder

COLLINS GLASS

2 parts Gin
1 part Blue Curaçao
1 part Triple Sec
fill with Orange Juice

Build over ice and stir.

Winter Breeze

BEER MUG

1 part Crème de Cacao (White)
1 part Vanilla Liqueur
1 part Irish Cream Liqueur
fill with Milk

Build over ice and stir.

Wobbly Knee

COLLINS GLASS

1½ parts Gin
1 part Blue Curaçao
1 part Orange Juice
1 part Lemon-Lime Soda

Build over ice and stir.

Wolf Blood
COLLINS GLASS
1 part Raspberry Liqueur
1½ parts Lime Juice
fill with Grape Soda
Build over ice and stir.

Wonder Woman®
HURRICANE GLASS
1 part Melon Liqueur
1 part Peach Schnapps
1 part Pineapple Juice
2 parts Cranberry Juice Cocktail
3 parts Orange Juice
Build over ice.

Woody Woodpecker®
COLLINS GLASS
1½ parts Cachaça
½ part Galliano®
fill with Orange Juice
Shake with ice and strain over ice.

Wrath of Grapes
COLLINS GLASS
1¼ parts Dark Rum
1 part Sweet & Sour Mix
fill with Grape Juice (Red)
Build over ice and stir.

Wrong Number
COLLINS GLASS
1 part Gin
1 part Rum
1 part Vodka
1 part Orange Juice
1 part Pineapple Juice
Build over ice and stir.

Xixu
COLLINS GLASS
1½ parts Vodka
½ part Campari®
½ part Melon Liqueur
splash Crème de Menthe (White)
fill with Cola
Build over ice and stir.

Yeah Dude
COLLINS GLASS
1 part Vodka
1 part Southern Comfort®
splash Tabasco® Sauce
fill with Cola
Build over ice and stir.

Yellow Bird
COLLINS GLASS
1½ parts Rum
½ part Banana Liqueur
½ part Galliano®
1 part Grapefruit Juice
1 part Orange Juice
Shake with ice and pour.

Yellow Fingers
COLLINS GLASS
1 part Southern Comfort®
1 part Vodka
½ part Galliano®
1 part Orange Juice
1 part Lemon-Lime Soda
Build over ice and stir.

Yellow Fun
COLLINS GLASS
1 part Peach Schnapps
1 part Passion Fruit Liqueur
2 parts Pear Juice
2 parts Passion Fruit Juice
1 part Lemon Juice
1 part Mango Juice
Shake with ice and strain over ice.

Yellow Screwdriver
COLLINS GLASS
2 parts Vodka
fill with Lemonade
Build over ice and stir.

Yellow Star

COLLINS GLASS

1 part Dry Gin
1 part Crème de Banane
1 part Pastis
½ part Passion Fruit Nectar
fill with Orange Juice

Shake with ice and strain over ice.

Yesterday Sun

COLLINS GLASS

1 part Pineapple Juice
1 part Mandarine Napoléon® Liqueur
½ part Melon Liqueur
½ part Bourbon
½ part Crème de Banane
¼ part Grenadine

Build over ice and stir.

You Never Can Tell

COLLINS GLASS

1½ parts Rum
½ part Crème de Banane
fill with Orange Juice

Build over ice and stir.

Yukon Dew Me

COLLINS GLASS

2 parts Yukon Jack®
fill with Mountain Dew®

Build over ice and stir.

Zagoskin

COLLINS GLASS

½ part Sloe Gin
⅔ part Peach Schnapps
splash Guava Juice
splash Lychee Liqueur
fill with Pineapple Juice

Shake with ice and pour.

Zambeer

COLLINS GLASS

1½ parts Sambuca
fill with Root Beer

Build over ice and stir.

Zoot Liscious

COLLINS GLASS

1 part Rum
½ part Grenadine
fill with Cola

Build over ice.

Zula Lake Slammer

COLLINS GLASS

1 part Light Rum
1 part Sambuca
fill with Cola

Build over ice and stir.

Zulu

COLLINS GLASS

1 part Dark Rum
1 part Crème de Cacao (Dark)
½ part Crème de Banane
1 part Lime Juice
splash Grenadine
dash Pernod
fill with Cola

Shake all but Cola with ice and strain over ice. Fill with Cola.

Zyphar

COLLINS GLASS

2 parts Vodka
1 part Maraschino Cherry Juice
fill with Mountain Dew®

Build over ice and stir.

BEER DRINKS

Take the goodness of beer—ginger, root, or otherwise—and have fun with it.

101 Degrees in the Shade

COLLINS G-LASS

1 part Absolut® Peppar Vodka
1 part Beer
1 part Tomato Juice
Tabasco® Sauce

Build over ice and stir. Add Tabasco® to taste.

3-Week Vacation

HIGHBALL GLASS

1 part Raspberry Liqueur
½ part Cranberry Juice Cocktail
½ part Pineapple Juice
fill with Beer

Build over ice and stir.

666

COLLINS GLASS

1 part Banana Liqueur
1 part Blue Curaçao
fill with Beer

Build over ice and stir.

Aaron

BEER MUG

1 part Beer
1 part Lemonade

Build in the mug with no ice.

Abre Piernas

COLLINS GLASS

2 parts Lemon-Lime Soda
1 part Melon Liqueur
1 part Tequila
1 part White Wine
fill with Beer

Build over ice and stir.

Absolut® Beast

1 part Absolut® Citron Vodka
1 can Beer

Open the can of Beer, drink a little, and pour in the Vodka.

Adam's Lunch Box

BEER MUG

1½ parts Amaretto
2 parts Beer
3 parts Orange Juice

Build in the glass with no ice.

Aespec

BEER MUG

1 part Beer
1 part Gin

Build in the glass with no ice.

AJ's Bubbling Brew

BEER MUG

1 part Tequila
1 part Southern Comfort®
1 part 100-Proof Peppermint Schnapps
1 part 151-Proof Rum
fill with Beer

Carefully pour the Tequila, Southern Comfort®, Peppermint Schnapps, and Rum into the glass and light on fire. Quickly add the Beer, stir, and watch it bubble and froth.

Ambassador

HIGHBALL GLASS

1½ parts Rum
1 part Limeade
1 part Ginger Beer

Build over ice and stir.

Anus on Fire

BEER MUG

1 part Jack Daniel's®
1 part Sloe Gin
1 part Southern Comfort®
1 part Jägermeister®
fill with Beer

Build over ice and stir.

Apple Cider Slider

BEER MUG

1 part Sour Apple Schnapps
fill with Beer

Pour the Schnapps in a Beer mug and fill with Beer.

Asphalt

BEER MUG

1½ parts Blackberry Liqueur
1 part Chocolate Syrup
fill with Dark Beer

Build in the glass with no ice.

Bad-Ass Brew

COLLINS GLASS

1 part Vodka
1½ parts Beer
2 parts Tomato Juice
dash Salt

Build in the glass with no ice.

Baked Apple

BEER MUG

1 part Cinnamon Schnapps
fill with Hard Apple Cider

Pour the Schnapps into the mug first, then add the Cider. Serve cold.

Baltimore Zoo

HIGHBALL GLASS

1 part Light Rum
1 part Gin
1 part Vodka
½ part Triple Sec
1 part Sweet & Sour Mix
splash Grenadine
splash Beer

Build over ice and stir.

BB's Margarita

PITCHER

1 part Beer
1 part Tequila Reposado
1 part Frozen Limeade Concentrate
3 splashes Margarita Mix

Combine all ingredients in a blender with ice. Blend until smooth.

Beer Bloody Mary

BEER MUG

splash Worcestershire Sauce
dash Salt
dash Pepper
splash Lime Juice
fill with Beer

Build in the glass with no ice.

Beer Breezer

BEER MUG

2 parts Vodka
splash Tabasco® Sauce
dash Celery Salt
fill with Beer

Build in the glass with no ice.

Beer Buster

BEER MUG

1½ parts 100-Proof Vodka
fill with Beer
splash Tabasco® Sauce

Build in the glass with no ice.

Beer Garden

BEER MUG

1 part Vodka
1 part Triple Sec
1 part Lychee Liqueur
1 part Vanilla Liqueur
fill with Beer

Shake all but Beer with ice and strain. Top with Beer.

Beer Panache

COLLINS GLASS

splash Simple Syrup
1 part Lemon-Lime Soda
1 part Beer

Build in the glass with no ice.

Beer-a-Lade

BEER MUG

1 part Beer
1 part Lemon-Lime Gatorade®
splash Maple Syrup
splash Tabasco® Sauce

Build in the glass with no ice and stir.

Beeraquirilla

MARGARITA GLASS

½ part Tequila
½ part Light Rum
4 parts Beer
2 parts Strawberry Daiquiri Mix
2 parts Margarita Mix

Combine all ingredients in a blender with ice. Blend until smooth.

Beerdriver

BEER MUG

2 parts Vodka
1 part Orange Juice
1 part Beer

Build in the glass with no ice.

Belgian Waffle

BEER MUG

1 part Guinness Stout
1 part Belgian Ale

Build in a beer mug.

Big Belly

COLLINS GLASS

1 part Crème de Cassis
½ part Blackberry Liqueur
½ part Lemon Juice
fill with Beer

Shake all but Beer with ice and strain into a glass. Top with Beer.

Bionic Beaver

BEER MUG

1 part Vodka
1 part Southern Comfort®
1 part Sloe Gin
1 part Gin
splash Grenadine
fill with Beer

Build over ice and stir.

Black & Tan

BEER MUG

1 part Bass® Pale Ale
1 part Guinness® Stout

Layer in a beer mug or pint glass.

Black and Brown

BEER MUG

1 part Root Beer
1 part Guinness® Stout

Layer in a beer mug or pint glass.

Black Beerd

BEER MUG

1 part Blackberry Liqueur
fill with Beer

Build in the glass with no ice.

Black Cow

BEER MUG

2 scoops Vanilla Ice Cream
1 part Dark Rum
fill with Root Beer

Build in the glass with no ice.

Black Velvet

BEER MUG

1 part Rum
fill with Lager

Build in the glass with no ice.

Black Velvet (England)

BEER MUG

1 part Guinness® Stout
1 part Hard Apple Cider

Build in the glass with no ice.

Bloody Brew

COLLINS GLASS

1½ parts Vodka
1 part Beer
1 part Tomato Juice
dash Salt

Build over ice and stir.

Bloody Mary's White Trash Lover

BEER MUG

1 part Tomato Juice
1 part Beer
dash Salt
¼ part Lemon Juice

Build over ice and stir.

Blue Bear

BEER MUG

1 part Blue Curaçao
fill with Beer

Build in the glass with no ice.

Bluebeerd

BEER MUG

1 part Light Rum
fill with Beer
splash Blue Curaçao

Build in the glass with no ice.

British Snakebite

BEER MUG

1 part Beer
1 part Hard Cider

Build in the glass with no ice.

Brooklyn Zoo

COLLINS GLASS

1 part Rum
1 part Vodka
1 part Gin
splash Pineapple Juice
splash Raspberry Liqueur
splash Sweet & Sour Mix
fill with Beer

Build over ice and stir.

Brutus

COLLINS GLASS

1 part Beer
2 parts Clamato® Juice
dash Celery Salt

Build over ice and stir.

Butter Beer

BEER MUG

1 part Butterscotch Schnapps
fill with Beer

Build in the glass with no ice.

Clara

HIGHBALL GLASS

1 part Beer
1 part Lemon-Lime Soda

Build over ice and stir.

Concussion

ROCKS GLASS

1 part Beer
1 part Grain Alcohol
1 part Jack Daniel's®
dash Sugar

Shake with ice and strain.

Cranberry

BEER MUG

1 part Cranberry Juice Cocktail
fill with Beer

Build in the glass with no ice.

Cream de Spooge

BEER MUG

1 part Beer
1 part Cream Soda

Build in the glass with no ice.

Dark & Stormy

ROCKS GLASS

2 parts Gosling's Black Seal® Rum
fill with Ginger Beer

Build over ice.

Dead Penis

BEER MUG

1 part Light Rum
1 part Tequila
½ part Scotch
½ part Dark Rum
½ part Vodka
fill with Stout

Build in the glass with no ice.

Death Star

BEER MUG

1 part Irish Cream Liqueur
1½ parts Drambuie®
1 part Gin
2 parts Jägermeister®
fill with Beer
splash Crème de Menthe (Green)

Build in the glass with no ice.

Euthanasia

BEER MUG

1 part Southern Comfort®
1 part Jack Daniel's®
fill with Beer

Build in the glass with no ice.

The Field Camp

HURRICANE GLASS

1 part Blue Curaçao
1 part Whiskey
1 part Cola
fill with Beer

Build over ice and stir.

Flaming Firebeer

BEER MUG

1 part Amaretto
1 part Fireball Cinnamon Whiskey
1 pint Beer

Fill a shot glass with Amaretto and Rum, and a beer mug with beer. Light the Rum with a match or lighter and drop the flaming shot into the Beer. Drink quickly.

Flaming Orgasm

BEER MUG

1 shot 151-Proof Rum
Beer

Fill a shot glass with Rum and a beer mug with Beer. Light the Rum with a match or lighter and drop it into the Beer. Drink quickly.

A Furlong Too Late

HIGHBALL GLASS

1 part Light Rum
2 parts Ginger Beer

Build over ice and stir. Garnish with a Lemon Twist.

German Car Bomb

BEER MUG

1 shot Jägermeister®
Heineken®

Drop a shot of Jägermeister® into a beer mug filled with Heineken®. Drink quickly.

Ginger Mule

COLLINS GLASS

1½ parts Citrus Vodka
splash Parfait Amour
fill with Ginger Beer
splash Lime Juice

Build over ice and stir.

Graveyard

BEER MUG

1 part Triple Sec
1 part Light Rum
1 part Vodka
1 part Gin
1 part Tequila
1 part Scotch
2 parts Lager
2 parts Stout

Shake all the liquor with ice and strain. Top with Lager and Stout.

Graveyard Light

BEER MUG

1 part Triple Sec
1 part Light Rum
1 part Vodka
1 part Gin
1 part Tequila
2 parts Lager
2 parts Stout

Shake all the liquor with ice and strain. Top with Lager and Stout.

Green Goblin

BEER MUG

1 part Hard Apple Cider
1 part Lager
splash Blue Curaçao

Build over ice and stir.

Guinness® Shandy

BEER MUG

1 part Guinness® Stout
1 part Lemonade

Build in the glass with no ice.

Hard Eight

COLLINS GLASS

1½ parts Dark Rum
½ part Lime Juice
2 dashes Bitters
fill with Ginger Beer

Build over ice and stir.

Head Fake Jake

COUPETTE GLASS

1½ parts Beer
1 part Applejack
½ part Melon Liqueur
½ part Sweet & Sour Mix
2 scoops Ice Cream

Combine all ingredients in a blender with ice. Blend until smooth.

Hop, Skip, and Go Naked

COLLINS GLASS

1 part Vodka
1 part Gin
½ part Lime Juice
fill with Beer

Build over ice and stir.

Horse Jizz

BEER MUG

1 part Beer
1 part Milk

Build in the glass with no ice.

Jägerbeer Bomb

BEER MUG

1 shot Jägermeister®
Draft Beer

Drop a shot of Jägermeister® into a mug full of Beer. Drink quickly.

Jalisco Cooler

COLLINS GLASS

1½ parts Tequila Reposado
½ part Lime Juice
½ part Vanilla Liqueur
fill with Beer

Build over ice and stir.

Jamaican Mule

COLLINS GLASS

2 parts Light Rum
1 part Lime Juice
½ part Ginger Liqueur
splash 151-Proof Rum
fill with Ginger Beer

Build over ice and stir.

Järngrogg

BEER MUG

2 parts Vodka
fill with Beer

Build in the glass with no ice.

Lager & Lime

BEER MUG

fill with Lager
splash Lime Juice

Build in the glass with no ice.

Li'l Amick

BEER MUG

1 part Gin
½ part Lime Juice
fill with Beer

Build over ice.

Mead

BEER MUG

1½ parts Irish Mist®
fill with Beer

Build in the glass with no ice.

Mexican Iced Tea

COCKTAIL GLASS

1½ parts Tequila
fill with Beer
splash Lime Juice

Build in the glass with no ice.

Michelada

COLLINS GLASS

1 part Lemon Juice
2 splashes Worcestershire Sauce
splash Soy Sauce
splash Tabasco® Sauce
dash Salt
fill with Beer

Build over ice and stir.

Miner's Lung

BEER MUG

2 parts Vodka
fill with Guinness® Stout

Build in the glass with no ice.

Monaco

BEER MUG

1 part Beer
1 part Lemonade
splash Grenadine

Build in the glass with no ice.

Moscow Mule

HIGHBALL GLASS

1½ parts Vodka
1 part Lime Juice
fill with Ginger Beer

Build over ice. Garnish with a Lime Wedge.

Mosquito

BEER MUG

1½ parts Raspberry Liqueur
1 part Hard Cider
1 part Beer

Build in the glass with no ice.

Mule

HIGHBALL GLASS

1¼ parts Vodka
fill with Ginger Beer
splash Lime Juice

Build over ice and stir.

Musegg

COLLINS GLASS

1 part Orange Juice
1 part Apricot Brandy
1 part Triple Sec
fill with Beer

Build over ice and stir.

North Coast Dr. Pepper®

BEER MUG

1 part Amaretto
1 part Root Beer Schnapps
1 part 151-Proof Rum
fill with Beer

Pour the Amaretto, Schnapps, and Rum into a shot glass. Fill a beer mug ¾ full of Beer. Light the shot with a match or lighter and drop it into the Beer. Drink quickly.

Nuthugger

BEER MUG

1 part 151-Proof Rum
1 part Vodka
1 part Lime Juice
fill with Beer

Build in the glass with no ice.

Oyster Shooter

ROCKS GLASS

2 splashes Tabasco® Sauce
splash Horseradish
splash Cocktail Sauce
fill with Beer
1 Raw Oyster

Mix all but the Oyster in a rocks glass. Drop in the Oyster and drink.

Ozone

ROCKS GLASS

1½ parts Amaretto
splash Beer
fill with Sweet & Sour Mix
splash Lemon-Lime Soda

Build over ice and stir.

Pickled Beer

BEER MUG

1 part Pickle Juice
2 parts Beer

Build in the glass with no ice.

Pink Kangaroo

BEER MUG

1 part Tequila
2 parts Vodka
2 parts Hard Apple Cider
1 part Cranberry Juice Cocktail
1 part Orange Juice

Build over ice and stir.

Pond Water

BEER MUG

1 part Beer
1 part Cola
splash Blue Curaçao

Build in the glass with no ice.

Poolside Pleasure

COLLINS GLASSES

1 can Beer
6 parts Light Rum
1 can Frozen Limeade Concentrate

Combine in a pitcher and serve over ice.

Poor Man's Mimosa

HIGHBALL GLASS

1 part Beer
1 part Orange Juice

Build over ice and stir.

Pukemeister General

BEER MUG

1 part Tequila
1 part Rumple Minze®
1 part Hard Apple Cider
1 part Beer

Build in the glass with no ice.

Purple Velvet

BEER MUG

2 parts Port
fill with Guinness® Stout

Build in the glass with no ice.

Rabid Pitbull

COLLINS GLASS

2 parts Jack Daniel's®
2 dashes Bitters
1 part Lemon-Lime Soda
1 part Beer

Build over ice and stir.

Red Horn

BEER MUG

1 part RedRum®
fill with Hard Apple Cider

Build in the glass with no ice.

Red Eye

BEER MUG

3/4 pint Beer
1 part Vodka
fill with Tomato Juice

Build in a beer mug. Some like to add an egg as well.

Red Eye

COLLINS GLASS

1 part Rye Whiskey
1 part Beer
1 part Cola

Build over ice and stir.

Refajo

HIGHBALL GLASS

1 part Beer
1 part Cola

Build over ice and stir.

Rude Awakening

BEER MUG

1 part Jack Daniel's®
1 part Vodka
1 part Cinnamon Schnapps
1 part Orange Juice
1 part Beer

Build over ice and stir.

Schnider

BEER MUG

2 parts Peach Schnapps
fill with Hard Cider

Build over ice and stir.

Shady

BEER MUG

1 part Beer
1 part Lemonade

Build in the glass with no ice.

Shady Grove

HIGHBALL GLASS

1½ parts Gin
Juice of half a Lemon
dash Powdered Sugar
fill with Ginger Beer

Build over ice and stir.

Shandy

BEER MUG

1 part Beer
1 part Ginger Ale

Build in the glass with no ice.

Shanty

COLLINS GLASS

1 part Lemon-Lime Soda
1 part Beer

Build in the glass with no ice.

Sip and Get Funky

COLLINS GLASS

1 part Gin
½ part Grenadine
½ part Lemon-Lime Soda
fill with Beer

Build over ice and stir.

Skip and Go Naked

HIGHBALL GLASS

1 part Gin
1 part Apricot Brandy
1 part Cherry Juice
½ part Sweet & Sour Mix
fill with Beer

Build over ice and stir.

Skip, Run, and Go Naked

COLLINS GLASS

2 parts Tequila
dash Bitters
fill with Beer

Build over ice and stir.

Sloppy Seconds

BEER MUG

1 part Rum
splash Lime Juice
fill with Beer

Build in the glass with no ice.

Snakebite

BEER MUG

1 part Lager
1 part Hard Cider

Build in the glass with no ice.

Snake Venom

BEER MUG

1 part Lager
1 part Hard Apple Cider
1 part Pernod®

Build in the glass with no ice.

St. Paddy's Day Beer

HURRICANE GLASS

2 parts Melon Liqueur
fill with Beer

Build in the glass with no ice.

Stiff Pounder

BEER MUG

1 part Jägermeister®
fill with Beer

Build in the glass with no ice.

Stone Cold Stunner

COLLINS GLASS

1 part Vodka
1 part Beer
fill with Grapefruit Juice

Build over ice and stir.

Strip and Go Naked

COLLINS GLASS

2 parts Vodka
1 part Beer
1 part Lemonade

Build over ice and stir.

Sweaty Mexican

BEER MUG

1½ parts Tequila
splash 151-Proof Rum
fill with Beer

Build in the glass with no ice.

Toolbox Puker

BEER MUG

1 part Rum
1 part Vodka
fill with Beer

Build in the glass with no ice.

Tractor

BEER MUG

1 part Tia Maria®
1 part Guinness® Stout
1 part Hard Apple Cider

Build in the glass with no ice.

Tropical Fart

COLLINS GLASS

1 part Coconut Rum
1 part Peach Schnapps
1 part Orange Juice
1 part Pineapple Juice
splash Beer

Build over ice and stir.

Urine Sample with Gonorrhea

HIGHBALL GLASS

1 part Tequila
1 part Beer
splashes Tabasco® Sauce

Build in the glass with no ice.

V8® Beer

BEER MUG

2 parts Beer
1 part V8® Vegetable Juice Blend

Build in the glass with no ice.

Valley

COLLINS GLASS

2 parts Dark Rum
3 parts Apple Juice
1 part Beer

Build over ice and stir.

Vancouver in the Morning

COLLINS GLASS

1 part Vodka
1 part Pink Lemonade
1 part Beer

Shake with ice and strain over ice.

Wild Brew Yonder

HIGHBALL GLASS

1 part Vodka
½ part Blue Curaçao
fill with Beer

Build in the glass with no ice.

Yellow

BEER MUG

½ part Lemon Juice
fill with Beer

Build in the glass with no ice.

BOMBS, BOMBERS & DEPTH CHARGES

It all started with the Boilermaker: Drop a shot of whiskey into a glass of beer and chug it. Energy drinks such as Red Bull later replaced the beer. Whether you know them as bombs, bombers, or depth charges, here's a collection of drinks where you drop a shot into a glass of something else before downing it.

1.21 Gigawatts

SHOT GLASS, PINT GLASS

1 part Hpnotiq
1 part Raspberry Vodka
splash Grenadine
8 parts Red Bull Energy Drink

Layer the Hypnptiq, Vodka, and Grenadine in a shot glass. Drop the shot into the pint glass of Red Bull. Drink quickly.

110 in the Shade

SHOT GLASS, BEER MUG

1 shot Tequila
fill with Lager

Fill a shot glass with Tequila. Fill a beer mug with Lager. Drop the shot into the Beer and drink quickly.

Angry Balls

SHOT GLASS, PINT GLASS

1½ parts Fireball Cinnamon Whiskey
12 parts Angry Orchard Crisp Apple Hard Cider

Drop the shot into the pint glass of Cider and drink quickly.

Belfast Car Bomb

SHOT GLASS

1 pint Guinness® Stout
1 part Irish Cream Liqueur
1 part Scotch

Drop a shot glass filled with scotch into a pint of Guiness and float the Irish Cream Liqueur on top.

Beton

SHOT GLASS, BEER MUG

1 part Scotch
1 part Vodka
1 pint Beer

Place the Scotch and Vodka in a shot glass and drop it into the Beer. Drink quickly.

Boilermaker

SHOT GLASS, BEER MUG

1 shot Whiskey
Beer

Fill shot glass with Whiskey. Drop full shot into mug of Beer and drink immediately.

Bomber

SHOT GLASS, COLLINS GLASS

1 shot Tequila
1 pint Beer

Fill a shot glass with Tequila. Fill a Collins glass with Beer. Drop the shot into the Beer and drink quickly.

Burning Busch

SHOT GLASS, PINT GLASS

1½ parts Fireball Cinnamon Whiskey
8 parts Busch Beer

Drop the shot into the pint glass of Beer and drink quickly.

Car Bomb

SHOT GLASS, BEER MUG

1 part Irish Whiskey
1 part Irish Cream Liqueur
½ pint Guinness® Stout

Layer the Whiskey and Irish Cream in a shot glass. Drop the shot into the Beer and drink quickly.

Christmas Bomb

SHOT GLASS, PINT GLASS

1½ parts RumChata
8 parts Christmas Ale (Finger Lakes Brewing)

Drop the shot into the pint glass of Ale and drink quickly.

Crown the King

SHOT GLASS, PINT GLASS

1½ parts Crown Royal Canadian Whisky
1 pint Budweiser Beer

Drop the shot into the pint glass of Beer and drink quickly.

Dive Bomber

SHOT GLASS, BEER MUG

1 shot Amaretto
1 part Root Beer Schnapps
1 pint Beer

Fill shot glass with Amaretto and Root Beer Schnapps. Drop the shot into the Beer and drink quickly.

Dr. Pepper®

SHOT GLASS, BEER MUG

3 parts Amaretto
1 part 151-Proof Rum
1 pint Lager Beer

Fill a shot glass with Amaretto and 151-Proof Rum. Drop the shot into the Beer and drink quickly.

Dr. Pepper® #2

SHOT GLASS, BEER MUG

1 part 151-Proof Rum
1 part Amaretto
1 pint Beer

Fill a shot glass with 151-Proof Rum and Amaretto. Drop the shot into the Beer and drink quickly.

Drunk Driver

SHOT GLASS, BEER MUG

1 shot Jägermeister®
1 pint Guinness® Stout

Fill a shot glass with Jägermeister® and beer mug with Beer. Drop the shot into the Beer and drink quickly.

Flaming Cornholio

SHOT GLASS, BEER MUG

1 part Jack Daniel's®
4 parts Orange Juice
1 shot Cinnamon Schnapps

Combine Jack Daniel's® and Orange Juice in a beer mug. Drop a shot of Cinnamon Schnapps into the glass and drink quickly.

Flaming Depth Charge

SHOT GLASS, BEER MUG

1 shot 151-Proof Rum
Beer

Fill a beer mug with Beer and a shot glass with 151-Proof Rum. Light the Rum and drop the shot into the beer. Drink quickly.

Flaming Dr. Pepper®

SHOT GLASS, BEER MUG

3 parts Raspberry Liqueur
1 part 151-Proof Rum
Beer

Combine the Raspberry Liqueur and the 151-Proof Rum in a shot glass. Light the Rum and drop the shot into the Beer. Drink quickly.

Flaming Dr. Pepper® #2

SHOT GLASS, BEER MUG

3 parts Amaretto
1 part 151-Proof Rum
Beer

Combine the Amaretto and the 151-Proof Rum in a shot glass. Light the Rum and drop the shot into the Beer. Drink quickly.

Fuzzy Iranian

SHOT GLASS, BEER MUG

1 shot Peach Schnapps
Beer

Fill a shot glass with Peach Schnapps and a beer mug with Beer. Drop the shot into the Beer and drink quickly.

Green Bastard

SHOT GLASS, BEER MUG

1 part Sour Apple Schnapps
1 part Blue Curaçao
Beer

Combine Apple Schnapps and Blue Curaçao in a shot glass. Drop the shot into a pint of Beer and drink quickly.

Hairball

SHOT GLASS, COLLINS GLASS

1 shot Irish Whiskey
1 part Hard Apple Cider
1 part Guinness® Stout

Fill a shot glass with Irish Whiskey. Fill a Collins glass with Hard Cider and Guinness®. Drop the shot into the glass and drink quickly.

Irish Car Bomb

SHOT GLASS, BEER MUG

1 pint Guinness® Stout
1 part Irish Whiskey
1 part Coffee Liqueur
1 part Irish Cream Liqueur

Fill a mug with Guinness® and a shot glass with the liqueurs. Drop the shot into the Beer and drink quickly.

Lunch Box

SHOT GLASS, BEER MUG

1 part Beer
1 part Orange Juice
1 shot Amaretto

Fill a beer mug with Beer and Orange Juice. Fill a shot glass with Amaretto. Drop the shot into the beer mug and drink quickly.

Melon Squishy

SHOT GLASS, COLLINS GLASS

1 shot Melon Liqueur
1 part Pineapple Juice
1 part Orange Juice

Fill a shot glass with Melon Liqueur and a beer mug with Pineapple Juice and Orange Juice. Drop the shot into the mug and drink quickly.

Mexican Hillbilly

SHOT GLASS, BEER MUG

1 shot Jack Daniel's®
Corona® Beer

Fill a shot glass with Jack Daniel's®. Fill a beer mug with Corona®. Drop the shot into the Beer and drink quickly.

Minty Cum Shot

SHOT GLASS, BEER MUG

1 shot Peppermint Schnapps
fill with Mountain Dew®

Fill a shot glass with Peppermint Schnapps. Fill a beer mug with Mountain Dew®. Drop the shot into the mug and drink quickly.

Mountain Dew®

SHOT GLASS, BEER MUG

1 shot Melon Liqueur
1 part Beer
1 part Lemon-Lime Soda

Fill a shot glass with Melon Liqueur. Fill a beer mug with Beer and Lemon-Lime Soda. Drop the shot into the mug and drink quickly.

Orange Smarties

SHOT GLASS, PINT GLASS

3/4 part Jägermeister
3/4 part Orange Vodka
8 parts Red Bull Energy Drink

Combine the Jägermeister and Orange Vodka in a shot glass and drop it into the pint glass of Red Bull. Drink quickly.

Pap Smear

SHOT GLASS, BEER MUG

1 shot Smirnoff® Vodka
Pabst® Blue Ribbon Beer

Fill a shot glass with chilled Vodka. Fill a beer mug with Beer. Drop the shot into the Beer and drink quickly.

Peppermint Depth Charge

SHOT GLASS, BEER MUG

1 shot Peppermint Schnapps
Beer

Fill a shot glass with Peppermint Schnapps. Fill a beer mug with Beer. Drop the shot into the Beer and drink quickly.

Pumpkin Pie Splash

SHOT GLASS, PINT GLASS

1½ parts RumChata
8 parts Pumpkin Beer

Drop the shot into a the pint glass of beer and drink quickly.

Root Beer Barrel

SHOT GLASS, BEER MUG

1 shot Dark Rum
Root Beer

Fill a shot glass with Dark Rum. Fill a beer mug with Root Beer. Drop the shot into the Root Beer and drink quickly.

Russian Boilermaker

SHOT GLASS, BEER MUG

1 shot Vodka
Beer

Fill a shot glass with chilled Vodka. Fill a beer mug with Beer. Drop the shot into the Beer and drink quickly.

Sake Bomb

SHOT GLASS, BEER MUG

1 shot Sake
Beer

Fill a shot glass with Sake. Fill a beer mug with Beer. Drop the shot into the Beer and drink quickly.

Sambuca Depth Charge

SHOT GLASS, BEER MUG

1 shot Sambuca
Beer

Fill a shot glass with Sambuca. Fill a beer mug with Beer. Drop the shot into the Beer and drink quickly.

Samuel Jackson

SHOT GLASS, BEER MUG

1 shot 151-Proof Rum
Samuel Adams® Beer

Fill a shot glass with 151-Proof Rum. Fill a beer mug with Beer. Drop the shot into the Beer and drink quickly.

School Bus

SHOT GLASS, BEER MUG

1 shot Amaretto
1 part Beer
1 part Orange Juice

Fill a shot glass with chilled Amaretto. Combine the Beer and the Orange Juice in a beer mug. Drop the shot into the mug and drink quickly.

Sergeant Pepper

SHOT GLASS, BEER MUG

1 part Amaretto
1 part Beer
1 part Cola

Fill a shot glass with Amaretto. Fill a beer mug with Beer and Cola. Drop the shot into the mug and drink quickly.

Shoot the Root

SHOT GLASS, BEER MUG

1 shot Root Beer Schnapps
Beer

Fill a shot glass with Root Beer Schnapps. Fill a beer mug with Beer. Drop the shot into the Beer and drink quickly.

Strawberry

SHOT GLASS, BEER MUG

1 shot Strawberry Liqueur
Beer

Fill a shot glass with Strawberry Liqueur and a beer mug with Beer. Drop the shot into the Beer and drink quickly.

Strawberry #2

SHOT GLASS, BEER MUG

1 shot Strawberry Vodka
Beer

Fill a shot glass with Strawberry Liqueur and a beer mug with Beer. Drop the shot into the Beer and drink quickly.

Submarine

SHOT GLASS, BEER MUG

1 shot Jägermeister®
Beer

Fill a shot glass with Jägermeister. Fill a beer mug with Beer. Drop the shot into the Beer and drink quickly.

Tennessee Boilermaker

SHOT GLASS, BEER MUG

1 shot Whiskey
Beer

Fill a shot glass with Whiskey and a beer mug with Beer. Drop the shot into the Beer and drink quickly.

Tiajuana Car Bomb

SHOT GLASS, BEER MUG

1 shot Tequila
Beer

Fill a shot glass with Tequila and a beer mug with Beer. Drop the shot into the Beer and drink quickly.

Triple H

SHOT GLASS, BEER MUG

1 part Hennessy®
1 part Hpnotiq®
Heineken®

Fill a shot glass with Hennesy® and Hpnotiq® and a beer mug with Heineken®. Drop the shot into the Beer and drink quickly.

Whore in a Bucket

SHOT GLASS, BEER MUG

1 shot Southern Comfort®
Cranberry Juice Cocktail

Fill a shot glass with Southern Comfort® and a beer mug with Cranberry Juice. Drop the shot into the Cranberry Juice and drink quickly.

Wildfire

SHOT GLASS, PINT GLASS

½ part Tequila
½ part Peppermint Schnapps
½ part Tabasco Sauce
8 parts Beer

Fill a shot glass with Tequila, Peppermint Schnapps, and Tabasco Sauce. Drop the shot into the pint glass of beer and drink quickly.

Wisconsin Lunch Box

SHOT GLASS, BEER MUG

1 shot Amaretto
1 part Orange Juice
2 parts Beer

Fill a shot glass with Amaretto and a beer mug with Orange Juice and Beer. Drop the shot into the Beer and drink quickly.

CHAMPAGNE DRINKS

Combine the elegance of Champagne or other sparkling wine–including Prosecco or Cava–with a rotating combination of juices and liqueurs, and you'll have a collection of effervescent libations sure to please even the most discerning palate.

7 Miles

CHAMPAGNE FLUTE

1 part Pear Juice
1 part Grenadine
dash Orange Bitters
fill with Champagne

Shake all but Champange with ice and strain. Top with ice-cold Champagne.

'78 Camaro

HIGHBALL GLASS

1 part Yukon Jack®
1 part Rum
1 part Apricot Brandy
1½ parts Pineapple Juice
fill with Champagne

Shake all but Champagne with ice and strain. Fill with Champagne.

Absent-Minded

COCKTAIL GLASS

1 part Peach Schnapps
1 part Absinthe
1 part Champagne
1 part Orange Juice
splash Raspberry Juice

Shake with ice and strain.

Absinthe Groseille

COCKTAIL GLASS

1 part Absinthe
2/3 part Cointreau®
2 part Champagne
2/3 part Black Currant Juice
splash Crème de Cassis

Shake with ice and strain.

Absinth Kir

HIGHBALL GLASS

splash Crème de Cassis
splash Absinthe
fill with Champagne

Build over ice and stir.

Absolut® Champagne

COLLINS GLASS

1 part Vodka
splash Cream
fill with Champagne

Build in the glass with no ice.

Absolution

CHAMPAGNE FLUTE

1 part Vodka
fill with Champagne

Build in the glass with no ice.

Adol-Mari

CHAMPAGNE FLUTE

½ part Vodka
½ part Rum
½ part Apricot Brandy
½ part Campari®
½ part Pineapple Juice
fill with Champagne

Build in the glass with no ice.

Adria Look

CHAMPAGNE FLUTE

1 part Blue Curaçao
1 part Dry Gin
fill with Champagne

Build in the glass with no ice.

Adria Wixcey

CHAMPAGNE FLUTE

¾ parts Dry Vermouth
½ tbsp sugar
fill with Champagne

Build in the glass with no ice.

Always Together

CHAMPAGNE FLUTE

1 part Amaretto
1 part Brandy
fill with Champagne

Build in the glass with no ice.

Ambrosia

HIGHBALL GLASS

1 part Applejack
1 part Brandy
splash Triple Sec
splash Lemon Juice
fill with Champagne

Shake all but Champagne with ice and strain over ice. Top with Champagne.

American Flyer

CHAMPAGNE FLUTE

2 parts Light Rum
1 part Lime Juice
dash Sugar
fill with Champagne

Shake all but Champagne with ice. Strain and top with Champagne.

American Glory

HIGHBALL GLASS

1 part Sparkling Wine
1 part Orange Juice
1 part Lemonade

Build over ice.

American Rose

CHAMPAGNE FLUTE

1 part Cognac
½ part Peach Puree
splash Grenadine
splash Pastis
fill with Champagne

Shake all but Champagne with ice. Strain and top with Champagne.

American Rose #2

CHAMPAGNE FLUTE

1½ parts Brandy
½ part Grenadine
½ part Pastis
fill with Champagne

Shake all but Champagne with ice. Strain and top with Champagne.

Amy Jane

COLLINS GLASS

½ part Vodka
1 part Blue Curaçao
1 part Melon Liqueur
2 parts Pineapple Juice
fill with Champagne

Build over ice and stir.

Anadulsa

HIGHBALL GLASS

1 part Cherry Brandy
2½ parts Champagne
1 part Cranberry Juice Cocktail

Build over ice and stir.

Apricot Velvet

HIGHBALL GLASS

1 part Vodka
1 part Apricot Brandy
fill with Champagne

Build over ice and stir.

Aqua Marina

CHAMPAGNE FLUTE

1 part Vodka
½ part Crème de Menthe (Green)
fill with Champagne

Build in the glass with no ice.

Arctic Kiss

CHAMPAGNE FLUTE

2 parts Cranberry Vodka
fill with Champagne

Build in the glass with no ice.

Arise My Love

CHAMPAGNE FLUTE

splash Crème de Menthe (Green)
fill with Champagne

Build in the glass with no ice.

Aruban Angel

WHITE WINE GLASS

1 part Dry Gin
1 part Apricot Brandy
1 part Cherry Brandy
fill with Champagne

Shake all but Champagne with ice and strain into glass. Top with Champagne.

Atheist's Best

CHAMPAGNE FLUTE

2 parts Vodka
1 part Cherry Juice
1 part Lemon Juice
fill with Champagne

Shake all but Champagne with ice and strain into glass. Top with Champagne.

Austrian Airlines

CHAMPAGNE FLUTE

1 part Orange Vodka
1 part Red Bull
fill with Champagne

Build in the glass with no ice.

Axis Kiss

CHAMPAGNE FLUTE

splash Amaretto
splash Crème de Cassis
fill with Champagne

Build in the glass with no ice.

Balalaika Cocktail

COCKTAIL GLASS

2 parts Vodka
1 part Champagne
1 part Orange Juice

Shake with ice and strain.

Bartini

COCKTAIL GLASS

1 part Blue Curaçao
2 parts Champagne
1 part Papaya Juice

Shake with ice and strain.

Be Back Soon

COLLINS GLASS

1 part Vodka
½ part Mandarine Napoléon® Liqueur
½ part Strawberry Liqueur
1 part Lime Juice
fill with Champagne

Build over ice and stir.

Bellini

RED WINE GLASS

3 parts Peach Puree
splash Lemon Juice
splash Maraschino Liqueur
fill with Champagne

Build in the glass with no ice.

Bellini #2

CHAMPAGNE FLUTE

1 part Peach Schnapps
fill with Champagne

Build in the glass with no ice.

Bentley's Bubbles

HIGHBALL GLASS

1 part Blackberry Liqueur
1 part Cranberry Juice Cocktail
1 part Orange Juice
fill with Champagne

Build over ice.

Beverly Hills Iced Tea

COLLINS GLASS

1 part Vodka
1 part Triple Sec
1 part Gin
3 dashes Sugar
fill with Champagne

Build over ice and stir.

Big Flirt

COLLINS GLASS

1 part Vodka
1 part Champagne
½ part Raspberry Liqueur
1½ parts Pineapple Juice
½ part Strawberry Puree

Combine all ingredients in a blender with ice. Blend until smooth.

Bitchass

HIGHBALL GLASS

1 part Tequila
1 part Brandy
1 part Champagne
1 part Strawberry Liqueur

Build over ice and stir.

Black Pearl

CHAMPAGNE FLUTE

1 part Coffee Liqueur
1 part Cognac
fill with Champagne

Build in the glass with no ice.

Black Velvet

CHAMPAGNE FLUTE

1 part Chilled Stout
1 part Chilled Champagne

Build in the glass with no ice.

Blow Blue Bubbles

CHAMPAGNE FLUTE

1 part Blueberry Schnapps
fill with Champagne

Build in a glass with no ice.

Blue Gecko

CHAMPAGNE FLUTE

1 part Blue Curaçao
1 part Crème de Cacao (White)
fill with Champagne

Build in the glass with no ice.

Blue Parisian

CHAMPAGNE FLUTE

¼ part Blue Curaçao
splash Triple Sec
splash Lime Juice
dash Sugar
fill with Champagne

Build in the glass with no ice.

Blue Tahoe

COLLINS GLASS

1 part Blue Curaçao
1 part Tequila
1 part Lime Juice
fill with Champagne

Build over ice and stir. Garnish with a Lemon Slice, an Orange Slice, and a Cherry.

Bois de Rose

CHAMPAGNE FLUTE

1 part Gin
1 part St-Germain
splash Aperol
splash Lemon Juice
Brut Rose Champagne

Shake all but the Champagne with ice and strain. Fill with the Champagne and garnish with an Orange Peel or Twist.

Bonecrusher

HIGHBALL GLASS

1 part Champagne
½ part Triple Sec
½ part Tequila
½ part Vodka
½ part Gin
fill with Sweet & Sour Mix
splash Grenadine

Build over ice and stir.

Bubble Bath

CHAMPAGNE FLUTE

1 part Gin
1 part Campari®
1 part Strawberry Liqueur
2 parts Orange Juice
fill with Champagne

Shake all but Champagne with ice and strain into glass. Top with Champagne.

Bubbles 'n' Bells

HIGHBALL GLASS

1½ parts Raspberry Liqueur
fill with Champagne
splash Drambuie®

Build over ice and stir.

Bubblin' Blue

HIGHBALL GLASS

1 part Vodka
1 part Blue Curaçao
fill with Champagne
splash Cranberry Juice Cocktail
splash Sweet & Sour Mix

Build over ice and stir.

Buzz Bomb

HIGHBALL GLASS

1 part Vodka
1 part Cointreau®
1 part Cognac
1 part Bénédictine®
1 part Lime Juice
splash Champagne

Build over ice and stir.

Cameron Diaz

COLLINS GLASS

2 parts Vodka
2 parts Orange Juice
1 part Campari®
fill with Champagne
dash Orange Bitters

Build over ice and stir.

Camp Champ

WHITE WINE GLASS

1 part Campari®
1 part Orange
fill with Champagne

Build over ice.

Canadian Dollar

ROCKS GLASS

1 part Strawberry Vodka
fill with Champagne
dash Grenadine

Build over ice. Top with Grenadine.

Cara Bonita

CHAMPAGNE FLUTE

1 part Light Rum
1 part Blue Curaçao
1 part Pineapple Juice
2 splashes Lemon Juice
fill with Champagne

Shake all but Champagne with ice and strain. Top with Champagne.

Caribbean Champagne

CHAMPAGNE FLUTE

splash Rum
fill with Champagne
splash Crème de Banane

Build in the glass with no ice.

Cha Cha Cha L'Amour

HIGHBALL GLASS

½ part Chambord®
splash Chartreuse®
fill with Champagne

Build over ice and stir.

Champagne Berry

COCKTAIL GLASS

1 part Raspberry Liqueur
1 part Kirschwasser
fill with Champagne

Build over ice.

Champagne Bibaly

CHAMPAGNE FLUTE

1 Sugar Cube
dash Bitters
fill with Champagne

Soak the Sugar Cube with Bitters. Place the cube in the bottom of the glass and fill with Champagne.

Champagne Blitz

CHAMPAGNE FLUTE

1 part Crème de Menthe (White)
fill with Champagne

Build in the glass with no ice.

Champagne Gem

CHAMPAGNE FLUTE

splash Crème de Menthe (Green)
fill with Champagne

Build in the glass with no ice.

Champagne Polonaise

CHAMPAGNE FLUTE

½ part Blackberry Liqueur
splash Brandy
fill with Champagne

Build in the glass with no ice.

Champagne Royale

CHAMPAGNE FLUTE

splash Raspberry Liqueur
fill with Champagne

Build in the glass with no ice.

Champagne Smiler

CHAMPAGNE FLUTE

1 part Cherry Brandy
splash Lemon Juice
fill with Champagne

Build in the glass with no ice.

Cherub's Cup

COLLINS GLASS

1 Strawberry
1 part St-Germain
2 parts Gin
1 part Lemon Juice
splash Simple Syrup
Brut Champagne

In a shaker, muddle the Strawberry with the St-Germain. Add ice then the Gin, Lemon Juice, and Simple Syrup. Shake and strain over ice. Top with Brut Champagne (blanc or rosé). Garnish with a Strawberry.

A Christmas Ball

ROCKS GLASS

3 parts Champagne
1 part Raspberry Liqueur
1 part Triple Sec

Build over ice.

Citrus Champagne

CHAMPAGNE FLUTE

1 part Orange Juice
1 part Mandarine Napoléon® Liqueur
dash Orange Bitters
fill with Champagne

Build in the glass with no ice.

Count Currey

CHAMPAGNE FLUTE

1 part Gin
dash Powdered Sugar
fill with Champagne

Build in the glass with no ice.

Cristal Fizz

CHAMPAGNE FLUTE

½ part Pear Liqueur
dash Triple Sec
fill with Champagne

Build in the glass with no ice.

Danube Valley

WHITE WINE GLASS

1 part Apricot Brandy
1 part Apricot Juice
fill with Champagne

Build in the glass with no ice.

Death in the Afternoon

CHAMPAGNE FLUTE

1½ part Pernod
fill with Champagne

Build in the glass with no ice.

Deep Blue

CHAMPAGNE FLUTE

1 part Blue Curaçao
½ part Amer Picon®
fill with Champagne

Build in the glass with no ice.

Deep River

HIGHBALL GLASS

½ part Blue Curaçao
3 parts Champagne
⅔ part Mango Juice
⅔ part Passion Fruit Juice

Build over ice and stir.

Delta Force

HIGHBALL GLASS

½ part Blackberry Liqueur
½ part Vanilla Liqueur
fill with Champagne
½ part Lemon Juice
1½ parts Apple Juice

Build over ice and stir.

Diamond Fizz

HIGHBALL GLASS

2 parts Gin
½ part Lemon Juice
dash Powdered Sugar
fill with Champagne

Build over ice and stir.

Down in the Caribbean

COLLINS GLASS

splash Dark Rum
splash Mango Juice
splash Passion Fruit Nectar
splash Lemon Juice
fill with Champagne

Build over ice and stir.

Duke Cocktail

CHAMPAGNE FLUTE

1/2 part Triple Sec
1/12 part Maraschino Liqueur
1/3 part Lemon Juice
1/6 part Orange Juice
1 Egg
4 parts Sparkling Wine

Shake all but Sparkling Wine with ice and strain. Fill with Sparkling Wine and stir.

Emerald Eunuch

CHAMPAGNE FLUTE

1 part Blue Curaçao
fill with Champagne

Build in the glass with no ice.

Erotica

CHAMPAGNE FLUTE

1 part Gin
1/4 part Lemon Juice
2 dashes Sugar
fill with Champagne

Build in the glass with no ice.

Fancy Balls

CHAMPAGNE FLUTE

1 part Fireball Cinnamon Whiskey
fill with Champagne

Build in order.

Fantasy

CHAMPAGNE FLUTE

1 part Champagne
1 part Grapefruit Juice
1 part Aperol™
1/2 part Goldschläger®

Fill in a champagne glass.

Finesse

CHAMPAGNE FLUTE

1 part Kiwi Schnapps
1/2 part Crème de Coconut
fill with Champagne

Build in the glass with no ice.

First Love

HIGHBALL GLASS

1 part Gin
dash Powdered Sugar
2 splashes Cherry Heering®
fill with Champagne

Build over ice and stir.

Fizzgig

CHAMPAGNE FLUTE

1 part Blue Curaçao
1 part Amaretto
2 splashes Lemon Juice
fill with Champagne

Build in the glass with no ice.

Flaming Fire

CHAMPAGNE FLUTE

1 1/2 parts Strawberry Liqueur
1/2 part Vodka
1/2 part Strawberry Juice
fill with Champagne

Build in the glass with no ice.

Fleur de Savane

COCKTAIL GLASS

1/2 part Lychee Liqueur
3 parts Champagne
splash Lemon Juice
1 part Passion Fruit Juice
splash Kiwi Syrup

Shake with ice and strain.

Flirtini

CHAMPAGNE FLUTE

1 part Orange Vodka
1 part Pineapple Juice
fill with Champagne

Build in the glass with no ice.

Flirtini #2

COCKTAIL GLASS

1/2 part Vodka
1/2 part Triple Sec
splash Pineapple Juice
splash Lime Juice
fill with Champagne

Shake all but Champagne with ice and strain. Top with Champagne.

Flirtini #3

COCKTAIL GLASS

1 part Vodka
1 part Champagne
1/2 part Maraschino Liqueur
2 parts Pineapple Juice

Shake all but Champagne with ice and strain. Top with Champagne.

Forty-Seven-Eleven

COUPETTE GLASS

1 part Blue Curaçao
1 1/2 parts Pineapple Juice
1 1/2 parts Orange Juice
fill with Champagne

Shake all but Champagne with ice and strain. Fill with Champagne.

Fraise de Champagne

CHAMPAGNE FLUTE

1 part Strawberry Liqueur
1/2 part Cognac
fill with Champagne

Build in the glass with no ice.

Fraise Royale

CHAMPAGNE FLUTE

1 part Strawberry Liqueur
1 part Raspberry Liqueur
fill with Champagne

Build in the glass with no ice.

Freedom

HIGHBALL GLASS

1/2 part Crème de Coconut
2/3 part Melon Liqueur
2/3 part Pineapple Juice
fill with Champagne

Build over ice and stir.

French 125

COLLINS GLASS

2 parts Sweet & Sour Mix
1 part Brandy
fill with Champagne

Build over ice and stir.

French 25

COLLINS GLASS

1 part Tequila Reposado
splash Maple Syrup
fill with Champagne

Build over ice and stir.

French 75

COLLINS GLASS

1 1/2 parts Gin
2 dashes Powdered Sugar
1 1/2 parts Lemon Juice
fill with Champagne

Build over ice and stir. Garnish with an Orange Slice and a Maraschino Cherry.

French 85

COLLINS GLASS

1 1/2 parts Brandy
1 part Lemon Juice
dash Powdered Sugar
fill with Champagne

Build over ice and stir.

French Foam

COLLINS GLASS

½ part Brandy
½ part Kirschwasser
1½ parts Simple Syrup
3 dashes Bitters
fill with Champagne
1 scoop Orange Sorbet

Build over ice.

French Lover

HIGHBALL GLASS

½ part Peach Schnapps
⅔ part Plum Brandy
fill with Champagne

Build over ice and stir.

French Pirate

CHAMPAGNE FLUTE

½ part Blue Curaçao
1 part Dark Rum
fill with Champagne

Build in the glass with no ice.

Friar Delight

HIGHBALL GLASS

1 part Triple Sec
½ part Currant Vodka
2 parts Champagne
1 part Pineapple Juice

Build over ice and stir.

Fruity Bubbles

CHAMPAGNE FLUTE

1 part Apricot Brandy
1 part Banana Liqueur
fill with Champagne

Build in the glass with no ice.

Funny People

HIGHBALL GLASS

1 part Raspberry Liqueur
1 part Apricot Brandy
fill with Champagne

Build over ice and stir.

Gatita Mimosa

CHAMPAGNE FLUTE

1 part Scotch
1 part Triple Sec
fill with Champagne

Build in the glass with no ice.

Girlie Martini

COCKTAIL GLASS

splash Dry Vermouth
4 parts Vodka
3 parts Champagne
splash Maraschino Liqueur

Shake with ice and strain.

Glory

HIGHBALL GLASS

splash Crème de Cassis
splash Kiwi Schnapps
fill with Champagne
splash Lime Juice

Build over ice and stir.

Golden Bear

ROCKS GLASS

1 part Rum
1 part Vodka
1 part Champagne
1 part Orange Juice

Build over ice and stir.

Golden Lady

CHAMPAGNE FLUTE

1 part Triple Sec
1 part Orange Juice
1 part Cognac
fill with Champagne

Shake all but Champagne with ice and strain. Top with Champagne.

A Goodnight Kiss

CHAMPAGNE FLUTE

dash Bitters
1 Sugar Cube
fill with Champagne
splash Campari®

Put dash of Bitters on Sugar Cube and drop it in flute. Add the Champagne and the splash of Campari®.

Grand Champagner

CHAMPAGNE FLUTE

1 part Orange Juice
1 part Triple Sec
fill with Champagne

Build in the glass with no ice.

Green Dragon

CHAMPAGNE FLUTE

1 part Melon Liqueur
fill with Sparkling Wine

Build in order. Garnish with a green Maraschino Cherry.

Green Eagle

HIGHBALL GLASS

1 part Blue Curaçao
1 part Orange Juice
fill with Champagne

Build in the glass with no ice.

Grimosa

COLLINS GLASS

1 part Tequila
2 parts Orange Juice
fill with Champagne

Build over ice and stir.

Guadalajara

HIGHBALL GLASS

½ part Kiwi Schnapps
1 part Tequila
fill with Champagne
½ part Lime Juice

Build over ice and stir.

Gulf Stream

HURRICANE GLASS

1 part Blue Curaçao
½ part White Rum
½ part Brandy
1 part Lime Juice
1 part Lemonade
1 part Sparkling Wine

Build over ice and stir.

Hairspray

CHAMPAGNE FLUTE

1 part Gin
splash Blue Curaçao
splash Pernod®
fill with Champagne

Build in the glass with no ice.

Happy Birthday

CHAMPAGNE FLUTE

3 parts Blackberry Liqueur
1 part Light Rum
1 part Pineapple Juice
1 part Triple Sec
1 part Peach Juice
fill with Champagne

Build in the glass with no ice.

Happy Hollander

CHAMPAGNE FLUTE

1 part Mango Juice
¼ part Maraschino Liqueur
dash Powdered Sugar
fill with Champagne

Build in the glass with no ice.

Happy New Year

CHAMPAGNE FLUTE

1 part Orange Juice
1 part Port
½ part Brandy
fill with Champagne

Build in the glass with no ice.

Hard Day

HIGHBALL GLASS

2 parts Amaretto
fill with Champagne
splash Lemon Juice

Build over ice and stir.

Harlem Mugger

COLLINS GLASS

1 part Vodka
1 part Gin
1 part Light Rum
1 part Tequila
fill with Champagne
splash Cranberry Juice Cocktail

Build over ice.

Harvard Graduation

HIGHBALL GLASS

1 part Melon Liqueur
fill with Champagne
½ part Lime Juice

Build over ice and stir.

Head Case

CHAMPAGNE FLUTE

1 part Blue Curaçao
splash Crème de Cassis
fill with Champagne

Build in the glass with no ice.

Heather Blush

CHAMPAGNE FLUTE

1 part Scotch
1 part Strawberry Liqueur
fill with Champagne

Build in the glass with no ice.

Hemingway

CHAMPAGNE FLUTE

1 part Anisette
fill with Champagne

Build in the glass with no ice.

High Heels

CHAMPAGNE FLUTE

1 part Kirschwasser
½ part Vanilla Liqueur
fill with Champagne

Build in the glass with no ice.

Honeydew

HIGHBALL GLASS

1 part Melon Liqueur
1 part Lemonade
1 part Champagne

Build over ice and stir.

Hotel California

HURRICANE GLASS

1 part Gold Tequila
2 parts Orange Juice
2 parts Pineapple Juice
fill with Sparkling Wine

Build over ice and stir.

Hour of a Star

COCKTAIL GLASS

1½ parts Orange Juice
1½ parts Southern Comfort®
1 part Champagne

Shake all but Champagne with ice and strain. Top with Champagne.

Ichirose

HIGHBALL GLASS

½ part Vodka
½ part Peach Schnapps
½ part Blackberry Liqueur
½ part Raspberry Liqueur
1½ parts Champagne
1 part Sweet & Sour Mix

Build over ice and stir.

Indiana Jones®

HIGHBALL GLASS

1 part Tequila
1 part Whiskey
fill with Champagne

Build over ice and stir.

Irish Lady

CHAMPAGNE FLUTE

1 part Melon Liqueur
1 part Orange Juice
fill with Champagne

Build in the glass with no ice.

Jacuzzi®

CHAMPAGNE FLUTE

½ part Gin
1 part Passion Fruit Liqueur
2 parts Orange Juice
fill with Champagne

Build in the glass with no ice.

Jadranka

CHAMPAGNE FLUTE

1 part Blue Curaçao
1 part Dry Gin
1 part Maraschino Liqueur
fill with Champagne

Build in the glass with no ice.

Jäger Royale

CHAMPAGNE FLUTE

1½ parts Jägermeister®
fill with Champagne

Build in the glass with no ice.

Ja-Mora

CHAMPAGNE FLUTE

1 part Vodka
1 part Orange Juice
1 part Apple Juice
fill with Champagne

Build in the glass with no ice.

Jonathan Strange

CHAMPAGNE FLUTE

1 part Sparkling Wine
1 part Guinness Stout

Build in a champagne flute.

King's Peg

CHAMPAGNE FLUTE

1 part Cognac
fill with Champagne

Build in the glass with no ice.

Kir Empereur

CHAMPAGNE FLUTE

1 part Pastis
1 part Raspberry Liqueur
fill with Champagne

Build in the glass with no ice.

Kir Royale

CHAMPAGNE FLUTE

splash Crème de Cassis
fill with Champagne

Build in the glass with no ice.

Kordulas Special

CHAMPAGNE FLUTE

1 Sugar Cube
dash Bitters
fill with Champagne

Soak the Sugar Cube with Bitters. Place the Cube in the bottom of the glass and fill with Champagne.

L'Aiglon

CHAMPAGNE FLUTE

1 part Mandarine Napoléon® Liqueur
fill with Champagne

Build in the glass with no ice.

Leaping Lizard

CHAMPAGNE FLUTE

1 part Blue Curaçao
1 part Crème de Cacao (White)
fill with Champagne

Build in the glass with no ice.

Lemon Celebration
COCKTAIL GLASS

1 part Raspberry Liqueur
1 part Bacardi® Limón Rum
fill with Champagne

Stir gently with ice and strain.

Lemon Mimosa
WHITE WINE GLASS

½ part Lemon Juice
dash Powdered Sugar
fill with Champagne

Build in the glass with no ice.

Liberty Blue Champagne
CHAMPAGNE FLUTE

splash Blue Curaçao
splash Grand Marnier®
½ part Lemon Juice
1 part Vodka
fill with Champagne

Build in the glass with no ice.

Lion
CHAMPAGNE FLUTE

½ part Silver Tequila
½ part Peach Schnapps
1 part Passion Fruit Juice
splash Grenadine
fill with Champagne

Shake all but Champagne with ice and strain. Top with Champagne.

Lolala
HIGHBALL GLASS

½ part Gin
½ part Parfait Amour
2 parts Champagne
2 parts Apple Juice

Build over ice and stir.

London Sunset
CHAMPAGNE FLUTE

1 part Brandy
1 part Cherry Brandy
fill with Champagne

Build in the glass with no ice.

Lost Temple
HIGHBALL GLASS

splash Blue Curaçao
½ part Armagnac
1½ parts Orange Juice
fill with Champagne

Build over ice.

Lozana
CHAMPAGNE FLUTE

1 part Bourbon
½ part Strawberry Liqueur
½ part Crème de Menthe (White)
fill with Champagne

Build in the glass with no ice.

Lush
CHAMPAGNE FLUTE

1 part Vodka
fill with Champagne

Build in the glass with no ice.

Luxury Cocktail
CHAMPAGNE FLUTE

1 part Brandy
fill with Chilled Champagne
2 dashes Orange Bitters

Build in the glass with no ice.

Lychee Lover
HIGHBALL GLASS

1 part Lychee Liqueur
1 part Crème de Cassis
fill with Champagne

Build over ice.

Magnolia
HIGHBALL GLASS

⅔ part Maraschino Liqueur
½ part Silver Tequila
1 part Apple Juice
fill with Champagne

Build over ice and stir.

Manaus Nights

CHAMPAGNE FLUTE

1 part Passion Fruit Liqueur
1 part Cachaça
fill with Champagne

Build in the glass with no ice.

The Man-Mosa

CHAMPAGNE FLUTE

2 parts Fireball Cinnamon Whiskey
fill with Champagne
top with Orange Juice

Build in order.

Marilyn Monroe

CHAMPAGNE FLUTE

1 part Apple Brandy
1/6 part Grenadine
fill with Sparkling Wine

Build in order.

Mauve Sunset

CHAMPAGNE FLUTE

splash Parfait Amour
fill with Champagne

Build in the glass with no ice.

Metropolis

CHAMPAGNE FLUTE

1 part Vodka
1/2 part Strawberry Liqueur
fill with Champagne

Build in the glass with no ice.

Mexican Firewater

ROCKS GLASS

2 parts Tequila Reposado
1 part Coffee Liqueur
fill with Champagne

Build over ice and stir.

Millennium Cocktail

COCKTAIL GLASS

1/2 part Melon Liqueur
1/2 part Gin
1 part Champagne
2/3 parts Mango Juice
splash Lemon Syrup

Shake with ice and strain.

Mimosa

CHAMPAGNE FLUTE

2 parts Orange Juice
fill with Champagne

Build in the glass with no ice.

Mimosa-Super

CHAMPAGNE FLUTE

1 1/2 parts Orange Juice
1/2 part Triple Sec
fill with Champagne

Build in the glass with no ice.

Mint Champagne

CHAMPAGNE FLUTE

1 part Crème de Menthe (Green)
1 part Orange Juice
1 part Gin
fill with Champagne

Build in the glass with no ice.

Money Talk

COCKTAIL GLASS

1/2 part Passion Fruit Liqueur
1/2 part Dark Rum
2/3 part Orange Juice
fill with Champagne

Build in the glass with no ice.

Monte Carlo Imperial Highball

CHAMPAGNE FLUTE

2 parts Gin
1/2 part Crème de Menthe (White)
1/2 part Lemon Juice
fill with Champagne

Build in order.

Monte Carlo Imperial

HIGHBALL GLASS

1½ parts Gin
½ part Crème de Menthe (White)
splash Lemon Juice
fill with Champagne

Build over ice and stir.

Morning Champagne

CHAMPAGNE FLUTE

½ part Apricot Brandy
fill with Champagne

Build in the glass with no ice.

Morning Kiss

WHITE WINE GLASS

¾ part Brandy
¾ part Gin
1 part Orange Juice
fill with Champagne

Shake all but Champagne with ice and strain. Top with Champagne.

Mortal's Nectar

COCKTAIL GLASS

1 part Brandy
½ part Raspberry Liqueur
1 part Apple Brandy
1 part Champagne

Shake with ice and strain.

Moscow Mimosa

CHAMPAGNE FLUTE

3 parts Orange Juice
½ part Vodka
fill with Champagne

Build in the glass with no ice.

My Sister-in-Law

CHAMPAGNE FLUTE

1 part Scotch
½ part Triple Sec
fill with Champagne

Build in the glass with no ice.

Night and Day

WHITE WINE GLASS

1 part Cognac
½ part Apricot Brandy
1½ parts Orange Juice
fill with Champagne

Build over ice.

Night Flight

CHAMPAGNE FLUTE

1 part Amaretto
1 part Peach Schnapps
1 part Blackberry Liqueur
2 parts Orange Juice
fill with Champagne

Shake all but Champagne with ice and strain. Top with Champagne.

Noblesse

COCKTAIL GLASS

1½ parts Champagne
⅔ part Dark Rum
⅔ part Pear Syrup
splash Melon Liqueur

Stir gently with ice and strain.

Norma Jean

CHAMPAGNE FLUTE

1 part Blue Curaçao
fill with Champagne

Build in the glass with no ice.

The Odyssey

HIGHBALL GLASS

½ part Lychee Liqueur
1½ parts Vodka
2½ parts Champagne
dash Peychauds® Bitters

Build over ice and stir.

Ohio
CHAMPAGNE FLUTE

1 part Whiskey
½ part Triple Sec
½ part Sweet Vermouth
fill with Champagne
dash Bitters

Build over ice and stir.

Operation Greenpeace
HIGHBALL GLASS

1 part Melon Liqueur
1 part Passion Fruit Juice
fill with Champagne

Build over ice and stir.

Original Sin
BRANDY SNIFTER

1 part Brandy
1 part Cherry Heering®
½ shot Triple Sec
splash Sweet & Sour Mix
splash Grenadine
fill with Champagne

Build over ice and stir.

Oriole
HIGHBALL GLASS

1 part Peach Schnapps
1 part Champagne
1 part Orange Juice
1 part Pineapple Juice

Build over ice and stir.

Pamperito
CHAMPAGNE FLUTE

¾ part Pineapple Juice
½ part Gin
¼ part Triple Sec
splash Lemon Juice
fill with Champagne

Build in the glass with no ice.

Paradise
CHAMPAGNE FLUTE

1 part Raspberry Liqueur
fill with Champagne

Build in the glass with no ice.

Paris, Texas
CHAMPAGNE FLUTE

1 part Bourbon
1 part Blackberry Liqueur
fill with Champagne

Build in the glass with no ice.

Passat
CHAMPAGNE FLUTE

1 part Triple Sec
1 part Apricot Brandy
1½ parts Passion Fruit Juice
splash Orange Juice
fill with Champagne

Shake all but Champagne with ice and strain. Top with Champagne.

Peach Mimosa
CHAMPAGNE FLUTE

½ part Peach Schnapps
1 part Orange Juice
fill with Champagne

Build in the glass with no ice.

Peach Treat
COLLINS GLASS

1 part Peach Brandy
2 parts Orange Juice
fill with Chilled Champagne

Build over ice and stir.

Peppermint Peace
CHAMPAGNE FLUTE

1 part Crème de Cacao (White)
1 part Crème de Menthe (White)
fill with Champagne

Build in the glass with no ice.

Pilot House Fizz

WHITE WINE GLASS

1 part Vodka
1 part Grand Marnier®
splash Sweetened Lime Juice
dash Orange Bitters
fill with Champagne

Build over ice and stir.

Pimm's® Royal

CHAMPAGNE FLUTE

1½ parts Pimm's® No. 1 Cup
fill with Champagne

Build in the glass with no ice.

Pink California Sunshine

COCKTAIL GLASS

½ part Crème de Cassis
1 part Pink Champagne
1 part Orange Juice

Build over ice.

Pink Chevrolet

CHAMPAGNE FLUTE

1 part Strawberry Liqueur
fill with Champagne

Build in the glass with no ice.

Pink Millennium

CHAMPAGNE FLUTE

1 part Citrus Vodka
1 part Cranberry Juice Cocktail
splash Simple Syrup
fill with Champagne

Shake all but Champagne with ice and strain. Top with Champagne.

Pink Tail

CHAMPAGNE FLUTE

1 part Triple Sec
1 part Strawberry Liqueur
1 part Orange Juice
1 part Grape Juice (White)
fill with Champagne

Shake all but Champagne with ice and strain. Top with Champagne.

Plain White T

COLLINS GLASS

2 parts Vodka
2 parts Sparkling Wine
fill with Red Bull Energy Drink

Build over ice.

Player's Passion

HIGHBALL GLASS

1 part Alizé®
1 part Cognac
fill with Champagne

Build over ice and stir.

Poinsettia

CHAMPAGNE FLUTE

½ part Triple Sec
3 parts Champagne

Build in the glass with no ice.

Poinsettia #2

HIGHBALL GLASS

½ part Triple Sec
1 part Champagne
1 part Cranberry Juice Cocktail

Build over ice and stir.

Prince of Wales

CHAMPAGNE FLUTE

1 part Cognac
½ part Triple Sec
dash Bitters
fill with Champagne

Shake all but Champagne with ice and strain. Top with Champagne.

Qi Spring Punch

CHAMPAGNE FLUTE

1 part Vodka
1 part Strawberry Liqueur
fill with Champagne

Build in the glass with no ice.

Que Pasion

CHAMPAGNE FLUTE

1 part Southern Comfort®
1 part Passion Fruit Liqueur
fill with Champagne

Build in the glass with no ice.

Ray Gun

CHAMPAGNE FLUTE

1 part Blue Curaçao
1 part Melon Liqueur
fill with Champagne

Build in the glass with no ice.

Recife Real

CHAMPAGNE FLUTE

1 part Passion Fruit Liqueur
splash Crème de Cacao (White)
1 part Orange Juice
1 part Champagne

Shake all but Champagne with ice and strain. Top with Champagne.

Red Kiss

CHAMPAGNE FLUTE

1 part Dark Rum
1 part Cherry Brandy
1 part Pineapple Juice
fill with Champagne

Build in the glass with no ice.

Ritz Cocktail

CHAMPAGNE FLUTE

1 part Triple Sec
1 part Orange Juice
1 part Cognac
fill with Champagne

Shake all but Champagne with ice and strain. Top with Champagne.

Romy

CHAMPAGNE FLUTE

1½ parts Advocaat
fill with Champagne

Build in the glass with no ice.

Rosanna

CHAMPAGNE FLUTE

1½ parts Orange Juice
1 part Cinzano®
½ part Triple Sec
fill with Champagne

Shake all but Champagne with ice and strain. Top with Champagne.

Roses Are Red

CHAMPAGNE FLUTE

1½ parts Parfait Amour
½ part Grenadine
fill with Champagne

Shake all but Champagne with ice and strain. Top with Champagne.

Rototo

CHAMPAGNE FLUTE

1 part Cognac
1 part Triple Sec
1 part Maraschino Liqueur
fill with Champagne

Build in the glass with no ice.

Royal Bill

CHAMPAGNE FLUTE

½ part Pear Brandy
fill with Champagne

Build in the glass with no ice.

Royal Screw

HIGHBALL GLASS

1 part Cognac
1 part Orange Juice
fill with Champagne

Build over ice and stir.

Royal Starboard

HIGHBALL GLASS

1 part Raspberry Liqueur
1 part Blackberry Liqueur
3 parts Cranberry Juice Cocktail
fill with Champagne

Build over ice and stir.

Rue Royal

CHAMPAGNE FLUTE

1 part Strawberry Liqueur
½ part Cognac
fill with Champagne

Build in the glass with no ice.

Russian Spring Punch

COLLINS GLASS

2 parts Vodka
½ part Crème de Cassis
dash Powdered Sugar
fill with Champagne

Shake all but Champagne with ice and strain. Top with Champagne.

Rusty Betty

COLLINS GLASS

1 part Grand Marnier®
½ part Raspberry Liqueur
2 parts Pineapple Juice
fill with Champagne

Build over ice and stir.

Saiki

HIGHBALL GLASS

1 part Champagne
splash Crème de Banane
splash Frangelico®
½ part Orange Juice
splash Lemon Juice

Build over ice and stir.

Saint Germain

HIGHBALL GLASS

1 part Cherry Brandy
1 part Champagne

Build over ice and stir.

Saint Royal

CHAMPAGNE FLUTE

1 part Strawberry Liqueur
1 part Strawberry Puree
1 part Vanilla Vodka
fill with Champagne

Shake all but Champagne with ice and strain. Top with Champagne.

San Remo

WHITE WINE GLASS

1 part Triple Sec
1 part Apricot Brandy
1 part Grapefruit Juice
1 part Champagne

Build over ice.

Savoy 90

CHAMPAGNE FLUTE

1 part Amaretto
splash Orange Flower Water
fill with Champagne

Build in the glass with no ice.

Scotch Royale

CHAMPAGNE FLUTE

1 Sugar Cube
1½ parts Scotch
dash Bitters
fill with Champagne

Place Sugar Cube in a champagne flute and add Scotch and Bitters. Fill with Champagne.

Sea of Love

HURRICANE GLASS

1 part Crème de Coconut
1 part Strawberry Puree
½ part Rum
fill with Champagne

Shake all but Champagne with ice and strain. Top with Champagne.

Seelbach Cocktail

CHAMPAGNE FLUTE

1 part Bourbon
½ part Triple Sec
7 dashes Peychaud's® Bitters
7 dashes Angostura® Bitters
fill with Champagne

Shake all but Champagne with ice and strain. Top with Champagne.

Sexy Seville

HIGHBALL GLASS

1 part Peach Schnapps
1 part Cranberry Juice Cocktail
fill with Champagne

Build over ice and stir.

Shake

CHAMPAGNE FLUTE

1 part Apricot Brandy
½ part Kirschwasser
fill with Champagne

Build in the glass with no ice.

Silvester Königlich

CHAMPAGNE FLUTE

1 part Passion Fruit Liqueur
1 part Cachaça
1½ parts Orange Juice
fill with Champagne

Shake all but Champagne with ice and strain. Top with Champagne.

Singapore Fizz

CHAMPAGNE FLUTE

1 part Gin
½ part Cherry Brandy
splash Simple Syrup
fill with Champagne

Shake all but Champagne with ice and strain. Top with Champagne.

Sinus Dream

WHITE WINE GLASS

1 part Blue Curaçao
1 part Vodka
1 part Advocaat
fill with Champagne

Shake all but Champagne with ice and strain. Top with Champagne.

Sir Henry

COLLINS GLASS

1 part Peach Schnapps
1 part Orange Juice
fill with Champagne

Shake all but Champagne with ice and strain. Top with Champagne.

Southern Bubbles

CHAMPAGNE FLUTE

½ part Southern Comfort®
fill with Champagne

Build in the glass with no ice.

Space Journey

CHAMPAGNE FLUTE

1 part Vodka
½ part Cherry Brandy
fill with Champagne

Build in the glass with no ice.

Sparkling Kiwi

CHAMPAGNE FLUTE

1½ parts Kiwi Schnapps
fill with Champagne

Build in the glass with no ice.

Sparkling Strawberry

COLLINS GLASS

1 part Remy Martin® VSOP
splash Cherry Brandy
1½ parts Pineapple Juice
splash Strawberry Syrup
fill with Champagne

Build over ice and stir.

Sparks

CHAMPAGNE FLUTE

1 part Peppar Vodka
fill with Champagne

Build in the glass with no ice.

Spotlight

CHAMPAGNE FLUTE

1 part Cherry Brandy
splash Dry Gin
splash Dry Vermouth
splash Campari®
fill with Champagne

Shake all but Champagne with ice and strain. Top with Champagne.

Spring into Summer

CHAMPAGNE FLUTE

½ part Apricot Brandy
splash Crème de Menthe (Green)
fill with Champagne

Build in the glass with no ice.

Spring Sun

CHAMPAGNE FLUTE

1 part Triple Sec
1 part Orange Juice
fill with Champagne

Build in the glass with no ice.

Springtime

CHAMPAGNE FLUTE

1 part Gordon's® Orange Vodka
1 part Lychee Liqueur
splash Lime Juice
fill with Champagne

Build in the glass with no ice.

St. Champagne

CHAMPAGNE FLUTE

1½ parts St-Germain
fill with Champagne

Build in order and garnish with a Strawberry Slice.

St-Germain Cocktail

COLLINS GLASS

2 parts Champagne
1½ parts St-Germain
fill with Club Soda

Build over ice and stir.

St-Germain French 77

CHAMPAGNE FLUTE

1 part St-Germain
¼ part Lemon Juice
fill with Champagne

Shake the St-Germian and Juice with ice and strain. Fill with Champagne and garnish with a Lemon Twist.

Stockholm 75

CHAMPAGNE FLUTE

1 part Citrus Vodka
1 part Simple Syrup
1 part Lemon Juice
fill with Champagne

Shake all but Champagne with ice and strain. Top with Champagne.

Storm's a Brewing

HIGHBALL GLASS

1 part Cherry Brandy
½ part Kiwi Schnapps
1 part Orange Juice
1 part Pineapple Juice
1 part Sweet & Sour Mix
fill with Champagne

Build over ice and stir.

Strawberry Blonde Champagne

CHAMPAGNE FLUTE

2 parts Strawberry Liqueur
1 part Irish Mist®
fill with Champagne

Shake all but Champagne with ice and strain. Top with Champagne.

Sunny Side

CHAMPAGNE FLUTE

1 part Vodka
½ part Grenadine
½ part Raspberry Liqueur
fill with Champagne

Shake all but Champagne with ice and strain. Top with Champagne.

Sunset in a Glass

CHAMPAGNE FLUTE

2 parts Peach Schnapps
1 part Cranberry Juice Cocktail
splash Orange Juice
fill with Champagne

Shake all but Champagne with ice and strain. Top with Champagne.

Sunshine Smile

CHAMPAGNE FLUTE

1 part Vodka
1 part Orange Juice
fill with Champagne

Shake all but Champagne with ice and strain. Top with Champagne.

Sweet Thing

CHAMPAGNE FLUTE

1 part Melon Liqueur
1 part Peach Schnapps
fill with Champagne

Shake all but Champagne with ice and strain. Top with Champagne.

Sweetest Taboo

CHAMPAGNE FLUTE

splash Blue Curaçao
1½ parts Orange Juice
fill with Champagne

Shake all but Champagne with ice and strain. Top with Champagne.

Tahiti

WHITE WINE GLASS

1 part Dry Gin
1 part Triple Sec
fill with Champagne

Build in the glass with no ice.

Think I Love You

CHAMPAGNE FLUTE

1 part Strawberry Puree
1 part Pineapple Juice
½ part Red Curaçao
½ part Simple Syrup
fill with Champagne

Shake all but Champagne with ice and strain. Top with Champagne.

Titiani

CHAMPAGNE FLUTE

2 parts Grape Juice (Red)
splash Grenadine
fill with Champagne

Build in the glass with no ice.

Torque Wrench

SHOT GLASS

1 part Champagne
1 part Orange Juice
1 part Melon Liqueur

Build in the glass with no ice.

Tropical Bellini

COLLINS GLASS

1 part Peach Schnapps
1 scoop Peach Sorbet
1 part Pineapple Juice
fill with Champagne

Shake all but Champagne with ice and strain. Top with Champagne.

Tropical Champagne

CHAMPAGNE FLUTE

½ part Dark Rum
1 part Passion Fruit Liqueur
1½ parts Pineapple Juice
fill with Champagne

Shake all but Champagne with ice and strain. Top with Champagne.

True Lies

CHAMPAGNE FLUTE

1 part Triple Sec
1 part Strawberry Syrup
fill with Champagne

Build in the glass with no ice.

Tryst & Shout

CHAMPAGNE FLUTE

1½ parts Amaretto
2 parts Sweet & Sour Mix
fill with Champagne

Shake all but Champagne with ice and strain. Top with Champagne.

The Twist

CHAMPAGNE FLUTE

¾ parts Vermouth
½ part Crème de Menthe (White)
1 scoop Orange Sorbet
fill with Champagne

Shake all but Champagne with ice and strain. Top with Champagne.

Typhoon

COLLINS GLASS

1 part Gin
½ part Anisette
1 part Lime Juice
fill with Champagne

Shake all but Champagne with ice and strain. Top with Champagne.

Ultra-Marine

CHAMPAGNE FLUTE

½ part Blue Curaçao
fill with Champagne

Build in the glass with no ice.

Uptown Girl

COUPETTE GLASS

1½ parts Maraschino Liqueur
fill with Champagne

Build in the glass with no ice.

Valencia Fizz

CHAMPAGNE FLUTE

1 part Apricot Brandy
1 part Orange Juice
fill with Champagne

Shake all but Champagne with ice and strain. Top with Champagne.

Virginia Asshole

HURRICANE GLASS

1 part Blue Curaçao
1 part Vodka
fill with Champagne

Build over ice and stir.

Volcano Fizz

CHAMPAGNE FLUTE

1 part Raspberry Liqueur
1 part Blue Curaçao
fill with Champagne

Build in the glass with no ice.

Wayamata

CHAMPAGNE FLUTE

1 part Dark Rum
½ part Strawberry juice
¼ part Triple Sec
fill with Champagne

Shake all but Champagne with ice and strain. Top with Champagne.

Weirdness

HIGHBALL GLASS

1 part Peach Schnapps
1 part Crème de Banane
fill with Champagne

Build over ice and stir.

Wild Hibiscus Motherly Love Mimosa Punch

PUNCH BOWL, CHAMPAGNE FLUTE

5 parts St-Germain
5 parts Pink Grapefruit Juice
2½ parts Wild Hibiscus Syrup
1 bottle Sparkling Wine

Mix all ingredients in punch bowl with large block of ice. Garnish each flute with a Wild Hibiscus Flower and Grapefruit Twist.

Wings of Tenderness

CHAMPAGNE FLUTE

1 part Vodka
1 part Campari®
fill with Champagne

Shake all but Champagne with ice and strain. Top with Champagne.

Winter 42

COUPETTE GLASS

1½ part Vodka
1 part Light Rum
dash Bitters
fill with Champagne

Shake all but Champagne with ice and strain. Top with Champagne.

Y2K

CHAMPAGNE FLUTE

1 part Vodka
1 part Melon Liqueur
½ part Melon Puree
½ part Simple Syrup
fill with Champagne

Shake all but Champagne with ice and strain. Top with Champagne.

Yellow Cat

CHAMPAGNE FLUTE

1 part Orange Juice
1 part Dry Vermouth
1 part Crème de Coconut
fill with Champagne

Shake all but Champagne with ice and strain. Top with Champagne.

WINE DRINKS

These drinks fall somewhere between a wine cooler and a wicked hangover.

8th Wonder

WHITE WINE GLASS

2 parts White Wine
1 part Brandy
1 part Triple Sec
1 part Maraschino Liqueur
1 part Sweet & Sour Mix

Shake with ice and strain over ice.

Adler's OJ

COLLINS GLASS

1 part Red Wine
3 parts Orange Juice
3 parts Orange Soda

Build over ice and stir.

Amaretto Flirt

CHAMPAGNE FLUTE

3 parts Sparkling White Wine
1 part Amaretto
1 part Orange Juice

Build in the glass with no ice.

Amaretto Sangria

HIGHBALL GLASS

2 parts Amaretto
1 part Red Wine
1 part Orange Juice
1 part Pineapple Juice

Build over ice and stir.

Amaretto Wine Cooler

HIGHBALL GLASS

2 parts Amaretto
1 part White Wine
1 part Lemon-Lime Soda

Build over ice and stir.

Amaretto Wine Fizz

HIGHBALL GLASS

2 parts Amaretto
1 part Sweet & Sour Mix
1 part Orange Juice
1 part White Wine
1 part Lemon-Lime Soda

Build over ice and stir.

Anime Sailor

COLLINS GLASS

1 part Light Rum
1 part Advocaat
½ part Galliano®
¾ part Lemon Juice
fill with White Wine

Build over ice and stir.

Apple Wine Cooler

HIGHBALL GLASS

2 parts Sour Apple Schnapps
1 part White Wine
1 part Lemon-Lime Soda

Build over ice and stir.

Apple Wine Spritzer

HIGHBALL GLASS

2 parts Sour Apple Schnapps
1 part White Wine
1 part Club Soda

Build over ice and stir.

Australian Virgin

HIGHBALL GLASS

2 parts White Wine
1 part Dark Rum
3 parts Pineapple Juice
dash Grenadine

Shake with ice and strain over ice.

Balalaika Magika

WHITE WINE GLASS

½ part Creme de Menthe (White)
1 part Lemonade
fill with White Wine

Build over ice.

Balaton

WHITE WINE GLASS

1 part Apricot Brandy
1 part Peach Schnapps
fill with Sparkling White Wine

Shake all but Wine with ice and strain into glass. Top with Sparkling Wine.

Balla Balla

WHITE WINE GLASS

1 part Dry Gin
1 part Triple Sec
1 part Campari®
fill with Sparkling White Wine

Build over ice.

Balthazar

COLLINS GLASS

½ part Vanilla Liqueur
½ part Lemon Juice
2 parts Raspberry Seltzer
3 parts Red Wine

Build over ice and stir.

Bambi

COLLINS GLASS

1 part White Wine
1 part Ginger Ale
splash Lime Juice

Build over ice and stir.

Beach Cooler

COLLINS GLASS

1 part Vodka
1 part Red Wine
1 part Cola
1 part Orange Juice
1 part Passion Fruit Juice

Build over ice and stir.

Beach Peach

HIGHBALL GLASS

1 part Apricot Brandy
2 parts Peach Wine
2 parts Orange Juice

Shake with ice and strain.

Bermuda Blanc

WHITE WINE GLASS

1 part Light Rum
1 part Lime Cordial
fill with White Wine

Build over ice and stir.

Bernetto

HIGHBALL GLASS

1 part Currant Vodka
½ part Blackberry Liqueur
½ part Vanilla Liqueur
fill with Sparkling Wine

Build over ice and stir.

Berry Wine Cooler

HIGHBALL GLASS

1 part Blackberry Liqueur
4 parts White Wine
2 parts Pineapple Juice
1 part Cranberry Juice Cocktail
1 part Club Soda

Build over ice and stir.

Better Breezer
HIGHBALL GLASS

1/2 part Scotch
1 part Crème de Cassis
1/2 part Orange Liqueur
3 parts Sparkling Wine

Build over ice and stir.

The Big Shamble
HIGHBALL GLASS

splash Vanilla Liqueur
1/2 part Chambord®
1/2 part Hazelnut Liqueur
2 parts Red Wine
2 parts Raspberry Seltzer
1/2 part Lemon Juice

Build over ice and stir.

Bishop
HIGHBALL GLASS

1/4 part Lemon Juice
1/2 part Orange Juice
dash Powdered Sugar
fill with Red Wine

Shake all but Wine with ice and strain. Top with Red Wine.

Blackberry Wine Cooler
HIGHBALL GLASS

2 parts Blackberry Liqueur
1 part White Wine
1 part Lemon-Lime Soda

Build over ice and stir.

Bloody Pepper
RED WINE GLASS

1 part Red Wine
1 part Dr. Pepper®

Build over ice and stir.

Boston Bottle Rocket
ROCKS GLASS

1 part White Wine
1/2 part Lemon Juice
dash Sugar
fill with Orange Juice

Shake with ice and pour.

Burgundy Bishop
HIGHBALL GLASS

1 part Light Rum
1/4 part Lemon Juice
dash Powdered Sugar
fill with Red Wine

Shake all but Wine with ice and strain. Top with Red Wine.

Butterfly
ROCKS GLASS

1 part Sweet Vermouth
1 part Dry Vermouth
1/2 part Orange Juice
1/2 part Red Wine

Shake with ice and strain.

Cactus Berry
COUPETTE GLASS

1 1/4 parts Tequila
1 1/4 parts Red Wine
1 part Triple Sec
fill with Sweet & Sour Mix
splash Lemon-Lime Soda
splash Lime Juice

Shake with ice and strain.

Calimocho Blanco
HIGHBALL GLASS

1 part White Wine
1 part Lemon-Lime Soda

Build over ice and stir.

Captain with a Skirt
COLLINS GLASS

2 parts Spiced Rum
2 parts White Wine
fill with Cola

Build over ice and stir. Garnish with a Lime Slice.

Cliffhanger
CHAMPAGNE FLUTE

1 part Vanilla Liqueur
1/2 part Passion Fruit Liqueur
fill with White Wine

Build in the glass with no ice.

Cocomacoque

COLLINS GLASS

1½ parts Light Rum
2 parts Red Wine
½ part Lemon Juice
2 parts Pineapple Juice
2 parts Orange Juice

Shake with ice and pour.

Czar

HIGHBALL GLASS

1 part Vodka
1 part Grand Marnier®
½ part Lime Juice
fill with Dry Sparkling White Wine
dash Orange Bitters

Build over ice and stir.

Damn Yankees

HIGHBALL GLASS

1 part Triple Sec
2 parts White Wine
1½ parts Lemon-Lime Soda
1 part Pineapple Juice

Build over ice and stir.

Dog Day Cooler

ROCKS GLASS

1½ parts Gin
1 part Orange Juice
1 part Red Wine
1 part Lime Cordial

Shake with ice and pour.

Fernando

COLLINS GLASS

1½ parts Triple Sec
1½ parts Strawberry Liqueur
1 part White Wine
1 part Orange Juice

Shake with ice and strain over ice.

A Fruity Fuck Face

ROCKS GLASS

4 parts Vodka
2 parts Rum
1 part White Wine
3 parts Orange Juice

Build over ice and stir.

Green Pineapple

WHITE WINE GLASS

1½ parts Pineapple Juice
1 part Blue Curaçao
fill with Sparkling White Wine

Build over ice and stir.

Hillary Wallbanger

COLLINS GLASS

4 parts Dry White Wine
½ part Galliano®
fill with Orange Juice

Build over ice and stir.

Hokkaido Highball

HIGHBALL GLASS

1½ parts Gin
1 part Sake Rice Wine
½ part Triple Sec

Build over ice and stir.

Imperial Czar

WHITE WINE GLASS

1½ parts White Wine
½ part Vodka
½ part Triple Sec
¼ part Lime Cordial
2 dashes Orange Bitters

Shake with ice and strain.

Italian Perfume

WHITE WINE GLASS

1 part Brandy
1 part Amaretto
fill with White Wine

Build over ice and stir.

Kalimotxo

COLLINS GLASS

1 part Red Wine
1 part Cola

Build over ice and stir.

Laguna

COLLINS GLASS

½ part Blue Curaçao
1 part Pineapple Juice
1 part Sparkling White Wine

Build over ice and stir.

Lemon Wine Cooler

HIGHBALL GLASS

1 part White Wine
1 part Lemonade
1 part Lemon-Lime Soda

Build over ice and stir.

May Day

HIGHBALL GLASS

1½ parts Bourbon
splash Kirschwasser
splash Strawberry Liqueur
fill with Red Wine

Build over ice and stir.

My Best Friend's Girl

HIGHBALL GLASS

1 part Peach Schnapps
1 part White Wine
1 part Club Soda

Shake with ice and pour.

Paparazzi

WHITE WINE GLASS

½ part Dark Rum
¼ part Lime Juice
1 part Pineapple Juice
fill with Sparkling White Wine

Build over ice and stir.

Peach Bottom

BEER MUG

1 part Peach Schnapps
1 part Vodka
fill with White Wine
splash Lemon Juice

Build over ice and stir.

Peep Hole

COLLINS GLASS

1 part Orange Juice
1 part Brandy
½ part Simple Syrup
fill with White Zinfandel Wine

Build over ice and stir.

Queen Charlotte

COLLINS GLASS

2 parts Red Wine
1 part Grenadine
fill with Lemon-Lime Soda

Build over ice and stir.

Quick Thrill

WHITE WINE GLASS

½ part Dark Rum
1 part Red Wine
1 part Cola

Build over ice and stir.

Red Rover

COLLINS GLASS

1 part Dark Rum
½ part Raspberry Syrup
1 part Red Wine
1 part Club Soda

Build over ice and stir.

Red Wine Cobbler

COLLINS GLASS

1 part Orange Juice
1 part Maraschino Liqueur
1 part Lime Juice
fill with Red Wine

Build over ice and stir.

Red Wine Cooler

HIGHBALL GLASS

2 parts Red Wine
1 part Lemon-Lime Soda
1 part Ginger Ale

Build over ice and stir.

Regal Fizz

HIGHBALL GLASS

1 part Cherry Brandy
1 part Kirschwasser
fill with Sparkling White Wine

Build over ice and stir.

Regatta

HIGHBALL GLASS

1 part Vodka
1 part Triple Sec
fill with Sparkling White Wine

Build over ice and stir.

Rembrandt

WHITE WINE GLASS

1 part Apricot Brandy
fill with White Wine

Build in the glass with no ice.

Rhine Cooler

COLLINS GLASS

1 part Lime Juice
1 part White Wine
1 part Club Soda
dash Sugar

Build over ice and stir.

Royal Peach Freeze

COUPETTE GLASS

½ part Lime Juice
2 parts Orange Juice
2 parts Peach Schnapps
1½ parts Dry Sparkling White Wine

Combine all ingredients in a blender with ice. Blend until smooth.

Sangre de Toro

HIGHBALL GLASS

splash Apricot Brandy
fill with Red Wine

Build over ice and stir.

Smurf® Juice

COLLINS GLASS

splash Blue Curaçao
1 part White Wine
1 part Ginger Ale

Build over ice and stir.

Smut

BEER MUG

1 part Peach Schnapps
1 part Red Wine
1 part Cola
1 part Orange Juice

Build over ice and stir.

Sparkling Wine Polonaise

WHITE WINE GLASS

½ part Blackberry Liqueur
splash Cognac
fill with Dry Sparkling White Wine

Build in the glass with no ice.

Stab in the Back

HIGHBALL GLASS

½ part Brandy
1½ parts Orange Juice
2 parts Dry White Wine
2 parts Club Soda

Build over ice and stir.

Sunny Sex

COUPETTE GLASS

1 part Coconut Rum
1 part Fire Water®
½ part Vodka
½ part Red Wine
1 part Orange Juice

Shake with ice and pour.

Sunset Horizon

WHITE WINE GLASS

2/3 part Gin
2/3 part Cherry Liqueur
2 parts Vegetable Juice Blend
fill with White Wine

Build over ice and stir.

Talisman

ROCKS GLASS

1/2 part Crème de Cassis
3 parts White Wine
1 part Strawberry Juice
splash Orange Juice

Shake with ice and strain over ice.

Teacher's Pet

HIGHBALL GLASS

2/3 part Advocaat
2/3 part Calvados Apple Brandy
3 parts White Wine
1 part Lemon-Lime Soda

Shake with ice and strain over ice.

Urbinos

WHITE WINE GLASS

1 part Cognac
1/2 part Red Curacao
fill with White Wine

Build over ice and stir.

Webmaster Wine

HIGHBALL GLASS

1 1/2 parts Blackberry Liqueur
1 part White Wine
1 part Lemon-Lime Soda
1 part Cranberry Juice Cocktail

Build over ice and stir.

White Whine

HIGHBALL GLASS

1 part White Wine
1 part Ginger Ale
splash Lime Juice

Build over ice and stir.

White Wine Cooler

HIGHBALL GLASS

2 parts White Wine
1 part Lemon-Lime Soda
1 part Ginger Ale

Build over ice and stir.

White Wine Spritzer

WHITE WINE GLASS

1 part White Wine
1 part Club Soda

Build over ice and stir.

Wine Cooler

HIGHBALL GLASS

1 part White Wine
2 parts Lemon-Lime Soda

Build over ice and stir.

Wine Spritzer

WHITE WINE GLASS

3 parts White Wine
1 part Club Soda

Build over ice and stir.

Yellow-Bellied Chupacabra

BRANDY SNIFTER

1 part Red Wine
1 part Tequila
splash Sweet Vermouth

Build in the glass with no ice.

COFFEE DRINKS

Most of these drinks combine coffee with a liqueur or liquor and are served hot. The classic example is the Irish Coffee, which combines coffee with Irish whiskey, but here are plenty more to warm you up.

Alaskan Coffee

IRISH COFFEE CUP

3 parts Coffee
1½ parts Brandy
2 parts Vanilla Ice Cream

Build in a heat-proof cup or mug. Float Ice Cream on top.

All-Canadian Coffee

IRISH COFFEE CUP

¾ part Whipped Cream
⅓ part Maple Syrup
1 part Rye Whiskey
3 parts Coffee

Combine Whipped Cream with 4 teaspoons Maple Syrup until it forms soft mounds; set aside. Divide remaining Maple Syrup and Whiskey among 4 Irish coffee cups. Pour in coffee and top with Whipped Cream.

Almond Chocolate Coffee

IRISH COFFEE CUP

¾ part Amaretto
½ part Crème de Cacao (Dark)
fill with Coffee

Build in a heat-proof cup or mug. Top with Whipped Cream and Chocolate Shavings.

Amaretto Café

IRISH COFFEE CUP

1 part Coffee
1 part Amaretto

Fill coffee mug or cup with Hot Coffee. Stir in Amaretto. Top with Whipped Cream.

Anatole Coffee

IRISH COFFEE CUP

1 part Courvoisier®
1 part Tia Maria®
1 part Frangelico®
fill with Coffee

Build in a heat-proof cup or mug. Top with Whipped Cream and Chocolate Shavings.

Anders

IRISH COFFEE CUP

1 part Amaretto
½ part Brandy
½ part Coffee Liqueur
fill with Coffee

Build in a heat-proof cup or mug.

Anise Almond Coffee

IRISH COFFEE CUP

1 part Amaretto
1 part Crème de Cacao (Dark)
1 part Sambuca
fill with Coffee

Build in a heat-proof cup or mug.

Apocalypse

IRISH COFFEE CUP

1 part Peppermint Schnapps
3/4 part Vodka
1/2 part Coffee Liqueur
1/2 part Old Grand-Dad®
1 part Crème de Menthe (White)
3/4 part Southern Comfort®
fill with Hot Cocoa

Build in a heat-proof cup or mug.

Aqualung

IRISH COFFEE CUP

2 parts Coffee Liqueur
fill with Espresso
splash Chocolate Syrup

Build in a heat-proof cup or mug.

Bad Apple

COFFEE CUP OR HEAT-PROOF MUG

1 part Fireball Cinnamon Whiskey
1 cup Coffee

Build in order.

Baileys® Cup of Coffee

IRISH COFFEE CUP

1 part Baileys® Irish Cream Liqueur
1 part Coffee

Build in a heat-proof cup or mug.

Belgian Coffee

IRISH COFFEE CUP

1 part Triple Sec
1 part Irish Cream Liqueur
fill with Coffee

Build in a heat-proof cup or mug.

Berliner Mélange

IRISH COFFEE CUP

2 parts Cherry Brandy
1/2 part Simple Syrup
fill with Coffee

Build in a heat-proof cup or mug.

Berries 'n' Cream Coffee

IRISH COFFEE CUP

1 part Irish Cream Liqueur
1 part Raspberry Liqueur
fill with Coffee

Build in a heat-proof cup or mug.
Top with Whipped Cream.

Black Gold

IRISH COFFEE CUP

1 part Triple Sec
1 part Amaretto
1 part Irish Cream Liqueur
1 part Frangelico®
splash Cinnamon Schnapps
fill with Coffee

Build in a heat-proof cup or mug.

Black Maria

IRISH COFFEE CUP

1 part Light Rum
1 part Coffee Brandy
2 dashes Powdered Sugar
fill with Strong Black Coffee

Build in a heat-proof cup or mug.

Black Rose

IRISH COFFEE CUP

2 parts Dark Rum
1/2 part Simple Syrup
fill with Coffee

Build in a heat-proof cup or mug.

Blackjack

IRISH COFFEE CUP

1 1/2 parts Kirschwasser
1/2 part Cherry Brandy
1/2 part Simple Syrup
fill with Coffee

Build in a heat-proof cup or mug.

Boston-Baked Brandy

IRISH COFFEE CUP

1½ parts Brandy
¾ part Triple Sec
1 part Hot Coffee
1 part Hot Cocoa
splash Honey

Build in a heat-proof cup or mug.

Boston Caribbean Coffee

IRISH COFFEE CUP

1 part Crème de Cacao (Dark)
1 part Dark Rum
fill with Coffee

Build in a heat-proof cup or mug.

Bounce

IRISH COFFEE CUP

1½ parts Crème de Coconut
½ part Almond Syrup
fill with Coffee

Build in a heat-proof cup or mug.

Breathtaking

IRISH COFFEE CUP

1 part Amaretto
splash Frangelico®
fill with Coffee

Build in a heat-proof cup or mug.

Buie Coffee

IRISH COFFEE CUP

1 part Drambuie®
½ part Crème de Cacao (Dark)
2 parts Cream
fill with Black Coffee

Build in a heat-proof cup or mug.

Butternut Coffee

IRISH COFFEE CUP

1 part Butterscotch Schnapps
1 part Amaretto
fill with Coffee

Build in a heat-proof cup or mug.

Café Alpine

IRISH COFFEE CUP

1 part Peppermint Schnapps
fill with Coffee

Build in a heat-proof cup or mug.

Café Amaretto

IRISH COFFEE CUP

1 part Amaretto
fill with Coffee

Build in a heat-proof cup or mug.

Café Boom Boom

IRISH COFFEE CUP

1 part Frangelico®
1 part Irish Cream Liqueur
fill with Coffee

Build in a heat-proof cup or mug.

Café Caribbean

IRISH COFFEE CUP

1 part Rum
1 part Amaretto
fill with Coffee
dash Sugar

Build in a heat-proof cup or mug.
Top with Whipped Cream.

Café Curatao

IRISH COFFEE CUP

1½ parts Triple Sec
½ dash Powdered Sugar
fill with Hot Coffee

Build in a heat-proof cup or mug.
Top with Whipped Cream.

Café d'Amour

COFFEE CUP OR HEAT-PROOF MUG

1¼ parts Cognac
5 parts Hot Black Coffee
1 Cinnamon Stick

Rim the cup or mug with Lemon Juice and Sugar, then build the drink in order.

Café Di Limoni
IRISH COFFEE CUP

1 part Limoncello
fill with Coffee

Build in a heat-proof cup or mug.

Café Foster
COFFEE CUP OR HEAT-PROOF MUG

1 part Banana Liqueur
½ part Black Rum
5 parts Coffee

Build in order and garnish with Whipped Cream.

Café French
IRISH COFFEE CUP

1 part Triple Sec
1 part Amaretto
½ part Irish Cream Liqueur
fill with Coffee

Build in a heat-proof cup or mug.

Café Gates
IRISH COFFEE CUP

1 part Brandy
1 part Crème de Cacao (Dark)
fill with Coffee

Build in a heat-proof cup or mug.

Café Grog
IRISH COFFEE CUP

1½ parts Dark Rum
1 part Brandy
fill with Coffee

Build in a heat-proof cup or mug.

Café Imperial
COFFEE CUP OR HEAT-PROOF MUG

¾ part Mandarine Napoleon Orange Liqueur
5 parts Hot Black Coffee
Sugar

Build in order, add Sugar to taste, and garnish with Whipped Cream.

Café Jeavons
IRISH COFFEE CUP

1 part Dark Rum
1 part Cognac
splash Cream of Coconut
½ part Vanilla Ice Cream
fill with Black Coffee
dash Cinnamon

Build in a heat-proof cup or mug. Garnish with an Orange Peel.

Café Joy
IRISH COFFEE CUP

1 part Frangelico®
1 part Coconut Rum
1 part Irish Cream Liqueur
fill with Coffee

Build in a heat-proof cup or mug.

Café King Royale
IRISH COFFEE CUP

1 part Coffee Brandy
splash Galliano®
splash Grand Marnier®
fill with Coffee

Build in a heat-proof cup or mug.

Café L'Orange
IRISH COFFEE CUP

½ part Cognac
½ part Cointreau®
1 part Grand Marnier®
fill with Coffee

Build in a heat-proof cup or mug.

Café Mazatlan
IRISH COFFEE CUP

1 part Dark Rum
1 part Coffee Liqueur
fill with Coffee
dash Brown Sugar

Build in a heat-proof cup or mug. Top with Whipped Cream.

Café Nelson
IRISH COFFEE CUP

3/4 part Frangelico®
4 parts Coffee

Build in a heat-proof cup or mug.

Café Oscar
IRISH COFFEE CUP

1 part Amaretto
1 part Crème de Cacao (Dark)
fill with Coffee

Build in a heat-proof cup or mug.

Café Romano
IRISH COFFEE CUP

1 part Sambuca
fill with Coffee

Build in a heat-proof cup or mug.

Café Royale
IRISH COFFEE CUP

1 Sugar Cube
1 part Brandy
1 part Coffee Liqueur
fill with Coffee

Soak the Sugar Cube in Brandy. Place the Coffee Liqueur in a heat-proof cup or mug and fill with Coffee. Place the Brandy-soaked sugar in a teaspoon. Hold the teaspoon above the Coffee and ignite the Brandy on the sugar. Hold it until flame burns out and drop contents into the cup.

Café Seattle
IRISH COFFEE CUP

1 part Irish Cream Liqueur
1 part Absolut® Vodka
1 part Chocolate Syrup
fill with Coffee

Build in a heat-proof cup or mug.

Café Sonia
IRISH COFFEE CUP

3/4 part Metaxa®
1/2 part Amaretto
1/2 part Tia Maria®
splash Heavy Cream
splash Vanilla Extract
fill with Coffee

Build in a heat-proof cup or mug.

Café Toledo
IRISH COFFEE CUP

1 part Coffee Liqueur
1/2 part Chocolate Syrup
fill with Coffee

Build in a heat-proof cup or mug.

Café Wellington
IRISH COFFEE CUP

Whipped Cream
dash Instant Coffee
2 splashes Cream of Coconut
1 part Light Rum
fill with Coffee

Blend Whipped Cream with Instant Coffee until stiff peaks form. In a heat-proof cup or mug add Cream of Coconut and Rum and stir well while filling the cup with Coffee. Top with prepared Whipped Cream.

Café Zurich
IRISH COFFEE CUP

1 part Sambuca
1 part Cognac
1/2 part Amaretto
splash Honey
fill with Coffee

Build in a heat-proof cup or mug.

Calypso
IRISH COFFEE CUP

1 part Rum
1 part Tia Maria®
fill with Coffee

Build in a heat-proof cup or mug.

Calypso Coffee

COFFEE CUP OR HEAT-PROOF MUG

½ part White Rum
½ part Crème de Cacao (Dark)
5 parts hot black Coffee
dash Amaretto
1 tsp Sugar

Build in order. Top with Whipped Cream.

Candle in the Window

IRISH COFFEE CUP

2 parts Light Rum
splash Crème de Cacao (Dark)
splash Cherry Brandy
fill with Black Coffee

Build in a heat-proof cup or mug.

Cappuccino Sausalito

IRISH COFFEE CUP

½ part Amaretto
½ part Coffee Liqueur
1 part Coffee
1 part Hot Cocoa

Build in a heat-proof cup or mug.

Capriccio

IRISH COFFEE CUP

1 Sugar Cube
½ part Brandy
½ part Coffee Liqueur
1 part Amaretto
fill with Coffee

Build in a heat-proof cup or mug.

Caracof

IRISH COFFEE CUP

1½ parts Coffee Liqueur
1 part Caramel Syrup
fill with Hot Cocoa

Build in a heat-proof cup or mug.

Caribbean Coffee

IRISH COFFEE CUP

2 parts Dark Rum
dash Sugar
2 parts Cream
fill with Black Coffee

Build in a heat-proof cup or mug.

Casino Coffee

COFFEE CUP OR HEAT-PROOF MUG

½ part Amaretto
½ part Brandy
½ part Crème de Cacao (Dark)
5 parts Hot Black Coffee
Sugar

Build in order, add Sugar to taste, and garnish with Whipped Cream.

Charro

IRISH COFFEE CUP

1 part Tequila
1 part Evaporated Milk
fill with Coffee

Build in a heat-proof cup or mug.

Chocolate Coffee Kiss

IRISH COFFEE CUP

1 part Coffee Liqueur
1 part Irish Cream Liqueur
splash Crème de Cacao (Dark)
splash Grand Marnier®
1 part Chocolate Syrup
fill with Coffee

Build in a heat-proof cup or mug.

Chocolate Strawberry

IRISH COFFEE CUP

1 part Tequila Rose®
½ part Chocolate Liqueur
fill with Coffee

Build in a heat-proof cup or mug.

Chump
IRISH COFFEE CUP

1½ parts Dark Rum
½ part Tia Maria®
1 part Light Cream
fill with Coffee

Build in a heat-proof cup or mug.

Co-Co-Mo
IRISH COFFEE CUP

2 parts Coconut Rum
1 part Hot Cocoa
1 part Coffee

Build in a heat-proof cup or mug.

Coffee 43
IRISH COFFEE CUP

1 part Licor 43®
fill with Coffee

Build in a heat-proof cup or mug.

Coffee Fling
IRISH COFFEE CUP

1 part Scotch
splash Lemon Juice
fill with Coffee

Build in a heat-proof cup or mug.

Coffee Kisses
COFFEE CUP OR HEAT-PROOF MUG

½ part Chambord
½ part Irish Cream Liqueur
fill with Hot Black Coffee

Build in order and garnish with Whipped Cream.

Coffee Nudge
IRISH COFFEE CUP

¾ part Crème de Cacao (Dark)
¾ part Coffee Liqueur
½ part Brandy
fill with Coffee

Build in a heat-proof cup or mug.

Coffee Royale
IRISH COFFEE CUP

1½ parts Brandy
fill with Coffee

Build in a heat-proof cup or mug.

Coffee RumChata
COFFEE CUP OR HEAT-PROOF MUG

1 part Coconut Rum
1 part RumChata
fill with Hot Black Coffee

Build in order.

Comforting Coffee
IRISH COFFEE CUP

1 part Southern Comfort®
2 splashes Crème de Cacao (Dark)
2 parts Cream
fill with Black Coffee

Build in a heat-proof cup or mug.

Cossack
IRISH COFFEE CUP

1 part Vodka
1 part Coffee Liqueur
1 part Godiva® Liqueur
fill with Warm Milk

Build in a heat-proof cup or mug.

Dangerous Minds
IRISH COFFEE CUP

1 part Vodka
1 part Crème de Cacao (Dark)
fill with Coffee

Build in a heat-proof cup or mug.

Doublemint
IRISH COFFEE CUP

1 part Dr. McGillicuddy's®
Mentholmint Schnapps
fill with Coffee
splash Crème de Menthe (Green)

Build in a heat-proof cup or mug.

Dutch Coffee

IRISH COFFEE CUP

1½ parts Chocolate Mint Liqueur
fill with Coffee

Build in a heat-proof cup or mug.

Finals Night

IRISH COFFEE CUP

2 parts Tequila
½ part Crème de Cacao (Dark)
½ part Lemon Juice
fill with Coffee

Build in a heat-proof cup or mug.

French Coffee

IRISH COFFEE CUP

1 Sugar Cube
1 part Grand Marnier®
fill with Coffee

Build in a heat-proof cup or mug.

Fritzes Coffee

IRISH COFFEE CUP

1 part Frangelico®
1 part Irish Cream Liqueur
fill with Coffee

Build in a heat-proof cup or mug.

Fuzzy Asshole

IRISH COFFEE CUP

1 part Coffee
1 part Peach Schnapps

Build in a heat-proof cup or mug.

Fuzzy Dick

IRISH COFFEE CUP

1 part Coffee Liqueur
1 part Grand Marnier®
fill with Coffee

Build in a heat-proof cup or mug.

Galliano® Hotshot

IRISH COFFEE CUP

1 part Galliano®
fill with Coffee

Build in a heat-proof cup or mug.

Good Golly

IRISH COFFEE CUP

1½ parts Dark Rum
½ part Galliano®
2 splashes Crème de Cacao (Dark)
1 part Heavy Cream
fill with Black Coffee

Build over ice and stir.

Guapo

IRISH COFFEE CUP

1 part Irish Cream Liqueur
1 part Coffee Liqueur
2 splashes Butterscotch Schnapps
fill with Coffee

Build in a heat-proof cup or mug.

Handicapper's Choice

IRISH COFFEE CUP

1 part Irish Whiskey
1 part Amaretto
fill with Coffee

Build in a heat-proof cup or mug.

Heart Warmer

IRISH COFFEE CUP

1 part Vanilla Liqueur
1 part Peppermint Liqueur
1 part Amaretto
fill with Coffee

Build in a heat-proof cup or mug.

Henry III Coffee

IRISH COFFEE CUP

1 part Brandy
1 part Coffee
1 part Mandarine Napoléon® Liqueur
fill with Coffee

Build in a heat-proof cup or mug.

Hot Bush

IRISH COFFEE CUP

1 part Irish Whiskey
1 part Irish Cream Liqueur
fill with Coffee

Build in a heat-proof cup or mug.

Hot Butterscotch Cocoa

IRISH COFFEE CUP

1 part Butterscotch Schnapps
1 part Coffee Liqueur
fill with Hot Cocoa

Build in a heat-proof cup or mug.

Hot Coconut

IRISH COFFEE CUP

1 part Crème de Coconut
½ part Simple Syrup
fill with Coffee

Build in a heat-proof cup or mug.

Hot Irish Nut

IRISH COFFEE CUP

1 part Irish Cream Liqueur
1 part Frangelico®
1 part Amaretto
fill with Coffee

Build in a heat-proof cup or mug.

Hot Kiss

IRISH COFFEE CUP

1 part Irish Whiskey
½ part Crème de Cacao (White)
fill with Coffee

Build in a heat-proof cup or mug.

Hot Mollifier

IRISH COFFEE CUP

1½ parts Dark Rum
½ part Tia Maria®
2 parts Heavy Cream
fill with Coffee

Build in a heat-proof cup or mug.

Hot Piper

IRISH COFFEE CUP

2 parts Tequila
½ part Crème de Cacao (Dark)
2 splashes Lemon Juice
fill with Black Coffee

Build in a heat-proof cup or mug.

Hot Pleasure

IRISH COFFEE CUP

1 part Bourbon
½ part Amaretto
splash Cream
dash Brown Sugar
fill with Coffee

Build in a heat-proof cup or mug.

Hot Siberian Almond

IRISH COFFEE CUP

1 part Cream
1 part Amaretto
½ part Vodka
fill with Coffee

Build in a heat-proof cup or mug.

Irish '49

IRISH COFFEE CUP

1 part Irish Mist®
dash Sugar
fill with Coffee

Build in a heat-proof cup or mug.
Top with Whipped Cream.

Irish Coffee

IRISH COFFEE CUP

1½ parts Irish Whiskey
dash Sugar
fill with Coffee

Build in a heat-proof cup or mug.

Irish Coffee #2

IRISH COFFEE CUP

1 part Irish Whiskey
dash Sugar
2 parts Cream
fill with Black Coffee

Build in a heat-proof cup or mug.

An Irish Kiss

IRISH COFFEE CUP

1 part Irish Cream Liqueur
1 part Coffee Liqueur
fill with Coffee

Build in a heat-proof cup or mug.

Italian Amaretto Coffee

IRISH COFFEE CUP

1½ parts Amaretto
½ part Cream
fill with Coffee

Build in a heat-proof cup or mug. Top with Whipped Cream.

Italian Coffee

IRISH COFFEE CUP

1½ parts Amaretto
fill with Coffee

Build in a heat-proof cup or mug.

Jamaica Me Hot

IRISH COFFEE CUP

¾ part Dark Rum
¾ part Coffee Liqueur
1 part Milk
1 part Coffee

Build in a heat-proof cup or mug.

Jamaican Coffee

IRISH COFFEE CUP

1 part Brandy
1 part Rum
fill with Coffee

Build in a heat-proof cup or mug.

Jamaican Coffee #2

IRISH COFFEE CUP

1½ parts Rum
½ part Coffee Liqueur
fill with Coffee

Build in a heat-proof cup or mug.

Jamaican Coffee #3

IRISH COFFEE CUP

1 part Cognac
1 part Tia Maria®
1 part Dark Rum
fill with Coffee
dash Cinnamon
dash Ginger

Build in a heat-proof cup or mug.

Javameister

IRISH COFFEE CUP

1½ parts Jägermeister®
fill with Black Coffee

Build in a heat-proof cup or mug.

Jungle Coffee

IRISH COFFEE CUP

1 part Southern Comfort®
1 part Brandy
1 part Crème de Cacao (Dark)
1 part Crème de Banane
fill with Coffee

Build in a heat-proof cup or mug.

Kentucky Coffee

IRISH COFFEE CUP

1 part Bourbon
fill with Coffee

Build in a heat-proof cup or mug. Top with Whipped Cream.

Keoke Coffee

IRISH COFFEE CUP

1 part Rum
1 part Brandy
1 part Coffee Liqueur
fill with Coffee

Build in a heat-proof cup or mug.

Keoke Mocha

IRISH COFFEE CUP

1 part Chocolate Liqueur
1 part Frangelico
1 part Amaretto
fill with Coffee

Build in a heat-proof cup or mug. Top with Whipped Cream.

Kong Coffee

IRISH COFFEE CUP

1 part Whiskey
1 part Crème de Banane
fill with Coffee

Build in a heat-proof cup or mug. Top with Whipped Cream.

Last Dance

IRISH COFFEE CUP

1 part Vanilla Liqueur
1 part Almond Syrup
1 part Milk
fill with Coffee

Build in a heat-proof cup or mug.

Lebanese Coffee

IRISH COFFEE CUP

2 parts Apricot Brandy
1 part Coffee Liqueur
fill with Coffee

Build in a heat-proof cup or mug.

Lift

IRISH COFFEE CUP

1 part Amaretto
1 part Drambuie®
1 part Tia Maria®
fill with Coffee

Build in a heat-proof cup or mug.

Liquid Speedball

IRISH COFFEE CUP

1½ parts Vodka
1 part Espresso
fill with Black Coffee
dash Cinnamon

Build in a heat-proof cup or mug.

Loco Cocoa Mocha

IRISH COFFEE CUP

¾ part Coffee Liqueur
2 parts Heavy Cream
fill with Coffee
dash Hot Chocolate Mix

Build in a heat-proof cup or mug.

Mexican Coffee

IRISH COFFEE CUP

1 part Coffee Liqueur
1 part Cream
fill with Coffee

Build in a heat-proof cup or mug.

Mex-Italy Coffee

IRISH COFFEE CUP

1 part Coffee Liqueur
1 part Amaretto
fill with Coffee

Build in a heat-proof cup or mug.

Midnight in Malibu

IRISH COFFEE CUP

2 parts Coconut Rum
fill with Coffee

Build in a heat-proof cup or mug. Top with Whipped Cream.

Millionaire's Coffee

IRISH COFFEE CUP

1 part Irish Cream Liqueur
1 part Coffee Liqueur
1 part Frangelico®
fill with Coffee

Build in a heat-proof cup or mug.

Mocha Almond Fudge

IRISH COFFEE CUP

1 part Amaretto
1 part Coffee Liqueur
1 part Crème de Cacao (White)
fill with Coffee

Build in a heat-proof cup or mug.

Mocha Nut

IRISH COFFEE CUP

1½ parts Frangelico®
½ part Crème de Cacao (White)
2 parts Cream
fill with Coffee

Build in a heat-proof cup or mug.

Monastery Coffee

IRISH COFFEE CUP

2 parts Bénédictine®
2 parts Heavy Cream
fill with Black Coffee
dash Sugar

Build in a heat-proof cup or mug.

Monte Cristo

IRISH COFFEE CUP

1 part Coffee Liqueur
½ part Grand Marnier®
fill with Coffee

Build in a heat-proof cup or mug.
Top with Whipped Cream.

Morley's Driver

IRISH COFFEE CUP

1½ parts Dark Rum
½ part Cherry Brandy
2 splashes Crème de Cacao (Dark)
fill with Coffee

Build in a heat-proof cup or mug.
Top with Heavy Cream.

My Passion in a Cup

IRISH COFFEE CUP

1½ parts Butterscotch Schnapps
1 part Chocolate Syrup
fill with Coffee

Build in a heat-proof cup or mug.

Newport Coffee

IRISH COFFEE CUP

¾ part Crème de Menthe (White)
fill with Coffee

Build in a heat-proof cup or mug.
Top with Whipped Cream.

Night Train

IRISH COFFEE CUP

1 part Vodka
1 part Frangelico®
½ part Simple Syrup
fill with Coffee

Build in a heat-proof cup or mug.

Nikki Coffee

IRISH COFFEE CUP

1 part Irish Cream Liqueur
1 part Butterscotch Schnapps
fill with Coffee

Build in a heat-proof cup or mug.

Nudge

IRISH COFFEE CUP

1 part Coffee Liqueur
1 part Crème de Cacao (White)
1 part Vodka
fill with Coffee

Build in a heat-proof cup or mug.

Nutty Irish Coffee

IRISH COFFEE CUP

1 part Irish Cream Liqueur
1 part Frangelico®
splash Chocolate Syrup
fill with Coffee

Build in a heat-proof cup or mug.

Old Town

IRISH COFFEE CUP

1 part Rum
½ part Tia Maria®
1 tbsp brown sugar
fill with Coffee

Build in a heat-proof cup or mug.

Oslo Coffee

IRISH COFFEE CUP

½ part Goldschläger®
fill with Coffee

Build in a heat-proof cup or mug.

Ostrich Shit

IRISH COFFEE CUP

1 part Peppermint Schnapps
2 dashes Sugar
fill with Coffee

Build in a heat-proof cup or mug.

Peach Truffle

IRISH COFFEE CUP

1 part Peach Schnapps
1 part Crème de Cacao (White)
fill with Coffee

Build in a heat-proof cup or mug.

Peppermint Coffee

IRISH COFFEE CUP

1 part Crème de Menthe (Green)
1 part Cream
½ part Crème de Cacao (White)
fill with Coffee

Build in a heat-proof cup or mug.

Pike's Peak

IRISH COFFEE CUP

1 part Peppermint Schnapps
1 part Coffee Liqueur
fill with Coffee

Build in a heat-proof cup or mug.

Piper

COFFEE CUP OR HEAT-PROOF MUG

2 parts Tequila
½ part Crème de Cacao (Dark)
½ part Lemon Juice
fill with Strong Hot Black Coffee

Build in order.

Psycho Joe

IRISH COFFEE CUP

1 part Jägermeister®
1 part Rumchata
fill with Coffee

Build in a heat-proof cup or mug.

Puppet Master

IRISH COFFEE CUP

1 part Whiskey
½ part Coffee Liqueur
fill with Coffee

Build in a heat-proof cup or mug.

Randy's Special

IRISH COFFEE CUP

1 part Irish Cream Liqueur
1 part Frangelico®
1 part Amaretto
fill with Coffee

Build in a heat-proof cup or mug.

Raspberry Cappuccino

IRISH COFFEE CUP

2 parts Raspberry Liqueur
fill with Espresso

Build in a heat-proof cup or mug.

Razzmatazz

IRISH COFFEE CUP

1 part Blackberry Liqueur
½ part Crème de Cassis
½ part Coffee Liqueur
fill with Coffee

Build in a heat-proof cup or mug.

Rhode Island Iced Coffee

ROCKS GLASS

1 part Coffee Liqueur
1 part Vodka
½ part Brandy
2 parts Cream

Shake with ice and strain over ice.

Roman Coffee

IRISH COFFEE CUP

1 part Galliano®
fill with Coffee

Build in a heat-proof cup or mug.

Saturday Morning Special

IRISH COFFEE CUP

1 part Rum
2 splashes Chocolate Syrup
fill with Coffee

Build in a heat-proof cup or mug.

Schuylkill Pudding

IRISH COFFEE CUP

1 1/2 parts Dark Rum
1/2 part Cherry Brandy
1/4 part Crème de Cacao (Dark)
fill with Coffee

Build in a heat-proof cup or mug.

Scottish Coffee

IRISH COFFEE CUP

1 1/2 parts Drambuie®
fill with Coffee

Build in a heat-proof cup or mug.

Secret Place

IRISH COFFEE CUP

1 1/2 parts Dark Rum
1/2 part Cherry Brandy
2 splashes Crème de Cacao (Dark)
fill with Coffee

Build in a heat-proof cup or mug.

Sly Ol' Bastard

IRISH COFFEE CUP

1 part Cream
1 part Amaretto
fill with Coffee
top with Guinness® Stout

Build in a heat-proof cup or mug.

Snowball

IRISH COFFEE CUP

1 part Cinnamon Schnapps
1 part Coffee Liqueur
fill with Coffee

Build in a heat-proof cup or mug.

Sorrento Café

IRISH COFFEE CUP

1 part Limoncello
1 part Grand Marnier®
fill with Coffee

Build in a heat-proof cup or mug.

Southfork Coffee

IRISH COFFEE CUP

1/2 part Crème de Cacao (Dark)
2 parts Heavy Cream
fill with Black Coffee

Build in a heat-proof cup or mug.

Stanley Steamer

COFFEE CUP OR HEAT-PROOF MUG

1/2 part Coffee Liqueur
1/2 part Irish Cream Liqueur
1/2 part Cognac
fill with Hot Black Coffee
dash Grand Marnier

Build in order. Top with Whipped Cream.

Sudden Struck

IRISH COFFEE CUP

1 part Crème de Cacao (Dark)
1/2 part Sambuca
fill with Coffee

Build in a heat-proof cup or mug.

Super Coffee

IRISH COFFEE CUP

1 part Brandy
1 part Coffee Liqueur
fill with Coffee

Build in a heat-proof cup or mug. Top with Whipped Cream.

Swedish Coffee

IRISH COFFEE CUP

1 part Aquavit
fill with Coffee
dash Sugar

Build in a heat-proof cup or mug.

Tennessee Mud

IRISH COFFEE CUP

1 part Amaretto
1 part Whiskey
fill with Coffee

Build in a heat-proof cup or mug.

To Die For

IRISH COFFEE CUP

1 part Whiskey
1/4 part Crème de Cacao (Dark)
fill with Coffee

Build in a heat-proof cup or mug.

Torrence Coffee

IRISH COFFEE CUP

1 part Crème de Menthe (White)
1 part Irish Cream Liqueur
fill with Coffee

Build in a heat-proof cup or mug.

Triple Irish Coffee

IRISH COFFEE CUP

1 part Irish Whiskey
1 part Irish Cream Liqueur
1 part Irish Mist®
fill with Coffee

Build in a heat-proof cup or mug.
Top with Whipped Cream.

Tropical Clarkson

IRISH COFFEE CUP

1 1/2 parts Coffee Liqueur
fill with Hot Cocoa

Build in a heat-proof cup or mug.

Ukrainian Coffee

IRISH COFFEE CUP

1 part Coffee Liqueur
1/2 part Amaretto
1/2 part Mandarine Napoléon® Liqueur
fill with Coffee

Build in a heat-proof cup or mug.

Vanilla 49

IRISH COFFEE CUP

1 part Vanilla Liqueur
fill with Coffee

Build in a heat-proof cup or mug.
Top with Heavy Cream.

Venetian Coffee

IRISH COFFEE CUP

1 part Brandy
1 Sugar Cube
fill with Coffee

Build in a heat-proof cup or mug.
Top with Whipped Cream.

Virgin Mocha Almond Fudge

IRISH COFFEE CUP

2 splashes Chocolate Syrup
splash Almond Syrup
fill with Coffee

Build in a heat-proof cup or mug.

Warm Feelings

IRISH COFFEE CUP

1 part Crème de Cacao (Dark)
1 part Dark Rum
fill with Coffee

Build in a heat-proof cup or mug.

Zorro

IRISH COFFEE CUP

1 part Sambuca
1 part Irish Cream Liqueur
1 part Crème de Menthe (White)
fill with Coffee

Build in a heat-proof cup or mug.

OTHER HOT DRINKS

What to call drinks served hot but that don't contain coffee? These will also warm you up.

5 P.M.

IRISH COFFEE CUP

1 part Dark Rum
1/2 part Cointreau®
fill with Hot Tea
splash Milk

Build in a heat-proof cup or mug.

A.D.M. (After Dinner Mint)

IRISH COFFEE CUP

1/2 part Crème de Menthe (White)
3/4 part Southern Comfort®
1/2 part Vodka
fill with Hot Cocoa

Build in a heat-proof cup or mug.

Aberdeen Angus

IRISH COFFEE CUP

1/2 part Lime Juice
1/2 part Heather Honey
fill with Boiling Water
2 parts Scotch
1 part Drambuie®

Pour Lime Juice and Honey into a heat-proof mug. Add a little Boiling Water and stir until the Honey is dissolved. Add Scotch. Warm Drambuie® in a ladle over hot water, ignite, and pour into mug while burning. Fill with boiling water and stir.

Absinthe High Tea

COFFEE CUP OR HEAT-PROOF MUG

1 part Absinthe
3 parts Cranberry Juice
splash Lemon Juice
dash Honey
fill with Boiling Water
1 Cinnamon Stick

Combine all ingredients and stir with the Cinnamon Stick.

Adult Hot Chocolate

IRISH COFFEE CUP

1 1/2 parts Peppermint Schnapps
1 part Hot Cocoa

Build in a heat-proof cup or mug. Top with Whipped Cream.

After Dinner Mint Julep

IRISH COFFEE CUP

3/4 part Crème de Menthe (White)
1 part Southern Comfort®
1/2 part Whiskey
fill with Hot Cocoa

Combine in a heat-proof cup or mug. If desired, garnish with Whipped Cream and an Andes® Mint.

After Walk

IRISH COFFEE CUP

2 parts Citrus Vodka
1 part Vanilla Syrup
1 part Brown Sugar
fill with Club Soda

Combine in an Irish coffee cup and warm it in the microwave until hot.

Alhambra Royale

IRISH COFFEE CUP

1 part Hot Cocoa
1½ parts Cognac

Fill heat-proof cup nearly full of Hot Cocoa and add Orange Peel. Warm Cognac in a ladle over hot water, ignite, and pour into cup of Hot Cocoa while burning. Stir well and top with Whipped Cream.

Almond Hot Chocolate

IRISH COFFEE CUP

1 part Dark Rum
1 part Amaretto
fill with Hot Cocoa

Build in a heat-proof cup or mug.

American Grog

IRISH COFFEE CUP

1½ parts Rum
dash Powdered Sugar
½ part Lemon Juice
fill with Hot Water

Build in a heat-proof cup or mug.

Apple Skag

IRISH COFFEE CUP

1 part Sour Apple Schnapps
1 part Apple Brandy
fill with Apple Juice (Heated)

Build in a heat-proof cup or mug.

Apple Toddy

IRISH COFFEE CUP

1½ parts Apple Brandy
fill with Hot Apple Cider

Build in a heat-proof cup or mug.

Aprihot

IRISH COFFEE CUP

1 part Apricot Brandy
1 part Boiling Water

Build in a heat-proof cup or mug.

Bacardi® Fireside

IRISH COFFEE CUP

1½ parts Dark Rum
dash Sugar
fill with Hot Tea

Build in a heat-proof cup or mug. Garnish with a Lemon Slice.

Back Burner

IRISH COFFEE CUP

2 parts Tequila
½ part Galliano®
fill with Cold Hot Chocolate

Shake with ice and strain over ice. This may not be a hot drink, but it will still warm you up.

Barn Burner

IRISH COFFEE CUP

1½ parts Southern Comfort®
fill with Hot Apple Cider

Build in a heat-proof cup or mug. Stir with a Cinnamon Stick and garnish with a Lemon Twist.

Beam of Chocolate

IRISH COFFEE CUP

3 parts Jim Beam®
fill with Hot Cocoa

Build in a heat-proof cup or mug.

Bedroom Farce

IRISH COFFEE CUP

1 part Dark Rum
2 splashes Galliano®
fill with Hot Cocoa

Build in a heat-proof cup or mug. Top with Whipped Cream and Chocolate Shavings.

Big Hug

COFFEE CUP OR HEAT-PROOF MUG

1 part Irish Cream Liqueur
1 part Crème de Cacao (Dark)
fill with Hot Cocoa

Build in order and garnish with Whipped Cream.

Black Flag

IRISH COFFEE CUP

2 parts Dark Rum
½ part Molasses
splash Honey
fill with Boiling Water

Build in a heat-proof cup or mug.

Blueberry Tea

IRISH COFFEE CUP

1 part Amaretto
½ part Grand Marnier®
fill with Black Currant Tea

Build in a heat-proof cup or mug.

Bun Warmer

IRISH COFFEE CUP

1 part Apricot Brandy
1 part Southern Comfort®
fill with Hot Apple Cider

Build in a heat-proof cup or mug.

Butter Cup

IRISH COFFEE CUP

2 parts Butterscotch Schnapps
fill with Hot Cocoa

Build in a heat-proof cup or mug.

Butter Milk

IRISH COFFEE CUP

1 part Butterscotch Schnapps
fill with Warm Milk

Build over ice and stir.

Butterscotch Benchwarmer

IRISH COFFEE CUP

2 parts Butterscotch Schnapps
fill with Hot Milk
splash Honey

Build in a heat-proof cup or mug.

Café Mocha

IRISH COFFEE CUP

1 part Crème de Cacao (Dark)
1 part Cream
fill with Espresso

Build in a heat-proof cup or mug.

Cappuccino

IRISH COFFEE CUP

1 part Brandy
fill with Cappuccino

Build in a heat-proof cup or mug.

Caribbean Hot Chocolate

IRISH COFFEE CUP

1½ parts Dark Rum
½ part Crème de Cacao (Dark)
fill with Hot Cocoa

Build in a heat-proof cup or mug.

Chill Out

IRISH COFFEE CUP

1 part Crème de Coconut
1 part Amaretto
fill with Hot Cocoa

Build in a heat-proof cup or mug.

Chocolate Nemesis

IRISH COFFEE CUP

1 part Godiva® Liqueur
1 part Irish Cream Liqueur
fill with Hot Cocoa

Build in a heat-proof cup or mug.

Chocolate Raspberry Dream

IRISH COFFEE CUP

1 part Crème de Cacao (White)
1 part Vodka
1 part Raspberry Liqueur
fill with Hot Cocoa

Build in a heat-proof cup or mug.

Chocolingus

IRISH COFFEE CUP

1 part Rum
2 parts Godiva® Liqueur
3 dashes Hot Chocolate Mix
fill with Hot Milk

Build in a heat-proof cup or mug.

Cocomeister

IRISH COFFEE CUP

1½ parts Jägermeister®
fill with Hot Cocoa

Build in a heat-proof cup or mug.

Cure for What Ails Ya

IRISH COFFEE CUP

2 parts Brandy
1 part Honey
fill with Hot Tea

Build in a heat-proof cup or mug.

Dark Continent

IRISH COFFEE CUP

2 parts Dark Rum
1 part Cream
½ part Crème de Cacao (Dark)
fill with Hot Cocoa

Build in a heat-proof cup or mug.

Dreamy Winter Delight

IRISH COFFEE CUP

2 parts Irish Cream Liqueur
fill with Hot Cocoa

Build in a heat-proof cup or mug.

Fire-Cider

COFFEE CUP OR HEAT-PROOF MUG

1 part Fireball Cinnamon Whiskey
1 part Hot Apple Cider

Build in order.

Fireside Chat

IRISH COFFEE CUP

1 part Vanilla Liqueur
1 part Dark Rum
fill with Hot Tea

Build in a heat-proof cup or mug.

First Frost

IRISH COFFEE CUP

2 parts Cherry Brandy
splash Goldschläger®
fill with Hot Apple Cider
dash Powdered Sugar

Build in a heat-proof cup or mug.

Frenchman

IRISH COFFEE CUP

1 part Dark Rum
½ part Triple Sec
splash Honey
fill with Hot Tea

Build in a heat-proof cup or mug.

Fuzzy Nut

IRISH COFFEE CUP

1 part Peach Schnapps
1 part Amaretto
fill with Hot Cocoa

Build in a heat-proof cup or mug.

Girl Scout® Thinned Mint

IRISH COFFEE CUP

1 part Crème de Menthe (Green)
1 part Rumchata
fill with Hot Cocoa

Build in a heat-proof cup or mug.

Golden Apple Cider

IRISH COFFEE CUP

1 part Goldschläger®
fill with Hot Apple Cider

Build in a heat-proof cup or mug.

Golden Grog

IRISH COFFEE CUP

1 part Rye Whiskey
1 part Dark Rum
1 part Cointreau®
splash Amaretto
fill with Boiling Water

Build in a heat-proof cup or mug. Stir with a Cinnamon Stick and garnish with a Lemon Slice.

Gunfire

IRISH COFFEE CUP

1 part Dark Rum
fill with Hot Tea

Build in a heat-proof cup or mug.

Heat Wave

IRISH COFFEE CUP

1 part Dark Rum
1/2 part Triple Sec
1/2 part Rock & Rye
splash Lemon Juice
fill with Boiling Water

Build in a heat-proof cup or mug.

Hershey® Squirts

IRISH COFFEE CUP

1 1/2 parts Whiskey
fill with Hot Cocoa

Build in a heat-proof cup or mug.

Homemade Heaven

IRISH COFFEE CUP

1 1/2 parts Vanilla Liqueur
2/3 part Goldschläger®
fill with Hot Cocoa

Build in a heat-proof cup or mug.

Hot and Bothered

COFFEE CUP OR HEAT-PROOF MUG

2 parts Butterscotch Liqueur
1 part Godiva Chocolate Liqueur
1 part Irish Cream Liqueur
fill with Hot Cocoa

Build in order.

Hot Brandy Toddy

IRISH COFFEE CUP

2 parts Brandy
1 Sugar Cube
fill with Boiling Water

Build in a heat-proof cup or mug.

Hot Buttered Rum

IRISH COFFEE CUP

2 parts Dark Rum
dash Brown Sugar
fill with Boiling Water
dash Ground Cloves
dash Butter

Build in a heat-proof cup or mug.

Hot Buttery Goose Nipples

IRISH COFFEE CUP

1 part Butterscotch Schnapps
1 part Irish Cream Liqueur
fill with Hot Cocoa

Build in a heat-proof cup or mug.

Hot Chocolate Almond

IRISH COFFEE CUP

2 parts Amaretto
1/2 part Butterscotch Schnapps
fill with Hot Cocoa

Build in a heat-proof cup or mug.

Hot Chocolate Butternut

IRISH COFFEE CUP

2 parts Butterscotch Schnapps
½ part Amaretto
fill with Hot Cocoa

Build in a heat-proof cup or mug.

Hot Chocolate Monk

IRISH COFFEE CUP

1 part Tuaca®
1 part Frangelico®
fill with Hot Cocoa

Build in a heat-proof cup or mug.

Hot Cinnamon Roll

IRISH COFFEE CUP

1½ parts Cinnamon Schnapps
fill with Hot Apple Cider

Build in a heat-proof cup or mug.

Hot Dick

IRISH COFFEE CUP

1 part Irish Cream Liqueur
1 part Grand Marnier®
fill with Espresso

Build in a heat-proof cup or mug. Top with Whipped Cream.

Hot Gin Toddy

IRISH COFFEE CUP

2 parts Gin
1 Sugar Cube
fill with Boiling Water

Build in a heat-proof cup or mug.

Hot Girl Scout®

IRISH COFFEE CUP

1 part Crème de Menthe (White)
fill with Hot Cocoa

Build in a heat-proof cup or mug.

Hot Irish Chocolate

IRISH COFFEE CUP

1 part Whiskey
fill with Hot Cocoa

Build in a heat-proof cup or mug.

Hot Nun

COFFEE CUP OR HEAT-PROOF MUG

1½ parts Frangelico
½ part Honey
3 Whole Cloves
fill with Hot Water

Build in order and garnish with a Lemon Twist.

Hot Peppermint Pattie®

IRISH COFFEE CUP

1 part Peppermint Schnapps
fill with Hot Cocoa

Build in a heat-proof cup or mug.

Hot Zultry Zoe

IRISH COFFEE CUP

1½ parts Tequila
½ part Galliano®
2 parts Heavy Cream
fill with Hot Cocoa

Build in a heat-proof cup or mug.

Indian Summer

IRISH COFFEE CUP

1 part Rum
fill with Hot Apple Cider
dash Cinnamon

Build in a heat-proof cup or mug.

Jersey Toddy

IRISH COFFEE CUP

3 parts Applejack
splash Honey
2 dashes Bitters
fill with Boiling Water

Build in a heat-proof cup or mug.

Kirchoff's Rule

IRISH COFFEE CUP

1 part Irish Cream Liqueur
½ part Godiva® Liqueur
½ part Amaretto
fill with Hot Cocoa

Build in a heat-proof cup or mug. Top with Whipped Cream.

Kurant Tea

IRISH COFFEE CUP

1 part Currant Vodka
fill with Hot Tea

Build in a heat-proof cup or mug.

Long Island Hot Tea

COLLINS GLASS

1 part Peppar Vodka
1 part Tequila
1 part Rum
1 part Gin
1 part Triple Sec
fill with Hot Tea
splash Cola

Build in a heat-proof cup or mug.

Mexican Hot Chocolate

IRISH COFFEE CUP

1½ parts Tequila
½ part Coffee Liqueur
2 parts Cream
fill with Hot Cocoa

Build in a heat-proof cup or mug.

Nightgown

IRISH COFFEE CUP

½ part Chocolate Mint Liqueur
1½ parts Butterscotch Schnapps
fill with Hot Cocoa

Build in a heat-proof cup or mug.

Peppermint Hot Chocolate

IRISH COFFEE CUP

1 part Rumple Minze®
fill with Hot Cocoa

Build in a heat-proof cup or mug.

Ponche de Leche

IRISH COFFEE CUP

1½ parts Light Rum
½ part Cognac
½ part Triple Sec
dash Powdered Sugar
fill with Hot Milk

Build in a heat-proof cup or mug.

Raspberry Truffle

IRISH COFFEE CUP

1 part Raspberry Liqueur
1 part Crème de Cacao (White)
fill with Hot Milk

Build in a heat-proof cup or mug.

Royal Hot Chocolate

IRISH COFFEE CUP

1 part Raspberry Liqueur
1 part Crème de Cacao (White)
fill with Hot Cocoa

Build in a heat-proof cup or mug.

Rummy

IRISH COFFEE CUP

1 part Dark Rum
splash Honey
dash Brown Sugar
fill with Hot Water

Build in a heat-proof cup or mug.

Shocking Chocolate

IRISH COFFEE CUP

1 part Cinnamon Schnapps
fill with Hot Cocoa

Build in a heat-proof cup or mug.

Siperia

IRISH COFFEE CUP

1 part Vodka
1 part Goldschläger®
½ part Raspberry Syrup
fill with Hot Tea

Build in a heat-proof cup or mug.

Ski Lift

IRISH COFFEE CUP

1 part Peach Schnapps
½ part CocoRibe®
fill with Hot Cocoa
dash Cinnamon

Build in a heat-proof cup or mug.
Top with Whipped Cream.

Skier's Toddy

IRISH COFFEE CUP

1 part Coffee Liqueur
1 part Triple Sec
fill with Hot Cocoa

Build in a heat-proof cup or mug.
Top with Marshmallows.

Snow Bunny

IRISH COFFEE CUP

1½ parts Triple Sec
fill with Hot Cocoa

Build in a heat-proof cup or mug.

Snow Warmer

IRISH COFFEE CUP

2 parts Rumple Minze®
fill with Hot Cocoa

Build in a heat-proof cup or mug.

Snowball Melted

IRISH COFFEE CUP

1 part Brandy
1 part Peppermint Schnapps
1 part Crème de Cacao (White)
fill with Hot Cocoa

Build in a heat-proof cup or mug.

Snowplow

IRISH COFFEE CUP

1 part Irish Cream Liqueur
1 part Coconut Rum
½ part Crème de Cacao (White)
dash Cinnamon
fill with Hot Cocoa

Build in a heat-proof cup or mug.

Snuggler

IRISH COFFEE CUP

1½ parts Peppermint Schnapps
fill with Hot Cocoa

Build in a heat-proof cup or mug.

Spicy Scot

IRISH COFFEE CUP

1 part Butterscotch Schnapps
1 part Spiced Rum
fill with Hot Cocoa

Build in a heat-proof cup or mug.

Squire Racine

IRISH COFFEE CUP

1½ parts Dark Rum
½ part Southern Comfort®
fill with Hot Malted Milk

Build in a heat-proof cup or mug.

Tantalus

IRISH COFFEE CUP

1½ parts Triple Sec
½ part Peach Schnapps
½ part Vanilla Liqueur
fill with Hot Apple Juice

Build in a heat-proof cup or mug.

Tea & Sympathy

IRISH COFFEE CUP

1 part Grand Marnier®
fill with Hot Tea

Build in a heat-proof cup or mug.

Tea Off

IRISH COFFEE CUP

½ part Amaretto
splash Goldschläger®
splash Peppermint Liqueur
fill with Hot Tea
splash Honey

Build in a heat-proof cup or mug.

Tropical Heat

IRISH COFFEE CUP

1 part Cinnamon Schnapps
fill with Hot Apple Cider

Build in a heat-proof cup or mug.

Vacuum Bottle

IRISH COFFEE CUP

1 part Peppermint Liqueur
1 part Chocolate Liqueur
fill with Hot Cocoa

Build in a heat-proof cup or mug.

Voyager

IRISH COFFEE CUP

1 part Spiced Rum
1/4 part Crème de Banane
fill with Hot Apple Cider

Build in a heat-proof cup or mug.

Warm Woolly Sheep

IRISH COFFEE CUP

1 part Scotch
1 1/2 shots Drambuie®
fill with Warm Milk

Build in a heat-proof cup or mug.

Whiskey-All-In

IRISH COFFEE CUP

2 parts Whiskey
dash Sugar
2 splashes Lemon Juice
fill with Boiling Water
dash Ground Cloves

Build in a heat-proof cup or mug.

White Ape

IRISH COFFEE CUP

1 1/2 parts Irish Cream Liqueur
dash Cinnamon
fill with Hot Cocoa

Build in a heat-proof cup or mug.

White Hot Chocolate

IRISH COFFEE CUP

1 part Crème de Cacao (White)
fill with Hot Cocoa

Build in a heat-proof cup or mug.

Wooly Mitten

IRISH COFFEE CUP

1 1/2 parts Southern Comfort®
1 part Peppermint Schnapps
1 1/2 parts Irish Cream Liqueur
fill with Hot Cocoa

Build in a heat-proof cup or mug.
Top with Whipped Cream.

Zultry Zoe

IRISH COFFEE CUP

2 parts Tequila
1/2 part Galliano®
fill with Hot Cocoa

Build in a heat-proof cup or mug.

ACKNOWLEDGMENTS

This book wouldn't have been possible without the help, guidance, and support of a few key people:

Jill Quigley, my better half, for her constant support, kindness, and love and for *almost* never saying no when I hand her a glass and say, "Here, try this!"

My wonderful children, Camryn, Colby, and Cooper, for their understanding and patience while dad was writing. It won't be long now before they'll be old enough to read what dad has been writing about!

Carlo DeVito, who has brought sanity and order to this wild world of publishing and has been a friend since the very first book.

James Jayo and all the people at Sterling who worked tirelessly to transform my incoherent ramblings into the book you're holding now.

Thank you, all.

Credit where credit is due, some of the drinks in this book require a special thank you:

Amatitan Monk: Partida Tequila

Añejo Highball: ale DeGroff, author and master bartender.

Avion El Humo de Mexico: Avion Tequila

Estridentista: Ancho Reyes Chili Licor

Peruvian Elder Sour: Gary Regan through the St-Germain cocktail collection.

St. Zipang and St. Zipaine: Zipang Sake

Wild Hibiscus Motherly Love Mimosa Punch: Wild Hibiscus Flower Co.

Many of the Fireball Cinnamon Whiskey cocktails are courtesy of the Fireball website, FireballWhisky.com, part of the Sazerac Company.

Many of the St-Germain cocktails are courtesy of the St-Germain web site, www.stgermain.fr, part of Bacardi Global Brands Limited.

INDEX BY MAIN INGREDIENT

11,000 DRINKS
INDEX BY MAIN INGREDIENT

Blue Hawaiian Schnapps

Blue Maui

Blue Raspberry Liqueur

11,000 DRINKS INDEX BY MAIN INGREDIENT

Coconut Vodka

Coffee Brandy

Coffee Liqueur

Coffee Tequila

Coffee Vodka

Cognac, xxi

11,000 DRINKS INDEX BY MAIN INGREDIENT

J

K

L

11,000 DRINKS | INDEX BY MAIN INGREDIENT

11,000 DRINKS
INDEX BY MAIN INGREDIENT

INDEX BY DRINK NAME

11,000 DRINKS
INDEX BY DRINK NAME